NEPA DESKBOOK

4TH EDITION

Nicholas C. Yost

DENTONS US LLP

ENVIRONMENTAL LAW INSTITUTE

Washington, D.C.

Table of Contents

Contents

Appendices

Policy Guidance

CEQ Guidance

EPA Guidance

Other Helpful Materials

About the Author

Nicholas C. Yost is a Partner at Dentons US LLP in San Francisco, California, from which he directs the firm's practice of environmental and natural resources law with a focus on the National Environmental Policy Act (NEPA). His practice includes counseling clients on environmental leadership and compliance with state and federal environmental laws, obtaining permits and authorizations, litigation, and representing clients before federal and state agencies on environmental matters. Mr. Yost was General Counsel of the Counsel on Environmental Quality from 1977 until 1981, where he had lead responsibility for the development and drafting of NEPA's implementing regulations. He has also served in the California Department of Justice, forming and heading the Environmental Section, as a private interest lawyer, as a visiting scholar at the Environmental Law Institute, and as a private practitioner in Washington, D.C. Mr. Yost holds an L.L.B. from the School of Law, University of California at Berkeley (Boalt Hall), and an A.B. from Princeton University's Woodrow Wilson School of Public and International Affairs. He has chaired the Standing Committee on Environmental Law of the American Bar Association and the Committee on the Environment of the California State Bar, and has also co-chaired the Environment, Energy, and Natural Resources Section of the District of Columbia Bar. In 2010, he received the ABA's Award for Distinguished Achievement in Environmental Law and Policy.

Acknowledgments

The author wishes to acknowledge the contributions of James W. Rubin and Sarah Ratcliffe Choi, both with Dentons, and Kathleen Boergers, to earlier versions of this Deskbook, and that of Jessica Duggan, who assisted with the current appendices.

Foreword

The Environmental Law Institute (ELI) has a special interest in the National Environmental Policy Act that dates back to our shared birth date in December 1969. This *Deskbook*, now updated, is one of the most popular resources for environmental professionals in the United States and abroad. I was recently asked which statute I thought had the greatest impact on environmental law. Although there are many candidates for this honor, my own candidate is clear: NEPA. Not only did the statute revolutionize federal decisionmaking, but it has been replicated countless times in state statutes and exported to numerous foreign governments to guide their decisionmaking. We should always be proud of our nation's contribution to the worldwide use of NEPA-like statutes to advance environmental action.

Over the years, the Environmental Law Institute and the Council on Environmental Quality (CEQ) have cooperated in conference and research projects. We've watched the birth and application of NEPA, its inculcation into the fabric of the federal government's decisionmaking process, and its journey through many courts, creating a nearly unparalleled body of environmental law. Without question, NEPA has been highly successful in assuring that environmental considerations are factored into federal planning and decisionmaking.

NEPA is a statute of productive dimensions because it impacts the relationships of the body politic. It clearly directs coordination among federal, state, municipal, and private agencies that would not occur otherwise. Even when there is gridlock elsewhere, NEPA has often acted as a consensus-building tool to provide real options that take into account environmental protection. It also empowers citizens to participate directly in environmental planning. In fact, NEPA has been the single most useful development in opening up federal agency decisionmaking to groups that do not have budgets or staff to investigate projects. Citizen groups find environmental impact statements (EISs) particularly useful because they include key information about projects in one, easily accessible document. And, decisionmakers rely on NEPA impact statements, knowing that they must be both comprehensive and balanced to be effective.

The brilliance of NEPA is that it calls for active citizen and interest group participation to forge consensus and wise environmental decisions. And, it provides a record in one place for key decisions. In this effort, there is much work for lawyers. The *NEPA Deskbook* is designed to assist practitioners by assembling the necessary legal materials in one place.

The introductory chapter of the *Deskbook* presents a detailed analysis of the statute by the leading U.S. expert on NEPA. As General Counsel of the CEQ from 1977 until 1981, Nicholas C. Yost led the successful effort to write regulations that put administrative flesh on the bare bones of the statute. This expert legal commentary is accompanied by the text of the statute, the regulations, key policy guidance that gives insight into NEPA's implementation, and sample documents prepared under the statute. An especially useful feature of the *Deskbook* is its collection of summaries of U.S. Supreme Court cases prepared by the staff of ELI's highly regarded *Environmental Law Reporter (ELR)*.

Most of the lawsuits filed under NEPA have arisen from its statutory requirement that the lead agency file an EIS for each "major Federal action significantly affecting the quality of the human environment." These few words, each of them with independent meaning, have become the workhorse of environmental litigation, and lawyers play a key role in assuring compliance with its requirements. Knowledge of case law is especially essential in this area, and the *Deskbook* excels in presenting cases in a clear and understandable fashion.

As with all ELI Deskbooks, the *NEPA Deskbook* is an extremely valuable resource for a skilled practitioner. Keep it by your desk. Carry it to meetings. Our editors have carefully screened materials to include only the information environmental professionals need most.

The Deskbook series is a spinoff of *ELR*'s work in tracking and analyzing legislative, regulatory, and judicial developments. Companion Deskbooks—the *Environmental Law Deskbook*, the *TSCA Deskbook*, the *Wetlands Deskbook*, the *RCRA Permitting Deskbook*, the *Environmental Crimes Deskbook*, the *Natural Resource Damage Assessment Deskbook*, the *Superfund Deskbook*, and the *Oil Pollution Deskbook*—have drawn an enthusiastic response from environmental law practitioners.

As a national environmental research and publishing organization dedicated to the development of more effective and more efficient environmental protection efforts, ELI is pleased to present the fourth edition of the *NEPA Deskbook*. We hope that it will assist environmental lawyers and managers in their efforts to make this central and most important statute work to protect the environment.

— John C. Cruden, President
Environmental Law Institute

I. Overview

Introduction

The National Environmental Policy Act[1] (NEPA) is the most pervasive of America's panoply of environmental laws. Other statutes seek to conserve specific media (such as air, water, or land), to regulate specific endeavors (such as surface mining or introduction of new chemicals), or to protect specific places or flora or fauna (such as wilderness areas or endangered species). In contrast, NEPA involves all these areas, seeking to balance a broad range of environmental factors as well as "other essential considerations of national policy."[2] An understanding of NEPA and its processes is a necessary predicate to the practice of environmental law. This chapter is intended to provide that understanding.

The chapter is organized as a reference for practitioners working with NEPA as well as for others seeking an explanation of the law's requirements and operation. Section I of this Chapter provides an overview of the legislation, examining the U.S. Congress' intent in passing it, its stated purposes, and the institutional actors responsible for its implementation. Section II analyzes NEPA's administrative process, placing special emphasis on the stages leading to preparation of an environmental impact statement (EIS), NEPA's most conspicuous requirement. Finally, Section III examines the role of the courts in enforcing NEPA and reviewing agency decisions.

NEPA's Purposes

NEPA is "our basic national charter for protection of the environment."[3] Its purposes and policy, as declared in §§2 and 101,[4] are broadly worded, demonstrating the Act's wide reach and intent.[5] It is "the centerpiece of environmental regulations in the United States . . . ."[6] As noted above, the breadth of its stated goals sets NEPA apart from all other environmental statutes, which regulate specific aspects of our environment. NEPA encompasses all environmental values and forces the federal government and its permittees to bear those values in mind as they plan ahead. To accomplish this task, NEPA sets out two basic and related objectives: Preventing environmental damage and ensuring that agency decisionmakers take environmental factors into account.

---

1. 42 U.S.C. §§4321-4347, ELR Stat. NEPA §§2-209.
2. *Id.* §4331(b), ELR Stat. NEPA §101(b). "NEPA is the broadest and perhaps most important of the environmental statutes." Oregon Nat. Desert Ass'n. v. Bureau of Land Management, 531 F.3d 1114, 1121 (9th Cir. 2008).
3. 40 C.F.R. §1500.1(a); People of the State of California v. U.S. Department of Agriculture, 575 F.3d 999, 1012 (9th Cir. 2009).
4. 42 U.S.C. §§4321, 4331, ELR Stat. NEPA §§2, 101.
5. CEQ's NEPA regulations describe the Act's purposes and organizational scheme:
   The National Environmental Policy Act (NEPA) is our basic national charter for protection of the environment. It establishes policy, sets goals (section 101), and provides means (section 102) for carrying out the policy. Section 102(2) contains "action-forcing" provisions to make sure that federal agencies act according to the letter and spirit of the Act. The regulations that follow implement section 102(2). Their purpose is to tell federal agencies what they must do to comply with the procedures and achieve the goals of the Act. The President, the federal agencies, and the courts share responsibility for enforcing the Act so as to achieve the substantive requirements of section 101.
   40 C.F.R. §1500.1(a).
6. State of New Mexico v. Bureau of Land Management, 565 F.3d 683, 703 (10th Cir. 2009).

The First Objective: Preventing Environmental Damage

Section 2 of NEPA expressly declares a purpose of promoting efforts that "will prevent or eliminate damage to the environment" while encouraging productive and enjoyable harmony between people and their environment.[7] Section 101 pursues this objective, declaring it the national environmental policy that the federal government use all practicable means to "fulfill the responsibilities of each generation as trustee of the environment for succeeding generations."[8]

Federal agencies' slighting of these responsibilities and overall lack of concern for environmental protection occasioned NEPA's passage. Congress had seen accumulating "evidence of environmental mismanagement,"[9] and it viewed increasing citizen indignation and protest over federal agency action or inaction as indicative of the "public's growing concern" about this mismanagement. Congress responded by enacting what NEPA's Senate author, the late Sen. Henry Jackson (D-Wash.), described as "the most important and far-reaching environmental and conservation measure ever enacted."[10] NEPA's House author was no less eloquent in his description of the Act's protective purpose. Rep. John Dingell (D-Mich.) spoke of man's exploitation and free use of the resources provided by his natural environment, "secure in his belief that nature's bounty would last forever, heedless of any consequences in his headlong push toward greater power and prosperity."[11] Dingell continued, "[w]e have not yet learned that we must consider the natural environment as a whole and assess its quality continuously if we really wish to make strides in improving and preserving it."[12] Congress determined that federal agencies would never again act without heed to the environment, declaring a "national policy to guide Federal activities which are involved with or related to the management of the environment or which have an impact on the quality of the environment."[13]

To ensure that federal agencies follow this policy, Congress created in NEPA a statute regulating those agencies.[14] Congress was aware that "if goals and principles are to be effective, they must be capable of being applied in action."[15] Hence, Congress incorporated "certain 'action-forcing' provisions and procedures . . . designed to assure that all Federal agencies plan and work toward meeting the challenge of a better environment."[16] The most important of these "action-forcing" devices is the EIS.[17]

---

7. 42 U.S.C. §4321, ELR Stat. NEPA §2.
8. *Id.* §4331, ELR Stat. NEPA §101.
9. *See* S. Rep. No. 296, 91st Cong., at 8 (1969). The report listed numerous examples of mismanagement, including both federal activities and federally authorized private activities. *Id.*
10. 115 Cong. Rec. 40416 (1969). Rep. Gordon Allott (R-Colo.), ranking House minority member and later Senator, stressed that it was "significant [that NEPA] enjoys the sponsorship of every single member of the Senate Interior Committee." 115 Cong. Rec. 40422 (1969). President Nixon dramatized NEPA's significance by signing it on January 1, 1970, as "my first official act of the decade." CEQ, Environmental Quality 1970, at viii (1970); *see* Nicholas C. Yost, *Streamlining NEPA—An Environmental Success Story*, 9 B.C. Envtl. Aff. L. Rev. 507 (1981-1982).
11. 115 Cong. Rec. 26571 (1969).
12. *Id.*
13. S. Rep. No. 296, *supra* note 9, at 8. Senator Jackson explained the national policy to the Senate before its final passage of NEPA: A statement of environmental policy is more than a statement of what we believe as a people and as a Nation. It establishes priorities and gives expression to our national goals and aspirations. It provides a statutory foundation to which administrators may refer... for guidance in making decisions which find environmental values in conflict with other values. What is involved is a congressional declaration that we do not intend, as a government or as a people, to initiate actions which endanger the continued existence or the health of mankind: That we will not intentionally initiate actions which will do irreparable damage to the air, land, and water which support life on earth. An environmental policy is for people. Its primary concern is with man and his future. The basic principle of the policy is that we must strive in all that we do, to achieve a standard of excellence in man's relationships to his physical surroundings. If there are to be departures from this standard of excellence they should be exceptions to the rule and the policy. And as exceptions, they will have to be justified in the light of the public scrutiny as required by section 102.
    115 Cong. Rec. 40416 (1969).
14. In cases involving federal permitting, leasing, or finding, the law necessarily affects private, state and local government, and tribal applicants to federal agencies as well as the agencies themselves.
15. S. Rep. No. 296, *supra* note 9, at 9.
16. *Id.* As the final bill came out of conference, Senator Jackson explained that "to insure that the policies and goals defined in this act are infused into the ongoing programs and actions of the Federal Government, the Act . . . establishes some important 'action-forcing' procedures." 115 Cong. Rec. 40416 (1969). According to CEQ's NEPA regulations, "section 102(2) contains 'action-forcing' provisions to make sure that federal agencies act according to the letter and spirit of the Act." 40 C.F.R. §1500.1(a). The "action-forcing" provisions of NEPA, particularly the EIS requirement, were part of the Senate bill, but not of the House bill; the legislative history of the EIS is found only in the Senate report. *See* S. Rep. No. 296, *supra* note 9; *see also* H.R. Conf. Rep. No. 765, 91st Cong. (1969), *reprinted in* 1969 U.S.C.C.A.N. 2767. *See generally* Robertson v. Methow Valley Citizens Council, 490 U.S. 332, 19 ELR 20743 (1989); Andrus v. Sierra Club, 442 U.S. 347, 350, 9 ELR 20390, 20391 (1979); Kleppe v. Sierra Club, 427 U.S. 390, 409, 6 ELR 20532, 20536-37 (1976).
17. According to CEQ's NEPA regulations, "the primary purpose of an environmental impact statement is to serve as an action-forcing device to insure that the policies and goals defined in the Act are infused into the ongoing programs and actions of the Federal Government."

The Second Objective: Ensuring That Agency Decisionmakers Take Environmental Factors Into Account

NEPA's "action-forcing" provisions, particularly those requiring EIS preparation, express Congress' second objective: Ensuring that federal agency decisionmakers give environmental factors appropriate consideration and weight. Informed, environmentally responsible decisionmaking is an objective in itself as well as the means by which Congress sought to achieve its other NEPA objective—environmental protection.[18] As the U.S. Court of Appeals for the District of Columbia Circuit has observed, uninformed decisionmaking is itself a harm that NEPA was meant to address and for which relief may be granted:

> The harm against which NEPA's impact statement requirement was directed was not solely or even primarily adverse consequences to the environment; such consequences may ensue despite the fullest compliance. Rather NEPA was intended to ensure that decisions about federal actions would be made only after responsible decision-makers had fully adverted to the environmental consequences of the actions, and had decided that the public benefits flowing from the actions outweighed their environmental costs. Thus, the harm with which courts must be concerned in NEPA cases is not, strictly speaking, harm to the environment, but rather the failure of decision-makers to take environmental factors into account in the way that NEPA mandates. And, for purposes of deciding whether equitable relief is appropriate, we think that this harm matures simultaneously with NEPA's requirements, i.e., at the time the agency is, under NEPA, obliged to file the impact statement and fails to do so.[19]

More recently the same court has accurately observed that "The idea behind NEPA is that if the agency's eyes are open to the environmental consequences of its actions, and it considers options that entail less environmental damage, it may be persuaded to alter what it proposed."[20] Or, as articulated by another circuit, NEPA's purpose is realized not through substantive mandates but through procedures which are "almost certain to affect the agency's substantive decision[s]."[21] That Court continued: "NEPA is not just a paper exercise, and new analyses may point in new directions."[22] The U.S. Supreme Court has long emphasized the procedural nature of NEPA's obligations. In that Court's words, "NEPA does set forth significant substantive goals for the Nation, but its mandate to the agencies is essentially procedural."[23]

---

40 C.F.R. §1502.1. The regulations also state that "ultimately, of course, it is not better documents but better decisions that count. NEPA's purpose is not to generate paperwork—even excellent paperwork—but to foster excellent action." *Id.* §1500.1(c).

18. As the U.S. Supreme Court has stated in *Robertson*, "[B]y focusing the agency's attention on the environmental consequences of a proposed project, NEPA ensures that important effects will not be over-looked or underestimated only to be discovered after resources have been committed or the die otherwise cast." 490 U.S. at 349, 19 ELR at 20746; *see also* Marsh v. Oregon Natural Resources Council (ONRC), 490 U.S. 360, 19 ELR 20749 (1989).

19. Jones v. District of Columbia Redev. Land Agency, 499 F.2d 502, 512, 4 ELR 20479, 20483 (D.C. Cir. 1974), *cert. denied*, 423 U.S. 937 (1975) (footnote omitted). Unlike the substantive policy of the Act, which is flexible and allows for responsible exercise of discretion, "the Act also contains very important 'procedural' provisions—provisions which are designed to see that all federal agencies do in fact exercise substantive discretion given them." Calvert Cliffs Coord. Comm., Inc. v. Atomic Energy Comm'n, 449 F.2d 1109, 1112, 1 ELR 20346, 20347 (D.C. Cir. 1971), *cert. denied*, 404 U.S. 942 (1972); *see* Sierra Club v. Sigler, 695 F.2d 957, 965-67, 13 ELR 20210, 20214 (5th Cir. 1983). These procedural provisions "are not highly flexible." *Calvert Cliffs*, 449 F.2d at 1112, 1 ELR at 20347. "Indeed, they establish a strict standard of compliance." *Id.* Specifically, the decision to prepare an EIS "is not committed to the agency's discretion." Foundation for N. Am. Wild Sheep v. Department of Agric., 681 F.2d 1172, 1177 n.24, 12 ELR 20968, 20969 n.24 (9th Cir. 1982). NEPA's importance lies not only in the aid it gives the agency's decisionmaking process, but also in the notice it gives the public of environmental issues, both those that the agency is aware of and those that it has missed. Illinois Commerce Comm'n v. Interstate Commerce Comm'n, 848 F.2d 1246, 1260 (D.C. Cir. 1968), *cert. denied*, 488 U.S. 1004 (1989). In the Supreme Court's words, the EIS
> ensures that the agency, in reaching its decision, will have available and will carefully consider detailed information concerning significant environmental impacts; it also guarantees that the relevant information will be made available to the larger audience that may also play a role in both the decisionmaking process and the implementation of that decision. . . . Publication of an EIS, both in draft and final form, also serves a larger informational role. It gives the public the assurance that the agency "has indeed considered environmental concerns in its decisionmaking process," and, perhaps more significantly, provides a springboard for public comment.
Robertson, 490 U.S. at 349, 19 ELR at 20746 (citation omitted); *see ONRC*, 490 U.S. at 372-73, 19 ELR at 20752.

20. Lemon v. Geren, 514 F.3d 1312, 1315 (D.C. Cir. 2008).

21. Oregon Natural Desert Ass'n. v. Bureau of Land Management, 531 F.3d 1114, 1121 (9th Cir. 2008).

22. *Id.* at 1145.

23. Vermont Yankee Nuclear Power Corp. v. Natural Resources Defense Council, 435 U.S. 519, 558, 8 ELR 20288, 20297 (1978). The Court continued that administrative decisions should be set aside "only for substantial procedural or substantive reasons as mandated by statute." *Id.*; *see Robertson*, 490 U.S. at 350, 19 ELR at 20747.

In crafting these "action-forcing procedures," Congress envisioned a scheme of agency self-regulation; it did not create a regulatory body to enforce compliance.[24] This is why judicial enforcement of the Act is so important. The binding Council on Environmental Quality's (CEQ's) NEPA regulations clearly make all federal actors joint partners in implementing NEPA, stating that "[t]he President, the federal agencies, and the courts share responsibility for enforcing the Act."[25]

Agency Responsibilities Under NEPA

NEPA and subsequent legislation establish different roles for different agencies. The Act created the CEQ.[26] Since NEPA is directed at "all agencies of the Federal Government,"[27] however, every federal agency plays a role in its implementation. One such agency occupies a special dual position: The U.S. Environmental Protection Agency (EPA) is both an entity regulated under NEPA and a co-participant with the CEQ in the process of overseeing NEPA compliance by other federal agencies.

CEQ

NEPA's House sponsors considered creation of the CEQ the landmark achievement of the new legislation.[28] Congress modeled the new agency on the Council of Economic Advisers (CEA), an organization within the Executive Office of the President (EOP) that gives the President general advice on economic issues. Congress intended that the CEQ provide the same sort of pervasive advice concerning the environment.[29] The "only precedent and parallel to what is proposed," said Senator Jackson, was the Full Employment Act of 1946 which declared the national economic policy and established the CEA.[30]

President Richard M. Nixon originally charged the CEQ with various environmental oversight responsibilities, including adoption of "guidelines" for all agencies' implementation of NEPA's EIS requirement.[31] President Jimmy Carter strengthened the CEQ's role and authority: The CEQ "guidelines" became mandatory regulations, and their scope was broadened beyond EISs to include all "the procedural provisions of the Act."[32] The regulations, which in large part codified existing case law, became effective in 1979.[33] The Supreme Court subsequently described the new measures as a "single set of uniform, mandatory regulations" adopted through a "detailed and comprehensive process, ordered by the President, of transforming advisory guidelines into mandatory regulations applicable to all Federal agencies."[34] Those regulations

24. The CEQ does have NEPA oversight responsibilities, but, as a modestly sized agency within the Executive Office of the President (EOP), it does not have the resources to become involved in individual cases, except in the rare instance when, based on an EIS, an agency head believes that another agency's proposal is so environmentally harmful that EOP resolution of the issue is merited. The project is then referred to the CEQ, whose power depends largely on persuasion. 40 C.F.R. pt. 1504. *See* 42 U.S.C. §7609, ELR Stat. CAA §309; *infra* notes 265-71 and accompanying text.

25. 40 C.F.R. §1500.1(a); *see id.* §1500.6. Despite the mandate on all federal participants, "the substantive backbone of NEPA ultimately is dependent upon the courts' willingness to order agencies to change their plans or to abandon some pursuits." William H. Rodgers Jr., Handbook on Environmental Law 805 (1977).

26. 42 U.S.C. §4341, ELR Stat. NEPA §201.

27. *Id.* §4332(2), ELR Stat. NEPA §102(2).

28. Senate sponsors, on the other hand, viewed as the critical accomplishment of the new Act the linkage between the congressional statement of policy and the "action-forcing procedures devised to achieve that policy." *Compare* 115 Cong. Rec. 26571-91 (1969) (remarks of Representative Dingell) *and* H.R. Rep. No. 378, 91st Cong. (1969), *reprinted in* 1969 U.S.C.C.A.N. 2751, *with* 115 Cong. Rec. 40416 (1969) (remarks of Senator Jackson).

29. *See* S. Rep. No. 296, *supra* note 9, at 10; H.R. Rep. No. 378, *supra* note 28, at 9, *reprinted in* 1969 U.S.C.C.A.N. at 2759; *see also* Pacific Legal Found. v. Council on Envtl. Quality, 636 F.2d 1259, 1263-64, 10 ELR 20919, 20920 (D.C. Cir. 1980).

30. 115 Cong. Rec. 40416 (1969) (remarks of Senator Jackson).

31. Exec. Order No. 11514, §3(h), 3 C.F.R. pt. 904, Admin. Mat. 45001.

32. Exec. Order No. 11991, §2(g) ¶ 3(h), 3 C.F.R. pts. 124-125.

33. 40 C.F.R. §§1500-1508. The regulatory history of CEQ's NEPA regulations appears largely in the preamble that accompanied their publication in the *Federal Register*. 43 Fed. Reg. 55978 (Nov. 29, 1978). CEQ published its official explanations of the meaning of certain provisions in *Forty Most Asked Questions Concerning CEQ's National Environmental Policy Act Regulations.* 46 Fed. Reg. 18026 (Mar. 23, 1981) [hereinafter *Forty Questions*] (available from the ELR Document Service, ELR Order No. AD-00629); *see* 51 Fed. Reg. 15618 (Apr. 25, 1986) (question 20 withdrawn). CEQ has since issued further guidance, some of which appears in this volume. For further background see *Hearings on Implementation of the National Environmental Policy Act by the Council on Environmental Quality, Subcomm. on Toxic Substances and Envtl. Oversight,* Senate Comm. on Env't and Pub. Works, 97th Cong. 77-83 (1983); *Hearings on Council on Environmental Quality Reauthorization and Oversight, Subcomm. on Fisheries and Wildlife Conservation and the Env't, Comm. on Merchant Marine and Fisheries,* 98th Cong. 40-42 (1984) [hereinafter *CEQ Reauthorization and Oversight Hearing*]; Yost, *supra* note 10.

34. Andrus v. Sierra Club, 442 U.S. 347, 357-58, 9 ELR 20390, 20393(1979); *see* Robertson v. Methow Valley Citizens Council, 490 U.S. 332, 348-53, 19 ELR 20743, 20746-48 (1989).

remain in effect today, with only one section having been amended in the more than two decades since their adoption.[35]

The Supreme Court stated that the "CEQ's interpretation of NEPA is entitled to substantial deference."[36] As a corollary to that deference owing the CEQ, it is important to keep in mind that no deference is due to other agencies' interpretations of NEPA.[37] The agencies undertaking the action that is the subject of the NEPA analysis are the very agencies being regulated by NEPA—hardly the entities to which to defer in interpreting the statute.

The CEQ is an organization of modest size within the EOP,[38] and its limited resources preclude extensive involvement in individual NEPA problems. Thus, its participation in the NEPA process is largely generic. The CEQ adopts regulations applicable to all agencies and oversees adoption of individual agency implementing procedures.[39] It gets directly involved with individual issues only on rare occasions, such as when it receives "referrals" from EPA under §309 of the Clean Air Act (CAA) or from other agencies under part 1504 of the CEQ regulations.[40] The CEQ will also involve itself in an occasional project or program visible enough to warrant a diversion of its limited resources.[41]

From time to time CEQ issues informal "guidance," usually in the form of Memoranda to the Heads of Agencies, on the implementation of NEPA. (These documents are available at http://energy.gov/nepa/council-environmental-quality).[42] Three recent instances involve such memoranda addressing:

- Improving the Process for Preparing Efficient and Timely Environmental Reviews under NEPA (reprinted as App. 26 to this Deskbook).

- Use of Mitigation and Monitoring and Mitigated Findings of No Significant Impact (App. 27).

- Use of Categorical Exclusions (App. 28).

It is important to bear in mind that while these guidance documents do not establish new law, they d perform the valuable functions of both marshalling references to the appropriate regulations and indicating areas which an Administration chooses to emphasize in implementing NEPA.

EPA

EPA occupies a position somewhere between the CEQ and other federal agencies. Like the CEQ, EPA is a participant in the process of overseeing other agencies' preparation of EISs. Yet EPA is also a federal agency regulated under NEPA, so it must prepare EISs for certain of its own environmentally protective actions.[43]

EPA came to play this unique role partly as a result of a statutory attempt to bridge two approaches to environmental legislation. Under Senator Jackson's environmental charter approach, embodied in NEPA, Congress gave an all-embracing directive and left administrators to fill in the details. Under Senator

35. 40 C.F.R. §1502.22, dealing with "Incomplete or Unavailable Information," was amended in 1986. 51 Fed. Reg. 15625 (Apr. 25, 1986).
36. *Andrus*, 442 U.S. at 358, 9 ELR at 20393; *see also Robertson*, 490 U.S. at 355-56, 19 ELR at 20748; Marsh v. Oregon Natural Resources Council, 490 U.S. 360, 377, 19 ELR 20749, 20753 (1989).
37. Citizens Against Rails-to-Rails v. Surface Transp. Bd., 267 F.3d 1144, 1155 (D.C. Cir. 2001); American Airlines v. Department of Transp., 202 F.3d 788, 803 (5th Cir. 2000); Alaska Ctr. for the Env't v. West, 31 F. Supp. 2d. 714, 721 (D. Alaska 1988), *aff'd*, 157 F.3d 680, 29 ELR 20001 (9th Cir. 1998).
38. While Presidents Nixon, Ford, Carter, and Reagan appointed the full Council of three members, the two Presidents Bush and President Clinton have appointed only the chair. The size of the staff has varied from about 10 (under President Reagan) to about 70 (under Presidents Nixon, Ford, and Carter).
39. 40 C.F.R. §1507.3.
40. 42 U.S.C. §7609, ELR Stat. CAA §309; 40 C.F.R. pt. 1504; *see infra* Ch. 2 notes 207-13 and accompanying text.
41. For example, the CEQ has been involved in the U.S. Department of the Army's decisionmaking process regarding disposal of chemical weapons stockpiles. *See* CEQ, Environmental Quality 1985, at 149-58 (1986). For a discussion of the range of the CEQ's responsibilities, see generally *CEQ Reauthorization and Oversight Hearing, supra* note 33, at 34-36.
42. The NEPA.gov website contains the comprehensive compendium of NEPA documents, but the site is currently down and is being reconstructed.
43. While in 1986 EPA ranked fifth, tied with the Department of Housing and Urban Development, in production of EISs, CEQ, Environmental Quality 1986, at 245-47 tbl. B-6 (1988), it ranked only 15th in 1992, CEQ, Environmental Quality 1993, at 351 (1994). In the CEQ's last report, that for 1997, EPA produced only five EISs. CEQ, Environmental Quality 1997, at 357 (1998). Many EPA impact statements are occasioned by sewage treatment plant construction or issuance of national pollution discharge elimination system permits under the Clean Water Act (CWA). Other EPA actions have been either statutorily exempted from NEPA or found by courts to be exempt because they provide "functional equivalents" of NEPA procedures. *See infra* Ch. 3, notes 45-47 and accompanying text.

Muskie's approach, embodied in the CAA, a wary Congress gave far more detailed directives and left considerably less scope for agency discretion. In the CAA, passed one year after NEPA, Congress expressly made EPA the environmental evaluator of all agencies' actions by requiring it to review and comment on the environmental impact of other agencies' projects subject to the EIS requirement.[44] Under this authority, EPA not only comments generally on the impact of other agencies' proposals, but publicly rates the quality of their EISs.[45] EPA also coordinates EIS public notice and distribution procedures by publishing notices of all EISs when they are filed with it.[46] EPA must refer other agencies' actions to the CEQ if it finds them environmentally unsound.[47]

Other Federal Agencies

NEPA makes "all agencies of the Federal Government" participants in pursuing the goal of environmental protection.[48] Only Congress,[49] the judiciary, and the President are excluded from this broad mandate.[50] NEPA §102 requires that agencies "to the fullest extent possible" administer their laws in accordance with the national environmental policy and implement the action-forcing provisions of the Act.[51] According to the conference committee report on NEPA, this phrase means that agencies are expected to comply with the Act to the fullest extent possible under their statutory authorizations. They are not to interpret the words so as to avoid compliance, nor are they to construe their statutory authorizations excessively narrowly.[52] Indeed, the Act states that its policies and goals are supplementary to those in agencies' existing statutory authorizations.[53] NEPA thus makes environmental protection the mandate of every federal agency.[54] Each agency must adopt its own NEPA procedures consistent with and to assist in implementing CEQ's NEPA regulations.[55]

---

44. Section 309 provides:

    Policy Review. (a) The Administrator shall review and comment in writing on the environmental impact of any matter relating to duties and responsibilities granted pursuant to this chapter or other provisions of the authority of the Administrator, contained in any (1) legislation proposed by any federal department or agency, (2) newly authorized federal projects for construction and any major federal agency action (other than a project for construction) to which section 4332(2)(C) of this title applies, and (3) proposed regulations published by any department or agency of the Federal Government. Such written comment shall be made public at the conclusion of any such review.

    (b) In the event the Administrator determines that any such legislation, action, or regulation is unsatisfactory from the standpoint of public health or welfare or environmental quality, he shall publish his determination and the matter shall be referred to the Council on Environmental Quality.

    42 U.S.C. §7609, ELR Stat. CAA §309. For discussion of Senator Muskie's intentions regarding this important section, see Fred R. Anderson, NEPA in the Courts 230-31 (1973); Fred R. Anderson, Federal Environmental Law 268-69 (1974).

45. *See, e.g.,* 49 Fed. Reg. 41108 (Oct. 19, 1984). These ratings, of course, can be and are used by litigants to bolster their cases. At the same time, while an agency must consider and explain why it considers EPA's comments unpersuasive, the agency is not obliged to defer to those comments. Alaska Survival v. Surface Transportation Board, 705 F.3d 1073, 1087 (9th Cir. 2013).

46. 40 C.F.R. §1506.9-.10.

47. 42 U.S.C. §7609(b), ELR Stat. CAA §309(b); *see infra* Ch. 2 notes 207-13 and accompanying text.

48. 42 U.S.C. §4332(2), ELR Stat. NEPA §102(2).

49. In some situations, a proposal to Congress by the executive branch or an independent regulatory agency requires an EIS. 42 U.S.C. §4332(2)(C), ELR Stat. NEPA §102(2)(C); 40 C.F.R. §§1506.8, 1508.17.

50. *See* Public Citizen v. U.S. Trade Representative, 5 F.3d 549, 23 ELR 21471 (D.C. Cir. 1993). Performance of staff functions for the President in the EOP is also excluded. 40 C.F.R. §1508.12. For NEPA purposes a "federal agency" may include a state or local government or an Indian tribe that assumes NEPA responsibilities as a condition of receiving funds under §104(h) of the Housing and Community Development Act of 1974, 42 U.S.C. §5304(a). 40 C.F.R. §1508.12.

51. The Supreme Court has interpreted the term "fullest extent possible" as furthering NEPA's environmental mandate. *See* Flint Ridge Dev. Co. v. Scenic Rivers Ass'n, 426 U.S. 776, 6 ELR 20528 (1976).

52. H.R. Conf. Rep. No. 765, *supra* note 16, at 3, *reprinted in* 1969 U.S.C.C.A.N. at 2770.

53. 42 U.S.C. §4335, ELR Stat. NEPA §105. A more ambiguous provision was intended to harmonize NEPA and the pollution abatement legislation simultaneously considered by Congress. *Id.* §4334, ELR Stat. NEPA §104. The somewhat uneasy result is discussed *infra* Ch. 3 note 1 and accompanying text.

54. Calvert Cliffs Coordinating Comm., Inc. v. Atomic Energy Comm'n, 449 F.2d 1109, 1112, 1 ELR 20346, 20347 (D.C. Cir. 1971). For examples of judicial approval of agencies' use of NEPA to expand their mandates, see Detroit Edison Co. v. Nuclear Regulatory Comm'n, 630 F.2d 540, 10 ELR 20879 (6th Cir. 1980); Gulf Oil Corp. v. Morton, 493 F.2d 141, 4 ELR 20086 (9th Cir. 1973); Zabel v. Tabb, 430 F.2d 199, 1 ELR 20023 (5th Cir. 1970), *cert. denied,* 401 U.S. 910 (1971).

55. 40 C.F.R. §1507.3. The CEQ must, in turn, approve these agency procedures. *Id. See* Piedmont Environmental Council v. FERC, 558 F.3d 304, 317-19 (4th Cir. 2009) (an agency's procedures revised without consulting CEQ are invalid); Michigan Gaming Opposition v. Kempthorne, 525 F.3d 23, 28-29 (D.C. Cir. 2008) (agency not bound to follow its "checklist," which was not part of its CEQ-approved procedures). Each agency has its own NEPA liaison, the most recent listing of whom appears at CEQ, *Federal NEPA Contacts, at* http://energy.gov/nepa/downloads/federal-nepa-contacts (last visited Dec. 19, 2013).

Numbers of Environmental Documents Prepared

In analyzing NEPA's application to the range of federal activity, the number of documents prepared gives some indication of its pervasive nature as well as the rigor of the law's enforcement. Throughout it is important to bear in mind that vastly more environmental assessments (EAs) are prepared than are EISs. The average number of draft, revised, supplemental, and final EISs prepared annually has declined from approximately 2,000 in the early 1970s[56] to approximately 450 in the late 1990s.[57] By way of contrast, CEQ estimates that roughly 50,000 EAs are prepared annually.[58]

---

56. CEQ, ENVIRONMENTAL QUALITY 1994-1995, at 51 (1996).
57. CEQ, *Considering Cumulative Impacts Under the National Environmental Policy Act*, at 4 (1997), available at http://energy.gov/nepa/downloads/considering-cumulative-effects-under-national-environmental-policy-act.
58. *Id.*

II. The Administrative Process Under NEPA

Introduction

NEPA's administrative process is most easily understood when it is examined chronologically. Because the EIS is the most conspicuous part of the process,[1] the following discussion is organized chronologically by reference to the EIS. The discussion first covers prestatement procedures—early planning, followed by the decision on whether and when an EIS is required. It then proceeds through preparation of the statement, and finally describes post-statement procedures. This approach parallels the organization of the CEQ regulations, which trace the NEPA administrative process chronologically from agency planning,[2] through EIS preparation,[3] to commenting[4] and referrals of environmentally unsatisfactory projects to the CEQ,[5] and finally to agency decisions and their implementation.[6]

Other procedural requirements are also summarized throughout the discussion, for while litigation has concentrated largely on the EIS requirement and on the requirement of considering alternatives in less detail in EAs,[7] the administrative process shaping all federal agency activity in light of environmental considerations is pervasive. CEQ's NEPA regulations encapsulate the various procedural requirements, in large part codifying case law and the administrative experience of NEPA's early years. Those regulations discuss NEPA's purpose,[8] provide uniform terminology,[9] make clear what agencies must do to comply with NEPA,[10] and summarize various other NEPA requirements.[11] Throughout the analysis of NEPA's administrative process, it is important to remember that all of NEPA's procedural requirements must be strictly observed.[12]

It is also useful to remember that the procedural requirements are to be interpreted in light of NEPA's purposes.[13] The procedures of §102 are, after all, merely means of carrying out the policies of §101.[14] Ulti-

---

1. 42 U.S.C. §4332(2)(C), ELR Stat. NEPA §102(2)(C). While NEPA §102(2)(E) also requires agencies to consider alternatives, independent of the requirement that they prepare EISs, it is the EIS process that has occasioned the bulk of the litigation under NEPA. 42 U.S.C. §4332(2)(E), ELR Stat. NEPA §102(2)(E).
2. 40 C.F.R. pt. 1501.
3. *Id.* pt. 1502.
4. *Id.* pt. 1503.
5. *Id.* pt. 1504.
6. *Id.* pt. 1505.
7. *Id.* §1508.9.
8. *Id.* pt. 1500.
9. *Id.* pt. 1508.
10. *Id.* pt. 1507.
11. *Id.* pt. 1506.
12. Calvert Cliffs Coordinating Comm., Inc. v. Atomic Energy Comm'n, 449 F.2d 1109, 1112, 1 ELR 20346, 20347 (D.C. Cir. 1971). The NEPA regulations do caution that "trivial violations" are not intended to give rise to independent causes of action. 40 C.F.R. §1500.3.
13. *See generally* 40 C.F.R. pt. 1500.
14. *See* NEPA §102(1), 42 U.S.C. §4332(1) ("the policies, regulations, and public laws of the United States shall be interpreted and administered in accordance with the policies set forth in this Act . . ."). 40 C.F.R. §1500.1. The CEQ regulations stress that the President, federal agencies, and the courts share responsibility for enforcing the Act so as to achieve the substantive requirements of §101. *Id.* §1500.1(a).

mately, the regulations caution that "it is not better documents but better decisions that count."[15] NEPA's purpose is "not to generate paperwork—even excellent paperwork—but to foster excellent action."[16]

Above all, it should be stressed that although the Act forces decisionmakers to pay heed to environmental factors, CEQ's NEPA regulations are also designed to reduce paperwork[17] and delay.[18] Implementation of NEPA's administrative procedures must be sensitive to these two goals.[19]

Prestatement Procedures

Procedures for Determining Whether an EIS Is Required

The NEPA process begins with agency planning[20] and requires that environmental considerations be integrated into that planning.[21] CEQ's NEPA regulations give agencies detailed guidance on how to accomplish this integration.[22] They also provide direction for situations in which an applicant, rather than a federal agency, is developing a proposal.[23]

Once an agency begins to plan an action, it must determine whether it must complete an EIS on the proposed action. This threshold determination is governed by NEPA, CEQ's NEPA regulations, and the agency's own procedures. Agency actions can be divided into three categories.[24] First, agency procedures may provide for "categorical exclusions"[25] of categories of actions that individually or cumulatively do not have significant effects on the environment.[26] Since actions in these categories do not require EISs, the agency may simply proceed with them.[27] Second, agency procedures may specify cases that normally do require EISs; in such cases, the agency undertakes the process leading to EIS preparation.[28] Third, an agency may not have decided in advance whether a given type of action requires an EIS. In such a situation—the occasion for both disputes and litigation—the agency is to prepare an EA before proceeding.[29]

While CEQ's NEPA regulations set out the minimum requirements for considering environmental impacts, NEPA always permits agencies to do more if they choose. Thus, if a situation is categorically excluded, an agency could decide to prepare an EA or EIS anyway. Similarly, if an EA would initially suffice, the agency could nonetheless undertake an EIS directly without first preparing an EA. Agencies may do this to address or avoid controversy, or when they genuinely desire the additional environmental analysis that more complete documentation would provide. Conversely, once an agency has completed its "action," NEPA imposes no ongoing obligation to continue to document environmental impacts.[30]

- *The Categorical Exclusion.* As noted above, the use of categorical exclusions enables an agency, in advance of the subject action, to adopt procedures that provide that actions that individually and

---

15. 40 C.F.R. §1500.1(c).
16. *Id.*
17. *Id.* §1500.4.
18. *Id.* §1500.5.
19. *See* Exec. Order No. 11991; *see* the CEQ memorandum on efficient and timely environmental reviews, which appears as App. 26 to this Deskbook.
20. 40 C.F.R. pt. 1501.
21. *Id.* §1501.1(a).
22. *Id.* §1501.2.
23. *Id.* §1501.2(d).
24. Of course, for NEPA to apply, there must be an underlying "action." *See* Grand Canyon Trust v. U.S. Bureau of Reclamation, 691 F.3d 1008, 1022 (9th Cir. 2012) (NEPA doesn't apply to routine annual reporting); Minard Run Oil Co. v. U.S. Forest Services, 670 F.3d 236, 242 (3d Cir. 2011) (in a split estate context, NEPA does not apply to notice to proceed with respect to privately owned mineral rights); *but see* Karuk Tribe v. U.S. Forest Service, 681 F.3d 1006, 1021-22 (9th Cir. 2012) (en banc) (Court construes "agency action" broadly in Endangered Species Act context.).
25. 40 C.F.R. §1507.3(b)(2)(ii); *see* Sierra Club v. Bosworth, 510 F.3d 1016, 1027 (9th Cir. 2007) (allowing challenge to categorical exclusion); Wong v. Bush, 542 F.3d 732, 737 (9th Cir. 2008) (if categorically excluded, EIS requirements inapplicable).
26. 40 C.F.R. §1508.4.
27. *Id.* §1501.4(a)(2). *See infra* notes 30-33 and accompanying text.
28. 40 C.F.R. §1507.3(b)(2)(i); *see id.* §§1501.3(a), 1501.4(a)(1).
29. *Id.* §§1501.4(b), 1508.9.
30. Norton v. Southern Utah Wilderness Alliance, 124 S.Ct. 2373, 2384-85 (2004). Of course, if the criteria for a supplemental EIS are met (40 C.F.R. §1502.9(c)) or if ongoing monitoring or mitigation has been provided (40 C.F.R. §§1505.2, 1505.3), then the agencies' duties are ongoing.

cumulatively have no significant environmental impacts require neither an EA nor an EIS.[31] However, in its procedures the agency must provide for "extraordinary circumstances" in which a normally excluded action may have a significant environmental effect warranting further NEPA analysis.[32] Generally deference is due to an agency in its construction of its own categorical exclusions,[33] but courts have been increasingly apt to scrutinize agencies' use of categorical exclusions.[34]

- *The EA.* The EA is a concise public document designed to provide sufficient evidence and analysis for an agency to determine whether to prepare an EIS or a finding of no significant impact (FONSI).[35] An EA may also help an agency comply with NEPA when no EIS is needed,[36] and may facilitate preparation of an EIS when one is needed.[37] An EA must include brief discussions of the need for the proposed action, the alternatives required under NEPA §102(2)(E), and the environmental impacts of both the proposed action and the alternatives.[38] The EA must also list the agencies and persons consulted during its preparation.[39]

- *The FONSI.* Preparation of an EA can lead to one of two results. If the agency finds, based on the EA, that its proposal will have no significant impact on the environment, it prepares a FONSI, and no EIS is required.[40] A FONSI is a document briefly explaining why the proposal will have no such impact. A FONSI must include the EA or a summary of it and must note any other environmental documents related to the EA.[41]

If, however, the agency determines in its EA that there may or will be a significant environmental impact, it takes the first steps toward preparing an EIS.[42]

Definitions of Terms Regarding When an EIS Is Required: Proposals for Major Federal Actions Significantly Affecting the Quality of the Human Environment

NEPA never actually uses the phrase "environmental impact statement." Rather, it requires a "detailed statement" that includes discussions of various environmental impacts.[43] This statement is to be included by all agencies in "every recommendation or report on proposals for legislation and other major Federal actions significantly affecting the quality of the human environment."[44] CEQ's NEPA regulations elaborate on every word or phrase in this, the most litigated language in NEPA.

- *"Proposal."* The regulations define the term "proposal" largely in terms of timing. A "proposal" exists when an agency has a goal and is actively preparing to make a decision on one or more means of

---

31. 40 C.F.R. §§1507.3(b)(2)(ii), 1508.4; *see* the CEQ memorandum on Categorical Exclusions, which appears as App. 28.
32. 40 C.F.R. §1508.4; *see* Rhodes v. Johnson, 153 F.3d 785, 29 ELR 20092 (7th Cir. 1998) (court concludes that since "extraordinary circumstances" under agency's own regulations are present, the categorical exclusion found by the agency is invalid and an EA must be prepared).
33. City of Alexandria v. Federal Highway Admin., 756 F.2d 1014, 1020-21 (4th Cir. 1985); *see* Cellular Phone Task Force v. Federal Communications Comm'n, 205 F.3d 82, 30 ELR 20402 (2d Cir. 2000) (categorical exclusion upheld).
34. *See* West v. Secretary of the Dep't of Transp., 206 F.3d 920, 30 ELR 20444 (9th Cir. 2000) (use of categorical exclusions overruled because a project cannot be said to relieve traffic congestion while simultaneously having no impact); Save Our Heritage v. Federal Aviation Admin., 269 F.3d 49, 32 ELR 20290 (1st Cir. 2001) (categorical exclusion upheld but only after close judicial scrutiny); People of the State of California v. U.S. Department of Agriculture, 575 F.3d 999 (9th Cir. 2009) (court rejects agency's use of categorical exclusion).
35. 40 C.F.R. §1508.9(a)(1). The EA finds its statutory basis in §102(2)(E) of NEPA, which imposes its own alternative analysis requirement distinct from that imposed by §102(2)(C) for EISs. Surfrider Found. v. Dalton, 989 F. Supp. 1309, 1325 (S.D. Cal. 1998), *aff'd* on the basis of the District Court opinion sub nom. San Diego Chapter of the Surfrider Found. v. Dalton, 196 F.3d 1057 (9th Cir. 1997). Generally an EA must include sufficient analytical data to support the decision. Idaho Sporting Congress v. Thomas, 137 F.2d 1146, 28 ELR 21044 (9th Cir. 1998).
36. 40 C.F.R. §1508.9(a)(2).
37. *Id.* §1508.9(a)(3).
38. One circuit has observed that in the context of an EA, if there are fewer environmental consequences, fewer alternatives need be examined to address those consequences. Save Our Cumberland Mountains v. Kempthorne, 453 F.3d 334 (6th Cir. 2006).
39. 40 C.F.R. §1508.9(b). Whether public comment is required on an EA depends on the circumstances of the action involved. Bering Straits Citizens for Responsible Resource Development v. U.S. Army Corps of Engineers, 511 F.3d 1011, 1025 (9th Cir. 2008).
40. 40 C.F.R. §1501.4(e).
41. *Id.* §1508.13. A FONSI that includes an EA need not repeat the discussion in the EA but may incorporate it by reference. *Id.*; *see* the CEQ memorandum on mitigated FONSIs, which appears as App. 27.
42. 40 C.F.R. §§1501.4(d), 1508.3, 1508.11.
43. 42 U.S.C. §4332(2)(C), ELR Stat. NEPA §102(2)(C); *see* 40 C.F.R. §1508.11.
44. 42 U.S.C. §4332(2)(C), ELR Stat. NEPA §102(2)(C); *see* 40 C.F.R. §1502.3.

accomplishing it, and the effects of that decision can be meaningfully evaluated.[45] This definition essentially steers a line between two sets of concerns. First, the Supreme Court has held that EISs are not required until prospective proposals are more concrete than mere contemplation.[46] Second, both administrators and applicants share a concern that a delayed start on an EIS can delay the project, while those concerned with the environment want to ensure that environmental factors are incorporated as part of project development. The regulations require that an EIS be timed so that it will be complete and ready to be included in the agency's report or recommendation on the proposal.[47]

Proposals for legislation differ from other agency proposals for action in that the agency has no control over the action that is the subject of the EIS—the legislation. Rather, that control lies with a congressional committee. CEQ's NEPA regulations reflect this difference by providing a modified set of administrative procedures for legislative proposals, integrating the NEPA process with the legislative process.[48] On a related matter, the Supreme Court has upheld the CEQ's determination that NEPA's legislative EIS requirement does not extend to requests for appropriations.[49]

• *"Other Major Federal Actions."* In contrast to the modified requirements for proposals for legislation, the NEPA procedures for proposals for "other major Federal actions"[50] are more commonly used because these actions occasion the preparation of most EISs. "Other major Federal actions" are defined broadly to include "projects and programs entirely or partly financed, assisted, conducted, regulated, or approved by federal agencies; new or revised agency rules, regulations, plans, policies, or procedures; and legislative proposals."[51] Federal activities that may occasion EISs thus fall into four categories, sometimes known as the "four Ps"—policies, plans, programs, and projects.[52]

CEQ's NEPA regulations further define the term to include actions potentially subject to federal control and responsibility.[53] The regulations also state that "major" reinforces but has no meaning independent of "significantly."[54] This CEQ determination follows a well-reasoned line of cases[55] and was quoted with apparent approval by the Supreme Court in *Andrus v. Sierra Club*.[56] Finally, the regulations provide that in certain circumstances, a failure to act can also be an "action."[57]

---

45. 40 C.F.R. §1508.23.
46. Kleppe v. Sierra Club, 427 U.S. 390, 6 ELR 20532 (1976); *see also* Montana Ecosystems Defense Council v. Espy, 15 F.3d 1087, 24 ELR 20501 (9th Cir. 1994).
47. 40 C.F.R. §1508.23.
48. *Id.* §§1506.8, 1508.17, 1508.18(a). Only a limited number of EISs are prepared on proposals for legislation. *See* Dinah Bear, *NEPA at 19: A Primer*, 19 ELR 10060, 10067-68 (Feb. 1989) (discussing inattention to legislative EISs).
49. *See* Andrus v. Sierra Club, 442 U.S. 347, 9 ELR 20390 (1979); 40 C.F.R. §1508.17.
50. 42 U.S.C. §4332(2)(C), ELR STAT. NEPA §102(2)(C); 40 C.F.R. §1508.18.
51. 40 C.F.R. §1508.18(a).
52. *Id.* §1508.18(b).
53. *Id.* §1508.18. Ramsey v. Kantor, 96 F.3d 434, 445, 27 ELR 20158, 20161 (9th Cir. 1996). For a discussion of what is "federal," see WILLIAM H. RODGERS JR., HANDBOOK ON ENVIRONMENTAL LAW 761 (1977); William B. Ellis & Turner T. Smith Jr., *The Limits of Federal Environmental Responsibility and Control Under the National Environmental Policy Act*, 18 ELR 10055 (Feb. 1988). By way of examples when federal involvement was held to be so minimal as not to constitute major federal action, see Macht v. Skinner, 916 F.2d 13, 21 ELR 20004 (D.C. Cir. 1990) (Urban Mass Transportation Authority funding of preliminary studies does not rise to the level of major federal action); *see also* Maryland Conservation Council v. Gilchrist, 408 F.2d 1039, 17 ELR 20499 (4th Cir. 1986) (need for at least one federal approval); Village of Los Ranchos de Albuquerque v. Barnhart, 906 F.2d 1477, 20 ELR 21433 (10th Cir. 1990) (though eligible for federal funding, did not seek it; federal location study funds minuscule proportion of total); United States v. 0.95 Acres of Land, 994 F.2d 696, 23 ELR 20997 (9th Cir. 1993) (filing of condemnation proceeding not a major federal action); Foundation for Horses & Other Wild Animals v. Babbitt, 154 F.3d 1103, 29 ELR 20099 (9th Cir. 1998) (no federal involvement making NEPA applicable); Ross v. Federal Highway Admin., 162 F.3d 1046, 29 ELR 20342 (10th Cir. 1998) (disallows state attempt to defederalize portions of project to avoid NEPA); Southwest Williamson County Community Ass'n v. Slater, 243 F.3d 270, 279-86, 31 ELR 20504 (6th Cir. 2000) (court applies two-part test of restricting alternatives and agency responsibility). The courts have also discussed the related legal issue whether a "small [federal] handle" is sufficient to invoke federal responsibility under NEPA. *See* Sylvester v. U.S. Army Corps of Eng'rs, 884 F.2d 394, 19 ELR 20652 (9th Cir. 1989).
54. 40 C.F.R. §1508.18; *see infra* notes 57-71 and accompanying text.
55. *See, e.g.*, Minnesota Pub. Interest Research Group v. Butz, 498 F.2d 1314, 4 ELR 20700 (8th Cir. 1974) (en banc), *permanent injunction issued*, 401 F. Supp. 1276, 6 ELR 20133 (D. Minn. 1975), *injunction dissolved*, 541 F.2d 1292, 6 ELR 20736 (8th Cir. 1975). By following this line of cases, the CEQ rejected cases following a different interpretation. *See, e.g.*, NAACP v. Wilmington Medical Ctr., Inc., 584 F.2d 619, 8 ELR 20699 (3d Cir. 1978).
56. 442 U.S. 347, 361 n.20, 9 ELR 20390, 20394 n.20 (1979). For the legislative history of CEQ's NEPA regulations, see 43 Fed. Reg. 55978, 55989 (Nov. 29, 1978).
57. 40 C.F.R. §1508.18; *see Ramsey*, 96 F.3d at 445, 27 ELR at 20161.

- *"Significantly."* The term "significantly" presents the threshold for the EIS requirement, and no other term in NEPA has been the subject of more attention. Although there has been much litigation on the meaning of the word, the cases have been very fact-specific.[58] As a result, rather than formulating a universal interpretation, the CEQ regulations distill generalized direction from case law, and present this direction as a nonexclusive checklist.[59]

   The regulations define "significantly" in terms of both "context"[60] and "intensity."[61] The former term recognizes that significance varies with the setting of the proposed action and also indicates that an action should be viewed from several different perspectives, e.g., local, regional, and national.[62] The latter term refers to severity of impact and is to be evaluated according to various listed factors, including beneficial as well as adverse impacts[63]; effects on public health or safety[64]; unique characteristics of a geographic area[65]; whether the effects are highly controversial[66]; whether there are highly uncertain effects or unique or unknown risks[67]; whether the action may establish a precedent[68]; whether the action is related to other actions with individually insignificant but cumulatively significant effects[69]; whether historic, cultural, or scientific resources are affected[70]; whether endangered or threatened species are involved[71]; and whether the action threatens to violate federal, state, or local requirements protecting the environment.[72] In NEPA litigation, factual showings are likely to revolve around one or more of these factors.

- *"Affecting."* The regulations define "affecting" to mean "will or may have an effect on."[73] The rationale for this definition lies in the phraseology of NEPA itself and is supported by case law.[74] If there will be no significant environmental impact, no EIS is required. An EIS is required, however, both when a significant impact is certain and when it is not known whether there will be such an impact.[75]

   The regulations define "effects" to include both "direct effects," those that are caused by the action and occur at the same time and place,[76] and "indirect effects," those that are caused by the action and occur later or farther away but are still reasonably foreseeable.[77] Indirect effects may include growth

58. For summaries of some of these cases, see RODGERS, *supra* note 53, at 750-61.
59. 40 C.F.R. §1508.27; *see also* North Carolina v. Federal Aviation Admin., 957 F.2d 1125 (4th Cir. 1992).
60. 40 C.F.R. §1508.27(a).
61. *Id.* §1508.27(b).
62. *Id.* §1508.27(a).
63. *Id.* §1508.27(b)(1).
64. *Id.* §1508.27(b)(2).
65. *Id.* §1508.27(b)(3). These unique characteristics include proximity to historic or cultural resources, park lands, prime farmlands, wetlands, wild and scenic rivers, or ecologically critical areas. *Id.*
66. *Id.* §1508.27(b)(4); *see* Greenpeace Action v. Franklin, 982 F.2d 1342, 23 ELR 20639 (9th Cir. 1992).
67. 40 C.F.R. §1508.27(b)(5).
68. *Id.* §1508.27(b)(6).
69. *Id.* §1508.27(b)(7). Significance cannot be avoided by terming an action temporary or by breaking it down into small component parts. *Id.*; *see also id.* §1508.7. Named Individual Members of the San Antonio Conservation Soc'y v. Texas Highway Dep't, 446 F.2d 1013, 1 ELR 20379 (5th Cir. 1971), *cert. denied*, 406 U.S. 933 (1972); Conservation Law Found. v. Federal Highway Admin., 24 F.3d 1465, 24 ELR 21196 (Cir. 1994); Preserve Endangered Areas of Cobb's History, Inc. v. U.S. Army Corps of Eng'rs, 87 F.3d 1242, 26 ELR 21449 (11th Cir. 1996).
70. 40 C.F.R. §1508.27(b)(8).
71. *Id.* §1508.27(b)(9).
72. *Id.* §1508.27(b)(10).
73. *Id.* §1508.3.
74. *See, e.g.*, Save Our Ten Acres v. Kreger, 472 F.2d 463, 3 ELR 20041 (5th Cir. 1973); Lockhart v. Kenops, 927 F.2d 1028, 1033, 21 ELR 20994, 20996 (8th Cir. 1991).
75. *See* National Audubon Soc'y v. Hoffman, 132 F.3d 7, 18, 28 ELR 20318, 20322-23 (2d Cir. 1997); Louisiana v. Lee, 758 F.2d 1081, 1084-85, 15 ELR 20609, 20610-11 (5th Cir. 1985), *cert. denied sub nom.* Dravo Basic Materials Co. v. Louisiana, 475 U.S. 1044 (1986); *see also* Sierra Club v. Marsh, 769 F.2d 868, 871, 15 ELR 20911, 20912 (1st Cir. 1985); Foundation for N. Am. Wild Sheep v. Department of Agric., 681 F.2d 1172, 1178, 12 ELR 20968, 20969 (9th Cir. 1982); Minnesota Pub. Interest Research Group v. Butz, 498 F.2d 1314, 1320, 4 ELR 20700, 20702-03 (8th Cir. 1974) (en banc); Hanly v. Kleindienst, 471 F.2d 823, 831, 2 ELR 20717, 20720-21 (2d Cir. 1972), *cert. denied*, 412 U.S. 908 (1973); *see also* RODGERS, *supra* note 53, at 754-55.
76. 40 C.F.R. §1508.8(a).
77. *Id.* §1508.8(b). By way of examples of courts dealing with the reach of required analysis of impacts under NEPA, see *Lockhart*, 927 F.2d at 1028, 21 ELR at 20994 (when exchanging land with a private party an agency must examine the impacts of that party's use of the land acquired from the government, but, absent sham, need not look at potential uses by subsequent purchasers); Hoosier Envtl. Council, Inc. v. U.S. Army Corps of Eng'rs, 105 F. Supp. 2d 953, 975-76, 30 ELR 20788 (S.D. Ind. 2000) (finding that Corps was justified in not considering additional development around a riverboat casino in the EA when no additional development was proposed or foreseeable).

inducing effects and other effects of induced changes in land use patterns.[78] Environmental "effects" are generally synonymous with environmental "impacts" and encompass a broad range—ecological, aesthetic, historic, cultural, economic, social, health, and cumulative effects.[79] Socioeconomic impacts may only be considered, however, if they accompany physical impacts.[80] "Effects" include both the beneficial and the detrimental effects of an action, even if an agency considers the overall impact beneficial.[81]

Cumulative impacts merit special mention. They include those impacts that result from the environmental impact of the action in question when added to other past, present, and reasonably foreseeable future actions regardless of who is undertaking those actions.[82] Cumulative impacts can result from individually minor but cumulatively significant actions taking place over a period of time.[83] Allegations of failure to address appropriately cumulative impacts have become increasingly important in NEPA litigation.[84] There are, however, important distinctions to be drawn. While the analysis of cumulative impacts is often of high importance, the potential for cumulative impact in deciding whether to prepare an EIS cannot in and of itself require such preparation when the proposed action's impact is itself insignificant because that would delete the congressionally imposed threshold of significance from the calculus.

- *"The Quality of the Human Environment."* The final term in §102(2)(C)'s description of when an EIS is required is "the quality of the human environment." The regulations interpret this term comprehensively "to include the natural and physical environment and the relationship of people with that environment."[85] Economic and social effects by themselves do not require preparation of an EIS. When an EIS is prepared and economic or social and natural or physical environmental effects are interrelated, however, the EIS must discuss all of them.[86] In appropriate cases, this includes environmental justice impacts.[87]

Scoping

Once an agency determines through preparation of an EA or otherwise that a proposal may significantly affect the environment, it must prepare an EIS. The next step is "scoping," defined by the regulations as "an early and open process for determining the scope of issues to be addressed and for identifying the significant issues related to a proposed action."[88]

78. 40 C.F.R. §1508.8(b). These indirect effects were sometimes called "secondary impacts" prior to adoption of CEQ's NEPA regulations. The regulations opted for the direct-indirect distinction rather than the primary-secondary one because the latter sometimes led to the note necessarily accurate conclusion meant less important.
79. *Id.*
80. *Id.* §1508.14; *see* Douglas County v. Babbitt, 48 F.3d 1495, 25 ELR 20631 (9th Cir. 1995).
81. 40 C.F.R. §1508.8(b). One case, however, held that no EIS is required when all the effects are beneficial. Friends of the Fiery Gizzard v. Farmers Home Admin., 61 F.3d 501, 25 ELR 21536 (6th Cir. 1995).
82. 40 C.F.R. §1508.7. *See* CEQ, Considering Cumulative Impacts Under NEPA (1997); U.S. EPA, Consideration of Cumulative Impacts in EPA Review of NEPA Documents (1999).
83. 40 C.F.R. §1508.7.
84. *See* Fritiofson v. Alexander, 772 F.2d 1225, 15 ELR 21070 (5th Cir. 1985), *abrogated sub nom.* Sabine River Auth. v. U.S. Dep't of the Interior, 951 F.2d 669, 22 ELR 20633 (5th Cir. 1992); Conservation Law Found. v. Federal Highway Admin., 24 F.3d 1465, 24 ELR 21196 (1st Cir. 1994); Airport Neighbors Alliance v. United States, 90 F.3d 426, 27 ELR 20214 (10th Cir. 1996); Neighbors of Cuddy Mountain v. U.S. Forest Serv., 137 F.3d 1372, 28 ELR 21073 (9th Cir. 1998).
85. 40 C.F.R. §1508.14.
86. *See* Baltimore Gas & Elec. Co. v. Natural Resources Defense Council, 462 U.S. 87, 13 ELR 20544 (1983) (EIS must disclose significant socioeconomic impacts).
87. *Id.* On February 11, 1994, President Clinton issued Executive Order 12898 relating to environmental justice. Exec. Order No. 12898, 59 Fed. Reg. 7629 (Feb. 11, 1994). While this executive order is silent as to NEPA, in a memorandum for the heads of all departments and agencies of the same date the President said that, when feasible, NEPA documents should address the effects of federal actions on minority and low-income communities. White House, Memorandum for all Heads of all Departments and Agencies Regarding Executive Order on Federal Actions to Address Environmental Justice in Minority Populations and Low-Income Populations (Feb. 11, 1994) (available from the ELR Document Service, ELR Order No. AD-01134). President Bush has elected to keep that executive order in place. Various federal agencies have now proposed their own implementing guidance. *See, e.g.,* U.S. EPA, Final Guidance for Consideration of Environmental Justice in Clean Air Act Section 309 Reviews (1999) (available from the ELR Document Service, ELR Order No. AD-04219). Goshen Rd. Envtl. Action Team v. U.S. Dep't of Agric., 176 F.3d 475, 29 ELR 21243 (4th Cir. 1999) (unpublished decision) (EA, no requirement for disparate impact analysis).
88. 40 C.F.R. §§1501.7, 1508.25. *See generally* CEQ, Memorandum From CEQ to General Counsel, NEPA Liaisons, and Participants in Scoping (Apr. 30, 1981) (available from the ELR Document Service, ELR Order No. AD-00633). No scoping is required for EISs on

The initiative will have been taken by the lead agency,[89] assisted by other agencies with jurisdiction or expertise, called cooperating agencies.[90]

One purpose of scoping is to notify and involve all agencies and individuals concerned about the proposed action. Another is to identify issues that should be analyzed in-depth and eliminate from study those that are not significant.[91] To help achieve these purposes, the regulations encourage, but do not require, agencies to hold scoping meetings.[92] Finally, scoping is the appropriate occasion for an agency to set time limits for the entire NEPA process.[93] The agency may do this on its own, and "shall" do it if an applicant so requests.[94]

Preparation of the Statement

The next step in the NEPA process is preparation of the EIS itself.[95] At the outset, it is important to stress several aspects of the EIS. First and foremost, the EIS is not an end in itself, but rather a tool to promote environmentally sensitive decisionmaking.[96] Second, the document is to be analytic rather than encyclopedic.[97] It is to be concise—no longer than absolutely necessary to meet the law's requirements.[98] The regulations, in fact, impose a page limit of 150 pages, although they allow up to 300 pages for proposals of unusual scope or complexity.[99] Third, the statement should indicate how the proposal will achieve the policies of NEPA.[100] Above all, the EIS should be used to assess environmental impacts, not to justify decisions already made.[101]

With these considerations in mind, we now review the actual process of preparing an EIS, first determining who prepares the statement and then analyzing the chronological sequence of preparation.

Who Prepares the EIS

It is important to emphasize that NEPA requires federal agencies to be the entities preparing EISs, but, as will appear below, others may prepare supporting documents. When applicants are involved, two desirable goals conflict—eliminating duplication between the work done by the agency and that done by the applicants or their consultants, and ensuring that the agency exercises independent judgment by doing its own work either directly or through its consultant. The applicable regulation tracks case law on this issue[102] but gives deference to both considerations.[103]

The regulation provides different treatment for information and for EAs, as distinct from EISs. An applicant may submit[104] information to an agency either on its own or at the agency's request.[105] If an agency requests information, however, it must evaluate that information independently and is responsible for its accuracy. It is the regulation's intent that agencies verify, but not redo, acceptable work.[106]

---

legislative proposals. 40 C.F.R. §1506.8.
89. 40 C.F.R. §1501.5.
90. *Id.* §§1501.6, 1508.5; *see* North Buckhead Civic Ass'n v. Skinner, 903 F.2d 1533, 20 ELR 21061 (11th Cir. 1990).
91. 40 C.F.R. §1501.7; *see* Northwest Coalition for Alternatives to Pesticides v. Lyng, 844 F.2d 588, 594-95, 18 ELR 20738, 20741-42 (9th Cir. 1988) (agency violated spirit and letter of CEQ scoping regulations by failing to involve environmental organization that had previously enjoined agency's proposal).
92. 40 C.F.R. §1501.7(b)(4).
93. *Id.* §§1501.7(b)(2), 1501.8.
94. *Id.* §1501.8(a).
95. *Id.* pt. 1502.
96. *Id.* §§1500.1, 1502.1.
97. *Id.* §1502.2(a).
98. *Id.* §1502.2(c).
99. *Id.* §1502.7.
100. *Id.* §1502.2(d).
101. *Id.* §1502.2(g).
102. *See, e.g.,* Greene County Planning Bd. v. Federal Power Comm'n, 455 F.2d 412, 2 ELR 20017 (2d Cir. 1972), *cert. denied*, 490 U.S. 849 (1972), *stay granted*, 490 F.2d 256, 4 ELR 20080 (2d Cir. 1973).
103. 40 C.F.R. §1506.5.
104. *Id.* §1506.5(a), (c).
105. *Id.* §1506.5(a).
106. *Id.; see* People ex rel. Van de Kamp v. Marsh, 687 F. Supp. 495, 499, 19 ELR 20165, 20166 (N.D. Cal. 1988).

An agency may permit an applicant to prepare an EA. However, the agency must make its own evaluation of the environmental issues and take responsibility for the document's scope and content.[107]

Finally, an applicant cannot prepare an EIS; that document is solely the responsibility of the agency.[108] Thus, the EIS may only be prepared directly by the agency or by a contractor selected "solely" by an agency.[109] The process is designed to avoid the potential conflict of interest arising from an applicant's selection of a consultant whose analysis could serve the applicant's own interests. A contractor selected by an agency must execute a disclosure statement specifying that it has no financial or other interest in the outcome of the project.[110] Further, the agency must furnish guidance to the contractor and must independently evaluate and take responsibility for the document.[111]

It is important to discuss the roles agencies play when more than one is expected to be heavily involved in the EIS process. In this situation, the NEPA regulations provide for a "lead agency"[112] to take "primary responsibility"[113] for preparation of the EIS and to supervise the process.[114] This simplifies EIS preparation and avoids duplication.

The regulations further allow the lead agency to designate as "cooperating agencies" other agencies that have jurisdiction by law over a project.[115] The lead agency may also so designate other agencies with special expertise on any environmental issues that the EIS should discuss.[116] This mechanism is designed to promote agency cooperation early in the NEPA process, hopefully ensuring that all agencies' concerns are addressed and averting subsequent squabbles.

The EIS

The lead agency preparing the EIS must address the following issues:

- *Determining the Scope of the EIS.* Although the lead agency should already have considered the scope of the EIS during the scoping process,[117] the regulations require that it further define that scope as it prepares the EIS.[118] Questions of scope cannot be manipulated so as to avoid the EIS process; for example, an agency may not segment an environmentally significant project into less significant portions that do not require EISs.[119] On the other hand, proposals or parts of proposals that are so closely related as to be, in effect, a single course of action may be treated as such in a single EIS.[120] EISs may also be prepared for broad proposals. Such statements may, for example, evaluate similar actions generically, or consider all actions that occur within given geographic areas.[121]

---

107. 40 C.F.R. §1506.5(b).
108. *Id.* §1506.5(c).
109. *Id.* In *Citizens Against Burlington v. Busey*, the court found that the Federal Aviation Administration had violated this section. Although the court chastised the agency, it declined to reverse on that ground. 938 F.2d 190, 21 ELR 21142 (D.C. Cir. 1991).
110. 40 C.F.R. §1506.5(c).
111. *Id.* A provision does not exist for an agency to select a contractor whom the applicant then pays. *Forty Most Asked Questions Concerning CEQ's National Environmental Policy Act Regulations.* 46 Fed. Reg. 18026, 18031 (Mar. 23, 1981) [hereinafter *Forty Questions*] (available as App. 19). In some cases this procedure, known as a "third party contract," will expedite the processing of the application.
112. 40 C.F.R. §§1501.5, 1508.16. When there is a dispute over which agency is to be the lead agency, the regulations provide criteria for resolution, *id.* §1501.5(c), and, if necessary, a mechanism for an independent and final determination by the CEQ. *Id.* §1501.5(d)-(f).
113. *Id.* §1508.16.
114. *Id.* §1501.5.
115. *Id.* §§1501.6, 1508.5. Other agencies may opt out of the cooperating agency role based on other program commitments. *Id.* §1501.6(c). The provision empowering lead agencies to appoint cooperating agencies is designed, however, to stimulate agencies with jurisdiction to cooperate with the lead agency from the beginning, rather than holding fire until they see a draft EIS and then taking pot shots at it.
116. *Id.* §1501.6. A state or local agency or Indian tribe possessing jurisdiction by law or special expertise may also, by agreement with the lead agency, become a cooperating agency. *Id.* §1508.5.
117. *Id.* §§1502.4, 1508.25.
118. *Id.*
119. Named Individual Members of the San Antonio Conservation Soc'y v. Texas Highway Dep't, 446 F.2d 1013, 1 ELR 20379 (5th Cir. 1971), *cert. denied*, 406 U.S. 933 (1972) (segmentation of major highway project into less significant portions does not allow agency to avoid EIS process); *see also* Taxpayers Watchdog, Inc. v. Stanley, 819 F.2d 294, 299, 17 ELR 20905, 20906-07 (D.C. Cir. 1987); Conservation Law Found. v. Federal Highway Admin., 24 F.3d 1465, 24 ELR 21196 (1st Cir. 1994); Preserve Endangered Areas of Cobb's History, Inc. v. U.S. Army Corps of Eng'rs, 87 F.3d 1242, 26 ELR 21449 (11th Cir. 1996).
120. 40 C.F.R. §1502.4(a); Pacific Coast Federation v. Blank, 693 F.3d 1084, 1097-1101 (9th Cir. 2012); Great Basin Mine Watch v. Hankins, 456 F.3d 955 (9th Cir. 2006).
121. 40 C.F.R. §1502.4(b), (c). As examples of broad programs, the regulations cite adoption of new agency programs or regulations. *Id.*; *see id.* §1508.18.

- *Tiering.* In some instances, the regulations suggest that agencies employ "tiering" to help them focus on those issues ripe for decision."[122] Tiering is appropriate when different stages of development—such as a nationwide program and a specific project under that program—are the subjects of separate EISs. Tiering is a method of gearing each EIS to the appropriate stage of development, incorporating by reference what has gone before. Each EIS therefore avoids addressing issues that are premature or that have already been analyzed.[123]

- *Timing, Interdisciplinary Approach, and Plain Language.* CEQ's NEPA regulations provide, as a general rule, that EISs are to be prepared earlier rather than later to eliminate subsequent delay and to integrate environmental considerations most effectively into the decisionmaking process.[124] The timing of a statement, while usually obvious, can present difficult issues. The regulations address these specifically, providing different rules for federally undertaken projects,[125] applications to agencies,[126] adjudication,[127] and rulemaking.[128]

  EISs are to be prepared using an interdisciplinary approach, integrating whenever appropriate the natural and social sciences and the environmental design arts.[129] The statements are to be prepared in language that can be readily understood.[130]

- *Stages and Format of the EIS.* EISs are almost always prepared in two stages, draft and final.[131] The one exception to this rule is for EISs for legislative proposals, which need only be prepared as draft statements.[132] For a nonlegislative proposal, the lead agency, in conjunction with any cooperating agencies, prepares a draft EIS and circulates it for comment.[133] After receiving comments, the lead agency prepares a final EIS, indicating its responses to any issues raised by the comments and discussing any responsible opposing views that were not adequately discussed in the draft.[134] An EIS may be supplemented,[135] and must be if the agency makes "substantial changes in the proposed action" that are relevant to environmental concerns, or if there are "significant new circumstances or information relevant to environmental concerns and bearing on the proposed action or its impacts."[136]

---

122. *Id.* §§1502.4(d), 1502.20, 1508.28; *see* Idaho Conservation League v. Mumma, 956 F.2d 1508, 1511-12, 22 ELR 20569, 20569-79 (9th Cir. 1992) (staged decisionmaking); San Juan Citizens Alliance v. Stiles, 654 F.3d 1038 (10th Cir. 2011) (EIS upheld because subsequent EIS or EA would tier from it); Theodore Roosevelt Conservation Partnership v. Salazar, 616 F.3d 497, 511-2 (D.C. Cir. 2010) (tiering allowed from EIS even though newer information available). *See also* CEQ, Guidance Regarding NEPA Regulations, 48 Fed. Reg. 34263, 34268 (July 28, 1983) (supporting tiering) (available as App. 20). While tiering was specifically directed at EISs, there is no reason why tiering cannot also be employed with EAs in appropriate cases, particularly when the EA being tiered from has undergone an EIS-like review.
123. 40 C.F.R. §§1502.4(d), 1502.20, 1508.28.
124. *Id.* §1502.5.
125. *Id.* §1502.5(a).
126. *Id.* §1502.5(b).
127. *Id.* §1502.5(c). By adjudication, the regulations primarily mean actions undertaken by independent regulatory agencies. *Id.*
128. *Id.* §1502.5(d).
129. *Id.* §1502.6. NEPA specifically mentions these professional disciplines. 42 U.S.C. §4332(2)(A), ELR Stat. NEPA §102(2)(A).
130. 40 C.F.R. §1502.8; *see* Oregon Envtl. Council v. Kunzman, 817 F.2d 484, 493-94, 17 ELR 20756, 20759-60 (9th Cir. 1987); Texas Comm'n on Natural Resources v. Van Winckle, 197 F. Supp. 2d 586, 600, 32 ELR 20639 (N.D. Tex. 2002).
131. 40 C.F.R. §§1502.9, 1506.8. Concerning supplemental EISs, see *Coker v. Skidmore*, 941 F.2d 1306, 21 ELR 21481 (5th Cir. 1991).
132. 40 C.F.R. §1502.9. This exception is itself subject to four exceptions requiring preparation of both draft and final statements. *Id.*
133. *Id.* §1502.9(a), pt. 1503.
134. *Id.* §1502.9(b).
135. *Id.* §1502.9(c).
136. *Id.* §1502.9(c)(1). Preparation of a supplemental statement "is at times necessary to satisfy the Act's 'action-forcing' purpose." Marsh v. Oregon Natural Resources Council, 490 U.S. 360, 371, 19 ELR 20749, 20752 (1989). In the Supreme Court's words:
    It would be incongruous with [NEPA's] approach to environmental protection, and with the Act's manifest concern with preventing uninformed action, for the blinders to adverse environmental effects, once unequivocally removed, to be restored prior to the completion of agency action simply because the relevant proposal has received initial approval.
    Id.; *see also* Sierra Club v. Van Antwerp, 526 F.3d 1353, 1360 (11th Cir. 2008) (changes that minimize impacts are apt to be encompassed within the original EIS and do not require supplementation); Upper Snake River Chapter of Trout Unlimited v. Hodel, 921 F.2d 232, 21 ELR 20347 (9th Cir. 1990) (periodic adjustment of water flow from dam does not require EIS); Coker v. Skidmore, 744 F. Supp. 121, 21 ELR 20657 (S.D. Miss. 1990) (an EIS can become outdated and no longer provide a basis for tiering), *aff'd*, 941 F.2d 1306, 21 ELR 21481 (5th Cir. 1991); South Trenton Residents Against 29 v. Federal Highway Admin., 176 F.3d 658, 29 ELR 21229 (3d Cir. 1999) (a seriously different picture of the environmental impact is needed to require a supplemental EIS); Davis v. Latschar, 202 F.3d 359, 30 ELR 20364 (D.C. Cir. 2000) (no supplemental EIS required because effects to be caused not different from those already studied); *but see* Town of Winthrop v. Federal Aviation Administration, 535 F.3d 1 (1st Cir. 2008) (mere passage of time does not render an analysis invalid).

The regulations recommend that statements follow a format[137] consisting of a cover sheet[138]; a summary not to exceed 15 pages[139]; a brief recitation of the purpose of and need for the proposed action[140]; analyses of the alternatives[141]; the affected environment that exists before the action[142] and the environmental consequences[143]; a list of preparers[144]; and an optional appendix.[145]

- *Purpose and Need.* EISs also must include a brief discussion specifying the underlying purpose and need of the proposal.[146] For many years this provision received little judicial attention, but in the 1990s that changed. The developing case law is consistent in asserting that the purpose and need for the proposed action delineates the range of alternatives to be discussed, and while the cases also uniformly assert that the purpose may not be inappropriately skewed so as to eliminate otherwise reasonable alternatives, some cases have followed the logic of that analysis in their conclusions[147] while other have not.[148]

- *Environmental Consequences and Alternatives.* The discussions of the environmental consequences of, and the alternatives to, a proposal are the most critical sections of the EIS.[149] The environmental consequences section is intended to form "the scientific and analytic basis for the comparisons" in the alternatives section,[150] and to incorporate the discussions required by various subparagraphs of NEPA §102(2)(C). Hence, the regulations require the environmental consequences section to discuss: the direct[151] and indirect effects[152] of the proposal and alternatives[153]; possible conflicts with land use plans[154]; energy requirements and conservation potential[155]; natural or depletable resources requirements and conservation potential[156]; effects on the urban, historic, and built environment, and the reuse and conservation potential[157]; and means of mitigating adverse environmental effects.[158] The discussion of cumulative impacts is often a vital part of the EIS.[159]

---

137. 40 C.F.R. §1502.10.

138. *Id.* §1502.11.

139. *Id.* §1502.12.

140. *Id.* §1502.13. The regulations as originally proposed limited this section to one page under normal circumstances, 43 Fed. Reg. 25230, 25237 (June 9, 1978), but the final regulations removed this limitation, 43 Fed. Reg. 55978, 55996 (Nov. 29, 1978), on the ground that in "some cases" more than one page would be needed. *Id.* at 55983.

141. 40 C.F.R. §1502.14.

142. *Id.* §1502.15.

143. *Id.* §1502.16. This section represents the principal analytic discussion. The regulations require the section to include discussions of eight factors. *Id.* §1502.16(a)-(h); *see infra* notes 149-157 and accompanying text.

144. 40 C.F.R. §1502.17.

145. *Id.* §1502.18.

146. 40 C.F.R. §1502.13; Alaska Survival v. Surface Transportation Board, 705 F.3d 1073, 1084-87 (9th Cir. 2013).

147. *See, e.g.,* Simmons v. U.S. Army Corps of Eng'rs, 120 F.3d 664, 27 ELR 21204 (7th Cir. 1997).

148. *See, e.g.,* Citizens Against Burlington, Inc. v. Busey, 938 F.2d 190, 21 ELR 21142 (D.C. Cir. 1991).

149. The description of the "affected environment" is consciously down-graded. The notorious "dandelion counts," overly descriptive discussions that accounted for much of the unneeded bulk of many early EISs, are discouraged. In the regulation's own words, "[v]erbose descriptions of the affected environment are themselves no measure of the adequacy of an environmental impact statement." 40 C.F.R. §1502.15. As a generality, if the affected environment description in an EIS is longer than the two analytic sections (*id.* §§1502.14, 1502.16), one may justifiably look askance at undue padding of the former at the expense of the latter.

150. *Id.* §1502.16.

151. *Id.* §1502.16(a).

152. *Id.* §1502.16(b). Indirect effects include off-site impacts. Robertson v. Methow Valley Citizens Council, 490 U.S. 332, 339, 350, 19 ELR 20743, 20744, 20747 (1989).

153. 40 C.F.R. §1502.16(d).

154. *Id.* §1502.16(c).

155. *Id.* §1502.16(e); *see* All Indian Pueblo Council v. United States, 975 F.2d 1437, 23 ELR 20473 (10th Cir. 1992).

156. 40 C.F.R. §1502.16(f).

157. *Id.* §1502.16(g).

158. *Id.* §1502.16(h). NEPA §102(2)(C)(ii) specifically requires discussion of adverse impacts that "cannot be avoided should the proposal be implemented." 42 U.S.C. §4332(2)(C)(ii), ELR Stat. NEPA §102(2)(C)(ii). In the Supreme Court's words, "one important ingredient of an EIS is the discussion of steps that can be taken to mitigate adverse environmental consequences." Robertson v. Methow Valley Citizens Council, 490 U.S. 332, 351, 19 ELR 20743, 20747 (1989) (footnote omitted). Indeed, "omission of a reasonably complete discussion of possible mitigation measures would undermine the 'action-forcing' function of NEPA." *Id.* While *Robertson* holds that a full mitigation plan need not be adopted, such a plan is enforceable once it is adopted by the agency in its record of decision. 40 C.F.R. §§1505.2(c), 1505.3.

159. 40 C.F.R. §§1508.7, 1508.25; *see* Resources Ltd. v. Robertson, 8 F.3d 1394, 1400, 24 ELR 20026, 20028 (9th Cir. 1993) (requiring consideration of cumulative impacts not under federal control); Great Basin Mine Watch v. Hankins, 456 F.3d 955, 972-74 (9th Cir. 2006) (obligation to consider cumulative impacts not satisfied by "conclusory statements"); Te-Moak Tribe v. U.S. Dep't of the Interior, 608 F.3d 592, 602-07 (9th Cir. 2010) (invalidated EA because cumulative impacts evaluated in conclusory fashion).

The alternatives section is based on the information and analysis in the environmental consequences section, but should not duplicate that section.[160] Described as the "heart of the environmental impact statement," the alternatives section is to "present the environmental impacts of the proposal and the alternatives in comparative form, thus sharply defining the issues and providing a clear basis for choice among options by the decisionmakers and the public."[161] The discussion is to "[r]igorously explore and objectively evaluate all reasonable alternatives," giving "substantial treatment" to each alternative that is considered in detail.[162] The agency is required to consider alternatives not within the jurisdiction of the lead agency[163] and must always consider the "no action" alternative.[164] The agency is to identify its "preferred alternative," if it has one, at the draft stage, and must identify that alternative when it prepares the final statement.[165]

- *Mitigation.* CEQ's NEPA regulations require a discussion of mitigation, which can be part of the original proposal or discussed as part of the environmental consequences or as part of the alternatives analysis.[166] The Supreme Court has held that NEPA does not require adoption of a mitigation plan as part of an EIS.[167] Nevertheless, if mitigation is adopted by an agency, it is enforceable.[168] Clearly if an EA shows potentially significant impacts that are then mitigated below the threshold of significance—a so-called "mitigated Finding of No Significant Impact" or "mitigated FONSI"—the mitigation becomes mandatory in that it is a condition of non-preparation of an EIS.[169]

- *Incomplete or Unavailable Information.* One provision of the regulations, while only occasionally applied, excited considerable controversy—the section on "incomplete or unavailable information."[170] According to the CEQ, "incomplete information" is that which cannot be obtained because the over-

---

160. 40 C.F.R. §1502.14.

161. *Id. See* Surfrider Found. v. Dalton, 989 F. Supp. 1309 (S.D. Cal. 1998), *aff'd on the basis of the district court opinion sub nom.* San Diego Chapter of the Surfrider Found. v. Dalton, 196 F.3d 1057, 1058 (9th Cir. 1999) (failure to consider a viable alternative renders an alternatives analysis invalid); Friends of Yosemite Valley v. Kempthorne, 520 F.3d 1024, 1038-39 (9th Cir. 2008) (alternatives with essentially identical components invalid).

162. 40 C.F.R. §1502.14(d); League of Wilderness Defenders v. U.S. Forest Service, 689 F.3d 1060, 1076-77 (9th Cir. 2012) (existence of a viable but unexamined alternative renders an EIS invalid). "Substantial treatment," rather than equal treatment, is required, since the treatment must necessarily vary with the degree of impact. For an example of case law construing what alternatives must be considered as "reasonable alternatives," see *City of Tenakee Springs v. Clough*, 915 F.2d 1308, 21 ELR 20001 (9th Cir. 1990) (the existence of a contract between the agency and the applicant that constrained consideration of certain alternatives did not prevent such alternatives from being reasonable ones that had to be considered). For a contrasting case in which a court upheld an agency's finding that only one alternative was reasonable because the others were infeasible, see *Tongass Conservation Soc'y v. Cheney*, 924 F.2d 1137, 21 ELR 20558 (D.C. Cir. 1991). See Dubois v. U.S. Department of Agric., 102 F.3d 1273, 27 ELR 20622 (1st Cir. 1996), *cert. denied sub nom.* Loon Mountain Recreation Corp. v. Dubois, 117 S. Ct. 2510 (1997) (alternatives analysis invalidated for failure to examine reasonable alternative suggested by commenters).

163. 40 C.F.R. §1502.14(c). Similarly, an agency may not ignore an otherwise reasonable alternative because of a contractual bar since the contract may be amended. *Tenakee Springs*, 915 F.2d at 1308, 21 ELR at 20001; *see also Tongass Conservation Soc'y*, 924 F.2d at 1137, 21 ELR at 20558; Idaho Conservation League v. Mumma, 956 F.2d 1508, 22 ELR 20569 (9th Cir. 1992); Alaska Wilderness Recreation & Tourism Ass'n v. Morrison, 67 F.3d 723, 730, 26 ELR 20065, 20069 (9th Cir. 1995).

164. 40 C.F.R. §1502.14(d).

165. *Id.* §1502.14(e). An exception is made for situations in which other laws may prohibit expression of such a preference at this stage. *Id.* This exception was designed to cover independent regulatory agencies. In such agencies, staff may prepare a draft and final EIS, but only the commissioners may express an agency preference, and they may not do so until after the final EIS is prepared.

166. *Id.* §1502.14(e), (h). For a case discussing the importance of mitigation to the NEPA process, see *C.A.R.E. NOW, Inc. v. Federal Aviation Admin.*, 844 F.2d 1569, 18 ELR 21081 (11th Cir. 1988).

167. Robertson v. Methow Valley Citizens Council, 490 U.S. 332, 19 ELR 20743 (1989); Pacific Coast Federation of Fishermen, 693 F.3d at 1103; *see also* Colorado Environmental Coalition v. Dombeck, 185 F.3d 1162 (10th Cir. 1999) (mitigation upheld); South Fork Band v. U.S. Dep't of the Interior, 588 F.3d 718, 722 (9th Cir. 2009) (mitigation held to be inadequate). Recently the D.C. Circuit has upheld mitigation, which included an "adaptive management plan" whereby the measures employed by the agency were adapted to developments that would become apparent as the project proceeded. Theodore Roosevelt Conservation Partnership v. Salazar, 616 F.3d 497, 515-17 (D.C. Cir. 2010).

168. Tyler v. Cisneros, 136 F.3d 603, 28 ELR 20540 (9th Cir. 1998).

169. *See* Cabinet Mountains Wilderness v. Peterson, 685 F.2d 678, 12 ELR 21058 (D.C. Cir. 1982); *C.A.R.E. Now, Inc.*, 844 F.2d 1569, 18 ELR 21081.

170. 40 C.F.R. §1502.22. *See generally Robertson*, 490 U.S. at 332, 19 ELR at 20743; Friends of Endangered Species v. Jantzen, 760 F.2d 976, 15 ELR 20455 (9th Cir. 1985); Save Our Ecosystems v. Clark, 747 F.2d 1240, 15 ELR 20035 (9th Cir. 1984); Southern Or. Citizens Against Toxic Sprays, Inc. v. Clark, 720 F.2d 1475, 14 ELR 20061 (9th Cir. 1983), *cert. denied*, 469 U.S. 1028 (1984); City of New York v. Department of Transp., 715 F.2d 732, 13 ELR 20823 (2d Cir. 1983), *appeal dismissed, cert. denied*, 465 U.S. 1055 (1984); Sierra Club v. Sigler, 695 F.2d 957, 13 ELR 20210 (5th Cir. 1983); Oregon Envtl. Council v. Kunzman, 614 F. Supp. 657, 15 ELR 20499 (D. Or. 1985), *injunction dissolved*, 636 F. Supp. 632, 16 ELR 20658 (D. Or. 1986), *aff'd*, 817 F.2d 484, 17 ELR 20756 (9th Cir. 1987); Vicki O'Meara Masterman, *Worst Case Analysis: The Final Chapter?*, 19 ELR 10026 (Jan. 1989); Nicholas C. Yost, *Don't Gut Worst Case Analysis*, 13 ELR 10394 (Dec. 1983).

all costs of obtaining it are exorbitant.[171] "Unavailable information" is that which cannot be obtained because the means of obtaining it are not known.[172]

The CEQ regulations provide that when information on reasonably foreseeable adverse impacts evaluated in an EIS is essential to making a reasoned choice and the costs of obtaining it are not exorbitant, the agency must secure it.[173] However, if this information is incomplete or unavailable—that is, if the costs of obtaining it are exorbitant or the means of obtaining it are beyond the state of the art—the agency must "make clear that such information is lacking."[174] The agency must follow four prescribed steps.[175] First, it must state that the information is incomplete or unavailable.[176] Second, it must state the relevance of the missing information.[177] Third, it must summarize the existing credible scientific evidence relevant to its evaluation of reasonably foreseeable impacts.[178] Fourth, it must analyze those impacts based on theoretical approaches or scientific methods generally accepted in the scientific community.[179] The regulation clearly states that agencies must consider impacts with low probability but catastrophic consequences as long as the analysis "is supported by credible scientific evidence, is not based on pure conjecture, and is within the rule of reason."[180]

Risk analysis of improbable but highly significant impacts is not a new concept.[181] As articulated by the U.S. Court of Appeals for the First Circuit in *Massachusetts v. Andrus*:

---

171. 51 Fed. Reg. 15618, 15621 (Apr. 25, 1986).

172. *Id.* Indeed, in case of uncertainty concerning impacts or conflicting data, at minimum an EA must be prepared. American Bird Conservancy v. Federal Communications Comm'n, 516 F.3d 1027, 1032-33 (D.C. Cir. 2008).

173. 40 C.F.R. §1502.22(a).

174. *Id.* §1502.22; *see* Scientists' Inst. for Pub. Info. v. Atomic Energy Comm'n, 481 F.2d 1079, 1091-92, 3 ELR 20525, 20531-32 (D.C. Cir. 1973). In that case, the court stated:

> It must be remembered that the basic thrust of an agency's responsibilities under NEPA is to predict the environmental effects of a proposed action *before* the action is taken and those effects fully known. *Reasonable forecasting and speculation is thus implicit in NEPA* and we must reject any attempt by agencies to shirk their responsibilities under NEPA by labeling any and all discussion of future environmental effects a "crystal ball inquiry."

Id. at 1092, 3 ELR at 20531-32 (emphasis added); *see also* Kleppe v. Sierra Club, 427 U.S. 390, 410 n.21, 6 ELR 20532, 20537 n.21 (1976); Massachusetts v. Andrus, 594 F.2d 872, 892, 9 ELR 20162, 20173 (1st Cir. 1979); Alaska v. Andrus, 580 F.2d 465, 473-74, 8 ELR 20237, 20242 (D.C. Cir. 1978), *vacated on other grounds sub nom.* Western Oil & Gas Ass'n v. Alaska, 439 U.S. 922 (1978); Ethyl Corp. v. EPA, 541 F.2d 1, 18, 6 ELR 20267, 20279 (D.C. Cir. 1976) (en banc), *cert. denied*, 426 U.S. 941 (1976); I-291 Why? Ass'n v. Burns, 517 F.2d 1077, 1081, 5 ELR 20430, 20432 (2d Cir. 1975) (per curiam).

175. 40 C.F.R. §1502.22. This is the only regulation that the CEQ has amended since it promulgated NEPA regulations. The regulation as amended in 1986 shares certain goals with the prior regulation: Disclosure that information is missing, acquisition of that information, and evaluation of impacts in the absence of all information. *See* 51 Fed. Reg. at 15619, 15620.

The amendment does, however, make one significant change in the method by which agencies consider incomplete or unavailable information. The earlier regulation provided that when cost or lack of appropriate methodology precluded acquisition of relevant information, the agency had to weigh the need for the action against the risk and severity of possible adverse impacts were the action to proceed in the face of uncertainty. Before proceeding, an agency had to perform a "worst case analysis," indicating both the probability and the improbability of the occurrence of that worst case. Application of worst case analysis, particularly by the Ninth Circuit in *Save Our Ecosystems v. Clark* and *Southern Or. Citizens Against Toxic Sprays, Inc. v. Clark*, engendered a certain unhappiness among some government agencies that thought they had to go beyond reasonable limits to develop a "worst case scenario." Save Our Ecosystems v. Clark, 747 F.2d 1240, 15 ELR 20035 (9th Cir. 1984); Southern Or. Citizens Against Toxic Sprays, Inc. v. Clark, 720 F.2d 1475, 14 ELR 20061 (9th Cir. 1983).

The CEQ amended the regulation to delete the worst case analysis requirement. The amendment was to apply to all EISs for which a notice of intent was published in the *Federal Register* on or after May 27, 1986. For EISs in progress before then, the agency may choose to comply with either the original or the amended regulation. 40 C.F.R. §1502.22(c). The Supreme Court has upheld the new regulation as within the deference to be accorded to the CEQ (while suggesting that the former regulation was also within that deference). *See* Robertson v. Methow Valley Citizens Council, 490 U.S. 332, 19 ELR 20743 (1989); *see also* Marsh v. Oregon Natural Resources Council, 490 U.S. 360, 19 ELR 20749 (1989).

176. 40 C.F.R. §1502.22(b)(1).

177. *Id.* §1502.22(b)(2).

178. *Id.* §1502.22(b)(3).

179. *Id.* §1502.22(b)(4). The CEQ intends for evaluations of reasonably foreseeable significant impacts to be carefully conducted and based on credible scientific evidence. All scientific evidence must be disclosed, including responsible opposing views supported by generally accepted theoretical approaches or scientific methods. 51 Fed. Reg. 15618, 15621 (Apr. 25, 1986).

180. This portion of the amended regulation is specifically intended to substitute for worst case analysis.

181. Both the prior regulation and the amended regulation incorporate this concept. Moreover, a pre-amendment Supreme Court case recognized the difference between considering the impacts of improbable but possible occurrences should they actually occur, and considering the more speculative impacts generated by apprehension of those occurrences. In *Metropolitan Edison Co. v. People Against Nuclear Energy*, the Court declined to apply NEPA to the psychological fears generated by the "risk" of a nuclear accident at Three Mile Island (TMI), but acknowledged the need to consider improbable but possible accidents, stating:

> We emphasize that in this case we are considering effects caused by the risk of an accident. The situation where an agency is asked to consider effects that will occur if a risk is realized, for example, if an accident occurs at TMI-1, is an entirely different case. The [Nuclear Regulatory Commission] considered, in the original EIS and in the most recent EIA for TMI-1, the possible adverse effects of a number of accidents that might occur at TMI-1.

If it were 100% certain that particular precautions would obviate all danger, the task would be simple; but there is a large element of the unknown created by gaps in science, by possible human error, and by freak weather conditions. Thus, the Secretary must engage in an uneasy calculus akin to that described by Judge Learned Hand, weighing "the probability" of accident, "the gravity of the resulting injury" and "the burden of adequate precautions."[182]

The District of Columbia Circuit made the same point in *Ethyl Corp. v. U.S. Environmental Protection Agency*:

Danger . . . is not set by a fixed probability of harm, but rather is composed of reciprocal elements of risk and harm, or probability and severity. . . . That is to say, the public health may properly be found endangered both by a lesser risk of a greater harm and by a greater risk of a lesser harm.[183]

NEPA essentially requires analysis of both the lesser risks of greater harms and the greater risks of lesser harms before actions are taken to bring about the risks. As courts recognize, such "[r]easonable forecasting and speculation is thus implicit in NEPA."[184]

- *Methodology.* Agencies are required to specify the methodology used and to identify scientific sources relied upon in the statement.[185] At the same time, if an agency has given thoughtful consideration to the views of opposing experts, it may at the end of the day, particularly when the area of expertise is one within the scope of the agency's mission, rely on its own experts in the face of conflicting views expressed by other experts.[186]

- *Streamlining.* As noted above, the NEPA regulations set out as goals the reduction of both paperwork[187] and delay in the NEPA process.[188] The procedures accordingly contain certain streamlining provisions designed to simplify NEPA's implementation and to mesh its application with that of other laws. For example, one section permits EISs to incorporate certain material by reference when this will cut down on their bulk.[189] The incorporated information must be cited, briefly described, and made publicly available, however, so as not to impede review by other agencies and the public.[190] Another provision allows an agency to "adopt" in whole or in part another EIS prepared by the same or a different federal agency, thus eliminating unnecessary duplication of work.[191]

Similarly, the regulations seek to eliminate duplication with state environmental procedures,[192] specifically directing federal agencies to prepare joint statements in cooperation with states that themselves have EIS requirements.[193] Indeed, the regulations allow an EIS to be combined with any other environmental

---

460 U.S. 766, 775 n.9, 13 ELR 20515, 20518 n.9 (1983).

182. 594 F.2d 872, 892, 9 ELR 20162, 20173 (1st Cir. 1979), Evaluation of uncertainties has always been a part of the legal process. "Certainty," in Justice Holmes' famous phrase, "generally is illusion." OLIVER WENDELL HOLMES, COLLECTED LEGAL PAPERS 181 (1920). Nevertheless, in the absence of certainty we do the best we can. As lucidly put by Justice Cardozo: "The law is not an exact science, we are told, and there the matter ends, if we are willing to end it . . . . Exactness may be impossible, but that is not enough to cause the mind to acquiesce in a predestined incoherence," BENJAMIN CARDOZO, THE PARADOXES OF LEGAL SCIENCE 2-3 (1928).

183. 541 F.2d 1, 18, 6 ELR 20267, 20279 (D.C. Cir. 1976).

184. Scientists' Inst. for Pub. Info. v. Atomic Energy Comm'n, 481 F.2d 1079, 1092, 3 ELR 20525, 20532 (D.C. Cir. 1973); *see also* Kleppe v. Sierra Club, 427 U.S. 390, 410 n.21, 6 ELR 20532, 20537 n.21 (1976); Alaska v. Andrus, 580 F.2d 465, 473-74, 8 ELR 20237, 20242 (D.C. Cir. 1978), *vacated on other grounds sub nom.* Western Oil & Gas Ass'n v. Alaska, 439 U.S. 922 (1978); I-291 Why? Ass'n v. Burns, 517 F.2d 1077, 1081, 5 ELR 20430, 20432 (2d Cir. 1975) (per curiam).

185. 40 C.F.R. §1502.24.

186. Wyoming Farm Bureau Fed'n v. Babbitt, 199 F.3d 1224, 30 ELR 20289 (10th Cir. 2000); Central S. Dakota Co-Op. Grazing Dist. v. Secretary of U.S. Dep't of Agric., 266 F.3d 889, 32 ELR 20192 (8th Cir. 2001); Earth Island Institute v. U.S. Forest Service, 697 F.3d 1010, 1019-20 (9th Cir. 2012); Native Ecosystems Council v. Weldon, 697 F.3d 1043, 1051-52 (9th Cir. 2012). While deferring to agency expertise, the 9th Circuit particularly takes care to examine the underlying scientific integrity of the decision. League of Wilderness Defenders v. U.S. Forest Service, 689 F.3d 1060, 1073 (9th Cir. 2012),

187. 40 C.F.R. §1500.4.

188. *Id.* §1500.5.

189. *Id.* §1502.21.

190. *Id.* Material based on proprietary data that is itself not available for public review cannot be incorporated by reference. *Id.*

191. *Id.* §1506.3. This section requires that the adopted EIS meet the standards of an adequate EIS, and specifically describes the kind of circulation necessary for an adopted statement. *Id.*

192. *Id.* §1506.2(b).

193. *Id.* §1506.2(c).

document to reduce paperwork and duplication.[194] When streamlining is appropriate, agencies must nevertheless ensure the professional and scientific integrity of environmental analyses.[195]

Commenting

Once the draft EIS is prepared, it is to be circulated for comment to all relevant federal, state, and local agencies; to applicants, if any; and to members of the public who request it.[196] Both the Act[197] and the regulations[198] mandate that lead agencies "obtain" comments from federal agencies with jurisdiction by law over a project or with special expertise. Lead agencies generally need only "request" comments from other federal agencies, state and local agencies, affected Indian tribes, applicants, and the public.[199] Agency comments are to be as specific as possible, and agencies making critical comments must specify what they believe should be done to address the problems they identify.[200] The usual comment period on a draft EIS is not less than 45 days,[201] although provisions exist for both reducing and extending that period.[202]

Response to Comments and the Final EIS

Consistent with NEPA's goal of public-private cooperation in environmental protection,[203] the regulations impose a requirement unique among environmental and, perhaps, all governmental obligations: In the final EIS, the lead agency must explain its position in writing to any member of the public who chooses to comment. When preparing its final EIS, the agency "shall respond" to comments by adding to or modifying its analyses, by making factual corrections, or by explaining why the comments do not warrant these actions, citing "the sources, authorities, or reasons" supporting its position.[204]

After responding to comments, the agency must circulate its final EIS in much the same manner as it did its draft EIS.[205] Although agencies do not usually request additional comments on final EISs, they may do so and anyone can still comment on a final statement before the agency makes its final decision.[206] The regulations require that the agency make no decision until 30 days after the final EIS is filed. This allows time for comment and ensures that the agency has adequate time to consider the statement.[207]

---

194. *Id.* §1506.4. Environmental statements are to be integrated to the fullest extent possible with other environmental analyses required by the Fish and Wildlife Coordination Act, the National Historic Preservation Act, and the Endangered Species Act, as well as other environmental review laws. *Id.* §1502.25(a). The draft EIS must also list all other federal permits that will be required. *Id.* §1502.25(b).

195. *Id.* §1502.24. CEQ's NEPA regulations do not require cost-benefit analyses, but give specific guidance as to the contents of such analyses if they are included. *Id.* §1502.23.

196. 40 C.F.R. §1502.19. Section 1506.6 is the provision governing public involvement throughout the NEPA process. This involvement is extensive. *Id.* §1506.6.

197. 42 U.S.C. §4332(2)(C), ELR Stat. NEPA §102(2)(C).

198. 40 C.F.R. §§1503.1(a)(1), 1503.2.

199. *Id.* §1503.1(a)(2).

200. *Id.* §1503.3.

201. *Id.* §1506.10(c).

202. *Id.* §1506.10(d).

203. 42 U.S.C. §4331(a), ELR Stat. NEPA §101(a).

204. 40 C.F.R. §1503.4. An agency is not bound to follow other agencies' comments, but it must consider them. Custer County Action Ass'n v. Garvey, 256 F.3d 1024, 1038, 31 ELR 20804, 20808 (10th Cir. 2001). Indeed, failure to respond to a comment may result in invalidation of the EIS. Dubois v. U.S. Dep't of Agric., 102 F.3d 1273, 1288, 27 ELR 20622, 20628-29 (1st Cir. 1996). At the same time, however, it is up to the lead agency to determine the value of another agency's comments. Missouri Coalition for the Environment v. FERC, 544 F.3d 955, 959 (8th Cir. 2008); Alaska Survival v. Surface Transportation Board, 705 F.3d 1073, 1087 (9th Cir. 2013). 42 U.S.C. §4332a, enacted in 2012, elaborates on the mechanics of finalizing an FEIS.

205. 40 C.F.R. §1502.19.

206. *Id.* §1503.1(b). On the rare occasion when a draft EIS is "so inadequate as to preclude meaningful analysis," the agency is required to recirculate a revised draft. *Id.* §1502.9(a).

207. *Id.* §1506.10(b)(2). The decision must also be made at least 90 days after the draft EIS. *Id.* §1506.10(b)(1). All dates are measured from the date an EIS is filed with EPA in Washington, D.C. *Id.* §§1506.9, 1506.10. That filing date is not the actual date of receipt, but the date of public notice by EPA in the *Federal Register* of the statements received during the preceding week. *Id.* §1506.10(a). The applicable regulation has specific provisions governing special timing situations, such as agency rulemaking and decisions subject to internal appeal, in which the normal time limits may be adjusted. *Id.* §1506.10(b). If the final EIS is filed within 90 days after the draft EIS is filed, the minimum 30-day and minimum 90-day periods may run concurrently, although agencies cannot allow less than 45 days for comments on the draft statement. *Id.* §1506.10(c). Lead agencies may also extend prescribed periods; EPA may, on a showing of need by the lead agency, reduce them. *Id.* §1506.10(d).

Post-Statement Procedures

CEQ Referrals

After an EIS is complete but before a decision is made on the proposal, an infrequent but important procedure may intervene: Referral to the CEQ of environmentally unsatisfactory federal action.[208] Under §309 of the CAA,[209] EPA may refer any proposed federal agency action to the CEQ if EPA determines that the action is environmentally unsatisfactory.[210] Under NEPA, other agencies may refer allegedly unsatisfactory proposed actions to the CEQ as well.[211] Only a small number of visible and significant agency proposals are referred to the CEQ.[212] As of 2002, the CEQ had received 27 referrals.[213]

A 1986 report concluded that the referral process causes agencies to consider the environmental impacts of their proposals more fully, and facilitates interagency communication and dispute resolution. The report concluded that the effectiveness of the process depends substantially on, and varies with, the CEQ's perceived competence, objectivity, and White House backing. Earlier CEQ involvement in potential disputes and increased monitoring of CEQ recommendations on referrals, the report continued, could enhance that effectiveness further.[214]

Agency Decisionmaking and the Record of Decision

The NEPA process is to be thoroughly integrated into agency decisionmaking, and CEQ's NEPA regulations are designed to ensure this integration. For example, the regulations require each agency to adopt procedures ensuring that its decisions accord with the policies and processes of NEPA.[215] In addition, the regulations require agencies to prepare a document, second in importance only to the EIS, which is designed to ensure that agency decisionmakers respect the environment: The record of decision (ROD).[216] An agency must prepare a concise and public ROD whenever it makes a decision following preparation of a final EIS.[217] The ROD must state the decision[218] and identify all alternatives. It must specify the alternative or alternatives "considered to be environmentally preferable"[219] and may specify alternatives considered to be preferable from the point of view of other "essential considerations of national policy."[220] The agency is to discuss these considerations in explaining how it reached its decision. The ROD must also state "whether all practicable means to avoid or minimize environmental harm from the alternative selected have been adopted and if not, why they were not."[221] Finally, a ROD must adopt and summarize a monitoring and enforcement program, if applicable, for any mitigation.[222]

---

208. *Id.* pt. 1504.
209. 42 U.S.C. §7609, ELR Stat. CAA §309.
210. 40 C.F.R. §1504.1(b).
211. *Id.* §§1504.1-.2.
212. The CEQ referral process is not discussed in detail because it is used so infrequently. Any agency or person affected, however, should become closely familiar with the regulations. *See id.* §§1504.2-.3.
213. *See* CEQ, *Federal NEPA Contacts, at* http://energy.gov/sites/prod/files/2013/10/f3/Federal_NEPA_Contacts-Updated_21Oct2013.pdf (last visited Dec. 19, 2013). Environmental Law Institute, Environmental Referrals and the Council on Environmental Quality (1986), *reprinted in* CEQ, Environmental Quality 1986, at 252 (1988). One reason for the paucity of referrals may be that lead agencies seek to avoid them by working more closely with other involved agencies at earlier stages. The very existence of the referral process may thus increase interagency cooperation, even if the process is not actually used much. *Id.* at 253.
214. CEQ, Environmental Quality 1986, at 253 (1988). The possibility that the CEQ will publish findings that do not support an agency's position and that can be used in litigation also serves as an impetus to agencies to pay heed to environmental factors.
215. 40 C.F.R. §1505.1.
216. *Id.* §1505.2.
217. *Id.*
218. *Id.* §1505.2(a).
219. *Id.* §1505.2(b).
220. 42 U.S.C. §4331(b), ELR Stat. NEPA §101(b); 40 C.F.R. §1505.2(b).
221. 40 C.F.R. §1505.2(c).
222. *Id.* The regulations provide specific guidance for implementation of mitigation and post-decision monitoring. *Id.* §1505.3.

As a general rule, agencies may not take any action concerning a proposal while an EIS is pending. The regulations address this important issue with specificity,[223] tracking both case law[224] and administrative practice. When, as is usually the case, a proposal is not part of an overall program, the applicable regulation prohibits taking any action on the proposal before issuance of a ROD if the action would have an adverse environmental impact or limit the choice of reasonable alternatives.[225] An individual action that is part of a larger program[226] cannot proceed while the program's EIS is pending unless the action meets three criteria: (1) it is justified independently of the program; (2) it is itself accompanied by an adequate EIS; and (3) it will not prejudice the ultimate decision on the program.[227] The regulation also specifically addresses situations involving applications to agencies both in general[228] and when applicants are developing plans or designs or are performing other work necessary to support their applications.[229]

---

223. 40 C.F.R. §1506.1.
224. The most important case in this regard is *Kleppe v. Sierra Club.* 427 U.S. 390, 6 ELR 20532 (1976).
225. 40 C.F.R. §1506.1(a).
226. The regulations refer to a program for which an EIS is "required" in order to ensure that individual actions are not held up when an agency voluntarily (without being required to do so, but in furtherance of good environmental practice) undertakes preparation of a program EIS. *Id.* §1506.1(c).
227. *Id.* "Prejudice to the ultimate decision on the program" is defined as a tendency to determine subsequent development or to limit alternatives. *Id.*
228. *Id.* §1506.l(b). If an agency considering an application becomes aware that an applicant is about to take an action that may adversely impact the environment or limit the choice of reasonable alternatives, the agency must promptly notify the applicant that it will "take appropriate action to insure that the objectives and procedures of NEPA are achieved." *Id.*
229. *Id.* §1506.1(d). Such actions are not precluded.

III. Judicial Review

Introduction

The Importance of Courts in the NEPA Process

It is judicial review that has given NEPA its significance. The Act places regulatory obligations on agencies without apparent means of oversight. By the conscious choice of its drafters, NEPA internalizes each agency's environmental obligations and is thus essentially self-regulatory in nature. Rather than relying on an outside agency for environmental analysis, each agency is to consider the environmental impacts of its own actions. While NEPA supplies a pervasive impetus for environmentally responsible decisionmaking throughout the government, the absence of institutional enforcement invites administrative inattention and noncompliance.[1] The CEQ, as a White House agency, is too small to get involved in numerous individual projects. EPA's leverage under §309 of the CAA is murky at best, and the Agency is no disinterested party, given its conflicting role as a principal preparer of EISs on its own actions. Clearly, successful implementation of NEPA must depend on some other institution removed from the administrative process.

NEPA's enforcement ultimately depends on the courts. Fortunately, the action-forcing provisions of the Act neatly lend themselves to judicial enforcement. The importance of the role these provisions have played in fostering judicial acceptance of the Act cannot be overemphasized. Judges may, and usually should, reasonably question their competence to second-guess the scientific determinations of administrative agencies. Judges may also lack understanding of or sympathy for claimants' environmental goals. But all judges understand procedure. The requirement that an EIS must be filed as a condition precedent to an action is just the sort of requirement that taps familiar judicial strains. Implementation of the procedural provisions of NEPA is judicially comfortable. It has also ensured the success of the Act.

NEPA Litigation in the Courts

NEPA litigation, while not extensive, constitutes a significant proportion of the environmental litigation against the government. In 1980, for example, the United States was a party to 63,628 actions commenced in federal district court.[2] Of these, 26,835 actions were brought under statutes[3]; of these, the United States was plaintiff in 8,600 cases and defendant in 18,235.[4] The United States was defendant in 201 of the 457 statutory cases that involved environmental causes of action.[5] In that same year, the CEQ reported that 140

---

1. Sen. Edmund Muskie (D-Me.) was somewhat leery of NEPA's self-scrutiny approach. As part of the negotiation between Sens. Henry Jackson (D. Wash.) and Muskie, the requirements of a "detailed statement"—the NEPA term for what has become popularly known as the EIS—was substituted for a requirement of "findings" because Senator Muskie believed that such findings would too strongly reflect self-serving agencies' mission-oriented priorities. 115 Cong. Rec. 29053 (1969).
2. Annual Report of the Director of the Administrative Office of the United States Courts 1980, at 376, tbl. C3 (1981).
3. The nonstatutory cases were overwhelmingly actions under contracts, while the balance primarily involved torts and real property. *Id.*
4. *Id.* at 374, tbl. C2.
5. *Id.* Less than 1% (0.716%) of the cases to which the United States was a party were environmental in nature. Of the statutory actions in which the United States as a defendant, 1.102% were environmental.

cases were brought challenging federal actions under NEPA.[6] In the most recent year for which statistics are available, 2011, 94 cases were brought under NEPA.[7] During that same year 146 NEPA cases were disposed of, 79 with judgment for the government and 29 with judgment for the complaining party.[8] The remaining cases were settled.

Overview of the Judicial Process in NEPA Cases

The Complaint

A typical NEPA case begins with a plaintiff filing a complaint in federal court seeking both declaratory and injunctive relief.[9] Typically the complaint is filed in federal district court, but there are agencies whose organic statutes require challenges to their actions to be filed in a circuit court of appeals, e.g., the Federal Aviation Administration, the Federal Energy Regulatory Commission, and the Nuclear Regulatory Commission. The complaint will typically name as defendants the various federal agency officials in the chain of command responsible for the proposed action that is alleged to violate NEPA. A complaint should also name state officials if their agencies are involved in joint lead capacities.[10] Private applicants need not be named as defendants since an injunction barring issuance of a permit will necessarily prevent the private action. Should a plaintiff be concerned that a private party might proceed with a plan in spite of injunctive relief against the agency, the plaintiff can name the private party as a co-defendant; this does not preclude the plaintiff from seeking an injunction against the private party in a separate proceeding.[11] In any event, as a practical matter, a private applicant will probably seek to intervene in an action against an agency.[12]

Venue

A limited measure of forum shopping is available under NEPA in that naming a particular official as a defendant may establish venue in a desirable locale. Venue in NEPA cases is determined under the general venue statute for suits against the federal government.[13] That statute is permissive and allows the plaintiff wide leeway in the initial choice of forum. As in other suits against the government, that choice is subject to a motion to change venue for the convenience of the parties and in the interest of justice.[14]

Discovery

Discovery is more limited in NEPA litigation than in litigation generally because judicial review is ordinarily confined to the administrative record.[15] However, it is sometimes necessary to look outside the record

6. CEQ, Environmental Quality 1981, at 183 (1982). The total includes lawsuits with causes of action in addition to those under NEPA. The CEQ maintains and annually reports statistics concerning all NEPA actions—the number of cases, the nature of the causes of action, the nature of relief, and the institutional identity (environmentalists, states, businesses, and so on) of the plaintiffs.
7. CEQ, at NEPA.gov.
8. Id.
9. For what may constitute "final agency action" under NEPA for purposes of making litigation ripe, see Association of Citizens to Protect and Preserve the Environment v. Federal Aviation Administration, 2008 WL 2751300 (11th Cir. 2008) (not published); City of Dania Beach, Fla. v. Federal Aviation Administration, 485 F.3d 1181, 1188 (D.C. Cir. 2007); and Oregon Natural Desert Ass'n v. Bureau of Land Management, 531 F.3d 1114, 1139-40 (9th Cir. 2008).
10. State officials might also be involved in highway construction projects under NEPA §102(2)(D). 42 U.S.C. §4332(2)(D), ELR Stat. NEPA §102(2)(D).
11. See Fed. R. Civ. P. 65(d); see also Foundation on Economic Trends v. Heckler, 756 F.2d 143, 155, 15 ELR 20248, 20254 (D.C. Cir. 1985).
12. An applicant will usually find it important to intervene, since its interests and the agency's may not coincide. A plaintiff generally will not resist such intervention.
13. 28 U.S.C. §1391(e). This provision allows a plaintiff to bring suit:
    (1) where a defendant resides; (2) where the cause of action arose; (3) where the real property involved in the action is situated; or (4) where the plaintiff resides if real property is not involved. Id. Section 1391 also provides for nationwide service of process.
14. 28 U.S.C. §1404(a).
15. Citizens to Preserve Overton Park v. Volpe, 401 U.S. 402, 1 ELR 20110 (1971). Of course, the alert participant in the NEPA process places all he or she wishes in the administrative record when the structure of the proceeding so permits. When an EIS is prepared, the commenting process provides the usual occasion to place such information in the record. See generally Richard McMillan & Todd D. Peterson, The Permissible Scope of Hearings, Discovery, and Additional Factfinding During Judicial Review of Informal Agency Action, 1982 Duke L.J. 333 (1982).

in order to properly evaluate what information the agency did not consider.[16] The limitations on what may be added to the record will determine what information the government will seek or divulge during discovery. In some cases, the government may assert a deliberative process privilege. In any event, the plaintiff should still press its discovery program if it is critical or useful to the case. Defendants typically have less to gain from discovery, except that discovery may bolster defenses such as standing, and, if plaintiffs have succeeded in introducing further evidence, discovery may enable defendants to examine that evidence or its presenting witnesses.

The Course of Litigation

In a NEPA case, either the U.S. Department of Justice or the local U.S. Attorney represents the federal agency, although the agency itself may answer the complaint and proceed through discovery to trial.[17] As with discovery, the usual course of NEPA litigation is more abbreviated than that of general litigation because of the time pressures that typify projects reviewed under NEPA. A plaintiff may take several steps to expedite the litigation. For example, the plaintiff may move for a preliminary injunction. As a practical matter, the case may end if the plaintiff loses at this stage and the project proceeds in the interim between the ruling and trial. Alternatively, the plaintiff can seek to have the hearing on the preliminary injunction consolidated with an advanced trial on the merits.[18] Often the plaintiff will move for summary judgment based on the administrative record, since that record was generated by the agency and purportedly contains undisputed facts. The defendant agency or intervening applicant will probably file a motion or cross-motion for summary judgment or dismissal. At any rate, most NEPA actions are resolved on motion.

Remedies

"When a court has found that a party is in violation of NEPA," the U.S. Court of Appeals for the Fifth Circuit has said, "the remedy should be shaped so as to fulfill the objectives of the statute as closely as possible, consistent with the broader public interest."[19] As stated at the outset of this Chapter, those objectives are to prevent or eliminate damage to the environment and to ensure environmentally responsible decisionmaking by agencies. In order to achieve these objectives, plaintiff may ask for, and courts may grant, preliminary or permanent injunctive relief.

Preliminary Relief

In the Supreme Court's words:

> A Plaintiff seeking a preliminary injunction must establish that he is likely to succeed on the merits, that he is likely to suffer irreparable harm in the absence of preliminary relief, that the balance of equities tips in his favor, and that an injunction is in the public interest.[20]

In so holding the Court emphasized that the irreparable harm must be "likely" and that the mere "possibility" of such harm is insufficient to warrant preliminary injunctive relief.[21] To the extent not inconsistent with *Winter*, there remain the general judicial policy of shaping injunctions to implement NEPA's objectives, rather than thwart them.[22] That said, the Supreme Court has emphasized that the traditional tests for injunctive relief remain under NEPA. There is no "thumbs on the scales" in NEPA cases.[23]

---

16. County of Suffolk v. Secretary of the Interior, 562 F.2d 1368, 1384, 7 ELR 20637, 20644 (2d Cir. 1977); *see* Animal Defense Council v. Hodel, 840 F.2d 1432, 1436-37, 18 ELR 20497, 20409-500 (9th Cir. 1988); Friends of the Payette v. Horseshoe Bend Hydroelectric Co., 988 F.2d 989, 997, 23 ELR 20530, 20534 (9th Cir. 1993); National Audubon Soc'y v. U.S. Forest Serv., 4 F.3d 832, 841-42, 23 ELR 21520, 21525 (9th Cir. 1993); Greenpeace v. Evans, 688 F. Supp. 579, 584-85, 17 ELR 21207, 21209 (W.D. Wash. 1987).
17. Note that when U.S. officers are parties in a NEPA case, the government has 60 days to file its answer. Fed. R. Civ. P. 12(a).
18. Fed. R. Civ. P. 65(a)(2).
19. Environmental Defense Fund v. Marsh, 651 F.2d 983, 1005, 11 ELR 21012, 21022 (5th Cir. 1981).
20. Winter v. Natural Resources Defense Counsel, 129 S. Ct. 365, 374 (2008); *see* Sierra Forest Legacy v. Rey, 577 F.3d 1015, 1021-24 (9th Cir. 2009).
21. *Winter*, 129 S. Ct, at 375.
22. *See* Foundation on Economic Trends v. Heckler, 756 F.2d 143, 157, 15 ELR 20248, 20255 (D.C. Cir. 1985).
23. Monsanto Co. v. Geertson Seed Farms, 130 S. Ct. 2743, 2757 (2010).

Permanent Relief

Once a violation of NEPA has been established, a plaintiff faces a somewhat lesser burden in seeking permanent injunctive relief, particularly since it need no longer show a probability of success on the merits. Nevertheless, both preliminary and permanent injunctions are equitable in nature and the considerations for whether they should issue have much in common.[24]

In the Supreme Court's words:

> [A] plaintiff seeking a permanent injunction must satisfy a four-factor test before a court may grant such relief. A plaintiff must demonstrate: (1) that is has suffered an irreparable injury; (2) that remedies available at law, such as monetary damages, are inadequate to compensate for that injury; (3) that, considering the balance of hardships between the plaintiff and defendant, a remedy in equity is warranted; and (4) that the public interest would not be disserved by a permanent injunction.[25]

When a NEPA violation has been found, the court typically shapes the injunction to remedy it. For example, if a court determines that an EIS should have been prepared, it will order the agency to prepare one.[26]

Prior to *Winter* and *Monsanto* many courts had presumed or otherwise favored injunctive relief in NEPA cases as a matter of course,[27] however, *Monsanto* has made clear that an injunction should issue only if the traditional four part test is met.[28]

That said, injunctive relief, when granted in a NEPA case, is designed to maintain the status quo until the appropriate NEPA document has been prepared.[29]

In the 1980s two Supreme Court cases gave some indication that the Court preferred appellate courts to defer to trial courts' traditional balancing of equitable factors rather than to apply presumptions necessitating injunctive relief. Those cases, *Weinberger v. Romero-Barcelo*[30] and *Amoco Production Co. v. Village of Gambell*,[31] held that violations of federal environmental statutes did not necessarily compel injunctions or raise presumptions of irreparable harm. While neither case explicitly addressed injunctive relief under NEPA, they led some lower courts to question whether Congress intended NEPA to limit traditional equitable discretion in enforcing the statute.[32] *Winter* and *Monsanto* have now given direction as to the parameters within which NEPA injunctive relief is now to be administered.

---

24. *See* CHARLES A. WRIGHT & ARTHUR R. MILLER, FEDERAL PRACTICE AND PROCEDURE §2942 (1973).
25. *Monsanto Co.*, 130 S. Ct. at 2756, *quoting* eBay Inc. v. MercExchange, L.L.C., 126 S. Ct. 1837 (2008).
26. *See, e.g.*, Environmental Defense Fund v. Marsh, 651 F.2d 983, 1005-06, 11 ELR 21012, 21022 (5th Cir. 1981).
27. *See* Environmental Defense Fund v. Froehlke, 477 F.2d 1033, 1037, 3 ELR 20383, 20384 (8th Cir. 1973); Realty Income Trust v. Eckerd, 564 F.2d 447, 456, 7 ELR 20541, 20545 (D.C. Cir. 1977); American Motorcyclist Ass'n v. Watt, 714 F.2d 962, 966, 15 ELR 20735 (9th Cir. 1983); Thomas v. Peterson, 253 F.2d 754, 764, 15 ELR 20225, 20230 (9th Cir. 1985).
28. *Monsanto Co.*, 130 S. Ct. at 2757.
29. *See Environmental Defense Fund*, 651 F.2d at 1005-06; Natural Resources Defense Council v. Calloway, 524 F.2d 79, 95, 5 ELR 20640, 20648 (2d Cir. 1975); Jones v. District of Columbia Redev. Land Agency, 499 F.2d 502, 512-13, 4 ELR 20479, 20483 (D.C. Cir. 1974). Relicensing is more akin to an irreversible and irretrievable commitment of resources that a mere continuation of the status quo. *See* Confederated Tribes & Bands of the Yakima Indian Nation v. Federal Energy Regulatory Comm'n., 746 F.2d 466, 475-76, 14 ELR 20593, 2597-98 (9th Cir. 1984), *cert. denied*, 471 U.S. 1116 (1985). For examples of the numerous cases granting injunctive relief to bar or severely limit an action pending completion of an adequate EIS, see *Save Our Ecosystems v. Clark*, 747 F.2d 1240, 1250, 15 ELR 20035, 20040 (9th Cir. 1984); *Sierra Club v. U.S. Army Corps. of Eng'rs*, 701 F.2d 1011, 1034, 13 ELR 20326, 20337-38 (2d Cir. 1983); *Environmental Defense Fund*, 651 F.2d at 1005-06; *Natural Resources Defense Council*, 524 F.2d at 94-95; *Manatee County v. Gorsuch*, 554 F. Supp. 778, 794, 13 ELR 20180, 20187-88 (M.D. Fla. 1982); *Montgomery v. Ellis*, 364 F. Supp. 517, 535, 3 ELR 20845, 20852-53 (N.D. Ala. 1973); *see also Lemon v. Geren*, 514 F.3d 1312, 1315-16 (D.C. Cir. 2008) (if unraveling a transfer is necessary, it is in the court's power to do so).
30. 456 U.S. 305, 12 ELR 20538 (1982). In *Romero-Barcelo*, the Court held that federal courts are not compelled to issue injunctions against violators of CWA §402 because the Act provided for alternative means of enforcement.
31. 480 U.S. 531, 17 ELR 20574 (1987). In *Gambell*, the Court held that the U.S. Court of Appeals for the Ninth Circuit erroneously applied a presumption of irreparable injury to the questions of whether injunctive relief was appropriate for a violation of §810 of the Alaska National Interests Lands Conservation Act (ANILCA). ANILCA §810(a) requires an evaluation of any decision relating to the use or disposition of public lands or the impact on Alaskan native subsistence uses and needs before that decision is made. If the evaluation indicates that the proposed use would significantly restrict subsistence uses, the proposal may not be implemented until certain notice and mitigation measures are met. 16 U.S.C. §3120(a). Concluding that the environment can be protected without a presumption of irreparable harm, the Court questioned the Ninth Circuit's adherence to the principal that "[i]rreparable damage is presumed when an agency fails to evaluate thoroughly the environmental impact of a proposed action." 480 U.S. at 544-45, 17 ELR at 20577.
32. *See* Northern Cheyenne Tribe v. Hodel, 815 F.2d 1152, 1158, 18 ELR 20865, 20867 (9th Cir. 1988); Save the Yaak Comm. v. Block, 840 F.2d 714, 722, 18 ELR 20869, 20873 (9th Cir. 1988); *see also* Town of Huntington v. Marsh, 884 F.2d 648, 19 ELR 21350 (2d Cir.

Defenses

Before plaintiffs can obtain temporary or permanent injunctive relief, they may have to overcome defenses typically raised by defendants or interveners in NEPA cases. These defenses are lack of standing, inapplicability of NEPA, and certain procedural defenses not specifically related to the Act.

* *Standing.* Provided that the facts are suitable and the complaint is properly worded, a standing defense should not present a significant hurdle to the plaintiff.[33] The leading case on standing in environmental litigation, *Sierra Club v. Morton*,[34] made clear that environmental as well as economic interests allow a plaintiff to meet this threshold requirement as long as injury to those interests is particularized to the plaintiff. Thus, it is insufficient for a plaintiff to assert a general interest in protecting the environment. Rather, the complaint must state that the plaintiff in fact uses and enjoys the environmental amenity alleged to be threatened. If the plaintiff is an organization, it must allege that some of its members use and enjoy that amenity. In *Morton*, for example, it was not enough for the plaintiffs to allege that they were interested in protecting the Mineral King Valley in California. Instead, they had to allege that they used and enjoyed the valley.[35]

  As another early NEPA case, *United States v. Students Challenging Regulatory Agency Procedures (SCRAP I)*,[36] made clear, the Supreme Court's broad view of standing is not diminished by pervasiveness of the alleged environmental injury. In *SCRAP I*, the Court found that plaintiffs had standing to challenge nationwide freight rates for recycled goods. The environmental injury alleged—damage to plaintiffs' recreational use and enjoyment of forests, streams, mountains, and other resources in the Washington, D.C., metropolitan region—was widely shared, but still gave plaintiffs standing to sue.[37]

  In a significant opinion dealing with standing under NEPA, *Lujan v. National Wildlife Federation*,[38] the Supreme Court took a more constrained view of standing. The Court held that plaintiffs, through their limited affidavits, lacked standing to challenge as a nationwide program what in reality the Court found to be many hundreds of separate actions.

  Given these and subsequent cases, plaintiffs who are individuals affected by a proposed action, organizations whose members include such individuals, or state or local governments[39] whose citizens are so affected should not have difficulty establishing standing if the required injury-in-fact exists and is set out with sufficient particularity. The Supreme Court has made very clear its insistence

---

1989); Sierra Club v. U.S. Forest Serv., 843 F.2d 1190, 1195, 18 ELR 20749, 20752 (9th Cir. 1988); Crutchfield v. U.S. Army Corps of Eng'rs, 192 F. Supp. 2d 444, 453 (E.D. Va. 2001).

33. *See generally* FRED R. ANDERSON, FEDERAL ENVIRONMENTAL LAW 283 (1974); WILLIAM H. RODGERS JR., HANDBOOK ON ENVIRONMENTAL LAW 22-30 (1977).

34. 405 U.S. 727, 2 ELR 20192 (1972); *see* Defenders of Wildlife v. Hodel, 851 F.2d 1035, 1039-40, 18 ELR 21343, 21345-46 (8th Cir. 1988). The injury may be threatened or contingent. *Id.*

35. The Supreme Court held that the Sierra Club's allegation of interest in environmental protection was insufficient for standing, but noted in a footnote that actual use would suffice. 405 U.S. at 735 n.8, 2 ELR at 20194 n.8. On remand, the appropriate allegations of use were made and standing was achieved. Sierra Club v. Morton, 348 F. Supp. 219, 2 ELR 20576 (N.D. Cal. 1972); *see also* Sierra Club v. SCM Corp., 747 F.2d 99, 14 ELR 20890 (2d Cir. 1984).

36. 412 U.S. 669, 3 ELR 20536 (1973); *see also* Oregon Envtl. Council v. Kunzman, 817 F.2d 484, 491-92, 17 ELR 20756, 20758 (9th Cir. 1987) (plaintiffs have standing to challenge nationwide spraying program because they live in state that is part of program, and thus have "geographical nexus"). *But see* Lujan v. National Wildlife Fed'n, 497 U.S. 871, 20 ELR 20962 (1990), discussed *infra* note 38 and accompanying text.

37. *See* Resources Ltd. v. Robertson, 8 F.3d 1394, 24 ELR 20026 (9th Cir. 1993).

38. *Lujan*, 497 U.S. at 871, 20 ELR at 20962.

39. A significant percentage of NEPA litigation typically includes state or local governmental plaintiffs. The proportion has ranged from 28% of the cases filed in 1978, CEQ, ENVIRONMENTAL QUALITY 1979, at 589 (1979); to 14 % of those filed in 1982, CEQ, ENVIRONMENTAL QUALITY 1983, at 266, tbl. 7-2 (1984); to 30% of those filed in 1985, CEQ, ENVIRONMENTAL QUALITY 1986, at 243, tbl. B-4 (1988); to 6% of those filed in 1989, CEQ, ENVIRONMENTAL QUALITY 1990, at 235, tbl. 5-4 (1991); to 8% of those filed in 1991, CEQ, ENVIRONMENTAL QUALITY 1992, at 167 (1993); to 16% of those filed in 1992, CEQ, ENVIRONMENTAL QUALITY 1993, at 371 (1994); 10% in 1997, CEQ, ENVIRONMENTAL QUALITY 1997, at 355 (1998); and 6% in 2011, CEQ, *supra* note 6.

   These percentages were computed by comparing the number of plaintiffs by category to the total number of suits filed. *See* City of Davis v. Coleman, 521 F.2d 661, 5 ELR 20633 (9th Cir. 1975); *see also* Michigan v. United States, 994 F.2d 1197, 23 ELR 21003 (6th Cir. 1993); Louisiana v. Lee, 596 F. Supp. 645, 649-50, 15 ELR 20141, 20142 (E.D. La. 1984), *rev'd*, 758 F.2d 1081, 15 ELR 20609 (5th Cir. 1985).

on the fact of injury and the connection of the plaintiff to it.[40] Some business plaintiffs, however, may have difficulty establishing that their interests are within the zone of interests protected by NEPA, a prerequisite to standing under the Act,[41] or that the injuries suffered are sufficient to confer standing.[42] Business plaintiffs are a significant proportion of the parties filing NEPA cases,[43] though, and in some of these cases environmental and business interests coincide, so that the two types of organizations join as plaintiffs.[44]

- *Inapplicability of NEPA.* Defendants and intervenors have attempted to escape judicial enforcement of NEPA by arguing that their proposals lie outside the coverage of the Act. Again, such arguments may be easily overcome and have met with little success. This is due largely to NEPA's broad mandate as affirmed by the Supreme Court; the Act applies to all agency actions, absent clear conflicts of statutory authority.[45] Only one significant exception has been carved into NEPA's reach, partly by Congress[46] and partly by the courts.[47] Certain limited regulatory activities conducted for purposes of environmental protection are said to constitute the "functional equivalents" of EISs. Additionally, the courts have generally been unsympathetic to the application of NEPA to Superfund cleanups.[48]

- *Procedural Defenses.* NEPA defendants and intervenors may raise general procedural defenses not directly related to NEPA, such as ripeness, exhaustion, laches, and mootness. These defenses, like those discussed above, have rarely been successful.[49]

---

40. Lujan v. National Wildlife Fed'n, 497 U.S. 871, 20 ELR 20962 (1990); Lujan v. Defenders of Wildlife, 504 U.S. 555, 22 ELR 20913 (1992). *But see* Resources Ltd. v. Robertson, 8 F.3d 1394, 24 ELR 20026 (9th Cir. 1993). For an exceptionally restricted view of standing see *Florida Audubon Soc'y v. Bentsen*, 94 F.3d 685 (D.C. Cir. 1996). For more traditional holdings allowing citizen standing, see *Committee to Save the Rio Hondo v. Lucero*, 102 F.3d 455, 27 ELR 20576 (10th Cir. 1996), *Dubois v. U.S. Department of Agriculture*, 102 F.3d 1273, 27 ELR 20622 (1st Cir. 1996); *Lemon v. Geren*, 514 F.3d 1312, 1315 (D.C. Cir. 2008) (an agency's failure to follow NEPA's procedures creates a procedural injury, which in turn creates standing).

41. While one circuit has held that purely economic interest does not establish standing for NEPA purposes (*ANR Pipeline Co. v. Federal Energy Regulatory Comm'n*, 205 F.3d 403, 30 ELR 20421 (D.C. Cir. 2000)), another has allowed a business concern having only economic interests to intervene in support of the government (*Kleissler v. U.S. Forest Serv.*, 157 F.3d 964, 29 ELR 20152 (3d Cir. 1998)). Yet another circuit has held that an applicant, as the one with the immediate stake in the NEPA process, may intervene as a matter of right (*Wildearth Guardians v. United State Forest Service*, 573 F.3d 992, 995-97 (10th Cir. 2009)).

42. Region 8 Forest Serv. Timber Purchasers Council v. Alcock, 993 F.2d 800, 23 ELR 21051 (11th Cir. 1993); Nevada Land Action Ass'n v. U.S. Forest Service, 8 F.3d 713, 24 ELR 20100 (9th Cir. 1993).

43. Business and industry plaintiffs were involved in 19% of the NEPA cases filed in 1978, CEQ, Environmental Quality 1979, at 589 (1979); in 12% in 1983, CEQ, Environmental Quality 1984, at 523, tbl. 12-2 (1986); in 7.4% in 1985, CEQ, Environmental Quality 1986, at 243, tbl. B-4 (1988); in 4.4 % in 1991, CEQ, Environmental Quality 1992, at 167 (1993); in 12% in 1992, CEQ, Environmental Quality 1993, at 371 (1994); in 7% in 1997, CEQ, Environmental Quality 1997, at 355 (1998); and 5% in 2011, NEPA.gov.

44. For example, NEPA litigation challenging construction of locks and dams that facilitate barge traffic on rivers may be brought both by environmental groups and by railroads, whose interests can be assumed to be at least partly competitive. *See* Environmental Defense Fund v. Marsh, 651 F.2d 983, 11 ELR 21012 (5th Cir. 1981) (Environmental Defense Fund joined with Louisville & Nashville Railroad Company in litigation over Tennessee-Tombigbee Waterway); Izaak Walton League v. Marsh, 655 F.2d 346, 11 ELR 20707 (D.C. Cir. 1981) (environmental organization joined with Atcheson, Topeka & Santa Fe Railway in suit concerning locks on Mississippi River), *cert. denied*, 454 U.S. 1092 (1981).

45. Flint Ridge Dev. Co. v. Scenic Rivers Ass'n, 426 U.S. 776, 777-78, 6 ELR 20528, 20529 (1976); *see also* Concerned About Trident v. Rumsfeld, 555 F.2d 817, 823, 6 ELR 20787, 20789-90 (D.C. Cir. 1977); Douglas County v. Babbitt, 48 F.3d 1495, 25 ELR 20631 (9th Cir. 1995). *Cf.* William B. Ellis & Turner T. Smith Jr., *The Limits of Federal Environmental Responsibility and Control Under the National Environmental Policy Act*, 18 ELR 10055 (Feb. 1988) (analyzing scope of "federal action" subject to NEPA).

46. All of EPA's actions under the CAA, and some of those under the CWA, are exempted. 15 U.S.C. §793(c)(1) (no action taken under CAA is "major Federal action" within the meaning of NEPA); 33 U.S.C. §1371(c)(1), ELR Stat. FWPCA §511 (only construction of publicly owned treatment works under §201 and issuance of new pollution source permits under §306 and §402 are not exempted from NEPA).

47. *See* Portland Cement Ass'n v. Ruckelshaus, 486 F.2d 375, 3 ELR 20642 (D.C. Cir. 1973), *cert. denied*, 417 U.S. 921 (1974); Alabama v. EPA, 911 F.2d 499, 21 ELR 20107 (11th Cir. 1990); *see also* Rodgers, *supra* note 33, at 764.

48. *See, e.g.*, Oil, Chem. & Atomic Workers Int'l Union v. Richardson, 214 F.3d 1379, 30 ELR 20754 (D.C. Cir. 2000); Farmers Against Irresponsible Remediation v. EPA, 165 F. Supp. 2d 253 (N.D.N.Y. 2001) (federal courts do not have jurisdiction over challenges to removal actions, including under NEPA); *but see* Lone Pine Steering Comm. v. EPA, 600 F. Supp. 1487, 1488, 15 ELR 20109, 20110 (D.N.J. 1985). A state court in California has applied the state's NEPA equivalent to a Superfund cleanup. *See* County of Kern v. State Dep't of Health Servs., No. 190784, slip op. (Cal. Super. Ct. 1985). The legislative history of Superfund makes clear the intent that NEPA apply in some, but not all, situations. *See generally* S. Rep. No. 948, 96th Cong., at 61 (1980).

49. *See, e.g.*, Concerned Citizens on I-190 v. Secretary of Transp., 641 F.2d 1, 2-8, 11 ELR 20087, 20087-91 (1st Cir. 1981) (laches); Park County Resources Council v. U.S. Dep't of Agric., 817 F.2d 609, 617, 17 ELR 20851, 20854 (10th Cir. 1987) (laches); Alaska Ctr. for the Env't v. U.S. Forest Serv., 189 F.3d 851, 30 ELR 20105 (9th Cir. 1999) (mootness); Lujan v. National Wildlife Fed'n, 497 U.S. 871, 894, 20 ELR 20962, 20968 (1990) (ripeness); Foundation on Economic Trends v. Heckler, 756 F.2d 143, 156, 15 ELR 20248, 20254-55 (D.C. Cir. 1985) (exhaustion).

Two NEPA regulations bear directly on the procedural aspects of judicial relief. Both were adopted to assuage apprehensions that the new regulations—designed in part to relieve delay in the NEPA process—could, paradoxically, have the opposite effect. Fears were expressed that because the regulations had a greater number of explicit commands, there would be more provisions to violate, and there would therefore be earlier and more frequent litigation that could undermine the delay reducing purpose of the regulations. The CEQ responded by adding the two provisions on judicial relief. The first directly addresses the issue of ripeness and provides that it is the

> Council's intention that judicial review of agency compliance with these regulations not occur before any agency has filed the final environmental impact statement or has made a final finding of no significant impact (when such a finding will result in action affecting the environment), or takes action that will result in irreparable injury.[50]

The second provision asserts the CEQ's intention that a "trivial violation" of the regulation "not give rise to any independent cause of action."[51] Litigation prior to an agency's final decision and litigation on minor technical flaws in the agency's procedure under NEPA are thus discouraged. The doctrine of exhaustion of administrative remedies raises the question of the degree to which objectors must make their environmental reservations known to an agency as a condition of later asserting them in court. There is a certain tension between an agency's NEPA obligations and this more traditional doctrine of administrative law. NEPA obligates an agency to gather information itself to protect the public rather than to act as an umpire between opposing parties, but a basic tenet of administrative law demands that one who has information bring it to that agency's attention before seeking judicial review.[52] Given NEPA's mandate that agencies consider all pertinent environmental impacts, courts have favored demanding more from agencies than from plaintiffs and have quite properly been reluctant to penalize plaintiffs for tardily bringing to an agency's attention what the agency itself should have known from its own studies.[53]

Standards of Review of NEPA Cases

The majority of NEPA cases filed allege that an EIS should have been prepared but was not, or that an EIS that was prepared was inadequate.[54] Hence, most substantive reviews of NEPA cases involve these issues. A smaller number of cases allege inadequate EAs or other violations of the Act.[55] The following discussion briefly analyzes the standards of review employed by courts examining these various claims.

---

50. 40 C.F.R. §1500.3. A case is not ripe when the lead agency's conditional approval depends upon the approvals of other agencies that have not acted. City of Fall River, Mass. v. FERC, 507 F.3d 1, 7 (1st Cir. 2007).

51. 40 C.F.R. §1500.3; see 43 Fed. Reg. 55978, 55981 (Nov. 29, 1978). Of course the converse is also the case—significant violations of the regulations do provide grounds for judicial relief. This is precisely how NEPA and its regulations are enforced. The question of ripeness overlaps with that of when a "proposal" exists that may require an EIS. This issue is discussed supra Ch. 2, notes 103-07, and accompanying text; see also FRED R. ANDERSON, NEPA IN THE COURTS 46-47 (1973).

52. See Greene County Planning Bd. v. Federal Power Comm'n, 455 F.2d 412, 419, 2 ELR 20017, 20019-20 (2d Cir. 1972); NEPA IN THE COURTS, supra note 51, at 45-46. In adopting its "scoping" regulation, see supra Ch. 2, notes 146-52 and accompanying text, the CEQ clearly intended to make sure that interested persons or groups are alerted to pending federal proposals before NEPA studies are undertaken. In this way, the concerns of these parties can be known and addressed. Other implications also follow, however: The opportunity to comment makes it more difficult for a person or group who is given notice but does not participate to come to court later and complain.

53. See Park County Resources Council v. U.S. Dep't of Agric., 817 F.2d 609, 619, 17 ELR 20851, 20854 (10th Cir. 1987). Anderson quite appropriately suggests a greater obligation to exhaust remedies when "extensive administrative proceedings" precede the agency's action. NEPA IN THE COURTS, supra note 51, at 46.

Courts have been as reluctant to apply the doctrine of laches to preclude NEPA claims as they have been to dismiss for failure to exhaust administrative remedies. See, e.g., Park County Resources Council, 817 F.2d at 617-19, 17 ELR at 20854; Headwaters, Inc. v. Bureau of Land Management, Medford Dist., 665 F. Supp. 873, 876, 18 ELR 21370, 21371 (D. Or. 1987). But see National Parks & Conservation Ass'n v. Hodel, 679 F. Supp. 49, 54 (D.D.C. 1987) (laches bars action).

Courts may also be reluctant to declare a NEPA complaint moot when an agency has produced an inadequate EIS, but indicates it will not implement the decision it made based on that statement, if the agency's NEPA violation is capable of repetition but evading review. See Oregon Envtl. Council v. Kunzman, 817 F.2d 484, 492, 17 ELR 20756, 20758 (9th Cir. 1987); Apache Survival Coalition v. United States, 21 F.3d 895, 24 ELR 20854 (9th Cir. 1994).

54. CEQ, ENVIRONMENTAL QUALITY 1990, 235, tbl. 5-3 (1991); CEQ, ENVIRONMENTAL QUALITY 1993, 371 (1994).

55. CEQ, ENVIRONMENTAL QUALITY 1994-95, 543 (1996); NEPA.gov.

Failure to Prepare an EIS

Since NEPA's enactment, courts have applied various standards in reviewing complaints alleging that EISs should have been prepared. Until recently, the majority employed a "reasonableness" standard, applying searching scrutiny to an agency's determination that no EIS was required.[56] A minority employed the "arbitrary and capricious" standard, a standard typically applied in the field of administrative law.[57] A few courts took middle positions.[58]

The Supreme Court, while stating that it was only deciding the "narrow question" of what standard of review governed failure to supplement an EIS, appears to have come down on the side of the arbitrary and capricious standard.[59] In doing so, however, the Court stressed that a "searching and careful" inquiry must be made[60] and observed that the difference between the two standards "is not of great pragmatic consequence."[61] "Accordingly," the Court continued, "our decision today will not require a substantial reworking of long-established NEPA law."[62] After the Supreme Court applied the arbitrary and capricious standard of review to supplementation decisions, several courts abandoned the reasonableness standard for review of an agency's threshold decision on whether to prepare an EIS in favor of the more deferential arbitrary and capricious standard.[63] The rationale for a searching and careful review of such decisions remains valid, however. That rationale was clearly articulated by the Fifth Circuit in *Save Our Ten Acres v. Kreger*[64]:

> NEP was intended not only to insure that the appropriate responsible official considered the environmental effects of the project, but also provided Congress (and others receiving such recommendation or proposal) with a sound basis for evaluating the environmental aspects of the particular project or program. The spirit of the Act would die aborning if a facile, ex parte decision that the project was minor or did not significantly affect the environment were too well shielded from impartial review. Every such decision pretermits all consideration of that which Congress has directed be considered "to the fullest extent possible." The primary decision to give or bypass the consideration required by the Act must be subject to inspection under a more searching standard.[65]

This guidance retains its wisdom. The threshold determination of whether to prepare an EIS is not the informed exercise of agency discretion, which should properly receive considerable deference. Rather, that determination is the agency's decision whether or not to inform its discretion by preparing an EIS that will provide the information it needs to evaluate the environmental consequences of a project. Judicial solicitude for agency discretion is proper when, based on whatever record the law requires, the agency exercises *informed* discretion. An agency's decision not to prepare an EIS, however, is a decision not to inform its

---

56. *See* E. David Hoskins, *Judicial Review of an Agency's Decision Not to Prepare an Environmental Impact Statement*, 18 ELR 10331, 10339-45 (Sept. 1988) (analyzing cases applying reasonableness standard).
57. *Id.* at 10336-39 (analyzing cases applying arbitrary and capricious standard).
58. Several courts have questioned whether there is any difference between the standards. *See* Sierra Club v. Marsh, 769 F.2d 868, 871, 15 ELR 20911, 20912 (1st Cir. 1985); River Road Alliance v. U.S. Army Corps of Eng'rs, 764 F.2d 445, 449, 15 ELR 20518, 20519 (7th Cir. 1985); Quinonez-Lopez v. Coco Lagoon Dev. Corp., 733 F.2d 1, 3, 14 ELR 20445, 20446 (1st Cir. 1984); The Township of Lower Alloways Creek v. Public Serv. Elec. & Gas Co., 687 F.2d 732, 742, 12 ELR 21029, 21033-34 (3d Cir. 1982); Boles v. Onton Dock, Inc., 659 F.2d 74, 75, 11 ELR 20986, 20987 (6th Cir. 1981); *see also* Marsh v. Oregon Natural Resources Council (ONRC), 490 U.S. 360, 377 n.23, 19 ELR 20749, 20753 n.23 (1989); City of Alexandria v. Federal Highway Admin., 756 F.2d 1014, 1017 (4th Cir. 1985); Committee for Auto Responsibility v. Solomon, 603 F.2d 992, 9 ELR 20575 (D.C. Cir. 1973); Peshlakai v. Duncan, 476 F. Supp. 1247, 1252, 9 ELR 20690, 20692 (D.D.C. 1979), *cert. denied*, 445 U.S. 915 (1980).
59. *ONRC*, 490 U.S. at 376, 19 ELR at 20753. However, at least one circuit has held that when the question is primarily legal rather than factual, the reasonableness standard is the appropriate one. Alaska Wilderness Recreation & Tourism Ass'n v. Morrison, 67 F.3d 723, 727, 26 ELR 20065, 20067 (9th Cir. 1995); Northcoast Envtl. Ctr. v. Glickman, 136 F.3d 660, 28 ELR 20632 (9th Cir. 1998).
60. *ONRC*, 490 U.S. at 376, 19 ELR at 20753.
61. *Id.* at 377 n.23, 19 ELR at 20753 n.23. *But see* National Audubon Soc'y v. U.S. Forest Serv., 4 F.3d 832, 840, 23 ELR 21520, 21524 (9th Cir. 1993).
62. *ONRC*, 490 U.S. at 377 n.23, 19 ELR at 20753 n.23.
63. *See, e.g.*, Greenpeace Action v. Franklin, 982 F.2d 1342, 23 ELR 20639 (9th Cir. 1992); Friends of the Payette v. Horseshoe Bend Hydroelectric Co., 988 F.2d 989, 23 ELR 20530 (9th Cir. 1993); *see also* Sabine River Auth. v. Department of the Interior, 951 F.2d 669, 22 ELR 20633 (5th Cir. 1992); Village of Los Ranchos de Albuquerque v. Marsh, 956 F.2d 970, 22 ELR 21033 (10th Cir. 1992); Lockhart v. Kenops, 927 F.2d 1028, 21 ELR 20994 (8th Cir. 1991); Committee to Preserve Boomer Lake Park v. Department of Transp., 4 F.3d 1543, 24 ELR 20142 (10th Cir. 1993). Each of these cases involved review of an agency's decision not to prepare an EIS after the agency had prepared an EA that resulted in a FONSI. The Ninth Circuit holds that when a question is primarily legal rather than factual, the reasonableness standard applies (Northcoast Envt'l Ctr. v. Glickman, 136 F.3d 660, 28 ELR 20632 (9th Cir. 1998)), while the Eighth Circuit does not apply the arbitrary and capricious standard to the threshold question whether NEPA applies (Goos v. ICC, 911 F.2d 1283, 1292 (8th Cir. 1990)).
64. 472 F.2d 463, 3 ELR 20041 (5th Cir. 1973).
65. *Id.* at 466, 3 ELR at 20042.

discretion and therefore invites more exacting judicial scrutiny. An agency should not be enabled to bypass the entire EIS requirement with a cursory assessment to which a court gives an equally cursory review. Conversely, some EAs are EISs in all but name only (both in detail and in use of the comment process), and such EAs may properly be found not to evade the fuller responsibility mandated for EISs.

Inadequacy of an EIS or EA

Cases challenging the adequacy of EISs or EAs are reviewed under a less disputed standard than decisions on whether to prepare EISs.[66] This is primarily due to the fact that such cases present factual rather than legal issues, and courts traditionally afford substantial deference to agency determinations of fact. While NEPA does not specifically provide for judicial review of EISs, these documents are usually reviewed under the Administrative Procedure Act[67] standard for review of agency actions: an agency action is to be set aside if found to be "arbitrary, capricious, an abuse of discretion, or otherwise not in accordance with law,"[68] or "without observance of procedure as required by law."[69] EAs are also judicially reviewable under this standard[70] and allegations of EA inadequacy form a significant portion of NEPA litigation.[71]

Other Nontrivial Violations of NEPA

While the CEQ does not intend for trivial violations of its regulations to give rise to independent actions,[72] nontrivial violations of the law or regulations may do so. These violations constitute the third most frequent group of allegations made in NEPA suits.[73] Where agency decisionmaking is alleged to violate NEPA regulations, the same standard applies as in cases alleging inadequate EISs—the arbitrary and capricious standard.[74]

Substantive Review of NEPA Actions

One final issue concerning judicial review merits attention—the degree to which a court can reverse an agency decision made in compliance with NEPA procedures. NEPA and its procedures seek to ensure environmentally responsible decisionmaking, but an agency may quite possibly comply with the Act and still fail to choose the action most consistent with the national environmental policy stated in §§101 and 102(1) of the Act. Early in NEPA's development there were considerable indications that the judiciary would go beyond procedure and show a greater willingness to conduct substantive review of final agency decisions.[75] The Supreme Court has limited, but has not completely foreclosed, such developments. In *Vermont Yankee Nuclear Power Corp. v. Natural Resources Defense Council*,[76] the Court said that NEPA sets forth "significant substantive goals" for the nation, but that its mandate to the agencies is "essentially

---

66. Indeed, the standard of judicial review in this area has been accurately described as "relatively stable." DANIEL MANDELKER, NEPA LAW AND LITIGATION §10.13, at 30 (1984); *see* FEDERAL ENVIRONMENTAL LAW, *supra* note 33, at 375.
67. 5 U.S.C. §706.
68. *Id.* §706(2)(A); *see* Oregon Envtl. Council v. Kunzman, 817 F.2d 484, 492, 17 ELR 20756, 20759 (9th Cir. 1987); Sierra Club v. U.S. Army Corps of Eng'rs, 772 F.2d 1043, 1050, 15 ELR 20998, 21001 (2d Cir. 1985).
69. 5 U.S.C. §706(2)(D); *see Oregon Envtl. Council*, 817 F.2d at 492, 17 ELR at 20759; Natural Resources Defense Council v. Securities & Exchange Comm'n, 606 F.2d 1031, 9 ELR 20367 (D.C. Cir. 1979); *see also* 5 U.S.C. §706(2)(C) ("in excess of statutory jurisdiction, authority, or limitation").
70. Hanly v. Kleindienst, 471 F.2d 823, 2 ELR 20717 (2d Cir. 1972), *cert. denied*, 412 U.S. 908 (1973).
71. Of the NEPA suits filed in 1992, 21% alleged this ground while 13% alleged that an EA should have been prepared but was not. CEQ, ENVIRONMENTAL QUALITY 1993, at 371 (1994). Of the NEPA cases involving EAs that were resolved in 2007, 52% were found to be inadequate (as opposed to 55% of the EISs), while in 2011, 20% of the EAs were found to be inadequate (as were 33% of the EISs). CEQ, NEPA.gov.
72. 40 C.F.R. §1500.3.
73. In 1992, six of 112 causes of action brought under NEPA were filed on bases other than those mentioned above. An additional five concerned the filing of supplemental EISs. CEQ, ENVIRONMENTAL QUALITY 1993, at 371 (1994).
74. *See supra* notes 56-65 and accompanying text.
75. *See* RODGERS, *supra* note 33, at 738-50; *see also* CEQ, ENVIRONMENTAL QUALITY 1978, at 403-05 (1979) (summarizing cases).
76. 435 U.S. 519, 8 ELR 20288 (1978).

procedural."[77] That remains an accurate statement.[78] Even acknowledging the deference properly due to agencies in their decisionmaking, the CEQ has taken the view that their actions can be so violative of NEPA's "substantive requirements"[79] as to merit review under the arbitrary and capricious standard.[80]

---

77. *Id.* at 558, 8 ELR at 20297; *see* Baltimore Gas & Elec. Co. v. Natural Resources Defense Council, 462 U.S. 87, 13 ELR 20544 (1983); Strycker's Bay Neighborhood Council v. Karlen, 444 U.S. 223, 10 ELR 20079 (1980); Paul Weinstein, *Substantive Review Under NEPA After* Vermont Yankee IV, 36 Syracuse L. Rev. 837 (1985).

   The Court has defined the judicial role as that of ensuring that agencies take a "hard look" at environmental consequences in their actions under NEPA. Kleppe v. Sierra Club, 427 U.S. 390, 6 ELR 20532 (1976); Seattle Community Council Fed'n v. Federal Aviation Admin., 961 F.2d 829 (9th Cir. 1992). This means that a reviewing court must make a pragmatic judgment as to whether the form, content, and preparation of the EIS foster "both informed decisionmaking and informed public participation." Northwest Coalition for Alternatives to Pesticides v. Lyng, 844 F.2d 588, 590-91, 18 ELR 20738, 20739 (9th Cir. 1988).

78. Robertson v. Methow Valley Citizens Council, 490 U.S. 332, 348-53, 19 ELR 20743, 20746-48 (1989).

79. 40 C.F.R. §1500.1(a).

80. *See* Federal Environmental Law, *supra* note 33; Rodgers, *supra* note 33, §7.5; Weinstein, *supra* note 77; *see also* 40 C.F.R. §§1500.1, 1502.2(d), 1505.1(a), 1505.2(b). The most recent Supreme Court discussion of this issue, however, further narrows the opportunity for review beyond the essentially procedural. *Robertson*, 490 U.S. at 332, 19 ELR at 20743. For a criticism of the Supreme Court's increasingly narrow reading of NEPA, see Nicholas C. Yost, *NEPA's Promise—Partially Fulfilled*, 20 Envtl. L. 533 (1990). While federal court rulings do not oblige a reluctant agency to make a particular decision on overt substantive NEPA grounds, the courts do force reexamination. For instance, the Nuclear Regulatory Commission decision to allow 90% of a decommissioning to occur without NEPA compliance was set aside as arbitrary and capricious and lacking a rational basis. Citizens Awareness Network, Inc. v. U.S. Nuclear Regulatory Comm'n, 59 F.3d 284, 293, 25 ELR 21564, 21568 (1st Cir. 1995).

IV. Conclusion

NEPA's congressional framers sought to change the way the federal government operates. After three decades of experience, it may fairly be concluded that they succeeded. Federal officials know that they must consider the environment in all that they do. Those who care about the environment are armed with NEPA's action-forcing provisions. Those less environmentally inclined are brought into line by this congressional enactment, buttressed by the ever-present prospect of litigation. In short, NEPA works.

IV. Conclusion

Glossary

CAA	Clean Air Act
CEA	Council of Economic Advisers
CEQ	Council on Environmental Quality
EA	environmental assessment
EIS	environmental impact statement
EOP	Executive Office of the President
EPA	U.S. Environmental Protection Agency
FONSI	finding of no significant impact
NEPA	National Environmental Policy Act
ROD	record of decision

NEPA Deskbook

Statutes

**Appendix 1   National Environmental Policy Act
42 U.S.C. §§4321-4347**

National Environmental Policy Act 42 U.S.C. §§4321-4347

§4321.   Congressional declaration of purpose

The purposes of this chapter are: To declare a national policy which will encourage productive and enjoyable harmony between man and his environment; to promote efforts which will prevent or eliminate damage to the environment and biosphere and stimulate the health and welfare of man; to enrich the understanding of the ecological systems and natural resources important to the Nation; and to establish a Council on Environmental Quality.

(Pub. L. 91–190, §2, Jan. 1, 1970, 83 Stat. 852.)

Short Title

Section 1 Pub. L. 91–190 provided: "That this Act [enacting this chapter] may be cited as the 'National Environmental Policy Act of 1969'."

Transfer of Functions

Enforcement functions of Secretary or other official in Department of the Interior related to compliance with system activities requiring coordination and approval under this chapter, and enforcement functions of Secretary or other official in Department of Agriculture, insofar as they involve lands and programs under jurisdiction of that Department, related to compliance with this chapter with respect to pre-construction, construction, and initial operation of transportation system for Canadian and Alaskan natural gas transferred to Federal Inspector, Office of Federal Inspector for Alaska Natural Gas Transportation System, until first anniversary of date of initial operation of Alaska Natural Gas Transportation System, see Reorg. Plan No. 1 of 1979, §§102(e), (f), 203(a), 44 F.R. 33663, 33666, 93 Stat. 1373, 1376, effective July 1, 1979, set out in the Appendix to Title 5, Government Organization and Employees. Office of Federal Inspector for the Alaska Natural Gas Transportation System abolished and functions and authority vested in Inspector transferred to Secretary of Energy by section 3012(b) of Pub. L. 102–486, set out as an Abolition of Office of Federal Inspector note under section 719e of Title 15, Commerce and Trade. Functions and authority vested in Secretary of Energy subsequently transferred to Federal Coordinator for Alaska Natural Gas Transportation Projects by section 720d(f) of Title 15.

Emergency Preparedness Functions

For assignment of certain emergency preparedness functions to Administrator of Environmental Protection Agency, see Parts 1, 2, and 16 of Ex. Ord. No. 12656, Nov. 18, 1988, 53 F.R. 47491, set out as a note under section 5195 of this title.

Modification or Replacement of Executive Order No. 13423

Pub. L. 111–117, div. C, title VII, §742(b), Dec. 16, 2009, 123 Stat. 3216, provided that: "Hereafter, the President may modify or replace Executive Order No. 13423 [set out as a note under this section] if the President determines that a revised or new executive order will achieve equal or better environmental or energy efficiency results."

Pub. L. 111–8, div. D, title VII, §748, Mar. 11, 2009, 123 Stat. 693, which provided that Ex. Ord. No. 13423 (set out as a note under this section) would remain in effect on and after Mar. 11, 2009, except as otherwise provided by law after Mar. 11, 2009, was repealed by Pub. L. 111–117, div. C, title VII, §742(a), Dec. 16, 2009, 123 Stat. 3216.

Necessity of Military Low-Level Flight Training To Protect National Security and Enhance Military Readiness

Pub. L. 106–398, §1 [[div. A], title III, §317], Oct. 30, 2000, 114 Stat. 1654, 1654A–57, provided that: "Nothing in the National Environmental Policy Act of 1969 (42 U.S.C. 4321 et seq.) or the regulations implementing such law shall require the Secretary of Defense or the Secretary of a military department to prepare a programmatic, nation-wide environmental impact statement for low-level flight training as a precondition to the use by the Armed Forces of an airspace for the performance of low-level training flights."

Pollution Prosecution

Pub. L. 101–593, title II, Nov. 16, 1990, 104 Stat. 2962, provided that:

"SEC. 201. SHORT TITLE.

"This title may be cited as the 'Pollution Prosecution Act of 1990'.

"SEC. 202. EPA OFFICE OF CRIMINAL INVESTIGATION.

"(a) The Administrator of the Environmental Protection Agency (hereinafter referred to as the 'Administrator') shall increase the number of criminal investigators assigned to the Office of Criminal Investigations by such numbers as may be necessary to assure that the number of criminal investigators assigned to the office—

"(1) for the period October 1, 1991, through September 30, 1992, is not less than 72;

"(2) for the period October 1, 1992, through September 30, 1993, is not less than 110;

"(3) for the period October 1, 1993, through September 30, 1994, is not less than 123;

"(4) for the period October 1, 1994, through September 30, 1995, is not less than 160;

"(5) beginning October 1, 1995, is not less than 200.

"(b) For fiscal year 1991 and in each of the following 4 fiscal years, the Administrator shall, during each such fiscal year, provide increasing numbers of additional support staff to the Office of Criminal Investigations.

"(c) The head of the Office of Criminal Investigations shall be a position in the competitive service as defined in 2102 of title 5 U.S.C. or a career reserve [reserved]

position as defined in 3132(A) [3132(a)] of title 5 U.S.C. and the head of such office shall report directly, without intervening review or approval, to the Assistant Administrator for Enforcement.

"SEC. 203. CIVIL INVESTIGATORS.

"The Administrator, as soon as practicable following the date of the enactment of this Act [Nov. 16, 1990], but no later than September 30, 1991, shall increase by fifty the number of civil investigators assigned to assist the Office of Enforcement in developing and prosecuting civil and administrative actions and carrying out its other functions.

"SEC. 204. NATIONAL TRAINING INSTITUTE.

"The Administrator shall, as soon as practicable but no later than September 30, 1991 establish within the Office of Enforcement the National Enforcement Training Institute. It shall be the function of the Institute, among others, to train Federal, State, and local lawyers, inspectors, civil and criminal investigators, and technical experts in the enforcement of the Nation's environmental laws.

"SEC. 205. AUTHORIZATION.

"For the purposes of carrying out the provisions of this Act [probably should be "this title"], there is authorized to be appropriated to the Environmental Protection Agency $13,000,000 for fiscal year 1991, $18,000,000 for fiscal year 1992, $20,000,000 for fiscal year 1993, $26,000,000 for fiscal year 1994, and $33,000,000 for fiscal year 1995."

Subchapter I—Policies and Goals

§4331.   *Congressional declaration of national environmental policy*

(a) The Congress, recognizing the profound impact of man's activity on the interrelations of all components of the natural environment, particularly the profound influences of population growth, high-density urbanization, industrial expansion, resource exploitation, and new and expanding technological advances and recognizing further the critical importance of restoring and maintaining environmental quality to the overall welfare and development of man, declares that it is the continuing policy of the Federal Government, in cooperation with State and local governments, and other concerned public and private organizations, to use all practicable means and measures, including financial and technical assistance, in a manner calculated to foster and promote the general welfare, to create and maintain conditions under which man and nature can exist in productive harmony, and fulfill the social, economic, and other requirements of present and future generations of Americans.

(b) In order to carry out the policy set forth in this chapter, it is the continuing responsibility of the Federal Government to use all practicable means, consistent with other essential considerations of national policy, to improve and coordinate Federal plans, functions, programs, and resources to the end that the Nation may—

(1) fulfill the responsibilities of each generation as trustee of the environment for succeeding generations;

(2) assure for all Americans safe, healthful, productive, and esthetically and culturally pleasing surroundings;

(3) attain the widest range of beneficial uses of the environment without degradation, risk to health or safety, or other undesirable and unintended consequences;

(4) preserve important historic, cultural, and natural aspects of our national heritage, and maintain, wherever possible, an environment which supports diversity and variety of individual choice;

(5) achieve a balance between population and resource use which will permit high standards of living and a wide sharing of life's amenities; and

(6) enhance the quality of renewable resources and approach the maximum attainable recycling of depletable resources.

(c) The Congress recognizes that each person should enjoy a healthful environment and that each person has a responsibility to contribute to the preservation and enhancement of the environment.

(Pub. L. 91–190, title I, §101, Jan. 1, 1970, 83 Stat. 852.)

Commission on Population Growth and the American Future

Pub. L. 91–213, §§1–9, Mar. 16, 1970, 84 Stat. 67–69, established the Commission on Population Growth and the American Future to conduct and sponsor such studies and research and make such recommendations as might be necessary to provide information and education to all levels of government in the United States, and to our people regarding a broad range of problems associated with population growth and their implications for America's future; prescribed the composition of the Commission; provided for the appointment of

its members, and the designation of a Chairman and Vice Chairman; required a majority of the members of the Commission to constitute a quorum, but allowed a lesser number to conduct hearings; prescribed the compensation of members of the Commission; required the Commission to conduct an inquiry into certain prescribed aspects of population growth in the United States and its foreseeable social consequences; provided for the appointment of an Executive Director and other personnel and prescribed their compensation; authorized the Commission to enter into contracts with public agencies, private firms, institutions, and individuals for the conduct of research and surveys, the preparation of reports, and other activities necessary to the discharge of its duties, and to request from any Federal department or agency any information and assistance it deems necessary to carry out its functions; required the General Services Administration to provide administrative services for the Commission on a reimbursable basis; required the Commission to submit an interim report to the President and the Congress one year after it was established and to submit its final report two years after Mar. 16, 1970; terminated the Commission sixty days after the date of the submission of its final report; and authorized to be appropriated, out of any money in the Treasury not otherwise appropriated, such amounts as might be necessary to carry out the provisions of Pub. L. 91–213.

Executive Order No. 11507

Ex. Ord. No. 11507, eff. Feb. 4, 1970, 35 F.R. 2573, which related to prevention, control, and abatement of air and water pollution at federal facilities was superseded by Ex. Ord. No. 11752, eff. Dec. 17, 1973, 38 F.R. 34793, formerly set out below.

Executive Order No. 11752

Ex. Ord. No. 11752, Dec. 17, 1973, 38 F.R. 34793, which related to the prevention, control, and abatement of environmental pollution at Federal facilities, was revoked by Ex. Ord. No. 12088, Oct. 13, 1978, 43 F.R. 47707, set out as a note under section 4321 of this title.

§4332. *Cooperation of agencies; reports; availability of information; recommendations; international and national coordination of efforts*

The Congress authorizes and directs that, to the fullest extent possible: (1) the policies, regulations, and public laws of the United States shall be interpreted and administered in accordance with the policies set forth in this chapter, and (2) all agencies of the Federal Government shall—

(A) utilize a systematic, interdisciplinary approach which will insure the integrated use of the natural and social sciences and the environmental design arts in planning and in decisionmaking which may have an impact on man's environment;

(B) identify and develop methods and procedures, in consultation with the Council on Environmental Quality established by subchapter II of this chapter, which will insure that presently unquantified environmental amenities and values may be given appropriate consideration in decisionmaking along with economic and technical considerations;

(C) include in every recommendation or report on proposals for legislation and other major Federal actions significantly affecting the quality of the human environment, a detailed statement by the responsible official on—

(i) the environmental impact of the proposed action,

(ii) any adverse environmental effects which cannot be avoided should the proposal be implemented,

(iii) alternatives to the proposed action,

(iv) the relationship between local short-term uses of man's environment and the maintenance and enhancement of long-term productivity, and

(v) any irreversible and irretrievable commitments of resources which would be involved in the proposed action should it be implemented.

Prior to making any detailed statement, the responsible Federal official shall consult with and obtain the comments of any Federal agency which has jurisdiction by law or special expertise with respect to any environmental impact involved. Copies of such statement and the comments and views of the appropriate Federal, State, and local agencies, which are authorized to develop and enforce environmental standards, shall be made available to the President, the Council on Environmental Quality and to the public as provided by section 552 of title 5, and shall accompany the proposal through the existing agency review processes;

(D) Any detailed statement required under subparagraph (C) after January 1, 1970, for any major Federal action funded under a program of grants to States shall not be deemed to be legally insufficient solely by reason of having been prepared by a State agency or official, if:

(i) the State agency or official has statewide jurisdiction and has the responsibility for such action,

(ii) the responsible Federal official furnishes guidance and participates in such preparation,

(iii) the responsible Federal official independently evaluates such statement prior to its approval and adoption, and

(iv) after January 1, 1976, the responsible Federal official provides early notification to, and solicits the views of, any other State or any Federal land management entity of any action or any alternative thereto which may have significant impacts upon such State or affected Federal land management entity and, if there is any disagreement on such impacts, prepares a written assessment of such impacts and views for incorporation into such detailed statement.

The procedures in this subparagraph shall not relieve the Federal official of his responsibilities for the scope, objectivity, and content of the entire statement or of any other responsibility under this chapter; and further, this subparagraph does not affect the legal sufficiency of statements prepared by State agencies with less than statewide jurisdiction.[1]

(E) study, develop, and describe appropriate alternatives to recommended courses of action in any proposal which involves unresolved conflicts concerning alternative uses of available resources;

(F) recognize the worldwide and long-range character of environmental problems and, where consistent with the foreign policy of the United States, lend appropriate support to initiatives, resolutions, and programs designed to maximize international cooperation in anticipating and preventing a decline in the quality of mankind's world environment;

(G) make available to States, counties, municipalities, institutions, and individuals, advice and information useful in restoring, maintaining, and enhancing the quality of the environment;

(H) initiate and utilize ecological information in the planning and development of resource-oriented projects; and

(I) assist the Council on Environmental Quality established by subchapter II of this chapter.

(Pub. L. 91–190, title I, §102, Jan. 1, 1970, 83 Stat. 853; Pub. L. 94–83, Aug. 9, 1975, 89 Stat. 424.)

---

[1] So in original. The period probably should be a semicolon.

Amendments

1975—Subpars. (D) to (I). Pub. L. 94–83 added subpar. (D) and redesignated former subpars. (D) to (H) as (E) to (I), respectively.

Certain Commercial Space Launch Activities

Pub. L. 104–88, title IV, §401, Dec. 29, 1995, 109 Stat. 955, provided that: "The licensing of a launch vehicle or launch site operator (including any amendment, extension, or renewal of the license) under chapter 701 of title 49, United States Code, shall not be considered a major Federal action for purposes of section 102(C) of the National Environmental Policy Act of 1969 (42 U.S.C. 4332(C)) if—

"(1) the Department of the Army has issued a permit for the activity; and

"(2) the Army Corps of Engineers has found that the activity has no significant impact."

Ex. Ord. No. 13352. Facilitation of Cooperative Conservation

Ex. Ord. No. 13352, Aug. 26, 2004, 69 F.R. 52989, provided:

By the authority vested in me as President by the Constitution and the laws of the United States of America, it is hereby ordered as follows:

Section 1. *Purpose.* The purpose of this order is to ensure that the Departments of the Interior, Agriculture, Commerce, and Defense and the Environmental Protection Agency implement laws relating to the environment and natural resources in a manner that promotes cooperative conservation, with an emphasis on appropriate inclusion of local participation in Federal decisionmaking, in accordance with their respective agency missions, policies, and regulations.

Sec. 2. *Definition.* As used in this order, the term "cooperative conservation" means actions that relate to use, enhancement, and enjoyment of natural resources, protection of the environment, or both, and that involve collaborative activity among Federal, State, local, and tribal governments, private for-profit and nonprofit institutions, other nongovernmental entities and individuals.

Sec. 3. *Federal Activities.* To carry out the purpose of this order, the Secretaries of the Interior, Agriculture, Commerce, and Defense and the Administrator of the Environmental Protection Agency shall, to the extent permitted by law and subject to the availability of appropriations and in coordination with each other as appropriate:

(a) carry out the programs, projects, and activities of the agency that they respectively head that implement laws relating to the environment and natural resources in a manner that:

(i) facilitates cooperative conservation;

(ii) takes appropriate account of and respects the interests of persons with ownership or other legally recognized interests in land and other natural resources;

(iii) properly accommodates local participation in Federal decisionmaking; and

(iv) provides that the programs, projects, and activities are consistent with protecting public health and safety;

(b) report annually to the Chairman of the Council on Environmental Quality on actions taken to implement this order; and

(c) provide funding to the Office of Environmental Quality Management Fund (42 U.S.C. 4375) for the Conference for which section 4 of this order provides.

Sec. 4. *White House Conference on Cooperative Conservation.* The Chairman of the Council on Environmental Quality shall, to the extent permitted by law and subject to the availability of appropriations:

(a) convene not later than 1 year after the date of this order, and thereafter at such times as the Chairman deems appropriate, a White House Conference on Cooperative Conservation (Conference) to facilitate the exchange of information and advice relating to (i) cooperative conservation and (ii) means for achievement of the purpose of this order; and

(b) ensure that the Conference obtains information in a manner that seeks from Conference participants their individual advice and does not involve collective judgment or consensus advice or deliberation.

Sec. 5. *General Provision.* This order is not intended to, and does not, create any right or benefit, substantive or procedural, enforceable at law or in equity by any party against the United States, its departments, agencies, instrumentalities or entities, its officers, employees or agents, or any other person.

George W. Bush.

§4332a. Accelerated decisionmaking in environmental reviews

(a) In general In preparing a final environmental impact statement under the National Environmental Policy Act of 1969 (42 U.S.C. 4321 et seq.), if the lead agency modifies the statement in response to comments that are minor and are confined to factual corrections or explanations of why the comments do not warrant additional agency response, the lead agency may write on errata sheets attached to the statement instead of rewriting the draft statement, subject to the condition that the errata sheets—

(1) cite the sources, authorities, or reasons that support the position of the agency; and

(2) if appropriate, indicate the circumstances that would trigger agency reappraisal or further response.

(b) Incorporation To the maximum extent practicable, the lead agency shall expeditiously develop a single document that consists of a final environmental impact statement and a record of decision, unless—

(1) the final environmental impact statement makes substantial changes to the proposed action that are relevant to environmental or safety concerns; or

(2) there are significant new circumstances or information relevant to environmental concerns and that bear on the proposed action or the impacts of the proposed action.

(Pub. L. 112–141, div. A, title I, § 1319, July 6, 2012, 126 Stat. 551.)

References in Text

The National Environmental Policy Act of 1969, referred to in subsec. (a), is Pub. L. 91–190, Jan. 1, 1970, 83 Stat. 852, which is classified generally to this chapter. For complete classification of this Act to the Code, see Short Title note set out under section 4321 of this title and Tables.

Codification

Section was enacted as part of the Moving Ahead for Progress in the 21st Century Act, also known as the MAP–21, and not as part of the National Environmental Policy Act of 1969 which comprises this chapter.

Effective Date

Section effective Oct. 1, 2012, see section 3(a) of Pub. L. 112–141, set out as an Effective and Termination

Dates of 2012 Amendment note under section 101 of Title 23, Highways.

§4333. Conformity of administrative procedures to national environmental policy

All agencies of the Federal Government shall review their present statutory authority, administrative regulations, and current policies and procedures for the purpose of determining whether there are any deficiencies or inconsistencies therein which prohibit full compliance with the purposes and provisions of this chapter and shall propose to the President not later than July 1, 1971, such measures as may be necessary to bring their authority and policies into conformity with the intent, purposes, and procedures set forth in this chapter.

(Pub. L. 91–190, title I, §103, Jan. 1, 1970, 83 Stat. 854.)

§4334. Other statutory obligations of agencies

Nothing in section 4332 or 4333 of this title shall in any way affect the specific statutory obligations of any Federal agency (1) to comply with criteria or standards of environmental quality, (2) to coordinate or consult with any other Federal or State agency, or (3) to act, or refrain from acting contingent upon the recommendations or certification of any other Federal or State agency.

(Pub. L. 91–190, title I, §104, Jan. 1, 1970, 83 Stat. 854.)

§4335. Efforts supplemental to existing authorizations

The policies and goals set forth in this chapter are supplementary to those set forth in existing authorizations of Federal agencies.

(Pub. L. 91–190, title I, §105, Jan. 1, 1970, 83 Stat. 854.)

Subchapter II—Council on Environmental Quality

§4341. Omitted

Codification

Section, Pub. L. 91–190, title II, §201, Jan. 1, 1970, 83 Stat. 854, which required the President to transmit to Congress annually an Environmental Quality Report, terminated, effective May 15, 2000, pursuant to section 3003 of Pub. L. 104–66, as amended, set out as a note under section 1113 of Title 31, Money and Finance. See, also, item 1 on page 41 of House Document No. 103–7.

§4342. Establishment; membership; Chairman; appointments

There is created in the Executive Office of the President a Council on Environmental Quality (hereinafter referred to as the "Council"). The Council shall be composed of three members who shall be appointed by the President to serve at his pleasure, by and with the advice and consent of the Senate. The President shall designate one of the members of the Council to serve as Chairman. Each member shall be a person who, as a result of his training, experience, and attainments, is exceptionally well qualified to analyze and interpret environmental trends and information of all kinds; to appraise programs and activities of the Federal Government in the light of the policy set forth in subchapter I of this chapter; to be conscious of and responsive to the scientific, economic, social, esthetic, and cultural needs and interests of the Nation; and to formulate and recommend national policies to promote the improvement of the quality of the environment.

(Pub. L. 91–190, title II, §202, Jan. 1, 1970, 83 Stat. 854.)

Council on Environmental Quality; Reduction of Members

Provisions stating that notwithstanding this section, the Council was to consist of one member, appointed by the President, by and with the advice and consent of the Senate, serving as chairman and exercising all powers, functions, and duties of the Council, were contained in the Department of the Interior, Environment, and Related Agencies Appropriations Act, 2006, Pub. L. 109–54, title III, Aug. 2, 2005, 119 Stat. 543, and were repeated in provisions of subsequent appropriations acts which are not set out in the Code. Similar provisions were also contained in the following prior appropriations acts:

Pub. L. 108–447, div. I, title III, Dec. 8, 2004, 118 Stat. 3332.

Pub. L. 108–199, div. G, title III, Jan. 23, 2004, 118 Stat. 408.

Pub. L. 108–7, div. K, title III, Feb. 20, 2003, 117 Stat. 514.

Pub. L. 107–73, title III, Nov. 26, 2001, 115 Stat. 686.

Pub. L. 106–377, §1(a)(1) [title III], Oct. 27, 2000, 114 Stat. 1441, 1441A–45.

Pub. L. 106–74, title III, Oct. 20, 1999, 113 Stat. 1084.

Pub. L. 105–276, title III, Oct. 21, 1998, 112 Stat. 2500.

Pub. L. 105–65, title III, Oct. 27, 1997, 111 Stat. 1375.

§4343. Employment of personnel, experts and consultants

(a) The Council may employ such officers and employees as may be necessary to carry out its functions under this chapter. In addition, the Council may employ and fix the compensation of such experts and consultants as may be necessary for the carrying out of its functions under this chapter, in accordance with section 3109 of title 5 (but without regard to the last sentence thereof).

(b) Notwithstanding section 1342 of title 31, the Council may accept and employ voluntary and uncompensated services in furtherance of the purposes of the Council.

(Pub. L. 91–190, title II, §203, Jan. 1, 1970, 83 Stat. 855; Pub. L. 94–52, §2, July 3, 1975, 89 Stat. 258.)

References in Text

The last sentence of section 3109 of title 5, referred to in subsec. (a), probably means the last sentence of section 3109(b) of title 5, which was the last sentence of that section when the reference was enacted. Since then, section 3109 of title 5 has been amended to add subsecs. (c) to (e) at the end.

Codification

In subsec. (b), "section 1342 of title 31" substituted for "section 3679(b) of the Revised Statutes (31 U.S.C. 665(b))" on authority of Pub. L. 97–258, §4(b), Sept. 13, 1982, 96 Stat. 1067, the first section of which enacted Title 31, Money and Finance.

Amendments

1975—Pub. L. 94–52 designated existing provisions as subsec. (a) and added subsec. (b).

§4344. Duties and functions

It shall be the duty and function of the Council—

(1) to assist and advise the President in the preparation of the Environmental Quality Report required by section 4341[1] of this title;

---

[1] See References in Text note below.

(2) to gather timely and authoritative information concerning the conditions and trends in the quality of the environment both current and prospective, to analyze and interpret such information for the purpose of determining whether such conditions and trends are interfering, or are likely to interfere, with the achievement of the policy set forth in subchapter I of this chapter, and to compile and submit to the President studies relating to such conditions and trends;

(3) to review and appraise the various programs and activities of the Federal Government in the light of the policy set forth in subchapter I of this chapter for the purpose of determining the extent to which such programs and activities are contributing to the achievement of such policy, and to make recommendations to the President with respect thereto;

(4) to develop and recommend to the President national policies to foster and promote the improvement of environmental quality to meet the conservation, social, economic, health, and other requirements and goals of the Nation;

(5) to conduct investigations, studies, surveys, research, and analyses relating to ecological systems and environmental quality;

(6) to document and define changes in the natural environment, including the plant and animal systems, and to accumulate necessary data and other information for a continuing analysis of these changes or trends and an interpretation of their underlying causes;

(7) to report at least once each year to the President on the state and condition of the environment; and

(8) to make and furnish such studies, reports thereon, and recommendations with respect to matters of policy and legislation as the President may request.

(Pub. L. 91–190, title II, §204, Jan. 1, 1970, 83 Stat. 855.)

References in Text

Section 4341 of this title, referred to in par. (1), was omitted from the Code.

Transfer of Functions

So much of functions of Council on Environmental Quality under par. (5) of this section as pertains to ecological systems transferred to Administrator of Environmental Protection Agency by Reorg. Plan No. 3 of 1970, §2(a)(5), eff. Dec. 2, 1970, 35 F.R. 15623, 84 Stat. 2086, set out under section 4321 of this title.

§4345. Consultation with Citizens' Advisory Committee on Environmental Quality and other representatives

In exercising its powers, functions, and duties under this chapter, the Council shall—

(1) consult with the Citizens' Advisory Committee on Environmental Quality established by Executive Order numbered 11472, dated May 29, 1969, and with such representatives of science, industry, agriculture, labor, conservation organizations, State and local governments and other groups, as it deems advisable; and

(2) utilize, to the fullest extent possible, the services, facilities, and information (including statistical information) of public and private agencies and organizations, and individuals, in order that duplication of effort and expense may be avoided, thus assuring that the Council's activities will not unnecessarily overlap or conflict with similar activities authorized by law and performed by established agencies.

(Pub. L. 91–190, title II, §205, Jan. 1, 1970, 83 Stat. 855.)

References in Text

Executive Order numbered 11472, dated May 29, 1969, referred to in par. (1), is set out as a note under section 4321 of this title.

Citizens' Advisory Committee on Environmental Quality

For provisions relating to termination of Citizens' Advisory Committee on Environmental Quality, see Ex. Ord. No. 12007, Aug. 22, 1977, 42 F.R. 42839, set out as a note under section 14 of the Federal Advisory Committee Act in the Appendix to Title 5, Government Organization and Employees.

§4346. Tenure and compensation of members

Members of the Council shall serve full time and the Chairman of the Council shall be compensated at the rate provided for Level II of the Executive Schedule Pay Rates (5 U.S.C. 5313). The other members of the Council shall be compensated at the rate provided for Level IV or[1] the Executive Schedule Pay Rates (5 U.S.C. 5315).

(Pub. L. 91–190, title II, §206, Jan. 1, 1970, 83 Stat. 856.)

---

[1] So in original. Probably should be "of".

§4346a. Travel reimbursement by private organizations and Federal, State, and local governments

The Council may accept reimbursements from any private nonprofit organization or from any department, agency, or instrumentality of the Federal Government, any State, or local government, for the reasonable travel expenses incurred by an officer or employee of the Council in connection with his attendance at any conference, seminar, or similar meeting conducted for the benefit of the Council.

(Pub. L. 91–190, title II, §207, as added Pub. L. 94–52, §3, July 3, 1975, 89 Stat. 258.)

§4346b. Expenditures in support of international activities

The Council may make expenditures in support of its international activities, including expenditures for: (1) international travel; (2) activities in implementation of international agreements; and (3) the support of international exchange programs in the United States and in foreign countries.

(Pub. L. 91–190, title II, §208, as added Pub. L. 94–52, §3, July 3, 1975, 89 Stat. 258.)

§4347. Authorization of appropriations

There are authorized to be appropriated to carry out the provisions of this chapter not to exceed $300,000 for fiscal year 1970, $700,000 for fiscal year 1971, and $1,000,000 for each fiscal year thereafter.

(Pub. L. 91–190, title II, §209, formerly §207, Jan. 1, 1970, 83 Stat. 856, renumbered §209, Pub. L. 94–52, §3, July 3, 1975, 89 Stat. 258.)

NEPA Deskbook

NEPA Deskbook

Appendix 1: Environmental Quality Improvement Act
42 U.S.C. §§4371-4375

Environmental Quality Improvement Act 42 U.S.C. §§4371-4375

§4371.   Congressional findings, declarations, and purposes

(a) The Congress finds—

(1) that man has caused changes in the environment;

(2) that many of these changes may affect the relationship between man and his environment; and

(3) that population increases and urban concentration contribute directly to pollution and the degradation of our environment.

(b)(1) The Congress declares that there is a national policy for the environment which provides for the enhancement of environmental quality. This policy is evidenced by statutes heretofore enacted relating to the prevention, abatement, and control of environmental pollution, water and land resources, transportation, and economic and regional development.

(2) The primary responsibility for implementing this policy rests with State and local government.

(3) The Federal Government encourages and supports implementation of this policy through appropriate regional organizations established under existing law.

(c) The purposes of this chapter are—

(1) to assure that each Federal department and agency conducting or supporting public works activities which affect the environment shall implement the policies established under existing law; and

(2) to authorize an Office of Environmental Quality, which, notwithstanding any other provision of law, shall provide the professional and administrative staff for the Council on Environmental Quality established by Public Law 91–190.

(Pub. L. 91–224, title II, §202, Apr. 3, 1970, 84 Stat. 114.)

References in Text

Public Law 91–190, referred to in subsec. (c)(2), is Pub. L. 91–190, Jan. 1, 1970, 83 Stat. 852, as amended, known as the National Environmental Policy Act of 1969, which is classified generally to chapter 55 (§4321 et seq.) of this title. For complete classification of this Act to the Code, see Short Title note set out under section 4321 of this title and Tables.

Short Title

Section 201 of Pub. L. 91–224 provided that: "This title [enacting this chapter] may be cited as the 'Environmental Quality Improvement Act of 1970'."

§4372.   Office of Environmental Quality

(a) Establishment; Director; Deputy Director

There is established in the Executive Office of the President an office to be known as the Office of Environmental Quality (hereafter in this chapter referred to as the "Office"). The Chairman of the Council on Environmental Quality established by Public Law 91–190 shall be the Director of the Office. There shall be in the Office a Deputy Director who shall be appointed by the President, by and with the advice and consent of the Senate.

(b) Compensation of Deputy Director

The compensation of the Deputy Director shall be fixed by the President at a rate not in excess of the annual rate of compensation payable to the Deputy Director of the Office of Management and Budget.

(c) Employment of personnel, experts, and consultants; compensation

The Director is authorized to employ such officers and employees (including experts and consultants) as may be necessary to enable the Office to carry out its functions under this chapter and Public Law 91–190, except that he may employ no more than ten specialists and other experts without regard to the provisions of title 5, governing appointments in the competitive service, and pay such specialists and experts without regard to the provisions of chapter 51 and subchapter III of chapter 53 of such title relating to classification and General Schedule pay rates, but no such specialist or expert shall be paid at a rate in excess of the maximum rate for GS–18 of the General Schedule under section 5332 of title 5.

(d) Duties and functions of Director

In carrying out his functions the Director shall assist and advise the President on policies and programs of the Federal Government affecting environmental quality by—

(1) providing the professional and administrative staff and support for the Council on Environmental Quality established by Public Law 91–190;

(2) assisting the Federal agencies and departments in appraising the effectiveness of existing and proposed facilities, programs, policies, and activities of the Federal Government, and those specific major projects designated by the President which do not require individual project authorization by Congress, which affect environmental quality;

(3) reviewing the adequacy of existing systems for monitoring and predicting environmental changes in order to achieve effective coverage and efficient use of research facilities and other resources;

(4) promoting the advancement of scientific knowledge of the effects of actions and technology on the environment and encourage[1] the development of the means to prevent or reduce adverse effects that endanger the health and well-being of man;

(5) assisting in coordinating among the Federal departments and agencies those programs and activities which affect, protect, and improve environmental quality;

(6) assisting the Federal departments and agencies in the development and interrelationship of environmental quality criteria and standards established through the Federal Government;

(7) collecting, collating, analyzing, and interpreting data and information on environmental quality, ecological research, and evaluation.

(e) Authority of Director to contract

The Director is authorized to contract with public or private agencies, institutions, and organizations and with individuals without regard to section 3324(a) and (b) of title 31 and section 5 of title 41 in carrying out his functions.

(Pub. L. 91–224, title II, §203, Apr. 3, 1970, 84 Stat. 114; 1970 Reorg. Plan No. 2, §102, eff. July 1, 1970, 35 F.R. 7959, 84 Stat. 2085.)

References in Text

Public Law 91–190, referred to in subsecs. (a), (c), and (d), is Pub. L. 91–190, Jan. 1, 1970, 83 Stat. 852, as amended, known as the National Environmental Policy Act of 1969, which is classified generally to chapter 55 (§4321 et seq.) of this title. For complete classification of this Act to the Code, see Short Title note set out under section 4321 of this title and Tables.

The provisions of title 5, governing appointments in the competitive service, referred to in subsec. (c), are classified to section 3301 et seq. of Title 5, Government Organization and Employees.

The General Schedule, referred to in subsec. (c), is set out under section 5332 of Title 5.

Codification

In subsec. (e), "section 3324(a) and (b) of title 31" substituted for reference to section 3648 of the Revised Statutes (31 U.S.C. 529) on authority of Pub. L. 97–258, §4(b), Sept. 13, 1982, 96 Stat. 1067, the first section of which enacted Title 31, Money and Finance.

Transfer of Functions

Functions vested by law (including reorganization plan) in Bureau of the Budget or Director of Bureau of the Budget transferred to President by section 101 of Reorg. Plan No. 2 of 1970, eff. July 1, 1970, 35 F.R. 7959, 84 Stat. 2085, set out in the Appendix to Title 5, Government Organization and Employees. Section 102 of Reorg. Plan No. 2 of 1970, redesignated Bureau of the Budget as Office of Management and Budget.

References in Other Laws to GS–16, 17, or 18 Pay Rates

References in laws to the rates of pay for GS–16, 17, or 18, or to maximum rates of pay under the General Schedule, to be considered references to rates payable under specified sections of Title 5, Government Organization and Employees, see section 529 [title I, §101(c)(1)] of Pub. L. 101–509, set out in a note under section 5376 of Title 5.

§4373. Referral of Environmental Quality Reports to standing committees having jurisdiction

Each Environmental Quality Report required by Public Law 91–190 shall, upon transmittal to Congress, be referred to each standing committee having jurisdiction over any part of the subject matter of the Report.

---

1 So in original. Probably should be "encouraging".

(Pub. L. 91–224, title II, §204, Apr. 3, 1970, 84 Stat. 115.)

References in Text

Public Law 91–190, referred to in text, is Pub. L. 91–190, Jan. 1, 1970, 83 Stat. 852, as amended, known as the National Environmental Policy Act of 1969, which is classified generally to chapter 55 (§4321 et seq.) of this title. For complete classification of this Act to the Code, see Short Title note set out under section 4321 of this title and Tables.

§4374. Authorization of appropriations

There are hereby authorized to be appropriated for the operations of the Office of Environmental Quality and the Council on Environmental Quality not to exceed the following sums for the following fiscal years which sums are in addition to those contained in Public Law 91–190:

(a) $2,126,000 for the fiscal year ending September 30, 1979.

(b) $3,000,000 for each of the fiscal years ending September 30, 1980, and September 30, 1981.

(c) $44,000 for the fiscal years ending September 30, 1982, 1983, and 1984.

(d) $480,000 for each of the fiscal years ending September 30, 1985 and September 30, 1986.

(Pub. L. 91–224, title II, §205, Apr. 3, 1970, 84 Stat. 115; Pub. L. 93–36, May 18, 1973, 87 Stat. 72; Pub. L. 94–52, §1, July 3, 1975, 89 Stat. 258; Pub. L. 94–298, May 29, 1976, 90 Stat. 587; Pub. L. 95–300, June 26, 1978, 92 Stat. 342; Pub. L. 97–350, §1, Oct. 18, 1982, 96 Stat. 1661; Pub. L. 98–581, §1, Oct. 30, 1984, 98 Stat. 3093.)

References in Text

Public Law 91–190, referred to in text, is Pub. L. 91–190, Jan. 1, 1970, 83 Stat. 852, as amended, known as the National Environmental Policy Act of 1969, which is classified generally to chapter 55 (§4321 et seq.) of this title. For complete classification of this Act to the Code, see Short Title note set out under section 4321 of this title and Tables.

Amendments

1984—Cl. (d). Pub. L. 98–581 added cl. (d).

1982—Cl. (c). Pub. L. 97–350 added cl. (c).

1978—Pub. L. 95–300 added cls. (a) and (b). Former cls. (a) to (d), which authorized appropriations of $2,000,000 for fiscal year ending June 30, 1976, $500,000 for transition period of July 1, 1976 to Sept. 30, 1976, $3,000,000 for fiscal year ending Sept. 30, 1977, and $3,000,000 for fiscal year ending Sept. 30, 1978, respectively, were struck out.

1976—Pub. L. 94–298 made changes in structure by designating existing provisions as cls. (a) and (b) and adding cls. (c) and (d).

1975—Pub. L. 94–52 substituted "$2,000,000 for the fiscal year ending June 30, 1976, and not to exceed $500,000 for the transition period (July 1, 1976 to September 30, 1976)" for "$1,500,000 for the fiscal year ending June 30, 1974, and $2,000,000 for the fiscal year ending June 30, 1975".

1973—Pub. L. 93–36 substituted provisions authorizing to be appropriated for operations of the Office of Environmental Quality and the Council on Environmental Quality $1,500,000 for fiscal year ending June 30, 1974, and $2,000,000 for fiscal year ending June 30, 1975, for provisions authorizing to be appropriated not to exceed $500,000 for fiscal year ending June 30, 1970, not to exceed $750,000 for fiscal year ending June 30, 1971, not to exceed $1,250,000 for fiscal year ending June 30, 1972, and not to exceed $1,500,000 for fiscal year ending June 30, 1973.

§4375. Office of Environmental Quality Management Fund

(a) Establishment; financing of study contracts and Federal interagency environmental projects

There is established an Office of Environmental Quality Management Fund (hereinafter referred to as the "Fund") to receive advance payments from other agencies or accounts that may be used solely to finance—

(1) study contracts that are jointly sponsored by the Office and one or more other Federal agencies; and

(2) Federal interagency environmental projects (including task forces) in which the Office participates.

(b) Study contract or project initiative

Any study contract or project that is to be financed under subsection (a) of this section may be initiated only with the approval of the Director.

(c) Regulations

The Director shall promulgate regulations setting forth policies and procedures for operation of the Fund.

(Pub. L. 91–224, title II, §206, as added Pub. L. 98–581, §2, Oct. 30, 1984, 98 Stat. 3093.)

NEPA Deskbook

Appendix 3 **Clean Air Act §309**
42 U.S.C. §7609

Clean Air Act §309
42 U.S.C. §7609

§7609.   *Policy review*

(a) Environmental impact

The Administrator shall review and comment in writing on the environmental impact of any matter relating to duties and responsibilities granted pursuant to this chapter or other provisions of the authority of the Administrator, contained in any (1) legislation proposed by any Federal department or agency, (2) newly authorized Federal projects for construction and any major Federal agency action (other than a project for construction) to which section 4332(2)(C) of this title applies, and (3) proposed regulations published by any department or agency of the Federal Government. Such written comment shall be made public at the conclusion of any such review.

(b) Unsatisfactory legislation, action, or regulation

In the event the Administrator determines that any such legislation, action, or regulation is unsatisfactory from the standpoint of public health or welfare or environmental quality, he shall publish his determination and the matter shall be referred to the Council on Environmental Quality.

(July 14, 1955, ch. 360, title III, §309, as added Pub. L. 91–604, §12(a), Dec. 31, 1970, 84 Stat. 1709.)

Codification

Section was formerly classified to section 1857h–7 of this title.

Prior Provisions

A prior section 309 of act July 14, 1955, ch. 360, title III, formerly §13, as added Dec. 17, 1963, Pub. L. 88–206, §1, 77 Stat. 401; renumbered §306, Oct. 20, 1965, Pub. L. 89–272, title I, §101(4), 79 Stat. 992; renumbered §309, Nov. 21, 1967, Pub. L. 90–148, §2, 81 Stat. 506; renumbered §316, Dec. 31, 1970, Pub. L. 91–604, §12(a), 84 Stat. 1705, related to appropriations and was classified to section 1857*l* of this title, prior to repeal by section 306 of Pub. L. 95–95. See section 7626 of this title.

Modification or Rescission of Rules, Regulations, Orders, Determinations, Contracts, Certifications, Authorizations, Delegations, and Other Actions

All rules, regulations, orders, determinations, contracts, certifications, authorizations, delegations, or other actions duly issued, made, or taken by or pursuant to act July 14, 1955, the Clean Air Act, as in effect immediately prior to the date of enactment of Pub. L. 95–95 [Aug. 7, 1977] to continue in full force and effect until modified or rescinded in accordance with act July 14, 1955, as amended by Pub. L. 95–95 [this chapter], see section 406(b) of Pub. L. 95–95, set out as an Effective Date of 1977 Amendment note under section 7401 of this title.

NEPA Deskbook

Appendix 4   State "Mini-NEPAs" and Other State Environmental Review Requirements

State "Mini-NEPAs" and Other State Environmental Review Requirements

States with Environmental Policy Acts

Fifteen states, the District of Columbia, and Puerto Rico have environmental policy acts or "little NEPAs."

State	Citation
Arkansas	Ark. Stat. Ann. §8-1-101 (1987)
California	Cal. Pub. Res. Code §§21000 et seq. (West 1982)
Connecticut	Conn. Gen. Stat. Ann. §§22a-14 to 22a-20 (West Supp. 1974-1975)
District of Columbia	D.C. Code Ann. 1981 §§6-981 et seq.
Hawaii	Hawaii Rev. Stat. §§343-1 to 343-8 (1985)
Indiana	Ind. Code Ann. §§13-1-10-1 to 13-1-10-8 (West 1987)
Maryland	Md. Nat. Res. Code Ann. §§1-301 to 1-305 (1983 and Supp. 1987)
Massachusetts	Mass. Gen. Laws Ann. Ch. 30, §§61-62H
Minnesota	Minn. Stat. Ann. §§116D.01 et seq. (West 1977 and Supp. 1981)
Montana	Mont. Code Ann. §§75-1-101 to -105; §75-1-201 (1981)
New York	N.Y. Envtl. Conserv. Law §§8-0101 to 8-0117 (McKinney 1984)
North Carolina	N.C. Gen. Stat. §§113A-1 to 10 (1978)
Puerto Rico	P.R. Laws Ann. Tit. 12, §§1121-1127
South Dakota	S.D. Codified Laws Ann. §§34A-9-1 to 34A-9-12
Virginia	Va. Code §§10.1-1200 through 10.1-1212 (Subject to redefinition by the Virginia General Assembly in 1992)
Washington	Wash. Rev. Code §§43.21C.010-43.21C.910 (1974); Wash. Admin. Code R. 197-11
Wisconsin	Wis. Stat. §§1.11 et seq.; Department of Natural Resources WEPA rules are found in Wis. Admin. Code NR 150.01-40

States With Limited Environmental Review Requirements Established by Statute, Executive Order, or Other Administrative Directives

Eighteen states and the District of Columbia have limited environmental review requirements established by statute, Executive Order, or other administrative directives.

State	Requirement
Arizona	An Executive Order mandates that the Governor's Commission on Arizona Environment evaluate environmental problems, make recommendations to the Governor, and establish a clearinghouse for the exchange of information relating to environmental problems and their solutions.
Arkansas	In addition to a "little NEPA," Ark. Code Ann. §15-41-108 provides that the Arkansas Game and Fish Commission must prepare an EIS for cutting timber on Commission land.

State	Requirement
California	In addition to a "little NEPA," the following California Codes require environmental impact reports: Cal. Food & Agric. Code §33487 (new construction or repairs of dairy farms) Cal. Gov. Code §7075 (establishment of enterprise zones) Cal. Gov. §7087.5 (initial study and notice of preparation under Employment and Economic Incentive Act) Cal. Gov. Code §51119 (timberland production zones; exemption) Cal. Gov. Code §65950.1 (extension of time for EIR for planning and zoning of development projects) Cal. Health & Safety Code §33333.3 (preparation and adoption of community redevelopment plans) Cal. Health & Safety Code §56040 (implementation and administration for large-scale urban development) Cal. Pub. Res. Code §6873.2 (oil and gas leases on tide and submerged lands and beds of navigable rivers and lakes) Cal. Pub. Res. Code §25540.4 (power facility and site certification) Cal. Pub. Res. Code §30718 (implementation of port development under California Coastal Act) Cal. Str. & H. Code §199.9 (mass transit guideway system) Cal. Water Code §13389 (applicability of EISs to Clean Water Act)
Delaware	In the Del. Code Ann. Tit. 7, Chapter 66 concerns wetlands permits, and Chapter 20, coastal zone permits.
District of Columbia	In addition to a "little NEPA," D.C. Code Ann. §43.1903 involves public utility environmental impact statements.
Georgia	The Code of Georgia provides that on certain types of actions on a case-by-case basis, the state may require that an environmental assessment be prepared; EAs would be reviewed by the state Department of Natural Resources, Environmental Protection Division.
Louisiana	La. Rev. Stat. Ann. §30:2021 (West 1991) covers interstate compacts on environmental control, for which the Louisiana Department of Environmental Quality serves as a clearinghouse for all statements of environmental impact to be prepared or reviewed by state agencies (other than Department of Transportation and Development), in accordance with NEPA. The Department of Wildlife and Fisheries is responsible for review and comment on any EIS regarding fish and wildlife resources or their habitat, as well as the discharge of dredge and fill material into state waters. The Department of Health and Human Resources is responsible for EISs regarding public health.
Massachusetts	In addition to a "little NEPA," Mass. Gen. Laws Ann. ch. 111H, §30 concern low-level radioactive waste facility licensing.
Michigan	Executive Order 1974-4 requires each state agency to prepare a formal environmental assessment for all major activities of the agency having a possible significant impact on the environment or human life. Mich. Comp. Laws Ann. §§281.655 et seq. covers EISs for sand dune mining and model zoning plans under the Lakes and Rivers Sand Dune Protection and Management Act.
New Jersey	Executive Order No. 53 (1973) requires all state agencies and departments to submit to the Department of Environmental Protection a description of the environmental impact of all major construction projects. N.J. Rev. Stat. §13:19-7 provides for EISs for such projects as coastal protection, N.J. Rev. Stat. §27:23-23-5 covers EISs for the New Jersey Turnpike authority (highways and turnpikes). N.J. Rev. Stat. §52:13F-4 refers to environmental impact statements on specific legislative bills.
North Carolina	In addition to a "little NEPA," N.C. Gen. Stat. §104G-11 concerns low-level radioactive waste management technology licensing.

State	Requirement
North Dakota	N.D. Century Code §§54-01-05.4 provides that the Governor may require EISs of a limited nature prior to the transfer of any interest in state-owned land to federal agencies.
Oregon	Although Oregon Rev. Stat. ch. 46 does not require EISs for major actions having a significant impact on the environment, permit applications for siting of major energy-generating facilities must include a background report addressing various anticipated environmental impacts.
Pennsylvania	Executive Order requires Environmental Assessments for all transportation projects. Various state regulations require EAs for other state actions.
Rhode Island	R.I. Gen. Laws §23-63-3 provides that a facility which plans to export tires for burning must submit an EIS conforming to the EPA standards.
South Dakota	In addition to a "little NEPA," S.D. Codified Laws Ann. §§49-41B-21 et seq. concern agency conversion and transmission facilities.
Utah	State of Utah Exec. Order (Aug. 27, 1974).
Washington	In addition to a "little NEPA," Wash. Rev. Code Ann. §78.52.125 (oil and gas conservation drilling that affects surface waters), Wash. Rev. Code Ann. §70.95.700 (solid waste incineration or energy recovery facility).
Wisconsin	In addition to a "little NEPA," Wis. Stat. Ann. §144.68 (solid waste, hazardous waste, and refuse).

NEPA Deskbook

Executive Orders

**Appendix 5   Executive Order 11514
Protection and Enhancement of
Environmental Quality**

Executive Order 11514

Protection and Enhancement of Environmental Quality

3 C.F.R. 902 (1966-70); as amended by Executive Order 11991, 3 C.F.R. 123 (1978)

By virtue of the authority vested in me as President of the United States and in furtherance of the purpose and policy of the National Environmental Policy Act of 1969 (Public Law No. 91-190, approved January 1, 1970), it is ordered as follows:

SECTION 1. *Policy.* The Federal Government shall provide leadership in protecting and enhancing the quality of the Nation's environment to sustain and enrich human life. Federal agencies shall initiate measures needed to direct their policies, plans and programs so as to meet national environmental goals. The Council on Environmental Quality, through the Chairman, shall advise and assist the President in leading this national effort.

SEC. 2. *Responsibilities of Federal agencies.* Consonant with Title I of the National Environmental Policy Act of 1969, hereinafter referred to as the "Act", the heads of Federal agencies shall:

(a) Monitor, evaluate, and control on a continuing basis their agencies' activities so as to protect and enhance the quality of the environment. Such activities shall include those directed to controlling pollution and enhancing the environment and those designed to accomplish other program objectives which may affect the quality of the environment. Agencies shall develop programs and measures to protect and enhance environmental quality and shall assess progress in meeting the specific objectives of such activities. Heads of agencies shall consult with appropriate Federal, State and local agencies in carrying out their activities as they affect the quality of the environment.

(b) Develop procedures to ensure the fullest practicable provision of timely public information and understanding of Federal plans and programs with environmental impact in order to obtain the views of interested parties. These procedures shall include, whenever appropriate, provision for public hearings, and shall provide the public with relevant information, including information on alternative courses of action. Federal agencies shall also encourage State and local agencies to adopt similar procedures for informing the public concerning their activities affecting the quality of the environment.

(c) Insure that information regarding existing or potential environmental problems and control methods developed as part of research, development, demonstration, test, or evaluation activities is made available to Federal agencies, States, counties, municipalities, institutions, and other entities, as appropriate.

(d) Review their agencies' statutory authority, administrative regulations, policies, and procedures, including those relating to loans, grants, contracts, leases, licenses, or permits, in order to identify any deficiencies or inconsistencies therein which prohibit or limit full compliance with the purposes and provisions of the Act. A report on this review and the corrective actions taken or planned, including such measures to be proposed to the President as may be necessary to bring their authority and policies into conformance with the intent, purposes and procedures of the Act, shall be provided to the Council on Environmental Quality not later than September 1, 1970.

(e) Engage in exchange of data and research results, and cooperate with agencies of other governments to foster the purposes of the Act.

(f) Proceed, in coordination with other agencies, with actions required by section 102 of the Act.

(g) In carrying out their responsibilities under the Act and this Order, comply with the regulations issued by the Council except where such compliance would be inconsistent with statutory requirements.

[SEC. 2(g) added by Executive Order 11991.]

SEC. 3. *Responsibilities of Council on Environmental Quality.* The Council on Environmental Quality shall:

(a) Evaluate existing and proposed policies and activities of the Federal Government directed to the control of pollution and the enhancement of the environment and to the accomplishment of other objectives which affect the quality of the environment. This shall include continuing review of procedures employed in the development and enforcement of Federal standards affecting environmental quality. Based upon such evaluations the Council shall, where appropriate, recommend to the President policies of environmental quality and shall, where appropriate, seek resolution of significant environmental issues.

(b) Recommend to the President and to the agencies priorities among programs designed for the control of pollution and for enhancement of the environment.

(c) Determine the need for new policies and programs for dealing with environmental problems not being adequately addressed.

(d) Conduct, as it determines to be appropriate, public hearings or conferences on issues of environmental significance.

(e) Promote the development and use of indices and monitoring systems (1) to assess environmental conditions and trends, (2) to predict the environmental impact of proposed public and private actions, and (3) to determine the effectiveness of programs of protecting and enhancing environmental quality.

(f) Coordinate Federal programs related to environmental quality.

(g) Advise and assist the President and the agencies in achieving international cooperation for dealing with environmental problems, under the foreign policy guidance of the Secretary of State.

(h) Issue regulations to Federal agencies for the implementation of the procedural provisions of the Act (42 U.S.C. 4332(2)). Such regulations shall be developed after consultation with affected agencies and after such public hearings as may be appropriate. They will be designed to make the environmental impact statement process more useful to decisionmakers and the public; and to reduce paperwork and the accumulation of extraneous background data, in order to emphasize the need to focus on real environmental issues and alternatives. They will require impact statements to be con-

cise, clear, and to the point, and supported by evidence that agencies have made the necessary environmental analyses. The Council shall include in its regulations procedures (1) for the early preparation of environmental impact statements, and (2) for the referral to the Council of conflicts between agencies concerning the implementation of the National Environmental Policy Act of 1969, as amended, and Section 309 of the Clean Air Act, as amended, for the Council's recommendation as to their prompt resolution.

[SEC. 3(h) revised by Executive Order 11991.]

(i) Issue such other instructions to agencies, and request such reports and other information from them, as may be required to carry out the Council's responsibilities under the Act.

(j) Assist the President in preparing the annual Environmental Quality Report provided for in section 201 of the Act.

(k) Foster investigations, studies, surveys, research, and analyses relating to (i) ecological systems and environmental quality, (ii) the impact of new and changing technologies thereon, and (iii) means of preventing or reducing adverse effects from such technologies.

SEC. 4. *Amendments of E.O. 11472. [Omitted -- Ed.].*

RICHARD NIXON
The White House
March 5, 1970

NEPA Deskbook

Appendix 6 **Executive Order 12114**
Environmental Effects Abroad of
Major Federal Actions

Executive Order 12114

Environmental Effects Abroad of Major Federal Actions

3 C.F.R. 356 (1980)

By virtue of the authority vested in me by the Constitution and the laws of the United States, and as President of the United States, in order to further environmental objectives consistent with the foreign policy and national security policy of the United States, it is ordered as follows:

SEC. 1.

1-1. *Purpose and Scope.* The purpose of this Executive Order is to enable responsible officials of Federal agencies having ultimate responsibility for authorizing and approving actions encompassed by this Order to be informed of pertinent environmental considerations and to take such considerations into account, with other pertinent considerations of national policy, in making decisions regarding such actions. While based on independent authority, this Order furthers the purpose of the National Environmental Policy Act and the Marine Protection Research and Sanctuaries Act and the Deepwater Port Act consistent with the foreign policy and national security policy of the United States, and represents the United States government's exclusive and complete determination of the procedural and other actions to be taken by Federal agencies to further the purpose of the National Environmental Policy Act, with respect to the environment outside the United States, its territories and possessions.

SEC. 2.

2-1. *Agency Procedures.* Every Federal agency taking major Federal actions encompassed hereby and not exempted herefrom having significant effects on the environment outside the geographical borders of the United States and its territories and possessions shall within eight months after the effective date of this Order have in effect procedures to implement this Order. Agencies shall consult with the Department of State and the Council on Environmental Quality concerning such procedures prior to placing them in effect.

2-2. *Information Exchange.* To assist in effectuating the foregoing purpose, the Department of State and the Council on Environmental Quality in collaboration with other interested Federal agencies and other nations shall conduct a program for exchange on a continuing basis of information concerning the envi-

ronment. The objectives of this program shall be to provide information for use by decisionmakers, to heighten awareness of and interest in environmental concerns and, as appropriate, to facilitate environmental cooperation with foreign nations.

2-3. *Actions Included.* Agencies in their procedures under Section 2-1 shall establish procedures by which their officers having ultimate responsibility for authorizing and approving actions in one of the following categories encompassed by this Order, take into consideration in making decisions concerning such actions, a document described in Section 2-4(a):

(a) major Federal actions significantly affecting the environment of the global commons outside the jurisdiction of any nation (e.g., the oceans or Antarctica);

(b) major Federal actions significantly affecting the environment of a foreign nation not participating with the United States and not otherwise involved in the action;

(c) major Federal actions significantly affecting the environment of a foreign nation which provide to that nation:

(1) a product, or physical project producing a principal product or an emission or effluent, which is prohibited or strictly regulated by Federal law in the United States because its toxic effects on the environment create a serious public health risk; or

(2) a physical project which in the United States is prohibited or strictly regulated by Federal law to protect the environment against radioactive substances.

(d) major Federal actions outside the United States, its territories and possessions which significantly affect natural or ecological resources of global importance designated for protection under this subsection by the President, or, in the case of such a resource protected by international agreement binding on the United States, by the Secretary of State. Recommendations to the President under this subsection shall be accompanied by the views of the Council on Environmental Quality and the Secretary of State.

2-4. *Applicable Procedures.* (a) There are the following types of documents to be used in connection with actions described in Section 2-3:

(i) environmental impact statements (including generic, program and specific statements);

(ii) bilateral or multilateral environmental studies, relevant or related to the proposed action, by the United

States and one or more foreign nations, or by an international body or organization in which the United States is a member or participant; or

(iii) concise reviews of the environmental issues involved, including environmental assessments, summary environmental analyses or other appropriate documents.

(b) Agencies shall in their procedures provide for preparation of documents described in Section 2-4(a), with respect to actions described in Section 2-3, as follows:

(i) for effects described in Section 2-3(a), an environmental impact statement described in Section 2-4(a)(i);

(ii) for effects described in Section 2-3(b), a document described in Section 2-4(a)(ii) or (iii), as determined by the agency;

(iii) for effects described in Section 2-3(c), a document described in Section 2-4(a)(ii) or (iii), as determined by the agency;

(iv) for effects described in Section 2-3(d), a document described in Section 2-4(a)(i), (ii) or (iii), as determined by the agency.

Such procedures may provide that an agency need not prepare a new document when a document described in Section 2-4(a) already exists.

(c) Nothing in this Order shall serve to invalidate any existing regulations of any agency which have been adopted pursuant to court order or pursuant to judicial settlement of any case or to prevent any agency from providing in its procedures for measures in addition to those provided for herein to further the purpose of the National Environmental Policy Act and other environmental laws, including the Marine Protection Research and Sanctuaries Act and the Deepwater Port Act, consistent with the foreign and national security policies of the United States.

(d) Except as provided in Section 2-5(b), agencies taking action encompassed by this Order shall, as soon as feasible, inform other Federal agencies with relevant expertise of the availability of environmental documents prepared under this Order.

Agencies in their procedures under Section 2-1 shall make appropriate provision for determining when an affected nation shall be informed in accordance with Section 3-2 of this Order of the availability of environmental documents prepared pursuant to those procedures.

In order to avoid duplication of resources, agencies in their procedures shall provide for appropriate utilization of the resources of other Federal agencies with relevant environmental jurisdiction or expertise.

2-5. *Exemptions and Considerations.*

(a) Notwithstanding Section 2-3, the following actions are exempt from this Order:

(i) actions not having a significant effect on the environment outside the United States as determined by the agency;

(ii) actions taken by the President;

(iii) actions taken by or pursuant to the direction of the President or Cabinet officer when the national security or interest is involved or when the action occurs in the course of an armed conflict;

(iv) intelligence activities and arms transfers;

(v) export licenses or permits or export approvals, and actions relating to nuclear activities except actions providing to a foreign nation a nuclear production or utilization facility as defined in the Atomic Energy Act of 1954, as amended, or a nuclear waste management facility;

(vi) votes and other actions in international conferences and organizations;

(vii) disaster and emergency relief action.

(b) Agency procedures under Section 2-1 implementing Section 2-4 may provide for appropriate modifications in the contents, timing and availability of documents to other affected Federal agencies and affected nations, where necessary to:

(i) enable the agency to decide and act promptly as and when required;

(ii) avoid adverse impacts on foreign relations or infringement in fact or appearance of other nations' sovereign responsibilities; or

(iii) ensure appropriate reflection of:

(1) diplomatic factors;

(2) international commercial, competitive and export promotion factors;

(3) needs for governmental or commercial confidentiality;

(4) national security considerations;

(5) difficulties of obtaining information and agency ability to analyze meaningfully environmental effects of a proposed action; and

(6) the degree to which the agency is involved in or able to affect a decision to be made.

(c) Agency procedures under Section 2-1 may provide for categorical exclusions and for such exemptions in addition to those specified in subsection (a) of this Section as may be necessary to meet emergency circumstances, situations involving exceptional foreign policy and national security sensitivities and other such special circumstances. In utilizing such additional exemptions agencies shall, as soon as feasible, consult with the Department of State and the Council on Environmental Quality.

(d) The provisions of Section 2-5 do not apply to actions described in Section 2-3(a) unless permitted by law.

SEC. 3.

3-1. *Rights of Action.* This Order is solely for the purpose of establishing internal procedures for Federal agencies to consider the significant effects of their actions on the environment outside the United States, its territories and possessions, and nothing in this Order shall be construed to create a cause of action.

3-2. *Foreign Relations.* The Department of State shall coordinate all communications by agencies with foreign governments concerning environmental agreements and other arrangements in implementation of this Order.

3-3. *Multi-Agency Actions.* Where more than one Federal agency is involved in an action or program, a lead agency, as determined by the agencies involved, shall have responsibility for implementation of this Order.

3-4. *Certain Terms.* For purposes of this Order, "environment" means the natural and physical environment and excludes social, economic and other environments; and an action significantly affects the environment if it does significant harm to the environment even though on balance the agency believes the action to be beneficial to the environment. The term "export approvals" in Section 2-5(a)(v) does not mean or include direct loans to finance exports.

3-5. *Multiple Impacts.* If a major Federal action having effects on the environment of the United States or the global commons requires preparation of an environmental impact statement, and if the action also has effects on the environment of a foreign nation, an environmental impact statement need not be prepared with respect to the effects on the environment of the foreign nation.

JIMMY CARTER
The White House,
January 4, 1979.

[Filed with the Office of the Federal Register, 3:38 p.m., January 5, 1979]

NEPA Deskbook

Regulations

Appendix 7   Council on Environmental Quality NEPA Regulations, 40 C.F.R. Pts. 1500-1508

Council on Environmental Quality

NEPA Regulations

40 C.F.R. Pts. 1500-1508

Pt. 1500

Part 1500—Purpose, Policy, and Mandate

Authority:
NEPA, the Environmental Quality Improvement Act of 1970, as amended (42 U.S.C. 4371 et seq.), sec. 309 of the Clean Air Act, as amended (42 U.S.C. 7609) and E.O. 11514, Mar. 5, 1970, as amended by E.O. 11991, May 24, 1977).

Source:
43 FR 55990, Nov. 28, 1978, unless otherwise noted.

§1500.1   Purpose.

(a) The National Environmental Policy Act (NEPA) is our basic national charter for protection of the environment. It establishes policy, sets goals (section 101), and provides means (section 102) for carrying out the policy. Section 102(2) contains "action-forcing" provisions to make sure that federal agencies act according to the letter and spirit of the Act. The regulations that follow implement section 102(2). Their purpose is to tell federal agencies what they must do to comply with the procedures and achieve the goals of the Act. The President, the federal agencies, and the courts share responsibility for enforcing the Act so as to achieve the substantive requirements of section 101.

(b) NEPA procedures must insure that environmental information is available to public officials and citizens before decisions are made and before actions are taken. The information must be of high quality. Accurate scientific analysis, expert agency comments, and public scrutiny are essential to implementing NEPA. Most important, NEPA documents must concentrate on the issues that are truly significant to the action in question, rather than amassing needless detail.

(c) Ultimately, of course, it is not better documents but better decisions that count. NEPA's purpose is not to generate paperwork—even excellent paperwork—but to foster excellent action. The NEPA process is intended to help public officials make decisions that are based on understanding of environmental consequences, and take actions that protect, restore, and enhance the environment. These regulations provide the direction to achieve this purpose.

§1500.2   Policy.

Federal agencies shall to the fullest extent possible:

(a) Interpret and administer the policies, regulations, and public laws of the United States in accordance with the policies set forth in the Act and in these regulations.

(b) Implement procedures to make the NEPA process more useful to decisionmakers and the public; to reduce paperwork and the accumulation of extraneous background data; and to emphasize real environmental issues and alternatives. Environmental impact statements shall be concise, clear, and to the point, and shall be supported by evidence that agencies have made the necessary environmental analyses.

(c) Integrate the requirements of NEPA with other planning and environmental review procedures required by law or by agency practice so that all such procedures run concurrently rather than consecutively.

(d) Encourage and facilitate public involvement in decisions which affect the quality of the human environment.

(e) Use the NEPA process to identify and assess the reasonable alternatives to proposed actions that will avoid or minimize adverse effects of these actions upon the quality of the human environment.

(f) Use all practicable means, consistent with the requirements of the Act and other essential considerations of national policy, to restore and enhance the quality of the human environment and avoid or minimize any possible adverse effects of their actions upon the quality of the human environment.

§1500.3   Mandate.

Parts 1500 through 1508 of this title provide regulations applicable to and binding on all Federal agencies for implementing the procedural provisions of the National Environmental Policy Act of 1969, as amended (Pub. L. 91-190, 42 U.S.C. 4321 et seq.) (NEPA or the Act) except where compliance would be inconsistent with other statutory requirements. These regulations are issued pursuant to NEPA, the Environmental Quality Improvement Act of 1970, as amended (42 U.S.C. 4371 et seq.) section 309 of the Clean Air Act, as amended (42 U.S.C. 7609) and Executive Order 11514, Protection and Enhancement of Environmental Quality (March 5, 1970, as amended by Executive Order 11991, May 24, 1977). These regulations, unlike the predecessor guidelines, are not confined to sec. 102(2)(C) (environmental impact statements). The regulations apply to the whole of section 102(2). The provisions of the Act and of these regulations must be read together as a whole in order to comply with the spirit and letter of the law. It is the Council's intention that judicial review of agency compliance with these regulations not occur before an agency has filed the final environmental impact statement, or has made a final finding of no significant impact (when such a finding will result in action affecting the environment), or takes action that will result in irreparable injury. Furthermore, it is the Council's intention that any trivial violation of these regulations not give rise to any independent cause of action.

§1500.4   Reducing paperwork.

Agencies shall reduce excessive paperwork by:

(a) Reducing the length of environmental impact statements (§ 1502.2(c)), by means such as setting appropriate page limits (§§ 1501.7(b)(1) and 1502.7).

(b) Preparing analytic rather than encyclopedic environmental impact statements (§ 1502.2(a)).

(c) Discussing only briefly issues other than significant ones (§ 1502.2(b)).

(d) Writing environmental impact statements in plain language (§ 1502.8).

(e) Following a clear format for environmental impact statements (§ 1502.10).

(f) Emphasizing the portions of the environmental impact statement that are useful to decisionmakers and the public (§§ 1502.14 and 1502.15) and reducing emphasis on background material (§ 1502.16).

(g) Using the scoping process, not only to identify significant environmental issues deserving of study, but also to deemphasize insignificant issues, narrowing the scope of the environmental impact statement process accordingly (§ 1501.7).

(h) Summarizing the environmental impact statement (§ 1502.12) and circulating the summary instead of the entire environmental impact statement if the latter is unusually long (§ 1502.19).

(i) Using program, policy, or plan environmental impact statements and tiering from statements of broad scope to those of narrower scope, to eliminate repetitive discussions of the same issues (§§ 1502.4 and 1502.20).

(j) Incorporating by reference (§ 1502.21).

(k) Integrating NEPA requirements with other environmental review and consultation requirements (§ 1502.25).

(l) Requiring comments to be as specific as possible (§ 1503.3).

(m) Attaching and circulating only changes to the draft environmental impact statement, rather than rewriting and circulating the entire statement when changes are minor (§ 1503.4(c)).

(n) Eliminating duplication with State and local procedures, by providing for joint preparation (§ 1506.2), and with other Federal procedures, by providing that an agency may adopt appropriate environmental documents prepared by another agency (§ 1506.3).

(o) Combining environmental documents with other documents (§ 1506.4).

(p) Using categorical exclusions to define categories of actions which do not individually or cumulatively have a significant effect on the human environment and which are therefore exempt from requirements to prepare an environmental impact statement (§ 1508.4).

(q) Using a finding of no significant impact when an action not otherwise excluded will not have a significant effect on the human environment and is therefore exempt from requirements to prepare an environmental impact statement (§ 1508.13).

[43 FR 55990, Nov. 29, 1978; 44 FR 873, Jan. 3, 1979]

§1500.5   Reducing delay.

Agencies shall reduce delay by:

(a) Integrating the NEPA process into early planning (§ 1501.2).

(b) Emphasizing interagency cooperation before the environmental impact statement is prepared, rather than submission of adversary comments on a completed document (§ 1501.6).

(c) Insuring the swift and fair resolution of lead agency disputes (§ 1501.5).

(d) Using the scoping process for an early identification of what are and what are not the real issues (§ 1501.7).

(e) Establishing appropriate time limits for the environmental impact statement process (§§ 1501.7(b)(2) and 1501.8).

(f) Preparing environmental impact statements early in the process (§ 1502.5).

(g) Integrating NEPA requirements with other environmental review and consultation requirements (§ 1502.25).

(h) Eliminating duplication with State and local procedures by providing for joint preparation (§ 1506.2) and with other Federal procedures by providing that an agency may adopt appropriate environmental documents prepared by another agency (§ 1506.3).

(i) Combining environmental documents with other documents (§ 1506.4).

(j) Using accelerated procedures for proposals for legislation (§ 1506.8).

(k) Using categorical exclusions to define categories of actions which do not individually or cumulatively have a significant effect on the human environment (§ 1508.4) and which are therefore exempt from requirements to prepare an environmental impact statement.

(l) Using a finding of no significant impact when an action not otherwise excluded will not have a significant effect on the human environment (§ 1508.13) and is therefore exempt from requirements to prepare an environmental impact statement.

§1500.6   Agency authority.

Each agency shall interpret the provisions of the Act as a supplement to its existing authority and as a mandate to view traditional policies and missions in the light of the Act's national environmental objectives. Agencies shall review their policies, procedures, and regulations accordingly and revise them as necessary to insure full compliance with the purposes and provisions of the Act. The phrase "to the fullest extent possible" in section 102 means that each agency of the Federal Government shall comply with that section unless existing law applicable to the agency's operations expressly prohibits or makes compliance impossible.

Pt. 1501

Part 1501—NEPA and Agency Planning

Sec.
1501.1   Purpose.
1501.2   Apply NEPA early in the process.
1501.3   When to prepare an environmental assessment.
1501.4   Whether to prepare an environmental impact statement.
1501.5   Lead agencies.
1501.6   Cooperating agencies.
1501.7   Scoping.
1501.8   Time limits.

Authority:
NEPA, the Environmental Quality Improvement Act of 1970, as amended (42 U.S.C. 4371 et seq.), sec. 309 of the Clean Air Act, as amended (42 U.S.C. 7609, and E.O. 11514 (Mar. 5, 1970, as amended by E.O. 11991, May 24, 1977).

Source:
43 FR 55992, Nov. 29, 1978, unless otherwise noted.

§1501.1   Purpose.

The purposes of this part include:

(a) Integrating the NEPA process into early planning to insure appropriate consideration of NEPA's policies and to eliminate delay.

(b) Emphasizing cooperative consultation among agencies before the environmental impact statement is prepared rather than submission of adversary comments on a completed document.

(c) Providing for the swift and fair resolution of lead agency disputes.

(d) Identifying at an early stage the significant environmental issues deserving of study and deemphasizing insignificant issues, narrowing the scope of the environmental impact statement accordingly.

(e) Providing a mechanism for putting appropriate time limits on the environmental impact statement process.

§1501.2   Apply NEPA early in the process.

Agencies shall integrate the NEPA process with other planning at the earliest possible time to insure that planning and decisions reflect environmental values, to avoid delays later in the process, and to head off potential conflicts. Each agency shall:

(a) Comply with the mandate of section 102(2)(A) to "utilize a systematic, interdisciplinary approach which will insure the integrated use of the natural and social sciences and the environmental design arts in planning and in decisionmaking which may have an impact on man's environment," as specified by § 1507.2.

(b) Identify environmental effects and values in adequate detail so they can be compared to economic and technical analyses. Environmental documents and appropriate analyses shall be circulated and reviewed at the same time as other planning documents.

(c) Study, develop, and describe appropriate alternatives to recommended courses of action in any proposal which involves unresolved conflicts concerning alternative uses of available resources as provided by section 102(2)(E) of the Act.

(d) Provide for cases where actions are planned by private applicants or other non-Federal entities before Federal involvement so that:

(1) Policies or designated staff are available to advise potential applicants of studies or other information foreseeably required for later Federal action.

(2) The Federal agency consults early with appropriate State and local agencies and Indian tribes and with interested private persons and organizations when its own involvement is reasonably foreseeable.

(3) The Federal agency commences its NEPA process at the earliest possible time.

§1501.3　When to prepare an environmental assessment.

(a) Agencies shall prepare an environmental assessment (§ 1508.9) when necessary under the procedures adopted by individual agencies to supplement these regulations as described in § 1507.3. An assessment is not necessary if the agency has decided to prepare an environmental impact statement.

(b) Agencies may prepare an environmental assessment on any action at any time in order to assist agency planning and decisionmaking.

§1501.4　Whether to prepare an environmental impact statement.

In determining whether to prepare an environmental impact statement the Federal agency shall:

(a) Determine under its procedures supplementing these regulations (described in § 1507.3) whether the proposal is one which:

(1) Normally requires an environmental impact statement, or

(2) Normally does not require either an environmental impact statement or an environmental assessment (categorical exclusion).

(b) If the proposed action is not covered by paragraph (a) of this section, prepare an environmental assessment (§ 1508.9). The agency shall involve environmental agencies, applicants, and the public, to the extent practicable, in preparing assessments required by § 1508.9(a)(1).

(c) Based on the environmental assessment make its determination whether to prepare an environmental impact statement.

(d) Commence the scoping process (§ 1501.7), if the agency will prepare an environmental impact statement.

(e) Prepare a finding of no significant impact (§ 1508.13), if the agency determines on the basis of the environmental assessment not to prepare a statement.

(1) The agency shall make the finding of no significant impact available to the affected public as specified in § 1506.6.

(2) In certain limited circumstances, which the agency may cover in its procedures under § 1507.3, the agency shall make the finding of no significant impact available for public review (including State and areawide clearinghouses) for 30 days before the agency makes its final determination whether to prepare an environmental impact statement and before the action may begin. The circumstances are:

(i) The proposed action is, or is closely similar to, one which normally requires the preparation of an environmental impact statement under the procedures adopted by the agency pursuant to § 1507.3, or

(ii) The nature of the proposed action is one without precedent.

§1501.5　Lead agencies.

(a) A lead agency shall supervise the preparation of an environmental impact statement if more than one Federal agency either:

(1) Proposes or is involved in the same action; or

(2) Is involved in a group of actions directly related to each other because of their functional interdependence or geographical proximity.

(b) Federal, State, or local agencies, including at least one Federal agency, may act as joint lead agencies to prepare an environmental impact statement (§ 1506.2).

(c) If an action falls within the provisions of paragraph (a) of this section the potential lead agencies shall determine by letter or memorandum which agency shall be the lead agency and which shall be cooperating agencies. The agencies shall resolve the lead agency question so as not to cause delay. If there is disagreement among the agencies, the following factors (which are listed in order of descending importance) shall determine lead agency designation:

(1) Magnitude of agency's involvement.

(2) Project approval/disapproval authority.

(3) Expertise concerning the action's environmental effects.

(4) Duration of agency's involvement.

(5) Sequence of agency's involvement.

(d) Any Federal agency, or any State or local agency or private person substantially affected by the absence of lead agency designation, may make a written request to the potential lead agencies that a lead agency be designated.

(e) If Federal agencies are unable to agree on which agency will be the lead agency or if the procedure described in paragraph (c) of this section has not resulted within 45 days in a lead agency designation, any of the agencies or persons concerned may file a request with the Council asking it to determine which Federal agency shall be the lead agency.

A copy of the request shall be transmitted to each potential lead agency. The request shall consist of:

(1) A precise description of the nature and extent of the proposed action.

(2) A detailed statement of why each potential lead agency should or should not be the lead agency under the criteria specified in paragraph (c) of this section.

(f) A response may be filed by any potential lead agency concerned within 20 days after a request is filed with the Council. The Council shall determine as soon as possible but not later than 20 days after receiving the request and all responses to it which Federal agency shall be the lead agency and which other Federal agencies shall be cooperating agencies.

[43 FR 55992, Nov. 29, 1978; 44 FR 873, Jan. 3, 1979]

§ 1501.6   Cooperating agencies.

The purpose of this section is to emphasize agency cooperation early in the NEPA process. Upon request of the lead agency, any other Federal agency which has jurisdiction by law shall be a cooperating agency. In addition any other Federal agency which has special expertise with respect to any environmental issue, which should be addressed in the statement may be a cooperating agency upon request of the lead agency. An agency may request the lead agency to designate it a cooperating agency.

(a) The lead agency shall: (1) Request the participation of each cooperating agency in the NEPA process at the earliest possible time.

(2) Use the environmental analysis and proposals of cooperating agencies with jurisdiction by law or special expertise, to the maximum extent possible consistent with its responsibility as lead agency.

(3) Meet with a cooperating agency at the latter's request.

(b) Each cooperating agency shall:

(1) Participate in the NEPA process at the earliest possible time.

(2) Participate in the scoping process (described below in § 1501.7).

(3) Assume on request of the lead agency responsibility for developing information and preparing environmental analyses including portions of the environmental impact statement concerning which the cooperating agency has special expertise.

(4) Make available staff support at the lead agency's request to enhance the latter's interdisciplinary capability.

(5) Normally use its own funds. The lead agency shall, to the extent available funds permit, fund those major activities or analyses it requests from cooperating agencies. Potential lead agencies shall include such funding requirements in their budget requests.

(c) A cooperating agency may in response to a lead agency's request for assistance in preparing the environmental impact statement (described in paragraph (b)(3), (4), or (5) of this section) reply that other program commitments preclude any involvement or the degree of involvement requested in the action that is the subject of the environmental impact statement. A copy of this reply shall be submitted to the Council.

§1501.7   Scoping.

There shall be an early and open process for determining the scope of issues to be addressed and for identifying the significant issues related to a proposed action. This process shall be termed scoping. As soon as practicable after its decision to prepare an environmental impact statement and before the scoping process the lead agency shall publish a notice of intent (§ 1508.22) in the Federal Register except as provided in § 1507.3(e).

(a) As part of the scoping process the lead agency shall:

(1) Invite the participation of affected Federal, State, and local agencies, any affected Indian tribe, the proponent of the action, and other interested persons (including those who might not be in accord with the action on environmental grounds), unless there is a limited exception under § 1507.3(c). An agency may give notice in accordance with § 1506.6.

(2) Determine the scope (§ 1508.25) and the significant issues to be analyzed in depth in the environmental impact statement.

(3) Identify and eliminate from detailed study the issues which are not significant or which have been covered by prior environmental review (§ 1506.3), narrowing the discussion of these issues in the statement to a brief presentation of why they will not have a significant effect on the human environment or providing a reference to their coverage elsewhere.

(4) Allocate assignments for preparation of the environmental impact statement among the lead and cooperating agencies, with the lead agency retaining responsibility for the statement.

(5) Indicate any public environmental assessments and other environmental impact statements which are being or will be prepared that are related to but are not part of the scope of the impact statement under consideration.

(6) Identify other environmental review and consultation requirements so the lead and cooperating agencies may prepare other required analyses and studies con-

currently with, and integrated with, the environmental impact statement as provided in § 1502.25.

(7) Indicate the relationship between the timing of the preparation of environmental analyses and the agency's tentative planning and decisionmaking schedule.

(b) As part of the scoping process the lead agency may:

(1) Set page limits on environmental documents (§ 1502.7).

(2) Set time limits (§ 1501.8).

(3) Adopt procedures under § 1507.3 to combine its environmental assessment process with its scoping process.

(4) Hold an early scoping meeting or meetings which may be integrated with any other early planning meeting the agency has. Such a scoping meeting will often be appropriate when the impacts of a particular action are confined to specific sites.

(c) An agency shall revise the determinations made under paragraphs (a) and (b) of this section if substantial changes are made later in the proposed action, or if significant new circumstances or information arise which bear on the proposal or its impacts.

§1501.8   Time limits.

Although the Council has decided that prescribed universal time limits for the entire NEPA process are too inflexible, Federal agencies are encouraged to set time limits appropriate to individual actions (consistent with the time intervals required by § 1506.10). When multiple agencies are involved the reference to agency below means lead agency.

(a) The agency shall set time limits if an applicant for the proposed action requests them: Provided, That the limits are consistent with the purposes of NEPA and other essential considerations of national policy.

(b) The agency may:

(1) Consider the following factors in determining time limits:

(i) Potential for environmental harm.

(ii) Size of the proposed action.

(iii) State of the art of analytic techniques.

(iv) Degree of public need for the proposed action, including the consequences of delay.

(v) Number of persons and agencies affected.

(vi) Degree to which relevant information is known and if not known the time required for obtaining it.

(vii) Degree to which the action is controversial.

(viii) Other time limits imposed on the agency by law, regulations, or executive order.

(2) Set overall time limits or limits for each constituent part of the NEPA process, which may include:

(i) Decision on whether to prepare an environmental impact statement (if not already decided).

(ii) Determination of the scope of the environmental impact statement.

(iii) Preparation of the draft environmental impact statement.

(iv) Review of any comments on the draft environmental impact statement from the public and agencies.

(v) Preparation of the final environmental impact statement.

(vi) Review of any comments on the final environmental impact statement.

(vii) Decision on the action based in part on the environmental impact statement.

(3) Designate a person (such as the project manager or a person in the agency's office with NEPA responsibilities) to expedite the NEPA process.

(c) State or local agencies or members of the public may request a Federal Agency to set time limits.

Pt. 1502

Part 1502—Environmental Impact Statement

Authority:
NEPA, the Environmental Quality Improvement Act of 1970, as amended (42 U.S.C. 4371 et seq.), sec. 309 of the Clean Air Act, as amended (42 U.S.C. 7609), and E.O. 11514 (Mar. 5, 1970, as amended by E.O. 11991, May 24, 1977).

Source:
43 FR 55994, Nov. 29, 1978, unless otherwise noted.

§1502.1   Purpose.

The primary purpose of an environmental impact statement is to serve as an action-forcing device to insure that the policies and goals defined in the Act are infused into the ongoing programs and actions of the Federal Government. It shall provide full and fair discussion of significant environmental impacts and shall inform decisionmakers and the public of the reasonable alternatives which would avoid or minimize adverse impacts or enhance the quality of the human environment. Agencies shall focus on significant environmental issues and alternatives and shall reduce paperwork and the accumulation of extraneous background data. Statements shall be concise, clear, and to the point, and shall be supported by evidence that the agency has made the necessary environmental analyses. An environmental impact statement is more than a disclosure document. It shall be used by Federal officials in conjunction with other relevant material to plan actions and make decisions.

§1502.2   Implementation.

To achieve the purposes set forth in § 1502.1 agencies shall prepare environmental impact statements in the following manner:

(a) Environmental impact statements shall be analytic rather than encyclopedic.

(b) Impacts shall be discussed in proportion to their significance. There shall be only brief discussion of other than significant issues. As in a finding of no significant impact, there should be only enough discussion to show why more study is not warranted.

(c) Environmental impact statements shall be kept concise and shall be no longer than absolutely necessary to comply with NEPA and with these regulations. Length should vary first with potential environmental problems and then with project size.

(d) Environmental impact statements shall state how alternatives considered in it and decisions based on it will or will not achieve the requirements of sections 101 and 102(1) of the Act and other environmental laws and policies.

(e) The range of alternatives discussed in environmental impact statements shall encompass those to be considered by the ultimate agency decisionmaker.

(f) Agencies shall not commit resources prejudicing selection of alternatives before making a final decision (§ 1506.1).

(g) Environmental impact statements shall serve as the means of assessing the environmental impact of proposed agency actions, rather than justifying decisions already made.

§1502.3   Statutory requirements for statements.

As required by sec. 102(2)(C) of NEPA environmental impact statements (§ 1508.11) are to be included in every recommendation or report.

On proposals (§ 1508.23).

For legislation and (§ 1508.17).

Other major Federal actions (§ 1508.18).

Significantly (§ 1508.27).

Affecting (§§ 1508.3, 1508.8).

The quality of the human environment (§ 1508.14).

§1502.4   Major Federal actions requiring the preparation of environmental impact statements.

(a) Agencies shall make sure the proposal which is the subject of an environmental impact statement is properly defined. Agencies shall use the criteria for scope (§ 1508.25) to determine which proposal(s) shall be the subject of a particular statement. Proposals or parts of proposals which are related to each other closely enough to be, in effect, a single course of action shall be evaluated in a single impact statement.

(b) Environmental impact statements may be prepared, and are sometimes required, for broad Federal actions such as the adoption of new agency programs or regulations (§ 1508.18). Agencies shall prepare statements on broad actions so that they are relevant to policy and are timed to coincide with meaningful points in agency planning and decisionmaking.

(c) When preparing statements on broad actions (including proposals by more than one agency), agencies may find it useful to evaluate the proposal(s) in one of the following ways:

(1) Geographically, including actions occurring in the same general location, such as body of water, region, or metropolitan area.

(2) Generically, including actions which have relevant similarities, such as common timing, impacts, alternatives, methods of implementation, media, or subject matter.

(3) By stage of technological development including federal or federally assisted research, development or demonstration programs for new technologies which, if applied, could significantly affect the quality of the human environment. Statements shall be prepared on such programs and shall be available before the program has reached a stage of investment or commitment to implementation likely to determine subsequent development or restrict later alternatives.

(d) Agencies shall as appropriate employ scoping (§ 1501.7), tiering (§ 1502.20), and other methods listed in §§ 1500.4 and 1500.5 to relate broad and narrow actions and to avoid duplication and delay.

§1502.5   Timing.

An agency shall commence preparation of an environmental impact statement as close as possible to the time the agency is developing or is presented with a proposal (§ 1508.23) so that preparation can be completed in time for the final statement to be included in any recommendation or report on the proposal. The statement shall be prepared early enough so that it can serve practically as an important contribution to the decisionmaking process and will not be used to rationalize or justify decisions already made (§§ 1500.2(c), 1501.2, and 1502.2). For instance:

(a) For projects directly undertaken by Federal agencies the environmental impact statement shall be prepared at the feasibility analysis (go-no go) stage and may be supplemented at a later stage if necessary.

(b) For applications to the agency appropriate environmental assessments or statements shall be commenced no later than immediately after the application is received. Federal agencies are encouraged to begin preparation of such assessments or statements earlier, preferably jointly with applicable State or local agencies.

(c) For adjudication, the final environmental impact statement shall normally precede the final staff recommendation and that portion of the public hearing related to the impact study. In appropriate circumstances the statement may follow preliminary hearings designed to gather information for use in the statements.

(d) For informal rulemaking the draft environmental impact statement shall normally accompany the proposed rule.

§1502.6   Interdisciplinary preparation.

Environmental impact statements shall be prepared using an inter-disciplinary approach which will insure the integrated use of the natural and social sciences and the environmental design arts (section 102(2)(A) of the Act). The disciplines of the preparers shall be appropriate to the scope and issues identified in the scoping process (§ 1501.7).

§1502.7   Page limits.

The text of final environmental impact statements (e.g., paragraphs (d) through (g) of § 1502.10) shall normally be less than 150 pages and for proposals of unusual scope or complexity shall normally be less than 300 pages.

§1502.8   Writing.

Environmental impact statements shall be written in plain language and may use appropriate graphics so that decisionmakers and the public can readily understand them. Agencies should employ writers of clear prose or editors to write, review, or edit statements, which will be based upon the analysis and supporting data from the natural and social sciences and the environmental design arts.

§1502.9   Draft, final, and supplemental statements.

Except for proposals for legislation as provided in § 1506.8 environmental impact statements shall be prepared in two stages and may be supplemented.

(a) Draft environmental impact statements shall be prepared in accordance with the scope decided upon in the scoping process. The lead agency shall work with the cooperating agencies and shall obtain comments as required in part 1503 of this chapter. The draft statement must fulfill and satisfy to the fullest extent possible the requirements established for final statements in section 102(2)(C) of the Act. If a draft statement is so inadequate as to preclude meaningful analysis, the agency shall prepare and circulate a revised draft of the appropriate portion. The agency shall make every effort to disclose and discuss at appropriate points in the draft statement all major points of view on the environmental impacts of the alternatives including the proposed action.

(b) Final environmental impact statements shall respond to comments as required in part 1503 of this chapter. The agency shall discuss at appropriate points in the final statement any responsible opposing view which was not adequately discussed in the draft statement and shall indicate the agency's response to the issues raised.

(c) Agencies:

(1) Shall prepare supplements to either draft or final environmental impact statements if:

(i) The agency makes substantial changes in the proposed action that are relevant to environmental concerns; or

(ii) There are significant new circumstances or information relevant to environmental concerns and bearing on the proposed action or its impacts.

(2) May also prepare supplements when the agency determines that the purposes of the Act will be furthered by doing so.

(3) Shall adopt procedures for introducing a supplement into its formal administrative record, if such a record exists.

(4) Shall prepare, circulate, and file a supplement to a statement in the same fashion (exclusive of scoping) as a draft and final statement unless alternative procedures are approved by the Council.

§1502.10 Recommended format.

Agencies shall use a format for environmental impact statements which will encourage good analysis and clear presentation of the alternatives including the proposed action. The following standard format for environmental impact statements should be followed unless the agency determines that there is a compelling reason to do otherwise:

(a) Cover sheet.

(b) Summary.

(c) Table of contents.

(d) Purpose of and need for action.

(e) Alternatives including proposed action (sections 102(2)(C)(iii) and 102(2)(E) of the Act).

(f) Affected environment.

(g) Environmental consequences (especially sections 102(2)(C)(i), (ii), (iv), and (v) of the Act).

(h) List of preparers.

(i) List of Agencies, Organizations, and persons to whom copies of the statement are sent.

(j) Index.

(k) Appendices (if any).

If a different format is used, it shall include paragraphs (a), (b), (c), (h), (i), and (j), of this section and shall include the substance of paragraphs (d), (e), (f), (g), and (k) of this section, as further described in §§ 1502.11 through 1502.18, in any appropriate format.

§1502.11 Cover sheet.

The cover sheet shall not exceed one page. It shall include:

(a) A list of the responsible agencies including the lead agency and any cooperating agencies.

(b) The title of the proposed action that is the subject of the statement (and if appropriate the titles of related cooperating agency actions), together with the State(s) and county(ies) (or other jurisdiction if applicable) where the action is located.

(c) The name, address, and telephone number of the person at the agency who can supply further information.

(d) A designation of the statement as a draft, final, or draft or final supplement.

(e) A one paragraph abstract of the statement.

(f) The date by which comments must be received (computed in cooperation with EPA under § 1506.10).

The information required by this section may be entered on Standard Form 424 (in items 4, 6, 7, 10, and 18).

§1502.12 Summary.

Each environmental impact statement shall contain a summary which adequately and accurately summarizes the statement. The summary shall stress the major conclusions, areas of controversy (including issues raised by agencies and the public), and the issues to be resolved (including the choice among alternatives). The summary will normally not exceed 15 pages.

§1502.13 Purpose and need.

The statement shall briefly specify the underlying purpose and need to which the agency is responding in proposing the alternatives including the proposed action.

§1502.14 Alternatives including the proposed action.

This section is the heart of the environmental impact statement. Based on the information and analysis presented in the sections on the Affected Environment (§ 1502.15) and the Environmental Consequences (§ 1502.16), it should present the environmental impacts of the proposal and the alternatives in comparative form, thus sharply defining the issues and providing a clear basis for choice among options by the decisionmaker and the public. In this section agencies shall:

(a) Rigorously explore and objectively evaluate all reasonable alternatives, and for alternatives which were eliminated from detailed study, briefly discuss the reasons for their having been eliminated.

(b) Devote substantial treatment to each alternative considered in detail including the proposed action so that reviewers may evaluate their comparative merits.

(c) Include reasonable alternatives not within the jurisdiction of the lead agency.

(d) Include the alternative of no action.

(e) Identify the agency's preferred alternative or alternatives, if one or more exists, in the draft statement and identify such alternative in the final statement unless another law prohibits the expression of such a preference.

(f) Include appropriate mitigation measures not already included in the proposed action or alternatives.

§1502.15 Affected environment.

The environmental impact statement shall succinctly describe the environment of the area(s) to be affected or created by the alternatives under consideration. The descriptions shall be no longer than is necessary to understand the effects of the alternatives. Data and analyses in a statement shall be commensurate with the importance of the impact, with less important material summarized, consolidated, or simply referenced. Agencies shall avoid useless bulk in statements and shall concentrate effort and attention on important issues. Verbose descriptions of the affected environment are themselves no measure of the adequacy of an environmental impact statement.

§1502.16 Environmental consequences.

This section forms the scientific and analytic basis for the comparisons under § 1502.14. It shall consolidate the discussions of those elements required by sections 102(2)(C)(i), (ii), (iv), and (v) of NEPA which are within the scope of the statement and as much of section 102(2)(C)(iii) as is necessary to support the comparisons. The discussion will include the environmental impacts of the alternatives including the proposed action, any adverse environmental effects which cannot be avoided should the proposal be implemented, the relationship between short-term uses of man's environment and the maintenance and enhancement of long-term productivity, and any irreversible or irretrievable commitments of resources which would be involved in the proposal should it be implemented. This section should not duplicate discussions in § 1502.14. It shall include discussions of:

(a) Direct effects and their significance (§ 1508.8).

(b) Indirect effects and their significance (§ 1508.8).

(c) Possible conflicts between the proposed action and the objectives of Federal, regional, State, and local (and in the case of a reservation, Indian tribe) land use plans, policies and controls for the area concerned. (See § 1506.2(d).)

(d) The environmental effects of alternatives including the proposed action. The comparisons under § 1502.14 will be based on this discussion.

(e) Energy requirements and conservation potential of various alternatives and mitigation measures.

(f) Natural or depletable resource requirements and conservation potential of various alternatives and mitigation measures.

(g) Urban quality, historic and cultural resources, and the design of the built environment, including the reuse and conservation potential of various alternatives and mitigation measures.

(h) Means to mitigate adverse environmental impacts (if not fully covered under § 1502.14(f)).

[43 FR 55994, Nov. 29, 1978; 44 FR 873, Jan. 3, 1979]

§1502.17 List of preparers.

The environmental impact statement shall list the names, together with their qualifications (expertise, experience, professional disciplines), of the persons who were primarily responsible for preparing the environmental impact statement or significant background papers, including basic components of the statement (§§ 1502.6 and 1502.8). Where possible the persons who are responsible for a particular analysis, including analyses in background papers, shall be identified. Normally the list will not exceed two pages.

§1502.18 Appendix.

If an agency prepares an appendix to an environmental impact statement the appendix shall:

(a) Consist of material prepared in connection with an environmental impact statement (as distinct from material which is not so prepared and which is incorporated by reference (§ 1502.21)).

(b) Normally consist of material which substantiates any analysis fundamental to the impact statement.

(c) Normally be analytic and relevant to the decision to be made.

(d) Be circulated with the environmental impact statement or be readily available on request.

§1502.19 Circulation of the environmental impact statement.

Agencies shall circulate the entire draft and final environmental impact statements except for certain appendices as provided in § 1502.18(d) and unchanged statements as provided in § 1503.4(c). However, if the statement is unusually long, the agency may circulate the summary instead, except that the entire statement shall be furnished to:

(a) Any Federal agency which has jurisdiction by law or special expertise with respect to any environmental impact involved and any appropriate Federal, State or local agency authorized to develop and enforce environmental standards.

(b) The applicant, if any.

(c) Any person, organization, or agency requesting the entire environmental impact statement.

(d) In the case of a final environmental impact statement any person, organization, or agency which submitted substantive comments on the draft.

If the agency circulates the summary and thereafter receives a timely request for the entire statement and for additional time to comment, the time for that requestor only shall be extended by at least 15 days beyond the minimum period.

§1502.20   Tiering.

Agencies are encouraged to tier their environmental impact statements to eliminate repetitive discussions of the same issues and to focus on the actual issues ripe for decision at each level of environmental review (§ 1508.28). Whenever a broad environmental impact statement has been prepared (such as a program or policy statement) and a subsequent statement or environmental assessment is then prepared on an action included within the entire program or policy (such as a site specific action) the subsequent statement or environmental assessment need only summarize the issues discussed in the broader statement and incorporate discussions from the broader statement by reference and shall concentrate on the issues specific to the subsequent action. The subsequent document shall state where the earlier document is available. Tiering may also be appropriate for different stages of actions. (Section 1508.28).

§1502.21   Incorporation by reference.

Agencies shall incorporate material into an environmental impact statement by reference when the effect will be to cut down on bulk without impeding agency and public review of the action. The incorporated material shall be cited in the statement and its content briefly described. No material may be incorporated by reference unless it is reasonably available for inspec-

tion by potentially interested persons within the time allowed for comment. Material based on proprietary data which is itself not available for review and comment shall not be incorporated by reference.

§1502.22   Incomplete or unavailable information.

When an agency is evaluating reasonably foreseeable significant adverse effects on the human environment in an environmental impact statement and there is incomplete or unavailable information, the agency shall always make clear that such information is lacking.

(a) If the incomplete information relevant to reasonably foreseeable significant adverse impacts is essential to a reasoned choice among alternatives and the overall costs of obtaining it are not exorbitant, the agency shall include the information in the environmental impact statement.

(b) If the information relevant to reasonably foreseeable significant adverse impacts cannot be obtained because the overall costs of obtaining it are exorbitant or the means to obtain it are not known, the agency shall include within the environmental impact statement:

(1) A statement that such information is incomplete or unavailable; (2) a statement of the relevance of the incomplete or unavailable information to evaluating reasonably foreseeable significant adverse impacts on the human environment; (3) a summary of existing credible scientific evidence which is relevant to evaluating the reasonably foreseeable significant adverse impacts on the human environment, and (4) the agency's evaluation of such impacts based upon theoretical approaches or research methods generally accepted in the scientific community. For the purposes of this section, "reasonably foreseeable" includes impacts which have catastrophic consequences, even if their probability of occurrence is low, provided that the analysis of the impacts is supported by credible scientific evidence, is not based on pure conjecture, and is within the rule of reason.

(c) The amended regulation will be applicable to all environmental impact statements for which a Notice of Intent (40 CFR 1508.22) is published in the Federal Register on or after May 27, 1986. For environmental impact statements in progress, agencies may choose to comply with the requirements of either the original or amended regulation.

[51 FR 15625, Apr. 25, 1986]

§1502.23 Cost-benefit analysis.

If a cost-benefit analysis relevant to the choice among environmentally different alternatives is being considered for the proposed action, it shall be incorporated by reference or appended to the statement as an aid in evaluating the environmental consequences. To assess the adequacy of compliance with section 102(2)(B) of the Act the statement shall, when a cost-benefit analysis is prepared, discuss the relationship between that analysis and any analyses of unquantified environmental impacts, values, and amenities. For purposes of complying with the Act, the weighing of the merits and drawbacks of the various alternatives need not be displayed in a monetary cost-benefit analysis and should not be when there are important qualitative considerations. In any event, an environmental impact statement should at least indicate those considerations, including factors not related to environmental quality, which are likely to be relevant and important to a decision.

§1502.24 Methodology and scientific accuracy.

Agencies shall insure the professional integrity, including scientific integrity, of the discussions and analyses in environmental impact statements. They shall identify any methodologies used and shall make explicit reference by footnote to the scientific and other sources relied upon for conclusions in the statement. An agency may place discussion of methodology in an appendix.

§1502.25 Environmental review and consultation requirements.

(a) To the fullest extent possible, agencies shall prepare draft environmental impact statements concurrently with and integrated with environmental impact analyses and related surveys and studies required by the Fish and Wildlife Coordination Act (16 U.S.C. 661 et seq.), the National Historic Preservation Act of 1966 (16 U.S.C. 470 et seq.), the Endangered Species Act of 1973 (16 U.S.C. 1531 et seq.), and other environmental review laws and executive orders.

(b) The draft environmental impact statement shall list all Federal permits, licenses, and other entitlements which must be obtained in implementing the proposal. If it is uncertain whether a Federal permit, license, or other entitlement is necessary, the draft environmental impact statement shall so indicate.

Pt. 1503

Part 1503—Commenting

Sec.
1503.1   Inviting comments.
1503.2   Duty to comment.
1503.3   Specificity of comments.
1503.4   Response to comments.

Authority:
NEPA, the Environmental Quality Improvement Act of 1970, as amended (42 U.S.C. 4371 et seq.), sec. 309 of the Clean Air Act, as amended (42 U.S.C. 7609), and E.O. 11514 (Mar. 5, 1970, as amended by E.O. 11991, May 24, 1977).

Source:
43 FR 55997, Nov. 29, 1978, unless otherwise noted.

§1503.1   Inviting comments.

(a) After preparing a draft environmental impact statement and before preparing a final environmental impact statement the agency shall:

(1) Obtain the comments of any Federal agency which has jurisdiction by law or special expertise with respect to any environmental impact involved or which is authorized to develop and enforce environmental standards.

(2) Request the comments of:

(i) Appropriate State and local agencies which are authorized to develop and enforce environmental standards;

(ii) Indian tribes, when the effects may be on a reservation; and

(iii) Any agency which has requested that it receive statements on actions of the kind proposed.

Office of Management and Budget Circular A-95 (Revised), through its system of clearinghouses, provides a means of securing the views of State and local environmental agencies. The clearinghouses may be used, by mutual agreement of the lead agency and the clearinghouse, for securing State and local reviews of the draft environmental impact statements.

(3) Request comments from the applicant, if any.

(4) Request comments from the public, affirmatively soliciting comments from those persons or organizations who may be interested or affected.

(b) An agency may request comments on a final environmental impact statement before the decision is finally made. In any case other agencies or persons may make comments before the final decision unless a different time is provided under § 1506.10.

§1503.2 Duty to comment.

Federal agencies with jurisdiction by law or special expertise with respect to any environmental impact involved and agencies which are authorized to develop and enforce environmental standards shall comment on statements within their jurisdiction, expertise, or authority. Agencies shall comment within the time period specified for comment in § 1506.10. A Federal agency may reply that it has no comment. If a cooperating agency is satisfied that its views are adequately reflected in the environmental impact statement, it should reply that it has no comment.

§1503.3 Specificity of comments.

(a) Comments on an environmental impact statement or on a proposed action shall be as specific as possible and may address either the adequacy of the statement or the merits of the alternatives discussed or both.

(b) When a commenting agency criticizes a lead agency's predictive methodology, the commenting agency should describe the alternative methodology which it prefers and why.

(c) A cooperating agency shall specify in its comments whether it needs additional information to fulfill other applicable environmental reviews or consultation requirements and what information it needs. In particular, it shall specify any additional information it needs to comment adequately on the draft statement's analysis of significant site-specific effects associated with the granting or approving by that cooperating agency of necessary Federal permits, licenses, or entitlements.

(d) When a cooperating agency with jurisdiction by law objects to or expresses reservations about the proposal on grounds of environmental impacts, the agency expressing the objection or reservation shall specify the mitigation measures it considers necessary to allow the agency to grant or approve applicable permit, license, or related requirements or concurrences.

§1503.4 Response to comments.

(a) An agency preparing a final environmental impact statement shall assess and consider comments both individually and collectively, and shall respond by one or more of the means listed below, stating its response in the final statement. Possible responses are to:

(1) Modify alternatives including the proposed action.

(2) Develop and evaluate alternatives not previously given serious consideration by the agency.

(3) Supplement, improve, or modify its analyses.

(4) Make factual corrections.

(5) Explain why the comments do not warrant further agency response, citing the sources, authorities, or reasons which support the agency's position and, if appropriate, indicate those circumstances which would trigger agency reappraisal or further response.

(b) All substantive comments received on the draft statement (or summaries thereof where the response has been exceptionally voluminous), should be attached to the final statement whether or not the comment is thought to merit individual discussion by the agency in the text of the statement.

(c) If changes in response to comments are minor and are confined to the responses described in paragraphs (a)(4) and (5) of this section, agencies may write them on errata sheets and attach them to the statement instead of rewriting the draft statement. In such cases only the comments, the responses, and the changes and not the final statement need be circulated (§ 1502.19). The entire document with a new cover sheet shall be filed as the final statement (§ 1506.9).

Pt. 1504

Part 1504—Predecision Referrals to the Council of Proposed Federal Actions Determined To Be Environmentally Unsatisfactory

Sec.
1504.1   Purpose.
1504.2   Criteria for referral.
1504.3   Procedure for referrals and response.

Authority:
NEPA, the Environmental Quality Improvement Act of 1970, as amended (42 U.S.C. 4371 et seq.), sec. 309 of the Clean Air Act, as amended (42 U.S.C. 7609), and E.O. 11514 (Mar. 5, 1970, as amended by E.O. 11991, May 24, 1977).

§1504.1 Purpose.

(a) This part establishes procedures for referring to the Council Federal interagency disagreements concerning proposed major Federal actions that might cause unsatisfactory environmental effects. It provides means for early resolution of such disagreements.

(b) Under section 309 of the Clean Air Act (42 U.S.C. 7609), the Administrator of the Environmental Protection Agency is directed to review and comment publicly on the environmental impacts of Federal activities, including actions for which environmental impact statements are prepared. If after this review the Administrator determines that the matter is "unsatisfactory from the standpoint of public health or welfare or environmental quality," section 309 directs that the matter be referred to the Council (hereafter "environmental referrals").

(c) Under section 102(2)(C) of the Act other Federal agencies may make similar reviews of environmental impact statements, including judgments on the acceptability of anticipated environmental impacts. These reviews must be made available to the President, the Council and the public.

[43 FR 55998, Nov. 29, 1978]

§1504.2   Criteria for referral.

Environmental referrals should be made to the Council only after concerted, timely (as early as possible in the process), but unsuccessful attempts to resolve differences with the lead agency. In determining what environmental objections to the matter are appropriate to refer to the Council, an agency should weigh potential adverse environmental impacts, considering:

(a) Possible violation of national environmental standards or policies.

(b) Severity.

(c) Geographical scope.

(d) Duration.

(e) Importance as precedents.

(f) Availability of environmentally preferable alternatives.

[43 FR 55998, Nov. 29, 1978]

§1504.3   Procedure for referrals and response.

(a) A Federal agency making the referral to the Council shall:

(1) Advise the lead agency at the earliest possible time that it intends to refer a matter to the Council unless a satisfactory agreement is reached.

(2) Include such advice in the referring agency's comments on the draft environmental impact statement, except when the statement does not contain adequate information to permit an assessment of the matter's environmental acceptability.

(3) Identify any essential information that is lacking and request that it be made available at the earliest possible time.

(4) Send copies of such advice to the Council.

(b) The referring agency shall deliver its referral to the Council not later than twenty-five (25) days after the final environmental impact statement has been made available to the Environmental Protection Agency, commenting agencies, and the public. Except when an extension of this period has been granted by the lead agency, the Council will not accept a referral after that date.

(c) The referral shall consist of:

(1) A copy of the letter signed by the head of the referring agency and delivered to the lead agency informing the lead agency of the referral and the reasons for it, and requesting that no action be taken to implement the matter until the Council acts upon the referral. The letter shall include a copy of the statement referred to in (c)(2) of this section.

(2) A statement supported by factual evidence leading to the conclusion that the matter is unsatisfactory from the standpoint of public health or welfare or environmental quality. The statement shall:

(i) Identify any material facts in controversy and incorporate (by reference if appropriate) agreed upon facts,

(ii) Identify any existing environmental requirements or policies which would be violated by the matter,

(iii) Present the reasons why the referring agency believes the matter is environmentally unsatisfactory,

(iv) Contain a finding by the agency whether the issue raised is of national importance because of the threat to national environmental resources or policies or for some other reason,

(v) Review the steps taken by the referring agency to bring its concerns to the attention of the lead agency at the earliest possible time, and

(vi) Give the referring agency's recommendations as to what mitigation alternative, further study, or other course of action (including abandonment of the matter) are necessary to remedy the situation.

(d) Not later than twenty-five (25) days after the referral to the Council the lead agency may deliver a response to the Council, and the referring agency. If the lead agency requests more time and gives assurance that the matter will not go forward in the interim, the Council may grant an extension. The response shall:

(1) Address fully the issues raised in the referral.

(2) Be supported by evidence.

(3) Give the lead agency's response to the referring agency's recommendations.

(e) Interested persons (including the applicant) may deliver their views in writing to the Council. Views in support of the referral should be delivered not later than the referral. Views in support of the response shall be delivered not later than the response.

(f) Not later than twenty-five (25) days after receipt of both the referral and any response or upon being informed that there will be no response (unless the lead agency agrees to a longer time), the Council may take one or more of the following actions:

(1) Conclude that the process of referral and response has successfully resolved the problem.

(2) Initiate discussions with the agencies with the objective of mediation with referring and lead agencies.

(3) Hold public meetings or hearings to obtain additional views and information.

(4) Determine that the issue is not one of national importance and request the referring and lead agencies to pursue their decision process.

(5) Determine that the issue should be further negotiated by the referring and lead agencies and is not appropriate for Council consideration until one or more heads of agencies report to the Council that the agencies' disagreements are irreconcilable.

(6) Publish its findings and recommendations (including where appropriate a finding that the submitted evidence does not support the position of an agency).

(7) When appropriate, submit the referral and the response together with the Council's recommendation to the President for action.

(g) The Council shall take no longer than 60 days to complete the actions specified in paragraph (f)(2), (3), or (5) of this section.

(h) When the referral involves an action required by statute to be determined on the record after opportunity for agency hearing, the referral shall be conducted in a manner consistent with 5 U.S.C. 557(d) (Administrative Procedure Act).

[43 FR 55998, Nov. 29, 1978; 44 FR 873, Jan. 3, 1979]

Pt. 1505

Part 1505—NEPA and Agency Decisionmaking

Sec.
1505.1   Agency decisionmaking procedures.
1505.2   Record of decision in cases requiring environmental impact statements.
1505.3   Implementing the decision.

Authority:
NEPA, the Environmental Quality Improvement Act of 1970, as amended (42 U.S.C. 4371 et seq.), sec. 309 of the Clean Air Act, as amended (42 U.S.C. 7609), and E.O. 11514 (Mar. 5, 1970, as amended by E.O. 11991, May 24, 1977).

Source:
43 FR 55999, Nov. 29, 1978, unless otherwise noted.

§1505.1   Agency decisionmaking procedures.

Agencies shall adopt procedures (§ 1507.3) to ensure that decisions are made in accordance with the policies and purposes of the Act. Such procedures shall include but not be limited to:

(a) Implementing procedures under section 102(2) to achieve the requirements of sections 101 and 102(1).

(b) Designating the major decision points for the agency's principal programs likely to have a significant effect on the human environment and assuring that the NEPA process corresponds with them.

(c) Requiring that relevant environmental documents, comments, and responses be part of the record in formal rulemaking or adjudicatory proceedings.

(d) Requiring that relevant environmental documents, comments, and responses accompany the proposal through existing agency review processes so that agency officials use the statement in making decisions.

(e) Requiring that the alternatives considered by the decisionmaker are encompassed by the range of alternatives discussed in the relevant environmental documents and that the decisionmaker consider the alternatives described in the environmental impact statement. If another decision document accompanies the relevant environmental documents to the decisionmaker, agencies are encouraged to make available to the public before the decision is made any part of that document that relates to the comparison of alternatives.

§1505.2   Record of decision in cases requiring environmental impact statements.

At the time of its decision (§ 1506.10) or, if appropriate, its recommendation to Congress, each agency shall prepare a concise public record of decision. The record, which may be integrated into any other record prepared by the agency, including that required by OMB Circular A-95 (Revised), part I, sections 6(c) and (d), and part II, section 5(b)(4), shall:

(a) State what the decision was.

(b) Identify all alternatives considered by the agency in reaching its decision, specifying the alternative or alternatives which were considered to be environmentally preferable. An agency may discuss preferences among alternatives based on relevant factors including economic and technical considerations and agency statutory missions. An agency shall identify and discuss all such factors including any essential considerations of national policy which were balanced by the agency in making its decision and state how those considerations entered into its decision.

(c) State whether all practicable means to avoid or minimize environmental harm from the alternative selected have been adopted, and if not, why they were not. A monitoring and enforcement program shall be adopted and summarized where applicable for any mitigation.

§1505.3   Implementing the decision.

Agencies may provide for monitoring to assure that their decisions are carried out and should do so in important cases. Mitigation (§ 1505.2(c)) and other conditions established in the environmental impact statement or during its review and committed as part of the decision shall be implemented by the lead agency or other appropriate consenting agency. The lead agency shall:

(a) Include appropriate conditions in grants, permits or other approvals.

(b) Condition funding of actions on mitigation.

(c) Upon request, inform cooperating or commenting agencies on progress in carrying out mitigation measures which they have proposed and which were adopted by the agency making the decision.

(d) Upon request, make available to the public the results of relevant monitoring.

Pt. 1506

Part 1506—Other Requirements of NEPA

Sec.

Authority:
NEPA, the Environmental Quality Improvement Act of 1970, as amended (42 U.S.C. 4371 et seq.), sec. 309 of the Clean Air Act, as amended (42 U.S.C. 7609), and E.O. 11514 (Mar. 5, 1970, as amended by E.O. 11991, May 24, 1977).

Source:
43 FR 56000, Nov. 29, 1978, unless otherwise noted.

§1506.1   Limitations on actions during NEPA process.

(a) Until an agency issues a record of decision as provided in § 1505.2 (except as provided in paragraph (c) of this section), no action concerning the proposal shall be taken which would:

(1) Have an adverse environmental impact; or

(2) Limit the choice of reasonable alternatives.

(b) If any agency is considering an application from a non-Federal entity, and is aware that the applicant is about to take an action within the agency's jurisdiction that would meet either of the criteria in paragraph (a) of this section, then the agency shall promptly notify the applicant that the agency will take appropriate action to insure that the objectives and procedures of NEPA are achieved.

(c) While work on a required program environmental impact statement is in progress and the action is not covered by an existing program statement, agencies shall not undertake in the interim any major Federal action covered by the program which may significantly affect the quality of the human environment unless such action:

(1) Is justified independently of the program;

(2) Is itself accompanied by an adequate environmental impact statement; and

(3) Will not prejudice the ultimate decision on the program. Interim action prejudices the ultimate decision on the program when it tends to determine subsequent development or limit alternatives.

(d) This section does not preclude development by applicants of plans or designs or performance of other work necessary to support an application for Federal, State or local permits or assistance. Nothing in this section shall preclude Rural Electrification Administration approval of minimal expenditures not affecting the environment (e.g. long leadtime equipment and purchase options) made by non-governmental entities seeking loan guarantees from the Administration.

§1506.2   *Elimination of duplication with State and local procedures.*

(a) Agencies authorized by law to cooperate with State agencies of statewide jurisdiction pursuant to section 102(2)(D) of the Act may do so.

(b) Agencies shall cooperate with State and local agencies to the fullest extent possible to reduce duplication between NEPA and State and local requirements, unless the agencies are specifically barred from doing so by some other law. Except for cases covered by paragraph (a) of this section, such cooperation shall to the fullest extent possible include:

(1) Joint planning processes.

(2) Joint environmental research and studies.

(3) Joint public hearings (except where otherwise provided by statute).

(4) Joint environmental assessments.

(c) Agencies shall cooperate with State and local agencies to the fullest extent possible to reduce duplication between NEPA and comparable State and local requirements, unless the agencies are specifically barred from doing so by some other law. Except for cases covered by paragraph (a) of this section, such cooperation shall to the fullest extent possible include joint environmental impact statements. In such cases one or more Federal agencies and one or more State or local agencies shall be joint lead agencies. Where State laws or local ordinances have environmental impact statement requirements in addition to but not in conflict with those in NEPA, Federal agencies shall cooperate in fulfilling these requirements as well as those of Federal laws so that one document will comply with all applicable laws.

(d) To better integrate environmental impact statements into State or local planning processes, statements shall discuss any inconsistency of a proposed action with any approved State or local plan and laws (whether or not federally sanctioned). Where an inconsistency exists, the statement should describe the extent to which the agency would reconcile its proposed action with the plan or law.

§1506.3   *Adoption.*

(a) An agency may adopt a Federal draft or final environmental impact statement or portion thereof provided that the statement or portion thereof meets the standards for an adequate statement under these regulations.

(b) If the actions covered by the original environmental impact statement and the proposed action are substantially the same, the agency adopting another agency's statement is not required to recirculate it except as a final statement. Otherwise the adopting agency shall treat the statement as a draft and recirculate it (except as provided in paragraph (c) of this section).

(c) A cooperating agency may adopt without recirculating the environmental impact statement of a lead agency when, after an independent review of the statement, the cooperating agency concludes that its comments and suggestions have been satisfied.

(d) When an agency adopts a statement which is not final within the agency that prepared it, or when the action it assesses is the subject of a referral under part 1504, or when the statement's adequacy is the subject of a judicial action which is not final, the agency shall so specify.

§1506.4   Combining documents.

Any environmental document in compliance with NEPA may be combined with any other agency document to reduce duplication and paperwork.

§1506.5   Agency responsibility.

(a) Information. If an agency requires an applicant to submit environmental information for possible use by the agency in preparing an environmental impact statement, then the agency should assist the applicant by outlining the types of information required. The agency shall independently evaluate the information submitted and shall be responsible for its accuracy. If the agency chooses to use the information submitted by the applicant in the environmental impact statement, either directly or by reference, then the names of the persons responsible for the independent evaluation shall be included in the list of preparers (§ 1502.17). It is the intent of this paragraph that acceptable work not be redone, but that it be verified by the agency.

(b) Environmental assessments. If an agency permits an applicant to prepare an environmental assessment, the agency, besides fulfilling the requirements of paragraph (a) of this section, shall make its own evaluation of the environmental issues and take responsibility for the scope and content of the environmental assessment.

(c) Environmental impact statements. Except as provided in §§ 1506.2 and 1506.3 any environmental impact statement prepared pursuant to the requirements of NEPA shall be prepared directly by or by a contractor selected by the lead agency or where appropriate under § 1501.6(b), a cooperating agency. It is the intent of these regulations that the contractor be chosen solely by the lead agency, or by the lead agency in cooperation with cooperating agencies, or where appropriate by a cooperating agency to avoid any conflict of interest. Contractors shall execute a disclosure statement prepared by the lead agency, or where appropriate the cooperating agency, specifying that they have no financial or other interest in the outcome of the project. If the document is prepared by contract, the responsible Federal official shall furnish guidance and participate in the preparation and shall independently evaluate the statement prior to its approval and take responsibility for its scope and contents. Nothing in this section is intended to prohibit any agency from requesting any person to submit information to it or to prohibit any person from submitting information to any agency.

§1506.6   Public involvement.

Agencies shall:

(a) Make diligent efforts to involve the public in preparing and implementing their NEPA procedures.

(b) Provide public notice of NEPA-related hearings, public meetings, and the availability of environmental documents so as to inform those persons and agencies who may be interested or affected.

(1) In all cases the agency shall mail notice to those who have requested it on an individual action.

(2) In the case of an action with effects of national concern notice shall include publication in the Federal Register and notice by mail to national organizations reasonably expected to be interested in the matter and may include listing in the 102 Monitor. An agency engaged in rulemaking may provide notice by mail to national organizations who have requested that notice regularly be provided. Agencies shall maintain a list of such organizations.

(3) In the case of an action with effects primarily of local concern the notice may include:

(i) Notice to State and areawide clearinghouses pursuant to OMB Circular A-95 (Revised).

(ii) Notice to Indian tribes when effects may occur on reservations.

(iii) Following the affected State's public notice procedures for comparable actions.

(iv) Publication in local newspapers (in papers of general circulation rather than legal papers).

(v) Notice through other local media.

(vi) Notice to potentially interested community organizations including small business associations.

(vii) Publication in newsletters that may be expected to reach potentially interested persons.

(viii) Direct mailing to owners and occupants of nearby or affected property.

(ix) Posting of notice on and off site in the area where the action is to be located.

(c) Hold or sponsor public hearings or public meetings whenever appropriate or in accordance with statutory requirements applicable to the agency. Criteria shall include whether there is:

(1) Substantial environmental controversy concerning the proposed action or substantial interest in holding the hearing.

(2) A request for a hearing by another agency with jurisdiction over the action supported by reasons why a hearing will be helpful. If a draft environmental impact statement is to be considered at a public hearing, the agency should make the statement available to the public at least 15 days in advance (unless the purpose of the hearing is to provide information for the draft environmental impact statement).

(d) Solicit appropriate information from the public.

(e) Explain in its procedures where interested persons can get information or status reports on environmental impact statements and other elements of the NEPA process.

(f) Make environmental impact statements, the comments received, and any underlying documents available to the public pursuant to the provisions of the Freedom of Information Act (5 U.S.C. 552), without regard to the exclusion for interagency memoranda where such memoranda transmit comments of Federal agencies on the environmental impact of the proposed action. Materials to be made available to the public shall be provided to the public without charge to the extent practicable, or at a fee which is not more than the actual costs of reproducing copies required to be sent to other Federal agencies, including the Council.

§1506.7   Further guidance.

The Council may provide further guidance concerning NEPA and its procedures including:

(a) A handbook which the Council may supplement from time to time, which shall in plain language provide guidance and instructions concerning the application of NEPA and these regulations.

(b) Publication of the Council's Memoranda to Heads of Agencies.

(c) In conjunction with the Environmental Protection Agency and the publication of the 102 Monitor, notice of:

(1) Research activities;

(2) Meetings and conferences related to NEPA; and

(3) Successful and innovative procedures used by agencies to implement NEPA.

§1506.8   Proposals for legislation.

(a) The NEPA process for proposals for legislation (§ 1508.17) significantly affecting the quality of the human environment shall be integrated with the legislative process of the Congress. A legislative environmental impact statement is the detailed statement required by law to be included in a recommendation or report on a legislative proposal to Congress. A legislative environmental impact statement shall be considered part of the formal transmittal of a legislative proposal to Congress; however, it may be transmitted to Congress up to 30 days later in order to allow time for completion of an accurate statement which can serve as the basis for public and Congressional debate. The statement must be available in time for Congressional hearings and deliberations.

(b) Preparation of a legislative environmental impact statement shall conform to the requirements of these regulations except as follows:

(1) There need not be a scoping process.

(2) The legislative statement shall be prepared in the same manner as a draft statement, but shall be considered the "detailed statement" required by statute; Provided, That when any of the following conditions exist both the draft and final environmental impact statement on the legislative proposal shall be prepared and circulated as provided by §§ 1503.1 and 1506.10.

(i) A Congressional Committee with jurisdiction over the proposal has a rule requiring both draft and final environmental impact statements.

(ii) The proposal results from a study process required by statute (such as those required by the Wild and Scenic Rivers Act (16 U.S.C. 1271 et seq.) and the Wilderness Act (16 U.S.C. 1131 et seq.)).

(iii) Legislative approval is sought for Federal or federally assisted construction or other projects which the agency recommends be located at specific geographic locations. For proposals requiring an environmental impact statement for the acquisition of space by the General Services Administration, a draft statement shall accompany the Prospectus or the 11(b) Report of Building Project Surveys to the Congress, and a final statement shall be completed before site acquisition.

(iv) The agency decides to prepare draft and final statements.

(c) Comments on the legislative statement shall be given to the lead agency which shall forward them along with its own responses to the Congressional committees with jurisdiction.

§1506.9 Filing requirements.

(a) Environmental impact statements together with comments and responses shall be filed with the Environmental Protection Agency, attention Office of Federal Activities, EIS Filing Section, Ariel Rios Building (South Oval Lobby), Mail Code 2252-A, Room 7220, 1200 Pennsylvania Ave., NW., Washington, DC 20460. This address is for deliveries by US Postal Service (including USPS Express Mail).

(b) For deliveries in-person or by commercial express mail services, including Federal Express or UPS, the correct address is: US Environmental Protection Agency, Office of Federal Activities, EIS Filing Section, Ariel Rios Building (South Oval Lobby), Room 7220, 1200 Pennsylvania Avenue, NW., Washington, DC 20004.

(c) Statements shall be filed with the EPA no earlier than they are also transmitted to commenting agencies and made available to the public. EPA shall deliver one copy of each statement to the Council, which shall satisfy the requirement of availability to the President. EPA may issue guidelines to agencies to implement its responsibilities under this section and § 1506.10.

[70 FR 41148, July 18, 2005]

§1506.10 Timing of agency action.

(a) The Environmental Protection Agency shall publish a notice in the Federal Register each week of the environmental impact statements filed during the preceding week. The minimum time periods set forth in this section shall be calculated from the date of publication of this notice.

(b) No decision on the proposed action shall be made or recorded under § 1505.2 by a Federal agency until the later of the following dates:

(1) Ninety (90) days after publication of the notice described above in paragraph (a) of this section for a draft environmental impact statement.

(2) Thirty (30) days after publication of the notice described above in paragraph (a) of this section for a final environmental impact statement.

An exception to the rules on timing may be made in the case of an agency decision which is subject to a formal internal appeal. Some agencies have a formally established appeal process which allows other agencies or the public to take appeals on a decision and make their views known, after publication of the final environmental impact statement. In such cases, where a real opportunity exists to alter the decision, the decision may be made and recorded at the same time the environmental impact statement is published. This means that the period for appeal of the decision and the 30-day period prescribed in paragraph (b)(2) of this section may run concurrently. In such cases the environmental impact statement shall explain the timing and the public's right of appeal. An agency engaged in rulemaking under the Administrative Procedure Act or other statute for the purpose of protecting the public health or safety, may waive the time period in paragraph (b)(2) of this section and publish a decision on the final rule simultaneously with publication of the notice of the availability of the final environmental impact statement as described in paragraph (a) of this section.

(c) If the final environmental impact statement is filed within ninety (90) days after a draft environmental impact statement is filed with the Environmental Protection Agency, the minimum thirty (30) day period and the minimum ninety (90) day period may run concurrently. However, subject to paragraph (d) of this section agencies shall allow not less than 45 days for comments on draft statements.

(d) The lead agency may extend prescribed periods. The Environmental Protection Agency may upon a showing by the lead agency of compelling reasons of national policy reduce the prescribed periods and may upon a showing by any other Federal agency of compelling reasons of national policy also extend prescribed periods, but only after consultation with the lead agency. (Also see § 1507.3(d).) Failure to file timely comments shall not be a sufficient reason for extending a period. If the lead agency does not concur with the extension of time, EPA may not extend it for more than 30 days. When the Environmental Protection Agency reduces or extends any period of time it shall notify the Council.

[43 FR 56000, Nov. 29, 1978; 44 FR 874, Jan. 3, 1979]

§1506.11 Emergencies.

Where emergency circumstances make it necessary to take an action with significant environmental impact without observing the provisions of these regulations, the Federal agency taking the action should consult with the Council about alternative arrangements. Agencies and the Council will limit such arrangements to actions necessary to control the immediate impacts of the emergency. Other actions remain subject to NEPA review.

§1506.12 Effective date.

The effective date of these regulations is July 30, 1979, except that for agencies that administer programs that qualify under section 102(2)(D) of the Act or under section 104(h) of the Housing and Community Development Act of 1974 an additional four months shall be allowed for the State or local agencies to adopt their implementing procedures.

(a) These regulations shall apply to the fullest extent practicable to ongoing activities and environmental documents begun before the effective date. These regulations do not apply to an environmental impact statement or supplement if the draft statement was filed before the effective date of these regulations. No completed environmental documents need be redone by reasons of these regulations. Until these regulations are applicable, the Council's guidelines published in the Federal Register of August 1, 1973, shall continue to be applicable. In cases where these regulations are applicable the guidelines are superseded. However, nothing shall prevent an agency from proceeding under these regulations at an earlier time.

(b) NEPA shall continue to be applicable to actions begun before January 1, 1970, to the fullest extent possible.

Pt. 1507

Part 1507—Agency Compliance

Sec.
1507.1   Compliance.
1507.2   Agency capability to comply.
1507.3   Agency procedures.

Authority:
NEPA, the Environmental Quality Improvement Act of 1970, as amended (42 U.S.C. 4371 et seq.), sec. 309 of the Clean Air Act, as amended (42 U.S.C. 7609), and E.O. 11514 (Mar. 5, 1970, as amended by E.O. 11991, May 24, 1977).

Source:
43 FR 56002, Nov. 29, 1978, unless otherwise noted.

§1507.1 Compliance.

All agencies of the Federal Government shall comply with these regulations. It is the intent of these regulations to allow each agency flexibility in adapting its

implementing procedures authorized by § 1507.3 to the requirements of other applicable laws.

§1507.2 Agency capability to comply.

Each agency shall be capable (in terms of personnel and other resources) of complying with the requirements enumerated below. Such compliance may include use of other's resources, but the using agency shall itself have sufficient capability to evaluate what others do for it. Agencies shall:

(a) Fulfill the requirements of section 102(2)(A) of the Act to utilize a systematic, interdisciplinary approach which will insure the integrated use of the natural and social sciences and the environmental design arts in planning and in decisionmaking which may have an impact on the human environment. Agencies shall designate a person to be responsible for overall review of agency NEPA compliance.

(b) Identify methods and procedures required by section 102(2)(B) to insure that presently unquantified environmental amenities and values may be given appropriate consideration.

(c) Prepare adequate environmental impact statements pursuant to section 102(2)(C) and comment on statements in the areas where the agency has jurisdiction by law or special expertise or is authorized to develop and enforce environmental standards.

(d) Study, develop, and describe alternatives to recommended courses of action in any proposal which involves unresolved conflicts concerning alternative uses of available resources. This requirement of section 102(2)(E) extends to all such proposals, not just the more limited scope of section 102(2)(C)(iii) where the discussion of alternatives is confined to impact statements.

(e) Comply with the requirements of section 102(2)(H) that the agency initiate and utilize ecological information in the planning and development of resource-oriented projects.

(f) Fulfill the requirements of sections 102(2)(F), 102(2)(G), and 102(2)(I), of the Act and of Executive Order 11514, Protection and Enhancement of Environmental Quality, Sec. 2.

§1507.3 Agency procedures.

(a) Not later than eight months after publication of these regulations as finally adopted in the Federal Register, or five months after the establishment of an agency, whichever shall come later, each agency shall as necessary adopt procedures to supplement these regulations. When the agency is a department, major subunits are encouraged (with the consent of the department) to adopt their own procedures. Such procedures shall not paraphrase these regulations. They shall confine themselves to implementing procedures. Each agency shall consult with the Council while developing its procedures and before publishing them in the Federal Register for comment. Agencies with similar programs should consult with each other and the Council to coordinate their procedures, especially for programs requesting similar information from applicants. The procedures shall be adopted only after an opportunity for public review and after review by the Council for conformity with the Act and these regulations. The Council shall complete its review within 30 days. Once in effect they shall be filed with the Council and made readily available to the public. Agencies are encouraged to publish explanatory guidance for these regulations and their own procedures. Agencies shall continue to review their policies and procedures and in consultation with the Council to revise them as necessary to ensure full compliance with the purposes and provisions of the Act.

(b) Agency procedures shall comply with these regulations except where compliance would be inconsistent with statutory requirements and shall include:

(1) Those procedures required by §§ 1501.2(d), 1502.9(c)(3), 1505.1, 1506.6(e), and 1508.4.

(2) Specific criteria for and identification of those typical classes of action:

(i) Which normally do require environmental impact statements.

(ii) Which normally do not require either an environmental impact statement or an environmental assessment (categorical exclusions (§ 1508.4)).

(iii) Which normally require environmental assessments but not necessarily environmental impact statements.

(c) Agency procedures may include specific criteria for providing limited exceptions to the provisions of these regulations for classified proposals. They are proposed actions which are specifically authorized under criteria established by an Executive Order or statute to be kept secret in the interest of national defense or foreign policy and are in fact properly classified pursuant to such Executive Order or statute. Environmental assessments and environmental impact statements which address classified proposals may be safeguarded and restricted from public dissemination in accordance with agencies' own regulations applicable to classified information. These documents may be organized so that classified portions can be included as annexes, in order that the unclassified portions can be made available to the public.

(d) Agency procedures may provide for periods of time other than those presented in § 1506.10 when necessary to comply with other specific statutory requirements.

(e) Agency procedures may provide that where there is a lengthy period between the agency's decision to prepare an environmental impact statement and the time of actual preparation, the notice of intent required by § 1501.7 may be published at a reasonable time in advance of preparation of the draft statement.

Pt. 1508

Part 1508—Terminology and Index

Authority:
NEPA, the Environmental Quality Improvement Act of 1970, as amended (42 U.S.C. 4371 et seq.), sec. 309 of the Clean Air Act, as amended (42 U.S.C. 7609), and E.O. 11514 (Mar. 5, 1970, as amended by E.O. 11991, May 24, 1977).

Source:
43 FR 56003, Nov. 29, 1978, unless otherwise noted.

§1508.1   Terminology.

The terminology of this part shall be uniform throughout the Federal Government.

§1508.2   Act.

Act means the National Environmental Policy Act, as amended (42 U.S.C. 4321, et seq.) which is also referred to as "NEPA."

§1508.3   Affecting.

Affecting means will or may have an effect on.

§1508.4   Categorical exclusion.

Categorical exclusion means a category of actions which do not individually or cumulatively have a significant effect on the human environment and which have been found to have no such effect in procedures adopted by a Federal agency in implementation of these regulations (§ 1507.3) and for which, therefore, neither an environmental assessment nor an environmental impact statement is required. An agency may decide in its procedures or otherwise, to prepare environmental assessments for the reasons stated in § 1508.9 even though it is not required to do so. Any procedures under this section shall provide for extraordinary circumstances in which a normally excluded action may have a significant environmental effect.

§1508.5   Cooperating agency.

Cooperating agency means any Federal agency other than a lead agency which has jurisdiction by law or special expertise with respect to any environmental impact involved in a proposal (or a reasonable alternative) for legislation or other major Federal action significantly affecting the quality of the human environment. The selection and responsibilities of a cooperating agency are described in § 1501.6. A State or local agency of similar qualifications or, when the effects are on a reservation, an Indian Tribe, may by agreement with the lead agency become a cooperating agency.

§1508.6   Council.

Council means the Council on Environmental Quality established by title II of the Act.

§1508.7   Cumulative impact.

Cumulative impact is the impact on the environment which results from the incremental impact of the action when added to other past, present, and reasonably foreseeable future actions regardless of what agency (Federal or non-Federal) or person undertakes such other actions. Cumulative impacts can result from individually minor but collectively significant actions taking place over a period of time.

§1508.8   Effects.

Effects include:

(a) Direct effects, which are caused by the action and occur at the same time and place.

(b) Indirect effects, which are caused by the action and are later in time or farther removed in distance, but are still reasonably foreseeable. Indirect effects may include growth inducing effects and other effects related to induced changes in the pattern of land use, population density or growth rate, and related effects on air and water and other natural systems, including ecosystems.

Effects and impacts as used in these regulations are synonymous. Effects includes ecological (such as the effects on natural resources and on the components, structures, and functioning of affected ecosystems), aesthetic, historic, cultural, economic, social, or health, whether direct, indirect, or cumulative. Effects may also include those resulting from actions which may have both beneficial and detrimental effects, even if on balance the agency believes that the effect will be beneficial.

§1508.9   Environmental assessment.

(a) Means a concise public document for which a Federal agency is responsible that serves to:

(1) Briefly provide sufficient evidence and analysis for determining whether to prepare an environmental impact statement or a finding of no significant impact.

(2) Aid an agency's compliance with the Act when no environmental impact statement is necessary.

(3) Facilitate preparation of a statement when one is necessary.

(b) Shall include brief discussions of the need for the proposal, of alternatives as required by section 102(2)(E), of the environmental impacts of the proposed action and alternatives, and a listing of agencies and persons consulted.

§1508.10 Environmental document.

Environmental document includes the documents specified in § 1508.9 (environmental assessment),

§ 1508.11 (environmental impact statement), § 1508.13 (finding of no significant impact), and § 1508.22 (notice of intent).

§1508.11 Environmental impact statement.

Environmental impact statement means a detailed written statement as required by section 102(2)(C) of the Act.

§1508.12 Federal agency.

Federal agency means all agencies of the Federal Government. It does not mean the Congress, the Judiciary, or the President, including the performance of staff functions for the President in his Executive Office. It also includes for purposes of these regulations States and units of general local government and Indian tribes assuming NEPA responsibilities under section 104(h) of the Housing and Community Development Act of 1974.

§1508.13 Finding of no significant impact.

Finding of no significant impact means a document by a Federal agency briefly presenting the reasons why an action, not otherwise excluded (§ 1508.4), will not have a significant effect on the human environment and for which an environmental impact statement therefore will not be prepared. It shall include the environmental assessment or a summary of it and shall note any other environmental documents related to it (§ 1501.7(a)(5)). If the assessment is included, the finding need not repeat any of the discussion in the assessment but may incorporate it by reference.

§1508.14 Human environment.

Human environment shall be interpreted comprehensively to include the natural and physical environment and the relationship of people with that environment. (See the definition of "effects" (§ 1508.8).) This means that economic or social effects are not intended by themselves to require preparation of an environmental impact statement. When an environmental impact statement is prepared and economic or social and natural or physical environmental effects are interrelated, then the environmental impact statement will discuss all of these effects on the human environment.

§1508.15 Jurisdiction by law.

Jurisdiction by law means agency authority to approve, veto, or finance all or part of the proposal.

§1508.16 Lead agency.

Lead agency means the agency or agencies preparing or having taken primary responsibility for preparing the environmental impact statement.

§1508.17 Legislation.

Legislation includes a bill or legislative proposal to Congress developed by or with the significant cooperation and support of a Federal agency, but does not include requests for appropriations. The test for significant cooperation is whether the proposal is in fact predominantly that of the agency rather than another source. Drafting does not by itself constitute significant cooperation. Proposals for legislation include requests for ratification of treaties. Only the agency which has primary responsibility for the subject matter involved will prepare a legislative environmental impact statement.

§1508.18 Major Federal action.

Major Federal action includes actions with effects that may be major and which are potentially subject to Federal control and responsibility. Major reinforces but does not have a meaning independent of significantly (§ 1508.27). Actions include the circumstance where the responsible officials fail to act and that failure to act is reviewable by courts or administrative tribunals under the Administrative Procedure Act or other applicable law as agency action.

(a) Actions include new and continuing activities, including projects and programs entirely or partly financed, assisted, conducted, regulated, or approved by federal agencies; new or revised agency rules, regulations, plans, policies, or procedures; and legislative proposals (§§ 1506.8, 1508.17). Actions do not include funding assistance solely in the form of general revenue sharing funds, distributed under the State and Local Fiscal Assistance Act of 1972, 31 U.S.C. 1221 et seq., with no Federal agency control over the subsequent use of such funds. Actions do not include bringing judicial or administrative civil or criminal enforcement actions.

(b) Federal actions tend to fall within one of the following categories:

(1) Adoption of official policy, such as rules, regulations, and interpretations adopted pursuant to the Administrative Procedure Act, 5 U.S.C. 551 et seq.; treaties and international conventions or agreements; formal documents establishing an agency's policies which will result in or substantially alter agency programs.

(2) Adoption of formal plans, such as official documents prepared or approved by federal agencies which guide or prescribe alternative uses of Federal resources, upon which future agency actions will be based.

(3) Adoption of programs, such as a group of concerted actions to implement a specific policy or plan; systematic and connected agency decisions allocating agency resources to implement a specific statutory program or executive directive.

(4) Approval of specific projects, such as construction or management activities located in a defined geographic area. Projects include actions approved by permit or other regulatory decision as well as federal and federally assisted activities.

§1508.19 Matter.

Matter includes for purposes of part 1504:

(a) With respect to the Environmental Protection Agency, any proposed legislation, project, action or regulation as those terms are used in section 309(a) of the Clean Air Act (42 U.S.C. 7609).

(b) With respect to all other agencies, any proposed major federal action to which section 102(2)(C) of NEPA applies.

§1508.20 Mitigation.

Mitigation includes:

(a) Avoiding the impact altogether by not taking a certain action or parts of an action.

(b) Minimizing impacts by limiting the degree or magnitude of the action and its implementation.

(c) Rectifying the impact by repairing, rehabilitating, or restoring the affected environment.

(d) Reducing or eliminating the impact over time by preservation and maintenance operations during the life of the action.

(e) Compensating for the impact by replacing or providing substitute resources or environments.

§1508.21 NEPA process.

NEPA process means all measures necessary for compliance with the requirements of section 2 and title I of NEPA.

§1508.22 Notice of intent.

Notice of intent means a notice that an environmental impact statement will be prepared and considered. The notice shall briefly:

(a) Describe the proposed action and possible alternatives.

(b) Describe the agency's proposed scoping process including whether, when, and where any scoping meeting will be held.

(c) State the name and address of a person within the agency who can answer questions about the proposed action and the environmental impact statement.

§1508.23 Proposal.

Proposal exists at that stage in the development of an action when an agency subject to the Act has a goal and is actively preparing to make a decision on one or more alternative means of accomplishing that goal and the effects can be meaningfully evaluated. Preparation of an environmental impact statement on a proposal should be timed (§ 1502.5) so that the final statement may be completed in time for the statement to be included in any recommendation or report on the proposal. A proposal may exist in fact as well as by agency declaration that one exists.

§1508.24 Referring agency.

Referring agency means the federal agency which has referred any matter to the Council after a determination that the matter is unsatisfactory from the standpoint of public health or welfare or environmental quality.

§1508.25 Scope.

Scope consists of the range of actions, alternatives, and impacts to be considered in an environmental impact statement. The scope of an individual statement may depend on its relationships to other statements (§§ 1502.20 and 1508.28). To determine the scope of environmental impact statements, agencies shall consider 3 types of actions, 3 types of alternatives, and 3 types of impacts. They include:

(a) Actions (other than unconnected single actions) which may be:

(1) Connected actions, which means that they are closely related and therefore should be discussed in the same impact statement. Actions are connected if they:

(i) Automatically trigger other actions which may require environmental impact statements.

(ii) Cannot or will not proceed unless other actions are taken previously or simultaneously.

(iii) Are interdependent parts of a larger action and depend on the larger action for their justification.

(2) Cumulative actions, which when viewed with other proposed actions have cumulatively significant impacts and should therefore be discussed in the same impact statement.

(3) Similar actions, which when viewed with other reasonably foreseeable or proposed agency actions, have similarities that provide a basis for evaluating their environmental consequencies together, such as common timing or geography. An agency may wish to analyze these actions in the same impact statement. It should do so when the best way to assess adequately the combined impacts of similar actions or reasonable alternatives to such actions is to treat them in a single impact statement.

(b) Alternatives, which include:

(1) No action alternative.

(2) Other reasonable courses of actions.

(3) Mitigation measures (not in the proposed action).

(c) Impacts, which may be: (1) Direct; (2) indirect; (3) cumulative.

§1508.26 Special expertise.

Special expertise means statutory responsibility, agency mission, or related program experience.

§1508.27 Significantly.

Significantly as used in NEPA requires considerations of both context and intensity:

(a) Context. This means that the significance of an action must be analyzed in several contexts such as society as a whole (human, national), the affected region, the affected interests, and the locality. Significance varies with the setting of the proposed action. For instance, in the case of a site-specific action, significance would usually depend upon the effects in the locale rather than in the world as a whole. Both short- and long-term effects are relevant.

(b) Intensity. This refers to the severity of impact. Responsible officials must bear in mind that more than one agency may make decisions about partial aspects of a major action. The following should be considered in evaluating intensity:

(1) Impacts that may be both beneficial and adverse. A significant effect may exist even if the Federal agency believes that on balance the effect will be beneficial.

(2) The degree to which the proposed action affects public health or safety.

(3) Unique characteristics of the geographic area such as proximity to historic or cultural resources, park lands, prime farmlands, wetlands, wild and scenic rivers, or ecologically critical areas.

(4) The degree to which the effects on the quality of the human environment are likely to be highly controversial.

(5) The degree to which the possible effects on the human environment are highly uncertain or involve unique or unknown risks.

(6) The degree to which the action may establish a precedent for future actions with significant effects or represents a decision in principle about a future consideration.

(7) Whether the action is related to other actions with individually insignificant but cumulatively significant impacts. Significance exists if it is reasonable to anticipate a cumulatively significant impact on the environment. Significance cannot be avoided by terming an action temporary or by breaking it down into small component parts.

(8) The degree to which the action may adversely affect districts, sites, highways, structures, or objects listed in or eligible for listing in the National Register of Historic Places or may cause loss or destruction of significant scientific, cultural, or historical resources.

(9) The degree to which the action may adversely affect an endangered or threatened species or its habitat that has been determined to be critical under the Endangered Species Act of 1973.

(10) Whether the action threatens a violation of Federal, State, or local law or requirements imposed for the protection of the environment.

[43 FR 56003, Nov. 29, 1978; 44 FR 874, Jan. 3, 1979]

§1508.28 Tiering.

Tiering refers to the coverage of general matters in broader environmental impact statements (such as national program or policy statements) with subsequent narrower statements or environmental analyses (such as regional or basinwide program statements or ultimately site-specific statements) incorporating by reference the general discussions and concentrating solely on the issues specific to the statement subsequently prepared. Tiering is appropriate when the sequence of statements or analyses is:

(a) From a program, plan, or policy environmental impact statement to a program, plan, or policy statement or analysis of lesser scope or to a site-specific statement or analysis.

(b) From an environmental impact statement on a specific action at an early stage (such as need and site selection) to a supplement (which is preferred) or a subsequent statement or analysis at a later stage (such as environmental mitigation). Tiering in such cases is appropriate when it helps the lead agency to focus on the issues which are ripe for decision and exclude from consideration issues already decided or not yet ripe.

NEPA Deskbook

Appendix 8   NEPA Implementation Procedures, Appendices I, II, and III

49750   Federal Register / Vol. 49, No. 247 / Friday, December 21, 1984 / Rules and Regulations

COUNCIL ON ENVIRONMENTAL QUALITY

40 CFR Ch. V

National Environmental Policy Act (NEPA) Implementation Procedures; Appendices I, II, and III

AGENCY: Council on Environmental Quality, Executive Office of the President.

ACTION: Appendices to regulations.

SUMMARY: These appendices are intended to improve public participation and facilitate agency compliance with the National Environmental Policy Act (NEPA) and the Council on Environmental Quality's NEPA Regulations.

Appendix I updates and replaces the Federal and Federal-State Agency NEPA Contacts that appeared in Appendix I in the Federal Register of Thursday, August 28, 1980 (45 FR 57488).

Appendix II updates and replaces the compilation of Federal and Federal-State Agencies With Jurisdiction by Law or Special Expertise on Environmental Quality Issues that appeared in Appendix II in the Federal Register of Thursday, August 28, 1980 (45 FR 57491).

Appendix III is reinstated as, and is an update of, the listing of Federal and Federal-State Agency Offices for Receiving and Commenting on Other Agencies' Environmental Documents. Appendix III last appeared in the Federal Register of August 1, 1973 (38 FR 20559).

EFFECTIVE DATE: December 21, 1984.

ADDRESSES: Comments should be addressed to General Counsel, Council on Environmental Quality, 722 Jackson Place, NW., Washington, DC 20006-4978.

FOR INFORMATION CONTACT: Dinah Bear, General Counsel, Council on Environmental Quality, 722 Jackson Place, NW, Washington, DC 20006-4978 (202) 395-5754.

SUPPLEMENTARY INFORMATION:

Appendix I—Federal and Federal-State Agency National Environmental Policy Act (NEPA) Contacts

Section 1507.2 of the Council's regulations for implementing the procedural provisions of the National Environmental Policy Act requires agencies to have an individual responsible for overall NEPA compliance. This appendix identifies the individual within each agency that is responsible for coordinating with the Council on behalf of that agency and for exercising NEPA oversight within that agency. This person can provide basic information about the agency's NEPA

activities and about the procedures which the agency has adopted to supplement the Council regulations (40 CFR 1507.3).

To ascertain the proper office in an agency for receiving and commenting on other agencies' environmental documents, refer to Appendix III of this issuance.

Appendix II—Federal and Federal-State Agencies With Jurisdiction by Law or Special Expertise on Environmental Quality Issues

This appendix is a compilation of Federal and Federal-State agencies with jurisdiction by law, a statutorily mandated consultative role, or special expertise on environmental quality issues. Both the public and private sectors and governmental agencies can use this list as a reference guide to facilitate their participation in and compliance with NEPA process.

The appendix is organized into four broad categories: pollution control, energy, land use, and natural resource management. Because most actions involve environmental issues falling into more than one of these categories, users should consult all pertinent entries.

The areas of special expertise are listed in parentheses *following* the agency name. They are intended to provide examples rather than define the limits of an agency's total expertise in that area.

The areas of jurisdiction by law and statutorily mandated consultations are listed *below* each appropriate agency or component. Entries dealing with jurisdiction by law relate to that agency's authority to approve, deny, or finance all or part of a proposal and include permits and licenses. Because experience in implementing NEPA has proven that identification of an agency's statutorily mandated consultative role is of equal significance to users of this list, those responsibilities are now specifically cited and include such authorities as the National Historic Preservation Act of 1966 (16 U.S.C. Sec. 470 *et seq.*), the Fish and Wildlife Coordination Act (16 U.S.C. Sec. 661 *et seq.*), and the Endangered Species Act of 1973 (16 U.S.C. Sec. 1531 *et seq.*). Because laws are amended and new laws enacted, the responsibilities identified in this appendix may change or new ones may be added. Hence, the definitive responsibility of an agency depends on the then current law and not on this index.

The Council on Environmental Quality has prepared this list to supplement its NEPA regulations and believes that it will be helpful in the following ways:

First, the Council's NEPA regulations require the Federal agency having primary responsibility for preparing an environmental impact statement (EIS) under NEPA (the lead agency) to determine whether any other Federal agencies have jurisdiction by law or special expertise with respect to any environmental effects involved in a proposal for legislation or other major Federal action significantly affecting the human environment. 40 CFR 1501.5(a), 1501.6(a), 1501.7(a). The Federal lead agency must, early in the NEPA process, request the participation of Federal cooperating agencies with jurisdiction by law or special expertise concerning the proposal. 40 CFR 1501.6(a), 1501.7(a). The lead agency and those involved in the "scoping process" (see 40 CFR 1501.7) may use this list to help determine which other Federal agencies should be requested to participate as cooperating agencies in the NEPA process. The list will also be helpful to the lead agency in determining which agencies should receive copies of the draft environmental impact statement for review and comment. 40 CFR 1503.1.

Second, this compilation will prove useful to those whose activities or proposed actions require Federal regulatory approvals by facilitating the identification of:

a. Those Federal agencies with the authority to issue applicable permits, licenses or other Federal regulatory approvals, and

b. Those Federal agencies that have a statutorily mandated consultative role that must be carried out before a decision is made.

Third, a major goal of NEPA and the CEQ regulations is to encourage public participation in agency decisionmaking. 40 CFR 1500.2(d). Individuals, citizen groups and State and local governments who are interested in an environmental issue may use the list to help identify those agencies that have jurisdiction by law over or special expertise in the subject matter of a proposal. Those interested may then contact the potentially involved agencies to obtain information on the issues and to participate in the NEPA process.

Appendix III—Federal and Federal-State Agency Offices for Receiving and Commenting on Other Agencies' Environmental Documents

Section 1503.1 of the Council's regulations for implementing the procedural provisions of the National Environmental Policy Act requires the agency that has prepared a draft environmental impact statement to "obtain the comments of any Federal

Federal Register / Vol. 49, No. 247 / Friday, December 21, 1984 / Rules and Regulations   **49751**

agency which has jurisdiction by law or special expertise with respect to any environmental impact involved or which is authorized to develop and enforce environmental standards." Section 1503.2 discusses the "Duty to Comment" by those Federal agencies. This appendix identifies the location of the Federal and Federal-State agency offices for receiving and commenting on other agencies' environmental documents. The agency distributing the environmental document should give special attention to the instruction immediately following the agency name to ensure that the comment request and document(s) are sent to the correct office, e.g., some agencies ask that documents concerning legislation, regulations, national program proposals and other major policy issues be sent only to its headquarters office with all other documents to be sent to a regional office. If a transmitting agency has questions about where to send a document, consult the Federal agency NEPA contact listed in Appendix I.

Other Information

Since agency responsibilities, legal authorities, programs, and other data appearing in these Appendices change regularly, the Council will update the Appendices periodically. Agencies and the public are strongly encouraged to send comments noting changes or corrections that should be made to any Appendix.

Dated: December 14, 1984.

Dinah Bear,

General Counsel.

Editorial Note: The following appendices will not appear in the CFR.

Appendix I—Federal and Federal-State Agency National Environmental Policy Act (NEPA) Contacts

DEPARTMENTS

Department of Agriculture

Assistant Secretary for Natural Resources and Environment, Department of Agriculture; Attn: Executive Secretary, Natural Resources and Environment Committee: Room 242 W, Administration Bldg., 14th St. and Independence Ave., SW, Wash., D.C. 20250-0001. (202) 447-5166.

Department of Agriculture Components

Agricultural Research Service: Deputy Administrator, National Program Staff, Agricultural Research Service, Department of Agriculture: Room 125, Bldg. 005, Agricultural Research Center-West, Beltsville, MD 20705-2350. (301) 344-3064.

Agricultural Stabilization and Conservation Service: Chief, Planning and Evaluation Branch, Conservation and Environmental Protection Division; Agricultural Stabilization and Conservation Service, Department of Agriculture, Room

4714, South Agriculture Bldg., 14th St. and Independence Ave., SW, P.O. Box 2415, Wash., D.C. 20013-2415. (202) 447-3264.

Animal and Plant Health Inspection Service: Environmental Coordinator, Animal and Plant Health Inspection Service, Department of Agriculture: Room 600, Federal Bldg., 6505 Belcrest Road, Hyattsville, MD 20782-2058. (301) 436-8896.

Economic Research Service: Director, Natural Resource Economics Division, Economic Research Service, Department of Agriculture, Room 412, GHI Bldg., 500 12th St, SW, Wash., D.C. 20250-0001. (202) 447-6239.

Extension Service: Deputy Administrator, Natural Resources and Rural Development, Extension Service, Department of Agriculture, Room 3909, South Agriculture Bldg., 14th St. and Independence Ave., SW, Wash., D.C. 20250-0001. (202) 447-7947.

Farmers Home Administration: Environmental Protection Specialist, Program Support Staff; Farmers Home Administration, Department of Agriculture, Room 6309, South Agriculture Bldg., 14th St. and Independence Ave., SW, Wash., D.C. 20250-0001. (202) 382-9619.

Food Safety and Inspection Service: Director, Regulations Office, Food Safety and Inspection Service, Department of Agriculture, Room 2940, South Agriculture Bldg., 14th St. and Independence Ave., SW, Wash., D.C. 20250-0001. (202) 447-3317.

Forest Service: Director, Environmental Coordination Staff, Forest Service, Department of Agriculture: Room 4204, South Agriculture Bldg., 14th St. and Independence Ave., SW, P.O. Box 2417, Wash., D.C. 20013-2417. (202) 447-4708.

Rural Electrification Administration: Environmental Policy Specialist, Engineering Standards Division, Rural Electrification Administration, Department of Agriculture, Room 1257, South Agriculture Bldg., 14th St. and Independence Ave., SW, Wash., D.C. 20250-0001. (202) 382-0097.

Soil Conservation Service: National Environmental Coordinator, Environmental Activities Branch, Ecological Sciences Division, Soil Conservation Service, Department of Agriculture, Room 6156, South Agriculture Bldg., 14th St. and Independence Ave., SW, P.O. Box 2890, Wash., D.C. 20013-2890. (202) 447-4912.

Department of Commerce

Chief, Ecology and Conservation Division, Office of Policy and Planning, National Oceanic and Atmospheric Administration, Department of Commerce, Room H-6111, Herbert Hoover Bldg., 14th St. and Constitution Ave., NW, Wash., D.C. 20230-0001. (202) 377-5181.

Department of Commerce Components

Economic Development Administration: Associate Director for Environment, Economic Development Adminstration, Department of Commerce, Room 7319, Herbert Hoover Bldg., 14th St. and Constitution Ave., NW, Wash., D.C. 20230-0001. (202) 377-4208.

National Oceanic and Atmospheric Administration: Chief, Ecology and Conservation Division, Office of Policy and Planning, National Oceanic and Atmospheric

Administration, Department of Commerce, Room H-6111, Herbert Hoover Bldg., 14th St. and Constitution Ave., NW, Wash., D.C. 20230-0001. (202) 377-5181.

Department of Defense

Director, Environmental Policy, Office of the Assistant Secretary of Defense (Manpower, Installations and Logistics), Department of Defense, Room 3D833, The Pentagon, Wash., D.C. 20301-0001. (202) 695-7820.

Department of Defense Components

Defense Logistics Agency: Staff Director, Office of Installation Services and Environmental Protection, Defense Logistics Agency, Department of Defense, Cameron Station, Room 4D448, Alexandria, VA 22304-6100. (202) 274-6124.

Department of the Air Force: Deputy for Environment and Safety, Office of the Deputy Assistant Secretary for Installations, Environment and Safety, Department of the Air Force, Room 4C916, The Pentagon, Wash., D.C. 20330-0001. (202) 697-9297.

Department of the Army: Chief, Army Environmental Office, Attn: HQDA (DAEN-ZCE); Department of the Army, Room 1E678, The Pentagon, Wash., D.C. 20310-2600. (202) 694-3434.

Corps of Engineers: Assistant Director of Civil Works, Environmental Programs (DAEN-CWZ-P), Office of the Chief of Engineers, Room 7233, Pulaski Bldg., 20 Massachusetts Avenue, NW, Wash., D.C. 20314-1000. (202) 272-0103.

Department of the Navy: Director, Environmental Protection and Occupational Safety and Health Division (OP-453), Office of the Chief of Naval Operations, Department of the Navy, Bldg. 200, Room S-3, Washington Navy Yard, Wash., D.C. 20374-0001. (202) 433-2428.

U.S. Marine Corps: Head, Land Resources and Environmental Branch, Code: LFL, U.S. Marine Corps, Commonwealth Bldg., Room 614, 1300 Wilson Blvd., Arlington, VA. (202) 694-9237/38. MAILING ADDRESS: Commandant, U.S. Marine Corps, ATTN: Land Resources and Environmental Branch, Code: LFL, Wash., D.C. 20380-0001.

Department of Energy

Director, Office of Environmental Compliance (PE-25), Department of Energy, Room 4G-085, Forrestal Building, 1000 Independence Ave., SW, Wash., D.C. 20585-0001. (202) 252-4600.

Department of Health and Human Services

Departmental Environmental Officer, Office of the Assistant Secretary for Management Analysis and Systems, Department of Health and Human Services, Room 542 E. Hubert H. Humphrey Bldg., 200 Independence Ave., SW, Wash., D.C. 20201-0001. (202) 245-7354.

Department of Health and Human Services Components

Center for Disease Control: Chief, Environmental Affairs Group, Center for Environmental Health, Center for Disease Control, Room 1015, Bldg.: Chamblee-9,

49752 Federal Register / Vol. 49, No. 247 / Friday, December 21, 1984 / Rules and Regulations

Atlanta. GA 30329–4018. (404) 452-4257; (FTS) 236-4257.

Food and Drug Administration: Chief. Environmental Impact Staff (HFV–310) Food and Drug Administration. Parklawn Bldg.. Room 7–89. 5600 Fishers Lane. Rockville, MD 20857–0001. (301) 443-1880.

Health Resources and Services Administration: Chief Environmental Health Branch. Division of Clinical and Environmental Services. Indian Health Service. Health Resources and Services Administration. Parklawn Building, Room 6A–54, 5600 Fishers Lane, Rockville, MD 20857–0001. (301) 443-1043.

National Institutes of Health: Chief. Environmental Protection Branch. National Institutes of Health, Bldg. 13, Room 2E55, 9100 Rockville Pike. Bethesda, MD 21205–0001. (301) 496-3537.

Office of Community Services: Director, Office of State Project Assistance, Office of Community Services, Room 500, Brown Bldg., 1200 19th St.. NW.. Wash.. D.C. 20506–0007. (202) 653-5875.

Department of Housing and Urban Development

Director, Office of Environment and Energy, Department of Housing and Urban Development, Room 7154, HUD Building, 451 Seventh St., SW., Wash., D.C. 20410–0001. (202) 755-7894.

Department of the Interior

Director, Office of Environmental Project Review, Department of the Interior. Room 4260. Interior Bldg., 18th and C Sts.. NW. Wash.. D.C. 20240–0001. (202) 343-3891.

Department of the Interior Components

Fish and Wildlife Services: Chief, Division of Environmental Coordination, Fish and Wildlife Service. Department of the Interior. Room 402, Hamilton Bldg., 1375 K St., NW. Wash.. D.C. (202) 343-5685. MAILING ADDRESS: 18th & C Sts.. NW. Wash.. D.C. 20240–0001.

Geological Survey: Chief. Review Unit, Environmental Affairs Program (MS–423), U.S. Geological Survey. Department of the Interior. Room 2D318. 12201 Sunrise Valley Drive. Reston. VA 22092–9998. (703) 860-7568.

Bureau of Indian Affairs: Chief. Environmental Services Staff, Office of Trust Responsibilities. Bureau of Indian Affairs. Department of the Interior. Room 4560, Interior Bldg., 18th and C Sts., NW. Wash., D.C. 20245–0001. (202) 343-6574.

Bureau of Land Management: Chief, Office of Planning and Environmental Coordination, Bureau of Land Management, Department of the Interior. Room 906, Premier Bldg., 1725 I St., NW. Wash., D.C. 20240–0001. (202) 653-8830.

Minerals Management Service: Chief. Offshore Environmental Assessment Division. Mineral Management Service. Department of the Interior, Room 2044, Interior Bldg., 18th and C Sts.. NW. Wash.. D.C. 20240–0001 (202) 343-2097.

Bureau of Mines: Special Assistant for Environmental Assessment, Bureau of Mines. Department of the Interior, Room 1004, Columbia Plaza Bldg., 2401 E St., NW. Wash., D.C. 20241–0001. (202) 634-1310.

National Park Service: Chief. Environmental Compliance Division (782). National Park Service, Department of the Interior. Room 1210. Interior Bldg., 18th and C Sts.. NW. Wash.. D.C. 20240–0001. (202) 343-2163.

Bureau of Reclamation: Director. Office of Environmental Affairs, Bureau of Reclamation. Department of the Interior. Room 7622, Interior Bldg., 18th and C Sts., NW., Wash., D.C. 20240–0001. (202) 343-4991.

Office of Surface Mining: Chief, Division of Permits and Environmental Analysis, Office of Surface Mining Reclamation and Enforcement, Department of the Interior. Room 134, Interior-South Bldg., 1951 Constitution Ave.. NW., Wash., D.C. 20240–0001. (202) 343-5261.

Department of Justice

Assistant Chief, General Litigation Section. Land and Natural Resources Division. Department of Justice. Room 2133, Justice Bldg., 9th St. and Pennsylvania Ave., NW. Wash., D.C. 20530–0001. (202) 633-2704.

Department of Justice Components

Bureau of Prisons: Chief. Office of Facilities Development and Operations. Bureau of Prisons, Department of Justice, 320 First St., NW, Wash., D.C. 20534–0001. (202) 724-3232.

Drug Enforcement Administration: Deputy Assistant Administrator, Office of Science and Technology. Drug Enforcement Administration. Department of Justice, 1405 Eye St.. NW, Wash., D.C. 20537–0001. (202) 633-1211.

Immigration and Naturalization Service: Chief, Facilities and Engineering Branch. Immigration and Naturalization Service. Department of Justice, 425 Eye St., NW, Wash., D.C. 20536–0001. (202) 633-4448.

Office of Justice Assistance. Research and Statistics: Director, Office of Justice Assistance, Research and Statistics; Department of Justice. Room 1300, 633 Indiana Ave., NW, Wash., D.C. 20531–0001. (202) 724-5933.

Office of Legal Counsel: Assistant Attorney General. Office of Legal Counsel, Department of Justice, Room 5214, Justice Bldg., 9th St. and Pennsylvania Ave., NW, Wash., D.C. 20530–0001. (202) 633-2041.

Department of Labor

Director, Office of Regulatory Economics, Assistant Secretary for Policy, Department of Labor, Room S–2312, Frances Perkins Bldg., 200 Constitution Ave., NW, Wash., D.C. 20210–0001. (202) 523-6197.

Department of Labor Components

Mine Safety and Health Administration: Chief. Office of Standards, Regulations and Variances. Mine Safety and Health Administration. Department of Labor, Room 627. Ballston Tower #3, 4015 Wilson Blvd., Arlington, VA 22203–1923. (703) 235-1910.

Occupational Safety and Health Administration: Director, Office of Regulatory Analysis, Occupational Safety and Health Administration. Department of Labor, Room N–3635, Frances Perkins Bldg., 200 Constitution Ave., NW, Wash., D.C. 20210–0001. (202) 523-8017.

Department of State

Director. Office of Environment and Health. Department of State. Room 4325, State Department Bldg.. 21st and C Sts.. NW Wash.. D.C. 20520–0001. (202) 632-9266.

Department of Transportation

Deputy Director for Environment and Policy Review, Office of Economics, Department of Transportation, Room 10309 Nassif Bldg., 400 Seventh St., SW, Wash.. D.C. 20590–0001. (202) 426-4357.

Department of Transportation Components

Federal Aviation Administration: Director. Office of Environment and Energy (AEE–1). Federal Aviation Administration, Room 432. FOB–10A. 800 Independence Ave., SW. Wash., D.C. 20591–0001. (202) 426-8406.

Federal Highway Administration: Director. Office of Environmental Policy (HEV–1), Federal Highway Administration, Room 3222, Nassif Bldg., 400 Seventh St., SW. Wash.. D.C. 20590–0001. (202) 426-0351.

Federal Railroad Administration: Director. Office of Economic Analysis (RRP–30), Federal Railroad Administration. Room 8300, Nassif Bldg., 400 Seventh St., SW. Wash.. D.C. 20590–0001. (202) 426-7391.

Maritime Administration: Head, Environmental Activities Group (MAR–700.4). Maritime Administration, Room 2120, Nassif Bldg.. 400 Seventh St., SW. Wash., D.C. 20590–0001. (202) 426-5739.

National Highway Traffic Safety Administration: Assistant Chief Counsel for General Law, Office of Chief Counsel (NOA–33). National Highway Traffic Safety Administration, Room 5219, Nassif Bldg., 400 Seventh St., SW. Wash.. D.C. 20590–0001. (202) 426-1834.

Research and Special Programs Administration (includes Materials Transportation Bureau): Chief, Environmental Technology Division (UTS–48), Research and Special Programs Administration, US-DOT. Transportation Systems Center, Room 3–55. Kendall Square, Cambridge, MA 02142-1001. (617) 494-2018; (FTS) 837-2018.

St. Lawrence Seaway Development Corporation: Deputy Chief Engineer, St. Lawrence Seaway Development Corporation. Seaway Administration Bldg.. 180 Andrews St.. P.O. Box 520. Massena. NY 13662-1760. (315) 764-3256; (FTS) 953-0256.

United States Coast Guard: Chief, Environmental Compliance and Review Branch (G-WP-3), Office of Marine Environment and Systems. U.S. Coast Guard. 2100 2nd St., SW. Wash.. D.C. 20593–0001. (202) 426-3300.

Urban Mass Transportation Administration: Director. Office of Planning Assistance (UGM–20). Urban Mass Transportation Administration, Room 9311. Nassif Bldg., 400 Seventh St., SW. Wash.. D.C. 20590–0001. (202) 426-2360.

Department of Treasury

Manager. Environmental Quality. Physical Security and Safety Division. Department of the Treasury. Room 800, Treasury Bldg.. 1331 G St. NW, Wash., D.C. 20220–0001. (202) 376-0260.

Federal Register / Vol. 49, No. 247 / Friday, December 21, 1984 / Rules and Regulations   **49753**

INDEPENDENT AGENCIES

ACTION

Assistant Director, Office of Policy and Planning, ACTION, Room M-606, 806 Connecticut Ave., NW, Wash., D.C. 20525-0001. (202) 634-9304; WATS #800-424-8580, ext. 81.

Advisory Council on Historic Preservation

Director, Office of Cultural Resource Preservation, Advisory Council on Historic Preservation, Old Post Office Building, Suite 803, 1100 Pennsylvania Ave., NW, Wash., D.C. 20004-2590. (202) 786-0505.

Appalachian Regional Commission

Director, Division of Housing and Community Development, Appalachian Regional Commission, 1666 Connecticut Ave., NW, Wash., D.C. 20235-0001. (202) 673-7845.

Arms Control and Disarmament Agency

General Counsel, Arms Control and Disarmament Agency, Room 5534, 320 21st St., NW, Wash., D.C. 20451-0001. (202) 632-3582.

Central Intelligence Agency

Chief, Real Estate and Construction Division, Office of Logistics, Central Intelligence Agency, Room 2FO9, Page Bldg., 803 Follin Lane, Vienna, VA. (703) 281-8111. MAILING ADDRESS: Washington, D.C. 20505-0001.

Civil Aeronautics Board

Chief, Environmental and Energy Programs (B-60C), Civil Aeronautics Board, Room 909, Universal Bldg., 1825 Connecticut Ave., NW, Wash., D.C. 20428-0001. (202) 426-9622.

Consumer Product Safety Commission

Assistant General Counsel, Office of the General Counsel, Consumer Product Safety Commission, Room 200, 5401 Westbard Ave., Bethesda, MD. (301) 492-6550. MAILING ADDRESS: Washington, D.C. 20207-0001.

Delaware River Basin Commission

Executive Director, Delaware River Basin Commission, 25 State Police Drive, P.O. Box 7360, West Trenton, NJ 08628-0340. (609) 883-9500; (FTS) 483-2077.

Environmental Protection Agency

Director, Office of Federal Activities (A-104), Environmental Protection Agency, Room 2119-I, 401 M St., SW, Wash., D.C. 20460-0001. (202) 382-5053.

Export-Import Bank of the United States

General Counsel, Export-Import Bank of the United States, Room 947, Lafayette Bldg., Room 947, 811 Vermont Ave., NW, Wash., D.C. 20571-0001. (202) 566-8334.

Farm Credit Administration

Deputy Governor—Region I, Office of Examination and Supervision, Farm Credit Administration, 1501 Farm Credit Drive, McLean, VA 22102-5090. (703) 883-4181.

Federal Communications Commission

Staff Attorney, Legal Counsel Division, Office of General Counsel, Federal Communications Commission, Room 621,

---

1919 M St., NW, Wash., D.C. 20554-0001. (202) 632-6990.

Federal Deposit Insurance Corporation

Director, Division of Accounting and Corporate Services, Federal Deposit Insurance Corporation, Room 6120, 550 Seventeenth St., NW, Wash., D.C. 20429-0001. (202) 389-4891.

Federal Emergency Management Agency

Associate General Counsel, Federal Emergency Management Agency, Room 840, 500 C St., SW, Wash., D.C. 20472-0001. (202) 287-0387.

Federal Energy Regulatory Commission

(1) Legal Matters: Deputy Assistant General Counsel, Division of Rulemaking and Policy Coordination, Office of General Counsel, Federal Energy Regulatory Commission, Room 6600A, 825 N. Capitol St., NE, Wash., D.C. 20426-0001. (202) 357-8033.

(2) Natural Gas Matters: Chief, Environmental Evaluation Branch, Office of Pipeline and Producer Regulation, Federal Energy Regulatory Commission, Room 7102A, 825 N. Capitol St., NE, Wash., D.C. 20426-0001. (202) 357-8098.

(3) Electric and Hydroelectric Matters: Director, Division of Environmental Analysis, Office of Hydropower Licensing, Federal Energy Regulatory Commission, Room 308, Railway Labor Building, 400 First St., NW, Wash., D.C. 20426-0001. (202) 376-1768.

Federal Home Loan Bank Board

Deputy Director for Corporate, Corporate and Securities Division, Office of General Counsel, Federal Home Loan Bank Board, Third Floor, East Wing, 1700 G St., NW, Wash., D.C. 20552-0001. (202) 377-6411.

Federal Maritime Commission

Director, Office of Energy and Environmental Impact, Federal Maritime Commission, 1100 L St., NW, Wash., D.C. 20573-0001. (202) 523-5835.

Federal Reserve Board

Senior Attorney, Office of General Counsel, Federal Reserve Board, Room B-1016E, 20th St. and Constitution Ave., NW, Wash., D.C. 20551-0001. (202) 452-3734.

Federal Trade Commission

Deputy Assistant General Counsel, Federal Trade Commission, Room 582, 6th St. and Pennsylvania Ave., NW, Wash., D.C. 20580-0001. (202) 523-1928.

General Services Administration

Director, Environmental Affairs Staff (PRE), Office of Space Management, Public Buildings Service, General Services Administration, Room 2323, 18th and F Sts., NW, Wash., D.C. 20405-0001. (202) 566-0854.

International Boundary and Water Commission, United States Section

Principal Engineer, Investigations and Planning Division, International Boundary and Water Commission, United States Section, IBWC Bldg., 4110 Rio Bravo, El Paso, TX 79902-1091. (915) 541-7304; (FTS) 572-7304.

Interstate Commerce Commission

Chief, Section of Energy and Environment, Office of Transportation Analysis, Interstate Commerce Commission, Room 4143, 12th St. and Constitution Ave., NW, Wash., D.C. 20423-0001. (202) 275-0800.

Lowell Historic Preservation Commission

Planning Director, Lowell Historic Preservation Commission, 204 Middle Street, Lowell, MA 01852-1815. (617) 459-7653; (FTS) 829-0766.

Marine Mammal Commission

General Counsel, Marine Mammal Commission, Room 307, 1625 Eye St., NW, Wash., D.C. 20006-3954. (202) 653-6237.

National Academy of Sciences

Staff Director, Environmental Studies Board, National Academy of Sciences, Room JH-604, 2101 Constitution Ave., NW, Wash., D.C. 20418-0001. (202) 334-3060.

National Aeronautics and Space Administration

Environmental Compliance Officer, Facilities Engineering Division (NXG), National Aeronautics and Space Administration, Room 5031, 600 Maryland Ave., SW, Wash., D.C. 20546-0001. (202) 453-1958.

National Capital Planning Commission

Environmental/Energy Officer, Division of Planning Services, National Capital Planning Commission, Room 1024, 1325 G St., NW, Wash., D.C. 20576-0001. (202) 724-0178.

National Credit Union Administration

Director, Department of Legal Services, National Credit Union Administration, Room 8261, 1776 G St., NW, Wash., D.C. 20456-0001. (202) 357-1030.

National Science Foundation

Chairman and Staff Associate, Committee on Environmental Matters, Office of Astronomical, Atmospheric, Earth and Ocean Sciences, National Science Foundation, Room 641, 1800 G St., NW, Wash., D.C. 20550-0001. (202) 357-7615.

Nuclear Regulatory Commission

(1) Director, Division of Engineering, Office of Nuclear Reactor Regulation, Nuclear Regulatory Commission, Room P-202, Phillips Bldg., 7920 Norfolk Ave., Bethesda, MD 20814-2587. (301) 492-7207.

(2) Director, Division of Fuel Cycle and Materials Safety, Office of Nuclear Material Safety and Safeguards, Nuclear Regulatory Commission, Room 562, Willste Building, 7915 Eastern Ave., Silver Spring, MD 20910-4898. (301) 427-4485.

Pennsylvania Avenue Development Corporation

Director of Development, Pennsylvania Avenue Development Corporation, Suite 1248, 425 13th St., NW, Wash., D.C. 20004-1850. (202) 523-5477.

Securities and Exchange Commission

Special Counsel, Office of Public Utility Regulation, Securities and Exchange

49754 **Federal Register** / Vol. 49, No. 247 / Friday, December 21, 1984 / Rules and Regulations

Commission. Room 7012. 450 Fifth St., NW. Wash., D.C. 20549–0001. (202) 272–7648.

Small Business Administration

Director. Office of Business Loans, Small Business Administration. Room 804–C, 1441 L St., NW. Wash., D.C. 20416–0001. (202) 653–6696.

Susquehanna River Basin Commission

Executive Director, Susquehanna River Basin Commission. 1721 N. Front St., Harrisburg. PA. 17102–2391. (717) 238–0422.

Tennessee Valley Authority

Director, Environmental Quality Staff. Tennessee Valley Authority, 201 Summer Place Building, 309 Walnut St., Knoxville, TN 37902–1411. (615) 632–6578; (FTS) 856–6578.

United States Information Agency

Assistant General Counsel. United States Information Agency, 301 Fourth St., SW. Wash., D.C. 20547–0001. (202) 485–7976.

United States International Development Cooperation Agency

(1) Environmental Affairs Coordinator, Office of External Affairs, U.S. Agency for International Development. Department of State Bldg., 320 21st St., NW. Wash., D.C. 20523–0001. (202) 632–8268.

(2) International Economist/Environmental Officer, Office of Development, Overseas Private Investment Corporation, 1129 20th St., NW, Wash., D.C. 20527–0001. (202) 653–2904.

United States Postal Service

Director, Office of Program Planning. Real Estate and Buildings Department, United States Postal Service, Room 4014, 475 L'Enfant Plaza West, SW, Wash., D.C. 20260–6420. (202) 245–4304.

Veterans Administration

Director, Environmental Affairs, Veterans Administration, Code 005, 810 Vermont Ave. NW, Wash., D.C. 20420–0001. (202) 389–2192.

Appendix II—Federal and Federal-State Agencies With Jurisdiction by Law or Special Expertise on Environmental Quality Issues

I. POLLUTION CONTROL

A. Air Quality

Department of Agriculture

• Agricultural Research Service (effects of air pollution on vegetative growth).
• Farmers Home Administration (effects of air pollution on housing. community, and business loan programs. and farmer loan programs).
• Forest Service (effects of air pollution on vegetation and visibility; fire smoke management on National Forest and Grasslands).
• Rural Electrification Administration (electric power plant emissions).
• Soil Conservation Service (effects of air pollution on vegetation; wind erosion).

Department of Commerce

• National Bureau of Standards (air quality measurements. standards, data and methods).
• National Oceanic and Atmospheric Administration (meteorological and climatological research and monitoring in relation to urban air pollution; incorporation of national air quality standards in Coastal Zone Management Plans for management and protection of coastal and marine resources).

Department of Defense

• Department of the Air Force (air pollution from military aircraft).
• Department of the Army (emissions from military vehicles).

Department of Energy

• Economic Regulatory Administration (emissions from power plants and other major fuel-burning installations):
—Exemptions from prohibitions against burning of natural gas and oil in power plants and major fuel-burning installations. 42 U.S.C 7101 and 8301 (10 CFR Part 500, et seq.).
• Office of Policy, Safety, and Environment (air quality in relation to general energy policies, programs, and projects: emissions from energy sources).

Department of Health and Human Services

• Public Health Service: Center for Disease Control (effects of air pollution on health); National Institutes of Health (effects of air pollution on health).

Department of Housing and Urban Development

• Office of Community Planning and Development (effects of air pollution on the built environment: air pollution abatement: energy costs and State Implementation Plans).
• Office of Housing (effect of air pollution on housing values and marketability: economic impacts).

Department of the Interior

• Fish and Wildlife Service (effects of air pollution, including acid rain, on endangered species and critical habitats; National Wildlife Refuge System areas; and other fish and wildlife resources).
• Geological Survey (effects of acid rain on surface and ground waters).
• Bureau of Indian Affairs (effects of etr pollution on Indian lands).
• Bureau of Land Management (effects of air pollution, including smoke from forest fires and prescribed burning, on public lands, vegetation and visibility).
• Minerals Management Service (emissions from outer continental shelf lease operations):
—Oil, gas, and sulphur operations on the outer continental shelf—air quality. 43 U.S.C. 1331. et seq., and 42 U.S.C. 7411 (30 CFR Part 250.57).
• Bureau of Mines (air pollution from mining and minerals processing).
• National Park Service (visibility and other effects of air pollution on National Park System areas; effects of air pollution on recreation areas and historic, archeological and architectural sites).
• Office of Surface Mining Reclamation and Enforcement (air pollution from surface coal mining and reclamation operations; control of wind erosion at surface coal mines: control of coal waste fires).

Department of Labor

• Mine Safety and Health Administration (airborne hazards in mining operations).
• Occupational Safety and Health Administration (airborne hazards in the workplace):
—Air contaminants, toxic and hazardous substances. 29 U.S.C. 655, et seq. (29 CFR Part 1910, Subpart Z).
Department of State (international aspects of air pollution).

Department of Transportation

• Coast Guard (cargo tank venting and vapor recovery systems).
• Federal Aviation Administration (aircraft emissions):
—Fuel venting and exhaust emission requirements for turbine engine powered airplanes. Special Federal Aviation Regulation 27 (SFAR). 42 U.S.C. 1857, et seq., 7671 and 7601; 49 U.S.C. 1345, 1348, 1421, 1423 and 1655 (14 CFR Part 11; 40 CFR Part 87).
• Federal Highway Administration (highway related air quality impacts; vehicle emissions):

—Air quality conformity of highway projects. 23 U.S.C. 109; 42 U.S.C. 7401, *et seq.*, and 7506 (23 CFR Part 770).

• Federal Railroad Administration (locomotive emissions).

• Urban Mass Transportation Administration (air quality effects of urban transportation systems):

—Air quality conformity of transit projects. 42 U.S.C. 7401, *et seq.*, and 7506 (49 CFR Part 623).

Advisory Council on Historic Preservation (effects of air pollution on historic districts, buildings and monuments).

Consumer Product Safety Commission (toxic emissions from consumer products and household substances):

—Consumer products and household substances regulations. 15 U.S.C. 1261, *et seq.*, and 2051, *et seq.* (16 CFR Part 1000, *et seq.*).

Environmental Protection Agency (effect of air pollution on public health and welfare; air quality criteria and standards; air pollution control and abatement technologies; transportation emissions and air quality impacts; stationary source emissions; monitoring technology):

—Air quality programs in general. 42 U.S.C. 1857, *et seq.*; 7401, *et seq.*; 7501, *et seq.*; and 7601, *et seq.* (40 CFR Parts 50–87).

—Prevention of significant air quality deterioration. 42 U.S.C. 7470, *et seq.* (40 CFR Parts 51, 52 and 124).

—Approval of State Implementation Plans (SIPs) for National primary and secondary ambient air quality standards. 42 U.S.C. 7410 (40 CFR Parts 51 and 52).

—Approval of State plans for standards of performance for new stationary emission sources (NSPS). 42 U.S.C. 7411 (40 CFR Part 60).

—Applications for primary non-ferrous smelter orders. 42 U.S.C. 7419 (40 CFR Part 57).

—Assuring that Federal projects conform with State Implementation Plans. 42 U.S.C. 7616 (40 CFR Part 20).

—Certification of new emission sources for conformance with National Emission Standards for Hazardous Air Pollutants including radioactive materials. 42 U.S.C. 7412(c) (40 CFR Part 61).

Interstate Commerce Commission (air pollution from trucks and railroads).

National Aeronautics and Space Administration (advanced technology for remote sensing of air quality parameters and for reduction of aircraft engine emissions).

Nuclear Regulatory Commission (radioactive substances in air pollution):

—For jurisdictional reapponsibilities see Part I.E—Radiation.

Tennessee Valley Authority (air quality in the Tennessee Valley region; measurement and control of air pollution from fossil-fueled steamplants; effects on vegetation).

B. Water Quality

Department of Agriculture

• Agricultural Research Service (research on erosion and sediment control, pesticide degradation and runoff, and salinity).

• Agricultural Stabilization and Conservation Service (water quality on agricultural lands; Water Bank Program).

• Farmers Home Administration (water quality in relation to housing, community, and business loan programs, and farmer loan programs).

• Forest Service (effects of water pollution on National Forests and Grasslands, and on forest and range land in general):

—Consultation regarding effects of pollution on rivers established as units of the National Wild and Scenic Rivers System and on those rivers designated for study as potential additions to that System. 16 U.S.C. 1278, *et seq.*

—Management of municipal watersheds on National Forest lands. (36 CFR Parts 251.9 and 251.35).

• Soil Conservation Service (water quality in relation to agricultural waste management, erosion and sediment control and stabilization of rural abandoned mines; salinity control; pesticides in conservation systems):

—Reclamation of rural abandoned mined land. 30 U.S.C. 1201 *et seq.* (7 CFR Part 632).

—Program for land conservation and utilization, and aquaculture. 7 U.S.C. 1011(e).

Department of Commerce

• National Bureau of Standards (water quality measurements, standards, data, and methods).

• National Oceanic and Atmospheric Administration (water quality in the management and protection of coastal and marine resources, marine pollution research and monitoring for ocean mining):

—National Ocean Pollution Planning Act. 33 U.S.C. 1701, *et seq.*

—Marine Protection, Research, and Sanctuaries Act. 16 U.S.C. 1431. *et seq.* 15 CFR Part 922, *et seq.*).

Department of Defense

• Army Corps of Engineers (water pollution from activities in navigable waters):

—Rules governing work or structure in or affecting navigable waters of the United States. 33 U.S.C. 401 and 403 (33 CFR Parts 321 and 322).

—Authority to enjoin dumping of, or force removal of, refuse placed in or on the banks of a navigable water or tributary of a navigable water. 33 U.S.C. 407 (33 CFR Part 320.2(d)).

—Permits for discharges of dredged or fill materials into waters of the United States. 33 U.S.C. 1344 (33 CFR Part 323).

—Guidelines controlling discharge of dredged or fill material in waters of the U.S. including wetlands. 33 U.S.C. 1344(b) and 1361(a) (40 CFR Part 230).

—Permits for transportation of dredged materials for dumping into ocean waters. 33 U.S.C. 1413 (33 CFR Part 324).

—Regulation of artificial islands, installations and devices on the outer continental shelf. 43 U.S.C. 1333(e). (33 CFR Part 320.2(b)).

• Department of Navy (water pollution control for ships and naval installations; oceanography).

Department of Energy

• Office of Policy, Safety, and Environment (water quality and marine pollution in relation to general energy policies, programs and projects).

Department of Health and Human Services

• Center for desease Control (effects of water quality on health).

• Food and Drug Administration (shellfish sanitation; contamination of fish and shellfish with toxics).

Department of Housing and Urban Development

• Office of Community Planning and Development (effects of water pollution community planning and on sole source aquifers, floodplains, wetlands, and urban coastal zones).

Department of the Interior

• Fish and Wildlife Service (effects of water pollution on National Wildlife Refuge and National Fish Hatchery System areas, endangered species and their critical habitats, migratory waterfowl, floodplains, wetlands, estuarine areas, marine sanctuaries, barrier islands, and sport fisheries and wildlife resources).

• Geological Survey (general hydrology and water quality; National Water Summary; National Stream Quality Accounting Network [NASQAN]).

• Bureau of Indian Affairs (water quality on Indian lands).

• Bureau of Land Management (water quality on public lands):

—Permits and leases for facilities to control/reduce water pollution. 43 U.S.C. 1732(b) and 1761(a)(1) (43 CFR Part 2800).

• Minerals Management Service (effects of marine pollution on the outer continental shelf and coastal waters):

—Control of pollution from mineral mining, including oil and gas development, on the outer continental shelf. 43 U.S.C. 1331–1343. (30 CFR Parts 250, 251, 252 and 256).

• Bureau of Mines (water pollution from mining and mineral processing; acid mine drainage).

• National Park Service (effects of water pollution on National Park System areas including National Seashores and Lakeshores, on outdoor recreational values, and on historic, archeological, and architectural resources):

—Consultations regarding effects of pollution on rivers established as units of the National Wild and Scenic Rivers System and on those rivers designated for study as potential additions to that System. 16 U.S.C. 1278, *et seq.*

• Bureau of Reclamation (effects of public works, salinity control, sedimentation, and irrigation on water quality; effects of water developments on estuarine areas; research in weather modification, water quality and quantity, and desalinization).

• Office of Surface Mining Reclamation and Enforcement (effects of surface coal mining and reclamation operations on water quality and hydrologic balance).

Department of State (international aspects of water pollution):

—Facilities for export/import of water and sewage. Executive Order 11423.

49756   **Federal Register** / Vol. 49, No. 247 / Friday, December 21, 1984 / Rules and Regulations

Department of Transportation

• Coast Guard (effects of oil spills and ship sanitation on water quality; ocean dumping enforcement; marine resource protection):

—Tanker construction, equipment, manning operation. 46 U.S.C. 391(a) (33 CFR Part 157).

—Control of pollution by oil and hazardous substance discharges in ports, waterways, and offshore facilities. 33 U.S.C. 1008–1011, 1221, and 1321; 50 U.S.C. 191 (33 CFR Parts 151and 154-156).

—Certification of marine sanitation devices 33 U.S.C. 1322 (33 CFR Part 159).

• Federal Highway Administration (effects of highways, traffic and use of salt on water quality).

• Maritime Administration (water pollution from ships; destruction/treatment of wastes at sea):

—Merchant vessels, polluting discharges and dumping. 46 U.S.C. 1101, *et seq.*

—Port operations, polluting discharges and dumping. 46 U.S.C. 867.

• Research and Special Programs Administration; Materials Transportation Bureau (effects of hazardous substances transportation on water quality).

Advisory Council on Historic Preservation (effects of water pollution on historic districts, buildings and monuments).

Environmental Protection Agency (waste water treatment works; effluent limitations; oil and hazardous substance discharges; protection of drinking water supplies; thermal discharges; ocean dumping; monitoring technology):

—Water quality programs in general. 33 U.S.C. 1160, *et seq.*, and 1251, *et seq.*; 42 U.S.C. 300f, *et seq.*, and 6901, *et seq.* (40 CFR Parts 100–149).

—Effluent guidelines and standards. 33 U.S.C. 1251, *et seq.* (40 CFR Part 401, *et seq.*).

—Ocean dumping in general. 33 U.S.C. 1344, 1361 and 1412–1418 (40 CFR Parts 220-231).

—Permits for discharge of specific pollutants from aqoaculture projects. 33 U.S.C.1328 (40 CFR Parts 122–124).

—Review of permits for transportation of dredged material for ocean dumping. 33 U.S.C. 1413 (40 CFR Parts 220–229).

—Permits for transportation of materials (other than dredged material) for ocean dumping. 33 U.S.C. 1412 and 1414 (40 CFR Parts 220-229).

—Permits for disposal of sewage sludge. 33 U.S.C. 1345 (40 CFR Parts 122–125).

—Permits for ocean discharges. 33 U.S.C. 1343 (40 CFR Parts 125.120-125.124).

—Regulation of discharges of oil and hazardous substances in waters of the United States. 33 U.S.C. 1321 and 1361 (40 CFR Part 112).

—Permits for treatment, storage or disposal of hazardous wastes. 2 U.S.C. 6925 (40 CFR Parts 124, 270, and 271).

—Review of permits for discharges of dredged or fill materials into navigable waters. 33 U.S.C. 1344(c) (40 CFR Part 230).

—Guidelines controlling the discharge of dredged or fill material in waters of the U.S. including wetlands. 33 U.S.C. 1344(b) and 1361(a) (40 CFR Part 230).

—Assistance for construction of publicly-owned waste water treatment works. 33 U.S.C. 1281 (40 CFR Parts 30 and 35).

—Underground injection control permits. 42 U.S.C. 300f. *et seq.* (40CFR Parts 122-124 and 144-146).

—National Pollutant Discharge Elimination System (NPDES) wastewater permits. 33 U.S.C. 1342 (40 CFR Parts 122-125, 129, 133 and 136).

—Designation of Sole Source Aquifers. 42 U.S.C. 300f and h-3(e) (40 CFR Part 148).

Federal Emergency Management Agency (water quality in floodplain management).

Federal Maritime Commission (vessel certification with respect to liability for water pollution):

—Certificates of financial responsibility for water pollution. 33 U.S.C. 1321 (46 CFR Part 542); 42 U.S.C. 1643 (46 CFR Part 543); 43 U.S.C.1815 (46 CFR Part 544).

International Boundary and Water Commission, United States Section (U.S.-Mexico border water quality, salinity, and sanitation problems).

National Aeronautics and Space Administration (advanced technology for remote sensing of water quality and marine pollution).

Nuclear Regulatory Commission (radioactive substances in water pollution):

—For jurisdictional responsibilities, see PART I. E—Radiation.

Tennessee Valley Authority (water quality in the Tennessee Valley; effects of chemical and thermal effluents).

C. Waste Disposal on Land

Department of Agriculture

• Agricultural Research Service (effects of agricultural wastes and sludge on cropland).

• Agriculture Stabilization and Conservation Service (effects of solid waste, especially sludge disposal, on cropland).

• Forest Service (effects of solid and liquid wastes on National Forests and Grasslands):

—Permits for disposal sites on National Forest System lands. 16 U.S.C. 495, 497, 532–538 and 580 (36 CFR Part 251).

• Rural Electrification Administration (solid waste disposal from electric power plants).

• Soil Conservation Service (agriculture waste management; siting of disposal areas; sludge application on cropland for beneficial purposes).

Department of Commerce

• National Bureau of Standards (measurements, standards, data, and methods relating to solid and liquid wastes).

• National Oceanic and Atmospheric Administration (disposal of solid wastes in the management and protection of coastal end marine resources).

Department of Health and Human Services

• Center for Disease Control (effects of wastes on health).

• Food and Drug Administration (contamination of food resulting from disposal of municipal and industrial waste treatment sludge).

Department of the Interior

• Fish and Wildlife Service (effects of solid wastes on National Wildlife Refuge and National Fish Hatchery System areas,

endangered species and their critical habitats, and other fish and wildlife resources).

• Geological Survey (geologic and hydrologic effects of solid and liquid wastes)

• Bureau of Indian Affairs (effects of solid wastes on Indian lands).

• Bureau of Land Management (effects of solid wastes on public lands):

—Sale or lease of land for solid waste disposal sites. 43 U.S.C. 669, *et seq.* (for sale—43 CFR Part 2740; for lease—43 CFR Part 2912).

• Bureau of Mines (mine wastes; mineral processing wastes; tailings stabilization; impoundment structures; municipal solid wastes; recycling).

• National Park Service (effects of solid wastes on National Park System areas).

• Office of Surface Mining Reclamation and Enforcement (surface coal mining and reclamation operation wastes).

Department of Labor

• Mine Safety and Health Administration (mine waste control).

Department of Transportation

• Maritime Administration (destruction/ treatment of wastes at sea).

• Research and Special Programs Administration; Materials Transportation Bureau (transport of hazardous wastes):

—Hazardous materials regulations. (49 CFR Part 171, *et seq.*).

Environmental Protection Agency (solid wastes; hazardous waste; resource conservation and recovery; removal and remedial actions; environmental effects):

Solid wastes in general. 42 U.S.C. 3251, *et seq.*, and 6901, *et seq.* (40 CFR Parts 240–271) 42 U.S.C. 9601 *et seq.* (40 CFR Part 300, *et seq.*).

—Permits for disposal of sewage sludge. 33 U.S.C. 1345 (40 CFR Parts 122–125).

—Solid Waste Disposal Act permits. 42 U.S.C. 3251, *et seq.*, and 6901, *et seq.* (40 CFR Parts 124, 257, 270, 271 and 350).

—Criteria for classification of solid waste disposal facilities and practices. 42 U.S.C. 6907(a)(3) and 6944(a); 33 U.S.C. 1345 (40 CFR Part 257).

—Identification and listing of hazardous westes. 42 U.S.C. 6921 (40 CFR Part 281).

—Standards applicable to generators and transporters of hazardous waste, and for owners and operators of hazardous waste treatment, storage, and disposal facilities. 42 U.S.C. 6922–6924 (40 CFR Parts 260–267)

—Permits for hazardous waste treatment, storage, and disposal facilities. 42 U.S.C. 6925 (40 CFR Parts 123, 124, 270 and 271).

—Preliminary notification of hazardous waste activities. 42 U.S.C. 6930 (40 CFR Parts 281.5, 282.12, and 263.11).

—Removal and remedial actions taken in response to the release or threatened release of hazardous substances. 42 U.S.C. 9601 (23) and (24) 40 CFR Part 300).

—National Contingency plan for the release of oil and hazardous substances into the environment. 42 U.S.C. 9605 (40 CFR Part 300).

Federal Register / Vol. 49, No. 247 / Friday, December 21, 1984 / Rules and Regulations   49757

—Notification requirements for the release of hazardous substances into the environment. 42 U.S.C. 9605 (10 CFR Part 302).

—Assistance for construction and waste disposal facilities. 42 U.S.C. 6901, et seq. (40 CFR Parts 30 and 35).

Federal Emergency Management Agency (hazardous materials emergency management and disaster relief assistance).

General Services Administration (wastes in public buildings).

Nuclear Regulatory Commission (radioactive waste disposal):

—For jurisdictional responsibilities, see PART I. E—Radiation.

Tennessee Valley Authority (coal combustion products).

D. Noise

Department of Agriculture

• Farmers Home Administration (noise in relation to housing, community, and business loan programs, and farmer loan programs).
• Forest Service (noise effects on National Forests and Grasslands).
• Rural Electrification Administration (electric generating facility, powerline, and substation noise).

Department of Commerce

• National Oceanic and Atmospheric Administration (effects of noise on marine mammals).

Department of Defense

• Department of the Air Force (military aircraft noise).
• Department of the Army (noise from rotary wing aircraft and other military vehicles).

Department of Health and Human Services

• Public Health Service (effects of noise on health).

Department of Housing and Urban Development

• Office of Community Planning and Development (aircraft and vehicular noise and land use compatibility):
—Noise abatement and control. (24 CFR Part 51, Subpart B).
—Siting of HUD assisted projects in runway clear zones (civil airports) and clear zones and accident potential zones (military airfields). (24 CFR Part 51, Subpart D).
• Office of Housing (noise standards for housing; noise abatement and control).

Department of Interior

• Fish and Wildlife Service (effects of noise on endangered species and their critical habitats, National Wildlife Refuge System areas, and other fish and wildlife resources).
• Bureau of Indian Affairs (noise effects on Indian lands).
• Bureau of Land Management (noise effects on public lands; noise abatement and control).
• Minerals Management Service (effects of noise on marine mammals).
• Bureau of Mines (mine noise, blasting and vibration).
• National Park Service (effects of noise on National Parks system areas, including off-road vehicular noise; effects of noise and vibration on historic, archeological, and architectural sites, and recreational resources).
• Bureau of Reclamation (effects of noise on reclamation project lands).
• Office of Surface Mining Reclamation and Enforcement (noise from surface coal mining and reclamation operations, and from the use of explosives).

Department of Labor

• Mining Safety and Health Administration (noise in mining operations).
• Occupational Safety and Health Administration (noise in the workplace):
—Occupational noise exposure. 29 U.S.C. 655, et seq. (29 CFR Part 1910.95).

Department of Transportation

• Federal Aviation Administration (aircraft noise and land use compatibility):
—Airport noise compatibility planning. 49 U.S.C. 1341, 1354, 1421, 1431, 1655 and 2101–2104 (14 CFR Part 150).
—Noise standards. Aircraft type and airworthiness certification. 49 U.S.C. 1354, 1421, 1423, 1431 and 1655 (14 CFR Part 36).
—Operating noise limits. 49 U.S.C. 1344, et seq.; 1421, et seq., and 1655 (14 CFR Part 91, Subpart E).
—Civil aircraft sonic boom. (14 CFR Part 91.55).
• Federal Highway Administration (traffic and motor vehicle noise):
—Procedures for abatement of highway traffic and construction noise. 23 U.S.C. 109 (23 CFR Part 772).
• Federal Railroad Administration (railroad noise):
—Railroad noise emission compliance regulation. 42 U.S.C. 4901, et seq. (49 CFR Part 210).
—Noise standards for railroad employees. (49 CFR Parts 228–229).
• Urban Mass Transportation Administration (urban transportation system noise).

Advisory Council on Historic Preservation (effects of noise and vibration on historic districts, buildings and monuments).

Consumer Products Safety Commission (hazardous noise from consumer products):
—Consumer products regulations. 15 U.S.C. 1261, et seq., and 2051, et seq. (16 CFR Part 1000, et seq.).

Environmental Protection Agency (noise exposure standards; noise abatement and control techniques; noise impact assessment techniques; environmental effects):
—Noise abatement programs. 42 U.S.C. 4901, et seq. (40 CFR Part 201, et seq.).

Interstate Commerce Commission (noise effects from trucks and railroads).

National Aeronautics and Space Administration (advanced technology for reduction of aircraft noise).

E. Radiation

Department of Agriculture

• Agricultural Research Service (effects of irradiation on insects and microorganisms in food).

Forest Service (disposal of radioactive materials in National forests and Grasslands; electromagnetic radiation from powerlines, radio transmission systems).

Rural Electrification Administration (electromagnetic radiation from high voltage sources).

Department of Commerce

• National Bureau of Standards (radiation measurements, standards, methods and data).
• National Oceanic and Atmospheric Administration (electromagnetic radiation from radar systems and telecommunications)

Department of Energy

• Office of Civilian Radioactive Waste Management (storage and disposal of commercial high-level radioactive waste and spent nuclear fuel).
• Office of Defense Programs (storage and disposal of Defense nuclear waste).
• Office of Energy Research (health effects of radiation and nuclear energy).
• Office of Policy, Safety, and Environment (nuclear energy and radioactive waste disposal; radiation effects).

Department of Health and Human Services

• Food and Drug Administration (effects of radiation on health and safety; contamination of food with radioactive materials).
• National Institutes of Health (effects of radiation on health).

Department of Housing and Urban Development

• Office of Community Planning and Development (radiation health and safety factors; siting and distance criteria):
—Policy guidance on problems posed by toxic chemicals and radioactive materials (HUD Notice 79–33 of Sept. 10, 1979).
• Office of Housing (radiation location factors affecting value and marketability).

Department of the Interior

• Fish and Wildlife Service (effects of radiation on National Wildlife Refuges, endangered species and their critical habitats, and other fish and wildlife resources).
• Geological Survey (effects of radioactive waste disposal).
• Bureau of Indian Affairs (effects of radiation on Indian lands).
• Bureau of Land Management (effects of radiation on public lands):
—Withdrawal of public lands for deep-burial depositories for radioactive waste. 43 U.S.C. 1714 (43 CFR Part 2300, et seq.).
• Bureau of Mines (radiation from uranium mines).
• National Park Service (effects of radiation on National Park System areas).

Department of Labor

• Mining Safety and Health Administration (worker protection from radiation exposure in mining).
• Occupational Safety and Health Administration (worker protection from exposure to sources of radiation not covered by other Federal agencies):

49758 **Federal Register** / Vol. 49, No. 247 / Friday. December 21, 1984 / Rules and Regulations

—Ionizing and nonionizing radiation. 29 U.S.C. 655. *et seq.* [29 CFR Parts 1910.96 and 1910.97).

Department of Transportation

• Federal Aviation Administration (radiation effects on air traffic; transport of radioactive materials).
• Federal Highway Administration: Bureau of Motor Carrier Safety [radioactive material transaportation in interstale commerce):
—Hazardous materials tables and communications regulations. (49 CFR Part 172).
• Research and Special Programs Administration: Materials Transportation Bureau (transportation of radioactive materials);
—Hazardous materials regulations. 49 U.S.C. 1801, *et seq.* (49 CFR Part 171. *et seq.*).

Consumer Product Safety Commission (radiation from consumer products and household substances):
—Consumer products and household substances regulations. 15 U.S.C. 1261, *et seq.*; 2051, *et seq.*, and 2080 [16 CFR Part 1000. *et seq.*).

Environmental Protection Agency (radiation protection standards and guidance; radioactive air emissions; ocean disposal of radioactive waste; radiation limits for drinking water; radiation monitoring):
—Radiation protection programs. 42 U.S.C. 2011. *et seq.* (40 CFR Part 190, *et seq.*).
—Standards for the uranium fuel cycle. 42 U.S.C. 2011. *et seq.* (40 CFR Part 190).
—Standards for uranium mill tailings. 42 U.S.C. 2022. (40 CFR Part 192).
—Radiation standards for drinking water. 42 U.S.C. 300f, *et seq.* (40 CFR Part 141).
—Guidance to other Federal agencies for environmental radiation standards. 42 U.S.C. 2021(h).

Federal Emergency Management Agency (review and approval of state and local nuclear incident emergency response plans; Federal contingency plans; radiation hazards emergency management),

Nuclear Regulatory Commission (radioactive wastes, radiation effects in general):
—Standards for protection against radiation. 42 U.S.C. 2073, *et seq.*, and 5841, *et seq.* (10 CFR Part 20).
—Licensing of byproduct material. 42 U.S.C. 2014. *et seq.*, and 5841, *et seq.* (10 CFR Parts 30–33 and 35).
—Licensing and radiation safety requirements for radiography. 42 U.S.C. 2111, *et seq.*, and 5841, *et seq.* (10 CFR Part 34).
—Licensing of source material. 42 U.S.C. 2014 *et seq.*, and 5841, *et seq.* (10 CFR Part 40).
—Licensing of production and utilization facilities. 42 U.S.C. 2073, *et seq.*, and 5841, *et seq.* (10 CFR Parts 50, 51 and 55).
—Disposal of high level radioactive waste. 42 U.S.C. 2021, *et seq.*, and 5842, *et seq.* (10 CFR Parts 60 and 61).
—Licensing of special nuclear material. 42 U.S.C. 2014. *et seq.*, and 5841, *et seq.* (10 CFR Part 70).
—Packaging and transportation of radioactive material. 42 U.S.C. 2073, *et seq.*, and 5841 *et seq.* (10 CFR Part 71).

—Licensing for storage of spent fuel. 42 U.S.C. 2021. *et seq.*. and 5872 *et seq.* (10 CFR Part 72).
—Reactor site criteria. 42 U.S.C. 2133, *et seq.*, and 5841, *et seq.* (10 CFR Part 100).
—Export and import of nuclear material. 42 U.S.C. 2073, *et seq.*, and 5841 [10 CFR Part 110).
—Licenses for Department of Energy demonstration reactors. 42 U.S.C. 5842 (1) and (2).
—Licenses for receipt and long-term storage of high-level radioactive wastes at Department of Energy facilities. 42 U.S.C. 5842 (3) and (4).

Tennessee Valley Authority (nuclear power plant planning; radiation monitoring).

F. Hazardous Substances

(1) Toxic, Explosive, and Flammable Materials

Department of Agriculture

• Agricultural Marketing Services (toxic materials and consumer protection).
• Animal and Plant Health Inspection Service (toxic materials in the control of plant pests, noxious weeds, animal diseases, and vectors).
• Food Safety and Inspection Service (toxic materials and consumer protection).
• Forest Service (effects of toxic materials on National Forests and Grasslands).
• Soil Conservation Service (toxic materials in the control of insects and other plant pests).

Department of Commerce

• National Bureau of Standards (toxic material measurements, standards, methods and data).
• National Oceanic and Atmospheric Administration (toxic materials in coastal and marine resources management and protection; ocean pollution research and monitoring).

Department of Defense (toxic materials in military operations).

Department of Health and Human Services

• Center for Disease Control (toxic materials and health issues).
• Food and Drug Administration (toxic materials and contamination of food).
• National Institutes of Health (toxic materials and health issues).

Department of Housing and Urban Development

• Office of Community Planning and Development (hazardous waste disposal, treatment, and compatible land use):
—Assurances that HUD assisted projects are located in a safe and healthful environment. 42 U.S.C. 1441. *et seq.*
—Policy guidance on problems posed by toxic chemicals and radioactive materials. (HUD Notice 79–33 of Sept. 10, 1979).
—Siting of HUD assisted projects near hazardous operations handling explosive or flammable materials. (24 CFR Part 51. Subpart C).

• Office of Housing (lead-based paint poisoning prevention; hazardous material storage and effects on property values).

Department of the Interior

• Fish and Wildlife Service (effects of toxic materials, including lead shot. on endangered species and critical habitats. National Wildlife Refuge and National Fish Hatchery System areas. and other fish and wildlife resources).
• Geological Survey (effects of the disposal of toxic wastes).
• Bureau of Indian Affairs (toxic materials on Indian lands).
• Bureau of Land Management (toxic materials on public lands).
• Minerals Management Service (toxic materials from outer continental shelf mineral, including oil and gas, operations):
—Discharges from outer continental shelf mineral, including oil and gas, operations. 43 U.S.C. 1331. *et seq.* (30 CFR Part 250).
• Bureau of Mines (disposal methods for selected milling and mine wastes).
• National Park Service (effects of toxic materials on National Park System areas).
• Bureau of Reclamation (effects of toxic materials on water storage and delivery projects).
• Office of Surface Mining Reclamation and Enforcement (toxic materials from surface coal mining and reclamation wastes).

Department of Labor

• Mining Safety and Health Administration (toxic materials in mining).
• Occupational Safety and Health Administration (toxic materials in the workplace):
—Hazardous and toxic materials and substances. 29 U.S.C. 655, *et seq.* [29 CFR Part 1910, Subparts H and Z).

Department of Transportation

• Coast Guard (transportation of toxic materials by vessel; discharges to navigable waters):
—Transportation of hazardous materials by vessel. 46 U.S.C. 170, 375, 391(a) and 416(j); 49 U.S.C. 1655, 1803, 1804 and 1808(j); 50 U.S.C. 191 (33 CFR Parts 151. *et seq.*, and 160, *et seq.* (46 CFR Chapter I).
—Hazardous substance discharge in navigable waters. 33 U.S.C. 1321 (33 CFR Parts 25 and 151, *et seq.*; 46 CFR Part 542 *et seq.*).
• Federal Aviation Administration (hazardous aircraft cargo).
• Federal Highway Administration: Bureau of Motor Carrier Safety (hazardous material transportation in interstate commerce):
—Hazardous materials tables and communications regulations. (49 CFR Part 172).
—Transportation of hazardous materials— driving and parking rules. (49 CFR Part 397).
• Federal Railroad Administration (railroad transport of hazardous materials).
• Maritime Administration (port, coastal and ocean pollution from hazardous materials):
—Merchant vessels, polluting discharges, dumping, and destruction/treatment of wastes at sea. 46 U.S.C. 1101, *et seq.*

• Research and Special Programs Administration: Materials Transportation Bureau (hazardous-cargo; hazardous materials in pipelines):

—Transportation of hazardous materials. 49 U.S.C. 1801. *et seq.* (49 CFR Part 171. *et seq.*, and 190, *et seq.*).

—Approval for shipments of Class A explosives. 49 U.S.C.1707 (7).

—Permits for facilities to handle hazardous materials. 49 U.S.C. 1801, *et seq.*

Consumer Product Safety Commission (toxic consumer products and hazardous household substances):

—Consumer product and household substances regulations. 15 U.S.C. 1261, *et seq.*: 1471, *et seq.*; and 2051. *et seq.* (16 CFR Part 1000. *et seq.*).

Environmental Protection Agency (hazardous material pollution control and environmental effects):

—Permits for the treatment. storage and disposal of hazardous wastes. 42 U.S.C. 6901. *et se* 40 CFR Parts 122–124, 257, 270, and 2 .

—Criteria for classification of hazardous waste disposal facilities and practices. 42 U.S.C. 6907(a)(3) and 6944(a); 33 U.S.C. 1345 (40 CFR Part 257).

—Identification and listing of hazardous waste. 42 U.S.C. 6921 (40 CFR Part 261).

—Standards applicable to generators and transporters of hazardous wastes and for owners and operators of hazardous waste treatment, storage and disposal facilities. 42 U.S.C. 6901. *et seq.* (40 CFR Parts 260–287).

—Preliminary notification of hazardous waste activities. 42 U.S.C. 6930 (40 CFR Parts 261.5, 262.12 and 263.11).

—National emission standards for hazardous air pollutants (NESHAP). 42 U.S.C. 1857, *et seq.* General provisions: (40 CFR Part 61).

—Hazardous substances in water. 33 U.S.C. 1251, *et seq.* (40 CFR Parts 116 and 117).

—Toxic effluent standards. 33 U.S.C. 1251, *et seq.* (40 CFR Part 129).

—Control of toxic substances in general. 15 U.S.C. 2601, *et seq.* (40 CFR Part 702, *et seq.*).

—Regulation of hazardous chemical substances and mixtures. 15 U.S.C. 2605 (40 CFR Part 750).

—Reporting of toxic substances inventory and retention of information. 15 U.S.C. 2607 (40 CFR Parts 710, 716, 761 and 763).

—Testing of chemical substances and mixtures. 15 U.S.C. 2603.

Federal Emergency Management Agency (evacuations and relocations resulting from hazardous materials released into the environment):

—Temporary evacuation and housing and permanent relocation due to hazardous substances pollution. 42 U.S.C. 9604(a)(1) and 9607 (23) and (24).

(2) Food Additives and Contamination of Food

Department of Agriculture

• Agricultural Research Service (detection of additives and contaminants in food).
• Agricultural Marketing Service (food quality standards).

• Food Safety and Inspection Service (contamination of meat and poultry products).

Department of Commerce

• National Oceanic and Atmospheric Administration (seafood quality).

Department of Health and Human Services

• Food and Drug Administration (effects of food additives and contamination on health).

Department of the Interior

• Fish and Wildlife Service (effects of contaminated food on endangered and threatened species and other Federally protected fish and wildlife).

Environmental Protection Agency (contamination of the environment and food from pesticide use and other toxic materials).

(3) Pesticides

Department of Agriculture

• Agricultural Research Service (biological controls; pesticides in food and fiber production).
• Animal Plant Health and Inspection Service (pesticides in the control of animal and plant pests and exotic noxious weeds).
• Food Safety and Inspection Service (pesticide residues and consumer protection).
• Forest Service (pesticides in the control of animal and plant pests; pesticide use on National Forests and Grasslands).
• Soil Conservation Service (pesticides in conservation systems; watershed resource protection).

Department of Commerce

• National Oceanic and Atmospheric Administration (effects of pesticides on marine life, the coastal zone, and seafood quality; ocean pollution research and monitoring).

Department of Defense

• Armed Forces Pest Management Board (pesticide use on military lands, facilities and equipment; control of disease vectors).

Department of Health and Human Services

• Center for Disease Control (effects of pesticides on health).
• Food and Drug Administration (pesticide contamination of food).

Department of the Interior

• Fish and Wildlife Service (pesticide use on National Wildlife Refuge and National Fish Hatchery System lands; effects of pesticides on endangered species and their critical habitats, and other fish and wildlife resources).
• Geological Survey (effects of pesticides on water quality).
• Bureau of Indian Affairs (pesticide use on Indian lands).
• Bureau of Land Management (pesticide use on public lands).
• Bureau of Reclamation (pesticide use on irrigated lands and other project lands, facilities and rights-of-way).
• National Park Service (pesticide use in National Park System areas).

Department of Labor

• Occupational Safety and Health Administration (worker exposures during manufacture of pesticides):

—Hazardous and toxic materials and substances. 29 U.S.C. 655, *et seq.* (29 CFR Part 1910, Subparts H and Z).

Department of Transportation

• Coast Guard (transportation of pesticides by vessel):

—Permits for transportation of hazardous substances by vessel. 46 U.S.C. 170, and 391a (33 CFR Parts 151, *et seq.*, and 160, *et seq.*; 46 CFR Chapter I).

• Federal Aviation Administration (transport and use of pesticides by aircraft).

• Federal Highway Administration: Bureau of Motor Carrier Safety (pesticide transport in interstate commerce):

—Hazardous materials tables and communications regulations. (49 CFR Part 172).

• Federal Railroad Administration (transport of pesticides by railroads).

• Research and Special Programs Administration: Materials Transportation Bureau (transport of pesticides):

—Transportation of hazardous materials. 49 U.S.C. 1801. *et seq.* (49 CFR Part 171, *et seq.*).

Environmental Protection Agency (pollution control and environmental effects of pesticides):

—Pesticide programs in general. 7 U.S.C. 136, *et seq.*; 21 U.S.C. 346a (40 CFR Part 162, *et seq.*).

—Certification of pesticide applicators. 7 U.S.C. 136b (40 CFR Part 171).

—Registration of pesticides. 7 U.S.C. 136a (40 CFR Part 162).

—Experimental pesticide use permits. 7 U.S.C. 136c (40 CFR Part 172).

—Establishment of pesticide tolerances. 21 U.S.C. 346a (40 CFR Part 180 and 21 CFR Part 193).

—Pesticide disposal and transportation. 7 U.S.C. 136q (40 CFR Part 165).

—Worker protection standards for agricultural pesticides. 7 U.S.C. 136 (40 CFR Part 170).

—Emergency exemptions for pesticides use. 7 U.S.C. 136p (40 CFR Part 166).

Tennessee Valley Authority (pesticide use on public lands and waters in Tennessee Valley region).

II. ENERGY

A. Electric Power (Development, Generation, Transmission, and Use)

Department of Agriculture

• Farmers Home Administration (small hydro, solar, and wind projects):

—Approval of plans and specifications for FMHA funded projects. 7 U.S.C. 1942 (7 CFR Parts 1924, 1942 and 1944).

• Forest Service (power development in National Forests and Grasslands):

—Permits, easements, and leases for power transmission, road, and hydro

developments. 16 U.S.C. 522. *et seq.*: 43 U.S.C. 1761 (36 CFR Part 251.50, *et seq.*)
—Permits for commercial use of existing roads. 16 U.S.C. 537 (37 CFR Part 212)
—Consultations regarding power developments on rivers established as units of the National Wild and Scenic Rivers System and on those rivers designated for study as potential additions to that System. 16 U.S.C. 1278, *et seq.*

• Rural Electrification Administration (power development in and for rural areas):
—Electrical generation and transmission projects. 7 U.S.C. 901 *et seq.* (7 CFR Part 1700, *et seq.*

Department of Commerce

• National Oceanic and Atmospheric Administration (coastal energy facility planning and siting):
—Approval of licenses for siting, design, and operation of ocean-thermal energy facilities. 42 U.S.C. 9101, *et seq.* (15 CFR Part 981).

Department of Defense

• Army Corps of Engineers (hydroelectric projects; effects of power development on navigable waters):
—For jurisdictional responsibilities, see PART I. B.—Water Quality.

Department of Energy

• Economic Regulatory Administration (regulation of power plants and other major fuel-burning installations):
—Exemptions from prohibitions against the burning of natural gas and petroleum in power plants and major fuel burning installations. 42 U.S.C. 7101 and 8301 (10 CFR Part 500, *et seq.*).
—Transmission of electric energy to a foreign country. 16 U.S.C. 824a(e); E.O. 10485 and E.O. 12038 (18 CFR Parts 32.30-32.38 and 10 CFR Parts 205.300-205.309).

• Office of Policy, Safety, and Environment (general energy policies, programs and projects).

• Alaska Power Administration (hydroelectric generation and transmission systems in Alaska).

• Bonneville Power Administration (electric transmission systems in the Pacific northwest).

• Southeastern Power Administration (electric transmission systems in the southeastern States).

• Southwestern Power Administration (electric transmission systems in the southwestern States).

• Western Area Power Administration (electric transmission systems in the western States).

Department of Housing and Urban Development

• Office of Community Planning and Development (energy policy; demonstration programs; research; assistance for community and economic development; assistance for energy efficiency):
—Housing and Community Development Act of 1974. 42 U.S.C. 5301. *et seq.* (24 CFR Part 570).

• Office of Housing (energy factors in rehabilitation and retrofitting).

• Office of Policy Development and Research (building energy technology; urban energy studies).

• Office of Solar Energy and Conservation (new technologies and research)

Department of the Interior

• Fish and Wildlife Service (effects of power development, including transmission line and tower construction, on endangered species and their critical habitats. National Wildlife Refuge and National Fish Hatchery System areas, and other fish and wildlife resources):
—Easements/permits for transmission line rights-of-way across National Wildlife Refuge and National Fish Hatchery System land. For refuges—16 U.S.C. 668dd; for hatcheries—43 U.S.C. 931 c and d (50 CFR Part 29.21).
—Permits for rights-of-way on National Wildlife Monuments (Alaska only). 16 U.S.C. 432. 460(k)-3 and 742(f) (50 CFR Part 96).
—For additional jurisdictional responsibilities, see PART IV. C— Water Resources Development.

• Geological Survey (geologic and hydrologic siting constraints for power developments: National Water Summary).

• Bureau of Indian Affairs (power development on Indian lands):
—Approval of leases and permits for Indian lands. 25 U.S.C. 380, 393-395, 397, 402-403, 413, 415, 477 and 635 (25 CFR Part 162).
—Rights-of-way over Indian lands. 25 U.S.C. 311-321 and 323-328 (25 CFR Part 169).
—Specific power systems. (25 CFR Parts 175-177).

• Bureau of Land Management (power development on public lands):
—Easements/permits for rights-of-way. 30 U.S.C. 185 and 43 U.S.C. 1701, *et seq.* (43 CFR Parts 2800-2887).
—Exchange of Federal lands to facilitate energy development. 43 U.S.C. 1716 (43 CFR Parts 2200-2270).

• National Park Service (effects of power development on National Park System lands; on historic archeologic and architectural sites; and on recreational values):
—Easements for rights-of-way across National Park system land. 16 U.S.C. 5 (36 CFR Parts 7 and 14).
—Consultations about extent to which proposed recreational developments at hydroelectric projects conform to and are in accord with the Statewide Comprehensive Outdoor Recreation Plans 16 U.S.C. 460.
—Consultations regarding power developments on rivers established as units of the National Wild and Scenic Rivers System and on those rivers designated for study as potential additions to that System. 16 U.S.C. 1278, *et seq.*

• Bureau of Reclamation (hydroelectric power development in the 17 contiguous western states, impact of power development on State water laws; analysis of cost sharing).
—Easements/permits for powerline rights-of-way. 43 U.S.C. 3871.

Department of Labor

• Occupational Safety and Health Administration (workers safety and health issues):
—Construction, transmission and distribution facilities. 29 U.S.C. 655, *et seq.* (29 CFR Part 1926, Subpart V).

Department of Transportation

• Federal Highway Administration (highways and electric utility facilities):
—Relocation and accommodation of utility facilities on highway rights-of-way. 23 U.S.C. 109(1), 116 and 123 (23 CFR Part 645).

Advisory Council on Historic Preservation (effects of power developments on historic properties).

Environmental Protection Agency (pollution control and environmental effects of power development):
—For jurisdictional responsibilities see PART I.A.—Air Quality, PART I.B.—Water Quality, and PART I.C.—Waste Disposal on Land.

Federal Emergency Management Agency (review and approval of state and local nuclear incident emergency response plans).

Federal Energy Regulatory Commission (hydroelectric power projects; electric transmission; electric supply; facility siting):
—Regulation of interconnection of electric transmission facilities and regulation of enlargement of electric transmission facilities. 18 U.S.C. 824-825K (18 CFR Part 32).
—Regulation of the development of water power including the licensing of non-Federal hydroelectric power projects. 16 U.S.C. 791-825r (18 CFR Parts 4-25, 36, 131 and 141).
—Application for order directing the establishment of physical connection facilities. 16 U.S.C. 834(h).
—Withdrawal of Federal lands for power and powersite development purposes. 16 U.S.C. 618 (43 CFR Part 2344, *et seq.*).

International Boundary and Water Commission, United States Section (hydroelectric power installations on the Rio Grande).

Nuclear Regulatory Commission (nuclear power development in general):
—Licensing of production and utilization facilities. 42 U.S.C. 2073. *et seq.*. and 5841. *et seq.* (10 CFR Parts 50 and 51).
—Nuclear power reactor operators' licenses. 42 U.S.C. 2137. *et seq.*, and 5841, *et seq.* (10 CFR Part 55).
—Reactor site criteria. 42 U.S.C. 2133, *et seq.*, and 5841, *et seq.* (10 CFR Part 100).
—For other jurisdictional responsibilities, see PART I.E.—Radiation.

Tennessee Valley Authority (power development in the Tennessee Valley Region).

B. Oil and Gas (Development, Extraction, Refining, Transport and Use)

Department of Agriculture

• Forest Service (effects of oil and gas development on National Forests and Grasslands):

—Permits and rights-of-way on National Forest System lands. 16 U.S.C. 471-472, 478, 495, 497-498, 528, 531-538, 551, 572 and 580 (36 CFR Parts 212, 251 and 261).

Department of Commerce

• National Oceanic and Atmospheric Administration (effects of oil and gas development and coastal and marine resources, management, and protection).

Department of Defense

• Army Corps of Engineers (effects of oil and gas development on navigable waters):

—For jurisdictional responsibilities, see PART I.B—Water Quality.

Department of Energy

• Economic Regulatory Administration (regulation of power plants and other major fuel-burning installations):

—Exemptions from prohibitions against the burning of petroleum in power plants and major fuel-burning installations. 42 U.S.C. 7101 and 6301 (10 CFR Part 500, *et seq.*).

• Office of Policy, Safety, and Environment (general energy policies, programs, and projects).

Department of Housing and Urban Development

• Office of Community Planning and Development (health and safety standards; distance factors for pipeline, storage, and production facilities including sour gas wells; assistance for community and economic development assistance to conserve petroleum and natural gas energy efficiency):

—Assurances that HUD assisted projects are located in a safe and healthful environment. 42 U.S.C. 1441, *et seq.*

—Siting of HUD assisted projects near hazardous operations handling petroleum products or chemicals of an explosive or flammable nature. (24 CFR Part 51, Subpart C).

—Housing and Community Development Act of 1974. 42 U.S.C. 5301, *et seq.* (24 CFR Part 570).

• Office of Housing (siting standards and effects on housing values and marketability).

Department of the Interior

• Fish and Wildlife Service (effects of oil and gas development on endangered species and their critical habitats, National Wildlife Refuge and National Fish Hatchery System areas, and other fish and wildlife resources):

—Permits for oil and gas pipeline rights-of-way across National Wildlife Refuge and National Fish Hatchery Systems lands. For refuges—16 U.S.C. 668dd; for hatcheries—43 U.S.C. 931c and d (50 CFR Part 29.21).

—Permits for rights-of-way across National Wildlife Monuments (Alaska only). 16 U.S.C. 432, 460(k)-3 and 742(f) (50 CFR Part 36).

• Geological Survey (oil and gas resources in general).

• Bureau of Indian Affairs (oil and gas development on Indian lands):

—Leases and permits on Indian lands. 25 U.S.C. 380, 393-395, 397, 402-408, 413, 415, 477 and 635 (25 CFR Part 182).

—Rights-of-way over Indian lands. 25 U.S.C. 311-321 and 323-328 (25 CFR Part 169).

—Mining leases (including oil and gas) on Indian lands. 25 U.S.C. 378, 396, 476-477 and 509 (25 CFR Parts 211-215 and 226-227).

• Bureau of Land Management (oil and gas development on public lands):

—Leases for oil and gas deposits:

(a) Public domain lands. 30 U.S.C. 181, *et seq.*; 43 CFR Parts 3100, *et seq.*, and 3160.

(b) Acquired lands. 30 U.S.C. 351-359 (43 CFR Parts 3100, *et seq.*, and 3160).

(c) In and under railroad and other rights-of-way acquired under laws of the United States. 30 U.S.C. 301-306 (43 CFR Part 3100).

(d) Indian lands. 25 U.S.C. 396a, *et seq.* (25 CFR Parts 211, 213, 226 and 227).

—Leases and land exchanges for oil shale, native asphalt, solid and semisolid bitumen and bituminous rock. For leases—30 U.S.C. 241 (43 CFR Part 3500); for exchanges—43 U.S.C. 1716 (43 CFR Parts 2200-2270).

—Easements/permits for oil and gas pipeline rights-of-way. 30 U.S.C. 185 and 43 U.S.C. 1701, *et seq.* (43 CFR Parts 2800-2867).

—Easements/leases/permits for use, occupancy and development of public lands. 43 U.S.C. 1732 (43 CFR Subchapters 2000 and 3000).

—Disposal of government royalty oil (non-OCS oil). 30 U.S.C. 189, 192 and 359 (30 CFR Part 208).

—Exchange of non-OCS Federal lands with oil and gas deposits. 43 U.S.C. 1716 (43 CFR Parts 2200-2207).

• Minerals Management Service (oil and gas development on the outer continental shelf).

—Leases for minerals on the outer continental shelf. 43 U.S.C. 1331-1343 (30 CFR Parts 250, 251, 252 and 256).

—Permits/easements for rights-of-way for "common carrier" oil gas pipelines on the outer continental shelf. 43 U.S.C. 1331 (30 CFR Part 256, Subpart N).

—Permits for exploration and development activities on Federal leases on the outer continental shelf. 43 U.S.C. 1331, *et seq.* (30 CFR Parts 250 and 251).

—Easements/rights-of-way for gathering pipelines, artificial islands, platforms, and other fixed structures on any Federal or State outer continental shelf oil and gas lease. 43 U.S.C. 1334-1335 (30 CFR Parts 250.16-250.19).

—Applications for purchase of government royalty oil from the outer continental shelf. 43 U.S.C. 1334 (30 CFR Part 225a).

—Permits for geological and geophysical exploration on the outer continental shelf. 43 U.S.C. 1334 and 1340 (30 CFR Part 251).

—Drilling permits. 43 U.S.C. 1351.

• Bureau of Mines (environmental, health, and safety aspects of mining oil, tar sands, and oil shale; coalbed methane control and recovery; helium conservation).

• National Park Service (effects of oil and gas development on National Park System areas on historic, archeological, and architectural sites, and on recreational values):

—Permits for oil and gas operations on National Park system areas. 16 U.S.C. 1 (36 CFR Part 9).

—Determination of significance of effects for combined hydrocarbon lease conversions

in Glen Canyon NRA. (43 CFR Parts 3140.7 and 3141.2).

• Bureau of Reclamation (effects of oil and gas development on water storage and delivery systems):

—Easements/permits for pipeline rights-of-way. 43 U.S.C. 3871.

Department of Labor

• Occupational Safety and Health Administration (general worker safety and health issues):

—Oil and gas well drilling. 29 U.S.C. 655, *et seq.* (29 CFR Part 1910.270).

Department of State (international aspects of oil and gas development):

—Facilities for export/import of petroleum and petroleum products. E.O. 11423.

Department of Transportation

• Coast Guard (oil and gas transport by vessel):

—Tank vessel regulation. 46 U.S.C. 391(a) (33 CFR Part 157).

—Ports and waterways safety. 33 U.S.C. 1221 (33 CFR Part 160, *et seq.*).

—Construction and alteration of bridges for pipelines over navigable waters. 33 U.S.C. 491, *et seq.*; 511, *et seq.*; 525, *et seq.*, and 535 (33 CFR Part 114, *et seq.*).

—Outer continental shelf structures. 43 U.S.C. 1331 (33 CFR Part 140, *et seq.*).

• Maritime Administration (effects of oil and gas development on port, coastal and ocean pollution):

—Merchant vessels, including liquefied natural gas vessels. 42 U.S.C. 1101, *et seq.* (46 CFR Part 250, *et seq.*).

—Port operations, including loading/unloading of liquefied natural gas vessels. 42 U.S.C. 867 (46 CFR Part 346, *et seq.*).

• Federal Highway Administration (pipelines and highway rights-of-way):

—Relocation and accommodation of pipelines on highway rights-of-way. U.S.C. 109(1), 116 and 123 (23 CFR 645).

• Federal Railroad Administration (railroad transport of oil and gas).

• Research and Special Programs Administration: Materials Transportation Bureau (pipeline safety; oil and gas shipments; natural gas marine terminals):

—Pipeline safety. 49 U.S.C. 1671, *et seq.*, and 2001, *et seq.* (49 CFR Part 190, *et seq.*).

Advisory Council on Historic Preservation (effects of oil and gas development on historic properties):

Environmental Protection Agency (pollution control and environmental effects of oil and gas development):

—For jurisdictional responsibilities, see PART I.A.—Air Quality, PART I.B.—Water Quality, and PART I.C.—Waste Disposal on Land.

Federal Energy Regulatory Commission (charges/rates for transportation of oil and gas by pipeline; transportation, storage, and sale of natural gas):

—Certificates for natural gas facilities (underground storage fields, LNG facilities, and transmission pipeline facilities); sale, exchange and transportation of gas;

49762 Federal Register / Vol. 49, No. 247 / Friday, December 21, 1984 / Rules and Regulations

abandonment of facilities and curtailment of natural gas service; authorization to import and export natural gas. 15 U.S.C. 717–717(w); E.O. 10485 and E.O. 12038 (18 CFR Part 152. *et seq.*).

—Authorization compelling the expansion, improvement or connection of natural gas facilities. 15 U.S.C. 717f(a) (18 CFR Part 156).

Interstate Commerce Commission (regulation of petroleum and natural gas carriers).

C. Coal (Development, Mining, Conversion, Processing, Transport and Use)

Department of Agriculture

• Forest Service (effects of coal development on National Forests and Grasslands):

—Permits and rights-of-way on National Forest System lands. 16 U.S.C. 471–472, 478, 495, 497–498, 525, 526, 531–538, 551, 572 and 580 (36 CFR Parts 212, 251 and 261).

—Coal leasing. 30 U.S.C. 201–352.

—Surface coal mining operations. 30 U.S.C. 1272.

• Rural Electrification Administration (coal development in relation to rural electrification):

—Financial assistance for purchase of coal mines and mining facilities. 7 U.S.C. 901, *et seq.* (7 CFR Part 1700, *et seq.*).

• Soil Conservation Service (abandoned rural mined land, mine reclamation, and transportation):

—Reclamation of rural abandoned mined land. 30 U.S.C. 1201, *et seq.* (7 CFR Part 632).

Department of Commerce

• National Oceanic and Atmospheric Administration (atmospheric dispersion of effluents; acid rain; management and protection of coastal and marine resources; air and water pollution from mining; offshore and coastal mining; port planning).

Department of Defense

• Army Corps of Engineers (effects of coal development on navigable waters):

—For jurisdictional responsibilities, see PART I. B.—Water Quality.

Department of Energy

• Economic Regulatory Administration (regulation of powerplants and other major fuel-burning installations):

—Exemption from prohibitions against burning of natural gas and oil in powerplants and major fuel-burning installations. 42 U.S.C. 7101 and 8301 (10 CFR Part 500, *et seq.*).

• Office of Policy, Safety, and Environment (general energy policies, programs, and projects).

• Office of Fossil Energy (coal research, coal liquification projects, and emerging coal technologies).

Department of Housing and Urban Development

• Office of Community Planning and Development (assistance for community impacts due to rapid development):

—Housing and Community Development Act of 1974. 42 U.S.C. 5301. *et seq.* (24 CFR Part 570).

• Office of Housing (subsidence from mining operations and soil factors related to housing).

Department of the Interior

• Fish and Wildlife Service (effects of coal development on endangered species and their critical habitats, National Wildlife Refuge and National Fish Hatchery System areas, and other fish and wildlife resources):

—Permits for use of National Wildlife Refuge and National Fish Hatchery System lands. For refuges—16 U.S.C. 668 dd and ee; for hatcheries—43 U.S.C. 931 c and d (50 CFR Parts 25.41 and 29.21).

—Permits for rights-of-way across National Wildlife Monuments (Alaska only). 16 U.S.C. 432, 460(k–3) and 742(f) (50 CFR Part 86).

• Geological Survey (coal resources in general; hydrologic effects of coal mining and reclamation).

• Bureau of Indian Affairs (coal development on Indian lands):

—Leases and permits on Indian lands. 25 U.S.C. 380, 393–395, 397, 402–403, 413, 415, 477 and 635 (25 CFR Part 182).

—Rights-of-way over Indian lands. 25 U.S.C. 311–321 and 328 (25 CFR Part 169).

—Mining leases on Indian lands. U.S.C. 356, 396, 476–477 and 509 (25 CFR Parts 211–215 and 226–227).

—Surface exploration and reclamation. 25 U.S.C. 355, 396, 473 and 501–502 (25 CFR Part 216).

• Bureau of Land Management (coal development on public lands):

—Exploration licenses for coal deposits on unleased lands. 30 U.S.C. 181 and 201(b) (43 CFR Part 3400).

—Leases/permits for recovery of coal deposits. 30 U.S.C. 181, *et seq.*, 201b and 202a; 43 U.S.C. 1701, *et seq.* (43 CFR Parts 3400 and 3480).

—Easements/lease/permits for use, occupancy and development of public lands. 43 U.S.C. 1732 (43 CFR Subchapters 2000 and 3000).

—Permits to mine coal for domestic needs. 30 U.S.C. 208 (43 CFR Part 3440).

—Easements/permits for rights-of-way. 30 U.S.C. 185 and 43 U.S.C. 1701, *et seq.* (43 CFR Parts 2800–2887).

—Exchange of Federal lands with coal or uranium deposits. 43 U.S.C. 1716 (43 CFR Parts 2200–2270).

• Bureau of Mines (mining technology, health and safety, subsidence prediction and control, and land reclamation).

• National Park Service (effects of coal development on National Park System areas and on historic and recreational values):

—Leases, permits and licenses for mining on National Park System lands involved in Wild and Scenic River Systems. 16 U.S.C. 1280.

—Access permits for mining activity within the National Park System. 16 U.S.C. 1902 and 1908 (36 CFR Part 9).

—Easements for rights-of-way across National Park System land. 16 U.S.C. 1, *et seq.* (36 CFR Part 9, *et seq.*).

• Bureau of Reclamation (effects of coal development on water storage and delivery projects):

—Easement/permits for access rights-of-way 43 U.S.C. 3871.

• Office of Surface Mining Reclamation and Enforcement (surface coal mining and reclamation; general effects of surface coal mining operations):

—Identification of certain lands considered unsuitable for surface coal mining operations. 30 U.S.C. 1272 (30 CFR Chapter 7, Subchapter F).

—Permits for coal exploration operations on Federal lands within an approved mining permit area, and, if there is no approved State Coal Mining Regulatory Program, on non-Federal and non-Indian lands. 30 U.S.C. 1262 (30 CFR Chapter VII and 43 CFR Part 3400).

—Permits for surface coal mining and reclamation operations (includes underground mines with surface effects) on Federal lands except the States may do this when there is both an approved State Coal Mining Regulatory Program and a Cooperative Agreement between the State and the Secretary of the Interior. 30 U.S.C. 1256, 1267, 1268, 1271 and 1273 (30 CFR Chapter VII).

—Permits for surface coal mining and reclamation operations (includes underground mines with surface effects) on non-Federal lands in those States where there is no approved State Coal Mining Regulatory Program. 30 U.S.C. 1256–1262 (30 CFR Chapter VII).

—Permits for surface coal mining and reclamation operations (includes underground mines with surface effects) on Indian lands. 30 U.S.C. 1300 (30 CFR Chapter VII and 25 CFR Part 216).

—Grants for reclamation of abandoned mined lands. 30 U.S.C. 1231–1235 and 1237–1243 (30 CFR Chapter VII).

Department of Labor

• Mining Safety and Health Administration (safety and health issues in mining operations).

• Occupational Safety and Health Administration (worker safety and health issues):

—Coal tar pitch volatiles. 29 U.S.C. 655, *et seq.* (29 CFR Part 1910.1002).

Department of State (international aspects of coal development):

—Facilities for export/import of coal. E.O. 11423.

Department of Transportation

• Coast Guard (vessel transport of coal):

—Construction and alterations of bridges and causeways over navigable waters. 33 U.S.C. 491, *et seq.*; 511, *et seq.*; 525, *et seq.*, and 535 (33 CFR Part 114, *et seq.*).

—Ports and waterways safety. 33 U.S.C. 1221 (33 CFR Part 160, *et seq.*).

• Federal Highway Administration (coal haul roads; effects of railroad coal transport on roads and streets).

• Federal Railroad Administration (railroad transport of coal).

• Maritime Administration (bulk shipping of coal and other minerals in the inland waterways, domestic oceans, Great Lakes, and U.S. foreign trade)

Advisory Council on Historic Preservation (effects of coal development on historic properties).

Environmental Protection Agency (pollution control and environmental effects of coal development):

—For jurisdictional responsibilities see PART I. A.—Air Quality, PART I. B.—Water Quality, and PART I. C.—Waste Disposal on Land.

Interstate Commerce Commission (regulation of coal rail-carriers and rates; impacts from railroad construction for moving coal, including downline impacts).

Tennessee Valley Authority (coal development in the Tennessee Valley region).

D. Uranium (Exploration, Mining, Transport and Use)

Department of Agriculture

• Forest Service (uranium on National Forests and Grasslands).

—Permits and rights-of-way on National Forest System lands. 16 U.S.C. 471–472, 478, 495, 497–498, 525, 528, 531–538, 551, 572 and 580 (36 CFR Parts 212, 251 and 261).

—Surface use of public domain lands under U.S. mining laws. 16 U.S.C. 478 and 551 (36 CFR Part 228).

—Mineral development on acquired lands. For solid (hardrock) minerals—16 U.S.C. 520 (43 CFR Part 3500); for phosphate, sodium, potassium and sulphur—30 U.S.C. 351, *et seq.*

• Soil Conservation Service (abandoned mine land, mine reclamation, and transportation).

Department of Commerce

• National Oceanic and Atmospheric Administration (air and water pollution from mining; offshore and coastal mining; port planning; management and protection of coastal and marine resources):

—Approval of licenses for deep seabed hard mineral exploration and development. 30 U.S.C. 1401, *et seq.* (15 CFR Part 970).

Department of Defense

• Army Corps of Engineers (effects of uranium mining on navigable waters):

—For jurisdictional responsibilities, see PART I.B.—Water Quality.

Department of Energy

• Office of Policy, Safety, and Environment (general energy policies, programs and projects).

• Office of Civilian Radioactive Waste Management (management of commercial radioactive wastes).

• Office of Defense Programs (management of Defense radioactive wastes)

• Office of Nuclear Energy (nuclear energy in general).

Department of Housing and Urban Development

• Office of Housing (subsidence from mining operations and soil factors related to housing).

Department of the Interior

• Fish and Wildlife Service (effects of uranium mining on endangered species and their critical habitats, National Wildlife Refuge and National Fish Hatchery System areas, and other fish and wildlife resources):

—Easements/permits on National Wildlife Refuge and National Fish Hatchery System land. 16 U.S.C. 668 dd, *et seq.*; 43 U.S.C. 931 c and d (50 CFR Parts 25.41 and 29.21).

—Permits for rights-of-way across National Wildlife Monuments (Alaska only). 16 U.S.C. 432, 460(k–3) and 742(f) (50 CFR Part 96).

• Geological Survey (uranium resources in general).

• Bureau of Indian Affairs (uranium on Indian lands):

—Leases and permits on Indian lands. 25 U.S.C. 380, 393–395, 397, 402–403, 413, 415, 477 and 635 (25 CFR Part 162).

—Rights-of-way over Indian lands. 25 U.S.C. 311–321 and 323–328 (25 CFR Part 169).

—Mining leases on Indian lands. 25 U.S.C. 356, 396, 476–477 and 509 (25 CFR Parts 211–215 and 226–227).

—Surface exploration and reclamation. 25 U.S.C. 355, 396, 473 and 501–502 (25 CFR Part 216).

• Bureau of Land Management (uranium on public lands):

—Exchange of Federal lands with coal or uranium deposits. 43 U.S.C. 1716 (43 CFR Parts 2200–2270).

—Leases for uranium exploration and mining. 30 U.S.C. 181, 351–359 and 1201, *et seq.* (43 CFR Parts 3500–3800).

—Approval of plan of operations in connection with uranium leases. 30 U.S.C. 22, *et seq.*; 30 U.S.C. 181, *et seq.*; and 43 U.S.C. 1701, *et seq.* (43 CFR Parts 3570 and 3802).

—Easements/leases/permits for use, occupancy and development of public lands. 43 U.S.C. 1732 (43 CFR Subchapter 2000 and 3000).

—Exploration licenses to explore for uranium and other leasable minerals on unleased lands. 30 U.S.C. 181, *et seq.*, and 201(b) (43 CFR Parts 3400 and 3480).

—Leases, permits and licenses for mining in Wild and Scenic River System areas. 16 U.S.C. 1280 (each area has special Federal Regulations).

—Concurrence for mining use of public lands withdrawn or reserved for power development or for a power site. 30 U.S.C. 621 (43 CFR Part 3730).

—Easements/permits for rights-of-way. 30 U.S.C. 185 and 43 U.S.C. 1701, *et seq.* (43 CFR Parts 2800–2900).

• Bureau of Mines (uranium mining in general).

• National Park Service (effects of uranium mining on public park and recreation values; on historic, archeological and architectural sites; and on National Park System areas):

—Permits, leases, and easements for rights-of-way. 16 U.S.C. 1, *et seq.* (36 CFR Part 9, *et seq.*).

—Leases, permits and license for mining on National Park System lands involved in Wild and Scenic River Systems. 16 U.S.C. 1280.

—Access permits for mining activity within the National Park System. 16 U.S.C. 1902 and 1908; 30 U.S.C. 21, *et seq.* (36 CFR Part 9).

• Bureau of Reclamation (effects of uranium mining on water storage and delivery projects):

—Easements/permits for access, pipeline, and other rights-of-way. 43 U.S.C. 3571.

Department of Labor

• Mining Safety and Health Administration (safety and health issues in mining operations).

• Occupational Safety and Health Administration (general worker safety and health issues):

—General industrial, and construction standards. 29 U.S.C. 655, *et seq.* (29 CFR Parts 1910 and 1926).

Department of State (international aspects of uranium mining):

—Facilities for export/import of minerals. E.O. 11423.

Department of Transportation

• Coast Guard (vessel transport of minerals):

—Construction and alterations of bridges and causeways over navigable waters. 33 U.S.C. 491, *et seq.*; 511, *et seq.*; 525, *et seq.*, and 535 (33 CFR Part 114, *et seq.*).

—Ports and waterways safety. 33 U.S.C. 1221 (33 CFR Part 160, *et seq.*).

Advisory Council on Historic Preservation (effects of uranium mining on historic properties).

Environmental Protection Agency (pollution control and environmental effects of uranium mining):

—For jurisdictional responsibilities, see Part I.A.—Air Quality, PART I. B.—Water Quality, PART I. C.—Waste Disposal on Land, and PART I. E.—Radiation.

Nuclear Regulatory Commission (nuclear power development in general):

—Licensing uranium milling operations. 42 U.S.C. 2091 *et seq.* (10 CFR Part 40).

Tennessee Valley Authority (uranium mining and milling).

E. Geothermal Resources (Development, Transmission, and Use)

Department of Agriculture

• Forest Service (effects of geothermal resource development on National Forests and Grasslands):

—Leases for geothermal resource development. 30 U.S.C. 1014.

—Permits and rights-of-way on National Forest System lands. 16 U.S.C. 471–472, 478, 495, 497–498, 525, 528, 531–538, 551, 572 and 580 (36 CFR Parts 212, 251 and 261).

Department of Commerce

• National Oceanic and Atmospheric Administration (air and water pollution from geothermal development).

Department of Defense

• Army Corps of Engineers (effects of geothermal development on navigable waters):

49764   Federal Register / Vol. 49, No. 247 / Friday, December 21, 1984 / Rules and Regulations

—For jurisdictional responsibilities, see PART I. B.—Water Quality.

Department of Energy

• Office of Policy, Safety, and Environment (general energy policies, programs and projects).
• Office of Conservation and Renewable Energy (research and development on geothermal energy sources).

Department of the Interior

• Fish and Wildlife Service (effects of geothermal development on endangered species and their critical habitats, National Wildlife Refuge and National Fish Hatchery System areas, and other fish and wildlife resources):

—Easements/permits on National Wildlife Refuge and National Fish Hatchery System land. For refuges—16 U.S.C. 668 dd, et seq., for hatcheries—43 U.S.C. 931 c and d (50 CFR Parts 25.41 and 29.21).
—Permits for rights-of-way across National Wildlife Monuments (Alaska only). 16 U.S.C. 432, 460(k–3) and 742(f) (50 CFR Part 96).

• Geological Survey (geothermal resources in general).
• Bureau of Indian Affairs (geothermal development on Indian lands):

—Leases and permits on Indian lands. 25 U.S.C. 380, 393–395, 397, 402–403, 413, 415, 477 and 635 (25 CFR Part 162).
—Rights-of-way over Indian lands, 25 U.S.C. 311–321 and 323–328 (25 CFR Part 169).

• Bureau of Land Management (geothermal development on public lands):

—Permits for geothermal resources exploration. 30 U.S.C.1023 (43 CFR Part 3260).
—Leases for geothermal resources recovery. 30 U.S.C. 1001–1025 (43 CFR Parts 3200–3250, 3260 and 3280).
—Licenses for geothermal powerplants. 30 U.S.C. 1001–1025 (43 CFR Part 3250).
—Easements/leases/permits for use, occupancy and development of public lands. 43 U.S.C 1732 (43 CFR Subchapter 2000 and 3000).

Easements/permits for rights-of-way. 30 U.S.C. 185 and 43 U.S.C 1701, et seq. (43 CFR Parts 2800–2900).

• Bureau of Mines (recovery of mineral values in geothermal operations; materials for construction of geothermal facilities).
• National Park Service (effects of geothermal development on public park and recreation values, on historic, archeological and architectural sites, and on National Park System areas).
• Bureau of Reclamation (alternative energy studies; coordination of geothermal operations with hydroelectric generation):

—Easements/permits for access, pipeline, and other rights-of-way. 43 U.S.C. 387.

Department of Labor

• Occupational Safety and Health Administration (worker safety and health issues):

—General industrial and construction standards. 29 U.S.C. 655, et seq. (29 CFR Parts 1910 and 1926).

Advisory Council on Historic Preservation (effects of geothermal development on historic properties).

Environmental Protection Agency (pollution control and environmental effects of geothermal development).

—For jurisdictional responsibilities, see PART I. A.—Air Quality, PART I. B.—Water Quality, and PART I. C.—Waste Disposal on Land.

F. Other Energy Sources—Solar, Wind, Biomass, etc. (Development and Use)

Department of Agriculture

• Agricultural Research Service (utilization of biomass, wastes, solar, and wind energy sources in agricultural production).
• Farmers Home Administration (small hydro, solar, and wind projects):

—Approval of plans and specifications for FMHA-funded projects. 7 U.S.C. 1942 (7 CFR Parts 1924, 1942 and 1944).

• Forest Service (uses and rights-of-way on National Forests and Grasslands):

—Permits and rights-of-way on National Forest System lands. 16 U.S.C. 471–472, 478, 495, 497–498, 525, 528, 531–538, 551, 572 and 580 (36 CFR Parts 212, 251 and 281).

• Office of Energy (general energy policies related to agriculture):

—Solar and wind energy facility siting. 16 U.S.C. 470 (36 CFR Part 200).

Department of Commerce

• National Oceanic and Atmospheric Administration (coastal energy facility planning and siting; basic weather data and research):

—Approval of licenses for siting, design, and operation of ocean-thermal energy facilities, 42 U.S.C. 9101, et seq. (15 CFR Part 981).

Department of Energy

• Office of Policy, Safety, and Environment (general energy policies, programs and projects).
• Office of Conservation and Renewable Energy (research and development programs on alternative energy sources).

Department of Housing and Urban Development

• Office of Community Planning and Development (alternative energy policy, including district heating and cogeneration; demonstration programs; research; technical assistance and feasibility studies; building rehabilitation and retrofit; assistance for community and economic development):

—Housing and Community Development Act of 1974. 42 U.S.C. 5301, et seq. (24 CFR Part 570).
—Urban Development Action Grant Handbook. HUD 6050.1 of Oct. 1982.

• Solar Energy and Energy Conservation Bank (assistance for energy conservation improvements to residential, commercial, and agricultural buildings, including solar energy systems):

—Energy Security Act of 1980. 12 U.S.C. 3601, et seq. (24 CFR Part 1800, et seq.).

Department of the Interior

• Fish and Wildlife Service (effects of alternative energy development on endangered species and their critical habitats, National Wildlife Refuge and National Fish Hatchery System areas, and other fish and wildlife resources).
• Geological Survey (geology and hydrologic siting constraints for alternative energy development).
• Bureau of Indian Affairs (alternative energy development on Indian lands).
• Bureau of Land Management (alternative energy development on public lands):

—Licenses for synthetic liquid fuel facilities 30 U.S.C. 323.
—Solar energy facility siting. 43 U.S.C. 1781

• National Park Service (effects of alternative energy development on park and recreation values on historic, archeological and architectural sites, and on National Park System areas).
• Bureau of Reclamation (alternative energy studies; coordination of operations with hydroelectric generation).

Department of Labor

• Occupational Health and Safety Administration (worker safety and health issues):

—General industrial and construction standards. 29 U.S.C. 655, et seq. (29 CFR Parts 1910 and 1926).

Advisory Council on Historic Preservation (effects of alternative energy development on historic properties).

Environmental Protection Agency (pollution control and environmental effects of alternative energy development):

—For jurisdictional responsibilities, see PART I.—POLLUTION CONTROL.

G. Energy Conservation

Department of Agriculture

• Extension Service (rural family energy conservation).
• Farmers Home Administration (energy conservation in relation to agency funded projects).
• Forest Service (energy conservation in National Forests and Grasslands).
• Office of Energy (general agricultural energy policies).
• Rural Electrification Administration (energy conservation in relation to power development in rural areas).

Department of Commerce

• National Bureau of Standards (energy efficiency objectives and standards).
• National Oceanic and Atmospheric Administration (heating fuel usage forecasting; weather forecasting in relation to energy conservation).

Department of Energy

• Office of Policy, Safety, and Environment (general energy policies, programs and projects).
• Office of Conservation and Renewable Energy (energy efficiency of transportation, building, and industrial systems; assistance programs for energy planning and conservation):

—Energy conservation standards for new buildings. 42 U.S.C. 6834 (10 CFR Part 450 *et seq.*).

• Bonneville Power Administration (energy conservation studies in the Pacific Northwest):

—Regional planning and conservation. 16 U.S.C. 839, *et seq.*

Department of Housing and Urban Development

• Office of Community Planning and Development (energy conservation policy. demonstration and research programs; technical assistance; assistance for community and neighborhood development. economic development, public facilities, residential and commercial rehabilitation and retrofit for energy efficiency; comprehensive energy use strategies):

—Housing and Community Development Act of 1974. 42 U.S.C. 5301. *et seq.* (24 CFR Part 570).

—Urban Development Action Grant Handbook. HUD 6050.1 of Oct. 1982.

—Housing Act of 1937. 42 U.S.C. 1401, *et seq.*

• Solar Energy and Energy Conservation Bank (assistance for energy conservation improvements to residential, commercial, and agricultural buildings. including solar energy systems):

—Energy Security Act of 1980. 12 U.S.C. 3601. *et seq.* (24 CFR Part 1800, *et seq.*).

• Office of Manufactured Housing and Construction Standards (building materials; new materials standards and performance criteria).

• Office of Policy Development and Research (building energy technology).

• Office of Public Housing (energy factors in rehabilitation and retrofitting: urban energy studies).

Department of the Interior

• Fish and Wildlife Service (energy conservation in National Wildlife Refuge and National Fish Hatchery System areas, and effects of energy conservation projects on endangered species and critical habitats).

• Bureau of Indian Affairs (energy conservation on Indian lands).

• Bureau of Land Management (energy conservation on public lands).

• National Park Service (energy conservation in National Park System areas: effects of energy conservation on historic, archeological, and architectural sites, and on park and recreation values).

• Bureau of Reclamation (energy conservation in relation to hydroelectric power development, and water storage and delivery systems).

Department of Transportation

• Federal Aviation Administration (aviation energy conservation and energy-use assessments).

• Federal Highway Administration (energy conservation in relation to highway systems).

• National Highway Traffic Safety Administration (fuel economy standards for motor vehicles):

—Fuel economy standards. 15 U.S.C. 2001. *et seq.* (49 CFR Parts 525–527, 531, 533 and 537.

• Research and Special Programs Administration: Transportation Systems Center (energy conservation and transportation systems in general).

• Urban Mass Transportation Administration (energy conservation in relation to urban transportation systems).

Advisory Council on Historic Preservation (effects of energy conservation on historic properties).

Interstate Commerce Commission (assessment of differences in energy efficiencies between transport modes).

Tennessee Valley Authority (energy conservation in general).

III. LAND USE

A. Land Use Planning, Regulation, and Development

Department of Agriculture

• Agricultural Research Service (effects of agricultural practices, resource quality and off-farm pollution).

• Agricultural Stabilization and Conservation Service (federally subsidized agricultural conservation and land use programs).

• Economic. Research Service and Statistical Reporting Service (data on natural resources; analysis of the economic impacts of agriculturally related pollution and resource degradation; interactions of environmental programs with other Federal farm policy objectives).

• Extension Service (rural and community development).

• Farmers Home Administration (farmland protection; rural and community development):

—Farmland Protection Policy Act. Secretary's Memorandum 9500–2, *Statement on Land Use Policy* (7 CFR Part 1940).

• Forest Service (effects of adjacent land uses on National Forests and Grasslands):

—Coordination with other public planning efforts. (36 CFR Part 219.7).

• Soil Conservation Service (land use data; soil and water resource condition data and related natural resources data; resource management technology and technical planning assistance for watershed protection):

—Soil. water, and related resource data. 7 U.S.C. 1010a.

—Program for land conservation and utilization. 7 U.S.C. 1011(e).

Department of Commerce

• National Oceanic and Atmospheric Administration (management and protection of coastal and marine resources).

Department of Defense

• Army Corps of Engineers (land use in flood plains and wetlands):

—For jurisdictional responsibilities see PART I.B.—Water Quality.

• Department of the Air Force (land use around military airfields).

Department of Energy

• Office of Policy, Safety, and Environment (effects of energy policies, programs, and projects on adjacent land uses).

Department of Housing and Urban Development

• Office of Community Planning and Development (land use planning; environmental criteria and compatible uses near hazards; noise abatement and mitigation measures):

—Assurances that HUD assisted projects are located in a safe and healthful environment. 42 U.S.C. 1441. *et seq.*

—Siting of HUD assisted projects near hazardous operations handling explosive or flammable materials. (24 CFR Part 51. Subpart C).

—Siting of HUD assisted projects in runway clear zones (civil airports) and clear zones and accident potential zones (military airfields). (24 CFR Part 51, Subpart D).

• Office of Interstate Land Sales (subdivided land sales):

—Subdivided land sales, registration, and disclosure statements. 15 U.S.C. 1701 (24 CFR Part 1700, *et seq.*).

Department of the Interior

• Fish and Wildlife Service (effects of land use on endangered species and their critical habitats. other fish and wildlife resources, and components of the National Wildlife Refuge and National Fish Hatchery Systems):

—Approval of conversion of use for State lands acquired, developed or improved with grants under the: (1) Pittman-Robertson Act. (2) Dingell-Johnson Act. (3) Endangered Species Act and/or (4) Anadromous Fish Conservation Act. For (1)–16 U.S.C. 669 (50 CFR Parts 80.4 and 80.14); for (2)–16 U.S.C. 777 (50 CFR Parts 80.4 and 80.14); for (3)–16 U.S.C. 1535; and for (4)–16 U.S.C. 757(a) and (b).

—Consultation regarding any Federal actions that may directly or indirectly affect a designated coastal barrier. 16 U.S.C. 3501 (for advisory guidelines. see 48 FR 45664 of Oct. 6. 1983).

—Consultation concerning the protection of fish and wildlife refuges. which may be impacted by transportation projects. 49 U.S.C. 303.

—For jurisdictional responsibilities of the Fish and Wildlife Service on Federal lands see PART III. B.—Federal Land Management.

• Geological Survey (land use planning: geologic and hydrologic hazards: flood studies: geologic, topographic, land use, and photographic mapping).

• Bureau of Indian Affairs (effects of land uses on Indian lands):

—Approval of leases and permits on Indian lands. 25 U.S.C. 380, 393–395, 397, 402–403, 413, 415, 477 and 635 (25 CFR Part 162).

—Sale of Indian land. 25 U.S.C. 293–294, 355, 372–73, 378–79, 385–386, 404–405, 483–484, 483 and 608 (25 CFR Parts 152 and 159-160).

—Rights-of-way over Indian lands. 25 U.S.C. 311–321 and 323–328 (25 CFR Part 169).

—Permits concessions and leases on lands withdrawn or acquired in connection with Indian irrigation projects. 25 U.S.C. 390 (25 CFR Part 173).

—For jurisdictional responsibilities on Federal lands administered by Bureau of

49766 Federal Register / Vol. 49, No. 247 / Friday, December 21, 1984 / Rules and Regulations

Indian Affairs, see PART III B.—Federal Land Management.

• Bureau of Land Management (effects of land uses on public lands):

-For jurisdiction responsibilities on Federal lands administered by the Bureau of Land Management, see PART III. B.—Federal Land Management.

• Bureau of Mines (mineral resources and land use).

• National Park Service (effects of land uses on National Park System areas; National Trails System; Wild and Scenic River System; park and recreation areas and values; and historic, archeological and architectural sites):

—Approval of a conversion to a non-designated use for State and local lands acquired or developed, in whole or in part, with a Land and Water Conservation Fund Act grant. 16 U.S.C. 4601.

—Assistance to State and local agencies, through an Urban Park and Recreation Recovery Act grant, for the development and/or improvement of park and recreation areas. 16 U.S.C. 2504 (36 CFR Part 69).

—Approval of a conversion to other than public recreation uses for State and local areas developed or improved with an Urban Park and Recreation Recovery Act grant. 16 U.S.C. 2504 (36 CFR Part 69).

—Consultations regarding land uses and effects on rivers established as units of the National Wild and Scenic Rivers System and on those rivers designated for study as potential additions to that System. 16 U.S.C. 1276, et seq.

—Permits for use of National Historic and National Scenic Trails administered by the National Park Service. 16 U.S.C. 1246.

—Approval of a conversion to a non-designated use for lands deeded by the Federal government to State and local entities as park demonstration areas, as recreation areas, as wildlife conservation preserves and refuges and as historic monuments and properties under: (1) Recreation Demonstration Act of 1942 and (2) Federal Property and Administrative Services Act of 1949. For (1)-16 U.S.C. 459 (r-t); for (2)-40 U.S.C. 484(k)(2) (41 CFR Part 101-47).

—Approval of a conversion to a non-designated use of abandoned railroad rights-of-way acquired by State and local governments under Section 809(b) of the Railroad Revitalization and Regulatory Reform Act of 1976. 49 U.S.C. 1(a) (36 CFR Part 64).

—Consultation concerning the protection of park, recreation, and cultural resources which may be impacted by transportation projects. 49 U.S.C. 303.

—For other jurisdictional responsibilities of the National Park Service, see PART III. B.—Federal Land Management.

• Bureau of Reclamation (effects of land use on Federal water storage and distribution projects; planning for water development projects; basin-wide water studies and land use aspects of the National Water Summary):

—Sale of farm units on Federal irrigation projects. (Statutory authority appears in individual project authorizations.)

—Administration of excess lands and residency requirements. 43 U.S.C. 371.

• Office of Surface Mining Reclamation and Enforcement (land use and surface coal mining and reclamation operations):

—For jurisdictional responsibilities of the Office of Surface Mining, see PART II. C.—Coal.

Department of Transportation

Office of the Secretary (general effects of transportation projects on land use):

—Approval of transportation programs or projects that require the use of or have significant impacts on park and recreation areas, fish and wildlife refuges, and historic sites. 49 U.S.C. 303.

• Coast Guard (effects of bridges on land use):

—Permits for bridges and causeways over navigable waters. 33 U.S.C. 491, et seq.; 511, et seq.; 525, et seq.; end 535 (33 CFR Part 114 et seq.).

• Federal Aviation Administration (airport land use compatibility):

—Airport aid program. 49 U.S.C. 1711-1727 (14 CFR Part 152).

—Acquisition of U.S. land for public airports. 49 U.S.C. 1723 (14 CFR Part 154).

—Notice of construction, alteration, activation, and deactivation of airports 49 U.S.C. 1350, 1354 and 1355 (14 CFR Part 157).

—Objects affecting navigable airspace. 49 U.S.C. 1655 (14 CFR Part 77).

—Release of airport property from surplus property disposal restrictions. 49 U.S.C. 1101-1119 (14 CFR Part 155).

• Federal Highway Administration (effects of highways on land use):

—Approval of highway projects and programs. 23 U.S.C. 101-156, generally, and 23 U.S.C. 201-219.

—Consultations, in cooperation with the Urban Mass Transportation Administration, with State and local officials concerning urban transportation related systems. 23 U.S.C. 105(d) and 134(a); 49 U.S.C. 1604(g) (23 CFR Part 450).

—Regulation of highway-related land use. For highway beautification—23 U.S.C. 131 (23 CFR Part 750); for junkyard control and acquisition—23 U.S.C. 136 (23 CFR Part 751); for landscape and roadside development—23 U.S.C. 131 and 319 (23 CFR Part 752); for protection of parklands, recreation areas, wildlife refuges, end historic sites—23 U.S.C. 138 (23 CFR Part 771).

• Urban Mass Transportation Administration (effects of urban transportation systems on land use):

—Consultation, in cooperation with the Federal Highway Administration, with State and local officials concerning urban transportation related systems. 23 U.S.C. 105(d) and 134(a); 49 U.S.C. 1604(g) (49 CFR Part 613).

—Approval for substituting mass transit or other transit projects in lieu of an interstate highway project. 23 U.S.C. 103(e)(4).

Advisory Council on Historic Preservation (effects of land use planning on historic properties).

Environmental Protection Agency (effects of land use on pollution control and environmental quality):

—For jurisdictional responsibilities see PART I. A.—Air Quality, PART I. B.—Water Quality, and PART I. C.—Waste Disposal on Land.

Federal Emergency Management Agency (national flood insurance program; disaster relief assistance; mitigation of natural hazards).

Federal Energy Regulatory Commission (effects of power projects on land use):

—Regulation of development of water resources. 16 U.S.C. 791-825(r) (18 CFR Parts 4-25, 36, 131 and 141).

International Boundary and Water Commission, United States Section (land use along international boundary with Mexico).

Interstate Commerce Commission (land use and Interstate commerce):

—Approval of Public Convenience and Necessity Certificate for new railroad lines 49 U.S.C. 10901.

National Aeronautics and Space Administration (remote sensing of land use and land cover).

National Capital Planning Commission (land use in the National Capital Region).

—Approval of land-use plans and construction in National Capital Region. 40 U.S.C. 74a (DC Code 9-404, DC Code 8-102); 40 U.S.C. 122 (DC Code 8-111, DC Code 5-432).

Tennessee Valley Authority (land use planning on public lands in Tennessee Valley region; assistance to local planning organizations).

B. Federal Land Management

Department of Agriculture

• Forest Service (National Forests and Grasslands management, including fire management):

—National Forest System Management Planning. 16 U.S.C. 1604 and 1613 (36 CFR Part 219).

—Special use permits, archeological permits, leases and easements. 16 U.S.C. 497 and 580(d); 43 U.S.C. 1761 and 46 U.S.C. 341 (36 CFR Parts 251 and 291).

—Easement and road rights-of-way on National Forests and other lands. 16 U.S.C. 533 (36 CFR Part 212.10).

—Permits for commercial use of existing roads. 16 U.S.C. 537 (36 CFR Part 212).

—Bankhead-Jones Farm Tenant Act. Title III permits on National Grasslands. 7 U.S.C. 1010-12 (36 CFR Part 213.3).

Department of Commerce

• National Oceanic and Atmospheric Administration (consistency of Federal land uses with coastal zone management programs).

Department of Defense (overall management of Department of Defense lands).

• Department of the Army (management of Army lands):

—Permits and leases for use of Army reservations.

—Permits and leases for use and occupancy of lands at water development projects of the Corps of Engineers.

Federal Register / Vol. 49, No. 247 / Friday, December 21, 1984 / Rules and Regulations   **49767**

- Department of the Air Force (management of Air Force lands):

—Permits and leases for use of Air Force reservations.

- Department of the Navy (management of Navy and Marine Corps lands):

—Permits and leases for uses of naval reservations.

Department of the Interior

- Fish and Wildlife Service (effects of Federal land management on endangered species and their critical habitats and other fish and wildlife resources, management of National Wildlife Refuge and National Fish Hatchery System areas):

—Easements/permits for right-of-way across National Wildlife Refuge and National Fish Hatchery System land. For refuges—16 U.S.C. 668dd, et seq.; for hatcheries—43 U.S.C. 931 c and d (50 CFR Parts 25.41 and 29.21).

—Permits for rights-of-way across National Wildlife Monuments (Alaska only). 16 U.S.C. 432, 460k-3 and 742(f) (50 CFR Part 96).

—Permits for off-road vehicular use on National Wildlife Refuge System areas. E.O. 11644 (50 CFR Part 26.34).

—Consultation concerning the protection of fish and wildlife refuges which may be impacted by transportation projects. 49 U.S.C. 303.

- Geological Survey (Federal land mineral resource potential: wilderness reviews, land-use planning; geologic and hydrologic hazards; flood studies; geologic, topographic, land use, and photographic mapping).

- Bureau of Indian Affairs (effects of Federal land management on Indian lands; management of Bureau of Indian Affairs lands):

—Sale of Federal land purchased for Indian administrative uses. 25 U.S.C. 293.

—Rights-of-way over Federal lands under BIA jurisdiction. 25 U.S.C. 323-328 (25 CFR Part 160).

—Leases for mining, oil and gas, coal, farming and other uses on Federal lands under BIA jurisdiction. 5 U.S.C. 301 and 25 U.S.C. 393, et seq. (25 CFR Part 162).

—For the trust responsibilities of the Bureau of Indian Affairs for Indian lands, see PART III. A.—Land Use Planning, etc.

- Bureau of Land Management (management of Federal lands):

—Easements/permits for rights-of-way. 43 U.S.C. 9 and 1701, et seq. (43 CFR Parts 2800-2900).

—Special land-use permits for habitation, occupation and other purposes. 43 U.S.C. 1732(b) (43 CFR Part 2920).

—Conditions and standards for off-road vehicle use on BLM lands. 43 U.S.C. 1201; E.O. 11644 (43 CFR Part 8340).

—Permits for off-road vehicular use special events, i.e., tours and competitions. 43 U.S.C. 1701, et seq., and 16 U.S.C. 460(1-6a) (43 CFR Part 6372).

—Exchange of Federal lands for other property. 43 U.S.C. 1716 (43 CFR Parts 2200-2270).

—Leases/transfers of public lands for a public airport. 43 U.S.C. 1201 and 49 U.S.C. 1115 (43 CFR Part 2640).

—Sales/leases of Federal land to State and local agencies and non-profit groups for recreational and public purposes. 43 U.S.C. 869, et seq. for sales—43 CFR Part 2740; for leases—43 CFR Part 2912).

—Permits for commercial recreational use of public lands. 43 U.S.C. 1701, et seq. (43 CFR Part 8370).

- Bureau of Mines (mineral land assessment).

- National Park Service (management of National Park System areas; units of the National Wild and Scenic Rivers System; National Trails System):

—Permits, leases, and easements of rights-of-way and other uses of National Park System areas. 16 U.S.C. 1, et seq. (36 CFR Parts 9 and 14).

—Permits for commercial operations on National Park System areas. 16 U.S.C. 1, et seq. (36 CFR Parts 7, 14, 50 and 51).

—Permits for off-road vehicular use in National Park System areas. E.O. 11644 (36 CFR Part 7).

—Consultations regarding use of and effect on rivers established as units of the National Wild and Scenic Rivers System and on those rivers designated for study as potential additions to that System. 16 U.S.C. 1278, et seq.

—Permits for use of National Historic and National Scenic Trails administered by the National Park Service. 16 U.S.C. 1246.

—Consultation concerning the protection of park, recreation, and cultural resources which may be impacted by transportation projects. 49 U.S.C. 303.

- Bureau of Reclamation (management of public water storage and delivery projects and recreational developments; irrigation; and impacts of Federal land management of State water planning):

—Sale or lease of project lands to a governmental entity or a non-profit group for recreational or other public purposes. 43 U.S.C. 869.

—Lease of project lands for commercial recreational developments. 43 U.S.C. 391, et seq.

Department of Transportation

- Office of the Secretary (effects of transportation projects on Federal land):

—Approval of transportation programs and projects which use a publicly owned park and recreation area, wildlife or waterfowl refuge, or any historic site. 49 U.S.C. 303.

- Federal Highway Administration (construction and management of Federal Lands Highways, including forest highways and National Park Service roads and parkways):

—Federal Lands Highways Program. 23 U.S.C. 204 (23 CFR Parts 660 and 667).

Advisory Council on Historic Preservation (effects of Federal land management on historic properties).

Environmental Protection Agency (effects of Federal land management on pollution control and environmental quality; pesticide use and integrated pest management on public lands):

—Underground injection control permits on Indian lands. 42 U.S.C. 300(f), et seq.

—Air emissions from Federal facilities. 42 U.S.C. 7418.

—Wastewater discharges from Federal facilities. 33 U.S.C. 1323.

—Solid wastes and hazardous wastes from Federal facilities. 42 U.S.C. 6961.

—Pesticide use of public lands. 7 U.S.C. 136.

—For other jurisdictional responsibilities, see PART I.—POLLUTION CONTROL.

Federal Emergency Management Agency (effects of the National Flood Insurance Program and disaster relief assistance on Federal land management).

General Services Administration

- Public Buildings Service (management of public buildings and property).

- Federal Property Resources Service (public land disposal).

National Aeronautics and Space Administration (advanced technology for remote sensing of land use and land cover).

Tennessee Valley Authority (TVA reservoir property, secondary use of reservoir property, and reservation planning).

C. Coastal Areas

Department of Agriculture

- Farmers Home Administration (housing, community, and business loan programs; and farmer loan programs in coastal areas).

- Forest Service (National Forests in coastal areas).

—Consultations regarding uses and effects on rivers established as units of the National Wild and Scenic Rivers System and on those rivers designated for study as potential additions to that System. 16 U.S.C. 1278, et seq.

- Soil Conservation Service (coastal soil stabilization).

Department of Commerce

- National Oceanic and Atmospheric Administration (coastal and marine resources and protection):

—Permits for activities in designated marine sanctuaries. 16 U.S.C. 143, et seq. (15 CFR Part 922).

—Approval and funding of State coastal management programs. 16 U.S.C. 1451, et seq. (15 CFR Parts 923 and 930).

—Establishment of estuarine sanctuaries. 16 U.S.C. 1461 (15 CFR Part 921).

—Determinations to insure Federal development projects and federally permitted or funded projects are consistent with an approved State coastal zone management plan. 16 U.S.C. 1451 (15 CFR Part 930).

—Grants and loans under Coastal Energy Impact Program. 16 U.S.C. 1456(a) (15 CFR Part 931).

Department of Defense

- Army Corps of Engineers (beach erosion and stabilization; dredge and fill permits; ocean dumping; Refuse Act permits):

—For jurisdictional responsibilities, see PART I. B.—Water Quality.

49768   Federal Register / Vol. 49, No. 247 / Friday, December 21, 1984 / Rules and Regulations

Department of Energy

• Office of Policy, Safety, and Environment (effects of energy policies, programs and projects on coastal areas).

Department of Housing and Urban Development

• Office of Housing and Office of Community Planning and Development (development in coastal areas; consistency with coastal zone management plans; consistency with Coastal Barrier Resources Act).

Department of the Interior

• Fish and Wildlife Service (effects of coastal land uses on endangered species and their critical habitats, National Wildlife Refuge and National Fish Hatchery System areas, and other fish and wildlife resources):

—Consultation regarding any Federal actions that may directly or indirectly affect a designated coastal barrier. 16 U.S.C. 3501. (For advisory guidelines, see 48 FR 45664 of Oct. 6, 1983).

—Consultation regarding Federal projects that may affect an estuarine area 15 U.S.C. 1224.

—Consultation regarding Federal or Federally permitted projects that affect fish and wildlife resources under the Fish and Wildlife Coordination Act. 16 U.S.C. 661, *et seq.*

—U.S. Fish and Wildlife Service Mitigation Policy. 16 U.S.C. 661, *et seq.*; 742(a)–754 and 1001–1009 (46 FR 7644 of Jan. 23, 1981).

• Geological Survey (land use planning; geologic and hydrologic hazards; geologic, topographic, land use, and photographic mapping, including areas of the outer continental shelf and Exclusive Economic Zone).

• Bureau of Indian Affairs (Indian lands in coastal areas).

• Bureau of Land Management (public land management in coastal areas).

• Minerals Management Service (coastal zone planning and management; outer continental shelf lands):

—Oil, gas, and sulphur exploration, development, and production on the outer continental shelf. (30 CFR Part 250.34).

• National Park Service (effects of coastal land use on National Park System areas, park and recreation areas, and historical, archeological and architectural sites; barrier island ecology and coastal processes):

—Identification and listing on the National Registry of Natural Landmarks of nationally significant natural areas in the United States. 16 U.S.C. 461 (36 CFR Part 62).

—Consultations regarding use of and effects on rivers established as units of the National Wild and Scenic Rivers System and on those rivers designated for study as potential additions to that System. 16 U.S.C. 1276, *et seq.*

• Bureau of Reclamation (water development projects in coastal areas, effects of water developments and irrigation on estuarine areas).

Department of Transportation

• Coast Guard (bridges, pipelines and transmission lines crossing navigable waters; navigation and deep water ports):

—Permits for bridges and causeways over navigable waters. 33 U.S.C. 491, *et seq.*; 511, *et seq.*; 525, *et seq.*, and 535 (33 CFR Part 114, *et seq.*).

—Permits for waterfront facilities. 33 U.S.C. 1221, *et seq.* (33 CFR Parts 125 and 126).

—Deepwater port regulation and licensing. 33 U.S.C. 1503–1524 (33 CFR Parts 148–150).

• Maritime Administration (coastal land use in relation to ports).

Advisory Council on Historic Preservation (effects of coastal land uses on historic properties).

Environmental Protection Agency (effects of coastal land uses on pollution control and environmental quality):

—For jurisdictional responsibilities see PART I.B.—Water Quality.

Federal Emergency Management Agency (National Flood Insurance Program; floodplain management; uses on sand dunes, mangrove forests and barrier islands; disaster relief assistance).

Federal Energy Regulatory Commission (effects of natural gas transportation, storage, and sale on coastal areas).

Marine Mammal Commission (conservation and protection of marine mammals and their habitat in coastal areas):

—Conservation and oversight responsibility for activities affecting marine mammals. 16 U.S.C. 1402.

National Aeronautics and Space Administration (advanced technology for remote sensing of land use and land cover).

D. Environmentally Sensitive Areas (Wilderness Areas, Wild and Scenic Rivers, Floodplains [see Executive Order 11988], Wetlands [see Executive Order 11990], Barrier Islands, Beaches and Dunes, Unstable Soils, Steep Slopes, Aquifer Recharge Areas, Tundra, etc.)

Department of Agriculture

• Agricultural Research Service (research activities to conserve and assist environmentally sensitive areas).

• Agricultural Stabilization and Conservation Service (commodity and land use programs; Water Bank).

• Farmers Home Administration (housing, community, and business loan programs; farmer loan programs in environmentally sensitive areas).

• Forest Service (management of environmentally sensitive areas on National Forest and Grassland System lands, including fire management):

—Permits for use of wilderness areas. 16 U.S.C. 472 and 551 (36 CFR Part 293).

—Consultations regarding use of and effects on rivers established as units of the National Wild and Scenic Rivers System and on those rivers designated for study as potential additions to that System. 16 U.S.C. 1276, *et seq.*

• Soil Conservation Service (conservation and protection of environmentally sensitive areas in rural regions).

Department of Commerce

• National Oceanic and Atmospheric Administration (management and protection of environmentally sensitive coastal and marine areas):

—Consultations concerning the protection of threatened and endangered marine species and their critical habitats. 16 U.S.C. 1531, *et seq.* (50 CFR Part 222).

—Permits for activities in designated marine sanctuaries. 16 U.S.C. 1431, *et seq.* (15 CFR Part 922).

—Establishment of estuarine sanctuaries. 16 U.S.C. 1461 (15 CFR Part 921).

—Habitat Conservation Policy (48 FR 53142 of Nov. 25, 1983).

Department of Defense

• Army Corps of Engineers (protection of beaches, wetlands, floodplains, barrier islands):

—For jurisdictional responsibilities, see PART I.B.—Water Quality.

Department of Health and Human Services

• Public Health Service: Center for Disease Control (environmentally sensitive areas in relation to human health issues).

Department of Housing and Urban Development

• Office of Community Planning and Development (locational criteria for floodplain and wetland development; sole source aquifer and critical habitat; development affecting endangered species and their critical habitats).

• Office of Housing (developable slope and soils criteria).

Department of Interior

• Fish and Wildlife Service (protection of endangered species and their critical habitats; conservation of environmentally sensitive areas in National Wildlife Refuges and National Fish Hatcheries):

—Consultations regarding any Federal actions that may directly or indirectly affect a designated coastal barrier. 16 U.S.C. 3501 (for advisory guidelines, see 48 FR 45664 of Oct. 6, 1983).

—Consultations concerning the protection of endangered species and their critical habitats. 16 U.S.C. 1531–1543 (50 CFR Part 402).

—Determination of critical habitats for endangered and threatened species of fish and wildlife and plants. 16 U.S.C. 1533 (50 CFR Parts 17, 402 and 424).

• Geological Survey (geologic and hydrologic assessments of sensitive areas, including energy and mineral resources in wilderness areas; earthquake, volcanic and other natural hazards).

• Bureau of Indian Affairs (environmentally sensitive areas on Indian lands).

• Bureau of Land Management (environmentally sensitive areas on public lands; management of special areas):

—Leases, permits and licenses for mining in Wild and Scenic Rivers System areas. 16 U.S.C. 1280 (each area has special Federal Regulations).

Federal Register / Vol. 49, No. 247 / Friday, December 21, 1984 / Rules and Regulations

49769

—Approval of plan of operations for a mining lease in a wilderness study area. 43 U.S.C. 1701, et seq. and 1782; 12 U.S.C. 1201, et seq. (43 CFR Part 3802).

—Permits for use of a designated "special area" as defined in 43 CFR Part 8372.0–5(g). 43 U.S.C. 1701, et seq.; 16 U.S.C. 460 (1–6a) and 670 (g–n) (43 CFR Part 8370 et seq.).

—Restrictions on use of "outstanding natural areas" and "primitive areas." 43 U.S.C. 1701, et seq. (43 CFR Subpart 8352).

• National Park Service (historical and recreational values; Wild and Scenic Rivers System; National Trails System; National Park System areas):

—Identification and listing on the National Registry of Natural Landmarks of nationally significant natural areas in the United States. 16 U.S.C. 461 (36 CFR Part 62).

—Leases, permits, and licenses for mining on National Park System lands involved in Wild and Scenic Rivers System. 16 U.S.C. 1280.

—Consultations regarding use of and effect on rivers established as units of the National Wild and Scenic Rivers System and on those rivers designated for study as potential additions to that System. 16 U.S.C. 1276, et seq.

—Permits for use of National Historic and National Scenic Trails administered by the National Park Service. 16 U.S.C. 1246.

• Bureau of Reclamation (water resource planning and water storage and delivery projects in environmentally sensitive areas; National Water Summary).

• Office of Surface Mining Reclamation and Enforcement (surface coal mining and reclamation operations in environmentally sensitive areas):

—Identification of lands considered unsuitable for all or certain stipulated methods of coal mining involving surface coal mining operations. 30 U.S.C. 1272(e) (30 CFR Chapter 7, Subchapter F).

—Protection of prime farmlands during surface coal mining and reclamation operations. 30 U.S.C. 1266 (30 CFR Parts 785.17 and 823).

Department of Transportation

• Office of Secretary (effects of all types of transportation projects on environmentally sensitive areas).

• Coast Guard (port facilities and bridges in environmentally sensitive areas):

—Establishment of port access routes in environmentally sensitive areas. 33 U.S.C. 1221.

• Federal Highway Administration (highways in environmentally sensitive areas):

—Mitigation of impacts to privately owned wetlands. 23 U.S.C. 109; Executive Order 11990 (23 CFR Part 777).

Advisory Council on Historic Preservation (effects of activities in sensitive areas on historic properties).

Environmental Protection Agency (pollution control and environmental effects on wetlands, floodplains, prime agricultural lands, and other environmentally sensitive areas):

—For jurisdictional responsibilities, see PART I. A.—Air Quality, PART I. B.—Water Quality, and PART I. C.—Waste disposal on Land.

Federal Emergency Management Agency (National Flood Insurance Program; floodplain management: uses on sand dunes, mangrove forests, and barrier islands; disaster relief assistance).

National Science Foundation (conservation of Antarctic animals, plants, and ecosystems):

—Permits for the taking or collecting of Antarctic animals and plants, and for entry into certain designated areas. 16 U.S.C. 2401, et seq. (45 CFR Part 670).

Tennessee Valley Authority (Protection and management of environmentally sensitive areas in the Tennessee Valley region).

E. Outdoor Recreation

Department of Agriculture

• Forest Service (recreation in National Forests and Grasslands):

—Use of recreation areas. (36 CFR Parts 291, 292 and 294).

—Permits for use of wilderness areas. 16 U.S.C. 472 and 551 (36 CFR Part 293).

—Conditions and requirements for use of National Forest road and trail system. 16 U.S.C. 537 (36 CFR Part 212).

—Permits for use of National Scenic Trails administered by Forest Service. 16 U.S.C. 1246.

—Permits for hunting and fishing in fish and wildlife refuge lands. 16 U.S.C. 551 and 683.

—Conditions and standards for off-road vehicle use on National Forest System lands. 16 U.S.C. 551; E.O. 11644 (36 CFR Part 295).

—Consultations regarding use of and effects on rivers established as units of the National Wild and Scenic Rivers System and on those rivers designated for study as potential additions to that System. 16 U.S.C. 1276, et seq.

• Soil Conservation Service (recreation and watershed protection; planning assistance to private landowners):

—Assistance to State and local sponsors, through a Small Watershed Program grant, for reservoir and stream modification projects including development of basic public recreation facilities. 16 U.S.C. 1001, et seq. and 33 U.S.C. 701–1.

Department of Commerce

• National Oceanic and Atmospheric Administration (marine recreational fishing; coastal access planning in State coastal zone management programs).

Department of Defense

• Army Corps of Engineers (recreational areas on Corps project lands):

—Permits for activities and developments on water resources development projects. 16 U.S.C. 460(d) (36 CFR Parts 313 and 327).

Department of Health and Human Services

• Public Health Service: Center for Disease Control (outdoor recreation and health).

Department of Housing and Urban Development

• Office of Community Planning and Development (outdoor recreation in urban areas):

—Approval of a conversion to a non-designated use for State and local lands acquired or developed in whole or in part, with an Open Space Land Program grant. 42 U.S.C. 1500–1500e.

Department of the Interior

• Fish and Wildlife Service (effects of recreation on endangered species and their critical habitats, and other fish and wildlife resources; recreation on National Wildlife Refuge and National Fish Hatchery System lands):

—Permits for special uses including concessions and other recreational facilities on National Wildlife Refuge System lands. 16 U.S.C. 668dd, et seq. (50 CFR 25.41, et seq.).

—Permits for off-road vehicular use on National Wildlife Refuge System lands. E.O. 11644 (50 CFR Part 28.34).

—Consultation concerning the protection of fish and wildlife refuges which may be impacted by transportation projects. 49 U.S.C. 303.

• Geological Survey (effects of water quality and erosion on recreation).

• Bureau of Indian Affairs (outdoor recreation on Indian lands).

• Bureau of Land Management (outdoor recreation on public lands generally, including ORV use and river management):

—Leases and sale of Federal land to State and local agencies and non-profit groups for recreational and public purposes. 43 U.S.C. 869, et seq. (For sales—43 CFR Part 2740; for leases—43 CFR Part 2912).

—Conditions and standards for off-road vehicle use on BLM lands. 43 U.S.C. 1201; E.O. 11644 (43 CFR Part 8340).

—Permits for off-road vehicular use special events, i.e., tours and competitions. 43 U.S.C. 1701, et seq., and 16 U.S.C. 460 (1–6a) (43 CFR Part 8372).

—Permits for use of a national trail, developed facility and a designated "special area" as defined in 43 CFR Part 8372.0–5(g). 43 U.S.C. 1701, et seq.; 16 U.S.C. 460 (1–6a) and 670 (g–n) (43 CFR Part 8370).

—Permits for commercial recreation use of public lands. 43 U.S.C. 1701, et seq. (43 CFR Part 8370).

• National Park Service (outdoor recreation, urban parks, Wild and Scenic Rivers System, National Trails System; recreation in National Park System areas):

—Assistance to State and local agencies, through Land and Water Conservation Fund Act grants, for the acquisition and/or development of park and recreation areas and/or facilities. 16 U.S.C. 4601.

—Approval of a conversion to a non-designated use for State and local lands acquired or developed, in whole or in part, with a Land and Water Conservation Fund Act grant. 16 U.S.C. 4601.

—Assistance to State and local agencies, through Urban Park and Recreation Recovery Act grants, for the development

49770 Federal Register / Vol. 49, No. 247 / Friday, December 21, 1984 / Rules and Regulations

and/or improvement of park and recreation areas. 16 U.S.C. 2504 (36 CFR Part 1228).

—Approval of a conversion to other than public recreation uses for State and local areas developed or improved with an Urban Park and Recreation Recovery Act grant. 16 U.S.C. 2504 (36 CFR Part 69).

—Consultations regarding use of and effects on rivers established as units of the National Wild and Scenic Rivers System and on those rivers designated for study as potential additions to that System. 16 U.S.C. 1278. *et seq.*

—Permits for use of National Historic and National Scenic Trails administered by the National Park Service. 16 U.S.C.1246.

—Approval of a conversion to a non-designated use for lands deeded by the Federal government to State and local entities as park demonstration areas, recreation areas, wildlife conservation preserves and refuges and as historic monuments and properties under the (1) Recreation Demonstration Act of 1942 and (2) Federal Property and Administrative Services Act of 1949. For (1)—16 U.S.C. 459 r–t; for (2)—40 U.S.C. 484(k)(2) (41 CFR Part 101–47).

—Approval of a conversion to a non-designated use of abandoned railroad rights-of-way acquired by State and local governments under Section 809(b) of the Railroad Revitalization and Regulatory Reform Act of 1976. 49 U.S.C. 1a (38 CFR Part 64).

—Consultation concerning the protection of park, recreation, and cultural resources which may be impacted by transportation projects. 49 U.S.C. 303.

—Consultations about extent to which proposed recreational developments at hydroelectric projects conform to and are in accord with the Statewide Comprehensive Outdoor Recreation Plans. 16 U.S.C. 460.

—Permits for off-road vehicle use on National Park System lands. 16 U.S.C. 1. *et seq.;* E.O. 11644 (36 CFR Part 7).

• Bureau of Reclamation (recreation on water storage and delivery projects):

—Sale or lease of project lands to a governmental entity or a non-profit group for recreational purposes. 43 U.S.C. 869.

—Lease of project lands for commercial recreational developments. 43 U.S.C. 391. *et seq.*

—Permits for organized off-road vehicular events. (43 CFR Part 420.24).

• Office of Surface Mining Reclamation and Enforcement (use of abandoned mined lands for recreational purposes):

—Identification of park and recreation lands considered unsuitable for surface coal mining operations. 30 U.S.C. 1272(e) (30 CFR Chapter 7, Subchapter F).

Department of Transportation

• Office of the Secretary (general effects of transportation projects on parks and recreation areas):

—Approval of transportation programs or projects that require the use of or have significant impact on park and recreation areas. 49 U.S.C. 303.

• Coast Guard (recreational boating):

—Recreational boating regulations and permits. 46 U.S.C. 1451 (33 CFR Part 173. *et seq.*).

• Federal Highway Administration (effects of highways on parks and recreation areas):

—Special protection considerations for public park and recreation areas. 23 U.S.C.138 and 49 U.S.C. 303 (23 CFR Part 771).

—Access highways to public recreation areas on lakes. 23 U.S.C. 155.

Advisory Council on Historic Preservation (effects of recreational activities and development on historic properties).

Environmental Protection Agency (pollution control and environmental quality in relation to outdoor recreation):

—For jurisdictional responsibilities, see PART I—POLLUTION CONTROL.

National Capital Planning Commission (recreation in the Washington, D.C. area):

—Approval of land use plans and construction in the National Capital Region. 40 U.S.C. 74a (D.C. Code 9-404, D.C. Code 8-102); 40 U.S.C. 122 (D.C. Code 8-11, D.C. Code 5-432).

Tennessee Valley Authority (recreation on public lands and waters in Tennessee Valley Region).

F. Community Development

Department of Agriculture

• Agricultural Stabilization and Conservation Service (rural development and farm programs).

• Extension Service (rural and community development programs).

• Farmers Home Administration (rural and community development programs).

• Forest Service (programs to assist in coordinating development of communities in and adjacent to National Forest System areas; urban forestry).

• Soil Conservation Service (soil and related resource surveys; land conservation and utilization):

—Soil, water, and related resource data. 7 U.S.C. 1010a.

—Program for land conservation and utilization. 7 U.S.C. 1011(e).

Department of Commerce

• Economic Development Administration (community development programs in designated areas).

• National Oceanic and Atmospheric Administration (energy development impacts on communities):

—Approval and funding of State coastal zone management programs. 16 U.S.C. 1451, *et seq.* (15 CFR Parts 130 and 923).

Department of Health and Human Services

• Center for Disease Control (community health issues).

• Office of Human Development Services (problems of handicapped, aged, children and Native Americans).

Department of Housing and Urban Development

• Office of Community Planning and Development (community development; effects on low income populations; economic revitalization in distressed areas; density and

congestion mitigation; rehabilitation and urban homesteading):

—Assurances that HUD assisted projects are located in a safe and healthful environment. 42 U.S.C. 1441, *et seq.*

—Housing and Community Development Act of 1974. 42 U.S.C. 5301, *et seq.* (24 CFR Part 570).

—Approval of a conversion to a non-designated use for State and local lands acquired or developed, in whole or in part, with an Open Space Land Program grant. 42 U.S.C. 1500–1500e.

Department of the Interior

• Fish and Wildlife Service (effects of community developments on endangered species and their critical habitats, other fish and wildlife resources, and National Wildlife Refuge and National Fish Hatchery System areas).

• Geological Survey (effects of development on water resources and erosion; geologic and hydrologic hazards, including floods, subsidence, sink holes, landslides, and earthquakes).

• Bureau of Indian Affairs (community development for Indian peoples and on Indian lands).

• Bureau of Land Management (community developments on public lands):

—Leases and sale of Federal land to State and local agencies and non-profit groups for recreational and public purposes. 43 U.S.C. 869, *et seq.* (For sales—43 CFR Part 2740, for leases—43 CFR Part 2912).

—Leases/transfers of public lands for a public airport. 49 U.S.C. 1115 (43 CFR Part 2640).

—Exchange of Federal lands for other property. 43 U.S.C. 1716 (43 CFR Part 2200–2270).

• National Park Service (effects of community developments on natural and historic landmarks, archeological remains, outdoor recreation, urban parks, historic preservation, and National Park System areas):

—Approval of a conversion to a non-designated use for State and local lands acquired or developed, in whole or in part, with a Land and Water Conservation Fund Act grant. 16 U.S.C. 4601.

—Approval of a conversion to other than a public recreation use for State and local areas developed or improved with an Urban Park and Recreation Recovery Act grant. 16 U S.C. 2504 (38 CFR Part 69).

—Approval of a conversion to a non-designated use for lands deeded by the Federal government to State and local entities as park demonstration areas, recreation areas, wildlife conservation preserves and refuges and as historic monuments and properties under the (1) Recreation Demonstration Act of 1942 and (2) Federal Property and Administrative Services Act of 1949. For (1)—16 U.S.C. 459 r–t; for (2)—40 U.S.C. 484(k)(2) (41 CFR Part 101–47).

—Approval of a conversion to a non-designated use of abandoned railroad right-of-way acquired by State and local governments under Section 809(b) of the

Federal Register / Vol. 49, No. 247 / Friday, December 21, 1984 / Rules and Regulations   49771

Railroad Revitalization and Regulatory Reform Act of 1976. 49 U.S.C. 1a (36 CFR Part 64).
—Assistance for the acquisition, rehabilitation, restoration and reconstruction of historic properties. 16 U.S.C. 470, *et seq.* (36 CFR Parts 60.3 and 68).
• Bureau of Reclamation (water storage, delivery, and irrigation systems for community development purposes):
—Sales of farm units on Federal irrigation projects (Statutory jurisdiction appears in individual project authorizations).
—Sale or lease of project lands to a governmental entity or nonprofit group for recreational or other public purposes. 43 U.S.C. 869.
• Office of Surface Mining Reclamation and Enforcement (effects of surface mining and reclamation operations on community development).

Department of Transportation
• Federal Aviation Administration (effects of airport development and use on communities):
—Approval of an airport noise compatibility program. 49 U.S.C. 2101, *et seq.* (14 CFR Part 150).
• Federal Highway Administration (effects of highways on communities):
—Relocation assistance in connection with highway projects. 42 U.S.C. 4601 *et seq.* (23 CFR Part 740 and 49 CFR Part 25).
—Grants for economic growth center development highways. 23 U.S.C. 143.
• Urban Mass Transportation Administration (effects of urban transportation systems on communities):
—Grants for Urban Mass Transportation Act projects. 49 U.S.C. 1610, *et seq.*
ACTION (effects of community development on low income populations).
Advisory Council on Historic Preservation (effects of community development on historic properties).
Environmental Protection Agency (air, noise, and water pollution control relating to community development):
—For jurisdictional responsibilities, see PART I.—POLLUTION CONTROL.
Federal Emergency Management Agency (National Flood Insurance Program; disaster relief assistance; mitigation of natural hazards).

General Services Administration
• Public Building Service (building design, construction, and use).
Interstate Commerce Commission (effects of rail line construction and abandonment on community development).
National Capital Planning Commission (community developments in the Washington, D.C. area):
—Approval of land use plans and construction in the National Capital Region. 40 U.S.C. 74a (DC Code 9–404, DC Code 8–102); 40 U.S.C. 122 (D.C. Code 8–111, DC Code 5–432).
National Endowment for the Arts (effects of development on artistic values).

G. Historic, Architectual, and Archeological Resources

Department of Agriculture
• Office of the Secretary (protection of archeological resources):
—Permits and procedures for the recovery and preservation of archeological resources on Department of Agriculture lands. 16 U.S.C. 470 aa–ll (36 CFR Part 296).
• Agricultural Stabilization and Conservation Service (effects on historic and archeological resources from agriculture).
• Farmers Home Administration (effects of housing, community, and business programs, and farmer programs on cultural resources).
• Forest Service (protection of historic and archeological resources in National Forests and Grasslands):
—Special-use permits, archeological permits, leases and easements. 16 U.S.C. 497 and 580(d); 43 U.S.C. 1761; 48 U.S.C. 341 (36 CFR Parts 251 and 261).
• Soil Conservation Service (effects of agriculture on cultural resources).

Department of Commerce
• National Oceanic and Atmospheric Administration (areas for preservation and restoration under State coastal zone management programs):
—National Marine Sanctuaries. 16 U.S.C. 1431 (15 CFR Part 922).
—National Estuarine Sanctuaries. 16 U.S.C. 1461 (15 CFR Part 921).

Department of Defense
• Office of the Secretary (protection of archeological resources):
—Permits/procedures for recovery and preservation of archeological resources on Department of Defense lands. 16 U.S.C. 470 aa–ll (32 CFR Part 229).

Department of Housing and Urban Development
• Office of Community Planning and Development (protection of historic and architectural resources in developed areas):
—Housing and Community Development Act of 1974. 42 U.S.C. 5304(f) (24 CFR Part 58).

Department of the Interior
• Fish and Wildlife Service (cultural resource management on National Wildlife Refuge and National Fish Hatchery System lands, and affects of cultural resource management on endangered species and critical habitats):
—Special use permit for antiquities search and collection activities—in addition to an antiquity permit. 16 U.S.C. 668(dd), *et seq.* (50 CFR Part 25.41): also see 16 U.S.C. 470 aa–ll (43 CFR Part 7).
• Geological Survey (paleontological resources in general).
• Bureau of Indian Affairs (protection of historic and archeological resources on Indian and Native American lands):
—Concurrence for issuance and supervision of antiquity permits on Indian lands. 16 U.S.C. 432 (25 CFR Part 261); also see 16 U.S.C. 470 aa–ll (43 CFR Part 7).
—Protection of access to sacred sites, use and possession of sacred objects and other rights of the American Indian, Eskimo, Aleut, and Native Hawaiian. 42 U.S.C. 1996.
• Bureau of Land Management (cultural resource management on public lands):
—Concurrence for issuance and supervision of antiquity permits. 16 U.S.C. 432 (43 CFR Part 3); also see 16 U.S.C. 470 aa–ll (43 CFR Part 7).
• Minerals Management Service (protection of cultural resources on outer continental shelf lands):
—Outer Continental Shelf Lands Act. 43 U.S.C. 1331 (30 CFR Parts 250 and 251).
• National Park Service (protection of historic, archeological, architectual and paleontological properties; cultural resource management on National Park System lands):
—Nominations to and determinations of eligibility of properties for inclusion in the National Register of Historic Places. 16 U.S.C. 470, *et seq.* (36 CFR Part 60 and 63).
—Approval of procedures in State and local government historic preservation programs 16 U.S.C. 470, *et seq.* (36 CFR Part 61).
—National Historic Landmarks Program—nominations and designations. 16 U.S.C. 461, *et seq.* (36 CFR Part 65).
—Historic Preservation Certifications pursuant to the Tax Reform Act of 1976, the Revenue Act of 1978, the Tax Treatment Extension Act of 1980, and the Economic Recovery Tax Act of 1981. 16 U.S.C. 470, *et seq.*; 90 Stat. 1519; 92 Stat. 2828; 94 Stat. 3204; 95 Stat. 172 (36 CFR Part 67).
—The Secretary of the Interior's Standards and Guidelines for Historic Preservation Projects. 16 U.S.C. 470, *et seq.*; Executive Order 11593 (36 CFR Part 68).
—The Secretary of the Interior's Standards and Guidelines for Archeology and Historic Preservation pursuant to Sections 101 and 110 of the National Historic Preservation Act. 16 U.S.C. 470, *et seq.* (48 FR 44716 of Sept. 29 1983).
—Waiver Federal Agency Responsibilities under section 110 of the National Historic Preservation Act. 16 U.S.C. 470, *et seq.* (36 CFR Part 78).
—Protection of the world's cultural and natural heritage: the World Heritage Convention. 16 U.S.C. 470a–1 and 2–2d (36 CFR Part 73).
—Permits and procedures for the recovery and preservation of archeological resource on Department of the Interior lands. 16 U.S.C. 470 aa–ll (43 CFR Part 7).
—Permits to examine ruins, excavate archeological sites and gather objects of antiquity on Federal and Indian lands (Antiquity permits issued by the Departmental Consulting Archeologist). 16 U.S.C. 432 (43 CFR Part 3; 36 CFR Parts 2.20 and 2.25); also see 16 U.S.C. 470 aa–ll (43 CFR Part 7).
—Approval of a conversion to a non-designated use for lands deeded by the Federal government to State and local entities as park demonstration areas, recreation areas, wildlife conservation preserves and refuges and as historic monuments and properties under the (1) Recreation Demonstration Act of 1942 and (2) Federal Property and Administrative

49772   Federal Register / Vol. 49, No. 247 / Friday, December 21, 1984 / Rules and Regulations

Services Act of 1949. For (1)—16 U.S.C. 459 r–t; for (2)—40 U.S.C. 484(k)(2) (41 CFR Part 101–47).

—Consultation concerning the protection of any historic site which may be impacted by a transportation project. 49 U.S.C. 303.

• Bureau of Reclamation (protection of cultural resources on water storage and delivery project lands):

—Procedures for the administration and protection of cultural resources. E.O. 11593 (43 CFR Part 422).

—Concurrence for issuance and supervision of antiquity permits. 16 U.S.C. 432 (43 CFR Part 3); also see 16 U.S.C. 470 aa–ll (43 CFR Part 7).

• Office of Surface Mining Reclamation and Enforcement (protection of important historic, cultural, scientific, and aesthetic resources in surface coal mining and reclamation operations):

—Concurrence for issuance and the supervision of antiquity permits. 16 U.S.C. 432 (43 CFR Part 3); also see 16 U.S.C. 470 aa–ll (43 CFR Part 7).

Department of Transportation

• Office of the Secretary (general effects of transportation projects on cultural resources):

—Approval of transportation programs or projects that require the use of or have significant impacts on historic sites. 49 U.S.C. 303.

• Coast Guard (effects of bridges on cultural resources):

—Construction and alterations on bridges and causeways over navigable waters that are or require the use of or have significant impacts on historic sites. 33 U.S.C. 491, et seq.; 511, et seq.; 525, et seq., and 535 (33 CFR Part 114, et seq.).

• Federal Aviation Administration (effects of airport developments and air traffic on cultural resources; sonic boom impacts).

• Federal Highway Administration (effects of highway projects on cultural resources):

—Approval of transportation programs or projects that require the use of or have significant impacts on historic sites. 23 U.S.C. 138 and 49 U.S.C. 303 (23 CFR Part 771).

—Archeological and paleontological salvage on Federal and Federal-aid highway projects. 23 U.S.C. 305.

• Federal Railroad Administration (effects of railroad projects on cultural resources).

• Urban Mass Transportation Administration (effects of urban transportation projects on architectural and historic resources).

Advisory Council on Historic Preservation

(effects of development or other actions on historic properties):

—Consultation concerning the effects of any Federal, federally assisted, or federally regulated activity on historic properties. 16 U.S.C. 470, et seq. (36 CFR Part 800).

General Services Administration

• Public Buildings Service (effects of development and pollution on architectural and historic resources in urban areas).

Interstate Commerce Commission (effects of rail line construction and abandonment on cultural resources).

National Capital Planning Commission

(effects of development and pollution on architectural, historic and archeological resources in the Washington, D.C. area):

—Approval of land use plans and construction in the National Capital Region. 40 U.S.C. 74a (D.C. Code 9–404, D.C. Code 8–102); 40 U.S.C. 122 (D.C. Code 6–111, D.C. Code 5–432).

Tennessee Valley Authority (effects of development and other actions on historic and archeological resources in the Tennessee Valley region):

—Permits and procedures for the recovery and preservation of archeological resources on TVA lands. 16 U.S.C. 470 aa–ll (18 CFR Part 1312).

IV. NATURAL RESOURCES MANAGEMENT

A. Weather Modification

Department of Agriculture

• Forest Service (effects of weather modification on National Forests and Grasslands).

• Soil Conservation Service (snow surveys and soil moisture monitoring).

• World Agricultural Outlook Board (data relating to weather and agricultural commodities).

Department of Commerce

• National Oceanic and Atmospheric Administration (weather research and development):

—Records and reports or weather modification activities. 85 Stat. 735 (15 CFR Part 908).

Department of Defense

• Department of the Air Force (fog dissipation).

Department of the Interior

• Bureau of Indian Affairs (effects of weather modification on Indian Lands).

• Bureau of Land Management (effects of weather modification on public lands).

• Fish and Wildlife Service (effects of weather modification on endangered species and their critical habitats, other fish and wildlife resources, and National Wildlife Refuge and National Fish Hatchery System areas).

• Geological Survey (effects of weather modification on water resources; paleoclimatic studies).

• National Park Service (effects of weather modification on National Park System areas).

• Bureau of Reclamation (effects of weather modification on water storage and delivery projects; research in relation to water resources):

—Precipitation augmentation through cloud seeding. 43 U.S.C. 377.

Environmental Protection Agency (effects of weather modification on pollution control and environmental quality).

B. Marine Resources

Department of Commerce

• National Oceanic and Atmospheric Administration (meteorological and oceanographic research and monitoring;

management and protection of coastal and marine resources; marine pollution research and monitoring; ocean pollution; ocean mining, ocean dumping, seafood quality; regulation of marine fisheries):

—Establishment of estuarine sanctuaries. 16 U.S.C. 1461 (15 CFR Part 921).

—Permits for activities in designated marine sanctuaries. 16 U.S.C. 1431, et seq. (15 CFR Part 922).

—Consultations regarding Federal or federally permitted projects affecting fish and wildlife habitat in coastal and offshore areas under the Fish and Wildlife Coordination Act. 16 U.S.C. 661, et seq.

—Consultations regarding projects which may effect any threatened or endangered marine species or its critical habitat. 16 U.S.C. 1531, et seq. (50 CFR Parts 222 and 402).

—Permits for scientific research and display of marine mammals. 16 U.S.C. 1374 (50 CFR Parts 216.31, 220 and 618).

—Permits to enhance the propagation or survival of endangered or threatened marine species. 16 U.S.C. 1531 (50 CFR Part 222.21).

—Control of fishing by foreign and domestic vessels in the 3–200 mile Fishery Conservation Zone. 16 U.S.C. 1801, et seq. (50 CFR Chapter VI).

—Permits for importing marine mammals or products thereof. 16 U.S.C. 1361 and 1371–74 (50 CFR Parts 18 and 216).

—Licenses for siting, design, and operation of ocean-thermal energy facilities. 42 U.S.C. 9101, et seq. (15 CFR Part 981).

—Licenses and permits for deep seabed hard mineral resource exploration or recovery. 30 U.S.C. 1401, et seq. (15 CFR Part 970).

—Approval of fishery management plans. 16 U.S.C. 1801, et seq. (50 CFR Part 601).

—Permits for scientific research, propagation and survival of marine reptiles. 16 U.S.C. 1538 (50 CFR Part 223.23).

—Permits for whaling for scientific and subsistence purposes. 16 U.S.C. 916 (50 CFR Part 216).

Department of Defense

• Army Corps of Engineers (effects of activities in navigable waters on marine resources):

—Regulation of artificial islands, installations and devices on the outer continental shelf. 43 U.S.C. 1333(e) (33 CFR Part 320.2(b)).

—For other jurisdictional responsibilities, see PART I. B.—Water Quality.

• Department of the Navy (oceanography and hydrographic mapping; ship pollution).

Department of Energy

• Office of Policy, Safety, and Environment (effects of energy programs on marine resources).

Department of Health and Human Services

• Public Health Service (effects of marine pollution on health).

• Food and Drug Administration (shellfish sanitation; contamination of fish and shellfish with toxics).

Department of the Interior

• Fish and Wildlife Service (effec marine pollution on endangered spec d their critical habitats, estuarine areas arine sanctuaries, sport fisheries, migratory waterfowl, barrier islands, and coastal National Wildlife Refuges):

—Consultation regarding Federal projects that may affect an estuarine area. 15 U.S.C. 1224.

—Habitat acquisition and improvement for designated marine mammals. 16 U.S.C. 136. *et seq.*

• Geological Survey (marine geophysical surveys, including assessment of marine energy and mineral deposits; offshore geologic studies).

• Minerals Management Service (emissions from outer continental shelf lease operations; effects of pollution from outer continental shelf mineral lease operations; protection of marine biological resources on outer continental shelf leases; management of outer continental shelf lands):

—For jurisdictional responsibilities see PART II. B.—Oil and Gas and PART IV. G—Non-energy Mineral Resources.

• Bureau of Mines (pollution from ocean mining).

• National Park Service (marine pollution affecting National Park System areas, especially National Seashores; marine recreational resources; historic and archeological sites in coastal areas and on the continental shelf).

• *Department of State* (international aspects of water pollution and marine resources, including migratory birds and marine mammals).

Department of Transportation

• Coast Guard (ocean dumping enforcement and marine resource protection; discharges of toxic materials in navigable waters; recreational boating):

—Transportation of hazardous materials by vessel. 46 U.S.C. 170, 375, 391(a) and 416(j); 49 U.S.C. 1655, 1603, 1804 and 1808(j); 50 U.S.C. 191 (33 CFR Parts 151, *et seq.;* and 160, *et seq.;* 46 CFR Chapter I).

—Hazardous substance discharge to navigable waters. 33 U.S.C. 1321 (33 CFR Parts 25 and 151, *et seq.;* 46 CFR Part 542, *et seq.*).

—Navigation and waterfront facility regulation. 33 U.S.C. 1221, *et seq.* (33 CFR Parts 125 and 126).

—Outer continental shelf structures. 43 U.S.C. 1331 (33 CFR Part 140, *et seq.*).

—Ports and waterways safety. 33 U.S.C. 1221 (33 CFR Part 160, *et seq.*).

—Deepwater port regulation and licensing. 33 U.S.C. 1503–1524 (33 CFR Parts 148–150).

—Recreational boating regulation. 46 U.S.C. 1451 (33 CFR Part 173, *et seq.*).

• Maritime Administration (port, coastal, and ocean pollution; marine pollution from ships; destruction/treatment of wastes at sea):

—Merchant vessels: polluting, discharging and dumping. 46 U.S.C. 1101, *et seq.*

—Port operations: polluting, discharging and dumping. 46 U.S.C. 867.

Advisory Council on Historic Preservation (effects of activities in coastal and marine areas on historic properties).

Environmental Protection Agency (marine discharges, oil spills, ocean dumping; environmental effects; ocean disposal of radioactive waste and hazardous materials):

—For jurisdictional responsibilities, see PART I. B.—Water Quality.

Federal Maritime Commission (vessel certification with respect to liability for water pollution):

—Certificates of financial responsibility for water pollution. 33 U.S.C. 1321 (46 CFR Part 542); 42 U.S.C. 1643 (46 CFR Part 543); 43 U.S.C. 1815 (46 CFR Part 544).

Marine Mammal Commission (conservation and protection of marine mammals and their habitat):

—Consultation and oversight responsibility for activities affecting marine mammals. 16 U.S.C. 1402.

—Review of permit applications for taking and importation of marine mammals and marine mammal products. 16 U.S.C. 1371(a).

National Aeronautics and Space Administration (advanced technology for remote sensing in oceanography and marine resource conservation).

Nuclear Regulatory Commission (radioactive substances in the marine environment).

C. Water Resources Development and Regulation

Department of Agriculture

• Agricultural Stabilization and Conservation Service (water resource conservation; Water Bank program).

• Animal and Plant Health Inspection Service (control of exotic noxious weeds in waterways and streams).

• Forest Service (effects of water resource developments on National Forests and Grasslands):

—Water resource development in wilderness areas. (36 CFR Part 293.15).

—Consultations regarding water resource development and effects on rivers established as units of the National Wild and Scenic Rivers System and on those rivers designated for study as potential additions to that System. 16 U.S.C. 1278, *et seq.*

• Agricultural Research Service (research on soil and water conservation).

• Soil Conservation Service (watershed protection; river basin studies; flood prevention; and habitat analysis):

—Assistance to State and local sponsors, through a Small Watershed Program grant, for watershed, reservoir, flood-control and drainage projects. 16 U.S.C. 1001, *et seq.;* 33 U.S.C. 701–1 and 42 U.S.C. 1962, *et seq.* (7 CFR Parts 620, *et seq.;* and 660).

Department of Commerce

• National Oceanic and Atmospheric Administration (estuarine and anadromous fish habitat; review of Federal permits affecting water resources and management; protection of coastal and marine resources; river and flood forecasting).

Department of Defense

• Army Corps of Engineers (water resource development and regulation activities in water of the United States):

—Rules governing work or structures in or affecting navigable waters of the United States. 33 U.S.C. 401, 403, and 419 (33 CFR Part 322).

—Permits for discharges of dredged or fill materials into waters of the United States. 33 U.S.C. 1344 (33 CFR Part 323).

—Guidelines controlling the discharge of dredged or fill material in waters of the United States including wetlands. (40 CFR Part 230).

—Permits for uses at Corps reservoirs managed by a lakeshore management plan. 33 U.S.C. 1251.

—Permits for use of river or harbor improvements built by United States. 33 U.S.C. 408 (33 CFR Part 320.2(e).

—For o ı̇riadictional responsibilities, see PART —Water Quality.

Department of Energy

• Office of Policy, Safety, and Environment (effect of energy policies, programs, and projects).

Department of the Interior

• Fish and Wildlife Service (effects of water resource developments on endangered species and their critical habitats, other fish and wildlife resources, and National Wildlife Refuge and National Fish Hatchery System areas):

—Consultation regarding Federal or Federally permitted projects which affect streams and water bodies. 16 U.S.C. 661, *et seq.*

—U. S. Fish and Wildlife Service Mitigation Policy. 16 U.S.C. 661–667(e), 742(a)–754 and 1001–1009 (46 FR 7644 of Jan. 23, 1981).

—Consultation regarding Federal projects that may affect an estuerine area under the Estuarine Protection Act. 15 U.S.C. 1224.

• Geological Survey (hydrologic research; collection, analysis, and dissemination of data on quantity and quality of surface and ground water; National Water Summary).

• Bureau of Indian Affairs (effects of water resources developments on Indian lands):

—Permits, concessions, and leases on lands withdrawn or acquired in connection with Indian irrigation projects. 25 U.S.C. 390 (25 CFR Part 173).

• Bureau of Land Management (effects of water resource developments on public lands):

—Permits, leases, and easements for water control projects. 43 U.S.C. 1732(b) and 1761(a)(1) (43 CFR Part 2800).

• Bureau of Mines (effects of water resource developments and regulation on mineral resources, production and transportation).

• National Park Service (effects of water resource developments on Wild and Scenic River System, outdoor recreation areas, and National Park System areas):

—Consultations regarding water resource developments and effects on rivers established as units of the National Wild

49774 Federal Register / Vol. 49, No. 247 / Friday, December 21, 1984 / Rules and Regulations

and Scenic Rivers System and on those rivers designated for study as potential additions to that System. 16 U SC. 1278, *et seq.*
—Consultations about extent to which proposed recreational developments at hydroelectric projects conform to and are in accord with the State Comprehensive Outdoor Recreation Plan. 16 U.S.C. 470.

• Bureau of Reclamation (water storage and delivery projects and their effects: water policy analysis: impacts on State water management):
—Construction and operation of works and structures for storage, diversion and development of waters, including flood control, navigation and river-flow regulation and control in the 17 contiguous western States. 43 U.S.C. 391 *et seq.*

• Office of Surface Mining Reclamation and Enforcement (effects of water resource developments on surface coal mining and reclamation operations).

Department of Transportation

• Coast Guard (vessel, bridge, port, and waterway regulation and safety; navigational aids):
—Ports and waterways safety. 33 U.S.C. 1221 (33 CFR Part 160, *et seq.*).
—Construction and alterations of bridges and causeways over navigable waters. 33 U.S.C. 491, *et seq.;* 511, *et seq.;* 525, *et seq.,* and 535 (33 CFR Part 114, *et seq.*).

• Federal Highway Administration (effects of water resource developments on highways):
—Approval of Federal-aid highway end bridge projects involving navigable waters and channel changes. 23 U.S.C. 144 (23 CFR Part 650).
—Approval of toll bridge and ferry projects. 23 U.S.C. 129.

• Saint Lawrence Seaway Development Corporation (Seaway regulation):
—Construction, development, operation, and maintenance of the United States part of the Seaway. 33 U.S.C. 981–990 (33 CFR Parts 401–403).

Advisory Council on Historic Preservation (effects of water resource developments on historic properties).

Delaware River Basin Commission (management of water resources in the Delaware River basin):
—Review and approval of water resource projects. 75 Stat. 706 (18 CFR Parts 401–430).

Environmental Protection Agency (effects of water resource developments on pollution control):
—Review of permits for discharge of dredged or fill materials into waters of the United States. 33 U.S.C. 1344 (40 CFR Part 230).
—Guidelines controlling the discharge of dredged or fill material in waters of the U.S. including wetlands. (40 CFR Part 230).
—For other jurisdictional responsibilities, see PART I. B.—Water Quality.

Federal Emergency Management Agency (floodplain mapping and floodplain management; dam and levee safety; mitigation of natural hazards).

Federal Energy Regulatory Commission (effects of power projects):
—Regulation of development of water resources. 16 U.S.C. 791–825(r) (18 CFR Parts 4–25, 36, 131 and 141).

International Boundary and Water Commission, United States Section (maintenance, restoration and protection of banks of Rio Grande and Colorado River where they form the international boundary with Mexico; construction and operation of works and structures for storage and diversion of waters, including flood control on the Rio Grande and Colorado Rivers).

National Capital Planning Commission (water resource developments in Washington, D.C. area):
—Approval of taking lines end general development plans for parks in stream valleys in Maryland and Virginia tributaries to the Potomac and Anacostia Rivers. Act of May 29, 1930; 46 Stat. 482 as amended.

Susquehanna River Basin Commission (management of water resources in the Susquehanna River basin):
—Review and approval of water resource projects. 84 Stat. 1509 *et seq.* (18 CFR Parts 801–803).

Tennessee Valley Authority (water resource developments and regulation in the Tennessee Valley region):
—Construction of dams, appurtenant works, or other waterway improvement activities affecting navigation, flood control, public lands or reservations on the Tennessee River System. 16 U.S.C. 831(y–1).

D. Watershed Protection and Soil Conservation

Department of Agriculture

• Agricultural Research Service (technical aspects of water and soil conservation).
• Agricultural Stabilization and Conservation Service (soil conservation; cost-sharing farm and forest conservation programs).
• Extension Service (extension programs in agricultural conservation).
• Farmers Home Administration (effects of housing, community, and business programs, and farmer programs on soil and water conservation; conservation loan programs).
• Forest Service (soil and water conservation, and their effects on National Forests and Grasslands; forest and range soil rehabilitation):
—Emergency soil and water conservation programs. 16 U.S.C. 2202, *et seq.*
• Soil Conservation Service (soil surveys; technical assistance in areas of soil, water, and related resource conservation for landowners and landusers through several multi-functional programs):
—Grants for Watershed Protection and Flood Prevention Act activities. 16 U.S.C. 1001, *et seq.* (7 CFR Part 620, *et seq.*, and 660).
—Land conservation and land utilization program. 7 U.S.C. 1010, *et seq.*

Department of Commerce

• National Oceanic and Atmospheric Administration (weather research, river and flood forecasting).

Department of Defense

• Army Corps of Engineers (dredging, flood control, control of aquatic plants, shoreline stabilization):
—For jurisdictional responsibilities, see PART I. B.—Water Quality.

Department of Energy

• Office of Policy, Safety, and Environment (effects of energy policies, programs and projects on watersheds).

Department of the Interior

• Fish and Wildlife Service (effects of soil erosion end watershed protection on endangered species end critical habitats, and on fish and wildlife resources in general):
—Consultation regarding small watershed projects of the Soil Conservation Service under the Watershed Protection and Flood Protection and Flood Prevention Act. 16 U.S.C. 1006.
• Geological Survey (geology and hydrology in general; National Water Summary; erosion and sedimentation; engineering geology).
• Bureau of Indian Affairs (soil conservation and watershed protection on Indian lands).
• Bureau of Land Management (watershed protection and soil conservation on public lands).
• Bureau of Mines (hydraulic impacts of mining; revegetation end reclamation after mining).
• National Park Service (watershed protection and soil conservation on National Park System lands):
—Special use permits, grazing permits, permits to collect soil, rock, water, and plant specimens. 16 U.S.C. 1, *et seq.* (36 CFR Parts 1, 2 and 7).
• Bureau of Reclamation (soil and moisture conservation; hydrology; erosion control on public lands; water storage and delivery project; water resources research; analysis of Federal role in groundwater management).
• Office of Surface Mining Reclamation and Enforcement (effects of surface coal mining and reclamation operations on erosion, aquifers and alluvial valley floors).

Department of Transportation

• Federal Highway Administration (erosion control on highway projects; vegetation management on highway rights-of-way; highway drainage problems on watersheds).

Advisory Council on Historic Preservation (effects of watershed protection activities on historic properties).

Environmental Protection Agency (watershed protection and soil conservation in relation to pollution control).

Federal Emergency Management Agency (floodplain mapping and management, mitigation of natural hazards).

Federal Energy Regulatory Commission (effects of power projects):
—Regulation of development of water resources. 16 U.S.C. 791–825(r) (18 CFR Parts 4–25, 36, 131 and 141).

Federal Register / Vol. 49, No. 247 / Friday, December 21, 1984 / Rules and Regulations   **49775**

National Aeronautics and Space Administration (advanced technology for remote sensing of watersheds and soils).

Tennessee Valley Authority (watershed protection and soil conservation in the Tennessee Valley region).

E. Forest, Range, and Vegetative Resources (Includes Development, Production, Harvest and Transport of These Renewable Resources)

Department of Agriculture

• Agricultural Research Service (forest and range management).
• Agricultural Stabilization and Conservation Service (renewable resource conservation programs; Forestry Incentivee Program; Water Bank Program).
• Economic Research Service and Statistical Reporting Service (economic and statistical data on renewable resources).
• Extension Service (rural extension programs in renewable resource conservation and management).
• Farmers Home Administration (resource conservation and development loan programs).
• Forest Service (forest and grassland productivity in general; fire management; timber sale, free use of timber and other renewable resources. timber management activities and grazing habitat management in National Forests and Grasslands):
—Timber management. 16 U.S.C. 472, 528–531 and 1600–1614 (36 CFR Part 222).
—Grazing permits. 43 U.S.C. 1901 (36 CFR Part 222).
—Management and disposal of wild free-roaming horses and burros. 16 U.S.C. 1331–1340 (36 CFR Part 222, Subpart B).
• Soil Conservation Service (watershed resources protection; soil conservation technology).

Department of Commerce

• National Oceanic and Atmospheric Administration (coastal and marine resources management and development).

Department of Defense

• Army Corps of Engineers (effects of activities in the waters of the U.S. on renewable resources):
—For jurisdictional responsibilities, see PART I. B.—Water Quality.

Department of Energy

• Bonneville Power Administration (renewable resource development in the Pacific Northwest):
—Regional planning and conservation. 16 U.S.C. 839. *et seq.*

Department of the Interior

• Fish and Wildlife Service (effects of agriculture, forestry, and other renewable resource activities on endangered species and their critical habitats, National Wildlife Refuges and National Fish Hatchery systems, and other fish and wildlife resources).
• Geological Survey (effects of renewable resource activities on water resources and erosion; remote sensing of vegetation).
• Bureau of Indian Affairs (forest, range, and vegetative resources on Indian lands):

—Permits for grazing on Indian lands and on Federal lands under BIA jurisdiction. 5 U.S.C. 301; 25 U.S.C. 179, 345, 380, 393–394, 397, 402–403 and 413 (25 CFR Parts 166–166).
—Sale of timber from tribal and allotted lands. 25 U.S.C. 406–407, 413 and 466 (25 CFR Part 163).
—Permits, concessions, and leases on lands withdrawn or acquired in connection with Indian irrigation projects. 25 U.S.C. 390 (25 CFR Part 173).
—Leases for farming and other uses on Federal lands under BIA jurisdiction. 5 U.S.C. 301; 25 U.S.C. 380, 393–395, 397, 402–403, 413, 415, 477 and 635 (25 CFR Part 162).
• Bureau of Land Management (forest, range and vegetative resources on public lands):
—Permits for use of rangelands. 43 U.S.C. 315 (43 CFR Group 4100).
—Sale by contract of timber and other forest products. 30 U.S.C. 601, *et seq.*; 43 U.S.C. 315, 423, and 1181(a) (43 CFR Group 5400).
—Permits for free use of timber. 16 U.S.C. 604, *et seq.*; 30 U.S.C. 189; 48 U.S.C. 423 (43 CFR Part 5510).
—Management and control of wild free-roaming horses and burros and agreements for their adoption. 16 U.S.C. 1331–1340 (43 CFR Group 4700).
• National Park Service (effects of forest, range, and other vegetative resource activities on historical and recreational values and on National Park System areas):
—Permits for farming and grazing. 16 U.S.C. Chapter 1, *et seq.* (36 CFR Parts 1, 2 and 7).
• Bureau of Reclamation (water storage and delivery projects and irrigation projects in relation to forest, range, and other vegetative resource activities; evaluation of water policy alternatives):
—Sale of farm units on Federal irrigation projects (statutory authority appears in individual project authorizations).
• Office of Surface Mining Reclamation and Enforcement (effects of surface coal mining and reclamation operations on renewable resources):
—Protection of prime farmlands during surface coal mining and reclamation operations. 30 U.S.C. 1265 (30 CFR Parts 785.17 and 823).

Department of Transportation

• Federal Highway Administration (development of forest haul and access roads. effects of highway projects on forest, range, and other vegetative resources).

Advisory Council on Historic Preservation (effects of renewable resource activities on historic properties).

Environmental Protection Agency (effects of pollution, pesticide, and other environmental quality controls on forest, range, and other vegetative resources).

Interstate Commerce Commission (freight rates for renewable resources).

Tennessee Valley Authority (effects of hydro-electric and other power developments on forest, range, and other vegetative resources; biomass production and use).

F. Fish and Wildlife

Department of Agriculture

• Agricultural Research Service (basic and applied research in animal and plant protection).
• Agricultural Stabilization and Conservation Service (fish and wildlife in relation to agricultural conservation and the Water Bank Program).
• Animal and Plant Health Inspection Service (animal and plant health in general; control of pests and diseases):
—Prevention of importation or exportation of diseased livestock, or poultry. 21 U.S.C. 102–105, 111 and 132(a)–134(f).
• Farmers Home Administration (effects of farm housing, community, and business programs on fish and wildlife; conservation loan programs).
• Forest Service (fish and wildlife habitat management in National Forests and Grasslands; use of fire in habitat management):
—Fish and wildlife management (36 CFR Part 219.19).
—Management and disposal of wild free-roaming horses and burros. 16 U.S.C. 1331–1340 (36 CFR Part 222, Subpart B).
—Permits for hunting and fishing in refuge areas. 16 U.S.C. 551 and 683.
• Soil Conservation Service (fish and wildlife habitat, fish ponds, and raceways):
—Assistance to State and local sponsors, through a Small Watershed Program grant, for reservoir developments and stream modification projects including specific fish and wildlife habitat improvements. 16 U.S.C. 1001, *et seq.*, and 33 U.S.C. 701–1.

Department of Commerce

• National Oceanic and Atmospheric Administration (endangered species and critical habitats; coastal fish and wildlife management and protection):
—Approval and funding of State coastal zone management programs. 16 U.S.C. 1451, *et seq.* (15 CFR Parts 923 and 930).
—For other jurisdictional responsibilities, see PART IV. B.—Marine Resources.

Department of Defense

• Army Corps of Engineers (fish and wildlife mitigation measures at public works and navigable waterway projects, dredge and fill permits):
—For jurisdictional responsibilities, see PART I. B.—Water Quality.
• Department of the Air Force (bird/aircraft strike hazard reduction).

Department of Energy

• Bonneville Power Administration (fish and wildlife management and enhancement on power projects in the Pacific Northwest):
—Regional planning and conservation. 16 U.S.C. 839, *et seq.*

Department of the Interior

• Fish and Wildlife Service (endangered species and their critical habitats; management of effects on fish and wildlife in general):

49776   Federal Register / Vol. 49, No. 247 / Friday, December 21, 1984 / Rules and Regulations

—Permits to take bald and golden eagles for scientific, religious and other purposes. 16 U.S.C. 668(a) (50 CFR Part 22).

—Permits for the taking and importation of marine mammals. 16 U.S.C. 1361, et seq. (50 CFR Part 18).

—Permits to export/import and to take for scientific and other purposes endangered or threatened wildlife and plants. 16 U.S.C. 1531, et seq. (50 CFR Part 17).

—Permits for the importation of injurious mammals, birds, fish and other wildlife. 18 U.S.C. 42-44 (40 CFR Part 16.22).

—Permits for export/import and interstate transportation of wildlife. 18 U.S.C. 42, et seq. (50 CFR Part 14).

—Permits for the banding and marking of migratory birds. 16 U.S.C. 703-711 (50 CFR Part 21.22).

—Consultations regarding Federal projects that may affect an estuarine area. 15 U.S.C. 1224.

—Permits to perform taxidermy services on migratory birds, nests and eggs for commercial uses. 16 U.S.C. 704 (50 CFR Part 21.24).

—Permits for special purpose uses of migratory birds. 16 U.S.C. 701, et seq. (50 CFR Part 21.27).

—Certificates or permits of exception to Convention on International Trade in Endangered Species. 16 U.S.C. 1531-1543 (50 CFR Part 23).

—Consultations regarding projects which may effect any threatened or endangered species or its critical habitats. 16 U.S.C. 1531, et seq. (50 CFR Part 402).

—Determination of critical habitats for endangered and threatened species of fish, wildlife, and plants. 16 U.S.C. 1531, et seq. (50 CFR Parts 17, 402 and 424).

—Endangered species exemption process. 16 U.S.C. 1531, et seq. (50 CFR Parts 450-453).

—Consultation regarding Federal or federally permitted projects which affect fish and wildlife resources under the Fish and Wildlife Coordination Act. 16 U.S.C. 661, et seq.

—U.S. Fish and Wildlife Service Mitigation Policy. 16 U.S.C. 661-687(e), 742(a)-754 and 1001-1009 (see 46 FR 7644 of Jan. 23, 1981).

—Restoration and enhancement of anadromous fishery resources through grants for fish ladders, new anadromous fish hatcheries, new fishways, etc. 16 U.S.C. 742(a)-742(j) (50 CFR Part 401).

—Improvement of sport fishery resources through grants to States under the Dingell-Johnson (D–J) Program. 16 U.S.C. 777-777(k) (50 CFR Part 80).

—Restoration and enhancement of wildlife populations and resources through grants to States under the Pittman-Robertson (P-R) Program. 16 U.S.C. 669, et seq. (50 CFR Part 80).

—Approval of conversion of use for State lands acquired, developed or improved with grants under the (1) Pittman-Robertson Act, (2) Dingell-Johnson Act, (3) Endangered Species Act and/or (4) Anadromous Fish Conservation Act. For (1)—16 U.S.C. 669 (50 CFR Parts 80.4 and 80.14); for (2)—16 U.S.C. 777 (50 CFR Parts 80.4 and 80.14); (3)—16 U.S.C. 1535; and for (4)—16 U.S.C. 757 (a) and (b).

—Land acquisition, management and other activities for endangered and threatened

species through grants to States. 16 U.S.C. 1531-1543 (50 CFR Part 81).

—Consultation concerning the protection of fish and wildlife which may be impacted by transportation projects. 49 U.S.C. 303.

• Geological Survey (water quality and quantity in relation to fish and wildlife resources).

• Bureau of Indian Affairs (fish and wildlife resource management on Indian lands; off-reservation treaty fishing).

• Bureau of Land Management (fish and wildlife management on public lands; wild horses and burros; endangered species and raptors; effects on fish and wildlife of power lines and other major projects crossing public lands):

—Management and disposal of wild free-roaming horses and burros. 16 U.S.C. 1331-1340 (43 CFR Part 4700).

• National Park Service (fishing, hunting and other outdoor recreational pursuits, fish and wildlife management in National Park System areas):

—Permits for collecting animal specimens from National Park System areas. 16 U.S.C. 1, et seq. (36 CFR Part 2).

—Licenses and permits for sport or commercial fishing in certain National Park System areas. (36 CFR Part 2).

—Disposition of surplus animals from National Park System areas. (36 CFR Part 10).

• Bureau of Reclamation (fish and wildlife management on water storage and delivery projects; hunting and fishing on project lands; mitigation measures; limnology).

• Office of Surface Mining Reclamation and Enforcement (effects of surface mining and reclamation operations on fish and wildlife).

Department of Health and Human Services

• Public Health Service: Centers for Disease Control (fish and wildlife in relation to human health); Food and Drug Administration (contamination of fish and shellfish with toxics).

Department of State (international issues concerning fish and wildlife, including migratory birds and marine mammals).

Department of Transportation

• Office of the Secretary (general effects of transportation projects on fish and wildlife refuges):

—Approval of transportation programs or projects that require the use of or have a significant impact on wildlife and waterfowl refuges. 49 U.S.C. 303.

• Federal Highway Administration (effects of highway projects on fish and wildlife habitat, and wildlife and waterfowl refuges):

—Preservation of park and recreation areas, and wildlife and waterfowl refuges: 23 U.S.C. 136 (23 CFR Part 771).

• Federal Aviation Administration (bird-aircraft strike hazard reduction).

• Coast Guard (enforcement of laws affecting Fishery Management Zones).

Environmental Protection Agency (effects of pollution control and water quality on fish and wildlife).

Marine Mammal Commission (conservation and protection of marine mammals and their habitat):

—Consultation and oversight responsibility for activities affecting marine mammals. 16 U.S.C. 1402.

—Review of permit applications for taking and importation of marine mammals and marine mammal products. 16 U.S.C. 1371(a).

National Science Foundation (conservation of antarctic animals, plants, and ecosystems):

—Permits for the taking or collecting of Antarctic animals and plants, and for entry into certain designated areas. 16 U.S.C. 2401, et seq. (45 CFR Part 670)

Tennessee Valley Authority (fish and wildlife management and conservation in the Tennessee Valley).

G. Non-Energy Mineral Resources

Department of Agriculture

• Forest Service (mineral resources development in National Forests and Grasslands; reclamation of disturbed lands):

—Permits and rights-of-way on National Forest System lands. 16 U.S.C. 471-472, 476, 495, 497-498, 525, 528, 531-538, 551, 572 and 580 (36 CFR Parts 212, 251 and 261).

—Surface use of public domain lands under U.S. mining laws. 16 U.S.C. 478 and 551 (36 CFR Part 228).

—Mineral development on acquired lands. For solid (hardrock) minerals—16 U.S.C. 520 (43 CFR Part 3500); for phosphate, sodium, potassium and sulphur—30 U.S.C. 351, et seq.

• Soil Conservation Service (abandoned mine land and mine reclamation).

Department of Commerce

• National Oceanic and Atmospheric Administration (air and water pollution from mining, offshore and coastal mining; port planning, management and protection of coastal and marine resources):

—Approval of licenses for deep seabed hard mineral exploration and development. 30 U.S.C. 1401, et seq. (15 CFR Part 970).

Department of Defense

• Army Corps of Engineers (effects of mineral development on navigable waters):

—For jurisdictional responsibilities, see PART I, B.—Water Quality.

Department of Housing and Urban Development

• Office of Housing (subsidence from mining operations and soil factors related to housing).

Department of the Interior

• Fish and Wildlife Service (effects of mineral development on endangered species and their critical habitats, National Wildlife Refuge and National Fish Hatchery Systems, and other fish and wildlife resources):

—Easements/permits for transmission line, pipelines and other rights-of-way across National Wildlife Refuge and National Fish Hatchery System land. For refuges—16 U.S.C. 668 dd, et seq.; for hatcheries—43

U.S.C. 931 c and (50 CFR Parts 25.41 and 29.21).
—Permits for rights-of-way across National Wildlife Monuments (Alaska only). 16 U.S.C. 432, 460(k-3) and 742(f) (50 CFR Part 96).
• Geological Survey (mineral resources in general, with emphasis on strategic and critical minerals; mineral resources assessment on public lands).
• Bureau of Indian Affairs (affects on Indian lands of mineral operations):
—Leases and permits on Indian lands. 25 U.S.C. 380, 393-395, 397, 402-403, 413, 415, 477 and 635 (25 CFR Part 162).
—Rights-of-way over Indian lands. 25 U.S.C. 311-321 and 323-328 (25 CFR Part 169).
—Mining leases on Indian lands. 25 U.S.C. 358, 396, 476-477 and 509 (25 CFR Parts 211-215 and 226-227).
—Permits for surface exploration and reclamation. 25 U.S.C. 355, 396, 473 and 501-502 (25 CFR Part 216).
• Bureau of Land Management (mineral development on public lands):
—Easements/leases/permits for use, occupancy and development of public lands. 43 U.S.C. 1732 (43 CFR Subchapters 2000 and 3000).
—Exploration licenses for leasable minerals on unleased land. 30 U.S.C. 181. et seq. and 201(b) (43 CFR Parts 3400 and 3480).
—Leases for phosphate, sodium, potassium, etc., exploration and mining. 30 U.S.C. 181, et seq. (43 CFR Group 3500 and Part 3570).
—Permits for sand, stone and gravel. 30 U.S.C. 601 and 602.
—Leases, permits and licenses for mining in Wild and Scenic River System areas. 16 U.S.C. 1280 (each area has special Federal Regulations).
—Concurrence for placer mining use of the surface of public lands withdrawn or reserved for power development or for a power site. 30 U.S.C. 621 (43 CFR Part 3730).
—Leases and permits for sulfur in Louisiana and New Mexico. 30 U.S.C. 271, et seq. (43 CFR Group 3500).
—Easements/permits for rights-of-way. 30 U.S.C. 185 and 43 U.S.C. 1701, et seq. (43 CFR Parts 2800-2880).
• Minerals Management Service (mineral development on the outer continental shelf):
—Leases for minerals on the outer continental shelf. 43 U.S.C. 1331-1343 (30 CFR Parts 250, 251, 252 and 256).
—Permits for exploration and development activities on Federal leases on the outer continental shelf. 43 U.S.C. 1331, et seq. (30 CFR Parts 250 and 251).
—Permits for geological and geophysical exploration on the outer continental shelf. 43 U.S.C. 1334 (30 CFR Part 251).
—Approval of geological geophysical exploration plans. 43 U.S.C. 1340 (30 CFR Part 251).
—Permits for artificial islands, platforms, and other fixed structures on any Federal or State outer continental shelf lease. 43 U.S.C. 1334-1335 (30 CFR 250.16 and 250.19).
• Bureau of Mines (mining, milling, and mineral land assessments):

—Agreements to dispose of helium of the United States. 43 U.S.C. 1201 and 30 U.S.C. 1 et seq. (43 CFR Part 16).
• National Park Service (effects of mineral development on public, park, recreation and cultural/historical resources and values, and on National Park System areas):
—Permits, leases and easements for rights-of-way, grazing and other uses on National Park System areas. 16 U.S.C. 1, et seq. (36 CFR Parts 9 and 14).
—Leases, permits and licenses for mining on National Park System lands involved in National Wild and Scenic Rivers System. 16 U.S.C. 1280.
—Access permits for mining activity within the National Park System. 16 U.S.C. 1902 and 1908; 30 U.S.C. 21, et seq. (36 CFR Part 9).
• Bureau of Reclamation (effects of mineral development on water storage and delivery projects):
—Easements/permits for access, pipeline, and other rights-of-way. 43 U.S.C. 3571.

Department of Labor
• Mining Safety and Health Administration (safety and health issues in mining operations).
• Occupational Safety and Health Administration (general worker safety and health issues).
Department of State (international aspects of mineral development):
—Facilities for export/import of minerals. Executive Order 11423.

Department of Transportation
• Coast Guard (vessel transport of minerals):
—Ports and waterways safety. 33 U.S.C. 1221 (33 CFR Part 160, et seq.).
• Maritime Administration (dry bulk shipping of coal and other minerals in the inland waterways, domestic ocean, Great Lakes, and U.S. foreign trades).
Advisory Council on Historic Preservation (effects of mineral development activities on historic properties).

Environmental Protection Agency (pollution control and other environmental effects of minerals development):
—For jurisdictional responsibilities, see PART I—POLLUTION CONTROL.

H. Natural Resource Conservation

Department of Agriculture
• Agricultural Stabilization and Conservation Service (natural resource conservation programs; Forestry Incentives Program; Water Bank Program).
• Agricultural Research Service (research in technical aspects of soil and water conservation and forest and range management).
• Extension Service (rural area extension programs in conservation).
• Farmers Home Administration (farmer loan programs related to natural resource conservations).
• Forest Service (conservation of forest and rangeland resources; use of fire as a management tool).

• Soil Conservation Service (soil, water, and related resources conservation technology):
—Land conservation and utilization program. 7 U.S.C. 1010, et seq.
—Watershed protection, conservation and utilization of land and water resources. 16 U.S.C. 1001, et seq.
—Soil and water resources conservation. 16 U.S.C. 2001, et seq.

Department of Commerce
• National Oceanic and Atmospheric Administration (coastal and marine resources management and protection; national estuarine and marine sanctuaries; coastal energy facility planning and siting in State coastal zone management programs).

Department of Energy
• Bonneville Power Administration (resource conservation in the Pacific Northwest):
—Regional planning and conservation. 16 U.S.C. 839, et seq.
• Office of Policy, Safety, and Environment (general energy policies, programs and projects in relation to conservation).

Department of the Interior
• Fish and Wildlife Service (conservation of, and effects of conservation on, endangered species and their critical habitats, and other fish and wildlife resources; conservation in National Wildlife Refuge and National Fish Hatchery System areas).
• Geological Survey (conservation of water and mineral resources).
• Bureau of Indian Affairs (conservation of Indian lands).
• Bureau of Land Management (conservation on public lands).
• Minerals Management Service (conservation in relation to minerals management activities on the outer continental shelf).
• Bureau of Mines (conservation of mineral resources and land, air, and water resources associated with mineral deposits).
• National Park Service (conservation in relation to urban parks, outdoor recreation, historical and cultural resources, National Trails System, Wild and Scenic Rivers System, and the National Park System).
• Bureau of Reclamation (conservation in relation to water storage and delivery projects, water resources, and desalinization; Soil and Moisture Conservation Program; development of water policy options; National Water Summary).
• Office of Surface Mining Reclamation and Enforcement (conservation in relation to surface coal mining and reclamation operations).
Environmental Protection Agency (resource recovery from wastes; pollution and other environmental controls):
—Solid Waste Disposal Act permits. 42 U.S.C. 321 et seq., and 6901, et seq. (40 CFR Parts 122, 123 and 124).
—Guidelines on solid waste collection and storage for Federal assistance. 42 U.S.C. 6907 (40 CFR Part 243).

49778 **Federal Register** / Vol. 49, No. 247 / Friday, December 21, 1984 / Rules and Regulations

—Resource recovery facilities. 42 U.S.C. 6907 (40 CFR Part 245).
—Materials recovery and solid waste management guidelines for source separation. 42 U.S.C. 6907 (40 CFR Part 246).
—Solid waste management guidelines for beverage containers. 42 U.S.C. 6907 (40 CFR Part 244).

Federal Energy Regulatory Commission (relation of conservation to hydroelectric power development and natural gas facilities).

National Science Foundation (conservation of antarctic animals, plants, and ecosystems):
—Permits for the taking or collecting of antarctic animals and plants, and for entry into certain designated areas. 16 U.S.C. 2401, *et seq.* (45 CFR Part 670).

Tennessee Valley Authority (soil and other natural resource conservation in the Tennessee Valley region).

Appendix III—Federal and Federal-State Agency Offices for Receiving and Commenting on Other Agencies' Environmental Documents

DEPARTMENTS

Department of Agriculture

Send request to the Departmental office for comments on environmental documents about legislation, regulations, national program proposals or other major policy issues. For other comment requests, send to the listed office of the departmental components.

Assistant Secretary for Natural Resources and Environment, Department of Agriculture; Attn: Executive Secretary, Natural Resources and Environment Committee; Room 242-W, Administration Bldg., 14th St. and Independence Ave., SW. Wash., D.C. 20250-0001. (202) 447-5166.

Department of Agriculture Components

Agricultural Research Service: Deputy Administrator, National Program Staff, Agricultural Research Service, Department of Agriculture, Room 125, Bldg. 005, Agricultural Research Center-West, Beltsville, MD 20705-2350. (301) 344-3084.

Agricultural Stabilization and Conservation Service: Chief, Planning and Evaluation Branch, Conservation and Environmental Protection Division, Agricultural Stabilization and Conservation Service, Department of Agriculture, Room 4714, South Agriculture Bldg., P.O. Box 2415; Wash., D.C. 20013-2415. (202) 447-3264.

Animal and Plant Health Inspection Service: Environmental Coordinator, Animal and Plant Health Inspection Service, Department of Agriculture, Room 600, Federal Bldg., 6505 Belcrest Road, Hyattsville, MD 20782-2058. (301) 436-8896.

Economic Research Service: Director, Natural Resource Economics Division, Economic Research Service, Department of Agriculture, Room 412, GHI Bldg., 500 12th St., SW, Wash., D.C. 20250-0001. (202) 447-8239.

Extension Service: Deputy Administrator, Natural Resources and Rural Development, Extension Service, Department of Agriculture,

Room 3909, South Agriculture Bldg., 14th St. and Independence Ave., SW, Wash., D.C. 20250-0001. (202) 447-7947.

Farmers Home Administration: Environmental Protection Specialist, Program Support Staff, Farmers Home Administration, Department of Agriculture, Room 6309, South Agriculture Bldg., 14th St. and Independence Ave., SW, Wash., D.C. 20250-0001. (202) 382-9819.

Food Safety and Inspection Service: Director, Regulations Office, Food Safety and Inspection Service, Department of Agriculture, Room 2940, South Agriculture Bldg., 14th St. and Independence Ave., SW, Wash., D.C. 20250-0001. (202) 447-3317.

Rural Electrification Administration: Environmental Policy Specialist, Engineering Standards Division, Rural Electrification Administration, Department of Agriculture, Room 1257, South Agriculture Bldg., 14th St. and Independence Ave., SW, Wash., D.C. 20250-0001. (202) 382-0097.

Soil Conservation Service: National Environmental Coordinator, Environmental Activities Branch, Ecological Sciences Division, Soil Conservation Service, Department of Agriculture, Room 6155, South Agriculture Bldg., P.O. Box 2890, Wash., D.C. 20013-2890. (202) 447-4912.

U.S. Forest Service

For actions of national or inter-regional scope, send comment request and documents to Wash., D.C. For actions of a regional, State or local scope, send comment request and documents to the Regional Forester and Area Director in whose area the proposed action (e.g., highway or water resource construction project) will take place.

Director, Environmental Coordination Staff, Forest Service, Department of Agriculture, Room 4204, South Agriculture Bldg., P.O. Box 2417, Wash., D.C. 20013-2417. (202) 447-4708.

Region 1. Northern Region (northern ID, MT, ND, and northwest SD): Regional Forester, Northern Region, Forest Service, USDA, Federal Bldg., P.O. Box 7669, Missoula, MT 59807-7669. (406) 329-3011; (FTS) 585-3316.

Region 2. Rocky Mountain Region (CO, KS, NE, SD, and eastern WY): Regional Forester, Rocky Mountain Region, Forest Service, USDA, 11177 W. 8th Ave., Box 25127, Lakewood, CO 80225-0127. (303) 234-3711.

Region 3. Southwestern Region (AZ, and NM): Regional Forester, Southwestern Region, Forest Service, USDA, Federal Bldg., 517 Gold Ave., SW, Albuquerque, NM 87102-3156. (505) 476-3300.

Region 4. Intermountain Region (southern ID, NV, UT, and western WY): Regional Forester, Intermountain Region, Forest Service, USDA, Federal Bldg., 324 25th St., Ogden, UT 84401-2310. (801) 625-5605; (FTS) 586-5605.

Region 5. Pacific Southwest Region (CA and HI): Regional Forester, Pacific Southwest Region, Forest Service, USDA, 630 Sansome St., San Francisco, CA 94111-2206. (415) 556-4310.

Region 6. Pacific Northwest Region (OR and WA): Regional Forester, Pacific Northwest Region, Forest Service, USDA, 319 SW Pine St., P.O. Box 3623, Portland, OR 97208-3623. (503) 221-3625; (FTS) 423-3625.

Region 8. Southern Region (AL, AR, FL, GA, KY, LA, MS, NC, OK, SC, TN, TX, VA, PR, and VI): Regional Forester, Southern Region, Forest Service, USDA, 1720 Peachtree Road, NW, Atlanta, GA 30367-9101. (404) 881-4177; (FTS) 257-4177.

Region 9. Eastern Region (CT, DE, IA, IL, IN, MA, MD, ME, MI, MN, MO, NH, NJ, NY, OH, PA, RI, VT, WI, and WV): Regional Forester, Eastern Region, Forest Service, USDA, Henry S. Reuss Federal Plaza, Suite 500, 310 W. Wisconsin Ave., Milwaukee, WI 53203-2211. (414) 291-3693; (FTS) 362-3600.

Region 10. Alaska Region (AK): Regional Forester, Alaska Region, Forest Service, USDA, Federal Office Building, Box 1628, Juneau, AK 99802-1628. (907) 586-7263.

Northeastern State and Private Forestry Area (Same as Region 9, above): Director, Northeastern State and Private Forestry Area, Forest Service, USDA, 370 Reed Road, Broomall, PA 19008-4088. (215) 461-3125; (FTS) 489-3125.

(In Regions 1 through 6, 8 and 10, State and private activities of the Forest Service are handled at regional offices.)

Department of Commerce

Chief, Ecology and Conservation Division, Office of Policy and Planning, National Oceanic and Atmospheric Administration, Department of Commerce, Room H6111, Herbert Hoover Bldg., 14th St. and Constitution Ave., NW, Wash., D.C. 20230-0001. (202) 377-5181.

Department of Defense

Send comment request and documents about legislation, regulations, national program proposals or other major policy issues to Department of Defense, except for the Corps of Engineers. For other comment requests, send to the listed office of the departmental components.

Director, Environmental Policy, Office of the Assistant Secretary of Defense (Manpower, Installations and Statistics), Department of Defense, Room 3D833, The Pentagon, Wash., D.C. 20301-0001. (202) 695-7820.

Department of Defense Components

Defense Logistics Agency: Staff Director, Office of Installation Services and Environmental Protection, Defense Logistics Agency, Department of Defense, Cameron Station, Room 4D446, Alexandria, VA 22304-6100. (202) 274-6124.

Department of the Air Force: Deputy for Environment and Safety, Office of the Deputy Assistant Secretary for Installations, Environment and Safety, Department of the Air Force, Room 4C916, The Pentagon, Wash., D.C. 20330-0001. (202) 697-9297.

Department of the Army: Chief, Army Environmental Office; Attn: HQDA (DAEN-ZCE); Department of the Army, Room 1E676, The Pentagon, Wash., D.C. 20310-2600. (202) 694-3434.

Department of the Navy: Director, Environmental Protection and Occupational Safety and Health Division (OP-453), Office of the Chief of Naval Operations, Department of the Navy, Bldg. 200, Room S-3, Washington Navy Yard, Wash., D.C. 20374-0001. (202) 433-2428.

U.S. Marine Corps: Head, Land Resources and Environmental Branch, Code: LFL, U.S. Marine Corps, Commonwealth Bldg., Room 614, 1300 Wilson Blvd., Arlington, VA. (202) 694-9237/38. MAILING ADDRESS: Commandant, U.S. Marine Corps; ATTN: Land Resources and Environmental Branch, Code: LFL; Wash., D.C. 20380-0001.

Corps of Engineers

Send comment request and documents about legislation, regulations, national program proposals or other major policy issues to:

Assistant Director of Civil Works, Environmental Programs (DAEN-CWZ-P), Office of the Chief of Engineers, Room 7233, Pulaski Bldg., 20 Massachusetts Ave., NW, Wash., D.C. 20314-1000. (202) 272-0103.

Send comment request and documents for other Federal actions to the Corps' District Engineer or the Division Engineer, in the case of Pacific Ocean and New England Division, in whose area the action will take place. If the action involves more than one Corps District, increase number of copies accordingly but send all to District Engineer primarily involved. For a map showing the Corps' Division and District Boundaries, contact the Director of Civil Works cited above.

• Division Engineer, U.S. Army Corps of Engineers, New England Division, 424 Trapelo Rd., Waltham, MA 02254-9194. (617) 647-8220; (FTS) 839-7220.

• District Engineer, U.S. Army Corps of Engineers, New York District, 26 Federal Plaza, New York, NY 10278-0022. (212) 264-0100.

• District Engineer, U.S. Army Corps of Engineers, Philadelphia District, U.S. Custom House, 2nd and Chestnut Sts., Philadelphia, PA 19106-2912. (215) 597-4848.

• District Engineer, U.S. Army Corps of Engineers, Baltimore District, P.O. Box 1715, Baltimore MD 21203-1715. (301) 962-4545; (FTS) 922-4545.

• District Engineer, U.S. Army Corps of Engineers, Norfolk District, 803 Front St., Norfolk, VA 23510-1096. (804) 441-3601; (FTS) 827-3601.

• District Engineer, U.S. Army Corps of Engineers, Wilmington District, P.O. Box 1890, Wilmington, NC 28402-1890. (919) 343-4501; (FTS) 671-4501.

• District Engineer, U.S. Army Corps of Engineers, Charleston District, P.O. Box 919, Charleston, SC 29402-0919. (803) 724-4229; (FTS) 677-4229.

• District Engineer, U.S. Army Corps of Engineers, Savannah District, P.O. Box 889, Savannah, GA 31402-0889. (912) 944-5224; (FTS) 248-5224.

• District Engineer, U.S. Army Corps of Engineers, Jacksonville District, P.O. Box 4970, Jacksonville, FL 32201-4970. (904) 791-2241; (FTS) 946-2241.

• District Engineer, U.S. Army Corps of Engineers, Mobile District, P.O. Box 2288, Mobile, AL 36628-0001. (205) 690-2511; (FTS) 537-2511.

• District Engineer, U.S. Army Corps of Engineers, Vicksburg District, P.O. Box 60, Vicksburg, MS 39180-0060. (601) 634-5010; (FTS) 542-5010.

• District Engineer, U.S. Army Corps of Engineers, New Orleans District, P.O. Box 60267, New Orleans, LA 70160-0267. (504) 838-2204.

• District Engineer, U.S. Army Corps of Engineers, Memphis District, B-314 Clifford Davis Federal Bldg., Memphis, TN 38103-1816. (901) 521-3221; (FTS) 222-3221.

• District Engineer, U.S. Army Corps of Engineers, St. Louis District, 210 Tucker Blvd. North, St. Louis, MO 63101-1947. (314) 263-5660; (FTS) 273-5660.

• District Engineer, U.S. Army Corps of Engineers, Nashville District, P.O. Box 1070, Nashville, TN 37202-1070. (615) 251-5626; (FTS) 852-5626.

• District Engineer, U.S. Army Corps of Engineers, Louisville District, P.O. Box 59, Louisville, KY 40201-0059. (502) 582-5601; (FTS) 352-5601.

• District Engineer, U.S. Army Corps of Engineers, Huntington District, 502 8th St., Huntington, WV 25701-2070. (304) 529-5395; (FTS) 942-5395.

• District Engineer, U.S. Army Corps of Engineers, Pittsburgh District, William S. Moorehead Federal Bldg., 1000 Liberty Ave., Pittsburgh, PA 15222-4004. (412) 644-6800; (FTS) 722-6800.

• District Engineer, U.S. Army Corps of Engineers, Buffalo District, 1776 Niagara St. Buffalo, NY 14207-3199. (716) 876-5454, x2200; (FTS) 473-2200.

• District Engineer, U.S. Army Corps of Engineers, Chicago District, 219 S. Dearborn St., Chicago, IL 60604-1702. (312) 353-6400; (FTS) 353-6400.

• District Engineer, U.S. Army Corps of Engineers, Rock Island District, Clock Tower Bldg., P.O. Box 2004, Rock Island, IL 61204-2004. (309) 788-6361, x8224; (FTS) 386-6011.

• District Engineer, U.S. Army Corps of Engineers, Detroit District, P.O. Box 1027, Detroit, MI 48231-1027. (313) 226-6762.

• District Engineer, U.S. Army Corps of Engineers, St. Paul District, 1135 USPO & Custom House, St. Paul, MN 55101-1479. (612) 725-7501.

• District Engineer, U.S. Army Corps of Engineers, Kansas City District, 700 Federal Bldg., 601 E. 12th St., Kansas City, MO 64106-2826. (816) 374-3201; (FTS) 758-3201.

• District Engineer, U.S. Army Corps of Engineers, Omaha District, 6014 USPO and Courthouse, Omaha, NE 68102-4910. (402) 221-3900; (FTS) 864-3900.

• District Engineer, U.S. Army Corps of Engineers, Little Rock District, P.O. Box 867, Little Rock, AR 72203-0867. (501) 378-5531; (FTS) 740-5531.

• District Engineer, U.S. Army Corps of Engineers, Tulsa District, P.O. Box 61, Tulsa, OK 74121-0061. (918) 581-7311; (FTS) 745-7311.

• District Engineer, U.S. Army Corps of Engineers, Galveston District, P.O. Box 1229, Galveston, TX 77553-1229. (409) 766-3006; (FTS) 527-6006.

• District Engineer, U.S. Army Corps of Engineers, Fort Worth District, P.O. Box 17300, Fort Worth, TX 76102-0300. (817) 334-2300.

• District Engineer, U.S. Army Corps of Engineers, Albuquerque District, P.O. Box 1580, Albuquerque, NM 87103-1580. (505) 766-2732; (FTS) 474-2732.

• District Engineer, U.S. Army Corps of Engineers, Los Angeles District, P.O. Box 2711, Los Angeles, CA 90053-2325. (213) 688-5300; (FTS) 798-5300.

• District Engineer, U.S. Army Corps of Engineers, San Francisco District, 211 Main Street, San Francisco, CA 94105-1905. (415) 974-0358; (FTS) 454-0358.

• District Engineer, U.S. Army Corps of Engineers, Sacramento District, 650 Capitol Mall, Sacramento, CA 95814-4708. (916) 440-2232; (FTS) 448-2232.

• District Engineer, U.S. Army Corps of Engineers, Portland District, P.O. Box 2946, Portland, OR 97208-2946. (503) 221-6000; (FTS) 423-6000.

• District Engineer, U.S. Army Corps of Engineers, Walla Walla District, Bldg. 602, City-County Airport, Walla Walla, WA 99362-9265. (509) 525-6509, ext. 100; (FTS) 434-6509.

• District Engineer, U.S. Army Corps of Engineers, Seattle District, P.O. Box C-3755, Seattle, WA 98124-2255. (206) 764-3690; (FTS) 399-3690.

• District Engineer, U.S. Army Corps of Engineers, Alaska District, Pouch 898, Anchorage, AK 99506-0001. (907) 279-1132.

• Division Engineer, U.S. Army Corps of Engineers, Pacific Ocean Division, Building 230, Ft. Shafter, HA. 96858-4910. (808) 438-1500.

Department of Energy

Director, Office of Environmental Compliance (PE-25), Department of Energy, Room 4G-085, Forrestal Building, 1000 Independence Ave., SW, Wash., D.C. 20585-0001. (202) 252-4600.

Department of Health and Human Services

Departmental Environmental Officer, Office of Management Analysis and Systems, Department of Health and Human Services, Room 542 E. Hubert H. Humphrey Bldg., 200 Independence Ave., SW, Wash., D.C. 20201-0001. (202) 245-7354.

Department of Housing and Urban Development

Send comment request and documents about legislation, regulations, national program proposals and other major policy issues to Wash., D.C. Send comment request and documents about other Federal actions to the Regional Environmental Officer in whose area the action will take place.

Director, Office of Environment and Energy, Department of Housing and Urban Development, Room 7154, HUD Bldg., 451 Seventh St., SW, Wash., D.C. 20410-0001, (202) 755-7894.

Federal Region I: Regional Environmental Officer, U.S. Department of Housing and Urban Development, Bulfinch Bldg., 15 New Chardon St., Boston, MA 02114-7596, (617) 223-1620.

Federal Region II: Regional Environmental Officer, U.S. Department of Housing and Urban Development, 26 Federal Plaza, New York, NY 10278-0022, (212) 264-5806.

Federal Region III: Regional Environmental Officer, U.S. Department of Housing and Urban Development, Curtis Building, 148 S. 6th St., Philadelphia, PA 19106-3313, (215) 597-3903.

Federal Region IV: Regional Environmental Officer, U.S. Department of Housing and Urban Development, Richard B. Russell

49780   Federal Register / Vol. 49, No. 247 / Friday, December 21, 1984 / Rules and Regulations

Federal Bldg., 75 Spring St., SW, Atlanta, GA 30303-3309, (404) 221-5197; (FTS) 242-5197.

Federal Region V: Regional Environmental Officer, U.S. Department of Housing and Urban Development, 300 S. Wacker Dr., Chicago, IL 60606-6606, (312) 353-1696.

Federal Region VI: Regional Environmental Officer, U.S. Department of Housing and Urban Development, 221 W. Lancaster Ave., P.O. Box 2905, Ft. Worth, TX 76113-2905, (817) 870-5482; (FTS) 728-5482.

Federal Region VII: Regional Environmental Officer, U.S. Department of Housing and Urban Development, Professional Bldg., 1103 Grand Ave., Kansas City, MO 64106-2496, (816) 374-3192; (FTS) 758-3192.

Federal Region VIII: Regional Environmental Officer, U.S. Department of Housing and Urban Development, Executive Tower Bldg., 1405 Curtis St., Denver, CO 80202-2394, (303) 837-3102; (FTS) 327-3102.

Federal Region IX: Regional Environmental Officer, U.S. Department of Housing and Urban Development, 450 Golden Gate Ave., P.O. Box 36003, San Francisco, CA 94102-3448, (415) 556-6642.

Federal Region X: Regional Environmental Officer, U.S. Department of Housing and Urban Development, 3051 Arcade Plaza Building, 1321 Second Ave., Seattle, WA 98101-2058, (206) 442-4521; (FTS) 399-4521.

Department of the Interior

Director, Office of Environmental Project Review, Department of the Interior, Room 4241, Interior Bldg., 18th and C Sts., NW, Wash., D.C. 20240-0001, (202) 343-3891.

Department of Labor

Director, Office of Regulatory Economics, Assistant Secretary for Policy, Department of Labor, Room S-2312, Frances Perkins Bldg., 200 Constitution Ave., NW, Wash., D.C. 20210-0001, (202) 523-6197.

Department of State

Director, Office of Environment and Health, Department of State, Room 4325, State Department Bldg., 21st and C Sts., NW, Wash., D.C. 20520-0001, (202) 632-9266.

Department of Transportation

For documents about legislation, regulations, national program proposals and any action with national policy implications, send comment request and documents to DOT's Office of Economics shown below. For an action which may involve more than one modal administration within DOT, send comment request and documents to the DOT Regional Secretarial Representative in whose area the action will take place. If the action involves more than one region, send request to each Regional Secretarial Representative (DOT will coordinate to provide a consolidated response). For an action which may involve only one modal administration, send comment request and documents to the regional office of the modal administration in whose area the action will take place but, if in doubt, send material to DOT's Regional Secretarial Representative.

Deputy Director for Environment and Policy Review, Office of Economics, Department of Transportation, Room 10309,

Nassif Bldg., 400 Seventh St., SW, Wash., D.C. 20590-0001, (202) 426-4357.

DOT Regional Secretarial Representatives

Federal Regions I, II and III: Secretarial Representative, U.S. Department of Transportation, Independence Bldg., Suite 1000, 430 Walnut St., Philadelphia, PA 19106-3714, (215) 597-9430.

Federal Region IV: Secretarial Representative, U.S. Department of Transportation, Suite 515, 1720 Peachtree Rd., NW, Atlanta, GA 30309-2405, (404) 881-3738; (FTS) 257-3738.

Federal Region V: Secretarial Representative, U.S. Department of Transportation, Room 700, 300 S. Wacker Dr., Chicago, IL 60606-6607, (312) 353-4000.

Federal Region VI: Secretarial Representative, U.S. Department of Transportation, Room 7A29, 819 Taylor St., Fort Worth, TX 76102-6114, (817) 334-2725.

Federal Regions VII and VIII: Secretarial Representative, U.S. Department of Transportation, Room 634, 601 E. 12th St., Room 634, Kansas City, MO 64106-2878, (816) 374-5801; (FTS) 758-5801.

Federal Regions IX and X: Secretarial Representative, U.S. Department of Transportation, Room 1005, 211 Main St., San Francisco, CA 94105-1924, (415) 974-8464; (FTS) 454-8464.

Federal Aviation Administration

New England Region (CT, ME, MA, NH, RI, and VT): Regional Director, Federal Aviation Administration, 12 New England Executive Park, P.O. Box 510, Burlington, MA 01803-0933, (617) 273-7244; (FTS) 836-1244.

Eastern Region (DE, DC, MD, NJ, NY, PA, VA, and WV): Regional Director, Federal Aviation Administration, Fitzgerald Building, JFK International Airport, Jamaica, NY 11430-2181, (212) 917-1005; (FTS) 667-1005.

Southern Region (AL, FL, GA, KY, MS, NC, PR, Republic of Panama, SC, and TN): Regional Director, Federal Aviation Administration, P.O. Box 20636, Atlanta, GA 30320-0636, (404) 763-7222; (FTS) 246-7222.

Great Lakes Region (IL, IN, MI, MN, ND, OH, SD, and WI): Regional Director, Federal Aviation Administration, 2300 East Devon Ave., Des Plaines, IL 60018-4686, (312) 694-7294; (FTS) 384-7294.

Southwest Region (AR, LA, NM, OK, and TX): Regional Director, Federal Aviation Administration, P.O. Box 1689, Fort Worth, TX 76101-1689, (817) 877-2100; (FTS) 734-2100.

Central Region (IA, KS, MO, and NE): Regional Director, Federal Aviation Administration, 601 E. 12th St., Kansas City, MO 64106-2894, (816) 374-5626; (FTS) 758-5626.

Western-Pacific Region (AZ, CA, HI, and NV): Regional Director, Federal Aviation Administration, P.O. Box 92007, World Way Postal Center, Los Angeles, CA 90009-2007, (213) 536-6427; (FTS) 966-6427.

Northwest Mountain Region (CO, ID, MT, OR, UT, WA, and WY): Regional Director, Federal Aviation Administration, 17900 Pacific Highway South, Seattle, WA 98188-0966, (206) 431-2001; (FTS) 446-2001.

Alaskan Region (AK): Regional Director, Federal Aviation Administration, P.O. Box 14,

701 C St., Anchorage, AK 99513-0001, (907) 271-5645.

Federal Highway Administration

Federal Regions I and II: Regional Administrator, Federal Highway Administration, 729 Leo W. O'Brien Federal Bldg., Clinton Ave. and N. Pearl St., Albany, NY, 12207-2396, (518) 472-6476; (FTS) 562-6476.

Federal Region III: Regional Administrator, Federal Highway Administration, Room 1633, George H. Fallon Federal Office Building, 31 Hopkins Plaza, Baltimore, MD 21201-2825, (301) 962-0093; (FTS) 922-2773.

Federal Region IV: Regional Administrator, Federal Highway Administration, Suite 200, 1720 Peachtree Road, NW, Atlanta, GA 30309-2405, (404) 881-4078; (FTS) 257-4078.

Federal Region V: Regional Administrator, Federal Highway Administration, 18209 Dixie Highway, Homewood, IL 60430-2206, (312) 799-6300; (FTS) 370-9102.

Federal Region VI: Regional Administrator, Federal Highway Administration, 819 Taylor St., Fort Worth, TX 76102-6187 (817) 334-3908; (FTS) 334-3232.

Federal Region VII: Regional Administrator, Federal Highway Administration, 6301 Rockhill Rd., Kansas City, MO 64131-1117, (816) 926-7563; (FTS) 926-7490.

Federal Region VIII: Regional Administrator, Federal Highway Administration, 555 Zang St., P.O. Box 25246, Denver, CO 80225-0246, (303) 234-4051.

Federal Region IX: Regional Administrator, Federal Highway Administration, 211 Main St., Room 1100, San Francisco, CA 94105-1905, (415) 974-8450; (FTS) 454-8450.

Federal Region X: Regional Administrator, Federal Highway Administration, Room 412, Mohawk Building, 708 S.W. Third St., Portland, OR 97204-2469, (503) 221-2053; (FTS) 423-2065.

Federal Railroad Administration: Director, Office of Economic Analysis (RRP-30), Federal Railroad Administration, Room 5300, Nassif Bldg., 400 Seventh St., SW, Wash., D.C. 20590-0001, (202) 426-7391.

Maritime Administration: Head, Environmental Activities Group (MAR-700.4), Maritime Administration, Room 2120, Nassif Bldg., 400 Seventh St., SW, Wash., D.C. 20590-0001, (202) 426-5738.

National Highway Traffic Safety Administration: Assistant Chief Counsel for General Law, Office of Chief Counsel (NOA-33), National Highway Traffic Safety Administration, Room 5219, Nassif Bldg., 400 Seventh St., SW, Wash., D.C. 20590-0001, (202) 426-1834.

Research and Special Programs Administration (includes Materials Transportation Bureau): Chief, Environmental Technology Division (DTS-48), Research and Special Programs Administration, US-DOT, Transportation Systems Center, Room 3-55, Kendall Square, Cambridge, MA 02142-1001, (617) 494-2018; (FTS) 837-2018.

St. Lawrence Seaway Development Corporation: Deputy Chief Engineer, St. Lawrence Seaway Development Corporation, Seaway Administration Bldg., 180 Andrews

St., P.O. Box 520, Massena, NY 13662-1760. (315) 764-3256; (FTS) 953-0256.

United States Coast Guard: Chief, Environmental Compliance and Review Branch (G-WP-3), Office of Marine Environment and Systems, U.S. Coast Guard, 2100 2nd St., SW, Wash., D.C. 20593-0001. (202) 426-3300.

District I (MA, ME, NH, RI, and eastern VT): Commander, First Coast Guard District, 150 Causeway St., Boston, MA 02114-1391. (617) 223-3603; (FTS) 223-3644.

District II (Northern AL, AR, CO, IL, IN, KY, KS, MN, MO, northern MS, ND, NE, OH, OK, western PA, SD, TN, WI, WV, and WY (except Great Lakes Area)): Commander, Second Coast Guard District, 1430 Olive St., St. Louis, MO 63103-2398. (314) 425-4601; (FTS) 279-4601.

District III (CT, DE, NJ, eastern NY, eastern PA, and western VT): Commander, Third Coast Guard District, Governors Island, New York, NY 10004-5000. (212) 668-7196; (FTS) 664-7196.

District V (DC, MD, NC, and VA): Commander, Fifth Coast Guard District, Federal Bldg., 431 Crawford St., Portsmouth, VA 23704-5000. (804) 398-6000; (FTS) 827-9000.

District VII (Eastern FL, eastern GA, PR, SC, and VI): Commander, Seventh Coast Guard District, Room 1018, Federal Bldg., 51 SW 1st Ave., Miami, FL 33130-1608. (305) 350-5654.

District VIII (Southern AL, western FL, western GA, LA, southern MS, NM, and TX): Commander, Eighth Coast Guard District, Hale Boggs Federal Bldg., 500 Camp St., New Orleans, LA 70130-3313. (504) 589-6298; (FTS) 682-6298.

District IX (Great Lakes Area): Commander, Ninth Coast Guard District, 1240 E. 9th St., Cleveland, OH 44199-2060. (216) 522-3910; (FTS) 293-3910.

District XI (AZ, southern CA, southern NV, and southern UT): Commander, Eleventh Coast Guard District, Union Bank Bldg., 400 Oceangate Blvd., Long Beach, CA 90822-5399. (213) 590-2311; (FTS) 984-9311.

District XII (northern CA, northern NV, and northern UT): Commander, Twelfth Coast Guard District, Government Island, Alameda, CA 94501-9991. (415) 437-3196; (FTS) 536-3196.

District XIII (ID, MT, OR, and WA): Commander, Thirteenth Coast Guard District, Federal Bldg., 915 2nd Ave., Seattle, WA 98174-1001. (206) 442-5078; (FTS) 399-5078.

District XIV (AS, GU, HI, and TP): Commander, Fourteenth Coast Guard District, 9th Floor Prince Kalanianaole Federal Bldg., 300 Ala Moana Blvd., Honolulu, HI 96813-4982. (808) 546-5531.

District XVII (AK): Commander, Seventeenth Coast Guard District, P.O. Box 3-5000, Juneau, AK 99802-1217. (907) 586-2680.

Urban Mass Transportation Administration

Federal Region I: Regional Administrator, Urban Mass Transportation Administration, Transportation Systems Center, Room 921 55 Broadway, Cambridge, MA 02142-1001. (617) 494-2055; (FTS) 837-2055.

Federal Region II: Regional Administrator, Urban Mass Transportation Administration,

26 Federal Plaza, Suite 14-110, New York, NY 10278-0022. (212) 264-8162.

Federal Region III: Regional Administrator, Urban Mass Transportation Administration, Suite 1010, 434 Walnut St., Philadelphia, PA 19106-3790. (215) 597-6098.

Federal Region IV: Regional Administrator, Urban Mass Transportation Administration, Suite 400, 1720 Peachtree Road, NW, Atlanta, GA 30309-2472. (404) 881-3948; (FTS) 257-3948.

Federal Region V: Regional Administrator, Urban Mass Transportation Administration, Suite 1720, 300 S. Wacker Dr., Chicago, IL 60606-6755. (312) 353-2789.

Federal Region VI: Regional Administrator, Urban Mass Transportation Administration, Suite 9A32, 819 Taylor St., Dallas, TX 76102-8180. (817) 334-3787.

Federal Region VII: Regional Administrator, Urban Mass Transportation Administration, Suite 100, 6301 Rockhill, Rd., Kansas City, MO 64131-1117. (816) 926-5053.

Federal Region VIII: Regional Administrator, Urban Mass Transportation Administration, Prudential Plaza, Suite 1822, 1050 17th Street, Denver, CO 80285-1898. (303) 837-3242; (FTS) 327-3242.

Federal Region IX: Regional Administrator, Urban Mass Transportation, Room 1160, 211 Main St., San Francisco, CA 94105-1971. (415) 974-7313; (FTS) 454-7313.

Federal Region X: Regional Administrator, Urban Mass Transportation Administration, Suite 3142, 915 Second Avenue, Seattle, WA 98174-1001. (206) 442-4210; (FTS) 399-4210.

Department of Treasury

Manager, Environmental Quality, Physical Security and Safety Division, Department of the Treasury, Room 800, Treasury Bldg., 1331 G St., NW, Wash., D.C. 20220-0001. (202) 376-0289.

INDEPENDENT AGENCIES

ACTION

Assistant Director, Office of Policy and Planning, ACTION, Room M-806, 806 Connecticut Ave., NW, Wash., D.C. 20525-0001. (202) 634-9304; WATS #800-424-8580, ext. 81.

Advisory Council on Historic Preservation

Director, Office of Cultural Resource Preservation, Advisory Council on Historic Preservation, Old Post Office Building, Suite 803, 1100 Pennsylvania Ave., NW, Wash., D.C. 20004-2590. (202) 786-0505.

Appalachian Regional Commission

Director, Division of Housing and Community Development, Appalachian Regional Commission, 1666 Connecticut Ave., NW, Wash., D.C. 20235-0001. (202) 673-7845.

Civil Aeronautics Board

Chief, Environmental and Energy Programs (B-60C), Civil Aeronautics Board, Room 909, Universal Bldg., 1825 Connecticut Ave., NW, Wash., D.C. 20428-0001. (202) 426-9622.

Consumer Product Safety Commission

Assistant General Counsel, Office of the General Counsel, Consumer Product Safety Commission, Room 200, 5401 Westbard Ave., Bethesda, MD. (301) 492-6980. MAILING ADDRESS: Washington, D.C. 20207-0001.

Delaware River Basin Commission

Executive Director, Delaware River Basin Commission, 25 State Police Drive, P.O. Box 7360, West Trenton, NJ 08628-0360. (609) 883-9500; (FTS) 483-2877.

Environmental Protection Agency

Send comment request and documents about legislation, regulations, national program proposals and other major policy issues to Wash., D.C. Send comment request and documents about other Federal actions to the Federal Regional Administrator in whose area the action will take place. If the action involves more than one region, increase number of copies accordingly but send to the region primarily involved.

Director, Office of Federal Activities, Environmental Protection Agency, Room 2119-I, 401 M St., SW, Wash., D.C. 20460-0001. (202) 382-5053.

Federal Region I: Regional Administrator, U.S. Environmental Protection Agency, Room 2203, John F. Kennedy Federal Bldg., Boston, MA 02203-0001. (617) 223-7210.

Federal Region II: Regional Administrator, U.S. Environmental Protection Agency, Room 900, 26 Federal Plaza, New York, NY, 10278-0014. (212) 264-2525.

Federal Region III: Regional Administrator, U.S. Environmental Protection Agency, Curtis Bldg., 6th and Walnut Sts., Philadelphia, PA 19106-3310. (215) 597-9800.

Federal Region IV: Regional Administrator, U.S. Environmental Protection Agency, 345 Courtland Street, NE, Atlanta, GA 30365-2401. (404) 257-4727.

Federal Region V: Regional Administrator, U.S. Environmental Protection Agency, 230 S. Dearborn St., Chicago, IL 60604-1590. (312) 353-2000.

Federal Region VI: Regional Administrator, U.S. Environmental Protection Agency, 1201 Elm St., Dallas, TX 75270-2180. (214) 767-2600; (FTS) 729-2600.

Federal Region VII: Regional Administrator, U.S. Environmental Protection Agency, 324 E. 11th St., Kansas City, MO 64106-2467. (816) 374-5493; (FTS) 758-5493.

Federal Region VIII: Regional Administrator, U.S. Environmental Protection Agency, Suite 900, Lincoln Tower, 1660 Lincoln Street, Denver, CO 80295-0699. (303) 837-3895; (FTS) 327-3895.

Federal Region IX: Regional Administrator, U.S. Environmental Protection Agency, 215 Freemont St., San Francisco, CA 94105-2399. (415) 974-8153; (FTS) 454-8153.

Federal Region X: Regional Administrator, U.S. Environmental Protection Agency, 1200 Sixth Ave., Seattle, WA 98101-3188. (206) 442-5810; (FTS) 399-5810.

Federal Emergency Management Agency

Associate General Counsel, Federal Emergency Management Agency, Room 840, 500 C St., SW, Wash., D.C. 20472-0001. (202) 287-0387.

Federal Energy Regulatory Commission

Send comment requests and documents about legislation, regulations, national program proposals, major policy issues and Federal actions to:

49782 Federal Register / Vol. 49, No. 247 / Friday, December 21, 1984 / Rules and Regulations

For electric and hydroelectric matters—Director, Division of Environmental Analysis, Office of Hydropower Licensing, Federal Energy Regulatory Commission, Room 308, Railway Labor Building, 400 First St., NW, Wash., D.C. 20426–0001. (202) 376–1768.

For natural gas matters—Chief, Environmental Evaluation Branch, Office of Pipeline and Producer Regulation, Federal Energy Regulatory Commission, Room 7102A, 825 N. Capitol St., NE, Wash., D.C. 20426–0001. (202) 357–8098.

Federal Maritime Commission

Director, Office of Energy and Environmental Impact, Federal Maritime Commission, 1100 L St., NW, Wash., D.C. 20573–0001. (202) 523–5835.

Federal Trade Commission

Deputy Assistant General Counsel, Federal Trade Commission, Room 582, 6th St. and Pennsylvanie Ave., NW, Wash., D.C. 20580–0001. (202) 523–1926.

General Services Administration

Send comment requests and documents about legislation, regulations, national program proposals and other major policy issues to Washington, D.C. Send comment requests and documents about other Federal actions to the regional office having responsibility for the area in which the action will take place.

Director, Environmental Affairs Staff (PRE), Office of Space Management, Public Buildings Service, General Services Administration, Room 2323, 18th and F Sts., NW, Wash., D.C. 20405–0001. (202) 566–0654.

Federal Region I: Chief, Planning Staff (1PEP) Public Buildings and Real Property, General Services Administration, John W. McCormack Post Office and Courthouse, Boston, MA 02109–4559. (617) 223–2707.

Federal Region II: Chief, Planning Staff (2PEP) Public Buildings and Real Property, General Services Administration, 26 Federal Plaza, New York, NY 10278–0022. (212) 264–3544.

Federal Region III: Chief, Planning Staff (3PEP) Public Buildings and Real Property, General Services Administration, 9th and Market Sts., Philadelphia, PA 19107–4268. (215) 597–0268.

Federal Region IV: Chief, Planning Staff (4PEP) Public Buildings and Reel Property, General Services Administration, 75 Spring St., SW, Atlanta, GA 30303–3309. (404) 221–3080; (FTS) 242–3080.

Federal Region V: Chief, Planning Staff (5PEP) Public Buildings and Real Property, General Services Administration, 230 S. Dearborn St., Chicago, IL 60604–1602. (312) 353–5610.

Federal Region VI: Chief, Planning Staff (6PEP) Public Buildings and Real Property, General Services Administration, 1500 E.

Bannister Rd., Kansas City, MO 64131–3087. (816) 926–7240.

Federal Region VII: Chief, Planning Staff (7PEP) Public Buildings and Real Property, General Services Administration, 819 Taylor St., Fort Worth, TX 76102–6114. (817) 334–2531.

Federal Region VIII: Chief, Planning Staff (8PEP) Public Buildings end Real Property, General Services Administration, Building 41, Denver Federal Center Lakewood, CO 80225–0001. (303) 776–7244.

Federal Region IX: Chief, Planning Staff (9PEP) Public Buildings and Real Property, General Services Administration, 525 Market St., San Francisco, CA 94105–2708. (415) 974–7623; (FTS) 454–7623.

Federal Region X: Chief, Planning Staff (10PEP) Public Buildings and Real Property, General Services Administration, GSA Center, 1501 G St., SW, Auburn, WA 98001–6599. (206) 931–7265; (FTS) 396–7265.

Federal National Capital Region: Chief, Planning Staff (WPJ) Public Buildings and Real Property, General Services Administration, 7th & D Sts., SW, Wash., D.C. 20407–0001. (202) 472–1479.

International Boundary and Water Commission, United States Section

Principal Engineer, Investigations end Planning Division, International Boundary and Water Commission, United States Section, IBWC Bldg., 4110 Rio Bravo, El Paso, TX 79902–1091. (915) 541–7304; (FTS) 572–7304.

Interstate Commerce Commission

Chief, Section of Energy and Environment, Office of Transportation Analysis, Interstate Commerce Commission, Room 4143, 12th St. and Constitution Ave., NW, Wash., D.C. 20423–0001. (202) 275–0800.

Marine Mammal Commission

General Counsel, Marine Mammal Commission, Room 307, 1625 Eye St., NW, Wash., D.C. 20006–3164. (202) 653–6237.

National Aeronautics and Space Administration

Environmental Compliance Officer, Facilities Engineering Division, National Aeronautics and Space Administration, Code NXG, Room 5031, 400 Maryland Ave., SW, Wash., D.C. 20546–0001. (202) 453–1958.

National Capital Planning Commission

Environmental/Energy Officer, Division of Planning Services, National Capital Planning Commission, Room 1024, 1325 G St., NW, Wash., D.C. 20576–0001. (202) 724–0179.

National Science Foundation

Chairman and Staff Associate, Committee on Environmental Matters; Office of Astronomical, Atmospheric, Earth and Ocean Sciences; National Science Foundation, Room

641, 1800 G St., NW, Wash., D.C. 20550–0001. (202) 357–7615.

Nuclear Regulatory Commission:

Chief, Environmental and Hydrologic Engineering Branch, Division of Engineering, Office of Nuclear Reactor Regulation, Nuclear Regulatory Commission, Room P–312, Phillips Bldg., 7920 Norfolk Ave., Bethesda, MD 20814–2587. (301) 492–7972.

Pennsylvania Avenue Development Corporation

Director of Development, Pennsylvania Avenue Development Corporation, Suite 1248, 425 13th St., NW, Wash., D.C. 20004–1856. (202) 523–5477.

Small Business Administration

Chief, Loan Processing Branch, Office of Business Loans, Small Business Administration, Room 804–B, 1441 L St., NW, Wash., D.C. 20416–0001. (202) 653–6470.

Susquehanna River Basin Commission

Executive Director, Susquehanna River Basin Commission, 1721 N. Front St., Harrisburg, PA. 17102–2391. (717) 238–0422.

Tennessee Valley Authority

Director, Environmental Quality Staff, Tennessee Valley Authority, 201 Summer Place Building, 309 Walnut St., Knoxville, TN 37902–1411. (615) 632–6578; (FTS) 856–6578.

United States Information Agency

Assistant General Counsel, United States Information Agency, 301 Fourth St., SW, Wash., D.C. 20547–0001. (202) 485–7976.

United States International Development Cooperation Agency:

For USAID matters, send to—Environmental Affairs Coordinator, Office of External Affairs, U.S. Agency for International Development, Department of State Bldg., 320 Twenty-First St., NW, Wash., D.C. 20523–0001. (202) 632–6298.

For OPIC matters, send to—International Economist/Environmental Officer, Office of Development, Overseas Private Investment Corporation, 1129 Twentieth St., NW, Wash., D.C. 20527–0001. (202) 653–2904.

United States Postal Service

Director, Office of Program Planning, Real Estate and Building Department, United States Postal Service, Room 4014, 475 L'Enfant Plaza West, SW, Wash., D.C. 20260–6420. (202) 245–4304.

Veterans Administration

Director, Office of Environmental Affairs, Veterans Administration, Code 088C, 810 Vermont Ave., NW, Wash., D.C. 20420–0001. (202) 389–3316.

[FR Doc. 84–32983 Filed 12–20–84; 8:45 em]

BILLING CODE 3125-01-M

NEPA Deskbook

Appendix 9   List of Agency NEPA Regulations and Procedures

Agency NEPA Procedures

Each agency of the Federal government is required to comply with the CEQ Regulations for implementing the procedural provisions of the Act, and, in consultation with CEQ, to develop their agency specific procedures to ensure that environmental information is available to the public and the agency decision makers before decisions are made and actions taken.

This resource is a compendium of Federal agency NEPA procedures. The procedures are listed alphabetically by the responsible agency. Some agencies issue their procedures as regulations, others issue them as agency guidance documents. Those that are codified as regulations appear in the Code of Federal Regulations (CFR). Where appropriate, the CFR and Federal Register citations providing notice of the agencies NEPA procedures are provided.

DEPARTMENT OF AGRICULTURE		
Agriculture Research Service	---	7 CFR 520
Animal and Plant Health Inspection Service	Environmental Services	7 CFR 372 / 60 FR 6000
National Institute of Food and Agriculture	Natural Resources and Environmental Unit	7 CFR 3407
Economic Research Service	Resource Economic Division	7 CFR 1b
Farms Service Agency	Conservation and Env. Programs Division, Env. Activities Branch	7 CFR 799
Food Safety and Inspection Service	Policy Evaluation and Planning	7 CFR 372
Forest Service	Ecosystem Management Coordination	36 CFR 220 / 73 FR 43084
Natural Resources Conservation Service	---	7 CFR 650
Rural Business-Cooperative Service	Rural Housing Staff, Program Support Staff/Technical Support Branch	7 CFR 1940.301-.336 Subpart G / 65 FR 55784
Rural Housing Service	Program Support Staff/Technical Support Branch	7 CFR 1940 Subpart G
Rural Utilities Service	Engineering and Environmental Staff	7 CFR 1794 / 63 FR 68648
DEPARTMENT OF COMMERCE		
Economic Development Administration	Compliance Review Division	48 FR 14734
National Oceanic and Atmospheric Administration	Office of Policy and Strategic Planning	48 FR 14734, NAO 216-6
DEPARTMENT OF DEFENSE		
Defense Logistics Agency	Environmental Safety Policy Office	76 FR 72391
Department of Air Force	Environmental Planning, Education and Training	32 CFR 989 / 64 FR 38127
Department of Army	U.S. Army Corps of Engineers	33 CFR 230
Department of Army	Deputy Assistant Secretary of the Army for Environment, Safety and Occupational Health	32 CFR 651 / 65 FR 54348
Department of Defense	Environmental Security-EQ	32 CFR 188
Department of Navy	U.S. Marine Corps	
Department of Navy	Office of the Chief of Naval Operations	32 CFR 775 / 64 FR 37069

Department of Navy	Office of the Assistant Secretary of the Navy for Environment and Safety	32 CFR 775 / 64 FR 37069
DEPARTMENT OF ENERGY		
Office of Environment, Safety and Health	Office of NEPA Policy and Compliance	10 CFR 1021 / 61 FR 64603
DEPARTMENT OF HEALTH AND HUMAN SERVICES		
Centers for Disease Control	---	65 FR 10230
Food and Drug Administration	Office of Science	21 CFR 25 / 65 FR 30352
Indian Health Service	Sanitation Facilities Construction Program, Engineering/ Environmental Branch	58 FR 569
National Institute of Health	---	65 FR 2977
Office of Facility Services	---	45 CFR 76519 / 65 FR 10230
DEPARTMENT OF HOMELAND SECURITY		
Department of Homeland Security	---	71 FR 16790
Federal Emergency Management Agency	---	44 CFR 10
U.S. Coast Guard	---	Coast Guard NEPA Handbook, available at http://www.uscg.mil/ hq/cg4/cg443/docs/ NEPA_handbook.pdf
DEPARTMENT OF HOUSING AND URBAN DEVELOPMENT		
Housing and Urban Development	Office of Community Viability	24 CFR 50 / 53 FR 11224
DEPARTMENT OF INTERIOR		
Bureau of Indian Affairs	---	53 FR 10439
Bureau of Land Management	Planning, Assessment, and Community Support	
Bureau of Reclamation	---	
National Park Service	Environmental Quality Division	
Office of Environmental Affairs	Office of Environmental Policy and Compliance	43 CFR 46 / 73 FR 61291
Office of Surface Mining	---	
U.S. Fish and Wildlife Service	---	
U.S. Geological Survey	Environmental Affairs Program	
DEPARTMENT OF JUSTICE		
Drug Enforcement Administration	Civil Litigation Section (CCL)	28 CFR 61, Appendix B
Environment and Natural Resources Division	General Litigation Section	28 CFR 61
Federal Bureau of Prisons	Site Selection and Environmental Review Branch	28 CFR 61, Appendix A / 63 FR 11120

Immigration and Naturalization Service	Headquarters, Facilities Office	28 CFR 61, Appendix C
Office of Justice Assistance, Research, and Statistics	---	28 CFR 61, Appendix D
Office of Justice Programs	Office of General Counsel	28 CFR 61
DEPARTMENT OF LABOR		
Mine Safety and Health Administration	Office of Standards, Regulations, and Variances	29 CFR 11
Occupational Safety and Health Administration	Directorate of Safety Standards Programs	
DEPARTMENT OF STATE		
Bureau of Oceans and International Environmental and Scientific Affairs	Office of Environmental Policy	22 CFR 161 / 44 FR 65560
DEPARTMENT OF TRANSPORTATION		
Federal Aviation Administration	Office of Environment and Energy	64 FR 55526
Federal Aviation Administration	Office of Environment and Energy (AEE-300)	45 FR 2244
Federal Highway Administration	Office of NEPA Facilitation	23 CFR 771 / 65 FR 33960
Federal Railroad Administration	Office of Policy and Program Development	64 FR 28545
Federal Transit Administration	Office of Planning (TPL-22)	49 CFR 622
John A. Volpe National Transportation Systems Center	Environmental Preservation and Systems Modernization Office	
Maritime Administration	Office of Environmental Activities	
National Highway Traffic Safety Administration	General Law	49 CFR 520
Office of Assistant Secretary for Transportation Policy	---	44 FR 56420
Saint Lawrence Seaway Development Corporation	---	
Surface Transportation Board	Environmental Analysis Section	49 CFR 1105
U.S. Coast Guard (Headquarters)	Environmental Management Division (G-SEC-3)	50 FR 32944
DEPARTMENT OF TREASURY		
Office of Asset Management	Environment and Planning	45 FR 1828
DEPARTMENT OF VETERANS AFFAIRS		
Office of Facilities Quality Service	---	38 CFR 26
INDEPENDENT AGENCIES		
Advisory Council on Historic Preservation	Office of Planning and Review	36 CFR 805 / 64 FR 27044
Appalachian Regional Commission	Program Operations Division	
Board of Governors of the Federal Reserve System	---	

Committee for Purchase From People Who Are Blind or Severely Disabled	---	
Delaware River Basin Commission	---	18 CFR 401
Export-Import Bank of the United States	---	12 CFR 408
Farm Credit Administration	Office of General Counsel	45 FR 81733
Federal Communications Commission	Common Carrier Bureau	47 CFR
Federal Communications Commission	Mass Media Bureau	47 CFR
Federal Communications Commission	Office of Engineering and Technology	47 CFR
Federal Communications Commission	---	47 CFR 1.1301
Federal Communications Commission	Wireless Telecommunications Bureau	47 CFR
Federal Deposit Insurance Corporation	Health, Safety & Environmental Programs Unit/Administration Division/Corporate Services Branch	63 FR 63474
Federal Emergency Management Agency	---	44 CFR 10
Federal Energy Regulatory Commission	Office of Energy Projects	18 CFR 380 / 64 FR 26572
Federal Energy Regulatory Commission	Office of Pipeline Regulation/ Environmental and Engineering Review and Compliance Branch II	18 CFR 2.80, 380 / 64 FR 26572
Federal Maritime Commission	---	46 CFR 504
Federal Trade Commission	Litigation	16 CFR 1
General Services Administration	Public Buildings Service, PXE	50 CFR 7648 / 65 FR 69558
International Boundary and Water Commission	Engineering Department, United States Section	46 FR 44083
Marine Mammal Commission	---	50 CFR 530
National Aeronautics and Space Administration	Environmental Management Division	14 CFR 1216 / 77 FR 3102
National Capital Planning Commission	Office of Plans Review	69 FR 41299
National Credit Union Administration	Division of Operations/Office of General Counsel	
National Indian Gaming Commission	---	
National Science Foundation	Office of General Counsel	45 CFR 640; 641
Overseas Private Investment Corporation	Investment Development Department	44 FR 51385
Securities and Exchange Commission	Office of Public Utility Regulation	17 CFR 200
Small Business Administration	Office of Financial Assistance	
Tennessee Valley Authority	Environmental Policy and Planning	48 FR 19264
U.S. Access Board	---	
U.S. Agency for International Development	Bureau for Policy and Program Coordination	22 CFR 216
U.S. Consumer Product Safety Commission	Directorate for Health Sciences	16 CFR 1021

U.S. Environmental Protection Agency	Office of Federal Activities	40 CFR 6
U.S. Nuclear Regulatory Commission	Office of State and Tribal Programs	10 CFR 51 / 64 FR 48496
U.S. Postal Service Headquarters	---	39 CFR 775 / 65 FR 41011
Water Resources Council	---	18 CFR 707
Presidio Trust	---	36 CFR 1010 / 65 FR 55896
Council on Environmental Quality	Chair	40 CFR 1500 / 43 FR 55990
Presidio Trust	---	36 CFR 1010 / 65 FR 55896
Armed Forces Retirement Home	---	38 CFR 200
Community Development Financial Institutions Fund	---	12 CFR 1815

NEPA Deskbook

Appendix 10 **Department of Agriculture Regulations and Procedures (USDA Part 1b and USDA Part 3100)**

Part 1b—National Environmental Policy Act

Sec.
1b.1   Purpose.
1b.2   Policy.
1b.3   Categorical exclusions.
1b.4   Exclusion of agencies.

Authority:
5 U.S.C. 301; 42 U.S.C. 4321 et seq.; E.O. 11514, 3 CFR, 1966-1970 Comp., p. 902, as amended by E.O. 11991, 3 CFR, 1978 Comp., p. 123; E.O. 12114, 3 CFR, 1980 Comp., p. 356; 40 CFR 1507.3.

Source:
48 FR 11403, Mar. 18, 1983, unless otherwise noted.

§1b.1   Purpose.

(a) This part supplements the regulations for implementation of the National Environmental Policy Act (NEPA), for which regulations were published by the Council on Environmental Quality (CEQ) in 40 CFR parts 1500 through 1508. This part incorporates and adopts those regulations.

(b) This part sets forth Departmental policy concerning NEPA, establishes categorical exclusions of actions carried out by the Department and its agencies, and sets forth those USDA agencies which are excluded from the requirement to prepare procedures implementing NEPA.

[48 FR 11403, Mar. 18, 1983, as amended at 60 FR 66481, Dec. 22, 1995]

§1b.2   Policy.

(a) All policies and programs of the various USDA agencies shall be planned, developed, and implemented so as to achieve the goals and to follow the procedures declared by NEPA in order to assure responsible stewardship of the environment for present and future generations.

(b) Each USDA agency is responsible for compliance with this part, the regulations of CEQ, and NEPA. Compliance will include the preparation and implementation of specific procedures and processes relating to the programs and activities of the individual agency, as necessary.

(c) The Under Secretary, Natural Resources and Environment (NR&E), is responsible for ensuring that agency implementing procedures are consistent with CEQ's NEPA regulations and for coordinating NEPA compliance for the Department. The Under Secretary, NR&E, through the Agricultural Council on Environmental Quality, will develop the necessary processes to be used by the Office of the Secretary in reviewing, implementing, and planning its NEPA activities, determinations, and policies.

(d) In connection with the policies and requirements set forth in this part, all USDA agencies are responsible for compliance with Executive Order 12114, "Environmental Effects Abroad of Major Federal Actions." Compliance will include the preparation and implementation of specific procedures and processes relative to the programs and activities of the individual agencies, as necessary. Agencies shall consult with the Department of State; the Council on Environmental Quality; and the Under Secretary, NR&E, prior to placing procedures and processes in effect.

[48 FR 11403, Mar. 18, 1983, as amended at 60 FR 66481, Dec. 22, 1995]

§1b.3   Categorical exclusions.

(a) The following are categories of activities which have been determined not to have a significant individual or cumulative effect on the human environment and are excluded from the preparation of environmental assessment (EA's) or environmental impact statement (EIS's), unless individual agency procedures prescribed otherwise.

(1) Policy development, planning and implementation which relate to routine activities, such as personnel, organizational changes, or similar administrative functions;

(2) Activities which deal solely with the funding of programs, such as program budget proposals, disbursements, and transfer or reprogramming of funds;

(3) Inventories, research activities, and studies, such as resource inventories and routine data collection when such actions are clearly limited in context and intensity;

(4) Educational and informational programs and activities;

(5) Civil and criminal law enforcement and investigative activities;

(6) Activities which are advisory and consultative to other agencies and public and private entities, such as legal counselling and representation;

(7) Activities related to trade representation and market development activities abroad.

(b) Agencies will identify in their own procedures the activities which normally would not require an environmental assessment or environmental impact statement.

(c) Notwithstanding the exclusions listed in paragraphs (a) of this section and § 1b.4, or identified in agency procedures, agency heads may determine that circumstances dictate the need for preparation of an EA or EIS for a particular action. Agencies shall continue to scrutinize their activities to determine continued eligibility for categorical exclusion.

[48 FR 11403, Mar. 18, 1983, as amended at 60 FR 66481, Dec. 22, 1995]

§1b.4   *Exclusion of agencies.*

(a) The USDA agencies and agency units listed in paragraph (b) of this section conduct programs and activities that have been found to have no individual or cumulative effect on the human environment. The USDA agencies and agency units listed in paragraph (b) of this section are excluded from the requirements of preparing procedures to implement NEPA. Actions of USDA agencies and agency units listed in paragraph

(b) of this section are categorically excluded from the preparation of an EA or EIS unless the agency head determines that an action may have a significant environmental effect.

(b)(1) Agricultural Marketing Service

(2) Economic Research Service

(3) Extension Service

(4) Federal Corp Insurance Corporation

(5) Food and Consumer Service

(6) Food Safety and Inspection Service

(7) Foreign Agricultural Service

(8) Grain Inspection, Packers and Stockyards Administration

(9) National Agricultural Library

(10) National Agricultural Statistics Service

(11) Office of the General Counsel

(12) Office of the Inspector General

[60 FR 66481, Dec. 22, 1995]

Part 3100—Cultural and Environmental Quality

Subparts A-B [Reserved]

Subpart C—Enhancement, Protection, and Management of the Cultural Environment

Sec.
3100.40 Purpose.
3100.41 Authorities.
3100.42 Definitions.
3100.43 Policy.
3100.44 Implementation.
3100.45 Direction to agencies.
3100.46 Responsibilities of the Department of Agriculture.

Subparts A-B [Reserved]

Subpart C—Enhancement, Protection, and Management of the Cultural Environment

Authority:
Sec. 106, National Historic Preservation Act, as amended (16 U.S.C. 470f); National Environmental Policy Act, as amended (42 U.S.C. 4321 et seq.); E.O. 11593, 36 FR 8921, May 13, 1971.

Source:
44 FR 66181, Nov. 19, 1979, unless otherwise noted.

§3100.40 Purpose.

(a) This subpart establishes USDA policy regarding the enhancement, protection, and management of the cultural environment.

(b) This subpart establishes procedures for implementing Executive Order 11593, and regulations promulgated by the Advisory Council on Historic Preservation (ACHP) "Protection of Historical and Cultural Properties" in 36 CFR part 800 as required by § 800.10 of those regulations.

(c) Direction is provided to the agencies of USDA for protection of the cultural environment.

§3100.41 Authorities.

These regulations are based upon and implement the following laws, regulations, and Presidential directives:

(a) Antiquities Act of 1906 (Pub. L. 59-209; 34 Stat. 225; 16 U.S.C. 431 et seq.) which provides for the protection of historic or prehistoric remains or any object

of antiquity on Federal lands; establishes criminal sanctions for unauthorized destruction or appropriation of antiquities; and authorizes scientific investigation of antiquities on Federal lands, subject to permit and regulations. Paleontological resources also are considered to fall within the authority of this Act.

(b) Historic Sites Act of 1935 (Pub. L. 74-292; 49 Stat. 666; 16 U.S.C. 461 et seq.) which authorizes the establishment of National Historic Sites and otherwise authorizes the preservation of properties of national historical or archeological significance; authorizes the designation of National Historic Landmarks; establishes criminal sanctions for violation of regulations pursuant to the Act; authorizes interagency, intergovernmental, and interdisciplinary efforts for the preservation of cultural resources; and other provisions.

(c) Reservoir Salvage Act of 1960 (Pub. L. 86-521; 74 Stat. 220; 16 U.S.C. 469-469c.) which provides for the recovery and preservation of historical and archeological data, including relics and specimens, that might be lost or destroyed as a result of the construction of dams, reservoirs, and attendant facilities and activities.

(d) The National Historic Preservation Act of 1966 as amended (16 U.S.C. 470), which establishes positive national policy for the preservation of the cultural environment, and sets forth a mandate for protection in section 106. The purpose of section 106 is to protect properties on or eligible for the National Register of Historic Places through review and comment by the ACHP of Federal undertakings that affect such properties. Properties are listed on the National Register or declared eligible for listing by the Secretary of the Interior. As developed through the ACHP's regulations, section 106 establishes a public interest process in which the Federal agency proposing an undertaking, the State Historic Preservation Officer, the ACHP, interested organizations and individuals participate. The process is designed to insure that properties, impacts on them, and effects to them are identified, and that alternatives to avoid or mitigate an adverse effect on property eligible for the National Register are adequately considered in the planning process.

(e) The National Environmental Policy Act of 1969 (NEPA) (Pub. L. 91-190; 83 Stat. 852; 42 U.S.C. 4321 et seq.) which declares that it is the policy of the Federal Government to preserve important historic, cultural, and natural aspects of our national heritage. Compliance with NEPA requires consideration of all environmental concerns during project planning and execution.

(f) Executive Order 11593, "Protection and Enhancement of the Cultural Environment", which gives the Federal Government the responsibility for stewardship of our nation's heritage resources and charges Federal agencies with the task of inventorying historic and prehistoric sites on their lands. E.O. 11593 also charges agencies with the task of identifying and nominating all historic properties under their jurisdiction, and exercising caution to insure that they are not transferred, sold, demolished, or substantially altered.

(g) Historical and Archeological Data Preservation Act of 1974. (Pub. L. 93-291; 88 Stat. 174.) which amends the Reservoir Salvage Act of 1960 to extend its provisions beyond the construction of dams to any alteration of the terrain caused as a result of any Federal construction project or federally licensed activity or program. In addition, the Act provides a mechanism for funding the protection of historical and archeological data.

(h) Presidential memorandum of July 12, 1978, "Environmental Quality and Water Resource Management" which directs the ACHP to publish final regulations, implementing section 106 of the National Historic Preservation Act (NHPA), and further directs each agency with water and related land resources responsibilities to publish procedures implementing those regulations.

(i) 36 CFR part 800, "Protection of Historic and Cultural Properties" which establishes procedures for the implementation of section 106 of the NHPA, and directs publication of agency implementing procedures.

(j) Land use policy of the USDA (Secretary's Memorandum No. 1827 Revised, with Supplement) which establishes a commitment by the Department to the preservation of farms, rural communities, and rural landscapes.

(k) Public Buildings Cooperative Use Act of 1976 (40 U.S.C. 611) and Executive Order 12072 (Federal Space Management). The Act encourages adaptive use of historic buildings as administrative facilities for Federal agencies and activities; the Executive Order directs Federal agencies to locate administrative and other facilities in central business districts.

(l) American Indian Religious Freedom Act of 1978 (42 U.S.C. 1996) which declares it to be the policy of the United States to protect and preserve for American Indians their inherent right of freedom to believe, express, and exercise the traditional religions of the American Indian, Eskimo, Aleut, and Native Hawaiians.

§3100.42 Definitions.

All definitions are those which appear in 36 CFR part 800. In addition, the following apply in this rule:

Cultural resources (heritage resources) are the remains or records of districts, sites, structures, buildings, networks, neighborhoods, objects, and events from the past. They may be historic, prehistoric, archeological, or architectural in nature. Cultural resources are an irreplaceable and nonrenewable aspect of our national heritage.

Cultural environment is that portion of the environment which includes reminders of the rich historic and prehistoric past of our nation.

§3100.43 Policy.

(a) The nonrenewable cultural environment of our country constitutes a valuable and treasured portion of the national heritage of the American people. The Department of Agriculture is committed to the management—identification, protection, preservation, interpretation, evaluation and nomination—of our prehistoric and historic cultural resources for the benefit of all people of this and future generations.

(b) The Department supports the cultural resource goals expressed in Federal legislation. Executive orders, and regulations.

(c) The Department supports the preservation and protection of farms, rural landscapes, and rural communities.

(d) The Department is committed to consideration of the needs of American Indians, Eskimo, Aleut, and Native Hawaiians in the practice of their traditional religions.

(e) The Department will aggressively implement these policies to meet goals for the positive management of the cultural environment.

§3100.44 Implementation.

(a) It is the intent of the Department to carry out its program of management of the cultural environment in the most effective and efficient manner possible. Implementation must consider natural resource utilization, must exemplify good government, and must constitute a noninflationary approach which makes the best use of tax dollars.

(b) The commitment to cultural resource protection is vital. That commitment will be balanced with the multiple departmental goals of food and fiber production, environmental protection, natural resource and energy conservation, and rural development. It is essential that all of these be managed to reduce conflicts between programs. Positive management of the cultural environment can contribute to achieving better land use, protection of rural communities and farm lands, conservation of energy, and more efficient use of resources.

(c) In reaching decisions, the long-term needs of society and the irreversible nature of an action must be considered. The Department must act to preserve future options; loss of important cultural resources must be avoided except in the face of overriding national interest where there are no reasonable alternatives.

(d) To assure the protection of Native American religious practices, traditional religious leaders and other native leaders (or their representatives) should be consulted about potential conflict areas in the management of the cultural environment and the means to reduce or eliminate such conflicts.

§3100.45 Direction to agencies.

(a) Each agency of the Department shall consult with OEQ to determine whether its programs and activities may affect the cultural environment. Then, if needed, the agency, in consultation with the OEQ, shall develop its own specific procedures for implementing section 106 of the National Historic Preservation Act, Executive Order 11593, the regulations of the ACHP (36 CFR part 800), the American Indian Religious Freedom Act of 1978 and other relevant legislation and regulations in accordance with the agency's programs, mission and authorities. Such implementing procedures shall be published as proposed and final procedures in the Federal Register, and must be consistent with the requirements of 36 CFR part 800 and this subpart. Where applicable, each agency's procedures must contain mechanisms to insure:

(1) Compliance with section 106 of NHPA and mitigation of adverse effects to cultural properties on or eligible for the National Register of Historic Places;

(2) Clear definition of the kind and variety of sites and properties which should be managed;

(3) Development of a long-term program of management of the cultural environment on lands administered by USDA as well as direction for project-specific protection;

(4) Identification of all properties listed on or eligible for listing in the National Register that may be affected directly or indirectly by a proposed activity;

(5) Location, identification and nomination to the Register of all sites, buildings, objects, districts, neighborhoods, and networks under its management which appear to qualify (in compliance with E.O. 11593);

(6) The exercise of caution to assure that properties managed by USDA which may qualify for nomination are not transferred, sold, demolished, or substantially altered;

(7) Early consultation with, and involvement of, the State Historic Preservation Officer(s), the ACHP, Native American traditional religious leaders and appropriate tribal leaders, and others with appropriate interests or expertise;

(8) Early notification to insure substantive and meaningful involvement by the public in the agency's decisionmaking process as it relates to the cultural environment;

(9) Identification and consideration of alternatives to a proposed undertaking that would mitigate or minimize adverse effects to a property identified under paragraph (a)(4) of this section;

(10) Funding of mitigation measures where required to minimize the potential for adverse effects on the cultural environment. Funds for mitigation shall be available and shall be spent when needed during the life of the project to mitigate the expected loss; and

(11) Development of plans to provide for the management, protection, maintenance and/or restoration of Register sites under its management.

(b) Each agency of the Department which conducts programs or activities that may have an effect on the cultural environment shall recruit, place, develop, or otherwise have available, professional expertise in anthropology, archeology, history, historic preservation, historic architecture, and/or cultural resource management (depending upon specific need). Such arrangements may include internal hiring, Intergovernmental Personnel Act assignments, memoranda of agreement with other agencies or Departments, or other mechanisms which insure a professionally directed program. Agencies should use Department of the Interior professional standards (36 CFR 61.5) as guidelines to insure Departmentwide competence and consistency.

(c) Compliance with cultural resource legislation is the responsibility of each individual agency. Consideration of cultural resource values must begin during the earliest planning stages of any undertaking.

(d) Agency heads shall insure that cultural resource management activities meet professional standards as promulgated by the Department of the Interior (e.g., 36 CFR parts 60, 63, 66, 1208).

(e) Cultural resource review requirements and compliance with section 106 of NHPA and Executive Order 11593 shall be integrated and run concurrently, rather than consecutively, with the other environmental considerations under NEPA regulations. As such, direct and indirect impacts on cultural resources must be addressed in the environmental assessment for every agency undertaking. In meeting these requirements, agencies shall be guided by regulations implementing the procedural provisions of NEPA (40 CFR parts 1500-1508) and Department of Agriculture regulations (7 CFR part 3100, subpart B).

(f) Each agency shall work closely with the appropriate State Historic Preservation Officer(s) in their preparation of State plans, determination of inventory needs, and collection of data relevant to general plans or specific undertakings in carrying out mutual cultural resource responsibilities.

(g) Each agency shall, to the maximum extent possible, use existing historic structures for administrative purposes in compliance with Public Buildings Cooperative Use Act of 1976 and Executive Order 12072, "Federal Space Management".

(h) Each agency should consult with Native American traditional religious leaders or their representatives and other native leaders in the development and implementation of cultural resource programs which may affect their religious customs and practices.

§3100.46 Responsibilities of the Department of Agriculture.

(a) Within the Department, the responsibility for the protection of the cultural environment is assigned to the Office of Environmental Quality (OEQ). The Office is responsible for reviewing the development and implementation of agency procedures and insuring Departmental commitment to cultural resource goals.

(b) The Director of the OEQ is the Secretary's Designee to the ACHP.

(c) In order to carry out cultural resource responsibilities, there will be professional expertise within the OEQ to advise agencies, aid the Department in meeting its cultural resource management goals, and to insure that all Departmental and agency undertakings comply with applicable cultural resource protection legislation and regulations.

(d) The OEQ will be involved in individual compliance cases only where resolution cannot be reached at the agency level. Prior to the decision to refer a matter to the full Council of the ACHP, the OEQ will review the case and make recommendations to the Secretary regarding the position of the Department. The agency also will consult with the OEQ before reaching a final decision in response to the Council's comments. Copies of correspondence relevant to compliance with Section 106 shall be made available to OEQ.

7 CFR Ch. XXXII (1-1-08 Edition)

Office of Procurement and Property Management, USDA

NEPA Deskbook

Appendix 11 **U.S. Army Corps of Engineers Regulations and Procedures (Corps Part 230 and Corps Part 325)**

33 C.F.R. Pt. 230

Part 230—Procedures for Implementing NEPA

Contents

AUTHORITY: National Environmental Policy Act (NEPA) (42 U.S.C. 4321 *et seq.*); E.O. 11514, Protection and Enhancement of Environmental Quality, March 5, 1970, as amended by E.O. 11991, May 24, 1977; and CEQ Regulations Implementing the Procedural Provisions of NEPA (40 CFR 1507.3).

SOURCE: 53 FR 3127, Feb. 3, 1988, unless otherwise noted.

§230.1   Purpose.

This regulation provides guidance for implementation of the procedural provisions of the National Environmental Policy Act (NEPA) for the Civil Works Program of the U.S. Army Corps of Engineers. It supplements Council on Environmental Quality (CEQ) regulations 40 CFR parts 1500 through 1508, November 29, 1978, in accordance with 40 CFR 1507.3, and is intended to be used only in conjunction with the CEQ regulations. Whenever the guidance in this regulation is unclear or not specific the reader is referred to the CEQ regulations. Appendix A provides guidance on processing NEPA documents except for those concerning regulatory actions. Appendix C (formally ER 200-2-1) has been added to provide guidance on preparing and processing a notice of intent to prepare an EIS for publication in the FEDERAL REGISTER for all types of Corps actions. 33 CFR part 325, Appendix B provides procedural guidance for preparing and processing NEPA documents for regulatory actions.

§230.2   Applicability.

This regulation is applicable to all HQUSACE elements and all Field Operating Activities (FOAs) having responsibility for preparing and processing environmental documents in support of Civil Works functions.

§230.3   References.

(a) Executive Order 12291, Federal Regulation, February 17, 1981 (46 FR 13193, February 19, 1981).

(b) Executive Order 12114, Environmental Effects Abroad of Major Federal Actions, January 4, 1979 (44 FR 1957, January 9, 1979).

(c) Clean Water Act (formerly known as the Federal Water Pollution Control Act) 33 U.S.C. 1344 (hereinafter referred to as section 404).

(d) Endangered Species Act of 1973, as amended, 16 U.S.C. 1531 *et seq.*

(e) Environmental Effects Abroad of Major Department of Defense Actions; Policies and Procedures 32 CFR part 197 (44 FR 21786-92, April 12, 1979).

(f) Fish and Wildlife Coordination Act, 16 U.S.C. 661 *et seq.*

(g) National Environmental Policy Act of 1969, as amended, 42 U.S.C. 4321 *et seq.*

(h) National Historic Preservation Act of 1966, as amended, 16 U.S.C. 470 *et seq.*

(i) "Regulations for Implementing the Procedural Provisions of the National Environmental Policy Act of 1969," (40 CFR parts 1500 through 1508, November 29, 1978), Council on Environmental Quality.

(j) Economic and Environmental Principles and Guidelines for Water and Related Land Resource Implementation Studies (48 CFR parts 10249 through 10258, March 10, 1983).

(k) Regulatory Programs of the Corps of Engineers 33 CFR parts 320 through 330, and 334.

(l) CEQ Information Memorandum to Agencies Containing Answers to 40 Most Asked Questions on NEPA Regulations (46 FR 34263-68, July 28, 1983).

(m) ER 310-1-5. Federal Register Act Requisitioning.

(n) ER 1105-2-10 thru 60. Planning Regulations.

§230.4   Definitions.

Refer to 40 CFR part 1508; other definitions may be found in the references given above.

§230.5   Responsible officials.

The district commander is the Corps NEPA official responsible for compliance with NEPA for actions within district boundaries. The district commander also provides agency views on other agencies' environmental impact statements (EIS). The Office of Environmental Policy HQUSACE (CECW-RE) WASH DC 20314-1000 (phone number 202-272-0166) is the point of contact for information on Corps NEPA documents, NEPA oversight activities, review of other agencies' EISs and NEPA documents about legislation, regulations, national program proposals or other major policy issues. The Assistant Chief Counsel for Environmental Law and Regulatory Programs, HQUSACE (CECC-E) WASH DC 20314-1000, is the point of contact for legal questions involving environmental matters. Requests for information on regulatory permit actions should be directed to HQUSACE (CECW-OR) WASH DC 20314-1000.

§230.6   Actions normally requiring an EIS.

Actions normally requiring an EIS are:

(a) Feasibility reports for authorization and construction of major projects;

(b) Proposed changes in projects which increase size substantially or add additional purposes; and

(c) Proposed major changes in the operation and/or maintenance of completed projects.

District commanders may consider the use of an environmental assessment (EA) on these types of actions if early studies and coordination show that a particular action is not likely to have a significant impact on the quality of the human environment.

§230.7   Actions normally requiring an Environmental Assessment (EA) but not necessarily an EIS.

Actions normally requiring an EA, but not an EIS, are listed below:

(a) *Regulatory Actions.* Most permits will normally require only an EA.

(b) *Authorized Projects and Projects Under Construction.* Changes which may be approved under the discretionary authority of the Secretary of the Army.

(c) *Continuing Authorities Program.* Projects recommended for approval of the Chief of Engineers under the following authorities:

(1) Section 205, Small Flood Control Authority;

(2) Section 208, Snagging and Clearing for Flood Control Authority;

(3) Section 107, Small Navigation Project Authority;

(4) Section 103, Small Beach Erosion Control Project Authority; and

(5) Section 111, Mitigation of Shore Damages Attributable to Navigation Projects.

(d) *Construction and Operations and Maintenance.* Changes in environmental impacts which were not considered in the project EIS or EA. Examples are changes in pool level operations, use of new disposal areas, location of bank protection works, etc.

(e) *Real Estate Management and Disposal Actions.*
(1) Disposal of a Civil Works project or portions of project properties not reported as excess to the General Services Administration.

(2) Disposal of real property for public port and industrial purposes.

(3) Grants of leases or easements for other than minor oil and gas transmission lines, electric power transmission lines, road and highway rights-of-way, and sewage or water treatment facilities and land fills.

§230.8   Emergency actions.

In responding to emergency situations to prevent or reduce imminent risk of life, health, property, or severe economic losses, district commanders may proceed without the specific documentation and procedural requirements of other sections of this regulation. District commanders shall consider the probable environmental consequences in determining appropriate emergency actions and when requesting approval to proceed on emergency actions, will describe proposed NEPA documentation or reasons for exclusion from documentation. NEPA documentation should be accomplished prior to initiation of emergency work if time constraints render this practicable. Such documentation may also be accomplished after the completion of emergency work, if appropriate. Emergency actions include Flood Control and Coastal Emergencies Activities pursuant to Pub. L. 84-99, as amended, and projects constructed under sections 3 of the River and Harbor Act of 1945 or 14 of the Flood Control Act of 1946 of the Continuing Authorities Program. When possible, emergency actions considered major in scope with potentially significant environmental impacts shall be referred through the division commanders to HQUSACE (CECW-RE) for consultation with CEQ about NEPA arrangements.

§230.9   Categorical exclusions.

Actions listed below when considered individually and cumulatively do not have significant effects on the quality of the human environment and are categorically excluded from NEPA documentation. However, district commanders should be alert for extraordinary circumstances which may dictate the need to prepare an EA or an EIS. Even though an EA or EIS is not indicated for a Federal action because of a "categorical exclusion", that fact does not exempt the action from compliance with any other Federal law. For example, compliance with the Endangered Species Act, the Fish and Wildlife Coordination Act, the National Historic Preservation Act, the Clean Water Act, etc., is always mandatory, even for actions not requiring an EA or EIS.

(a) For a period of one year from the effective date of these regulations, district commanders should maintain an information list on the type and number of categorical exclusion actions which due to extraordinary circumstances triggered the need for an EA and finding of no significant impact (FONSI) or an EIS. If a district commander determines that a categorical exclusion should be modified, the information will be furnished to the division commander, who will review and analyze the actions and circumstances to determine if there is a basis for recommending a modification to the list of categorical exclusions. HQUSACE (CECW-RE) will review recommended changes for Corps-wide consistency and revise the list accordingly.

See 33 CFR part 325, appendix B for categorical exclusions for regulatory actions.

(b) Activities at completed Corps projects which carry out the authorized project purposes. Examples include routine operation and maintenance actions, general administration, equipment purchases, custodial actions, erosion control, painting, repair, rehabilitation, replacement of existing structures and facilities such as buildings, roads, levees, groins and utilities, and installation of new buildings utilities, or roadways in developed areas.

(c) Minor maintenance dredging using existing disposal sites.

(d) Planning and technical studies which do not contain recommendations for authorization or funding for construction, but may recommend further study. This does not exclude consideration of environmental matters in the studies.

(e) All Operations and Maintenance grants, general plans, agreements, etc., necessary to carry out land use, development and other measures proposed in project authorization documents, project design memoranda, master plans, or reflected in the project NEPA documents.

(f) Real estate grants for use of excess or surplus real property.

(g) Real estate grants for Government-owned housing.

(h) Exchanges of excess real property and interests therein for property required for project purposes.

(i) Real estate grants for rights-of-way which involve only minor disturbances to earth, air, or water:

(1) Minor access roads, streets and boat ramps.

(2) Minor utility distribution and collection lines, including irrigation.

(3) Removal of sand, gravel, rock, and other material from existing borrow areas.

(4) Oil and gas seismic and gravity meter survey for exploration purposes.

(j) Real estate grants of consent to use Government-owned easement areas.

(k) Real estate grants for archeological and historical investigations compatible with the Corps Historic Preservation Act responsibilities.

(l) Renewal and minor amendments of existing real estate grants evidencing authority to use Government-owned real property.

(m) Reporting excess real property to the General Services Administration for disposal.

(n) Boundary line agreements and disposal of lands or release of deed restrictions to cure encroachments.

(o) Disposal of excess easement interest to the underlying fee owner.

(p) Disposal of existing buildings and improvements for off-site removal.

(q) Sale of existing cottage site areas.

(r) Return of public domain lands to the Department of the Interior.

(s) Transfer and grants of lands to other Federal agencies.

§230.10   Environmental Assessments (EA).

(a) *Purpose.* An EA is a brief document which provides sufficient information to the district commander on potential environmental effects of the proposed action and, if appropriate, its alternatives, for determining whether to prepare an EIS or a FONSI (40 CFR 1508.9). The district commander is responsible for making this determination and for keeping the public informed of the availability of the EA and FONSI.

(b) *Format.* While no special format is required, the EA should include a brief discussion of the need for the proposed action, or appropriate alternatives if there are unresolved conflicts concerning alternative uses of available resources, of the environmental impacts of the proposed action and alternatives and a list of the agencies, interested groups and the public consulted. The document is to be concise for meaningful review and decision.

(c) *Integration with Corps Reports.* In the case of planning and/or engineering reports not requiring an EIS, the EA may be combined with or integrated into the report. The same guidance on combining or integrating an EIS within the report shall apply equally to an EA. Where the EA is combined with a Corps report or prepared as a separate document in the case of construction, operating projects and real estate actions requiring an EA, the EA normally should not exceed 15 pages.

§230.11   Finding of No Significant Impact (FONSI).

A FONSI shall be prepared for a proposed action, not categorically excluded, for which an EIS will not be prepared. The FONSI will be a brief summary document as noted in 40 CFR 1508.13. In the case of feasibility, continuing authority, or special planning reports and certain planning/engineering reports, the draft FONSI and EA should be included within the draft report and circulated for a minimum 30-day review to concerned agencies, organizations and the interested public (40 CFR 1501.4(e)(2)). In the case of operation and maintenance activities involving the discharge of dredged or fill material requiring a public notice, the notice will indicate the availability of the EA/FONSI. For all other Corps project actions a notice of availability of the FONSI will be sent to concerned agencies, organizations and the interested public (40 CFR 1501.4(e)(1)).

§230.12   Notice of intent and scoping.

As soon as practicable after a decision is made to prepare an EIS or supplement, the scoping process for the draft EIS or supplement will be announced in a notice of intent. Guidance on preparing a notice of intent to prepare an EIS for publication in the FEDERAL REGISTER is discussed in Appendix C. Also, a public notice will be widely distributed inviting public participation in the scoping process. As described in 40 CFR 1501.7 and reference 3(m), this process is the key to preparing a concise EIS and clarifying the significant issues to be analyzed in depth. Public concerns on issues, studies needed, alternatives to be examined, procedures and other related matters will be addressed during scoping.

§230.13   Environmental Impact Statement (EIS).

An EIS for feasibility or continuing authority reports and certain planning/engineering reports may be combined with or integrated into the report in accordance with 40 CFR 1500.4(o) and 1506.4. An EIS combined with the report shall follow the format in 40 CFR 1502.10, follow the main report, use colored paper and not be an attachment or appendix. An EIS integrated within the report may follow the instructions in the last paragraph of 40 CFR 1502.10. Additional guidance on combining and integrating EISs is located in ER 1105-2-60. Where the EIS is not combined with or integrated into the project document, the EIS shall be a separate document and follow the format in 40 CFR 1502.10. CEQ regulations suggest maximum lengths for the text of an EIS at 40 CFR 1502.07. An effort should be exerted to cover the substantive topics simply and concisely to the extent practicable, and consistent with producing a legally and technically adequate EIS. Normally, the CEQ page limits should be met.

(a) *Draft and final EISs.* Guidance on EISs prepared for planning and certain planning/engineering studies is contained in ER 1105-2-10 thru 60. 33 CFR part 325, appendix B contains guidance for regulatory actions. For final EISs which are not combined with or integrated into the report, the final EIS may take the form of an "abbreviated" document described in 40 CFR 1503.4(c). An abbreviated final EIS should consist of a new title page, summary, errata or correction sheet(s) and comments and responses. In filing the abbreviated final EIS with EPA (Washington Office), five copies of the draft EIS shall be included in the transmittal. District commanders shall be responsible for determining the type of final EIS to prepare.

(b) *Supplements.* A supplement to the draft or final EIS should be prepared whenever required as discussed in 40 CFR 1502.09(c). A supplement to a draft EIS should be prepared and filed in the same manner as a draft EIS and should be titled "Supplement I", "Supplement II", etc. The final EIS should address the changes noted in the supplement and substantive comments received as a result of circulation of the document. A supplement to a final EIS should be prepared and filed first as a *draft* supplement and then as a *final* supplement. Supplements will be filed and circulated in the same manner as a draft and final EIS (including the abbreviated procedure discussed in 13a. above). Supplements to a draft or final EIS filed before 30 July 1979 may follow the format of the previously filed EIS. Supplements to a draft EIS filed after this date will follow the format outlined in 40 CFR 1502.10. References to the draft or final EIS being supplemented should be used to eliminate repetitive discussions in order to focus on the important issues and impacts. The transmittal letter to EPA as well as the cover sheet should clearly identify the title and purpose of the document as well as the title and filing date of the previous EIS being supplemented and how copies can be obtained. The decision may be made on the proposed action by the appropriate Corps official no sooner than 30 days after the final supplement has been on file. A record of decision will be signed when the decision is made.

(c) *Tiering.* Tiering is discussed in 40 CFR 1502.20 and 1508.28 and should be used in appropriate cases. The initial broad or programmatic EIS must present sufficient information regarding overall impacts of the proposed action so that the decision-makers can make a reasoned judgment on the merits of the action at the present stage of planning or development and exclude from consideration issues already decided or not ready for decision. The initial broad EIS should also identify data gaps and discuss future plans to supplement the data and prepare and circulate site specific EISs or EAs as appropriate.

(d) *Other Reports.* District commanders may also publish periodic fact sheets and/or other supplemental information documents on long-term or complex EISs to keep the public informed on the status of the proposed action. These documents will not be filed officially with EPA.

§230.14   Record of decision and implementation.

A record of decision shall be prepared by the district commander, in accordance with 40 CFR 1505.2, for the signature of the final decisionmaker as prescribed by applicable Corps regulations. Procedures implementing the decision are discussed in 40 CFR 1505.3. Incoming letters of comment on the final EIS will be furnished for review by the decisionmaker who signs the record of decision. For example, the record of decision for feasibility reports will be signed by the ASA(CW) at the time the report is transmitted to Congress for authorization.

§230.15   Mitigation and monitoring.

See 40 CFR 1505.2(c) and 1505.3. District commanders shall, upon request from interested agencies or the public, provide reports on the progress and status of required mitigation and other provisions of their decisions on Corps projects. The term monitoring will be interpreted as that oversight activity necessary to ensure that the decision, including required mitigation measures, is implemented.

§230.16   Lead and cooperating agencies.

Lead agency, joint lead agency, and cooperating agency designation and responsibilities are covered in 40 CFR 1501.5 and 1501.6. The district commander is authorized to enter into agreements with regional offices of other agencies as required by 40 CFR 1501.5(c). District or division commanders will consult with HQUSACE (CECW-RE), WASH DC 20314-1000 prior to requesting resolution by CEQ as outlined by 40 CFR 1501.5 (e) and (f).

(a) *Lead Agency.* The Corps will normally be lead agency for Corps civil works projects and will normally avoid joint lead agency arrangements. Lead agency status for regulatory actions will be determined on the basis of 40 CFR 1501.5(c).

(b) *Corps as a Cooperating Agency.* For cooperating agency designation the Corps area of expertise or jurisdiction by law is generally flood control, navigation, hydropower and Corps regulatory responsibilities. See Appendix II of CEQ regulations (49 FR 49750, December 21, 1984).

§230.17   Filing requirements.

Five copies of draft, final and supplement EISs should be sent to: Director, Office of Federal Activities (A-104), Environmental Protection Agency, 401 M Street SW., Washington, DC 20460. District commanders should file draft EISs and draft supplements directly with EPA. Final EISs and final supplements should be filed by appropriate elements within HQUSACE for feasibility and reevaluation reports requiring Congressional authorization. Division commanders should file final EISs and final supplements for all other Corps actions except for final EISs or final supplements for permit actions which should be filed by the district commander after appropriate reviews by division and the incorporation of division's comments in the EIS. HQUSACE and/or division will notify field office counterparts when to circulate the final EIS or final supplement and will file the final document with EPA after notified that distribution of the document has been accomplished.

(a) *Timing requirements.* Specific timing requirements regarding the filing of EISs with EPA are discussed in 40 CFR 1506.10. District commanders will forward any expedited filing requests with appropriate supporting information through channels to CECW-RE. Once a decision is reached to prepare an EIS or supplement, district commanders will establish a time schedule for each step of the process based upon considerations listed in 40 CFR 1501.8 and upon other management considerations. The time required from the decision to prepare an EIS to filing the final EIS normally should not exceed one year (46 FR 18037, March 23, 1981). For feasibility, continuing authority, or reevaluation studies, where the project's study time is expected to exceed 12 months, the timing of the EIS should be commensurate with the study time. In appropriate circumstances where the costs of completing studies or acquiring information for an EIS (*i.e.,* cost in terms of money, time, or other resources) would be exorbitant, the district commander should consider using the mechanism described in 40 CFR 1502.22, as amended. In all cases, however, it is the district commander's responsibility to assure that the time-limit

established for the preparation of an EIS or supplement is consistent with the purposes of NEPA.

(b) *Timing requirements on supplements.* Minimum review periods will be observed for draft and final supplements covering actions not having a bearing on the overall project for which a final EIS has been filed. Such supplements should not curtail other ongoing or scheduled actions on the overall project which have already complied with the procedural requirements of NEPA.

§230.18   Availability.

Draft and final EISs and supplements will be available to the public as provided in 40 CFR 1502.19 and 1506.6. A summary may be circulated in lieu of the EIS, as provided in 40 CFR 1502.19, if the statement is unusually long. These documents will normally be made available without charge except that, in unusual circumstances, reproduction costs may be recovered in accordance with 40 CFR 1506.6(f) from recipients other than those required by CEQ to receive the complete EIS.

§230.19   Comments.

District commanders shall request comments as set forth in 40 CFR 1503 and 1506.6. A lack of response may be presumed to indicate that the party has no comment to make.

(a) *Time extensions.* District commanders will consider and act on requests for time extensions to review and comment on an EIS based on timeliness of distribution of the document, prior agency involvement in the proposed action, and the action's scope and complexity.

(b) *Public meetings and hearings.* See 40 CFR 1506.6(c). Refer to paragraph 12, 33 CFR part 325, appendix B for regulatory actions.

(c) *Comments received on the draft EIS.* See 40 CFR 1503.4. District commanders will pay particular attention to the display in the final EIS of comments received on the draft EIS. In the case of abbreviated final EISs, follow 40 CFR 1503.4(c). For all other final EISs, comments and agency responses thereto will be placed in an appendix in a format most efficient for users of the final EIS to understand the nature of public input and the district commander's consideration thereof. District commanders will avoid lengthy or repetitive verbatim reporting of comments and will keep responses clear and concise.

(d) *Comments received on the final EIS.* Responses to comments received on the final EIS are required only when substantive issues are raised which have not been addressed in the EIS. In the case of feasibility reports where the final report and EIS, Board of Engineers for Rivers and Harbors (CEBRH) or Mississippi River Commission (CEMRC) report, and the proposed Chief's report are circulated for review, incoming comment letters will normally be answered, if appropriate, by CECW-P. After the review period is over, CECW-P will provide copies of all incoming comments received in HQUSACE to the district commander for use in preparing the draft record of decision. For all other Corps actions except regulatory actions (See 33 CFR part 325, appendix B), two copies of all incoming comment letters (even if the letters do not require an agency response) together with the district commander's responses (if appropriate) and the draft record of decision will be submitted through channels to the appropriate decision authority. In the case of a letter recommending a referral under 40 FR part 1504, reporting officers will notify CECW-RE and request further guidance. The record of decision will not be signed nor any action taken on the proposal until the referral case is resolved.

(e) *Commenting on other agencies' EISs.* See 40 CFR 1503.2 and 1503.3. District commanders will provide comments directly to the requesting agency. CECW-RE will provide comments about legislation, national program proposals, regulations or other major policy issues to the requesting agency. See appendix III of CEQ regulations. When the Corps is a cooperating agency, the Corps will provide comments on another Federal agency's draft EIS even if the response is no comment. Comments should be specific and restricted to areas of Corps jurisdiction by law and special expertise as defined in 40 CFR 1508.15 and 1508.26, generally including flood control, navigation, hydropower, and regulatory responsibilities. See appendix II of CEQ regulations.

§230.20　Integration with State and local procedures.

See 40 CFR 1506.2.

§230.21　Adoption.

See 40 CFR 1506.3. A district commander will normally adopt another Federal agency's EIS and consider it to be adequate unless the district commander finds substantial doubt as to technical or procedural adequacy or omission of factors important to the Corps decision. In such cases, the district commander will prepare a draft and final supplement noting in the draft supplement why the EIS was considered inadequate. In all cases, except where the document is not

recirculated as provided in 40 CFR 1506.3 (b) or (c), the adopted EIS with the supplement, if any, will be processed in accordance with this regulation. A district commander may also adopt another agency's EA/FONSI.

§230.22　Limitations on actions during the NEPA process.

See 40 CFR 1506.1.

§230.23　Predecision referrals.

See 40 CFR part 1504. If the district commander determines that a predecision referral is appropriate, the case will be sent through division to reach CECW-RE not later than 15 days after the final EIS was filed with EPA. Corps actions referred to CEQ by another Federal agency shall be transmitted to CECW-RE for further guidance. See paragraph 19, 33 CFR part 325, appendix B, for guidance on predecision referrals affecting regulatory permit actions.

§230.24　Agency decision points.

The timing and processing of NEPA documents in relation to major decision points are addressed in paragraphs 11 and 14 and appendix A for studies and projects and 33 CFR part 320 through 330 for regulatory actions.

§230.25　Environmental review and consultation requirements.

See 40 CFR 1502.25.

(a) For Federal projects, NEPA documents shall be prepared concurrently with and utilize data from analyses required by other environmental laws and executive orders. A listing of environmental laws and orders is contained in table 3.4.3 of Economic and Environmental Principles and Guidelines for Water and Related Land Resources Implementation Studies. Reviews and consultation requirements, analyses, and status of coordination associated with applicable laws, executive orders and memoranda will be summarized in the draft document. The results of the coordination completed or underway pursuant to these authorities will be summarized in the final document. Where the results of the ongoing studies are not expected to materially affect the decision on the proposed action, the filing of the final EIS need not be delayed.

(b) *Executive Order 12114, Environmental Effects Abroad of Major Federal Actions, 4 January 1979.* For general policy guidance, see FEDERAL REGISTER of April 12, 1979, 32 CFR part 197. Procedural requirements for Civil Works studies and projects are discussed below.

(1) The district commander through the division commander will notify CECW-PE, PN, PS or PW as appropriate, of an impending action which may impact on another country and for which environmental studies may be necessary to determine the extent and significance of the impact. The district commander will inform CECW-P whether entry into the country is necessary to study the base condition.

(2) CECW-P will notify the State Department, Office of Environment and Health (OES/ENH) of the district commander's concern, and whether a need exists at this point to notify officially the foreign nation of our intent to study potential impacts. Depending on expected extent and severity of impacts, or if entry is deemed necessary, the matter will be referred to the appropriate foreign desk for action.

(3) As soon as it becomes evident that the impacts of the proposed actions are considered significant, CECW-P will notify the State Department. The State Department will determine whether the foreign embassy needs to be notified, and will do so if deemed appropriate, requesting formal discussions on the matter. When the International Joint Commission (IJC) or the International Boundary and Water Commission, United States and Mexico (IBWC) is involved in a study, the State Department should be consulted to determine the foreign policy implications of any action and the proper course of action for formal consultations.

(4) Prior to public dissemination, press releases or reports dealing with impact assessments in foreign nations should be made available to the appropriate foreign desk at the State Department for clearance and coordination with the foreign embassy.

§230.26   General considerations in preparing Corps EISs.

(a) *Interdisciplinary preparation.* See (40 CFR 1502.6).

(b) *Incorporation by reference.* To the maximum extent practicable, the EIS should incorporate material by reference in accordance with 40 CFR 1502.21. Footnotes should be used only where their use greatly aids the reader's understanding of the point discussed. Citation in the EIS of material incorporated by reference should be made by indicating an author's last name and date of the reference in parentheses at the appropriate location in the EIS. The list of references will be placed at the end of the EIS. Only information sources actually

cited in the text should appear in the reference list. The reference list should include the author's name, the date and title of the publication, personal communications and type of communication (e.g., letter, telephone, interview, etc.).

Appendix A to Part 230—Processing Corps NEPA Documents

NEFA documents for Civil Works activities other than permits will be processed in accordance with the instructions contained in this appendix and applicable paragraphs in the regulation.

Table of Contents

Title
1. Feasibility Studies
2. Continuing Authorities Program Studies
3. Projects in Preconstruction Engineering, and Design, Construction, and Completed Projects in an Operations and Maintenance Category
4. Other Corps Projects

1.   Feasibility Studies

a. *Preparation and Draft Review.* During the reconnaissance phase, the district commander should undertake environmental studies along with engineering, economic and other technical studies to determine the probable environmental effects of alternatives and the appropriate NEPA document to accompany the feasibility report. This environmental evaluation should be continued in the feasibility phase, and if the need for an EIS develops the district commander will issue a notice of intent as early in the feasibility phase as possible. Following the guidance in ER 1105-2-10 through 60, the district commander will prepare a draft feasibility report combining or integrating the draft EIS or EA and draft FONSI (as appropriate), or a separate NEPA document and circulate it to agencies, organizations and members of the public known to have an interest in the study. Five copies of the draft EIS and report will be mailed to Director, Office of Federal Activities (A-104), Environmental Protection Agency, 401 M Street SW., Washington, DC 20460 for filing after distribution has been accomplished. After receipt and evaluation of comments received, the district commander will prepare the final report and EIS or EA and FONSI and submit it to the division commander for review.

b. *Division Review.* After review, the division commander will issue a public notice of report issuance and transmit the report to the CEBRH. On Mississippi River and Tributaries projects, the district commander will issue a public notice and submit the report to the

CEMRC. For the purpose of this regulation, only the acronym CEBRH will be used since the review functions of CEMRC and CEBRH are similar. The notice will provide a 30-day period for comments to be submitted to CEBRH on the report and EIS. Although the EIS in the report is identified as "final" at this stage of processing, it should be made clear to all those requesting a copy that it is an "Interim Document under Agency Review—Subject to Revision" and will become the agency's final EIS when it is filed after CEBRH review.

c. *CEBRH Review.* CEBRH will review the EIS at the same time it reviews the final feasibility report. The report and EIS should be compatible. If the CEBRH review requires minor revisions (with insignificant impacts) to the plan as recommended by the division and district commanders, these changes and impacts shall be noted in the CEBRH report. If the CEBRH action results in major revisions to the recommended plan and revisions are variants of the plan or are within the range of alternatives considered and discussed in the draft EIS, an addendum to the final EIS will be prepared by CEBRH (with assistance from the district commander, as required). This addendum "package" will be identified as an "Addendum to the Final EIS— Environmental Consequences of the Modifications Recommended by the Board of Engineers for Rivers and Harbors—project name." The format shall include an abstract on the cover page; recommended changes to the division/district commander's proposed plan; rationale for the recommended changes; environmental consequences of the recommended changes; and the name, expertise/discipline, experience, and role of the principal preparer(s) of the addendum. Letters received during CEBRH review which provide new pertinent information having a bearing on the modifications recommended by CEBRH will be attached to the addendum. If CEBRH proposes to recommend a major revision or a new alternative to the plan recommended by the division and district commanders with significant impacts which were not discussed in the draft EIS, a supplement to the draft EIS will be required. After consultation with CEBRH and the division commander, the district commander will prepare and circulate the supplement to the draft EIS in accordance with paragraph 13(b). The supplement together with incoming letters of comment and Corps responses to substantive issues shall be incorporated into the existing final report and EIS with a minimum of page changes or revisions to reflect the modified or new proposed plan. CEBRH will review its proposed action in light of the comments received prior to taking final action on the report and EIS.

d. *Departmental Review.* The report and final EIS, together with the proposed report of the Chief of Engineers and the CEBRH report, will be filed with EPA at about the same time as it is circulated for the 90-day departmental review by Federal agencies at the Washington level and the concerned state(s). District commanders will circulate the proposed Chief's report, CEBRH report, and the report and final EIS to parties on the project mailing list not contacted by HQUSACE (groups and individuals known to have an interest in the study or who provided comments on the draft EIS) allowing the normal 30-day period of review. HQUSACE will provide a standard letter for the district to use to transmit these documents which explains the current status of the report and EIS and directs all comments to be sent to HQUSACE (CECW-P). Copies of the report appendices circulated with the draft need not be circulated with the report and final EIS. All letters of comment received on the report and final EIS together with HQUSACE responses and the draft record of decision (to be provided by the district commander) will be included with other papers furnished at the time the final Chief's report is transmitted to ASA(CW) for further review and processing.

e. *Executive Reviews.* After completion of review, the Chief of Engineers will sign his final report and transmit the report and accompanying documents to ASA(CW). After review ASA(CW) will transmit the report to OMB requesting its views in relation to the programs of the President. After OMB provides its views, ASA(CW) will sign the record of decision (ROD) and transmit the report to Congress. In situations where Congress has acted to authorize construction of a project prior to receiving ASA(CW) recommendations, the Director of Civil Works is the designated official to sign the ROD. In this case the ROD should only address the project as authorized by the Congress and not attempt to provide any additional justification of the Congressional action.

2. Continuing Authorities Program Studies

a. *Preparation and Draft Review.* During the reconnaissance phase, the district commander should undertake environmental studies along with engineering, economic and other technical studies to determine the probable environmental effects of alternatives and the appropriate NEPA document to accompany the detailed project report (DPR). If the results of the reconnaissance phase warrant preparation of an EIS, the district commander will issue a notice of intent early in the ensuing feasibility study. Following the guidance in ER 1105-2-10 through 60 the district commander will prepare the draft DPR incorporating the EA and draft FONSI or draft EIS (as appropriate), and circulate it to agencies, organizations and members of the public known to have an interest in the study. If an EIS is prepared, five copies of the draft EIS and report will be mailed to Director, Office of Federal Activities (A-104), Environmental Protection Agency, 401 M Street SW, Washington, DC 20460 for filing after distribution has been accomplished.

b. *Agency Review.* After receipt and evaluation of comments the district commander will prepare the final DPR and EA/FONSI or final EIS and submit eight (8) copies to the division commander for review and approval. After review, the division commander will file five (5) copies of the final DPR and EIS with the Washington office of EPA. The division commander will not file the final EIS until notified by the district commander that distribution has been accomplished.

c. *Final Review.* Letters of comment on the final DPR including the final EIS will be answered by the district commander on an individual basis if appropriate. Two (2) copies of all incoming letters and the district commander's reply together with five copies of the final DPR and EIS and a draft of the record of decision will be submitted through division to the appropriate element within CECW-P. After review of the DPR and NEPA documents, the Director of Civil Works or Chief, Planning Division will approve the project and sign the record of decision if an EIS was prepared for the DPR.

3. Projects in Preconstruction Engineering and Design, Construction, and Completed Projects in an Operations and Maintenance Category

a. *General.* District commanders will review the existing NEPA document(s) to determine if there are new circumstances or significant impacts which warrant the preparation of a draft and final supplement to the EIS. If the proposed changes and new impacts are not significant an EA and FONSI may be used.

b. *Preparation and Draft Review.* As soon as practicable after the district commander makes a determination to prepare an EIS or supplement for the proposed project, a notice of intent will be issued. The district commander will, in accordance with 40 CFR 1506.6, prepare and circulate the draft EIS or supplement for review and comment to agencies, groups and individuals known who may be interested or affected. Five (5) copies will be sent to Director, Office of Federal activities (A-104), Environmental Protection Agency, 401 M Street SW., Washington, DC 20460 for filing after distribution has been accomplished.

c. *Agency Review.* The district commander will prepare the final EIS or supplement after receipt and evaluation of comments. Eight (8) copies will be transmitted to the division commander for review. After review the division commander will file five (5) copies with the Washington office of EPA. A copy of the final EIS or supplement and transmittal letter to EPA will be provided to the appropriate counterpart office within HQUSACE. The division commander will file the final EIS when the district commander has made distribution.

d. *Final Review.* Letters of comment on the final EIS or supplement will be answered by the district commander on an individual basis as appropriate. Two (2) copies of the incoming letters and the district commander's reply together with two copies of the final EIS or supplement and a draft of the record of decision will be submitted to the appropriate Corps official having approval authority. After review of the NEPA documents and letters, the appropriate approving official will sign the record of decision.

4. *Other Corps Projects.* Draft and final EISs for other Civil Works projects or activities having significant environmental impacts which may be authorized by Congress without an EIS having been previously filed and for certain real estate management and disposal actions which may require an EIS should be processed in a manner similar to that discussed in paragraph 3 of this appendix except that CERE-MC will be the coordinating office within HQUSACE for real estate actions.

Appendix B to Part 230 [Reserved]

Appendix C to Part 230—Notice of Intent To Prepare a Draft EIS

1. *Purpose.* This appendix provides guidance on the preparation and processing of a notice of intent to prepare a draft EIS for publication in the FEDERAL REGISTER. A notice of intent to prepare a draft EIS or a draft supplement is discussed in 40 CFR 1508.22.

2. *Procedure.* District commanders shall publish a notice of intent in the FEDERAL REGISTER as soon as practicable after a decision is made to prepare a draft EIS or draft supplement. See 40 CFR 1507.3(e) for timing of notice of intent for Corps feasibility studies. Guidance on the format and content of the notice in the form of a sample notice of intent is contained in paragraph 4 of this appendix. District commanders shall also follow this guidance when publishing a notice of intent to withdraw a notice of intent when a decision has been made to terminate the EIS process.

3. *Publishing Documents in the Federal Register.* The following information is furnished for preparation and publication of notices of intent in the FEDERAL REGISTER:

a. A brief transmittal letter inclosing three (3) signed copies of the notice of intent should be processed through local Chief, Information Management channels to: HQDA, SFIS-APP, ATTN: Department of the Army Liaison Officer with the Office of the Federal Register, Alexandria, VA 22331-0302. This office will review and correct (if needed) all documents prior to publication in the FEDERAL REGISTER.

b. The notice must be signed by the official issuing the document along with the signer's typed name, rank and position title for military officials or name and position title for civilian officials. A signer cannot sign "as acting" or "for" if another name is shown in the signature block. All three copies sent forward must be signed in ink. A xerox copy of the signature is not allowed.

c. A six-digit billing code number must be typed or handwritten in ink at the top of the first page on all three copies of a notice. This billing code number can be found on GPO bills, GPO Form 400, in the upper left corner opposite the address. The billing code number will be indicated as 3710-XX. FOAs must submit an open-end printing and binding requisition, Standard Form 1, each fiscal year to cover FEDERAL REGISTER printing costs (reference 3(n)). Completed requisitions (SF-1) must be forwarded to reach HQUSACE (CEIM-SP) WASH DC 20314-1000 by 1 June of each year. Consult the local chief, Information Management for Assistance.

4. *Sample Notice of Intent.* The following is a sample notice of intent to be used by district commanders:

Department of Defense

Corps of Engineer, Department of the Army, 3710-XX (Use Local Billing Code Number)

Intent To Prepare a Draft Environment Impact Statement (DEIS) For a Proposed (*Name and location of project, permit or activity*).

Agency: U.S. Army Corps of Engineers, DoD.

Action: Notice of Intent.

Summary: The summary should briefly state in simple language what action is being taken, why the action is necessary, and the intended effect of the action. Extensive discussion belongs under the Supplementary Information caption.

For Further Information Contact: Questions about the proposed action and DEIS can be answered by: (Provide name, telephone number, and address of the person in the district or division who can answer questions about the proposed action and the DEIS).

Supplementary Information: The Supplementary Information should contain the remainder of the necessary information of the document. It should contain any authority citation, FEDERAL REGISTER citation to a previously published document, or CFR citation when appropriate and include a discussion of the following topics:

1. Briefly describe the proposed action.

2. Briefly describe reasonable alternatives.

3. Briefly describe the Corps' scoping process which is reasonably foreseeable for the DEIS under consideration. The description:

a. Shall discuss the proposed public involvement program and invite the participation of affected Federal, state and local agencies, affected Indian tribes, and other interested private organizations and parties.

b. Shall identify significant issues to be analyzed in depth in the DEIS.

c. May discuss possible assignments for input into the EIS under consideration among the lead and cooperating agencies.

d. Shall identify other environmental review and consultation requirements.

4. Indicate whether or not a scoping meeting will be held. Indicate time, date and location if a meeting is scheduled.

5. Provide an estimated date when the DEIS will be made available to the public.

(Provide date)

_____

(Signature)

_____

See par. 3.b. for instructions on signature

Note

- Text to be double-spaced. Use block format.

- Place local billing code number at the top of the first page on all three copies.

- Margins—one inch on top, bottom and right side; and one and one-half inches on the left side.

- Pages must be numbered consecutively.

- Text should be typed on one side only.

- Use 8½ by 11 inch bond paper or photocopy paper.

33 CFR Pt. 325

Part 325—Processing of Department of the Army Permits

Contents

AUTHORITY: 33 U.S.C. 401 *et seq.;* 33 U.S.C. 1344; 33 U.S.C. 1413.

SOURCE: 51 FR 41236, Nov. 13, 1986, unless otherwise noted.

§325.1   Applications for permits.

(a) *General.* The processing procedures of this part apply to any Department of the Army (DA) permit. Special procedures and additional information are contained in 33 CFR parts 320 through 324, 327 and part 330. This part is arranged in the basic timing sequence used by the Corps of Engineers in processing applications for DA permits.

(b) *Pre-application consultation for major applications.* The district staff element having responsibility for administering, processing, and enforcing federal laws and regulations relating to the Corps of Engineers regulatory program shall be available to advise potential applicants of studies or other information foreseeably required for later federal action. The district engineer will establish local procedures and policies including appropriate publicity programs which will allow potential applicants to contact the district engineer or the regulatory staff element to request pre-application consultation. Upon receipt of such request, the district engineer will assure the conduct of an orderly process which may involve other staff elements and affected agencies (Federal, state, or local) and the public. This early process should be brief but thorough so that the potential applicant may begin to assess the viability of some of the more obvious potential alternatives in the application. The district engineer will endeavor, at this stage, to provide the potential applicant with all helpful information necessary in pursuing the application, including factors which the Corps must consider in its permit decision making process. Whenever the district engineer becomes aware of planning for work which may require a DA permit and which may involve the preparation of an environmental document, he shall contact the principals involved to advise them of the requirement for the permit(s) and the attendant public interest review including the development of an environmental document. Whenever a potential applicant indicates the intent to submit an application for work which may require the preparation of an environmental document, a single point of contact shall be designated within the district's regulatory staff to effectively coordinate the regulatory process, including the National Environmental Policy Act (NEPA) procedures and all attendant reviews, meetings, hearings, and other actions, including the scoping process if appropriate, leading to a decision by the district engineer. Effort devoted to this process should be commensurate with the likelihood of a permit application actually being submitted to the Corps. The regulatory staff coordinator shall maintain an open relationship with each potential applicant or his consultants so as to assure that the potential applicant is fully aware of the substance (both quantitative and qualitative) of the data required by the district engineer for use in preparing an environmental assessment or an environmental impact statement (EIS) in accordance with 33 CFR part 230, Appendix B.

(c) *Application form.* Applicants for all individual DA permits must use the standard application form (ENG Form 4345, OMB Approval No. OMB 49-R0420). Local variations of the application form for purposes of facilitating coordination with federal, state and local agencies may be used. The appropriate form may be obtained from the district office having jurisdiction over the waters in which the activity is proposed to be located. Certain activities have been authorized by general permits and do not require submission of an application form but may require a separate notification.

(d) *Content of application.* (1) The application must include a complete description of the proposed activity including necessary drawings, sketches, or plans sufficient for public notice (detailed engineering plans and specifications are not required); the location, purpose and need for the proposed activity; scheduling of the activity; the names and addresses of adjoining property owners; the location and dimensions of adjacent structures; and a list of authorizations required by other federal, interstate, state, or local agencies for the work, including all approvals received or denials already made. See §325.3 for information required to be in public notices. District and division engineers are not authorized to develop additional information forms but may request specific information on a case-by-case basis. (See §325.1(e)).

(2) All activities which the applicant plans to undertake which are reasonably related to the same project and for which a DA permit would be required should be included in the same permit application. District engineers should reject, as incomplete, any permit application which fails to comply with this requirement. For example, a permit application for a marina will include dredging required for access as well as any fill associated with construction of the marina.

(3) If the activity would involve dredging in navigable waters of the United States, the application must include a description of the type, composition and quantity of the material to be dredged, the method of dredging, and the site and plans for disposal of the dredged material.

(4) If the activity would include the discharge of dredged or fill material into the waters of the United States or the transportation of dredged material for the purpose of disposing of it in ocean waters the application must include the source of the material; the purpose of the discharge, a description of the type, composition and quantity of the material; the method of transportation and disposal of the material; and the location of the disposal site. Certification under section 401 of the Clean Water Act is required for such discharges into waters of the United States.

(5) If the activity would include the construction of a filled area or pile or float-supported platform the project description must include the use of, and specific structures to be erected on, the fill or platform.

(6) If the activity would involve the construction of an impoundment structure, the applicant may be required to demonstrate that the structure complies with established state dam safety criteria or that the structure has been designed by qualified persons and, in appropriate cases, independently reviewed (and modified as the review would indicate) by similarly qualified persons. No specific design criteria are to be prescribed nor is an independent detailed engineering review to be made by the district engineer.

(7) For activities involving discharges of dredged or fill material into waters of the United States, the application must include a statement describing how impacts to waters of the United States are to be avoided and minimized. The application must also include either a statement describing how impacts to waters of the United States are to be compensated for or a statement explaining why compensatory mitigation should not be required for the proposed impacts. (See §332.4(b)(1) of this chapter.)

(8) *Signature on application.* The application must be signed by the person who desires to undertake the proposed activity (*i.e.*, the applicant) or by a duly authorized agent. When the applicant is represented by an agent, that information will be included in the space provided on the application or by a separate written statement. The signature of the applicant or the agent will be an affirmation that the applicant possesses or will possess the requisite property interest to undertake the activity proposed in the application, except where the lands are under the control of the Corps of Engineers, in which cases the district engineer will coordinate the transfer of the real estate and the permit action. An application may include the activity of more than one owner provided the character of the activity of each owner is similar and in the same general area and each owner submits a statement designating the same agent.

(9) If the activity would involve the construction or placement of an artificial reef, as defined in 33 CFR 322.2(g), in the navigable waters of the United States or in the waters overlying the outer continental shelf, the application must include provisions for siting, constructing, monitoring, and managing the artificial reef.

(10) *Complete application.* An application will be determined to be complete when sufficient information is received to issue a public notice (See 33 CFR 325.1(d) and 325.3(a).) The issuance of a public notice will not be delayed to obtain information necessary to evaluate an application.

(e) *Additional information.* In addition to the information indicated in paragraph (d) of this section, the applicant will be required to furnish only such additional information as the district engineer deems essential to make a public interest determination including, where applicable, a determination of compliance with the section 404(b)(1) guidelines or ocean dumping criteria. Such additional information may include environmental data and information on alternate methods and sites as may be necessary for the preparation of the required environmental documentation.

(f) *Fees.* Fees are required for permits under section 404 of the Clean Water Act, section 103 of the Marine Protection, Research and Sanctuaries Act of 1972, as amended, and sections 9 and 10 of the Rivers and Harbors Act of 1899. A fee of $100.00 will be charged when the planned or ultimate purpose of the project is commercial or industrial in nature and is in support of operations that charge for the production, distribution or sale of goods or services. A $10.00 fee will be charged for permit applications when the proposed work is non-commercial in nature and would provide personal benefits that have no connection with a commercial enterprise. The final decision as to the basis for a fee (commercial vs. non-commercial) shall be solely the responsibility of the district engineer. No fee will be charged if the applicant withdraws the application at any time prior to issuance of the permit or if the permit is denied. Collection of the fee will be deferred until the proposed activity has been determined to be not contrary to the public interest. Multiple fees are not to be charged if more than one law is applicable. Any modification significant enough to require publication of a public notice will also require a fee. No fee will be assessed when a permit is transferred from one property owner to another. No fees will be charged for time extensions, general permits or letters of permission. Agencies or instrumentalities of federal, state or local governments will not be required to pay any fee in connection with permits.

[51 FR 41236, Nov. 13, 1986, as amended at 73 FR 19670, Apr. 10, 2008]

§325.2   Processing of applications.

(a) *Standard procedures.* (1) When an application for a permit is received the district engineer shall immediately assign it a number for identification, acknowledge receipt thereof, and advise the applicant of the number assigned to it. He shall review the application for completeness, and if the application is incomplete, request from the applicant within 15 days of receipt of the application any additional information necessary for further processing.

(2) Within 15 days of receipt of an application the district engineer will either determine that the application is complete (see 33 CFR 325.1(d)(9) and issue a public notice as described in §325.3 of this part, unless specifically exempted by other provisions of this regulation or that it is incomplete and notify the applicant of the information necessary for a complete application. The district engineer will issue a supplemental, revised, or corrected public notice if in his view there is a change in the application data that would affect the public's review of the proposal.

(3) The district engineer will consider all comments received in response to the public notice in his subsequent actions on the permit application. Receipt of the comments will be acknowledged, if appropriate, and they will be made a part of the administrative record of the application. Comments received as form letters or petitions may be acknowledged as a group to the person or organization responsible for the form letter or petition. If comments relate to matters within the special expertise of another federal agency, the district engineer may seek the advice of that agency. If the district engineer determines, based on comments received, that he must have the views of the applicant on a particular issue to make a public interest determination, the applicant will be given the opportunity to furnish his views on such issue to the district engineer (see §325.2(d)(5)). At the earliest practicable time other substantive comments will be furnished to the applicant for his information and any views he may wish to offer. A summary of the comments, the actual letters or portions thereof, or representative comment letters may be furnished to the applicant. The applicant may voluntarily elect to contact objectors in an attempt to resolve objections but will not be required to do so. District engineers will ensure that all parties are informed that the Corps alone is responsible for reaching a decision on the merits of any application. The district engineer may also offer Corps regulatory staff to be present at meetings between applicants and objectors, where appropriate, to provide information on the process, to mediate differences, or to gather information to aid in the decision process. The district engineer should not delay processing of the application unless the applicant requests a reasonable delay, normally not to exceed 30 days, to provide additional information or comments.

(4) The district engineer will follow Appendix B of 33 CFR part 230 for environmental procedures and documentation required by the National Environmental Policy Act of 1969. A decision on a permit application will require either an environmental assessment or an environmental impact statement unless it is included within a categorical exclusion.

(5) The district engineer will also evaluate the application to determine the need for a public hearing pursuant to 33 CFR part 327.

(6) After all above actions have been completed, the district engineer will determine in accordance with the record and applicable regulations whether or not the permit should be issued. He shall prepare a statement of findings (SOF) or, where an EIS has been prepared, a record of decision (ROD), on all permit decisions. The SOF or ROD shall include the district engineer's views on the probable effect of the proposed work

on the public interest including conformity with the guidelines published for the discharge of dredged or fill material into waters of the United States (40 CFR part 230) or with the criteria for dumping of dredged material in ocean waters (40 CFR parts 220 to 229), if applicable, and the conclusions of the district engineer. The SOF or ROD shall be dated, signed, and included in the record prior to final action on the application. Where the district engineer has delegated authority to sign permits for and in his behalf, he may similarly delegate the signing of the SOF or ROD. If a district engineer makes a decision on a permit application which is contrary to state or local decisions (33 CFR 320.4(j) (2) & (4)), the district engineer will include in the decision document the significant national issues and explain how they are overriding in importance. If a permit is warranted, the district engineer will determine the special conditions, if any, and duration which should be incorporated into the permit. In accordance with the authorities specified in §325.8 of this part, the district engineer will take final action or forward the application with all pertinent comments, records, and studies, including the final EIS or environmental assessment, through channels to the official authorized to make the final decision. The report forwarding the application for decision will be in a format prescribed by the Chief of Engineers. District and division engineers will notify the applicant and interested federal and state agencies that the application has been forwarded to higher headquarters. The district or division engineer may, at his option, disclose his recommendation to the news media and other interested parties, with the caution that it is only a recommendation and not a final decision. Such disclosure is encouraged in permit cases which have become controversial and have been the subject of stories in the media or have generated strong public interest. In those cases where the application is forwarded for decision in the format prescribed by the Chief of Engineers, the report will serve as the SOF or ROD. District engineers will generally combine the SOF, environmental assessment, and findings of no significant impact (FONSI), 404(b)(1) guideline analysis, and/or the criteria for dumping of dredged material in ocean waters into a single document.

(7) If the final decision is to deny the permit, the applicant will be advised in writing of the reason(s) for denial. If the final decision is to issue the permit and a standard individual permit form will be used, the issuing official will forward the permit to the applicant for signature accepting the conditions of the permit. The permit is not valid until signed by the issuing official. Letters of permission require only the signature of the issuing official. Final action on the permit application is the signature on the letter notifying the applicant of the denial of the permit or signature of the issuing official on the authorizing document.

(8) The district engineer will publish monthly a list of permits issued or denied during the previous month. The list will identify each action by public notice number, name of applicant, and brief description of activity involved. It will also note that relevant environmental documents and the SOF's or ROD's are available upon written request and, where applicable, upon the payment of administrative fees. This list will be distributed to all persons who may have an interest in any of the public notices listed.

(9) Copies of permits will be furnished to other agencies in appropriate cases as follows:

(i) If the activity involves the construction of artificial islands, installations or other devices on the outer continental shelf, to the Director, Defense Mapping Agency, Hydrographic Center, Washington, DC 20390 Attention, Code NS12, and to the National Ocean Service, Office of Coast Survey, N/CS261, 1315 East West Highway, Silver Spring, Maryland 20910-3282.

(ii) If the activity involves the construction of structures to enhance fish propagation (e.g., fishing reefs) along the coasts of the United States, to the Defense Mapping Agency, Hydrographic Center and National Ocean Service as in paragraph (a)(9)(i) of this section and to the Director, Office of Marine Recreational Fisheries, National Marine Fisheries Service, Washington, DC 20235.

(iii) If the activity involves the erection of an aerial transmission line, submerged cable, or submerged pipeline across a navigable water of the United States, to the National Ocean Service, Office of Coast Survey, N/CS261, 1315 East West Highway, Silver Spring, Maryland 20910-3282.

(iv) If the activity is listed in paragraphs (a)(9) (i), (ii), or (iii) of this section, or involves the transportation of dredged material for the purpose of dumping it in ocean waters, to the appropriate District Commander, U.S. Coast Guard.

(b) *Procedures for particular types of permit situations—* (1) *Section 401 Water Quality Certification.* If the district engineer determines that water quality certification for the proposed activity is necessary under the provisions of section 401 of the Clean Water Act, he shall so notify the applicant and obtain from him or the certifying agency a copy of such certification.

(i) The public notice for such activity, which will contain a statement on certification requirements (see §325.3(a)(8)), will serve as the notification to the Administrator of the Environmental Protection Agency (EPA) pursuant to section 401(a)(2) of the Clean Water Act. If EPA determines that the proposed discharge may affect the quality of the waters of any state other than the state in which the discharge will originate, it will so notify such other state, the district engineer, and the applicant. If such notice or a request for supplemental information is not received within 30 days of issuance of the public notice, the district engineer will assume EPA has made a negative determination with respect to section 401(a)(2). If EPA determines another state's waters may be affected, such state has 60 days from receipt of EPA's notice to determine if the proposed discharge will affect the quality of its waters so as to violate any water quality requirement in such state, to notify EPA and the district engineer in writing of its objection to permit issuance, and to request a public hearing. If such occurs, the district engineer will hold a public hearing in the objecting state. Except as stated below, the hearing will be conducted in accordance with 33 CFR part 327. The issues to be considered at the public hearing will be limited to water quality impacts. EPA will submit its evaluation and recommendations at the hearing with respect to the state's objection to permit issuance. Based upon the recommendations of the objecting state, EPA, and any additional evidence presented at the hearing, the district engineer will condition the permit, if issued, in such a manner as may be necessary to insure compliance with applicable water quality requirements. If the imposition of conditions cannot, in the district engineer's opinion, insure such compliance, he will deny the permit.

(ii) No permit will be granted until required certification has been obtained or has been waived. A waiver may be explicit, or will be deemed to occur if the certifying agency fails or refuses to act on a request for certification within sixty days after receipt of such a request unless the district engineer determines a shorter or longer period is reasonable for the state to act. In determining whether or not a waiver period has commenced or waiver has occurred, the district engineer will verify that the certifying agency has received a valid request for certification. If, however, special circumstances identified by the district engineer require that action on an application be taken within a more limited period of time, the district engineer shall determine a reasonable lesser period of time, advise the certifying agency of the need for action by a particular date, and that, if certification is not received by that date, it will be considered that the requirement for

certification has been waived. Similarly, if it appears that circumstances may reasonably require a period of time longer than sixty days, the district engineer, based on information provided by the certifying agency, will determine a longer reasonable period of time, not to exceed one year, at which time a waiver will be deemed to occur.

(2) *Coastal Zone Management consistency.* If the proposed activity is to be undertaken in a state operating under a coastal zone management program approved by the Secretary of Commerce pursuant to the Coastal Zone Management (CZM) Act (see 33 CFR 320.3(b)), the district engineer shall proceed as follows:

(i) If the applicant is a federal agency, and the application involves a federal activity in or affecting the coastal zone, the district engineer shall forward a copy of the public notice to the agency of the state responsible for reviewing the consistency of federal activities. The federal agency applicant shall be responsible for complying with the CZM Act's directive for ensuring that federal agency activities are undertaken in a manner which is consistent, to the maximum extent practicable, with approved CZM Programs. (See 15 CFR part 930.) If the state coastal zone agency objects to the proposed federal activity on the basis of its inconsistency with the state's approved CZM Program, the district engineer shall not make a final decision on the application until the disagreeing parties have had an opportunity to utilize the procedures specified by the CZM Act for resolving such disagreements.

(ii) If the applicant is not a federal agency and the application involves an activity affecting the coastal zone, the district engineer shall obtain from the applicant a certification that his proposed activity complies with and will be conducted in a manner that is consistent with the approved state CZM Program. Upon receipt of the certification, the district engineer will forward a copy of the public notice (which will include the applicant's certification statement) to the state coastal zone agency and request its concurrence or objection. If the state agency objects to the certification or issues a decision indicating that the proposed activity requires further review, the district engineer shall not issue the permit until the state concurs with the certification statement or the Secretary of Commerce determines that the proposed activity is consistent with the purposes of the CZM Act or is necessary in the interest of national security. If the state agency fails to concur or object to a certification statement within six months of the state agency's receipt of the certification statement, state agency concurrence with the certification statement shall be conclusively presumed. District engineers will seek agreements with state CZM agencies that the agency's failure to provide comments during the public notice comment period will be considered as a concurrence with the certification or waiver of the right to concur or non-concur.

(iii) If the applicant is requesting a permit for work on Indian reservation lands which are in the coastal zone, the district engineer shall treat the application in the same manner as prescribed for a Federal applicant in paragraph (b)(2)(i) of this section. However, if the applicant is requesting a permit on non-trust Indian lands, and the state CZM agency has decided to assert jurisdiction over such lands, the district engineer shall treat the application in the same manner as prescribed for a non-Federal applicant in paragraph (b)(2)(ii) of this section.

(3) *Historic properties.* If the proposed activity would involve any property listed or eligible for listing in the National Register of Historic Places, the district engineer will proceed in accordance with Corps National Historic Preservation Act implementing regulations.

(4) *Activities associated with Federal projects.* If the proposed activity would consist of the dredging of an access channel and/or berthing facility associated with an authorized federal navigation project, the activity will be included in the planning and coordination of the construction or maintenance of the federal project to the maximum extent feasible. Separate notice, hearing, and environmental documentation will not be required for activities so included and coordinated, and the public notice issued by the district engineer for these federal and associated non-federal activities will be the notice of intent to issue permits for those included non-federal dredging activities. The decision whether to issue or deny such a permit will be consistent with the decision on the federal project unless special considerations applicable to the proposed activity are identified. (See §322.5(c).)

(5) *Endangered Species.* Applications will be reviewed for the potential impact on threatened or endangered species pursuant to section 7 of the Endangered Species Act as amended. The district engineer will include a statement in the public notice of his current knowledge of endangered species based on his initial review of the application (see 33 CFR 325.2(a)(2)). If the district engineer determines that the proposed activity would not affect listed species or their critical habitat, he will include a statement to this effect in the public notice. If he finds the proposed activity may affect an endangered or threatened species or their critical habitat, he will initiate formal consultation procedures with the U.S. Fish and Wildlife Service or National

Marine Fisheries Service. Public notices forwarded to the U.S. Fish and Wildlife Service or National Marine Fisheries Service will serve as the request for information on whether any listed or proposed to be listed endangered or threatened species may be present in the area which would be affected by the proposed activity, pursuant to section 7(c) of the Act. References, definitions, and consultation procedures are found in 50 CFR part 402.

(c) [Reserved]

(d) *Timing of processing of applications.* The district engineer will be guided by the following time limits for the indicated steps in the evaluation process:

(1) The public notice will be issued within 15 days of receipt of all information required to be submitted by the applicant in accordance with paragraph 325.1.(d) of this part.

(2) The comment period on the public notice should be for a reasonable period of time within which interested parties may express their views concerning the permit. The comment period should not be more than 30 days nor less than 15 days from the date of the notice. Before designating comment periods less than 30 days, the district engineer will consider: (i) Whether the proposal is routine or noncontroversial,

(ii) Mail time and need for comments from remote areas,

(iii) Comments from similar proposals, and

(iv) The need for a site visit. After considering the length of the original comment period, paragraphs (a)(2) (i) through (iv) of this section, and other pertinent factors, the district engineer may extend the comment period up to an additional 30 days if warranted.

(3) District engineers will decide on all applications not later than 60 days after receipt of a complete application, unless (i) precluded as a matter of law or procedures required by law (see below),

(ii) The case must be referred to higher authority (see §325.8 of this part),

(iii) The comment period is extended,

(iv) A timely submittal of information or comments is not received from the applicant,

(v) The processing is suspended at the request of the applicant, or

(vi) Information needed by the district engineer for a decision on the application cannot reasonably be obtained within the 60-day period. Once the cause for preventing the decision from being made within the normal 60-day period has been satisfied or eliminated, the 60-day clock will start running again from where it was suspended. For example, if the comment period is extended by 30 days, the district engineer will, absent other restraints, decide on the application within 90 days of receipt of a complete application. Certain laws (e.g., the Clean Water Act, the CZM Act, the National Environmental Policy Act, the National Historic Preservation Act, the Preservation of Historical and Archeological Data Act, the Endangered Species Act, the Wild and Scenic Rivers Act, and the Marine Protection, Research and Sanctuaries Act) require procedures such as state or other federal agency certifications, public hearings, environmental impact statements, consultation, special studies, and testing which may prevent district engineers from being able to decide certain applications within 60 days.

(4) Once the district engineer has sufficient information to make his public interest determination, he should decide the permit application even though other agencies which may have regulatory jurisdiction have not yet granted their authorizations, except where such authorizations are, by federal law, a prerequisite to making a decision on the DA permit application. Permits granted prior to other (non-prerequisite) authorizations by other agencies should, where appropriate, be conditioned in such manner as to give those other authorities an opportunity to undertake their review without the applicant biasing such review by making substantial resource commitments on the basis of the DA permit. In unusual cases the district engineer may decide that due to the nature or scope of a specific proposal, it would be prudent to defer taking final action until another agency has acted on its authorization. In such cases, he may advise the other agency of his position on the DA permit while deferring his final decision.

(5) The applicant will be given a reasonable time, not to exceed 30 days, to respond to requests of the district engineer. The district engineer may make such requests by certified letter and clearly inform the applicant that if he does not respond with the requested information or a justification why additional time is necessary, then his application will be considered withdrawn or a final decision will be made, whichever is appropriate. If additional time is requested, the district engineer will either grant the time, make a final decision, or consider the application as withdrawn.

(6) The time requirements in these regulations are in terms of calendar days rather than in terms of working days.

(e) *Alternative procedures.* Division and district engineers are authorized to use alternative procedures as follows:

(1) *Letters of permission.* Letters of permission are a type of permit issued through an abbreviated processing procedure which includes coordination with Federal and state fish and wildlife agencies, as required by the Fish and Wildlife Coordination Act, and a public interest evaluation, but without the publishing of an individual public notice. The letter of permission will not be used to authorize the transportation of dredged material for the purpose of dumping it in ocean waters. Letters of permission may be used:

(i) In those cases subject to section 10 of the Rivers and Harbors Act of 1899 when, in the opinion of the district engineer, the proposed work would be minor, would not have significant individual or cumulative impacts on environmental values, and should encounter no appreciable opposition.

(ii) In those cases subject to section 404 of the Clean Water Act after:

(A) The district engineer, through consultation with Federal and state fish and wildlife agencies, the Regional Administrator, Environmental Protection Agency, the state water quality certifying agency, and, if appropriate, the state Coastal Zone Management Agency, develops a list of categories of activities proposed for authorization under LOP procedures;

(B) The district engineer issues a public notice advertising the proposed list and the LOP procedures, requesting comments and offering an opportunity for public hearing; and

(C) A 401 certification has been issued or waived and, if appropriate, CZM consistency concurrence obtained or presumed either on a generic or individual basis.

(2) *Regional permits.* Regional permits are a type of general permit as defined in 33 CFR 322.2(f) and 33 CFR 323.2(n). They may be issued by a division or district engineer after compliance with the other procedures of this regulation. After a regional permit has been issued, individual activities falling within those categories that are authorized by such regional permits do not have to be further authorized by the procedures of this regulation. The issuing authority will determine and add appropriate conditions to protect the public interest. When the issuing authority determines on

a case-by-case basis that the concerns for the aquatic environment so indicate, he may exercise discretionary authority to override the regional permit and require an individual application and review. A regional permit may be revoked by the issuing authority if it is determined that it is contrary to the public interest provided the procedures of §325.7 of this part are followed. Following revocation, applications for future activities in areas covered by the regional permit shall be processed as applications for individual permits. No regional permit shall be issued for a period of more than five years.

(3) *Joint procedures.* Division and district engineers are authorized and encouraged to develop joint procedures with states and other Federal agencies with ongoing permit programs for activities also regulated by the Department of the Army. Such procedures may be substituted for the procedures in paragraphs (a)(1) through (a)(5) of this section provided that the substantive requirements of those sections are maintained. Division and district engineers are also encouraged to develop management techniques such as joint agency review meetings to expedite the decision-making process. However, in doing so, the applicant's rights to a full public interest review and independent decision by the district or division engineer must be strictly observed.

(4) *Emergency procedures.* Division engineers are authorized to approve special processing procedures in emergency situations. An "emergency" is a situation which would result in an unacceptable hazard to life, a significant loss of property, or an immediate, unforeseen, and significant economic hardship if corrective action requiring a permit is not undertaken within a time period less than the normal time needed to process the application under standard procedures. In emergency situations, the district engineer will explain the circumstances and recommend special procedures to the division engineer who will instruct the district engineer as to further processing of the application. Even in an emergency situation, reasonable efforts will be made to receive comments from interested Federal, state, and local agencies and the affected public. Also, notice of any special procedures authorized and their rationale is to be appropriately published as soon as practicable.

[51 FR 41236, Nov. 13, 1986, as amended at 62 FR 26230, May 13, 1997]

§325.3   *Public notice.*

(a) *General.* The public notice is the primary method of advising all interested parties of the proposed activity for which a permit is sought and of soliciting comments and information necessary to evaluate the prob-

able impact on the public interest. The notice must, therefore, include sufficient information to give a clear understanding of the nature and magnitude of the activity to generate meaningful comment. The notice should include the following items of information:

(1) Applicable statutory authority or authorities;(2) The name and address of the applicant;

(3) The name or title, address and telephone number of the Corps employee from whom additional information concerning the application may be obtained;

(4) The location of the proposed activity;

(5) A brief description of the proposed activity, its purpose and intended use, so as to provide sufficient information concerning the nature of the activity to generate meaningful comments, including a description of the type of structures, if any, to be erected on fills or pile or float-supported platforms, and a description of the type, composition, and quantity of materials to be discharged or disposed of in the ocean;

(6) A plan and elevation drawing showing the general and specific site location and character of all proposed activities, including the size relationship of the proposed structures to the size of the impacted waterway and depth of water in the area;

(7) If the proposed activity would occur in the territorial seas or ocean waters, a description of the activity's relationship to the baseline from which the territorial sea is measured;

(8) A list of other government authorizations obtained or requested by the applicant, including required certifications relative to water quality, coastal zone management, or marine sanctuaries;

(9) If appropriate, a statement that the activity is a categorical exclusion for purposes of NEPA (see paragraph 7 of Appendix B to 33 CFR part 230);

(10) A statement of the district engineer's current knowledge on historic properties;

(11) A statement of the district engineer's current knowledge on endangered species (see §325.2(b)(5));

(12) A statement(s) on evaluation factors (see §325.3(c));

(13) Any other available information which may assist interested parties in evaluating the likely impact of the proposed activity, if any, on factors affecting the public interest;

(14) The comment period based on §325.2(d)(2);

(15) A statement that any person may request, in writing, within the comment period specified in the notice, that a public hearing be held to consider the application. Requests for public hearings shall state, with particularity, the reasons for holding a public hearing;

(16) For non-federal applications in states with an approved CZM Plan, a statement on compliance with the approved Plan; and

(17) In addition, for section 103 (ocean dumping) activities:

(i) The specific location of the proposed disposal site and its physical boundaries;

(ii) A statement as to whether the proposed disposal site has been designated for use by the Administrator, EPA, pursuant to section 102(c) of the Act;

(iii) If the proposed disposal site has not been designated by the Administrator, EPA, a description of the characteristics of the proposed disposal site and an explanation as to why no previously designated disposal site is feasible;

(iv) A brief description of known dredged material discharges at the proposed disposal site;

(v) Existence and documented effects of other authorized disposals that have been made in the disposal area (e.g., heavy metal background reading and organic carbon content);

(vi) An estimate of the length of time during which disposal would continue at the proposed site; and

(vii) Information on the characteristics and composition of the dredged material.

(b) *Public notice for general permits.* District engineers will publish a public notice for all proposed regional general permits and for significant modifications to, or reissuance of, existing regional permits within their area of jurisdiction. Public notices for statewide regional permits may be issued jointly by the affected Corps districts. The notice will include all applicable information necessary to provide a clear understanding of the proposal. In addition, the notice will state the availability of information at the district office which reveals the Corps' provisional determination that the proposed activities comply with the requirements for issuance of general permits. District engineers will publish a public notice for nationwide permits in accordance with 33 CFR 330.4.

(c) *Evaluation factors.* A paragraph describing the various evaluation factors on which decisions are based shall be included in every public notice.

(1) Except as provided in paragraph (c)(3) of this section, the following will be included:

"The decision whether to issue a permit will be based on an evaluation of the probable impact including cumulative impacts of the proposed activity on the public interest. That decision will reflect the national concern for both protection and utilization of important resources. The benefit which reasonably may be expected to accrue from the proposal must be balanced against its reasonably foreseeable detriments. All factors which may be relevant to the proposal will be considered including the cumulative effects thereof; among those are conservation, economics, aesthetics, general environmental concerns, wetlands, historic properties, fish and wildlife values, flood hazards, floodplain values, land use, navigation, shoreline erosion and accretion, recreation, water supply and conservation, water quality, energy needs, safety, food and fiber production, mineral needs, considerations of property ownership and, in general, the needs and welfare of the people."

(2) If the activity would involve the discharge of dredged or fill material into the waters of the United States or the transportation of dredged material for the purpose of disposing of it in ocean waters, the public notice shall also indicate that the evaluation of the inpact of the activity on the public interest will include application of the guidelines promulgated by the Administrator, EPA, (40 CFR part 230) or of the criteria established under authority of section 102(a) of the Marine Protection, Research and Sanctuaries Act of 1972, as amended (40 CFR parts 220 to 229), as appropriate. (See 33 CFR parts 323 and 324).

(3) In cases involving construction of artificial islands, installations and other devices on outer continental shelf lands which are under mineral lease from the Department of the Interior, the notice will contain the following statement: "The decision as to whether a permit will be issued will be based on an evaluation of the impact of the proposed work on navigation and national security."

(d) *Distribution of public notices.* (1) Public notices will be distributed for posting in post offices or other appropriate public places in the vicinity of the site of the proposed work and will be sent to the applicant, to appropriate city and county officials, to adjoining property owners, to appropriate state agencies, to appropriate Indian Tribes or tribal representatives, to concerned Federal agencies, to local, regional and national shipping and other concerned business and conservation organizations, to appropriate River Basin Commissions, to appropriate state and areawide clearing houses as prescribed by OMB Circular A-95, to local news media and to any other interested party. Copies of public notices will be sent to all parties who have specifically requested copies of public notices, to the U.S. Senators and Representatives for the area where the work is to be performed, the field representative of the Secretary of the Interior, the Regional Director of the Fish and Wildlife Service, the Regional Director of the National Park Service, the Regional Administrator of the Environmental Protection Agency (EPA), the Regional Director of the National Marine Fisheries Service of the National Oceanic and Atmospheric Administration (NOAA), the head of the state agency responsible for fish and wildlife resources, the State Historic Preservation Officer, and the District Commander, U.S. Coast Guard.

(2) In addition to the general distribution of public notices cited above, notices will be sent to other addressees in appropriate cases as follows:

(i) If the activity would involve structures or dredging along the shores of the seas or Great Lakes, to the Coastal Engineering Research Center, Washington, DC 20016.

(ii) If the activity would involve construction of fixed structures or artificial islands on the outer continental shelf or in the territorial seas, to the Assistant Secretary of Defense (Manpower, Installations, and Logistics (ASD(MI&L)), Washington, DC 20310; the Director, Defense Mapping Agency (Hydrographic Center) Washington, DC 20390, Attention, Code NS12; and the National Ocean Service, Office of Coast Survey, N/CS261, 1315 East West Highway, Silver Spring, Maryland 20910-3282, and to affected military installations and activities.

(iii) If the activity involves the construction of structures to enhance fish propagation (e.g., fishing reefs) along the coasts of the United States, to the Director, Office of Marine Recreational Fisheries, National Marine Fisheries Service, Washington, DC 20235.

(iv) If the activity involves the construction of structures which may affect aircraft operations or for purposes associated with seaplane operations, to the Regional Director of the Federal Aviation Administration.

(v) If the activity would be in connection with a foreign-trade zone, to the Executive Secretary, Foreign-Trade Zones Board, Department of Commerce, Washington, DC 20230 and to the appropriate District Director of Customs as Resident Representative, Foreign-Trade Zones Board.

(3) It is presumed that all interested parties and agencies will wish to respond to public notices; therefore, a lack of response will be interpreted as meaning that there is no objection to the proposed project. A copy of the public notice with the list of the addresses to whom the notice was sent will be included in the record. If a question develops with respect to an activity for which another agency has responsibility and that other agency has not responded to the public notice, the district engineer may request its comments. Whenever a response to a public notice has been received from a member of Congress, either in behalf of a constituent or himself, the district engineer will inform the member of Congress of the final decision.

(4) District engineers will update public notice mailing lists at least once every two years.

§325.4   Conditioning of permits.

(a) District engineers will add special conditions to Department of the Army permits when such conditions are necessary to satisfy legal requirements or to otherwise satisfy the public interest requirement. Permit conditions will be directly related to the impacts of the proposal, appropriate to the scope and degree of those impacts, and reasonably enforceable.

(1) Legal requirements which may be satisfied by means of Corps permit conditions include compliance with the 404(b)(1) guidelines, the EPA ocean dumping criteria, the Endangered Species Act, and requirements imposed by conditions on state section 401 water quality certifications.

(2) Where appropriate, the district engineer may take into account the existence of controls imposed under other federal, state, or local programs which would achieve the objective of the desired condition, or the existence of an enforceable agreement between the applicant and another party concerned with the resource in question, in determining whether a proposal complies with the 404(b)(1) guidelines, ocean dumping criteria, and other applicable statutes, and is not contrary to the public interest. In such cases, the Department of the Army permit will be conditioned to state that material changes in, or a failure to implement and enforce such program or agreement, will be grounds for modifying, suspending, or revoking the permit.

(3) Such conditions may be accomplished on-site, or may be accomplished off-site for mitigation of significant losses which are specifically identifiable, reasonably likely to occur, and of importance to the human or aquatic environment.

(b) District engineers are authorized to add special conditions, exclusive of paragraph (a) of this section, at the applicant's request or to clarify the permit application.

(c) If the district engineer determines that special conditions are necessary to insure the proposal will not be contrary to the public interest, but those conditions would not be reasonably implementable or enforceable, he will deny the permit.

(d) *Bonds.* If the district engineer has reason to consider that the permittee might be prevented from completing work which is necessary to protect the public interest, he may require the permittee to post a bond of sufficient amount to indemnify the government against any loss as a result of corrective action it might take.

§325.5   Forms of permits.

(a) *General discussion.* (1) DA permits under this regulation will be in the form of individual permits or general permits. The basic format shall be ENG Form 1721, DA Permit (Appendix A).

(2) The general conditions included in ENG Form 1721 are normally applicable to all permits; however, some conditions may not apply to certain permits and may be deleted by the issuing officer. Special conditions applicable to the specific activity will be included in the permit as necessary to protect the public interest in accordance with §325.4 of this part.

(b) *Individual permits*—(1) *Standard permits.* A standard permit is one which has been processed through the public interest review procedures, including public notice and receipt of comments, described throughout this part. The standard individual permit shall be issued using ENG Form 1721.

(2) *Letters of permission.* A letter of permission will be issued where procedures of §325.2(e)(1) have been followed. It will be in letter form and will identify the permittee, the authorized work and location of the work, the statutory authority, any limitations on the work, a construction time limit and a requirement for a report of completed work. A copy of the relevant general conditions from ENG Form 1721 will be attached and will be incorporated by reference into the letter of permission.

(c) *General permits*—(1) *Regional permits.* Regional permits are a type of general permit. They may be issued by a division or district engineer after compliance with the other procedures of this regulation. If the public interest so requires, the issuing authority may condition the regional permit to require a case-by-case reporting and acknowledgment system. However, no separate applications or other authorization documents will be required.

(2) *Nationwide permits.* Nationwide permits are a type of general permit and represent DA authorizations that have been issued by the regulation (33 CFR part 330) for certain specified activities nationwide. If certain conditions are met, the specified activities can take place without the need for an individual or regional permit.

(3) *Programmatic permits.* Programmatic permits are a type of general permit founded on an existing state, local or other Federal agency program and designed to avoid duplication with that program.

(d) *Section 9 permits.* Permits for structures in interstate navigable waters of the United States under section 9 of the Rivers and Harbors Act of 1899 will be drafted at DA level.

§325.6   Duration of permits.

(a) *General.* DA permits may authorize both the work and the resulting use. Permits continue in effect until they automatically expire or are modified, suspended, or revoked.

(b) *Structures.* Permits for the existence of a structure or other activity of a permanent nature are usually for an indefinite duration with no expiration date cited. However, where a temporary structure is authorized, or where restoration of a waterway is contemplated, the permit will be of limited duration with a definite expiration date.

(c) *Works.* Permits for construction work, discharge of dredged or fill material, or other activity and any construction period for a structure with a permit of indefinite duration under paragraph (b) of this section will specify time limits for completing the work or activity. The permit may also specify a date by which the work must be started, normally within one year from the date of issuance. The date will be established by the issuing official and will provide reasonable times based on the scope and nature of the work involved. Permits issued for the transport of dredged material for the purpose of disposing of it in ocean waters will specify a completion date for the disposal not to exceed three years from the date of permit issuance.

(d) *Extensions of time.* An authorization or construction period will automatically expire if the permittee fails to request and receive an extension of time. Extensions of time may be granted by the district engineer. The permittee must request the extension and explain the basis of the request, which will be granted unless the district engineer determines that an extension would be contrary to the public interest. Requests for extensions will be processed in accordance with the regular procedures of §325.2 of this part, including issuance of a public notice, except that such processing is not required where the district engineer determines that there have been no significant changes in the attendant circumstances since the authorization was issued.

(e) *Maintenance dredging.* If the authorized work includes periodic maintenance dredging, an expiration date for the authorization of that maintenance dredging will be included in the permit. The expiration date, which in no event is to exceed ten years from the date of issuance of the permit, will be established by the issuing official after evaluation of the proposed method of dredging and disposal of the dredged material in accordance with the requirements of 33 CFR parts 320 to 325. In such cases, the district engineer shall require notification of the maintenance dredging prior to actual performance to insure continued compliance with the requirements of this regulation and 33 CFR parts 320 to 324. If the permittee desires to continue maintenance dredging beyond the expiration date, he must request a new permit. The permittee should be advised to apply for the new permit six months prior to the time he wishes to do the maintenance work.

§325.7   Modification, suspension, or revocation of permits.

(a) *General.* The district engineer may reevaluate the circumstances and conditions of any permit, including regional permits, either on his own motion, at the request of the permittee, or a third party, or as the result of periodic progress inspections, and initiate action to modify, suspend, or revoke a permit as may be made necessary by considerations of the public interest. In the case of regional permits, this reevaluation may cover individual activities, categories of activities, or geographic areas. Among the factors to be considered are the extent of the permittee's compliance with the terms and conditions of the permit; whether or not circumstances relating to the authorized activity have changed since the permit was issued or extended, and the continuing adequacy of or need for the permit conditions; any significant objections to the authorized

activity which were not earlier considered; revisions to applicable statutory and/or regulatory authorities; and the extent to which modification, suspension, or other action would adversely affect plans, investments and actions the permittee has reasonably made or taken in reliance on the permit. Significant increases in scope of a permitted activity will be processed as new applications for permits in accordance with §325.2 of this part, and not as modifications under this section.

(b) *Modification.* Upon request by the permittee or, as a result of reevaluation of the circumstances and conditions of a permit, the district engineer may determine that the public interest requires a modification of the terms or conditions of the permit. In such cases, the district engineer will hold informal consultations with the permittee to ascertain whether the terms and conditions can be modified by mutual agreement. If a mutual agreement is reached on modification of the terms and conditions of the permit, the district engineer will give the permittee written notice of the modification, which will then become effective on such date as the district engineer may establish. In the event a mutual agreement cannot be reached by the district engineer and the permittee, the district engineer will proceed in accordance with paragraph (c) of this section if immediate suspension is warranted. In cases where immediate suspension is not warranted but the district engineer determines that the permit should be modified, he will notify the permittee of the proposed modification and reasons therefor, and that he may request a meeting with the district engineer and/or a public hearing. The modification will become effective on the date set by the district engineer which shall be at least ten days after receipt of the notice by the permittee unless a hearing or meeting is requested within that period. If the permittee fails or refuses to comply with the modification, the district engineer will proceed in accordance with 33 CFR part 326. The district engineer shall consult with resource agencies before modifying any permit terms or conditions, that would result in greater impacts, for a project about which that agency expressed a significant interest in the term, condition, or feature being modified prior to permit issuance.

(c) *Suspension.* The district engineer may suspend a permit after preparing a written determination and finding that immediate suspension would be in the public interest. The district engineer will notify the permittee in writing by the most expeditious means available that the permit has been suspended with the reasons therefor, and order the permittee to stop those activities previously authorized by the suspended permit. The permittee will also be advised that following this suspension a decision will be made to either reinstate, modify, or revoke the permit, and that he may within 10 days of receipt of notice of the suspension, request a meeting with the district engineer and/or a public hearing to present information in this matter. If a hearing is requested, the procedures prescribed in 33 CFR part 327 will be followed. After the completion of the meeting or hearing (or within a reasonable period of time after issuance of the notice to the permittee that the permit has been suspended if no hearing or meeting is requested), the district engineer will take action to reinstate, modify, or revoke the permit.

(d) *Revocation.* Following completion of the suspension procedures in paragraph (c) of this section, if revocation of the permit is found to be in the public interest, the authority who made the decision on the original permit may revoke it. The permittee will be advised in writing of the final decision.

(e) *Regional permits.* The issuing official may, by following the procedures of this section, revoke regional permits for individual activities, categories of activities, or geographic areas. Where groups of permittees are involved, such as for categories of activities or geographic areas, the informal discussions provided in paragraph (b) of this section may be waived and any written notification nay be made through the general public notice procedures of this regulation. If a regional permit is revoked, any permittee may then apply for an individual permit which shall be processed in accordance with these regulations.

§325.8   *Authority to issue or deny permits.*

(a) *General.* Except as otherwise provided in this regulation, the Secretary of the Army, subject to such conditions as he or his authorized representative may from time to time impose, has authorized the Chief of Engineers and his authorized representatives to issue or deny permits for dams or dikes in intrastate waters of the United States pursuant to section 9 of the Rivers and Harbors Act of 1899; for construction or other work in or affecting navigable waters of the United States pursuant to section 10 of the Rivers and Harbors Act of 1899; for the discharge of dredged or fill material into waters of the United States pursuant to section 404 of the Clean Water Act; or for the transportation of dredged material for the purpose of disposing of it into ocean waters pursuant to section 103 of the Marine Protection, Research and Sanctuaries Act of 1972, as amended. The authority to issue or deny permits in interstate navigable waters of the United States pursuant to section 9 of the Rivers and Harbors Act of March 3, 1899 has not been delegated to the Chief of Engineers or his authorized representatives.

(b) *District engineer's authority.* District engineers are authorized to issue or deny permits in accordance with these regulations pursuant to sections 9 and 10 of the Rivers and Harbors Act of 1899; section 404 of the Clean Water Act; and section 103 of the Marine Protection, Research and Sanctuaries Act of 1972, as amended, in all cases not required to be referred to higher authority (see below). It is essential to the legality of a permit that it contain the name of the district engineer as the issuing officer. However, the permit need not be signed by the district engineer in person but may be signed for and in behalf of him by whomever he designates. In cases where permits are denied for reasons other than navigation or failure to obtain required local, state, or other federal approvals or certifications, the Statement of Findings must conclusively justify a denial decision. District engineers are authorized to deny permits without issuing a public notice or taking other procedural steps where required local, state, or other federal permits for the proposed activity have been denied or where he determines that the activity will clearly interfere with navigation except in all cases required to be referred to higher authority (see below). District engineers are also authorized to add, modify, or delete special conditions in permits in accordance with §325.4 of this part, except for those conditions which may have been imposed by higher authority, and to modify, suspend and revoke permits according to the procedures of §325.7 of this part. District engineers will refer the following applications to the division engineer for resolution:

(1) When a referral is required by a written agreement between the head of a Federal agency and the Secretary of the Army;

(2) When the recommended decision is contrary to the written position of the Governor of the state in which the work would be performed;

(3) When there is substantial doubt as to authority, law, regulations, or policies applicable to the proposed activity;

(4) When higher authority requests the application be forwarded for decision; or

(5) When the district engineer is precluded by law or procedures required by law from taking final action on the application (e.g. section 9 of the Rivers and Harbors Act of 1899, or territorial sea baseline changes).

(c) *Division engineer's authority.* Division engineers will review and evaluate all permit applications referred by district engineers. Division engineers may authorize the issuance or denial of permits pursuant to section

10 of the Rivers and Harbors Act of 1899; section 404 of the Clean Water Act; and section 103 of the Marine Protection, Research and Sanctuaries Act of 1972, as amended; and the inclusion of conditions in accordance with §325.4 of this part in all cases not required to be referred to the Chief of Engineers. Division engineers will refer the following applications to the Chief of Engineers for resolution:

(1) When a referral is required by a written agreement between the head of a Federal agency and the Secretary of the Army;

(2) When there is substantial doubt as to authority, law, regulations, or policies applicable to the proposed activity;

(3) When higher authority requests the application be forwarded for decision; or

(4) When the division engineer is precluded by law or procedures required by law from taking final action on the application.

§325.9   Authority to determine jurisdiction.

District engineers are authorized to determine the area defined by the terms "navigable waters of the United States" and "waters of the United States" except:

(a) When a determination of navigability is made pursuant to 33 CFR 329.14 (division engineers have this authority); or

(b) When EPA makes a section 404 jurisdiction determination under its authority.

§325.10   Publicity.

The district engineer will establish and maintain a program to assure that potential applicants for permits are informed of the requirements of this regulation and of the steps required to obtain permits for activities in waters of the United States or ocean waters. Whenever the district engineer becomes aware of plans being developed by either private or public entities which might require permits for implementation, he should advise the potential applicant in writing of the statutory requirements and the provisions of this regulation. Whenever the district engineer is aware of changes in Corps of Engineers regulatory jurisdiction, he will issue appropriate public notices.

Appendix A to Part 325—Permit Form and Special Conditions

A. Permit Form

Department of the Army Permit

Permittee _____

Permit No. _____

Issuing Office _____

NOTE: The term "you" and its derivatives, as used in this permit, means the permittee or any future transferee. The term "this office" refers to the appropriate district or division office of the Corps of Engineers having jurisdiction over the permitted activity or the appropriate official of that office acting under the authority of the commanding officer.

You are authorized to perform work in accordance with the terms and conditions specified below.

Project Description: (Describe the permitted activity and its intended use with references to any attached plans or drawings that are considered to be a part of the project description. Include a description of the types and quantities of dredged or fill materials to be discharged in jurisdictional waters.)

Project Location: (Where appropriate, provide the names of and the locations on the waters where the permitted activity and any off-site disposals will take place. Also, using name, distance, and direction, locate the permitted activity in reference to a nearby landmark such as a town or city.)

Permit Conditions:

General Conditions:

1. The time limit for completing the work authorized ends on _____. If you find that you need more time to complete the authorized activity, submit your request for a time extension to this office for consideration at least one month before the above date is reached.

2. You must maintain the activity authorized by this permit in good condition and in conformance with the terms and conditions of this permit. You are not relieved of this requirement if you abandon the permitted activity, although you may make a good faith transfer to a third party in compliance with General Condition 4 below. Should you wish to cease to maintain the authorized activity or should you desire to abandon it without a good faith transfer, you must

obtain a modification of this permit from this office, which may require restoration of the area.

3. If you discover any previously unknown historic or archeological remains while accomplishing the activity authorized by this permit, you must immediately notify this office of what you have found. We will initiate the Federal and state coordination required to determine if the remains warrant a recovery effort or if the site is eligible for listing in the National Register of Historic Places.

4. If you sell the property associated with this permit, you must obtain the signature of the new owner in the space provided and forward a copy of the permit to this office to validate the transfer of this authorization.

5. If a conditioned water quality certification has been issued for your project, you must comply with the conditions specified in the certification as special conditions to this permit. For your convenience, a copy of the certification is attached if it contains such conditions.

6. You must allow representatives from this office to inspect the authorized activity at any time deemed necessary to ensure that it is being or has been accomplished in accordance with the terms and conditions of your permit.

Special Conditions: (Add special conditions as required in this space with reference to a continuation sheet if necessary.)

Further Information:

1. Congressional Authorities: You have been authorized to undertake the activity described above pursuant to:

(   ) Section 10 of the Rivers and Harbors Act of 1899 (33 U.S.C. 403).

(   ) Section 404 of the Clean Water Act (33 U.S.C. 1344).

(   ) Section 103 of the Marine Protection, Research and Sanctuaries Act of 1972 (33 U.S.C. 1413).

2. Limits of this authorization.

a. This permit does not obviate the need to obtain other Federal, state, or local authorizations required by law.

b. This permit does not grant any property rights or exclusive privileges.

c. This permit does not authorize any injury to the property or rights of others.

d. This permit does not authorize interference with any existing or proposed Federal project.

3. Limits of Federal Liability. In issuing this permit, the Federal Government does not assume any liability for the following:

a. Damages to the permitted project or uses thereof as a result of other permitted or unpermitted activities or from natural causes.

b. Damages to the permitted project or uses thereof as a result of current or future activities undertaken by or on behalf of the United States in the public interest.

c. Damages to persons, property, or to other permitted or unpermitted activities or structures caused by the activity authorized by this permit.

d. Design or construction deficiencies associated with the permitted work.

e. Damage claims associated with any future modification, suspension, or revocation of this permit.

4. Reliance on Applicant's Data: The determination of this office that issuance of this permit is not contrary to the public interest was made in reliance on the information you provided.

5. Reevaluation of Permit Decision. This office may reevaluate its decision on this permit at any time the circumstances warrant. Circumstances that could require a reevaluation include, but are not limited to, the following:

a. You fail to comply with the terms and conditions of this permit.

b. The information provided by you in support of your permit application proves to have been false, incomplete, or inaccurate (See 4 above).

c. Significant new information surfaces which this office did not consider in reaching the original public interest decision.

Such a reevaluation may result in a determination that it is appropriate to use the suspension, modification, and revocation procedures contained in 33 CFR 325.7 or enforcement procedures such as those contained in 33 CFR 326.4 and 326.5. The referenced enforcement procedures provide for the issuance of an administrative order requiring you to comply with the terms and conditions of your permit and for the initiation of legal action where appropriate. You will be required to pay for any corrective measures ordered by this office, and if you fail to comply with such directive, this office may in certain situations (such as those specified in 33 CFR 209.170) accomplish the corrective measures by contract or otherwise and bill you for the cost.

6. Extensions. General condition 1 establishes a time limit for the completion of the activity authorized by this permit. Unless there are circumstances requiring either a prompt completion of the authorized activity or a reevaluation of the public interest decision, the Corps will normally give favorable consideration to a request for an extension of this time limit.

Your signature below, as permittee, indicates that you accept and agree to comply with the terms and conditions of this permit.

_____

(Permittee)

_____

(Date)

This permit becomes effective when the Federal official, designated to act for the Secretary of the Army, has signed below.

_____

(District Engineer)

_____

(Date)

When the structures or work authorized by this permit are still in existence at the time the property is transferred, the terms and conditions of this permit will continue to be binding on the new owner(s) of the property. To validate the transfer of this permit and the associated liabilities associated with compliance with its terms and conditions, have the transferee sign and date below.

_____

(Transferee)

_____

(Date)

B. Special Conditions. No special conditions will be preprinted on the permit form. The following and

other special conditions should be added, as appropriate, in the space provided after the general conditions or on a referenced continuation sheet:

1. Your use of the permitted activity must not interfere with the public's right to free navigation on all navigable waters of the United States.

2. You must have a copy of this permit available on the vessel used for the authorized transportation and disposal of dredged material.

3. You must advise this office in writing, at least two weeks before you start maintenance dredging activities under the authority of this permit.

4. You must install and maintain, at your expense, any safety lights and signals prescribed by the United States Coast Guard (USCG), through regulations or otherwise, on your authorized facilities. The USCG may be reached at the following address and telephone number:

_____

5. The condition below will be used when a Corps permit authorizes an artificial reef, an aerial transmission line, a submerged cable or pipeline, or a structure on the outer continental shelf.

National Ocean Service (NOS) has been notified of this authorization. You must notify NOS and this office in writing, at least two weeks before you begin work and upon completion of the activity authorized by this permit. Your notification of completion must include a drawing which certifies the location and configuration of the completed activity (a certified permit drawing may be used). Notifications to NOS will be sent to the following address: National Ocean Service, Office of Coast Survey, N/CS261, 1315 East West Highway, Silver Spring, Maryland 20910-3282.

6. The following condition should be used for every permit where legal recordation of the permit would be reasonably practicable and recordation could put a subsequent purchaser or owner of property on notice of permit conditions.

You must take the actions required to record this permit with the Registrar of Deeds or other appropriate official charged with the responsibility for maintaining records of title to or interest in real property.

[51 FR 41236, Nov. 13, 1986, as amended at 62 FR 26230, May 13, 1997]

Appendix B to Part 325—NEPA Implementation Procedures for the Regulatory Program

1. *Introduction.* In keeping with Executive Order 12291 and 40 CFR 1500.2, where interpretive problems arise in implementing this regulation, and consideration of all other factors do not give a clear indication of a reasonable interpretation, the interpretation (consistent with the spirit and intent of NEPA) which results in the least paperwork and delay will be used. Specific examples of ways to reduce paperwork in the NEPA process are found at 40 CFR 1500.4. Maximum advantage of these recommendations should be taken.

2. *General.* This Appendix sets forth implementing procedures for the Corps regulatory program. For additional guidance, see the Corps NEPA regulation 33 CFR part 230 and for general policy guidance, see the CEQ regulations 40 CFR 1500-1508.

3. *Development of Information and Data.* See 40 CFR 1506.5. The district engineer may require the applicant to furnish appropriate information that the district engineer considers necessary for the preparation of an Environmental Assessment (EA) or Environmental Impact Statement (EIS). See also 40 CFR 1502.22 regarding incomplete or unavailable information.

4. *Elimination of Duplication with State and Local Procedures.* See 40 CFR 1506.2.

5. *Public Involvement.* Several paragraphs of this appendix (paragraphs 7, 8, 11, 13, and 19) provide information on the requirements for district engineers to make available to the public certain environmental documents in accordance with 40 CFR 1506.6.

6. *Categorical Exclusions*—a. *General.* Even though an EA or EIS is not legally mandated for any Federal action falling within one of the "categorical exclusions," that fact does not exempt any Federal action from procedural or substantive compliance with any other Federal law. For example, compliance with the Endangered Species Act, the Clean Water Act, etc., is always mandatory, even for actions not requiring an EA or EIS. The following activities are not considered to be major Federal actions significantly affecting the quality of the human environment and are therefore categorically excluded from NEPA documentation:

(1) Fixed or floating small private piers, small docks, boat hoists and boathouses.

(2) Minor utility distribution and collection lines including irrigation;

(3) Minor maintenance dredging using existing disposal sites;

(4) Boat launching ramps;

(5) All applications which qualify as letters of permission (as described at 33 CFR 325.5(b)(2)).

b. *Extraordinary Circumstances.* District engineers should be alert for extraordinary circumstances where normally excluded actions could have substantial environmental effects and thus require an EA or EIS. For a period of one year from the effective data of these regulations, district engineers should maintain an information list on the type and number of categorical exclusion actions which, due to extraordinary circumstances, triggered the need for an EA/FONSI or EIS. If a district engineer determines that a categorical exclusion should be modified, the information will be furnished to the division engineer who will review and analyze the actions and circumstances to determine if there is a basis for recommending a modification to the list of categorical exclusions. HQUSACE (CECW-OR) will review recommended changes for Corps-wide consistency and revise the list accordingly.

7. *EA/FONSI Document.* (See 40 CFR 1508.9 and 1508.13 for definitions)—a. *Environmental Assessment (EA) and Findings of No Significant Impact (FONSI).* The EA should normally be combined with other required documents (EA/404(b)(1)/SOF/FONSI). "EA" as used throughout this Appendix normally refers to this combined document. The district engineer should complete an EA as soon as practicable after all relevant information is available (*i.e.*, after the

comment period for the public notice of the permit application has expired) and when the EA is a separate document it must be completed prior to completion of the statement of finding (SOF). When the EA confirms that the impact of the applicant's proposal is not significant and there are no "unresolved conflicts concerning alternative uses of available resources * * *" (section 102(2)(E) of NEPA), and the proposed activity is a "water dependent" activity as defined in 40 CFR 230.10(a)(3), the EA need not include a discussion on alternatives. In all other cases where the district engineer determines that there are unresolved conflicts concerning alternative uses of available resources, the EA shall include a discussion of the reasonable alternatives which are to be considered by the ultimate decision-maker. The decision options available to the Corps, which embrace all of the applicant's alternatives, are issue the permit, issue with modifications or deny the permit. Modifications are limited to those project modifications within the scope of established permit conditioning policy (See 33 CFR 325.4). The decision option to deny the permit results in the "no action" alternative (*i.e.,* no activity requiring a Corps permit). The combined document normally should not exceed 15 pages and shall conclude with a FONSI (See 40 CFR 1508.13) or a determination that an EIS is required. The district engineer may delegate the signing of the NEPA document. Should the EA demonstrate that an EIS is necessary, the district engineer shall follow the procedures outlined in paragraph 8 of this Appendix. In those cases where it is obvious an EIS is required, an EA is not required. However, the district engineer should document his reasons for requiring an EIS.

b. *Scope of Analysis.* (1) In some situations, a permit applicant may propose to conduct a specific activity requiring a Department of the Army (DA) permit (e.g., construction of a pier in a navigable water of the United States) which is merely one component of a larger project (e.g., construction of an oil refinery on an upland area). The district engineer should establish the scope of the NEPA document (e.g., the EA or EIS) to address the impacts of the specific activity requiring a DA permit and those portions of the entire project over which the district engineer has sufficient control and responsibility to warrant Federal review.

(2) The district engineer is considered to have control and responsibility for portions of the project beyond the limits of Corps jurisdiction where the Federal involvement is sufficient to turn an essentially private action into a Federal action. These are cases where the environmental consequences of the larger project are essentially products of the Corps permit action.

Typical factors to be considered in determining whether sufficient "control and responsibility" exists include:

(i) Whether or not the regulated activity comprises "merely a link" in a corridor type project (e.g., a transportation or utility transmission project).

(ii) Whether there are aspects of the upland facility in the immediate vicinity of the regulated activity which affect the location and configuration of the regulated activity.

(iii) The extent to which the entire project will be within Corps jurisdiction.

(iv) The extent of cumulative Federal control and responsibility.

A. Federal control and responsibility will include the portions of the project beyond the limits of Corps jurisdiction where the cumulative Federal involvement of the Corps and other Federal agencies is sufficient to grant legal control over such additional portions of the project. These are cases where the environmental consequences of the additional portions of the projects are essentially products of Federal financing, assistance, direction, regulation, or approval (not including funding assistance solely in the form of general revenue sharing funds, with no Federal agency control over the subsequent use of such funds, and not including judicial or administrative civil or criminal enforcement actions).

B. In determining whether sufficient cumulative Federal involvement exists to expand the scope of Federal action the district engineer should consider whether other Federal agencies are required to take Federal action under the Fish and Wildlife Coordination Act (16 U.S.C. 661 *et seq.*), the National Historic Preservation Act of 1966 (16 U.S.C. 470 *et seq.*), the Endangered Species Act of 1973 (16 U.S.C. 1531 *et seq.*), Executive Order 11990, Protection of Wetlands, (42 U.S.C. 4321 91977), and other environmental review laws and executive orders.

C. The district engineer should also refer to paragraphs 8(b) and 8(c) of this appendix for guidance on determining whether it should be the lead or a cooperating agency in these situations.

These factors will be added to or modified through guidance as additional field experience develops.

(3) *Examples:* If a non-Federal oil refinery, electric generating plant, or industrial facility is proposed to be built on an upland site and the only DA permit

requirement relates to a connecting pipeline, supply loading terminal or fill road, that pipeline, terminal or fill road permit, in and of itself, normally would not constitute sufficient overall Federal involvement with the project to justify expanding the scope of a Corps NEPA document to cover upland portions of the facility beyond the structures in the immediate vicinity of the regulated activity that would effect the location and configuration of the regulated activity.

Similarly, if an applicant seeks a DA permit to fill waters or wetlands on which other construction or work is proposed, the control and responsibility of the Corps, as well as its overall Federal involvement would extend to the portions of the project to be located on the permitted fill. However, the NEPA review would be extended to the entire project, including portions outside waters of the United States, only if sufficient Federal control and responsibility over the entire project is determined to exist; that is, if the regulated activities, and those activities involving regulation, funding, etc. by other Federal agencies, comprise a substantial portion of the overall project. In any case, once the scope of analysis has been defined, the NEPA analysis for that action should include direct, indirect and cumulative impacts on all Federal interests within the purview of the NEPA statute. The district engineer should, whenever practicable, incorporate by reference and rely upon the reviews of other Federal and State agencies.

For those regulated activities that comprise merely a link in a transportation or utility transmission project, the scope of analysis should address the Federal action, *i.e.,* the specific activity requiring a DA permit and any other portion of the project that is within the control or responsibility of the Corps of Engineers (or other Federal agencies).

For example, a 50-mile electrical transmission cable crossing a $1\frac{1}{4}$ mile wide river that is a navigable water of the United States requires a DA permit. Neither the origin and destination of the cable nor its route to and from the navigable water, except as the route applies to the location and configuration of the crossing, are within the control or responsibility of the Corps of Engineers. Those matters would not be included in the scope of analysis which, in this case, would address the impacts of the specific cable crossing.

Conversely, for those activities that require a DA permit for a major portion of a transportation or utility transmission project, so that the Corps permit bears upon the origin and destination as well as the route of the project outside the Corps regulatory boundaries, the scope of analysis should include those portions of the project outside the boundaries of the Corps section 10/404 regulatory jurisdiction. To use the same example, if 30 miles of the 50-mile transmission line crossed wetlands or other "waters of the United States," the scope of analysis should reflect impacts of the whole 50-mile transmission line.

For those activities that require a DA permit for a major portion of a shoreside facility, the scope of analysis should extend to upland portions of the facility. For example, a shipping terminal normally requires dredging, wharves, bulkheads, berthing areas and disposal of dredged material in order to function. Permits for such activities are normally considered sufficient Federal control and responsibility to warrant extending the scope of analysis to include the upland portions of the facility.

In all cases, the scope of analysis used for analyzing both impacts and alternatives should be the same scope of analysis used for analyzing the benefits of a proposal.

8. *Environmental Impact Statement—General—a. Determination of Lead and Cooperating Agencies.* When the district engineer determines that an EIS is required, he will contact all appropriate Federal agencies to determine their respective role(s), *i.e.,* that of lead agency or cooperating agency.

b. *Corps as Lead Agency.* When the Corps is lead agency, it will be responsible for managing the EIS process, including those portions which come under the jurisdiction of other Federal agencies. The district engineer is authorized to require the applicant to furnish appropriate information as discussed in paragraph 3 of this appendix. It is permissable for the Corps to reimburse, under agreement, staff support from other Federal agencies beyond the immediate jurisdiction of those agencies.

c. *Corps as Cooperating Agency.* If another agency is the lead agency as set forth by the CEQ regulations (40 CFR 1501.5 and 1501.6(a) and 1508.16), the district engineer will coordinate with that agency as a cooperating agency under 40 CFR 1501.6(b) and 1508.5 to insure that agency's resulting EIS may be adopted by the Corps for purposes of exercising its regulatory authority. As a cooperating agency the Corps will be responsible to the lead agency for providing environmental information which is directly related to the regulatory matter involved and which is required for the preparation of an EIS. This in no way shall be construed as lessening the district engineer's ability to request the applicant to furnish appropriate information as discussed in paragraph 3 of this appendix.

When the Corps is a cooperating agency because of a regulatory responsibility, the district engineer should, in accordance with 40 CFR 1501.6(b)(4), "make available staff support at the lead agency's request" to enhance the latter's interdisciplinary capability provided the request pertains to the Corps regulatory action covered by the EIS, to the extent this is practicable. Beyond this, Corps staff support will generally be made available to the lead agency to the extent practicable within its own responsibility and available resources. Any assistance to a lead agency beyond this will normally be by written agreement with the lead agency providing for the Corps expenses on a cost reimbursable basis. If the district engineer believes a public hearing should be held and another agency is lead agency, the district engineer should request such a hearing and provide his reasoning for the request. The district engineer should suggest a joint hearing and offer to take an active part in the hearing and ensure coverage of the Corps concerns.

d. *Scope of Analysis.* See paragraph 7b.

e. *Scoping Process.* Refer to 40 CFR 1501.7 and 33 CFR 230.12.

f. *Contracting.* See 40 CFR 1506.5.

(1) The district engineer may prepare an EIS, or may obtain information needed to prepare an EIS, either with his own staff or by contract. In choosing a contractor who reports directly to the district engineer, the procedures of 40 CFR 1506.5(c) will be followed.

(2) Information required for an EIS also may be furnished by the applicant or a consultant employed by the applicant. Where this approach is followed, the district engineer will (i) advise the applicant and/or his consultant of the Corps information requirements, and (ii) meet with the applicant and/or his consultant from time to time and provide him with the district engineer's views regarding adequacy of the data that are being developed (including how the district engineer will view such data in light of any possible conflicts of interest).

The applicant and/or his consultant may accept or reject the district engineer's guidance. The district engineer, however, may after specifying the information in contention, require the applicant to resubmit any previously submitted data which the district engineer considers inadequate or inaccurate. In all cases, the district engineer should document in the record the Corps independent evaluation of the information and its accuracy, as required by 40 CFR 1506.5(a).

g. *Change in EIS Determination.* If it is determined that an EIS is not required after a notice of intent has been published, the district engineer shall terminate the EIS preparation and withdraw the notice of intent. The district engineer shall notify in writing the appropriate division engineer; HQUSACE (CECW-OR); the appropriate EPA regional administrator, the Director, Office of Federal Activities (A-104), EPA, 401 M Street SW., Washington, DC 20460 and the public of the determination.

h. *Time Limits.* For regulatory actions, the district engineer will follow 33 CFR 230.17(a) unless unusual delays caused by applicant inaction or compliance with other statutes require longer time frames for EIS preparation. At the outset of the EIS effort, schedule milestones will be developed and made available to the applicant and the public. If the milestone dates are not met the district engineer will notify the applicant and explain the reason for delay.

9. *Organization and Content of Draft EISs—a. General.* This section gives detailed information for preparing draft EISs. When the Corps is the lead agency, this draft EIS format and these procedures will be followed. When the Corps is one of the joint lead agencies, the joint lead agencies will mutually decide which agency's format and procedures will be followed.

b. *Format—*(1) *Cover Sheet.* (a) Ref. 40 CFR 1502.11.

(b) The "person at the agency who can supply further information" (40 CFR 1502.11(c) is the project manager handling that permit application.

(c) The cover sheet should identify the EIS as a Corps permit action and state the authorities (sections 9, 10, 404, 103, etc.) under which the Corps is exerting its jurisdiction.

(2) *Summary.* In addition to the requirements of 40 CFR 1502.12, this section should identify the proposed action as a Corps permit action stating the authorities (sections 9, 10, 404, 103, etc.) under which the Corps is exerting its jurisdiction. It shall also summarize the purpose and need for the proposed action and shall briefly state the beneficial/adverse impacts of the proposed action.

(3) *Table of Contents.*

(4) *Purpose and Need.* See 40 CFR 1502.13. If the scope of analysis for the NEPA document (see paragraph 7b) covers only the proposed specific activity requiring a Department of the Army permit, then the underlying purpose and need for that specific activity should be stated. (For example, "The purpose and need

for the pipe is to obtain cooling water from the river for the electric generating plant.") If the scope of analysis covers a more extensive project, only part of which may require a DA permit, then the underlying purpose and need for the entire project should be stated. (For example, "The purpose and need for the electric generating plant is to provide increased supplies of electricity to the (named) geographic area.") Normally, the applicant should be encouraged to provide a statement of his proposed activity's purpose and need from his perspective (for example, "to construct an electric generating plant"). However, whenever the NEPA document's scope of analysis renders it appropriate, the Corps also should consider and express that activity's underlying purpose and need from a public interest perspective (to use that same example, "to meet the public's need for electric energy"). Also, while generally focusing on the applicant's statement, the Corps, will in all cases, exercise independent judgment in defining the purpose and need for the project from both the applicant's and the public's perspective.

(5) *Alternatives.* See 40 CFR 1502.14. The Corps is neither an opponent nor a proponent of the applicant's proposal; therefore, the applicant's final proposal will be identified as the "applicant's preferred alternative" in the final EIS. Decision options available to the district engineer, which embrace all of the applicant's alternatives, are issue the permit, issue with modifications or conditions or deny the permit.

(a) Only reasonable alternatives need be considered in detail, as specified in 40 CFR 1502.14(a). Reasonable alternatives must be those that are feasible and such feasibility must focus on the accomplishment of the underlying purpose and need (of the applicant or the public) that would be satisfied by the proposed Federal action (permit issuance). The alternatives analysis should be thorough enough to use for both the public interest review and the 404(b)(1) guidelines (40 CFR part 230) where applicable. Those alternatives that are unavailable to the applicant, whether or not they require Federal action (permits), should normally be included in the analysis of the no-Federal-action (denial) alternative. Such alternatives should be evaluated only to the extent necessary to allow a complete and objective evaluation of the public interest and a fully informed decision regarding the permit application.

(b) The "no-action" alternative is one which results in no construction requiring a Corps permit. It may be brought by (1) the applicant electing to modify his proposal to eliminate work under the jurisdiction of the Corps or (2) by the denial of the permit. District engi-

neers, when evaluating this alternative, should discuss, when appropriate, the consequences of other likely uses of a project site, should the permit be denied.

(c) The EIS should discuss geographic alternatives, e.g., changes in location and other site specific variables, and functional alternatives, e.g., project substitutes and design modifications.

(d) The Corps shall not prepare a cost-benefit analysis for projects requiring a Corps permit. 40 CFR 1502.23 states that the weighing of the various alternatives need not be displayed in a cost-benefit analysis and "* * * should not be when there are important qualitative considerations." The EIS should, however, indicate any cost considerations that are likely to be relevant to a decision.

(e) Mitigation is defined in 40 CFR 1508.20, and Federal action agencies are directed in 40 CFR 1502.14 to include appropriate mitigation measures. Guidance on the conditioning of permits to require mitigation is in 33 CFR 320.4(r) and 325.4. The nature and extent of mitigation conditions are dependent on the results of the public interest review in 33 CFR 320.4.

(6) *Affected Environment.* See Ref. 40 CFR 1502.15.

(7) *Environmental Consequences.* See Ref. 40 CFR 1502.16.

(8) *List of Preparers.* See Ref. 40 CFR 1502.17.

(9) *Public Involvement.* This section should list the dates and nature of all public notices, scoping meetings and public hearings and include a list of all parties notified.

(10) *Appendices.* See 40 CFR 1502.18. Appendices should be used to the maximum extent practicable to minimize the length of the main text of the EIS. Appendices normally should not be circulated with every copy of the EIS, but appropriate appendices should be provided routinely to parties with special interest and expertise in the particular subject.

(11) *Index.* The Index of an EIS, at the end of the document, should be designed to provide for easy reference to items discussed in the main text of the EIS.

10. *Notice of Intent.* The district engineer shall follow the guidance in 33 CFR part 230, Appendix C in preparing a notice of intent to prepare a draft EIS for publication in the FEDERAL REGISTER.

11. *Public Hearing.* If a public hearing is to be held pursuant to 33 CFR part 327 for a permit application

requiring an EIS, the actions analyzed by the draft EIS should be considered at the public hearing. The district engineer should make the draft EIS available to the public at least 15 days in advance of the hearing. If a hearing request is received from another agency having jurisdiction as provided in 40 CFR 1506.6(c)(2), the district engineer should coordinate a joint hearing with that agency whenever appropriate.

12. *Organization and Content of Final EIS.* The organization and content of the final EIS including the abbreviated final EIS procedures shall follow the guidance in 33 CFR 230.14(a).

13. *Comments Received on the Final EIS.* For permit cases to be decided at the district level, the district engineer should consider all incoming comments and provide responses when substantive issues are raised which have not been addressed in the final EIS. For permit cases decided at higher authority, the district engineer shall forward the final EIS comment letters together with appropriate responses to higher authority along with the case. In the case of a letter recommending a referral under 40 CFR part 1504, the district engineer will follow the guidance in paragraph 19 of this appendix.

14. *EIS Supplement.* See 33 CFR 230.13(b).

15. *Filing Requirements.* See 40 CFR 1506.9. Five (5) copies of EISs shall be sent to Director, Office of Federal Activities (A-104), Environmental Protection Agency, 401 M Street SW., Washington, DC 20460. The official review periods commence with EPA's publication of a notice of availability of the draft or final EISs in the FEDERAL REGISTER. Generally, this notice appears on Friday of each week. At the same time they are mailed to EPA for filing, one copy of each draft or final EIS, or EIS supplement should be mailed to HQUSACE (CECW-OR) WASH DC 20314-1000.

16. *Timing.* 40 CFR 1506.10 describes the timing of an agency action when an EIS is involved.

17. *Expedited Filing.* 40 CFR 1506.10 provides information on allowable time reductions and time extensions associated with the EIS process. The district engineer will provide the necessary information and facts to HQUSACE (CECW-RE) WASH DC 20314-1000 (with copy to CECW-OR) for consultation with EPA for a reduction in the prescribed review periods.

18. *Record of Decision.* In those cases involving an EIS, the statement of findings will be called the record of

decision and shall incorporate the requirements of 40 CFR 1505.2. The record of decision is not to be included when filing a final EIS and may not be signed until 30 days after the notice of availability of the final EIS is published in the FEDERAL REGISTER. To avoid duplication, the record of decision may reference the EIS.

19. *Predecision Referrals by Other Agencies.* See 40 CFR part 1504. The decisionmaker should notify any potential referring Federal agency and CEQ of a final decision if it is contrary to the announced position of a potential referring agency. (This pertains to a NEPA referral, not a 404(q) referral under the Clean Water Act. The procedures for a 404(q) referral are outlined in the 404(q) Memoranda of Agreement. The potential referring agency will then have 25 calendar days to refer the case to CEQ under 40 CFR part 1504. Referrals will be transmitted through division to CECW-RE for further guidance with an information copy to CECW-OR.

20. *Review of Other Agencies' EISs.* District engineers should provide comments directly to the requesting agency specifically related to the Corps jurisdiction by law or special expertise as defined in 40 CFR 1508.15 and 1508.26 and identified in Appendix II of CEQ regulations (49 FR 49750, December 21, 1984). If the district engineer determines that another agency's draft EIS which involves a Corps permit action is inadequate with respect to the Corps permit action, the district engineer should attempt to resolve the differences concerning the Corps permit action prior to the filing of the final EIS by the other agency. If the district engineer finds that the final EIS is inadequate with respect to the Corps permit action, the district engineer should incorporate the other agency's final EIS or a portion thereof and prepare an appropriate and adequate NEPA document to address the Corps involvement with the proposed action. See 33 CFR 230.21 for guidance. The agency which prepared the original EIS should be given the opportunity to provide additional information to that contained in the EIS in order for the Corps to have all relevant information available for a sound decision on the permit.

21. *Monitoring.* Monitoring compliance with permit requirements should be carried out in accordance with 33 CFR 230.15 and with 33 CFR part 325.

[53 FR 3134, Feb. 3, 1988]

Appendix C to Part 325—Procedures for the Protection of Historic Properties

1.   Definitions

a. *Designated historic property* is a historic property listed in the National Register of Historic Places (National Register) or which has been determined eligible for listing in the National Register pursuant to 36 CFR part 63. A historic property that, in both the opinion of the SHPO and the district engineer, appears to meet the criteria for inclusion in the National Register will be treated as a "designated historic property."

b. *Historic property* is a property which has historical importance to any person or group. This term includes the types of districts, sites, buildings, structures or objects eligible for inclusion, but not necessarily listed, on the National Register.

c. *Certified local government* is a local government certified in accordance with section 101(c)(1) of the NHPA (See 36 CFR part 61).

d. The term "criteria for inclusion in the National Register" refers to the criteria published by the Department of Interior at 36 CFR 60.4.

e. An "effect" on a "designated historic property" occurs when the undertaking may alter the characteristics of the property that qualified the property for inclusion in the National Register. Consideration of effects on "designated historic properties" includes indirect effects of the undertaking. The criteria for effect and adverse effect are described in Paragraph 15 of this appendix.

f. The term "undertaking" as used in this appendix means the work, structure or discharge that requires a Department of the Army permit pursuant to the Corps regulations at 33 CFR 320-334.

g. Permit area.

(1) The term "permit area" as used in this appendix means those areas comprising the waters of the United States that will be directly affected by the proposed work or structures and uplands directly affected as a result of authorizing the work or structures. The following three tests must all be satisfied for an activity undertaken outside the waters of the United States to be included within the "permit area":

(i) Such activity would not occur but for the authorization of the work or structures within the waters of the United States;

(ii) Such activity must be integrally related to the work or structures to be authorized within waters of the United States. Or, conversely, the work or structures to be authorized must be essential to the completeness of the overall project or program; and

(iii) Such activity must be directly associated (first order impact) with the work or structures to be authorized.

(2) For example, consider an application for a permit to construct a pier and dredge an access channel so that an industry may be established and operated on an upland area.

(i) Assume that the industry requires the access channel and the pier and that without such channel and pier the project would not be feasible. Clearly then, the industrial site, even though upland, would be within the "permit area." It would not be established "but for" the access channel and pier; it also is integrally related to the work and structure to be authorized; and finally it is directly associated with the work and structure to be authorized. Similarly, all three tests are satisfied for the dredged material disposal site and it too is in the "permit area" even if located on uplands.

(ii) Consider further that the industry, if established, would cause local agencies to extend water and sewer lines to service the area of the industrial site. Assume that the extension would not itself involve the waters of the United States and is not solely the result of the industrial facility. The extensions would not be within the "permit area" because they would not be directly associated with the work or structure to be authorized.

(iii) Now consider that the industry, if established, would require increased housing for its employees, but that a private developer would develop the housing. Again, even if the housing would not be developed but for the authorized work and structure, the housing would not be within the permit area because it would not be directly associated with or integrally related to the work or structure to be authorized.

(3) Consider a different example. This time an industry will be established that requires no access to the navigable waters for its operation. The plans for the facility, however, call for a recreational pier with an access channel. The pier and channel will be used for the company-owned yacht and employee recreation. In the example, the industrial site is not included within the permit area. Only areas of dredging, dredged material disposal, and pier construction would be within the permit area.

(4) Lastly, consider a linear crossing of the waters of the United States; for example, by a transmission line, pipeline, or highway.

(i) Such projects almost always *can* be undertaken without Corps authorization, if they are designed to avoid affecting the waters of the United States. Corps authorization is sought because it is less expensive or more convenient for the applicant to do so than to avoid affecting the waters of the United States. Thus the "but for" test is not met by the entire project right-of-way. The "same undertaking" and "integral relationship" tests are met, but this is not sufficient to make the whole right-of-way part of the permit area. Typically, however, some portion of the right-of-way, approaching the crossing, would not occur in its given configuration "but for" the authorized activity. This portion of the right-of-way, whose location is determined by the location of the crossing, meets all three tests and hence is part of the permit area.

(ii) Accordingly, in the case of the linear crossing, the permit area shall extend in either direction from the crossing to that point at which alternative alignments leading to reasonable alternative locations for the crossing can be considered and evaluated. Such a point may often coincide with the physical feature of the waterbody to be crossed, for example, a bluff, the limit of the flood plain, a vegetational change, etc., or with a jurisdictional feature associated with the waterbody, for example, a zoning change, easement limit, etc., although such features should not be controlling in selecting the limits of the permit area.

2. General Policy

This appendix establishes the procedures to be followed by the U.S. Army Corps of Engineers (Corps) to fulfill the requirements set forth in the National Historic Preservation Act (NHPA), other applicable historic preservation laws, and Presidential directives as they relate to the regulatory program of the Corps of Engineers (33 CFR parts 320-334).

a. The district engineer will take into account the effects, if any, of proposed undertakings on historic properties both within and beyond the waters of the U.S. Pursuant to section 110(f) of the NHPA, the district engineer, where the undertaking that is the subject of a permit action may directly and adversely affect any National Historic Landmark, shall, to the maximum extent possible, condition any issued permit as may be necessary to minimize harm to such landmark.

b. In addition to the requirements of the NHPA, all historic properties are subject to consideration under the National Environmental Policy Act, (33 CFR part 325, appendix B), and the Corps' public interest review requirements contained in 33 CFR 320.4. Therefore, historic properties will be included as a factor in the district engineer's decision on a permit application.

c. In processing a permit application, the district engineer will generally accept for Federal or Federally assisted projects the Federal agency's or Federal lead agency's compliance with the requirements of the NHPA.

d. If a permit application requires the preparation of an Environmental Impact Statement (EIS) pursuant to the National Environmental Policy Act, the draft EIS will contain the information required by paragraph 9.a. below. Furthermore, the SHPO and the ACHP will be given the opportunity to participate in the scoping process and to comment on the Draft and Final EIS.

e. During pre-application consultations with a prospective applicant the district engineer will encourage the consideration of historic properties at the earliest practical time in the planning process.

f. This appendix is organized to follow the Corps standard permit process and to indicate how historic property considerations are to be addressed during the processing and evaluating of permit applications. The procedures of this Appendix are not intended to diminish the full consideration of historic properties in the Corps regulatory program. Rather, this appendix is intended to provide for the maximum consideration of historic properties within the time and jurisdictional constraints of the Corps regulatory program. The Corps will make every effort to provide information on historic properties and the effects of proposed undertakings on them to the public by the public notice within the time constraints required by the Clean Water Act. Within the time constraints of applicable laws, executive orders, and regulations, the Corps will provide the maximum coordination and comment opportunities to interested parties especially the SHPO and ACHP. The Corps will discuss with and encourage the applicant to avoid or minimize effects on historic properties. In reaching its decisions on permits, the Corps will adhere to the goals of the NHPA and other applicable laws dealing with historic properties.

3.   Initial Review

a. Upon receipt of a completed permit application, the district engineer will consult district files and records, the latest published version(s) of the National Register, lists of properties determined eligible, and other appropriate sources of information to determine if there are any designated historic properties which may be affected by the proposed undertaking. The district engineer will also consult with other appropriate sources of information for knowledge of undesignated historic properties which may be affected by the proposed undertaking. The district engineer will establish procedures (e.g., telephone calls) to obtain supplemental information from the SHPO and other appropriate sources. Such procedures shall be accomplished within the time limits specified in this appendix and 33 CFR part 325.

b. In certain instances, the nature, scope, and magnitude of the work, and/or structures to be permitted may be such that there is little likelihood that a historic property exists or may be affected. Where the district engineer determines that such a situation exists, he will include a statement to this effect in the public notice. Three such situations are:

(1) Areas that have been extensively modified by previous work. In such areas, historic properties that may have at one time existed within the permit area may be presumed to have been lost unless specific information indicates the presence of such a property (e.g., a shipwreck).

(2) Areas which have been created in modern times. Some recently created areas, such as dredged material disposal islands, have had no human habitation. In such cases, it may be presumed that there is no potential for the existence of historic properties unless specific information indicates the presence of such a property.

(3) Certain types of work or structures that are of such limited nature and scope that there is little likelihood of impinging upon a historic property even if such properties were to be present within the affected area.

c. If, when using the pre-application procedures of 33 CFR 325.1(b), the district engineer believes that a designated historic property may be affected, he will inform the prospective applicant for consideration during project planning of the potential applicability of the Secretary of the Interior's Standards and Guidelines for Archeology and Historic Preservation (48 FR 44716). The district engineer will also inform the prospective applicant that the Corps will consider any effects on historic properties in accordance with this appendix.

d. At the earliest practical time the district engineer will discuss with the applicant measures or alternatives to avoid or minimize effects on historic properties.

4.   Public Notice.

a. Except as specified in subparagraph 4.c., the district engineer's current knowledge of the presence or absence of historic properties and the effects of the undertaking upon these properties will be included in the public notice. The public notice will be sent to the SHPO, the regional office of the National Park Service (NPS), certified local governments (see paragraph (1.c.) and Indian tribes, and interested citizens. If there are designated historic properties which reasonably may be affected by the undertaking or if there are undesignated historic properties within the affected area which the district engineer reasonably expects to be affected by the undertaking and which he believes meet the criteria for inclusion in the National Register, the public notice will also be sent to the ACHP.

b. During permit evaluation for newly designated historic properties or undesignated historic properties which reasonably may be affected by the undertaking and which have been newly identified through the public interest review process, the district engineer will immediately inform the applicant, the SHPO, the appropriate certified local government and the ACHP of the district engineer's current knowledge of the effects of the undertaking upon these properties. Commencing from the date of the district engineer's letter, these entities will be given 30 days to submit their comments.

c. Locational and sensitive information related to archeological sites is excluded from the Freedom of Information Act (Section 304 of the NHPA and Section 9 of ARPA). If the district engineer or the Secretary of the Interior determine that the disclosure of information to the public relating to the location or character of sensitive historic resources may create a substantial risk of harm, theft, or destruction to such resources or to the area or place where such resources are located, then the district engineer will not include such information in the public notice nor otherwise make it available to the public. Therefore, the district engineer will furnish such information to the ACHP and the SHPO by separate notice.

5.   Investigations

a. When initial review, addition submissions by the applicant, or response to the public notice indicates the existence of a potentially eligible property, the district engineer shall examine the pertinent evidence to determine the need for further investigation. The evidence must set forth specific reasons for the need to further investigate within the permit area and may consist of:

(1) Specific information concerning properties which may be eligible for inclusion in the National Register and which are known to exist in the vicinity of the project; and

(2) Specific information concerning known sensitive areas which are likely to yield resources eligible for inclusion in the National Register, particularly where such sensitive area determinations are based upon data collected from other, similar areas within the general vicinity.

b. Where the scope and type of work proposed by the applicant or the evidence presented leads the district engineer to conclude that the chance of disturbance by the undertaking to any potentially eligible historic property is too remote to justify further investigation, he shall so advise the reporting party and the SHPO.

c. If the district engineer's review indicates that an investigation for the presence of potentially eligible historic properties on the upland locations of the permit area (see paragraph 1.g.) is justified, the district engineer will conduct or cause to be conducted such an investigation. Additionally, if the notification indicates that a potentially eligible historic property may exist within waters of the U.S., the district engineer will conduct or cause to be conducted an investigation to determine whether this property may be eligible for inclusion in the National Register. Comments or information of a general nature will not be considered as sufficient evidence to warrant an investigation.

d. In addition to any investigations conducted in accordance with paragraph 6.a. above, the district engineer may conduct or cause to be conducted additional investigations which the district engineer determines are essential to reach the public interest decision . As part of any site visit, Corps personnel will examine the permit area for the presence of potentially eligible

historic properties. The Corps will notify the SHPO, if any evidence is found which indicates the presence of potentially eligible historic properties.

e. As determined by the district engineer, investigations may consist of any of the following: further consultations with the SHPO, the State Archeologist, local governments, Indian tribes, local historical and archeological societies, university archeologists, and others with knowledge and expertise in the identification of historical, archeological, cultural and scientific resources; field examinations; and archeological testing. In most cases, the district engineer will require, in accordance with 33 CFR 325.1(e), that the applicant conduct the investigation at his expense and usually by third party contract.f. The Corps of Engineers' responsibilities to seek eligibility determinations for potentially eligible historic properties is limited to resources located within waters of the U.S. that are directly affected by the undertaking. The Corps responsibilities to identify potentially eligible historic properties is limited to resources located within the permit area that are directly affected by related upland activities. The Corps is not responsible for identifying or assessing potentially eligible historic properties outside the permit area, but will consider the effects of undertakings on any known historic properties that may occur outside the permit area.

6.   Eligibility determinations

a. For a historic property within waters of the U.S. that will be directly affected by the undertaking the district engineer will, for the purposes of this Appendix and compliance with the NHPA:

(1) Treat the historic property as a "designated historic property," if both the SHPO and the district engineer agree that it is eligible for inclusion in the National Register; or

(2) Treat the historic property as not eligible, if both the SHPO and the district engineer agree that it is not eligible for inclusion in the National Register; or

(3) Request a determination of eligibility from the Keeper of the National Register in accordance with applicable National Park Service regulations and notify the applicant, if the SHPO and the district engineer disagree or the ACHP or the Secretary of the Interior so request. If the Keeper of the National Register determines that the resources are not eligible for listing in the National Register or fails to respond within 45 days of receipt of the request, the district engineer may proceed to conclude his action on the permit application.

b. For a historic property outside of waters of the U.S. that will be directly affected by the undertaking the district engineer will, for the purposes of this appendix and compliance with the NHPA:

(1) Treat the historic property as a "designated historic property," if both the SHPO and the district engineer agree that it is eligible for inclusion in the National Register; or

(2) Treat the historic property as not eligible, if both the SHPO and the district engineer agree that it is not eligible for inclusion in the National Register; or

(3) Treat the historic property as not eligible unless the Keeper of the National Register determines it is eligible for or lists it on the National Register. (See paragraph 6.c. below.)

c. If the district engineer and the SHPO do not agree pursuant to paragraph 6.b.(1) and the SHPO notifies the district engineer that it is nominating a potentially eligible historic property for the National Register that may be affected by the undertaking, the district engineer will wait a reasonable period of time for that determination to be made before concluding his action on the permit. Such a reasonable period of time would normally be 30 days for the SHPO to nominate the historic property plus 45 days for the Keeper of the National Register to make such determination. The district engineer will encourage the applicant to cooperate with the SHPO in obtaining the information necessary to nominate the historic property.

7. Assessing Effects

a. *Applying the Criteria of Effect and Adverse Effect.* During the public notice comment period or within 30 days after the determination or discovery of a designated history property the district engineer will coordinate with the SHPO and determine if there is an effect and if so, assess the effect. (See Paragraph 15.)

b. *No Effect.* If the SHPO concurs with the district engineer's determination of no effect or fails to respond within 15 days of the district engineer's notice to the SHPO of a no effect determination, then the district engineer may proceed with the final decision.

c. *No Adverse Effect.* If the district engineer, based on his coordination with the SHPO (see paragraph 7.a.), determines that an effect is not adverse, the district engineer will notify the ACHP and request the comments of the ACHP. The district engineer's notice will include a description of both the project and the designated historic property; both the district engineer's and the SHPO's views, as well as any views of affected local governments, Indian tribes, Federal agencies, and the public, on the no adverse effect determination; and a description of the efforts to identify historic properties and solicit the views of those above. The district engineer may conclude the permit decision if the ACHP does not object to the district engineer's determination or if the district engineer accepts any conditions requested by the ACHP for a no adverse effect determination, or the ACHP fails to respond within 30 days of the district engineer's notice to the ACHP. If the ACHP objects or the district engineer does not accept the conditions proposed by the ACHP, then the effect shall be considered as adverse.

d. *Adverse Effect.* If an adverse effect on designated historic properties is found, the district engineer will notify the ACHP and coordinate with the SHPO to seek ways to avoid or reduce effects on designated historic properties. Either the district engineer or the SHPO may request the ACHP to participate. At its discretion, the ACHP may participate without such a request. The district engineer, the SHPO or the ACHP may state that further coordination will not be productive. The district engineer shall then request the ACHP's comments in accordance with paragraph 9.

8. Consultation

At any time during permit processing, the district engineer may consult with the involved parties to discuss and consider possible alternatives or measures to avoid or minimize the adverse effects of a proposed activity. The district engineer will terminate any consultation immediately upon determining that further consultation is not productive and will immediately notify the consulting parties. If the consultation results in a mutual agreement among the SHPO, ACHP, applicant and the district engineer regarding the treatment of designated historic properties, then the district engineer may formalize that agreement either through permit conditioning or by signing a Memorandum of Agreement (MOA) with these parties. Such MOA will constitute the comments of the ACHP and the SHPO, and the district engineer may proceed with the permit decision. Consultation shall not continue beyond the comment period provided in paragraph 9.b.

9. ACHP Review and Comment

a. If: (i) The district engineer determines that coordination with the SHPO is unproductive; or (ii) the ACHP, within the appropriate comment period, requests additional information in order to provide its comments; or (iii) the ACHP objects to any agreed resolution of impacts on designated historic properties; the district engineer, normally within 30 days, shall provide the ACHP with:

(1) A project description, including, as appropriate, photographs, maps, drawings, and specifications (such as, dimensions of structures, fills, or excavations; types of materials and quantity of material);

(2) A listing and description of the designated historic properties that will be affected, including the reports from any surveys or investigations;

(3) A description of the anticipated adverse effects of the undertaking on the designated historic properties and of the proposed mitigation measures and alternatives considered, if any; and

(4) The views of any commenting parties regarding designated historic properties.

In developing this information, the district engineer may coordinate with the applicant, the SHPO, and any appropriate Indian tribe or certified local government.

Copies of the above information also should be forwarded to the applicant, the SHPO, and any appropriate Indian tribe or certified local government. The district engineer will not delay his decision but will consider any comments these parties may wish to provide.

b. The district engineer will provide the ACHP 60 days from the date of the district engineer's letter forwarding the information in paragraph 9.a., to provide its comments. If the ACHP does not comment by the end of this comment period, the district engineer will complete processing of the permit application. When the permit decision is otherwise delayed as provided in 33 CFR 325.2(d) (3) & (4), the district engineer will provide additional time for the ACHP to comment consistent with, but not extending beyond that delay.

10.   District Engineer Decision

a. In making the public interest decision on a permit application, in accordance with 33 CFR 320.4, the district engineer shall weigh all factors, including the effects of the undertaking on historic properties and any comments of the ACHP and the SHPO, and any views of other interested parties. The district engineer will add permit conditions to avoid or reduce effects on historic properties which he determines are necessary in accordance with 33 CFR 325.4. In reaching his determination, the district engineer will consider the Secretary of the Interior's Standards and Guidelines for Archeology and Historic Preservation (48 FR 44716).

b. If the district engineer concludes that permitting the activity would result in the irrevocable loss of important scientific, prehistoric, historical, or archeological data, the district engineer, in accordance with the Archeological and Historic Preservation Act of 1974, will advise the Secretary of the Interior (by notifying the National Park Service (NPS)) of the extent to which the data may be lost if the undertaking is permitted, any plans to mitigate such loss that will be implemented, and the permit conditions that will be included to ensure that any required mitigation occurs.

11.   Historic Properties Discovered During Construction

After the permit has been issued, if the district engineer finds or is notified that the permit area contains a previously unknown potentially eligible historic property which he reasonably expects will be affected by the undertaking, he shall immediately inform the Department of the Interior Departmental Consulting Archeologist and the regional office of the NPS of the current knowledge of the potentially eligible historic property and the expected effects, if any, of the undertaking on that property. The district engineer will seek voluntary avoidance of construction activities that could affect the historic property pending a recommendation from the National Park Service pursuant to the Archeological and Historic Preservation Act of 1974. Based on the circumstances of the discovery, equity to all parties, and considerations of the public interest, the district engineer may modify, suspend or revoke a permit in accordance with 33 CFR 325.7.

12.   Regional General Permits

Potential impacts on historic properties will be considered in development and evaluation of general permits. However, many of the specific procedures contained in this appendix are not normally applicable to general permits. In developing general permits, the district engineer will seek the views of the SHPO and, the ACHP and other organizations and/or individuals with expertise or interest in historic properties. Where designated historic properties are reasonably likely to be affected, general permits shall be conditioned to protect such properties or to limit the applicability of the permit coverage.

13.   Nationwide General Permit

a. The criteria at paragraph 15 of this Appendix will be used for determining compliance with the nationwide permit condition at 33 CFR 330.5(b)(9) regarding the effect on designated historic properties. When making this determination the district engineer may consult with the SHPO, the ACHP or other interested parties.

b. If the district engineer is notified of a potentially eligible historic property in accordance with nationwide permit regulations and conditions, he will immediately notify the SHPO. If the district engineer believes that the potentially eligible historic property meets the criteria for inclusion in the National Register and that it may be affected by the proposed undertaking then he may suspend authorization of the nationwide permit until he provides the ACHP and the SHPO the opportunity to comment in accordance with the provisions of this Appendix. Once these provisions have been satisfied, the district engineer may notify the general permittee that the activity is authorized including any special activity specific conditions identified or that an individual permit is required.

14. Emergency Procedures

The procedures for processing permits in emergency situations are described at 33 CFR 325.2(e)(4). In an emergency situation the district engineer will make every reasonable effort to receive comments from the SHPO and the ACHP, when the proposed undertaking can reasonably be expected to affect a potentially eligible or designated historic property and will comply with the provisions of this Appendix to the extent time and the emergency situation allows.

15. Criteria of Effect and Adverse Effect

(a) An undertaking has an effect on a designated historic property when the undertaking may alter characteristics of the property that qualified the property for inclusion in the National Register. For the purpose of determining effect, alteration to features of a property's location, setting, or use may be relevant, and depending on a property's important characteristics, should be considered.

(b) An undertaking is considered to have an adverse effect when the effect on a designated historic property may diminish the integrity of the property's location, design, setting, materials, workmanship, feeling, or

association. Adverse effects on designated historic properties include, but are not limited to:

(1) Physical destruction, damage, or alteration of all or part of the property;

(2) Isolation of the property from or alteration of the character of the property's setting when that character contributes to the property's qualification for the National Register;

(3) Introduction of visual, audible, or atmospheric elements that are out of character with the property or alter its setting;

(4) Neglect of a property resulting in its deterioration or destruction; and

(5) Transfer, lease, or sale of the property.

(c) Effects of an undertaking that would otherwise be found to be adverse may be considered as being not adverse for the purpose of this appendix:

(1) When the designated historic property is of value only for its potential contribution to archeological, historical, or architectural research, and when such value can be substantially preserved through the conduct of appropriate research, and such research is conducted in accordance with applicable professional standards and guidelines;

(2) When the undertaking is limited to the rehabilitation of buildings and structures and is conducted in a manner that preserves the historical and architectural value of affected designated historic properties through conformance with the Secretary's "Standards for Rehabilitation and Guidelines for Rehabilitating Historic Buildings", or

(3) When the undertaking is limited to the transfer, lease, or sale of a designated historic property, and adequate restrictions or conditions are included to ensure preservation of the property's important historic features.

[55 FR 27003, June 29, 1990]

NEPA Deskbook

Appendix 12 Environmental Protection Agency Regulations and Procedures (EPA Part 6)

40 CFR Pt. 6

Part 6—Procedures for Implementing the Requirements of the Council on Environmental Quality on the National Environmental Policy Act

Subpart J—Assessing the Environmental Effects Abroad of EPA Actions

Appendix A to Part 6—Statement of Procedures on Floodplain Management and Wetlands Protection

Authority:
42 U.S.C. 4321 et seq., 7401-7671q; 40 CFR part 1500.

Source:
44 FR 64177, Nov. 6, 1979, unless otherwise noted.

Subpart A—General

§6.100   Purpose and policy.

(a) The National Environmental Policy Act of 1969 (NEPA), 42 U.S.C. 4321 et seq., as implemented by Executive Orders 11514 and 11991 and the Council on Environmental Quality (CEQ) Regulations of November 29, 1978 (43 FR 55978) requires that Federal agencies include in their decision-making processes appropriate and careful consideration of all environmental effects of proposed actions, analyze potential environmental effects of proposed actions and their alternatives for public understanding and scrutiny, avoid or minimize adverse effects of proposed actions, and restore and enhance environmental quality as much as possible. The Environmental Protection Agency (EPA) shall integrate these NEPA factors as early in the Agency planning processes as possible. The environmental review process shall be the focal point to assure NEPA considerations are taken into account. To the extent applicable, EPA shall prepare environmental impact statements (EISs) on those major actions determined to have significant impact on the quality of the human environment. This part takes into account the EIS exemptions set forth under section 511(c)(1) of the Clean Water Act (Pub. L. 92-500) and section 7(c)(1) of the Energy Supply and Environmental Coordination Act of 1974 (Pub. L. 93-319).

(b) This part establishes EPA policy and procedures for the identification and analysis of the environmental impacts of EPA-related activities and the preparation and processing of EISs.

§6.101   Definitions.

(a) Terminology. All terminology used in this part will be consistent with the terms as defined in 40 CFR part 1508 (the CEQ Regulations). Any qualifications will be provided in the definitions set forth in each subpart of this regulation.

(b) The term CEQ Regulations means the regulations issued by the Council on Environmental Quality on November 29, 1978 (see 43 FR 55978), which implement Executive Order 11991. The CEQ Regulations will often be referred to throughout this regulation by reference to 40 CFR part 1500 et al.

(c) The term environmental review means the process whereby an evaluation is undertaken by EPA to determine whether a proposed Agency action may have a significant impact on the environment and therefore require the preparation of the EIS.

(d) The term environmental information document means any written analysis prepared by an applicant, grantee or contractor describing the environmental impacts of a proposed action. This document will be of sufficient scope to enable the responsible official to prepare an environmental assessment as described in the remaining subparts of this regulation.

(e) The term grant as used in this part means an award of funds or other assistance by a written grant agreement or cooperative agreement under 40 CFR chapter I, subpart B.

§6.102   Applicability.

(a) Administrative actions covered. This part applies to the activities of EPA in accordance with the outline of the subparts set forth below. Each subpart describes the detailed environmental review procedures required for each action.

(1) Subpart A sets forth an overview of the regulation. Section 6.102(b) describes the requirements for EPA legislative proposals.

(2) Subpart B describes the requirements for the content of an EIS prepared pursuant to subparts E, F, G, H, and I.

(3) Subpart C describes the requirements for coordination of all environmental laws during the environmental review undertaken pursuant to subparts E, F, G, H, and I.

(4) Subpart D describes the public information requirements which must be undertaken in conjunc-

tion with the environmental review requirements under subparts E, F, G, H, and I.

(5) Subpart E describes the environmental review requirements for the wastewater treatment construction grants program under Title II of the Clean Water Act.

(6) Subpart F describes the environmental review requirements for new source National Pollutant Discharge Elimination System (NPDES) permits under section 402 of the Clean Water Act.

(7) Subpart G describes the environmental review requirements for research and development programs undertaken by the Agency.

(8) Subpart H describes the environmental review requirements for solid waste demonstration projects undertaken by the Agency.

(9) Subpart I describes the environmental review requirements for construction of special purpose facilities and facility renovations by the Agency.

(b) Legislative proposals. As required by the CEQ Regulations, legislative EISs are required for any legislative proposal developed by EPA which significantly affects the quality of the human environment. A preliminary draft EIS shall be prepared by the responsible EPA office concurrently with the development of the legislative proposal and contain information required under subpart B. The EIS shall be processed in accordance with the requirements set forth under 40 CFR 1506.8.

(c) Application to ongoing activities—(1) General. The effective date for these regulations is December 5, 1979. These regulations do not apply to an EIS or supplement to that EIS if the draft EIS was filed with the Office of External Affairs, (OEA) before July 30, 1979. No completed environmental documents need be redone by reason of these regulations.

(2) With regard to activities under subpart E, these regulations shall apply to all EPA environmental review procedures effective December 15, 1979. However, for facility plans begun before December 15, 1979, the responsible official shall impose no new requirements on the grantee. Such grantees shall comply with requirements applicable before the effective date of this regulation. Notwithstanding the above, this regulation shall apply to any facility plan submitted to EPA after September 30, 1980.

[44 FR 64177, Nov. 6, 1979, as amended at 47 FR 9829, Mar. 8, 1982]

§6.103 Responsibilities.

(a) General responsibilities. (1) The responsible official's duties include:

(i) Requiring applicants, contractors, and grantees to submit environmental information documents and related documents and assuring that environmental reviews are conducted on proposed EPA projects at the earliest possible point in EPA's decision-making process. In this regard, the responsible official shall assure the early involvement and availability of information for private applicants and other non-Federal entities requiring EPA approvals.

(ii) When required, assuring that adequate draft EISs are prepared and distributed at the earliest possible point in EPA's decision-making process, their internal and external review is coordinated, and final EISs are prepared and distributed.

(iii) When an EIS is not prepared, assuring documentation of the decision to grant a categorical exclusion, or assuring that findings of no significant impact (FNSIs) and environmental assessments are prepared and distributed for those actions requiring them.

(iv) Consulting with appropriate officials responsible for other environmental laws set forth in subpart C.

(v) Consulting with the Office of External Affairs (OEA) on actions involving unresolved conflicts concerning this part or other Federal agencies.

(vi) When required, assuring that public participation requirements are met.

(2) Office of External Affairs duties include: (i) Supporting the Administrator in providing EPA policy guidance and assuring that EPA offices establish and maintain adequate administrative procedures to comply with this part.

(ii) Monitoring the overall timeliness and quality of the EPA effort to comply with this part.

(iii) Providing assistance to responsible officials as required, i.e., preparing guidelines describing the scope of environmental information required by private applicants relating to their proposed actions.

(iv) Coordinating the training of personnel involved in the review and preparation of EISs and other associated documents.

(v) Acting as EPA liaison with the Council on Environmental Quality and other Federal and State entities on matters of EPA policy and administrative mechanisms to facilitate external review of EISs, to determine lead agency and to improve the uniformity of the NEPA procedures of Federal agencies.

(vi) Advising the Administrator and Deputy Administrator on projects which involve more than one EPA office, are highly controversial, are nationally significant, or pioneer EPA policy, when these projects have had or should have an EIS prepared on them.

(vii) Carrying out administrative duties relating to maintaining status of EISs within EPA, i.e., publication of notices of intent in the Federal Register and making available to the public status reports on EISs and other elements of the environmental review process.

(3) Office of an Assistant Administrator duties include: (i) Providing specific policy guidance to their respective offices and assuring that those offices establish and maintain adequate administrative procedures to comply with this part.

(ii) Monitoring the overall timeliness and quality of their respective office's efforts to comply with this part.

(iii) Acting as liaison between their offices and the OEA and between their offices and other Assistant Administrators or Regional Administrators on matters of agencywide policy and procedures.

(iv) Advising the Administrator and Deputy Administrator through the OEA on projects or activities within their respective areas of responsibilities which involve more than one EPA office, are highly controversial, are nationally significant, or pioneer EPA policy, when these projects will have or should have an EIS prepared on them.

(v) Pursuant to § 6.102(b) of this subpart, preparing legislative EISs as appropriate on EPA legislative initiatives.

(4) The Office of Policy, Planning, and Evaluation duties include: responsibilities for coordinating the preparation of EISs required on EPA legislative proposals in accordance with § 6.102(b).

(b) Responsibilities for subpart E—(1) Responsible official. The responsible official for EPA actions covered by this subpart is the Regional Administrator.

(2) Assistant Administrator. The responsibilities of the Assistant Administrator, as described in § 6.103(a)(3), shall be assumed by the Assistant Administrator for Water for EPA actions covered by this subpart.

(c) Responsibilities for subpart F—(1) Responsible official. The responsible official for activities covered by this subpart is the Regional Administrator.

(2) Assistant Administrator. The responsibilities of the Assistant Administrator, as described in § 6.103(a)(3), shall be assumed by the Assistant Administrator for Enforcement and Compliance Monitoring for EPA actions covered by this subpart.

(d) Responsibilities for subpart G. The Assistant Administrator for Research and Development will be the responsible official for activities covered by this subpart.

(e) Responsibilities for subpart H. The Assistant Administrator for Solid Waste and Emergency Response will be the responsible official for activities covered by this subpart.

(f) Responsibilities for subpart I. The responsible official for new construction and modification of special purpose facilities is as follows:

(1) The Chief, Facilities Engineering and Real Estate Branch, Facilities and Support Services Division, Office of the Assistant Administrator for Administration and Resource Management (OARM) shall be the responsible official on all new construction of special purpose facilities and on all new modification projects for which the Facilities Engineering and Real Estate Branch has received a funding allowance and for all other field components not covered elsewhere in paragraph (f) of this section.

(2) The Regional Administrator shall be the responsible official on all improvement and modification projects for which the regional office has received the funding allowance.

[44 FR 64177, Nov. 6, 1979, as amended at 47 FR 9829, Mar. 8, 1982; 50 FR 26315, June 25, 1985; 51 FR 32609, Sept. 12, 1986]

§6.104 Early involvement of private parties.

As required by 40 CFR 1501.2(d) and § 6.103(a)(3)(v) of this regulation, responsible officials must ensure early involvement of private applicants or other non-Federal entities in the environmental review process related to EPA grant and permit actions set forth under subparts E, F, G, and H. The responsible official in conjunction with OEA shall:

(a) Prepare where practicable, generic guidelines describing the scope and level of environmental information required from applicants as a basis for evaluating their proposed actions, and make these guidelines available upon request.

(b) Provide such guidance on a project-by-project basis to any applicant seeking assistance.

(c) Upon receipt of an application for agency approval, or notification that an application will be filed, consult as required with other appropriate parties to initiate and coordinate the necessary environmental analyses.

[44 FR 64177, Nov. 6, 1979, as amended at 47 FR 9829, Mar. 8, 1982]

§6.105　Synopsis of environmental review procedures.

(a) Responsible official. The responsible official shall utilize a systematic, interdisciplinary approach to integrate natural and social sciences as well as environmental design arts in planning programs and making decisions which are subject to environmental review. The respective staffs may be supplemented by professionals from other agencies (see 40 CFR 1501.6) or consultants whenever in-house capabilities are insufficiently interdisciplinary.

(b) Environmental information documents (EID). Environmental information documents (EIDs) must be prepared by applicants, grantees, or permittees and submitted to EPA as required in subparts E, F, G, H, and I. EIDs will be of sufficient scope to enable the responsible official to prepare an environmental assessment as described under § 6.105(d) of this part and subparts E through I. EIDs will not have to be prepared for actions where a categorical exclusion has been granted.

(c) Environmental reviews. Environmental reviews shall be conducted on the EPA activities outlined in § 6.102 of this part and set forth under subparts E, F, G, H and I. This process shall consist of a study of the action to identify and evaluate the related environmental impacts. The process shall include a review of any related environmental information document to determine whether any significant impacts are anticipated and whether any changes can be made in the proposed action to eliminate significant adverse impacts; when an EIS is required, EPA has overall responsibility for this review, although grantees, applicants, permittees or contractors will contribute to the review through submission of environmental information documents.

(d) Environmental assessments. Environmental assessments (i.e., concise public documents for which EPA is responsible) are prepared to provide sufficient data and

analysis to determine whether an EIS or finding of no significant impact is required. Where EPA determines that a categorical exclusion is appropriate or an EIS will be prepared, there is no need to prepare a formal environmental assessment.

(e) Notice of intent and EISs. When the environmental review indicates that a significant environmental impact may occur and significant adverse impacts can not be eliminated by making changes in the project, a notice of intent to prepare an EIS shall be published in the Federal Register, scoping shall be undertaken in accordance with 40 CFR 1501.7, and a draft EIS shall be prepared and distributed. After external coordination and evaluation of the comments received, a final EIS shall be prepared and disseminated. The final EIS shall list any mitigation measures necessary to make the recommended alternative environmentally acceptable.

(f) Finding of no significant impact (FNSI). When the environmental review indicates no significant impacts are anticipated or when the project is altered to eliminate any significant adverse impacts, a FNSI shall be issued and made available to the public. The environmental assessment shall be included as a part of the FNSI. The FNSI shall list any mitigation measures necessary to make the recommended alternative environmentally acceptable.

(g) Record of decision. At the time of its decision on any action for which a final EIS has been prepared, the responsible official shall prepare a concise public record of the decision. The record of decision shall describe those mitigation measures to be undertaken which will make the selected alternative environmentally acceptable. Where the final EIS recommends the alternative which is ultimately chosen by the responsible official, the record of decision may be extracted from the executive summary to the final EIS.

(h) Monitoring. The responsible official shall provide for monitoring to assure that decisions on any action where a final EIS has been prepared are properly implemented. Appropriate mitigation measures shall be included in actions undertaken by EPA.

[44 FR 64177, Nov. 6, 1979, as amended at 50 FR 26315, June 25, 1985; 51 FR 32610, Sept. 12, 1986]

§6.106　Deviations.

(a) General. The Assistant Administrator, OEA, is authorized to approve deviations from these regulations. Deviation approvals shall be made in writing by the Assistant Administrator, OEA.

(b) Requirements. (1) Where emergency circumstances make it necessary to take an action with significant environmental impact without observing the substantive provisions of these regulations or the CEQ Regulations, the responsible official shall notify the Assistant Administrator, OEA, before taking such action. The responsible official shall consider to the extent possible alternative arrangements; such arrangements will be limited to actions necessary to control the immediate impacts of the emergency; other actions remain subject to the environmental review process. The Assistant Administrator, OEA, after consulting CEQ, will inform the responsible official, as expeditiously as possible of the disposition of his request.

(2) Where circumstances make it necessary to take action without observing procedural provisions of these regulations, the responsible official shall notify the Assistant Administrator, OEA, before taking such action. If the Assistant Administrator, OEA, determines such a deviation would be in the best interest of the Government, he shall inform the responsible official, as soon as possible, of his approval.

(3) The Assistant Administrator, OEA, shall coordinate his action on a deviation under § 6.106(b) (1) or (2) of this part with the Director, Grants Administration Division, Office of Planning and Management, for any required grant-related deviation under 40 CFR 30.1000, as well as the appropriate Assistant Administrator.

[44 FR 64177, Nov. 6, 1979, as amended at 47 FR 9829, Mar. 8, 1982]

§6.107   *Categorical exclusions.*

(a) General. Categories of actions which do not individually, cumulatively over time, or in conjunction with other Federal, State, local, or private actions have a significant effect on the quality of the human environment and which have been identified as having no such effect based on the requirements in § 6.505, may be exempted from the substantive environmental review requirements of this part. Environmental information documents and environmental assessments or environmental impact statements will not be required for excluded actions.

(b) Determination. The responsible official shall determine whether an action is eligible for a categorical exclusion as established by general criteria in § 6.107 (d) and (e) and any applicable criteria in program specific subparts of part 6 of this title. A determination shall be made as early as possible following the receipt of an application. The responsible official shall document the decision to issue or deny an exclusion as soon as practicable following review in accordance with § 6.400(f). For qualified actions, the documentation shall include the application, a brief description of the proposed action, and a brief statement of how the action meets the criteria for a categorical exclusion without violating criteria for not granting an exclusion.

(c) Revocation. The responsible official shall revoke a categorical exclusion and shall require a full environmental review if, subsequent to the granting of an exclusion, the responsible official determines that: (1) The proposed action no longer meets the requirements for a categorical exclusion due to changes in the proposed action; or (2) determines from new evidence that serious local or environmental issues exist; or (3) that Federal, State, local, or tribal laws are being or may be violated.

(d) General categories of actions eligible for exclusion. Actions consistent with any of the following categories are eligible for a categorical exclusion:

(1) Actions which are solely directed toward minor rehabilitation of existing facilities, functional replacement of equipment, or towards the construction of new ancillary facilities adjacent or appurtenant to existing facilities;

(2) Other actions specifically allowed in program specific subparts of this regulation; or

(3) Other actions developed in accordance with paragraph (f) of this section.

(e) General criteria for not granting a categorical exclusion. (1) The full environmental review procedures of this part must be followed if undertaking an action consistent with allowable categories in paragraph (d) of this section may involve serious local or environmental issues, or meets any of the criteria listed below:

(i) The action is known or expected to have a significant effect on the quality of the human environment, either individually, cumulatively over time, or in conjunction with other Federal, State, local, tribal or private actions;

(ii) The action is known or expected to directly or indirectly affect:

(A) Cultural resource areas such as archaeological and historic sites in accordance with § 6.301,

(B) Endangered or threatened species and their critical habitats in accordance with § 6.302 or State lists,

(C) Environmentally important natural resource areas such as floodplains, wetlands, important farmlands, aquifer recharge zones in accordance with § 6.302, or

(D) Other resource areas identified in supplemental guidance issued by the OEA;

(iii) The action is known or expected not to be cost-effective or to cause significant public controversy; or

(iv) Appropriate specialized program specific criteria for not granting an exclusion found in other subparts of this regulation are applicable to the action.

(2) Notwithstanding the provisions of paragraph (d) of this section, if any of the conditions cited in paragraph (e)(1) of this section exist, the responsible official shall ensure:

(i) That a categorical exclusion is not granted or, if previously granted, that it is revoked according to paragraph (c) of this section;

(ii) That an adequate EID is prepared; and

(iii) That either an environmental assessment and FNSI or a notice of intent for an EIS and ROD is prepared and issued.

(f) Developing new categories of excluded actions. The responsible official, or other interested parties, may request that a new general or specialized program specific category of excluded actions be created, or that an existing category be amended or deleted. The request shall be in writing to the Assistant Administrator, OEA, and shall contain adequate information to support the request. Proposed new categories shall be developed by OEA and published in the Federal Register as a proposed rule, amending paragraph (d) of this section when the proposed new category applies to all eligible programs or, amending appropriate paragraphs in other subparts of this part when the proposed new category applies to one specific program. The publication shall include a thirty (30) day public comment period. In addition to criteria for specific programs listed in other subparts of this part, the following general criteria shall be considered in evaluating proposals for new categories:

(1) Any action taken seldom results in the effects identified in general or specialized program specific criteria identified through the application of criteria for not granting a categorical exclusion;

(2) Based upon previous environmental reviews, actions consistent with the proposed category have not required the preparation of an EIS; and

(3) Whether information adequate to determine if a potential action is consistent with the proposed category will normally be available when needed.

[50 FR 26315, June 25, 1985, as amended at 51 FR 32610, Sept. 12, 1986]

§6.108   Criteria for initiating an EIS.

The responsible official shall assure that an EIS will be prepared and issued for actions under subparts E, G, H, and I when it is determined that any of the following conditions exist:

(a) The Federal action may significantly affect the pattern and type of land use (industrial, commercial, agricultural, recreational, residential) or growth and distribution of population;

(b) The effects resulting from any structure or facility constructed or operated under the proposed action may conflict with local, regional or State land use plans or policies;

(c) The proposed action may have significant adverse effects on wetlands, including indirect and cumulative effects, or any major part of a structure or facility constructed or operated under the proposed action may be located in wetlands;

(d) The proposed action may significantly affect threatened and endangered species or their habitats identified in the Department of the Interior's list, in accordance with § 6.302, or a State's list, or a structure or a facility constructed or operated under the proposed action may be located in the habitat;

(e) Implementation of the proposed action or plan may directly cause or induce changes that significantly:

(1) Displace population;

(2) Alter the character of existing residential areas;

(3) Adversely affect a floodplain; or

(4) Adversely affect significant amounts of important farmlands as defined in requirements in § 6.302(c), or agricultural operations on this land.

(f) The proposed action may, directly, indirectly or cumulatively have significant adverse effect on parklands, preserves, other public lands or areas of recognized scenic, recreational, archaeological, or historic value; or

(g) The Federal action may directly or through induced development have a significant adverse effect upon local ambient air quality, local ambient noise levels, surface water or groundwater quality or quantity, water supply, fish, shellfish, wildlife, and their natural habitats.

[50 FR 26315, June 25, 1985, as amended at 51 FR 32611, Sept. 12, 1986]

Subpart B—Content of EISs

§6.200   The environmental impact statement.

Preparers of EISs must conform with the requirements of 40 CFR part 1502 in writing EISs.

§6.201   Format.

The format used for EISs shall encourage good analysis and clear presentation of alternatives, including the proposed action, and their environmental, economic and social impacts. The following standard format for EISs should be used unless the responsible official determines that there is a compelling reason to do otherwise:

(a) Cover sheet;

(b) Executive Summary;

(c) Table of contents;

(d) Purpose of and need for action;

(e) Alternatives including proposed action;

(f) Affected environment;

(g) Environmental consequences of the alternatives;

(h) Coordination (includes list of agencies, organizations, and persons to whom copies of the EIS are sent);

(i) List of preparers;

(j) Index (commensurate with complexity of EIS);

(k) Appendices.

§6.202   Executive summary.

The executive summary shall describe in sufficient detail (10-15 pages) the critical facets of the EIS so that the reader can become familiar with the proposed project or action and its net effects. The executive summary shall focus on:

(a) The existing problem;

(b) A brief description of each alternative evaluated (including the preferred and no action alternatives)

along with a listing of the environmental impacts, possible mitigation measures relating to each alternative, and any areas of controversy (including issues raised by governmental agencies and the public); and

(c) Any major conclusions.

A comprehensive summary may be prepared in instances where the EIS is unusually long in nature. In accordance with 40 CFR 1502.19, the comprehensive summary may be circulated in lieu of the EIS; however, both documents shall be distributed to any Federal, State and local agencies who have EIS review responsibilities and also shall be made available to other interested parties upon request.

§6.203   Body of EISs.

(a) Purpose and need. The EIS shall clearly specify the underlying purpose and need to which EPA is responding. If the action is a request for a permit or a grant, the EIS shall clearly specify the goals and objectives of the applicant.

(b) Alternatives including the proposed action. In addition to 40 CFR 1502.14, the EIS shall discuss:

(1) Alternatives considered by the applicant. This section shall include a balanced description of each alternative considered by the applicant. These discussions shall include size and location of facilities, land requirements, operation and maintenance requirements, auxiliary structures such as pipelines or transmission lines, and construction schedules. The alternative of no action shall be discussed and the applicant's preferred alternative(s) shall be identified. For alternatives which were eliminated from detailed study, a brief discussion of the reasons for their having been eliminated shall be included.

(2) Alternatives available to EPA. EPA alternatives to be discussed shall include: (i) Taking an action; or (ii) taking an action on a modified or alternative project, including an action not considered by the applicant; and (iii) denying the action.

(3) Alternatives available to other permitting agencies. When preparing a joint EIS, and if applicable, the alternatives available to other Federal and/or State agencies shall be discussed.

(4) Identifying preferred alternative. In the final EIS, the responsible official shall signify the preferred alternative.

(c) Affected environment and environmental consequences of the alternatives. The affected environment on which the evaluation of each alternative shall be based includes, for example, hydrology, geology, air quality, noise, biology, socioeconomics, energy, land use, and archeology and historic subjects. The discussion shall be structured so as to present the total impacts of each alternative for easy comparison among all alternatives by the reader. The effects of a "no action" alternative should be included to facilitate reader comparison of the beneficial and adverse impacts of other alternatives to the applicant doing nothing. A description of the environmental setting shall be included in the "no action" alternative for the purpose of providing needed background information. The amount of detail in describing the affected environment shall be commensurate with the complexity of the situation and the importance of the anticipated impacts.

(d) Coordination. The EIS shall include:

(1) The objections and suggestions made by local, State, and Federal agencies before and during the EIS review process must be given full consideration, along with the issues of public concern expressed by individual citizens and interested environmental groups. The EIS must include discussions of any such comments concerning our actions, and the author of each comment should be identified. If a comment has resulted in a change in the project or the EIS, the impact statement should explain the reason.

(2) Public participation through public hearings or scoping meetings shall also be included. If a public hearing has been held prior to the publication of the EIS, a summary of the transcript should be included in this section. For the public hearing which shall be held after the publication of the draft EIS, the date, time, place, and purpose shall be included here.

(3) In the final EIS, a summary of the coordination process and EPA responses to comments on the draft EIS shall be included.

[44 FR 64177, Nov. 6, 1979, as amended at 50 FR 26316, June 25, 1985]

§6.204   Incorporation by reference.

In addition to 40 CFR 1502.21, material incorporated into an EIS by reference shall be organized to the extent possible into a Supplemental Information Document and be made available for review upon request. No material may be incorporated by reference unless it is reasonably available for inspection by potentially interested persons within the period allowed for comment.

§6.205   List of preparers.

When the EIS is prepared by contract, either under direct contract to EPA or through an applicant's or grantee's contractor, the responsible official must independently evaluate the EIS prior to its approval and take responsibility for its scope and contents. The EPA officials who undertake this evaluation shall also be described under the list of preparers.

Subpart C—Coordination With Other Environmental Review and Consultation Requirements

§6.300   General.

Various Federal laws and executive orders address specific environmental concerns. The responsible official shall integrate to the greatest practicable extent the applicable procedures in this subpart during the implementation of the environmental review process under subparts E through I. This subpart presents the central requirements of these laws and executive orders. It refers to the pertinent authority and regulations or guidance that contain the procedures. These laws and executive orders establish review procedures independent of NEPA requirements. The responsible official shall be familiar with any other EPA or appropriate agency procedures implementing these laws and executive orders.

[44 FR 64177, Nov. 6, 1979, as amended at 50 FR 26316, June 25, 1985]

§6.301   Landmarks, historical, and archeological sites.

EPA is subject to the requirements of the Historic Sites Act of 1935, 16 U.S.C. 461 et seq., the National Historic Preservation Act of 1966, as amended, 16 U.S.C. 470 et seq., the Archaeological and Historic Preservation Act of 1974, 16 U.S.C. 469 et seq., and Executive Order 11593, entitled "Protection and Enhancement of the Cultural Environment." These statutes, regulations and executive orders establish review procedures independent of NEPA requirements.

(a) National natural landmarks. Under the Historic Sites Act of 1935, the Secretary of the Interior is authorized to designate areas as national natural landmarks for listing on the National Registry of Natural Landmarks. In conducting an environmental review of a proposed EPA action, the responsible official shall consider the existence and location of natural landmarks using information provided by the National Park Service pursuant to 36 CFR 62.6(d) to avoid undesirable impacts upon such landmarks.

(b) Historic, architectural, archeological, and cultural sites. Under section 106 of the National Historic Preservation Act and Executive Order 11593, if an EPA undertaking affects any property with historic, architectural, archeological or cultural value that is listed on or eligible for listing on the National Register of Historic Places, the responsible official shall comply with the procedures for consultation and comment promulgated by the Advisory Council on Historic Preservation in 36 CFR part 800. The responsible official must identify properties affected by the undertaking that are potentially eligible for listing on the National Register and shall request a determination of eligibility from the Keeper of the National Register, Department of the Interior, under the procedures in 36 CFR part 63.

(c) Historic, prehistoric and archeological data. Under the Archeological and Historic Preservation Act, if an EPA activity may cause irreparable loss or destruction of significant scientific, prehistoric, historic or archeological data, the responsible official or the Secretary of the Interior is authorized to undertake data recovery and preservation activities. Data recovery and preservation activities shall be conducted in accordance with implementing procedures promulgated by the Secretary of the Interior. The National Park Service has published technical standards and guidelines regarding archeological preservation activities and methods at 48 FR 44716 (September 29, 1983).

[44 FR 64177, Nov. 6, 1979, as amended at 50 FR 26316, June 25, 1985]

§6.302 *Wetlands, floodplains, important farmlands, coastal zones, wild and scenic rivers, fish and wildlife, and endangered species.*

The following procedures shall apply to EPA administrative actions in programs to which the pertinent statute or executive order applies.

(a) Wetlands protection. Executive Order 11990, Protection of Wetlands, requires Federal agencies conducting certain activities to avoid, to the extent possible, the adverse impacts associated with the destruction or loss of wetlands and to avoid support of new construction in wetlands if a practicable alternative exists. EPA's Statement of Procedures on Floodplain Management and Wetlands Protection (dated January 5, 1979, incorporated as appendix A hereto) requires EPA programs to determine if proposed actions will be in or will affect wetlands. If so, the responsible official shall

prepare a floodplains/wetlands assessment, which will be part of the environmental assessment or environmental impact statement. The responsible official shall either avoid adverse impacts or minimize them if no practicable alternative to the action exists.

(b) Floodplain management. Executive Order 11988, Floodplain Management, requires Federal agencies to evaluate the potential effects of actions they may take in a floodplain to avoid, to the extent possible, adverse effects associated with direct and indirect development of a floodplain. EPA's Statement of Procedures on Floodplain Management and Wetlands Protection (dated January 5, 1979, incorporated as appendix A hereto), requires EPA programs to determine whether an action will be located in or will affect a floodplain. If so, the responsible official shall prepare a floodplain/wetlands assessment. The assessment will become part of the environmental assessment or environmental impact statement. The responsible official shall either avoid adverse impacts or minimize them if no practicable alternative exists.

(c) Important farmlands. It is EPA's policy as stated in the EPA Policy To Protect Environmentally Significant Agricultural Lands, dated September 8, 1978, to consider the protection of the Nation's significant/important agricultural lands from irreversible conversion to uses which result in its loss as an environmental or essential food production resource. In addition the Farmland Protection Policy Act, (FPPA) 7 U.S.C. 4201 et seq., requires Federal agencies to use criteria developed by the Soil Conservation Service, U.S. Department of Agriculture, to:

(1) Identify and take into account the adverse effects of their programs on the preservation of farmlands from conversion to other uses;

(2) Consider alternative actions, as appropriate, that could lessen such adverse impacts; and

(3) Assure that their programs, to the extent possible, are compatible with State and local government and private programs and policies to protect farmlands. If an EPA action may adversely impact farmlands which are classified prime, unique or of State and local importance as defined in the Act, the responsible official shall in all cases apply the evaluative criteria promulgated by the U.S. Department of Agriculture at 7 CFR part 658. If categories of important farmlands, which include those defined in both the FPPA and the EPA policy, are identified in the project study area, both direct and indirect effects of the undertaking on the remaining farms and farm support services within the project area and immediate environs shall be evalu-

ated. Adverse effects shall be avoided or mitigated to the extent possible.

(d) Coastal zone management. The Coastal Zone Management Act, 16 U.S.C. 1451 et seq., requires that all Federal activities in coastal areas be consistent with approved State Coastal Zone Management Programs, to the maximum extent possible. If an EPA action may affect a coastal zone area, the responsible official shall assess the impact of the action on the coastal zone. If the action significantly affects the coastal zone area and the State has an approved coastal zone management program, a consistency determination shall be sought in accordance with procedures promulgated by the Office of Coastal Zone Management in 15 CFR part 930.

(e) Wild and scenic rivers. (1) The Wild and Scenic Rivers Act, 16 U.S.C. 1274 et seq., establishes requirements applicable to water resource projects affecting wild, scenic or recreational rivers within the National Wild and Scenic Rivers system as well as rivers designated on the National Rivers Inventory to be studied for inclusion in the national system. Under the Act, a Federal agency may not assist, through grant, loan, license or otherwise, the construction of a water resources project that would have a direct and adverse effect on the values for which a river in the National System or study river on the National Rivers Inventory was established, as determined by the Secretary of the Interior for rivers under the jurisdiction of the Department of the Interior and by the Secretary of Agriculture for rivers under the jurisdiction of the Department of Agriculture. Nothing contained in the foregoing sentence, however, shall:

(i) Preclude licensing of, or assistance to, developments below or above a wild, scenic or recreational river area or on any stream tributary thereto which will not invade the area or unreasonably diminish the scenic, recreational, and fish and wildlife values present in the area on October 2, 1968; or

(ii) Preclude licensing of, or assistance to, developments below or above a study river or any stream tributary thereto which will not invade the area or diminish the scenic, recreational and fish and wildlife values present in the area on October 2, 1968.

(2) The responsible official shall:

(i) Determine whether there are any wild, scenic or study rivers on the National Rivers Inventory or in the planning area, and

(ii) Not recommend authorization of any water resources project that would have a direct and adverse effect on the values for which such river was established, as determined by the administering Secretary in request of appropriations to begin construction of any such project, whether heretofore or hereafter authorized, without advising the administering Secretary, in writing of this intention at least sixty days in advance, and without specifically reporting to the Congress in writing at the time the recommendation or request is made in what respect construction of such project would be in conflict with the purposes of the Wild and Scenic Rivers Act and would affect the component and the values to be protected by the Responsible Official under the Act.

(3) Applicable consultation requirements are found in section 7 of the Act. The Department of Agriculture has promulgated implementing procedures, under section 7 at 36 CFR part 297, which apply to water resource projects located within, above, below or outside a wild and scenic river or study river under the Department's jurisdiction.

(f) Barrier islands. The Coastal Barrier Resources Act, 16 U.S.C. 3501 et seq., generally prohibits new Federal expenditures or financial assistance for any purpose within the Coastal Barrier Resources System on or after October 18, 1982. Specified exceptions to this prohibition are allowed only after consultation with the Secretary of the Interior. The responsible official shall ensure that consultation is carried out with the Secretary of the Interior before making available new expenditures or financial assistance for activities within areas covered by the Coastal Barriers Resources Act in accord with the U.S. Fish and Wildlife Service published guidelines defining new expenditures and financial assistance, and describing procedures for consultation at 48 FR 45664 (October 6, 1983).

(g) Fish and wildlife protection. The Fish and Wildlife Coordination Act, 16 U.S.C. 661 et seq., requires Federal agencies involved in actions that will result in the control or structural modification of any natural stream or body of water for any purpose, to take action to protect the fish and wildlife resources which may be affected by the action. The responsible official shall consult with the Fish and Wildlife Service and the appropriate State agency to ascertain the means and measures necessary to mitigate, prevent and compensate for project-related losses of wildlife resources and to enhance the resources. Reports and recommendations of wildlife agencies should be incorporated into the environmental assessment or environmental impact statement. Consultation procedures are detailed in 16 U.S.C. 662.

(h) Endangered species protection. Under the Endangered Species Act, 16 U.S.C. 1531 et seq., Federal agencies are prohibited from jeopardizing threatened or endangered species or adversely modifying habitats essential to their survival. The responsible official shall identify all designated endangered or threatened species or their habitat that may be affected by an EPA action. If listed species or their habitat may be affected, formal consultation must be undertaken with the Fish and Wildlife Service or the National Marine Fisheries Service, as appropriate. If the consultation reveals that the EPA activity may jeopardize a listed species or habitat, mitigation measures should be considered. Applicable consultation procedures are found in 50 CFR part 402.

[44 FR 64177, Nov. 6, 1979, as amended at 50 FR 26316, June 25, 1985]

§6.303   Air quality.

(a) The Clean Air Act, as amended in 1990, 42 U.S.C. 7476(c), requires Federal actions to conform to any State implementation plan approved or promulgated under section 110 of the Act. For EPA actions, the applicable conformity requirements specified in 40 CFR part 51, subpart W, 40 CFR part 93, subpart B, and the applicable State implementation plan must be met.

(b) In addition, with regard to wastewater treatment works subject to review under subpart E of this part, the responsible official shall consider the air pollution control requirements specified in section 316(b) of the Clean Air Act, 42 U.S.C. 7616, and Agency implementation procedures.

(c)-(g) [Reserved]

[58 FR 63247, Nov. 30, 1993]

Subpart D—Public and Other Federal Agency Involvement

§6.400   Public involvement.

(a) General. EPA shall make diligent efforts to involve the public in the environmental review process consistent with program regulations and EPA policies on public participation. The responsibile official shall ensure that public notice is provided for in accordance with 40 CFR 1506.6(b) and shall ensure that public involvement is carried out in accordance with EPA

Public Participation Regulations, 40 CFR part 25, and other applicable EPA public participation procedures.

(b) Publication of notices of intent. As soon as practicable after his decision to prepare an EIS and before the scoping process, the responsible official shall send the notice of intent to interested and affected members of the public and shall request the OEA to publish the notice of intent in the Federal Register. The responsible official shall send to OEA the signed original notice of intent for Federal Register publication purposes. The scoping process should be initiated as soon as practicable in accordance with the requirements of 40 CFR 1501.7. Participants in the scoping process shall be kept informed of substantial changes which evolve during the EIS drafting process.

(c) Public meetings or hearings. Public meetings or hearings shall be conducted consistent with Agency program requirements. There shall be a presumption that a scoping meeting will be conducted whenever a notice of intent has been published. The responsible official shall conduct a public hearing on a draft EIS. The responsible official shall ensure that the draft EIS is made available to the public at least 30 days in advance of the hearing.

(d) Findings of no significant impact (FNSI). The responsible official shall allow for sufficient public review of a FNSI before it becomes effective. The FNSI and attendant publication must state that interested persons disagreeing with the decision may submit comments to EPA. The responsible official shall not take administrative action on the project for at least thirty (30) calendar days after release of the FNSI and may allow more time for response. The responsible official shall consider, fully, comments submitted on the FNSI before taking administrative action. The FNSI shall be made available to the public in accordance with the requirements and all appropriate recommendations contained in § 1506.6 of this title.

(e) Record of Decision (ROD). The responsible official shall disseminate the ROD to those parties which commented on the draft or final EIS.

(f) Categorical exclusions. (1) For categorical exclusion determinations under subpart E (Wastewater Treatment Construction Grants Program), an applicant who files for and receives a determination of categorical exclusion under § 6.107(a), or has one rescinded under § 6.107(c), shall publish a notice indicating the determination of eligibility or rescission in a local newspaper of community-wide circulation and indicate the availability of the supporting documentation for public inspection. The responsible official shall, concurrent with the publication of the notice, make the documentation as outlined in § 6.107(b) available to the public and distribute the notice of the determination to all known interested parties.

(2) For categorical exclusion determinations under other subparts of this regulation, no public notice need be issued; however, information regarding these determinations may be obtained by contacting the U.S. Environmental Protection Agency's Office of Research Program Management for ORD actions, or the Office of Federal Activities for other program actions.

[44 FR 64177, Nov. 6, 1979, as amended at 51 FR 32611, Sept. 12, 1986; 56 FR 20543, May 6, 1991]

§6.401　　Official filing requirements.

(a) General. OEA is responsible for the conduct of the official filing system for EISs. This system was established as a central repository for all EISs which serves not only as means of advising the public of the availability of each EIS but provides a uniform method for the computation of minimum time periods for the review of EISs. OEA publishes a weekly notice in the Federal Register listing all EISs received during a given week. The 45-day and 30-day review periods for draft and final EISs, respectively, are computed from the Friday following a given reporting week. Pursuant to 40 CFR 1506.9, responsible officials shall comply with the guidelines established by OEA on the conduct of the filing system.

(b) Minimum time periods. No decision on EPA actions shall be made until the later of the following dates:

(1) Ninety (90) days after the date established in § 6.401(a) of this part from which the draft EIS review time period is computed.

(2) Thirty (30) days after the date established in § 6.401(a) of this part from which the final EIS review time period is computed.

(c) Filing of EISs. All EISs, including supplements, must be officially filed with OEA. Responsible officials shall transmit each EIS in five (5) copies to the Director, Office of Environmental Review, EIS Filing Section (A-104). OEA will provide CEQ with one copy of each EIS filed. No EIS will be officially filed by OER unless the EIS has been made available to the public. OEA will not accept unbound copies of EISs for filing.

(d) Extensions or waivers. The responsible official may independently extend review periods. In such cases, the responsible official shall notify OEA as soon as possible

so that adequate notice may be published in the weekly Federal Register report. OEA upon a showing of compelling reasons of national policy may reduce the prescribed review periods. Also, OEA upon a showing by any other Federal agency of compelling reasons of national policy may extend prescribed review periods, but only after consultation with the responsible official. If the responsible official does not concur with the extension of time, OEA may not extend a prescribed review period more than 30 days beyond the minimum prescribed review period.

(e) Rescission of filed EISs. The responsible official shall file EISs with OEA at the same time they are transmitted to commenting agencies and made available to the public. The responsible official is required to reproduce an adequate supply of EISs to satisfy these distribution requirements prior to filing an EIS. If the EIS is not made available, OEA will consider retraction of the EIS or revision of the prescribed review periods based on the circumstances.

[44 FR 64177, Nov. 6, 1979, as amended at 47 FR 9829, Mar. 8, 1982]

§6.402　　Availability of documents.

(a) General. The responsible official will ensure sufficient copies of the EIS are distributed to interested and affected members of the public and are made available for further public distribution. EISs, comments received, and any underlying documents should be available to the public pursuant to the provisions of the Freedom of Information Act (5 U.S.C. 552(b)), without regard to the exclusion for interagency memoranda where such memoranda transmit comments of Federal agencies on the environmental impact of the proposed actions. To the extent practicable, materials made available to the public shall be provided without charge; otherwise, a fee may be imposed which is not more than the actual cost of reproducing copies required to be sent to another Federal agency.

(b) Public information. Lists of all notices, determinations and other reports/documentation, related to these notices and determinations, involving CEs, EAs, FNSIs, notices of intent, EISs, and RODs prepared by EPA shall be available for public inspection and maintained by the responsible official as a monthly status report. OEA shall maintain a comprehensive list of notices of intent and draft and final EISs provided by all responsible officials for public inspection including publication in the Federal Register. In addition, OEA will make copies of all EPA-prepared EISs available for public inspection; the responsible official shall do the same for any EIS he/she undertakes.

[44 FR 64177, Nov. 6, 1979, as amended at 51 FR 32611, Sept. 12, 1986]

§6.403   The commenting process.

(a) Inviting comments. After preparing a draft EIS and before preparing a final EIS, the responsible official shall obtain the comments of Federal agencies, other governmental entities and the public in accordance with 40 CFR 1503.1.

(b) Response to comments. The responsible official shall respond to comments in the final EIS in accordance with 40 CFR 1503.4.

§6.404   Supplements.

(a) General. The responsible official shall consider preparing supplements to draft and final EISs in accordance with 40 CFR 1502.9(c). A supplement shall be prepared, circulated and filed in the same fashion (exclusive of scoping) as draft and final EISs.

(b) Alternative procedures. In the case where the responsible official wants to deviate from existing procedures, OEA shall be consulted. OEA shall consult with CEQ on any alternative arrangements.

[44 FR 64177, Nov. 6, 1979, as amended at 47 FR 9829, Mar. 8, 1982]

Subpart E—Environmental Review Procedures for Wastewater Treatment Construction Grants Program

Source:
50 FR 26317, June 25, 1985, unless otherwise noted.

§6.500   Purpose.

This subpart amplifies the procedures described in subparts A through D with detailed environmental review procedures for the Municipal Wastewater Treatment Works Construction Grants Program under Title II of the Clean Water Act.

§6.501   Definitions.

(a) Step 1 facilities planning means preparation of a plan for facilities as described in 40 CFR part 35, subpart E or I.

(b) Step 2 means a project to prepare design drawings and specifications as described in 40 CFR part 35, subpart E or I.

(c) Step 3 means a project to build a publicly owned treatment works as described in 40 CFR part 35, subpart E or I.

(d) Step 2+3 means a project which combines preparation of design drawings and specifications as described in § 6.501(b) and building as described in § 6.501(c).

(e) Applicant means any individual, agency, or entity which has filed an application for grant assistance under 40 CFR part 35, subpart E or I.

(f) Grantee means any individual, agency, or entity which has been awarded wastewater treatment construction grant assistance under 40 CFR part 35, subpart E or I.

(g) Responsible Official means a Federal or State official authorized to fulfill the requirements of this subpart. The responsible Federal official is the EPA Regional Administrator and the responsible State official is as defined in a delegation agreement under 205(g) of the Clean Water Act. The responsibilities of the State official are subject to the limitations in § 6.514 of this subpart.

(h) Approval of the facilities plan means approval of the facilities plan for a proposed wastewater treatment works pursuant to 40 CFR part 35, subpart E or I.

§6.502   Applicability and limitations.

(a) Applicability. This subpart applies to the following actions:

(1) Approval of a facilities plan or an amendment to the plan;

(2) Award of grant assistance for a project where signficant change has occurred in the project or its impact since prior compliance with this part; and

(3) Approval of preliminary Step 3 work prior to the award of grant assistance pursuant to 40 CFR part 35, subpart E or I.

(b) Limitations. (1) Except as provided in § 6.504(c), all recipients of Step 1 grant assistance must comply with the requirements, steps, and procedures described in this subpart.

(2) As specified in 40 CFR 35.2113, projects that have not received Step 1 grant assistance must comply with the requirements of this subpart prior to submission of an application for Step 3 or Step 2+3 grant assistance.

(3) Except as otherwise provided in § 6.507, no step 3 or 2=3 grant assistance may be awarded for the

construction of any component/portion of a proposed wastewater treatment system(s) until the responsible official has:

(i) Completed the environmental review for all complete wastewater treatment system alternatives under consideration for the facilities planning area, or any larger study area identified for the purposes of conducting an adequate environmental review as required under this subpart; and

(ii) Recorded the selection of the preferred alternative(s) in the appropriate decision document (ROD for EISs, FNSI for environmental assessments, or written determination for categorical exclusions).

(4) In accord with § 6.302(f), on or after October 18, 1982, no new expenditures or financial assistance involving the construction grants program can be made within the Coastal Barrier Resource System, or for projects outside the system which would have the effect of encouraging development in the system, other than specified exceptions made by the EPA after consultation with the Secretary of the Interior.

[50 FR 26317, June 25, 1985, as amended at 51 FR 32611, Sept. 12, 1986]

§6.503　Overview of the environmental review process.

The process for conducting an environmental review of wastewater treatment construction grant projects includes the following steps:

(a) Consultation. The Step 1 grantee or the potential Step 3 or Step 2+3 applicant is encouraged to consult with the State and EPA early in project formulation or the facilities planning stage to determine whether a project is eligible for a categorical exclusion from the remaining substantive environmental review requirements of this part (§ 6.505), to determine alternatives to the proposed project for evaluation, to identify potential environmental issues and opportunities for public recreation and open space, and to determine the potential need for partitioning the environmental review process and/or the need for an Environmental Impact Statement (EIS).

(b) Determining categorical exclusion eligibility. At the request of a potential Step 3 or Step 2+3 grant applicant, or a Step 1 facilities planning grantee, the responsible official will determine if a project is eligible for a categorical exclusion in accordance with § 6.505. A Step 1 facilities planning grantee awarded a Step 1 grant on or before December 29, 1981 may request a categorical exclusion at any time during Step 1 facili-

ties planning. A potential Step 3 or Step 2+3 grant applicant may request a categorical exclusion at any time before the submission of a Step 3 or Step 2+3 grant application.

(c) Documenting environmental information. If the project is determined to be ineligible for a categorical exclusion, or if no request for a categorical exclusion is made, the potential Step 3 or Step 2+3 applicant or the Step 1 grantee subsequently prepares an Environmental Information Document (EID) (§ 6.506) for the project.

(d) Preparing environmental assessments. Except as provided in § 6.506(c)(4) and following a review of the EID by EPA or by a State with delegated authority, EPA prepares an environmental assessment (§ 6.506), or a State with delegated authority (§ 6.514) prepares a preliminary environmental assessment. EPA reviews and finalizes any preliminary assessments. EPA subsequently:

(1) Prepares and issues a Finding of No Significant Impact (FNSI) (§ 6.508); or

(2) Prepares and issues a Notice of Intent to prepare an original or supplemental EIS (§ 6.510) and Record of Decision (ROD) (§ 6.511).

(e) Monitoring. The construction and post-construction operation and maintenance of the facilities are monitored (§ 6.512) to ensure implementation of mitigation measures (§ 6.511) identified in the FNSI or ROD.

[50 FR 26317, June 25, 1985, as amended at 51 FR 32611, Sept. 12, 1986]

§6.504　Consultation during the facilities planning process.

(a) General. Consistent with 40 CFR 1501.2 and 35.2030(c), the responsible official shall initiate the environmental review process early to identify environmental effects, avoid delays, and resolve conflicts. The environmental review process should be integrated throughout the facilities planning process. Two processes for consultation are described in this section to meet this objective. The first addresses projects awarded Step 1 grant assistance on or before December 29, 1981. The second applies to projects not receiving grant assistance for facilities planning on or before December 29, 1981 and, therefore, subject to the regulations implementing the Municipal Wastewater Treatment Construction Grant Amendments of 1981 (40 CFR part 35, subpart I).

(b) Projects receiving Step 1 grant assistance on or before December 29, 1981. (1) During facilities planning, the grantee shall evaluate project alternatives and the existence of environmentally important resource areas including those identified in § 6.108 and § 6.509 of this subpart, and potential for open space and recreation opportunities in the facilities planning area. This evaluation is intended to be brief and concise and should draw on existing information from EPA, State agencies, regional planning agencies, areawide water quality management agencies, and the Step 1 grantee. The Step 1 grantee should submit this information to EPA or a delegated State at the earliest possible time during facilities planning to allow EPA to determine if the action is eligible for a categorical exclusion. The evaluation and any additional analysis deemed necessary by the responsible official may be used by EPA to determine whether the action is eligible for a categorical exclusion from the substantive environmental review requirements of this part. If a categorical exclusion is granted, the grantee will not be required to prepare a formal EID nor will the responsible official be required to prepare an environmental assessment under NEPA. If an action is not granted a categorical exclusion, this evaluation may be used to determine the scope of the EID required of the grantee. This information can also be used to make an early determination of the need for partitioning the environmental review or for an EIS. Whenever possible, the Step 1 grantee should discuss this initial evaluation with both the delegated State and EPA.

(2) A review of environmental information developed by the grantee should be conducted by the responsible official whenever meetings are held to assess the progress of facilities plan development. These meetings should be held after completion of the majority of the EID document and before a preferred alternative is selected. Since any required EIS must be completed before the approval of a facilities plan, a decision whether to prepare an EIS is encouraged early during the facilities planning process. These meetings may assist in this early determination. EPA should inform interested parties of the following:

(i) The preliminary nature of the Agency's position on preparing an EIS;

(ii) The relationship between the facilities planning and environmental review processes;

(iii) The desirability of public input; and

(iv) A contact person for further information.

(c) Projects not receiving grant assistance for Step 1 facilities planning on or before December 29, 1981. Potential Step 3 or Step 2+3 grant applicants should, in accordance with § 35.2030(c), consult with EPA and the State early in the facilities planning process to determine the appropriateness of a categorical exclusion, the scope of an EID, or the appropriateness of the early preparation of an environmental assessment or an EIS. The consultation would be most useful during the evaluation of project alternatives prior to the selection of a preferred alternative to assist in resolving any identified environmental problems.

§6.505 Categorical exclusions.

(a) General. At the request of an existing Step 1 facilities planning grantee or of a potential Step 3 or Step 2+3 grant applicant, the responsible official, as provided for in §§ 6.107(b), 6.400(f) and 6.504(a), shall determine from existing information and document whether an action is consistent with the categories eligible for exclusion from NEPA review identified in § 6.107(d) or § 6.505(b) and not inconsistent with the criteria in § 6.107(e) or § 6.505(c).

(b) Specialized categories of actions eligible for exclusion. For this subpart, eligible actions consist of any of the categories in § 6.107(d), or:

(1) Actions for which the facilities planning is consistent with the category listed in § 6.107(d)(1) which do not affect the degree of treatment or capacity of the existing facility including, but not limited to, infiltration and inflow corrections, grant-eligible replacement of existing mechanical equipment or structures, and the construction of small structures on existing sites;

(2) Actions in sewered communities of less than 10,000 persons which are for minor upgrading and minor expansion of existing treatment works. This category does not include actions that directly or indirectly involve the extension of new collection systems funded with Federal or other sources of funds;

(3) Actions in unsewered communities of less than 10,000 persons where on-site technologies are proposed; or

(4) Other actions are developed in accordance with § 6.107(f).

(c) Specialized Criteria for not granting a categorical exclusion. (1) The full environmental review procedures of this part must be followed if undertaking an action consistent with the categories described in paragraph (b) of this section meets any of the criteria listed in § 6.107(e) or when:

(i) The facilities to be provided will (A) create a new, or (B) relocate an existing, discharge to surface or ground waters;

(ii) The facilities will result in substantial increases in the volume of discharge or the loading of pollutants from an existing source or from new facilities to receiving waters; or

(iii) The facilities would provide capacity to serve a population 30% greater than the existing population.

(d) Proceeding with grant awards. (1) After a categorical exclusion on a proposed treatment works has been granted, and notices published in accordance with § 6.400(f), grant awards may proceed without being subject to any further environmental review requirements under this part, unless the responsible official later determines that the project, or the conditions at the time the categorical determination was made, have changed significantly since the independent EPA review of information submitted by the grantee in support of the exclusion.

(2) For all categorical exclusion determinations:

(i) That are five or more years old on projects awaiting Step 2+3 or Step 3 grant funding, the responsible official shall re-evaluate the project, environmental conditions and public views and, prior to grant award, either:

(A) Reaffirm—issue a public notice reaffirming EPA's decision to proceed with the project without need for any further environmental review;

(B) Supplement—update the information in the decision document on the categorically excluded project and prepare, issue, and distribute a revised notice in accordance with § 6.107(f); or

(C) Reassess—revoke the categorical exclusion in accordance with § 6.107(c) and require a complete environmental review to determine the need for an EIS in accordance with § 6.506, followed by preparation, issuance and distribution of an EA/FNSI or EIS/ROD.

(ii) That are made on projects that have been awarded a Step 2+3 grant, the responsible official shall, at the time of plans and specifications review under § 35.2202(b) of this title, assess whether the environmental conditions or the project's anticipated impact on the environment have changed and, prior to plans and specifications approval, advise the Regional Administrator if additional environmental review is necessary.

[50 FR 26317, June 25, 1985, as amended at 51 FR 32611, Sept. 12, 1986]

§6.506　Environmental review process.

(a) Review of completed facilities plans. The responsible official shall ensure a review of the completed facilities plan with particular attention to the EID and its utilization in the development of alternatives and the selection of a preferred alternative. An adequate EID shall be an integral part of any facilities plan submitted to EPA or to a State. The EID shall be of sufficient scope to enable the responsible official to make determinations on requests for partitioning the environmental review process in accordance with § 6.507 and for preparing environmental assessments in accordance with § 6.506(b).

(b) Environmental assessment. The environmental assessment process shall cover all potentially significant environmental impacts. The responsible official shall prepare a preliminary environmental assessment on which to base a recommendation to finalize and issue the environmental assessment/FNSI. For those States delegated environmental review responsibilities under § 6.514, the State responsible official shall prepare the preliminary environmental assessment in sufficient detail to serve as an adequate basis for EPA's independent NEPA review and decision to finalize and issue an environmental assessment/FNSI or to prepare and issue a notice of intent for an EIS/ROD. The EPA also may require submission of supplementary information before the facilities plan is approved if needed for its independent review of the State's preliminary assessment for compliance with environmental review requirements. Substantial requests for supplementary information by EPA, including the review of the facilities plan, shall be made in writing. Each of the following subjects outlined below, and requirements of subpart C of this part, shall be reviewed by the responsible official to identify potentially significant environmental concerns and their associated potential impacts, and the responsible official shall furthermore address these concerns and impacts in the environmental assessment:

(1) Description of the existing environment. For the delineated facilities planning area, the existing environmental conditions relevant to the analysis of alternatives, or to determining the environmental impacts of the proposed action, shall be considered.

(2) Description of the future environment without the project. The relevant future environmental conditions shall be described. The no action alternative should be discussed.

(3) Purpose and need. This should include a summary discussion and demonstration of the need, or absence of need, for wastewater treatment in the facilities planning area, with particular emphasis on existing public health or water quality problems and their severity and extent.

(4) Documentation. Citations to information used to describe the existing environment and to assess future environmental impacts should be clearly referenced and documented. These sources should include, as appropriate but not limited to, local, tribal, regional, State, and Federal agencies as well as public and private organizations and institutions with responsibility or interest in the types of conditions listed in § 6.509 and in subpart C of this part.

(5) Analysis of alternatives. This discussion shall include a comparative analysis of feasible alternatives, including the no action alternative, throughout the study area. The alternatives shall be screened with respect to capital and operating costs; direct, indirect, and cumulative environmental effects; physical, legal, or institutional constraints; and compliance with regulatory requirements. Special attention should given to: the environmental consequences of long-term, irreversible, and induced impacts; and for projects initiated after September 30, 1978, that grant applicants have satisfactorily demonstrated analysis of potential recreation and open-space opportunities in the planning of the proposed treatment works. The reasons for rejecting any alternatives shall be presented in addition to any significant environmental benefits precluded by rejection of an alternative. The analysis should consider when relevant to the project:

(i) Flow and waste reduction measures, including infiltration/inflow reduction and pretreatment requirements;

(ii) Appropriate water conservation measures;

(iii) Alternative locations, capacities, and construction phasing of facilities;

(iv) Alternative waste management techniques, including pretreatment, treatment and discharge, wastewater reuse, land application, and individual systems;

(v) Alternative methods for management of sludge, other residual materials, including utilization options such as land application, composting, and conversion of sludge for marketing as a soil conditioner or fertilizer;

(vi) Improving effluent quality through more efficient operation and maintenance;

(vii) Appropriate energy reduction measures; and

(viii) Multiple use including recreation, other open space, and environmental education.

(6) Evaluating environmental consequences of proposed action. A full range of relevant impacts of the proposed action shall be discussed, including measures to mitigate adverse impacts, any irreversible or irretrievable commitments of resources to the project and the relationship between local short-term uses of the environment and the maintenance and enhancement of long-term productivity. Any specific requirements, including grant conditions and areawide waste treatment management plan requirements, should be identified and referenced. In addition to these items, the responsible official may require that other analyses and data in accordance with subpart C which are needed to satisfy environmental review requirements be included with the facilities plan. Such requirements should be discussed whenever meetings are held with Step 1 grantees or potential Step 3 or Step 2 = 3 applicants.

(7) Minimizing adverse effects of the proposed action. (i) Structural and nonstructural measures, directly or indirectly related to the facilities plan, to mitigate or eliminate adverse effects on the human and natural environments, shall be identified during the environmental review. Among other measures, structual provisions include changes in facility design, size, and location; non-structural provisions include staging facilities, monitoring and enforcement of environmental regulations, and local commitments to develop and enforce land use regulations.

(ii) The EPA shall not accept a facilities plan, nor award grant assistance for its implementation, if the applicant/grantee has not made, or agreed to make, changes in the project, in accordance with determinations made in a FNSI based on its supporting environmental assessment or the ROD for a EIS. The EPA shall condition a grant, or seek other ways, to ensure that the grantee will comply with such environmental review determinations.

(c) FNSI/EIS determination. The responsible official shall apply the criteria under § 6.509 to the following:

(1) A complete facilities plan;

(2) The EID;

(3) The preliminary environmental assessment; and

(4) Other documentation, deemed necessary by the responsible official adequate to make an EIS determination by EPA. Where EPA determines that an EIS

is to be prepared, there is no need to prepare a formal environmental assessment. If EPA or the State identifies deficiencies in the EID, preliminary environmental assessment, or other supporting documentation, necessary corrections shall be made to this documentation before the conditions of the Step 1 grant are considered satisfied or before the Step 3 or Step 2+3 application is considered complete. The responsible official's determination to issue a FNSI or to prepare an EIS shall constitute final Agency action, and shall not be subject to administrative review under 40 CFR part 30, subpart L.

[50 FR 26317, June 25, 1985, as amended at 51 FR 32612, Sept. 12, 1986]

§6.507 Partitioning the environmental review process.

(a) Purpose. Under certain circumstances the building of a component/portion of a wastewater treatment system may be justified in advance of completing all NEPA requirements for the remainder of the system(s). When there are overriding considerations of cost or impaired program effectiveness, the responsible official may award a construction grant, or approve procurement by other than EPA funds, for a discrete component of a complete wastewater treatment system(s). The process of partitioning the environmental review for the discrete component shall comply with the criteria and procedures described in paragraph (b) of this section. In addition, all reasonable alternatives for the overall wastewater treatment works system(s) of which the component is a part shall have been previously identified, and each part of the environmental review for the remainder of the overall facilities system(s) in the planning area in accordance with § 6.502(b)(3) shall comply with all requirements under § 6.506.

(b) Criteria for partitioning. (1) Projects may be partitioned under the following circumstances:

(i) To overcome impaired program effectiveness, the project component, in addition to meeting the criteria listed in paragraph (b)(2) of this section, must immediately remedy a severe public health, water quality or other environmental problem; or

(ii) To significantly reduce direct costs on EPA projects, or other related public works projects, the project component (such as major pieces of equipment, portions of conveyances or small structures) in addition to meeting the criteria listed in paragraph (b)(2) of this section, must achieve a cost savings to the Federal Government and/or to the grantee's or potential grantee's overall costs incurred in procuring the wastewater

treatment component(s) and/or the installation of other related public works projects funded in coordination with other Federal, State, tribal or local agencies.

(2) The project component also must:

(i) Not foreclose any reasonable alternatives identified for the overall wastewater treatment works system(s);

(ii) Not cause significant adverse direct or indirect environmental impacts including those which cannot be acceptably mitigated without completing the entire wastewater treatment system of which the component is a part; and

(iii) Not be highly controversial.

(c) Requests for partitioning. The applicant's or State's request for partitioning must contain the following:

(1) A description of the discrete component proposed for construction before completing the environmental review of the entire facilities plan;

(2) How the component meets the above criteria;

(3) The environmental information required by § 6.506 of this subpart for the component; and

(4) Any preliminary information that may be important to EPA in an EIS determination for the entire facilities plan (§ 6.509).

(d) Approval of requests for partitioning. The responsible official shall:

(1) Review the request for partitioning against all requirements of this subpart;

(2) If approvable, prepare and issue a FNSI in accordance with § 6.508;

(3) Include a grant condition prohibiting the building of additional or different components of the entire facilities system(s) in the planning area as described in § 6.502(b)(3)(i).

[50 FR 26317, June 25, 1985, as amended at 51 FR 32612, Sept. 12, 1986]

§6.508 Finding of No Significant Impact (FNSI) determination.

(a) Criteria for producing and distributing FNSIs. If, after completion of the environmental review, EPA determines that an EIS will not be required, the responsible official shall issue a FNSI in accordance with §§ 6.105(f) and 6.400(d). The FNSI will be based on EPA's independent review of the preliminary environmental assessment and any other environmental information deemed necessary by the responsible official consistent with the requirements of § 6.506(c). Following the Agency's independent review, the environmental assessment will be finalized and either be incorporated into, or attached to, the FNSI. The FNSI shall list all mitigation measures as defined in § 1508.20 of this title, and specifically identify those mitigation measures necessary to make the recommended alternative environmentally acceptable.

(b) Proceeding with grant awards. (1) Once an environmental assessment has been prepared and the issued FNSI becomes effective for the treatment works within the study area, grant awards may proceed without preparation of additional FNSIs, unless the responsible official later determines that the project or environmental conditions have changed significantly from that which underwent environmental review.

(2) For all environmental assessment/FNSI determinations:

(i) That are five or more years old on projects awaiting Step 2+3 or Step 3 grant funding, the responsible official shall re-evaluate the project, environmental conditions and public views and, prior to grant award, either:

(A) Reaffirm—issue a public notice reaffirming EPA's decision to proceed with the project without revising the environmental assessment;

(B) Supplement—update information and prepare, issue and distribute a revised EA/FNSI in accordance with §§ 6.105(f) and 6.400(d); or

(C) Reassess—withdraw the FNSI and publish a notice of intent to produce an EIS followed by the preparation, issuance and distribution of the EIS/ROD.

(ii) That are made on projects that have been awarded a Step 2+3 grant, the responsible official shall, at the time of plans and specifications review under § 35.2202(b) of this title, assess whether the environmental conditions or the project's anticipated impact on the environment have changed and, prior to plans and specifications approval, advise the Regional Administrator if additional environmental review is necessary.

[51 FR 32612, Sept. 12, 1986]

§6.509 Criteria for initiating Environmental Impact Statements (EIS).

(a) Conditions requiring EISs. (1) The responsible official shall assure that an EIS will be prepared and issued when it is determined that the treatment works or collector system will cause any of the conditions under § 6.108 to exist, or when

(2) The treated effluent is being discharged into a body of water where the present classification is too lenient or is being challenged as too low to protect present or recent uses, and the effluent will not be of sufficient quality or quantity to meet the requirements of these uses.

(b) Other conditions. The responsible official shall also consider preparing an EIS if: The project is highly controversial; the project in conjunction with related Federal, State, local or tribal resource projects produces significant cumulative impacts; or if it is determined that the treatment works may violate Federal, State, local or tribal laws or requirements imposed for the protection of the environment.

§6.510 Environmental Impact Statement (EIS) preparation.

(a) Steps in preparing EISs. In addition to the requirements specified in subparts A, B, C, and D of this part, the responsible official will conduct the following activities:

(1) Notice of intent. If a determination is made that an EIS will be required, the responsible official shall prepare and distribute a notice of intent as required in § 6.105(e) of this part.

(2) Scoping. As soon as possible, after the publication of the notice of intent, the responsible official will convene a meeting of affected Federal, State and local agencies, or affected Indian tribes, the grantee and other interested parties to determine the scope of the EIS. A notice of this scoping meeting must be made in accordance with § 6.400(a) and 40 CFR 1506.6(b). As part of the scoping meeting EPA, in cooperation with any delegated State, will as a minimum:

(i) Determine the significance of issues for and the scope of those significant issues to be analyzed in depth, in the EIS;

(ii) Identify the preliminary range of alternatives to be considered;

(iii) Identify potential cooperating agencies and determine the information or analyses that may be needed from cooperating agencies or other parties;

(iv) Discuss the method for EIS preparation and the public participation strategy;

(v) Identify consultation requirements of other environmental laws, in accordance with subpart C; and

(vi) Determine the relationship between the EIS and the completion of the facilities plan and any necessary coordination arrangements between the preparers of both documents.

(3) Identifying and evaluating alternatives. Immediately following the scoping process, the responsible official shall commence the identification and evaluation of all potentially viable alternatives to adequately address the range of issues identified in the scoping process. Additional issues may be addressed, or others eliminated, during this process and the reasons documented as part of the EIS.

(b) Methods for preparing EISs. After EPA determines the need for an EIS, it shall select one of the following methods for its preparation:

(1) Directly by EPA's own staff;

(2) By EPA contracting directly with a qualified consulting firm;

(3) By utilizing a third party method, whereby the responsible official enters into "third party agreements" for the applicant to engage and pay for the services of a third party contractor to prepare the EIS. Such agreement shall not be initiated unless both the applicant and the responsible official agree to its creation. A third party agreement will be established prior to the applicant's EID and eliminate the need for that document. In proceeding under the third party agreement, the responsible official shall carry out the following practices:

(i) In consultation with the applicant, choose the third party contractor and manage that contract;

(ii) Select the consultant based on ability and an absence of conflict of interest. Third party contractors will be required to execute a disclosure statement prepared by the responsible official signifying they have no financial or other conflicting interest in the outcome of the project; and

(iii) Specify the information to be developed and supervise the gathering, analysis and presentation of

the information. The responsible official shall have sole authority for approval and modification of the statements, analyses, and conclusions included in the third party EIS; or

(4) By utilizing a joint EPA/State process on projects within States which have requirements and procedures comparable to NEPA, whereby the EPA and the State agree to prepare a single EIS document to fulfill both Federal and State requirements. Both EPA and the State shall sign a Memorandum of Agreement which includes the responsibilities and procedures to be used by both parties for the preparation of the EIS as provided for in 40 CFR 1506.2(c).

§6.511   Record of Decision (ROD) for EISs and identification of mitigation measures.

(a) Record of Decision. After a final EIS has been issued, the responsible official shall prepare and issue a ROD in accordance with 40 CFR 1505.2 prior to, or in conjunction with, the approval of the facilities plan. The ROD shall include identification of mitigation measures derived from the EIS process including grant conditions which are necessary to minimize the adverse impacts of the selected alternative.

(b) Specific mitigation measures. Prior to the approval of a facilities plan, the responsible official must ensure that effective mitigation measures identified in the ROD will be implemented by the grantee. This should be done by revising the facilities plan, initiating other steps to mitigate adverse effects, or including conditions in grants requiring actions to minimize effects. Care should be exercised if a condition is to be imposed in a grant document to assure that the applicant possesses the authority to fulfill the conditions.

(c) Proceeding with grant awards. (1) Once the ROD has been prepared on the selected, or preferred, alternative(s) for the treatment works described within the EIS, grant awards may proceed without the preparation of supplemental EISs unless the responsible official later determines that the project or the environmental conditions described within the current EIS have changed significantly from the previous environmental review in accordance with § 1502.9(c) of this title.

(2) For all EIS/ROD determinations:

(i) That are five or more years old on projects awaiting Step 2+3 or Step 3 grant funding, the responsible official shall re-evaluate the project, environmental conditions and public views and, prior to grant award, either:

(A) Reaffirm—issue a public notice reaffirming EPA's decision to proceed with the project, and documenting that no additional significant impacts were identified during the re-evaluation which would require supplementing the EIS; or

(B) Supplement—conduct additional studies and prepare, issue and distribute a supplemental EIS in accordance with § 6.404 and document the original, or any revised, decision in an addendum to the ROD.

(ii) That are made on projects that have been awarded a Step 2+3 grant, the responsible official shall, at the time of plans and specifications review under § 35.2202(b) of this title, assess whether the environmental conditions or the project's anticipated impact on the environment have changed, and prior to plans and specifications approval, advise the Regional Administrator if additional environmental review is necessary.

[50 FR 26317, June 25, 1985, as amended at 51 FR 32613, Sept. 12, 1986]

§6.512　Monitoring for compliance.

(a) General. The responsible official shall ensure adequate monitoring of mitigation measures and other grant conditions identified in the FNSI, or ROD.

(b) Enforcement. If the grantee fails to comply with grant conditions, the responsible official may consider applying any of the sanctions specified in 40 CFR 30.900.

§6.513　Public participation.

(a) General. Consistent with public participation regulations in part 25 of this title, and subpart D of this part, it is EPA policy that certain public participation steps be achieved before the State and EPA complete the environmental review process. As a minimum, all potential applicants that do not qualify for a categorical exclusion shall conduct the following steps in accordance with procedures specified in part 25 of this title:

(1) One public meeting when alternatives have been developed, but before an alternative has been selected, to discuss all alternatives under consideration and the reasons for rejection of others; and

(2) One public hearing prior to formal adoption of a facilities plan to discuss the proposed facilities plan and any needed mitigation measures.

(b) Coordination. Public participation activities undertaken in connection with the environmental review process should be coordinated with any other applicable public participation program wherever possible.

(c) Scope. The requirements of 40 CFR 6.400 shall be fulfilled, and consistent with 40 CFR 1506.6, the responsible official may institute such additional NEPA-related public participation procedures as are deemed necessary during the environmental review process.

[50 FR 26317, June 25, 1985, as amended at 51 FR 32613, Sept. 12, 1986]

§6.514　Delegation to States.

(a) General. Authority delegated to the State under section 205(g) of the Clean Water Act to review a facilities plan may include all EPA activities under this part except for the following:

(1) Determinations of whether or not a project qualifies for a categorical exclusion;

(2) Determinations to partition the environmental review process;

(3) Finalizing the scope of an EID when required to adequately conclude an independent review of a preliminary environmental assessment;

(4) Finalizing the scope of an environmental assessment, and finalization, approval and issuance of a final environmental assessment;

(5) Determination to issue, and issuance of, a FNSI based on a completed (§ 6.508) or partitioned (§ 6.507(d)(2)) environmental review;

(6) Determination to issue, and issuance of, a notice of intent for preparing an EIS;

(7) Preparation of EISs under § 6.510(b) (1) and (2), final decisions required for preparing an EIS under § 6.510(b)(3), finalizing the agreement to prepare an EIS under § 6.510(b)(4), finalizing the scope of an EIS, and issuance of draft, final and supplemental EISs;

(8) Preparation and issuance of the ROD based on an EIS;

(9) Final decisions under other applicable laws described in subpart C of this part;

(10) Determination following re-evaluations of projects awaiting grant funding in the case of Step 3 projects whose existing evaluations and/or decision documents are five or more years old, or determinations following re-evaluations on projects submitted for plans and specifications review and approval in the case of awarded Step 2+3 projects where the EPA Regional Administrator has been advised that additional environmental review is necessary, in accordance with § 6.505(d)(2), § 6.508(b)(2) or § 6.511(c)(2); and

(11) Maintenance of official EPA monthly status reports as required under § 6.402(b).

(b) Elimination of duplication. The responsible official shall assure that maximum efforts are undertaken to minimize duplication within the limits described under paragraph (a) of this section. In carrying out requirements under this subpart, maximum consideration shall be given to eliminating duplication in accordance with § 1506.2 of this title. Where there are State or local procedures comparable to NEPA, EPA should enter into memoranda of understanding with these States concerning workload distribution and responsibilities not specifically reserved to EPA in paragraph (a) of this section for implementing the environmental review and facilities planning process.

[50 FR 26317, June 25, 1985, as amended at 51 FR 32613, Sept. 12, 1986]

Subpart F—Environmental Review Procedures for the New Source NPDES Program

§6.600   Purpose.

(a) General. This subpart provides procedures for carrying out the environmental review process for the issuance of new source National Pollutant Discharge Elimination System (NPDES) discharge permits authorized under section 306, section 402, and section 511(c)(1) of the Clean Water Act.

(b) Permit regulations. All references in this subpart to the permit regulations shall mean parts 122 and 124 of title 40 of the CFR relating to the NPDES program.

[44 FR 64177, Nov. 6, 1979, as amended at 47 FR 9831, Mar. 8, 1982]

§6.601   Definitions.

(a) The term administrative action for the sake of this subpart means the issuance by EPA of an NPDES permit to discharge as a new source, pursuant to 40 CFR 124.15.

(b) The term applicant for the sake of this subpart means any person who applies to EPA for the issuance of an NPDES permit to discharge as a new source.

[44 FR 64177, Nov. 6, 1979, as amended at 47 FR 9831, Mar. 8, 1982]

§6.602   Applicability.

(a) General. The procedures set forth under subparts A, B, C and D, and this subpart shall apply to the issuance of new source NPDES permits, except for the issuance of a new source NPDES permit from any State which has an approved NPDES program in accordance with section 402(b) of the Clean Water Act.

(b) New Source Determination. An NPDES permittee must be determined a new source before these procedures apply. New source determinations will be undertaken pursuant to the provisions of the permit regulations under § 122.29(a) and (b) of this chapter and § 122.53(h).

[44 FR 64177, Nov. 6, 1979, as amended at 47 FR 9831, Mar. 8, 1982; 51 FR 32613, Sept. 12, 1986]

§6.603   Limitations on actions during environmental review process.

The processing and review of an applicant's NPDES permit application shall proceed concurrently with the procedures within this subpart. Actions undertaken by the applicant or EPA shall be performed consistent with the requirements of § 122.29(c) of this chapter.

[47 FR 9831, Mar. 8, 1982, as amended at 51 FR 32613, Sept. 12, 1986]

§6.604   Environmental review process.

(a) New source. If EPA's initial determination under § 6.602(b) is that the facility is a new source, the responsible official shall evaluate any environmental information to determine if any significant impacts are anticipated and an EIS is necessary. If the permit applicant requests, the responsible official shall establish time limits for the completion of the environmental review process consistent with 40 CFR 1501.8.

(b) Information needs. Information necessary for a proper environmental review shall be provided by the permit applicant in an environmental information document. The responsible official shall consult with the applicant to determine the scope of an environmental information document. In doing this the responsible official shall consider the size of the new source and the extent to which the applicant is capable of providing the required information. The responsible official shall not require the applicant to gather data or perform analyses which unnecessarily duplicate either existing data or the results of existing analyses available to EPA. The responsible official shall keep requests for data to the minimum consistent with his responsibilities under NEPA.

(c) Environmental assessment. The responsible official shall prepare a written environmental assessment based on an environmental review of either the environmental information document and/or any other available environmental information.

(d) EIS determination. (1) When the environmental review indicates that a significant environmental impact may occur and that the significant adverse impacts cannot be eliminated by making changes in the proposed new source project, a notice of intent shall be issued, and a draft EIS prepared and distributed. When the environmental review indicates no significant impacts are anticipated or when the proposed project is changed to eliminate the significant adverse impacts, a FNSI shall be issued which lists any mitigation measures necessary to make the recommended alternative environmentally acceptable.

(2) The FNSI together with the environmental assessment that supports the finding shall be distributed in accordance with § 6.400(d) of this regulation.

(e) Lead agency. (1) If the environmental review reveals that the preparation of an EIS is required, the responsible official shall determine if other Federal agencies are involved with the project. The responsible official shall contact all other involved agencies and together the agencies shall decide the lead agency based on the criteria set forth in 40 CFR 1501.5.

(2) If, after the meeting of involved agencies, EPA has been determined to be the lead agency, the responsible official may request that other involved agencies be cooperating agencies. Cooperating agencies shall be chosen and shall be involved in the EIS preparation process in the manner prescribed in the 40 CFR 1501.6(a). If EPA has been determined to be a cooperating agency, the responsible official shall be involved in assisting in the preparation of the EIS in the manner prescribed in 40 CFR 1501.6(b).

(f) Notice of intent. (1) If EPA is the lead agency for the preparation of an EIS, the responsible official shall arrange through OER for the publication of the notice of intent in the Federal Register, distribute the notice

of intent and arrange and conduct a scoping meeting as outlined in 40 CFR 1501.7.

(2) If the responsible official and the permit applicant agree to a third party method of EIS preparation, pursuant to § 6.604(g)(3) of this part, the responsible official shall insure that a notice of intent is published and that a scoping meeting is held before the third party contractor begins work which may influence the scope of the EIS.

(g) EIS method. EPA shall prepare EISs by one of the following means:

(1) Directly by its own staff;

(2) By contracting directly with a qualified consulting firm; or

(3) By utilizing a third party method, whereby the responsible official enters into a third party agreement for the applicant to engage and pay for the services of a third party contractor to prepare the EIS. Such an agreement shall not be initiated unless both the applicant and the responsible official agree to its creation. A third party agreement will be established prior to the applicant's environmental information document and eliminate the need for that document. In proceeding under the third party agreement, the responsible official shall carry out the following practices:

(i) In consultation with the applicant, choose the third party contractor and manage that contract.

(ii) Select the consultant based on his ability and an absence of conflict of interest. Third party contractors will be required to execute a disclosure statement prepared by the responsible official signifying they have no financial or other conflicting interest in the outcome of the project.

(iii) Specify the information to be developed and supervise the gathering, analysis and presentation of the information. The responsible official shall have sole authority for approval and modification of the statements, analyses, and conclusions included in the third party EIS.

(h) Documents for the administrative record. Pursuant to 40 CFR 124.9(b)(6) and 124.18(b)(5) any environmental assessment, FNSI EIS, or supplement to an EIS shall be made a part of the administrative record related to permit issuance.

[44 FR 64177, Nov. 6, 1979, as amended at 47 FR 9831, Mar. 8, 1982]

§6.605   Criteria for preparing EISs.

(a) General guidelines. (1) When determining the significance of a proposed new source's impact, the responsible official shall consider both its short term and long term effects as well as its direct and indirect effects and beneficial and adverse environmental impacts as defined in 40 CFR 1508.8.

(2) If EPA is proposing to issue a number of new source NPDES permits during a limited time span and in the same general geographic area, the responsible official shall examine the possibility of tiering EISs. If the permits are minor and environmentally insignificant when considered separately, the responsible official may determine that the cumulative impact of the issuance of all these permits may have a significant environmental effect and require an EIS for the area. Each separate decision to issue an NPDES permit shall then be based on the information in this areawide EIS. Site specific EISs may be required in certain circumstances in addition to the areawide EIS.

(b) Specific criteria. An EIS will be prepared when:

(1) The new source will induce or accelerate significant changes in industrial, commercial, agricultural, or residential land use concentrations or distributions which have the potential for significant environmental effects. Factors that should be considered in determining if these changes are environmentally significant include but are not limited to: The nature and extent of the vacant land subject to increased development pressure as a result of the new source; the increases in population or population density which may be induced and the ramifications of such changes; the nature of land use regulations in the affected area and their potential effects on development and the environment; and the changes in the availability or demand for energy and the resulting environmental consequences.

(2) The new source will directly, or through induced development, have significant adverse effect upon local ambient air quality, local ambient noise levels, floodplains, surface or groundwater quality or quantity, fish, wildlife, and their natural habitats.

(3) Any major part of the new source will have significant adverse effect on the habitat of threatened or endangered species on the Department of the Interior's or a State's lists of threatened and endangered species.

(4) The environmental impact of the issuance of a new source NPDES permit will have significant direct and adverse effect on a property listed in or eligible for listing in the National Register of Historic Places.

(5) Any major part of the source will have significant adverse effects on parklands, wetlands, wild and scenic rivers, reservoirs or other important bodies of water, navigation projects, or agricultural lands.

§6.606   Record of decision.

(a) General. At the time of permit award, the responsible official shall prepare a record of decision in those cases where a final EIS was issued in accordance with 40 CFR 1505.2 and pursuant to the provisions of the permit regulations under 40 CFR 124.15 and 124.18(b)(5). The record of decision shall list any mitigation measures necessary to make the recommended alternative environmentally acceptable.

(b) Mitigation measures. The mitigation measures derived from the EIS process shall be incorporated as conditions of the permit; ancillary agreements shall not be used to require mitigation.

[44 FR 64177, Nov. 6, 1979, as amended at 47 FR 9831, Mar. 8, 1982]

§6.607   Monitoring.

In accordance with 40 CFR 1505.3 and pursuant to 40 CFR 122.66(c) and 122.10 the responsible official shall ensure that there is adequate monitoring of compliance with all NEPA related requirements contained in the permit.

[47 FR 9831, Mar. 8, 1982]

Subpart G—Environmental Review Procedures for Office of Research and Development Projects

Source:
56 FR 20543, May 6, 1991, unless otherwise noted.

§6.700   Purpose.

(a) This subpart amplifies the requirements described in subparts A through D by providing specific environmental review procedures for activities undertaken or funded by the Office of Research and Development (ORD).

(b) The ORD Program provides scientific support for setting environmental standards as well as the technology needed to prevent, monitor and control pollution. Intramural research is conducted at EPA laboratories and field stations throughout the United States. Extramural research is implemented through grants, cooperative agreements, and contracts. The majority of ORD's research is conducted within the confines of laboratories. Outdoor research includes monitoring, sampling, and environmental stress and ecological effects studies.

§6.701   Definition.

The term appropriate program official means the official at each decision level within ORD to whom the Assistant Administrator has delegated responsibility for carrying out the environmental review process.

§6.702   Applicability.

The requirements of this subpart apply to administrative actions undertaken to approve intramural and extramural projects under the purview of ORD.

§6.703   General.

(a) Environmental information. (1) For intramural research projects, information necessary to perform the environmental review shall be obtained by the appropriate program official.

(2) For extramural research projects, environmental information documents shall be submitted to EPA by applicants to facilitate the Agency's environmental review process. Guidance on environmental information documents shall be included in all assistance application kits and in contract proposal instructions. If there is a question concerning the preparation of an environmental information document, the applicant should consult with the project officer or contract officer for guidance.

(b) Environmental review. The diagram in figure 1 represents the various stages of the environmental review process to be undertaken for ORD projects.

(1) For intramural research projects, an environmental review will be performed for each laboratory's projects at the start of the planning year. The review will be conducted before projects are incorporated into the ORD program planning system. Projects added at a later date and, therefore, not identified at the start of the planning year, or any redirection of a project that could have significant environmental effects, also will be subjected to an environmental review. This review will be performed in accordance with the process set forth in this subpart and depicted in figure 1.

(2) For extramural research projects, the environmental review shall be conducted before an initial or continuing award is made. The appropriate program official will perform the environmental review in accordance with the process set forth in this subpart and depicted in figure 1. EPA form 5300-23 will be used to docu-

ment categorical exclusion determinations or, with appropriate supporting analysis, as the environmental assessment (EA). The completed form 5300-23 and any finding of no significant impact (FNSI) or environmental impact statement (EIS) will be submitted with the proposal package to the appropriate EPA assistance or contract office.

(c) Agency coordination. In order to avoid duplication of effort and ensure consistency throughout the Agency, environmental reviews of ORD projects will be coordinated, as appropriate and feasible, with reviews performed by other program offices. Technical support documents prepared for reviews in other EPA programs may be adopted for use in ORD's environmental reviews and supplemented, as appropriate.

§6.704   Categorical exclusions.

(a) At the beginning of the environmental review process (see Figure 1), the appropriate program official shall determine whether an ORD project can be categorically excluded from the substantive requirements of a NEPA review. This determination shall be based on general criteria in § 6.107(d) and specialized categories of ORD actions eligible for exclusion in § 6.704(b). If the appropriate program official determines that an ORD project is consistent with the general criteria and any of the specialized categories of eligible activities, and does not satisfy the criteria in § 6.107(e) for not granting a categorical exclusion, then this finding shall be documented and no further action shall be required. A categorical exclusion shall be revoked by the appropriate program official if it is determined that the project meets the criteria for revocation in § 6.107(c). Projects that fail to qualify for categorical exclusion or for which categorical exclusion has been revoked must undergo full environmental review in accordance with § 6.705 and § 6.706.

(b) The following specialized categories of ORD actions are eligible for categorical exclusion from a detailed NEPA review:

(1) Library or literature searches and studies;

(2) Computer studies and activities;

(3) Monitoring and sample collection wherein no significant alteration of existing ambient conditions occurs;

(4) Projects conducted completely within a contained facility, such as a laboratory or other enclosed building, where methods are employed for appropriate disposal of laboratory wastes and safeguards exist against hazardous, toxic, and radioactive materials entering the

environment. Laboratory directors or other appropriate officials must certify and provide documentation that the laboratory follows good laboratory practices and adheres to applicable Federal statutes, regulations and guidelines.

§6.705   Environmental assessment and finding of no significant impact.

(a) When a project does not meet any of the criteria for categorical exclusion, the appropriate program official shall undertake an environmental assessment in accordance with 40 CFR 1508.9 in order to determine whether an EIS is required or if a FNSI can be made. ORD projects which normally result in the preparation of an EA include the following:

(1) Initial field demonstration of a new technology;

(2) Field trials of a new product or new uses of an existing technology;

(3) Alteration of a local habitat by physical or chemical means.

(b) If the environmental assessment reveals that the research is not anticipated to have a significant impact on the environment, the appropriate program official shall prepare a FNSI in accordance with § 6.105(f). Pursuant to § 6.400(d), no administrative action will be taken on a project until the prescribed 30-day comment period for a FNSI has elapsed and the Agency has fully considered all comments.

(c) On actions involving potentially significant impacts on the environment, a FNSI may be prepared if changes have been made in the proposed action to eliminate any significant impacts. These changes must be documented in the proposal and in the FNSI.

(d) If the environmental assessment reveals that the research may have a significant impact on the environment, an EIS must be prepared. The appropriate program official may make a determination that an EIS is necessary without preparing a formal environmental assessment. This determination may be made by applying the criteria for preparation of an EIS in § 6.706.

§6.706   Environmental impact statement.

(a) Criteria for preparation. In performing the environmental review, the appropriate program official shall assure that an EIS is prepared when any of the conditions under § 6.108 (a) through (g) exist or when:

(1) The proposed action may significantly affect the environment through the release of radioactive, hazardous or toxic substances;

(2) The proposed action, through the release of an organism or organisms, may involve environmental effects which are significant;

(3) The proposed action involves effects upon the environment which are likely to be highly controversial;

(4) The proposed action involves environmental effects which may accumulate over time or combine with effects of other actions to create impacts which are significant;

(5) The proposed action involves uncertain environmental effects or highly unique environmental risks which may be significant.

(b) ORD actions which may require preparation of an EIS. There are no ORD actions which normally require the preparation of an EIS. However, each ORD project will be evaluated using the EIS criteria as stated in § 6.706(a) to determine whether an EIS must be prepared.

(c) Notice of intent. (1) If the environmental review reveals that a proposed action may have a significant effect on the environment and this effect cannot be eliminated by redirection of the research or other means, the appropriate program official shall issue a notice of intent to prepare an EIS pursuant to § 6.400(b).

(2) As soon as possible after release of the notice of intent, the appropriate program official shall ensure that a draft EIS is prepared in accordance with subpart B and that the public is involved in accordance with subpart D.

(3) Draft and final EISs shall be sent to the Assistant Administrator for ORD for approval.

(4) Pursuant to § 6.401(b), a decision on whether to undertake or fund a project must be made in conformance with the time frames indicated.

(d) Record of decision. Before the project is undertaken or funded, the appropriate program official shall prepare, in accordance with § 6.105 (g) and (h), a record of decision in any case where a final EIS has been issued.

Figure 1. Environmental review process for ORD projects

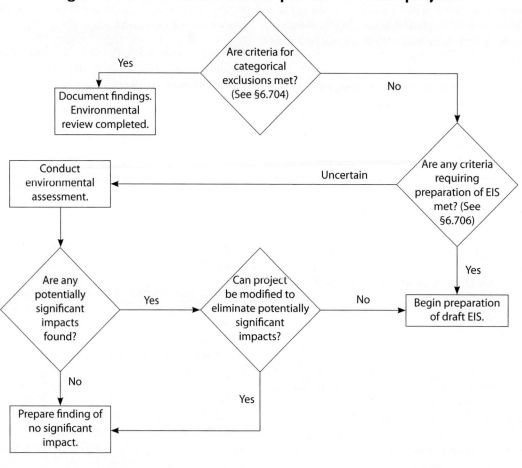

Subpart H—Environmental Review Procedures for Solid Waste Demonstration Projects

§6.800   Purpose.

This subpart amplifies the procedures described in subparts A through D by providing more specific environmental review procedures for demonstration projects undertaken by the Office of Solid Waste and Emergency Response.

[44 FR 64177, Nov. 6, 1979, as amended at 51 FR 32613, Sept. 12, 1986]

§6.801   Applicability.

The requirements of this subpart apply to solid waste demonstration projects for resource recovery systems and improved solid waste disposal facilities undertaken pursuant to section 8006 of the Resource Conservation and Recovery Act of 1976.

§6.802   Criteria for preparing EISs.

The responsible official shall assure that an EIS will be prepared when it is determined that any of the conditions in § 6.108 exist.

[44 FR 64177, Nov. 6, 1979, as amended at 50 FR 26323, June 25, 1985]

§6.803   Environmental review process.

(a) Environmental information. (1) Environmental information documents shall be submitted to EPA by grant applicants or contractors. If there is a question concerning the need for a document, the potential contractor or grantee should consult with the appropriate project officer for the grant or contract.

(2) The environmental information document shall contain the same sections specified for EIS's in subpart B. Guidance alerting potential grantees and contractors of the environmental information documents shall be included in all grant application kits, attached to

letters concerning the submission of unsolicited proposals, and included with all requests for proposal.

(b) Environmental review. An environmental review will be conducted before a grant or contract award is made. This review will include the preparation of an environmental assessment by the responsible official; the appropriate Regional Administrator's input will include his recommendations on the need for an EIS.

(c) Notice of intent and EIS. Based on the environmental review if the criteria in § 6.802 of this part apply, the responsible official will assure that a notice of intent and a draft EIS are prepared. The responsible official may request the appropriate Regional Administrator to assist him in the preparation and distribution of the environmental documents.

(d) Finding of no significant impact. If the environmental review indicated no significant environmental impacts, the responsible official will assure that a FNSI is prepared which lists any mitigation measures necessary to make the recommended alternative environmentally acceptable.

(e) Timing of action. Pursuant to § 6.401(b), in no case shall a contract or grant be awarded until the prescribed 30-day review period for a final EIS has elapsed. Similarly, no action shall be taken until the 30-day comment period for a FNSI is completed.

§6.804　Record of decision.

The responsible official shall prepare a record of decision in any case where final EIS has been issued in accordance with 40 CFR 1505.2. It shall be prepared at the time of contract or grant award. The record of decision shall list any mitigation measures necessary to make the recommended alternative environmentally acceptable.

Subpart I—Environmental Review Procedures for EPA Facility Support Activities

§6.900　Purpose.

This subpart amplifies the general requirements described in subparts A through D by providing environmental procedures for the preparation of EISs on construction and renovation of special purpose facilities.

§6.901　Definitions.

(a) The term special purpose facility means a building or space, including land incidental to its use, which is wholly or predominantly utilized for the special purpose of an agency and not generally suitable for other uses, as determined by the General Services Administration.

(b) The term program of requirements means a comprehensive document (booklet) describing program activities to be accomplished in the new special purpose facility or improvement. It includes architectural, mechanical, structural, and space requirements.

(c) The term scope of work means a document similar in content to the program of requirements but substantially abbreviated. It is usually prepared for small-scale projects.

§6.902　Applicability.

(a) Actions covered. These procedures apply to all new special purpose facility construction, activities related to this construction (e.g., site acquisition and clearing), and any improvements or modifications to facilities having potential environmental effects external to the facility, including new construction and improvements undertaken and funded by the Facilities Engineering and Real Estate Branch, Facilities and Support Services Division, Office of the Assistant Administrator for Administration and Resource Management; or by a regional office .

(b) Actions excluded. This subpart does not apply to those activities of the Facilities Engineering and Real Estate Branch, Facilities and Support Services Division, for which the branch does not have full fiscal responsibility for the entire project. This includes pilot plant construction, land acquisition, site clearing and access road construction where the Facilities Engineering and Real Estate Branch's activity is only supporting a project financed by a program office. Responsibility for considering the environmental impacts of such projects rests with the office managing and funding the entire project. Other subparts of this regulation apply depending on the nature of the project.

[44 FR 64177, Nov. 6, 1979, as amended at 51 FR 32613, Sept. 12, 1986]

§6.903　Criteria for preparing EISs.

(a) Preliminary information. The responsible official shall request an environmental information document from a construction contractor or consulting architect/engineer employed by EPA if he is involved in the planning, construction or modification of special purpose facilities when his activities have potential environmental effects external to the facility. Such modifications include but are not limited to facility additions, changes in central heating systems or waste-water treatment systems, and land clearing for access roads and parking lots.

(b) EIS preparation criteria. The responsible official shall conduct an environmental review of all actions involving construction of special purpose facilities and improvements to these facilities. The responsible official shall assure that an EIS will be prepared when it is determined that any of the conditions in § 6.108 of this part exist.

[44 FR 64177, Nov. 6, 1979, as amended at 50 FR 26323, June 25, 1985]

§6.904   Environmental review process.

(a) Environmental review. (1) An environmental review shall be conducted when the program of requirements or scope of work has been completed for the construction, improvements, or modification of special purpose facilities. For special purpose facility construction, the Chief, Facilities Engineering and Real Estate Branch, shall request the assistance of the appropriate program office and Regional Administrator in the review. For modifications and improvement, the appropriate responsible official shall request assistance in making the review from other cognizant EPA offices.

(2) Any environmental information documents requested shall contain the same sections listed for EISs in subpart B. Contractors and consultants shall be notified in contractual documents when an environmental information document must be prepared.

(b) Notice of intent, EIS, and FNSI. The responsible official shall decide at the completion of the Environmental review whether there may be any significant environmental impacts. If there could be significant environmental impacts, a notice of intent and an EIS shall be prepared according to the procedures under subparts A, B, C and D. If there are not any significant environmental impacts, a FNSI shall be prepared according to the procedures in subparts A and D. The FNSI shall list any mitigation measures necessary to make the recommended alternative environmentally acceptable.

(c) Timing of action. Pursuant to § 6.401(b), in no case shall a contract be awarded or construction activities begun until the prescribed 30-day wait period for a final EIS has elapsed. Similarly, under § 6.400(d), no action shall be taken until the 30-day comment period for FNSIs is completed.

§6.905   Record of decision.

At the time of contract award, the responsible official shall prepare a record of decision in those cases where a final EIS has been issued in accordance with 40 CFR 1505.2. The record of decision shall list any mitigation measures necessary to make the recommended alternative environmentally acceptable.

Subpart J—Assessing the Environmental Effects Abroad of EPA Actions

Authority:
Executive Order 12114, 42 U.S.C. 4321, note.

Source:
46 FR 3364, Jan. 14, 1981, unless otherwise noted.

§6.1001   Purpose and policy.

(a) Purpose. On January 4, 1979, the President signed Executive Order 12114 entitled "Environmental Effects Abroad of Major Federal Actions." The purpose of this Executive Order is to enable responsible Federal officials in carrying out or approving major Federal actions which affect foreign nations or the global commons to be informed of pertinent environmental considerations and to consider fully the environmental impacts of the actions undertaken. While based on independent authority, this Order furthers the purpose of the National Environmental Policy Act (NEPA) (42 U.S.C. 4321 et seq.) and the Marine Protection Research and Sanctuaries Act (MPRSA) (33 U.S.C. 1401 et seq.). It should be noted, however, that in fulfilling its responsibilities under Executive Order 12114, EPA shall be guided by CEQ regulations only to the extent that they are made expressly applicable by this subpart. The procedures set forth below reflect EPA's duties and responsibilities as required under the Executive Order and satisfy the requirement for issuance of procedures under section 2-1 of the Executive Order.

(b) Policy. It shall be the policy of this Agency to carry out the purpose and requirements of the Executive Order to the fullest extent possible. EPA, within the realm of its expertise, shall work with the Department of State and the Council on Environmental Quality to provide information to other Federal agencies and foreign nations to heighten awareness of and interest in the environment. EPA shall further cooperate to the extent possible with Federal agencies to lend special expertise and assistance in the preparation of required environmental documents under the Executive Order. EPA shall perform environmental reviews of activities significantly affecting the global commons and foreign nations as required under Executive Order 12114 and as set forth under these procedures.

§6.1002   Applicability.

(a) Administrative actions requiring environmental review. The environmental review requirements apply to the activities of EPA as set forth below:

(1) Major research or demonstration projects which affect the global commons or a foreign nation.

(2) Ocean dumping activities carried out under section 102 of the MPRSA which affect the related environment.

(3) Major permitting or licensing by EPA of facilities which affect the global commons or the environment of a foreign nation. This may include such actions as the issuance by EPA of hazardous waste treatment, storage, or disposal facility permits pursuant to section 3005 of the Resource Conservation and Recovery Act (42 U.S.C. 6925), NPDES permits pursuant to section 402 of the Clean Water Act (33 U.S.C. 1342), and prevention of significant deterioration approvals pursuant to Part C of the Clean Air Act (42 U.S.C. 7470 et seq.).

(4) Wastewater Treatment Construction Grants Program under section 201 of the Clean Water Act when activities addressed in the facility plan would have environmental effects abroad.

(5) Other EPA activities as determined by OER and OIA (see § 6.1007(c)).

§6.1003   Definitions.

As used in this subpart, environment means the natural and physical environment and excludes social, economic and other environments; global commons is that area (land, air, water) outside the jurisdiction of any nation; and responsible official is either the EPA Assistant Administrator or Regional Administrator as appropriate for the particular EPA program. Also, an action significantly affects the environment if it does significant harm to the environment even though on balance the action may be beneficial to the environment. To the extent applicable, the responsible official shall address the considerations set forth in the CEQ Regulations under 40 CFR 1508.27 in determining significant effect.

§6.1004   Environmental review and assessment requirements.

(a) Research and demonstration projects. The appropriate Assistant Administrator is responsible for perform-ing the necessary degree of environmental review on research and demonstration projects undertaken by EPA. If the research or demonstration project affects the environment of the global commons, the applicant shall prepare an environmental analysis. This will assist the responsible official in determining whether an EIS is necessary. If it is determined that the action significantly affects the environment of the global commons, then an EIS shall be prepared. If the undertaking significantly affects a foreign nation EPA shall prepare a unilateral, bilateral or multilateral environmental study. EPA shall afford the affected foreign nation or international body or organization an opportunity to participate in this study. This environmental study shall discuss the need for the action, analyze the environmental impact of the various alternatives considered and list the agencies and other parties consulted.

(b) Ocean dumping activities. (1) The Assistant Administrator for Water and Waste Management shall ensure the preparation of appropriate environmental documents relating to ocean dumping activities in the global commons under section 102 of the MPRSA. For ocean dumping site designations prescribed pursuant to section 102(c) of the MPRSA and 40 CFR part 228, EPA shall prepare an environmental impact statement consistent with the requirements of EPA's Procedures for the Voluntary Preparation of Environmental Impact Statements dated October 21, 1974 (see 39 FR 37419). Also EPA shall prepare an environmental impact statement for the establishment or revision of criteria under section 102(a) of MPRSA.

(2) For individual permits issued by EPA under section 102(b) an environmental assessment shall be made by EPA. Pursuant to 40 CFR part 221, the permit applicant shall submit with the application an environmental analysis which includes a discussion of the need for the action, an outline of alternatives, and an analysis of the environmental impact of the proposed action and alternatives consistent with the EPA criteria established under section 102(a) of MPRSA. The information submitted under 40 CFR part 221 shall be sufficient to satisfy the environmental assessment requirement.

(c) EPA permitting and licensing activities. The appropriate Regional Administrator is responsible for conducting concise environmental reviews with regard to permits issued under section 3005 of the Resource Conservation and Recovery Act (RCRA permits), section 402 of the Clean Water Act (NPDES permits), and section 165 of the Clean Air Act (PSD permits), for such actions undertaken by EPA which affect the global commons or foreign nations. The information submitted by applicants for such permits or approvals under the applicable consolidated permit regulations (40 CFR parts 122 and 124) and Prevention of Significant Deterioration (PSD) regulations (40 CFR part 52) shall satisfy the environmental document requirement under section 2-4(b) of Executive Order 12114. Compliance with applicable requirements in part 124 of the consolidated permit regulations (40 CFR part 124) shall be sufficient to satisfy the requirements to conduct a concise environmental review for permits subject to this paragraph.

(d) Wastewater treatment facility planning. 40 CFR 6.506 details the environmental review process for the facilities planning process under the wastewater treatment works construction grants program. For the purpose of these regulations, the facility plan shall also include a concise environmental review of those activities that would have environmental effects abroad. This shall apply only to the Step 1 grants awarded after January 14, 1981, but on or before December 29, 1981, and facilities plans developed after December 29, 1981. Where water quality impacts identified in a facility plan are the subject or water quality agreements with Canada or Mexico, nothing in these regulations shall impose on the facility planning process coordination and consultation requirements in addition to those required by such agreements.

(e) Review by other Federal agencies and other appropriate officials. The responsible officials shall consult with other Federal agencies with relevant expertise during the preparation of the environmental document. As soon as feasible after preparation of the environmental document, the responsible official shall make the document available to the Council on Environmental Quality, Department of State, and other appropriate officials. The responsible official with assistance from OIA shall work with the Department of State to establish procedures for communicating with and making documents available to foreign nations and international organizations.

[46 FR 3364, Jan. 14, 1981, as amended at 50 FR 26323, June 25, 1985]

§6.1005   Lead or cooperating agency.

(a) Lead Agency. Section 3-3 of Executive Order 12114 requires the creation of a lead agency whenever an action involves more than one Federal agency. In implementing section 3-3, EPA shall, to the fullest extent possible, follow the guidance for the selection of a lead agency contained in 40 CFR 1501.5 of the CEQ regulations.

(b) Cooperating Agency. Under section 2-4(d) of the Executive Order, Federal agencies with special expertise are encouraged to provide appropriate resources to the agency preparing environmental documents in order to avoid duplication of resources. In working with a lead agency, EPA shall to the fullest extent possible serve as a cooperating agency in accordance with 40 CFR 1501.6. When other program commitments preclude the degree of involvement requested by the lead agency, the responsible EPA official shall so inform the lead agency in writing.

§6.1006   Exemptions and considerations.

Under section 2-5 (b) and (c) of the Executive Order, Federal agencies may provide for modifications in the contents, timing and availability of documents or exemptions from certain requirements for the environmental review and assessment. The responsible official, in consultation with the Director, Office of Environmental Review (OER), and the Director, Office of International Activities (OIA), may approve modifications for situations described in section 2-5(b). The responsible official, in consultation with the Director, OER and Director OIA, shall obtain exemptions from the Administrator for situations described in section 2-5(c). The Department of State and the Council on Environmental Quality shall be consulted as soon as possible on the utilization of such exemptions.

§6.1007   Implementation.

(a) Oversight. OER is responsible for overseeing the implementation of these procedures and shall consult with OIA wherever appropriate. OIA shall be utilized for making formal contacts with the Department of State. OER shall assist the responsible officials in carrying out their responsibilities under these procedures.

(b) Information exchange. OER with the aid of OIA, shall assist the Department of State and the Council on Environmental Quality in developing the informational exchange on environmental review activities with foreign nations.

(c) Unidentified activities. The responsible official shall consult with OER and OIA to establish the type of environmental review or document appropriate for any new EPA activities or requirements imposed upon EPA by statute, international agreement or other agreements.

Pt. 6, App. A

Appendix A to Part 6—Statement of Procedures on Floodplain Management and Wetlands Protection

Contents:
Section 1 General
Section 2 Purpose
Section 3 Policy
Section 4 Definitions
Section 5 Applicability
Section 6 Requirements
Section 7 Implementation

Section 1 General

a. Executive Order 11988 entitled "Floodplain Management" dated May 24, 1977, requires Federal agencies to evaluate the potential effects of actions it may take in a floodplain to avoid adversely impacting floodplains wherever possible, to ensure that its planning programs and budget requests reflect consideration of flood hazards and floodplain management, including the restoration and preservation of such land areas as natural undeveloped floodplains, and to prescribe procedures to implement the policies and procedures of this Executive Order. Guidance for implementation of the Executive Order has been provided by the U.S. Water Resources Council in its Floodplain Management Guidelines dated February 10, 1978 (see 40 FR 6030).

b. Executive Order 11990 entitled "Protection of Wetlands", dated May 24, 1977, requires Federal agencies to take action to avoid adversely impacting wetlands wherever possible, to minimize wetlands destruction and to preserve the values of wetlands, and to prescribe procedures to implement the policies and procedures of this Executive Order.

c. It is the intent of these Executive Orders that, wherever possible, Federal agencies implement the floodplains/wetlands requirements through existing procedures, such as those internal procedures established to implement the National Environmental Policy Act (NEPA) and OMB A-95 review procedures. In those instances where the environmental impacts of a proposed action are not significant enough to require an environmental impact statement (EIS) pursuant to section 102(2)(C) of NEPA, or where programs are not subject to the requirements of NEPA, alternative but equivalent floodplain/wetlands evaluation and notice procedures must be established.

Section 2 Purpose

a. The purpose of this Statement of Procedures is to set forth Agency policy and guidance for carrying out the provisions of Executive Orders 11988 and 11990.

b. EPA program offices shall amend existing regulations and procedures to incorporate the policies and procedures set forth in this Statement of Procedures.

c. To the extent possible, EPA shall accommodate the requirements of Executive Orders 11988 and 11990 through the Agency NEPA procedures contained in 40 CFR part 6.

Section 3 Policy

a. The Agency shall avoid wherever possible the long and short term impacts associated with the destruction of wetlands and the occupancy and modification of floodplains and wetlands, and avoid direct and indirect support of floodplain and wetlands development wherever there is a practicable alternative.

b. The Agency shall incorporate floodplain management goals and wetlands protection considerations into its planning, regulatory, and decisionmaking processes. It shall also promote the preservation and restoration of floodplains so that their natural and beneficial values can be realized. To the extent possible EPA shall:

(1) Reduce the hazard and risk of flood loss and wherever it is possible to avoid direct or indirect adverse impact on floodplains;

(2) Where there is no practical alternative to locating in a floodplain, minimize the impact of floods on human safety, health, and welfare, as well as the natural environment;

(3) Restore and preserve natural and beneficial values served by floodplains;

(4) Require the construction of EPA structures and facilities to be in accordance with the standards and criteria, of the regulations promulgated pursuant to the National Flood Insurance Program;

(5) Identify floodplains which require restoration and preservation and recommend management programs necessary to protect these floodplains and to include such considerations as part of on-going planning programs; and

(6) Provide the public with early and continuing information concerning floodplain management and with opportunities for participating in decision making

including the (evaluation of) tradeoffs among competing alternatives.

c. The Agency shall incorporate wetlands protection considerations into its planning, regulatory, and decisionmaking processes. It shall minimize the destruction, loss, or degradation of wetlands and preserve and enhance the natural and beneficial values of wetlands. Agency activities shall continue to be carried out consistent with the Administrator's Decision Statement No. 4 dated February 21, 1973 entitled "EPA Policy to Protect the Nation's Wetlands."

Section 4 Definitions

a. Base Flood means that flood which has a one percent chance of occurrence in any given year (also known as a 100-year flood). This term is used in the National Flood Insurance Program (NFIP) to indicate the minimum level of flooding to be used by a community in its floodplain management regulations.

b. Base Floodplain means the land area covered by a 100-year flood (one percent chance floodplain). Also see definition of floodplain.

c. Flood or Flooding means a general and temporary condition of partial or complete inundation of normally dry land areas from the overflow of inland and/or tidal waters, and/or the unusual and rapid accumulation or runoff of surface waters from any source, or flooding from any other source.

d. Floodplain means the lowland and relatively flat areas adjoining inland and coastal waters and other floodprone areas such as offshore islands, including at a minimum, that area subject to a one percent or greater chance of flooding in any given year. The base floodplain shall be used to designate the 100-year floodplain (one percent chance floodplain). The critical action floodplain is defined as the 500-year floodplain (0.2 percent chance floodplain).

e. Floodproofing means modification of individual structures and facilities, their sites, and their contents to protect against structural failure, to keep water out or to reduce effects of water entry.

f. Minimize means to reduce to the smallest possible amount or degree.

g. Practicable means capable of being done within existing constraints. The test of what is practicable depends upon the situation and includes consideration of the pertinent factors such as environment, community welfare, cost, or technology.

h. Preserve means to prevent modification to the natural floodplain environment or to maintain it as closely as possible to its natural state.

i. Restore means to re-establish a setting or environment in which the natural functions of the floodplain can again operate.

j. Wetlands means those areas that are inundated by surface or ground water with a frequency sufficient to support and under normal circumstances does or would support a prevalence of vegetative or aquatic life that requires saturated or seasonally saturated soil conditions for growth and reproduction. Wetlands generally include swamps, marshes, bogs, and similar areas such as sloughs, potholes, wet meadows, river overflows, mud flats, and natural ponds.

Section 5 Applicability

a. The Executive Orders apply to activities of Federal agencies pertaining to (1) acquiring, managing, and disposing of Federal lands and facilities, (2) providing Federally undertaken, financed, or assisted construction and improvements, and (3) conducting Federal activities and programs affecting land use, including but not limited to water and related land resources planning, regulating, and licensing activities.

b. These procedures shall apply to EPA's programs as follows: (1) All Agency actions involving construction of facilities or management of lands or property. This will require amendment of the EPA Facilities Management Manual (October 1973 and revisions thereafter).

(2) All Agency actions where the NEPA process applies. This would include the programs under sections 306/402 of the Clean Water Act pertaining to new source permitting and section 201 of the Clean Water Act pertaining to wastewater treatment construction grants.

(3) All agency actions where there is sufficient independent statutory authority to carry out the floodplain/wetlands procedures.

(4) In program areas where there is no EIS requirement nor clear statutory authority for EPA to require procedural implementation, EPA shall continue to provide leadership and offer guidance so that the value of floodplain management and wetlands protection can be understood and carried out to the maximum extent practicable in these programs.

c. These procedures shall not apply to any permitting or source review programs of EPA once such authority has been transferred or delegated to a State.

However, EPA shall, to the extent possible, require States to provide equivalent effort to assure support for the objectives of these procedures as part of the State assumption process.

Section 6 Requirements

a. Floodplain/Wetlands review of proposed Agency actions.

(1) Floodplain/Wetlands Determination— Before undertaking an Agency action, each program office must determine whether or not the action will be located in or affect a floodplain or wetlands. The Agency shall utilize maps prepared by the Federal Insurance Administration of the Federal Emergency Management Agency (Flood Insurance Rate Maps or Flood Hazard Boundary Maps), Fish and Wildlife Service (National Wetlands Inventory Maps), and other appropriate agencies to determine whether a proposed action is located in or will likely affect a floodplain or wetlands. If there is no floodplain/wetlands impact identified, the action may proceed without further consideration of the remaining procedures set forth below.

(2) Early Public Notice—When it is apparent that a proposed or potential agency action is likely to impact a floodplain or wetlands, the public should be informed through appropriate public notice procedures.

(3) Floodplain/Wetlands Assessment—If the Agency determines a proposed action is located in or affects a floodplain or wetlands, a floodplain/wetlands assessment shall be undertaken. For those actions where an environmental assessment (EA) or environmental impact statement (EIS) is prepared pursuant to 40 CFR part 6, the floodplain/wetlands assessment shall be prepared concurrently with these analyses and shall be included in the EA or EIS. In all other cases, a floodplain/wetlands assessment shall be prepared. Assessments shall consist of a description of the proposed action, a discussion of its effect on the floodplain/wetlands, and shall also describe the alternatives considered.

(4) Public Review of Assessments—For proposed actions impacting floodplain/wetlands where an EA or EIS is prepared, the opportunity for public review will be provided through the EIS provisions contained in 40 CFR parts 6, 25, or 35, where appropriate. In other cases, an equivalent public notice of the floodplain/wetlands assessment shall be made consistent with the public involvement requirements of the applicable program.

(5) Minimize, Restore or Preserve—If there is no practicable alternative to locating in or affecting the floodplain or wetlands, the Agency shall act to minimize potential harm to the floodplain or wetlands. The Agency shall also act to restore and preserve the natural and beneficial values of floodplains and wetlands as part of the analysis of all alternatives under consideration.

(6) Agency Decision—After consideration of alternative actions, as they have been modified in the preceding analysis, the Agency shall select the desired alternative. For all Agency actions proposed to be in or affecting a floodplain/wetlands, the Agency shall provide further public notice announcing this decision. This decision shall be accompanied by a Statement of Findings, not to exceed three pages. This Statement shall include: (i) The reasons why the proposed action must be located in or affect the floodplain or wetlands; (ii) a description of significant facts considered in making the decision to locate in or affect the floodplain or wetlands including alternative sites and actions; (iii) a statement indicating whether the proposed action conforms to applicable State or local floodplain protection standards; (iv) a description of the steps taken to design or modify the proposed action to minimize potential harm to or within the floodplain or wetlands; and (v) a statement indicating how the proposed action affects the natural or beneficial values of the floodplain or wetlands. If the provisions of 40 CFR part 6 apply, the Statement of Findings may be incorporated in the final EIS or in the environmental assessment. In other cases, notice should be placed in the Federal Register or other local medium and copies sent to Federal, State, and local agencies and other entities which submitted comments or are otherwise concerned with the floodplain/wetlands assessment. For floodplain actions subject to Office of Management and Budget (OMB) Circular A-95, the Agency shall send the Statement of Findings to State and areawide A-95 clearinghouse in the geographic area affected. At least 15 working days shall be allowed for public and interagency review of the Statement of Findings.

(7) Authorizations/Appropriations—Any requests for new authorizations or appropriations transmitted to OMB shall include, a floodplain/wetlands assessment and, for floodplain impacting actions, a Statement of Findings, if a proposed action will be located in a floodplain or wetlands.

b. Lead agency concept. To the maximum extent possible, the Agency shall relay on the lead agency concept to carry out the provisions set forth in section 6.a of this appendix. Therefore, when EPA and another Federal agency have related actions, EPA shall work with the other agency to identify which agency shall take the lead in satisfying these procedural requirements and thereby avoid duplication of efforts.

c. Additional floodplain management provisions relating to Federal property and facilities.

(1) Construction Activities—EPA controlled structures and facilities must be constructed in accordance with existing criteria and standards set forth under the NFIP and must include mitigation of adverse impacts wherever feasible. Deviation from these requirements may occur only to the extent NFIP standards are demonstrated as inappropriate for a given structure or facility.

(2) Flood Protection Measures—If newly constructed structures or facilities are to be located in a floodplain, accepted floodproofing and other flood protection measures shall be undertaken. To achieve flood protection, EPA shall, wherever practicable, elevate structures above the base flood level rather than filling land.

(3) Restoration and Preservation—As part of any EPA plan or action, the potential for restoring and preserving floodplains and wetlands so that their natural and beneficial values can be realized must be considered and incorporated into the plan or action wherever feasible.

(4) Property Used by Public—If property used by the public has suffered damage or is located in an identified flood hazard area, EPA shall provide on structures, and other places where appropriate, conspicuous indicators of past and probable flood height to enhance public knowledge of flood hazards.

(5) Transfer of EPA Property—When property in flood plains is proposed for lease, easement, right-of-way, or disposal to non-Federal public or private parties, EPA shall reference in the conveyance those uses that are restricted under Federal, State and local floodplain regulations and attach other restrictions to uses of the property as may be deemed appropriate. Notwithstanding, EPA shall consider withholding such properties from conveyance.

Section 7 Implementation

a. Pursuant to section 2, the EPA program offices shall amend existing regulations, procedures, and guidance, as appropriate, to incorporate the policies and procedures set forth in this Statement of Procedures. Such amendments shall be made within six months of the date of these Procedures.

b. The Office of External Affairs (OEA) is responsible for the oversight of the implementation of this Statement of Procedures and shall be given advanced opportunity to review amendments to regulations, procedures, and guidance. OEA shall coordinate efforts with the program offices to develop necessary manuals and more specialized supplementary guidance to carry out this Statement of Procedures.

[44 FR 64177, Nov. 6, 1976, as amended at 50 FR 26323, June 25, 1985]

NEPA Deskbook

Appendix 13 Federal Energy Regulatory Commission Regulations and Procedures (FERC Part 380)

18 CFR Pt. 380

Part 380—Regulations Implementing the National Environmental Policy Act

Authority:
42 U.S.C. 4321-4370h, 7101-7352; E.O. 12009, 3 CFR 1978 Comp., p. 142.

Source:
Order 486, 52 FR 47910, Dec. 17, 1987, unless otherwise noted.

§380.1   Purpose.

The regulations in this part implement the Federal Energy Regulatory Commission's procedures under the National Environmental Policy Act of 1969 (NEPA). These regulations supplement the regulations of the Council on Environmental Quality, 40 CFR parts 1500 through 1508. The Commission will comply with the regulations of the Council on Environmental Quality except where those regulations are inconsistent with the statutory requirements of the Commission.

[Order 486, 52 FR 47910, Dec. 17, 1987, as amended by Order 756, 77 FR 4895, Feb. 1, 2012]

§380.2   Definitions and terminology.

For purposes of this part—

(a) Categorical exclusion means a category of actions described in § 380.4, which do not individually or cumulatively have a significant effect on the human environment and which the Commission has found to have no such effect and for which, therefore, neither an environmental assessment nor an environmental impact statement is required. The Commission may decide to prepare environmental assessments for the reasons stated in § 380.4(b).

(b) Commission means the Federal Energy Regulatory Commission.

(c) Council means the Council on Environmental Quality.

(d) Environmental assessment means a concise public document for which the Commission is responsible that serves to:

(1) Briefly provide sufficient evidence and analysis for determining whether to prepare an environmental impact statement or a finding of no significant impact.

(2) Aid the Commission's compliance with NEPA when no environmental impact statement is necessary.

(3) Facilitate preparation of a statement when one is necessary. Environmental assessments must include brief discussions of the need for the proposal, of alternatives as required by section 102(2)(E) of NEPA, of the environmental impacts of the proposed action and alternatives, and a listing of agencies and persons consulted.

(e) Environmental impact statement (EIS) means a detailed written statement as required by section 102(2)(C) of NEPA. DEIS means a draft EIS and FEIS means a final EIS.

(f) Environmental report or ER means that part of an application submitted to the Commission by an applicant for authorization of a proposed action which includes information concerning the environment, the applicant's analysis of the environmental impact of the action, or alternatives to the action required by this or other applicable statutes or regulations.

(g) Finding of no significant impact (FONSI) means a document by the Commission briefly presenting the reason why an action, not otherwise excluded by § 380.4, will not have a significant effect on the human environment and for which an environmental impact statement therefore will not be prepared. It must include the environmental assessment or a summary of it and must note other environmental documents related to it. If the assessment is included, the FONSI need not repeat any of the discussion in the assessment but may incorporate it by reference.

§380.3   Environmental information to be supplied by an applicant.

(a) An applicant must submit information as follows:

(1) For any proposed action identified in §§ 380.5 and 380.6, an environmental report with the proposal as prescribed in paragraph (c) of this section.

(2) For any proposal not identified in paragraph (a)(1) of this section, any environmental information that the Commission may determine is necessary for compliance with these regulations, the regulations of the Council, NEPA and other Federal laws such as the Endangered Species Act, the National Historic Preservation Act or the Coastal Zone Management Act.

(b) An applicant must also:

(1) Provide all necessary or relevant information to the Commission;

(2) Conduct any studies that the Commission staff considers necessary or relevant to determine the impact of the proposal on the human environment and natural resources;

(3) Consult with appropriate Federal, regional, State, and local agencies during the planning stages of the proposed action to ensure that all potential environmental impacts are identified. (The specific requirements for consultation on hydropower projects are contained in § 4.38 and § 16.8 of this chapter and in section 4(a) of the Electric Consumers Protection Act, Pub. L. No. 99-495, 100 Stat. 1243, 1246 (1986));

(4) Submit applications for all Federal and State approvals as early as possible in the planning process; and

(5) Notify the Commission staff of all other Federal actions required for completion of the proposed action so that the staff may coordinate with other interested Federal agencies.

(c) Content of an applicant's environmental report for specific proposals—1) Hydropower projects. The information required for specific project applications under part 4 or 16 of this chapter.

(2) Natural gas projects. (i) For any application filed under the Natural Gas Act for any proposed action

identified in §§ 380.5 or 380.6, except for prior notice filings under § 157.208, as described in § 380.5(b), the information identified in § 380.12 and Appendix A of this part.

(ii) For prior notice filings under § 157.208, the report described by § 157.208(c)(11) of this chapter.

(3) Electric transmission project. For pre-filing requests and applications filed under section 216 of the Federal Power Act identified in §§ 380.5(b)(14) and 380.6(a)(5).

[Order 486, 52 FR 47910, Dec. 17, 1987, as amended by Order 533, 56 FR 23155, May 20, 1991; Order 603, 64 FR 26611, May 14, 1999; Order 689, 71 FR 69470, Dec. 1, 2006; Order 756, 77 FR 4895, Feb. 1, 2012]

§380.4   Projects or actions categorically excluded.

(a) General rule. Except as stated in paragraph (b) of this section, neither an environmental assessment nor an environmental impact statement will be prepared for the following projects or actions:

(1) Procedural, ministerial, or internal administrative and management actions, programs, or decisions, including procurement, contracting, personnel actions, correction or clarification of filings or orders, and acceptance, rejection and dismissal of filings;

(2)(i) Reports or recommendations on legislation not initiated by the Commission, and

(ii) Proposals for legislation and promulgation of rules that are clarifying, corrective, or procedural, or that do not substantially change the effect of legislation or regulations being amended;

(3) Compliance and review actions, including investigations (jurisdictional or otherwise), conferences, hearings, notices of probable violation, show cause orders, and adjustments under section 502(c) of the Natural Gas Policy Act of 1978 (NGPA);

(4) Review of grants or denials by the Department of Energy (DOE) of any adjustment request, and review of contested remedial orders issued by DOE;

(5) Information gathering, analysis, and dissemination;

(6) Conceptual or feasibility studies;

(7) Actions concerning the reservation and classification of United States lands as water power sites and other actions under section 24 of the Federal Power Act;

(8) Transfers of water power project licenses and transfers of exemptions under Part I of the Federal Power Act and Part 9 of this chapter;

(9) Issuance of preliminary permits for water power projects under Part I of the Federal Power Act and Part 4 of this chapter;

(10) Withdrawals of applications for certificates under the Natural Gas Act, or for water power project preliminary permits, exemptions, or licenses under Part I of the Federal Power Act and Part 4 of this chapter;

(11) Actions concerning annual charges or headwater benefits, charges for water power projects under Parts 11 and 13 of this chapter and establishment of fees to be paid by an applicant for a license or exemption required to meet the terms and conditions of section 30(c) of the Federal Power Act;

(12) Approval for water power projects under Part I of the Federal Power Act, of "as built" or revised drawings or exhibits that propose no changes to project works or operations or that reflect changes that have previously been approved or required by the Commission;

(13) Surrender and amendment of preliminary permits, and surrender of water power licenses and exemptions where no project works exist or ground disturbing activity has occurred and amendments to water power licenses and exemptions that do not require ground disturbing activity or changes to project works or operation;

(14) Exemptions for small conduit hydroelectric facilities as defined in §§ 4.30(b)(26) of this chapter under Part I of the Federal Power Act and Part 4 of this chapter;

(15) Electric rate filings submitted by public utilities under sections 205 and 206 of the Federal Power Act, the establishment of just and reasonable rates, and confirmation, approval, and disapproval of rate filings submitted by Federal power marketing agencies under the Pacific Northwest Electric Power Planning and Conservation Act, the Department of Energy Organization Act, and DOE Delegation Order No. 0204-108.

(16) Approval of actions under sections 4(b), 203, 204, 301, 304, and 305 of the Federal Power Act relating to issuance and purchase of securities, acquisition or disposition of property, merger, interlocking directorates, jurisdictional determinations and accounting orders;

(17) Approval of electrical interconnections and wheeling under sections 202(b), 210, 211, and 212 of the Federal Power Act, that would not entail:

(i) Construction of a new substation or expansion of the boundaries of an existing substation;

(ii) Construction of any transmission line that operates at more than 115 kilovolts (KV) and occupies more than ten miles of an existing right-of-way; or

(iii) Construction of any transmission line more than one mile long if located on a new right-of-way;

(18) Approval of changes in land rights for water power projects under Part I of the Federal Power Act and Part 4 of this chapter, if no construction or change in land use is either proposed or known by the Commission to be contemplated for the land affected;

(19) Approval of proposals under Part I of the Federal Power Act and Part 4 of this chapter to authorize use of water power project lands or waters for gas or electric utility distribution lines, radial (sub-transmission) lines, communications lines and cables, storm drains, sewer lines not discharging into project waters, water mains, piers, landings, boat docks, or similar structures and facilities, landscaping or embankments, bulkheads, retaining walls, or similar shoreline erosion control structures;

(20) Action on applications for exemption under section 1(c) of the Natural Gas Act;

(21) Approvals of blanket certificate applications and prior notice filings under § 157.204 and §§ 157.209 through 157.218 of this chapter;

(22) Approvals of blanket certificate applications under §§ 284.221 through 284.224 of this chapter;

(23) Producers' applications for the sale of gas filed under §§ 157.23 through 157.29 of this chapter;

(24) Approval under section 7 of the Natural Gas Act of taps, meters, and regulating facilities located completely within an existing natural gas pipeline right-of-way or compressor station if company records show the land use of the vicinity has not changed since the original facilities were installed, and no significant nonjurisdictional facilities would be constructed in association with construction of the interconnection facilities;

(25) Review of natural gas rate filings, including any curtailment plans other than those specified in § 380.5(b)(5), and establishment of rates for transportation and sale of natural gas under sections 4 and 5 of the Natural Gas Act and sections 311 and 401 through 404 of the Natural Gas Policy Act of 1978;

(26) Review of approval of oil pipeline rate filings under Parts 340 and 341 of this chapter;

(27) Sale, exchange, and transportation of natural gas under sections 4, 5 and 7 of the Natural Gas Act that require no construction of facilities;

(28) Abandonment in place of a minor natural gas pipeline (short segments of buried pipe of 6-inch inside diameter or less), or abandonment by removal of minor surface facilities such as metering stations, valves, and taps under section 7 of the Natural Gas Act so long as appropriate erosion control and site restoration takes place;

(29) Abandonment of service under any gas supply contract pursuant to section 7 of the Natural Gas Act;

(30) Approval of filing made in compliance with the requirements of a certificate for a natural gas project under section 7 of the Natural Gas Act or a preliminary permit, exemption, license, or license amendment order for a water power project under Part I of the Federal Power Act;

(31) Abandonment of facilities by sale that involves only minor or no ground disturbance to disconnect the facilities from the system;

(32) Conversion of facilities from use under the NGPA to use under the NGA;

(33) Construction or abandonment of facilities constructed entirely in Federal offshore waters that has been approved by the Minerals Management Service and the Corps of Engineers, as necessary;

(34) Abandonment or construction of facilities on an existing offshore platform;

(35) Abandonment, construction or replacement of a facility (other than compression) solely within an existing building within a natural gas facility (other than LNG facilities), if it does not increase the noise or air emissions from the facility, as a whole; and

(36) Conversion of compression to standby use if the compressor is not moved, or abandonment of compression if the compressor station remains in operation.

(b) Exceptions to categorical exclusions. (1) In accordance with 40 CFR 1508.4, the Commission and its staff will independently evaluate environmental information supplied in an application and in comments by the public. Where circumstances indicate that an action may be a major Federal action significantly affecting the quality of the human environment, the Commission:

(i) May require an environmental report or other additional environmental information, and

(ii) Will prepare an environmental assessment or an environmental impact statement.

(2) Such circumstances may exist when the action may have an effect on one of the following:

(i) Indian lands;

(ii) Wilderness areas;

(iii) Wild and scenic rivers;

(iv) Wetlands;

(v) Units of the National Park System, National Refuges, or National Fish Hatcheries;

(vi) Anadromous fish or endangered species; or

(vii) Where the environmental effects are uncertain.

However, the existence of one or more of the above will not automatically require the submission of an environmental report or the preparation of an environmental assessment or an environmental impact statement.

[Order 486, 52 FR 47910, Dec. 17, 1987, as amended at 53 FR 8177, Mar. 14, 1988; Order 486-B, 53 FR 26437, July 13, 1988; 54 FR 48740, Nov. 27, 1989; Order 603, 64 FR 26611, May 14, 1999; Order 609, 64 FR 57392, Oct. 25, 1999; Order 756, 77 FR 4895, Feb. 1, 2012]

§380.5   Actions that require an environmental assessment.

(a) An environmental assessment will normally be prepared first for the actions identified in this section. Depending on the outcome of the environmental assessment, the Commission may or may not prepare an environmental impact statement. However, depending on the location or scope of the proposed action, or the resources affected, the Commission may in specific circumstances proceed directly to prepare an environmental impact statement.

(b) The projects subject to an environmental assessment are as follows:

(1) Except as identified in §§ 380.4, 380.6 and 2.55 of this chapter, authorization for the site of new gas import/export facilities under DOE Delegation No. 0204-112 and authorization under section 7 of the

Natural Gas Act for the construction, replacement, or abandonment of compression, processing, or interconnecting facilities, onshore and offshore pipelines, metering facilities, LNG peak-shaving facilities, or other facilities necessary for the sale, exchange, storage, or transportation of natural gas;

(2) Prior notice filings under § 157.208 of this chapter for the rearrangement of any facility specified in §§ 157.202 (b)(3) and (6) of this chapter or the acquisition, construction, or operation of any eligible facility as specified in §§ 157.202 (b)(2) and (3) of this chapter;

(3) Abandonment or reduction of natural gas service under section 7 of the Natural Gas Act unless excluded under § 380.4 (a)(21), (28) or (29);

(4) Except as identified in § 380.6, conversion of existing depleted oil or natural gas fields to underground storage fields under section 7 of the Natural Gas Act.

(5) New natural gas curtailment plans, or any amendment to an existing curtailment plan under section 4 of the Natural Gas Act and sections 401 through 404 of the Natural Gas Policy Act of 1978 that has a major effect on an entire pipeline system;

(6) Licenses under Part I of the Federal Power Act and part 4 of this chapter for construction of any water power project—existing dam;

(7) Exemptions under section 405 of the Public Utility Regulatory Policies Act of 1978, as amended, and §§ 4.30(b)(29) and 4.101-4.108 of this chapter for small hydroelectric power projects of 5 MW or less;

(8) Licenses for additional project works at licensed projects under Part I of the Federal Power Act whether or not these are styled license amendments or original licenses;

(9) Licenses under Part I of the Federal Power Act and part 4 of this chapter for transmission lines only;

(10) Applications for new licenses under section 15 of the Federal Power Act;

(11) Approval of electric interconnections and wheeling under section 202(b), 210, 211, and 212 of the Federal Power Act, unless excluded under § 380.4(a)(17);

(12) Regulations or proposals for legislation not included under § 380.4(a)(2);

(13) Surrender of water power licenses and exemptions where project works exist or ground disturbing activity has occurred and amendments to water power licenses

and exemptions that require ground disturbing activity or changes to project works or operations; and

(14) Except as identified in § 380.6, authorization to site new electric transmission facilities under section 216 of the Federal Power Act and DOE Delegation Order No. 00-004.00A.

[Order 486, 52 FR 47910, Dec. 17, 1987; Order 486, 53 FR 4817, Feb. 17, 1988, as amended by 53 FR 8177, Mar. 14, 1988; Order 486-B, 53 FR 26437, July 13, 1988; Order 689, 71 FR 69470, Dec. 1, 2006; Order 756, 77 FR 4895, Feb. 1, 2012]

§380.6   Actions that require an environmental impact statement.

(a) Except as provided in paragraph (b) of this section, an environmental impact statement will normally be prepared first for the following projects:

(1) Authorization under sections 3 or 7 of the Natural Gas Act and DOE Delegation Order No. 0204-112 for the siting, construction, and operation of jurisdictional liquefied natural gas import/export facilities used wholly or in part to liquefy, store, or regasify liquefied natural gas transported by water;

(2) Certificate applications under section 7 of the Natural Gas Act to develop an underground natural gas storage facility except where depleted oil or natural gas producing fields are used;

(3) Major pipeline construction projects under section 7 of the Natural Gas Act using rights-of-way in which there is no existing natural gas pipeline;

(4) Licenses under Part I of the Federal Power Act and part 4 of this chapter for construction of any unconstructed water power projects; and

(5) Major electric transmission facilities under section 216 of the Federal Power Act and DOE Delegation Order No. 00-004.00A using right-of-way in which there is no existing facility.

(b) If the Commission believes that a proposed action identified in paragraph (a) of this section may not be a major Federal action significantly affecting the quality of the human environment, an environmental assessment, rather than an environmental impact statement, will be prepared first. Depending on the outcome of the environmental assessment, an environmental impact statement may or may not be prepared.

(c) An environmental impact statement will not be required if an environmental assessment indicates that a proposal has adverse environmental affects and the proposal is not approved.

[Order 486, 52 FR 47910, Dec. 17, 1987, as amended at 53 FR 8177, Mar. 14, 1988; Order 486-B, 53 FR 26437, July 13, 1988; Order 689, 71 FR 69470, Dec. 1, 2006; Order 756, 77 FR 4895, Feb. 1, 2012]

§380.7 Format of an environmental impact statement.

In addition to the requirements for an environmental impact statement prescribed in 40 CFR 1502.10 of the regulations of the Council, an environmental impact statement prepared by the Commission will include a section on the literature cited in the environmental impact statement and a staff conclusion section. The staff conclusion section will include summaries of:

(a) The significant environmental impacts of the proposed action;

(b) Any alternative to the proposed action that would have a less severe environmental impact or impacts and the action preferred by the staff;

(c) Any mitigation measures proposed by the applicant, as well as additional mitigation measures that might be more effective;

(d) Any significant environmental impacts of the proposed action that cannot be mitigated; and

(e) References to any pending, completed, or recommended studies that might provide baseline data or additional data on the proposed action.

§380.8 Preparation of environmental documents.

The preparation of environmental documents, as defined in § 1508.10 of the regulations of the Council (40 CFR 1508.10), on hydroelectric projects, natural gas facilities, and electric transmission facilities in national interest electric transmission corridors is the responsibility of the Commission's Office of Energy Projects, 888 First Street NE., Washington, DC 20426, (202) 502-8700. Persons interested in status reports or information on environmental impact statements or other elements of the NEPA process, including the studies or other information the Commission may require on these projects, can contact this office.

[Order 689, 71 FR 69471, Dec. 1, 2006, as amended by Order 756, 77 FR 4895, Feb. 1, 2012]

§380.9 Public availability of NEPA documents and public notice of NEPA related hearings and public meetings.

(a)(1) The Commission will comply with the requirements of 40 CFR 1506.6 of the regulations of the Council for public involvement in NEPA.

(2) If an action has effects of primarily local concern, the Commission may give additional notice in a Commission order.

(b) The Commission will make environmental impact statements, environmental assessments, the comments received, and any underlaying documents available to the public pursuant to the provisions of the Freedom of Information Act (5 U.S.C. 552 (1982)). The exclusion in the Freedom of Information Act for interagency memoranda is not applicable where such memoranda transmit comments of Federal agencies on the environmental impact of the proposed action. Such materials will be made available to the public at the Commission's Public Reference Room at 888 First Street NE., Room 2A, Washington, DC 20426 at a fee and in the manner described in Part 388 of this chapter. A copy of an environmental impact statement or environmental assessment for hydroelectric projects may also be made available for inspection at the Commission's regional office for the region where the proposed action is located.

[Order 486, 52 FR 47910, Dec. 17, 1987, as amended by Order 603-A, 64 FR 54537, Oct. 7, 1999]

§380.10 Participation in Commission proceedings.

(a) Intervention proceedings involving a party or parties—1) Motion to intervene. (i) In addition to submitting comments on the NEPA process and NEPA related documents, any person may file a motion to intervene in a Commission proceeding dealing with environmental issues under the terms of § 385.214 of this chapter. Any person who files a motion to intervene on the basis of a draft environmental impact statement will be deemed to have filed a timely motion, in accordance with § 385.214, as long as the motion is filed within the comment period for the draft environmental impact statement.

(ii) Any person that is granted intervention after petitioning becomes a party to the proceeding and accepts the record as developed by the parties as of the time that intervention is granted.

(2)(i) Issues not set for trial-type hearing. An intervenor who takes a position on any environmental issue that has not yet been set for hearing must file a timely motion with the Secretary containing an analysis of its position on such issue and specifying any differences with the position of Commission staff or an applicant upon which the intervenor wishes to be heard at a hearing.

(ii) Issues set for trial-type hearing. (A) Any intervenor that takes a position on an environmental issue set for hearing may offer evidence for the record in support of such position and otherwise participate in accordance with the Commission's Rules of Practice and Procedure. Any intervenor must specify any differences from the staff's and the applicant's positions.

(B) To be considered, any facts or opinions on an environmental issue set for hearing must be admitted into evidence and made part of the record of the proceeding.

(iii) Commission pre-filing activities commenced under §§ 157.21 and 50.5 of this chapter, respectively, are not considered proceedings under part 385 of this chapter and are not open to motions to intervene. Once an application is filed under part 157 subpart A or part 50 of this chapter, any person may file a motion to intervene in accordance with §§ 157.10 or 50.10 of this chapter or in accordance with this section.

(b) Rulemaking proceedings. Any person may file comments on any environmental issue in a rulemaking proceeding.

[Order 486, 52 FR 47910, Dec. 17, 1987, as amended by Order 689, 71 FR 69471, Dec. 1, 2006]

§380.11　Environmental decisionmaking.

(a) Decision points. For the actions which require an environmental assessment or environmental impact statement, environmental considerations will be addressed at appropriate major decision points.

(1) In proceedings involving a party or parties and not set for trial-type hearing, major decision points are the approval or denial of proposals by the Commission or its designees.

(2) In matters set for trial-type hearing, the major decision points are the initial decision of an administrative law judge or the decision of the Commission.

(3) In a rulemaking proceeding, the major decision points are the Notice of Proposed Rulemaking and the Final Rule.

(b) Environmental documents as part of the record. The Commission will include environmental assessments, findings of no significant impact, or environmental impact statements, and any supplements in the record of the proceeding.

(c) Application denials. Notwithstanding any provision in this part, the Commission may dismiss or deny an application without performing an environmental impact statement or without undertaking environmental analysis.

§380.12　Environmental reports for Natural Gas Act applications.

(a) Introduction. (1) The applicant must submit an environmental report with any application that proposes the construction, operation, or abandonment of any facility identified in § 380.3(c)(2)(i). The environmental report shall consist of the thirteen resource reports and related material described in this section.

(2) The detail of each resource report must be commensurate with the complexity of the proposal and its potential for environmental impact. Each topic in each resource report shall be addressed or its omission justified, unless the resource report description indicates that the data is not required for that type of proposal. If material required for one resource report is provided in another resource report or in another exhibit, it may be incorporated by reference. If any resource report topic is required for a particular project but is not provided at the time the application is filed, the environmental report shall explain why it is missing and when the applicant anticipates it will be filed.

(3) The appendix to this part contains a checklist of the minimum filing requirements for an environmental report. Failure to provide at least the applicable checklist items will result in rejection of the application unless the Director of the Office of Energy Projects determines that the applicant has provided an acceptable reason for the item's absence and an acceptable schedule for filing it. Failure to file within the accepted schedule will result in rejection of the application.

(b) General requirements. As appropriate, each resource report shall:

(1) Address conditions or resources that might be directly or indirectly affected by the project;

(2) Identify significant environmental effects expected to occur as a result of the project;

(3) Identify the effects of construction, operation (including maintenance and malfunctions), and ter-

mination of the project, as well as cumulative effects resulting from existing or reasonably foreseeable projects;

(4) Identify measures proposed to enhance the environment or to avoid, mitigate, or compensate for adverse effects of the project;

(5) Provide a list of publications, reports, and other literature or communications, including agency contacts, that were cited or relied upon to prepare each report. This list should include the name and title of the person contacted, their affiliations, and telephone number;

(6) Whenever this section refers to "mileposts" the applicant may substitute "survey centerline stationing" if so desired. However, whatever method is chosen should be used consistently throughout the resource reports.

(c) Resource Report 1—General project description. This report is required for all applications. It will describe facilities associated with the project, special construction and operation procedures, construction timetables, future plans for related construction, compliance with regulations and codes, and permits that must be obtained. Resource Report 1 must:

(1) Describe and provide location maps of all jurisdictional facilities, including all aboveground facilities associated with the project (such as: meter stations, pig launchers/receivers, valves), to be constructed, modified, abandoned, replaced, or removed, including related construction and operational support activities and areas such as maintenance bases, staging areas, communications towers, power lines, and new access roads (roads to be built or modified). As relevant, the report must describe the length and diameter of the pipeline, the types of aboveground facilities that would be installed, and associated land requirements. It must also identify other companies that must construct jurisdictional facilities related to the project, where the facilities would be located, and where they are in the Commission's approval process.

(2) Identify and describe all nonjurisdictional facilities, including auxiliary facilities, that will be built in association with the project, including facilities to be built by other companies.

(i) Provide the following information:

(A) A brief description of each facility, including as appropriate: Ownership, land requirements, gas consumption, megawatt size, construction status, and an update of the latest status of Federal, state, and local permits/approvals;

(B) The length and diameter of any interconnecting pipeline;

(C) Current 1:24,000/1:25,000 scale topographic maps showing the location of the facilities;

(D) Correspondence with the appropriate State Historic Preservation Officer (SHPO) or duly authorized Tribal Historic Preservation Officer (THPO) for tribal lands regarding whether properties eligible for listing on the National Register of Historic Places (NRHP) would be affected;

(E) Correspondence with the U.S. Fish and Wildlife Service (and National Marine Fisheries Service, if appropriate) regarding potential impacts of the proposed facility on federally listed threatened and endangered species; and

(F) For facilities within a designated coastal zone management area, a consistency determination or evidence that the owner has requested a consistency determination from the state's coastal zone management program.

(ii) Address each of the following factors and indicate which ones, if any, appear to indicate the need for the Commission to do an environmental review of project-related nonjurisdictional facilities.

(A) Whether or not the regulated activity comprises "merely a link" in a corridor type project (e.g., a transportation or utility transmission project).

(B) Whether there are aspects of the nonjurisdictional facility in the immediate vicinity of the regulated activity which uniquely determine the location and configuration of the regulated activity.

(C) The extent to which the entire project will be within the Commission's jurisdiction.

(D) The extent of cumulative Federal control and responsibility.

(3) Provide the following maps and photos:

(i) Current, original United States Geological Survey (USGS) 7.5-minute series topographic maps or maps of equivalent detail, covering at least a 0.5-mile-wide corridor centered on the pipeline, with integer mileposts identified, showing the location of rights-of-way, new access roads, other linear construction areas, compressor stations, and pipe storage areas. Show nonlinear construction areas on maps at a scale of 1:3,600 or larger keyed graphically and by milepost to the right-of-way maps.

(ii) Original aerial images or photographs or photo-based alignment sheets based on these sources, not more than 1 year old (unless older ones accurately depict current land use and development) and with a scale of 1:6,000 or larger, showing the proposed pipeline route and location of major aboveground facilities, covering at least a 0.5 mile-wide corridor, and including mileposts. Older images/photographs/alignment sheets should be modified to show any residences not depicted in the original. Alternative formats (e.g., blue-line prints of acceptable resolution) need prior approval by the environmental staff of the Office of Energy Projects.

(iii) In addition to the copy required under § 157.6(a)(2) of this chapter, applicant should send two additional copies of topographic maps and aerial images/photographs directly to the environmental staff of the Office of Energy Projects.

(4) When new or additional compression is proposed, include large scale (1:3,600 or greater) plot plans of each compressor station. The plot plan should reference a readily identifiable point(s) on the USGS maps required in paragraph (c)(3) of this section. The maps and plot plans must identify the location of the nearest noise-sensitive areas (schools, hospitals, or residences) within 1 mile of the compressor station, existing and proposed compressor and auxiliary buildings, access roads, and the limits of areas that would be permanently disturbed.

(5)(i) Identify facilities to be abandoned, and state how they would be abandoned, how the site would be restored, who would own the site or right-of-way after abandonment, and who would be responsible for any facilities abandoned in place.

(ii) When the right-of-way or the easement would be abandoned, identify whether landowners were given the opportunity to request that the facilities on their property, including foundations and below ground components, be removed. Identify any landowners whose preferences the company does not intend to honor, and the reasons therefore.

(6) Describe and identify by milepost, proposed construction and restoration methods to be used in areas of rugged topography, residential areas, active croplands, sites where the pipeline would be located parallel to and under roads, and sites where explosives are likely to be used.

(7) Unless provided in response to Resource Report 5, describe estimated workforce requirements, including the number of pipeline construction spreads, average workforce requirements for each construction spread and meter or compressor station, estimated duration of construction from initial clearing to final restoration, and number of personnel to be hired to operate the proposed project.

(8) Describe reasonably foreseeable plans for future expansion of facilities, including additional land requirements and the compatibility of those plans with the current proposal.

(9) Describe all authorizations required to complete the proposed action and the status of applications for such authorizations. Identify environmental mitigation requirements specified in any permit or proposed in any permit application to the extent not specified elsewhere in this section.

(10) Provide the names and mailing addresses of all affected landowners specified in § 157.6(d) and certify that all affected landowners will be notified as required in § 157.6(d).

(d) Resource Report 2—Water use and quality. This report is required for all applications, except those which involve only facilities within the areas of an existing compressor, meter, or regulator station that were disturbed by construction of the existing facilities, no wetlands or waterbodies are on the site and there would not be a significant increase in water use. The report must describe water quality and provide data sufficient to determine the expected impact of the project and the effectiveness of mitigative, enhancement, or protective measures. Resource Report 2 must:

(1) Identify and describe by milepost perennial waterbodies and municipal water supply or watershed areas, specially designated surface water protection areas and sensitive waterbodies, and wetlands that would be crossed. For each waterbody crossing, identify the approximate width, state water quality classifications, any known potential pollutants present in the water or sediments, and any potable water intake sources within 3 miles downstream.

(2) Compare proposed mitigation measures with the staff's current "Wetland and Waterbody Construction and Mitigation Procedures," which are available from the Commission Internet home page or the Commission staff, describe what proposed alternative mitigation would provide equivalent or greater protection to the environment, and provide a description of site-specific construction techniques that would be used at each major waterbody crossing.

(3) Describe typical staging area requirements at waterbody and wetland crossings. Also, identify and describe waterbodies and wetlands where staging areas are likely to be more extensive.

(4) Include National Wetland Inventory (NWI) maps. If NWI maps are not available, provide the appropriate state wetland maps. Identify for each crossing, the milepost, the wetland classification specified by the U.S. Fish and Wildlife Service, and the length of the crossing. Include two copies of the NWI maps (or the substitutes, if NWI maps are not available) clearly showing the proposed route and mileposts directed to the environmental staff. Describe by milepost, wetland crossings as determined by field delineations using the current Federal methodology.

(5) Identify aquifers within excavation depth in the project area, including the depth of the aquifer, current and projected use, water quality and average yield, and known or suspected contamination problems.

(6) Describe specific locations, the quantity required, and the method and rate of withdrawal and discharge of hydrostatic test water. Describe suspended or dissolved material likely to be present in the water as a result of contact with the pipeline, particularly if an existing pipeline is being retested. Describe chemical or physical treatment of the pipeline or hydrostatic test water. Discuss waste products generated and disposal methods.

(7) If underground storage of natural gas is proposed:

(i) Identify how water produced from the storage field will be disposed of, and

(ii) For salt caverns, identify the source locations, the quantity required, and the method and rate of withdrawal of water for creating salt cavern(s), as well as the means of disposal of brine resulting from cavern leaching.

(8) Discuss proposed mitigation measures to reduce the potential for adverse impacts to surface water, wetlands, or groundwater quality to the extent they are not described in response to paragraph (d)(2) of this section. Discuss the potential for blasting to affect water wells, springs, and wetlands, and measures to be taken to detect and remedy such effects.

(9) Identify the location of known public and private groundwater supply wells or springs within 150 feet of proposed construction areas. Identify locations of EPA or state-designated sole-source aquifers and wellhead protection areas crossed by the proposed pipeline facilities.

(e) Resource Report 3—Fish, wildlife, and vegetation. This report is required for all applications, except those involving only facilities within the improved area of an existing compressor, meter, or regulator station. It must describe aquatic life, wildlife, and vegetation in the vicinity of the proposed project; expected impacts on these resources including potential effects on biodiversity; and proposed mitigation, enhancement or protection measures. Resource Report 3 must:

(1) Describe commercial and recreational warmwater, coldwater, and saltwater fisheries in the affected area and associated significant habitats such as spawning or rearing areas and estuaries.

(2) Describe terrestrial habitats, including wetlands, typical wildlife habitats, and rare, unique, or otherwise significant habitats that might be affected by the proposed action. Describe typical species that have commercial, recreational, or aesthetic value.

(3) Describe and provide the acreage of vegetation cover types that would be affected, including unique ecosystems or communities such as remnant prairie or old-growth forest, or significant individual plants, such as old-growth specimen trees.

(4) Describe the impact of construction and operation on aquatic and terrestrial species and their habitats, including the possibility of a major alteration to ecosystems or biodiversity, and any potential impact on state-listed endangered or threatened species. Describe the impact of maintenance, clearing and treatment of the project area on fish, wildlife, and vegetation. Surveys may be required to determine specific areas of significant habitats or communities of species of special concern to state or local agencies.

(5) Identify all federally listed or proposed endangered or threatened species and critical habitat that potentially occur in the vicinity of the project. Discuss the results of the consultation requirements listed in § 380.13(b) at least through § 380.13(b)(5)(i) and include any written correspondence that resulted from the consultation. The initial application must include the results of any required surveys unless seasonal considerations make this impractical. If species surveys are impractical, there must be field surveys to determine the presence of suitable habitat unless the entire project area is suitable habitat.

(6) Identify all federally listed essential fish habitat (EFH) that potentially occurs in the vicinity of the project. Provide information on all EFH, as identified by the pertinent Federal fishery management plans, that may be adversely affected by the project and the

results of abbreviated consultations with NMFS, and any resulting EFH assessments.

(7) Describe site-specific mitigation measures to minimize impacts on fisheries, wildlife, and vegetation.

(8) Include copies of correspondence not provided pursuant to paragraph (e)(5) of this section, containing recommendations from appropriate Federal and state fish and wildlife agencies to avoid or limit impact on wildlife, fisheries, and vegetation, and the applicant's response to the recommendations.

(f) Resource Report 4—Cultural resources. This report is required for all applications. In preparing this report, the applicant must follow the principles in § 380.14 of this part. Guidance on the content and the format for the documentation listed below, as well as professional qualifications of preparers, is detailed in " Office of Energy Projects' (OEP) Guidelines for Reporting on Cultural Resources Investigations," which is available from the Commission Internet home page or from the Commission staff.

(1) Resource Report 4 must contain:

(i) Documentation of the applicant's initial cultural resources consultation, including consultations with Native Americans and other interested persons (if appropriate);

(ii) Overview and Survey Reports, as appropriate;

(iii) Evaluation Report, as appropriate;

(iv) Treatment Plan, as appropriate; and

(v) Written comments from State Historic Preservation Officer(s) (SHPO), Tribal Historic Preservation Officers (THPO), as appropriate, and applicable land-managing agencies on the reports in paragraphs (f)(1)(i)-(iv) of this section.

(2) Initial filing requirements. The initial application must include the documentation of initial cultural resource consultation, the Overview and Survey Reports, if required, and written comments from SHPOs, THPOs and land-managing agencies, if available. The initial cultural resources consultations should establish the need for surveys. If surveys are deemed necessary by the consultation with the SHPO/THPO, the survey report must be filed with the application.

(i) If the comments of the SHPOs, THPOs, or land-management agencies are not available at the time the application is filed, they may be filed separately, but they must be filed before a final certificate is issued.

(ii) If landowners deny access to private property and certain areas are not surveyed, the unsurveyed area must be identified by mileposts, and supplemental surveys or evaluations shall be conducted after access is granted. In such circumstances, reports, and treatment plans, if necessary, for those inaccessible lands may be filed after a certificate is issued.

(3) The Evaluation Report and Treatment Plan, if required, for the entire project must be filed before a final certificate is issued.

(i) The Evaluation Report may be combined in a single synthetic report with the Overview and Survey Reports if the SHPOs, THPOs, and land-management agencies allow and if it is available at the time the application is filed.

(ii) In preparing the Treatment Plan, the applicant must consult with the Commission staff, the SHPO, and any applicable THPO and land-management agencies.

(iii) Authorization to implement the Treatment Plan will occur only after the final certificate is issued.

(4) Applicant must request privileged treatment for all material filed with the Commission containing location, character, and ownership information about cultural resources in accordance with § 388.112 of this chapter. The cover and relevant pages or portions of the report should be clearly labeled in bold lettering: "CONTAINS PRIVILEGED INFORMATION—DO NOT RELEASE."

(5) Except as specified in a final Commission order, or by the Director of the Office of Energy Projects, construction may not begin until all cultural resource reports and plans have been approved.

(g) Resource Report 5—Socioeconomics. This report is required only for applications involving significant aboveground facilities, including, among others, conditioning or liquefied natural gas (LNG) plants. It must identify and quantify the impacts of constructing and operating the proposed project on factors affecting towns and counties in the vicinity of the project. Resource Report 5 must:

(1) Describe the socioeconomic impact area.

(2) Evaluate the impact of any substantial immigration of people on governmental facilities and services and plans to reduce the impact on the local infrastructure.

(3) Describe on-site manpower requirements and payroll during construction and operation, including the

number of construction personnel who currently reside within the impact area, would commute daily to the site from outside the impact area, or would relocate temporarily within the impact area.

(4) Determine whether existing housing within the impact area is sufficient to meet the needs of the additional population.

(5) Describe the number and types of residences and businesses that would be displaced by the project, procedures to be used to acquire these properties, and types and amounts of relocation assistance payments.

(6) Conduct a fiscal impact analysis evaluating incremental local government expenditures in relation to incremental local government revenues that would result from construction of the project. Incremental expenditures include, but are not limited to, school operating costs, road maintenance and repair, public safety, and public utility costs.

(h) Resource Report 6—Geological resources. This report is required for applications involving LNG facilities and all other applications, except those involving only facilities within the boundaries of existing aboveground facilities, such as a compressor, meter, or regulator station. It must describe geological resources and hazards in the project area that might be directly or indirectly affected by the proposed action or that could place the proposed facilities at risk, the potential effects of those hazards on the facility, and methods proposed to reduce the effects or risks. Resource Report 6 must:

(1) Describe, by milepost, mineral resources that are currently or potentially exploitable;

(2) Describe, by milepost, existing and potential geological hazards and areas of nonroutine geotechnical concern, such as high seismicity areas, active faults, and areas susceptible to soil liquefaction; planned, active, and abandoned mines; karst terrain; and areas of potential ground failure, such as subsidence, slumping, and landsliding. Discuss the hazards posed to the facility from each one.

(3) Describe how the project would be located or designed to avoid or minimize adverse effects to the resources or risk to itself, including geotechnical investigations and monitoring that would be conducted before, during, and after construction. Discuss also the potential for blasting to affect structures, and the measures to be taken to remedy such effects.

(4) Specify methods to be used to prevent project-induced contamination from surface mines or from mine tailings along the right-of-way and whether the project would hinder mine reclamation or expansion efforts.

(5) If the application involves an LNG facility located in zones 2, 3, or 4 of the Uniform Building Code's Seismic Risk Map, or where there is potential for surface faulting or liquefaction, prepare a report on earthquake hazards and engineering in conformance with "Data Requirements for the Seismic Review of LNG Facilities," NBSIR 84-2833. This document may be obtained from the Commission staff.

(6) If the application is for underground storage facilities:

(i) Describe how the applicant would control and monitor the drilling activity of others within the field and buffer zone;

(ii) Describe how the applicant would monitor potential effects of the operation of adjacent storage or production facilities on the proposed facility, and vice versa;

(iii) Describe measures taken to locate and determine the condition of old wells within the field and buffer zone and how the applicant would reduce risk from failure of known and undiscovered wells; and

(iv) Identify and discuss safety and environmental safeguards required by state and Federal drilling regulations.

(i) Resource Report 7—Soils. This report is required for all applications except those not involving soil disturbance. It must describe the soils that would be affected by the proposed project, the effect on those soils, and measures proposed to minimize or avoid impact. Resource Report 7 must:

(1) List, by milepost, the soil associations that would be crossed and describe the erosion potential, fertility, and drainage characteristics of each association.

(2) If an aboveground facility site is greater than 5 acres:

(i) List the soil series within the property and the percentage of the property comprised of each series;

(ii) List the percentage of each series which would be permanently disturbed;

(iii) Describe the characteristics of each soil series; and

(iv) Indicate which are classified as prime or unique farmland by the U.S. Department of Agriculture, Natural Resources Conservation Service.

(3) Identify, by milepost, potential impact from: Soil erosion due to water, wind, or loss of vegetation; soil compaction and damage to soil structure resulting from movement of construction vehicles; wet soils and soils with poor drainage that are especially prone to structural damage; damage to drainage tile systems due to movement of construction vehicles and trenching activities; and interference with the operation of agricultural equipment due to the probability of large stones or blasted rock occurring on or near the surface as a result of construction.

(4) Identify, by milepost, cropland and residential areas where loss of soil fertility due to trenching and backfilling could occur.

(5) Describe proposed mitigation measures to reduce the potential for adverse impact to soils or agricultural productivity. Compare proposed mitigation measures with the staff's current "Upland Erosion Control, Revegetation and Maintenance Plan," which is available from the Commission Internet home page or from the Commission staff, and explain how proposed mitigation measures provide equivalent or greater protections to the environment.

(j) Resource Report 8—Land use, recreation and aesthetics. This report is required for all applications except those involving only facilities which are of comparable use at existing compressor, meter, and regulator stations. It must describe the existing uses of land on, and (where specified) within 0.25 mile of, the proposed project and changes to those land uses that would occur if the project is approved. The report shall discuss proposed mitigation measures, including protection and enhancement of existing land use. Resource Report 8 must:

(1) Describe the width and acreage requirements of all construction and permanent rights-of-way and the acreage required for each proposed plant and operational site, including injection or withdrawal wells.

(i) List, by milepost, locations where the proposed right-of-way would be adjacent to existing rights-of-way of any kind.

(ii) Identify, preferably by diagrams, existing rights-of-way that would be used for a portion of the construction or operational right-of-way, the overlap and how much additional width would be required.

(iii) Identify the total amount of land to be purchased or leased for each aboveground facility, the amount of land that would be disturbed for construction and operation of the facility, and the use of the remaining land not required for project operation.

(iv) Identify the size of typical staging areas and expanded work areas, such as those at railroad, road, and waterbody crossings, and the size and location of all pipe storage yards and access roads.

(2) Identify, by milepost, the existing use of lands crossed by the proposed pipeline, or on or adjacent to each proposed plant and operational site.

(3) Describe planned development on land crossed or within 0.25 mile of proposed facilities, the time frame (if available) for such development, and proposed coordination to minimize impacts on land use. Planned development means development which is included in a master plan or is on file with the local planning board or the county.

(4) Identify, by milepost and length of crossing, the area of direct effect of each proposed facility and operational site on sugar maple stands, orchards and nurseries, landfills, operating mines, hazardous waste sites, state wild and scenic rivers, state or local designated trails, nature preserves, game management areas, remnant prairie, old-growth forest, national or state forests, parks, golf courses, designated natural, recreational or scenic areas, or registered natural landmarks, Native American religious sites and traditional cultural properties to the extent they are known to the public at large, and reservations, lands identified under the Special Area Management Plan of the Office of Coastal Zone Management, National Oceanic and Atmospheric Administration, and lands owned or controlled by Federal or state agencies or private preservation groups. Also identify if any of those areas are located within 0.25 mile of any proposed facility.

(5) Identify, by milepost, all residences and buildings within 50 feet of the proposed pipeline construction right-of-way and the distance of the residence or building from the right-of-way. Provide survey drawings or alignment sheets to illustrate the location of the facilities in relation to the buildings.

(6) Describe any areas crossed by or within 0.25 mile of the proposed pipeline or plant and operational sites which are included in, or are designated for study for inclusion in: The National Wild and Scenic Rivers System (16 U.S.C. 1271); The National Trails System (16 U.S.C. 1241); or a wilderness area designated under the Wilderness Act (16 U.S.C. 1132).

(7) For facilities within a designated coastal zone management area, provide a consistency determination or evidence that the applicant has requested a consistency determination from the state's coastal zone management program.

(8) Describe the impact the project will have on present uses of the affected area as identified above, including commercial uses, mineral resources, recreational areas, public health and safety, and the aesthetic value of the land and its features. Describe any temporary or permanent restrictions on land use resulting from the project.

(9) Describe mitigation measures intended for all special use areas identified under paragraphs (j)(2) through (6) of this section.

(10) Describe proposed typical mitigation measures for each residence that is within 50 feet of the edge of the pipeline construction right-of-way, as well as any proposed residence-specific mitigation. Describe how residential property, including for example, fences, driveways, stone walls, sidewalks, water supply, and septic systems, would be restored. Describe compensation plans for temporary and permanent rights-of-way and the eminent domain process for the affected areas.

(11) Describe measures proposed to mitigate the aesthetic impact of the facilities especially for aboveground facilities such as compressor or meter stations.

(12) Demonstrate that applications for rights-of-way or other proposed land use have been or soon will be filed with Federal land-management agencies with jurisdiction over land that would be affected by the project.

(k) Resource Report 9—Air and noise quality. This report is required for applications involving compressor facilities at new or existing stations, and for all new LNG facilities. It must identify the effects of the project on the existing air quality and noise environment and describe proposed measures to mitigate the effects. Resource Report 9 must:

(1) Describe the existing air quality, including background levels of nitrogen dioxide and other criteria pollutants which may be emitted above EPA-identified significance levels.

(2) Quantitatively describe existing noise levels at noise-sensitive areas, such as schools, hospitals, or residences and include any areas covered by relevant state or local noise ordinances.

(i) Report existing noise levels as the Leq (day), Leq (night), and Ldn and include the basis for the data or estimates.

(ii) For existing compressor stations, include the results of a sound level survey at the site property line and nearby noise-sensitive areas while the compressors are operated at full load.

(iii) For proposed new compressor station sites, measure or estimate the existing ambient sound environment based on current land uses and activities.

(iv) Include a plot plan that identifies the locations and duration of noise measurements, the time of day, weather conditions, wind speed and direction, engine load, and other noise sources present during each measurement.

(3) Estimate the impact of the project on air quality, including how existing regulatory standards would be met.

(i) Provide the emission rate of nitrogen oxides from existing and proposed facilities, expressed in pounds per hour and tons per year for maximum operating conditions, include supporting calculations, emission factors, fuel consumption rates, and annual hours of operation.

(ii) For major sources of air emissions (as defined by the Environmental Protection Agency), provide copies of applications for permits to construct (and operate, if applicable) or for applicability determinations under regulations for the prevention of significant air quality deterioration and subsequent determinations.

(4) Provide a quantitative estimate of the impact of the project on noise levels at noise-sensitive areas, such as schools, hospitals, or residences.

(i) Include step-by-step supporting calculations or identify the computer program used to model the noise levels, the input and raw output data and all assumptions made when running the model, far-field sound level data for maximum facility operation, and the source of the data.

(ii) Include sound pressure levels for unmuffled engine inlets and exhausts, engine casings, and cooling equipment; dynamic insertion loss for all mufflers; sound transmission loss for all compressor building components, including walls, roof, doors, windows and ventilation openings; sound attenuation from the station to nearby noise-sensitive areas; the manufacturer's name, the model number, the performance rating; and a description of each noise source and noise control component to be employed at the proposed compressor station. For proposed compressors the initial filing must include at least the proposed horsepower, type of compression, and energy source for the compressor.

(iii) Far-field sound level data measured from similar units in service elsewhere, when available, may be substituted for manufacturer's far-field sound level data.

(iv) If specific noise control equipment has not been chosen, include a schedule for submitting the data prior to certification.

(v) The estimate must demonstrate that the project will comply with applicable noise regulations and show how the facility will meet the following requirements:

(A) The noise attributable to any new compressor station, compression added to an existing station, or any modification, upgrade or update of an existing station, must not exceed a day- night sound level (Ldn) of 55 dBA at any pre-existing noise-sensitive area (such as schools, hospitals, or residences).

(B) New compressor stations or modifications of existing stations shall not result in a perceptible increase in vibration at any noise-sensitive area.

(5) Describe measures and manufacturer's specifications for equipment proposed to mitigate impact to air and noise quality, including emission control systems, installation of filters, mufflers, or insulation of piping and buildings, and orientation of equipment away from noise-sensitive areas.

(l) Resource Report 10—Alternatives. This report is required for all applications. It must describe alternatives to the project and compare the environmental impacts of such alternatives to those of the proposal. The discussion must demonstrate how environmental benefits and costs were weighed against economic benefits and costs, and technological and procedural constraints. The potential for each alternative to meet project deadlines and the environmental consequences of each alternative shall be discussed. Resource Report 10 must:

(1) Discuss the "no action" alternative and the potential for accomplishing the proposed objectives through the use of other systems and/or energy conservation. Provide an analysis of the relative environmental benefits and costs for each alternative.

(2) Describe alternative routes or locations considered for each facility during the initial screening for the project.

(i) For alternative routes considered in the initial screening for the project but eliminated, describe the environmental characteristics of each route or site, and the reasons for rejecting it. Identify the location of such alternatives on maps of sufficient scale to depict their location and relationship to the proposed action, and the relationship of the pipeline to existing rights-of-way.

(ii) For alternative routes or locations considered for more in-depth consideration, describe the environmental characteristics of each route or site and the reasons for rejecting it. Provide comparative tables showing the differences in environmental characteristics for the alternative and proposed action. The location of any alternatives in this paragraph shall be provided on maps equivalent to those required in paragraph (c)(2) of this section.

(m) Resource Report 11—Reliability and safety. This report is required for applications involving new or recommissioned LNG facilities. Information previously filed with the Commission need not be refiled if the applicant verifies its continued validity. This report shall address the potential hazard to the public from failure of facility components resulting from accidents or natural catastrophes, how these events would affect reliability, and what procedures and design features have been used to reduce potential hazards. Resource Report 11 must:

(1) Describe measures proposed to protect the public from failure of the proposed facilities (including coordination with local agencies).

(2) Discuss hazards, the environmental impact, and service interruptions which could reasonably ensue from failure of the proposed facilities.

(3) Discuss design and operational measures to avoid or reduce risk.

(4) Discuss contingency plans for maintaining service or reducing downtime.

(5) Describe measures used to exclude the public from hazardous areas. Discuss measures used to minimize problems arising from malfunctions and accidents (with estimates of probability of occurrence) and identify standard procedures for protecting services and public safety during maintenance and breakdowns.

(n) Resource Report 12—PCB contamination. This report is required for applications involving the replacement, abandonment by removal, or abandonment in place of pipeline facilities determined to have polychlorinated biphenyls (PCBs) in excess of 50 ppm in pipeline liquids. Resource Report 12 must:

(1) Provide a statement that activities would comply with an approved EPA disposal permit, with the dates of issuance and expiration specified, or with the requirements of the Toxic Substances Control Act.

(2) For compressor station modifications on sites that have been determined to have soils contaminated with PCBs, describe the status of remediation efforts completed to date.

(o) Resource Report 13—Engineering and design material. This report is required for construction of new liquefied natural gas (LNG) facilities, or the recommissioning of existing LNG facilities. If the recommissioned facility is existing and is not being replaced, relocated, or significantly altered, resubmittal of information already on file with the Commission is unnecessary. Resource Report 13 must:

(1) Provide a detailed plot plan showing the location of all major components to be installed, including compression, pretreatment, liquefaction, storage, transfer piping, vaporization, truck loading/unloading, vent stacks, pumps, and auxiliary or appurtenant service facilities.

(2) Provide a detailed layout of the fire protection system showing the location of fire water pumps, piping, hydrants, hose reels, dry chemical systems, high expansion foam systems, and auxiliary or appurtenant service facilities.

(3) Provide a layout of the hazard detection system showing the location of combustible-gas detectors, fire detectors, heat detectors, smoke or combustion product detectors, and low temperature detectors. Identify those detectors that activate automatic shutdowns and the equipment that would shut down. Include all safety provisions incorporated in the plant design, including automatic and manually activated emergency shutdown systems.

(4) Provide a detailed layout of the spill containment system showing the location of impoundments, sumps, subdikes, channels, and water removal systems.

(5) Provide manufacturer's specifications, drawings, and literature on the fail-safe shut-off valve for each loading area at a marine terminal (if applicable).

(6) Provide a detailed layout of the fuel gas system showing all taps with process components.

(7) Provide copies of company, engineering firm, or consultant studies of a conceptual nature that show the engineering planning or design approach to the construction of new facilities or plants.

(8) Provide engineering information on major process components related to the first six items above, which include (as applicable) function, capacity, type, manufacturer, drive system (horsepower, voltage), operating pressure, and temperature.

(9) Provide manuals and construction drawings for LNG storage tank(s).

(10) Provide up-to-date piping and instrumentation diagrams. Include a description of the instrumentation and control philosophy, type of instrumentation (pneumatic, electronic), use of computer technology, and control room display and operation. Also, provide an overall schematic diagram of the entire process flow system, including maps, materials, and energy balances.

(11) Provide engineering information on the plant's electrical power generation system, distribution system, emergency power system, uninterruptible power system, and battery backup system.

(12) Identify all codes and standards under which the plant (and marine terminal, if applicable) will be designed, and any special considerations or safety provisions that were applied to the design of plant components.

(13) Provide a list of all permits or approvals from local, state, Federal, or Native American groups or Indian agencies required prior to and during construction of the plant, and the status of each, including the date filed, the date issued, and any known obstacles to approval. Include a description of data records required for submission to such agencies and transcripts of any public hearings by such agencies. Also provide copies of any correspondence relating to the actions by all, or any, of these agencies regarding all required approvals.

(14) Identify how each applicable requirement will comply with 49 CFR part 193 and the National Fire Protection Association 59A LNG Standards. For new facilities, the siting requirements of 49 CFR part 193, subpart B, must be given special attention. If applicable, vapor dispersion calculations from LNG spills over water should also be presented to ensure compliance with the U.S. Coast Guard's LNG regulations in 33 CFR part 127.

(15) Provide seismic information specified in Data Requirements for the Seismic Review of LNG facili-

ties (NBSIR 84-2833, available from FERC staff) for facilities that would be located in zone 2, 3, or 4 of the Uniform Building Code Seismic Map of the United States.

[Order 603, 64 FR 26611, May 14, 1999, as amended by Order 603-A, 64 FR 54537, Oct. 7, 1999; Order 609, 64 FR 57392, Oct. 25, 1999; Order 699, 72 FR 45328, Aug. 14, 2007; Order 756, 77 FR 4895, Feb. 1, 2012]

§380.13 Compliance with the Endangered Species Act.

(a) Definitions. For purposes of this section:

(1) Listed species and critical habitat have the same meaning as provided in 50 CFR 402.02.

(2) Project area means any area subject to construction activities (for example, material storage sites, temporary work areas, and new access roads) necessary to install or abandon the facilities.

(b) Procedures for informal consultation—(1) Designation of non-Federal representative. The project sponsor is designated as the Commission's non-Federal representative for purposes of informal consultations with the U.S. Fish and Wildlife Service (FWS) and the National Marine Fisheries Service (NMFS) under the Endangered Species Act of 1973, as amended (ESA).

(2) Consultation requirement. (i) Prior to the filing of the environmental report specified in § 380.12, the project sponsor must contact the appropriate regional or field office of the FWS or the NMFS, or both if appropriate, to initiate informal consultations, unless it is proceeding pursuant to a blanket clearance issued by the FWS and/or NMFS which is less than 1 year old and the clearance does not specify more frequent consultation.

(ii) If a blanket clearance is more than 1 year old or less than 1 year old and specifies more frequent consultations, or if the project sponsor is not proceeding pursuant to a blanket clearance, the project sponsor must request a list of federally listed or proposed species and designated or proposed critical habitat that may be present in the project area, or provide the consulted agency with such a list for its concurrence.

(iii) The consulted agency will provide a species and critical habitat list or concur with the species list provided within 30 days of its receipt of the initial request. In the event that the consulted agency does not provide this information within this time period, the project sponsor may notify the Director of the Office of

Energy Projects and continue with the remaining procedures of this section.

(3) End of informal consultation. (i) At any time during the informal consultations, the consulted agency may determine or confirm:

(A) That no listed or proposed species, or designated or proposed critical habitat, occurs in the project area; or

(B) That the project is not likely to adversely affect a listed species or critical habitat;

(ii) If the consulted agency provides the determination or confirmation described in paragraph (b)(3)(i) of this section, no further consultation is required.

(4) Potential impact to proposed species. (i) If the consulted agency, pursuant to informal consultations, initially determines that any species proposed to be listed, or proposed critical habitat, occurs in the project area, the project sponsor must confer with the consulted agency on methods to avoid or reduce the potential impact.

(ii) The project sponsor shall include in its proposal, a discussion of any mitigating measures recommended through the consultation process.

(5) Continued informal consultations for listed species. (i) If the consulted agency initially determines, pursuant to the informal consultations, that a listed species or designated critical habitat may occur in the project area, the project sponsor must continue informal consultations with the consulted agency to determine if the proposed project may affect the species or designated critical habitat. These consultations may include discussions with experts (including experts provided by the consulted agency), habitat identification, field surveys, biological analyses, and the formulation of mitigation measures. If the provided information indicates that the project is not likely to adversely affect a listed species or critical habitat, the consulting agency will provide a letter of concurrence which completes informal consultation.

(ii) The project sponsor must prepare a Biological Assessment unless the consulted agency indicates that the proposed project is not likely to adversely affect a specific listed species or its designated critical habitat. The Biological Assessment must contain the following information for each species contained in the consulted agency's species list:

(A) Life history and habitat requirements;

(B) Results of detailed surveys to determine if individuals, populations, or suitable, unoccupied habitat exists in the proposed project's area of effect;

(C) Potential impacts, both beneficial and negative, that could result from the construction and operation of the proposed project, or disturbance associated with the abandonment, if applicable; and

(D) Proposed mitigation that would eliminate or minimize these potential impacts.

(iii) All surveys must be conducted by qualified biologists and must use FWS and/or NMFS approved survey methodology. In addition, the Biological Assessment must include the following information:

(A) Name(s) and qualifications of person(s) conducting the survey;

(B) Survey methodology;

(C) Date of survey(s); and

(D) Detailed and site-specific identification of size and location of all areas surveyed.

(iv) The project sponsor must provide a draft Biological Assessment directly to the environmental staff of the Office of Energy Projects for review and comment and/or submission to the consulted agency. If the consulted agency fails to provide formal comments on the Biological Assessment to the project sponsor within 30 days of its receipt, as specified in 50 CFR 402.120, the project sponsor may notify the Director, OEP, and follow the procedures in paragraph (c) of this section.

(v) The consulted agency's comments on the Biological Assessment's determination must be filed with the Commission.

(c) Notification to Director. In the event that the consulted agency fails to respond to requests by the project sponsor under paragraph (b) of this section, the project sponsor must notify the Director of the Office of Energy Projects. The notification must include all information, reports, letters, and other correspondence prepared pursuant to this section. The Director will determine whether:

(1) Additional informal consultation is required;

(2) Formal consultation must be initiated under paragraph (d) of this section; or

(3) Construction may proceed.

(d) Procedures for formal consultation. (1) In the event that formal consultation is required pursuant to paragraphs (b)(5)(v) or (c)(2) of this section, the Commission staff will initiate formal consultation with the FWS and/or NMFS, as appropriate, and will request that the consulted agency designate a lead Regional Office, lead Field/District Office, and Project Manager, as necessary, to facilitate the formal consultation process. In addition, the Commission will designate a contact for formal consultation purposes.

(2) During formal consultation, the consulted agency, the Commission, and the project sponsor will coordinate and consult to determine potential impacts and mitigation which can be implemented to minimize impacts. The Commission and the consulted agency will schedule coordination meetings and/or field visits as necessary.

(3) The formal consultation period will last no longer than 90 days, unless the consulted agency, the Commission, and project sponsor mutually agree to an extension of this time period.

(4) The consulted agency will provide the Commission with a Biological Opinion on the proposed project, as specified in 50 CFR 402.14(e), within 45 days of the completion of formal consultation.

[Order 603, 64 FR 26617, May 14, 1999, as amended by Order 699, 72 FR 45328, Aug. 14, 2007]

§380.14 Compliance with the National Historic Preservation Act.

(a) Section 106 of the National Historic Preservation Act, as amended (16 U.S.C. 470(f)) (NHPA), requires the Commission to take into account the effect of a proposed project on any historic property and to afford the Advisory Council on Historic Preservation (Council) an opportunity to comment on projects if required under 36 CFR 800. The project sponsor, as a non-Federal party, assists the Commission in meeting its obligations under NHPA section 106 and the implementing regulations at 36 CFR part 800 by following the procedures at § 380.12(f). The project sponsor may contact the Commission at any time for assistance. The Commission will review the resultant filings.

(1) The Commission's NHPA section 106 responsibilities apply to public and private lands, unless subject to the provisions of paragraph (a)(2) of this section. The project sponsor will assist the Commission in taking into account the views of interested parties, Native Americans, and tribal leaders.

(2) If Federal or Tribal land is affected by a proposed project, the project sponsor shall adhere to any requirements for cultural resources studies of the applicable Federal land- managing agencies on Federal lands and any tribal requirements on Tribal lands. The project sponsor must identify, in Resource Report 4 filed with the application, the status of cultural resources studies on Federal or Tribal lands, as applicable.

(3) The project sponsor must consult with the SHPO(s) and THPOs, if appropriate. If the SHPO or THPO declines to consult with the project sponsor, the project sponsor shall not continue with consultations, except as instructed by the Director of the Office of Energy Projects.

(4) If the project is covered by an agreement document among the Commission, Council, SHPO(s), THPO(s), land-managing agencies, project sponsors, and interested persons, as appropriate, then that agreement will provide for compliance with NHPA section 106, as applicable.

(b) [Reserved]

[Order 603, 64 FR 26618, May 14, 1999, as amended by Order 699, 72 FR 45329, Aug. 14, 2007; Order 756, 77 FR 4895, Feb. 1, 2012]

§380.15 Siting and maintenance requirements.

(a) Avoidance or minimization of effects. The siting, construction, and maintenance of facilities shall be undertaken in a way that avoids or minimizes effects on scenic, historic, wildlife, and recreational values.

(b) Landowner consideration. The desires of landowners should be taken into account in the planning, locating, clearing, and maintenance of rights-of-way and the construction of facilities on their property, so long as the result is consistent with applicable requirements of law, including laws relating to land-use and any requirements imposed by the Commission.

(c) Safety regulations. The requirements of this paragraph do not affect a project sponsor's obligations to comply with safety regulations of the U.S. Department of Transportation and recognized safe engineering practices for Natural Gas Act projects and the National Electric Safety Code for section 216 Federal Power Act projects.

(d) Pipeline and electric transmission facilities construction. (1) The use, widening, or extension of existing rights-of-way must be considered in locating proposed facilities.

(2) In locating proposed facilities, the project sponsor shall, to the extent practicable, avoid places listed on, or eligible for listing on, the National Register of Historic Places; natural landmarks listed on the National Register of Natural Landmarks; officially designated parks; wetlands; and scenic, recreational, and wildlife lands. If rights-of-way must be routed near or through such places, attempts should be made to minimize visibility from areas of public view and to preserve the character and existing environment of the area.

(3) Rights-of-way should avoid forested areas and steep slopes where practical.

(4) Rights-of-way clearing should be kept to the minimum width necessary.

(5) In selecting a method to clear rights-of-way, soil stability and protection of natural vegetation and adjacent resources should be taken into account.

(6) Trees and vegetation cleared from rights-of-way in areas of public view should be disposed of without undue delay.

(7) Remaining trees and shrubs should not be unnecessarily damaged.

(8) Long foreground views of cleared rights-of-way through wooded areas that are visible from areas of public view should be avoided.

(9) Where practical, rights-of-way should avoid crossing hills and other high points at their crests where the crossing is in a forested area and the resulting notch is clearly visible in the foreground from areas of public view.

(10) Screen plantings should be employed where rights-of-way enter forested areas from a clearing and where the clearing is plainly visible in the foreground from areas of public view.

(11) Temporary roads should be designed for proper drainage and built to minimize soil erosion. Upon abandonment, the road area should be restored and stabilized without undue delay.

(e) Right-of-way maintenance. (1) Vegetation covers established on a right-of-way should be properly maintained.

(2) Access and service roads should be maintained with proper cover, water bars, and the proper slope to minimize soil erosion. They should be jointly used with other utilities and land-management agencies where practical.

(3) Chemical control of vegetation should not be used unless authorized by the landowner or land-managing agency. When chemicals are used for control of vegetation, they should be approved by EPA for such use and used in conformance with all applicable regulations.

(f) Construction of aboveground facilities. (1) Unobtrusive sites should be selected for the location of aboveground facilities.

(2) Aboveground facilities should cover the minimum area practicable.

(3) Noise potential should be considered in locating compressor stations, or other aboveground facilities.

(4) The exterior of aboveground facilities should be harmonious with the surroundings and other buildings in the area.

(5) For Natural Gas Act projects, the site of aboveground facilities which are visible from nearby residences or public areas, should be planted in trees and shrubs, or other appropriate landscaping and should be installed to enhance the appearance of the facilities, consistent with operating needs.

[Order 603, 64 FR 26619, May 14, 1999, as amended by Order 689, 71 FR 69741, Dec. 1, 2006; Order 756, 77 FR 4895, Feb. 1, 2012]

§380.16   Environmental reports for section 216 Federal Power Act Permits.

(a) Introduction. (1) The applicant must submit an environmental report with any application that proposes the construction or modification of any facility identified in § 380.3(c)(3). The environmental report must include the 11 resource reports and related material described in this section.

(2) The detail of each resource report must be commensurate with the complexity of the proposal and its potential for environmental impact. Each topic in each resource report must be addressed or its omission justified, unless the data is not required for that type of proposal. If material required for one resource report is provided in another resource report or in another exhibit, it may be cross referenced. If any resource report topic is required for a particular project but is not provided at the time the application is filed, the environmental report must explain why it is missing and when the applicant anticipates it will be filed.

(b) General requirements. As appropriate, each resource report must:

(1) Address conditions or resources that are likely to be directly or indirectly affected by the project;

(2) Identify significant environmental effects expected to occur as a result of the project;

(3) Identify the effects of construction, operation (including maintenance and malfunctions), as well as cumulative effects resulting from existing or reasonably foreseeable projects;

(4) Identify measures proposed to enhance the environment or to avoid, mitigate, or compensate for adverse effects of the project; and

(5) Provide a list of publications, reports, and other literature or communications, including agency contacts, that were cited or relied upon to prepare each report. This list must include the names and titles of the persons contacted, their affiliations, and telephone numbers.

(6) Whenever this section refers to "mileposts" the applicant may substitute "survey centerline stationing" if so preferred. However, whatever method is chosen must be used consistently throughout the resource reports.

(c) Resource Report 1—General project description. This report must describe facilities associated with the project, special construction and operation procedures, construction timetables, future plans for related construction, compliance with regulations and codes, and permits that must be obtained. Resource Report 1 must:

(1) Describe and provide location maps of all project facilities, include all facilities associated with the project (such as transmission line towers, substations, and any appurtenant facilities), to be constructed, modified, replaced, or removed, including related construction and operational support activities and areas such as maintenance bases, staging areas, communications towers, power lines, and new access roads (roads to be built or modified). As relevant, the report must describe the length and size of the proposed transmission line conductor cables, the types of appurtenant facilities that would be constructed, and associated land requirements.

(2) Provide the following maps and photos:

(i) Current, original United States Geological Survey (USGS) 7.5-minute series topographic maps or maps of equivalent detail, covering at least a 0.5-mile-wide corridor centered on the electric transmission facility centerline, with integer mileposts identified, showing the location of rights-of-way, new access roads, other linear construction areas, substations, and construction materials storage areas. Nonlinear construction areas must be shown on maps at a scale of 1:3,600 or larger keyed graphically and by milepost to the right-of-way maps. In areas where the facilities described in paragraph (j)(6) of this section are located, topographic map coverage must be expanded to depict those facilities.

(ii) Original aerial images or photographs or photo-based alignment sheets based on these sources, not more than one year old (unless older ones accurately depict current land use and development) and with a scale of 1:6,000, or larger, showing the proposed transmission line route and location of transmission line towers, substations and appurtenant facilities, covering at least a 0.5 mile-wide corridor, and including mileposts. The aerial images or photographs or photo-based alignment sheets must show all existing transmission facilities located in the area of the proposed facilities and the location of habitable structures, radio transmitters and other electronic installations, and airstrips. Older images/photographs/alignment sheets must be modified to show any residences not depicted in the original. In areas where the facilities described in paragraph (j)(6) of this section are located, aerial photographic coverage must be expanded to depict those facilities. Alternative formats (e.g., blue-line prints of acceptable resolution) need prior approval by the environmental staff of the Office of Energy Projects.

(iii) In addition to the copies required under § 50.3(b) of this chapter, the applicant must send three additional copies of topographic maps and aerial images/photographs directly to the environmental staff of the Commission's Office of Energy Projects.

(3) Describe and identify by milepost, proposed construction and restoration methods to be used in areas of rugged topography, residential areas, active croplands and sites where explosives are likely to be used.

(4) Identify the number of construction spreads, average workforce requirements for each construction spread and estimated duration of construction from initial clearing to final restoration, and any identified constraints to the timing of construction.

(5) Describe reasonably foreseeable plans for future expansion of facilities, including additional land requirements and the compatibility of those plans with the current proposal.

(6) Describe all authorizations required to complete the proposed action and the status of applications for such authorizations. Identify environmental mitigation

requirements specified in any permit or proposed in any permit application to the extent not specified elsewhere in this section.

(7) Provide the names and mailing addresses of all affected landowners identified in § 50.5(c)(4) of this chapter and certify that all affected landowners will be notified as required in § 50.4(c) of this chapter.

(d) Resource Report 2—Water use and quality. This report must describe water quality and provide data sufficient to determine the expected impact of the project and the effectiveness of mitigative, enhancement, or protective measures. Resource Report 2 must:

(1) Identify and describe by milepost waterbodies and municipal water supply or watershed areas, specially designated surface water protection areas and sensitive waterbodies, and wetlands that would be crossed. For each waterbody crossing, identify the approximate width, State water quality classifications, any known potential pollutants present in the water or sediments, and any potable water intake sources within three miles downstream.

(2) Provide a description of site-specific construction techniques that will be used at each major waterbody crossing.

(3) Describe typical staging area requirements at waterbody and wetland crossings. Also, identify and describe waterbodies and wetlands where staging areas are likely to be more extensive.

(4) Include National Wetland Inventory (NWI) maps. If NWI maps are not available, provide the appropriate State wetland maps. Identify for each crossing, the milepost, the wetland classification specified by the U.S. Fish and Wildlife Service, and the length of the crossing. Include two copies of the NWI maps (or the substitutes, if NWI maps are not available) clearly showing the proposed route and mileposts. Describe by milepost, wetland crossings as determined by field delineations using the current Federal methodology.

(5) Identify aquifers within excavation depth in the project area, including the depth of the aquifer, current and projected use, water quality, and known or suspected contamination problems.

(6) Discuss proposed mitigation measures to reduce the potential for adverse impacts to surface water, wetlands, or groundwater quality. Discuss the potential for blasting to affect water wells, springs, and wetlands, and measures to be taken to detect and remedy such effects.

(7) Identify the location of known public and private groundwater supply wells or springs within 150 feet of proposed construction areas. Identify locations of EPA or State-designated, sole-source aquifers and wellhead protection areas crossed by the proposed transmission line facilities.

(e) Resource Report 3—Fish, wildlife, and vegetation. This report must describe aquatic life, wildlife, and vegetation in the vicinity of the proposed project; expected impacts on these resources including potential effects on biodiversity; and proposed mitigation, enhancement, or protection measures. Resource Report 3 must:

(1) Describe commercial and recreational warmwater, coldwater, and saltwater fisheries in the affected area and associated significant habitats such as spawning or rearing areas and estuaries.

(2) Describe terrestrial habitats, including wetlands, typical wildlife habitats, and rare, unique, or otherwise significant habitats that might be affected by the proposed action. Describe typical species that have commercial, recreational, or aesthetic value.

(3) Describe and provide the affected acreage of vegetation cover types that would be affected, including unique ecosystems or communities such as remnant prairie or old-growth forest, or significant individual plants, such as old-growth specimen trees.

(4) Describe the impact of construction and operation on aquatic and terrestrial species and their habitats, including the possibility of a major alteration to ecosystems or biodiversity, and any potential impact on State-listed endangered or threatened species. Describe the impact of maintenance, clearing and treatment of the project area on fish, wildlife, and vegetation. Surveys may be required to determine specific areas of significant habitats or communities of species of special concern to State, Tribal, or local agencies.

(5) Identify all Federally-listed or proposed threatened or endangered species and critical habitat that potentially occur in the vicinity of the project. Discuss the results of the consultation requirements listed in § 380.13(b) through § 380.13(b)(5)(i) and include any written correspondence that resulted from the consultation. The initial application must include the results of any required surveys unless seasonal considerations make this impractical. If species surveys are impractical, there must be field surveys to determine the presence of suitable habitat unless the entire project area is suitable habitat.

(6) Identify all Federally-listed essential fish habitat (EFH) that potentially occurs in the vicinity of the project. Provide information on all EFH, as identified by the pertinent Federal fishery management plans, that may be adversely affected by the project and the results of abbreviated consultations with NMFS, and any resulting EFH assessments.

(7) Describe site-specific mitigation measures to minimize impacts on fisheries, wildlife, and vegetation.

(8) Include copies of correspondence not provided under paragraph (e)(5) of this section, containing recommendations from appropriate Federal and State fish and wildlife agencies to avoid or limit impact on wildlife, fisheries, and vegetation, and the applicant's response to the recommendations.

(f) Resource Report 4—Cultural resources. In order to prepare this report, the applicant must follow the principles in § 380.14.

(1) Resource Report 4 must contain:

(i) Documentation of the applicant's initial cultural resources consultations, including consultations with Native Americans and other interested persons (if appropriate);

(ii) Overview and Survey Reports, as appropriate;

(iii) Evaluation Report, as appropriate;

(iv) Treatment Plan, as appropriate; and

(v) Written comments from State Historic Preservation Officer(s) (SHPO), Tribal Historic Preservation Officers (THPO), as appropriate, and applicable land-managing agencies on the reports in paragraphs (f)(1)(i) through (iv) of this section.

(2) The initial application or pre-filing documents, as applicable, must include the documentation of initial cultural resource consultation(s), the Overview and Survey Reports, if required, and written comments from SHPOs, THPOs, and land-managing agencies, if available. The initial cultural resources consultations should establish the need for surveys. If surveys are deemed necessary by the consultation with the SHPO/THPO, the survey reports must be filed with the initial application or pre-filing documents.

(i) If the comments of the SHPOs, THPOs, or land-management agencies are not available at the time the application is filed, they may be filed separately, but they must be filed before a permit is issued.

(ii) If landowners deny access to private property and certain areas are not surveyed, the unsurveyed area must be identified by mileposts, and supplemental surveys or evaluations must be conducted after access is granted. In those circumstances, reports, and treatment plans, if necessary, for those inaccessible lands may be filed after a permit is issued.

(3) The Evaluation Report and Treatment Plan, if required, for the entire project must be filed before a permit is issued.

(i) In preparing the Treatment Plan, the applicant must consult with the Commission staff, the SHPO, and any applicable THPO and land-management agencies.

(ii) Authorization to implement the Treatment Plan will occur only after the permit is issued.

(4) Applicant must request privileged treatment for all material filed with the Commission containing location, character, and ownership information about cultural resources in accordance with § 388.112 of this chapter. The cover and relevant pages or portions of the report should be clearly labeled in bold lettering: "CONTAINS PRIVILEGED INFORMATION—DO NOT RELEASE."

(5) Except as specified in a final Commission order, or by the Director of the Office of Energy Projects, construction may not begin until all cultural resource reports and plans have been approved.

(g) Resource Report 5—Socioeconomics. This report must identify and quantify the impacts of constructing and operating the proposed project on factors affecting towns and counties in the vicinity of the project. Resource Report 5 must:

(1) Describe the socioeconomic impact area.

(2) Evaluate the impact of any substantial immigration of people on governmental facilities and services and plans to reduce the impact on the local infrastructure.

(3) Describe on-site manpower requirements and payroll during construction and operation, including the number of construction personnel who currently reside within the impact area, will commute daily to the site from outside the impact area, or will relocate temporarily within the impact area.

(4) Determine whether existing housing within the impact area is sufficient to meet the needs of the additional population.

(5) Describe the number and types of residences and businesses that will be displaced by the project, procedures to be used to acquire these properties, and types and amounts of relocation assistance payments.

(6) Conduct a fiscal impact analysis evaluating incremental local government expenditures in relation to incremental local government revenues that will result from construction of the project. Incremental expenditures include, but are not limited to, school operating costs, road maintenance and repair, public safety, and public utility costs.

(h) Resource Report 6—Geological resources. This report must describe geological resources and hazards in the project area that might be directly or indirectly affected by the proposed action or that could place the proposed facilities at risk, the potential effects of those hazards on the facility, and methods proposed to reduce the effects or risks. Resource Report 6 must:

(1) Describe, by milepost, mineral resources that are currently or potentially exploitable.

(2) Describe, by milepost, existing and potential geological hazards and areas of nonroutine geotechnical concern, such as high seismicity areas, active faults, and areas susceptible to soil liquefaction; planned, active, and abandoned mines; karst terrain; and areas of potential ground failure, such as subsidence, slumping, and landsliding. Discuss the hazards posed to the facility from each one.

(3) Describe how the project will be located or designed to avoid or minimize adverse effects to the resources or risk to itself, including geotechnical investigations and monitoring that would be conducted before, during, and after construction. Discuss also the potential for blasting to affect structures, and the measures to be taken to remedy such effects.

(4) Specify methods to be used to prevent project-induced contamination from surface mines or from mine tailings along the right-of-way and whether the project would hinder mine reclamation or expansion efforts.

(i) Resource Report 7—Soils. This report must describe the soils that will be affected by the proposed project, the effect on those soils, and measures proposed to minimize or avoid impact. Resource Report 7 must:

(1) List, by milepost, the soil associations that would be crossed and describe the erosion potential, fertility, and drainage characteristics of each association.

(2) Identify, by milepost, potential impact from: Soil erosion due to water, wind, or loss of vegetation; soil compaction and damage to soil structure resulting from movement of construction vehicles; wet soils and soils with poor drainage that are especially prone to structural damage; damage to drainage tile systems due to movement of construction vehicles and trenching activities; and interference with the operation of agricultural equipment due to the possibility of large stones or blasted rock occurring on or near the surface as a result of construction.

(3) Identify, by milepost, cropland, and residential areas where loss of soil fertility due to construction activity can occur. Indicate which are classified as prime or unique farmland by the U.S. Department of Agriculture, Natural Resources Conservation Service.

(j) Resource Report 8—Land use, recreation, and aesthetics. This report must describe the existing uses of land on, and (where specified) within 0.25 mile of, the edge of the proposed transmission line right-of-way and changes to those land uses that will occur if the project is approved. The report must discuss proposed mitigation measures, including protection and enhancement of existing land use. Resource Report 8 must:

(1) Describe the width and acreage requirements of all construction and permanent rights-of-way required for project construction, operation and maintenance.

(i) List, by milepost, locations where the proposed right-of-way would be adjacent to existing rights-of-way of any kind.

(ii) Identify, preferably by diagrams, existing rights-of-way that will be used for a portion of the construction or operational right-of-way, the overlap and how much additional width will be required.

(iii) Identify the total amount of land to be purchased or leased for each project facility, the amount of land that would be disturbed for construction, operation, and maintenance of the facility, and the use of the remaining land not required for project operation and maintenance, if any.

(iv) Identify the size of typical staging areas and expanded work areas, such as those at railroad, road, and waterbody crossings, and the size and location of all construction materials storage yards and access roads.

(2) Identify, by milepost, the existing use of lands crossed by the proposed transmission facility, or on or adjacent to each proposed project facility.

(3) Describe planned development on land crossed or within 0.25 mile of proposed facilities, the time frame (if available) for such development, and proposed coordination to minimize impacts on land use. Planned development means development which is included in a master plan or is on file with the local planning board or the county.

(4) Identify, by milepost and length of crossing, the area of direct effect of each proposed facility and operational site on sugar maple stands, orchards and nurseries, landfills, operating mines, hazardous waste sites, wild and scenic rivers, designated trails, nature preserves, game management areas, remnant prairie, old-growth forest, national or State forests, parks, golf courses, designated natural, recreational or scenic areas, or registered natural landmarks, Native American religious sites and traditional cultural properties to the extent they are known to the public at large, and reservations, lands identified under the Special Area Management Plan of the Office of Coastal Zone Management, National Oceanic and Atmospheric Administration, and lands owned or controlled by Federal or State agencies or private preservation groups. Also identify if any of those areas are located within 0.25 mile of any proposed facility.

(5) Tribal resources. Describe Indian tribes, tribal lands, and interests that may be affected by the project.

(i) Identify Indian tribes that may attach religious and cultural significance to historic properties within the project right-of-way or in the project vicinity, as well as available information on Indian traditional cultural and religious properties, whether on or off of any Federally-recognized Indian reservation.

(ii) Information made available under this section must delete specific site or property locations, the disclosure of which will create a risk of harm, theft, or destruction of archaeological or Native American cultural resources or to the site at which the resources are located, or which would violate any Federal law, including the Archaeological Resources Protection Act of 1979, 16 U.S.C. 470w-3, and the National Historic Preservation Act of 1966, 16 U.S.C. 470hh.

(6) Identify, by milepost, all residences and buildings within 200 feet of the edge of the proposed transmission line construction right-of-way and the distance of the residence or building from the edge of the right-of-way. Provide survey drawings or alignment sheets to illustrate the location of the transmission facilities in relation to the buildings.

(i) Buildings: List all single-family and multi-family dwellings and related structures, mobile homes, apartment buildings, commercial structures, industrial structures, business structures, churches, hospitals, nursing homes, schools, or other structures normally inhabited by humans or intended to be inhabited by humans on a daily or regular basis within a 0.5-mile-wide corridor centered on the proposed transmission line alignment. Provide a general description of each habitable structure and its distance from the centerline of the proposed project. In cities, towns, or rural subdivisions, houses can be identified in groups. Provide the number of habitable structures in each group and list the distance from the centerline to the closest habitable structure in the group.

(ii) Electronic installations: List all commercial AM radio Transmitters located within 10,000 feet of the centerline of the proposed project and all FM radio transmitters, microwave relay stations, or other similar electronic installations located within 2,000 feet of the centerline of the proposed project. Provide a general description of each installation and its distance from the centerline of the projects. Locate all installations on a routing map.

(iii) Airstrips: List all known private airstrips within 10,000 feet of the centerline of the project. List all airports registered with the Federal Aviation Administration (FAA) with at least one runway more than 3,200 feet in length that are located within 20,000 feet of the centerline of the proposed project. Indicate whether any transmission structures will exceed a 100:1 horizontal slope (one foot in height for each 100 feet in distance) from the closest point of the closest runway. List all airports registered with the FAA having no runway more than 3,200 feet in length that are located within 10,000 feet of the centerline of the proposed project. Indicate whether any transmission structures will exceed a 50:1 horizontal slope from the closest point of the closest runway. List all heliports located within 5,000 feet of the centerline of the proposed project. Indicate whether any transmission structures will exceed a 25:1 horizontal slope from the closest point of the closest landing and takeoff area of the heliport. Provide a general description of each private airstrip, registered airport, and registered heliport, and state the distance of each from the centerline of the proposed transmission line. Locate all airstrips, airports, and heliports on a routing map.

(7) Describe any areas crossed by or within 0.25 mile of the proposed transmission project facilities which are included in, or are designated for study for inclusion in: The National Wild and Scenic Rivers System

(16 U.S.C. 1271); The National Trails System (16 U.S.C. 1241); or a wilderness area designated under the Wilderness Act (16 U.S.C. 1132).

(8) For facilities within a designated coastal zone management area, provide a consistency determination or evidence that the applicant has requested a consistency determination from the State's coastal zone management program.

(9) Describe the impact the project will have on present uses of the affected areas as identified above, including commercial uses, mineral resources, recreational areas, public health and safety, and the aesthetic value of the land and its features. Describe any temporary or permanent restrictions on land use resulting from the project.

(10) Describe mitigation measures intended for all special use areas identified under this section.

(11) Describe the visual characteristics of the lands and waters affected by the project. Components of this description include a description of how the transmission line project facilities will impact the visual character of project right-of-way and surrounding vicinity, and measures proposed to lessen these impacts. Applicants are encouraged to supplement the text description with visual aids.

(12) Demonstrate that applications for rights-of-way or other proposed land use have been or soon will be filed with Federal land-management agencies with jurisdiction over land that would be affected by the project.

(k) Resource Report 9—Alternatives. This report must describe alternatives to the project and compare the environmental impacts of such alternatives to those of the proposal. It must discuss technological and procedural constraints, costs, and benefits of each alternative. The potential for each alternative to meet project purposes and the environmental consequences of each alternative must be discussed. Resource Report 9 must:

(1) Discuss the "no action" alternative and other alternatives given serious consideration to achieve the proposed objectives.

(2) Provide an analysis of the relative environmental benefits and impacts of each such alternative, including but not limited to:

(i) For alternatives considered in the initial screening for the project but eliminated, describe the environmental characteristics of each alternative, and the reasons for rejecting it. Where applicable, identify the location of such alternatives on maps of sufficient scale to depict their location and relationship to the proposed action, and the relationship of the transmission facilities to existing rights-of-way; and

(ii) For alternatives that were given more in-depth consideration, describe the environmental characteristics of each alternative and the reasons for rejecting it. Provide comparative tables showing the differences in environmental characteristics for the alternative and proposed action. The location, where applicable, of any alternatives in this paragraph shall be provided on maps equivalent to those required in paragraph (c)(2) of this section.

(l) Resource Report 10—Reliability and Safety. This report must address the potential hazard to the public from facility components resulting from accidents or natural catastrophes, how these events will affect reliability, and what procedures and design features have been used to reduce potential hazards. Resource Report 10 must:

(1) Describe measures proposed to protect the public from failure of the proposed facilities (including coordination with local agencies).

(2) Discuss hazards, the environmental impact, and service interruptions which could reasonably ensue from failure of the proposed facilities.

(3) Discuss design and operational measures to avoid or reduce risk.

(4) Discuss contingency plans for maintaining service or reducing downtime.

(5) Describe measures used to exclude the public from hazardous areas. Discuss measures used to minimize problems arising from malfunctions and accidents (with estimates of probability of occurrence) and identify standard procedures for protecting services and public safety during maintenance and breakdowns.

(6) Provide a description of the electromagnetic fields to be generated by the proposed transmission lines, including their strength and extent. Provide a depiction of the expected field compared to distance horizontally along the right-of-way under the conductors, and perpendicular to the centerline of the right-of-way laterally.

(7) Discuss the potential for acoustic and electrical noise from electric and magnetic fields, including shadowing and reradiation, as they may affect health or communication systems along the transmission right-of-way. Indicate the noise level generated by the line in both dB and dBA scales and compare this to any known noise ordinances for the zoning districts through which the transmission line will pass.

(8) Discuss the potential for induced or conducted currents along the transmission right-of-way from electric and magnetic fields.

(m) Resource Report 11—Design and Engineering. This report consists of general design and engineering drawings of the principal project facilities described under Resource Report 1—General project description. If the version of this report submitted with the application is preliminary in nature, applicant must state that in the application. The drawings must conform to the specifications determined in the initial consultation meeting required by § 50.5(b) of this chapter.

(1) The drawings must show all major project structures in sufficient detail to provide a full understanding of the project including:

(i) Plans (overhead view);

(ii) Elevations (front view);

(iii) Profiles (side view); and

(iv) Sections.

(2) The applicant may submit preliminary design drawings with the pre-filing documents or application. The final design drawings may be submitted during the construction permit process or after the Commission issues a permit and must show the precise plans and specifications for proposed structures. If a permit is granted on the basis of preliminary designs, the applicant must submit final design drawings for written approval by the Director of the Office of Energy Project's prior to commencement of any construction of the project.

(3) Supporting design report. The applicant must submit, at a minimum, the following supporting information to demonstrate that existing and proposed structures are safe and adequate to fulfill their stated functions and must submit such information in a separate report at the time the application is filed:

(i) An assessment of the suitability of the transmission line towers and appurtenant structures locations based on geological and subsurface investigations, including investigations of soils and rock borings and tests for the evaluation of all foundations and construction materials sufficient to determine the location and type of transmission line tower or appurtenant structures suitable for the site;

(ii) Copies of boring logs, geology reports, and laboratory test reports;

(iii) An identification of all borrow areas and quarry sites and an estimate of required quantities of suitable construction material;

(iv) Stability and stress analyses for all major transmission structures and conductors under all probable loading conditions, including seismic, wind, and ice loading, as appropriate, in sufficient detail to permit independent staff evaluation.

(4) The applicant must submit two copies of the supporting design report described in paragraph (m)(3) of this section at the time preliminary and final design drawings are filed. If the report contains preliminary drawings, it must be designated a "Preliminary Supporting Design Report."

[Order 689, 71 FR 69471, Dec. 1, 2006]

Pt. 380, App. A

Appendix A to Part 380—Minimum Filing Requirements for Environmental Reports Under the Natural Gas Act

Environmental Reports Under the Natural Gas Act.

Resource Report 1—General Project Description

1. Provide a detailed description and location map of the project facilities. (§ 380.12(c)(1)).

2. Describe any nonjurisdictional facilities that would be built in association with the project. (§ 380.12(c)(2)).

3. Provide current original U.S. Geological Survey (USGS) 7.5-minute-series topographic maps with mileposts showing the project facilities; (§ 380.12(c)(3)).

4. Provide aerial images or photographs or alignment sheets based on these sources with mileposts showing the project facilities; (§ 380.12(c)(3)).

5. Provide plot/site plans of compressor stations showing the location of the nearest noise-sensitive areas (NSA) within 1 mile. (§ 380.12(c)(3,4)).

6. Describe construction and restoration methods. (§ 380.12(c)(6)).

7. Identify the permits required for construction across surface waters. (§ 380.12(c)(9)).

8. Provide the names and address of all affected landowners and certify that all affected landowners will be notified as required in § 157.6(d). (§§ 380.12(c)(10))

Resource Report 2—Water Use and Quality

1. Identify all perennial surface waterbodies crossed by the proposed project and their water quality classification. (§ 380.12(d)(1)).

2. Identify all waterbody crossings that may have contaminated waters or sediments. (§ 380.12(d)(1)).

3. Identify watershed areas, designated surface water protection areas, and sensitive waterbodies crossed by the proposed project. (§ 380.12(d)(1)).

4. Provide a table (based on NWI maps if delineations have not been done) identifying all wetlands, by milepost and length, crossed by the project (including abandoned pipeline), and the total acreage and acreage of each wetland type that would be affected by construction. (§ 380.12(d)(1 & 4)).

5. Discuss construction and restoration methods proposed for crossing wetlands, and compare them to staff's Wetland and Waterbody Construction and Mitigation Procedures; (§ 380.12(d)(2)).

6. Describe the proposed waterbody construction, impact mitigation, and restoration methods to be used to cross surface waters and compare to the staff's Wetland and Waterbody Construction and Mitigation Procedures. (§ 380.12(d)(2)).

7. Provide original National Wetlands Inventory (NWI) maps or the appropriate state wetland maps, if NWI maps are not available, that show all proposed facilities and include milepost locations for proposed pipeline routes. (§ 380.12(d)(4)).

8. Identify all U.S. Environmental Protection Agency (EPA)- or state- designated aquifers crossed. (§ 380.12(d)(9)).

Resource Report 3—Vegetation and Wildlife

1. Classify the fishery type of each surface waterbody that would be crossed, including fisheries of special concern. (§ 380.12(e)(1)).

2. Describe terrestrial and wetland wildlife and habitats that would be affected by the project. (§ 380.12(e)(2)).

3. Describe the major vegetative cover types that would be crossed and provide the acreage of each vegetative cover type that would be affected by construction. (§ 380.12(e)(3)).

4. Describe the effects of construction and operation procedures on the fishery resources and proposed mitigation measures. (§ 380.12(e)(4)).

5. Evaluate the potential for short-term, long-term, and permanent impact on the wildlife resources and state-listed endangered or threatened species caused by construction and operation of the project and proposed mitigation measures. (§ 380.12(e)(4)).

6. Identify all federally listed or proposed endangered or threatened species that potentially occur in the vicinity of the project and discuss the results of the consultations with other agencies. Include survey reports as specified in § 380.12(e)(5).

7. Identify all federally listed essential fish habitat (EFH) that potentially occurs in the vicinity of the project and the results of abbreviated consultations with NMFS, and any resulting EFH assessments. (§ 380.12(e)(6))

8. Describe any significant biological resources that would be affected. Describe impact and any mitigation proposed to avoid or minimize that impact. (§§ 380.12(e)(4 & 7))

Resource Report 4—Cultural Resources

See § 380.14 and "OPR's Guidelines for Reporting on Cultural Resources Investigations" for further guidance.

1. Initial cultural resources consultation and documentation, and documentation of consultation with Native Americans. (§ 380.12(f)(1)(i) & (2)).

2. Overview/Survey Report(s). (§ 380.12(f)(1)(ii) & (2)).

Resource Report 5—Socioeconomics

1. For major aboveground facilities and major pipeline projects that require an EIS, describe existing socioeconomic conditions within the project area. (§ 380.12(g)(1)).

2. For major aboveground facilities, quantify impact on employment, housing, local government services, local tax revenues, transportation, and other relevant factors within the project area. (§ 380.12(g)(2-6)).

Resource Report 6—Geological Resources

1. Identify the location (by milepost) of mineral resources and any planned or active surface mines crossed by the proposed facilities. (§ 380.12(h)(1 & 2)).

2. Identify any geologic hazards to the proposed facilities. (§ 380.12(h)(2))

3. Discuss the need for and locations where blasting may be necessary in order to construct the proposed facilities. (§ 380.12(h)(3))

4. For LNG projects in seismic areas, the materials required by "Data Requirements for the Seismic Review of LNG Facilities," NBSIR84-2833. (§ 380.12(h)(5))

5. For underground storage facilities, how drilling activity by others within or adjacent to the facilities would be monitored, and how old wells would be located and monitored within the facility boundaries. (§ 380.12(h)(6))

Resource Report 7—Soils

1. Identify, describe, and group by milepost the soils affected by the proposed pipeline and aboveground facilities. (§ 380.12(i)(1))

2. For aboveground facilities that would occupy sites over 5 acres, determine the acreage of prime farmland soils that would be affected by construction and operation. (§ 380.12(i)(2))

3. Describe, by milepost, potential impacts on soils. (§ 380.12(i)(3,4))

4. Identify proposed mitigation to minimize impact on soils, and compare with the staff's Upland Erosion Control, Revegetation, and Maintenance Plan. (§ 380.12(i)(5))

Resource Report 8—Land Use, Recreation and Aesthetics

1. Classify and quantify land use affected by: (§ 380.12(j)(1))

a. Pipeline construction and permanent rights-of-way (§ 380.12(j)(1));

b. Extra work/staging areas (§ 380.12(j)(1));

c. Access roads (§ 380.12(j)(1));

d. Pipe and contractor yards (§ 380.12(j)(1)); and

e. Aboveground facilities (§ 380.12(j)(1)).

2. Identify by milepost all locations where the pipeline right-of-way would at least partially coincide with existing right-of-way, where it would be adjacent to existing rights-of-way, and where it would be outside of existing right-of-way. (§ 380.12(j)(1))

3. Provide detailed typical construction right-of-way cross-section diagrams showing information such as widths and relative locations of existing rights-of-way, new permanent right-of-way, and temporary construction right-of-way. (§ 380.12(j)(1))

4. Summarize the total acreage of land affected by construction and operation of the project. (§ 380.12(j)(1))

5. Identify by milepost all planned residential or commercial/business development and the time frame for construction. (§ 380.12(j)(3))

6. Identify by milepost special land uses (e.g., sugar maple stands, specialty crops, natural areas, national and state forests, conservation land, etc.). (§ 380.12(j)(4))

7. Identify by beginning milepost and length of crossing all land administered by Federal, state, or local agencies, or private conservation organizations. (§ 380.12(j)(4))

8. Identify by milepost all natural, recreational, or scenic areas, and all registered natural landmarks crossed by the project. (§ 380.12(j)(4 & 6))

9. Identify all facilities that would be within designated coastal zone management areas. Provide a consistency determination or evidence that a request for a consistency determination has been filed with the appropriate state agency. ((§ 380.12(j)(4 & 7))

10. Identify by milepost all residences that would be within 50 feet of the construction right-of-way or extra work area. (§ 380.12(j)(5))

11. Identify all designated or proposed candidate National or State Wild and Scenic Rivers crossed by the project. (§ 380.12(j)(6))

12. Describe any measures to visually screen aboveground facilities, such as compressor stations. (§ 380.12(j)(11))

13. Demonstrate that applications for rights-of-way or other proposed land use have been or soon will be filed with Federal land-managing agencies with jurisdiction over land that would be affected by the project. (§ 380.12(j)(12))

Resource Report 9—Air and Noise Quality

1. Describe existing air quality in the vicinity of the project. (§ 380.12(k)(1))

2. Quantify the existing noise levels (day-night sound level (Ldn) and other applicable noise parameters) at noise-sensitive areas and at other areas covered by relevant state and local noise ordinances. (§ 380.12(k)(2))

3. Quantify existing and proposed emissions of compressor equipment, plus construction emissions, including nitrogen oxides (NOX) and carbon monoxide (CO), and the basis for these calculations. Summarize anticipated air quality impacts for the project. (§ 380.12(k)(3))

4. Describe the existing compressor units at each station where new, additional, or modified compressor units are proposed, including the manufacturer, model number, and horsepower of the compressor units. For proposed new, additional, or modified compressor units include the horsepower, type, and energy source. (§ 380.12(k)(4)).

5. Identify any nearby noise-sensitive area by distance and direction from the proposed compressor unit building/enclosure. (§ 380.12(k)(4))

6. Identify any applicable state or local noise regulations. (§ 380.12(k)(4))

7. Calculate the noise impact at noise-sensitive areas of the proposed compressor unit modifications or additions, specifying how the impact was calculated, including manufacturer's data and proposed noise control equipment. (§ 380.12(k)(4))

Resource Report 10—Alternatives

1. Address the "no action" alternative. (§ 380.12(l)(1))

2. For large projects, address the effect of energy conservation or energy alternatives to the project. (§ 380.12(l)(1))

3. Identify system alternatives considered during the identification of the project and provide the rationale for rejecting each alternative. (§ 380.12(l)(1))

4. Identify major and minor route alternatives considered to avoid impact on sensitive environmental areas (e.g., wetlands, parks, or residences) and provide sufficient comparative data to justify the selection of the proposed route. (§ 380.12(l)(2)(ii))

5. Identify alternative sites considered for the location of major new aboveground facilities and provide sufficient comparative data to justify the selection of the proposed site. (§ 380.12(l)(2)(ii))

Resource Report 11—Reliability and Safety

Describe how the project facilities would be designed, constructed, operated, and maintained to minimize potential hazard to the public from the failure of project components as a result of accidents or natural catastrophes. (§ 380.12(m))

Resource Report 12—PCB Contamination

1. For projects involving the replacement or abandonment of facilities determined to have PCBs, provide a statement that activities would comply with an approved EPA disposal permit or with the requirements of the TSCA. (§ 380.12(n)(1))

2. For compressor station modifications on sites that have been determined to have soils contaminated with PCBs, describe the status of remediation efforts completed to date. (§ 380.12(n)(2))

Resource Report 13—Additional Information Related to LNG Plants

Provide all the listed detailed engineering materials. (§ 380.12(o))

[Order 603, 64 FR 26619, May 14, 1999, as amended by Order 603-A, 64 FR 54537, Oct. 7, 1999; Order 609, 64 FR 57392, Oct. 25, 1999; Order 609-A, 65 FR 15238, Mar. 22, 2000]

NEPA Deskbook

Appendix 14 Federal Highway Administration Regulations and Procedures (FHwA Part 771)

Federal Highway Administration

NEPA Regulations

23 CFR Pt 771

Part 771—Environmental Impact and Related Procedures

Contents

AUTHORITY: 42 U.S.C. 4321 *et seq.*; 23 U.S.C. 106, 109, 128, 138, 139, 315, 325, 326, and 327; 49 U.S.C. 303 and 5323(q); 40 CFR Parts 1500-1508; 49 CFR 1.81, 1.85, and 1.91; Pub. L. 109-59, 119 Stat. 1144, sections 6002 and 6010; Pub. L. 112-141, 126 Stat. 405, sections 1315, 1316 and 1317.

[79 FR 2118, Jan. 13, 2014].

SOURCE: 52 FR 32660, Aug. 28, 1987, unless otherwise noted.

§771.101 Purpose.

This regulation prescribes the policies and procedures of the Federal Highway Administration (FHWA) and the Federal Transit Administration (FTA) for implementing the National Environmental Policy Act of 1969 as amended (NEPA), and supplements the NEPA regulation of the Council on Environmental Quality (CEQ), 40 CFR parts 1500 through 1508 (CEQ regulation). Together these regulations set forth all FHWA, FTA, and Department of Transportation (DOT) requirements under NEPA for the processing of high-way and public transportation projects. This regulation also sets forth procedures to comply with 23 U.S.C. 109(h), 128, 138, 139, 325, 326, 327, and 49 U.S.C. 303, 5301, and 5323.

[74 FR 12527, Mar. 24, 2009, as amended at 78 FR 8982, Feb. 7, 2013]

§771.103 [Reserved]

§771.105 Policy.

It is the policy of the Administration that:

(a) To the fullest extent possible, all environmental investigations, reviews, and consultations be coordinated as a single process, and compliance with all applicable environmental requirements be reflected in the environmental review document required by this regulation.[1]

(b) Alternative courses of action be evaluated and decisions be made in the best overall public interest based upon a balanced consideration of the need for safe and efficient transportation; of the social, economic, and environmental impacts of the proposed transportation improvement; and of national, State, and local environmental protection goals.

(c) Public involvement and a systematic interdisciplinary approach be essential parts of the development process for proposed actions.

(d) Measures necessary to mitigate adverse impacts be incorporated into the action. Measures necessary to mitigate adverse impacts are eligible for Federal funding when the Administration determines that:

(1) The impacts for which the mitigation is proposed actually result from the Administration action; and

(2) The proposed mitigation represents a reasonable public expenditure after considering the impacts of the action and the benefits of the proposed mitigation measures. In making this determination, the Administration will consider, among other factors, the extent to which the proposed measures would assist in comply-

---

1.   FHWA and FTA have supplementary guidance on environmental documents and procedures for their programs. This guidance includes, but is not limited to: FHWA Technical Advisory T6640.8A, October 30, 1987; "SAFETEA-LU Environmental Review Process: Final Guidance," November 15, 2006; Appendix A of 23 CFR part 450, titled "Linking the Transportation Planning and NEPA Processes"; and "Transit Noise and Vibration Impact Assessment," May 2006. The FHWA and FTA supplementary guidance, and any updated versions of the guidance, are available from the respective FHWA and FTA headquarters and field offices as prescribed in 49 CFR part 7 and on their respective Web sites at *http://www.fhwa.dot.gov* and *http://www.fta.dot.gov*, or in hard copy by request.

ing with a Federal statute, Executive Order, or Administration regulation or policy.

(e) Costs incurred by the applicant for the preparation of environmental documents requested by the Administration be eligible for Federal assistance.

(f) No person, because of handicap, age, race, color, sex, or national origin, be excluded from participating in, or denied benefits of, or be subject to discrimination under any Administration program or procedural activity required by or developed pursuant to this regulation.

[52 FR 32660, Aug. 28, 1987; 53 FR 11065, Apr. 5, 1988, as amended at 70 FR 24469, May 9, 2005; 74 FR 12527, Mar. 24, 2009; 78 FR 8982, Feb. 7, 2013]

§771.107 Definitions.

The definitions contained in the CEQ regulation and in Titles 23 and 49 of the United States Code are applicable. In addition, the following definitions apply.

(a) *Environmental studies.* The investigations of potential environmental impacts to determine the environmental process to be followed and to assist in the preparation of the environmental document.

(b) *Action.* A highway or transit project proposed for FHWA or FTA funding. It also includes activities such as joint and multiple use permits, changes in access control, etc., which may or may not involve a commitment of Federal funds.

(c) *Administration action.* The approval by FHWA or FTA of the applicant's request for Federal funds for construction. It also includes approval of activities such as joint and multiple use permits, changes in access control, etc., which may or may not involve a commitment of Federal funds.

(d) *Administration.* The FHWA or FTA, whichever is the designated Federal lead agency for the proposed action. A reference herein to the Administration means the FHWA, or FTA, or a State when the State is functioning as the FHWA or FTA in carrying out responsibilities delegated or assigned to the State in accordance with 23 U.S.C. 325, 326, or 327, or other applicable law. A reference herein to the FHWA or FTA means the State when the State is functioning as the FHWA or FTA respectively in carrying out responsibilities delegated or assigned to the State in accordance with 23 U.S.C. 325, 326, or 327, or other applicable law. Nothing in this definition alters the scope of any delegation or assignment made by FHWA or FTA.

(e) *Section 4(f).* Refers to 49 U.S.C. 303 and 23 U.S.C. 138.[2]

(f) *Applicant.* Any State, local, or federally-recognized Indian tribal governmental unit that requests funding approval or other action by the Administration and that the Administration works with to conduct environmental studies and prepare environmental review documents. When another Federal agency, or the Administration itself, is implementing the action, then the lead agencies (as defined in this regulation) may assume the responsibilities of the applicant in this part. If there is no applicant, then the Federal lead agency will assume the responsibilities of the applicant in this part.

(g) *Lead agencies.* The Administration and any other agency designated to serve as a joint lead agency with the Administration under 23 U.S.C. 139(c)(3) or under the CEQ regulation.

(h) *Participating agency.* A Federal, State, local, or federally-recognized Indian tribal governmental unit that may have an interest in the proposed project and has accepted an invitation to be a participating agency, or, in the case of a Federal agency, has not declined the invitation in accordance with 23 U.S.C. 139(d)(3).

(i) *Project sponsor.* The Federal, State, local, or federally-recognized Indian tribal governmental unit, or other entity, including any private or public-private entity that seeks an Administration action.

[52 FR 32660, Aug. 28, 1987, as amended at 70 FR 24469, May 9, 2005; 74 FR 12527, Mar. 24, 2009; 78 FR 8982, Feb. 7, 2013]

§771.109 Applicability and responsibilities.

(a)(1) The provisions of this regulation and the CEQ regulation apply to actions where the Administration exercises sufficient control to condition the permit or project approval. Actions taken by the applicant which do not require Federal approvals, such as preparation of a regional transportation plan are not subject to this regulation.

(2) This regulation does not apply to, or alter approvals by the Administration made prior to the effective date of this regulation.

---

2. Section 4(f), which protected certain public lands and all historic sites, technically was repealed in 1983 when it was codified, without substantive change, as 49 U.S.C. 303. This regulation continues to refer to section 4(f) because it would create needless confusion to do otherwise; the policies section 4(f) engendered are widely referred to as "section 4(f)" matters. A provision with the same meaning is found at 23 U.S.C. 138 and applies only to FHWA actions.

(3) Environmental documents accepted or prepared after the effective date of this regulation shall be developed in accordance with this regulation.

(b) It shall be the responsibility of the applicant, in cooperation with the Administration to implement those mitigation measures stated as commitments in the environmental documents prepared pursuant to this regulation. The FHWA will assure that this is accomplished as a part of its program management responsibilities that include reviews of designs, plans, specifications, and estimates (PS&E), and construction inspections. The FTA will assure implementation of committed mitigation measures through incorporation by reference in the grant agreement, followed by reviews of designs and construction inspections.

(c) The following roles and responsibilities apply during the environmental review process:

(1) The lead agencies are responsible for managing the environmental review process and the preparation of the appropriate environmental review documents.

(2) Any applicant that is a State or local governmental entity that is, or is expected to be, a direct recipient of funds under title 23, U.S. Code, or chapter 53 of title 49 U.S. Code, for the action shall serve as a joint lead agency with the Administration in accordance with 23 U.S.C. 139, and may prepare environmental review documents if the Administration furnishes guidance and independently evaluates the documents.

(3) The Administration may invite other Federal, State, local, or federally-recognized Indian tribal governmental units to serve as joint lead agencies in accordance with the CEQ regulation. If the applicant is serving as a joint lead agency under 23 U.S.C. 139(c)(3), then the Administration and the applicant will decide jointly which other agencies to invite to serve as joint lead agencies.

(4) When the applicant seeks an Administration action other than the approval of funds, the role of the applicant will be determined by the Administration in accordance with the CEQ regulation and 23 U.S.C. 139.

(5) Regardless of its role under paragraphs (c)(2) through (c)(4) of this section, a public agency that has statewide jurisdiction (for example, a State highway agency or a State department of transportation) or a local unit of government acting through a statewide agency, that meets the requirements of section 102(2) (D) of NEPA, may prepare the EIS and other environmental review documents with the Administration fur-

nishing guidance, participating in the preparation, and independently evaluating the document. All FHWA applicants qualify under this paragraph.

(6) The role of a project sponsor that is a private institution or firm is limited to providing technical studies and commenting on environmental review documents.

(d) When entering into Federal-aid project agreements pursuant to 23 U.S.C. 106, it shall be the responsibility of the State highway agency to ensure that the project is constructed in accordance with and incorporates all committed environmental impact mitigation measures listed in approved environmental review documents unless the State requests and receives written FHWA approval to modify or delete such mitigation features.

[52 FR 32660, Aug. 28, 1987; 53 FR 11065, Apr. 5, 1988, as amended at 62 FR 6873, Feb. 14, 1997; 70 FR 24469, May 9, 2005; 74 FR 12527, Mar. 24, 2009; 78 FR 8982, Feb. 7, 2013]

§771.111 Early coordination, public involvement, and project development.

(a)(1) Early coordination with appropriate agencies and the public aids in determining the type of environmental review documents an action requires, the scope of the document, the level of analysis, and related environmental requirements. This involves the exchange of information from the inception of a proposal for action to preparation of the environmental review documents. Applicants intending to apply for funds should notify the Administration at the time that a project concept is identified. When requested, the Administration will advise the applicant, insofar as possible, of the probable class of action and related environmental laws and requirements and of the need for specific studies and findings which would normally be developed concurrently with the environmental review documents.

(2) The information and results produced by, or in support of, the transportation planning process may be incorporated into environmental review documents in accordance with 40 CFR 1502.21 and 23 CFR 450.212 or 450.318.[3]

3.　On February 14, 2007, FHWA and FTA issued guidance on incorporating products of the planning process into NEPA documents as Appendix A of 23 CFR part 450. This guidance, titled "Linking the Transportation Planning and NEPA Processes," is available on the FHWA Web site at *http://www.fhwa.dot.gov* or in hard copy upon request.

(b) The Administration will identify the probable class of action as soon as sufficient information is available to identify the probable impacts of the action.

(c) When both the FHWA and FTA are involved in the development of a project, or when the FHWA or FTA acts as a joint lead agency with another Federal agency, a mutually acceptable process will be established on a case-by-case basis.

(d) During the early coordination process, the lead agencies may request other agencies having an interest in the action to participate, and must invite such agencies if the action is subject to the project development procedures in 23 U.S.C. 139.[4] Agencies with special expertise may be invited to become cooperating agencies. Agencies with jurisdiction by law must be requested to become cooperating agencies.

(e) Other States, and Federal land management entities, that may be significantly affected by the action or by any of the alternatives shall be notified early and their views solicited by the applicant in cooperation with the Administration. The Administration will prepare a written evaluation of any significant unresolved issues and furnish it to the applicant for incorporation into the environmental assessment (EA) or draft EIS.

(f) In order to ensure meaningful evaluation of alternatives and to avoid commitments to transportation improvements before they are fully evaluated, the action evaluated in each EIS or finding of no significant impact (FONSI) shall:

(1) Connect logical termini and be of sufficient length to address environmental matters on a broad scope;

(2) Have independent utility or independent significance, i.e., be usable and be a reasonable expenditure even if no additional transportation improvements in the area are made; and

(3) Not restrict consideration of alternatives for other reasonably foreseeable transportation improvements.

(g) For major transportation actions, the tiering of EISs as discussed in the CEQ regulation (40 CFR 1502.20) may be appropriate. The first tier EIS would focus on broad issues such as general location, mode choice, and areawide air quality and land use implications of the major alternatives. The second tier would address site-specific details on project impacts, costs, and mitigation measures.

(h) For the Federal-aid highway program:

(1) Each State must have procedures approved by the FHWA to carry out a public involvement/public hearing program pursuant to 23 U.S.C. 128 and 139 and CEQ regulation.

(2) State public involvement/public hearing procedures must provide for:

(i) Coordination of public involvement activities and public hearings with the entire NEPA process.

(ii) Early and continuing opportunities during project development for the public to be involved in the identification of social, economic, and environmental impacts, as well as impacts associated with relocation of individuals, groups, or institutions.

(iii) One or more public hearings or the opportunity for hearing(s) to be held by the State highway agency at a convenient time and place for any Federal-aid project which requires significant amounts of right-of-way, substantially changes the layout or functions of connecting roadways or of the facility being improved, has a substantial adverse impact on abutting property, otherwise has a significant social, economic, environmental or other effect, or for which the FHWA determines that a public hearing is in the public interest.

(iv) Reasonable notice to the public of either a public hearing or the opportunity for a public hearing. Such notice will indicate the availability of explanatory information. The notice shall also provide information required to comply with public involvement requirements of other laws, Executive orders, and regulations.

(v) Explanation at the public hearing of the following information, as appropriate:

(A) The project's purpose, need, and consistency with the goals and objectives of any local urban planning,

(B) The project's alternatives, and major design features,

(C) The social, economic, environmental, and other impacts of the project,

(D) The relocation assistance program and the right-of-way acquisition process.

(E) The State highway agency's procedures for receiving both oral and written statements from the public.

(vi) Submission to the FHWA of a transcript of each public hearing and a certification that a required hearing or hearing opportunity was offered. The transcript

4.   The FHWA and FTA have developed guidance on 23 U.S.C. Section 139 titled "SAFETEA-LU Environmental Review Process: Final Guidance," November 15, 2006, and available at http://www. fhwa.dot.gov or in hard copy upon request.

will be accompanied by copies of all written statements from the public, both submitted at the public hearing or during an announced period after the public hearing.

(vii) An opportunity for public involvement in defining the purpose and need and the range of alternatives, for any action subject to the project development procedures in 23 U.S.C. 139.

(viii) Public notice and an opportunity for public review and comment on a Section 4(f) *de minimis* impact finding, in accordance with 49 U.S.C. 303(d).[5]

(3) Based on the reevaluation of project environmental documents required by §771.129, the FHWA and the State highway agency will determine whether changes in the project or new information warrant additional public involvement.

(4) Approvals or acceptances of public involvement/ public hearing procedures prior to the publication date of this regulation remain valid.

(i) Applicants for capital assistance in the FTA program:

(1) Achieve public participation on proposed projects through activities that engage the public, including public hearings, town meetings, and charettes, and seeking input from the public through the scoping process for environmental review documents. Project milestones may be announced to the public using electronic or paper media (e.g., newsletters, note cards, or emails) pursuant to 40 CFR 1506.6. For projects requiring EISs, an early opportunity for public involvement in defining the purpose and need for action and the range of alternatives must be provided, and a public hearing will be held during the circulation period of the draft EIS. For other projects that substantially affect the community or its public transportation service, an adequate opportunity for public review and comment must be provided.

(2) May participate in early scoping as long as enough project information is known so the public and other agencies can participate effectively. Early scoping constitutes initiation of NEPA scoping while local planning efforts to aid in establishing the purpose and need and in evaluating alternatives and impacts are underway. Notice of early scoping must be made to the public and other agencies. If early scoping is the start of the NEPA process, the early scoping notice must include language to that effect. After development of the proposed action at the conclusion of early scoping, FTA will publish the Notice of Intent if it is determined at that time that the proposed action requires an EIS. The Notice of Intent will establish a 30-day period for comments on the purpose and need and the alternatives.

(3) Are encouraged to post and distribute materials related to the environmental review process, including but not limited to, NEPA documents, public meeting announcements, and minutes, through publicly-accessible electronic means, including project Web sites. Applicants are encouraged to keep these materials available to the public electronically until the project is constructed and open for operations.

(4) Are encouraged to post all environmental impact statements and records of decision on a project Web site until the project is constructed and open for operation.

(j) Information on the FTA environmental process may be obtained from: Director, Office of Human and Natural Environment, Federal Transit Administration, Washington, DC 20590. Information on the FHWA environmental process may be obtained from: Director, Office of Project Development and Environmental Review, Federal Highway Administration, Washington, DC 20590.

[52 FR 32660, Aug. 28, 1987, as amended at 70 FR 24469, May 9, 2005; 74 FR 12528, Mar. 24, 2009; 78 FR 8982, Feb. 7, 2013]

§771.113 Timing of Administration activities.

(a) The lead agencies, in cooperation with the applicant (if not a lead agency), will perform the work necessary to complete a finding of no significant impact (FONSI) or a record of decision (ROD) and comply with other related environmental laws and regulations to the maximum extent possible during the NEPA process. This work includes environmental studies, related engineering studies, agency coordination and public involvement. However, final design activities, property acquisition, purchase of construction materials or rolling stock, or project construction shall not proceed until the following have been completed, except as otherwise provided in law or in paragraph (d) of this section:

(1)(i) The action has been classified as a categorical exclusion (CE), or

5.   The FHWA and FTA have developed guidance on Section 4(f) de minimis impact findings titled "Guidance for Determining *De Minimis* Impacts to Section 4(f) Resources," December 13, 2005, which is available at *http://www.fhwa.dot.gov* or in hard copy upon request.

(ii) A FONSI has been approved, or

(iii) A final EIS has been approved and available for the prescribed period of time and a record of decision has been signed;

(2) For actions proposed for FHWA funding, the Administration has received and accepted the certifications and any required public hearing transcripts required by 23 U.S.C. 128;

(3) For activities proposed for FHWA funding, the programming requirements of 23 CFR part 450, subpart B, and 23 CFR part 630, subpart A, have been met.

(b) Completion of the requirements set forth in paragraphs (a)(1) and (2) of this section is considered acceptance of the general project location and concepts described in the environmental review documents unless otherwise specified by the approving official.

(c) Letters of Intent issued under the authority of 49 U.S.C. 5309(g) are used by FTA to indicate an intention to obligate future funds for multi-year capital transit projects. Letters of Intent will not be issued by FTA until the NEPA process is completed.

(d) The prohibition in paragraph (a)(1) of this section is limited by the following exceptions:

(1) Exceptions for hardship and protective acquisitions of real property are addressed in paragraph (d)(12) of §771.117 for FHWA. Exceptions for the acquisitions of real property are addressed in paragraphs (c)(6) and (d)(3) of §771.118 for FTA.

(2) Paragraph (d)(4) of §771.118 contains an exception for the acquisition of right-of-way for future transit use in accordance with 49 U.S.C. 5323(q).

(3) FHWA regulations at 23 CFR 710.503 establish conditions for FHWA approval of Federal-aid highway funding for hardship and protective acquisitions.

(4) FHWA regulations at 23 CFR 710.501 address early acquisition of right-of-way by a State prior to the execution of a project agreement with the FHWA or completion of NEPA. In paragraphs (b) and (c) of §710.501, the regulation establishes conditions governing subsequent requests for Federal-aid credit or reimbursement for the acquisition. Any State-funded early acquisition for a Federal-aid highway project where there will not be Federal-aid highway credit or reimbursement for the early acquisition is subject to the limitations described in the CEQ regula-

tions at 40 CFR 1506.1 and other applicable Federal requirements.

(5) A limited exception for rolling stock is provided in 49 U.S.C. 5309(h)(6).

[52 FR 32660, Aug. 28, 1987; 53 FR 11066, Apr. 5, 1988, as amended at 70 FR 24469, May 9, 2005; 74 FR 12528, Mar. 24, 2009; 78 FR 8983, Feb. 7, 2013]

§771.115 Classes of actions.

There are three classes of actions which prescribe the level of documentation required in the NEPA process.

(a) *Class I (EISs)*. Actions that significantly affect the environment require an EIS (40 CFR 1508.27). The following are examples of actions that normally required an EIS:

(1) A new controlled access freeway.

(2) A highway project of four or more lanes on a new location.

(3) Construction or extension of a fixed transit facility (e.g., rapid rail, light rail, commuter rail, bus rapid transit) that will not be located within an existing transportation right-of-way.

(4) New construction or extension of a separate roadway for buses or high occupancy vehicles not located within an existing highway facility.

(b) Class II (CEs). Actions that do not individually or cumulatively have a significant environmental effect are excluded from the requirement to prepare an EA or EIS. A specific list of CEs normally not requiring NEPA documentation is set forth in §771.117(c) for FHWA actions or pursuant to §771.118(c) for FTA actions. When appropriately documented, additional projects may also qualify as CEs pursuant to §771.117(d) for FHWA actions or pursuant to §771.118(d) for FTA actions.

(c) *Class III (EAs)*. Actions in which the significance of the environmental impact is not clearly established. All actions that are not Class I or II are Class III. All actions in this class require the preparation of an EA to determine the appropriate environmental document required.

[52 FR 32660, Aug. 28, 1987, as amended at 74 FR 12529, Mar. 24, 2009; 78 FR 8983, Feb. 7, 2013]

§771.117 FHWA categorical exclusions.

Link to an amendment published at 79 FR 2118, January 13, 2014.

(a) Categorical exclusions (CEs) are actions which meet the definition contained in 40 CFR 1508.4, and, based on past experience with similar actions, do not involve significant environmental impacts. They are actions which: do not induce significant impacts to planned growth or land use for the area; do not require the relocation of significant numbers of people; do not have a significant impact on any natural, cultural, recreational, historic or other resource; do not involve significant air, noise, or water quality impacts; do not have significant impacts on travel patterns; or do not otherwise, either individually or cumulatively, have any significant environmental impacts.

(b) Any action which normally would be classified as a CE but could involve unusual circumstances will require the FHWA, in cooperation with the applicant, to conduct appropriate environmental studies to determine if the CE classification is proper. Such unusual circumstances include:

(1) Significant environmental impacts;

(2) Substantial controversy on environmental grounds;

(3) Significant impact on properties protected by section 4(f) of the DOT Act or section 106 of the National Historic Preservation Act; or

(4) Inconsistencies with any Federal, State, or local law, requirement or administrative determination relating to the environmental aspects of the action.

(c) The following actions meet the criteria for CEs in the CEQ regulations (40 CFR 1508.4) and §771.117(a) and normally do not require any further NEPA approvals by the FHWA:

(1) Activities which do not involve or lead directly to construction, such as planning and research activities; grants for training; engineering to define the elements of a proposed action or alternatives so that social, economic, and environmental effects can be assessed; and Federal-aid system revisions which establish classes of highways on the Federal-aid highway system.

(2) Approval of utility installations along or across a transportation facility.

(3) Construction of bicycle and pedestrian lanes, paths, and facilities.

(4) Activities included in the State's *highway safety plan* under 23 U.S.C. 402.

(5) Transfer of Federal lands pursuant to 23 U.S.C. 107(d) and/or 23 U.S.C. 317 when the land transfer is in support of an action that is not otherwise subject to FHWA review under NEPA.

(6) The installation of noise barriers or alterations to existing publicly owned buildings to provide for noise reduction.

(7) Landscaping.

(8) Installation of fencing, signs, pavement markings, small passenger shelters, traffic signals, and railroad warning devices where no substantial land acquisition or traffic disruption will occur.

(9) The following actions for transportation facilities damaged by an incident resulting in an emergency declared by the Governor of the State and concurred in by the Secretary, or a disaster or emergency declared by the President pursuant to the Robert T. Stafford Act (42 U.S.C. 5121):

(i) Emergency repairs under 23 U.S.C. 125; and

(ii) The repair, reconstruction, restoration, retrofitting, or replacement of any road, highway, bridge, tunnel, or transit facility (such as a ferry dock or bus transfer station), including ancillary transportation facilities (such as pedestrian/bicycle paths and bike lanes), that is in operation or under construction when damaged and the action:

(A) Occurs within the existing right-of-way and in a manner that substantially conforms to the preexisting design, function, and location as the original (which may include upgrades to meet existing codes and standards as well as upgrades warranted to address conditions that have changed since the original construction); and

(B) Is commenced within a 2-year period beginning on the date of the declaration.

(10) Acquisition of scenic easements.

(11) Determination of payback under 23 U.S.C. 156 for property previously acquired with Federal-aid participation.

(12) Improvements to existing rest areas and truck weigh stations.

(13) Ridesharing activities.

(14) Bus and rail car rehabilitation.

(15) Alterations to facilities or vehicles in order to make them accessible for elderly and handicapped persons.

(16) Program administration, technical assistance activities, and operating assistance to transit authorities to continue existing service or increase service to meet routine changes in demand.

(17) The purchase of vehicles by the applicant where the use of these vehicles can be accommodated by existing facilities or by new facilities which themselves are within a CE.

(18) Track and railbed maintenance and improvements when carried out within the existing right-of-way.

(19) Purchase and installation of operating or maintenance equipment to be located within the transit facility and with no significant impacts off the site.

(20) Promulgation of rules, regulations, and directives.

(21) Deployment of electronics, photonics, communications, or information processing used singly or in combination, or as components of a fully integrated system, to improve the efficiency or safety of a surface transportation system or to enhance security or passenger convenience. Examples include, but are not limited to, traffic control and detector devices, lane management systems, electronic payment equipment, automatic vehicle locaters, automated passenger counters, computer-aided dispatching systems, radio communications systems, dynamic message signs, and security equipment including surveillance and detection cameras on roadways and in transit facilities and on buses.

(22) Projects, as defined in 23 U.S.C. 101, that would take place entirely within the existing operational right-of-way. Existing operational right-of-way refers to right-of-way that has been disturbed for an existing transportation facility or is maintained for a transportation purpose. This area includes the features associated with the physical footprint of the transportation facility (including the roadway, bridges, interchanges, culverts, drainage, fixed guideways, mitigation areas, etc.) and other areas maintained for transportation purposes such as clear zone, traffic control signage, landscaping, any rest areas with direct access to a controlled access highway, areas maintained for safety and security of a transportation facility, parking facilities with direct access to an existing transportation facility, transit power substations, transit venting structures, and transit maintenance facilities. Portions of the right-of-way that have not been disturbed or that are not maintained for transportation purposes are not in the existing operational right-of-way.

(23) Federally-funded projects:

(i) That receive less than $5,000,000 of Federal funds; or

(ii) With a total estimated cost of not more than $30,000,000 and Federal funds comprising less than 15 percent of the total estimated project cost.

(d) Additional actions which meet the criteria for a CE in the CEQ regulations (40 CFR 1508.4) and paragraph (a) of this section may be designated as CEs only after the FHWA approval. The applicant shall submit documentation which demonstrates that the specific conditions or criteria for these CEs are satisfied and that significant environmental effects will not result. Examples of such actions include but are not limited to:

(1) Modernization of a highway by resurfacing, restoration, rehabilitation, reconstruction, adding shoulders, or adding auxiliary lanes (e.g., parking, weaving, turning, climbing).

(2) Highway safety or traffic operations improvement projects including the installation of ramp metering control devices and lighting.

(3) Bridge rehabilitation, reconstruction or replacement or the construction of grade separation to replace existing at-grade railroad crossings.

(4) Transportation corridor fringe parking facilities.

(5) Construction of new truck weigh stations or rest areas.

(6) Approvals for disposal of excess right-of-way or for joint or limited use of right-of-way, where the proposed use does not have significant adverse impacts.

(7) Approvals for changes in access control.

(8) Construction of new bus storage and maintenance facilities in areas used predominantly for industrial or transportation purposes where such construction is not inconsistent with existing zoning and located on or near a street with adequate capacity to handle anticipated bus and support vehicle traffic.

(9) Rehabilitation or reconstruction of existing rail and bus buildings and ancillary facilities where only minor amounts of additional land are required and there is not a substantial increase in the number of users.

(10) Construction of bus transfer facilities (an open area consisting of passenger shelters, boarding areas, kiosks and related street improvements) when located in a commercial area or other high activity center in which there is adequate street capacity for projected bus traffic.

(11) Construction of rail storage and maintenance facilities in areas used predominantly for industrial or transportation purposes where such construction is not inconsistent with existing zoning and where there is no significant noise impact on the surrounding community.

(12) Acquisition of land for hardship or protective purposes. Hardship and protective buying will be permitted only for a particular parcel or a limited number of parcels. These types of land acquisition qualify for a CE only where the acquisition will not limit the evaluation of alternatives, including shifts in alignment for planned construction projects, which may be required in the NEPA process. No project development on such land may proceed until the NEPA process has been completed.

(i) Hardship acquisition is early acquisition of property by the applicant at the property owner's request to alleviate particular hardship to the owner, in contrast to others, because of an inability to sell his property. This is justified when the property owner can document on the basis of health, safety or financial reasons that remaining in the property poses an undue hardship compared to others.

(ii) Protective acquisition is done to prevent imminent development of a parcel which may be needed for a proposed transportation corridor or site. Documentation must clearly demonstrate that development of the land would preclude future transportation use and that such development is imminent. Advance acquisition is not permitted for the sole purpose of reducing the cost of property for a proposed project.

(e) Where a pattern emerges of granting CE status for a particular type of action, the FHWA will initiate rulemaking proposing to add this type of action to the list of categorical exclusions in paragraph (c) or (d) of this section, as appropriate.

[52 FR 32660, Aug. 28, 1987; 53 FR 11066, Apr. 5, 1988, as amended at 70 FR 24469, May 9, 2005; 74 FR 12529, Mar. 24, 2009; 78 FR 8983, Feb. 7, 2013; 78 FR 11602, Feb. 19, 2013; 79 FR 2118, Jan. 13, 2014]

§771.118 FTA categorical exclusions

Link to an amendment published at 79 FR 2118, January 13, 2014.

(a) Categorical exclusions (CEs) are actions which meet the definition contained in 40 CFR 1508.4, and, based on past experience with similar actions, do not involve significant environmental impacts. They are actions which: do not induce significant impacts to planned growth or land use for the area; do not require the relocation of significant numbers of people; do not have a significant impact on any natural, cultural, recreational, historic or other resource; do not involve significant air, noise, or water quality impacts; do not have significant impacts on travel patterns; or do not otherwise, either individually or cumulatively, have any significant environmental impacts.

(b) Any action which normally would be classified as a CE but could involve unusual circumstances will require FTA, in cooperation with the applicant, to conduct appropriate environmental studies to determine if the CE classification is proper. Such unusual circumstances include:

(1) Significant environmental impacts;

(2) Substantial controversy on environmental grounds;

(3) Significant impact on properties protected by Section 4(f) of the DOT Act or Section 106 of the National Historic Preservation Act; or

(4) Inconsistencies with any Federal, State, or local law, requirement or administrative determination relating to the environmental aspects of the action.

(c) Actions that FTA determines fall within the following categories of FTA CEs and that meet the criteria for CEs in the CEQ regulation (40 CFR 1508.4) and paragraph (a) of this section normally do not require any further NEPA approvals by FTA.

(1) Acquisition, installation, operation, evaluation, replacement, and improvement of discrete utilities and similar appurtenances (existing and new) within or adjacent to existing transportation right-of-way, such as: utility poles, underground wiring, cables, and information systems; and power substations and utility transfer stations.

(2) Acquisition, construction, maintenance, rehabilitation, and improvement or limited expansion of stand-alone recreation, pedestrian, or bicycle facilities, such as: a multiuse pathway, lane, trail, or pedestrian bridge; and transit plaza amenities.

(3) Activities designed to mitigate environmental harm that cause no harm themselves or to maintain and enhance environmental quality and site aesthetics, and employ construction best management practices, such as: noise mitigation activities; rehabilitation of public transportation buildings, structures, or facilities; retrofitting for energy or other resource conservation; and landscaping or re-vegetation.

(4) Planning and administrative activities which do not involve or lead directly to construction, such as: training, technical assistance and research; promulgation of rules, regulations, directives, or program guidance; approval of project concepts; engineering; and operating assistance to transit authorities to continue existing service or increase service to meet routine demand.

(5) Activities, including repairs, replacements, and rehabilitations, designed to promote transportation safety, security, accessibility and effective communication within or adjacent to existing right-of-way, such as: the deployment of Intelligent Transportation Systems and components; installation and improvement of safety and communications equipment, including hazard elimination and mitigation; installation of passenger amenities and traffic signals; and retrofitting existing transportation vehicles, facilities or structures, or upgrading to current standards.

(6) Acquisition or transfer of an interest in real property that is not within or adjacent to recognized environmentally sensitive areas (e.g., wetlands, non-urban parks, wildlife management areas) and does not result in a substantial change in the functional use of the property or in substantial displacements, such as: acquisition for scenic easements or historic sites for the purpose of preserving the site. This CE extends only to acquisitions and transfers that will not limit the evaluation of alternatives for future FTA-assisted projects that make use of the acquired or transferred property.

(7) Acquisition, installation, rehabilitation, replacement, and maintenance of vehicles or equipment, within or accommodated by existing facilities, that does not result in a change in functional use of the facilities, such as: equipment to be located within existing facilities and with no substantial off-site impacts; and vehicles, including buses, rail cars, trolley cars, ferry boats and people movers that can be accommodated by existing facilities or by new facilities that qualify for a categorical exclusion.

(8) Maintenance, rehabilitation, and reconstruction of facilities that occupy substantially the same geographic footprint and do not result in a change in functional use, such as: improvements to bridges, tunnels, storage

yards, buildings, stations, and terminals; construction of platform extensions, passing track, and retaining walls; and improvements to tracks and railbeds.

(9) Assembly or construction of facilities that is consistent with existing land use and zoning requirements (including floodplain regulations) and uses primarily land disturbed for transportation use, such as: buildings and associated structures; bus transfer stations or intermodal centers; busways and streetcar lines or other transit investments within areas of the right-of-way occupied by the physical footprint of the existing facility or otherwise maintained or used for transportation operations; and parking facilities.

(10) Development of facilities for transit and non-transit purposes, located on, above, or adjacent to existing transit facilities, that are not part of a larger transportation project and do not substantially enlarge such facilities, such as: police facilities, daycare facilities, public service facilities, amenities, and commercial, retail, and residential development.

(11) The following actions for transportation facilities damaged by an incident resulting in an emergency declared by the Governor of the State and concurred in by the Secretary, or a disaster or emergency declared by the President pursuant to the Robert T. Stafford Act (42 U.S.C. 5121):

(i) Emergency repairs under 49 U.S.C. 5324; and

(ii) The repair, reconstruction, restoration, retrofitting, or replacement of any road, highway, bridge, tunnel, or transit facility (such as a ferry dock or bus transfer station), including ancillary transportation facilities (such as pedestrian/bicycle paths and bike lanes), that is in operation or under construction when damaged and the action:

(A) Occurs within the existing right-of-way and in a manner that substantially conforms to the preexisting design, function, and location as the original (which may include upgrades to meet existing codes and standards as well as upgrades warranted to address conditions that have changed since the original construction); and

(B) Is commenced within a 2-year period beginning on the date of the declaration.

(12) Projects, as defined in 23 U.S.C. 101, that would take place entirely within the existing operational right-of-way. Existing operational right-of-way refers to right-of-way that has been disturbed for an existing transportation facility or is maintained for a transportation purpose. This area includes the features associ-

ated with the physical footprint of the transportation facility (including the roadway, bridges, interchanges, culverts, drainage, fixed guideways, mitigation areas, etc.) and other areas maintained for transportation purposes such as clear zone, traffic control signage, landscaping, any rest areas with direct access to a controlled access highway, areas maintained for safety and security of a transportation facility, parking facilities with direct access to an existing transportation facility, transit power substations, transit venting structures, and transit maintenance facilities. Portions of the right-of-way that have not been disturbed or that are not maintained for transportation purposes are not in the existing operational right-of-way.

(13) Federally-funded projects:

(i) That receive less than $5,000,000 of Federal funds; or

(ii) With a total estimated cost of not more than $30,000,000 and Federal funds comprising less than 15 percent of the total estimated project cost.

(d) Additional actions which meet the criteria for a CE in the CEQ regulations (40 CFR 1508.4) and paragraph (a) of this section may be designated as CEs only after FTA approval. The applicant shall submit documentation which demonstrates that the specific conditions or criteria for these CEs are satisfied and that significant environmental effects will not result. Examples of such actions include but are not limited to:

(1) Modernization of a highway by resurfacing, restoring, rehabilitating, or reconstructing shoulders or auxiliary lanes (e.g., lanes for parking, weaving, turning, climbing).

(2) Bridge replacement or the construction of grade separation to replace existing at-grade railroad crossings.

(3) Acquisition of land for hardship or protective purposes. Hardship and protective buying will be permitted only for a particular parcel or a limited number of parcels. These types of land acquisition qualify for a CE only where the acquisition will not limit the evaluation of alternatives, including shifts in alignment for planned construction projects, which may be required in the NEPA process. No project development on such land may proceed until the NEPA process has been completed.

(i) Hardship acquisition is early acquisition of property by the applicant at the property owner's request to alleviate particular hardship to the owner, in contrast to others, because of an inability to sell his property. This is justified when the property owner can document on the basis of health, safety or financial reasons that remaining in the property poses an undue hardship compared to others.

(ii) Protective acquisition is done to prevent imminent development of a parcel which may be needed for a proposed transportation corridor or site. Documentation must clearly demonstrate that development of the land would preclude future transportation use and that such development is imminent. Advance acquisition is not permitted for the sole purpose of reducing the cost of property for a proposed project.

(4) Acquisition of right-of-way. No project development on the acquired right-of-way may proceed until the NEPA process for such project development, including the consideration of alternatives, has been completed.

(5) [Reserved].

(6) Facility modernization through construction or replacement of existing components.

(e) Where a pattern emerges of granting CE status for a particular type of action, FTA will initiate rulemaking proposing to add this type of action to the appropriate list of categorical exclusions in this section.

[78 FR 8983, Feb. 7, 2013, as amended at 78 FR 11602, Feb. 19, 2013; 79 FR 2118, Jan. 13, 2014]

§771.119 Environmental assessments.

(a) An EA shall be prepared by the applicant in consultation with the Administration for each action that is not a CE and does not clearly require the preparation of an EIS, or where the Administration believes an EA would assist in determining the need for an EIS.

(b) For actions that require an EA, the applicant, in consultation with the Administration, shall, at the earliest appropriate time, begin consultation with interested agencies and others to advise them of the scope of the project and to achieve the following objectives: determine which aspects of the proposed action have potential for social, economic, or environmental impact; identify alternatives and measures which might mitigate adverse environmental impacts; and identify other environmental review and consultation requirements which should be performed concurrently with the EA. The applicant shall accomplish this through an early coordination process (*i.e.*, procedures under §771.111) or through a scoping process. Public involvement shall be summarized and the results of agency coordination shall be included in the EA.

(c) The EA is subject to Administration approval before it is made available to the public as an Administration document.

(d) The EA need not be circulated for comment but the document must be made available for public inspection at the applicant's office and at the appropriate Administration field offices in accordance with paragraphs (e) and (f) of this section. Notice of availability of the EA, briefly describing the action and its impacts, shall be sent by the applicant to the affected units of Federal, State and local government. Notice shall also be sent to the State intergovernmental review contacts established under Executive Order 12372.

(e) When a public hearing is held as part of the application for Federal funds, the EA shall be available at the public hearing and for a minimum of 15 days in advance of the public hearing. The notice of the public hearing in local newspapers shall announce the availability of the EA and where it may be obtained or reviewed. Comments shall be submitted in writing to the applicant or the Administration within 30 days of the availability of the EA unless the Administration determines, for good cause, that a different period is warranted. Public hearing requirements are as described in §771.111.

(f) When a public hearing is not held, the applicant shall place a notice in a newspaper(s) similar to a public hearing notice and at a similar stage of development of the action, advising the public of the availability of the EA and where information concerning the action may be obtained. The notice shall invite comments from all interested parties. Comments shall be submitted in writing to the applicant or the Administration within 30 days of the publication of the notice unless the Administration determines, for good cause, that a different period is warranted.

(g) If no significant impacts are identified, the applicant shall furnish the Administration a copy of the revised EA, as appropriate; the public hearing transcript, where applicable; copies of any comments received and responses thereto; and recommend a FONSI. The EA should also document compliance, to the extent possible, with all applicable environmental laws and Executive orders, or provide reasonable assurance that their requirements can be met.

(h) When the Administration expects to issue a FONSI for an action described in §771.115(a), copies of the EA shall be made available for public review

(including the affected units of government) for a minimum of 30 days before the Administration makes its final decision (See 40 CFR 1501.4(e)(2).) This public availability shall be announced by a notice similar to a public hearing notice.

(i) If, at any point in the EA process, the Administration determines that the action is likely to have a significant impact on the environment, the preparation of an EIS will be required.

(j) If the Administration decides to apply 23 U.S.C. 139 to an action involving an EA, then the EA shall be prepared in accordance with the applicable provisions of that statute.

[52 FR 32660, Aug. 28, 1987, as amended at 70 FR 24470, May 9, 2005; 74 FR 12529, Mar. 24, 2009]

§771.121 Findings of no significant impact.

(a) The Administration will review the EA and any public hearing comments and other comments received regarding the EA. If the Administration agrees with the applicant's recommendations pursuant to §771.119(g), it will make a separate written FONSI incorporating by reference the EA and any other appropriate environmental documents.

(b) After a FONSI has been made by the Administration, a notice of availability of the FONSI shall be sent by the applicant to the affected units of Federal, State and local government and the document shall be available from the applicant and the Administration upon request by the public. Notice shall also be sent to the State intergovernmental review contacts established under Executive Order 12372.

(c) If another Federal agency has issued a FONSI on an action which includes an element proposed for Administration funding, the Administration will evaluate the other agency's FONSI. If the Administration determines that this element of the project and its environmental impacts have been adequately identified and assessed, and concurs in the decision to issue a FONSI, the Administration will issue its own FONSI incorporating the other agency's FONSI. If environmental issues have not been adequately identified and assessed, the Administration will require appropriate environmental studies.

§771.123 Draft environmental impact statements.

(a) A draft EIS shall be prepared when the Administration determines that the action is likely to cause significant impacts on the environment. When the applicant, after consultation with any project sponsor that is not the applicant, has notified the Administration in accordance with 23 U.S.C. 139(e) and the decision has been made by the Administration to prepare an EIS, the Administration will issue a Notice of Intent (40 CFR 1508.22) for publication in the FEDERAL REGISTER. Applicants are encouraged to announce the intent to prepare an EIS by appropriate means at the local level.

(b) After publication of the Notice of Intent, the lead agencies, in cooperation with the applicant (if not a lead agency), will begin a scoping process which may take into account any planning work already accomplished, in accordance with 23 CFR 450.212 or 450.318. The scoping process will be used to identify the purpose and need, the range of alternatives and impacts, and the significant issues to be addressed in the EIS and to achieve the other objectives of 40 CFR 1501.7. For the FHWA, scoping is normally achieved through public and agency involvement procedures required by §771.111. For FTA, scoping is achieved by soliciting agency and public responses to the action by letter or by holding scoping meetings. If a scoping meeting is to be held, it should be announced in the Administration's Notice of Intent and by appropriate means at the local level.

(c) The draft EIS shall be prepared by the lead agencies, in cooperation with the applicant (if not a lead agency). The draft EIS shall evaluate all reasonable alternatives to the action and discuss the reasons why other alternatives, which may have been considered, were eliminated from detailed study. The draft EIS shall also summarize the studies, reviews, consultations, and coordination required by environmental laws or Executive Orders to the extent appropriate at this stage in the environmental process.

(d) Any of the lead agencies may select a consultant to assist in the preparation of an EIS in accordance with applicable contracting procedures and with 40 CFR 1506.5(c).

(e) The Administration, when satisfied that the draft EIS complies with NEPA requirements, will approve the draft EIS for circulation by signing and dating the cover sheet.

(f) A lead, joint lead, or a cooperating agency shall be responsible for printing the EIS. The initial printing of the draft EIS shall be in sufficient quantity to meet requirements for copies which can reasonably be expected from agencies, organizations, and individuals. Normally, copies will be furnished free of charge. However, with Administration concurrence, the party requesting the draft EIS may be charged a fee which is not more than the actual cost of reproducing the copy or may be directed to the nearest location where the statement may be reviewed.

(g) The draft EIS shall be circulated for comment by the applicant on behalf of the Administration. The draft EIS shall be made available to the public and transmitted to agencies for comment no later than the time the document is filed with the Environmental Protection Agency in accordance with 40 CFR 1506.9. The draft EIS shall be transmitted to:

(1) Public officials, interest groups, and members of the public known to have an interest in the proposed action or the draft EIS;

(2) Federal, State and local government agencies expected to have jurisdiction or responsibility over, or interest or expertise in, the action. Copies shall be provided directly to appropriate State and local agencies, and to the State intergovernmental review contacts established under Executive Order 12372; and

(3) States and Federal land management entities which may be significantly affected by the proposed action or any of the alternatives. These copies shall be accompanied by a request that such State or entity advise the Administration in writing of any disagreement with the evaluation of impacts in the statement. The Administration will furnish the comments received to the applicant along with a written assessment of any disagreements for incorporation into the final EIS.

(h) The FTA requires a public hearing during the circulation period of all draft EISs. FHWA public hearing requirements are as described in §771.111(h). Whenever a public hearing is held, the draft EIS shall be available at the public hearing and for a minimum of 15 days in advance of the public hearing. The availability of the draft EIS shall be mentioned, and public comments requested, in any public hearing notice and at any public hearing presentation. If a public hearing on an action proposed for FHWA funding is not held, a notice shall be placed in a newspaper similar to a public hearing notice advising where the draft EIS is available for review, how copies may be obtained, and where the comments should be sent.

(i) The FEDERAL REGISTER public availability notice (40 CFR 1506.10) shall establish a period of not fewer than 45 days nor more than 60 days for the return of comments on the draft EIS unless a different period is established in accordance with 23 U.S.C. 139(g)(2)(A). The notice and the draft EIS transmittal letter shall identify where comments are to be sent.

[52 FR 32660, Aug. 28, 1987, as amended at 70 FR 24470, May 9, 2005; 74 FR 12529, Mar. 24, 2009; 78 FR 8984, Feb. 7, 2013]

§771.125 Final environmental impact statements.

(a)(1) After circulation of a draft EIS and consideration of comments received, a final EIS shall be prepared by the lead agencies, in cooperation with the applicant (if not a lead agency). The final EIS shall identify the preferred alternative and evaluate all reasonable alternatives considered. It shall also discuss substantive comments received on the draft EIS and responses thereto, summarize public involvement, and describe the mitigation measures that are to be incorporated into the proposed action. Mitigation measures presented as commitments in the final EIS will be incorporated into the project as specified in paragraphs (b) and (d) of §771.109. The final EIS should also document compliance, to the extent possible, with all applicable environmental laws and Executive Orders, or provide reasonable assurance that their requirements can be met.

(2) Every reasonable effort shall be made to resolve interagency disagreements on actions before processing the final EIS. If significant issues remain unresolved, the final EIS shall identify those issues and the consultations and other efforts made to resolve them.

(b) The final EIS will be reviewed for legal sufficiency prior to Administration approval.

(c) The Administration will indicate approval of the EIS for an action by signing and dating the cover page. Final EISs prepared for actions in the following categories will be submitted to the Administration's Headquarters for prior concurrence:

(1) Any action for which the Administration determines that the final EIS should be reviewed at the Headquarters office. This would typically occur when the Headquarters office determines that (i) additional coordination with other Federal, State or local governmental agencies is needed; (ii) the social, economic, or environmental impacts of the action may need to be more fully explored; (iii) the impacts of the proposed action are unusually great; (iv) major issues remain unresolved; or (v) the action involves national policy issues.

(2) Any action to which a Federal, State or local government agency has indicated opposition on environmental grounds (which has not been resolved to the written satisfaction of the objecting agency).

(d) The signature of the FTA approving official on the cover sheet also indicates compliance with 49 U.S.C. 5324(b) and fulfillment of the grant application requirements of 49 U.S.C. 5323(b).

(e) Approval of the final EIS is not an Administration action as defined in paragraph (c) of §771.107 and does not commit the Administration to approve any future grant request to fund the preferred alternative.

(f) The initial printing of the final EIS shall be in sufficient quantity to meet the request for copies which can be reasonably expected from agencies, organizations, and individuals. Normally, copies will be furnished free of charge. However, with Administration concurrence, the party requesting the final EIS may be charged a fee which is not more than the actual cost of reproducing the copy or may be directed to the nearest location where the statement may be reviewed.

(g) The final EIS shall be transmitted to any persons, organizations, or agencies that made substantive comments on the draft EIS or requested a copy, no later than the time the document is filed with EPA. In the case of lengthy documents, the agency may provide alternative circulation processes in accordance with 40 CFR 1502.19. The applicant shall also publish a notice of availability in local newspapers and make the final EIS available through the mechanism established pursuant to DOT Order 4600.13 which implements Executive Order 12372. When filed with EPA, the final EIS shall be available for public review at the applicant's offices and at appropriate Administration offices. A copy should also be made available for public review at institutions such as local government offices, libraries, and schools, as appropriate.

[52 FR 32660, Aug. 28, 1987, as amended at 70 FR 24470, May 9, 2005; 74 FR 12530, Mar. 24, 2009]

§771.127 Record of decision.

(a) The Administration will complete and sign a ROD no sooner than 30 days after publication of the final EIS notice in the FEDERAL REGISTER or 90 days after publication of a notice for the draft EIS, whichever is later. The ROD will present the basis for the decision as specified in 40 CFR 1505.2, summarize any mitigation measures that will be incorporated in the project and document any required Section 4(f) approval in accordance with part 774 of this title. Until any required ROD has been signed, no further approvals may be given except for administrative activities taken to secure further project funding and other activities consistent with 40 CFR 1506.1.

(b) If the Administration subsequently wishes to approve an alternative which was not identified as the preferred alternative but was fully evaluated in the final EIS, or proposes to make substantial changes to the mitigation measures or findings discussed in the ROD, a revised ROD shall be subject to review by those Administration offices which reviewed the final EIS under §771.125(c). To the extent practicable the approved revised ROD shall be provided to all persons, organizations, and agencies that received a copy of the final EIS pursuant to §771.125(g).

[52 FR 32660, Aug. 28, 1987, as amended at 73 FR 13395, Mar. 12, 2008; 74 FR 12530, Mar. 24, 2009]

§771.129 Re-evaluations.

(a) A written evaluation of the draft EIS shall be prepared by the applicant in cooperation with the Administration if an acceptable final EIS is not submitted to the Administration within three years from the date of the draft EIS circulation. The purpose of this evaluation is to determine whether or not a supplement to the draft EIS or a new draft EIS is needed.

(b) A written evaluation of the final EIS will be required before further approvals may be granted if major steps to advance the action (e.g., authority to undertake final design, authority to acquire a significant portion of the right-of-way, or approval of the plans, specifications and estimates) have not occurred within three years after the approval of the final EIS, final EIS supplement, or the last major Administration approval or grant.

(c) After approval of the ROD, FONSI, or CE designation, the applicant shall consult with the Administration prior to requesting any major approvals or grants to establish whether or not the approved environmental document or CE designation remains valid for the requested Administration action. These consultations will be documented when determined necessary by the Administration.

[52 FR 32660, Aug. 28, 1987; 53 FR 11066, Apr. 5, 1988, as amended at 74 FR 12530, Mar. 24, 2009]

§771.130 Supplemental environmental impact statements.

(a) A draft EIS, final EIS, or supplemental EIS may be supplemented at any time. An EIS shall be supplemented whenever the Administration determines that:

(1) Changes to the proposed action would result in significant environmental impacts that were not evaluated in the EIS; or

(2) New information or circumstances relevant to environmental concerns and bearing on the proposed action or its impacts would result in significant environmental impacts not evaluated in the EIS.

(b) However, a supplemental EIS will not be necessary where:

(1) The changes to the proposed action, new information, or new circumstances result in a lessening of adverse environmental impacts evaluated in the EIS without causing other environmental impacts that are significant and were not evaluated in the EIS; or

(2) The Administration decides to approve an alternative fully evaluated in an approved final EIS but not identified as the preferred alternative. In such a case, a revised ROD shall be prepared and circulated in accordance with §771.127(b).

(c) Where the Administration is uncertain of the significance of the new impacts, the applicant will develop appropriate environmental studies or, if the Administration deems appropriate, an EA to assess the impacts of the changes, new information, or new circumstances. If, based upon the studies, the Administration determines that a supplemental EIS is not necessary, the Administration shall so indicate in the project file.

(d) A supplement is to be developed using the same process and format (i.e., draft EIS, final EIS, and ROD) as an original EIS, except that scoping is not required.

(e) A supplemental draft EIS may be necessary for major new fixed guideway capital projects proposed for FTA funding if there is a substantial change in the level of detail on project impacts during project planning and development. The supplement will address site-specific impacts and refined cost estimates that have been developed since the original draft EIS.

(f) In some cases, a supplemental EIS may be required to address issues of limited scope, such as the extent of proposed mitigation or the evaluation of location or design variations for a limited portion of the overall project. Where this is the case, the preparation of a supplemental EIS shall not necessarily:

(1) Prevent the granting of new approvals;

(2) Require the withdrawal of previous approvals; or

(3) Require the suspension of project activities; for any activity not directly affected by the supplement. If the changes in question are of such magnitude to require

a reassessment of the entire action, or more than a limited portion of the overall action, the Administration shall suspend any activities which would have an adverse environmental impact or limit the choice of reasonable alternatives, until the supplemental EIS is completed.

[52 FR 32660, Aug. 28, 1987, as amended at 70 FR 24470, May 9, 2005; 74 FR 12530, Mar. 24, 2009]

§771.131 Emergency action procedures.

Requests for deviations from the procedures in this regulation because of emergency circumstances (40 CFR 1506.11) shall be referred to the Administration's headquarters for evaluation and decision after consultation with CEQ.

§771.133 Compliance with other requirements.

The final EIS or FONSI should document compliance with requirements of all applicable environmental laws, Executive orders, and other related requirements. If full compliance is not possible by the time the final EIS or FONSI is prepared, the final EIS or FONSI should reflect consultation with the appropriate agencies and provide reasonable assurance that the requirements will be met. Approval of the environmental document constitutes adoption of any Administration findings and determinations that are contained therein. The Administration's approval of an environmental document constitutes its finding of compliance with the report requirements of 23 U.S.C. 128.

[52 FR 32660, Aug. 28, 1987, as amended at 74 FR 12530, Mar. 24, 2009]

§771.137 International actions.

(a) The requirements of this part apply to:

(1) Administration actions significantly affecting the environment of a foreign nation not participating in the action or not otherwise involved in the action.

(2) Administration actions outside the U.S., its territories, and possessions which significantly affect natural resources of global importance designated for protection by the President or by international agreement.

(b) If communication with a foreign government concerning environmental studies or documentation is anticipated, the Administration shall coordinate such communication with the Department of State through the Office of the Secretary of Transportation.

§771.139 Limitations on actions.

Notices announcing decisions by the Administration or by other Federal agencies on a transportation project may be published in the FEDERAL REGISTER indicating that such decisions are final within the meaning of 23 U.S.C. 139(*l*). Claims arising under Federal law seeking judicial review of any such decisions are barred unless filed within 180 days after publication of the notice. This 180-day time period does not lengthen any shorter time period for seeking judicial review that otherwise is established by the Federal law under which judicial review is allowed.[6] This provision does not create any right of judicial review or place any limit on filing a claim that a person has violated the terms of a permit, license, or approval.

[74 FR 12530, Mar. 24, 2009]

---

6. The FHWA published a detailed discussion of US DOT's interpretation of 23 U.S.C. 139(*l*), together with information applicable to FHWA projects about implementation procedures for 23 U.S.C. 139(*l*), in appendix E to the "SAFETEA-LU Environmental Review Process: Final Guidance," dated November 15, 2006. The implementation procedures in appendix E apply only to FHWA projects. The section 6002 guidance, including appendix E, is available at *http://www.fhwa.dot.gov/*, or in hard copy by request.

NEPA Deskbook

Appendix 15 Department of the Interior Regulations and Procedures (Part 516)

Department of the Interior Departmental Manual

Effective Date: 9/1/09

Series: Environmental Quality Programs

Part 516: National Environmental Policy Act of 1969

Chapter 3: Managing the NEPA Process

Originating Office: Office of Environmental Policy and Compliance

516 DM 3

3.1 **Purpose**. This chapter provides supplementary instructions for implementing those provisions of the CEQ Regulations and the Department's National Environmental Policy Act (NEPA) Regulations pertaining to procedures for implementing and managing the NEPA process.

3.2 **Organizational Responsibilities for Environmental Quality**.

A. Office of Environmental Policy and Compliance (OEPC). The Director, OEPC, is responsible for providing advice and assistance to the Department on matters pertaining to environmental quality and for overseeing and coordinating the Department's compliance with NEPA. (See also 112 DM 4.)

B. Bureaus and Offices. Heads of bureaus and offices will designate organizational elements or individuals, as appropriate, at headquarters and regional levels to be responsible for overseeing matters pertaining to the environmental effects of the bureau's plans and programs. The individuals assigned these responsibilities should have management experience or potential, understand the bureau's planning and decision making processes, and be well trained in environmental matters, including the Department's policies and procedures so that their advice has significance in the bureau's planning and decisions. These organizational elements will be identified in chapters 8-15, which contain all bureau NEPA requirements.

3.3 **Approval of Environmental Impact Statements (EISs)**.

A. A program Assistant Secretary is authorized to approve an EIS in those cases where the responsibility for the decision for which the EIS has been prepared rests with the Assistant Secretary or below. The Assistant Secretary may further assign the authority to approve the EIS if he or she chooses. The AS/PMB will make certain that each program Assistant Secretary has adequate safeguards to ensure that the EISs comply with NEPA, the Council of Environmental Quality (CEQ) Regulations, the Department's NEPA Regulations, and the Departmental Manual (DM).

B. The AS/PMB is authorized to approve an EIS in those cases where the decision for which the EIS has been prepared will occur at a level in the Department above an individual program Assistant Secretary.

3.4 **List of Specific Compliance Responsibilities**.

A. Bureaus and offices shall:

(1) Prepare NEPA handbooks providing guidance on the interpretation of NEPA, the CEQ regulations, 43 CFR Part 46, and the applicable portions of this Part in principal program areas.

(2) Prepare program regulations or directives for applicants.

(3) Propose and apply categorical exclusions (CEs).

(4) Prepare and approve Environmental Assessments (EAs).

(5) Decide whether to prepare an EIS.

(6) Prepare and publish NOIs and FONSIs.

(7) Prepare and, when assigned, approve EISs.

B. Program Assistant Secretaries shall:

(1) Approve bureau and office handbooks.

(2) Approve regulations or directives for applicants.

(3) Approve proposed categorical exclusions.

(4) Approve EISs pursuant to 516 DM 3.3.

C. The AS/PMB shall:

(1) Concur with regulations or directives for applicants.

(2) Concur with proposed categorical exclusions.

(3) Approve EISs pursuant to 516 DM 3.3. (See also 43 CFR 46.150).

3.5 **Bureau Requirements**.

A. Requirements specific to bureaus appear as separate chapters beginning with chapter 8 of this Part and include the following:

(1) Identification of officials and organizational elements responsible for NEPA compliance.

(2) List of program regulations or directives which provide information to applicants.

(3) Identification of major decision points in principal programs for which an EIS is normally prepared.

(4) List of projects or groups of projects for which an EA is normally prepared.

(5) List of categorical exclusions.

B. Bureau requirements are found in the following chapters for the current bureaus:

(1) U.S. Fish and Wildlife Service (Chapter 8).

(2) U.S. Geological Survey (Chapter 9).

(3) Bureau of Indian Affairs (Chapter 10).

(4) Bureau of Land Management (Chapter 11).

(5) National Park Service (Chapter 12).

(6) Office of Surface Mining (Chapter 13).

(7) Bureau of Reclamation (Chapter 14).

(8) Minerals Management Service (Chapter 15).

C. Offices in the Office of the Secretary (O/S) must comply with the policy in this chapter and will consult with the OEPC about compliance activities.

3.6 **Information about the NEPA Process**. The OEPC will periodically publish a Departmental list of bureau contacts where information about the NEPA process and the status of EISs may be obtained. This list will be available on OEPC's website at: http://www.doi.gov/oepc/.

Department of the Interior Departmental Manual

Effective Date: 5/27/04

Series: Environmental Quality Programs

Part 516: National Environmental Policy Act of 1969

Chapter 8: Managing the NEPA Process—U.S. Fish and Wildlife Service

Originating Office: U.S. Fish and Wildlife Service

516 DM 8

8.1 **Purpose**. This Chapter provides supplementary requirements for implementing provisions of 516 DM 1 through 6 within the Department's U.S. Fish and Wildlife Service. This Chapter is referenced in 516 DM 6.5.

8.2 **NEPA Responsibility**.

A. The Director is responsible for NEPA compliance for U.S. Fish and Wildlife Service (Service) activities, including approving recommendations to the Assistant Secretary (FW) for proposed referrals to the Council on Environmental Quality (CEQ) of other agency actions under 40 CFR 1504.

B. Each Assistant Director (Refuges and Wildlife, Fisheries, International Affairs, External Affairs, and Ecological Services) is responsible for general guidance and compliance in their respective areas of responsibility.

C. The Assistant Director for Ecological Services has been delegated oversight responsibility for Service NEPA compliance.

D. The Division of Habitat Conservation (DHC--Washington), which reports to the Assistant Director for Ecological Services, is responsible for internal control of the environmental review and analysis of documents prepared by other agencies and environmental statements prepared by the various Service Divisions. This office is also responsible for preparing Service NEPA procedures, guidelines, and instructions, and for supplying technical assistance and specialized training in NEPA compliance, in cooperation with the Service Office of Training and Education, to Service entities. The Washington Office Environmental Coordinator, who reports to DHC, provides staff assistance on NEPA matters to the Director, Assistant Directors, and their divisions and offices, and serves as the Service NEPA liaison to the CEQ, the Department's Office of Environmental Policy and Compliance (OEPC), and NEPA liaisons in other Federal agencies, in accordance with 516 DM 6.2.

E. Each Regional Director is responsible for NEPA compliance in his/her area of responsibility. The Regional Director should ensure that Service decisionmakers in his/her area of responsibility contact affected Federal agencies and State, tribal and local governments when initiating an action subject to an EA or EIS. An individual in each Regional Office, named by title and reporting to the Assistant Regional Director for Ecological Services, other appropriate Assistant Regional Director, or the Regional Director, will have NEPA coordination duties with all program areas at the Regional level similar to those of the Washington Office Environmental Coordinator, in accordance with 516 DM 6.2.

8.3 **General Service Guidance**. Service guidance on internal NEPA matters is found in 30 AM 2-3 (organizational structure and internal NEPA compliance), 550 FW1-3 (in preparation), 550 FW 3 (documenting and implementing Service decisions on Service actions), and 550 FW 1-2 (replacement to 30 AM 2-3 in preparation). These guidance documents encourage Service participation as a cooperating agency with other Federal agencies, encourage early coordination with other agencies and the public to resolve issues in a timely manner, and provide techniques for streamlining the NEPA process and integrating the NEPA process with other Service programs, environmental laws, and Executive orders. Some Service programs have additional NEPA compliance information related to specific program planning and decisionmaking activities. Service program guidance on NEPA matters must be consistent with the Service Manual on NEPA guidance and Departmental NEPA procedures. For example, additional NEPA guidance is found in the Federal Aid Handbook (521-523 FW), refuge planning guidance (602 FW 1-3), Handbook for Habitat Conservation Planning and Incidental Take Processing, and North American Wetlands Conservation Act Grant Application Instructions.

8.4 **Guidance to Applicants**.

A. Service Permits. The Service has responsibility for issuing permits to Federal and State agencies and private parties for actions which would involve certain wildlife species and/or use of Service-administered lands. When applicable, the Service may require permit applicants to provide additional information on the proposal and on its environmental effects as may be necessary to satisfy the Service's requirements to comply with NEPA, other Federal laws, and Executive orders.

(1) Permits for the Taking, Possession, Transportation, Sale, Purchase, Barter, Exportation, or Importation of Certain Wildlife Species. The Code of Federal Regulations, Part 13, Title 50 (50 CFR 13) contains regulations for General Permit Procedures. Section 13.3 lists types of permits and the pertinent Parts of 50 CFR. These include: Importation, Exportation, and Transportation of Wildlife (Part 14); Exotic Wild Bird Conservation (Part 15); Injurious Wildlife (Part 16); Endangered and Threatened Wildlife and Plants (Part 17); Marine Mammals (Part 18); Migratory Bird Hunting (Part 20); Migratory Bird Permits (Part 21); Eagle Permits (Part 22); Endangered Species Convention (Part 23); and Importation and Exportation of Plants (Part 24). Potential permit applicants should request information from the appropriate Regional Director, or the Office of Management Authority, U.S. Fish and Wildlife Service, Department of the Interior, Washington, DC 20240, as outlined in the applicable regulation.

(2) Federal Lands Managed by the Service. Service lands are administered under the National Wildlife Refuge System Administration Act of 1966 (16 U.S.C. 668dd-668ee), the Refuge Recreation Act of 1962 (16 U.S.C. 460k-460k-4), and the Alaska National Interest Lands Conservation Act of 1980 (16 U.S.C. 410hh-3233, 43 U.S.C. 1602-1784). Inherent in these acts is the requirement that only those uses that are compatible with the purposes of the refuge system unit may be allowed on Service lands. The Service also complies with Executive Order 12996, signed March 25, 1996, entitled "Management and General Public Use of the National Wildlife Refuge System." This Executive Order identifies general public uses that will be given priority consideration in refuge planning and management, subject to meeting the compatibility requirement and if adequate funding is available to administer the use. Detailed procedures regarding comprehensive management planning and integration with NEPA are found in the Service Manual (602 FW 1-3). Reference to this and other National Wildlife Refuge System requirements are found in the Code of Federal Regulations, Title 50 parts 25-29, 31-36, 60, and 70-71. Under these regulations, these protections are extended to all Service-administered lands, including the National Fish Hatchery System.

B. Federal Assistance to States, Local or Private Entities.

(1) Federal Assistance Programs. The Service administers financial assistance (grants and/or cooperative agreements) to State, local, and private entities under the Anadromous Fish Conservation Act (CFDA #15.600); North American Wetlands Conservation Act; Fish and Wildlife Act of 1956; Migratory Bird Conservation Act; Food Security Act of 1985; Food, Agriculture, Conservation and Trade Act of 1990; Partnerships for Wildlife Act of 1992; and Consolidated Farm and Rural Development Act. The Service administers financial assistance to States under the Sport Fish Restoration Act (CFDA #15.605), Wildlife Restoration Act (CFDA #15.611), Endangered Species Act (CFDA #15.612 and 15.615), Coastal Wetlands Planning Protection and Restoration Act (CFDA #15.614), and Clean Vessel Act of 1992 (CFDA #15.616).

(2) Program Information and NEPA Compliance. Information on how State, local, and private entities may request funds and assist the Service in NEPA compliance relative to the Anadromous Fish Conservation Act may be obtained through the Division of Fish and Wildlife Management Assistance, U.S. Fish and Wildlife Service, Department of the Interior, Arlington Square Building, Room 840, Washington, D.C. 20240. Similar information regarding the North American Wetlands Conservation Act may be obtained through the North American Waterfowl and Wetlands Office, U.S. Fish and Wildlife Service, Department of the Interior, Arlington Square Building, Room 110, Washington, D.C. 20240. All other requests for information on how funds may be obtained and guidance on how to assist the Service in NEPA compliance may be obtained through the Chief, Division of Federal Aid, U.S. Fish and Wildlife Service, Department of the Interior, Arlington Square Building, Room 140, Washington, D.C. 20240.

8.5 **Categorical Exclusions**. Categorical exclusions are classes of actions which do not individually or cumulatively have a significant effect on the human environment. Categorical exclusions are not the equivalent of statutory exemptions. If exceptions to categorical exclusions apply, under 516 DM 2, Appendix 2 of the Departmental Manual, the Departmental categorical exclusions cannot be used. In addition to the actions listed in the Departmental categorical exclusions outlined in Appendix 1 of 516 DM 2, the following Service actions are designated categorical exclusions unless the action is an exception to the categorical exclusion.

A. General.

(1) Changes or amendments to an approved action when such changes have no or minor potential environmental impact.

(2) Personnel training, environmental interpretation, public safety efforts, and other educational activities, which do not involve new construction or major additions to existing facilities.

(3) The issuance and modification of procedures, including manuals, orders, guidelines, and field instructions, when the impacts are limited to administrative effects.

(4) The acquisition of real property obtained either through discretionary acts or when acquired by law, whether by way of condemnation, donation, escheat, right-of-entry, escrow, exchange, lapses, purchase, or transfer and that will be under the jurisdiction or control of the United States. Such acquisition of real property shall be in accordance with 602 DM 2 and the Service's procedures, when the acquisition is from a willing seller, continuance of or minor modification to the existing land use is planned, and the acquisition planning process has been performed in coordination with the affected public.

B. Resource Management. Prior to carrying out these actions, the Service should coordinate with affected Federal agencies and State, tribal, and local governments.

(1) Research, inventory, and information collection activities directly related to the conservation of fish and wildlife resources which involve negligible animal mortality or habitat destruction, no introduction of contaminants, or no introduction of organisms not indigenous to the affected ecosystem.

(2) The operation, maintenance, and management of existing facilities and routine recurring management activities and improvements, including renovations and replacements which result in no or only minor changes in the use, and have no or negligible environmental effects on-site or in the vicinity of the site.

(3) The construction of new, or the addition of, small structures or improvements, including structures and improvements for the restoration of wetland, riparian, instream, or native habitats, which result in no or only minor changes in the use of the affected local area. The following are examples of activities that may be included.

(a) The installation of fences.

(b) The construction of small water control structures.

(c) The planting of seeds or seedlings and other minor revegetation actions.

(d) The construction of small berms or dikes.

(e) The development of limited access for routine maintenance and management purposes.

(4) The use of prescribed burning for habitat improvement purposes, when conducted in accordance with local and State ordinances and laws.

(5) Fire management activities, including prevention and restoration measures, when conducted in accordance with Departmental and Service procedures.

(6) The reintroduction or supplementation (e.g., stocking) of native, formerly native, or established species into suitable habitat within their historic or established range, where no or negligible environmental disturbances are anticipated.

(7) Minor changes in the amounts or types of public use on Service or State-managed lands, in accordance with existing regulations, management plans, and procedures.

(8) Consultation and technical assistance activities directly related to the conservation of fish and wildlife resources.

(9) Minor changes in existing master plans, comprehensive conservation plans, or operations, when no or minor effects are anticipated. Examples could include minor changes in the type and location of compatible public use activities and land management practices.

(10) The issuance of new or revised site, unit, or activity-specific management plans for public use, land use, or other management activities when only minor changes are planned. Examples could include an amended public use plan or fire management plan.

(11) Natural resource damage assessment restoration plans, prepared under sections 107, 111, and 122(j) of the Comprehensive Environmental Response Compensation and Liability Act (CERCLA); section 311(f)(4) of the Clean Water Act; and the Oil Pollution Act; when only minor or negligible change in the use of the affected areas is planned.

C. Permit and Regulatory Functions.

(1) The issuance, denial, suspension, and revocation of permits for activities involving fish, wildlife, or plants regulated under 50 CFR Chapter 1, Subsection B, when such permits cause no or negligible environmental disturbance. These permits involve endangered and threatened species, species listed under the Convention on International Trade in Endangered Species of Wild

Fauna and Flora (CITES), marine mammals, exotic birds, migratory birds, eagles, and injurious wildlife.

(2) The issuance of ESA section 10(a)(1)(B) "low-effect" incidental take permits that, individually or cumulatively, have a minor or negligible effect on the species covered in the habitat conservation plan.

(3) The issuance of special regulations for public use of Service-managed land, which maintain essentially the permitted level of use and do not continue a level of use that has resulted in adverse environmental effects.

(4) The issuance or reissuance of permits for limited additional use of an existing right-of-way for underground or above ground power, telephone, or pipelines, where no new structures (i.e., facilities) or major improvement to those facilities are required; and for permitting a new right-of-way, where no or negligible environmental disturbances are anticipated.

(5) The issuance or reissuance of special use permits for the administration of specialized uses, including agricultural uses, or other economic uses for management purposes, when such uses are compatible, contribute to the purposes of the refuge system unit, and result in no or negligible environmental effects.

(6) The denial of special use permit applications, either initially or when permits are reviewed for renewal, when the proposed action is determined not compatible with the purposes of the refuge system unit.

(7) Activities directly related to the enforcement of fish and wildlife laws, not included in 516 DM 2, Appendix 1.4. These activities include:

(a) Assessment of civil penalties.

(b) Forfeiture of property seized or subject to forfeiture.

(c) The issuance or reissuance of rules, procedures, standards, and permits for the designation of ports, inspection, clearance, marking, and license requirements pertaining to wildlife and wildlife products, and for the humane and healthful transportation of wildlife.

(8) Actions where the Service has concurrence or coapproval with another agency and the action is a categorical exclusion for that agency. This would normally involve one Federal action or connected actions where the Service is a cooperating agency.

D. Recovery Plans. Issuance of recovery plans under section 4(f) of the ESA.

E. Financial Assistance.

(1) State, local, or private financial assistance (grants and/or cooperative agreements), including State planning grants and private land restorations, where the environmental effects are minor or negligible.

(2) Grants for categorically excluded actions in paragraphs A, B, and C, above; and categorically excluded actions in Appendix 1 of 516 DM 2.

8.6 **Actions Normally Requiring an EA**.

A. Proposals to establish most new refuges and fish hatcheries; and most additions and rehabilitations to existing installations.

B. Any habitat conservation plan that does not meet the definition of "low-effect" in the Section 10(a)(1)(B) Handbook.

C. If, for any of the above proposals, the EA determines that the proposal is a major Federal action significantly affecting the quality of the human environment, an EIS will be prepared. The determination to prepare an EIS will be made by a notice of intent in the Federal Register and by other appropriate means to notify the affected public.

8.7 **Major Actions Normally Requiring an EIS**.

A. The following Service proposals, when determined to be a major Federal action significantly affecting the quality of the human environment, will normally require the preparation of an EIS.

(1) Major proposals establishing new refuge system units, fish hatcheries, or major additions to existing installations, which involve substantive conflicts over existing State and local land use, significant controversy over the environmental effects of the proposal, or the remediation of major on-site sources of contamination.

(2) Master or comprehensive conservation plans for major new installations, or for established installations, where major new developments or substantial changes in management practices are proposed.

B. If, for any of the above proposals it is initially determined that the proposal is not a major Federal action significantly affecting the quality of the human environment, an EA will be prepared and handled in accordance with 40 CFR 1501.4(e)(2). If the EA subsequently indicates the proposed action will cause significant impacts, an EIS will be prepared.

5/27/04 #3618

Replaces 3/18/80 #3511

Department of the Interior Departmental Manual

Effective Date: 5/27/04

Series: Environmental Quality Programs

Part 516: National Environmental Policy Act of 1969

Chapter 9: Managing the NEPA Process— U.S. Geological Survey

Originating Office: U.S. Geological Survey

516 DM 9

9.1 **Purpose**. This Chapter provides supplementary requirements for implementing provisions of 516 DM 1 through 6 within the Department's U.S. Geological Survey. This Chapter is referenced in 516 DM 6.5.

9.2 **NEPA Responsibility.**

A. The Director of the U.S. Geological Survey (USGS) is responsible for National Environmental Policy Act (NEPA) compliance for USGS activities.

B. The Assistant Director for Engineering Geology produces policy guidance, direction and oversight for environmental activities including implementation of NEPA, and approves Environmental Impact Statements (EIS) prepared by the USGS. The Assistant Director is also responsible for approving USGS reviews of environmental documents, regulations or rules proposed by other agencies.

C. The Chief, Environmental Affairs Program (Reston, VA), is the focal point for NEPA matters and develops NEPA-related policy and guidance for the USGS. The Chief is responsible for: assuring the quality control of USGS environmental documents; monitoring USGS-wide activities to ensure NEPA compliance, reviewing and commenting on other bureaus' and agencies' environmental documents; managing the assignment of USGS personnel to assist other agencies in developing EISs; and assisting in the performance of specialized studies to support environmental analyses. Information about USGS environmental documents or the NEPA process can be obtained by contacting the Environmental Affairs Program.

D. The Chiefs of the Divisions or Independent Offices are responsible within their respective organizations for ensuring compliance with NEPA and applicable consultation requirements.

9.3 **Guidance to Applicants**. Because the USGS does not have any regulatory responsibilities in this area, the USGS has no applicable programs requiring guidance to applicants.

9.4 **Actions Normally Requiring an EIS or Environmental Assessment (EA).**

A. Approval of construction of major new USGS research centers or test facilities normally will require the preparation of an EIS.

B. An EA will be prepared to aid in deciding whether a finding of no significant impact is appropriate, or whether an EIS is required prior to implementing any action. The EA will be prepared in accordance with guidance provided in 516 DM 3.1. Specifically, an EA is required for all actions which are: (a) not categorically excluded; (b) listed as exceptions to the Departmental categorical exclusions in 516 DM 2, Appendix 2; (c) not being addressed by an EIS.

9.5 **Categorical Exclusions**. In addition to the actions listed in the Departmental categorical exclusions specified in Appendix 1 of 516 DM 2, many of which the USGS also performs, the following USGS actions are designated categorical exclusions unless the action qualifies as an exemption from the Department's categorical exclusions under Appendix 2 of 516 DM 2. The exclusions shall apply to internal program initiatives performed in the United States and its Trust Territories and Possessions, including Federal lands and the Outer Continental Shelf (OCS).

A. Topographic, land use and land cover, geological, mineralogic, resources evaluation, and hydrologic mapping activities, including aerial topographic surveying, photography, and geophysical surveying.

B. Collation of data and samples for geologic, paleontologic, hydrologic, mineralogic, geochemical and surface or subsurface geophysical investigations, and resource evaluation, including contracts therefor.

C. Acquisition of existing geological, hydrological or geophysical data from private exploration ventures.

D. Well logging, aquifer response testing, digital modeling, inventory of existing wells and water supplies, water-sample collection.

E. Operation, construction and installation of: (a) Water-level or water quality recording devices in wells; (b) pumps in wells; (c) surface-water flow measuring equipment such as weirs and stream-gaging stations, and (d) telemetry systems, including contracts therefor.

F. Routine exploratory or observation groundwater well drilling operations which do not require a special access road, and which use portable tanks to recycle and remove drilling mud, and create no significant surface disturbance.

G. Test or exploration drilling and downhole testing, including contracts therefor.

H. Establishment of survey marks, placement and operation of field instruments, and installation of any research/monitoring devices.

I. Digging of exploratory trenches requiring less than 20 cubic yards of excavation.

J. Establishment of seasonal and temporary field camps.

K. Off-road travel to drilling, data collection or observation sites which does not impact ecologically sensitive areas such as wilderness areas, wetlands, or areas of critical habitat for listed endangered or threatened species.

L. Hydraulic fracturing of rock formations for the singular purpose of in situ stress measurements.

M. Reports to Surface Management Agencies, or any State, Territorial, Commonwealth or Federal Agencies concerning mineral and water resources appraisals.

N. Other actions where USGS has concurrence or coapproval with another Department of the Interior bureau and the action is a categorical exclusion for that bureau.

O. Minor, routine, or preventive maintenance activities at USGS facilities and lands, and geological, hydrological, or geophysical data collection stations.

P. Minor activities required to gain or prepare access to sites selected for completion of exploration drilling operations or construction of stations for hydrologic, geologic, or geophysical data collection.

5/27/04 #3619

Replaces 3/18/80 #3511

Department of the Interior Departmental Manual

Effective Date: 5/27/04

Series: Environmental Quality Programs

Part 516: National Environmental Policy Act of 1969

Chapter 10: Managing the NEPA Process— Bureau of Indian Affairs

Originating Office: Bureau of Indian Affairs

516 DM 10

10.1 **Purpose**. This Chapter provides supplementary requirements for implementing provisions of 516 DM 1 through 6 within the Department's Bureau of Indian Affairs (BIA). This Chapter is referenced in 516 DM 6.5.

10.2 **NEPA Responsibility**.

A. Deputy Commissioner of Indian Affairs is responsible for NEPA compliance of BIA activities and programs.

B. Director, Office of Trust Responsibilities (OTR) is responsible for oversight of the BIA program for achieving compliance with NEPA, program direction, and leadership for BIA environmental policy, coordination and procedures.

C. Environmental Services Staff, reports to the Director (OTR). This office is the Bureau-wide focal point for overall NEPA policy and guidance and is responsible for advising and assisting Area Offices, Agency Superintendents, and other field support personnel in their environmental activities. The office also provides training and acts as the Central Office's liaison with Indian tribal governments on NEPA and other environmental compliance matters. Information about BIA NEPA documents or the NEPA process can be obtained by contacting the Environmental Services Staff.

D. Other Central Office Directors and Division Chiefs are responsible for ensuring that the programs and activities within their jurisdiction comply with NEPA.

E. Area Directors and Project Officers are responsible for assuring NEPA compliance with all activities under their jurisdiction and providing advice and assistance to Agency Superintendents and consulting with the Indian tribes on environmental matters related to NEPA. Area Directors and Project Officers are also responsible for assigning sufficient trained staff to ensure NEPA compliance is carried out. An Environmental Coordinator is located at each Area Office.

F. Agency Superintendents and Field Unit Supervisors are responsible for NEPA compliance and enforcement at the Agency or field unit level.

10.3 **Guidance to Applicants and Tribal Governments**.

A. Relationship with Applicants and Tribal Governments.

(1) Guidance to Applicants.

(a) An "applicant" is an entity which proposes to undertake any activity which will at some point require BIA action. These may include tribal governments, private entities, state and local governments or other Federal agencies. BIA compliance with NEPA is Congressionally mandated. Compliance is initiated when a BIA action is necessary in order to implement a proposal.

(b) Applicants should contact the BIA official at the appropriate level for assistance. This will be the Agency Superintendent, Area Director or the Director, Office of Trust Responsibilities.

(c) If the applicant's proposed action will affect or involve more than one tribal government, one government agency, one BIA Agency, or where the action may be of State-wide or regional significance, the applicant should contact the respective Area Director(s). The Area Director(s), using sole discretion, may assign the lead NEPA compliance responsibilities to one Area Office or, as appropriate, to one Agency Superintendent. From that point, the Applicant will deal with the designated lead office.

(d) Since much of the applicant's planning may take place outside the BIA system, it is the applicant's responsibility to prepare a milestone chart for BIA use at the earliest possible stage in order to coordinate the efforts of both parties. Early communication with the responsible BIA office will expedite determination of the appropriate type of NEPA documentation required. Other matters such as the scope, depth and sources of data for an environmental document will also be expedited and will help lead to a more efficient and more timely NEPA compliance process.

(2) Guidance to Tribal Governments.

(a) Tribal governments may be applicants, and/or be affected by a proposed action of BIA or another Federal agency. Tribal governments affected by a proposed action shall be consulted during the preparation of environmental documents and, at their option, may cooperate in the review or preparation of such documents. Notwithstanding the above, the BIA retains sole responsibility and discretion in all NEPA compliance matters.

(b) Any proposed tribal actions that do not require BIA or other Federal approval, funding or "actions" are not subject to the NEPA process.

B. Prepared Program Guidance. BIA has implemented regulations for environmental guidance for surface mining in 25 CFR Part 216 (Surface Exploration, Mining and Reclamation of Lands.) Environmental guidance for Forestry activities is found in 25 CFR 163.27 and 53 BIAM Supplements 2 and 3.

C. Other Guidance. Programs under 25 CFR for which BIA has not yet issued regulations or directives for environmental information for applicants are listed below. These programs may or may not require environmental documents and could involve submission of applicant information to determine NEPA applicability. Applicants for these types of programs should contact the appropriate BIA office for information and assistance:

(1) Partial payment construction charges on Indian irrigation projects (25 CFR Part 134).

(2) Construction assessments, Crow Indian irrigation project (25 CFR Part 135).

(3) Fort Hall Indian irrigation project, Idaho (25 CFR Part 136).

(4) Reimbursement of construction costs, San Carlos Indian irrigation project, Arizona (25 CFR Part 137).

(5) Reimbursement of construction costs, Ahtanum Unit, Wapato Indian irrigation project, Washington CFR Part 138).

(6) Reimbursement of construction costs, Wapato-Satus Unit, Wapato Indian Irrigation project, Washington (25 CFR Part 139).

(7) Land acquisitions (25 CFR Part 151).

(8) Leasing and permitting (Lands) (25 CFR Part 162).

(9) Sale of lumber and other forest products produced by Indian enterprises from the forests on Indian reservation (25 CFR Part 164).

(10) Sale of forest products, Red Lake Indian Reservation, Minn. (25 CFR Part 165).

(11) General grazing regulations (25 CFR Part 166).

(12) Navajo grazing regulations (25 CFR Part 167).

(13) Grazing regulations for the Hopi partitioned lands (25 CFR Part 168).

(14) Rights-of-way over Indian lands (25 CFR Part 169).

(15) Roads of the Bureau of Indian Affairs (25 CFR Part 170).

(16) Concessions, permits and leases on lands withdrawn or acquired in connection with Indian irrigation projects (25 CFR Part 173).

(17) Indian Electric Power Utilities (25 CFR Part 175).

(18) Resale of lands within the badlands Air Force Gunnery Range (Pine Ridge Aerial Gunnery Range) (25 CFR Part 178).

(19) Leasing of tribal lands for mining (25 CFR Part 211).

(20) Leasing of allotted lands for mining (25 CFR Part 212).

(21) Leasing of restricted lands of members of Five Civilized Tribes, Oklahoma, for mining (25 CFR Part 213).

(22) Leasing of Osage Reservation lands, Oklahoma, for mining, except oil and gas (25 CFR Part 214).

(23) Lead and zinc mining operations and leases, Quapaw Agency (25 CFR Part 215).

(24) Leasing of Osage Reservation lands for oil and gas mining (25 CFR Part 226).

(25) Leasing of certain lands in Wind River Indian Reservation, Wyoming, for oil and gas mining (25 CFR Part 227).

(26) Indian fishing in Alaska (25 CFR Part 241).

(27) Commercial fishing on Red Lake Indian Reservation (25 CFR 242).

(28) Use of Columbia River in-lieu fishing sites (25 CFR Part 248).

(29) Off-reservation treaty fishing (25 CFR Part 249).

(30) Indian fishing - Hoopa Valley Indian Reservation (25 CFR Part 150).

(31) Housing Improvement Program (25 CFR Part 256).

(32) Contracts under Indian Self-Determination Act (25 CFR Part 271).

(33) Grants under Indian Self-Determination Act 25 CFR Part 272).

(34) School construction or services for tribally operated previously private schools (25 CFR Part 274).

(35) Uniform administration requirements for grants (25 CFR 276).

(36) School construction contracts for public schools (25 CFR Part 277).

10.4 Major Actions Normally Requiring an EIS.

A. The following BIA actions normally require the preparation of an Environmental Impact Statement (EIS):

(1) Proposed mining contracts (for other than oil and gas), or the combination of a number of smaller contracts comprising a mining unit for:

(a) New mines of 640 acres or more, other than surface coal mines.

(b) New surface coal mines of 1,280 acres or more, or having an annual full production level of 5 million tons or more.

(2) Proposed water development projects which would, for example, inundate more than 1,000 acres, or store more than 30,000 acre-feet, or irrigate more than 5,000 acres of undeveloped land.

(3) Construction of a treatment, storage or disposal facility for hazardous waste or toxic substances.

(4) Construction of a solid waste facility for commercial purposes.

B. If, for any of these actions, it is proposed not to prepare an EIS, an Environmental Assessment (EA) will be developed in accordance with 40 CFR 1501.4(a)(2).

10.5 Categorical Exclusions. In addition to the actions listed in the Department's categorical exclusions in Appendix 1 of 516 DM 2, many of which the BIA also performs, the following BIA actions are hereby designated as categorical exclusions unless the action qualifies as an exception under Appendix 2 of 516 DM 2. These activities are single, independent actions not associated with a larger, existing or proposed, complex or facility. If cases occur that involve larger complexes or facilities, an EA or supplement should be accomplished.

A. Operation, Maintenance, and Replacement of Existing Facilities. Examples are

normal renovation of buildings, road maintenance and limited rehabilitation of irrigation structures.

B. Transfer of Existing Federal Facilities to Other Entities. Transfer of existing operation and maintenance activities of Federal facilities to tribal groups, water user organizations, or other entities where the anticipated operation and maintenance activities are agreed to in a contract, follow BIA policy, and no change in operations or maintenance is anticipated.

C. Human Resources Programs. Examples are social services, education services, employment assistance, tribal operations, law enforcement and credit and financing activities not related to development.

D. Administrative Actions and Other Activities Relating to Trust Resources. Examples are: Management of trust funds (collection and distribution), budget, finance, estate planning, wills and appraisals.

E. Self-Determination and Self-Governance.

(1) Self-Determination Act contracts and grants for BIA programs listed as categorical exclusions, or for programs in which environmental impacts are adequately addressed in earlier NEPA analysis.

(2) Self-Governance compacts for BIA programs which are listed as categorical exclusions or for programs in which environmental impacts are adequately addressed in earlier NEPA analysis.

F. Rights-of-Way.

(1) Rights-of-Way inside another right-of-way, or amendments to rights-of-way where no deviations from or additions to the original right-of-way are involved and where there is an existing NEPA analysis covering the same or similar impacts in the right-of-way area.

(2) Service line agreements to an individual residence, building or well from an existing facility where installation will involve no clearance of vegetation from the right-of-way other than for placement of poles, signs (including highway signs), or buried power/cable lines.

(3) Renewals, assignments and conversions of existing rights-of-way where there would be essentially no change in use and continuation would not lead to environmental degradation.

G. Minerals.

(1) Approval of permits for geologic mapping, inventory, reconnaissance and surface sample collecting.

(2) Approval of unitization agreements, pooling or communitization agreements.

(3) Approval of mineral lease adjustments and transfers, including assignments and subleases.

(4) Approval of royalty determinations such as royalty rate adjustments of an existing lease or contract agreement.

H. Forestry.

(1) Approval of free-use cutting, without permit, to Indian owners for on-reservation personal use of forest products, not to exceed 2,500 feet board measure when cutting will not adversely affect associated resources such as riparian zones, areas of special significance, etc.

(2) Approval and issuance of cutting permits for forest products not to exceed $5,000 in value.

(3) Approval and issuance of paid timber cutting permits or contracts for products valued at less than $25,000 when in compliance with policies and guidelines established by a current management plan addressed in earlier NEPA analysis.

(4) Approval of annual logging plans when in compliance with policies and guidelines established by a current management plan addressed in earlier NEPA analysis.

(5) Approval of Fire Management Planning Analysis detailing emergency fire suppression activities.

(6) Approval of emergency forest and range rehabilitation plans when limited to environmental stabilization on less than 10,000 acres and not including approval of salvage sales of damaged timber.

(7) Approval of forest stand improvement projects of less than 2000 acres when in compliance with policies and guidelines established by a current management plan addressed in earlier NEPA analysis.

(8) Approval of timber management access skid trail and logging road construction when consistent with policies and guidelines established by a current management plan addressed in earlier NEPA analysis.

(9) Approval of prescribed burning plans of less than 2000 acres when in compliance with policies and

guidelines established by a current management plan addressed in earlier NEPA analysis.

(10) Approval of forestation projects with native species and associated protection and site preparation activities on less than 2000 acres when consistent with policies and guidelines established by a current management plan addressed in earlier NEPA analysis.

I. Land Conveyance and Other Transfers. Approvals or grants of conveyances and other transfers of interests in land where no change in land use is planned.

J. Reservation Proclamations. Lands established as or added to a reservation pursuant to 25 U.S.C. 467, where no change in land use is planned.

K. Waste Management.

(1) Closure operations for solid waste facilities when done in compliance with other federal laws and regulations and where cover material is taken from locations which have been approved for use by earlier NEPA analysis.

(2) Activities involving remediation of hazardous waste sites if done in compliance with applicable federal laws such as the Resource Conservation and Recovery Act (P.L. 94-580), Comprehensive Environmental Response, Compensation, and Liability Act (P.L. 96-516) or Toxic Substances Control Act (P.L. 94-469).

L. Roads and Transportation.

(1) Approval of utility installations along or across a transportation facility located in whole within the limits of the roadway right-of-way.

(2) Construction of bicycle and pedestrian lanes and paths adjacent to existing highways and within the existing rights-of-way.

(3) Activities included in a "highway safety plan" under 23 CFR 402.

(4) Installation of fencing, signs, pavement markings, small passenger shelters, traffic signals, and railroad warning devices where no substantial land acquisition or traffic disruption will occur.

(5) Emergency repairs under 23 U.S.C. 125.

(6) Acquisition of scenic easements.

(7) Alterations to facilities to make them accessible for the elderly or handicapped.

(8) Resurfacing a highway without adding to the existing width.

(9) Rehabilitation, reconstruction or replacement of an existing bridge structure on essentially the same alignment or location (e.g., widening, adding shoulders or safety lanes, walkways, bikeways or guardrails).

(10) Approvals for changes in access control within existing right-of-ways.

(11) Road construction within an existing right-of-way which has already been acquired for a HUD housing project and for which earlier NEPA analysis has already been prepared.

M. Other.

(1) Data gathering activities such as inventories, soil and range surveys, timber cruising, geological, geophysical, archeological, paleontological and cadastral surveys.

(2) Establishment of non-disturbance environmental quality monitoring programs and field monitoring stations including testing services.

(3) Actions where BIA has concurrence or co-approval with another Bureau and the action is categorically excluded for that Bureau.

(4) Approval of an Application for Permit to Drill for a new water source or observation well.

(5) Approval of conversion of an abandoned oil well to a water well if water facilities are established only near the well site.

(6) Approval and issuance of permits under the Archaeological Resources Protection Act (16 U.S.C. 470aa-ll) when the permitted activity is being done as a part of an action for which a NEPA analysis has been, or is being prepared.

5/27/04 #3620

Replaces 3/18/80 #3511

Department of the Interior Departmental Manual

Effective Date: 5/8/08

Series: Environmental Quality Programs

Part 516: National Environmental Policy Act of 1969

Chapter 11: Managing the NEPA Process— Bureau of Land Management

Originating Office: Bureau of Land Management

516 DM 11

11.1 **Purpose**. This chapter provides supplementary requirements for implementing provisions of 516 DM Chapters 1 through 6 for the Department of the Interior's Bureau of Land Management (BLM). The BLM's National Environmental Policy Act (NEPA) Handbook (H-1790-1) provides additional guidance.

11.2 **NEPA Responsibilities.**

A. The Director and Deputy Director(s) are responsible for the BLM NEPA compliance activities.

B. The Assistant Director, Renewable Resources and Planning, is responsible for national NEPA compliance leadership and coordination, program direction, policy, and protocols development, and implementation of the same at the line management level. The Division of Planning and Science Policy, within the Assistant Directorate, Renewable Resources and Planning, has the BLM lead for the NEPA compliance program direction and oversight.

C. The BLM Office Directors and other Assistant Directors are responsible for cooperating with the Assistant Director, Renewable Resources and Planning, to ensure that the BLM NEPA compliance procedures operate as prescribed within their areas of responsibility.

D. The BLM Center Directors are responsible for cooperating with the Assistant Director, Renewable Resources and Planning, to ensure that the BLM NEPA compliance procedures operate as prescribed within their areas of responsibility.

E. The State Directors are responsible to the Director/ Deputy Director(s) for overall direction, integration and implementation of the BLM NEPA compliance procedures in their states. This includes managing for the appropriate level of public notification and partici-

pation, and ensuring production of quality environmental review and decision documents. Deputy State Directors serve as focal points for NEPA compliance matters at the state level.

F. The District and Field Managers are responsible for NEPA compliance at the local level.

11.3 **External Applicants' Guidance**.

A. General.

(1) For all external proposals, applicants should make initial contact with the Responsible Official (District Manager, Field Manager, or State Director) responsible for the affected public lands as soon as possible after determining the BLM's involvement. This early contact is necessary to allow the BLM to consult early with appropriate state and local agencies and tribes and with interested private persons and organizations, and to commence its NEPA process at the earliest possible time.

(2) When a proposed action has the potential to affect public lands in more than one administrative unit, the applicant may initially contact any Responsible Official whose jurisdiction is involved. The BLM may then designate a lead office to coordinate between BLM jurisdictions.

(3) Potential applicants may secure from the Responsible Official a list of NEPA and other relevant regulations and requirements for environmental review related to each applicant's proposed action. The purpose of making these regulations and requirements known in advance is to assist the applicant in the development of an adequate and accurate description of the proposed action when the applicant submits their project application. The list provided to the applicant may not fully disclose all relevant regulations and requirements because additional requirements could be identified after review of the applicant's proposal document(s) and as a result of the "scoping" process.

(4) The applicant is encouraged to advise the BLM of their intentions early on in their planning process. Early communication is necessary so that the BLM can efficiently advise the applicant on the anticipated type of NEPA review required, information needed, and potential data gaps that may or may not need to be filled, so that the BLM can describe the relevant regulations and requirements likely to affect the proposed action(s), and to discuss scheduling expectations.

B. Regulations. The following list of potentially relevant regulations should be considered at a minimum. Many other regulations affect public lands—some of which are specific to the BLM, while others are applicable across a broad range of federal programs (e.g., Protection of Historic and Cultural Programs—36 Code of Federal Regulations (CFR) Part 800).

(1) Resource Management Planning—43 CFR 1610;

(2) Withdrawals—43 CFR 2300;

(3) Land Classification—43 CFR 2400;

(4) Disposition: Occupancy and Use—43 CFR 2500;

(5) Disposition: Grants—43 CFR 2600;

(6) Disposition: Sales—43 CFR 2700;

(7) Use: Rights-of-Way—43 CFR 2800;

(8) Use: Leases and Permits—43 CFR 2900;

(9) Oil and Gas Leasing—43 CFR 3100;

(10) Geothermal Resources Leasing—43 CFR 3200;

(11) Coal Management—43 CFR 3400;

(12) Leasing of Solid Minerals Other than Coal/Oil Shale—43 CFR 3500;

(13) Mineral Materials Disposal—43 CFR 3600;

(14) Mining Claims Under the General Mining Laws—43 CFR 3800;

(15) Grazing Administration—43 CFR 4100;

(16) Wild Free-Roaming Horse and Burro Management—43 CFR 4700;

(17) Forest Management—43 CFR 5000;

(18) Wildlife Management—43 CFR 6000;

(19) Recreation Management—43 CFR 8300; and

(20) Wilderness Management—43 CFR 6300.

11.4 **General Requirements**. The Council on Environmental Quality (CEQ) regulations state that federal agencies shall reduce paperwork and delay (40 CFR 1500.4 and 1500.5) to the fullest extent possible. The information used in any NEPA analysis must be of high quality. Accurate scientific analysis, agency expert comments, and public scrutiny are essential to implementing the NEPA (40 CFR 1500.1(b)). Environmental documents should be concise and written in plain language (40 CFR 1502.8), so they can be understood and should concentrate on the issues that are truly sig-

nificant to the action in question rather than amassing needless detail (40 CFR 1500.1(b)).

A. Reduce paperwork and delays: The Responsible Official will avoid unnecessary duplication of effort and promote cooperation with other federal agencies that have permitting, funding, approving, or other consulting or coordinating requirements associated with the proposed action. The Responsible Official shall, as appropriate, integrate NEPA requirements with other environmental review and consultation requirements (40 CFR 1500.4(k)); tier to broader environmental review documents (40 CFR 1502.20); incorporate by reference relevant studies and analyses (40 CFR 1502.21); adopt other agency environmental analyses (40 CFR 1506.3); and supplement analyses with new information (40 CFR 1502.9).

B. Eliminate duplicate tribal, state, and local governmental procedures (40 CFR 1506.2): The Responsible Official will cooperate with other governmental entities to the fullest extent possible to reduce duplication between federal, state, local and tribal requirements in addition to, but not in conflict with, those in the NEPA. Cooperation may include the following: common databases; joint planning processes; joint science investigations; joint public meetings and hearings; and joint environmental assessment (EA) level and joint environmental impact statement (EIS) level analyses using joint lead or cooperating agency status.

C. Consult and coordinate: The Responsible Official will determine early in the process the appropriate type and level of consultation and coordination required with other federal agencies and with state, local and tribal governments. After the NEPA review is completed, coordination will often continue throughout project implementation, monitoring, and evaluation.

D. Involve the public: The public must be involved early and continuously, as appropriate, throughout the NEPA process. The Responsible Official shall ensure that:

(1) The type and level of public involvement shall be commensurate with the NEPA analysis needed to make the decision.

(2) When feasible, communities can be involved through consensus-based management activities. Consensus-based management includes direct community involvement in the BLM activities subject to NEPA analyses, from initial scoping to implementation and monitoring of the impacts of the decision. Consensus-based management seeks to achieve agreement from diverse interests on the goals, purposes, and needs of

the BLM plans and activities and the methods needed to achieve those ends. The BLM retains exclusive decision-making responsibility and shall exercise that responsibility in a timely manner.

E. Implement Adaptive Management: The Responsible Official is encouraged to build "Adaptive Management" practice in to their proposed actions and NEPA compliance activities and train personnel in this important environmental concept. Adaptive Management in the DOI is a system of management practices based on clearly identified outcomes, monitoring to determine if management actions are meeting outcomes, and the facilitation of management changes to ensure that outcomes are met, or reevaluated as necessary. Such reevaluation may require new or supplemental NEPA compliance. Adaptive Management recognizes that knowledge about natural resource systems is sometimes uncertain and is the preferred method for addressing these cases. The preferred alternative should include sufficient flexibility to allow for adjustments in implementation in response to monitoring results.

F. Train for public and community involvement: The BLM employee(s) that facilitate(s) public and community involvement in the NEPA process should have training in public involvement, alternative dispute resolution, negotiation, meeting facilitation, collaboration, and/or partnering.

G. Limitations on Actions during the NEPA process: The following guidance may aid in fulfilling the requirements of 40 CFR 1506.1. During the preparation of a program or plan NEPA document, the Responsible Official may undertake any major Federal action within the scope and analyzed in the existing NEPA document supporting the current plan or program, so long as there is adequate NEPA documentation to support the individual action.

11.5 **Plan Conformance**. Where a BLM land use plan (LUP) exists, a proposed action must be in conformance with the plan. This means that the proposed action must be specifically provided for in the plan, or if not specifically mentioned, the proposal must be clearly consistent with the terms, conditions, and decisions of the plan or plan as amended. If it is determined that the proposed action does not conform to the plan, the Responsible Official may:

A. reject the proposal,

B. modify the proposal to conform to the land use plan, or

C. complete appropriate plan amendments and associated NEPA compliance requirements prior to proceeding with the proposed action.

11.6 **Existing Documentation (Determination of NEPA Adequacy)**. The Responsible Official may consider using existing NEPA analysis for a proposed action when the record documents show that the following conditions are met.

A. The proposed action is adequately covered by (i.e., is within the scope of and analyzed in) relevant existing analyses, data, and records; and

B. There are no new circumstances, new information, or unanticipated or unanalyzed environmental impacts that warrant new or supplemental analysis. If the Responsible Official determines that existing NEPA documents adequately analyzed the effects of the proposed action, this determination, usually prepared in a Determination of NEPA Adequacy (DNA) worksheet to provide the administrative record support, serves as an interim step in the BLM's internal decision-making process. The DNA is intended to evaluate the coverage of existing documents and the significance of new information, but does not itself provide NEPA analysis. If the Responsible Official concludes that the proposed action(s) warrant additional review, information from the DNA worksheet may be used to facilitate the preparation of the appropriate level of NEPA analysis. The BLM's NEPA Handbook and program specific regulations and guidance describe additional steps needed to make and document the agency's final determination regarding a proposed action.

11.7 **Actions Requiring an Environmental Assessment (EA)**.

A. An EA is a concise public document that serves to:

(1) Provide sufficient evidence and analysis for determining whether to prepare an environmental impact statement (EIS) or a Finding of No Significant Impact (FONSI);

(2) Aid the BLM's compliance with NEPA when an EIS is not necessary; and

(3) Facilitate preparation of an EIS when one is necessary.

B. Unlike an EIS that requires much more, an EA must include the following four items identified in 40 CFR 1508.9(b):

(1) The need for the proposal.

(2) Alternatives as described in Section 102(2)(E) of NEPA.

(3) The environmental impacts of the proposed action and alternatives.

(4) A listing of agencies and persons consulted.

C. An EA is usually the appropriate NEPA document for:

(1) Land Use Plan Amendments;

(2) Land use plan implementation decisions, including but not limited to analysis for implementation plans such as watershed plans or coordinated resource activity plans, resource use permits (except for those that are categorically excludable), and site-specific project plans, such as construction of a trail.

D. An EA should be completed when the Responsible Official is uncertain of the potential for significant impacts and needs further analysis to make the determination.

E. If, for any of these actions, it is anticipated or determined that an EA is not appropriate because of potential significant impacts, an EIS will be prepared.

11.8 Major Actions Requiring an EIS.

A. An EIS level analysis should be completed when an action meets either of the two following criteria.

(1) If the impacts of a proposed action are expected to be significant; or

(2) In circumstances where a proposed action is directly related to another action(s), and cumulatively the effects of the actions taken together would be significant, even if the effects of the actions taken separately would not be significant,

B. The following types of BLM actions will normally require the preparation of an EIS:

(1) Approval of Resource Management Plans.

(2) Proposals for Wild and Scenic Rivers and National Scenic and Historic Trails.

(3) Approval of regional coal lease sales in a coal production region.

(4) Decisions to issue a coal preference right lease.

(5) Approval of applications to the BLM for major actions in the following categories:

(a) Sites for steam-electric powerplants, petroleum refineries, synfuel plants, and industrial facilities; and

(b) Rights-of-way for major reservoirs, canals, pipelines, transmission lines, highways, and railroads.

(6) Approval of operations that would result in liberation of radioactive tracer materials or nuclear stimulation.

(7) Approval of any mining operations where the area to be mined, including any area of disturbance, over the life of the mining plan, is 640 acres or larger in size.

C. If potentially significant impacts are not anticipated for these actions, an EA will be prepared.

11.9 Actions Eligible for a Categorical Exclusion (CX). The Departmental Manual (516 DM 2.3A(3) and 516 DM 2, Appendix 2) requires that before any action described in the following list of CXs is used, the list of "extraordinary circumstances" must be reviewed for applicability. If a CX does not pass the "extraordinary circumstances" test, the proposed action analysis defaults to either an EA or an EIS. When no "extraordinary circumstances" apply, the following activities do not require the preparation of an EA or EIS. In addition, see 516 DM 2, Appendix 1 for a list of DOI-wide categorical exclusions. As proposed actions are designed and then reviewed against the CX list, proposed actions or activities must be, at a minimum, consistent with the DOI and the BLM regulations, manuals, handbooks, policies, and applicable land use plans regarding design features, best management practices, terms and conditions, conditions of approval, and stipulations.

A. Fish and Wildlife.

(1) Modification of existing fences to provide improved wildlife ingress and egress.

(2) Minor modification of water developments to improve or facilitate wildlife use (e.g., modify enclosure fence, install flood valve, or reduce ramp access angle).

(3) Construction of perches, nesting platforms, islands, and similar structures for wildlife use.

(4) Temporary emergency feeding of wildlife during periods of extreme adverse weather conditions.

(5) Routine augmentations, such as fish stocking, providing no new species are introduced.

(6) Relocation of nuisance or depredating wildlife, providing the relocation does not introduce new species into the ecosystem.

(7) Installation of devices on existing facilities to protect animal life, such as raptor electrocution prevention devices.

B. Oil, Gas, and Geothermal Energy.

(1) Issuance of future interest leases under the Mineral Leasing Act for Acquired Lands, where the subject lands are already in production.

(2) Approval of mineral lease adjustments and transfers, including assignments and subleases.

(3) Approval of unitization agreements, communitization agreements, drainage agreements, underground storage agreements, development contracts, or geothermal unit or participating area agreements.

(4) Approval of suspensions of operations, force majeure suspensions, and suspensions of operations and production.

(5) Approval of royalty determinations, such as royalty rate reductions.

(6) Approval of Notices of Intent to conduct geophysical exploration of oil, gas, or geothermal, pursuant to 43 CFR 3150 or 3250, when no temporary or new road construction is proposed.

C. Forestry.

(1) Land cultivation and silvicultural activities (excluding herbicide application) in forest tree nurseries, seed orchards, and progeny test sites.

(2) Sale and removal of individual trees or small groups of trees which are dead, diseased, injured, or which constitute a safety hazard, and where access for the removal requires no more than maintenance to existing roads.

(3) Seeding or reforestation of timber sales or burn areas where no chaining is done, no pesticides are used, and there is no conversion of timber type or conversion of non-forest to forest land. Specific reforestation activities covered include: seeding and seedling plantings, shading, tubing (browse protection), paper mulching, bud caps, ravel protection, application of non-toxic big game repellant, spot scalping, rodent trapping, fertilization of seed trees, fence construction around out-planting sites, and collection of pollen, scions and cones.

(4) Pre-commercial thinning and brush control using small mechanical devices.

(5) Disposal of small amounts of miscellaneous vegetation products outside established harvest areas, such as Christmas trees, wildings, floral products (ferns, boughs, etc.), cones, seeds, and personal use firewood.

(6) Felling, bucking, and scaling sample trees to ensure accuracy of timber cruises. Such activities:

(a) Shall be limited to an average of one tree per acre or less,

(b) Shall be limited to gas-powered chainsaws or hand tools,

(c) Shall not involve any road or trail construction,

(d) Shall not include the use of ground based equipment or other manner of timber yarding, and

(e) Shall be limited to the Coos Bay, Eugene, Medford, Roseburg, and Salem Districts and Lakeview District, Klamath Falls Resource Area in Oregon.

(7) Harvesting live trees not to exceed 70 acres, requiring no more than 0.5 mile of temporary road construction. Such activities:

(a) Shall not include even-aged regeneration harvests or vegetation type conversions.

(b) May include incidental removal of trees for landings, skid trails, and road clearing.

(c) May include temporary roads which are defined as roads authorized by contract, permit, lease, other written authorization, or emergency operation not intended to be part of the BLM transportation system and not necessary for long-term resource management. Temporary roads shall be designed to standards appropriate for the intended uses, considering safety, cost of transportation, and impacts on land and resources; and

(d) Shall require the treatment of temporary roads constructed or used so as to permit the reestablishment by artificial or natural means, or vegetative cover on the roadway and areas where the vegetative cover was disturbed by the construction or use of the road, as necessary to minimize erosion from the disturbed area. Such treatment shall be designed to reestablish vegetative cover as soon as practicable, but at least within 10 years after the termination of the contract. Examples include, but are not limited to:

(i) Removing individual trees for sawlogs, specialty products, or fuelwood.

(ii) Commercial thinning of overstocked stands to achieve the desired stocking level to increase health and vigor.

(8) Salvaging dead or dying trees not to exceed 250 acres, requiring no more than 0.5 mile of temporary road construction. Such activities:

(a) May include incidental removal of live or dead trees for landings, skid trails, and road clearing.

(b) May include temporary roads which are defined as roads authorized by contract, permit, lease, other written authorization, or emergency operation not intended to be part of the BLM transportation system and not necessary for long-term resource management. Temporary roads shall be designed to standards appropriate for the intended uses, considering safety, cost of transportation, and impacts on land and resources; and

(c) Shall require the treatment of temporary roads constructed or used so as to permit the reestablishment, by artificial or natural means, of vegetative cover on the roadway and areas where the vegetative cover was disturbed by the construction or use of the road, as necessary to minimize erosion from the disturbed area. Such treatment shall be designed to reestablish vegetative cover as soon as practicable, but at least within 10 years after the termination of the contract.

(d) For this CX, a dying tree is defined as a standing tree that has been severely damaged by forces such as fire, wind, ice, insects, or disease, and that in the judgment of an experienced forest professional or someone technically trained for the work, is likely to die within a few years. Examples include, but are not limited to:

(i) Harvesting a portion of a stand damaged by a wind or ice event.

(ii) Harvesting fire damaged trees.

(9) Commercial and non-commercial sanitation harvest of trees to control insects or disease not to exceed 250 acres, requiring no more than 0.5 miles of temporary road construction. Such activities:

(a) May include removal of infested/infected trees and adjacent live uninfested/uninfected trees as determined necessary to control the spread of insects or disease; and

(b) May include incidental removal of live or dead trees for landings, skid trails, and road clearing.

(c) May include temporary roads which are defined as roads authorized by contract, permit, lease, other writ-

ten authorization, or emergency operation not intended to be part of the BLM transportation system and not necessary for long-term resource management. Temporary roads shall be designed to standards appropriate for the intended uses, considering safety, cost of transportation, and impacts on land and resources; and

(d) Shall require the treatment of temporary roads constructed or used so as to permit the reestablishment, by artificial or natural means, of vegetative cover on the roadway and areas where the vegetative cover was disturbed by the construction or use of the road, as necessary to minimize erosion from the disturbed area. Such treatment shall be designed to reestablish vegetative cover as soon as practicable, but at least within 10 years after the termination of the contract. Examples include, but are not limited to:

(i) Felling and harvesting trees infested with mountain pine beetles and immediately adjacent uninfested trees to control expanding spot infestations; and

(ii) Removing or destroying trees infested or infected with a new exotic insect or disease, such as emerald ash borer, Asian longhorned beetle, or sudden oak death pathogen.

D. Rangeland Management.

(1) Approval of transfers of grazing preference.

(2) Placement and use of temporary (not to exceed one month) portable corrals and water troughs, providing no new road construction is needed.

(3) Temporary emergency feeding of livestock or wild horses and burros during periods of extreme adverse weather conditions.

(4) Removal of wild horses or burros from private lands at the request of the landowner.

(5) Processing (transporting, sorting, providing veterinary care, vaccinating, testing for communicable diseases, training, gelding, marketing, maintaining, feeding, and trimming of hooves of) excess wild horses and burros.

(6) Approval of the adoption of healthy, excess wild horses and burros.

(7) Actions required to ensure compliance with the terms of Private Maintenance and Care agreements.

(8) Issuance of title to adopted wild horses and burros.

(9) Destroying old, sick, and lame wild horses and burros as an act of mercy.

(10) Vegetation management activities, such as seeding, planting, invasive plant removal, installation of erosion control devices (e.g., mats/straw/chips), and mechanical treatments, such as crushing, piling, thinning, pruning, cutting, chipping, mulching, mowing, and prescribed fire when the activity is necessary for the management of vegetation on public lands. Such activities:

(a) Shall not exceed 4,500 acres per prescribed fire project and 1,000 acres for other vegetation management projects;

(b) Shall not be conducted in Wilderness areas or Wilderness Study Areas;

(c) Shall not include the use of herbicides, pesticides, biological treatments or the construction of new permanent roads or other new permanent infrastructure;

(d) May include temporary roads which are defined as roads authorized by contract, permit, lease, other written authorization, or emergency operation not intended to be part of the BLM transportation system and not necessary for long-term resource management. Temporary roads shall be designed to standards appropriate for the intended uses, considering safety, cost of transportation, and impacts on land and resources; and

(e) Shall require the treatment of temporary roads constructed or used so as to permit the reestablishment, by artificial or natural means, of vegetative cover on the roadway and areas where the vegetative cover was disturbed by the construction or use of the road, as necessary to minimize erosion from the disturbed area. Such treatment shall be designed to reestablish vegetative cover as soon as practicable, but at least within 10 years after the termination of the contract.

(11) Issuance of livestock grazing permits/leases where:

(a) The new grazing permit/lease is consistent with the use specified on the previous permit/lease, such that

(i) the same kind of livestock is grazed,

(ii) the active use previously authorized is not exceeded, and

(iii) grazing does not occur more than 14 days earlier or later than as specified on the previous permit/lease, and

(b) The grazing allotment(s) has been assessed and evaluated and the Responsible Official has documented in a determination that the allotment(s) is

(i) meeting land health standards, or

(ii) not meeting land health standards due to factors that do not include existing livestock grazing.

E. Realty.

(1) Withdrawal extensions or modifications, which only establish a new time period and entail no changes in segregative effect or use.

(2) Withdrawal revocations, terminations, extensions, or modifications; and classification terminations or modifications which do not result in lands being opened or closed to the general land laws or to the mining or mineral leasing laws.

(3) Withdrawal revocations, terminations, extensions, or modifications; classification terminations or modifications; or opening actions where the land would be opened only to discretionary land laws and where subsequent discretionary actions (prior to implementation) are in conformance with and are covered by a Resource Management Plan/EIS (or plan amendment and EA or EIS).

(4) Administrative conveyances from the Federal Aviation Administration (FAA) to the State of Alaska to accommodate airports on lands appropriated by the FAA prior to the enactment of the Alaska Statehood Act.

(5) Actions taken in conveying mineral interest where there are no known mineral values in the land under Section 209(b) of the Federal Land Policy and Management Act of 1976 (FLPMA).

(6) Resolution of class one color-of-title cases.

(7) Issuance of recordable disclaimers of interest under Section 315 of FLPMA.

(8) Corrections of patents and other conveyance documents under Section 316 of FLPMA and other applicable statutes.

(9) Renewals and assignments of leases, permits, or rights-of-way where no additional rights are conveyed beyond those granted by the original authorizations.

(10) Transfer or conversion of leases, permits, or rights-of-way from one agency to another (e.g., conversion of Forest Service permits to a BLM Title V Right-of-way).

(11) Conversion of existing right-of-way grants to Title V grants or existing leases to FLPMA Section 302(b) leases where no new facilities or other changes are needed.

(12) Grants of right-of-way wholly within the boundaries of other compatibly developed rights-of-way.

(13) Amendments to existing rights-of-way, such as the upgrading of existing facilities, which entail no additional disturbances outside the right-of-way boundary.

(14) Grants of rights-of-way for an overhead line (no pole or tower on BLM land) crossing over a corner of public land.

(15) Transfers of land or interest in land to or from other bureaus or federal agencies where current management will continue and future changes in management will be subject to the NEPA process.

(16) Acquisition of easements for an existing road or issuance of leases, permits, or rights-of-way for the use of existing facilities, improvements, or sites for the same or similar purposes.

(17) Grant of a short rights-of-way for utility service or terminal access roads to an individual residence, outbuilding, or water well.

(18) Temporary placement of a pipeline above ground.

(19) Issuance of short-term (3 years or less) rights-of-way or land use authorizations for such uses as storage sites, apiary sites, and construction sites where the proposal includes rehabilitation to restore the land to its natural or original condition.

(20) One-time issuance of short-term (3 years or less) rights-of-way or land use authorizations which authorize trespass action where no new use or construction is allowed, and where the proposal includes rehabilitation to restore the land to its natural or original condition.

F. Solid Minerals.

(1) Issuance of future interest leases under the Mineral Leasing Act for Acquired Lands where the subject lands are already in production.

(2) Approval of mineral lease readjustments, renewals, and transfers including assignments and subleases.

(3) Approval of suspensions of operations, force majeure suspensions, and suspensions of operations and production.

(4) Approval of royalty determinations, such as royalty rate reductions and operations reporting procedures.

(5) Determination and designation of logical mining units.

(6) Findings of completeness furnished to the Office of Surface Mining Reclamation and Enforcement for Resource Recovery and Protection Plans.

(7) Approval of minor modifications to or minor variances from activities described in an approved exploration plan for leasable, salable, and locatable minerals (e.g., the approved plan identifies no new surface disturbance outside the areas already identified to be disturbed).

(8) Approval of minor modifications to or minor variances from activities described in an approved underground or surface mine plan for leasable minerals (e.g., change in mining sequence or timing).

(9) Digging of exploratory trenches for mineral materials, except in riparian areas.

(10) Disposal of mineral materials, such as sand, stone, gravel, pumice, pumicite, cinders, and clay, in amounts not exceeding 50,000 cubic yards or disturbing more than 5 acres, except in riparian areas.

G. Transportation.

(1) Incorporation of eligible roads and trails in any transportation plan when no new construction or upgrading is needed.

(2) Installation of routine signs, markers, culverts, ditches, waterbars, gates, or cattleguards on/or adjacent to roads and trails identified in any land use or transportation plan, or eligible for incorporation in such plan.

(3) Temporary closure of roads and trails.

(4) Placement of recreational, special designation, or information signs, visitor registers, kiosks, and portable sanitation devices.

H. Recreation Management. Issuance of Special Recreation Permits for day use or overnight use up to 14 consecutive nights; that impacts no more than 3 staging area acres; and/or for recreational travel along roads, trails, or in areas authorized in a land use plan. This CX cannot be used for commercial boating permits along Wild and Scenic Rivers. This CX cannot be used for the establishment or issuance of Special Recreation Permits for "Special Area" management (43 CFR 2932.5).

I. Emergency Stabilization. Planned actions in response to wildfires, floods, weather events, earthquakes, or landslips that threaten public health or safety, property, and/or natural and cultural resources, and that are necessary to repair or improve lands unlikely to recover to a management-approved condition as a result of the event. Such activities shall be limited to: repair and installation of essential erosion control structures; replacement or repair of existing culverts, roads, trails, fences, and minor facilities; construction of protection fences; planting, seeding, and mulching; and removal of hazard trees, rocks, soil, and other mobile debris from, on, or along roads, trails, campgrounds, and watercourses. These activities:

(1) Shall be completed within one year following the event;

(2) Shall not include the use of herbicides or pesticides;

(3) Shall not include the construction of new roads or other new permanent infrastructure;

(4) Shall not exceed 4,200 acres; and

(5) May include temporary roads which are defined as roads authorized by contract, permit, lease, other written authorization, or emergency operation not intended to be part of the BLM transportation system and not necessary for long-term resource management. Temporary roads shall be designed to standards appropriate for the intended uses, considering safety, cost of transportation, and impacts on land and resources; and

(6) Shall require the treatment of temporary roads constructed or used so as to permit the reestablishment by artificial or natural means, or vegetative cover on the roadway and areas where the vegetative cover was disturbed by the construction or use of the road, as necessary to minimize erosion from the disturbed area. Such treatment shall be designed to reestablish vegetative cover as soon as practicable, but at least within 10 years after the termination of the contract

J. Other.

(1) Maintaining land use plans in accordance with 43 CFR 1610.5-4.

(2) Acquisition of existing water developments (e.g., wells and springs) on public land.

(3) Conducting preliminary hazardous materials assessments and site investigations, site characterization studies and environmental monitoring. Included are siting, construction, installation and/or operation of small monitoring devices such as wells, particulate dust counters and automatic air or water samples.

(4) Use of small sites for temporary field work camps where the sites will be restored to their natural or original condition within the same work season.

(5) Reserved.

(6) A single trip in a one month period for data collection or observation sites.

(7) Construction of snow fences for safety purposes or to accumulate snow for small water facilities.

(8) Installation of minor devices to protect human life (e.g., grates across mines).

(9) Construction of small protective enclosures, including those to protect reservoirs and springs and those to protect small study areas.

(10) Removal of structures and materials of no historical value, such as abandoned automobiles, fences, and buildings, including those built in trespass and reclamation of the site when little or no surface disturbance is involved.

(11) Actions where the BLM has concurrence or co-approval with another DOI agency and the action is categorically excluded for that DOI agency.

(12) Rendering formal classification of lands as to their mineral character, waterpower, and water storage values.

Department of the Interior Departmental Manual

Effective Date: 5/27/04

Series: Environmental Quality Programs

Part 516: National Environmental Policy Act of 1969

Chapter 12: Managing the NEPA Process— National Park Service

Originating Office: National Park Service

516 DM 12

12.1 **Purpose.** This Chapter provides supplementary requirements for implementing provisions of 516 DM 1 through 6 within the Department's National Park Service. This Chapter is referenced in 516 DM 6.5.

12.2 **NEPA Responsibility.**

A. The Director is responsible for NEPA compliance for National Park Service (NPS) activities.

B. Regional Directors are responsible to the Director for integrating the NEPA process into all regional activities and for NEPA compliance in their regions.

C. The Denver Service Center performs most major planning efforts for the National Park Service and integrates NEPA compliance and environmental considerations with project planning, consistent with direction and oversight provided by the appropriate Regional Director.

D. The Environmental Compliance Division (Washington), which reports to the Associate Director-Planning and Development, serves as the focal point for all matters relating to NEPA compliance; coordinates NPS review of NEPA documents prepared by other agencies; and provides policy review and clearance for NPS EISs. Information concerning NPS NEPA documents or the NEPA process can be obtained by contacting this office.

12.3 **Guidance to Applicants.** Actions in areas of NPS jurisdiction that are initiated by private or non-Federal entities include the following:

A. <u>Minerals</u>. Mineral exploration, leasing and development activities are not permitted in most units of the National Park System. There are exceptions where mineral activities are authorized by law and all mineral activities conducted under these exceptions require consultation with and evaluation by officials of the NPS and are subject to NEPA compliance. Some procedures whereby mineral activities are authorized are outlined below. For site-specific proposals, interested parties should contact the appropriate NPS Regional Director for a determination of whether authorities for conducting other types of mineral activities in particular areas exist and, if so, how to obtain appropriate permits. For further information about NPS minerals policy, interested parties should contact the Energy, Mining, and Minerals Division (Denver, Colorado).

(1) Mining Claims and Associated Mining Operations. All Units of the National Park System are closed to mineral entry under the 1872 Mining Law, and mining operations associated with mining claims are limited to the exercise of valid prior existing rights. Prior to conducting mining operations on patented or unpatented mining claims within the National Park System, operators must obtain approval of the appropriate NPS Regional Director. The Regional Directors base approval on information submitted by potential operators that discusses the scope of the proposed operations, evaluates the potential impacts on park resources, identifies measures that will be used to mitigate adverse impacts, and meets other requirements contained in 36 CFR Part 9, Subpart A, which governs mining operations on mining claims under the authority of the Mining in the Parks Act of 1976.

(2) Non-Federal Mineral Rights. Privately held Oil, gas and mineral rights on private land or split estates (Federally-owned surface estate and non-Federally owned subsurface estate) exist within some park boundaries. Owners of outstanding subsurface oil and gas rights are granted reasonable access on or across park units through compliance with 36 CFR Part 9, Subpart B. These procedures require an operator to file a plan of operations for approval by the appropriate NPS Regional Director. An approved plan of operations serves as the operator's access permit.

(3) Federal Mineral Leasing and Mineral Operations.

(a) Leasing of Federally-owned minerals is restricted to five national recreation areas in the National Park System, where leasing is authorized in the enabling legislation of the units. According to current regulations (43 CFR 3100.0-3(g)(4); 43 CFR 3500.0-3(c)(7)). These areas are: Lake Mead, Glen Canyon, Ross Lake, Lake Chelan, and Whiskeytown National Recreation Areas. However, Lake Chelan was designated in 1981 as an "excepted" area under the regulations and is closed to mineral leasing. The Bureau of Land Management (BLM) issues leases on these lands and controls and monitors operations. Applicable general leasing and operating procedures for oil and gas are contained in 43 CFR Part 3100, et seq, and for minerals other than oil and gas in 43 CFR 3500 et seq. Within units of the National Park System, the NPS, as the surface management agency, must consent to the permitting and leasing of park lands and concur with operating conditions established in consultation with the BLM. Leases and permits can only be granted upon a finding by the NPS Regional Director that the activities authorized will not have a significant adverse effect on the resources and administration of the unit. The NPS can also require special lease and permit stipulations for protecting the environment and other park resources. In addition, the NPS participates with BLM in preparing environmental analyses of all proposed activities and in establishing reclamation requirements for park unit lands.

(b) Glen Canyon National Recreation Area is the only unit of the National Park System containing special tar sands areas as defined in the Combined Hydrocarbon Leasing Act of 1981. In accordance with the requirements of this Act, the BLM has promulgated regulations governing the conversion of existing oil and gas leases located in special tar sands areas to combined hydrocarbon (oil, gas, and tar sands) leases and for instituting a competitive combined hydrocarbon leasing program in the special tar sands areas. Both of these activities, lease conversions and new leasing, may occur within the Glen Canyon NRA provided that they take place commensurate with the unit's minerals management plan and that the Regional Director of the NPS makes a finding of no significant adverse impact on the resources and administration of the unit or on other contiguous units of the National Park System. If the Regional Director does not make such a finding, then the BLM cannot authorize lease conversions or issue new leases within the Glen Canyon NRA. The applicable regulations are contained in 43 CFR 3140.7 and 3141.4-2, respectively. Intra-Departmental procedures for processing conversion applications have been laid out in a Memorandum of Understanding (MOU) between the BLM and the NPS. For additional information about combined hydrocarbon leasing, interested parties should contact the Energy, Mining and Minerals Division (Denver, Colorado).

B. Grazing. Grazing management plans for NPS units subject to legislatively-authorized grazing are normally prepared by the NPS or jointly with the BLM. Applicants for grazing allotments must provide the NPS and/or the BLM with such information as may be required to enable preparation of environmental documents on grazing management plans. Grazing is also permitted in some NPS areas as a condition of land acquisition in instances where grazing rights were held prior to Federal acquisition. The availability of these grazing rights is limited and information should be sought through individual Park Superintendents.

C. Permits, Rights-of-Way, and Easements for Non-Park Uses. Informational requirements are determined on a case-by-case basis, and applicants should consult with the Park Superintendent before making formal application. The applicant must provide sufficient information on the proposed non-park use, as well as park resources and resource-related values to be affected directly and indirectly by the proposed use in order to allow the Service to evaluate the application, assess the impact of the proposed use on the NPS unit and other environmental values, develop restrictions/stipulations to mitigate adverse impacts, and reach a decision on issuance of the instrument. Authorities for such permits, rights-of-way, etc., are found in the enabling legislation for individual National Park System units and 16 U.S.C. 5 and 79 and 23 U.S.C. 317. Right-of-way and easement regulations are found at 36 CFR Part 14. Policies concerning regulation of special uses are described in the NPS Management Policies Notebook.

D. Archaeological Permits. Permits for the excavation or removal of archaeological resources on public and Indian lands owned or administered by the Department of the Interior, and by other agencies that may delegate this responsibility to the Secretary, are issued by the Director of the NPS. These permits are required pursuant to the Archaeological Resources Protection Act of 1979 (Pub. L. 96-95) and implementing regulations (43 CFR Part 7), whenever materials of archaeological interest are to be excavated or removed. These permits are not required for archaeological work that does not result in any subsurface testing and does not result in the collection of any surface or subsurface archaeological materials. Applicants should contact the Departmental Consulting Archaeologist in Washington about these permits.

E. Federal Aid. The NPS administers financial and land grants to States, local governments and private organizations/individuals for outdoor recreation acquisition, development and planning (Catalog of Federal Domestic Assistance (CFDA #15.916), historic preservation (CFDA #15.904), urban park and recreation recovery (CFDA #15.919) and Federal surplus real property for park recreation and historic monument use (CFDA #15.403). The following program guidelines and regulations list environmental requirements which applicants must meet:

(1) Land and Water Conservation Fund Grants Manual, Part 650.2;

(2) Historic Preservation Grants-in-Aid Manual, Chapter 4;

(3) Urban Park and Recreation Recovery Guidelines, NPS-37;

(4) Policies and Responsibilities for Conveying Federal Surplus Property Manual, Part 271.

Copies of documents related to the Land and Water Conservation Fund and the Historic Preservation Fund have been provided to all State Liaison Officers for outdoor recreation and all State Historic Preservation Officers. Copies of these documents related to the Urban Park and Recreation Recovery Program are available for inspection in each NPS Regional Office as well as the NPS Office of Public Affairs in Washington, D.C. Many State agencies which seek NPS grants may prepare related EISs pursuant to section 102(2)(D) of NEPA. Such agencies should consult with the NPS Regional Office.

F. Conversion of Acquired and Developed Recreation Lands. The NPS must approve the conversion of certain acquired and developed lands prior to conversion. These include:

(1) All State and local lands and interests therein, and certain Federal lands under lease to the States, acquired or developed in whole or in part with monies from the Land and Water Conservation Fund Act are subject to section 6(f) of the Act which requires approval of conversion of use.

(2) All recreation areas and facilities (as defined in section 1004), developed or improved, in whole or in part, with a grant under the Urban Park and Recreation Recovery Act of 1978 (Pub. L. 95-625, Title 10) are subject to section 1010 of the Act which requires approval for a conversion to other than public recreation uses.

(3) Most Federal surplus real property which has been conveyed to State and local governments for use as recreation demonstration areas, historic monuments or public park and recreation areas (under the Recreation Demonstration Act of 1942 or the Federal Property and Administrative Services Act of 1949, as amended) are subject to approval of conversion of use.

(4) All abandoned railroad rights-of-way acquired by State and local governments for recreational and/or conservation uses with grants under section 809(b) of the Railroad Revitalization and Regulatory Reform

Act of 1976, are subject to approval of conversion of use. Application for approval of conversion of the use of these lands must be submitted to the appropriate Regional Director of the NPS. Early consultation with the Regional Office is encouraged to insure that the application is accompanied by any required environmental documentation. If the property was acquired through the Land and Water Conservation Fund, then the application must be submitted through the appropriate State Liaison Officer for Outdoor Recreation. If the property was acquired under the Federal Property and Administrative Services Act of 1949, as amended, approval of an application for conversion of use must also be concurred in by the General Services Administration.

12.4 **Major Actions Normally Requiring Environmental Impact Statements**.

A. The following types of NPS proposals will normally require the preparation of an EIS:

(1) Wild and Scenic River proposals;

(2) National Trail proposals;

(3) Wilderness proposals;

(4) General Management Plans for major National Park System units;

(5) Grants, including multi-year grants, whose size and/or scope will result in major natural or physical changes, including interrelated social and economic changes and residential and land use changes within the project area or its immediate environs;

(6) Grants which foreclose other beneficial uses of mineral, agricultural, timber, water, energy or transportation resources important to National or State welfare.

B. If for any of these proposals it is initially decided not to prepare an EIS, an EA will be prepared and made available for public review in accordance with section 1501.4(e)(2).

12.5 **Categorical Exclusions**. In addition to the actions listed in the Departmental categorical exclusions in Appendix 1 of 516 DM 2, many of which the Service also performs, the following NPS actions are designated categorical exclusions unless the action qualifies as an exception under Appendix 2 to 516 DM 2.

A. Actions Related to General Administration.

(1) Changes or amendments to an approved action when such changes would cause no or only minimal environmental impact.

(2) Land and boundary surveys,

(3) Minor boundary changes,

(4) Reissuance/renewal of permits, rights-of-way or easements not involving new environmental impacts,

(5) Conversion of existing permits to rights-of-way, when such conversions do not continue or initiate unsatisfactory environmental conditions,

(6) Issuances, extensions, renewals, reissuances or minor modifications of concession contracts or permits not entailing new construction,

(7) Commercial use licenses involving no construction,

(8) Leasing of historic properties in accordance with 36 CFR Part 18 and NPS-38,

(9) Preparation and issuance of publications,

(10) Modifications or revisions to existing regulations, or the promulgation of new regulations for NPS-administered areas, provided the modifications, revisions or new regulations do not:

(a) Increase public use to the extent of compromising the nature and character of the area or causing physical damage to it,

(b) Introduce noncompatible uses which might compromise the nature and characteristics of the area, or cause physical damage to it,

(c) Conflict with adjacent ownerships or land uses, or

(d) Cause a nuisance to adjacent owners or occupants.

(11) At the direction of the NPS responsible official, actions where NPS has concurrence or coapproval with another bureau and the action is a categorical exclusion for that bureau.

B. Plans, Studies and Reports.

(1) Changes or amendments to an approved plan, when such changes would cause no or only minimal environmental impact.

(2) Cultural resources maintenance guides, collection management plans and historic furnishings reports.

(3) Interpretive plans (interpretive prospectuses, audiovisual plans, museum exhibit plans, wayside exhibit plans).

(4) Plans, including priorities, justifications and strategies, for non-manipulative research, monitoring, inventorying and information gathering.

(5) Statements for management, outlines of planning requirements and task directives for plans and studies.

(6) Technical assistance to other Federal, State and local agencies or the general public.

(7) Routine reports required by law or regulation.

(8) Authorization, funding or approval for the preparation of Statewide Comprehensive Outdoor Recreation Plans.

(9) Adoption or approval of surveys, studies, reports, plans and similar documents which will result in recommendations or proposed actions which would cause no or only minimal environmental impact.

(10) Preparation of internal reports, plans, studies and other documents containing recommendations for action which NPS develops preliminary to the process of preparing a specific Service proposal or set of alternatives for decision.

(11) Land protection plans which propose no significant change to existing land or visitor use.

(12) Documents which interpret existing mineral management regulations and policies, and do not recommend action.

C. Actions Related to Development.

(1) Land acquisition within established park boundaries.

(2) Land exchanges which will not lead to significant changes in the use of land.

(3) Routine maintenance and repairs to non-historic structures, facilities, utilities, grounds and trails.

(4) Routine maintenance and repairs to cultural resource sites, structures, utilities and grounds under an approved Historic Structures Preservation Guide or Cyclic Maintenance Guide; or if the action would not adversely affect the cultural resource.

(5) Installation of signs, displays, kiosks, etc.

(6) Installation of navigation aids.

(7) Establishment of mass transit systems not involving construction, experimental testing of mass transit systems, and changes in operation of existing systems (e.g., routes and schedule changes).

(8) Replacement in kind of minor structures and facilities with little or no change in location, capacity or appearance.

(9) Repair, resurfacing, striping, installation of traffic control devices, repair/replacement of guardrails, etc., on existing roads.

(10) Sanitary facilities operation.

(11) Installation of wells, comfort stations and pit toilets in areas of existing use and in developed areas.

(12) Minor trail relocation, development of compatible trail networks on logging roads or other established routes, and trail maintenance and repair.

(13) Upgrading or adding new overhead utility facilities to existing poles, or replacement poles which do not change existing pole line configurations.

(14) Issuance of rights-of-way for overhead utility lines to an individual building or well from an existing line where installation will not result in significant visual intrusion and will involve no clearance of vegetation other than for placement of poles.

(15) Issuance of rights-of-way for minor overhead utility lines not involving placement of poles or towers and not involving vegetation management or significant visual intrusion in an NPS-administered area.

(16) Installation of underground utilities in previously disturbed areas having stable soils, or in an existing utility right-of-way.

(17) Construction of minor structures, including small improved parking lots, in previously disturbed or developed areas.

(18) Construction or rehabilitation in previously disturbed or developed areas, required to meet health or safety regulations, or to meet requirements for making facilities accessible to the handicapped.

(19) Landscaping and landscape maintenance in previously disturbed or developed areas.

(20) Construction of fencing enclosures or boundary fencing posing no effect on wildlife migrations.

D. Actions Related to Visitor Use.

(1) Carrying capacity analysis.

(2) Minor changes in amounts or types of visitor use for the purpose of ensuring visitor safety or resource protection in accordance with existing regulations.

(3) Changes in interpretive and environmental education programs.

(4) Minor changes in programs and regulations pertaining to visitor activities.

(5) Issuance of permits for demonstrations, gatherings, ceremonies, concerts, arts and crafts shows, etc., entailing only short-term or readily mitigable environmental disturbance.

(6) Designation of trail side camping zones with no or minimal improvements.

E. Actions Related to Resource Management and Protection.

(1) Archeological surveys and permits involving only surface collection or small-scale test excavations.

(2) Day-to-day resource management and research activities.

(3) Designation of environmental study areas and research natural areas.

(4) Stabilization by planting native plant species in disturbed areas.

(5) Issuance of individual hunting and/or fishing licenses in accordance with State and Federal regulations.

(6) Restoration of noncontroversial native species into suitable habitats within their historic range and elimination of exotic species.

(7) Removal of park resident individuals of non-threatened/endangered species which pose a danger to visitors, threaten park resources or become a nuisance in areas surrounding a park, when such removal is included in an approved resource management plan.

(8) Removal of non-historic materials and structures in order to restore natural conditions.

(9) Development of standards for, and identification, nomination, certification and determination of eligibility of properties for listing in the National Register of Historic Places and the National Historic Landmark and National Natural Landmark Programs.

F. Actions Related to Grant Programs.

(1) Proposed actions essentially the same as those listed in paragraphs A-E above.

(2) Grants for acquisition of areas which will continue in the same or lower density use with no additional disturbance to the natural setting.

(3) Grants for replacement or renovation of facilities at their same location without altering the kind and amount of recreational, historical or cultural resources of the area; or the integrity of the existing setting.

(4) Grants for construction of facilities on lands acquired under a previous NPS or other Federal grant provided that the development is in accord with plans submitted with the acquisition grant.

(5) Grants for the construction of new facilities within an existing park or recreation area, provided that the facilities will not:

(a) Conflict with adjacent ownerships or land use, or cause a nuisance to adjacent owners or occupants; e.g., extend use beyond daylight hours;

(b) Introduce motorized recreation vehicles;

(c) Introduce active recreation pursuits into a passive recreation area;

(d) Increase public use or introduce noncompatible uses to the extent of compromising the nature and character of the property or causing physical damage to it; or

(e) Add or alter access to the park from the surrounding area.

(6) Grants for the restoration, rehabilitation, stabilization, preservation and reconstruction (or the authorization thereof) of properties listed on or eligible for listing on the National Register of Historic Places at their same location and provided that such actions:

(a) Will not alter the integrity of the property or its setting;

(b) Will not increase public use of the area to the extent of compromising the nature and character of the property; and

(c) Will not cause a nuisance to adjacent property owners or occupants.

5/27/04 #3622

Replaces 3/18/80 #3511

Department of the Interior Departmental Manual

Effective Date: 5/27/04

Series: Environmental Quality Programs

Part 516: National Environmental Policy Act of 1969

Chapter 13: Managing the NEPA Process— Office of Surface Mining

Originating Office: Office of Surface Mining

516 DM 13

13.1 **Purpose**. This Chapter provides supplementary requirements for implementing provisions of 516 DM 1 through 6 within the Department's Office of Surface Mining. This Chapter is referenced in 516 DM 6.5.

13.2 **NEPA Responsibility**.

A. <u>Director</u>. Is responsible for NEPA compliance for the Office of Surface Mining (OSM).

B. <u>Assistant Directors</u>.

(1) Are responsible to the Director for supervision and coordination of NEPA activities in their program areas of responsibility.

(2) Are responsible, within their program areas, for OSM Headquarters review of EISs for compliance with program area policy guidance.

(3) Are responsible for assuring that environmental concerns are identified early in the planning stages and appropriate policy and program guidance is disseminated.

C. <u>Regional Directors</u>.

(1) Are responsible to the Director for integrating the NEPA process into all Regional activities and for NEPA compliance activities in their Regions.

(2) Will designate a staff position to be responsible to the Regional Director for the consistency, adequacy, and quality of all NEPA documents prepared by the Region's staff. The position will also be responsible to the Regional Director for providing information, guidance, training, advice, and coordination on NEPA matters, and for oversight of the Region's NEPA process.

D. Chief, Branch of Environmental Analysis (Washington). Is designated by the Director to be responsible for overall policy guidance for NEPA compliance for OSM. Information about OSM NEPA documents or the NEPA process can be obtained by contacting this Branch.

13.3 **Guidance to Applicants**. OSM personnel are available to meet with all applicants for permits on Federal lands or under a Federal program for a State to provide guidance on the permitting procedures. Permit applications under approved State programs are excluded from NEPA compliance. In addition, OSM's regulations implementing the Surface Mining Control and Reclamation Act of 1977 (SMCRA) provide requirements for applicants to submit environmental information. The following parts of the regulations (30 CFR) describe the information requirements.

A. Parts 770 and 771 outline the content requirements of permit applications on Federal lands or under a Federal program for a State, including: the procedures for coal exploration operations required by 30 CFR 776; the permit application contents for surface coal mining activities required by 30 CFR 778, 779, and 780; the permit application contents for underground coal mining required by 30 CFR 782, 783, and 784; the requirements for special categories of surface coal mining required by 30 CFR 785; and the procedures for review, revision, and renewal of permits and for the transfer, sale, or assignment of rights granted under permits, as required by 30 CFR 788.

B. Part 776 identifies the minimum requirements for coal exploration activities outside the permit area. Part 776 is complemented by Part 815 of Subchapter K which provides environmental protection performance standards applicable to these operations.

C. Part 778 provides the minimum requirements for legal, financial, compliance, and general nontechnical information for surface mining activities applications. Information submitted in permit applications under Part 778 will be used primarily to enable the regulatory authority and interested members of the public to ascertain the particular nature of the entity which will mine the coal and those entities which have other financial interests and public record ownership interests in both the mining entity and the property which is to be mined.

D. Part 779 establishes the minimum standards for permit applications regarding information on existing environmental resources that may be impacted by the conduct and location of the proposed surface mining activities. With the information required under Part

779, the regulatory authority is to utilize information provided in mining and reclamation plans under Part 780, in order to determine what specific impacts the proposed surface mining activities will have on the environment.

E. Part 780 establishes the heart of the permit application: the mining operations and reclamation plan for surface mining activities. The regulatory authority will utilize this information, together with the description of the existing environmental resources obtained under Part 779, to predict whether the lands to be mined can be reclaimed as required by the Act.

F. Part 782 contains permit application requirements for underground mining activities. This corresponds to Part 778 for surface mining. As such, Part 782 sets forth the minimum requirements for general, legal, financial, and compliance information required to be contained in applications for permits.

G. Part 783 describes the minimum requirements for information on existing environmental resources required in the permit application for underground mining and corresponds to Part 779 for surface mining activities.

H. Part 784 contains a discussion of the minimum requirements for reclamation and operation plans related to underground mining permit applications and corresponds to Part 780 for surface mining activities.

I. Part 785 contains requirements for permits for special categories of mining, including anthracite, special bituminous, experimental practices, mountaintop removal, steep slope, variances from approximate original contour restoration requirements, prime farmlands, alluvial valley floors, augering operation, and insitu activities. The provisions of Part 785 are interrelated to the performance standards applicable to the special categories covered in Subchapter K and must be reviewed together with the preamble and text for Parts 818 through 828 of Subchapter K.

J. Part 788 specifies the responsibilities of persons conducting surface coal mining and reclamation operations with respect to changes, modifications, renewals, and revisions of permits after they are originally granted, and of persons who attempt to succeed to rights granted under permits by transfer, sale, or assignment of rights.

13.4 Major Actions Normally Requiring an EIS.

A. The following OSM actions will normally require the preparation of an EIS:

(1) Approval of the Abandoned Mine Lands Reclamation Program, (SMCRA, Title IV). Completed in March 1980.

(2) Promulgation of the permanent regulatory program for surface coal mining and reclamation operations (SMCRA, Title V). Completed in February 1979.

(3) Approval of a proposed mining and reclamation plan that includes any of the following:

(a) Mountaintop removal operations.

(b) Mining within high use recreation areas.

(c) Mining that will cause population increases that exceed the community's ability to absorb the growth.

(d) Mining that would require a major change in existing coal transportation facilities.

(4) Approval of a proposed mining and reclamation plan for a surface mining operation that meets the following:

(a) The environmental impacts of the proposed mining operation are not adequately analyzed in an earlier environmental document covering the specific leases or mining activity; and

(b) The area to be mined is 1280 acres or more, or the annual full production level is 5 million tons or more; and

(c) Mining and reclamation operations will occur for 15 years or more.

B. If for any of these actions it is proposed not to prepare an EIS, an EA will be prepared and handled in accordance with Section 1501.4(e)(2).

13.5 Categorical Exclusions.

A. The following OSM actions are deemed not to be major Federal actions within the meaning of Section 102(2)(C) of NEPA under Sections 501(a) or 702(d) of the SMCRA. They are hereby designated as categorical exclusions from the NEPA process and are exempt from the exceptions under 516 DM 2.3A(3):

(1) Promulgation of interim regulations.

(2) Approval of State programs.

(3) Promulgation of Federal programs where a State fails to submit, implement, enforce, or maintain an acceptable State program.

(4) Promulgation and implementation of the Federal lands program.

B. In addition to the actions listed in the Departmental categorical exclusions outlined in Appendix 1 of 516 DM 2, many of which OSM also performs, the following OSM actions (SMCRA sections are in parentheses) are designated categorical exclusions unless the actions qualify as an exception under 516 DM 2.3A(3):

(1) Monetary allotments to States for mining and mineral resources institutes (301).

(2) Allocation of research funds to institutes (302).

(3) Any research effort associated with ongoing abandoned mine land reclamation projects where the research is coincidental to the reclamation (401(c)(6)).

(4) Collection of reclamation fees from operators (402(a)).

(5) Findings of fact and entries on land adversely affected by past coal mining (407(a)).

(6) Acquisition of particular parcels of abandoned mine lands for reclamation (407(c)).

(7) Filing liens against property adversely affected by past coal mining (408).

(8) Interim regulatory grants (502(e)(4)).

(9) Disapproval of a proposed State program (503(c)).

(10) Review of permits issued under a previously approved State program (504(d)).

(11) Five-year permit renewal on life-of-mine plans under the Federal lands program or the Federal program for a State where the environmental impacts of continued mining are adequately analyzed in a previous environmental document for the mining operation (506(d)).

(12) Small operator assistance program (507(c)).

(13) Issuance of public notices and holding public hearings on permit applications involving Federal lands or under a Federal program for a State (513).

(14) Routine inspection and enforcement activities (517).

(15) Conflict of interest regulations (517(g)).

(16) Assessment of civil penalties (518).

(17) Releases of performance bonds or deposits for mining on Federal lands or under a Federal program for a State (519).

(18) Issuance of cessation orders for coal mining and reclamation operations (521(a)(2) and (3)).

(19) Suspension or revocation of permits (521(a)(4)).

(20) Federal oversight and enforcement of ineffective State programs (521(b)).

(21) Cooperative agreements between a state and the Secretary to provide for State regulation of surface coal mining and reclamation operations on Federal lands (523(c)).

(22) Development of a program to assure that, with respect to the granting of permits, leases, or contracts for Federally-owned coal, no one shall be unreasonably denied purchase of the mined coal (523(d)).

(23) Annual grants programs to States for program development, administration, and enforcement (705(a)).

(24) Assistance to States in the development, administration, and enforcement of State programs (705(b)).

(25) Increasing the amount of annual grants to States (705(c)).

(26) Submission of the Secretary's annual report to the Congress (706).

(27) The proposal of legislation to allow Indian tribes to regulate surface coal mining on Indian lands (710(a)).

(28) The certification and training of blasters (719).

(29) Approval of State Reclamation Plans for abandoned mine lands (405).

(30) Development of project proposals for AML grants, including field work only to the extent necessary for the preparation and design of the proposal.

(31) Use of AML funds to allow States or tribes to set aside State share funds in a special trust for future AML projects.

(32) Use of AML funds in an insurance pool for the purposes of compensation for damage caused by mining prior to the date of the Act.

(33) AML reclamation projects involving: No more than 100 acres; no hazardous wastes; no explosives; no hazardous or explosive gases; no dangerous impound-

ments; no mine fires and refuse fires; no undisturbed, noncommercial borrow or disposal sites, no dangerous slides where abatement has the potential for damaging inhabited property; no subsidences involving the placement of material into underground mine voids through drilled holes to address more than one structure, and no unresolved issues with agencies, persons, or groups or adverse effects requiring specialized mitigation. Departmental exceptions in 516 DM 2, Appendix 2 apply to this exclusion. All sites considered in this categorical exclusion would have to first meet the eligibility test in sections 404, 409 and 411 of SMCRA. Also projects that have been declared an emergency pursuant to section 410 of SMCRA, may be candidates for this exclusion.

5/27/04 #3623

Replaces 3/18/80 #3511

Department of the Interior Departmental Manual

Effective Date: 5/27/04

Series: Environmental Quality Programs

Part 516: National Environmental Policy Act of 1969

Chapter 14: Managing the NEPA Process— Bureau of Reclamation

Originating Office: Bureau of Reclamation

516 DM 14

14.1 **Purpose**. This Chapter provides supplementary requirements for implementing provisions of 516 DM 1 through 6 within the Department's Bureau of Reclamation. This Chapter is referenced in 516 DM 6.5.

14.2 **NEPA Responsibility**.

A. <u>Commissioner</u>. Is responsible for NEPA compliance for Bureau of Reclamation (BuRec) activities.

B. <u>Assistant Commissioners</u>.

(1) Are responsible to the Commissioner for supervising and coordinating NEPA activities in their assigned areas of responsibility.

(2) Are responsible, in assigned areas of responsibility, for the Washington level review of EISs prepared in the regions or E&R Center for compliance with program area policy guidance.

(3) Provide supervision and coordination in assigned areas of responsibility to insure that environmental concerns are identified in the planning stages and to see that Regional Directors follow through with environmental commitments during the construction and operation and maintenance stages.

(4) May designate a staff position to be responsible for NEPA oversight and coordination in their assigned areas of responsibility.

C. <u>Regional Directors</u>.

(1) Are fully responsible to the Commissioner for integrating the NEPA compliance activities in their regional area.

(2) Will designate a staff position with the full responsibility to the Regional Director for providing direction of the NEPA process including information, guidance,

training, advice, consistency, quality, adequacy, oversight, and coordination on NEPA documents or matters.

D. <u>Division and Office Chiefs in E&R Center</u>.

(1) Are responsible for integrating the NEPA process into their activities.

(2) Will designate a staff position to be responsible to the division or office chief for providing guidance, advice, consistency, quality, adequacy, oversight, and coordination on NEPA documents for matters originating in the E&R Center.

(3) Will provide a technical review within their area of expertise of environmental documents directed to their office for review and comment.

E. <u>Director, Office of Environmental Affairs (Washington)</u>. Is the position designated by the Commissioner to be responsible for overall policy review of BuRec NEPA compliance. Information about BuRec NEPA documents of the NEPA process can be obtained by contacting this office.

14.3 **Guidance to Applicants**.

A. <u>Types of Applicants</u>.

(1) Actions that are initiated by private or non-Federal entities through applications include the following: Repayment contracts, water service contracts, Small Reclamation Projects Act Loans, Emergency Loans, Rehabilitation and Betterment Loans, Distribution System Loans, land use permits, licenses, easements, crossing agreements, permits for removal of sand and gravel, renewal of grazing, recreation management, or cabin site leases.

(2) Applicants will be provided information by the regional office on what environmental reports, analysis, or information are needed when they initiate their application. The environmental information requested may, of necessity, be related to impacts on private lands or other lands not under the jurisdiction of the Bureau to allow the BuRec to meet its environmental responsibilities.

B. <u>Prepared Program Guidance for Applicants</u>.

(1) Loans under the Small Reclamation Projects Act of 1958, U.S. Department of the Interior, Bureau of Reclamation, March 1976 (35 pages).

(2) Guidelines for Preparing Applications for Loans and Grants under the Small Reclamation Projects Act, Public Law 84-984, U.S. Department of the Interior, Bureau of Reclamation, December 1973 (121 pages).

(3) The Rehabilitation and Betterment Program, U.S. Department of the Interior, Bureau of Reclamation, September 1978 (14 pages).

(4) Guidelines for Preparation of Reports to Support Proposed Rehabilitation and Betterment Programs, U.S. Department of the Interior, Bureau of Reclamation, September 1978 (8 pages).

14.4 Major Actions Normally Requiring an EIS.

A. The following types of BuRec proposals will normally require the preparation of an EIS:

(1) Proposed Feasibility Reports on water resources projects.

(2) Proposed Definite Plan Reports (DPR) on water resources projects if not covered by an EIS at the feasibility report stage or if there have been major changes in the project plan which may cause significantly different or additional new impacts.

(3) Proposed repayment contracts and water service contracts or amendments thereof or supplements thereto, for irrigation, municipal, domestic, or industrial water where NEPA compliance has not already been accomplished.

(4) Proposed modifications to existing projects or proposed changes in the programmed operation of an existing project that may cause a significant new impact.

(5) Proposed initiation of construction of a project or major unit thereof, if not already covered by an EIS, or if significant new impacts are anticipated.

(6) Proposed major research projects where there may be significant impacts resulting from experimentation or other such research activities.

B. If, for any of these proposals it is initially decided not to prepare an EIS, an EA will be prepared and handled in accordance with Section 1501.4(e)(2).

14.5 Categorical Exclusions. In addition to the actions listed in the Departmental categorical exclusions outlined in Appendix 1 of 516 DM 2, many of which the Bureau also performs, the following Bureau actions are designated categorical exclusions unless the action qualifies as an exception under 516 DM 2.3A(3):

A. General Activities.

(1) Changes in regulations or policy directives and legislative proposals where the impacts are limited to economic and/or social effects.

(2) Training activities of enrollees assigned to the various youth programs. Such training may include minor construction activities for other entities.

(3) Research activities, such as nondestructive data collection and analysis, monitoring, modeling, laboratory testing, calibration, and testing of instruments or procedures and nonmanipulative field studies.

B. Planning Activities.

(1) Routine planning investigation activities where the impacts are expected to be localized, such as land classification surveys, topographic surveys, archeological surveys, wildlife studies, economic studies, social studies, and other study activity during any planning, preconstruction, construction, or operation and maintenance phases.

(2) Special, status, concluding, or other planning reports that do not contain recommendations for action, but may or may not recommend further study.

(3) Data collection studies that involve test excavations for cultural resources investigations or test pitting, drilling, or seismic investigations for geologic exploration purposes where the impacts will be localized.

C. Project Implementation Activities.

(1) Classification and certification of irrigable lands.

(2) Minor acquisition of land and rights-of-way or easements.

(3) Minor construction activities associated with authorized projects which correct unsatisfactory environmental conditions or which merely augment or supplement, or are enclosed within existing facilities.

(4) Approval of land management plans where implementation will only result in minor construction activities and resultant increased operation and maintenance activities.

D. Operation and Maintenance Activities.

(1) Maintenance, rehabilitation, and replacement of existing facilities which may involve a minor change in size, location, and/or operation.

(2) Transfer of the operation and maintenance of Federal facilities to water districts, recreation agencies, fish and wildlife agencies, or other entities where the anticipated operation and maintenance activities are agreed to in a contract or a memorandum of agreement, follow approved Reclamation policy, and no major change in operation and maintenance is anticipated.

(3) Administration and implementation of project repayment and water service contracts, including approval of organizational or other administrative changes in contracting entities brought about by inclusion or exclusion of lands in these contracts.

(4) Approval, execution, and implementation of water service contracts for minor amounts of long-term water use or temporary or interim water use where the action does not lead to long-term changes and where the impacts are expected to be localized.

(5) Approval of changes in pumping power and water rates charged contractors by the Bureau for project water service or power.

(6) Execution and administration of recordable contracts for disposal of excess lands.

(7) Withdrawal, termination, modification, or revocation where the land would be opened to discretionary land laws and where such future discretionary actions would be subject to the NEPA process, and disposal and sale of acquired lands where no major change in usage is anticipated.

(8) Renewal of existing grazing, recreation management, or cabin site leases which do not increase the level of use or continue unsatisfactory environmental conditions.

(9) Issuance of permits for removal of gravel or sand by an established process from existing quarries.

(10) Issuance of permits, licenses, easements, and crossing agreements which provide right-of-way over Bureau lands where the action does not allow for or lead to a major public or private action.

(11) Implementation of improved appearance and soil and moisture conservation programs where the impacts are localized.

(12) Conduct of programs of demonstration, educational, and technical assistance to water user organizations for improvement of project and on-farm irrigation water use and management.

(13) Follow-on actions such as access agreements, contractual arrangements, and operational procedures for hydropower facilities which are on or appurtenant to Bureau facilities or lands which are permitted or licensed by the Federal Energy Regulatory Commission (FERC), when FERC has accomplished compliance with NEPA (including actions to be taken by the Bureau) and when the Bureau's environmental concerns have been accommodated in accordance with the Bureau/FERC Memorandum of Understanding of June 22, 1981.

(14) Approval, renewal, transfer, and execution of an original, amendatory, or supplemental water service or repayment contract where the only result will be to implement an administrative or financial practice or change.

(15) Approval of second party water sales agreements for small amounts of water (usually less than 10 acre-feet) where the Bureau has an existing water sales contract in effect.

(16) Approval and execution of contracts requiring the repayment of funds furnished or expended on behalf of an entity pursuant to the Emergency Fund Act of June 26, 1948 (43 U.S.C. 502), where the action taken is limited to the original location of the damaged facility.

(17) Minor safety of dams construction activities where the work is confined to the dam, abutment areas, or appurtenant features, and where no major change in reservoir or downstream operation is anticipated as a result of the construction activities.

E. Grant and Loan Activities.

(1) Rehabilitation and Betterment Act loans and contracts which involve repair, replacement, or modification of equipment in existing structures or minor repairs to existing dams, canals, laterals, drains, pipelines, and similar facilities.

(2) Small Reclamation Projects Act grants and loans where the work to be done is confined to areas already impacted by farming or development activities, work is considered minor, and where the impacts are expected to be localized.

(3) Distribution System Loans Act loans where the work to be done is confined to areas already impacted by farming or developing activities, work is considered minor, and where the impacts are expected to be localized.

5/27/04 #3624

Replaces 3/18/80 #3511

Department of the Interior Departmental Manual

Effective Date: 5/27/04

Series: Environmental Quality Programs

Part 516: National Environmental Policy Act of 1969

Chapter 15: Managing the NEPA Process— Minerals Management Service

Originating Office: Minerals Management Service

516 DM 15

15.1 **Purpose.** This Chapter provides supplementary requirements for implementing provisions of 516 DM 1 through 6 within the Department's Minerals Management Service. This Chapter is referenced in 516 DM 6.5.

15.2 **NEPA Responsibility.**

A. The Director/Deputy Director are responsible for NEPA compliance for Minerals Management Service (MMS) activities.

B. The Associate Director for Offshore Minerals Management is responsible for ensuring NEPA compliance for all offshore MMS activities.

C. The Chief, Offshore Environmental Assessment Division (OEAD), is responsible for NEPA-related policy and guidance for MMS activities, including monitoring MMS activities to ensure NEPA compliance, assuring the quality control of MMS environmental documents, and managing the review of non-MMS environmental documents. The office is the focal point for all NEPA matters and information about MMS environmental documents or the NEPA process can be obtained by contacting it or the appropriate Region.

D. The Regional Directors are responsible to the Associate Director for Offshore Minerals Management for overall direction and integration of the NEPA process into their activities and for NEPA compliance in their Regions.

15.3 **Guidance to Applicants.**

A. General.

(1) Applicants should make initial contact with the Regional Director of the office where the affected action is located.

(2) Potential applicants may secure from Regional Directors a list or program regulations or other directives/guidance providing advice or requirements for submission of environmental information. The purpose of making these regulations known to potential applicants in advance is to assist them in presenting a detailed, adequate, and accurate description of the proposal and alternatives when they file their application and to minimize the need to request additional information. This is a minimum list, and additional requirements may be identified after detailed review of the formal submission and during scoping.

B. Regulations. The following partial list identifies MMS Outer Continental Shelf (OCS) regulations and other guidance which may apply to a particular application.

(1) Grants of pipeline rights-of-way and related facilities on the OCS (30 CFR Part 256, Subpart N).

(2) Exploration, development and production activities, Environmental Report (30 CFR Part 250, Sec. 250.34-3).

(3) Air quality (30 CFR Part 250, Sec. 250,57).

(4) Geological and geophysical explorations of the OCS (30 CFR Part 251. Sec. 251.6-2(b)).

(5) OCS Pipelines Rights-of-Ways. A Procedure Handbook.

(6) Guidelines for Preparing OCS Environmental Reports.

15.4 **Major Actions Normally Requiring an EIS.**

A. The following proposals will normally require the preparation of an EIS:

(1) Approval of a 5-year offshore oil and gas leasing program.

(2) Approval of offshore lease sales.

(3) Approval of an offshore oil and gas development and production plan in any area or region of the offshore, other than the central or western Gulf of Mexico, when the plan is declared to be a major Federal action in accordance with section 25(e)(1) of the OCS Lands Act Amendments of 1978.

B. If, for any of these actions, it is proposed not to prepare an EIS, an environmental assessment will be prepared and handled in accordance with Section 1501.4(e)(2).

15.4 **Categorical Exclusions.** In addition to the actions listed in the Departmental categorical exclusions outlined in Appendix 1 of 516 DM 2, many of which the MMS also performs, the following MMS actions are designated categorical exclusions unless the action qualifies as an exception under Appendix 2 of 516 DM 2:

A. General.

(1) Inventory, data, and information collection, including the conduct of environmental monitoring and nondestructive research programs.

(2) Actions for which MMS has concurrence or co-approval with another Bureau if the action is a categorical exclusion for that Bureau.

B. Internal Program Initiatives.

(1) All resource evaluation activities including surveying, mapping, and geophysical surveying which do not use solid or liquid explosives.

(2) Collection of geologic data and samples including geologic, paleontologic, mineralogic, geochemical, and geophysical investigations which does not involve drilling beyond 50 feet of consolidated rock or beyond 300 feet of unconsolidated rock, including contracts therefor.

(3) Acquisition of existing geological or geophysical data from otherwise private exploration ventures.

(4) Well logging, digital modeling. inventory of existing wells, and installation of recording devices in wells.

(5) Establishment and installation of any research/monitoring devices.

(6) Test or exploration drilling and downhole testing included in a project previously subject to the NEPA process.

(7) Insignificant revisions to the approved 5-year leasing program.

(8) Prelease planning steps such as the Call for Information and Area Identification.

C. Permit and Regulatory Functions.

(1) Issuance and modification of regulations, Orders, Standards, Notices to Lessees and Operators. Guidelines and field rules for which the impacts are limited to administrative, economic, or technological effects and the environmental impacts are minimal.

(2) Approval of production measurement methods, facilities, and procedures.

(3) Approval of off-lease storage in existing facilities.

(4) Approval of unitization agreements, pooling, or communitization agreements.

(5) Approval of commingling of production.

(6) Approval of suspensions of operations and suspensions of production.

(7) Approval of lease consolidation applications, lease assignments or transfers, operating rights, operating agreements, lease extensions, lease relinquishments, and bond terminations.

(8) Administration decisions and actions and record keeping such as:

(a) Approval of applications for pricing determinations under the Natural Gas Policy Act.

(b) Approval of underground gas storage agreements from a presently or formerly productive reservoir.

(c) Issuance of paying well determinations and participating area approvals.

(d) Issuance of drainage determinations.

(9) Approval of offshore geological and geophysical mineral exploration activities, except when the proposed activity includes the drilling of deep stratigraphic test holes or uses solid or liquid explosives.

(10) Approval of an offshore lease or unit exploration. development/production plan or a Development Operation Coordination Document in the central or western Gulf of Mexico (30 CFR 250.2) except those proposing facilities: (1) In areas of high seismic risk or seismicity, relatively untested deep water, or remote areas, or (2) within the boundary of a proposed or established marine sanctuary, and/or within or near the boundary of a proposed or established wildlife refuge or areas of high biological sensitivity; or (3) in areas of hazardous natural bottom conditions; or (4) utilizing new or unusual technology.

(11) Approval of minor revisions of or minor variances from activities described in an approved offshore exploration or development/production plan, including pipeline applications.

(12) Approval of an Application for Permit to Drill (APD) an offshore oil and gas exploration or development well, when said well and appropriate mitigation

measures are described in an approved exploration plan, development plan, production plan, or Development Operations Coordination Document.

(13) Preliminary activities conducted on a lease prior to approval of an exploration or development/production plan or a Development Operations Coordination Plan. These are activities such as geological, geophysical, and other surveys necessary to develop a comprehensive exploration plan, development/production plan, or Development Operations Coordination Plan.

(14) Approval of Sundry Notices and Reports on Wells.

(15) Rights-of-ways, easements, temporary use permits, and any revisions thereto that do not result in a new pipeline corridor to shore.

D. Royalty Functions. All functions of the Associate Director for Royalty Management including, but not limited to, such activities as: approval of royalty payment procedures, including royalty oil contracts; and determinations concerning royalty quantities and values, such as audits, royalty reductions, collection procedures, reporting procedures, and any actions taken with regard to royalty collections (including similar actions relating to net profit and windfall profit taxes).

5/27/04 #3625

Replaces 3/18/80 #3511

NEPA Deskbook

Appendix 16 Department of Transportation Regulations and Procedures (Part 5610)

Department of Transportation

Office of the Secretary
Washington, D.C.

ORDER

> DOT 5610.1C

9-18-79

Chg 1 7-13-82
chg 2 7-30-85

SUBJECT: PROCEDURES FOR CONSIDERING ENVIRONMENTAL IMPACTS

INTRODUCTION.

1. PURPOSE. This Order establishes procedures for consideration of
    environmental impacts in decision making on proposed Department of
    Transportation (DOT) actions. The Order provides that information
    on environmental impacts of proposed actions will be made available
    to public officials and citizens through environmental impact statements,
    environmental assessments or findings of no significant impact. These
    documents serve as the single vehicle for environmental findings and
    coordination.

2. CANCELLATION. DOT 5610.1B, PROCEDURES FOR CONSIDERING
    ENVIRONMENTAL IMPACTS, dated September 30, 1974.

3. AUTHORITY. This Order provides instructions for implementing Section
    102(2) of the National Environmental Policy Act of 1969, as amended,
    (42 USC 4321-4347, hereinafter "NEPA") and the Regulations for Implementing
    NEPA issued by the Council on Environmental Quality, 11-29-78 (40 CFR
    1500-1508); Sections 2(b) and 4(f) of the Department of Transportation
    Act of 1966 (49 USC 1653, hereinafter "the DOT Act"); Sections 309
    and 176 of the Clean Air Act, as amended (42 USC 7401 et seq.); Section 106
    of the National Historic Preservation Act of 1966 (16 USC 470,
    hereinafter "the Historic Preservation Act"); Sections 303 and 307 of
    the Coastal Zone Management Act of 1972 (43 USC 1241); Section 2 of
    the Fish and Wildlife Coordination Act (16 USC 661 et seq.); Section 7
    of the Endangered Species Act, as amended (16 USC 1533); the Federal
    Water Pollution Control Act, as amended (33 USC 1314 et seq.); Executive
    Order 12114, Environmental Effects Abroad of Major Federal Actions;
    and various Executive Orders relating to environmental impacts.
    In addition, the Order provides instructions for implementing, where
    environmental statements are required, Sections 138 and 109 of Federal-
    aid highway legislation (Title 23, USC, hereinafter "the Highway Act);
    Sections 16 and 18(a) of the Airport and Airway Development Act of
    1970 (49 USC 1716, 1718, hereinafter "the Airport Act"); and Section 14
    of the Urban Mass Transportation Act of 1964 (49 USC Section 1601 et
    seq., hereinafter "the Urban Mass Transportation Act").

DISTRIBUTION: T-1 (All DOT Office and Regional
             Directors and Above), Including
             Coast Guard
             National Transportation Safety Board (Info)

OPI: Office of
     Environment
     and Safety

TABLE OF CONTENTS

Attachment 1
State and Localities with EIS Requirements

Attachment 2
Form and Content of Environmental Impact Statements

Vertical line denotes change.

1.   BACKGROUND.

The National Environmental Policy Act (NEPA) establishes a broad
national policy to promote efforts to improve the relationship between
man and his environment. NEPA sets out certain policies and goals
concerning the environment and requires that to the fullest extent
possible, the policies, regulations, and public laws of the United States
shall be interpreted and administered in accordance with those policies
and goals.

Section 102 of NEPA is designed to insure that environmental considerations are given careful attention and appropriate weight in all decisions
of the Federal Government. Section 102(2)(C) requires that all agencies of
the Federal Government shall

> include in every recommendation or report on proposals for legisla-
> tion and other major Federal actions significantly affecting the
> quality of the human environment, a detailed statement by the
> responsible official on —
>
> (i)   the environmental impact of the proposed action,
>
> (ii)   any adverse environmental effects which cannot be avoided
>   should the proposal be implemented,
>
> (iii) alternatives to the proposed action,
>
> (iv)   the relationship between local short-term uses of man's
>   environment and the maintenance and enhancement of long-
>   term productivity, and
>
> (v)   any irreversible and irretrievable commitments of resources
>   which would be involved in the proposed action should it be
>   implemented.

Section 102(2)(A) requires all agencies of the Federal Government to
"utilize a systematic, interdisciplinary approach which will insure the
integrated use of the natural and social sciences and the environmental
design arts in planning and decision making which may have an impact on
man's environment..."

The Council on Environmental Quality (CEQ) issued regulations for implementation of the procedural provisions of NEPA (40 CFR Parts 1500-1508) on 11-29-78. The CEQ regulations apply uniformly to and are binding upon all Federal agencies, and direct each agency to adopt implementing procedures which relate the CEQ regulations to the specific needs of that agency's programs and operating procedures.

This Order implements the mandate of NEPA, as defined and elaborated upon by CEQ's regulations, within the programs of the Department of Transportation. The Order is not a substitute for the regulations promulgated by CEQ, nor does it repeat or paraphrase the language of those regulations. Rather, the Order supplements the CEQ regulations by applying them to DOT programs. Therefore, all operating administrations and Secretarial Offices shall comply with both the CEQ regulations and the provisions of this Order.

This Order provides instructions for implementation of relevant environmental laws and executive orders in addition to NEPA. The environmental process established by this Order is intended to implement the Department's policy objective of one-stop environmental processing. To the maximum extent possible, a single process shall be used to meet requirements for environmental studies, consultations and reviews.

2.   POLICY AND INTENT.

   a.   It is the policy of the Department of Transportation to integrate national environmental objectives into the missions and programs of the Department and to:

      (1)   avoid or minimize adverse effects wherever possible;

      (2)   restore or enhance environmental quality to the fullest extent practicable;

      (3)   preserve the natural beauty of the countryside and public park and recreation lands, wildlife and waterfowl refuges, and historic sites;

      (4)   preserve, restore and improve wetlands;

      (5)   improve the urban physical, social and economic environment;

(6) increase access to opportunities for disadvantaged persons; and

(7) utilize a systematic, interdisciplinary approach in planning and decision making which may have an impact on the environment.

b. The purpose of the environmental procedures in this Order is to provide Department officials, other decision makers, and the public, as part of the decision making process, with an understanding of the potential effects of proposed actions significantly affecting the quality of the human environment. The environmental review process is to be used to explore and document alternative actions that will avoid or minimize adverse impacts.

c. The environmental impact statement (EIS), finding of no significant impact (FONSI, formerly "negative declaration") and determination that a proposed action is categorically excluded serve as the record of compliance with the policy and procedures of NEPA and the policy and procedures of other environmental statutes and executive orders. To the maximum extent possible, all environmental studies, reviews and consultations shall be coordinated into a single process, and compliance with all applicable environmental requirements shall be reflected in the EIS or FONSI.

3. PLANNING AND EARLY COORDINATION.

a. The identification and evaluation of the social, economic and environmental effects of a proposed action and the identification of all reasonable measures to mitigate adverse impacts shall be initiated in the early planning stages of the action, and shall be considered along with technical and economic studies. Assessment of environmental impacts should be a part of regional transportation system planning and broad transportation program development.

General criteria for identification of social, economic, and environmental impacts in DOT planning programs are set forth in subparagraph 10.e., DOT 1130.4, Intermodal Planning Groups and Unified Planning Work Programs, of 2-12-79. Other guidance may be identified in the implementing procedures of the administrations.

b. Where the DOT action is initiated by a State or local agency or a private applicant, the responsible operating administration shall assure that the applicant is advised of environmental assessment and review requirements and that consultation with appropriate agencies and interested parties is initiated at the earliest possible time. (See paragraph 20.b. below.)

c. Existing administration procedures for early consultation and citizen participation shall be modified to incorporate the scoping process (CEQ 1501.7). Implementing procedures shall assure that significant issues are identified and that all interested parties have an opportunity to participate in the scoping and early consultation process.

d. Where the proposed action is initiated by a State and may have significant impacts on a Federal land management entity or any other State, the responsible Federal official shall provide early notice to and solicit the views of that Federal land management entity or other State.

4. ENVIRONMENTAL PROCESSING CHOICE.

a. Actions covered. Except as provided in subparagraph c. below, the requirements of this Order apply to, but are not limited to, the following: all grants, loans, loan guarantees, construction, research activities, rulemaking and regulatory actions, certifications, licenses, permits, approval of policies and plans (including those submitted to the Department by State or local agencies), adoption or implementation of programs, legislation proposed by DOT, and any renewals or reapprovals of the foregoing. (CEQ 1508.18(b).)

b. Environmental Impact Statements. An EIS shall be prepared for any proposed major Federal action significantly affecting the environment. (See also: CEQ 1508.27, and paragraphs 7 and 20 of this Order.)

c. Categorical Exclusions. The following actions are not Federal actions with a significant impact on the environment, and do not require either an environmental assessment or an environmental impact statement:

(1) Administrative procurements (e.g. general supplies) and contracts for personal services;

(2) Personnel actions (e.g. promotions, hirings);

(3) Project amendments (e.g. increases in costs) which do not significantly alter the environmental impact of the action;

DOT 5610.1C Chg 2   Page 5
7-30-85

    (4) Operating or maintenance subsidies when the subsidy will not result in a change in the effect on the environment; and

    (5) Other actions identified by the administrations as categorical exclusions pursuant to paragraph 20.

    (6) The following actions relating to economic regulation of airlines:

      (a) Actions implementing the essential air service program;

      (b) Enforcement proceedings;

      (c) Actions approving a carrier agreement; acquisition of control, merger, consolidation, or interlocking relationship;

      (d) Finding a carrier fit under section 401 of the Federal Aviation Act of 1958, as amended;

      (e) Approving or setting carrier fares or rates;

      (f) Route awards involving turboprop aircraft having a capacity of 60 seats or less and a maximum payload capacity of 18,000 pounds or less;

      (g) Route awards that do not involve supersonic service and will not result in an increase in commercial aircraft operations of one or more percent;

      (h) Determinations on termination of airline employees;

      (i) Actions relating to consumer protection, including regulations;

      (j) Authorizing carriers to serve airports already receiving the type of service authorized;

      (k) Granting temporary or emergency authority;

      (l) Negotiating bilateral agreements;

      (m) Registration of an air taxi operator pursuant to the Department's Regulations (14 CFR Part 298); and

      (n) Granting of charter authority to a U.S. or foreign air carrier under sections 401, 402 or 416 of the Federal Aviation Act or the Department's Economic Regulations.

  d. Environmental Assessment. An environmental assessment or EIS shall be prepared for actions normally categorically excluded, but which are likely to involve (1) significant impacts on the environment; (2) substantial controversy on environmental grounds; (3) impacts which are more than minimal on properties protected by section 4(f) and sections 106 of the Historic Preservation Act; or (4) inconsistencies with any Federal, State or local law or administrative determination relating to the environment.

Vertical line denotes change.

    e.   Exemptions. The provisions of this Order do not apply to actions that have an impact primarily outside the United States, except for those actions significantly affecting the environment of a foreign nation not participating in the action, or ecological natural resources designated for protection by the President or the Secretary of State, or the global commons.

5.   FINDING OF NO SIGNIFICANT IMPACT.

    a.   The FONSI may be attached to an enviornmental assessment or the environmental assessment and FONSI may be combined into a single document.

    b.   Except as provided in subparagraph c. below, a FONSI or environmental assessemnt need not be coordinated outside the originating office, but must be made available to the public upon request. Notice of availability shall be provided (see suggestions for public notice in CEQ 1506.6(b)). In all cases, notice shall be provided to State and areawide clearinghouses.

    c.   In the circumstances defined in CEQ 1501.4(e)(2), a copy of the environmental assessment should be made available to the public for a period of not less than 30 days before the finding of no significant impact is made and the action is implemented. Consultation with other Federal agencies concerning section 4(f) of the DOT Act, the Historic Preservation Act, section 404 permits and other Federal requirements should be accomplished prior to or during this period.

6.   LEAD AGENCIES AND COOPERATING AGENCIES.

    a.   The appropriate Operating Administration or Secretarial Office shall serve as the lead agency or joint lead agency for preparing and processing environmental documents when that element has the primary Federal responsibility for the action.

    b.   An applicant should to the fullest extent possible serve as a joint lead agency if the applicant is a State agency with State-wide jurisdiction, or is a State or local agency, and the proposed action is subject to State requirements comparable to NEPA. (See CEQ 1506.2.)

    c.   Coordination with cooperating agencies shall be initiated early in project planning and shall be continued through all stages of development of the appropriate environmental document.

    d.   If an agency requested to be a cooperating agency replies that it will not participate, the agency shall be provided a copy of the draft EIS. If the agency makes adverse comments on the draft EIS (including the adequacy of the EIS or consideration of alternatives or of mitigating measures), or if the agency indicates that it may delay or withhold action on some aspect of the proposal, the matter may be discussed with CEQ,

    e.   Where a DOT element is requested to be a cooperating agency, it shall make every effort to participate.

7.   PREPARATION AND PROCESSING OF DRAFT ENVIRONMENTAL STATEMENTS.

    a.   Scope of Statement. The action covered by the statement should have significance, and must be broad enough in scope to avoid segmentation of projects and to ensure meaningful consideration of alternatives. The scope of the statement should be decided upon during the scoping process. (See also CEQ 1502.20 and para. 7.g. below.) A general class of actions may be covered in a single EIS when the environmental impacts of all the actions are similar.

Vertical line denotes change.

b. <u>Timing of Preparation of Draft Statements</u>. Draft statements shall be prepared at the earliest practical time prior to the first significant point of decision in the program or project development process. They should be prepared early enough in the process so that the analysis of the environmental effects and the exploration of alternatives are meaningful inputs to the decision making process. The implementing guidance (see paragraph 20) shall specify the point at which draft statements should be prepared for each type of action.

c. <u>Interdisciplinary Approach and Responsibilities for EIS Preparation</u>. An interdisciplinary approach should be used throughout planning and preparation of environmental documents to help assure a systematic evaluation of reasonable alternative courses of action and their potential social, economic, and environmental consequences. At a minimum, operating administrations should have staff capabilities adequate to evaluate environmental assessments and environmental documents so that DOT can take responsibility for their content. Secretarial Offices may request assistance from P-30. If the necessary disciplines are not represented on the staff of the administration, the responsible official should obtain professional services from other Federal, State or local agencies, universities, or consulting firms.

d. <u>Preparation of Draft</u>. Draft EISs shall be prepared concurrently with and integrated with environmental analyses required by other environmental review laws and executive orders. To the maximum extent possible, the EIS process shall be used to coordinate all studies, reviews and consultations. (See CEQ 1502.25.) The draft EIS should reflect the result of the scoping/early consultation process. Further guidance on compliance with the various environmental statutes is included in Attachment 2.

e. <u>Format and Content</u>. Further guidance on the format and content of EISs is provided in Attachment 2.

f. <u>Circulation of the Draft Environmental Impact Statement</u>.

    (I) The originating operating administration or Secretarial Office shall circulate the draft environmental statement or summary to the parties indicated in paragraph 8 below. Copies of the draft EIS should be filed with the Environmental Protection Agency (EPA). (See also CEQ 1506.9 and 1506.10.)

Vertical line denotes change.

(2)   If a State agency with statewide jurisdiction is functioning as a joint lead agency and has prepared the draft EIS, the draft statement may be circulated by the State agency after the operating administration has approved it.

g.   Tiering. Tiering of EISs as discussed in CEQ 1502.20 is encouraged when it will improve or simplify the environmental processing of proposed DOT actions. Preparation of tiered EISs should be considered for complex transportation proposals (e.g. major urban transportation investments, airport master plans, aid to navigation systems, etc.) or for a number of discrete but closely related Federal actions. The first tier EIS should focus on broad issues such as mode choice, general location and areawide air quality and land use implications of the alternative transportation improvements. System planning activities should encompass environmental studies, as noted in subparagraph 3.a., and the first tier EISs should use information from these system planning studies and appropriate corridor planning and other planning studies. A second tier, site specific EIS should focus on more detailed project impacts and detailed mitigation measures (e.g. addressing detailed location, transit station locations, highway interchange configurations, etc.).

8.   INVITING COMMENTS ON THE DRAFT EIS.

The draft EIS shall be circulated with an invitation to comment to (1) all agencies having jurisdiction by law or special expertise with respect to the environmental impact involved; (2) interested parties; (3) EPA Office of Federal Activities; (4) the Assistant Secretary for Policy and International Affairs (P-1); and (5) other elements of DOT, where appropriate. A reasonable number of copies shall be provided to permit agencies and interested parties to comment expeditiously.

a.   State and Local Review.

(1)   Review of the proposed action by State and local agencies, when appropriate, shall be obtained as follows:

(a)   Where review of draft Federal development projects, and of projects assisted under programs listed in Attachment D to revised OMB Circular A-95 (as implemented

DOT 5610.1C   Page 9
9-13-79

by DOT 4600.4C, Evaluation, Review and Coordination
of DOT Assistance Programs and Projects, of 4-12-79),
takes place prior to preparation of a draft environmental statement, comments of the reviewing
agencies on the environmental effects of the proposed
project shall be attached to the environmental statement. Copies of the draft and final environmental
statements shall be sent to clearinghouses and to the
applicant whose project is the subject of the statement.

(b)   Project applicants or administrations shall obtain
      comments directly from appropriate State and local
      agencies, except where review is secured by agreement
      through A-95 clearinghouses. Comments shall be
      solicited from all affected local governments.

(2)   At the time a draft or final environmental statement is filed
      with EPA, the availability of the statement should be
      announced through advertisements in local newspapers and
      other effective methods. Copies of EISs shall be provided to
      the public upon request and made available at appropriate
      public places.

b.   Review of EISs Prepared Pursuant to Section 102(2)(D) of NEPA. If
     the draft EIS is prepared by a State agency with statewide jurisdiction,
     and the proposed action will affect another State or Federal land
     management entity, the draft EIS shall be circulated to the affected
     State or Federal land management entity.

9.   REVIEW OF ENVIRONMENTAL STATEMENTS PREPARED BY OTHER
     AGENCIES.

     The purpose of DOT review and comment on environmental statements
     drafted by other agencies is to provide a competent and cooperative
     advisory and consultative service.

a.   Comments should be limited to the impacts on areas within the Department's functional responsibility, jurisdiction by law or expertise.

b.   DOT projects that are environmentally or functionally related to the action proposed in the EIS should be identified so that inter-relationships can be discussed in the final statement. In such cases, the DOT agency should consider serving as a joint lead agency or cooperating agency.

c.   Other agencies will generally be requested to forward their draft environmental statements directly to the appropriate regional offices of the Department. There are several types of proposals, however, that should be referred by regional offices to Departmental headquarters for comment. These generally include the following:

    (1)   Actions with national policy implications;

    (2)   Legislation, regulations having national impacts, or national program proposals.

Draft EISs in these categories are to be referred to P-1 for preparation of DOT comments and, where appropriate, to the headquarters of the operating administrations. In referring these matters to headquarters, the regional office is encouraged to prepare a proposed Departmental response.

d.   Draft EISs for actions which have impact on only one region or which do not fall within subparagraph c. above should be reviewed by regional offices of DOT administrations. Comments should be forwarded directly to the office designated by the originating agency. If the receiving office believes that another DOT office is in a better position to respond, it should send the statement to that office. If more than one administration is commenting at the regional level, the comments shall be coordinated by the Regional Representative or a designee.

e.   When appropriate, the commenting office should coordinate a response with other Departmental offices having special expertise in the subject matter. For example, comments on projects affecting the transportation of hazardous materials or natural gas and liquid-products pipelines should be coordinated with the Research and Special Programs Administration, Materials Transportation Bureau, and water resources projects should be coordinated with the U.S. Coast Guard, Ports and Waterways Planning Staff (G-WS/73).

f.   Copies of comments on another agency's EIS shall be provided to the requesting agency, to P-1, and to the Regional Representative if the comment is prepared by a regional office.

10.   PREDECISION REFERRALS TO THE COUNCIL ON ENVIRONMENTAL QUALITY.

The following specific procedures apply to referrals involving DOT elements:

a.   DOT Lead Agency Proposals.

(1)   An operating administration or Secretarial Office receiving a notice of intended referral from another agency with respect to a proposed DOT action shall provide P-30 with a copy of the notice. Every effort should be made to resolve the issues raised by the referring agency prior to processing the final EIS. These efforts should be documented in the EIS. P-1 will be available to assist in any such resolution, and should be notified of the results.

(2)   In the event of an actual referral, the lead agency shall obtain P-1's concurrence in the response to CEQ.

b.   DOT Referrals to CEQ on other Agencies' Proposals.

(1)   If upon reviewing a draft from another Federal agency, an operating administration or Secretarial Office believes a referral will be necessary, it should so advise P-30. If P-30 agrees, it will advise the lead agency that DOT intends to refer the proposal to CEQ unless the proposal is changed. P-30 will coordinate DOT comments on the draft EIS, including the notice of intended referral.

Vertical line denotes change

(2)   Environmental referrals should be avoided, where possible, through efforts to resolve the issues, after providing notice of intent to refer and prior to the lead agency's filing the final EIS.

(3)   In the event that the issues have not been resolved prior to filing of the final EIS with EPA, P-1 will deliver a referral to CEQ not later than 25 calendar days after the final EIS is made available to EPA, commenting agencies, and the public.

   (a)   Operating administrations and Secretarial Offices should submit proposed referrals to P-1 at least 5 days prior to the 25-day deadline. The proposed referral should include the information specified in section 1504.3(c) of the CEQ regulations.

   (b)   P-1 will inform the lead agency of the referral and the reasons for it, including a copy of the detailed statement developed pursuant to section 1504.3(c).

11.   FINAL ENVIRONMENTAL IMPACT STATEMENTS.

   a.   Preparation. The final EIS shall identify the preferred alternative, including measures to mitigate adverse impacts. In identifying the preferred alternative, the DOT element should consider the policies stated in paragraph 2 above. Every effort should be made to resolve significant issues raised through circulation of the draft EIS, the community involvement process and consultation with cooperating agencies before the EIS is put into final form for approval by the responsible official. The final statement shall reflect such issues, consultation and efforts to resolve the issues, including an explanation of why any remaining issues have not been resolved.

   b.   Compliance with other Requirements. The final EIS should reflect that there has been compliance with the requirements of all applicable environmental laws and orders, e.g. section 4(f) of the DOT Act, section 106 of the Historic Preservation Act, section 404 of the Clean Water Act, section 7 of the Endangered Species Act, the DOT Floodplain Management Order (5650.2) and the DOT Wetlands Order (5660.1A). If such compliance is not possible by the time of final EIS preparation, the EIS should reflect consultation with the appropriate agencies and provide reasonable assurance that the requirements can be met.

c.   Legal Review. All final environmental statements shall be reviewed for legal sufficiency by the Chief Counsel of the operating administration concerned, or by a designee. Final environmental statements prepared within the Office of the Secretary (OST) shall be reviewed for legal sufficiency by the General Counsel (C-I).

d.   Approval. Final environmental impact statements may be approved by the Administrator or Secretarial Officer (or a designee) originating the action. For highly controversial final EIS's that require approval or concurrence by the headquarters of the operating administration pursuant to Administration procedures for approval, P-I and C-I shall be notified that the final EIS is under review and will be provided a copy of the summary section contained in the final EIS. P-I and C-I will also be given at least two weeks notice before approval of the final environmental impact statement. For purposes of this paragraph a proposed Federal action is considered highly controversial when the action is opposed on environmental grounds by a Federal, state, or local government agency or by a substantial number of the persons affected by such action.

e.   Availability Pending Approval. Following the initial level of approval by the administration (for example, by the FHWA Division Administrator), proposed final statements should normally be made available for inspection during usual business hours by the public and Federal, State or local agencies. Such statements should carry a notation that the statement is not approved and filed.

f.   Availability of Statements to EPA and the Public. After approval, the originating office shall transmit copies of each final statement to EPA in accordance with instructions from EPA. The originating office shall send copies of the final statement to the applicant, P-I all Federal, State, and local agencies and private organizations which commented substantively on the draft statement or requested copies of the final statement, and to individuals who requested copies.

Vertical line denotes change

g.   Implementation of Representations in Environmental Statements.
The administrations shall assure, through funding agreements and
project review procedures, that applicants carry out any actions to
minimize adverse environmental effects set forth in the approved
statement. Any significant deviation from prescribed action that
may reduce protection to the environment must be submitted
for concurrence in accordance with Administration procedures for
final EIS approval.

h.   Supplemental Statements. The responsible official shall supplement
a draft EIS when either: (1) it is determined that a reasonable
alternative which is significantly different from alternatives considered in the draft EIS exists and will be considered, or (2) when
environmental conditions or data change significantly from those
presented in the statement. A final EIS shall be supplemented when
substantial changes are made in the proposed action, when conditions or data change significantly from that presented in the
statement, or if the responsible official determines that a supplement is necessary for some other reason. (The development of
additional data as a proposal moves through the implementation
process would not require a supplement if the data does not
materially conflict with the data in the EIS.) A supplemental EIS
may be prepared to address detailed information which was not
available at the time an EIS was prepared and approved, for
example, site or project specific impacts which have been discussed
only in general terms in a corridor or program EIS. (See also CEQ
1502.20 and paragraph 7.g.) A supplemental statement should be
prepared, circulated and approved in accordance with the provisions
of the CEQ regulations and paragraphs 7, 8, and 11 of this Order,
unless the responsible official believes there are compelling reasons
to do otherwise. In such cases, the operating administration or
Secretarial Office should consult with CEQ.

12.   DETERMINATIONS UNDER SECTION 4(f) OF THE DOT ACT.

a.   Any action having more than a minimal effect on lands protected
under section 4(f) of the DOT Act will normally require the
preparation of an environmental statement. In these cases, the
environmental statement shall include the material required by
paragraph 4 of Attachment 2. If in the preparation of the final EIS,
it is concluded that there is no feasible and prudent alternative to
the use of section 4(f) lands, the final EIS shall support a specific
determination to that effect, including evidence that there has been
all possible planning to minimize harm to the protected lands.

Vertical line denotes change

b.   If an environmental statement is not required, the material called for in paragraph 4 of Attachment 2 shall be set forth in a separate document, accompanied by a FONSI or a determination that the section 4(f) involvement is minimal and that the action is categorically excluded. The section 4(f) determination shall be reviewed for legal sufficiency by the Chief Counsel of the operating administration involved, or by a designee. The document must reflect consultation with the Department of the Interior, and where appropriate, the Departments of Agriculture or Housing and Urban Development.

13.   RESPONSIBILITY.

Where an operating administration or Secretarial Office serves as lead agency or joint lead agency, it shall be responsible for the scope, objectivity, accuracy and content of EISs and environmental assessments. The EIS or environmental assessment shall be prepared by the operating administration or secretarial office, by a contractor selected by DOT, or by the applicant, pursuant to the provisions of CEQ 1506.2 and 1506.5. In developing implementing instructions, administrations shall note the distinctions made in the CEQ regulations between State agencies with statewide jurisdiction, State and local agencies which must comply with State or local requirements comparable to NEPA, and other applicants. State and local governments with requirements comparable to NEPA are listed in Attachment 1.

14.   CITIZEN INVOLVEMENT PROCEDURES.

a.   Citizen involvement in the environmental assessment of Departmental actions is encouraged at each appropriate stage of development of the proposed action and should be sought as early as possible. Citizen involvement in the environmental process should be integrated with other citizen involvement procedures to the maximum extent possible. Attempts should be made to solicit the views of the public through hearings, personal contact, press releases, advertisements or notices in newspapers, including minority or foreign language papers, if appropriate, and other methods. A summary of citizen involvement and any environmental issues raised should be documented in the EIS.

b.   The administrations' implementing instructions shall provide (1) that interested parties and Federal, State, and local agencies receive early notification of the decision to prepare an environmental impact statement, including publication of a notice of intent in the Federal Register, and (2) that their comments on the environmental effects of the proposed Federal action are solicited at an early stage in the preparation of the draft impact statement.

c. Administrations are encouraged to develop lists of interested parties at the national, State and local levels. These would include individuals and community, environmental, conservation, public service, education, labor, or business organizations, who are affected by or known to have an interest in the project, or who can speak knowledgeably on the environmental impact of the proposed action.

d. Under OMB Circular A-95, (Revised) Evaluation, Review, and Coordination of Federal Assistance Programs and Projects, and DOT 4600.4C, Evaluation, Review and Coordination of DOT Assistance Programs and Projects, of 4-12-76, a grant applicant must notify the clearinghouse of its intention to apply for Federal program assistance. The administrations' implementing instructions should provide for the solicitation of comments from the clearinghouse on the environmental consequences of the proposed action.

e. Hearings.

   (1) In several instances, a public hearing is required by statute as a condition to Federal approval of a proposed action. Even where not required by statute, an informational hearing or meeting may serve as a useful forum for public involvement.

   (2) If a public hearing is to be held, the draft EIS or environmental assessment (or environmental analysis where the hearing is held by an applicant which is not a joint lead agency) should be made available to the public at least 30 days prior to the hearing.

f. Interested persons can get information on the DOT environmental process and on the status of EISs issued by the Office of the Secretary from: Deputy Director for Environment and Policy Review (P-32), Department of Transportation, Washington, D.C. 20590, telephone 202-~~426-4361.~~ 366-4898.

   Each administration shall indicate in its implementing instructions where interested persons can get information or status reports on EISs and other elements of the NEPA process.

Vertical line denotes change

15.   **PROPOSALS FOR LEGISLATION.**

    a.   **Preparation.** An EIS shall be prepared and circulated for any legislative proposal, or for any favorable report on proposed legislation, for which DOT is primarily responsible and which involves significant environmental impacts. The administration or Secretarial Office originating the legislation or developing the Departmental position on the report shall prepare the EIS.

    b.   **Processing.** The draft EIS shall be cleared with P-1 and submitted by the Assistant General Counsel for Legislation (C-40) to the Office of Management and Budget for circulation in the normal legislative clearance process. The EIS shall be transmitted to Congress no later than 30 days after transmittal of the legislative proposal, and must be available in time for Congressional hearings. Any comments received on the EIS shall be transmitted to Congress. Except as provided by CEQ 1506.8(b)(2), there need not be a final EIS.

16.   **INTERNATIONAL ACTIONS.**

    a.   Pursuant to Executive Order 12114, Environmental Effects Abroad of Major Federal Actions, the requirements of this Order apply to:

        (1)   Major Federal actions significantly affecting the environment of the global commons outside the jurisdiction of any nation (e.g. the oceans and Antarctica).

        (2)   Major Federal actions significantly affecting the environment of a foreign nation not participating in the action or otherwise involved in the action.

        (3)   Major Federal actions significantly affecting the environment of a foreign nation which provide a product or a project producing a toxic emission or effluent, which is prohibited or strictly regulated in the U.S. by Federal law.

        (4)   Major Federal actions outside the U.S., its territories and possessions which significantly affect natural resources of global importance designated for protection by the President or by international agreement.

    b.   If communication with a foreign government concerning environmental studies or documentation is anticipated, the responsible Federal official shall coordinate such communication with the State Department, through P-1.

17.   TIMING OF AGENCY ACTION.

A decision on the proposed action may not be made sooner than the times specified in CEQ 1506.10(b).

a.   Requests for reasonable extensions of the review period for the draft EISs shall be granted whenever possible, and particularly when warranted by the magnitude and complexity of the statement or the extent of citizen interest.

b.   If an administration or Secretarial Office believes it is necessary to reduce the prescribed time periods for EIS processing, it should request such a reduction from EPA. P-32 should be notified of such a request.

c.   Where emergency circumstances make it necessary to take an action with significant environmental impacts without observing the provisions of this Order and the CEQ regulations, the administration or Secretarial Office should consult with CEQ. P-32 should be notified of such consultation.

18.   EFFECTIVE DATE.

a.   This Order and attachments apply to all draft statements filed by DOT with EPA after 7-30-79, except as provided in paragraph 1506.12 of the CEQ regulations.

b.   For final statements whose drafts are filed by 7-30-79 (for FHWA, 11-30-79), paragraph 11 of this Order applies after 7-30-81. In the interim, final EISs shall be processed in accordance with the provisions of DOT 5610.1B.

19.   TIME IN EFFECT OF STATEMENTS.

a.   The draft EIS may be assumed valid for a period of three years. If the proposed final EIS is not submitted to the approving official within three years from the date of the draft EIS circulation, a written reevaluation of the draft shall be prepared by the responsible Federal official to determine whether the consideration of alternatives, impacts, existing environment and mitigation measures set forth in the draft EIS remain applicable, accurate and valid. If there have been changes in these factors which would be significant in the consideration of the proposed action, a supplement to the draft EIS or a new draft statement shall be prepared and circulated.

Vertical line denotes change

b.   If major steps toward implementation of the proposed action (such as the start of construction or substantial acquisition and relocation activities) have not commenced within three years from the date of approval of the final EIS, a written reevaluation of the adequacy, accuracy and validity of the EIS shall be prepared by the responsible Federal official unless tiering of EISs (as discussed in subparagraph 7.g.) is being used. If there have been significant changes in the proposed action, the affected environment, anticipated impacts, or proposed mitigation measures, a new or supplemental EIS shall be prepared and circulated.

c.   If major steps toward implementation of the proposed action have not occurred within five years from the date of approval of the final EIS, or within the time frame set forth in the final EIS, the responsible Federal official shall prepare a written reevaluation of the adequacy, accuracy, and validity of the EIS. This reevaluation shall be processed in accordance with subparagraph 11.d.

d.   If the proposed action is to be implemented in phases or requires successive Federal approvals, a written reevaluation of the continued adequacy, accuracy and validity of the EIS shall be made prior to Federal approval of each major stage which occurs more than three years after approval of the final EIS, and a new or supplemental EIS prepared, if necessary.

20.   IMPLEMENTING INSTRUCTIONS.

a.   Operating administrations shall issue instructions implementing this Order using one of the following options:

(1)   An operating administration may issue detailed instructions or regulations which incorporate the points of this Order and the CEQ regulations and provide guidance on applying the environmental process to the administration's programs; or

(2)   An operating administration may rely on this Order as its implementing procedures, provided it issues supplementary guidance which at a minimum applies the environmental process to the administration's programs, as described in the following subparagraph.

b.   Implementing instructions shall include the following information:

(1)   A list of actions which normally require preparation of an EIS.

(2)   A list of actions which are not normally major Federal actions significantly affecting the environment and as such do not normally require an environmental assessment or an environmental impact statement (i.e. categorical exclusions). These actions may include, but are not limited to, funding or authorizing: maintenance and modernization of existing facilities; minor safety improvements; equipment purchases; operating expenses; and planning grants which do not imply a project commitment. Instructions should provide for preparation of environmental assessments or EISs, as appropriate, for actions which would otherwise be classified as categorically excluded, but which are likely to involve: (1) significant impacts on the environment; (2) substantial controversy; (3) impacts which are more than minimal on properties protected by section 4(f) and section 106 of the Historic Preservation Act; or (4) inconsistencies with any Federal, State, or local law or administrative determination relating to the environment.

(3)   Identification of the decision making process, including timing for preparation of a draft and final environmental statement or a FONSI and designation of officials responsible for providing information on the administration's preparation, review and approval of environmental documents.

(4)   A description of the public participation process or reference to other administration guidance on the public participation process. (See paragraph 14, public participation.)

(5)   A description of the processes to be used to insure early involvement of DOT, other agencies and the public in the environmental review of actions proposed by nonfederal applicants (CEQ 1501.2(d)).

(6)   A description of the procedures for assuring implementation of mitigation measures identified in the EIS and the record of decision.

c. Proposed implementing instructions and any substantial amendments thereto shall be submitted to P-1 for review and concurrence. Consultation with CEQ will be assisted by P-1. Proposed and final implementing instructions shall be published in the Federal Register.

21.　RESPONSIBLE OFFICIAL FOR OFFICE OF THE SECRETARY ACTIONS. For the actions originating within the Office of the Secretary, the official responsible for approval of environmental documents is the Office Director of the office originating the action. The Director, Office of Transportation Regulatory Affairs, is responsible for general oversight and advice on environmental matters in liaison with the Assistant General Counsel for Environmental, Civil Rights, and General Law.

FOR THE SECRETARY OF TRANSPORTATION:

Robert L. Fairman
Deputy Assistant Secretary
 for Administration

Vertical line denotes change.

DOT 5610.1C
9-18-79

Attachment 1
Page 1

STATES AND LOCALITIES WITH EIS REQUIREMENTS

1.   States with Comprehensive Statutory Requirements:

California
Connecticut
Hawaii
Indiana
Maryland
Massachusetts
Minnesota
Montana
New York
New Jersey
North Carolina
South Dakota
Virginia
Washington
Wisconsin
Puerto Rico

2.   States with Comprehensive Executive or Administrative Orders:

Michigan
New Jersey
Texas
Utah

3.   Local EIS requirements:

Bowie, Maryland
New York, New York

Source:

Memorandum for NEPA Liaisons from the Council on Environmental Quality,
on agency implementing procedures under CEQ's NEPA regulations, dated
January 19, 1979. (Appendix D)

FORMAT AND CONTENT OF ENVIRONMENTAL IMPACT STATEMENTS

1. **Format.**

    a. The format recommended in CEQ 1502.10 should be used for DOT EISs:

        (a) Cover Sheet
        (b) Summary
        (c) Table of Contents
        (d) Purpose and Need for the Action
        (e) Alternatives Including the Proposed Action
        (f) Affected Environment
        (g) · Environmental Consequences
        (h) List of Preparers
        (i) List of Agencies, Organizations, and Persons to Whom Copies of the Statement Are Sent
        (j) Index
        (k) Appendices (if any)

    b. The cover sheet for each environmental impact statement will include the information identified in CEQ 1502.11 and will be headed as follows:

    Department of Transportation

    _____
    (operating administration)

    (Draft/Final) Environmental Impact Statement
    Pursuant to Section 102(2)(C), P.L. 91-190

    As appropriate, the heading will indicate that the EIS also covers the requirements of section 4(f) of the DOT Act, section 14 of the Mass Transportation Act, and/or sections 16 and 18(a)(4) of the Airport Act.

Attachment 2   DOT 5610.1C
Page 2   .   9-18-79

2.   Guidance as to Content of Statements.

    a.   Environmental impact statements shall include the information
          specified in CEQ 1502.11 through 1502.18. The following paragraphs
          of Attachment 2 are intended to be considered, where relevant,
          as guidance regarding the content of environmental statements.

    b.   Additional information contained in research reports, guidance
          on methodology, and other materials relating to consideration
          of environmental factors should be employed as appropriate in
          the preparation of EISs and environmental assessments. Examples
          of such materials include:

          ·   U.S. Department of Transportation, Environmental Assessment
               Notebook Series: Highways, 1975, Report No. DOT P 5600.4,
               available from the U.S. Government Printing Office, Washington,
               D.C. 20402, Stock Number 050-000-00109-1;

               U.S. DOT, Environmental Assessment Notebook Series:
               Airports, 1978, Report Number DOT P 5600.5, available from
               the U.S. Government Printing Office, Washington, D.C.
               20402, Stock Number 050-000-00138-5;

               U.S. DOT, FAA, Environmental Assessment of Airport Development
               Actions, 1977, available from the National Technical Information
               Service, 5284 Port Royal Road, Springfield, Virginia 22161,
               NTIS Catalog Number ADA-039274; and

               U.S. DOT, Guidelines for Assessing the Environmental Impact
               of Public Mass Transportation Projects, 1979, Report Number
               DOT P 79 001, available from the National Technical Information
               Service, Springfield, Virginia 22161.

3.   General Content. The following points are to be covered.

    a.   A description of the proposed Federal action (e.g. "The proposed
          Federal action is approval of location of highway..." or "The proposed
          Federal action is approval of a grant application to construct..."),
          and a statement of its purpose.

    b.   Alternatives, including the proposed action, and including, where
          relevant, those alternatives not within the existing authority of
          the responsible preparing office. Section 102(2)(E) of NEPA requires
          the responsible agency to "study, develop, and describe appropriate
          alternatives to recommended courses of action in any proposal
          which involves unresolved conflicts concerning alternative uses

of available resources." A rigorous exploration and an objective
evaluation of the environmental impacts of all reasonable alternative
actions, particularly those that might enhance environmental
quality or avoid some or all of the adverse environmental effects,
are essential. Sufficient analysis of such alternatives and their
environmental benefits, costs, and risks should accompany the
proposed action through the review process in order not to foreclose
prematurely options which might enhance environmental quality
or have less detrimental effects. Examples of such alternatives
include: the alternative of not taking any action or of postponing
action pending further study; alternatives requiring actions of
a significantly different nature which would provide similar benefits
with different environmental impacts, e.g. low capital intensive
improvements, mass transit alternatives to highway construction;
alternatives related to different locations or designs or details
of the proposed action which would present different environmental
impacts. In each case, the analysis should be sufficiently detailed
to reveal comparative evaluation of the environmental benefits,
costs, and risks of each reasonable alternative, including the proposed
action. Where an existing impact statement already contains
such an analysis, its treatment of alternatives may be incorporated,
provided such treatment is current and relevant to the precise
purpose of the proposed action.

c. Affected environment.

(1) The statement should succinctly describe the environment of the
area affected as it exists prior to a proposed action, including
other related Federal activities in the area, their interrelationships,
and cumulative environmental impact. The amount of detail provided
in such descriptions should be commensurate with the extent and
expected impact of the action, and with the amount of information
required at the particular level of decision making (planning, feasibility,
design, etc.).

(2) The statement should identify, as appropriate, population and
growth characteristics of the affected area and any population
and growth assumptions used to justify the project or program
or to determine secondary population and growth impacts resulting
from the proposed action and its alternatives (see paragraph 3e(2)).
In discussing these population aspects, the statement should give
consideration to using the rates of growth in the region of the
project contained in the projections compiled for the Water Resources
Council by the Bureau of Economic Analysis of the Department
of Commerce and the Economic Research Service of the Department
of Agriculture (the OBERS projection).

d. <u>The relationship of the proposed action</u> and how it may conform
to or conflict with adopted or proposed land use plans, policies,
controls, and goals and objectives as have been promulgated by
affected communities. Where a conflict or inconsistency exists,
the statement should describe the extent of reconciliation and
the reasons for proceeding notwithstanding the absence of full
reconciliation.

e. <u>The probable impact of the proposed action on the environment.</u>

(1) This requires assessment of the positive and negative effects
of the proposed action as it affects both national and international
human environment. The attention given to different environmental
factors will vary according to the nature, scale, and location
of proposed actions. Primary attention should be given in
the statement to discussing those factors most evidently
impacted by the proposed action.

(2) Secondary and other foreseeable effects, as well as primary
consequences for the environment, should be included in
the analysis. Secondary effects, such as impacts on existing
community facilities and activities inducing new facilities
and activities, may often be even more substantial than
the primary effects of the original action itself. For example,
the effects of the proposed action on population and growth
may be among the more significant secondary effects. Such
population and growth impacts should be estimated and an
assessment made on their effects upon the resource base,
including land use, water; and public services, of the area
in question.

f. <u>Any probable adverse environmental effects which cannot be avoided</u>
(such as water or air pollution, noise, undesirable land use patterns,
or impacts on public parks and recreation areas, wildlife and waterfowl
refuges, or on historic sites, damage to life systems, traffic congestion,
threats to health, or other consequences adverse to the environmental
goals set out in section 101(b) of NEPA). This should be a brief
summary of those effects discussed in paragraph 3c that are adverse and
unavoidable under the proposed action. Included for purposes
of contrast should be a clear statement of how all adverse effects
will be mitigated.

g. The relationship between local short-term uses of man's environment and the maintenance and enhancement of long-term productivity. This discussion should cover the extent to which the proposed action involves tradeoffs between short-term environmental gains at the expense of long-term losses, or vice versa, and a discussion of the extent to which the proposed action forecloses future options.

h. Any irreversible and irretrievable commitments of resources that would be involved in the proposed action should it be implemented. This requires identification of unavoidable impacts and the extent to which the action irreversibly curtails the range of potential uses of the environment. "Resources" means not only the labor and materials devoted to an action but also the natural and cultural resources lost or destroyed.

i. An indication of what other interests and considerations of Federal policy are thought to offset the adverse environmental effects of the proposed action identified pursuant to subparagraphs (e) and (f) of this paragraph. The statement should also indicate the extent to which these stated countervailing benefits could be realized by following reasonable alternatives to the proposed action (as identified in subparagraph (b) of this paragraph) that would avoid some or all of the adverse environmental effects. In this connection, cost-benefit analyses of proposed actions, if prepared, should be attached, or summaries thereof, to the environmental impact statement, and should clearly indicate the extent to which environmental costs have not been reflected in such analyses.

j. A discussion of problems and objections raised by other Federal agencies, State and local entities, and citizens in the review process, and the disposition of the issues involved and the reasons therefor. (This section may be added to the final environmental statement at the end of the review process.)

   .(1) The draft and final statements should document issues raised through consultations with Federal, State, and local agencies with jurisdiction or special expertise and with citizens, of actions taken in response to comments, public hearings, and other citizen involvement proceedings.

   (2) Any unresolved environmental issues and efforts to resolve them, through further consultations or otherwise, should be identified in the final statement. For instance, where

an agency comments that the statement has inadequate
analysis or that the agency has reservations concerning
the impacts, or believes that the impacts are too adverse
for approval, either the issue should be resolved or the final
statement should reflect efforts to resolve the issue and
set forth any action that will result.

(3)   The statement should reflect that every effort was made
to discover and discuss all major points of view on the environmental
effects of the proposed action and alternatives in the draft
statement. However, where opposing professional views
and responsible opinion have been overlooked in the draft
statement and are raised through the commenting process,
the environmental effects of the action should be reviewed
in light of those views. A meaningful reference should be
made in the final statement to the existence of any responsible
opposing view not adequately discussed in the draft statement
indicating responses to the issues raised.

(4)   All substantive comments received on the draft (or summaries
of responses from the public which have been exceptionally
voluminous) should be attached to the final statement, whether
or not each such comment is thought to merit individual
discussion in the text of the statement.

k.   Draft statements should indicate at appropriate points in the text
any underlying studies, reports, and other information obtained
and considered in preparing the statement, including any cost-
benefit analyses prepared. In the case of documents not likely
to be easily accessible (such as internal studies or reports), the
statement should indicate how such information may be obtained.
If such information is attached to the statement, care should be
taken to insure that the statement remains an essentially self-
contained instrument, capable of being understood by the reader
without the need for undue cross reference.

4.   Publicly Owned Parklands, Recreational Areas, Wildlife and Waterfowl
Refuges and Historic Sites. The following points are to be covered:

a.   Description of "any publicly owned land from a public park, recreational
area or wildlife and waterfowl refuge" or "any land from an historic
site" affected or taken by the project. This includes its size, available
activities, use, patronage, unique or irreplaceable qualities, relationship
to other similarly used lands in the vicinity of the project, maps,

plans, slides, photographs, and drawings showing in sufficient scale and detail the project. This also includes its impact on park, recreation, wildlife, or historic areas, and changes in vehicular or pedestrian access.

b. Statement of the "national, State or local significance" of the entire park, recreation area, refuge, or historic site "as determined by the Federal, State or local officials having jurisdiction thereof."

(1) In the absence of such a statement, lands will be presumed to be significant. Any statement of "insignificance" by the official having jurisdiction is subject to review by the Department as to whether such statement is capricious.

(2) Where Federal lands are administered for multiple uses, the Federal official having jurisdiction over the lands shall determine whether the subject lands are in fact being used for park, recreation, wildlife, waterfowl, or historic purposes.

c. Similar data, as appropriate, for alternative designs and locations, including detailed cost estimates (with figures showing percentage differences in total project costs) and technical feasibility, and appropriate analysis of the alternatives, including any unique problems present and evidence that the cost or community disruptions resulting from alternative routes reach extraordinary magnitudes. This portion of the statement should demonstrate compliance with the Supreme Court's statement in the Overton Park case, as follows:

"The very existence of the statute indicates that the protection of parklands was to be given paramount importance. The few green havens that are public parks were not to be lost unless there were truly unusual factors present in a particular case or the cost or community disruption resulting from alternative routes reached extraordinary magnitudes. If the statutes are to have any meaning, the Secretary cannot approve the destruction of parkland unless he finds that the alternative routes present unique problems."

d. If there is no feasible and prudent alternative, description of all planning undertaken to minimize harm to the protected area and statement of actions taken or to be taken to implement this planning, including measures to maintain or enhance the natural beauty of the lands traversed.

(1)   Measures to minimize harm may include replacement of
land and facilities, providing land or facilities, or provision
for functional replacement of the facility (see 49 C.F.R.
25.267).

(2)   Design measures to minimize harm; e.g. tunneling, cut
and cover, cut and fill, treatment of embankments, planting,
screening, maintenance of pedestrian or bicycle paths and
noise mitigation measures, all reflecting utilization of appropriate
interdisciplinary design personnel.

e.   Evidence of concurrence or description of efforts to obtain concurrence
of Federal, State or local officials having jurisdiction over the
section 4(f) property regarding the action proposed and the measures
planned to minimize harm.

f.   If Federally-owned properties are involved in highway projects,
the final statement shall include the action taken or an indication
of the expected action after filing a map of the proposed use of
the land or other appropriate documentation with the Secretary
of the Department supervising the land (23 U.S.C. 317).

g.   If land acquired with Federal grant money (Department of Housing
and Urban Development open space or Heritage Conservation
and Recreation Service land and water conservation funds) is involved,
the final statement shall include appropriate communications
with the grantor agency.

h.   The General Counsel will determine application of section 4(f)
to public interests in lands, such as easements, reversions, etc.

i.   A specific statement that there is no feasible and prudent alternative
and that the proposal includes all possible planning to minimize
harm to the "section 4(f) area" involved.

5.   Properties and Sites of Historic and Cultural Significance. The statement
should document actions taken to preserve and enhance districts, sites,
buildings, structures, and objects of historical, architectural, archaeological,
or cultural significance affected by the action.

a.   Draft environmental statements should include identification, through
consulting the State Historic Preservation Officer and the National
Register and applying the National Register Criteria (36 C.F.R. Part 800), of
properties that are included in or eligible for inclusion in the National Register

of Historic Places that may be affected by the project. The Secretary of the Interior will advise whether properties not listed are eligible for the National Register (36 C.F.R. Part 63).

b.   If application of the Advisory Council on Historic Preservation's (ACHP) Criteria of Effect (36 C.F.R. Part 800) indicates that the project will have an effect upon a property included in or eligible for inclusion in the National Register of Historic Places, the draft environmental statement should document the effect. Evaluation of the effect should be made in consultation with the State Historic Preservation Officer (SHPO) and in accordance with the ACHP's Criteria of Adverse Effect (36 C.F.R. Part 800).

c.   Determinations of no adverse effect should be documented in the draft statement with evidence of the application of the ACHP's Criteria of Adverse Effect, the views of the appropriate State Historic Preservation Officer, and submission of the determination to the ACHP for review.

d.   If the project will have an adverse effect upon a property included in or eligible for inclusion in the National Register of Historic Places, the final environmental statement should include either an executed Memorandum of Agreement or comments from the Council after consideration of the project at a meeting of the ACHP and an account of actions to be taken in response to the comments of the ACHP. Procedures for obtaining a Memorandum of Agreement and the comments of the Council are found in 36.C.F.R. Part 800.

e.   To determine whether the project will have an effect on properties of State or local historical, architectural, archaeological, or cultural significance not included in or eligible for inclusion in the National Register, the responsible official should consult with the State Historic Preservation Officer, with the local official having jurisdiction of the property, and, where appropriate, with historical societies, museums, or academic institutions having expertise with regard to the property. Use of land from historic properties of Federal, State and local significance as determined by the official having jurisdiction thereof involves section 4(f) of the DOT Act and documentation should include information necessary to consider a section 4(f) determination (see paragraph 4).

6. **Impacts of the Proposed Action on the Human Environment Involving Community Disruption and Relocation.**

   a. The statement should include a description of probable impact sufficient to enable an understanding of the extent of the environmental and social impact of the project alternatives and to consider whether relocation problems can be properly handled. This would include the following information obtainable by visual inspection of the proposed affected area and from secondary sources and community sources when available.

      (1) An estimate of the households to be displaced including the family characteristics (e.g. minorities, and income levels, tenure, the elderly, large families).

      (2) Impact on the human environment of an action which divides or disrupts an established community, including, where pertinent, the effect of displacement on types of families and individuals affected, effect of streets cut off, separation of residences from community facilities, separation of residential areas.

      (3) Impact on the neighborhood and housing to which relocation is likely to take place (e.g. lack of sufficient housing for large families, doublings up).

      (4) An estimate of the businesses to be displaced, and the general effect of business dislocation on the economy of the community.

      (5) A discussion of relocation housing in the area and the ability to provide adequate relocation housing for the types of families to be displaced. If the resources are insufficient to meet the estimated displacement needs, a description of the actions proposed to remedy this situation including, if necessary, use of housing of last resort.

      (6) Results of consultation with local officials and community groups regarding the impacts to the community affected. Relocation agencies and staff and other social agencies can help to describe probable social impacts of this proposed action.

      (7) Where necessary, special relocation advisory services to be provided the elderly, handicapped and illiterate regarding interpretations of benefits, assistance in selecting replacement

housing, and consultation with respect to acquiring, leasing, and occupying replacement housing.

    b.   This data should provide the preliminary basis for assurance of the availability of relocation housing as required by DOT 5620.1, Replacement Housing Policy, dated 6-24-70, and 49 C.F.R. 25.57.

7.   <u>Considerations Relating to Pedestrians and Bicyclists</u>. Where appropriate, the statement should discuss impacts on and consideration to be given in the development of the project to pedestrian and bicycle access, movement and safety within the affected area, particularly in medium and high density commercial and residential areas.

8.   <u>Other Social Impacts</u>. The general social groups specially benefitted or harmed by the proposed action should be identified in the statement, including the following:

    a.   Particular effects of a proposal on the elderly, handicapped, non-drivers, transit dependent, or minorities should be described to the extent reasonably predictable.

    b.   How the proposal will facilitate or inhibit their access to jobs, educational facilities, religious institutions, health and welfare services, recreational facilities, social and cultural facilities, pedestrian movement facilities, and public transit services.

9.   <u>Standards as to Noise, Air, and Water Pollution</u>. The statement shall reflect sufficient analysis of the effects of the proposed action on attainment and maintenance of any environmental standards established by law or administrative determination (e.g. noise, ambient air quality, water quality), including the following documentation:

    a.   With respect to water quality, there should be consultation with the agency responsible for the State water pollution control program as to conformity with standards and regulations regarding storm sewer discharge, sedimentation control, and other non-point source discharges.

    b.   The comments or determinations of the offices charged with administration of the State's implementation plan for air quality as to the consistency of the project with State plans for the implementation of ambient air quality standards.

    c.   Conformity to adopted noise standards, compatible, if appropriate, with different land uses.

10. Energy Supply and Natural Resources Development. Where applicable, the statement should reflect consideration of whether the project or program will have any effect on either the production or consumption of energy and other natural resources, and discuss such effects if they are significant.

11. Floodplain Management Evaluation. When an alternative under consideration encroaches on a base (100-year) floodplain, the statement should describe the anticipated impacts on natural and beneficial floodplain values, any risk to or resulting from the transportation action, and the degree to which the action facilitates additional development in the base floodplain. The necessary measures to address floodplain impacts, including an evaluation of alternatives to avoid the encroachment in appropriate cases, should be described in compliance with Executive Order 11988, "Floodplain Management," and DOT Order 5650.2, "Floodplain Management and Protection."

12. Considerations Relating to Wetlands or Coastal Zones. Where wetlands or coastal zones are involved, the statement should reflect compliance with Executive Order 11990, Protection of Wetlands, and DOT 5660.1A and should include:

a. Information on location, types, and extent of wetlands areas which might be affected by the proposed action.

b. An assessment of the impacts resulting from both construction and operation of the project on the wetlands and associated wildlife, and measures to minimize adverse impacts.

c. A statement by the local representative of the Department of the Interior, and any other responsible officials with special expertise, setting forth his views on the impacts of the project on the wetlands, the worth of the particular wetlands areas involved to the community and to the Nation, and recommendtions as to whether the proposed action should proceed, and, if applicable, along what alternative route.

d. Where applicable, a discussion of how the proposed project relates to the State coastal zone management program for the particular State in which the project is to take place.

13. __Construction Impacts.__ In general, adverse impacts during construction will be of less importance than long-term impacts of a proposal. Nonetheless, statements should appropriately address such matters as the following, identifying any special problem areas:

   a. Noise impacts from construction and any specifications setting maximum noise levels.

   b. Disposal of spoil and effect on borrow areas and disposal sites (include specifications where special problems are involved).

   c. Measures to minimize effects on traffic and pedestrians.

14. __Land Use and Urban Growth.__ The statement should include, to the extent relevant and predictable:

   a. The effect of the project on land use, development patterns, and urban growth.

   b. Where significant land use and development impacts are anticipated, identify public facilities needed to serve the new development and any problems or issues which would arise in connection with these facilities, and the comments of agencies that would provide these facilities.

15. (Deleted)

16. __Projects under Section 14 of the Mass Transportation Act: Mass Transit Projects with a Significant Impact on the Quality of the Human Environment:__ The statement should include:

   a. Evidence of the opportunity that was afforded for the presentation of views by all parties with a significant economic, social or environmental interest.

   b. Evidence that fair consideration has been given to the preservation and enhancement of the environment and to the interests of the community in which the project is located.

   c. If there is an adverse environmental effect and there is no feasible and prudent alternative, description of all planning undertaken to minimize such adverse environmental effect and statement of actions taken or to be taken to implement the planning; or a specific statement that there is no adverse environmental effect.

NEPA Deskbook

Policy Guidance

Appendix 17 Preamble to Proposed CEQ NEPA Regulations

Proposed Implementation of Procedural Provisions of NEPA (Preamble to Proposed Regulations)
(Council on Environmental Quality)
43 Fed. Reg. 25230 (June 9, 1978)

25230

PROPOSED RULES

[3125-01]

COUNCIL ON ENVIRONMENTAL QUALITY

[40 CFR Parts 1500, 1501, 1502, 1503, 1504, 1505, 1506, 1507, 1508]

NATIONAL ENVIRONMENTAL POLICY ACT— REGULATIONS

Proposed Implementation of Procedural Provisions

MAY 31, 1978.

AGENCY: Council on Environmental Quality, Executive Office of the President.

ACTION: Proposed regulations.

SUMMARY: These proposed regulations implementing procedural provisions of the National Environmental Policy Act are submitted for public comment. These regulations would provide Federal agencies with uniform procedures for implementing the law. The regulations would accomplish three principal aims: to reduce paperwork, to reduce delays, and to produce better decisions.

DATES: Comments must be received by August 11, 1978.

ADDRESSES: Comments should be addressed to: Nicholas C. Yost, General Counsel, Attention: NEPA Comments, Council on Environmental Quality, 722 Jackson Place NW., Washington, D.C. 20006.

FOR FURTHER INFORMATION CONTACT:

Nicholas C. Yost, General Council on Environmental Quality (address same as above), 202-633-7032.

SUPPLEMENTARY INFORMATION:

1. PURPOSE

We are publishing for public review draft regulations to implement the National Environmental Policy Act. Their purpose is to provide all Federal agencies with an efficient, uniform procedure for translating the law into practical action. We expect the new regulations to accomplish three principal aims: To reduce paperwork, to reduce delays, and at the same time to produce better decisions, thereby better accomplishing the law's objective, which is to protect and enhance the quality of the human environment.

These regulations replace the Guidelines issued by previous Councils, under Executive Order 11514 (1970), and apply more broadly. The Guidelines assist Federal agencies in carrying out NEPA's most conspicuous requirement, the preparation of environmental impact statements (EISs). These regulations were developed in response to Executive Order 11991 issued by President Carter in 1977, and

implement "the procedural provisions of the Act." They address all nine subdivisions of Section 102(2) of the Act, rather than just the EIS provision covered by the Guidelines, and they carry out the broad purposes and spirit of the Act.

President Carter instructed us that the regulations should be:

* * * designed to make the enviromental impact statement more useful to decisionmakers and the public; and to reduce paperwork and the accumulation of extraneous background data, in order to emphasize the need to focus on real environmental issues and alternatives.

The President has also signed Executive Order 12044, dealing with regulatory reform. It is our intention that that Order and these NEPA regulations be read together and implemented consistently.

2. SUMMARY OF CHANGES MADE BY THE REGULATIONS

Following this mandate in developing the new regulations, we have kept in mind the threefold objective of less paperwork, less delay, and better decisions.

A. REDUCING PAPERWORK

The measures to reduce paperwork are listed in sec. 1500.4 of the regulations. Neither NEPA nor these regulations impose paperwork requirements on the public. These regulations reduce such requirements on agencies of government.

i. *Reducing the length of environmental impact statements.* Agencies are directed to write concise EISs, which shall normally be less than 150 pages, or, for proposals of unusual scope and complexity, 300 pages.

ii. *Emphasize options among alternatives.* The regulations stress that the environmental analysis is to concentrate on alternatives, which are the heart of the matter; to treat peripheral matters briefly; and to avoid accumulating masses of background data which tend to obscure the important issues.

iii. *Using an early "scoping" process to determine what the important issues are.* To assist agencies in deciding what the central issues are, how long the EIS shall be, and how the responsibility for the EIS will be allocated among the lead agency and cooperating agencies, a new "scoping" procedure is established. Scoping meetings are to be held as early in the NEPA process as possible—in most cases, shortly after the decision to prepare an EIS—and shall be integrated with other planning.

iv. *Writing in plain language.* The regulations strongly advocate writing in plain, direct language.

v. *Following a clear format.* The regulations spell out a standard format

intended to eliminate repetitive discussion, stress the major conclusions, highlight the areas of controversy, and focus on the issues to be resolved.

vi. *Requiring summaries of environmental impact statements* to make the document more usable by more people.

vii. *Eliminating duplication.* To eliminate duplication, the regulations provide for Federal agencies to prepare EISs jointly with state and local units of government which have "little NEPA" requirements. They also permit a Federal agency to adopt another agency's EIS.

viii. *Consistent terminology.* The regulations provide a uniform terminology for the implementation of NEPA. For instance, the CEQ requirement for an environmental assessment will replace the following (nonexhaustive) list of comparable existing agency procedures: "survey" (Corps of Engineers), "environmental analysis" (Forest Service), "initial assessment" (Transportation), "normal or special clearance" (HUD), "environmental analysis report" (Interior), and "marginal impact statement" (HEW).)

ix. *Reducing paperwork requirements.* The regulations will reduce reporting paperwork requirements as summarized below. The existing Guidelines issued under Executive Order 11514 cover section 102(2)(C) of NEPA (environmental impact statements), and the new CEQ regulations cover sections 102(2) (A) through (I). The regulations replace not only the requirements of the Guidelines concerning environmental impact statements, but also replace more than 70 different sets of existing agency regulations, although each agency will issue its own implementing procedures to explain how these regulations apply to its particular programs.

Existing Requirements (Applicable Guidelines sections are noted.)	New Requirements (Applicable regulations sections are noted.)
Assessment (optional under Guidelines on a case-by-case basis; currently required, however by most major agencies in practice or in procedures) 1500.6.	*Assessment* (limited requirement: not required where there would not be environmental effects or where an EIS would normally be required) 1501.3, .4.
Notice of intent to prepare impact statement 1500.6.	*Notice of intent* to prepare EIS and commence scoping process 1501.7
Quarterly list of notices of intent 1500.6.	Requirement abolished.
Negative determination (decision not to prepare impact, statement) 1500.6.	*Finding of no significant impact* 1501.4.
Quarterly list of negative determinations 1500.6.	Requirement abolished.
Draft EIS 1500.7	*Draft EIS* 1502.9
Final EIS 1500.6, .10	*Final EIS* 1502.9
EISs on legislative reports ("agency reports on legislation initiated elsewhere") 1500.5(a)(1).	Requirement abolished.
Agency report to CEQ on implementation experience 1500.14(b).	Do.

Existing Requirements (Applicable Guidelines sections are noted.)	New Requirements (Applicable regulations sections are noted.)
Agency report to CEQ on substantive guidance 1500.6(c), .14.	Do.
Record of decision (no Guideline provision but required by many agencies' own procedures and in a wide range of cases generally under the Administrative Procedure Act and OMB Circular A-95, Part I, sec. 6(c) and (d), Part II, sec. 5(b)(4)).	*Record of decision* (brief explanation of decision EIS has been prepared; no circulation requirement) 1505.2.

B. REDUCING DELAY

The measures to reduce delay are listed in § 1500.5 of the regulations.

i. *Time limits on the NEPA process.* The regulations encourage lead agencies to set time limits on the NEPA process and require that they be set when requested by an applicant.

ii. *Integrating EIS requirements with other environmental review requirements.* Often the NEPA process and the requirements of other laws proceed separately, causing delay. The regulations provide for all agencies with jurisdiction over the project to cooperate so that all reviews may be conducted simultaneously.

iii. *Integrating the NEPA process into early planning.* If environmental review is tacked on to the end of the planning process, then the process is prolonged, or else the EIS is written to justify a decision that has already been made, and genuine consideration may not be given to environmental factors.

iv. *Emphasizing interagency cooperation before the EIS is drafted.* The regulations emphasize that other agencies should begin cooperating with the lead agency before the EIS is prepared in order to encourage early resolution of differences. By having the affected agencies cooperate early in preparing a draft EIS, we hope both to produce a better draft and to reduce delays caused by unnecessarily late criticism.

v. *Swift and fair resolution of lead agency disputes.* When agencies differ as to who shall take the lead in preparing an EIS or none is willing to take the lead, the regulations provide a means for prompt resolution of the dispute.

vi. *Prepare EISs on programs and not repeat the same material in project specific EISs.* Material common to many actions may be covered in a broad EIS, and then through "tiering" may be incorporated by reference rather than reiterated in each subsequent EIS.

vii. *Legal delays.* The regulations provide that litigation should come at the end rather than in the middle of the process.

viii. *Accelerated procedures for legislative proposals.* The regulations provide accelerated simplified procedures for environmental analysis of legislative proposals, to fit better with Congressional schedules.

C. BETTER DECISIONS

Most of the features described above will help to improve decisionmaking. This, of course, is the fundamental purpose of the NEPA process, the end to which the EIS is a means. Section 101 of NEPA sets forth the substantive requirements of the Act, the policy to be implemented by the "action-forcing" procedures of Section 102. These procedures must be tied to their intended purpose, otherwise they are indeed useless paper work and wasted time. A central purpose of these regulations is to tie means to ends.

i. *Securing more accurate, professional documents.* The regulations insist upon accurate documents as the basis for sound decisions. The documents should draw upon all the appropriate disciplines from the natural and social sciences, plus the environmental design arts. The lead agency is responsible for the professional integrity of reports, and care should be taken to keep any possible bias from data prepared by applicants out of the environmental analysis. A list of people who helped prepare documents, and their professional qualifications, should be included in the EIS.

ii. *Recording in the decision how the EIS was used.* The new regulations require agencies to point out in the EIS analysis of alternatives which one is preferable on environmental grounds—including the often-overlooked alternative of no action at all. (However, if "no action" is identified as environmentally preferable, a second-best alternative must also be pointed out.)

Agencies must also produce a concise public record, indicating how the EIS was used in arriving at the decision. If the EIS is disregarded, it really is useless paperwork. It only contributes if it is used by the decisionmaker and the pubic. The record must state what the final decision was; whether the environmentally preferable alternative was selected; and if not, what considerations of national policy led to another choice.

iii. *Insure follow-up of agency decisions.* When an agency requires environmentally protective mitigation measures in its decision, the regulations provide for means to ensure that these measures are monitored and implemented.

Taken altogether, the regulations aim for a streamlined process, but one which as a broader purpose than the Guidelines they replace. The Guidelines emphasized a single document, the EIS, while the regulations emphasize the entire NEPA process, from early planning through assessment and EIS preparation through provisions for follow-up. They attempt to gear means to ends—to insure that the action-forcing procedures of sec. 102(2) of NEPA are used by agencies to fulfill the requirements of the Congressionally mandated policy set out in sec. 101 of the Act. Furthermore, the regulations are uniform, applying in the same way to all federal agencies, although each agency will develop its own procedures for implementing the regulations. Our attempt has been with these new regulations to carry out as faithfully as possible the original intent of Congress in enacting NEPA.

3. BACKGROUND

We have been greatly assisted in our task by the hundreds of people who responded to our call for suggestions on how to make the NEPA process work better. In public hearings which we held in June 1977, we invited testimony from a broad array of public officials, organizations, and private citizens, affirmatively involving NEPA's critics as well as its friends.

Among those represented were the U.S. Chamber of Commerce, which coordinated testimony from business; the Building and Construction Trades Department of the AFL-CIO, for labor; the National Conference of State Legislatures, for state and local governments; the Natural Resources Defense Council, for environmental groups. Scientists, scholars, and the general public were there.

There was extraordinary consensus among these diverse witnesses. All, without exception, expressed the view that NEPA benefited the public. Equally widely shared was the view that the process had become needlessly cumbersome and should be trimmed down. Witness after witness said that the length and detail of EIS's made it extremely difficult to distinguish the important from the trivial. The degree of unanimity about the good and bad points of the NEPA process was such that at one point an official spokesman for the oil industry rose to say that he adopted in its entirety the presentation of the President of the Sierra Club.

After the hearings we culled the record to organize both the problems and the solutions proposed by witnesses into a 38-page "NEPA Hearing Questionnaire." The questionnaire was sent to all witnesses, every state governor, all federal agencies, and everyone who responded to an invitation in the FEDERAL REGISTER. We received more than 300 replies, from a broad cross section of groups and individuals. By the comments we received from respondents we gauged our success in faithfully presenting the results of the public hearings. One commenter, an

25232

PROPOSED RULES

electric utility official, said that for the first time in his life he knew the government was listening to him, because all the suggestions made at the hearing turned up in the questionnaire. We then collated all the responses for use in drafting the regulations.

We also met with every agency of the federal government to discuss what should be in the regulations. Guided by these extensive interactions with government agencies and the public, we prepared draft regulations which were circulated for comment to all federal agencies in December 1977. We then studied agency comments in detail, and consulted numerous federal officials with special experience in implementing the Act. Informal redrafts were circulated to the agencies with greatest experience in preparing environmental impact statements. Improvements from our December 12 draft reflect this process.

At the same time that federal agencies were reviewing the early draft, we continued to meet with, listen to, and brief members of the public, including representatives of business, labor, state and local governments, environmental groups and others. We also considered seriously and proposed in our regulations virtually every major recommendation made by the Commission on Federal Paperwork and the General Accounting Office in their recent studies on the environmental impact statement process. The studies by these two independent bodies were among the most detailed and informed reviews of the paperwork abuses of the impact statement process. In many cases, such as streamlining intergovernmental coordination, the proposed regulations go further than their recommendations.

4. EXCLUSION

It should be noted that the issue of application of NEPA to environmental effects occurring outside the United States is the subject of continued discussions within the government and is not addressed in these regulations. Affected agencies continue to hold different views on this issue. Nothing in these regulations should be construed as asserting that NEPA either does or does not apply in this situation.

5. ANALYSIS AND ASSESSMENT OF THE REGULATIONS

Since Executive Order 12044 became effective on March 23, 1978, after the Council's draft NEPA regulations had completed interagency review, the extent to which Executive Order 12044 applies to the Council's nearly completed process of developing NEPA regulations is not clear. Nevertheless, the requirements of Executive Order 12044 have been undertaken to the fullest extent possible. The analy-

ses required by sections 2 (b), (c), (d), and 3(b), to the extent they may apply to the Council's proposed NEPA regulations, are available on request.

The Council has prepared a special environmental assessment of these regulations to illustrate the analysis that is appropriate under NEPA. The assessment discusses alternative regulatory approaches. Some regulations lend themselves to an analysis of their environmental impacts, particularly regulations with substantive requirements of those which apply to a physical setting. Although the Council obviously believes that its regulations will work to improve environmental quality, the impacts of procedural regulations of this kind are not susceptible to detailed analysis beyond that set out in the assessment.

Both the analyses under Executive Order 12044 and the assessment described above are available on request. Comments may be made on both documents in the same manner and by the same time as the comments on the regulations.

6. ADDITIONAL SUBJECTS FOR COMMENTS

Several issues have been brought to our attention as appropriate subjects to be covered in the regulations. They are difficult issues on which we particularly solicit thoughtful views.

a. *Data bank.* Many were intrigued by the idea of a national data bank in which information developed in one EIS would be stored and become available for use in a subsequent EIS. Public comment on the questionnaire led us to conclude, reluctantly, that the idea is impractical. In practice most environmental information is specific to given areas or activities. To assemble a nationwide data bank would demand financial and other resources that are simply beyond the benefits that may be achieved. We have not included a data bank in these regulations but have instead tried to insure that in the scoping process the preparers of one EIS become aware of all related EISs so they can make use of the information in them. We would, however, welcome comment on this subject.

b. *Encouragement for agencies to fund public comments on EISs when an important viewpoint would otherwise not be presented.* The Council has been urged to provide either encouragement or direction to agencies, as part of their routine EIS preparation, to provide funds to responsible groups for public comments when important viewpoints would not otherwise be presented. Although we are acutely aware of the importance of comments to the success of the EIS process, we have not included such a provision. We would welcome comment on this subject also.

CONCLUSION

We look forward to your comments and help. To repeat, comments should be sent by August 11, 1978, to Nicholas C. Yost, General Counsel, Attention: NEPA Comments, Council on Environmental Quality, 722 Jackson Place NW., Washington, D.C. 20006.

Thank you for cooperating with us.

CHARLES WARREN,
Chairman.

NEPA Deskbook

Appendix 18 Preamble to Final CEQ NEPA Regulations

55978

[3125-01-M]

Title 40—Protection of Environment

CHAPTER V—COUNCIL ON ENVIRONMENTAL QUALITY

NATIONAL ENVIRONMENTAL POLICY ACT—REGULATIONS

Implementation of Procedural Provisions

AGENCY: Council on Environmental Quality, Exective Office of the President.

ACTION: Final regulations.

SUMMARY: These final regulations establish uniform procedures for implementing the procedural provisions of the National Environmental Policy Act. The regulations would accomplish three principal aims: to reduce paperwork, to reduce delays, and to produce better decisions. The regulations were issued in draft form in 43 FR 25230-25247 (June 9, 1978) for public review and comment and reflect changes made as a result of this process.

EFFECTIVE DATE: July 30, 1979. (See exceptions listed in § 1506.12.)

FOR FURTHER INFORMATION CONTACT:

Nicholas C. Yost, General Counsel, Council on Environmental Quality, Executive Office of the President, 722 Jackson Place NW., Washington, D.C. 20006 (telephone number 202-633-7032 or 202-395-5750).

SUPPLEMENTARY INFORMATION:

1. PURPOSE

We are publishing these final regulations to implement the procedural provisions of the National Environmental Policy Act. Their purpose is to provide all Federal agencies with efficient, uniform procedures for translating the law into practical action. We expect the new regulations to accomplish three principal aims: To reduce paperwork, to reduce delays, and at the same time to produce better decisions which further the national policy to protect and enhance the quality of the human environment.

The Council on Environmental Quality is responsbile for overseeing Federal efforts to comply with the National Environmental Policy Act ("NEPA"). In 1970, the Council issued Guidelines for the preparation of environmental impact statements (EISs) under Executive Order 11514 (1970). The 1973 revised Guidelines are now in effect. Although the Council conceived of the Guidelines as non-discretionary standards for agency decision-making, some agencies viewed them as advisory only. Similarly, courts dif-

RULES AND REGULATIONS

fered over the weight which should be accorded the Guidelines in evaluating agency compliance with the statute.

The result has been an evolution of inconsistent agency practices and interpretations of the law. The lack of a uniform, government-wide approach to implementing NEPA has impeded Federal coordination and made it more difficult for those outside government to understand and participate in the environmental review process. It has also caused unnecessary duplication, delay and paperwork.

Moreover, by the terms of Executive Order 11514, the Guidelines were confined to Subsection (C) of Section 102(2) of NEPA—the requirement for environmental impact statements. The Guidelines did not address Section 102(2)'s other important provisions for agency planning and decisionmaking. Consequently, the environmental impact statement has tended to become an end in itself, rather than a means to making better decisions. Environmental impact statements have often failed to establish the link between what is learned through the NEPA process and how the information can contribute to decisions which further national environmental policies and goals.

To correct these problems, the President issued Executive Order 11991 on May 24, 1977 directing the Council to issue the regulations. The Executive Order was based on the President's Constitutional and statutory authority, including NEPA, the Environmental Quality Improvement Act, and Section 309 of the Clean Air Act. The President has a constitutional duty to insure that the laws are faithfully executed (U.S. Const. art. II, sec. 3), which may be delegated to appropriate officials. (Title 3 U.S.C., Sec. 301). In signing Executive Order 11991, the President delegated this authority to the agency created by NEPA, the Council on Environmental Quality.

In accordance with this directive, the Council's regulations are binding on all Federal agencies, replace some seventy different sets of agency regulations, and provide uniform standards applicable throughout the Federal government for conducting environmental reviews. The regulations also establish formal guidance from the Council on the requirements of NEPA for use by the courts in interpreting this law. The regulations address all nine subdivisions of Section 102(2) of the Act, rather than just the EIS provision covered by the Guidelines. Finally, as mandated by President Carter's Executive Order, the regulations are

"* * * designed to make the environmental impact statement more useful to decisionmakers and the public; and to reduce paperwork and the accumulation of ex-

traneous background data, in order to emphasize the need to focus on real environmental issues and alternatives."

2. SUMMARY OF MAJOR INNOVATIONS IN THE REGULATIONS

Following this mandate in developing the new regulations, we have kept in mind the threefold objective of less paperwork, less delay, and better decisions.

A. REDUCING PAPERWORK

These regulations reduce paperwork requirements on agencies of government. Neither NEPA nor these regulations impose paperwork requirements on the public.

i. *Reducing the length of environmental impact statements.* Agencies are directed to write concise EISs (§ 1502.2(c)), which normally shall be less than 150 pages, or, for proposals of unusual scope or complexity, 300 pages (§ 1502.7).

ii. *Emphasizing real alternatives.* The regulations stress that the environmental analysis is to concentrate on alternatives, which are the heart of the process (§§ 1502.14, 1502.16); to treat peripheral matters briefly (§ 1502.2(b)); and to avoid accumulating masses of background data which tend to obscure the important issues (§§ 1502.1, 1502.15).

iii. *Using an early "scoping" process to determine what the important issues are.* A new "scoping" procedure is established to assist agencies in deciding what the central issues are, how long the EIS shall be, and how the responsibility for the EIS will be allocated among the lead agency and cooperating agencies (§ 1501.7). The scoping process is to begin as early in the NEPA process as possible—in most cases, shortly after the decision to prepare an EIS—and shall be integrated with other planning.

iv. *Using plain language.* The regulations strongly advocate writing in plain language (§ 1502.8).

v. *Following a clear format.* The regulations recommend a standard format intended to eliminate repetitive discussion, stress the major conclusions, highlight the areas of controversy, and focus on the issues to be resolved (§ 1502.10).

vi. *Requiring summaries of environmental impact statements.* The regulations are intended to make the document more usable by more people (§ 1502.12). With some exceptions, a summary may be circulated in lieu of the environmental impact statement if the latter is unusually long (§ 1502.19).

vii. *Eliminating duplication.* Under the regulations Federal agencies may prepare EISs jointly with State and local units of government which have "little NEPA" requirements (§ 1506.2).

They may also adopt another Federal agency's EIS (§ 1506.3).

viii. *Consistent terminology.* The regulations provide uniform terminology for the implementation of NEPA (§ 1508.1). For instance, the CEQ term "environmental assessment" will replace the following (nonexhaustive) list of comparable existing agency procedures: "survey" (Corps of Engineers), "environmental analysis" (Forest Service), "normal or special clearance" (HUD), "environmental analysis report" (Interior), and "marginal impact statement" (HEW) (§ 1508.9).

ix. *Incorporation by reference.* Agencies are encouraged to incorporate material by reference into the environmental impact statement when the material is not of central importance and when it is readily available for public inspection (§ 1502.21).

x. *Specific comments.* The regulations require that comments on environmental impact statements be as specific as possible to facilitate a timely and informative exchange of views among the lead agency and other agencies and the public (§ 1503.3).

xi. *Simplified procedures for making minor changes in environmental impact statements.* If comments on a draft environmental impact statement require only minor changes or factual corrections, an agency may circulate the comments, responses thereto, and the changes from language in the draft statement, rather than rewriting and circulating the entire document as a final environmental impact statement (§ 1506.4).

xii. *Combining documents.* Agencies may combine environmental impact statements and other environmental documents with any other document used in agency planning and decisionmaking (§ 1506.4).

xiii. *Reducing paperwork involved in reporting requirements.* The regulations will reduce the paperwork involved in reporting requirements as summarized below. In comparing the requirements under the existing Guidelines and the new CEQ regulations, it should be kept in mind that the regulations cover Sections 102(2)(A) through (I) of NEPA, while the Guidelines cover only Section 102(2)(C) (environmental impact statements). CEQ's new regulations will also replace more than 70 different existing sets of individual agency regulations. (Under the new regulations each agency will only issue implementing procedures to explain how the regulations apply to its particular policies and programs (§ 1507.3).)

Existing requirements (Applicable guidelines sections are noted)	New requirements (Applicable regulations sections are noted)
Assessment (optional under Guidelines on a case-by-case basis; currently required, however, by most major agencies in practice or in procedures) Sec. 1500.6.	*Assessment* (limited requirement: not required where there would not be environmental effects or where an EIS will be required) Secs. 1501.3, .4.
Notice of intent to prepare impact statement Sec. 1500.6.	*Notice of intent* to prepare EIS and commence scoping process Sec. 1501.7.
Quarterly list of notices of intent Sec. 1500.6.	Requirement abolished.
Negative determination (decision not to prepare impact statement) Sec. 1500.6.	*Finding of no significant impact* Sec. 1501.4.
Quarterly list of negative determinations Sec. 1500.6.	Requirement abolished.
Draft EIS Sec. 1500.7	*Draft EIS* Sec. 1502.9.
Final EIS Sec. 1500.6, .10	*Final EIS* Sec. 1502.9.
EISs on non-agency legislative reports ("agency reports on legislation initiated elsewhere") Sec. 1500.5(a)(1).	Requirement abolished.
Agency report to CEQ on implementation experience Sec. 1500.14(b).	Requirement abolished.
Agency report to CEQ on substantive guidance Secs. 1500.6(c), .14.	Requirement abolished.
Record of decision (no Guideline provision but required by many agencies' own procedures and in a wide range of cases generally under the Administrative Procedure Act and OMB Circular A-95, Part I, Sec. 6(e) and (d), Part II, Sec. 5(b)(4)).	*Record of decision* (brief explanation of decision based in part on EIS that was prepared; no circulation requirement) Sec. 1505.2.

B. REDUCING DELAY

The measures to reduce delay are listed below.

i. *Time limits on the NEPA process.* The regulations encourage lead agencies to set time limits on the NEPA process and require that time limits be set when requested by an applicant (§§ 1501.7(b)(2), 1501.8).

ii. *Integrating EIS requirements with other environmental review requirements.* Often the NEPA process and the requirements of other laws proceed separately, causing delay. The regulations provide for all agencies with jurisdiction over a proposal to cooperate so that all reviews may be conducted simultaneously (§§ 1501.7, 1502.25).

iii. *Integrating the NEPA process into early planning.* If environmental review is tacked on to the end of the planning process, then the process is prolonged, or else the EIS is written to justify a decision that has already been made and genuine consideration may not be given to environmental factors. The regulations require agencies to integrate the NEPA process

with other planning at the earliest possible time (§ 1501.2).

iv. *Emphasizing interagency cooperation before the EIS is drafted.* The regulations emphasize that other agencies should begin cooperating with the lead agency before the EIS is prepared in order to encourage early resolution of differences (§ 1501.6). We hope that early cooperation among affected agencies in preparing a draft EIS will produce a better draft and will reduce delays caused by unnecessarily late criticism.

v. *Swift and fair resolution of lead agency disputes.* When agencies differ as to who shall take the lead in preparing an EIS, or when none is willing to take the lead, the regulations provide a means for prompt resolution of the dispute (§ 1501.5).

vi. *Preparing EISs on programs and not repeating the same material in project specific EISs.* Material common to many actions may be covered in a broad EIS, and then through "tiering" may be summarized and incorporated by reference rather than reiterated in each subsequent EIS (§§ 1502.4, 1502.20, 1502.21, 1508.28).

vii. *Legal delays.* The regulations provide that litigation, if any, should come at the end rather than in the middle of the process (§ 1500.3).

viii. *Accelerated procedures for legislative proposals.* The regulations provide accelerated, simplified procedures for environmental analysis of legislative proposals, to fit better with Congressional schedules (§ 1506.8).

ix. *Categorical exclusions.* Under the regulations, categories of actions which do not individually or cumulatively have a significant effect on the human environment may be excluded from environmental review requirements (§ 1508.4).

x. *Finding of no significant impact.* If an action has not been categorically excluded from environmental review under § 1508.4, but nevertheless will not significantly affect the quality of the human environment, the agency will issue a finding of no significant impact as a basis for not preparing an EIS (§ 1508.13).

C. BETTER DECISIONS

Most of the features described above will help to improve decisionmaking. This, of course, is the fundamental purpose of the NEPA process the end to which the EIS is a means. Section 101 of NEPA sets forth the substantive requirements of the Act, the policy to be implemented by the "action-forcing" procedures of Section 102. These procedures must be tied to their intended purpose, otherwise they are indeed useless paperwork and wasted time.

i. *Recording in the decision how the EIS was used.* The new regulations re-

55980

RULES AND REGULATIONS

quire agencies to produce a concise public record, indicating how the EIS was used in arriving at the decision (§ 1505.2). This record of decision must indicate which alternative (or alternatives) considered in the EIS is preferable on environmental grounds. Agencies may also discuss preferences among alternatives based on relevant factors including economic and technical considerations and agency statutory missions. Agencies should identify those "essential considerations of national policy", including factors not related to environmental quality, which were balanced in making the decision.

ii. *Insure follow-up of agency decisions.* When an agency requires environmentally protective mitigation measures in its decisions, the regulations provide for means to ensure that these measures are implemented and monitored (§ 1505.3).

iii. *Securing more accurate, professional documents.* The regulations require accurate documents as the basis for sound decisions. As provided by Section 102(2)(A) of NEPA, the documents must draw upon all the appropriate disciplines from the natural and social sciences, plus the environmental design arts (§ 1502.6). The lead agency is responsible for the professional integrity of environmental documents and requirements are established to ensure this result, such as special provisions regarding the use of data provided by an applicant (§ 1506.5). A list of people who helped prepare documents, and their professional qualifications, shall be included in the EIS to encourage professional responsibility and ensure that an interdisciplinary approach was followed (§ 1502.17).

The regulations establish a streamlined process, and one which has a broader purpose than the Guidelines they replace. The Guidelines emphasized a single document, the EIS, while the regulations emphasize the entire NEPA process, from early planning through assessment and EIS preparation through decisions and provisions for follow-up. They are designed to gear means to ends—to ensure that the action-forcing procedures of Section 102(2) of NEPA are used by agencies to fulfill the requirements of the Congressionally mandated policy set out in Section 101 of the Act. Furthermore, the regulations are uniform, applying in the same way to all Federal agencies, although each agency will develop its own procedures for implementing the regulations. With these new regulations we seek to carry out as faithfully as possible the original intent of Congress in enacting NEPA.

3. BACKGROUND

The Council was greatly assisted by the hundreds of people who responded to our call for suggestions on how to make the NEPA process work better. In all, the Council sought the views of almost 12,000 private organizations, individuals, State and local agencies, and Federal agencies. In public hearings which we held in June 1977, we invited testimony from a broad array of public officials, organizations, and private citizens, affirmatively involving NEPA's critics as well as its friends.

Among those represented were the U.S. Chamber of Commerce, which coordinated testimony from business; the Building and Construction Trades Department of the AFL-CIO, which did so for labor; the National Conference of State Legislatures, for State and local governments; and the Natural Resources Defense Council, for environmental groups. Scientists, scholars, and the general public were also represented.

There was broad consensus among these diverse witnesses. All, without exception, expressed the view that NEPA benefited the public. Equally widely shared was the view that the process had become needlessly cumbersome and should be streamlined. Witness after witness said that the length and detail of EISs made it difficult to distinguish the important from the trivial. The degree of unanimity about the good and bad points of the NEPA process was such that at one point an official spokesperson for the oil inductry rose to say that he adopted in its entirety the presentation of the President of the Sierra Club.

After the hearings we culled the record to organize both the problems and the solutions proposed by witnesses into a 38-page "NEPA Hearing Questionnaire." The questionnaire was sent to all witnesses, every State governor, all Federal agencies, and everyone who responded to an invitation in the FEDERAL REGISTER. We received more than 300 replies, from a broad cross section of groups and individuals. By the comments we received from respondents we gauged our success in faithfully presenting the results of the public hearings. One commenter, an electric utility official, said that for the first time in his life he knew the government was listening to him, because all the suggestions made at the hearing turned up in the questionnaire. We then collated all the responses for use in drafting the regulations.

We also met with every agency of the Federal government to discuss what should be in the regulations. Guided by these extensive interactions with government agencies and the public, we prepared draft regulations which were circulated for comment to all Federal agencies in December, 1977. We then studied agency comments in detail, and consulted numerous Federal officials with special experience in implementing the Act. Informal redrafts were circulated to the agencies with greatest experience in preparing environmental impact statements.

At the same time that Federal agencies were reviewing the early draft, we continued to meet with, listen to, and brief members of the public, including representatives of business, labor, State and local governments, environmental groups, and others. Their views were considered during this early stage of the rulemaking. We also considered seriously and proposed in our regulations virtually every major recommendation made by the Commission on Federal Paperwork and the General Accounting Office in their recent studies on the environmental impact statement process. The studies by these two independent bodies were among the most detailed and informed reviews of the paperwork abuses in the impact statement process. In many cases, such as streamlining intergovernmental coordination, the proposed regulations go further than their recommendations.

On June 9, 1978 the regulations were proposed in draft form (43 FR at pages 25230-25247) and the Council announced that the period for public review of and comment on the draft regulations would extend for two months until August 11, 1978. During this period, the Council received almost 500 written comments on the draft regulations, most of which contained specific and detailed suggestions for improving them. These comments were again broadly representative of the various interests which are involved in the NEPA process.

The Council carefully reevaluated the regulations in light of the comments we received. The Council's staff read and analyzed each of the comments and developed recommendations for responding to them. A clear majority of the comments were favorable and expressed strong support for the draft regulations as a major improvement over the existing Guidelines. Some comments suggested further improvements through changes in the wording of specific provisions. A smaller number expressed more general concerns about the approach and direction taken by the regulations. In continuing efforts to resolve issues raised during the review, staff members conducted numerous meetings with individuals and groups who had offered comments and with representatives of affected Federal agencies. This process continued until most concerns with the proposals were alleviated or satisfied.

When, after discussions and review the Council determined that the comments raised valid concerns, we altered the regulations accordingly. When we decided that reasons supporting the regulations were stronger than those for challenging them, we left the regulations unchanged. Part 4 of the Preamble describes section by section the more significant comments we received, and how we responded to them.

4. COMMENTS AND THE COUNCIL'S RESPONSE

PART 1500—PURPOSE, POLICY AND MANDATE

Comments on § 1500.3: Mandate. Section 1500.3 of the draft regulations stated that it is the Council's intention that judicial review of agency compliance with the regulations not occur before an agency has filed the final environmental impact statement, causes irreparable injury, or has made a finding of no significant impact. Some comments expressed concern that court action might be commenced under this provision following a finding of no significant impact which was only tentative and did not represent a final determination that an environmental impact statement would not be prepared.

The Council made two changes in response to this concern: First, the word "final" was inserted before the phrase "finding of no significant impact." Thus, the Council eliminated the possibility of interpreting this phrase to mean a preliminary or tentative determination. Second, a clarification was added to this provision to indicate the Council's intention that judicial review would be appropriate only where the finding of no significant impact would lead to action affecting the environment.

Several comments on § 1500.3 expressed concern that agency action could be invalidated in court proceedings as the result of trivial departures from the requirements established by the Council's regulations. This is not the Council's intention. Accordingly, a sentence was added to indicate the Council's intention that a trivial departure from the regulations not give rise to an independent cause of action under law.

PART 1501—NEPA AND AGENCY PLANNING

Comments on § 1501.2: Apply NEPA early in process. Section (d)(1) of § 1501.2 stated that Federal agencies should take steps to ensure that private parties and State and local entities initiate environmental studies as soon as Federal involvement in their proposals can be foreseen. Several commenters raised questions concerning the authority of a Federal agency to require that environmental studies be initiated by private parties, for example, even before that agency had become officially involved in the review of the proposal.

The Council's intention in this provision is to ensure that environmental factors are considered at an early stage in the planning process. The Council recognizes that the authority of Federal agencies may be limited before their duty to review proposals initiated by parties outside the Federal government officially begins. Accordingly, the Council altered subsection (d)(1) of § 1501.2 to require that in such cases Federal agencies must ensure that "[p]olicies or designated staff are available to advise potential applicants of studies or other information foreseeably required by later Federal action." The purpose of the amended provision is to assure the full cooperation and support of Federal agencies for efforts by private parties and State and local entities in making an early start on studies for proposals that will eventually be reviewed by the agencies.

Comments on § 1501.3: When to prepare an environmental assessment. One commenter asked whether an environmental assessment would be required where an agency had already decided to prepare an environmental impact statement. This is not the Council's intention. To clarify this point, the Council added a sentence to this provision stating that an assessment is not necessary if the agency has decided to prepare an environmental impact statement.

Comments on § 1501.5: Lead agencies. The Council's proposal was designed to insure the swift and fair resolution of lead agency disputes. Section 1501.5 of the draft regulations established procedures for resolving disagreements among agencies over which of them must take the lead in preparing an environmental impact statement. Under subsection (d) of this section, persons and governmental entities substantially affected by the failure of Federal agencies to resolve this question may request these agencies in writing to designate a lead agency forthwith. If this request has not been met "within a reasonable period of time," subsection (e) authorizes such persons and governmental entities to petition the Council for a resolution of this issue.

Several comments objected to the phrase "within a reasonable time" because it was vague, and left it uncertain when concerned parties could file a request with the Council. The comments urged that a precise time period be fixed instead. The Council adopted this suggestion and substituted 45 days for the phrase "within a reasonable period of time." With this change, the regulations require that a lead agency be designated, if necessary by the Council, within a fixed period following a request from concerned parties that this be done.

Several commenters suggested that the Council take responsibility for designating lead agencies in every case to reduce delay. These commenters recommended that all preliminary steps be dropped in favor of immediate Council action whenever the lead agency issue arose.

The Council determined, however, that individual agencies are in the best position to decide these questions and should be given the opportunity to do so. In view of its limited resources, the Council does not have the capability to make lead agency designations for all proposals. As a result of these factors, the Council determined not to alter this provision.

Several commenters opposed the concept of joint lead agencies authorized by subsection (b) of this section, particularly where two or more of the agencies are Federal. These commenters expressed doubt that Federal agencies could cooperate in such circumstances and stated their view that the environmental review process will only work where one agency is given primary responsibility for conducting it.

In the Council's judgment, however, the designation of joint lead agencies may be the most efficient way to approach the NEPA process where more than one agency plays a significant role in reviewing proposed actions. The Council believes that Federal agencies should have the option to become joint lead agencies in such cases.

Comments on § 1501.6: Cooperating agencies. The Council developed proposals to emphasize interagency cooperation before the environmental impact statement was prepared rather than comments on a completed document. Section 1501.6 stated that agencies with jurisdiction by law over a proposal would be required to become "cooperating agencies" in the preparation of an EIS should the lead agency request that they do so. Under subsection (b) of this provision, "cooperating agencies" could be required to assume responsibility for developing information and analysis within their special competence and to make staff support available to enhance the interdisciplinary capability of the lead agency.

Several comments pointed out that principal authority for environmental matters resides in a small number of agencies in the Federal government. Concern was expressed that these few agencies could be inundated with requests for cooperation in the preparation of EISs and, if required to meet these requests in every case, drained of resources required to fulfill other statutory mandates.

The Council determined that this was a valid concern. Accordingly, it added a new subsection (c) to this sec-

55982

tion which authorizes a cooperating agency to decline to participate or otherwise limit its involvement in the preparation of an EIS where existing program commitments preclude more extensive cooperation.

Subsection (b)(5) of this section provided that a lead agency shall finance the major activities or analyses it requests from cooperating agencies to the extent available funds permit. Several commenters expressed opposition to this provision on grounds that a lead agency should conserve its funds for the fulfillment of its own statutory mandate rather than disburse funds for analyses prepared by other agencies.

The same considerations apply, however, to cooperating agencies. All Federal agencies are subject to the mandate of the National Environmental Policy Act. This provision of the regulations allows a lead agency to facilitate compliance with this statute by funding analyses prepared by cooperating agencies "to the extent available funds permit." In the Council's view, this section will enhance the ability of a lead agency to meet all of its obligations under law.

Section 1501.7: Scoping. The new concept of "scoping" was intended by the Council and perceived by the great preponderance of the commenters as a means for early identification of what are and what are not the important issues deserving of study in the EIS. Section 1501.7 of the draft regulations established a formal mechanism for agencies, in consultation with affected parties, to identify the significant issues which must be discussed in detail in an EIS, to identify the issues that do not require detailed study, and to allocate responsibilities for preparation of the document. The section provided that a scoping meeting must be held when practicable. One purpose of scoping is to encourage affected parties to identify the crucial issues raised by a proposal before an environmental impact statement is prepared in order to reduce the possibility that matters of importance will be overlooked in the early stages of a NEPA review. Scoping is also designed to ensure that agency resources will not be spent on analysis of issues which none concerned believe are significant. Finally, since scoping requires the lead agency to allocate responsibility for preparing the EIS among affected agencies and to identify other environmental review and consultation requirements applicable to the project, it will set the stage for a more timely, coordinated, and efficient Federal review of the proposal.

The concept of scoping was one of the innovations in the proposed regulations most uniformly praised by members of the public ranging from business to environmentalists. There was considerable discussion of the details of implementing the concept. Some commenters objected to the formality of the scoping process, expressing the view that compliance with this provision in every case would be time-consuming, would lead to legal challenges by citizens and private organizations with objections to the agency's way of conducting the process, and would lead to paperwork since every issue raised during the process would have to be addressed to some extent in the environmental impact statement. These commenters stated further that Federal agencies themselves were in the best position to determine matters of scope, and that public participation in these decisions was unnecessary because any scoping errors that were made by such agencies could be commented upon when the draft EIS was issued (as was done in the past) and corrected in the final document. These commenters urged that scoping at least be more open-ended and flexible and that agencies be merely encouraged rather than required to undertake the process.

Other commenters said that the Council had not gone for enough in imposing uniform requirements. These commenters urged the Council to require that a scoping meeting be held in every case, rather than only when practicable; that a scoping document be issued which reflected the decisions reached during the process; and that formal procedures be established for the resolution of disagreements over scope that arise during the scoping process. These commenters felt that more stringent requirements were necessary to ensure that agencies did not avoid the process.

In developing § 1501.7, the Council sought to ensure that the benefits of scoping would be widely realized in Federal decisionmaking; but without significant disruptions for existing procedures. The Council made the process itself mandatory to guarantee that early cooperation among affected parties would be initiated in every case. However, § 1501.7 left important elements of scoping to agency discretion. After reviewing the recommendations for more flexibility on the one hand, and more formality on the other, and while making several specific changes in response to specific comments, the Council determined that the proper balance had been struck in Section 1501.7 and did not change the basic outline of this provision. The Council did accept amendments to make clear that scoping meetings were permissive and that an agency might make provision for combining its scoping process with its environmental assessment process.

Comments on § 1501.8: Time limits. Reducing delay and uncertainty by the use of time limits is one of the Council's principal changes. Section 1501.8 of the draft regulations established criteria for setting time limits for completion of the entire NEPA process or any part of the process. These criteria include the size of the proposal and its potential for environmental harm, the state of the art, the number of agencies involved, the availability of relevant information and the time required to obtain it. Under this section, if a private applicant requests a lead agency to set time limits for an EIS review, the agency must do so provided that the time limits are consistent with the purposes of NEPA and other essential considerations of national policy. If a Federal agency is the sponsor of a proposal for major action, the lead agency is encouraged to set a timetable for the EIS review.

Several commenters objected to the concept of time limits for the NEPA process. In their opinion, the uncertainties involved in an EIS review and competing demands for limited Federal resources could make it difficult for agencies to predict how much time will be required to complete environmental impact statements on major proposals. These commenters were concerned that time limits could prompt agencies to forego necessary analysis in order to meet deadlines. In their view, the concept of time limits should be dropped from the regulations in favor of more flexible "targets" or "goals" which would be set only after consultation with all concerned parties.

On the other side of the question, the Council received several comments that the provision for time limits was not strict enough. These comments expressed concern that the criteria contained in the draft regulations were vague and would not serve effectively to encourage tight timetables for rapid completion of environmental reviews. The Council was urged to strengthen this section by including definite time limits for the completion of the EIS process in every case or by providing that CEQ itself set such limits for every environmental review, and by setting time limits for the establishment of time limits.

A primary goal of the Council's regulations is to reduce delays in the EIS process. The Council recognizes the difficulties of evaluating in advance the time required to complete environmental reviews. Nevertheless, the Council believes that a provision for time limits is necessary to concentrate agencies' attention on the timely completion of environmental impact statements and to provide private applicants with reasonable certainty as to how long the NEPA process will take. Section 1501.7(c) of the regulations allows revision of time limits if significant new circumstances (including information) arise which bear on the proposal or its impacts.

At the same time, the Council believes that precise time limits to apply uniformly across government would be unrealistic. The factors which determine the time needed to complete an environmental review are various, including the state of the art, the size and complexity of the proposal, the number of Federal agencies involved, and the presence of sensitive ecological conditions. These factors may differ significantly from one proposal to the next. The same law that applies to a Trans-Alaska pipeline may also apply to a modest federally funded building in a historic district. In the Council's judgment, individual agencies are in the best position to perform this function. The Council does not have the resources to weigh these factors for each proposal. Accordingly, the Council determined not to change these provisions of § 1501.8 of the regulations.

PART 1502—ENVIRONMENTAL IMPACT STATEMENT

Comments on Section 1502.5: Timing. Several commenters noted that it has become common practice in informal rulemaking for Federal agencies to issue required draft environmental impact statements at the same time that rules are issued in proposed form. These commenters expressed the view that this procedure was convenient, time-saving and consistent with NEPA, and urged that the regulations provide for it. The Council added a new subsection (d) to § 1502.5 on informal rulemaking stating that this procedure shall normally be followed.

Comments on section 1502.7: Page limits. A principal purpose of these regulations is to turn bulky, often unused EISs into short, usable documents which are in fact used. Section 1502.7 of the draft regulations provided that final environmental impact statements shall normally be less than 150 pages long and, for proposals of unusual scope or complexity, shall normally be less than 300 pages. Numerous commenters expressed strong support for the Council's decision to establish page limits for environmental impact statements.

Several commenters objected to the concept of page limits for environmental impact statements on grounds that it could constrain the thoroughness of environmental reviews. Some said that the limits were too short and would preclude essential analysis; others contended that they were too long and would encourage the inclusion of unnecessary detail. One commenter proposed a "sliding scale" for page limits;

another suggested that a limitation on the number of words would be more effective than a limitation on the number of pages. A number of commenters urged that page limits be simply recommended rather than established as standards that should normally be met.

The usefulness of the NEPA process to decisionmakers and the public has been jeopardized in recent years by the length and complexity of environmental impact statements. In accordance with the President's directive, a primary objective of the regulations is to insure that these documents are clear, concise, and to the point. Numerous provisions in the regulations underscore the importance of focusing on the major issues and real choices facing federal decisionmakers and excluding less important matters from detailed study. Other sections in the regulations provide that certain technical and background materials developed during the environmental review process may be appended but need not be presented in the body of an EIS.

The Council recognizes the tension between the requirement of a thorough review of environmental issues and a limitation on the number of pages that may be devoted to the analysis. The Council believes that the limits set in the regulations are realistic and will help to achieve the goal of more succinct and useful environmental documents. The Council also determined that a limitation on the number of words in an EIS was not required for accomplishing the objective of this provision. The inclusion of the term "normally" in this provision accords Federal agencies latitude if abnormal circumstances exist.

Others suggested that page limits might result in conflict with judicial precedents on adequacy of EISs, that the proverbial kitchen sink may have to be included to insure an adequate document, whatever the length. The Council trusts and intends that this not be the case. Based on its day-to-day experience in overseeing the administration of NEPA throughout the Federal government, the Council is acutely aware that in many cases bulky EISs are not read and are not used by decisionmakers. An unread and unused document quite simply cannot achieve the purpose Congress set for it. The only way to give greater assurance that EISs will be used is to make them usable and that means making them shorter. By way of analogy, judicial opinions are themselves often models of compact treatment of complex subjects. Departmental option documents often provide brief coverage of complicated decisions. Without sacrifice of analytical rigor, we see no reason why the material to be covered in an EIS cannot normally

be covered in 150 pages (or 300 pages in extraordinary circumstances).

Comments on § 1502.10: Recommended format. Section 1502.10 stated that agencies shall normally use a standard format for environmental impact statements. This provision received broad support from those commenting on the draft regulations.

As part of the recommended format, environmental impact statements would be required to describe the environmental consequences of a proposed action before they described the environment that would be affected. Many commenters felt that these elements of the EIS should be reversed so that a description of the environmental consequences of a proposal would follow rather than precede a description of the affected environment. The commenters stated their view that it would be easier for the reader to appreciate the nature and significance of environmental consequences if a description of the affected environment was presented first. The Council concurs in this view and adopted the suggested change.

Comments on § 1502.13: Purpose and need. This section of the draft regulations provided that agencies shall briefly specify—normally in one page or less—the underlying purpose and need to which the agency is responding in proposing alternatives for action. Many commenters stated that in some cases this analysis would require more than one page. The Council responded to these comments by deleting the one page limitation.

Comments on § 1502.14: Alternatives including the proposed action. Subsection (a) of this section of the draft regulations provided, among other things, that agencies shall rigorously explore and objectively evaluate all reasonable alternatives. This provision was strongly supported by a majority of those who commented on the provision.

A number of commenters objected to the phrase "all reasonable alternatives" on the grounds that it was unduly broad. The commenters suggested a variety of ways to narrow this requirement and to place limits on the range and type of alternatives that would have to be considered in an EIS.

The phrase "all reasonable alternatives" is firmly established in the case law interpreting NEPA. The phrase has not been interpreted to require that an infinite or unreasonable number of alternatives be analyzed. Accordingly, the Council determined not to alter this subsection of the regulations.

Subsection (c) requires Federal agencies to consider reasonable alternatives not within the jurisdiction of the lead agency. Subsection (d) requires consideration of the no action alternative. A

55984   RULES AND REGULATIONS

few commenters inquired into the basis for these provisions. Subsections (c) and (d) are declaratory of existing law.

Subsection (e) of this section required Federal agencies to designate the "environmentally preferable alternative (or alternatives, if two or more are equally preferable)" and the reasons for identifying it. While the purpose of NEPA is better environmental decisionmaking, the process itself has not always successfully focused attention on this central goal. The objective of this requirement is to ensure that Federal agencies consider which course of action available to them will most effectively promote national environmental policies and goals. This provision was strongly supported in many comments on the regulations.

Some commenters noted that a wide variety of decisionmaking procedures are employed by agencies which are subject to NEPA and recommended flexibility to accommodate these diverse agency practices. In particular, the commenters recommended that agencies be given latitude to determine at what stage in the NEPA process—from the draft EIS to the record of decision—the environmentally preferable alternative would be designated.

The Council adopted this recommendation and deleted this requirement from the EIS portion of the regulations (§ 1502.14), while leaving it in § 1505.2 regarding the record of decision. Nothing in these regulations would preclude Federal agencies from choosing to identify the environmentally preferable alternative or alternatives in the environmental impact statement.

Comments on § 1502.15: Environmental consequences. Subsection (e) of this section requires an environmental impact statement to discuss energy requirements and conservation potential of various alternatives and mitigation measures. One commenter asked whether the subsection would require agencies to analyze total energy costs, including possible hidden or indirect costs, and total energy benefits of proposed actions. The Council intends that the subsection be interpreted in this way.

Several commenters suggested that the regulations expressly mention the quality of the urban environment as an environmental consequence to be discussed in an environmental impact statement. The Council responded by adding a new subsection (g) to this section requiring that EISs include a discussion of urban quality, historic and cultural resources, and the design of the built environment, including the reuse and conservation potential of various alternatives and mitigation

measures. Section 1502.15 has been renumbered as § 1502.16.

Comments on § 1502.17: List of preparers. Section 1502.17 provided that environmental impact statements shall identify and describe the qualifications and professional disciplines of those persons who were primarily involved in preparing the document and background analyses. This section has three principal purposes: First, Section 102(2)(A) of NEPA requires Federal agencies to "utilize a systematic, interdisciplinary approach which will insure the integrated use of the natural and social sciences and the environmental design arts in planning and decisionmaking which may have an impact on man's environment." The list of preparers will provide a basis for evaluating whether such a "systematic interdisciplinary approach" was used in preparing the EIS. Second, publication of a list of preparers increases accountability for the analyses appearing in the EIS, and thus tends to encourage professional competence among those preparing them. Finally, publication of the list will enhance the professional standing of the preparers by giving proper attribution to their contributions, and making them a recognized part of the literature of their disciplines. This provision received broad support from those commenting on the regulations.

Some commenters felt that a list of preparers would be used as a list of witnesses by those challenging the adequacy of an EIS in court proceedings. However, this information would ordinarily be available anyway through normal discovery proceedings.

Section 1502.17 was also criticized for failing expressly to mention expertise and experience as "qualifications" for preparing environmental impact statements. The Council added these two terms to this section to insure that the term "qualifications" would be interpreted in this way.

Some commenters suggested that the list of preparers should also specify the amount of time that was spent on the EIS by each person identified. These commenters felt that such information was required as a basis for accurately evaluating whether an interdisciplinary approach had been employed. While the Council felt there was much to be said for this suggestion, it determined that the incremental benefits gained from this information did not justify the additional agency efforts that would be required to provide it.

Comments on § 1502.19: Circulation of the environmental impact statement. If an EIS is unusually long, Section 1502.19 provided, with certain exceptions, that a summary can be circulated in lieu of the entire document. Several commenters suggested that

private applicants sponsoring a proposal should receive the entire environmental impact statement in every case in view of their interest and probable involvement in the NEPA process. The Council concurs and altered this provision accordingly.

Comments on § 1502.20: Tiering. Section 1502.20 encouraged agencies to tier their environmental impact statements, to eliminate repetitive discussions and to focus on the actual issues ripe for decision at each level of environmental review. Some commenters objected to tiering on grounds that it was not required by NEPA and would add an additional unauthorized layer to the environmental review process.

Section 1502.20 authorizes tiering of EISs; it does not require that it be done. In addition, the purpose of tiering is to simplify the EIS process by providing that environmental analysis completed at a broad program level not be duplicated for site-specific project reviews. Many agencies have already used tiering successfully in their decisionmaking. In view of these and other considerations, the Council determined not to alter this provision.

Comments on § 1502.22: Incomplete or unavailable information. Section 1502.22 provided, among other things, that agencies prepare a worst case analysis of the risk and severity of possible adverse environmental impacts when it proceeds with a proposal in the face of uncertainty. This provision received strong support from many commenters.

Several commenters expressed concern that this requirement would place undue emphasis on the possible occurence of adverse environmental consequences regardless of how remote the possiblity might be. In response, the Council added a phrase designed to ensure that the improbability as well as the probability of adverse environmental consequences would be discussed in worst case analyses prepared under this section.

Section 1502.22 stated that if information is essential to a reasoned choice among alternatives and is not known and the costs of obtaining it are not exorbitant, the agency shall include the information in the environmental impact statement. Some commenters inquired into the meaning of the term "costs." The Council intends for this word to be interpreted as including financial and other costs and adopted the phrase "overall costs" to convey this meaning.

PART 1503—COMMENTING

Comments on § 1503.1: Inviting comments. Section 1503.1 set forth the responsibility of Federal agencies to solicit comments on environmental impact statements. Several commenters observed that may Federal agencies solicit comments from State and local environmental agencies through procedures established by Office of Management and Budget Circular A-95 and suggested that the Council confirm this approach in the regulations. The Council adopted this suggestion by adding an appropriate paragraph to the section.

Comments on § 1503.2: Duty to comment. Section 1503.2 set forth the responsibilities of Federal agencies to comment on environmental impact statements. Several commenters suggested reinforcing the requirement that Federal agencies are subject to the same time limits as those outside the Federal government in order to avoid delays. The Council concurred in this suggestion and amended the provision accordingly. The Council was constrained from further changes by the requirement of Section 102(2)(C) of NEPA that agencies "consult with and obtain" the comments of specified other agencies.

Comments on § 1503.3: Specificity of comments. Section 1503.3 of the draft regulations elaborated upon the responsibilities of Federal agencies to comment specifically upon draft environmental impact statements prepared by other agencies. Several commenters suggested that cooperating agencies should assume a particular obligation in this regard. They noted that cooperating agencies which are themselves required independently to evaluate and/or approve the proposal at some later stage in the Federal review process are uniquely qualified to advise the lead agency of what additional steps may be required to facilitate these actions. In the opinion of these commenters, cooperating agencies should be required to provide this information to lead agencies when they comment on draft EISs so that the final EIS can be prepared with further Federal involvement in mind.

The Council adopted this suggestion and amended § 1503.3 through the addition of new subsections (c) and (d). The new subsections require cooperating agencies, in their comments on draft EISs, to specify what additional information, if any, is required for them to fulfill other applicable environmental review and consultation requirements, and to comment adequately on the site-specific effects to be expected from issuance of subsequent Federal approvals for the proposal. In addition, if a cooperating agency criticizes the proposed action, this section now requires that it specify the mitigation measures which would be necessary in order for it to approve the proposal under its independent statutory authority.

Comments on § 1504.3: Procedure for referrals and response. Several commenters noted that § 1504.3 did not es-

tablish a role for members of the public or applicants in the referral process. The Council determined that such persons and organizations were entitled to a role and that their views would be helpful in reaching a proper decision on the referral. Accordingly, the Council added subsection (e) to this section, authorizing interested persons including the applicant to submit their views on the referral, and any response to the referral, in writing to the Council.

Subsection (d) of this section provided that the Council may take one of several actions within 25 days after the referral and agency responses to the referral, if any, are received. Several commenters observed, however, that this subsection did not establish a deadline for final action by the Council in cases where additional discussions, public meetings, or negotiations were deemed appropriate. These commenters expressed concern that the absence of a deadline could lead to delays in concluding the referral process. The Council concurred. Accordingly, the Council added subsection (g) to this section which requires that specified actions be completed within 60 days.

Several commenters noted that the procedures established by Section 1504.3 may be inappropriate for referrals which involve agency determinations required by statute to be made on the record after opportunity for public hearing. The Council agrees. The Council added subsection (h) to this section requiring referrals in such cases to be conducted in a manner consistent with 5 U.S.C. 557(d). Thus, communications to agency officials who made the decision which is the subject of the referral must be made on the public record and after notice to all parties to the referral proceeding. In other words, ex parte contacts with agency decisionmakers in such cases are prohibited.

PART 1505—NEPA AND AGENCY DECISIONMAKING

Comments on Section 1501.1: Agency decisionmaking procedures. Some commenters asked whether this or other sections of the regulations would allow Federal agencies to place responsibility for compliance with NEPA in the hands of those with decisionmaking authority at the field level. Nothing in the regulations would prevent this arrangement. By delegating authority in this way, agencies can avoid multiple approvals of environmental documents and enhance the role of those most directly involved in their preparation and use. For policy oversight and quality control, an environmental quality review office at the national level can, among other things, establish general proce-

dures and guidance for NEPA compliance, monitor agency performance through periodic review of selected environmental documents, and facilitate coordination among agency subunits involved in the NEPA process.

Comments on § 1505.2: Record of decision in those cases requiring environmental impact statements. Section 1505.2 provided that in cases where an environmental statement was prepared, the agency shall prepare a concise public record stating what its final decision was. If an environmentally preferable alternative was not selected, § 1505.2 required the record of decision to state why other specific considerations of national policy overrode those alternatives.

This requirement was the single provision most strongly supported by individuals and organizations commenting on the regulations. These commenters stated, among things, that the requirement for a record of decision would be the most significant improvement over the existing process, would procedurally link NEPA's documentation to NEPA's policy, would relate the EIS process to agency decisionmaking, would ensure that EISs are actually considered by Federal decisionmakers, and was required as sound administrative practice.

As noted above, the Council decided that agencies shall identify the environmentally preferable alternative and the reasons for identifying it in the record of decision. *See* Comments on § 1502.14. The Council's decision does not involve the preparation of additional analysis in the EIS process; it simply affects where the analysis will be presented.

Some commenters objected to the concept of a public record of decision on actions subject to NEPA review. In the Council's opinion, however, a public record of decision is essential for the effective implementation of NEPA. As previously noted, environmental impact statement preparation has too often become an end in itself with no necessary role in agency decisionmaking. One serious problem with the administration of NEPA has been the separation between an agency's NEPA process and its decisionmaking process. In too many cases bulky EISs have been prepared and transmitted but not used by the decisionmaker. The primary purpose of requiring that a decisionmaker concisely record his or her decision in those cases where an EIS has been prepared is to tie means to ends, to see that the decisionmaker considers and pays attention to what the NEPA process has shown to be an environmentally sensitive way of doing things. Other factors may, on balance, lead the decisionmaker to decide that other policies outweigh the environmental ones, but at least

55986

RULES AND REGULATIONS

the record of decision will have achieved the original Congressional purpose of ensuring that environmental factors are integrated into the agency's decisionmaking.

Some commenters expressed the opinion that it could be difficult for Federal agencies to identify the environmentally preferable alternative or alternatives because of the multitude of factors that would have to be weighed in any such determination and the subjective nature of the balancing process. By way of illustration, commenters asked: Is clean water preferable to clean air, or the preservation of prime farmland in one region preferable to the preservation of wildlife habitat in another?

In response, the Council has amended the regulations to permit agencies to identify more than one environmentally preferable alternative, regardless of whether they are "equally" preferable, as originally proposed. Moreover, the "environmentally preferable alternative" will be that alternative which best promotes the national, environmental policy as expressed in Section 101 of NEPA and most specifically in Section 101(b). Section 101(a) stresses that the policy is concerned with man and nature, to see that they exist in productive harmony and that the social, economic, and other requirements of present and future generations of Americans are fulfilled. Section 101(c) recognizes the need for a healthy environment and each person's responsibility to contribute to it. Section 101(b) contemplates Federal actions which will enable the Nation to fulfill the responsibilities of each generation as trustee for the environment for succeeding generations; to attain the widest range of beneficial uses of the environment; to preserve important historic, cultural and natural aspects of our national heritage; and to accomplish other important goals. The Council recognizes that the identification of the environmentally preferable alternative or alternatives may involve difficult assessments in some cases. The Council determined that the benefits of ensuring that decisionmakers consider and take account of environmental factors outweigh these difficulties. To assist agencies in developing and determining environmentally preferable alternatives, commenters on impact statements may choose to provide agencies with their views on this matter.

Several commenters expressed concern that the regulations did not authorize Federal agencies to express preferences based on factors other than environmental quality. In the opinion of these commenters, this emphasis on environmental considerations was misplaced and not consistent with the factors that agencies are

expected to consider in decisionmaking.

The Council responded to these comments by reference to the statute, recognizing that Title II of NEPA and especially Section 101 clearly contemplate balancing of essential considerations of national policy. We provided that agencies may discuss preferences they have among alternatives based on relevant factors, including economic and technical considerations and agency statutory mission. Agencies should identify those considerations, including factors not related to environmental quality, which were balanced in making the decision. Nothing in the final regulations precludes Federal agencies from choosing to discuss these preferences and identifying these factors in the environmental impact statement.

Some commenters objected to the word "overrode" in this provision. The language of the Act and its legislative history make clear that Federal agencies must act in an environmentally responsible fashion and not merely consider environmental factors. NEPA requires that each Federal agency use "all practicable means and measures" to protect and improve the environment "consistent with other essential considerations of national policy." Section 101(b). The Council determined to tie this provision of the regulations to NEPA's statutory provision in place of the "overrode" language.

Several commenters expressed concern that the phrase "national policy" would not allow agencies to refer to state and local policies in the record of decision. "National policy" is the phrase used by Congress in NEPA. However, in many cases specific statutory provisions require that Federal agencies adhere to or pay heed to State and local policies.

Finally, some commenters expressed concern that the requirement for a concise record of decision would involve additional agency efforts. The intention is not to require new efforts, but to see that environmental considerations are built into existing processes. Preparing such decision records is recognized as good administrative practice and the benefits of this requirement outweigh the difficulties of building environmental considerations into the decisionmaking process.

Subsection (c) of § 1505.2 states that for any mitigation adopted a monitoring and enforcement program where applicable shall be adopted and summarized in the record of decision. One commenter asked what the term "summarized" was intended to mean in this context. The Council intends this word to be interpreted as requiring a brief and concise statement describing the monitoring and enforcement program which has been adopted.

Comments on § 1505.3: Implementing the decision. Section 1505.3 provides for mitigation of adverse environmental effects. Several commenters expressed concern that this provision would grant broad authority to the lead agency for mandating that other agencies undertake and monitor mitigation measures without their consent. This is not the Council's intention and the language of the provision does not support this interpretation.

PART 1506—OTHER REQUIREMENTS OF NEPA

Comments on §1506.1: Limitations on actions during NEPA process. Section 1506.1 placed limitations on actions which can be taken before completion of the environmental review process because of the possibility of prejudicing or foreclosing important choices. Some commenters expressed concern that these limitations would impair the ability of those outside the Federal government to develop proposals for agency review and approval. Accordingly, the Council added a new paragraph (d) to this section which authorizes certain limited activities before completion of the environmental review process.

Comments on §1506.2: Elimination of duplication with State and local procedures. This section received strong support from many commenters. Several commenters sought clarification of the procedures established by this section. It provides for coordination among Federal, State and local agencies in several distinct situations. First, subsection (a) of this section simply confirms that Federal agencies funding State programs have been authorized by Section 102(2)(D) of NEPA to cooperate with certain State agencies with statewide jurisdiction in conducting environmental reviews. Second, subsection (b) provides generally for Federal cooperation with all States in environmental reviews such as joint planning processes, joint research, joint public hearings, and joint environmental assessments. Third, subsection (c) specifically provides for Federal cooperation with those States and localities which administer "little NEPA's." The Federal agencies are directed to the fullest extent possible to reduce duplication between NEPA and comparable State and local requirements. Approximately half the states now have some sort of environmental impact statement requirement either legislatively adopted or administratively promulgated. In these circumstances, Federal agencies are required to cooperate in fulfilling these requirements as well as those of Federal laws so that one document will comply with all applicable laws. Finally, subsection (d) provides that Federal agencies generally shall in environmental impact statements discuss any inconsistency between a proposed action and any approved State or local plan or laws, regardless of whether the latter are Federally sanctioned.

Comments on § 1506.3: Adoption. Section 1506.3 authorized one Federal agency to adopt an environmental impact statement prepared by another in prescribed circumstances, provided that the statement is circulated for public comment in the same fashion as a draft EIS. Several commenters stated their view that recirculation was unnecessary if the actions contemplated by both agencies were substantially the same. The Council concurs and added a new paragraph (b) which provides that recirculation is not required in these circumstances.

Comments on § 1506.4: Combining documents. Section 1506.4 provided for the combination of environmental documents with other agency documents. Some commenters expressed the view that this section should enumerate the types of agency documents which could be combined under this provision. The Council concluded that such a list was not necessary and that such matters were better left to agency discretion. Thus, agencies may choose to combine a regulatory analysis review document, an urban impact analysis, and final decision or option documents with environmental impact statements.

Comments on § 1506.5: Agency responsibility. NEPA is a law which imposes obligations on Federal agencies. This provision is designed to insure that those agencies meet those obligations and to minimize the conflict of interest inherent in the situation of those outside the government coming to the government for money, leases or permits while attempting impartially to analyze the environmental consequences of their getting it. § 1506.5 set forth the responsibility of Federal agencies for preparing environmental documents, and addressed the role of those outside the Federal government. As proposed, subsection (b) of this section provided that environmental impact statements shall be prepared either by Federal agencies or by parties under contract to and chosen solely by Federal agencies. The purpose of this provision is to ensure the objectivity of the environmental review process.

Some commenters expressed the view that requiring Federal agencies to be a formal party to every contract for the preparation of an environmental impact statement was not necessary to ensure objectivity so long as the contractor was chosen solely by Federal agencies. These commenters contended that a requirement for formal Federal involvement in all such contracts could cause delay. The

Council concurs and deleted the phrase "under contract" from this provision.

Several commenters noted that the existing procedures for a few Federal programs are not consistent with § 1506.5. The Council recognizes that this provision will in a few cases require additional agency efforts where, for example, agencies have relied on applicants for the preparation of environmental impact statements. The Council determined that such efforts were justified by the goal of this provision.

Several commenters expressed concern that environmental information provided by private applicants would not be adequately evaluated by Federal agencies before it was used in environmental documents. Other commenters wanted to insure that applicants were free to submit information to the agencies. Accordingly, the Council amended subsection (a) to allow receipt of such information while requiring Federal agencies to independently evaluate the information submitted and to be responsible for its accuracy. In cases where the information is used in an environmental impact statement, the persons responsible for that evaluation must be identified in the list of preparers required by § 1502.17.

Several commenters expressed the view that applicants should be allowed to prepare environmental assessments. These commenters noted that the number of assessments prepared each year is far greater than the number of environmental impact statements; that such authority was necessary to ensure environmental sensitivity was built into actions, which while ultimately Federal were planned outside the Federal government; that assessments are much shorter and less complex than EISs; and that it would be considerably less difficult for Federal agencies independently to evaluate the information submitted for an environmental assessment than for an environmental impact statement.

The Council concurs and has added a new subsection (b) to this section which authorizes the preparation of environmental assessments by applicants. The Council intends that this provision enable private and State and local applicants to build the environment into their own planning processes, while the Federal agency retains the obligation for the ultimate EIS. The Council emphasizes, however, that Federal agencies must independently evaluate the information submitted for environmental assessments and assume responsibility for its accuracy; make their own evaluation of environmental issues; and take responsibility for the scope and content of environmental assessments.

Comments on § 1506.6: Public involvement. Subsection (b)(3) of this section listed several means by which Federal agencies might provide notice of actions which have effects primarily of local concern. Several commenters urged that such notices be made mandatory, rather than permissive; other commenters felt these methods of public notice should not be listed at all. Some commenters suggested that additional methods be included in this subsection; others urged that one or more methods be deleted.

Subsection (b) of this section required agencies to provide public notice by means calculated to inform those persons and agencies who may be interested or affected. Paragraph 3 of the subsection merely identified alternative techniques that might be used for this purpose at the local level. Paragraph 3 is not intended to provide an exhaustive list of the means of providing adequate public notice. Nor are the measures it lists mandatory in nature. On the basis of these considerations, the Council determined not to alter this provision.

As proposed, subsection (f) of this section required Federal agencies to make comments on environmental impact statements available to the public. This subsection repeated the existing language on the subject that has been in the Guidelines since 1973 (40 CFR 1500.11(d)) relative to the public availability of comments. On the basis of comments received, the Council altered this provision to state that intra-agency documents need not be made available when the Freedom of Information Act allows them to be withheld.

Several commenters observed that subsection (f) did not establish limitations on charges for environmental impact statements as the Council's Guidelines had. Accordingly, the Council incorporated the standard of the Guidelines into this subsection. The standard provides that such documents shall be provided to the public without charge to the extent practicable, or at a fee which is not more than the actual costs incurred.

Comments on § 1506.8: Proposals for legislation. Section 1506.8 established modified procedures for the preparation of environmental impact statements on legislative proposals. Except in prescribed circumstances, this section provided for the transmittal of a single legislative EIS to the Congress and to Federal, State and local agencies and the public for review and comment. No revised EIS is required in such cases.

A few commenters objected to these procedures and urged that draft and final environmental impact statements be required for all legislative proposals. These commenters said that the

55988

conventional final environmental impact statement, including an agency's response to comments, was no less important in this context than in a purely administrative setting.

However, the Council views legislative proposals as different from proposed actions to be undertaken by agencies, in several important respects. Unlike administrative proposals, the timing of critical steps (hearings, votes) is not under the control of the administrative agency. Congress will hold its hearings or take its votes when it chooses, and if an EIS is to influence those actions, it must be there in time. Congress may request Federal agencies to provide any additional environmental information it needs following receipt of a legislative EIS. Administration proposals are considered alongside other proposals introduced by members of Congress and the final product, if any, may be substantially different from the proposal transmitted by the Federal agency. Congress may hold hearings on legislative proposals and invite testimony on all aspects of proposed legislation including its environmental impacts. On the basis of these considerations, the Council determined that it would be overly burdensome and unproductive to require draft and final legislative environmental impact statements for all legislation, wherever it originates.

Several commenters also expressed concern about the requirement that the legislative environmental impact statement actually accompany legislative proposals when they are transmitted to Congress. These commenters noted that such proposals are often transmitted on an urgent basis without advance warning. Accordingly, the Council amended this section to provide for a period of thirty days for transmittal of legislative environmental impact statements, except that agencies must always transmit such EISs before the Congress begins formal deliberations on the proposal.

Comments on § 1506.10: Timing of agency action. Subsection (c) of this section provided that agencies shall allow not less than 45 days for comments on draft environmental impact statements. Several commenters felt that this period was too long; others thought it too short.

The Council recognizes that a balance must be struck between an adequate period for public comment on draft EIS's and timely completion of the environmental review process. In the Council's judgment, 45 days has proven to be the proper balance. This period for public comment was established by the Guidelines in 1973, and the Council determined not to alter it. Subsection (e) of this section authorizes the Environmental Protection Agency to reduce time periods for

agency action for compelling reasons of national policy.

Comments on § 1506.11: Emergencies. Section 1506.11 provided for agency action in emergency circumstances without observing the requirements of the regulations. The section required the Federal agency "proposing to take the action" to consult with the Council about alternative arrangements.

Several commenters expressed concern that use of the phrase "proposing to take the action" would be interpreted to mean that agencies consult with the Council before emergency action was taken. In the view of these commenters, such a requirement might be impractical in emergency circumstances and could defeat the purpose of the section. The Council concurs and substituted the phrase "taking the action" for "proposing to take the action." Similarly, the Council amended the section to provide for consultation "as soon as feasible" and not necessarily before emergency action.

PART 1507—AGENCY COMPLIANCE

Comments on § 1507.2: Agency capability to comply. Section 1507.2 provided, among other things, that a Federal agency shall itself have "sufficient capability" to evaluate any analysis prepared for it by others. Several commenters expressed concern that this could be interpreted to mean that each agency must employ the full range of professionals including geologists, biologists, chemists, botanists and others to gain sufficient capability for evaluating work prepared by others. This is not the Council's intention. Agency staffing requirements will vary with the agency's mission and needs including the number of EIS's for which they are responsible.

Comments on § 1507.3: Agency procedures. Subsection (a) of § 1507.3 provided that agencies shall adopt procedures for implementation of the regulations within eight months after the regulations are published in the FEDERAL REGISTER. Several commenters noted that State and local agencies participating in the NEPA process under certain statutory highway and community development programs would also require implementing procedures but could not finally begin to develop them until the relevant Federal agencies had completed this task. Accordingly, the Council amended this provision to allow such state and local agencies an additional four months for the adoption of implementing procedures.

Several commenters suggested that agencies with similar programs should establish similar procedures, especially for the submission of information by applicants. The Council concurs and added a new sentence to subsection (a)

stating that agencies with similar programs should consult with each other and the Council to coordinate their procedures, especially for programs requesting similar information from applicants.

Several commenters suggested that a committee be established to review agency compliance with these regulations. Under subsection (a), the Council will review agency implementing procedures for conformity with the Act and the regulations. Moreover, the Council regularly consults with Federal agencies regarding their implementation of NEPA and conducts periodic reviews on how the process is working. On the basis of these considerations, the Council determined that a committee for the review of agency compliance with NEPA should not be established.

PART 1508—TERMINOLOGY AND INDEX

Comments on § 1508.8: Effects. Several commenters urged that the term "effects" expressly include aesthetic, historic and cultural impacts. The Council adopted this suggestion and altered this provision accordingly.

Comments on § 1508.12: Federal agency. Several commenters urged that States and units of general local government assuming NEPA responsibilities under Section 104(h) of the Housing and Community Development Act of 1974 be expressly recognized as Federal agencies for purposes of these regulations. The Council adopted this suggestion and amended this provision accordingly.

Comments on § 1508.14: Human environment. In its proposed form, § 1508.14 stated that the term "human environment" shall be interpreted comprehensively to include the natural and physical environment and the interaction of people with that environment. A few commenters expressed concern that this definition could be interpreted as being limited to the natural and physical aspects of the environment. This is not the Council's intention. See § 1508.8 (relating to effects) and our discussion of the environment in the portion of this Preamble relating to § 1505.2. The full scope of the environment is set out in Section 101 of NEPA. Human beings are central to that concept. In § 1508.14 the Council replaced the work "interaction" with the work "relationship" to ensure that the definition is interpreted as being inclusive of the human environment.

The only line we draw is one drawn by the cases. Section 1508.14 stated that economic or social effects are not intended by themselves to require preparation of an environmental impact statement. A few commenters sought further explanation of this provision. This provision reflects the

Council's determination, which accords with the case law, that NEPA was not intended to require an environmental impact statement where the closing of a military base, for example, only affects such things as the composition of the population or the level of personal income in a region.

Comments on § 1508.16: Legislation. Section 1508.16 defined legislation to exclude requests for appropriations. Some commenters felt that this exclusion was inappropriate. Others noted that environmental reviews for requests for appropriations had not been conducted in the eight years since NEPA was enacted. On the basis of traditional concepts relating to appropriations and the budget cycle, considerations of timing and confidentiality, and other factors, the Council decided not to alter the scope of this provision. The Council is aware that this is the one instance in the regulations where we assert a position opposed to that in the predecessor Guidelines. Quite simply, the Council in its experience found that preparation of EISs is ill-suited to the budget preparation process. Nothing in the Council's determination, however, relieves agencies of responsibility to prepare statements when otherwise required on the underlying program or other actions. (We note that a petition for certiorari on this issue is now pending before the Supreme Court.) This section was renumbered as § 1508.17.

Comments on § 1508.17: Major Federal action. Section 1508.17 of the draft regulations addressed the issue of NEPA's application to Federal programs which are delegated or otherwise transferred to State and local government. Some commenters said that the application of NEPA in such circumstances is a highly complicated issue; that its proper resolution depends on a variety of factors that may differ significantly from one program to the next and should be weighed on a case-by-case basis; and that agencies themselves should be accorded latitude in resolving this issue, subject to judicial review. The Council concurs and determined not to address this issue in this context at the present time. This determination should not be interpreted as a decision one way or the other on the merits of the issue.

Section 1508.17 also stated that the term "major" reinforces but does not have a meaning independent of the term "significantly" in NEPA's phrase "major Federal action significantly affecting the quality of the human environment." A few commenters noted that courts have differed over whether these terms should have independent meaning under NEPA. The Council determined that any Federal action which significantly affects the quality of the human environment is "major"

for purposes of NEPA. The Council's view is in accord with *Minnesota PIRG v. Butz*, 498 F. 2d 1314 (8th Cir., 1974). Section 1508.17 was renumbered as § 1508.18.

Comments on § 1508.22: Proposal. Section 1508.22 stated that a proposal exists when an agency is "actively considering" alternatives and certain other factors are present. Several commenters expressed the view that this phrase could be interpreted to mean that a proposal exists too early in planning and decisionmaking, before there is any likelihood that the agency will be making a decision on the matter. In response to this concern, and to emphasize the link between EISs and actual agency decisions, the Council deleted the phrase "actively considering" and replaced it with the phrase "actively preparing to make a decision on" alternatives. The Council does not intend the change to detract from the importance of integrating NEPA with agency planning as provided in § 1501.2 of the regulations.

This section was renumbered as § 1508.23.

OTHER COMMENTS

Comments on the application of NEPA abroad. Several commenters urged that the question of whether NEPA applies abroad be resolved by these regulations. However, the President has publicly announced his intention to address this issue in an Executive Order. The Executive Order, when issued, will represent the position of the Administration on that issue.

Comments on the role of Indian tribes in the NEPA process. Several commenters stated that the regulations should clarify the role of Indian Tribes in the NEPA process. Accordingly, the Council expressly identified Indian Tribes as participants in the NEPA process in §§ 1501.2(d)(2), 1501.7(a)(1), 1502.15(c) and 1503.1(a)(2)(ii).

Comments on the Council's special environmental assessment for the NEPA regulations. The Council prepared a special environmental assessment for these regulations and announced in the preamble to the draft regulations that the document was available to the public upon request. Some commenters expressed the view that it did not contain an adequate evaluation of the effects of the regulations. For the reasons set out in the assessment, and the preamble to the proposed regulations, the Council confirmed its earlier determination that the special environmental assessment did provide an adequate evaluation for these procedural regulations.

Comments on the President's authority to issue Executive Order 11991 and the Council's authority to issue regula-

tions. A few commenters questioned the authority of the President to issue Executive Order 11991, and the authority of the Council to issue the regulations. The President is empowered to issue regulations implementing the procedural provisions of NEPA by virtue of the authority vested in him as President of the United States under Article II, Section 3 of the Constitution and other provisions of the Constitution and laws of the United States. The President is empowered to delegate responsibility for performing this function to the Council on Environmental Quality under Section 301 of Title 3 of the United States Code and other laws of the United States.

Comments on the responsibilities of Federal agencies in the NEPA process. Agency responsibilities under the regulations often depend upon whether they have "jurisdiction by law" or "special expertise" with respect to a particular proposal. Several commenters noted that these terms were not defined in the regulations and could be subject to varying interpretations. Accordingly, the Council added definitions for these terms in §§ 1508.15 and 1508.26.

Comments on the role of State and areawide clearinghouses. At the request of several States, the Council recognized the role of state and areawide clearinghouses in distributing Federal documents to appropriate recipients. *See* e.g. §§ 1501.4(e)(2), 1503.1(2)(iii), and 1506.6(b)(3)(i).

Comments on the concept of a national data bank. When the Council issued the proposed regulations, it invited comment on the concept of a national data bank. The purpose of a data bank would be to provide for the storage and recall of information developed in one EIS for use in subsequent EISs. Most commenters expressed reservations about the idea on grounds of cost and practicality. The Council, while still intrigued by the concept did not change its initial conclusion that the financial and other resources that would be required are beyond the benefits that might be achieved.

Comments on Federal funding of public comments on EISs. The Council also invited comment on a proposal for encouraging Federal agencies to fund public comments on EISs when an important viewpoint would otherwise not be presented. Several commenters supported this proposal on grounds that it would broaden the range and improve the quality of public comments on EISs. Others doubted that the expenditure of Federal funds for this purpose would be worthwhile. Some felt that Congress should decide the question. The Council determined not to address the issue of Federal funding for public comments on EISs in the regu-

55990

lations, but to leave the matter to individual agencies' discretion.

5. REGULATORY ANALYSES

The final regulations implement the policy and other requirements of Executive Order 12044 to the fullest extent possible. We intend agencies in implementing these regulations to minimize burdens on the public. The determinations required by Section 2(d) of the Order have been made by the Council and are available on request.

It is our intention that a Regulatory Analysis required by Section 3 of the Order be undertaken concurrently with and, where appropriate, integrated with an environmental impact statement required by NEPA and these regulations.

6. CONCLUSION

We could not, of course, adopt every suggestion that was made on the regulations. We have tried to respond to the major concerns that were expressed. In the process, we have changed 74 of the 92 sections, making a total of 340 amendments to the regulations. We are confident that any issues which arise in the future can be resolved through a variety of mechanisms that exists for improving the NEPA process.

We appreciate the efforts of the many people who participated in developing the regulations and look forward to their cooperation as the regulations are implemented by individual agencies.

CHARLES WARREN,
Chairman.

NEPA Deskbook

Appendix 19 Forty Most Asked Questions Concerning CEQ's NEPA Regulations

Forty Most Asked Questions Concerning CEQ's National Environmental Policy Act Regulations
(Council on Environmental Quality)
46 Fed. Reg. 18026 (Mar. 23, 1981), as amended by 51 Fed. Reg. 15618 (Apr. 25, 1986)

18026   Federal Register / Vol. 46, No. 55 / Monday, March 23, 1981 / Rules and Regulations

COUNCIL ON ENVIRONMENTAL QUALITY

40 CFR Parts 1500, 1501, 1502, 1503, 1504, 1505, 1506, 1507, and 1508

Forty Most Asked Questions Concerning CEQ's National Environmental Policy Act Regulations

March 17, 1981.

AGENCY: Council on Environmental Quality, Executive Office of the President.

ACTION: Information Only: Publication of Memorandum to Agencies Containing Answers to 40 Most Asked Questions on NEPA Regulations.

SUMMARY: The Council on Environmental Quality, as part of its oversight of implementation of the National Environmental Policy Act, held meetings in the ten Federal regions with Federal, State, and local officials to discuss administration of the implementing regulations. The forty most asked questions were compiled in a memorandum to agencies for the information of relevant officials. In order efficiently to respond to public inquiries this memorandum is reprinted in this issue of the Federal Register.

FOR FURTHER INFORMATION CONTACT:
Nicholas C. Yost, General Counsel, Council on Environmental Quality, 722 Jackson Place NW., Washington D.C. 20006; 202–395–5750.

March 16, 1981.

Memorandum for Federal NEPA Liaisons, Federal, State, and Local Officials and Other Persons Involved in the NEPA Process

Subject: Questions and Answers About the NEPA Regulations

During June and July of 1980 the Council on Environmental Quality, with the assistance and cooperation of EPA's EIS Coordinators from the ten EPA regions, held one-day meetings with federal, state and local officials in the ten EPA regional offices around the country. In addition, on July 10, 1980, CEQ conducted a similar meeting for the Washington, D.C. NEPA liaisons and persons involved in the NEPA process. At these meetings CEQ discussed (a) the results of its 1980 review of Draft EISs issued since the July 30, 1979 effective date of the NEPA regulations, (b) agency compliance with the Record of Decision requirements in Section 1505 of the NEPA regulations, and (c) CEQ's preliminary findings on how the scoping process is working. Participants at these meetings received copies of materials prepared by CEQ summarizing its oversight and findings.

These meetings also provided NEPA liaisons and other participants with an opportunity to ask questions about NEPA and the practical application of the NEPA regulations. A number of these questions were answered by CEQ representatives at the regional meetings. In response to the many requests from the agencies and other participants, CEQ has compiled forty of the most important or most frequently asked questions and their answers and reduced them to writing. The answers were prepared by the General Counsel of CEQ in consultation with the Office of Federal Activities of EPA. These answers, of course, do not impose any additional requirements beyond those of the NEPA regulations. This document does not represent new guidance under the NEPA regulations, but rather makes generally available to concerned agencies and private individuals the answers which CEQ has already given at the 1980 regional meetings. The answers also reflect the advice which the Council has given over the past two years to aid agency staff and consultants in their day-to-day application of NEPA and the regulations.

CEQ has also received numerous inquiries regarding the scoping process. CEQ hopes to issue written guidance on scoping later this year on the basis of its special study of scoping, which is nearing completion.

Nicholas C. Yost,
General Counsel.

Index

Questions and Answers About the NEPA Regulations (1981)

1a. Q. What is meant by "range of alternatives" as referred to in Sec. 1505.1(e)? [1]

A. The phrase "range of alternatives" refers to the alternatives discussed in environmental documents. It includes all reasonable alternatives, which must be rigorously explored and objectively evaluated, as well as those other alternatives, which are eliminated from detailed study with a brief discussion of the reasons for eliminating them. Section 1502.14. A decisionmaker must not consider alternatives beyond the range of alternatives discussed in the relevant environmental documents. Moreover, a decisionmaker must, in fact, consider all the alternatives discussed in an EIS. Section 1505.1(e).

1b. Q. How many alternatives have to be discussed when there is an infinite number of possible alternatives?

---

[1] References throughout the document are to the Council on Environmental Quality's Regulations For Implementing The Procedural Provisions of the National Environmental Policy Act. 40 CFR Parts 1500–1508.

Federal Register / Vol. 46, No. 55 / Monday, March 23, 1981 / Rules and Regulations　18027

A. For some proposals there may exist a very large or even an infinite number of possible reasonable alternatives. For example, a proposal to designate wilderness areas within a National Forest could be said to involve an infinite number of alternatives from 0 to 100 percent of the forest. When there are potentially a very large number of alternatives, only a reasonable number of examples, covering the *full spectrum* of alternatives, must be analyzed and compared in the EIS. An appropriate series of alternatives might include dedicating 0, 10, 30, 50, 70, 90, or 100 percent of the Forest to wilderness. What constitutes a reasonable range of alternatives depends on the nature of the proposal and the facts in each case.

2a. Q. If an EIS is prepared in connection with an application for a permit or other federal approval, must the EIS rigorously analyze and discuss alternatives that are outside the capability of the applicant or can it be limited to reasonable alternatives that can be carried out by the applicant?

A. Section 1502.14 requires the EIS to examine all reasonable alternatives to the proposal. In determining the scope of alternatives to be considered, the emphasis is on what is "reasonable" rather than on whether the proponent or applicant likes or is itself capable of carrying out a particular alternative. Reasonable alternatives include those that are *practical or feasible* from the technical and economic standpoint and using common sense, rather than simply *desirable* from the standpoint of the applicant.

2b. Q. Must the EIS analyze alternatives outside the jurisdiction or capability of the agency or beyond what Congress has authorized?

A. An alternative that is outside the legal jurisdiction of the lead agency must still be analyzed in the EIS if it is reasonable. A potential conflict with local or federal law does not necessarily render an alternative unreasonable, although such conflicts must be considered. Section 1506.2(d). Alternatives that are outside the scope of what Congress has approved or funded must still be evaluated in the EIS if they are reasonable, because the EIS may serve as the basis for modifying the Congressional approval or funding in light of NEPA's goals and policies. Section 1500.1(a).

3. Q. What does the "no action" alternative include? If an agency is under a court order or legislative command to act, must the EIS address the "no action" alternative?

A. Section 1502.14(d) requires the alternatives analysis in the EIS to include the alternative of no action."

There are two distinct interpretations of "no action" that must be considered, depending on the nature of the proposal being evaluated. The first situation might involve an action such as updating a land management plan where ongoing programs initiated under existing legislation and regulations will continue, even as new plans are developed. In these cases "no action" is "no change" from current management direction or level of management intensity. To construct an alternative that is based on no management at all would be a useless academic exercise. Therefore, the "no action" alternative may be thought of in terms of continuing with the present course of action until that action is changed. Consequently, projected impacts of alternative management schemes would be compared in the EIS to those impacts projected for the existing plan. In this case, alternatives would include management plans of both greater and lesser intensity, especially greater and lesser levels of resource development.

The second interpretation of "no action" is illustrated in instances involving federal decisions on proposals for projects. "No action" in such cases would mean the proposed activity would not take place, and the resulting environmental effects from taking no action would be compared with the effects of permitting the proposed activity or an alternative activity to go forward.

Where a choice of "no action" by the agency would result in predictable actions by others, this consequence of the "no action" alternative should be included in the analysis. For example, if denial of permission to build a railroad to a facility would lead to construction of a road and increased truck traffic, the EIS should analyze this consequence of the "no action" alternative.

In light of the above, it is difficult to think of a situation where it would *not* be appropriate to address a "no action" alternative. Accordingly, the regulations require the analysis of the no action alternative even if the agency is under a court order or legislative command to act. This analysis provides a benchmark, enabling decisionmakers to compare the magnitude of environmental effects of the action alternatives. It is also an example of a reasonable alternative outside the jurisdiction of the agency which must be analyzed. Section 1502.14(c). See Question 2 above. Inclusion of such an analysis in the EIS is necessary to inform the Congress, the public, and the President as intended by NEPA. Section 1500.1(a).

4a. Q. What is the "agency's preferred alternative"?

A. The "agency's preferred alternative" is the alternative which the agency believes would fulfill its statutory mission and responsibilities, giving consideration to economic, environmental, technical and other factors. The concept of the "agency's preferred alternative" is different from the "environmentally preferable alternative," although in some cases one alternative may be both. See Question 6 below. It is identified so that agencies and the public can understand the lead agency's orientation.

4b. Q. Does the "preferred alternative" have to be identified in the Draft EIS and the Final EIS or just in the Final EIS?

A. Section 1502.14(e) requires the section of the EIS on alternatives to "identify the agency's preferred alternative if one or more exists, in the draft statement, and identify such alternative in the final statement . . . This means that if the agency has a preferred alternative at the Draft EIS stage, that alternative must be labeled or identified as such in the Draft EIS. If the responsible federal official in fact has no preferred alternative at the Draft EIS stage, a preferred alternative need not be identified there. By the time the Final EIS is filed, Section 1502.14(e) presumes the existence of a preferred alternative and requires its identification in the Final EIS "unless another law prohibits the expression of such a preference."

4c. Q. Who recommends or determines the "preferred alternative?"

A. The lead agency's official with line responsibility for preparing the EIS and assuring its adequacy is responsible for identifying the agency's preferred alternative(s). The NEPA regulations do not dictate which official in an agency shall be responsible for preparation of EISs, but agencies can identify this official in their implementing procedures, pursuant to Section 1507.3.

Even though the agency's preferred alternative is identified by the EIS preparer in the EIS, the statement must be objectively prepared and not slanted to support the choice of the agency's preferred alternative over the other reasonable and feasible alternatives.

5a. Q. Is the "proposed action" the same thing as the "preferred alternative"?

A. The "proposed action" may be, but is not necessarily, the agency's "preferred alternative." The proposed action may be a proposal in its initial form before undergoing analysis in the EIS process. If the proposed action is

18028   **Federal Register** / Vol. 46, No. 55 / Monday, March 23, 1981 / Rules and Regulations

internally generated, such as preparing a land management plan, the proposed action might end up as the agency's preferred alternative. On the other hand the proposed action may be granting an application to a non-federal entity for a permit. The agency may or may not have a "preferred alternative" at the Draft EIS stage (see Question 4 above). In that case the agency may decide at the Final EIS stage, on the basis of the Draft EIS and the public and agency comments, that an alternative other than the proposed action is the agency's "preferred alternative."

5b. Q. Is the analysis of the "proposed action" in an EIS to be treated differently from the analysis of alternatives?

A. The degree of analysis devoted to each alternative in the EIS is to be substantially similar to that devoted to the "proposed action." Section 1502.14 is titled "Alternatives including the proposed action" to reflect such comparable treatment. Section 1502.14(b) specifically requires "substantial treatment" in the EIS of each alternative including the proposed action. This regulation does not dictate an *amount* of information to be provided, but rather, prescribes a *level of treatment*, which may in turn require varying amounts of information, to enable a reviewer to evaluate and compare alternatives.

6a. Q. What is the meaning of the term "environmentally preferable alternative" as used in the regulations with reference to Records of Decision? How is the term "environment" used in the phrase?

A. Section 1505.2(b) requires that, in cases where an EIS has been prepared, the Record of Decision (ROD) must identify all alternatives that were considered, ". . . specifying the alternative or alternatives which were considered to be environmentally preferable." The environmentally preferable alternative is the alternative that will promote the national environmental policy as expressed in NEPA's Section 101. Ordinarily, this means the alternative that causes the least damage to the biological and physical environment; it also means the alternative which best protects, preserves, and enhances historic, cultural, and natural resources.

The Council recognizes that the identification of the environmentally preferable alternative may involve difficult judgments, particularly when one environmental value must be balanced against another. The public and other agencies reviewing a Draft EIS can assist the lead agency to develop and determine environmentally

preferable alternatives by providing their views in comments on the Draft EIS. Through the identification of the environmentally preferable alternative, the decisionmaker is clearly faced with a choice between that alternative and others, and must consider whether the decision accords with the Congressionally declared policies of the Act.

6b. Q. Who recommends or determines what is environmentally preferable?

A. The agency EIS staff is encouraged to make recommendations of the environmentally preferable alternative(s) during EIS preparation. In any event the lead agency official responsible for the EIS is encouraged to identify the environmentally preferable alternative(s) in the EIS. In all cases, commentors from other agencies and the public are also encouraged to address this question. The agency must identify the environmentally preferable alternative in the ROD.

7. Q. What is the difference between the sections in the EIS on "alternatives" and "environmental consequences"? How do you avoid duplicating the discussion of alternatives in preparing these two sections?

A. The "alternatives" section is the heart of the EIS. This section rigorously explores and objectively evaluates all reasonable alternatives including the proposed action. Section 1502.14. It should include relevant comparisons on environmental and other grounds. The "environmental consequences" section of the EIS discusses the specific environmental impacts or effects of each of the alternatives including the proposed action. Section 1502.16. In order to avoid duplication between these two sections, most of the "alternatives" section should be devoted to describing and comparing the alternatives. Discussion of the environmental impacts of these alternatives should be limited to a concise descriptive summary of such impacts in a comparative form, including charts or tables, thus sharply defining the issues and providing a clear basis for choice among options. Section 1502.14. The "environmental consequences" section should be devoted largely to a scientific analysis of the direct and indirect environmental effects of the proposed action and of each of the alternatives. It forms the analytic basis for the concise comparison in the "alternatives" section.

8. Q. Section 1501.2(d) of the NEPA regulations requires agencies to provide for the early application of NEPA to cases where actions are planned by

private applicants or non-Federal entities and are, at some stage, subject to federal approval of permits, loans, loan guarantees, insurance or other actions. What must and can agencies do to apply NEPA early in these cases?

A. Section 1501.2(d) requires federal agencies to take steps toward ensuring that private parties and state and local entities initiate environmental studies as soon as federal involvement in their proposals can be foreseen. This section is intended to ensure that environmental factors are considered at an early stage in the planning process and to avoid the situation where the applicant for a federal permit or approval has completed planning and eliminated all alternatives to the proposed action by the time the EIS process commences or before the EIS process has been completed.

Through early consultation, business applicants and approving agencies may gain better appreciation of each other's needs and foster a decisionmaking process which avoids later unexpected confrontations.

Federal agencies are required by Section 1507.3(b) to develop procedures to carry out Section 1501.2(d). The procedures should include an "outreach program", such as a means for prospective applicants to conduct pre-application consultations with the lead and cooperating agencies. Applicants need to find out, in advance of project planning, what environmental studies or other information will be required, and what mitigation requirements are likely in connecton with the later federal NEPA process. Agencies should designate staff to advise potential applicants of the agency's NEPA information requirements and should publicize their pre-application procedures and information requirements in newsletters or other media used by potential applicants.

Complementing Section 1501.2(d), Section 1506.5(a) requires agencies to assist applicants by outlining the types of information required in those cases where the agency requires the applicant to submit environmental data for possible use by the agency in preparing an EIS.

Section 1506.5(b) allows agencies to authorize preparation of environmental assessments by applicants. Thus, the procedures should also include a means for anticipating and utilizing applicants' environmental studies or "early corporate environmental assessments" to fulfill some of the federal agency's NEPA obligations. However, in such cases the agency must still evaluate independently the environmental issues and take responsibility for the environmental assessment.

These provisions are intended to encourage and enable private and other non-federal entities to build environmental considerations into their own planning processes in a way that facilitates the application of NEPA and avoids delay.

9. Q. To what extent must an agency inquire into whether an applicant for a federal permit, funding or other approval of a proposal will also need approval from another agency for the same proposal or some other related aspect of it?

A. Agencies must integrate the NEPA process into other planning at the earliest possible time to insure that planning and decisions reflect environmental values, to avoid delays later in the process, and to head off potential conflicts. Specifically, the agency must "provide for cases where actions are planned by . . . applicants," so that designated staff are available to advise potential applicants of studies or other information that will foreseeably be required for the later federal action; the agency shall consult with the applicant if the agency foresees its own involvement in the proposal; and it shall insure that the NEPA process commences at the earliest possible time. Section 1501.2(d). (See Question 8.)

The regulations emphasize agency cooperation early in the NEPA process. Section 1501.6. Section 1501.7 on "scoping" also provides that all affected Federal agencies are to be invited to participate in scoping the environmental issues and to identify the various environmental review and consultation requirements that may apply to the proposed action. Further, Section 1502.25(b) requires that the draft EIS list all the federal permits, licenses and other entitlements that are needed to implement the proposal.

These provisions create an affirmative obligation on federal agencies to inquire early, and to the maximum degree possible, to ascertain whether an applicant is or will be seeking other federal assistance or approval, or whether the applicant is waiting until a proposal has been substantially developed before requesting federal aid or approval.

Thus, a federal agency receiving a request for approval or assistance should determine whether the applicant has filed separate requests for federal approval or assistance with other federal agencies. Other federal agencies that are likely to become involved should then be contacted, and the NEPA process coordinated, to insure an early and comprehensive analysis of the

direct and indirect effects of the proposal and any related actions. The agency should inform the applicant that action on its application may be delayed unless it submits all other federal applications (where feasible to do so), so that all the relevant agencies can work together on the scoping process and preparation of the EIS.

10a. Q. What actions by agencies and/or applicants are allowed during EIS preparation and during the 30-day review period after publication of a final EIS?

A. No federal decision on the proposed action shall be made or recorded until at least 30 days after the publication by EPA of notice that the particular EIS has been filed with EPA. Sections 1505.2 and 1506.10. Section 1505.2 requires this decision to be stated in a public Record of Decision.

Until the agency issues its Record of Decision, no action by an agency or an applicant concerning the proposal shall be taken which would have an adverse environmental impact or limit the choice of reasonable alternatives. Section 1506.1(a). But this does not preclude preliminary planning or design work which is needed *to support an application* for permits or assistance. Section 1506.1(d).

When the impact statement in question is a program EIS, no major action concerning the program may be taken which may significantly affect the quality of the human environment, unless the particular action is justified independently of the program, is accompanied by its own adequate environmental impact statement and will not prejudice the ultimate decision on the program. Section 1506.1(c).

10b. Q. Do these limitations on action (described in Question 10a) apply to state or local agencies that have statutorily delegated responsibility for preparation of environmental documents required by NEPA, for example, under the HUD Block Grant program?

A. Yes, these limitations do apply, without any variation from their application to federal agencies.

11. Q. What actions must a lead agency take during the NEPA process when it becomes aware that a non-federal applicant is about to take an action within the agency's jurisdiction that would either have an adverse environmental impact or limit the choice of reasonable alternatives (e.g., prematurely commit money or other resources towards the completion of the proposal)?

A. The federal agency must notify the applicant that the agency will take strong affirmative steps to insure that the objectives and procedures of NEPA

are fulfilled. Section 1506.1(b). These steps could include seeking injunctive measures under NEPA, or the use of sanctions available under either the agency's permitting authority or statutes setting forth the agency's statutory mission. For example, the agency might advise an applicant that if it takes such action the agency will not process its application.

12a. Q. What actions are subject to the Council's new regulations, and what actions are grandfathered under the old guidelines?

A. The effective date of the Council's regulations was July 30, 1979 (except for certain HUD programs under the Housing and Community Development Act, 42 U.S.C. 5304(h), and certain state highway programs that qualify under Section 102(2)(D) of NEPA for which the regulations became effective on November 30, 1979). All the provisions of the regulations are binding as of that date, including those covering decisionmaking, public participation, referrals, limitations on actions, EIS supplements, etc. For example, a Record of Decision would be prepared even for decisions where the draft EIS was filed before July 30, 1979.

But in determining whether or not the new regulations apply to the preparation of a *particular environmental document*, the relevant factor is the date of filing of the draft of that document. Thus, the new regulations do not require the redrafting of an EIS or supplement if the draft EIS or supplement was filed before July 30, 1979. However, a supplement prepared after the effective date of the regulations for an EIS issued in final before the effective date of the regulations would be controlled by the regulations.

Even though agencies are not required to apply the regulations to an EIS or other document for which the draft was filed prior to July 30, 1979, the regulations encourage agencies to follow the regulations "to the fullest extent practicable," i.e., if it is feasible to do so, in preparing the final document. Section 1506.12(a).

12b. Q. Are projects authorized by Congress before the effective date of the Council's regulations grandfathered?

A. No. The date of Congressional authorization for a project is not determinative of whether the Council's regulations or former Guidelines apply to the particular proposal. No incomplete projects or proposals of any kind are grandfathered in whole or in part. Only certain environmental documents, for which the draft was issued before the effective date of the regulations, are grandfathered and

18030   Federal Register / Vol. 46, No. 55 / Monday, March 23, 1981 / Rules and Regulations

subject to the Council's former Guidelines.

12c. Q. Can a violation of the regulations give rise to a cause of action?

A. While a trivial violation of the regulations would not give rise to an independent cause of action, such a cause of action would arise from a substantial violation of the regulations. Section 1500.3.

13. Q. Can the scoping process be used in connection with preparation of an environmental assessment, i.e., before both the decision to proceed with an EIS and publication of a notice of intent?

A. Yes. Scoping can be a useful tool for discovering alternatives to a proposal, or significant impacts that may have been overlooked. In cases where an environmental assessment is being prepared to help an agency decide whether to prepare an EIS, useful information might result from early participation by other agencies and the public in a scoping process.

The regulations state that the scoping process is to be preceded by a Notice of Intent (NOI) to prepare an EIS. But that is only the minimum requirement. Scoping may be initiated earlier, as long as there is appropriate public notice and enough information available on the proposal so that the public and relevant agencies can participate effectively.

However, scoping that is done before the assessment, and in aid of its preparation, cannot *substitute* for the normal scoping process after publication of the NOI, unless the earlier public notice stated clearly that this possibility was under consideration, *and* the NOI expressly provides that written comments on the scope of alternatives and impacts will still be considered.

14a. Q. What are the respective rights and responsibilities of lead and cooperating agencies? What letters and memoranda must be prepared?

A. After a lead agency has been designated (Sec. 1501.5), that agency has the responsibility to solicit cooperation from other federal agencies that have jurisdiction by law or special expertise on any environmental issue that should be addressed in the EIS being prepared. Where appropriate, the lead agency should seek the cooperation of state or local agencies of similar qualifications. When the proposal may affect an Indian reservation, the agency should consult with the Indian tribe. Section 1508.5. The request for cooperation should come at the earliest possible time in the NEPA process.

After discussions with the candidate cooperating agencies, the lead agency and the cooperating agencies are to determine by letter or by memorandum which agencies will undertake cooperating responsibilities. To the extent possible at this stage, responsibilities for specific issues should be assigned. The allocation of responsibilities will be completed during scoping. Section 1501.7(a)(4).

Cooperating agencies must assume responsibility for the development of information and the preparation of environmental analyses at the request of the lead agency. Section 1501.6(b)(3). Cooperating agencies are now required by Section 1501.6 to devote staff resources that were normally primarily used to critique or comment on the Draft EIS after its preparation, much earlier in the NEPA process—primarily at the scoping and Draft EIS preparation stages. If a cooperating agency determines that its resource limitations preclude any involvement, or the degree of involvement (amount of work) requested by the lead agency, it must so inform the lead agency in writing and submit a copy of this correspondence to the Council. Section 1501.6(c).

In other words, the potential cooperating agency must decide early if it is able to devote any of its resources to a particular proposal. For this reason the regulation states that an agency may reply to a request for cooperation that "other program commitments preclude any involvement or the degree of involvement requested in the *action* that is the subject of the environmental impact statement." (Emphasis added). The regulation refers to the "action," rather than to the EIS, to clarify that the agency is taking itself out of all phases of the federal action, not just draft EIS preparation. This means that the agency has determined that it cannot be involved in the later stages of EIS review and comment, as well as decisionmaking on the proposed action. For this reason, cooperating agencies with jurisdiction by law (those which have permitting or other approval authority) cannot opt out entirely of the duty to cooperate on the EIS. See also Question 15, relating specifically to the responsibility of EPA.

14b. Q. How are disputes resolved between lead and cooperating agencies concerning the scope and level of detail of analysis and the quality of data in impact statements?

A. Such disputes are resolved by the agencies themselves. A lead agency, of course, has the ultimate responsibility for the content of an EIS. But it is supposed to use the environmental analysis and recommendations of cooperating agencies with jurisdiction by law or special expertise to the maximum extent possible, consistent with its own responsibilities as lead agency. Section 1501.6(a)(2).

If the lead agency leaves out a significant issue or ignores the advice and expertise of the cooperating agency, the EIS may be found later to be inadequate. Similarly, where cooperating agencies have their own decisions to make and they intend to adopt the environmental impact statement and base their decisions on it, one document should include all of the information necessary for the decisions by the cooperating agencies. Otherwise they may be forced to duplicate the EIS process by issuing a new, more complete EIS or Supplemental EIS, even though the original EIS could have sufficed if it had been properly done at the outset. Thus, both lead and cooperating agencies have a stake in producing a document of good quality. Cooperating agencies also have a duty to participate fully in the scoping process to ensure that the appropriate range of issues is determined early in the EIS process.

Because the EIS is not the Record of Decision, but instead constitutes the *information* and *analysis* on which to base a decision, disagreements about conclusions to be drawn from the EIS need not inhibit agencies from issuing a joint document, or adopting another agency's EIS, if the analysis is adequate. Thus, if each agency has its own "preferred alternative," both can be identified in the EIS. Similarly, a cooperating agency with jurisdiction by law may determine in its own ROD that alternative A is the environmentally preferable action, even though the lead agency has decided in its separate ROD that Alternative B is environmentally preferable.

14c. Q. What are the specific responsibilities of federal and state cooperating agencies to review draft EISs?

A. Cooperating agencies (i.e., agencies with jurisdiction by law or special expertise) and agencies that are authorized to develop or enforce environmental standards, must comment on environmental impact statements within their jurisdiction, expertise or authority. Sections 1503.2, 1508.5. If a cooperating agency is satisfied that its views are adequately reflected in the environmental impact statement, it should simply comment accordingly. Conversely, if the cooperating agency determines that a draft EIS is incomplete, inadequate or inaccurate, or it has other comments, it should promptly make such comments, conforming to the requirements of specificity in section 1503.3.

Federal Register / Vol. 46, No. 55 / Monday, March 23, 1981 / Rules and Regulations   **1803**

14d. Q. How is the lead agency to treat the comments of another agency with jurisdiction by law or special expertise which has failed or refused to cooperate or participate in scoping or EIS preparation?

A. A lead agency has the responsibility to respond to all substantive comments raising significant issues regarding a draft EIS. Section 1503.4. However, cooperating agencies are generally under an obligation to raise issues or otherwise participate in the EIS process during scoping and EIS preparation if they reasonably can do so. In practical terms, if a cooperating agency fails to cooperate at the outset, such as during scoping, it will find that its comments at a later stage will not be as persuasive to the lead agency.

15. Q. Are EPA's responsibilities to review and comment on the environmental effects of agency proposals under Section 309 of the Clean Air Act independent of its responsibility as a cooperating agency?

A. Yes. EPA has an obligation under Section 309 of the Clean Air Act to review and comment in writing on the environmental impact of any matter relating to the authority of the Administrator contained in proposed legislation, federal construction projects, other federal actions requiring EISs, and new regulations. 42 U.S.C. Sec. 7609. This obligation is independent of its role as a cooperating agency under the NEPA regulations.

16. Q. What is meant by the term "third party contracts" in connection with the preparation of an EIS? See Section 1506.5(c). When can "third party contracts" be used?

A. As used by EPA and other agencies, the term "third party contract" refers to the preparation of EISs by contractors paid by the applicant. In the case of an EIS for a National Pollution Discharge Elimination System (NPDES) permit, the applicant, aware in the early planning stages of the proposed project of the need for an EIS, contracts directly with a consulting firm for its preparation. See 40 C.F.R. 6.604(g). The "third party" is EPA which, under Section 1506.5(c), must select the consulting firm, even though the applicant pays for the cost of preparing the EIS. The consulting firm is responsible to EPA for preparing an EIS that meets the requirements of the NEPA regulations and EPA's NEPA procedures. It is in the applicant's interest that the EIS comply with the law so that EPA can take prompt action on the NPDES permit application. The "third party contract" method under EPA's NEPA procedures is purely voluntary, though most applicants have

found it helpful in expediting compliance with NEPA.

If a federal agency uses "third party contracting," the applicant may undertake the necessary paperwork for the solicitation of a field of candidates under the agency's direction, so long as the agency complies with Section 1506.5(c). Federal procurement requirements do not apply to the agency because it incurs no obligations or costs under the contract, nor does the agency procure anything under the contract.

17a. Q. If an EIS is prepared with the assistance of a consulting firm, the firm must execute a disclosure statement. What criteria must the firm follow in determining whether it has any "financial or other interest in the outcome of the project" which would cause a conflict of interest?

A. Section 1506.5(c), which specifies that a consulting firm preparing an EIS must execute a disclosure statement, does not define "financial or other interest in the outcome of the project." The Council interprets this term broadly to cover any known benefits other than general enhancement of professional reputation. This includes any financial benefit such as a promise of future construction or design work on the project, as well as indirect benefits the consultant is aware of (e.g., if the project would aid proposals sponsored by the firm's other clients). For example, completion of a highway project may encourage construction of a shopping center or industrial park from which the consultant stands to benefit. If a consulting firm is aware that it has such an interest in the decision on the proposal, it should be disqualified from preparing the EIS, to preserve the objectivity and integrity of the NEPA process.

When a consulting firm has been involved in developing initial data and plans for the project, but does not have any financial or other interest in the outcome of the decision, it need not be disqualified from preparing the EIS. However, a disclosure statement in the draft EIS should clearly state the scope and extent of the firm's prior involvement to expose any potential conflicts of interest that may exist.

17b. Q. If the firm in fact has no promise of future work or other interest in the outcome of the proposal, may the firm later bid in competition with others for future work on the project if the proposed action is approved?

A. Yes.

18. Q. How should uncertainties about indirect effects of a proposal be addressed, for example, in cases of disposal of federal lands, when the

identity or plans of future landowners is unknown?

A. The EIS must identify all the indirect effects that are known, and make a good faith effort to explain the effects that are not known but are "reasonably foreseeable." Section 1508.8(b). In the example, if there is total uncertainty about the identity of future land owners or the nature of future land uses, then of course, the agency is not required to engage in speculation or contemplation about their future plans. But, in the ordinary course of business, people do make judgments based upon reasonably foreseeable occurrences. It will often be possible to consider the likely purchasers and the development trends in that area or similar areas in recent years; or the likelihood that the land will be used for an energy project, shopping center, subdivision, farm or factory. The agency has the responsibility to make an informed judgment, and to estimate future impacts on that basis, especially if trends are ascertainable or potential purchasers have made themselves known. The agency cannot ignore these uncertain, but probable, effects of its decisions.

19a. Q. What is the scope of mitigation measures that must be discussed?

A. The mitigation measures discussed in an EIS must cover the range of impacts of the proposal. The measures must include such things as design alternatives that would decrease pollution emissions, construction impacts, esthetic intrusion, as well as relocation assistance, possible land use controls that could be enacted, and other possible efforts. Mitigation measures must be considered even for impacts that by themselves would not be considered "significant." Once the proposal itself is considered as a whole to have significant effects, all of its specific effects on the environment (whether or not "significant") must be considered, and mitigation measures must be developed where it is feasible to do so. Sections 1502.14(f), 1502.16(h), 1508.14.

19b. Q. How should an EIS treat the subject of available mitigation measures that are (1) outside the jurisdiction of the lead or cooperating agencies, or (2) unlikely to be adopted or enforced by the responsible agency?

A. All relevant, reasonable mitigation measures that could improve the project are to be identified, even if they are outside the jurisdiction of the lead agency or the cooperating agencies, and thus would not be committed as part of the RODs of these agencies. Sections 1502.16(h), 1505.2(c). This will serve to

18032 Federal Register / Vol. 46. No. 55 / Monday, March 23, 1981 / Rules and Regulations

alert agencies or officials who *can* implement these extra measures, and will encourage them to do so. Because the EIS is the most comprehensive environmental document, it is an ideal vehicle in which to lay out not only the full range of environmental impacts but also the full spectrum of appropriate mitigation.

However, to ensure that environmental effects of a proposed action are fairly assessed, the probability of the mitigation measures being implemented must also be discussed. Thus the EIS and the Record of Decision should indicate the likelihood that such measures will be adopted or enforced by the responsible agencies. Sections 1502.16(h), 1505.2. If there is a history of nonenforcement or opposition to such measures, the EIS and Record of Decision should acknowledge such opposition or nonenforcement. If the necessary mitigation measures will not be ready for a long period of time, this fact, of course, should also be recognized.

20a. Q. When must a worst case analysis be included in an EIS?

A. If there are gaps in relevant information or scientific uncertainty pertaining to an agency's evaluation of significant adverse impacts on the human environment, an agency must make clear that such information is lacking or that the uncertainty exists. An agency must include a worst case analysis of the potential impacts of the proposal and an indication of the probability or improbability of their occurence if (a) the information relevant to adverse impacts is essential to a reasoned choice among alternatives and the overall costs of obtaining the information are exorbitant, or (b) the information relevant to adverse impacts is important to the decision and the means to obtain it are not known.

NEPA requires that impact statements, at a minimum, contain information to alert the public and Congress to all known *possible* environmental consequences of agency action. Thus, one of the federal government's most important obligations is to present to the fullest extent possible the spectrum of consequences that may result from agency decisions, and the details of their potential consequences for the human environment.

20b. Q. What is the purpose of a worst case analysis? How is it formulated and what is the scope of the analysis?

A. The purpose of the analysis is to carry out NEPA's mandate for full disclosure to the public of the potential consequences of agency decisions, and

to cause agencies to consider those potential consequences when acting on the basis of scientific uncertainties or gaps in available information. The analysis is formulated on the basis of available information, using reasonable projections of the worst possible consequences of a proposed action.

For example, if there are scientific uncertainty and gaps in the available information concerning the numbers of juvenile fish that would be entrained in a cooling water facility, the responsible agency must disclose and consider the possibility of the loss of the commercial or sport fishery.

In addition to an analysis of a low probability/catastrophic impact event, the worst case analysis should also include a spectrum of events of higher probability but less drastic impact.

21. Q. Where an EIS or an EA is combined with another project planning document (sometimes called "piggybacking"), to what degree may the EIS or EA refer to and rely upon information in the project document to satisfy NEPA's requirements?

A. Section 1502.25 of the regulations requires that draft EISs be prepared concurrently and integrated with environmental analyses and related surveys and studies required by other federal statutes. In addition, Section 1506.4 allows any environmental document prepared in compliance with NEPA to be combined with any other agency document to reduce duplication and paperwork. However, these provisions were not intended to authorize the preparation of a short summary or outline EIS, attached to a detailed project report or land-use plan containing the required environmental impact data. In such circumstances, the reader would have to refer constantly to the detailed report to understand the environmental impacts and alternatives which should have been found in the EIS itself.

The EIS must stand on its own as an analytical document which fully informs decisionmakers and the public of the environmental effects of the proposal and those of the reasonable alternatives. Section 1502.1. But, as long as the EIS is clearly identified and is self-supporting, it can be physically included in or attached to the project report or land use plan, and may use attached report material as technical backup.

Forest Service environmental impact statements for forest management plans are handled in this manner. The EIS identifies the agency's preferred alternative, which is developed in detail as the proposed management plan. The detailed proposed plan accompanies the EIS through the review process, and the

documents are appropriately cross-referenced. The proposed plan is useful for EIS readers as an example, to show how one choice of management options translates into effects on-natural resources. This procedure permits initiation of the 90-day public review of proposed forest plans, which is required by the National Forest Management Act.

All the alternatives are discussed in the EIS, which can be read as an independent document. The details of the management plan are not repeated in the EIS, and vice versa. This is a reasonable functional separation of the documents: the EIS contains information relevant to the choice among alternatives; the plan is a detailed description of proposed management activities suitable for use by the land managers. This procedure provides for concurrent compliance with the public review requirements of both NEPA and the National Forest Management Act.

Under some circumstances, a project report or management plan may be totally merged with the EIS, and the one document labeled as both "EIS" and "management plan" or "project report." This may be reasonable where the documents are short, or where the EIS format and the regulations for clear, analytical EISs also satisfy the requirements for a project report.

22. Q. May state and federal agencies serve as joint lead agencies? If so, how do they resolve law, policy and resource conflicts under NEPA and the relevant state environmental policy act? How do they resolve differences in perspective where, for example, national and local needs may differ?

A. Under Section 1501.5(b), federal, state or local agencies, as long as they include at least one federal agency, may act as joint lead agencies to prepare an EIS. Section 1506.2 also strongly urges state and local agencies and the relevant federal agencies to cooperate fully with each other. This should cover joint research and studies, planning activities, public hearings, environmental assessments and the preparation of joint EISs under NEPA and the relevant "little NEPA" state laws, so that one document will satisfy both laws.

The regulations also recognize that certain inconsistencies may exist between the proposed federal action and any approved state or local plan or law. The joint document should discuss the extent to which the federal agency would reconcile its proposed action with such plan or law. Section 1506.2(d). (See Question 23).

Because there may be differences in perspective as well as conflicts among

Federal Register / Vol. 46, No. 55 / Monday, March 23, 1981 / Rules and Regulations   18033

federal, state and local goals for resources management, the Council has advised participating agencies to adopt a flexible, cooperative approach. The joint EIS should reflect all of their interests and missions, clearly identified as such. The final document would then indicate how state and local interests have been accommodated, or would identify conflicts in goals (e.g., how a hydroelectric project, which might induce second home development, would require new land use controls). The EIS must contain a complete discussion of scope and purpose of the proposal, alternatives, and impacts so that the discussion is adequate to meet the needs of local, state and federal decisionmakers.

23a. Q. How should an agency handle potential conflicts between a proposal and the objectives of Federal, state or local land use plans, policies and controls for the area concerned? See Sec. 1502.16(c).

A. The agency should first inquire of other agencies whether there are any potential conflicts. If there would be immediate conflicts, or if conflicts could arise in the future when the plans are finished (see Question 23(b) below), the EIS must acknowledge and describe the extent of those conflicts. If there are any possibilities of resolving the conflicts, these should be explained as well. The EIS should also evaluate the seriousness of the impact of the proposal on the land use plans and policies, and whether, or how much, the proposal will impair the effectiveness of land use control mechanisms for the area. Comments from officials of the affected area should be solicited early and should be carefully acknowleged and answered in the EIS.

23b. Q. What constitutes a "land use plan or policy" for purposes of this discussion?

A. The term "land use plans," includes all types of formally adopted documents for land use planning, zoning and related regulatory requirements. Local general plans are included, even though they are subject to future change. Proposed plans should also be addressed if they have been formally proposed by the appropriate government body in a written form, and are being actively pursued by officials of the jurisdiction. Staged plans, which must go through phases of development such as the Water Resources Council's Level A, B and C planning process should also be included even though they are incomplete.

The term "policies" includes formally adopted statements of land use policy as embodied in laws or regulations. It also includes proposals for action such as the initiation of a planning process, or a formally adopted policy statement of the local, regional or state executive branch, even if it has not yet been formally adopted by the local, regional or state legislative body.

23c. Q. What options are available for the decisionmaker when conflicts with such plans or policies are identified?

A. After identifying any potential land use conflicts, the decisionmaker must weigh the significance of the conflicts, among all the other environmental and non-environmental factors that must be considered in reaching a rational and balanced decision. Unless precluded by other law from causing or contributing to any inconsistency with the land use plans, policies or controls, the decisionmaker retains the authority to go forward with the proposal, despite the potential conflict. In the Record of Decision, the decisionmaker must explain what the decision was, how it was made, and what mitigation measures are being imposed to lessen adverse environmental impacts of the proposal, among the other requirements of Section 1505.2. This provision would require the decisionmaker to explain any decision to override land use plans, policies or controls for the area.

24a. Q. When are EISs required on policies, plans or programs?

A. An EIS must be prepared if an agency proposes to implement a specific policy, to adopt a plan for a group of related actions, or to implement a specific statutory program or executive directive. Section 1508.18. In addition, the adoption of official policy in the form of rules, regulations and interpretations pursuant to the Administrative Procedure Act, treaties, conventions, or other formal documents establishing governmental or agency policy which will substantially alter agency programs, could require an EIS. Section 1508.18. In all cases, the policy, plan, or program must have the potential for significantly affecting the quality of the human environment in order to require an EIS. It should be noted that a proposal "may exist in fact as well as by agency declaration that one exists." Section 1508.23.

24b. Q. When is an area-wide or overview EIS appropriate?

A. The preparation of an area-wide or overview EIS may be particularly useful when similar actions, viewed with other reasonably foreseeable or proposed agency actions, share common timing or geography. For example, when a variety of energy projects may be located in a single watershed, or when a series of new energy technologies may be developed through federal funding, the overview or area-wide EIS would serve as a valuable and necessary analysis of the affected environment and the potential cumulative impacts of the reasonably foreseeable actions under that program or within that geographical area.

24c. Q. What is the function of tiering in such cases?

A. Tiering is a procedure which allows an agency to avoid duplication of paperwork through the incorporation by reference of the general discussions and relevant specific discussions from an environmental impact statement of broader scope into one of lesser scope or vice versa. In the example given in Question 24b, this would mean that an overview EIS would be prepared for all of the energy activities reasonably foreseeable in a particular geographic area or resulting from a particular development program. This impact statement would be followed by site-specific or project-specific EISs. The tiering process would make each EIS of greater use and meaning to the public as the plan or program develops, without duplication of the analysis prepared for the previous impact statement.

25a. Q. When is it appropriate to use appendices instead of including information in the body of an EIS?

A. The body of the EIS should be a succinct statement of all the information on environmental impacts and alternatives that the decisionmaker and the public need, in order to make the decision and to ascertain that every significant factor has been examined. The EIS must explain or summarize methodologies of research and modeling, and the results of research that may have been conducted to analyze impacts and alternatives.

Lengthy technical discussions of modeling methodology, baseline studies, or other work are best reserved for the appendix. In other words, if only technically trained individuals are likely to understand a particular discussion then it should go in the appendix, and a plain language summary of the analysis and conclusions of that technical discussion should go in the text of the EIS.

The final statement must also contain the agency's responses to comments on the draft EIS. These responses will be primarily in the form of changes in the document itself, but specific answers to each significant comment should also be included. These specific responses may be placed in an appendix. If the comments are especially voluminous, summaries of the comments and responses will suffice. (See Question 29 regarding the level of detail required for responses to comments.)

18034   **Federal Register** / Vol. 46, No. 55 / Monday, March 23, 1981 / Rules and Regulations

25b. Q. How does an appendix differ from incorporation by reference?

A. First, if at all possible, the appendix accompanies the EIS, whereas the material which is incorporated by reference does not accompany the EIS. Thus the appendix should contain information that reviewers will be likely to want to examine. The appendix should include material that pertains to preparation of a particular EIS. Research papers directly relevant to the proposal, lists of affected species, discussion of the methodology of models used in the analysis of impacts, extremely detailed responses to comments, or other information, would be placed in the appendix.

The appendix must be complete and available at the time the EIS is filed. Five copies of the appendix must be sent to EPA with five copies of the EIS for filing. If the appendix is too bulky to be circulated, it instead must be placed in conveniently accessible locations or furnished directly to commentors upon request. If it is not circulated with the EIS, the Notice of Availability published by EPA must so state, giving a telephone number to enable potential commentors to locate or request copies of the appendix promptly.

Material that is not directly related to preparation of the EIS should be incorporated by reference. This would include other EISs, research papers in the general literature, technical background papers or other material that someone with technical training could use to evaluate the analysis of the proposal. These must be made available, either by citing the literature, furnishing copies to central locations, or sending copies directly to commentors upon request.

Care must be taken in all cases to ensure that material incorporated by reference, and the occasional appendix that does not accompany the EIS, are in fact available for the full minimum public comment period.

26a. Q. How detailed must an EIS index be?

A. The EIS index should have a level of detail sufficient to focus on areas of the EIS of reasonable interest to any reader. It cannot be restricted to the most important topics. On the other hand, it need not identify every conceivable term or phrase in the EIS. If an agency believes that the reader is reasonably likely to be interested in a topic, it should be included.

26b. Q. Is a keyword index required?

A. No. A keyword index is a relatively short list of descriptive terms that identifies the key concepts or subject areas in a document. For example it could consist of 20 terms which describe the most significant aspects of an EIS that a future researcher would need: type of proposal, type of impacts, type of environment, geographical area, sampling or modelling methodologies used. This technique permits the compilation of EIS data banks, by facilitating quick and inexpensive access to stored materials. While a keyword index is not required by the regulations, it could be a useful addition for several reasons. First, it can be useful as a quick index for reviewers of the EIS, helping to focus on areas of interest. Second, if an agency keeps a listing of the keyword indexes of the EISs it produces, the EIS preparers themselves will have quick access to similar research data and methodologies to aid their future EIS work. Third, a keyword index will be needed to make an EIS available to future researchers using EIS data banks that are being developed. Preparation of such an index now when the document is produced will save a later effort when the data banks become operational.

27a. Q. If a consultant is used in preparing an EIS, must the list of preparers identify members of the consulting firm as well as the agency NEPA staff who were primarily responsible?

A. Section 1502.17 requires identification of the names and qualifications of persons who were primarily responsible for preparing the EIS or significant background papers, including basic components of the statement. This means that members of a consulting firm preparing material that is to become part of the EIS must be identified. The EIS should identify these individuals even though the consultant's contribution may have been modified by the agency.

27b. Q. Should agency staff involved in reviewing and editing the EIS also be included in the list of preparers?

A. Agency personnel who wrote basic components of the EIS or significant background papers must, of course, be identified. The EIS should also list the technical editors who reviewed or edited the statements.

27c. Q. How much information should be included on each person listed?

A. The list of preparers should normally not exceed two pages. Therefore, agencies must determine which individuals had *primary* responsibility and need not identify individuals with minor involvement. The list of preparers should include a very brief identification of the individuals involved, their qualifications (expertise, professional disciplines) and the specific portion of the EIS for which they are responsible. This may be done in tabular form to cut down on length. A line or two for each person's qualifications should be sufficient.

28. Q. May an agency file xerox copies of an EIS with EPA pending the completion of printing the document?

A. Xerox copies of an EIS may be filed with EPA prior to printing only if the xerox copies are simultaneously made available to other agencies and the public. Section 1506.9 of the regulations, which governs EIS filing, specifically requires Federal agencies to file EISs with EPA no earlier than the EIS is distributed to the public. However, this section does not prohibit xeroxing as a form of reproduction and distribution. When an agency chooses xeroxing as the reproduction method, the EIS must be clear and legible to permit ease of reading and ultimate microfiching of the EIS. Where color graphs are important to the EIS, they should be reproduced and circulated with the xeroxed copy.

29a. Q. What response must an agency provide to a comment on a draft EIS which states that the EIS's methodology is inadequate or inadequately explained? For example, what level of detail must an agency include in its response to a simple postcard comment making such an allegation?

A. Appropriate responses to comments are described in Section 1503.4. Normally the responses should result in changes in the text of the EIS, not simply a separate answer at the back of the document. But, in addition, the agency must state what its response was, and if the agency decides that no substantive response to a comment is necessary, it must explain briefly why.

An agency is not under an obligation to issue a lengthy reiteration of its methodology for any portion of an EIS if the only comment addressing the methodology is a simple complaint that the EIS methodology is inadequate. But agencies must respond to comments, however brief, which are specific in their criticism of agency methodology. For example, if a commentor on an EIS said that an agency's air quality dispersion analysis or methodology was inadequate, and the agency had included a discussion of that analysis in the EIS, little if anything need be added in response to such a comment. However, if the commentor said that the dispersion analysis was inadequate because of its use of a certain computational technique, or that a dispersion analysis was inadequately explained because computational techniques were not included or referenced, then the agency would have to respond in a substantive and meaningful way to such a comment.

Federal Register / Vol. 46, No. 55 / Monday, March 23, 1981 / Rules and Regulations   **18035**

If a number of comments are identical or very similar, agencies may group the comments and prepare a single answer for each group. Comments may be summarized if they are especially voluminous. The comments or summaries must be attached to the EIS regardless of whether the agency believes they merit individual discussion in the body of the final EIS.

29b. Q. How must an agency respond to a comment on a draft EIS that raises a new alternative not previously considered in the draft EIS?

A. This question might arise in several possible situations. First, a commentor on a draft EIS may indicate that there is a possible alternative which, in the agency's view, is not a reasonable alternative. Section 1502.14(a). If that is the case, the agency must explain why the comment does not warrant further agency response, citing authorities or reasons that support the agency's position and, if appropriate, indicate those circumstances which would trigger agency reappraisal or further response. Section 1503.4(a). For example, a commentor on a draft EIS on a coal fired power plant may suggest the alternative of using synthetic fuel. The agency may reject the alternative with a brief discussion (with authorities) of the unavailability of synthetic fuel within the time frame necessary to meet the need and purpose of the proposed facility.

A second possibility is that an agency may receive a comment indicating that a particular alternative, while reasonable, should be modified somewhat, for example, to achieve certain mitigation benefits, or for other reasons. If the modification is reasonable, the agency should include a discussion of it in the final EIS. For example, a commentor on a draft EIS on a proposal for a pumped storage power facility might suggest that the applicant's proposed alternative should be enhanced by the addition of certain reasonable mitigation measures, including the purchase and setaside of a wildlife preserve to substitute for the tract to be destroyed by the project. The modified alternative including the additional mitigation measures should be discussed by the agency in the final EIS.

A third slightly different possibility is that a comment on a draft EIS will raise an alternative which is a minor variation of one of the alternatives discussed in the draft EIS, but this variation was not given any consideration by the agency. In such a case, the agency should develop and evaluate the new alternative, if it is reasonable, in the final EIS. If it is qualitatively within the spectrum of alternatives that were discussed in the draft, a supplemental draft will not be needed. For example, a commentor on a draft EIS to designate a wilderness area within a National Forest might reasonably identify a specific tract of the forest, and urge that it be considered for designation. If the draft EIS considered designation of a range of alternative tracts which encompassed forest area of similar quality and quantity, no supplemental EIS would have to be prepared. The agency could fulfill its obligation by addressing that specific alternative in the final EIS.

As another example, an EIS on an urban housing project may analyze the alternatives of constructing 2,000, 4,000, or 6,000 units. A commentor on the draft EIS might urge the consideration of constructing 5,000 units utilizing a different configuration of buildings. This alternative is within the spectrum of alternatives already considered, and, therefore, could be addressed in the final EIS.

A fourth possibility is that a commentor points out an alternative which is not a variation of the proposal or of any alternative discussed in the draft impact statement, and is a reasonable alternative that warrants serious agency response. In such a case, the agency must issue a supplement to the draft EIS that discusses this new alternative. For example, a commentor on a draft EIS on a nuclear power plant might suggest that a reasonable alternative for meeting the projected need for power would be through peak load management and energy conservation programs. If the permitting agency has failed to consider that approach in the Draft EIS, and the approach cannot be dismissed by the agency as unreasonable, a supplement to the Draft EIS, which discusses that alternative, must be prepared. (If necessary, the same supplement should also discuss substantial changes in the proposed action or significant new circumstances or information, as required by Section 1502.9(c)(1) of the Council's regulations.)

If the new alternative was not raised by the commentor during scoping, but could have been, commentors may find that they are unpersuasive in their efforts to have their suggested alternative analyzed in detail by the agency. However, if the new alternative is discovered or developed later, and it could not reasonably have been raised during the scoping process, then the agency must address it in a supplemental draft EIS. The agency is, in any case, ultimately responsible for preparing an adequate EIS that considers all alternatives.

30. Q. When a cooperating agency with jurisdiction by law intends to adopt a lead agency's EIS and it is not satisfied with the adequacy of the document, may the cooperating agency adopt only the part of the EIS with which it is satisfied? If so, would a cooperating agency with jurisdiction by law have to prepare a separate EIS or EIS supplement covering the areas of disagreement with the lead agency?

A. Generally, a cooperating agency may adopt a lead agency's EIS without recirculating it if it concludes that its NEPA requirements and its comments and suggestions have been satisfied. Section 1506.3(a), (c). If necessary, a cooperating agency may adopt only a portion of the lead agency's EIS and may reject that part of the EIS with which it disagrees, stating publicly why it did so. Section 1506.3(a).

A cooperating agency with jurisdiction by law (e.g., an agency with independent legal responsibilities with respect to the proposal) has an independent legal obligation to comply with NEPA. Therefore, if the cooperating agency determines that the EIS is wrong or inadequate, it must prepare a supplement to the EIS, replacing or adding any needed information, and must circulate the supplement as a draft for public and agency review and comment. A final supplemental EIS would be required before the agency could take action. The adopted portions of the lead agency EIS should be circulated with the supplement. Section 1506.3(b). A cooperating agency with jurisdiction by law will have to prepare its own Record of Decision for its action, in which it must explain how it reached its conclusions. Each agency should explain how and why its conclusions differ, if that is the case, from those of other agencies which issued their Records of Decision earlier.

An agency that did not cooperate in preparation of an EIS may also adopt an EIS or portion thereof. But this would arise only in rare instances, because an agency adopting an EIS for use in its own decision normally would have been a cooperating agency. If the proposed action for which the EIS was prepared is substantially the same as the proposed action of the adopting agency, the EIS may be adopted as long as it is recirculated as a final EIS and the agency announces what it is doing. This would be followed by the 30-day review period and issuance of a Record of Decision by the adopting agency. If the proposed action by the adopting agency is not substantially the same as that in

18036 **Federal Register** / Vol. 46, No. 55 / Monday, March 23, 1981 / Rules and Regulations

the EIS (i.e., if an EIS on one action is being adapted for use in a decision on another action), the EIS would be treated as a draft and circulated for the normal public comment period and other procedures. Section 1506.3(b).

31a. Q. Do the Council's NEPA regulations apply to independent regulatory agencies like the Federal Energy Regulatory Commission (FERC) and the Nuclear Regulatory Commission?

A. The statutory requirements of NEPA's Section 102 apply to "all agencies of the federal government." The NEPA regulations implement the procedural provisions of NEPA as set forth in NEPA's Section 102(2) for all agencies of the federal government. The NEPA regulations apply to independent regulatory agencies, however, they do not direct independent regulatory agencies or other agencies to make decisions in any particular way or in a way inconsistent with an agency's statutory charter. Sections 1500.3, 1500.6, 1507.1, and 1507.3.

31b. Q. Can an Executive Branch agency like the Department of the Interior adopt an EIS prepared by an independent regulatory agency such as FERC?

A. If an independent regulatory agency such as FERC has prepared an EIS in connection with its approval of a proposed project, an Executive Branch agency (e.g., the Bureau of Land Management in the Department of the Interior) may, in accordance with Section 1506.3, adopt the EIS or a portion thereof for its use in considering the same proposal. In such a case the EIS must, to the satisfaction of the adopting agency, meet the standards for an adequate statement under the NEPA regulations (including scope and quality of analysis of alternatives) and must satisfy the adopting agency's comments and suggestions. If the independent regulatory agency fails to comply with the NEPA regulations, the cooperating or adopting agency may find that it is unable to adopt the EIS, thus forcing the preparation of a new EIS or EIS Supplement for the same action. The NEPA regulations were made applicable to all federal agencies in order to avoid this result, and to achieve uniform application and efficiency of the NEPA process.

32. Q. Under what circumstances do old EISs have to be supplemented before taking action on a proposal?

A. As a rule of thumb, if the proposal has not yet been implemented, or if the EIS concerns an ongoing program, EISs that are more than 5 years old should be carefully reexamined to determine if the

criteria in Section 1502.9 compel preparation of an EIS supplement.

If an agency has made a substantial change in a proposed action that is relevant to environmental concerns, or if there are significant new circumstances or information relevant to environmental concerns and bearing on the proposed action or its impacts, a supplemental EIS must be prepared for an old EIS so that the agency has the best possible information to make any necessary substantive changes in its decisions regarding the proposal. Section 1502.9(c).

33a. Q. When must a referral of an interagency disagreement be made to the Council?

A. The Council's referral procedure is a *pre-decision* referral process for interagency disagreements. Hence, Section 1504.3 requires that a referring agency must deliver its referral to the Council not later than 25 days after publication by EPA of notice that the final EIS is available (unless the lead agency grants an extension of time under Section 1504.3(b)).

33b. Q. May a referral be made after this issuance of a Record of Decision?

A. No, except for cases where agencies provide an internal appeal procedure which permits simultaneous filing of the final EIS and the record of decision (ROD). Section 1506.10(b)(2). Otherwise, as stated above, the process is a pre-decision referral process. Referrals must be made within 25 days after the notice of availability of the final EIS, whereas the final decision (ROD) may not be made or filed until after 30 days from the notice of availability of the EIS. Sections 1504.3(b), 1506.10(b). If a lead agency has granted an extension of time for another agency to take action on a referral, the ROD may not be issued until the extension has expired.

34a. Q. Must Records of Decision (RODs) be made public? How should they be made available?

A. Under the regulations, agencies must prepare a "concise *public* record of decision," which contains the elements specified in Section 1505.2. This public record may be integrated into any other decision record prepared by the agency, or it may be separate if decision documents are not normally made public. The Record of Decision is intended by the Council to be an environmental document (even though it is not explicitly mentioned in the definition of "environmental document" in Section 1508.10). Therefore, it must be made available to the public through appropriate public notice as required by Section 1506.6(b). However, there is no specific requirement for publication of

the ROD itself, either in the **Federal Register** or elsewhere.

34b. Q. May the summary section in the final Environmental Impact Statement substitute for or constitute an agency's Record of Decision?

A. No. An environmental impact statement is supposed to inform the decisionmaker before the decision is made. Sections 1502.1, 1505.2. The Council's regulations provide for a 30-day period after notice is published that the final EIS has been filed with EPA before the agency may take final action. During that period, in addition to the agency's own internal final review, the public and other agencies can comment on the final EIS prior to the agency's final action on the proposal. In addition, the Council's regulations make clear that the requirements for the summary in an EIS are not the same as the requirements for a ROD. Sections 1502.12 and 1505.2.

34c. Q. What provisions should Records of Decision contain pertaining to mitigation and monitoring?

A. Lead agencies "shall include appropriate conditions [including mitigation measures and monitoring and enforcement programs] in grants, permits or other approvals" and shall "condition funding of actions on mitigation." Section 1505.3. Any such measures that are adopted must be explained and committed in the ROD.

The reasonable alternative mitigation measures and monitoring programs should have been addressed in the draft and final EIS. The discussion of mitigation and monitoring in a Record of Decision must be more detailed than a general statement that mitigation is being required, but not so detailed as to duplicate discussion of mitigation in the EIS. The Record of Decision should contain a concise summary identification of the mitigation measures which the agency has committed itself to adopt.

The Record of Decision must also state whether all practicable mitigation measures have been adopted, and if not, why not. Section 1505.2(c). The Record of Decision must identify the mitigation measures and monitoring and enforcement programs that have been selected and plainly indicate that they are adopted as part of the agency's decision. If the proposed action is the issuance of a permit or other approval, the specific details of the mitigation measures shall then be included as appropriate conditions in whatever grants, permits, funding or other approvals are being made by the federal agency. Section 1505.3 (a), (b). If the proposal is to be carried out by the federal agency itself, the Record of Decision should delineate the mitigation and monitoring measures in sufficient detail to constitute an enforceable commitment, or incorporate by reference the portions of the EIS that do so.

34d. Q. What is the enforceability of a Record of Decision?

A. Pursuant to generally recognized principles of federal administrative law, agencies will be held accountable for preparing Records of Decision that conform to the decisions actually made and for carrying out the actions set forth in the Records of Decision. This is based on the principle that an agency must comply with its own decisons and regulations once they are adopted. Thus, the terms of a Record of Decision are enforceable by agencies and private parties. A Record of Decision can be used to compel compliance with or execution of the mitigation measures identified therein.

35. Q. How long should the NEPA process take to complete?

A. When an EIS is required, the process obviously will take longer than when an EA is the only document prepared. But the Council's NEPA regulations encourage streamlined review, adoption of deadlines, elimination of duplicative work, eliciting suggested alternatives and other comments early through scoping, cooperation among agencies, and consultation with applicants during project planning. The Council has advised agencies that under the new NEPA regulations even large complex energy projects would require only about 12 months for the completion of the entire EIS process. For most major actions, this period is well within the planning time that is needed in any event, apart from NEPA.

The time required for the preparation of program EISs may be greater. The Council also recognizes that some projects will entail difficult long-term planning and/or the acquisition of certain data which of necessity will require more time for the preparation of the EIS. Indeed, some proposals should be given more time for the thoughtful preparation of an EIS and development of a decision which fulfills NEPA's substantive goals.

For cases in which only an environmental assessment will be prepared, the NEPA process should take no more than 3 months, and in many cases substantially less, as part of the normal analysis and approval process for the action.

36a. Q. How long and detailed must an environmental assessment (EA) be?

A. The environmental assessment is a concise public document which has three defined functions. (1) It briefly provides sufficient evidence and analysis for determining whether to prepare an EIS; (2) it aids an agency's compliance with NEPA when no EIS is necessary, i.e., it helps to identify better alternatives and mitigation measures; and (3) it facilitates preparation of an EIS when one is necessary. Section 1508.9(a).

Since the EA is a concise document, it should not contain long descriptions or detailed data which the agency may have gathered. Rather, it should contain a brief discussion of the need for the proposal, alternatives to the proposal, the environmental impacts of the proposed action and alternatives, and a list of agencies and persons consulted. Section 1508.9(b).

While the regulations do not contain page limits for EA's, the Council has generally advised agencies to keep the length of EAs to not more than approximately 10–15 pages. Some agencies expressly provide page guidelines (e.g., 10–15 pages in the case of the Army Corps). To avoid undue length, the EA may incorporate by reference background data to support its concise discussion of the proposal and relevant issues.

36b. Q. Under what circumstances is a lengthy EA appropriate?

A. Agencies should avoid preparing lengthy EAs except in unusual cases, where a proposal is so complex that a concise document cannot meet the goals of Section 1508.9 *and* where it is extremely difficult to determine whether the proposal could have significant environmental effects. In most cases, however, a lengthy EA indicates that an EIS is needed.

37a. Q. What is the level of detail of information that must be included in a finding of no significant impact (FONSI)?

A. The FONSI is a document in which the agency briefly explains the reasons why an action will not have a significant effect on the human environment and, therefore, why an EIS will not be prepared. Section 1508.13. The finding itself need not be detailed, but must succinctly state the reasons for deciding that the action will have no significant environmental effects, and, if relevant, must show which factors were weighted most heavily in the determination. In addition to this statement, the FONSI must include, summarize, or attach and incorporate by reference, the environmental assessment.

37b. Q. What are the criteria for deciding whether a FONSI should be made available for public review for 30 days before the agency's final determination whether to prepare an EIS?

A. Public review is necessary, for example, (a) if the proposal is a borderline case, i.e., when there is a reasonable argument for preparation of an EIS; (b) if it is an unusual case, a new kind of action, or a precedent setting case such as a first intrusion of even a minor development into a pristine area; (c) when there is either scientific or public controversy over the proposal; or (d) when it involves a proposal which is or is closely similar to one which normally requires preparation of an EIS. Sections 1501.4(e)(2), 1508.27. Agencies also must allow a period of public review of the FONSI if the proposed action would be located in a floodplain or wetland. E.O. 11988, Sec. 2(a)(4); E.O. 11990, Sec. 2(b).

38. Q. Must (EAs) and FONSIs be made public? If so, how should this be done?

A. Yes, they must be available to the public. Section 1506.6 requires agencies to involve the public in implementing their NEPA procedures, and this includes public involvement in the preparation of EAs and FONSIs. These are public "environmental documents" under Section 1506.6(b), and, therefore, agencies must give public notice of their availability. A combination of methods may be used to give notice, and the methods should be tailored to the needs of particular cases. Thus, a **Federal Register** notice of availability of the documents, coupled with notices in national publications and mailed to interested national groups might be appropriate for proposals that are national in scope. Local newspaper notices may be more appropriate for regional or site-specific proposals.

The objective, however, is to notify all interested or affected parties. If this is not being achieved, then the methods should be reevaluated and changed. Repeated failure to reach the interested or affected public would be interpreted as a violation of the regulations.

39. Q. Can an EA and FONSI be used to impose enforceable mitigation measures, monitoring programs, or other requirements, even though there is no requirement in the regulations in such cases for a formal Record of Decision?

A. Yes. In cases where an environmental assessment is the appropriate environmental document, there still may be mitigation measures or alternatives that would be desirable to consider and adopt even though the impacts of the proposal will not be "significant." In such cases, the EA should include a discussion of these measures or alternatives to "assist

18038 Federal Register / Vol. 46, No. 55 / Monday, March 23, 1981 / Rules and Regulations

agency planning and decisionmaking" and to "aid an agency's compliance with [NEPA] when no environmental impact statement is necessary." Section 1501.3(b), 1508.9(a)(2). The appropriate mitigation measures can be imposed as enforceable permit conditions, or adopted as part of the agency final decision in the same manner mitigation measures are adopted in the formal Record of Decision that is required in EIS cases.

40. Q. If an environmental assessment indicates that the environmental effects of a proposal are significant but that, with mitigation, those effects may be reduced to less than significant levels, may the agency make a finding of no significant impact rather than prepare an EIS? Is that a legitimate function of an EA and scoping?

A. Mitigation measures may be relied upon to make a finding of no significant impact only if they are imposed by statute or regulation, or submitted by an applicant or agency as part of the original proposal. As a general rule, the regulations contemplate that agencies should use a broad approach in defining significance and should not rely on the possibility of mitigation as an excuse to avoid the EIS requirement. Sections 1508.8, 1508.27.

If a proposal appears to have adverse effects which would be significant, and certain mitigation measures are then developed during the scoping or EA stages, the existence of such *possible* mitigation does not obviate the need for an EIS. Therefore, if scoping or the EA identifies certain mitigation possibilities without altering the nature of the overall proposal itself, the agency should continue the EIS process and submit the proposal, and the potential mitigation, for public and agency review and comment. This is essential to ensure that the final decision is based on all the relevant factors and that the full NEPA process will result in enforceable mitigation measures through the Record of Decision.

In some instances, where the proposal itself so integrates mitigation from the beginning that it is impossible to define the proposal without including the mitigation, the agency may then rely on the mitigation measures in determining that the overall effects would not be significant (e.g., where an application for a permit for a small hydro dam is based on a binding commitment to build fish ladders, to permit adequate down stream flow, and to replace any lost wetlands, wildlife habitat and recreational potential). In those instances, agencies should make the FONSI and EA available for 30 days of

public comment before taking action. Section 1501.4(e)(2).

Similarly, scoping may result in a redefinition of the entire project, as a result of mitigation proposals. In that case, the agency may alter its previous decision to do an EIS, as long as the agency or applicant resubmits the entire proposal and the EA and FONSI are available for 30 days of review and comment. One example of this would be where the size and location of a proposed industrial park are changed to avoid affecting a nearby wetland area.

[FR Doc. 81-8734 Filed 3-20-81; 8:45 am]

BILLING CODE 3125-01-M

DEPARTMENT OF TRANSPORTATION

National Highway Traffic Safety Administration

49 CFR Part 531

[Docket No. LVM 77-05; Notice 5]

Passenger Automobile Average Fuel Economy Standards; Exemption From Average Fuel Economy Standards

AGENCY: National Highway Traffic Safety Administration, Department of Transportation.

ACTION: Final decision to grant exemption from fuel economy standards.

SUMMARY: This notice exempts Excalibur Automobile Corporation (Excalibur) from the generally applicable average fuel economy standards of 19.0 miles per gallon (mpg) and 20.0 mpg for 1979 and 1980 model year passenger automobiles, respectively, and establishes alternative standards. The alternative standards are 11.5 mpg in the 1979 model year and 16.2 mpg in the 1980 model year.

DATES: The exemptions and alternative standards set forth in this notice apply in the 1979 and 1980 model years.

FOR FURTHER INFORMATION CONTACT: Robert Mercure, Office of Automotive Fuel Economy Standards, National Highway Traffic Safety Administration, 400 Seventh Street SW., Washington, D.C. 20590 (202-755-9384).

SUPPLEMENTARY INFORMATION: The National Highway Traffic Safety Administration (NHTSA) is exempting Excalibur from the generally applicable average fuel economy standards for the 1979 and 1980 model year and establishing alternative standards applicable to that company in those model years. This exemption is issued under the authority of section 502(c) of the Motor Vehicle Information and Cost

Savings Act, as amended (the Act) (15 U.S.C. 2002(c)). Section 502(c) provides that a manufacturer of passenger automobiles that manufactures fewer than 10,000 passenger automobiles annually may be exempted from the generally applicable average fuel economy standard for a particular model year if that standard is greater than the low volume manufacturer's maximum feasible average fuel economy and if the NHTSA establishes an alternative standard applicable to that manufacturer at the low volume manufacturer's maximum feasible average fuel economy. Section 502(e) of the Act (15 U.S.C. 2002(e)) requires the NHTSA to consider:

(1) Technological feasibility;

(2) Economic practicability;

(3) The effect of other Federal motor vehicle standards on fuel economy; and

(4) The need of the Nation to conserve energy.

This final rule was preceded by a notice announcing the NHTSA's proposed decision to grant an exemption to Excalibur for the 1979 and 1980 model years (45 FR 50840, July 31, 1980). No comments were received during the 45-day comment period.

Based on its conclusions that it is not technologically feasible and economically practicable for Excalibur to improve the fuel economy of its 1979 and 1980 model year automobiles above an average of 11.5 and 16.2 mpg, respectively, that other Federal automobile standards did not affect achievable fuel economy beyond the extent considered in this analysis, and that the national effort to conserve energy will be negligibly affected by the granting of the requested exemptions, this agency concludes that the maximum feasible average fuel economy for Excalibur in the 1979 and 1980 model years is 11.5 mpg and 16.2 mpg, respectively. Therefore, NHTSA is exempting Excalibur from the generally applicable standards and is establishing alternative standards of 11.5 mpg for the 1979 model year and 16.2 mpg for the 1980 model year.

In consideration of the foregoing, 49 CFR Part 531 is amended by revising § 531.5(b)(5) to read as follows:

§ 531.5 Fuel economy standards.

* * * * *

(b) The following manufacturers shall comply with the fuel economy standards indicated below for the specified model years:

* * * * *

(5) Excalibur Automobile Corporation.

NEPA Deskbook

Appendix 20 Guidance Regarding NEPA Regulations

Guidance Regarding NEPA Regulations
(Council on Environmental Quality)
48 Fed. Reg. 34263 (July 28, 1983)

Federal Register / Vol. 48, No. 146 / Thursday, July 28, 1983 / Rules and Regulations   **34263**

COUNCIL ON ENVIRONMENTAL QUALITY

40 CFR Part 1500

Guidance Regarding NEPA Regulations

AGENCY: Council on Environmental Quality, Executive Office of the President.

ACTION: Information Only, Publication of Memorandum to Agencies Containing Guidance on Agency Implementation of NEPA Regulations.

SUMMARY: The Council on Environmental Quality, as part of its oversight of implementation of the National Environmental Policy Act, on August 14, 1981 requested comments from the public on how the various federal agencies are implementing the regulations promulgated by the Council in 1978 (40 CFR 1500 *et seq.*). The Council received 142 comments. Sixty-nine commenters represented business groups; forty represented state and local governments; fifteen represented environmental groups; thirteen represented federal agencies; and, five represented other interest groups or individuals. The Council staff summarized the comments received in a document which was subsequently made available to the public. On July 12, 1982 the Council published notice of the availability of this summary document in the **Federal Register**. The summary document identified a number of areas in which the comments indicate that agencies need to better manage the NEPA process.

On August 12, 1982 the Council held a public meeting to discuss the issue areas

identifed in the summary document. At that time representatives of environmental groups, industry groups, other federal agencies and individuals testified. Subsequent to the meeting the Council received several additional comments addressing the problem areas identifed in the summary document.

Based on the public comments received during this process, the Council is issuing the following guidance document to help officials manage the NEPA process in a more efficient fashion.

DATE: July 22, 1983.

FOR FURTHER INFORMATION CONTACT: Dinah Bear, General Counsel, Council on Environmental Quality, 722 Jackson Place, NW., Washington, D.C. 20006. (202) 395-5754.

A. Alan Hill,

Chairman.

Executive Office of the President

Council on Environmental Quality

722 Jackson Place, N.W.

Washington, D.C. 20006

July 22, 1983.

Memorandum

For: Heads of Federal Agencies
From: A. Alan Hill, Chairman
Re: Guidance Regarding NEPA Regulations

The Council on Environmental Quality (CEQ) regulations implementing the National Environmental Policy Act (NEPA) were issued on November 29, 1978. These regulations became effective for, and binding upon, most federal agencies on July 30, 1979, and for all remaining federal agencies on November 30, 1979.

As part of the Council's NEPA oversight responsibilities it solicited through an August 14, 1981, notice in the **Federal Register** public and agency comments regarding a series of questions that were developed to provide information on the manner in which federal agencies were implementing the CEQ regulations. On July 12, 1982, the Council announced the availability of a document summarizing the comments received from the public and other agencies and also identifying issue areas which the Council intended to review. On August 12, 1982, the Council held a public meeting to address those issues and hear any other comments which the public or other interested agencies might have about the NEPA process. The issues addressed in this guidance were identified during this process.

There are many ways in which agencies can meet their responsibilities

under NEPA and the 1978 regulations. The purpose of this document is to provide the Council's guidance on various ways to carry out activities under the regulations.

Scoping

The Council on Environmental Quality (CEQ) regulations direct federal agencies which have made a decision to prepare an environmental impact statement to engage in a public scoping process. Public hearings or meetings, although often held, are not required; instead the manner in which public input will be sought is left to the discretion of the agency.

The purpose of this process is to determine the scope of the EIS so that preparation of the document can be effectively managed. Scoping is intended to ensure that problems are identified early and properly studied, that issues of little significance do not consume time and effort, that the draft EIS is thorough and balanced, and that delays occasioned by an inadequate draft EIS are avoided. The scoping process should identify the public and agency concerns; clearly define the environmental issues and alternatives to be examined in the EIS including the elimination of nonsignificant issues; identify related issues which originate from separate legislation, regulation, or Executive Order (e.g. historic preservation or endangered species concerns); and identify state and local agency requirements which must be addressed. An effective scoping process can help reduce unnecessary paperwork and time delays in preparing and processing the EIS by clearly identifying all relevant procedural requirements.

In April 1981, the Council issued a "Memorandum for General Counsels, NEPA Liaisons and Participants in Scoping" on the subject of Scoping Guidance. The purpose of this guidance was to give agencies suggestions as to how to more effectively carry out the CEQ scoping requirement. The availability of this document was announced in the **Federal Register** at 46 FR 25461. It is still available upon request from the CEQ General Counsel's office.

The concept of lead agency (§ 1508.16) and cooperating agency (§ 1508.5) can be used effectively to help manage the scoping process and prepare the environmental impact statement. The lead agency should identify the potential cooperating agencies. It is incumbent upon the lead agency to identify any agency which may ultimately be involved in the proposed action, including any subsequent permitting

34264   **Federal Register** / Vol. 48, No. 146 / Thursday, July 28, 1983 / Rules and Regulations

actions. Once cooperating agencies have been identified they have specific responsibility under the NEPA regulations (40 CFR 1501.6). Among other things cooperating agencies have responsibilities to participate in the scoping process and to help identify issues which are germane to any subsequent action it must take on the proposed action. The ultimate goal of this combined agency effort is to produce an EIS which in addition to fulfilling the basic intent of NEPA, also encompasses to the maximum extent possible all the environmental and public involvement requirements of state and federal laws, Executive Orders, and administrative policies of the involved agencies. Examples of these requirements include the Fish and Wildlife Coordination Act, the Clean Air Act, the Endangered Species Act, the National Historic Preservation Act, the Wild and Scenic Rivers Act, the Farmland Protection Policy Act, Executive Order 11990 (Protection of Wetlands), and Executive Order 11998 (Floodplain Management).

It is emphasized that cooperating agencies have the responsibility and obligation under the CEQ regulations to participate in the scoping process. Early involvement leads to early identification of significant issues, better decisionmaking, and avoidance of possible legal challenges. Agencies with "jurisdiction by law" must accept designation as a cooperating agency if requested (40 CFR 1501.6).

One of the functions of scoping is to identify the public involvement/public hearing procedures of all appropriate state and federal agencies that will ultimately act upon the proposed action. To the maximum extent possible, such procedures should be integrated into the EIS process so that joint public meetings and hearings can be conducted. Conducting joint meetings and hearings eliminates duplication and should significantly reduce the time and cost of processing an EIS and any subsequent approvals. The end result will be a more informed public cognizant of all facets of the proposed action.

It is important that the lead agency establish a process to properly manage scoping. In appropriate situations the lead agency should consider designating a project coordinator and forming an interagency project review team. The project coordinator would be the key person in monitoring time schedules and responding to any problems which may arise in both scoping and preparing the EIS. The project review team would be established early in scoping and maintained throughout the process of

preparing the EIS. This review team would include state and local agency representatives. The review team would meet periodically to ensure that the EIS is complete, concise, and prepared in a timely manner.

A project review team has been used effectively on many projects. Some of the more important functions this review team can serve include: (1) A source of information, (2) a coordination mechanism, and (3) a professional review group. As an information source, the review team can identify all federal, state, and local environmental requirements, agency public meeting and hearing procedures, concerned citizen groups, data needs and sources of existing information, and the significant issues and reasonable alternatives for detailed analysis, excluding the non-significant issues. As a coordination mechanism, the team can ensure the rapid distribution of appropriate information or environmental studies, and can reduce the time required for formal consultation on a number of issues (e.g., endangered species or historic preservation). As a professional review group the team can assist in establishing and monitoring a tight time schedule for preparing the EIS by identifying critical points in the process, discussing and recommending solutions to the lead agency as problems arise, advising whether a requested analysis or information item is relevant to the issues under consideration, and providing timely and substantive review comments on any preliminary reports or analyses that may be prepared during the process. The presence of professionals from all scientific disciplines which have a significant role in the proposed action could greatly enhance the value of the team.

The Council recognizes that there may be some problems with the review team concept such as limited agency travel funds and the amount of work necessary to coordinate and prepare for the periodic team meetings. However, the potential benefits of the team concept are significant and the Council encourages agencies to consider utilizing interdisciplinary project review teams to aid in EIS preparation. A regularly scheduled meeting time and location should reduce coordination problems. In some instances, meetings can be arranged so that many projects are discussed at each session. The benefits of the concept are obvious: timely and effective preparation of the EIS, early identification and resolution of any problems which may arise, and elimination, or at least reduction of, the need for additional environmental

studies subsequent to the approval of the EIS.

Since the key purpose of scoping is to identify the issues and alternatives for consideration, the scoping process should "end" once the issues and alternatives to be addressed in the EIS have been clearly identified. Normally this would occur during the final stages of preparing the draft EIS and before it is officially circulated for public and agency review.

The Council encourages the lead agency to notify the public of the results of the scoping process to ensure that all issues have been identified. The lead agency should document the results of the scoping process in its administrative record.

The NEPA regulations place a new and significant responsibility on agencies and the public alike during the scoping process to identify all significant issues and reasonable alternatives to be addressed in the EIS. Most significantly, the Council has found that scoping is an extremely valuable aid to better decisionmaking. Thorough scoping may also have the effect of reducing the frequency with which proposed actions are challenged in court on the basis of an inadequate EIS. Through the techniques identified in this guidance, the lead agency will be able to document that an open public involvement process was conducted, that all reasonable alternatives were identified, that significant issues were identified and non-significant issues eliminated, and that the environmental public involvement requirements of all agencies were met, to the extent possible, in a single "one-stop" process.

Categorical Exclusions

Section 1507 of the CEQ regulations directs federal agencies when establishing implementing procedures to identify those actions which experience has indicated will not have a significant environmental effect and to categorically exclude them from NEPA review. In our August 1981 request for public comments, we asked the question "Have categorical exclusions been adequately identified and defined?".

The responses the Council received indicated that there was considerable belief that categorical exclusions were not adequately identified and defined. A number of commentators indicated that agencies had not identified all categories of actions that meet the categorical exclusion definition (§ 1508.4) or that agencies were overly restrictive in their interpretations of categorical exclusions. Concerns were expressed that agencies were requiring

Federal Register / Vol. 48, No. 146 / Thursday, July 28, 1983 / Rules and Regulations   34265

too much documentation for projects that were not major federal actions with significant effects and also that agency procedures to add categories of actions to their existing lists of categorical exclusions were too cumbersome.

The National Environmental Policy Act and the CEQ regulations are concerned primarily with those "major federal actions signficantly affecting the quality of the human environment" (42 U.S.C. 4332). Accordingly, agency procedures, resources, and efforts should focus on determining whether the proposed federal action is a major federal action significantly affecting the quality of the human environment. If the answer to this question is yes, an environmental impact statement must be prepared. If there is insufficient information to answer the question, an environmental assessment is needed to assist the agency in determining if the environmental impacts are significant and require an EIS. If the assessment shows that the impacts are not significant, the agency must prepare a finding of no significant impact. Further stages of this federal action may be excluded from requirements to prepare NEPA documents.

The CEQ regulations were issued in 1978 and most agency implementing regulations and procedures were issued shortly thereafter. In recognition of the experience with the NEPA process that agencies have had since the CEQ regulations were issued, the Council believes that it is appropriate for agencies to examine their procedures to ensure that the NEPA process utilizes this additional knowledge and experience. Accordingly, the Council strongly encourages agencies to re-examine their environmental procedures and specifically those portions of the procedures where "categorical exclusions" are discussed to determine if revisions are appropriate. The specific issues which the Council is concerned about are (1) the use of detailed lists of specific activities for categorical exclusions, (2) the excessive use of environmental assessments/findings of no significant impact and (3) excessive documentation.

The Council has noted some agencies have developed lists of specific activities which qualify as categorical exclusions. The Council believes that if this approach is applied narrowly it will not provide the agency with sufficient flexibility to make decisions on a project-by-project basis with full consideration to the issues and impacts that are unique to a specific project. The Council encourages the agencies to consider broadly defined criteria which

characterize types of actions that, based on the agency's experience, do not cause significant environmental effects. If this technique is adopted, it would be helpful for the agency to offer several examples of activities frequently performed by that agency's personnel which would normally fall in these categories. Agencies also need to consider whether the cumulative effects of several small actions would cause sufficient environmental impact to take the actions out of the categorically excluded class.

The Council also encourages agencies to examine the manner in which they use the environmental assessment process in relation to their process for identifying projects that meet the categorical exclusion definition. A report(1) to the Council indicated that some agencies have a very high ratio of findings of no significant impact to environmental assessments each year while producing only a handful of EIS's. Agencies should examine their decisionmaking process to ascertain if some of these actions do not, in fact, fall within the categorical exclusion definition, or, conversely, if they deserve full EIS treatment.

As previously noted, the Council received a number of comments that agencies require an excessive amount of environmental documentation for projects that meet the categorical exclusion definition. The Council believes that sufficient information will usually be available during the course of normal project development to determine the need for an EIS and further that the agency's administrative record will clearly document the basis for its decision. Accordingly, the Council strongly discourages procedures that would require the preparation of additional paperwork to document that an activity has been categorically excluded.

Categorical exclusions promulgated by an agency should be reviewed by the Council at the draft stage. After reviewing comments received during the review period and prior to publication in final form, the Council will determine whether the categorical exclusions are consistent with the NEPA regulations.

Adoption Procedures

During the recent effort undertaken by the Council to review the current NEPA regulations, several participants indicated federal agencies were not utilizing the adoption procedures as authorized by the CEQ regulations. The concept of adoption was incorporated into the Council's NEPA Regulations (40 CFR 1506.3) to reduce duplicative EISs prepared by Federal agencies. The

experiences gained during the 1970's revealed situations in which two or more agencies had an action relating to the same project; however, the timing of the actions was different. In the early years of NEPA implementation, agencies independently approached their activities and decisions. This procedure lent itself to two or even three EISs on the same project. In response to this situation the CEQ regulations authorized agencies, in certain instances, to adopt environmental impact statements prepared by other agencies.

In general terms, the regulations recognize three possible situations in which adoption is appropriate. One is where the federal agency participated in the process as a cooperating agency. (40 CFR 1506.3(c)). In this case, the cooperating agency may adopt a final EIS and simply issue its record of decision.(2) However, the cooperating agency must independently review the EIS and determine that its own NEPA procedures have been satisfied.

A second case concerns the federal agency which was not a cooperating agency, but is, nevertheless, undertaking an activity which was the subject of an EIS. (40 CFR 1506.3(b)). This situation would arise because an agency did not anticipate that it would be involved in a project which was the subject of another agency's EIS. In this instance where the proposed action is substantially the same as that action described in the EIS, the agency may adopt the EIS and recirculate (file with EPA and distribute to agencies and the public) it as a final EIS. However, the agency must independently review the EIS to determine that it is current and that its own NEPA procedures have been satisfied. When recirculating the final EIS the agency should provide information which identifies what federal action is involved.

The third situation is one in which the proposed action is not substantially the same as that covered by the EIS. In this case, any agency may adopt an EIS or a portion thereof by circulating the EIS as a draft or as a portion of the agency's draft and preparing a final EIS. (40 CFR 1506.3(a)). Repetitious analysis and time consuming data collection can be easily eliminated utilizing this procedure.

The CEQ regulations specifically address the question of adoption only in terms of preparing EIS's. However, the objectives that underlie this portion of the regulations—i.e., reducing delays and eliminating duplication—apply with equal force to the issue of adopting other environmental documents. Consequently, the Council encourages agencies to put in place a mechanism for

34266   Federal Register / Vol. 48, No. 146 / Thursday, July 28, 1983 / Rules and Regulations

adopting environmental assessments prepared by other agencies. Under such procedures the agency could adopt the environmental assessment and prepare a Finding of No Significant Impact based on that assessment. In doing so, the agency should be guided by several principles:

—First, when an agency adopts such an analysis it must independently evaluate the information contained therein and take full responsibility for its scope and content.

—Second, if the proposed action meets the criteria set out in 40 CFR 1501.4(e)(2), a Finding of No Significant Impact would be published for 30 days of public review before a final determination is made by the agency on whether to prepare an environmental impact statement.

Contracting Provisions

Section 1506.5(c) of the NEPA regulations contains the basic rules for agencies which choose to have an environmental impact statement prepared by a contractor. That section requires the lead or cooperating agency to select the contractor, to furnish guidance and to participate in the preparation of the environmental impact statement. The regulation requires contractors who are employed to prepare an environmental impact statement to sign a disclosure statement stating that they have no financial or other interest in the outcome of the project. The responsible federal official must independently evaluate the statement prior to its approval and take responsibility for its scope and contents.

During the recent evaluation of comments regarding agency implementation of the NEPA process, the Council became aware of confusion and criticism about the provisions of Section 1506.5(c). It appears that a great deal of misunderstanding exists regarding the interpretation of the conflict of interest provision. There is also some feeling that the conflict of interest provision should be completely eliminated.(3)

Applicability of § 1506.5(c)

This provision is only applicable when a federal lead agency determines that it needs contractor assistance in preparing an EIS. Under such circumstances, the lead agency or a cooperating agency should select the contractor to prepare the EIS.(4)

This provision does not apply when the lead agency is preparing the EIS based on information provided by a private applicant. In this situation, the private applicant can obtain its information from any source. Such

sources could include a contractor hired by the private applicant to do environmental, engineering, or other studies necessary to provide sufficient information to the lead agency to prepare an EIS. The agency must independently evaluate the information and is responsible for its accuracy.

Conflict of Interest Provisions

The purpose of the disclosure statement requirement is to avoid situations in which the contractor preparing the environmental impact statement has an interest in the outcome of the proposal. Avoidance of this situation should, in the Council's opinion, ensure a better and more defensible statement for the federal agencies. This requirement also serves to assure the public that the analysis in the environmental impact statement has been prepared free of subjective, self-serving research and analysis.

Some persons believe these restrictions are motivated by undue and unwarranted suspicion about the bias of contractors. The Council is aware that many contractors would conduct their studies in a professional and unbiased manner. However, the Council has the responsibility of overseeing the administration of the National Environmental Policy Act in a manner most consistent with the statute's directives and the public's expectations of sound government. The legal responsibilities for carrying out NEPA's objectives rest solely with federal agencies. Thus, if any delegation of work is to occur, it should be arranged to be performed in as objective a manner as possible.

Preparation of environmental impact statements by parties who would suffer financial losses if, for example, a "no action" alternative were selected, could easily lead to a public perception of bias. It is important to maintain the public's faith in the integrity of the EIS process, and avoidance of conflicts in the preparation of environmental impact statements is an important means of achieving this goal.

The Council has discovered that some agencies have been interpreting the conflicts provision in an overly burdensome manner. In some instances, multidisciplinary firms are being excluded from environmental impact statements preparation contracts because of links to a parent company which has design and/or construction capabilities. Some qualified contractors are not bidding on environmental impact statement contracts because of fears that their firm may be excluded from future design or construction contracts. Agencies have also applied the selection

and disclosure provisions to project proponents who wish to have their own contractor for providing environmental information. The result of these misunderstandings has been reduced competition in bidding for EIS preparation contracts, unnecessary delays in selecting a contractor and preparing the EIS, and confusion and resentment about the requirement. The Council believes that a better understanding of the scope of § 1506.5(c) by agencies, contractors and project proponents will eliminate these problems.

Section 1506.5(c) prohibits a person or entity entering into a contract with a federal agency to prepare an EIS when that party has at that time and during the life of the contract pecuniary or other interests in the outcomes of the proposal. Thus, a firm which has an agreement to prepare an EIS for a construction project cannot, at the same time, have an agreement to perform the construction, nor could it be the owner of the construction site. However, if there are no such separate interests or arrangements, and if the contract for EIS preparation does not contain any incentive clauses or guarantees of any future work on the project, it is doubtful that an inherent conflict of interest will exist. Further, § 1506.5(c) does not prevent an applicant from submitting information to an agency. The lead federal agency should evaluate potential conflicts of interest prior to entering into any contract for the preparation of environmental documents.

Selection of Alternatives in Licensing and Permitting Situations

Numerous comments have been received questioning an agency's obligation, under the National Environmental Policy Act, to evaluate alternatives to a proposed action developed by an applicant for a federal permit or license. This concern arises from a belief that projects conceived and developed by private parties should not be questioned or second-guessed by the government. There has been discussion of developing two standards to determining the range of alternatives to be evaluated: The "traditional" standard for projects which are initiated and developed by a Federal agency, and a second standard of evaluating only those alternatives presented by an applicant for a permit or license.

Neither NEPA nor the CEQ regulations make a distinction between actions initiated by a Federal agency and by applicants. Early NEPA case law, while emphasizing the need for a rigorous examination of alternatives, did

Federal Register / Vol. 48, No. 146 / Thursday, July 28, 1983 / Rules and Regulations

34267

not specifically address this issue. In 1981, the Council addressed the question in its document, "Forty Most Asked Questions Concerning CEQ's National Environmental Policy Act Regulations".(5) The answer indicated that the emphasis in determining the scope of alternatives should be on what is "reasonable". The Council said that, "Reasonable alternatives include those that are *practical or feasible* from the technical and economic standpoint and using common sense rather than simply *desirable* from the standpoint of the applicant."

Since issuance of that guidance, the Council has continued to receive requests for further clarification of this question. Additional interest has been generated by a recent appellate court decision. *Roosevelt Campobello International Park Commission* v. *E P.A.*(6) dealt with EPA's decision of whether to grant a permit under the National Pollutant Discharge Elimination System to a company proposing a refinery and deep-water terminal in Maine. The court discussed both the criteria used by EPA in its *selecting* of alternative sites to evaluate, and the substantive standard used to *evaluate* the sites. The court determined that EPA's choice of alternative sites was "focused by the primary objectives of the permit applicant . . ." and that EPA had limited its consideration of sites to only those sites which were considered feasible, given the applicant's stated goals. The court found that EPA's criteria for selection of alternative sites was sufficient to meet its NEPA responsibilities.

This decision is in keeping with the concept that an agency's responsibilities to examine alternative sites has always been "bounded by some notion of feasibility" to avoid NEPA from becoming "an exercise in frivolous boilerplate".(7) NEPA has never been interpreted to require examination of purely conjectural possibilities whose implementation is deemed remote and speculative. Rather, the agency's duty is to consider "alternatives as they exist and are likely to exist."(8) In the *Roosevelt Campobello* case, for example, EPA examined three alternative sites and two alternative modifications of the project at the preferred alternative site. Other factors to be developed during the scoping process—comments received from the public, other government agencies and institutions, and development of the agency's own environmental data—should certainly be incorporated into the decision of which alternatives to seriously evaluate in the EIS. There is,

however, no need to disregard the applicant's purposes and needs and the common sense realities of a given situation in the development of alternatives.

Tiering

Tiering of environmental impact statements refers to the process of addressing a broad, general program, policy or proposal in an initial environmental impact statement (EIS), and analyzing a narrower site-specific proposal, related to the initial program, plan or policy in a subsequent EIS. The concept of tiering was promulgated in the 1978 CEQ regulations; the preceding CEQ guidelines had not addressed the concept. The Council's intent in formalizing the tiering concept was to encourage agencies, "to eliminate repetitive discussions and to focus on the actual issues ripe for decisions at each level of environmental review."(9)

Despite these intentions, the Council perceives that the concept of tiering has caused a certain amount of confusion and uncertainty among individuals involved in the NEPA process. This confusion is by no means universal; indeed, approximately half of those commenting in response to our question about tiering (10) indicated that tiering is effective and should be used more frequently. Approximately one-third of the commentators responded that they had no experience with tiering upon which to base their comments. The remaining commentators were critical of tiering. Some commentators believed that tiering added an additional layer of paperwork to the process and encouraged, rather than discouraged, duplication. Some commentators thought that the inclusion of tiering in the CEQ regulations added an extra legal requirement to the NEPA process. Other commentators said that an initial EIS could be prepared when issues were too broad to analyze properly for any meaningful consideration. Some commentators believed that the concept was simply not applicable to the types of projects with which they worked; others were concerned about the need to supplement a tiered EIS. Finally, some who responded to our inquiry questioned the courts' acceptance of tiered EISs.

The Council believes that misunderstanding of tiering and its place in the NEPA process is the cause of much of this criticism. Tiering, of course, is by no means the best way to handle all proposals which are subject to NEPA analysis and documentation. The regulations do not require tiering; rather, they authorize its use when an agency determines it is appropriate. It is an

option for an agency to use when the nature of the proposal lends itself to tiered EIS(s).

Tiering does not add an additional legal requirement to the NEPA process. An environmental impact statement is required for proposals for legislation and other major Federal actions significantly affecting the quality of the human environment. In the context of NEPA, "major Federal actions" include adoption of official policy, formal plans, and programs as well as approval of specific projects, such as construction activities in a particular location or approval of permits to an outside applicant. Thus, where a Federal agency adopts a formal plan which will be executed throughout a particular region, and later proposes a specific activity to implement that plan in the same region, both actions need to be analyzed under NEPA to determine whether they are major actions which will significantly affect the environment. If the answer is yes in both cases, both actions will be subject to the EIS requirement, whether tiering is used or not. The agency then has one of two alternatives: Either preparation of two environmental impact statements, with the second repeating much of the analysis and information found in the first environmental impact statement, or tiering the two documents. If tiering is utilized, the site-specific EIS contains a summary of the issues discussed in the first statement and the agency will incorporate by reference discussions from the first statement. Thus, the second, or site-specific statement, would focus primarily on the issues relevant to the specific proposal, and would not duplicate material found in the first EIS. It is difficult to understand, given this scenario, how tiering can be criticized for adding an unnecessary layer to the NEPA process; rather, it is intended to streamline the existing process.

The Council agrees with commentators who stated that there are stages in the development of a proposal for a program, plan or policy when the issues are too broad to lend themselves to meaningful analysis in the framework of an EIS. The CEQ regulations specifically define a "proposal" as existing at, "that stage in the development of an action when an agency subject to [NEPA] has a goal and is actively preparing to make a decision on one or more alternative means of accomplishing the goal *and the effects can be meaningfully evaluated.*"(11) Tiering is not intended to force an agency to prepare an EIS before this stage is reached; rather, it is a technique to be used once meaningful analysis can be performed. An EIS is not required before that stage in the development of a proposal, whether tiering is used or not.

The Council also realizes that tiering is not well suited to all agency programs. Again, this is why tiering has been established as an *option* for the agency to use, as opposed to a requirement.

A supplemental EIS is required when an agency makes substantial changes in the proposed action relevant to environmental concerns, or when there are signifcant new circumstances or information relevant to environmental concerns bearing on the proposed action, and is optional when an agency otherwise determines to supplement an EIS.(12) The standard for supplementing an EIS is not changed by the use of tiering; there will no doubt be occasions when a supplement is needed, but the use of tiering should reduce the number of those occasions.

Finally, some commentators raised the question of courts' acceptability of tiering. This concern is understandable, given several cases which have reversed agency decisions in regard to a particular programmatic EIS. However, these decisions have never invalidated the concept of tiering, as stated in the CEQ regulations and discussed above. Indeed, the courts recognized the usefulness of the tiering approach in case law before the promulgation of the tiering regulation. Rather, the problems appear when an agency determines not to prepare a site-specific EIS based on the fact that a programmatic EIS was prepared. In this situation, the courts carefully examine the analysis contained in the programmatic EIS. A court may or may not find that the programmatic EIS contains appropriate analysis of impacts and alternatives to meet the adequacy test for the site-specific proposal. A recent decision by the Ninth Circuit Court of Appeals (13) invalidated an attempt by the Forest Service to make a determination regarding wilderness and non-wilderness designations on the basis of a programmatic EIS for this reason. However, it should be stressed that this and other decisions are not a repudiation of the tiering concept. In these instances, in fact, tiering has *not* been used; rather, the agencies have attempted to rely exclusively on programmatic or "first level" EISs which did not have site-specific information. No court has found that the tiering process as provided for in the CEQ regulations is an improper manner of implementing the NEPA process.

In summary, the Council believes that tiering can be a useful method of reducing paperwork and duplication when used carefully for appropriate types of plans, programs and policies which will later be translated into site-specific projects. Tiering should not be viewed as an additional substantive requirement, but rather a means of accomplishing the NEPA requirements in an efficient manner as possible.

Footnotes

(1) Environmental Law Institute, *NEPA In Action Environmental Offices in Nineteen Federal Agencies.* A Report To the Council on Environmental Quality, October 1981.

(2) Records of decision must be prepared by each agency responsible for making a decision, and cannot be adopted by another agency.

(3) The Council also received requests for guidance on effective management of the third-party environmental impact statement approach. However, the Council determined that further study regarding the policies behind this technique is warranted, and plans to undertake that task in the future.

(4) There is no bar against the agency considering candidates suggested by the applicant, although the Federal agency must retain its independence. If the applicant is seen as having a major role in the selection of the contractor, contractors may feel the need to please both the agency and the applicant. An applicant's suggestion, if any, to the agency regarding the choice of contractors should be one of many factors involved in the selection process.

(5) 46 FR 18026 (1981).

(6) 684 F.2d 1041 (1st Cir. 1982).

(7) *Vermont Yankee Nuclear Power Corp. v. NRDC.* 435 U.S. 519, 551 (1978).

(8) *Monarch Chemical Works, Inc. v. Exon.* 466 F.Supp. 639, 650 (1979), quoting *Carolina Environmental Study Group v. U.S.,* 510 F.2d 796, 801 (1975).

(9) Preamble, FR, Vol. 43, No. 230, p. 55984, 11/29/78.

(10) "Is tiering being used to minimizes repetition in an environmental assessment and in environmental impact statements?", 46 FR 41131, August 14, 1981.

(11) 40 CFR 1508.23 (emphasis added).

(12) 40 CFR 1502.9(c).

(13) *California v. Block.* 18 ERC 1149 (1982).

[FR Doc. 83–20522 Filed 7–27–83; 8:45 am]

BILLING CODE 3125–01–M

NEPA Deskbook

Appendix 21 NEPA Regulations; Incomplete or Unavailable Information

National Environmental Policy Act Regulations; Incomplete or Unavailable Information
(Counsel on Environmental Quality)
51 Fed. Reg. 15618 (Apr. 25, 1986)

15618   Federal Register / Vol. 51. No. 80 / Friday, April 25, 1986 / Rules and Regulations

COUNCIL ON ENVIRONMENTAL QUALITY

40 CFR Part 1502

National Environmental Policy Act Regulations; Incomplete or Unavailable Information

AGENCY: Council on Environmental Quality. Executive Office of the President.

ACTION: Final rule.

SUMMARY: The Council on Environmental Quality (CEQ) promulgates regulations, binding on all federal agencies. to implement the procedural provisions of the National Environmental Policy Act (NEPA). The regulations address the administration of the NEPA process. including preparation of environmental impact statements for major federal actions which significantly affect the quality of the human environment. On August 9. 1985. CEQ published a proposed amendment to one of these regulations (40 CFR 1502.22), which addresses incomplete or unavailable information in an environmental impact statement (EIS). 50 FR 32234. After reviewing the comments received in response to that proposal, the CEQ now issues the final amendment to that regulation. The final amendment requires all federal agencies to disclose the fact of incomplete or unavailable information when evaluating reasonably foreseeable significant adverse impacts on the human environment in an EIS, and to obtain that information if the overall costs of doing so are not exorbitant. If the agency is unable to obtain the information because overall costs are exorbitant or because the means to obtain it are not known, the agency must (1) affirmatively disclose the fact that such information is unavailable; (2) explain the relevance of the unavailable information; (3) summarize the existing credible scientific evidence which is relevant to the agency's evaluation of significant adverse impacts on the human environment; and (4) evaluate the impacts based upon theoretical approaches or research methods generally accepted in the scientific community. The amendment also specifies that impacts which have a low probability of occurrence but catastrophic consequences if they do occur. should be evaluated if the analysis is supported by credible scientific evidence and is not based on pure conjecture, and is within the rule of reason. The requirement to prepare a "worst case analysis" is rescinded.

The existing guidance regarding 40 CFR 1502.22, found in Question 20 of *Forty Most Asked Questions Concerning CEQ's National Environmental Policy Act Regulations*, 46 FR 18032 (1981), is hereby withdrawn. Guidance relevant to the amended regulation will be published after the regulation becomes effective.

EFFECTIVE DATE: May 27, 1986.

FOR FURTHER INFORMATION CONTACT: Dinah Bear, General Counsel, Council on Environmental Quality, 722 Jackson Place NW., Washington, DC 20006. (202) 395-5754.

Federal Register / Vol. 51, No. 80 / Friday, April 25, 1986 / Rules and Regulations   15619

SUPPLEMENTARY INFORMATION:

Executive Order 12291

Under Executive Order 12291, CEQ must judge whether a regulation is major and, therfore, whether a Regulatory Impact Analysis must be prepared. This regulation does not satisfy any of the criteria specified in section 1(b) of the Executive Order and, as such, does not constitute a major rulemaking. As required by Executive Order 12291, this regulation was submitted to the Office of Management and Budget (OMB) for review. There were no comments from OMB to CEQ regarding compliance with Executive Order 12291 in relationship to amendment of 40 CFR 1502.22.

Paperwork Reduction Act

The information collection requirements in this proposed rule were submitted for approval to OMB under the Paperwork Reduction Act of 1980, 44 U.S.C. 3501 *et seq.* No comments were submitted by OMB or the public on the information collection requirements.

Regulatory Flexibility Act

Under the Regulatory Flexibility Act, 5 U.S.C. 601 *et seq.*, CEQ is required to prepare a Regulatory Flexibility Analysis for proposed regulations which would have a significant impact on a substantial number of small entities. No analysis is required, however, when the Chairman of the Council certifies that the rule will not have a significant economic impact on a substantial number of small entities. Accordingly, I hereby certify, pursuant to 5 U.S.C. 605(b), that this final amendment would not have a significant impact on a substantial number of small entities.

Environmental Assessment

Although there are substantial legal questions as to whether entities within the Executive Office of the President are required to prepare environmental assessments, CEQ, consistent with its practice in 1978, has prepared a special environmental assessment and a Finding of No Significant Impact regarding amendment of this regulation, which is available to the public upon request. For the reasons stated in the Finding of No Significant Impact, CEQ has concluded that the amendment to 40 CFR 1502.22 will not have a significant impact on the quality of the human environment.

Background

The National Environmental Policy Act, signed into law by President Nixon on January 1, 1970, articulated national policy and goals for the nation, established the Council on Environmental Quality, and, among other federal agencies to assess the environmental impacts of and, among other things, required all federal agencies to assess the environmental impacts of and alternatives to proposals for major federal actions significantly affecting the quality of the human environment. The Council on Environmental Quality, charged with the duty of overseeing the implementation of NEPA, developed guidelines to aid federal agencies in assessing the environmental impacts of their proposals. A combination of agency practice, judicial decisions and CEQ guidance resulted in the development of what is commonly referred to as "the NEPA process", which includes the preparation of environmental impact statements for certain types of federal actions.

Because of complaints about paperwork and delays in projects caused by the NEPA process, and a perception that the problem was caused in part by lack of a uniform, binding authority, CEQ was directed in 1977 to promulgate binding regulations implementing the procedural provisions of NEPA. (Executive Order 11991, 3 CFR 123 (1978). Council was directed to specifically: "make the environmental impact statement process more useful to decisionmakers and the public; and to reduce paperwork and the accumulation of extraneous background data, in order to emphasize the need to focus on real environmental issues and alternatives." After undertaking an extensive process of review and comment with federal, state and local governmental officials, private citizens, business and industry representatives, and public interest organizations, the Council issued the NEPA regulations on November 29, 1978. 40 CFR 1500–1508 (1958). The regulations were hailed as a "significant improvement on prior EIS guidelines", (Letter, Chamber of Commerce of the United States, January 8, 1979), and became effective for, and binding upon, most federal agencies on July 30, 1979, and for all remaining federal agencies on November 29, 1979.

Since promulgation of the NEPA regulations, the Council has continually reviewed the regulations to identify areas where further interpretation or guidance is required.[1] No broad support for amendment of the regulations surfaced during review under the 1981 Vice President's Regulatory Relief Task Force; indeed, some recommended that, "CEQ's streamlining regulations for the implementation of NEPA requirements should receive full support from the Administration and the federal agencies". (Letter, National League of Cities, May 14, 1981). Although continual attention is required to ensure that the mandate of the regulations is being fulfilled, the regulations appear to be generally working well.

During the past two and a half years, however, the Council has received numerous requests from both government agencies and private parties to review and amend the regulation which addresses "incomplete or unavailable information" in the EIS process. That regulation currently reads as follows:

"Section 1502.22. Incomplete or unavailable information.

"When an agency is evaluating significant adverse effects on the human environment in an environmental impact statement and there are gaps in relevant information or scientific uncertainty, the agency shall always make clear that such information is lacking or that uncertainty exists.

"(a) If the information relevant to adverse impacts is essential to a reasoned choice among alternatives and is not known and the overall costs of obtaining it are not exorbitant, the agency shall include the information in the environmental impact statement.

"(b) If (1) the information relevant to adverse impacts is essential to a reasoned choice among alternatives and is not known and the overall costs of obtaining it are exorbitant or (2) the information relevant to adverse impacts is important to the decision and the means to obtain it are not known (e.g., the means for obtaining it are beyond the state of the art) the agency shall weigh the need for the action against the risk and severity of possible adverse impacts were the action to proceed in the face of uncertainty. If the agency proceeds, it shall include a worst case analysis and an indication of the probability or improbability of its occurrence." 40 CFR 1502.22.

On August 11, 1983, the Council proposed guidance regarding the "worst case analysis" requirement and asked for comments on the proposed guidance 48 FR 36486 (1983). The draft guidance suggested that an initial threshold of probability should be crossed before the requirements in 40 CFR 1502.22 became applicable. Although some

---

[1] See, *Forty Most Asked Questions Concerning CEQ's National Environmental Policy Act Regulations,* 46 FR 18026 (1981); *Memorandum for General Counsels, NEPA Liaisons and Participants in Scoping.* April 30, 1981 (available upon request from the General Counsel's office, CEQ); *Guidance Regarding NEPA Regulations,* 48 FR 34263 (1983).

15620   **Federal Register** / Vol. 51, No. 80 / Friday, April 25, 1986 / Rules and Regulations

commentators agreed with the guidance, others believed that the proposed threshold would weaken analysis of low probability and severe consequences impacts. Other writers suggested different approaches to the issue, or advocated amendment of the regulation rather than guidance. After reviewing the comments received in response to that proposal, the Council withdrew the proposed guidance, stating its intent to give the matter additional examination before publishing a new proposal. 49 FR 4803 (1984).

After many discussions with federal agency representatives and other interested parties in state governments, public interest groups, and business and industry, the Council published an Advance Notice of Proposed Rulemaking (ANPRM) for 40 CFR 1502.22, and stated that it was considering the need to amend the regulation. 49 FR 50744 (1984). The ANPRM posed five questions about the issue of incomplete or unavailable information in an EIS and asked for thoughtful written responses to the questions. The Council received 161 responses to the ANPRM. A majority of the commentators cited problems with the "worst case analysis" requirement, but recognized the need to address potential impacts in the face of incomplete or unavailable information. Many commentators thought that either the regulation itself or recent judicial decisions required agencies to go beyond the "rule of reason". These commentators suggested that the "rule of reason" should be made specifically applicable to the requirements of the regulation. A minority of commentators felt strongly that the original regulation was adequate and should not be amended.

On March 18, 1985, the Council held a meeting, open to the public, to discuss the comments received in response to the Advance Notice of Proposed Rulemaking. 50 FR 9535 (1985). Shortly after that meeting, the Council voted to amend the regulation. On August 9, 1985, CEQ published a proposed amendment to 40 CFR 1502.22 which read as follows:

"Section 1502.22. Incomplete of unavailable information.

"In preparing an environmental impact statement, the agency shall make reasonable efforts, in light of overall costs and state of the art, to obtain missing information which, in its judgment, is important to evaluating significant adverse impacts on the human environment that are reasonably foreseeable. If, for the reasons stated above, the agency is unable to obtain this missing information, the agency

shall include within the environmental impact statement (a) a statement that such information is missing, (b) a statement of the relevance of the missing information to evaluating significant adverse impacts on the human environment, (c) a summary of existing credible scientific evidence which is relevant to evaluating the significant adverse impacts on the human environment, and (d) the agency's evaluation of such evidence. 'Reasonably foreseeable' includes impacts which have catastrophic consequences, even if their probability of occurrence is low, provided that they have credible scientific support, are not based on pure conjecture, and are within the rule of reason." 50 FR 32238 (1985).

The Council received 184 comments in response to the proposed amendment: 81 comments from business and industry; 39 comments from private citizens; 30 comments from public interest groups; 15 comments from federal agencies; 14 comments from state governments; 4 comments from local governments; and one comment from a Member of Congress.

A majority of the commentators favored an amendment to the regulation, and supported the general approach of the proposed amendment. However, many of these writers offered specific suggestions for improving the proposal. Many commentators asked for definitions of terms used in the proposal, particularly for the phrase "credible scientific evidence." Some commentators wanted the Council to specify a particular methodology, such as risk assessment, as a substitute for a worst case analysis. Many commentators had specific comments about particular words or phrases used in the proposed amendment. Many commentators asked CEQ to provide further guidance or monitoring after the regulation was issued in final form.

A minority of commentators strongly opposed the amendment. Some of these writers were concerned over perceived changes in the first two paragraphs of the original regulation—requirements to disclose the fact that information is missing, and to obtain that information, if possible. Some commentators opposed deletion of the "worst case analysis" requirement. Other commentators believed that the proposed amendment did not require agencies to analyze or evaluate impacts in the face of incomplete or unavailable information. These comments, and others, will be discussed below in the section "Comments and the Council's Response".

On January 9, 1986, CEQ held a meeting, open to the public, to discuss the comments received in response to the proposed amendment. 50 FR 53061 (1985). A summary of the presentation made at that meeting is available from the Office of the General Counsel. Shortly after that meeting, the Council voted to proceed to final amendment of the regulation.

Purpose and Analysis of Final Amendment

CEQ is amending this regulation because it has concluded that the new requirements provide a wiser and more manageable approach to the evaluation of reasonably foreseeable significant adverse impacts in the face of incomplete or unavailable information in an EIS. The new procedure for analyzing such impacts in the face of incomplete or unavailable information will better inform the decisionmaker and the public. The Council's concerns regarding the original wording of 40 CFR 1502.22 are discussed at length in the preamble to the proposed amendment. 50 FR 32234 (1985). It must again be emphasized that the Council concurs in the underlying goals of the original regulation—that is, disclosure of the fact of incomplete or unavailable information; acquisition of that information if reasonably possible; and evaluation of reasonably foreseeable significant adverse impacts even in the absence of all information. These goals are based on sound public policy and early NEPA case law.[2] Rather, the need for amendment is based upon the Council's perception that the "worst case analysis" requirement is an unproductive and ineffective method of achieving those goals; one which can breed endless hypothesis and speculation.

The amended regulation applies when a federal agency is preparing an EIS on a major federal action sigificantly affecting the quality of the human environment and finds that there is incomplete or unavailable information relating to reasonably foreseeable significant adverse impacts on the environment. It retains the legal requirements of the first paragraph and subsection (a) of the environment and finds that there is incomplete or unavailable information relating to reasonably foreseeable significant adverse impacts on the environment. It retains the legal requirements of the first paragraph and subsection (a) of the

[2] See, for example, *Scientists' Institute for Public Information, Inc. v. Atomic Energy Commission,* 481 F.2d 1079 (D.C. Cir. 1973).

Federal Register / Vol. 51, No. 80 / Friday, April 25, 1986 / Rules and Regulations   15621

original regulation. Thus, when preparing an EIS, agencies must disclose the fact that there is incomplete or unavailable information. The term "incomplete information" refers to information which the agency cannot obtain because the overall costs of doing so are exorbitant. The term "unavailable information" refers to information which cannot be obtained because the means to obtain it are not known. If the incomplete information relevant to adverse impacts is essential to a reasoned choice among alternatives and the overall costs of obtaining it are not exorbitant, the agency must include the information in the EIS. The first paragraph and subsection (a) of the original regulation have been amended only insofar as the phrases "incomplete or unavailable information" (title of the original regulation) or "incomplete information" are substituted for synonymous phrases and the term "reasonably foreseeable" is added to modify "significant adverse impacts". These changes are made for consistency, clarity and readability.

Subsection (b) is amended to require federal agencies to include four items in an EIS if the information relevant to reasonably foreseeable significant adverse impacts remains unavailable because the overall costs of obtaining it are exorbitant or the means to obtain it are not known. The first step is disclosure of the fact that such information is incomplete or unavailable; that is, "a statement that such information is incomplete or unavailable". The second step is to discuss why this incomplete or unavailable information is relevant to the task of evaluating reasonably foreseeable significant adverse impacts; thus, "a statement of the relevance of the incomplete or unavailable information to evaluating reasonably foreseeable relevant to evaluating the reasonably foreseeable significant adverse impacts, impacts on the human environment". Fourth, the agency must use sound scientific methods to evaluate the potential impacts; or in the words of the regulation, "the agency's evaluation of such impacts based upon theoretical approaches or research methods generally accepted in the scientific community".

The regulation also makes clear that the reasonably foreseeable potential impacts which the agency must evaluate include those which have a low probability of occurrence but which would be expected to result in catastrophic consequences if they do occur. However, the regulation specifies that the analysis must be supported by

credible scientific evidence, not based on pure conjecture, and be within the rule of reason.

Subsection (b) deletes two substantive requirements from the same subsection of the original regulation, promulgated in 1978. First, it eliminates the requirement for agencies to "weigh the need for the action against the risk and severity of possible adverse impacts were the action to proceed in the face of uncertainty" while in the process of preparing an EIS. The Council believes that the weighing of risks and benefits for the particular federal proposal at hand is properly done after completion of the entire NEPA process, and is reflected in the Record of Decision. Nothing, of course, prohibits a decisionmaker from withdrawing a proposal during the course of EIS preparation.

Second, the regulation eliminates the "worst case analysis" requirement. It does not, however, eliminate the requirement for federal agencies to evaluate the reasonably foreseeable significant adverse impacts of an action, even in the face of unavailable or incomplete information. Rather, it specifies that the evaluation must be carefully conducted, based upon credible scientific evidence, and must consider those reasonably foreseeable significant adverse impacts which are based upon scientific evidence. The requirement to disclose all credible scientific evidence extends to responsible opposing views which are supported by theoretical approaches or research methods generally accepted in the scientific community (in other words, credible scientific evidence).

The regulation also requires that analysis of impacts in the face of unavailable information be grounded in the "rule of reason". The "rule of reason" is basically a judicial device to ensure that common sense and reason are not lost in the rubric of regulation. The rule of reason has been cited in numerous NEPA cases for the proposition that, "An EIS need not discuss remote and highly speculative consequences. . . . This is consistent with the (CEQ) Council on Environmental Quality Guidelines and the frequently expressed view that adequacy of the content of the EIS should be determined through use of a rule of reason." *Trout Unlimited* v. *Morton,* 509 F.2d 1276, 1283 (9th Cir. 1974). In the seminal case which applied the rule of reason to the problem of unavailable information, the court stated that, "[NEPA's] requirement that the agency describe the anticipated environmental effects of a proposed

action is subject to a rule of reason. The agency need not foresee the unforeseeable, but by the same token, neither can it avoid drafting an impact statement simply because describing the environmental effects of alternatives to particular agency action involves some degree of forecasting . . . 'The statute must be construed in the light of reason if it is not to demand what is, fairly speaking, not meaningfully possible . . .'" *Scientists' Institute for Public Information, Inc.* v. *Atomic Energy Commission,* 481 F.2d 1079, 1092 (D.C. 1973), citing *Calvert Cliffs' Coordinating Committee* v. *Atomic Energy Commission,* 499 F.2d 1109, 1114 (D.C. Cir. 1971). The Council's amendment supports and conforms with this direction.

The evaluation of impacts under § 1502.22 is an integral part of an EIS and should be treated in the same manner as those impacts normally analyzed in an EIS. The information included in the EIS to fulfill the requirements of § 1502.22 is properly a part of the "Environmental Consequences" section of the EIS (40 CFR 1502.16). As with other portions of the EIS, material substantiating the analysis fundamental to the evaluation of impacts may properly be included in an appendix to the EIS.

Comments and the Council's Response

Comment: CEQ does not make clear the fact that the first paragraph and paragraph (a) of 1502.22 would be eliminated in the proposed amendment. The preamble says nothing about radical changes in the research requirements of the existing regulation.

Response: The changes to the first paragraph and subsection (a) of the existing regulation in the proposed amendment were made primarily for the purpose of attempting to clarify and simplify the existing requirements. However, in response to a number of concerns regarding perceived changes in the legal requirements of these paragraphs, the Council has chosen to retain the original format of the regulation. The Council intends that the substitution of the phrase "incomplete or unavailable information" and "incomplete information" are taken from the title of the regulation itself, and are being inserted for the sake of consistency of terms and clarity.

Comment: The term "reasonable efforts" should be defined.

Response: The term "reasonable efforts" does not appear in the final regulation.

Comment: The proposed amendment drops the standard of "exorbitant costs"

15622   Federal Register / Vol. 51, No. 80 / Friday, April 25, 1986 / Rules and Regulations

and substitutes "overall costs." Substantively, the current standard should be retained. It is a purposefully high standard, intended to counter agencies' demonstrated reluctance to seek out information. The proposed standard is lax and undefined.

Response: The final regulation retains the original standard.

Comment: The term "state of the art" should be replaced with "the availability of adequate scientific or other analytical techniques or equipment".

Response: The term has been deleted in the final regulation, and the phrase "the means to obtain it are not known" is substituted. That phrase is meant to include circumstances in which the unavailable information cannot be obtained because adequate scientific knowledge, expertise, techniques or equipment do not exist.

Comment: The regulation should make clear that "overall costs" include, among other things, all economic costs and delays in timing. The "overall cost" requirement needs to be further defined to reflect items such as comparing low cost/high cost risk (and vice versa), costs of time in obtaining information, costs of delaying projects, benefit/cost ratio and outyear impact cost.

Response: CEQ intends that the term "overall costs" encompasses financial costs and other costs such as costs in terms of time (delay) and personnel. It does not intend that the phrase be interpreted as a requirement to weigh the cost of obtaining the information against the severity of the impacts, or to perform a cost-benefit analysis. Rather, it intends that the agency interpret "overall costs" in light of overall program needs.

Comment: The term "missing information" should be clarified or changed.

Response: The term "missing information" is deleted in the final regulation, and is replaced with the terms "incomplete or unavailable information" and "incomplete information". These terms are consistent with the title of the regulation.

Comment: The word "material" should be substituted for the word "significant" because the word "significant" is a term of art and incorporates consideration of controversy surrounding a proposal. The word "material" would be more appropriate.

Response: The final regulation retains the term "significant". "Significant" is indeed a term of art which connotes the type of environmental impact which the agency is obligated to analyze in an EIS. Consideration of controversy is one of

many factors which must be considered in determining whether an impact is "significant"; others include the degree to which the proposed action affects public health or safety, unique characteristics of the geographic area such as wetlands, wild and scenic rivers, etc., the degree to which the possible effects on the human environment are highly uncertain or involve unique or unknown risks, the cumulative impacts of an action, whether the action may adversely affect an endangered species or critical habitat, the degree to which an action may adversely affect historic areas, and whether the proposed action would violate another federal, state or local environmental law. 40 CFR 1508.27. The 1978 CEQ regulations differed from the earlier CEQ Guidelines in stating that the fact of controversy does not, alone, require preparation of an EIS; rather, it is one of many factors which the responsible official must bear in mind in judging the context and intensity of the potential impacts.

Comment: The term "in its judgment" gives agencies the administrative discretion to limit the data needed to prepare an EIS. It gives too much discretionary authority to agency officials to decide if they need to obtain the information. Suggest deleting "in its judgment" or adding "and with the concurrence of appropriate federal or state resource agencies".

Related Comment: It is important to allow an agency discretion to determine the extent of the investigation required to obtain information.

Response: The term "in its judgment" is deleted from the final regulation. However, deletion of that phrase is not intended to change the discretion currently vested in the agencies to determine the extent of the investigation required to obtain information. The agency's discretion must be used to make judgments about cost and scientific availability of the information.

Comment: The proposed amendment's definition of "reasonably foreseeable" should be strengthened or clarified or the use of this phrase should be changed.

Response: The term "reasonably foreseeable" has a long history of use in the context of NEPA law, and is included elsewhere in the CEQ NEPA regulations. 40 CFR 1508.8(b). Generally, the term has been used to describe what kind of environmental impacts federal agencies must analyze in an EIS; for example, ". . . if the [agency] makes a good faith effort in the survey to describe the *reasonably foreseeable* environmental impact of the program, alternatives to the program and their

reasonably foreseeable environmental impact, and the irreversible and irretrievable commitment of resources the program involves, we see no reason why the survey will not fully satisfy the requirements of [NEPA] section 102(C)." *Sierra Club* v. *Morton*, 379 F. Supp. 1254, 1259 (D. Col. 1974) (emphasis added). *See also, Town of Orangetown* v. *Gorsuch*, 718 F.2d 29, 34 (2d Cir. 1983); *NRDC* v. *NRC*, 685 F.2d 459, 476 (D.C. Cir. 1982). The term has also been used in the context of incomplete or unavailable information. *See Scientists' Institute for Public Information* v. *Atomic Energy Commission*, 481 F.2d 1079, 1092 (D.C. Cir. 1973).

Because of the controversy and nature of this particular regulation, CEQ has specified that in the context of 40 CFR 1502.22, the term "reasonably foreseeable" includes low probability/severe consequence impacts, provided that the analysis of such impacts is supported by credible scientific evidence, is not based on pure conjecture, and is within the rule of reason.

Comment: To prevent confusion, the proposed amendment should use either the term "credible scientific evidence" or "credible scientific support"—not both.

Response: The final regulation uses the term "credible scientific evidence" and deletes the term "credible scientific support".

Comment: The term "credible scientific evidence" should be defined. (A number of commentators offered specific suggestions for such a definition).

Response: The final regulation states that the agency's evaluation of impacts in the face of incomplete or unavailable information should be based upon theoretical approaches or research methods generally accepted in the scientific community. While this is admittedly a broad and general direction, CEQ is concerned that a narrow definition of "credible scientific evidence" would prove inappropriate in some circumstances, given the wide variety of actions which potentially fall under the auspices of this regulation. In many cases, the Council expects that "theoretical approaches or research methods generally accepted in the scientific community" will include commonly accepted professional practices such as literature searches and peer review.

Comment: The term "credible" should be deleted from the regulation, and all information should be considered.

Response: The definition of the word "credible" is, "capable of being

Federal Register / Vol. 51, No. 80 / Friday, April 25, 1986 / Rules and Regulations   **15623**

believed". *Webster's II New Riverside University Dictionary*, 1984. Information which is unworthy of belief should not be included in an EIS.

Comment: The term "scientific" is overly restrictive since measurement of an action's environmental effects may be grounded in, among other things, economic, historical or sociological information.

Response: In an EIS, federal agencies are responsible for analysis of significant environmental effects which include "ecological, aesthetic, historic, cultural, economic, social, or health, whether direct, indirect, or cumulative." 40 CFR 1508.8(b). The requirement to analyze these potential impacts or effects are not modified in any manner by the qualified "scientific evidence" in 40 CFR 1502.22. Rather, the term "scientific" is meant to imply that the evidence presented about the possibility of a certain impact should be based upon methodological activity, discipline or study. *Webster's II New Riverside University Dictionary*, 1984.

Comment: The amendment should include some recognized scientific method for evaluating uncertainty, such as, perhaps, a risk assessment approach.

Response: Because of the wide variety of types of incomplete or unavailable information which may potentially fall within the scope of this regulation, CEQ does not choose to specify a particular methodology. Rather, each agency should select that approach which best meets the goals of evaluating potential impacts in the face of unavailable information. Further, a requirement that a particular methodology be utilized might be soon outdated by scientific developments in a particular field.

Comment: The draft preamble states that the summary of credible scientific evidence must include all information from all sources, including minority or opposing viewpoints. What are "minority views" as they relate to credible scientific evidence?

Response: The preamble to the proposed amendment states that the requirement to disclose all credible scientific evidence extends to those views which are generally regarded as "minority views" within the scientific community. The final preamble adopts the term "responsible opposing views" as the preferred term, consistent with 40 CFR 1502.9(b). The requirement to include responsible opposing views reflects the belief that many times, particularly when dealing with questions of incomplete or unavailable information, there will be more than one point of view about potential environmental impacts which has scientific credibility. The regulation

requires an agency to include information about such views which have scientific credibility, rather than simply selecting one concept which supports its particular view. The responsible opposing views, must, of course, meet the criteria set out in subsection (b) of the regulation. Once such information is set out in the EIA, the agency must then use its own judgment and discretion to determine which viewpoint it believes is the most worthy of acceptance.

Comment: CEQ should indicate in the preamble that along with available scientific evidence, the views and conclusions of other government agencies and departments may be considered.

Response: The views and conclusion of other government agencies and departments are appropriately considered throughout the EIS process, beginning with the scoping process. Section 1502.22 does not limit involvement by other federal agencies in that process. Special attention should be paid to the views of those agencies with special expertise or jurisdiction by law in a particular field of inquiry. 40 CFR 1503.1(a)(1). The views of the public, and indeed all interested parties, are, of course also to be considered throughout the EIS process.

Comment: It should be made clear that the summary should be limited to credible scientific evidence only.

Response: This is precisely the requirement of the regulation itself. Again, credible scientific evidence includes both majority views and responsible opposing views, so long as these views meet the criteria in the regulation.

Comment: The regulation should require agencies to state the probability or improbability of the occurrence of the impacts which are identified.

Response: Although this requirement is not part of the final regulation, agencies are free to include this information in the EIS. The Council encourages the inclusion of such data when it is relatively reliable and when such information would help to put the analysis in perspective for the decisionmaker and other persons who read and comment on the EIS.

Comment: The fourth requirement, to include the agency's "evaluation" of the scientific evidence is vague. Presumably, what is meant is not a critique of the evidence, but an application of the evidence to predict impacts.

Response: The fourth requirement has been reworded so that it is clear that the agency is required to evaluate reasonably foreseeable significant

adverse impacts which significantly affect the quality of the human environment.

Comment: There is no requirement for the agencies to analyze impacts—the basic purpose of the regulation.

Response: The fourth requirement clearly states a requirement for the agencies to evaluate the reasonably foreseeable significant adverse impacts.

Comment: The final amendment should require agencies to address high probability/low or chronic impacts, as well as low probability/catastrophic impacts.

Response: If there is a high probability of an impact occurring, an agency is probably not in the realm of incomplete or unavailable information; hence, the impacts would be analyzed under the ordinary requirements in the "Environmental consequences" section. This section includes the analysis of the environmental impacts of the proposal and the environmental impacts of alternatives to the proposed action. 40 CFR 1502.16.

Comment: The preamble to the draft amendment errs in asserting that case law has established a precedent to go beyond the rule of reason and it ignores subsequent Ninth Circuit case law which applies the rule of reason to find that agencies properly refused to prepare a worst case analysis.

Response: The Ninth Circuit decision referred to in this comment held that a worst case analysis was not required because the lead agency had obtained the information which it needed; thus there was no incomplete or unavailable information to trigger the worst case analysis requirement. *Friends of Endangered Species* v. *Jantzen*, 760 F.2d 976 (9th Cir. 1985).

Comment: The threshold triggering the agency's responsibility to comply with 40 CFR 1502.22(b) is actually the existance of incomplete or unavailable information. "Scientific credibility" is not a threshold, but rather a standard to be applied to the analysis once the duty to comply is triggered.

Response: This comment is correct.

Comment: The Council should make clear in the regulation itself that "scientific credibility" is the threshold which triggers the regulation.

Response: "Scientific credibility" is the criterion for the evidence which should be used to evaluate impacts in the face of incomplete or unavailable information. The trigger to comply with the regulation itself is incomplete or unavailable information.

Comment: If the phrase "worst case analysis" is unacceptable, the Council should consider replacing the term with

15624   Federal Register / Vol. 51, No. 80 / Friday, April 25, 1986 / Rules and Regulations

its functional equivalent, "spectrum of events".

Response: In the final regulation, a lead agency is required to evaluate "impacts". "Impacts" or "effects" (the two are synonymous under CEQ regulations) are the subject of analysis in an EIS, not "events". Indeed, the event to be anticipated is the proposed action itself.

Under the final regulation, agencies are required to evaluate impacts for which there is credible scientific evidence. In implementing this section, agencies will have to determine the appropriate range of analysis based on the unique facts of each particular proposal. In some cases, this may amount to a spectrum or range of impacts. In other cases, the scope of suggested impacts may be much more limited. Credible scientific evidence should determine the scope of the analysis, as opposed to a pre-determined number of impacts.

Comment: A careful reading of the case law reveals that neither the Ninth Circuit nor any other circuit has required worst case analysis in the absence of scientific opinion, evidence, and experience, as alleged in the draft preamble.

Response: Although CEQ was asked to consider this question by various persons who were concerned about the effect in future cases of possible interpretations of judicial decisions involving the worst case analysis requirement, CEQ has amended the regulation because it believes, based on further review, that the worst case analysis requirement is flawed, and the new requirements provide a better and more logical means of dealing with the analysis of impacts in the face of incomplete or unavailable information in an EIS.

Comment: Deletion of the worst case requirement will weaken environmental protection.

Response: This assertion is incorrect. The amended regulation establishes a better approach to dealing with the issue of incomplete and unavailable information in an EIS. It is a less sensational approach, but one which is a more careful and professional approach to the analysis of impacts in the face of incomplete or unavailable information. It should improve the quality of the EIS and the decision which follows, and, hence, strengthen environmental protection, in conformance with the purpose and goals of NEPA. 42 U.S.C. 4321, 4331. It will provide the public and the decisionmaker with an improved and more informed basis for the decision.

Comment: Before eliminating the term "worst case analysis", the Council should determine whether a worst case analysis is really impossible to prepare, or whether it is being resisted by agencies unwilling to learn because they do not want to admit the adverse impacts of their preferred programs.

Response: The Council does not maintain that a worst case analysis is impossible to prepare; however, it does view the worst case analysis requirement as a flawed technique to analyze impacts in the face of incomplete or unavailable information. The new requirement will provide more accurate and relevant information about reasonably foreseeable significant adverse impacts. To the extent that agencies were reluctant to discuss such impacts under the requirements of the original regulation, the amended regulation will not offer them an escape route.

Comment: The expressed need for clarification can be met by simply adding the "rule of reason" to the existing regulation.

Response: While the "rule of reason" is indeed added to the language of the regulation, CEQ believes that it is also important to amend the requirement to prepare a worst case analysis. The requirement that the analysis of impacts be based on credible scientific evidence is viewed as a specific component of the "rule of reason".

Comment: The proposal inappropriately removes the obligation to weigh the need for an action against its potential impacts.

Response: The regulation deletes this requirement because it is more properly accomplished at the conclusion of the entire NEPA process. A decisionmaker may, of course, decide to withdraw a proposal at any stage of the NEPA process for any reason, including the belief that the paucity of information undermines the wisdom of proceeding in the face of possibly severe impacts. However, such weighing and balancing in the middle of EIS preparation is a matter of policy, not law.

It is clear that, "one of the costs that must be weighed by decisionmakers is the cost of uncertainty—i.e., the costs of proceeding without more and better information." *Alaska v. Andrus,* 580 F.2d 465, 473 (D.C. Cir. 1978). However, that weighing takes place after completion of the EIS process, including the public comment process. Indeed, it would seem that the results of such a weighing process would naturally be more informed and wiser after the agency has completed the requirements of § 1502.22 to evaluate the potential impacts in the face of incomplete or unavailable

information. After completion of the EIS process, the responsible decisionmaker must then weigh the costs of proceeding in the face of uncertainty, "and where the responsible decision-maker has decided that it is outweighed by the benefits of proceeding with the project without further delay . . ." he may proceed to do so. *Id.* Similarly, he or she may also decide, with the benefit of the best possible information, to delay the project until further information is obtained or to cancel the project altogether.

Comment: CEQ should provide additional guidance about the new regulation, and oversee and actively monitor its implementation.

Response: CEQ plans to provide additional guidance about the new regulation in the form of an amended question 20 of *Forty Most Asked Questions Concerning CEQ's National Environmental Policy Act Regulations.* CEQ also plans to actively monitor the implementation of the amended regulation, and evaluate its effectiveness after it has been implemented for a sufficient period of time to make a reasonable assessment.

Comment: It is unclear in which situations the new rule would apply, and what specific information it mandates. CEQ should apply the rule to actual or hypothetical situations and explain how the rule will apply and how the agencies' obligations differ under the new rule from those of the old. Request the Council provide such an analysis for particular fact patterns.

Response: CEQ plans to provide specific examples of the application of the rule to hypothetical situations in its guidance, following issuance of the final rule. The amended regulation will apply, of course, to the very same situations to which the original regulation applies; that is, the existence of incomplete or unavailable information related to significant adverse impacts on the human environment. The modifications to the regulation are designed to better articulate the precise requirements with which an agency must comply once it finds itself in this situation.

Comment: It is essential to mention the Committee of Scientists which was instrumental in development of the proposed regulation.

Response: The writer is probably referring to a proposed Advisory Committee on Worst Case Analysis, which would have included scientists. The Committee was never formed, and thus had no role in developing the amended regulation. Instead, the Council sought public comment through the process of asking questions in the

Federal Register / Vol. 51, No. 80 / Friday, April 25, 1986 / Rules and Regulations   15625

Advance Notice of Proposed Rulemaking.

Comment: CEQ should state that this analysis is to be done only in conjunction with an EIS, as opposed to an environmental assessment.

Response: Section 1502.22 is part of the set of regulations which govern the EIS process, as opposed to the preparation of an environmental assessment. *It is only appropriate to require this level of analysis when an agency is preparing an EIS.* The type of analysis called for in § 1502.22 is clearly much more sophisticated and detailed than the scope of an environmental assessment. Environmental assessments should be concise public documents which *briefly* provide sufficient analysis for determining whether to prepare an EIS; and aid in an agency's compliance with NEPA when no EIS is necessary. "Since the EA [environmental assessment] is a concise document, it should not contain long descriptions or detailed data which the agency may have gathered". The Council's suggested page limit for environmental assessments are ten to fifteen pages. *Forty Most Asked Questions Concerning CEQ's National Environmental Policy Act Regulations,* Question 36a, 46 FR 18026, 18037 (1981).

Comment: CEQ should state clearly that the amendment is intended to repudiate and overrule the Ninth Circuit decisions on worst case analysis.

Response: The Ninth Circuit opinions are based on the requirements of former § 1502.22, or agency reflections thereof, and are inapplicable to this revision. The regulation is being amended to provide a better approach to the problem of analyzing environmental impacts in the face of incomplete or unavailable information. Because the requirements of the amended regulation are more clearly articulated and manageable than the "worst case analysis" requirement, CEQ expects that there will be less litigation based on § 1502.22 than the former version of § 1502.22 interpreted by the Ninth Circuit.

Comment: CEQ should withdraw the guidance contained in the 1981 publication. *Forty Most Asked Questions about CEQ's NEPA Regulations,* relating to worst case analysis.

Response: That guidance is withdrawn by this publication.

Comment: CEQ has not complied with its duties to assert its substantive powers over federal agencies to comply with NEPA, to coordinate programs, and to issue instructions to agencies, but has instead succumbed to pressure from defendant agencies and their attorneys

to amend the regulation. Further, CEQ is collaterally estopped from overruling the Ninth Circuit decisions.

Response: CEQ manifests its oversight of the NEPA process in a number of ways on a daily basis: for example, review of agency NEPA procedures, resolving referrals of proposals of major federal actions, and assisting parties on an individual basis in resolving difficulties with the NEPA process. The requirements of the amended regulation are a more productive use of the agencies' resources than attempting to prepare a worst case analysis. Collateral estoppel is a doctrine by which a party may be barred from relitigating a question decided in a prior case. It does not bar an agency from changing a regulation that the courts have interpreted.

Comment: Agencies should be required to present an evaluation of the existing evidence of the most likely outcome.

Response: Step four of subsection (b) requires agencies to evaluate potential impacts. The lead agency may wish to specify which of the impacts are the most likely to occur, and the Council encourages inclusion of such data when it is reliable information which would be useful to the decisionmaker and the public.

Comment: Case law required worst case analysis prior to adoption of 40 CFR 1502.22.

Response: This assertion is incorrect. Case law prior to the adoption of 40 CFR 1502.22 *did* require agencies to make a "good faith effort . . . to describe the reasonably foreseeable environmental impact(s)" of the proposal and alternatives to the proposal in the face of incomplete or unavailable information, consistent with the "rule of reason". *Scientists' Institute for Public Information* v. *Atomic Energy Commission,* 481 F.2d 1079, 1092 (D.C. Cir. 1973). The "worst case analysis" requirement was a technique adopted by CEQ as a means of achieving the goals enunciated in such case law. The "worst case" requirement itself, however, was clearly a "major innovation". Comment. *New Rules for the NEPA Process: CEQ Establishes Uniform Procedures to Improve Implementation,* 9 Envt'l L.Rep. 10.005, 10.008 (1979). The U.S. Court of Appeals for the Fifth Circuit, interpreting the "worst case analysis" requirement for the first time in a litigation context, recognized that it was an innovation of CEQ. *Sierra Club* v. *Sigler,* 695 F.2d 957, 972 (5th Cir. 1983). CEQ has since observed difficulties with the technique of "worst case analysis" and is replacing it with a better

approach to the problem of incomplete or unavailable information in an EIS.

List of Subjects in 40 CFR Part 1502

Environmental impact statements.

PART 1502—[Amended].

40 CFR Part 1502 is amended as follows:

1. The authority citation for Part 1502 continues to read:

Authority: NEPA, the Environmental Quality Improvement Act of 1970, as amended (42 U.S.C. 4371 *et seq.*), sec. 309 of the Clean Air Act, as amended (42 U.S.C. 7609), and E.O. 11514 (Mar. 5, 1970, as amended by E.O. 11991, May 24, 1977).

2. Section 1502.22 is revised to read as follows:

§ 1502.22 Incomplete or unavailable information.

When an agency is evaluating reasonably foreseeable significant adverse effects on the human environment in an environmental impact statement and there is incomplete or unavailable information. the agency shall always make clear that such information is lacking.

(a) If the incomplete information relevant to reasonably foreseeable significant adverse impacts is essential to a reasoned choice among alternatives and the overall costs of obtaining it are not exorbitant, the agency shall include the information in the environmental impact statement.

(b) If the information relevant to reasonably foreseeable significant adverse impacts cannot be obtained because the overall costs of obtaining it are exorbitant or the means to obtain it are not known, the agency shall include within the environmental impact statement: (1) A statement that such information is incomplete or unavailable; (2) a statement of the relevance of the incomplete or unavailable information to evaluating reasonably foreseeable significant adverse impacts on the human environment; (3) a summary of existing credible scientific evidence which is relevant to evaluating the reasonably foreseeable significant adverse impacts on the human environment, and (4) the agency's evaluation of such impacts based upon theoretical approaches or research methods generally accepted in the scientific community. For the purposes of this section, "reasonably foreseeable" includes impacts which have catastrophic consequences, even if their probability of occurrence is low, provided that the analysis of the impacts is supported by credible scientific evidence. is not based on pure

15626   Federal Register / Vol. 51, No. 80 / Friday, April 25, 1986 / Rules and Regulations

conjecture, and is within the rule of reason.

(c) The amended regulation will be applicable to all environmental impact statements for which a Notice of Intent (40 CFR 1508.22) is published in the **Federal Register** on or after May 27, 1986. For environmental impact statements in progress, agencies may choose to comply with the requirements of either the original or amended regulation.

Dated: April 21, 1986.

A. Alan Hill,

Chairman.

[FR Doc. 86-9270 Filed 4-24-86; 8:45 am]

BILLING CODE 3125-01-M

NEPA Deskbook

Appendix 22 Application of NEPA to Proposed Federal Actions in the United States With Transboundary Effects

EXECUTIVE OFFICE OF THE PRESIDENT
COUNCIL ON ENVIRONMENTAL QUALITY
WASHINGTON. D.C. 20503

MEMORANDUM TO HEADS OF AGENCIES ON THE APPLICATION OF THE
NATIONAL ENVIRONMENTAL POLICY ACT TO PROPOSED FEDERAL ACTIONS IN
THE UNITED STATES WITH TRANSBOUNDARY EFFECTS

FROM: KATHLEEN A. MCGINTY
          CHAIR

DATE: JULY 1, 1997

In recent months, the Council has been involved in discussions with several agencies concerning
the applicability of the National Environmental Policy Act (NEPA) to transboundary impacts
that may occur as the result of proposed federal actions in the United States. To set forth a
consistent interpretation of NEPA, CEQ is today issuing the attached guidance on NEPA
analysis for transboundary impacts. In it, we advise that NEPA requires analysis and disclosure
of transboundary impacts of proposed federal actions taking place in the United States.

We recommend that agencies which take actions with potential transboundary impacts consult as
necessary with CEQ concerning specific procedures, proposals or programs which may be
affected.

COUNCIL ON ENVIRONMENTAL QUALITY GUIDANCE ON NEPA ANALYSES FOR TRANSBOUNDARY IMPACTS

JULY 1, 1997

The purpose of this guidance is to clarify the applicability of the National Environmental Policy Act (NEPA) to proposed federal actions in the United States, including its territories and possessions, that may have

country's environment. While the guidance arises in the context of negotiations undertaken with the governments of Mexico and Canada to develop an agreement on transboundary environmental impact assessment in North America, [1] the guidance pertains to all federal agency actions that are normally subject to NEPA, whether covered by an international agreement or not.

It is important to state at the outset the matters to which this guidance is addressed and those to which it is not. This guidance does not expand the range of actions to which NEPA currently applies. An action that does not otherwise fall under NEPA would not now fall under NEPA by virtue of this guidance. Nor does this guidance apply NEPA to so-called "extraterritorial actions"; that is, U.S. actions that take place in another country or otherwise outside the jurisdiction of the United States[2]. The guidance pertains only to those proposed actions currently covered by NEPA that take place within the United States and its territories, and it does not change the applicability of NEPA law, regulations or case law to those actions. Finally, the guidance is consistent with long-standing principles of international law.

NEPA LAW AND POLICY

harmony between human beings and their environment, promotes efforts

stimulates the health and welfare of human beings, and enriches the understanding of ecological systems.[3] Section 102(1) of NEPA "authorizes and directs that, to the fullest extent possible . . . . the policies, regulations and public laws of the United States shall be interpreted and administered in accordance with the policies set forth in [the] Act."[4] NEPA's explicit statement of policies calls for the federal government "to use all practical

man and nature can exist in productive harmony . . . ."[5] In addition, Congress directed federal agencies to "use all practical means . . . . to

to the end that the Nation may . . . . attain the widest range of beneficial uses of the environment without degradation, risk to health or safety, or other undesirable and unintended consequences."[6] Section 102(2)(C) requires federal agencies to assess the environmental impacts of and alternatives to proposed major federal actions significantly affecting the quality of the human environment.[7] Congress also recognized the "worldwide and long-range character of environmental problems" in NEPA and directed agencies to assist other countries in anticipating and preventing a decline in the quality of the world environment.[8]

Neither NEPA nor the Council on Environmental Quality's (CEQ) regulations implementing the procedural provisions of NEPA define agencies'

Rather, the entire body of NEPA law directs federal agencies to analyze the effects of proposed actions to the extent they are reasonably foreseeable consequences of the proposed action, regardless of where those impacts

the action, are later in time or farther removed in distance, but are still reasonably foreseeable, including growth-inducing effects and related effects on the ecosystem,[9] as well as cumulative effects.[10] Case law interpreting

boundaries within the United States,[11] and has also assumed that NEPA requires analysis of major federal actions that take place entirely outside of

States.[12]

Courts that have addressed impacts across the United States' borders have

Swinomish Tribal Community v. Federal Energy Regulatory Commission,[13] Canadian intervenors were allowed to challenge the adequacy of an

its approval of an amendment to the City of Seattle's license that permitted raising the height of the Ross Dam on the Skagit River in Washington State.

concluded that the report had taken the requisite "hard look" at Canadian impacts. Similarly, in Wilderness Society v. Morton,[14] the court granted intervenor status to Canadian environmental organizations that were challenging the adequacy of the trans-Alaska pipeline EIS. The court granted intervenor status because it found that there was a reasonable possibility that oil spill damage could significantly affect Canadian resources, and that Canadian interests were not adequately represented by other parties in the case.

In sum, based on legal and policy considerations, CEQ has determined that agencies must include analysis of reasonably foreseeable transboundary

United States.

PRACTICAL CONSIDERATIONS

effects, and cautions agencies against creating boilerplate sections in NEPA

scoping process[15] to identify those actions that may have transboundary environmental effects and determine at that point their information needs, if any, for such analyses. Agencies should be particularly alert to actions that may affect migratory species, air quality, watersheds, and other components of the natural ecosystem that cross borders, as well as to interrelated social and economic effects.[16] Should such potential impacts be identified, agencies may rely on available professional sources of information and should contact agencies in the affected country with relevant expertise.

Agencies have expressed concern about the availability of information that would be adequate to comply with NEPA standards that have been developed through the CEQ regulations and through judicial decisions. Agencies do have a responsibility to undertake a reasonable search for relevant, current information associated with an identified potential effect.

actions in this respect, and do not require agencies to discuss "remote and highly speculative consequences".[17] Furthermore, CEQ's regulation at 40 CFR 1502.22 dealing with incomplete or unavailable information sets forth clear steps to evaluating effects in the context of an EIS when information is unobtainable.[18] Additionally, in the context of international agreements, the parties may set forth a specific process for obtaining information from the affected country which could then be relied upon in most circumstances to satisfy agencies' responsibility to undertake a reasonable search for information.

Agencies have also pointed out that certain federal actions that may cause transboundary effects do not, under U.S. law, require compliance with Sections 102(2)(C) and 102(2)(E) of NEPA. Such actions include actions that are statutorily exempted from NEPA, Presidential actions, and individual

by virtue of the CEQ regulations[19] and various judicial doctrines interpreting NEPA[20]. Nothing in this guidance changes the agencies' ability to rely on those rules and doctrines.

INTERNATIONAL LAW

It has been customary law since the 1905 Trail Smelter Arbitration that no nation may undertake acts on its territory that will harm the territory of another state[21]. This rule of customary law has been recognized as binding in Principle 21 of the Stockholm Declaration on the Human Environment and

This concept, along with the duty to give notice to others to avoid or avert such harm, is incorporated into numerous treaty obligations undertaken by the United States. Analysis of transboundary impacts of federal agency actions that occur in the United States is an appropriate step towards implementing those principles.

CONCLUSION

NEPA requires agencies to include analysis of reasonably foreseeable

actions in the United States. Such effects are best identified during the scoping stage, and should be analyzed to the best of the agency's ability using reasonably available information. Such analysis should be included in the EA or EIS prepared for the proposed action.

1

North American Free Trade Agreement. The guidance is also relevant to the ECE Convention on Environmental Impact Assessment in a Transboundary Context, signed in Espoo, Finland in February, 1991, but not yet in force.

[2] For example, NEPA does apply to actions undertaken by the National

Science Foundation in the Antarctica. <u>Environmental Defense Fund v. Massey</u>, 986 F.2d 528 (D.C. Cir. 1993).

3 42 USC 4321.

4 42 USC 4332(1).

5 42 USC 4331(a).

6 42 USC 4331(b)(3).

7 42 USC 4332(2)(C).

8 42 USC 4332(2)(F).

9 40 CFR 1508.8(b).

10 40 CFR 1508.7.

11 See, *for example*, <u>Sierra Club v. U.S.Forest Service</u>, 46 F.3d 835 (8th Cir. 1995); <u>Resources Ltd., Inc. v. Robertson</u>, 35 F.3d 1300 and 8 F.3d 1394 (9th Cir. 1993); <u>Natural Resources Defense Council v. Hodel</u>, 865 F.2d 288 (D.C. Cir. 1988); <u>County of Josephine v. Watt</u>, 539 F.Supp. 696 (N.D. Cal. 1982).

12 See <u>Sierra Club v. Adams</u>, 578 F.2d 389 (D.C. Cir. 1978); <u>NORML v. Dept. of State</u>, 452 F.Supp. 1226 (D.D.C. 1978).

13 627 F.2d 499 (D.C. Cir. 1980).

14 463 F.2d 1261 (D.C. Cir. 1972).

15 40 CFR 1501.7. Scoping is a process for determining the scope of the

process prior to writing the environmental analyses.

16

by themselves do not require preparation of an EIS. 40 CFR 1508.14.

17 <u>Trout Unlimited v. Morton</u>, 509 F.2d 1276, 1283 (9th Cir. 1974). <u>See</u> <u>also</u>, <u>Northern Alaska Environmental Center v. Lujan</u>, 961 F.2d 886, 890 (9th Cir. 1992); <u>Idaho Conservation League v. Mumma</u>, 956 F.2d 1508, 1519 (9th Cir. 1992); <u>San Luis Obispo Mothers for Peace v. N.R.C.</u>, 751 F.2d 1287, 1300 (D.C. Cir. 1984); <u>Scientists Institute for Public Information, Inc. v. Atomic Energy Commission</u>, 481 F.2d 1079, 1092 (D.C. Cir. 1973).

18 See Preamble to Amendment of 40 CFR 1502.22, deleting prior requirement for "worst case analysis" at 51 <u>Federal Register</u> 15625, April 25, 1986, for a detailed explanation of this regulation.

19 For example, agencies may contact CEQ for approval of alternative arrangements for compliance with NEPA in the case of emergencies. 40 CFR 1506.11.

20 For example, courts have recognized that NEPA does not require an

information for national security reasons, <u>Weinberger v. Cathollic Action of Hawaii</u>, 454 U.S. 139 (1981).

21 *Trail Smelter Arbitration*, <u>U.S. v. Canada</u>, 3 UN Rep. Int'l Arbit. Awards 1911 (1941). The case involved a smelter in British Columbia that was

that "under principles of International Law, as well as the law of the United States, no State has the right to use or permit the use of its territory in such a manner as to cause injury by fumes in or to the territory of another or the properties or persons therein, when the case is of serious consequence and the injury is described by clear and convincing injury." *Id*. at 1965). Also see the American Law Institute's Restatement of the Foreign Relations Law of the United States 3d, Section 601, ("State obligations with respect to environment of other States and the common environment").

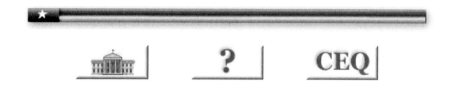

To submit questions and comments about CEQ NEPAnet,
please use the NEPAnet Feedback System.

NEPA Deskbook

Appendix 23 Designation of Non-Federal Agencies to Be Cooperative Agencies

EXECUTIVE OFFICE OF THE PRESIDENT
COUNCIL ON ENVIRONMENTAL QUALITY
WASHINGTON, D.C. 20503

July 28, 1999

MEMORANDUM FOR HEADS OF FEDERAL AGENCIES

FROM: GEORGE T. FRAMPTON, JR. GTFL.
             Acting Chair

SUBJECT: ATTACHED MEMORANDUM

Attached please find a memorandum regarding the designation of non-federal agencies to be
cooperating agencies in implementing the procedural requirements of the National
Environmental Policy Act. If you have any questions concerning this memorandum, please do
not hesitate to contact Dinah Bear, the Council on Environmental Quality's General Counsel, at
(202) 395-5750.

Attachment

EXECUTIVE OFFICE OF THE PRESIDENT
COUNCIL ON ENVIRONMENTAL QUALITY
WASHINGTON, D.C. 20503

July 28, 1999

MEMORANDUM FOR HEADS OF FEDERAL AGENCIES

FROM: GEORGE T. FRAMPTON, JR. GTFJr
             Acting Chair

SUBJECT: DESIGNATION OF NON-FEDERAL AGENCIES TO BE COOPERATING
           AGENCIES IN IMPLEMENTING THE PROCEDURAL REQUIREMENTS OF
           THE NATIONAL ENVIRONMENTAL POLICY ACT

The purpose of this Memorandum is to urge agencies to more actively solicit in the future

the participation of state, tribal and local governments as "cooperating agencies" in

implementing the environmental impact statement process under the National Environmental

Policy Act (NEPA). 40 C.F.R. §1508.5. As soon as practicable, but no later than the scoping

process, federal agency officials should identify state, tribal and local government agencies

which have jurisdiction by law and or special expertise with respect to reasonable alternatives or

significant environmental, social or economic impacts association with a proposed action that

requires the preparation of an environmental impact statement[1]. The federal agency should then

determine whether such non-federal agencies are interested in assuming the responsibilities of

becoming a cooperating agency under 40 C.F.R. §1501.6. Where invited tribal, state, or local

agencies choose not to become cooperators in the NEPA process, they may still be identified as

an internal party on the distribution list, if they so desire.

---

[1] While CEQ has not attempted to identify every state, tribal and local government agencies with jurisdiction by law
or special expertise (nor do we propose to do so), agencies may wish to refer to Appendix II to the CEQ regulations,
"Federal and Federal-State Agencies with Jurisdiction by Law or Special Expertise on Environmental Quality
Issues", Vol. 49 *Federal Register*,. No. 247, 49754-49778 (December 21, 1984), for guidance as to the types of
actions and expertise that are relevant in determining appropriate cooperating agencies. Please contact CEQ for
copies, if needed.

The benefits of granting cooperating agency status include disclosure of relevant information early in the analytical process, receipt of technical expertise and staff support, avoidance of duplication with state, tribal and local procedures, and establishment of a mechanism for addressing intergovernmental issues. If a non-federal agency agrees to become a cooperating agency, agencies are encouraged to document (e.g., in a memorandum of agreement) their specific expectations, roles and responsibilities, including such issues as preparation of analysis, schedules, availability of pre-decisional information and other issues. Cooperating agencies are normally expected to use their own funds for routine activities, but to the extent available funds permit, the lead agency should fund or include in its budget requests funding for major activities or analyses that it requests from cooperating agencies. 40 C.F.R. §1501.6(b)(5).

Agencies are reminded that cooperating agency status neither enlarges nor diminishes the decisionmaking authority of either federal or non-federal entities. However, cooperating agency relationships with state, tribal and local agencies help to achieve the direction set forth in NEPA to work with other levels of government "to promote the general welfare, to create and maintain conditions under which man and nature can exist in productive harmony, and fulfill the social, economic, and other requirements of present and future generations of Americans." Considering NEPA's mandate and the authority granted in federal regulation to allow for cooperating agency status for state, tribal and local agencies, cooperator status for appropriate non-federal agencies should be routinely solicited.

NEPA Deskbook

Appendix 24 Identifying Non-Federal Cooperating Agencies

September 25, 2000

MEMORANDUM FOR DEPUTY/ASSISTANT HEADS OF FEDERAL AGENCIES

FROM: HORST G. GRECZMIEL
               Associate Director for NEPA Oversight

SUBJECT: IDENTIFYING NON-FEDERAL COOPERATING AGENCIES IN
               IMPLEMENTING THE PROCEDURAL REQUIREMENTS OF
               THE NATIONAL ENVIRONMENTAL POLICY ACT

The purpose of this Memorandum is to ensure that all federal and non-federal cooperating agencies are identified on the cover sheet of each Environmental Impact Statement (EIS) prepared by your agency. In his Memorandum of July 28, 1999, George T. Frampton, Jr., the CEQ Chair, urged all agencies to more actively solicit the participation of state, tribal and local governments as cooperating agencies in implementing the environmental impact statement process under the National Environmental Policy Act (NEPA) (copy enclosed). Agencies are now implementing this policy and we expect that there will be more states, tribes and localities involved as cooperating agencies.

As a follow up to this policy, we want to be sure that the EIS database maintained for the Council on Environmental Quality (CEQ) by the Environmental Protection Agency (EPA) includes information on all non-federal and federal cooperating agencies. CEQ has been working to make this happen and on October 1, 2000, the EPA will begin entering the names of all cooperating agencies in the database. In order to ensure accurate information is collected, federal agencies must list all cooperating agencies (federal and non-federal) on the cover of each EIS as required by Section 1502.11 of the CEQ NEPA regulations. Please ensure that all cooperating agencies are identified on the cover sheet of every EIS issued by your agency.

If you have any questions concerning this memorandum, please contact me at 202-395-5750, or Anne Norton Miller, the Acting Director, Office of Federal Activities, EPA, at 202-564-2400.

NEPA Deskbook

Appendix 25 Cooperating Agencies in Implementing the Procedural Requirements of NEPA

January 30, 2002

MEMORANDUM FOR THE HEADS OF FEDERAL AGENCIES

FROM: JAMES CONNAUGHTON, Chair

SUBJECT: COOPERATING AGENCIES IN IMPLEMENTING THE
PROCEDURAL REQUIREMENTS OF THE NATIONAL ENVIRONMENTAL
POLICY ACT

The purpose of this Memorandum is to ensure that all Federal agencies are

agencies in the preparation of analyses and documentation required by the
National Environmental Policy Act (NEPA), and to ensure that Federal

NEPA processes. The CEQ regulations addressing cooperating agencies
status (40 C.F.R. §§ 1501.6 & 1508.5) implement the NEPA mandate that
Federal agencies responsible for preparing NEPA analyses and
documentation do so "in cooperation with State and local governments" and
other agencies with jurisdiction by law or special expertise. (42 U.S.C. §§
4331(a), 4332(2)). Despite previous memoranda and guidance from CEQ,
some agencies remain reluctant to engage other Federal and non-federal
agencies as a cooperating agency. In addition, some Federal agencies
remain reluctant to assume the role of a cooperating agency, resulting in an
inconsistent implementation of NEPA.

Studies regarding the efficiency, effectiveness, and value of NEPA analyses
conclude that stakeholder involvement is important in ensuring
decisionmakers have the environmental information necessary to make
informed and timely decisions efficiently. Cooperating agency status is a

nor diminishes the decisionmaking authority of any agency involved in the

beyond those found in current laws and regulations, nor does it require an
agency to provide financial assistance to a cooperating agency.

The benefits of enhanced cooperating agency participation in the
preparation of NEPA analyses include: disclosing relevant information early
in the analytical process; applying available technical expertise and staff
support; avoiding duplication with other Federal, State, Tribal and local
procedures; and establishing a mechanism for addressing intergovernmental
issues. Other benefits of enhanced cooperating agency participation include

governmental roles in the NEPA process, as well as enhancing agencies'
ability to adopt environmental documents. It is incumbent on Federal agency
officials to identify as early as practicable in the environmental planning

have jurisdiction by law and special expertise with respect to all reasonable
alternatives or significant environmental, social or economic impacts
associated with a proposed action that requires NEPA analysis.

The Federal agency responsible for the NEPA analysis should determine

responsibilities of becoming a cooperating agency under 40 C.F.R. § 1501.6.

become cooperating agencies, they should still be considered for inclusion in

lists for review and comment on the NEPA documents. Federal agencies
declining to accept cooperating agency status in whole or in part are
obligated to respond to the request and provide a copy of their response to

the Council. (40 C.F.R. § 1501.6(c)).

responsible for NEPA analysis are urged to set time limits, identify
milestones, assign responsibilities for analysis and documentation, specify
the scope and detail of the cooperating agency's contribution, and establish

to
consider documenting their expectations, roles and responsibilities (e.g.,
Memorandum of Agreement or correspondence). Establishing such a
relationship neither creates a requirement nor constitutes a presumption that
a lead agency provides financial assistance to a cooperating agency.

Once cooperating agency status has been extended and accepted,
circumstances may arise when it is appropriate for either the lead or
cooperating agency to consider ending cooperating agency status. This

accept or end cooperating agency status. These factors are neither intended
to be all-inclusive nor a rote test. Each determination should be made on a
case-by-case basis considering all relevant information and factors,

reasoned use of agency discretion and to articulate and document the bases
for extending, declining or ending cooperating agency status. The basis and
determination should be included in the administrative record.

CEQ regulations do not explicitly discuss cooperating agencies in the
context of Environmental Assessments (EAs) because of the expectation
that EAs will normally be brief, concise documents that would not warrant

particularly in the context of integrating compliance with other environmental
review laws – develop EAs of greater length and complexity than those
required under the CEQ regulations. While we continue to be concerned
about needlessly lengthy EAs (that may, at times, indicate the need to
prepare an Environmental Impact Statement (EIS)), we recognize that there
are times when cooperating agencies will be useful in the context of EAs.
For this reason, this guidance is recommended for preparing EAs. However,

set forth in the regulations or prior guidance.

To measure our progress in addressing the issue of cooperating agency
status, by October 31, 2002 agencies of the Federal government responsible
for preparing NEPA analyses (e.g., the lead agency) shall provide the first
bi-annual report regarding all EISs and EAs begun during the six-month
period between March 1, 2002 and August 31, 2002. This is a periodic

February 2003 period due on April 30, 2003. For EISs, the report shall

agency status; agencies which accepted cooperating agency status;
agencies whose cooperating agency status ended; and the current status of

shall provide the number of EAs and those involving cooperating agency(s)
as described in attachment 2. States, Tribes, and units of local governments
that have received authority by Federal law to assume the responsibilities for
preparing NEPA analyses are encouraged to comply with these reporting
requirements.

If you have any questions concerning this memorandum, please contact
Horst G. Greczmiel, Associate Director for NEPA Oversight at
202-395-5750, Horst_Greczmiel@ceq.eop.gov, or 202-456-0753 (fax).

# # #

**Factors for Determining Whether to Invite,
Decline or End Cooperating Agency Status**

1. Jurisdiction by law (40 C.F.R. § 1508.15) – for example, agencies

   agencies shall be a cooperating agency (1501.6); non-federal
   agencies may be invited (40 C.F.R. § 1508.5)]:

   ○ Does the agency have the authority to approve a proposal or a
   portion of a proposal?

   ○ Does the agency have the authority to veto a proposal or a
   portion of a proposal?

   ○ Does the agency have the authority to finance a proposal or a
   portion of a proposal?

2. Special expertise (40 C.F.R. § 1508.26) – cooperating agency status
   for specific purposes linked to special expertise requires more than
   an interest in a proposed action [federal and non-federal agencies
   may be requested (40 C.F.R. §§ 1501.6 & 1508.5)]:

   ○ Does the cooperating agency have the expertise needed to
   help the lead agency meet a statutory responsibility?

   ○ Does the cooperating agency have the expertise developed to
   carry out an agency mission?

   ○ Does the cooperating agency have the related program
   expertise or experience?

   ○ Does the cooperating agency have the expertise regarding the
   proposed actions' relationship to the objectives of regional,
   State and local land use plans, policies and controls
   (1502.16(c))?

3. Do the agencies understand what cooperating agency status means
   and can they legally enter into an agreement to be a cooperating
   agency?

4. Can the cooperating agency participate during scoping and/or
   throughout the preparation of the analysis and documentation as
   necessary and meet milestones established for completing the
   process?

5. Can the cooperating agency, in a timely manner, aid in:

   ○ identifying significant environmental issues [including aspects
   of the human environment (40 C.F.R. § 1508.14), including
   natural, social, economic, energy, urban quality, historic and
   cultural issues (40 C.F.R. § 1502.16)]?

   ○ eliminating minor issues from further study?

   ○ identifying issues previously the subject of environmental
   review or study?

   ○ identifying the proposed actions' relationship to the objectives
   of regional, State and local land use plans, policies and
   controls (1502.16(c))?

(40 C.F.R. §§ 1501.1(d) and 1501.7)

6. Can the cooperating agency assist in preparing portions of the review and analysis and resolving significant environmental issues to support scheduling and critical milestones?

7. Can the cooperating agency provide resources to support scheduling and critical milestones such as:

   ○ personnel? Consider all forms of assistance (e.g., data gathering; surveying; compilation; research.

   ○ expertise? This includes technical or subject matter expertise.

   ○ funding? Examples include funding for personnel, travel and studies. Normally, the cooperating agency will provide the funding; to the extent available funds permit, the lead agency shall fund or include in budget requests funding for an analyses the lead agency requests from cooperating agencies. Alternatives to travel, such as telephonic or video conferencing, should be considered especially when funding constrains participation.

   ○ models and databases? Consider consistency and compatibility with lead and other cooperating agencies' methodologies.

   ○ facilities, equipment and other services? This type of support is especially relevant for smaller governmental entities with limited budgets.

8. Does the agency provide adequate lead-time for review and do the other agencies provide adequate time for review of documents, issues and analyses? For example, are either the lead or cooperating

   a timely fashion after adequate time for review of documents, issues and analyses?

9. Can the cooperating agency(s) accept the lead agency's final decisionmaking authority regarding the scope of the analysis, including authority to define the purpose and need for the proposed action? For example, is an agency unable or unwilling to develop information/analysis of alternatives they favor and disfavor?

10. Are the agency(s) able and willing to provide data and rationale underlying the analyses or assessment of alternatives?

11. Does the agency release predecisional information (including working drafts) in a manner that undermines or circumvents the agreement to work cooperatively before publishing draft or final analyses and documents? Disagreeing with the published draft or final analysis should not be a ground for ending cooperating status. Agencies must

12. Does the agency consistently misrepresent the process or the findings presented in the analysis and documentation?

The factors provided for extending cooperating agency status are not intended to be all-inclusive. Moreover, satisfying all the factors is not required and satisfying one may be sufficient. Each determination should be made on a case-by-case basis considering all relevant information and factors.

**Sample Report to the Council on Environmental Quality
on Cooperating Agency (CA) Status**

March 1, 2002 to August 31, 2002

I. Environmental Impact Statements:

	1.	2.	etc.
EIS	(Title of EIS)		
Potential CA	(Name of potential CA)		
Invited CA	(Name of potential CA and basis – identify the jurisdiction by law or special expertise)		
Agency Requesting CA Status	(Name of potential CA and basis – identify the jurisdiction by law or special expertise)		
CAs	(Name of CA engaged in the EIS)		
CA Status not Initiated or Ended	(e.g., name of agency – reason status was not initiated or was ended – see examples listed below		
Status of EIS	(e.g., begun on mm/dd/yy; DEIS published mm/dd/yy; FEIS published mm/dd/yy; ROD published mm/dd/yy)		

Examples of reasons CA status was not initiated or why it ended:

1. Lack of special expertise – identify the expertise sought by the lead agency and/or offered by the potential cooperating agency).
2. State, Tribal or local entity lacks authority to enter into an agreement to be a CA.
3. Potential CA unable to agree to participate during scoping and/or throughout the preparation of the analysis and documentation as necessary and meet milestones established for completing the process.
4. Potential or active CA unable or unwilling to identify significant issues, eliminate minor issues, identify issues previously studied, or identify conflicts with the objectives of regional, State and local land use plans, policies and controls in a timely manner.
5. Potential or active CA unable or unwilling to assist in preparing portions of the review and analysis and resolving significant environmental issues in a timely manner.

6. Potential or active CA unable or unwilling to provide resources to support scheduling and critical milestones.
7. Agency unable or unwilling to consistently participate in meetings or respond in a timely fashion after adequate time for review of documents, issues and analyses.
8. CA unwilling or unable to accept the lead agency's decisionmaking authority regarding the scope of the analysis, including authority to define the purpose and need for the proposed action or to develop information/analysis of alternatives they favor and disfavor.
9. Agency unable or unwilling to provide data and rationale underlying the analyses or assessment of alternatives.
10. Agency releases predecisional information (including working drafts) in a manner that undermines or circumvents the agreement to work cooperatively before publishing draft or final analyses and documents.
11. Agency consistently misrepresents the process or the findings presented in the analysis and documentation.
12. Other. Identify the other:

II. Environmental Assessments:

	Total
Number of EAs started during the reporting period	
Number of EAs involving potential CAs	
Number of EAs where agencies were invited to participate	
Number of EAs where agencies requested CA status	
Number of EAs where a CA status was not initiated or was ended for the reasons identified	
Number of EAs involving CAs begun and ongoing during the reporting period	
Number of EAs involving CAs begun and completed during the reporting period	

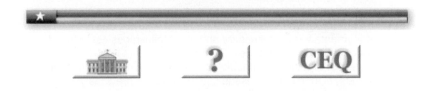

To submit questions and comments about CEQ NEPAnet, please use the NEPAnet Feedback System.

NEPAnet Privacy Statement

NEPA Deskbook

Appendix 26 Memorandum for Heads of
Federal Departments and
Agencies: Improving the Process
for Preparing Efficient and Timely
Environmental Reviews Under the
National Environmental Policy Act

EXECUTIVE OFFICE OF THE PRESIDENT
COUNCIL ON ENVIRONMENTAL QUALITY
WASHINGTON, D.C. 20503

March 6, 2012

MEMORANDUM FOR HEADS OF FEDERAL DEPARTMENTS AND AGENCIES

FROM: NANCY H SUTLEY
           Chair
           Council on Environmental Quality

SUBJECT: Improving the Process for Preparing Efficient and Timely Environmental
           Reviews under the National Environmental Policy Act

A wide array of tools is available to meet the goal of high quality, efficient, and timely environmental reviews under the National Environmental Policy Act (NEPA). The Council on Environmental Quality (CEQ) Regulations implementing NEPA contain a number of opportunities for achieving this goal. CEQ is issuing this guidance for Federal departments and agencies to emphasize and clarify those opportunities, fully consistent with a thorough and meaningful environmental review. The guidance also makes it clear that many of the provisions of the CEQ Regulations which specifically refer to an Environmental Impact Statement (EIS) provide efficiencies that can also be used to prepare an Environmental Assessment (EA). This guidance applies equally to the preparation of an EA or an EIS consistent with legal precedent and agency NEPA experience and practice.

In conducting all environmental reviews pursuant to NEPA, agencies should use the methods set out in the CEQ Regulations and in their own agency NEPA implementing procedures in a way that is mindful of the following basic principles:

- NEPA encourages straightforward and concise reviews and documentation that are proportionate to potential impacts and effectively convey the relevant considerations to the public and decisionmakers in a timely manner while rigorously addressing the issues presented;
- NEPA shall be integrated into project planning to ensure planning and decisions reflect environmental considerations, avoid delays later in the process, and anticipate and attempt to resolve potential issues rather than be an after-the-fact process that justifies a decision already made;
- NEPA reviews should coordinate and take appropriate advantage of existing documents and studies, including through adoption and incorporation by reference;

1

- Early and well-defined scoping can assist in focusing environmental reviews on appropriate issues that would be meaningful to a decision;
- Agencies are encouraged to develop meaningful and expeditious timelines for environmental reviews; and
- Agencies should respond to comments in proportion to the scope and scale of the environmental issues raised.

This guidance also reflects CEQ's continuing commitment to implement its Plan for Retrospective Review of Existing Regulations ("Plan") in accordance with Executive Order 13563.[1] Our ongoing review of the CEQ Regulations confirms the benefits of integrating environmental reviews into the decisionmaking process, coordinating multi-agency or multi-governmental reviews and approvals, and setting clear schedules for preparing EAs and EISs. This guidance promotes a sufficient and effective process that is tailored to avoid excessive burden. This guidance provides CEQ's interpretation of existing regulations promulgated under NEPA, and does not change agencies' obligations with regard to NEPA and the CEQ Regulations.[2]

Introduction and Steps to Date

CEQ was created by NEPA in 1970 and is charged with overseeing NEPA implementation by Federal agencies. In 1978, CEQ issued the CEQ Regulations implementing NEPA.[3] From time to time, CEQ issues guidance for the Federal agencies, to clarify the requirements and applicability of various provisions of NEPA and the CEQ Regulations, and to ensure that those requirements can be met in a timely and effective fashion.[4] These guidance

---

[1] Improving Regulation and Regulatory Review, Exec. Order No. 13,563, 76 Fed. Reg. 3,821 (Jan. 21, 2011), *available at* www.gpo.gov/fdsys/pkg/FR-2011-01-21/pdf/2011-1385.pdf.
[2] This guidance is not a rule or regulation, and the recommendations it contains may not apply to a particular situation based upon the individual facts and circumstances. This guidance does not change or substitute for any law, regulations, or any other legally binding requirement and is not legally enforceable. The use of non-mandatory terminology such as "guidance," "recommend," "may," "should," and "can," is intended to describe CEQ policies and recommendations. The use of mandatory terminology such as "shall," "must," and "required" is intended to describe controlling requirements under NEPA and the CEQ Regulations, but this document does not establish legally binding requirements in and of itself.
[3] The Council on Environmental Quality (CEQ) Regulations for Implementing the Procedural Provisions of the National Environmental Policy Act, 40 C.F.R. pts. 1500-1508 (2011) [hereinafter CEQ Regulations], *available on* www.nepa.gov *at* ceq.hss.doe.gov/ceq_regulations/regulations.html.
[4] These guidance documents are available online at ceq.hss.doe.gov/ceq_regulations/guidance.

2

documents represent CEQ's interpretation of NEPA, which the U.S. Supreme Court has said is "entitled to substantial deference."[5]

NEPA requires Federal agencies to consider the potential environmental consequences of their proposed action, and any reasonable alternatives, before deciding whether and in what form to take an action. Environmental reviews prepared under NEPA should provide a decisionmaker and the public with relevant and timely information, and the CEQ Regulations make it clear that "NEPA's purpose is not to generate paperwork--even excellent paperwork--but to foster excellent action."[6]

NEPA compliance can take three forms, a Categorical Exclusion, an EA, or an EIS:

- Categorical Exclusion (CE): A CE describes a category of actions that are expected not to have individually or cumulatively significant environmental impacts.[7] Each agency's procedures for implementing NEPA sets out that agency's CEs, which are established after CEQ and public review. A proposed action within such a category does not require further analysis and documentation in an EA or an EIS.[8] A CE can be used after determining that a proposed action falls within the categories of actions described in the CE and that there are no extraordinary circumstances indicating further environmental review is warranted..

- Environmental Assessment (EA): When a CE is not appropriate and the agency has not determined whether the proposed action will cause significant environmental effects, then an EA is prepared. If, as a result of the EA, a Finding of No Significant Impact (FONSI) is made, then the NEPA review process is completed with the FONSI, including documentation of its basis in the EA; otherwise an EIS is prepared.[9]

- Environmental Impact Statement (EIS): The most intensive level of analysis is the EIS, which is typically reserved for the analysis of proposed actions that are expected to result in significant environmental impacts. When an EIS is prepared, the NEPA review process is concluded when a record of decision (ROD) is issued.[10]

---

[5] *Andrus v. Sierra Club*, 442 U.S. 347, 358 (1979).
[6] 40 C.F.R. § 1500.1(c).
[7] Categorical exclusions can also be created legislatively.
[8] 40 C.F.R. §§ 1508.4, 1500.5(k).
[9] 40 C.F.R. § 1508.9.
[10] 40 C.F.R. § 1505.2.

3

CEQ has been working with agencies to modernize and reinvigorate NEPA implementation in several ways. CEQ issued guidance on the development and use of Categorical Exclusions in November 2010.[11] Properly developed and applied, CEs provide an efficient tool to complete the NEPA environmental review process for proposals that normally do not require more resource-intensive EAs or EISs. The use of CEs can reduce paperwork and delay for proposed actions that do not raise the potential for significant environmental effects.[12] In January 2011, CEQ provided guidance that specifically addressed the appropriate use of a FONSI or mitigated FONSI to conclude a NEPA review process relying on an EA. A mitigated FONSI is appropriate when mitigation is used to avoid or lessen potentially significant environmental effects of proposed actions that would otherwise need to be analyzed in an EIS.[13] In addition, in May 2010, CEQ issued guidance on ensuring efficient and expeditious compliance with NEPA when agencies must take exigent action to protect human health or safety and valued resources in a timeframe that does not allow sufficient time for the normal NEPA process.[14]

In August 2011 the President called for further steps to enhance the efficient and effective permitting and environmental review of infrastructure development "through such strategies as integrating planning and environmental reviews; coordinating multi-agency or multi-governmental reviews and approvals to run concurrently; setting clear schedules for completing steps in the environmental review and permitting process; and utilizing information technologies to inform the public about the progress of environmental reviews as well as the progress of Federal permitting and review processes."[15] This guidance sets forth straightforward means by which the CEQ Regulations support these strategies.

1.   Concise NEPA Documents

---

[11] CEQ, "Establishing, Applying, and Revising Categorical Exclusions under the National Environmental Policy Act" (Nov. 23, 2010), *available at* ceq.hss.doe.gov/ceq_regulations/NEPA_CE_Guidance_Nov232010.pdf.

[12] *See* 40 C.F.R. § 1500.4(p) (recommending categorical exclusions as a tool to reduce paperwork) and § 1500.5(k) (recommending categorical exclusions as a tool to reduce delay).

[13] CEQ, "Appropriate Use of Mitigation and Monitoring and Clarifying the Appropriate Use of Mitigated Findings of No Significant Impact" (Jan. 14, 2011), *available at* ceq.hss.doe.gov/current_developments/docs/Mitigation_and_Monitoring_Guidance_14Jan2011.pdf.

[14] CEQ, "Emergencies and the National Environmental Policy Act," (May 12, 2010), *available at* ceq.hss.doe.gov/ceq_regulations/Emergencies_and_NEPA_Memorandum_12May2010.pdf.

[15] Presidential Memorandum, "Speeding Infrastructure Development through More Efficient and Effective Permitting and Environmental Review" (Aug. 31, 2011), *available at* www.whitehouse.gov/the-press-office/2011/08/31/presidential-memorandum-speeding-infrastructure-development-through-more.

Agencies are encouraged to concentrate on relevant environmental analysis in their EAs and EISs, not to produce an encyclopedia of all applicable information.[16] Environmental analysis should focus on significant issues, discussing insignificant issues only briefly.[17] Impacts should be discussed in proportion to their significance, and if the impacts are not deemed significant there should be only enough discussion to show why more study is not warranted.[18] Scoping,[19] incorporation by reference,[20] and integration of other environmental analyses[21] are additional methods that may be used to avoid redundant or repetitive discussion of issues.[22]

All NEPA environmental documents, not just EISs, shall be written in plain language,[23] follow a clear format, and emphasize important impact analyses and relevant information necessary for those analyses, rather than providing extensive background material. Clarity and consistency ensure that the substance of the agency's analysis is understood, avoiding unnecessary confusion or risk of litigation that could result from an ambiguous or opaque analysis. The CEQ Regulations indicate that the text of a final EIS that addresses the purpose and need, alternatives, affected environment, and environmental consequences should normally be less than 150 pages and a final EIS for proposals of unusual scope or complexity should normally be less than 300 pages.[24]

In light of the growth of environmental requirements since the publication of the CEQ Regulations, and the desire to use the EIS to address, via integration, those requirements, it is recognized that there will be a range of appropriate lengths of EISs. Nevertheless, agencies should keep EISs as concise as possible (continuing to relegate to appendices the relevant studies and technical analyses used to support the determinations and conclusions reached in the EIS) and no longer than necessary to comply with NEPA and the other legal and regulatory requirements being addressed in the EIS, and to provide decision makers and the public with the information they need to assess the significant environmental effects of the action under review. Length should vary with the number, complexity and significance of potential environmental problems.[25]

---

[16] 40 C.F.R. §§ 1500.4(b), 1502.2(b).

[17] 40 C.F.R. § 1502.2(c); *see also* 40 C.F.R. § 1502.2(a) ("Environmental impact statements shall be analytic rather than encyclopedic.").

[18] 40 C.F.R. § 1502.2(b).

[19] 40 C.F.R. § 1500.4(g).

[20] 40 C.F.R. § 1500.4(j).

[21] 40 C.F.R. § 1500.4(k).

[22] *See generally* 40 C.F.R. § 1502.1 (EISs should be written in plain language so that decisionmakers and the public can understand them).

[23] 40 C.F.R. § 1502.8; *see also* www.plainlanguage.gov.

[24] 40 C.F.R. § 1502.7.

[25] 40 C.F.R. § 1502.2(c) (EISs "shall be kept concise and . . . . [l]ength should vary first with potential environmental problems and then with project size").

Similarly, the CEQ guidance issued in 1981 indicated that 10-15 pages is generally appropriate for EAs.[26] This guidance must be balanced with the requirement to take a hard look at the impacts of the proposed action. As with EISs, an EA's length should vary with the scope and scale of potential environmental problems as well as the extent to which the determination of no significant impact relies on mitigation, rather than just with the scope and scale of the proposed action.[27] The EA should be no more detailed than necessary to fulfill the functions and goals set out in the CEQ Regulations: (1) briefly provide sufficient evidence and analysis for determining whether to prepare an EIS; (2) aid an agency's compliance with NEPA when no EIS is necessary, i.e., the EA helps to identify and analyze better alternatives and mitigation measures; and (3) facilitate preparation of an EIS when one is necessary.[28]

2.   Early NEPA Integration in Planning

An agency should first consider integrating the NEPA process into planning when it structures its internal process for developing a proposed policy, program, management plan, or project. Agencies must integrate the NEPA process into their planning at the earliest possible time to ensure that planning and decisions reflect environmental values, avoid delays later in the process, and anticipate and attempt to resolve potential issues.[29] NEPA should not become an after-the-fact process that justifies decisions that have already been made.[30]

The CEQ Regulations emphasize early NEPA planning in the context of an EIS. The scoping process can be used before an agency issues a notice of intent to seek useful information

---

[26] See CEQ, "Forty Most Asked Questions Concerning CEQ's National Environmental Policy Act Regulations" (Mar. 16, 1981), available at ceq.hss.doe.gov/nepa/regs/40/30-40.HTM#36 (Question 36a and Answer). Note that at the time of Forty-Questions memorandum CEQ was of the opinion that mitigated Findings of No Significant Impact were only appropriate if the mitigation measures were imposed by statute or regulation, or submitted by an applicant or agency as part of the original proposal. See Id. (Question 40 and Answer). CEQ has since published guidance accepting mitigated FONSIs as another means of efficiently concluding the NEPA process without producing an EIS. CEQ, "Appropriate Use of Mitigation and Monitoring and Clarifying the Appropriate Use of Mitigated Findings of No Significant Impact" (Jan. 14, 2011), available at ceq.hss.doe.gov/current_developments/docs/Mitigation_and_Monitoring_Guidance_14Jan2011.pdf.
[27] See 40 C.F.R. § 1508.9 (stating the EA is "a concise public document") and 40 C.F.R. § 1502.2(c) (interpreting the conciseness requirement for an EIS to mean that "length should vary first with potential environmental problems and then with project size").
[28] 40 C.F.R. § 1508.9(a).
[29] 40 C.F.R. § 1501.2.
[30] 40 C.F.R. § 1502.2(g).

on a proposal from agencies and the public.[31] For example, agencies can commence the process to prepare an EIS during the early stages of development of a proposal, to ensure that the environmental analysis can be completed in time for the agency to consider the final EIS before making a decision on the proposal.[32] Further, an agency shall prepare an EIS so that it can inform the decisionmaking process in a timely manner "and will not be used to rationalize or justify decisions already made."[33]

To prepare efficient EAs, agencies should adhere to these same principles and ensure that the EA is prepared in conjunction with the development of the proposed action in time to inform the public and the decisionmaker. Agencies should review their NEPA implementing procedures as well as their NEPA practices to ensure that NEPA is integrated into overall project planning and management to the fullest extent possible.

The CEQ Regulations call upon agencies to provide for situations where the initial planning process is in the hands of an applicant or other non-Federal entity.[34] The Regulations require Federal agencies to address these situations in their NEPA implementing procedures.[35]

---

[31] *See* CEQ Memorandum to Agencies, "Forty Most Asked Questions Concerning CEQ's National Environmental Policy Act Regulations" (Mar. 16, 1981), *available at* ceq.hss.doe.gov/nepa/regs/40/11-19.HTM#13 (Question 13 and Answer).

[32] *See* 40 C.F.R. § 1508.23 (explaining that a proposal exists as soon as an agency "has a goal and is actively preparing to make a decision on one or more alternative means of accomplishing that goal and the effects can be meaningfully evaluated").

[33] 40 C.F.R. § 1502.5. For guidelines specific to different agency activities, see 40 C.F.R. § 1502.5(a)-(d). Misuse of the NEPA process to justify decisions already made is counterproductive and can result in litigation that could delay and ultimately prevent a proposed action from proceeding.

[34] *See* 40 C.F.R. § 1501.2(d) (non-Federal entities plan activities prior to Federal involvement that trigger NEPA requirements).

[35] 40 C.F.R. § 1507.3(b)(1). All agencies are required to adopt procedures that supplement the CEQ Regulations and provide NEPA implementing guidance that both provides agency personnel with additional, more specific direction for implementing the procedural provisions of NEPA and informs the public and State and local officials of how the CEQ Regulations will be implemented in agency decisionmaking. Agency procedures should therefore provide Federal personnel with the direction they need to implement NEPA on a day-to-day basis. The procedures must also provide a clear and uncomplicated picture of what those outside the Federal government may do to become involved in the environmental review process under NEPA. *See* CEQ, "Agency Implementing Procedures Under CEQ's NEPA Regulations" (Jan. 19, 1979), *available at* ceq.hss.doe.gov/nepa/regs/exec11979.html. Some examples of agency NEPA implementing procedures are the Department of the Interior, "Department Manual: Managing the NEPA Process--National Park Service" (May 27, 2004), *available at* http://206.131.241.18/app_dm/act_getfiles.cfm?relnum=3622 and the Department of the Interior, "Departmental Manual: Managing the NEPA Process--Bureau of Land Management" (May 8, 2008), *available at* http://elips.doi.gov/app_dm/act_getfiles.cfm?relnum=3799.

Consequently, agencies that have a reasonably foreseeable role in actions that are initially developed by private applicants or other non-Federal entities must plan for those situations. The NEPA implementing procedures for such agencies must provide access to designated staff or the policies that can inform applicants and other non-Federal entities of studies or other information foreseeably required for later Federal action.[36]

Advanced planning prior to Federal involvement in an action must also ensure that the Federal agency is able to initiate early consultation with appropriate Tribes, States, local agencies, and interested private persons and organizations when Federal involvement is reasonably foreseeable.[37] For actions initiated at the request of a non-Federal entity, Federal agencies should begin the NEPA process for preparing their EA or EIS as early as possible but no later than upon receipt of a complete application.[38] Federal agencies should, whenever possible, guide applicants to gather and develop the appropriate level of information and analyses in advance of submitting an application or other request for Federal agency action. For example, several agencies require an applicant to prepare and submit an environmental report to help prepare the NEPA analyses and documentation and facilitate the lead agency's independent environmental review of the proposal.

3.   Scoping

To effectuate integrated decisionmaking, avoid duplication, and focus the NEPA review, the CEQ Regulations provide for "scoping."[39] In scoping, the lead agency determines the issues that the EA or EIS will address and identifies the significant impacts related to the proposed action that will be considered in the analysis.[40] To increase efficiency, the lead agency can solicit cooperation at the earliest possible time from other agencies that have jurisdiction by law or special expertise on any environmental issue that should be considered. Cooperating agencies with jurisdiction by law or special expertise can work with the lead agency to ensure that,

---

[36] 40 C.F.R. § 1501.2(d)(1).

[37] 40 C.F.R. § 1501.2(d)(2). Agencies should be cognizant of their obligations under current Executive Orders 13175 (Consultation and Coordination with Indian Tribal Governments, Nov. 6, 2000) and 112898 (Federal Actions to Address Environmental Justice in Minority Populations and Low-Income Populations, Feb 11, 1994), *available at* ceq.hss.doe.gov/laws_and_executive_orders/executive_orders.html.

[38] 40 C.F.R. § 1501.2(d)(3).

[39] *See* 40 C.F.R. § 1501.7 ("There shall be an early and open process for determining the scope of issues to be addressed and for identifying the significant issues related to a proposed action. This process shall be termed scoping.").

[40] 40 C.F.R. §§ 1500.4(b), (g) and 1501.7.

whenever possible, one NEPA review process informs all the decisions needed to determine whether and, if so, how a proposed action will proceed.[41]

The CEQ Regulations explicitly address the role of scoping in preparation of an EIS. Agencies can also choose to take advantage of scoping whenever preparing an EA. Scoping can be particularly useful when an EA deals with uncertainty or controversy regarding potential conflicts over the use of resources or the environmental effects of the proposed action, or where mitigation measures are likely to play a large role in determining whether the impacts will be reduced to a level where a Finding of No Significant Impact can be made. A lead agency preparing an EA may use scoping to identify and eliminate from detailed study the issues that are not significant or that have been covered by prior environmental review.[42] The scoping process provides a transparent way to identify significant environmental issues *and* to deemphasize insignificant issues,[43] thereby focusing the analysis on the most pertinent issues and impacts.[44] We recommend that agencies review their NEPA implementing procedures, as well as their NEPA practices, to ensure they have the option of scoping for EAs.

The scoping process can be particularly helpful in identifying opportunities to coordinate reviews and related surveys and studies required by other laws or by executive orders. Scoping can also be used to begin inter- and intra-governmental coordination if it is not already ongoing. To accomplish these goals, the lead agency preparing an EA or an EIS can choose to invite the participation of affected Federal, State, and local agencies, any affected Indian tribe, the proponent of the action, and "other interested persons (including those who might not be in accord with the action on environmental grounds)."[45] In addition to facilitating coordination and

---

[41] *See* 40 C.F.R. §§ 1501.6, 1508.5 (responsibilities of the lead agency include the requirement to request the participation of any other Federal agency which has jurisdiction by law). CEQ has released previous guidance on engaging other agencies with jurisdiction over permits and other approvals required for a proposal to proceed. CEQ, "Cooperating Agencies in Implementing the Procedural Requirements of the National Environmental Policy Act" (Jan. 30, 2002), *available at* ceq.hss.doe.gov/nepa/regs/cooperating/cooperatingagenciesmemorandum.html; CEQ, "Forty Most Asked Questions Concerning CEQ's National Environmental Policy Act Regulations" (Mar. 16, 1981), *available at* ceq.hss.doe.gov/nepa/regs/40/11-19.HTM#14 (Question and Answer 14).
[42] 40 C.F.R. § 1501.7(a)(3).
[43] 40 C.F.R. § 1500.4(g).
[44] *See generally* 40 C.F.R. § 1501.4(b) (agencies are to involve the public in the preparation of EAs; the manner in which they do so is left to the agency).
[45] 40 C.F.R. §§ 1501.7(a)(1), 1501.4(b), 1506.6. Establishing cooperating agency status is discussed in greater detail in a CEQ memorandum addressed to the heads of Federal agencies, entitled "Cooperating Agencies in Implementing the Procedural Requirements of the National Environmental Policy Act." CEQ, "Cooperating Agencies in Implementing the Procedural Requirements of the National Environmental Policy Act" (Jan. 30, 2002), *available at* ceq.hss.doe.gov/nepa/regs/cooperating/cooperatingagenciesmemorandum.html.

the development of required environmental reviews, scoping will help to identify the universe of matters that need to be addressed with particular care and flag issues for thorough consideration, thereby defusing potential conflict that, absent early attention, could arise later and potentially delay the timely completion of the relevant NEPA review and agency decision.[46]

In sum, the scoping process provides an early opportunity to plan collaboration with other governments,[47] assign responsibilities,[48] and develop the planning and decisionmaking schedule.[49] It also affords lead agencies the option of setting page limits for environmental documents and setting time limits for the steps in the NEPA process.[50] Agencies may choose to use scoping whenever any of these techniques can provide for the more effective and efficient preparation of an EA.

4.   Inter-Governmental Coordination (State, Local, or Tribal Environmental Reviews)

CEQ encourages Federal agencies to collaborate with Tribal, State, and local governments to the fullest extent possible to reduce duplication, unless the agencies are specifically barred from doing so by some other law.[51] The CEQ Regulations explicitly provide for agencies to conduct joint planning processes, joint environmental research and studies, joint public hearings (except where otherwise precluded by statute), and joint environmental assessments.[52] Federal agencies should explore every reasonable opportunity to integrate the requirements of NEPA with the external planning and environmental reviews required on the

---

[46] In cases where a Federal agency uses scoping for an EA and subsequently determines it is necessary to conduct an EIS, the agency should refer to the guidance previously published by the CEQ. *See* CEQ, "Forty Most Asked Questions Concerning CEQ's National Environmental Policy Act Regulations" (Mar. 16, 1981), *available at* ceq.hss.doe.gov/nepa/regs/40/30-40.HTM#13 (Question 13 and the following answer state that scoping done before the assessment, and in aid of its preparation, cannot substitute for the normal scoping process after publication of the notice of intent, unless the earlier public notice stated clearly that this possibility was under consideration, and the notice of intent expressly provides that written comments on the scope of alternatives and impacts will still be considered).
[47] 40 C.F.R. §§ 1501.6, 1508.5. CEQ has published guidance encouraging lead agencies to establish a formal cooperating agency relationship with other Federal agencies as well as State, Tribal, and local governmental entities. CEQ, "Cooperating Agencies in Implementing the Procedural Requirements of the National Environmental Policy Act" (Jan. 30, 2002), *available at* ceq.hss.doe.gov/nepa/regs/cooperating/cooperatingagenciesmemorandum.html.
[48] *See, e.g.*, 40 C.F.R. § 1501.7(a)(4) (a lead agency may allocate responsibility for EIS preparation and analysis among cooperating agencies during scoping).
[49] 40 C.F.R. § 1501.7(a)(7).
[50] 40 C.F.R. §§ 1501.7(b)(1)-(2), 1501.8.
[51] 40 C.F.R. § 1506.2(b).
[52] 40 C.F.R. § 1506.2(b); *see also* 40 C.F.R. § 1500.4(n) (encouraging Federal agencies to eliminate duplication with State and local procedures through joint preparation of documents).

Federal as well as the State, Tribal, and local levels of government so that those reviews can run concurrently rather than consecutively.[53]

Where State law or local ordinances contain environmental impact analysis and documentation requirements in addition to, but not in conflict with, those in NEPA, the CEQ Regulations provide authority for producing joint EISs.[54] In such cases, Federal agencies shall cooperate with the State, Tribal, and local governments to integrate environmental impact analysis and documentation requirements so that one document will suffice for complying with as many applicable environmental laws and requirements as practicable. Agencies should adhere to these same principles when preparing an EA. Federal agencies should seek efficiencies and avoid delay by attempting to meet applicable non-Federal NEPA-like requirements in conjunction with either an EA or an EIS wherever possible.[55]

The CEQ Regulations also require that a Federal agency preparing an EIS better integrate the EIS into non-Federal planning processes by discussing and explaining any inconsistency of a proposed Federal action with any approved State or local plans and laws.[56] When preparing an EA or EIS, if an inconsistency with any approved Tribal, State, or local plan or law exists, the Federal agency should describe the extent to which it will reconcile its proposed action with the non-Federal plan or law.[57]

5.   Coordinating Reviews and Documents under Other Applicable Laws

Agencies must integrate, to the fullest extent possible, their draft EIS with environmental impact analyses and related surveys and studies required by other statutes or Executive Orders.[58] Coordinated and concurrent environmental reviews are appropriate whenever other analyses, surveys, and studies will consider the same issues and information as a NEPA analysis. Such coordination should be considered when preparing an EA as well as when preparing an EIS. Techniques available to agencies when coordinating a combined or a concurrent process include combining scoping, requests for public comment, and the subsequent preparation and display of responses to public comments.

---

[53] 40 C.F.R. § 1500.2(c). This point is reiterated throughout the CEQ Regulations.
[54] 40 C.F.R. § 1506.2(c).
[55] Although joint processes usually lead to greater efficiency and better decisionmaking, a joint process may become unwieldy and the result is that, for some projects, combining a State and Federal process is not practical.
[56] 40 C.F.R. § 1506.2(d).
[57] 40 C.F.R. § 1506.2(d).
[58] 40 C.F.R. § 1502.25(a). Examples provided in the Regulation are: the Fish and Wildlife Coordination Act (16 U.S.C. § 661 *et seq.*); the National Historic Preservation Act (16 U.S.C. §470 *et seq.*); and the Endangered Species Act (16 U.S.C. § 1531 *et seq.*).

The goal should be to conduct concurrent rather than sequential processes whenever appropriate. In situations where one aspect of a project is within the particular expertise or jurisdiction of another agency an agency should consider whether adoption or incorporation by reference of materials prepared by the other agency would be more efficient.

A coordinated or concurrent process may provide a better basis for informed decision making, or at least achieve the same result as separate or consecutive processes more quickly and with less potential for unnecessary duplication of effort. In addition to integrating the reviews and analyses, the CEQ Regulations allow an environmental document that complies with NEPA to be combined with a subsequent agency document to reduce duplication and paperwork.[59]

6.   Adoption

The adoption of one Federal agency's EIS, or a portion of that EIS, by another Federal agency is an efficiency that the CEQ Regulations provide.[60] An agency preparing an EA should similarly consider adopting another agency's EA or EIS when the EA or EIS, or a portion thereof, addresses the proposed action and meets the standards for an adequate analysis under NEPA, the CEQ's Regulations, and the adopting agency's NEPA implementing procedures.

The CEQ Regulations require agencies to involve agencies, applicants, and the public when preparing an EA; however, they do not require agencies to do so by preparing a draft or final EA for public review or comment.[61] If an agency's implementing NEPA procedures establish requirements for public review and comment when preparing an EA, then the agency must provide a similar process when it adopts another agency's EA, but may use the same efficiencies that are available when adopting another agency's EIS.

If the actions covered by the original EIS and the proposed action are substantially the same, the agency adopting the EIS is not required to recirculate the EIS as a draft for public review and comment.. This same holds true for the adoption of another agency's EA when the original and proposed actions are substantially the same. In addition, in cases where the adopting agency is also a cooperating agency in the preparation of an EIS, it may adopt the lead agency's EIS without recirculating the EIS as a draft or as a final EIS when, after an independent review, it concludes that the lead agency has adequately addressed the adopting agency's comments and suggestions.[62] Similarly, when the adopting agency was a cooperating agency in the preparation of an EA, it may adopt the EA without recirculating the EA.

---

[59] 40 C.F.R. §§ 1506.4, 1500.4(k) & (n).
[60] 40 C.F.R. § 1506.3.
[61] *See generally* 40 C.F.R. §§ 1501.4(b), 1506.6 (both regulations direct agencies to involve the public in the preparation of EAs; however, the manner in which they do so is left to the agency).
[62] 40 C.F.R. § 1506.3(c).

12

7.   Incorporation by Reference

Incorporation by reference is another method that provides efficiency and timesaving when preparing either an EA or an EIS.[63] The CEQ Regulations direct agencies to incorporate by reference material into an EIS to reduce the size of the EIS and avoid duplicative effort.[64] An agency must provide a citation that clearly identifies the incorporated material in an EIS and briefly describe the content.[65] The brief description should identify the referenced materials and the entity (Federal or non-Federal) that prepared the materials, inform the reader of the purpose and value of those materials (e.g., explain how the information or analyses are relevant to the issues associated with the proposal under review), and synopsize the basis provided in those materials that support any conclusions being incorporated. An agency may not incorporate any material by reference in an EIS unless the material is reasonably available for inspection by potentially interested persons within the time allowed for comment.[66] There are many techniques available to make the referenced material readily available such as: placing the relevant materials in an appendix; providing a hyperlink that provides internet access to the materials; and placing materials in local libraries or facilities accessible to the public. Agencies can, consistent with NEPA and the CEQ Regulations, incorporate by reference analyses and information from existing documents into an EA provided the material has been appropriately cited and described, and the materials are reasonably available for review by interested parties.

8.   Expediting Responses to Comments

Agencies should provide a reasonable and proportionate response to comments on a draft EIS by focusing on the environmental issues and information conveyed by the comments. When preparing a final EIS, if the draft EIS complies with NEPA, CEQ regulations, and agency implementing procedures, the agency may use the draft EIS as the final EIS under certain conditions. If changes in response to comments are minor and are limited to factual corrections and/or explanations of why the comments do not warrant further agency response, agencies may write them on errata sheets and attach them to the statement instead of rewriting the draft statement.[67] In such cases, the agency must circulate and make available for public review as the final EIS only the comments, the responses and the changes.[68] The comments, responses, and

---

[63] This guidance does not address tiering. Further guidance will be developed to address the use of broad, programmatic, analyses to focus future reviews and the subsequent, tiered, review of site- or project- specific proposed actions.
[64] 40 C.F.R. § 1502.21.
[65] 40 C.F.R. § 1502.21.
[66] *See* 40 C.F.R. § 1502.21 (material based on proprietary data which is itself not available for review and comment cannot be incorporated by reference).
[67] 40 C.F.R. §§ 1503.4(c), 1500.4(m).
[68] 40 C.F.R. § 1503.4(c).

changes, as well as the draft document and a new cover sheet need to be filed to make the EIS final, under those circumstances.[69]

Similarly, if an agency issues an EA for comment and the changes in response to comments are minor and limited to factual corrections and/or explanations of why the comments do not warrant further agency response, then the agency may prepare a similar cover and errata sheet and use its draft EA as the final EA. When circulating draft EAs or EISs for public review and comment, we recommend agencies facilitate public review and comment by also publishing the EISs and EAs, and subsequently the comments received, on agency websites.

9.   Clear Time Lines for NEPA Reviews

Establishing appropriate and predictable time limits promotes the efficiency of the NEPA process.[70] The CEQ Regulations recommend that agencies designate a person (such as a project manager or a person in the agency's office with NEPA responsibilities) to lead and shepherd the NEPA review to expedite the process.[71] The CEQ Regulations do not prescribe universal time limits for the entire NEPA process; instead they set certain minimum time limits for the various portions of the NEPA process.[72] The CEQ Regulations do encourage Federal agencies to set appropriate time limits for individual actions, however, and provide a list of factors to consider in establishing timelines.[73] Those factors include: the potential for environmental harm; the size of the proposed action; other time limits imposed on the action by other statutes, regulations, or Executive Orders; the degree of public need for the proposed action and the consequences of delay; and the need for a reasonable opportunity for public review.

The CEQ Regulations refer to the EIS process when describing the "constituent parts of the NEPA process" to which time limits may apply, require agencies to set time limits at the request of an applicant, and allow agencies to set time limits at the request of other interested parties.[74] It is entirely consistent with the purposes and goals of NEPA and with the CEQ Regulations for agencies to consider the same factors and determine appropriate time limits for the various phases of the EA process when requested by applicants, Tribes, States, local agencies, or members of the public.

---

[69] 40 C.F.R. § 1503.4(c).

[70] 40 C.F.R. § 1500.5(e).

[71] 40 C.F.R. § 1501.8(b)(3).

[72] See 40 C.F.R. § 1506.10 (setting 90 day time period between EPA publication of the notice of availability of a draft EIS and the Record of Decision, 30 day time period between EPA publication of the notice of availability of a final EIS and the Record of Decision, and 45 days for comment on a draft EIS).

[73] CEQ encourages Federal agencies to set time limits consistent with the time intervals required by § 1506.10. 40 C.F.R. § 1501.8.

[74] 40 C.F.R. § 1501.8(a), (c).

Conclusion

This guidance highlights for agencies preparing either an EA or an EIS the ability to employ all the methods provided in the CEQ regulations to prepare concise and timely NEPA reviews. Using methods such as integrating planning and environmental reviews and permitting, coordinating multi-agency or multi-governmental reviews and approvals, and setting schedules for completing the environmental review will assist agencies in preparing efficient and timely EAs and EISs consistent with legal precedent and agency NEPA experience and practice.

#   #   #

NEPA Deskbook

Appendix 27 **Memorandum for Heads of Federal Departments and Agencies: Appropriate Use of Mitigation and Monitoring and Appropriate Use of Mitigated Findings of No Significant Impact**

EXECUTIVE OFFICE OF THE PRESIDENT
COUNCIL ON ENVIRONMENTAL QUALITY
WASHINGTON, D.C. 20503

January 14, 2011

MEMORANDUM FOR HEADS OF FEDERAL DEPARTMENTS AND AGENCIES

FROM: NANCY H. SUTLEY
                  Chair

SUBJECT: Appropriate Use of Mitigation and Monitoring and Clarifying the
                  Appropriate Use of Mitigated Findings of No Significant Impact

        The Council on Environmental Quality (CEQ) is issuing this guidance for Federal
departments and agencies on establishing, implementing, and monitoring mitigation
commitments identified and analyzed in Environmental Assessments, Environmental
Impact Statements, and adopted in the final decision documents. This guidance also
clarifies the appropriate use of mitigated "Findings of No Significant Impact" under the
National Environmental Policy Act (NEPA). This guidance is issued in accordance with
NEPA, 42 U.S.C. § 4321 et seq., and the CEQ Regulations for Implementing the
Procedural Provisions of NEPA (CEQ Regulations), 40 CFR Parts 1500-1508.[1] The
guidance explains the requirements of NEPA and the CEQ Regulations, describes CEQ
policies, and recommends procedures for agencies to use to help them comply with the
requirements of NEPA and the CEQ Regulations when they establish mitigation planning
and implementation procedures.[2]

---

[1] The Council on Environmental Quality (CEQ) Regulations for Implementing the
Procedural Provisions of the National Environmental Policy Act (CEQ Regulations) are
available on www.nepa.gov at ceq.hss.doe.gov/ceq_regulations/regulations.html.

[2] CEQ is issuing this guidance as an exercise of its duties and functions under section
204 of the National Environmental Policy Act (NEPA), 42 U.S.C. § 4344, and Executive
Order No. 11,514, 35 Fed. Reg. 4,247 (Mar. 5, 1970), as amended by Executive Order
No. 11,991, 42 Fed. Reg. 26,927 (May 24, 1977). This guidance is not a rule or
regulation, and the recommendations it contains may not apply to a particular situation
based upon the individual facts and circumstances. This guidance does not change or
substitute for any law, regulation, or other legally binding requirement and is not legally
enforceable. The use of language such as "recommend," "may," "should," and "can" is
intended to describe CEQ policies and recommendations. The use of mandatory
terminology such as "must" and "required" is intended to describe controlling
requirements under the terms of NEPA and the CEQ Regulations, but this document does
not independently establish legally binding requirements.

1

NEPA was enacted to promote efforts that will prevent or eliminate damage to the human environment.[3] Mitigation measures can help to accomplish this goal in several ways. Many Federal agencies and applicants include mitigation measures as integral components of a proposed project's design. Agencies also consider mitigation measures as alternatives when developing Environmental Assessments (EA) and Environmental Impact Statements (EIS). In addition, agencies have increasingly considered mitigation measures in EAs to avoid or lessen potentially significant environmental effects of proposed actions that would otherwise need to be analyzed in an EIS.[4] This use of mitigation may allow the agency to comply with NEPA's procedural requirements by issuing an EA and a Finding of No Significant Impact (FONSI), or "mitigated FONSI," based on the agency's commitment to ensure the mitigation that supports the FONSI is performed, thereby avoiding the need to prepare an EIS.

This guidance addresses mitigation that an agency has committed to implement as part of a project design and mitigation commitments informed by the NEPA review process. As discussed in detail in Section I, below, agencies may commit to mitigation measures considered as alternatives in an EA or EIS so as to achieve an environmentally preferable outcome. Agencies may also commit to mitigation measures to support a mitigated FONSI, so as to complete their review of potentially significant environmental impacts without preparing an EIS. When agencies do not document and, in important cases, monitor mitigation commitments to determine if the mitigation was implemented or effective, the use of mitigation may fail to advance NEPA's purpose of ensuring informed and transparent environmental decisionmaking. Failure to document and monitor mitigation may also undermine the integrity of the NEPA review. These concerns and the need for guidance on this subject have long been recognized.[5] While

---

[3] 42 U.S.C. § 4321 (stating that the purposes of NEPA include promoting efforts which will prevent or eliminate damage to the environment).

[4] This trend was noted in CEQ's Twenty-Fifth Anniversary report on the effectiveness of NEPA implementation. *See* CEQ, "NEPA: A Study of its Effectiveness After Twenty-Five Years" 20 (1997), *available at* ceq.hss.doe.gov/nepa/nepa25fn.pdf.

[5] *See, e.g.,* CEQ, 1987-1988 Annual Report, *available at* www.slideshare.net/whitehouse/august-1987-1988-the-eighteenth-annual-report-of-the-council-on-environmental-quality (stating that CEQ would issue guidance on the propriety of an Environmental Assessment (EA) and Finding of No Significant Impact (FONSI) rather than requiring an Environmental Impact Statement (EIS) when the environmental effects of a proposal are significant but mitigation reduces those impacts to less than significant levels). In 2002, CEQ convened a Task Force on Modernizing NEPA Implementation, which recommended that CEQ issue guidance clarifying the requirements for public involvement, alternatives, and mitigation for actions that warrant longer EAs including those with mitigated FONSIs. CEQ NEPA Task Force, "Modernizing NEPA Implementation" 75 (2003), *available at* ceq.hss.doe.gov/ntf/report/totaldoc.html. NEPA experts and public stakeholders have expressed broad support for this recommendation, calling for consideration of monitoring and public involvement in the use of mitigated FONSIs. CEQ, "The Public and Experts'

2

this guidance is designed to address these concerns, CEQ also acknowledges that NEPA itself does not create a general substantive duty on Federal agencies to mitigate adverse environmental effects.[6]

Accordingly, in conjunction with the 40th Anniversary of NEPA, CEQ announced that it would issue this guidance to clarify the appropriateness of mitigated FONSIs and the importance of monitoring environmental mitigation commitments.[7] This new guidance affirms CEQ's support for the appropriate use of mitigated FONSIs, and accordingly amends and supplements previously issued guidance.[8] This guidance is intended to enhance the integrity and credibility of the NEPA process and the information upon which it relies.

CEQ provides several broad recommendations in Section II, below, to help improve agency consideration of mitigation in EISs and EAs. Agencies should not commit to mitigation measures considered in an EIS or EA absent the authority or expectation of resources to ensure that the mitigation is performed. In the decision documents concluding their environmental reviews, agencies should clearly identify any mitigation measures adopted as agency commitments or otherwise relied upon (to the extent consistent with agency authority or other legal authority), so as to ensure the integrity of the NEPA process and allow for greater transparency.

Review of the National Environmental Policy Act Task Force Report 'Modernizing NEPA Implementation'" 7 (2004), *available at* ceq.hss.doe.gov/ntf/CEQ_Draft_Final_Roundtable_Report.pdf; *see also* CEQ, "Rocky Mountain Roundtable Report" 8 (2004), *available at* ceq.hss.doe.gov/ntf/RockyMtnRoundTableReport.pdf (noting that participants in a regional roundtable on NEPA modernization identified "developing a means to enforce agency commitments to monitoring and mitigation" as one of the top five aspects of NEPA implementation needing immediate attention); "Eastern Round Table Report" 4 (2003), *available at* ceq.hss.doe.gov/ntf/EasternRoundTableReport.pdf (reporting that, according to several panelists at a regional roundtable, "parties responsible for monitoring the effects of . . . mitigation measures are rarely identified or easily held accountable," and that a lack of monitoring impedes agencies' ability to address the cumulative effects of EA actions).

[6] *Robertson v. Methow Valley Citizens Council*, 490 U.S. 332, 352 (1989).

[7] CEQ, "New Proposed NEPA Guidance and Steps to Modernize and Reinvigorate NEPA" (Feb. 18, 2010), *available at* www.whitehouse.gov/administration/eop/ceq/initiatives/nepa.

[8] This previous guidance is found in CEQ, "Forty Most Asked Questions Concerning CEQ's National Environmental Policy Act Regulations," 46 Fed. Reg. 18,026 (Mar. 23, 1981), *available at* ceq.eh.doe.gov/nepa/regs/40/40P1.htm (suggesting that the existence of mitigation measures developed during the scoping or EA stages "does not obviate the need for an EIS").

Section III emphasizes that agencies should establish implementation plans based on the importance of the project and its projected effects. Agencies should create new, or strengthen existing, monitoring to ensure that mitigation commitments are implemented. Agencies should also use effectiveness monitoring to learn if the mitigation is providing the benefits predicted. Importantly, agencies should encourage public participation and accountability through proactive disclosure of, and provision of access to, agencies' mitigation commitments as well as mitigation monitoring reports and related documents.

Although the recommendations in this guidance are broad in nature, agencies should establish, in their NEPA implementing procedures and/or guidance, specific procedures that create systematic accountability and the mechanisms to accomplish these goals.[9] This guidance is intended to assist agencies with the development and review of their NEPA procedures, by specifically recommending:

- How to ensure that mitigation commitments are implemented;
- How to monitor the effectiveness of mitigation commitments;
- How to remedy failed mitigation; and
- How to involve the public in mitigation planning.

Finally, to assist agencies in the development of their NEPA implementing procedures, an overview of relevant portions of the Department of the Army NEPA regulations is appended to this guidance as an example for agencies to consider when incorporating the recommendations of this guidance as requirements in their NEPA programs and procedures.[10]

I. THE IMPORTANCE OF MITIGATION UNDER NEPA

Mitigation is an important mechanism Federal agencies can use to minimize the potential adverse environmental impacts associated with their actions. As described in the CEQ Regulations, agencies can use mitigation to reduce environmental impacts in several ways. Mitigation includes:

- Avoiding an impact by not taking a certain action or parts of an action;
- Minimizing an impact by limiting the degree or magnitude of the action and its implementation;
- Rectifying an impact by repairing, rehabilitating, or restoring the affected environment;
- Reducing or eliminating an impact over time, through preservation and maintenance operations during the life of the action; and

---

[9] 40 CFR § 1507.3 (requiring agencies to issue, and continually review, policies and procedures to implement NEPA in conformity with NEPA and CEQ Regulations).

[10] *See id.*; *see also id.* § 1507.2 (requiring agencies to have personnel and other resources available to implement NEPA reviews and meet their NEPA responsibilities).

- Compensating for an impact by replacing or providing substitute resources or environments.[11]

Federal agencies typically develop mitigation as a component of a proposed action, or as a measure considered in the course of the NEPA review conducted to support agency decisionmaking processes, or both. In developing mitigation, agencies necessarily and appropriately rely upon the expertise and experience of their professional staff to assess mitigation needs, develop mitigation plans, and oversee mitigation implementation. Agencies may also rely on outside resources and experts for information about the ecosystem functions and values to be protected or restored by mitigation, to ensure that mitigation has the desired effects and to develop appropriate monitoring strategies. Any outside parties consulted should be neutral parties without a financial interest in implementing the mitigation and monitoring plans, and should have expert knowledge, training, and experience relevant to the resources potentially affected by the actions and—if possible—the potential effects from similar actions.[12] Further, when agencies delegate responsibility for preparing NEPA analyses and documentation, or when other entities (such as applicants) assume such responsibility, CEQ recommends that any experts employed to develop mitigation and monitoring should have the kind of expert knowledge, training, and experience described above.

The sections below clarify practices Federal agencies should use when they employ mitigation in three different contexts: as components of project design; as mitigation alternatives considered in an EA or an EIS and adopted in related decision documents; and as measures identified and committed to in an EA as necessary to support a mitigated FONSI. CEQ encourages agencies to commit to mitigation to achieve environmentally preferred outcomes, particularly when addressing unavoidable adverse environmental impacts. Agencies should not commit to mitigation, however, unless they have sufficient legal authorities and expect there will be necessary resources available to perform or ensure the performance of the mitigation. The agency's own underlying authority may provide the basis for its commitment to implement and monitor the mitigation. Alternatively, the authority for the mitigation may derive from legal requirements that are enforced by other Federal, state, or local government entities (e.g., air or water permits administered by local or state agencies).

A. Mitigation Incorporated into Project Design

Many Federal agencies rely on mitigation to reduce adverse environmental impacts as part of the planning process for a project, incorporating mitigation as integral components of a proposed project design before making a determination about the

---

[11] *Id.* § 1508.20 (defining mitigation to include these activities).

[12] *See id.* § 1506.5 (providing that agencies are responsible for the accuracy of environmental information submitted by applicants for use in EISs and EAs, and requiring contractors selected to prepare EISs to execute disclosure statement specifying that they have no financial or other interest in the outcome of the project).

5

significance of the project's environmental impacts.[13] Such mitigation can lead to an environmentally preferred outcome and in some cases reduce the projected impacts of agency actions to below a threshold of significance. An example of mitigation measures that are typically included as part of the proposed action are agency standardized best management practices such as those developed to prevent storm water runoff or fugitive dust emissions at a construction site.

Mitigation measures included in the project design are integral components of the proposed action, are implemented with the proposed action, and therefore should be clearly described as part of the proposed action that the agency will perform or require to be performed. Consequently, the agency can address mitigation early in the decisionmaking process and potentially conduct a less extensive level of NEPA review.

B. Mitigation Alternatives Considered in Environmental Assessments and Environmental Impact Statements

Agencies are required, under NEPA, to study, develop, and describe appropriate alternatives when preparing EAs and EISs.[14] The CEQ Regulations specifically identify procedures agencies must follow when developing and considering mitigation alternatives when preparing an EIS. When an agency prepares an EIS, it must include mitigation measures (not already included in the proposed action or alternatives) among the alternatives compared in the EIS.[15] Each EIS must contain a section analyzing the environmental consequences of the proposed action and its alternatives, including "[m]eans to mitigate adverse environmental impacts."[16]

When a Federal agency identifies a mitigation alternative in an EA or an EIS, it may commit to implement that mitigation to achieve an environmentally-preferable outcome. Agencies should not commit to mitigation measures considered and analyzed in an EIS or EA if there are insufficient legal authorities, or it is not reasonable to foresee the availability of sufficient resources, to perform or ensure the performance of the mitigation. Furthermore, the decision document following the EA should—and a Record of Decision (ROD) must—identify those mitigation measures that the agency is adopting

---

[13] CEQ NEPA Task Force, "Modernizing NEPA Implementation" at 69.

[14] 42 U.S.C. § 4332(2)(C) (mandating that agencies' detailed statements must include alternatives to the proposed action); *id.* § 4332(E) (requiring agencies to study, develop, and describe appropriate alternatives to recommended courses of action in any proposal which involves unresolved conflicts concerning alternative uses of available resources).

[15] 40 CFR § 1502.14(f) (listing mitigation measures as one of the required components of the alternatives included in an EIS); *id.* § 1508.25(b)(3) (defining the "scope" of an EIS to include mitigation measures).

[16] *Id.* § 1502.16(h).

and committing to implement, including any monitoring and enforcement program applicable to such mitigation commitments.[17]

C. Mitigation Commitments Analyzed in Environmental Assessments to Support a Mitigated FONSI

When preparing an EA, many agencies develop and consider committing to mitigation measures to avoid, minimize, rectify, reduce, or compensate for potentially significant adverse environmental impacts that would otherwise require full review in an EIS. CEQ recognizes the appropriateness, value, and efficacy of providing for mitigation to reduce the significance of environmental impacts. Consequently, when such mitigation measures are available and an agency commits to perform or ensure the performance of them, then these mitigation commitments can be used to support a FONSI, allowing the agency to conclude the NEPA process and proceed with its action without preparing an EIS.[18] An agency should not commit to mitigation measures necessary for a mitigated FONSI if there are insufficient legal authorities, or it is not reasonable to foresee the availability of sufficient resources, to perform or ensure the performance of the mitigation.[19]

Mitigation commitments needed to lower the level of impacts so that they are not significant should be clearly described in the mitigated FONSI document and in any other relevant decision documents related to the proposed action. Agencies must provide for appropriate public involvement during the development of the EA and FONSI.[20]

---

[17] *Id.* § 1505.2(c) (providing that a record of decision must state whether all practicable means to avoid or minimize environmental harm from the alternative selected have been adopted, and if not, why they were not; and providing that a monitoring and enforcement program must be adopted and summarized where applicable for any mitigation).

[18] This guidance approves of the use of the "mitigated FONSI" when the NEPA process results in *enforceable* mitigation measures. It thereby amends and supplements previously issued CEQ guidance that suggested that the existence of mitigation measures developed during the scoping or EA stages "does not obviate the need for an EIS." *See* CEQ, "Forty Most Asked Questions Concerning CEQ's National Environmental Policy Act Regulations," 46 Fed. Reg. 18,026 (Mar. 23, 1981), *available at* ceq.eh.doe.gov/nepa/regs/40/40P1.htm.

[19] When agencies consider and decide on an alternative outside their jurisdiction (as discussed in 40 CFR § 1502.14(c)), they should identify the authority for the mitigation and consider the consequences of it not being implemented.

[20] 40 CFR § 1501.4(b) (requiring agencies to involve environmental agencies, applicants, and the public, to the extent practicable); *id.* § 1501.4(e)(1) (requiring agencies to make FONSIs available to the affected public as specified in § 1506.6); *id.* § 1501.4(e)(2) (requiring agencies to make FONSIs available for public review for thirty days before making any final determination on whether to prepare an EIS or proceed with an action when the proposed action is, or is closely similar to, one which normally requires the

Furthermore, in addition to those situations where a 30-day public review of the FONSI is required,[21] agencies should make the EA and FONSI available to the public (e.g., by posting them on an agency website). Providing the public with clear information about agencies' mitigation commitments helps ensure the value and integrity of the NEPA process.

II. ENSURING THAT MITIGATION COMMITMENTS ARE IMPLEMENTED

Federal agencies should take steps to ensure that mitigation commitments are actually implemented. Consistent with their authority, agencies should establish internal processes to ensure that mitigation commitments made on the basis of any NEPA analysis are carefully documented and that relevant funding, permitting, or other agency approvals and decisions are made conditional on performance of mitigation commitments.

Agency NEPA implementing procedures should require clear documentation of mitigation commitments considered in EAs and EISs prepared during the NEPA process and adopted in their decision documents. Agencies should ensure that the expertise and professional judgment applied in determining the appropriate mitigation commitments are described in the EA or EIS, and that the NEPA analysis considers when and how those mitigation commitments will be implemented.

Agencies should clearly identify commitments to mitigation measures designed to achieve environmentally preferable outcomes in their decision documents. They should also identify mitigation commitments necessary to reduce impacts, where appropriate, to a level necessary for a mitigated FONSI. In both cases, mitigation commitments should be carefully specified in terms of measurable performance standards or expected results, so as to establish clear performance expectations.[22] The agency should also specify the

---

preparation of an EIS under agency NEPA implementing procedures, or when the nature of the proposed action is one without precedent); *id.* § 1506.6 (requiring agencies to make diligent efforts to involve the public in preparing and implementing their NEPA procedures).

[21] *Id.* § 1501.4(e)(2).

[22] In 2001, the Committee on Mitigating Wetland Losses, through the National Research Council (NRC), conducted a nationwide study evaluating compensatory mitigation, focusing on whether the process is achieving the overall goal of "restoring and maintaining the quality of the nation's waters." NRC Committee on Mitigating Wetland Losses, "Compensating for Wetland Losses Under the Clean Water Act" 2 (2001). The study's recommendations were incorporated into the 2008 Final Compensatory Mitigation Rule promulgated jointly by the U.S. Army Corps of Engineers and the U.S. Environmental Protection Agency. *See* U.S. Army Corps of Engineers & U.S. Environmental Protection Agency, "Compensatory Mitigation for Losses of Aquatic Resources," 73 Fed. Reg. 19,594 (Apr. 10, 2008).

timeframe for the agency action and the mitigation measures in its decision documents, to ensure that the intended start date and duration of the mitigation commitment is clear. When an agency funds, permits, or otherwise approves actions, it should also exercise its available authorities to ensure implementation of any mitigation commitments by including appropriate conditions on the relevant grants, permits, or approvals.

CEQ views funding for implementation of mitigation commitments as critical to ensuring informed decisionmaking. For mitigation commitments that agencies will implement directly, CEQ recognizes that it may not be possible to identify funds from future budgets; however, a commitment to seek funding is considered essential and if it is reasonably foreseeable that funding for implementation of mitigation may be unavailable at any time during the life of the project, the agency should disclose in the EA or EIS the possible lack of funding and assess the resultant environmental effects. If the agency has disclosed and assessed the lack of funding, then unless the mitigation is essential to a mitigated FONSI or necessary to comply with another legal requirement, the action could proceed. If the agency committing to implementing mitigation has not disclosed and assessed the lack of funding, and the necessary funding later becomes unavailable, then the agency should not move forward with the proposed action until funding becomes available or the lack of funding is appropriately assessed (*see* Section III, below).

A. Establishing a Mitigation Monitoring Program

Federal agencies must consider reasonably foreseeable future impacts and conditions in a constantly evolving environment. Decisionmakers will be better able to adapt to changing circumstances by creating a sound mitigation implementation plan and through ongoing monitoring of environmental impacts and their mitigation. Monitoring can improve the quality of overall agency decisionmaking by providing feedback on the effectiveness of mitigation techniques. A comprehensive approach to mitigation planning, implementation, and monitoring will therefore help agencies realize opportunities for reducing environmental impacts through mitigation, advancing the integrity of the entire NEPA process. These approaches also serve NEPA's goals of ensuring transparency and openness by making relevant and useful environmental information available to decisionmakers and the public.[23]

Adaptive management can help an agency take corrective action if mitigation commitments originally made in NEPA and decision documents fail to achieve projected environmental outcomes and there is remaining federal action. Agencies can, in their NEPA reviews, establish and analyze mitigation measures that are projected to result in the desired environmental outcomes, and can then identify those mitigation principles or measures that it would apply in the event the initial mitigation commitments are not implemented or effective. Such adaptive management techniques can be advantageous to both the environment and the agency's project goals.[24] Agencies can also, short of

---

[23] 40 CFR § 1500.1(b).

[24] *See* CEQ NEPA Task Force, "Modernizing NEPA Implementation" at 44.

adaptive management, analyze specific mitigation alternatives that could take the place of mitigation commitments in the event the commitment is not implemented or effective.

Monitoring is fundamental for ensuring the implementation and effectiveness of mitigation commitments, meeting legal and permitting requirements, and identifying trends and possible means for improvement. Under NEPA, a Federal agency has a continuing duty to ensure that new information about the environmental impact of its proposed actions is taken into account, and that the NEPA review is supplemented when significant new circumstances or information arise that are relevant to environmental concerns and bear on the proposed action or its impacts.[25] For agency decisions based on an EIS, the CEQ Regulations explicitly require that "a monitoring and enforcement program shall be adopted . . . where applicable for any mitigation."[26] In addition, the CEQ Regulations state that agencies may "provide for monitoring to assure that their decisions are carried out and should do so in important cases."[27] Accordingly, an agency should also commit to mitigation monitoring in important cases when relying upon an EA and mitigated FONSI. Monitoring is essential in those important cases where the mitigation is necessary to support a FONSI and thus is part of the justification for the agency's determination not to prepare an EIS.

Agencies are expected to apply professional judgment and the rule of reason when identifying those cases that are important and warrant monitoring, and when determining the type and extent of monitoring they will use to check on the progress made in implementing mitigation commitments as well as their effectiveness. In cases that are less important, the agency should exercise its discretion to determine what level of monitoring, if any, is appropriate. The following are examples of factors that agencies should consider to determine importance:

- Legal requirements of statutes, regulations, or permits;
- Human health and safety;
- Protected resources (e.g., parklands, threatened or endangered species, cultural or historic sites) and the proposed action's impacts on them;
- Degree of public interest in the resource or public debate over the effects of the proposed action and any reasonable mitigation alternatives on the resource; and
- Level of intensity of projected impacts.

Once an agency determines that it will provide for monitoring in a particular case, monitoring plans and programs should be described or incorporated by reference in the

---

[25] 40 CFR § 1502.9(c) (requiring supplementation of EISs when there are substantial changes to the proposed action, or significant new information or circumstances arise that are relevant to the environmental effects of the proposed action).

[26] *Id.* § 1505.2(c).

[27] *Id.* § 1505.3.

agency's decision documents.[28] Agencies have discretion, within the scope of their authority, to select an appropriate form and method for monitoring, but they should identify the monitoring area and establish the appropriate monitoring system.[29] The form and method of monitoring can be informed by an agency's past monitoring plans and programs that tracked impacts on similar resources, as well as plans and programs used by other agencies or entities, particularly those with an interest in the resource being monitored. For mitigation commitments that warrant rigorous oversight, an Environmental Management System (EMS), or other data or management system could serve as a useful way to integrate monitoring efforts effectively.[30] Other possible monitoring methods include agency-specific environmental monitoring, compliance assessment, and auditing systems. For activities involving third parties (e.g., permittees or grantees), it may be appropriate to require the third party to perform the monitoring as long as a clear accountability and oversight framework is established. The monitoring program should be implemented together with a review process and a system for reporting results.

Regardless of the method chosen, agencies should ensure that the monitoring program tracks whether mitigation commitments are being performed as described in the NEPA and related decision documents (i.e., implementation monitoring), and whether the mitigation effort is producing the expected outcomes and resulting environmental effects (i.e., effectiveness monitoring). Agencies should also ensure that their mitigation monitoring procedures appropriately provide for public involvement. These recommendations are explained in more detail below.

---

[28] The mitigation plan and program should be described to the extent possible based on available and reasonably foreseeable information in cases where the NEPA analysis and documentation are completed prior to final design of a proposed project.

[29] The Department of the Army regulations provide an example of this approach. *See* 32 CFR part 651 App. C. These regulations are summarized in the Appendix to this guidance.

[30] An EMS provides a systematic framework for a Federal agency to monitor and continually improve its environmental performance through audits, evaluations of legal and other requirements, and management reviews. The potential for EMS to support NEPA work is further addressed in CEQ, "Aligning National Environmental Policy Act Processes with Environmental Management Systems" 4 (2007) *available at* ceq.hss.doe.gov/nepa/nepapubs/Aligning_NEPA_Processes_with_Environmental_Manag ement_Systems_2007.pdf (discussing the use of EMSs to track implementation and monitoring of mitigation). In 2001, the Department of the Army announced that it would implement a recognized environmental management standard, ISO 14001, across Army installations. ISO 14001 represents a standardized system to plan, track, and monitor environmental performance within the agency's operations. To learn more about how EMS implementation has resulted in an effective EMS for monitoring purposes at an Army installation, see the Sustainability website for the Army's Fort Lewis installation, *available at* sustainablefortlewis.army.mil.

B. Monitoring Mitigation Implementation

A successful monitoring program will track the implementation of mitigation commitments to determine whether they are being performed as described in the NEPA documents and related decision documents. The responsibility for developing an implementation monitoring program depends in large part upon who will actually perform the mitigation—the lead Federal agency or cooperating agency; the applicant, grantee, or permit holder; another responsible entity or cooperative non-Federal partner; or a combination of these. The lead agency should ensure that information about responsible parties, mitigation requirements, as well as any appropriate enforcement clauses are included in documents such as authorizations, agreements, permits, financial assistance awards, or contracts.[31] Ultimate monitoring responsibility rests with the lead Federal agency or agencies to assure that monitoring is occurring when needed and that results are being properly considered. The project's lead agency can share monitoring responsibility with joint lead or cooperating agencies or other entities, such as applicants or grantees. The responsibility should be clearly described in the NEPA documents or associated decision documents, or related documents describing and establishing the monitoring requirements or expectations.

C. Monitoring the Effectiveness of Mitigation

Effectiveness monitoring tracks the success of a mitigation effort in achieving expected outcomes and environmental effects. Completing environmental data collection and analyses prior to project implementation provides an understanding of the baseline conditions for each potentially affected resource for reference when determining whether the predicted efficacy of mitigation commitments is being achieved. Agencies can rely on agency staff and outside experts familiar with the predicted environmental impacts to develop the means to monitor mitigation effectiveness, in the same way that they can rely on agency and outside experts to develop and evaluate the effectiveness of mitigation (*see* Section I, above).

When monitoring mitigation, agencies should consider drawing on sources of information available from the agency, from other Federal agencies, and from state, local, and tribal agencies, as well as from non-governmental sources such as local organizations, academic institutions, and non-governmental organizations. Agencies should especially consider working with agencies responsible for overseeing land management and impacts to specific resources. For example, agencies could consult with the U.S. Fish and Wildlife and National Marine Fisheries Services (for information to evaluate potential impacts to threatened and endangered species) and with State Historic Preservation Officers (for information to evaluate potential impacts to historic structures).

---

[31] Such enforcement clauses, including appropriate penalty clauses, should be developed as allowable under the applicable statutory and regulatory authorities.

D. The Role of the Public

Public involvement is a key procedural requirement of the NEPA review process, and should be fully provided for in the development of mitigation and monitoring procedures.[32] Agencies are also encouraged, as a matter of transparency and accountability, to consider including public involvement components in their mitigation monitoring programs. The agencies' experience and professional judgment are key to determining the appropriate level of public involvement. In addition to advancing accountability and transparency, public involvement may provide insight or perspective for improving mitigation activities and monitoring. The public may also assist with actual monitoring through public-private partnership programs.

Agencies should provide for public access to mitigation monitoring information consistent with NEPA and the Freedom of Information Act (FOIA).[33] NEPA and the CEQ Regulations incorporate the FOIA by reference to require agencies to provide public access to releasable documents related to EISs, which may include documents regarding mitigation monitoring and enforcement.[34] The CEQ Regulations also require agencies to involve the public in the EA preparation process to the extent practicable and in certain cases to make a FONSI available for public review before making its final determination on whether it will prepare an EIS or proceed with the action.[35] Consequently, agencies should involve the public when preparing EAs and mitigated FONSIs.[36] NEPA further requires all Federal agencies to make information useful for restoring, maintaining, and

---

[32] 40 CFR § 1506.6 (requiring agencies to make diligent efforts to involve the public in preparing and implementing their NEPA procedures).

[33] 5 U.S.C. § 552.

[34] 42 U.S.C. § 4332(2)(C) (requiring Federal agencies to make EISs available to the public as provided by the FOIA); 40 CFR § 1506.6(f) (requiring agencies to make EISs, comments received, and any underlying documents available to the public pursuant to the provisions of the FOIA without regard to the exclusion for interagency memoranda where such memoranda transmit comments of Federal agencies on the environmental impact of the proposed action).

[35] 40 CFR § 1501.4(b) (requiring agencies to involve environmental agencies, applicants, and the public, to the extent practicable); id. § 1501.4(e)(1) (requiring agencies to make FONSIs available to the affected public as specified in § 1506.6); id. § 1501.4(e)(2) (requiring agencies to make a FONSI available for public review for thirty days before making its final determination on whether it will prepare an EIS or proceed with the action when the nature of the proposed action is, or is similar to, an action which normally requires the preparation of an EIS); id. § 1506.6 (requiring agencies to make diligent efforts to involve the public in preparing and implementing their NEPA procedures).

[36] Id. § 1501.4.

enhancing the quality of the environment available to States, counties, municipalities, institutions, and individuals.[37] This requirement can include information on mitigation and mitigation monitoring.

Beyond these requirements, agencies are encouraged to make proactive, discretionary release of mitigation monitoring reports and other supporting documents, and to make responses to public inquiries regarding mitigation monitoring readily available to the public through online or print media. This recommendation is consistent with the President's Memorandum on Transparency and Open Government directing agencies to take affirmative steps to make information public without waiting for specific requests for information.[38] The Open Government Directive, issued by the Office of Management and Budget in accordance with the President's Memorandum, further directs agencies to use their web sites and information technology capabilities to disseminate, to the maximum extent practicable, useful information under FOIA, so as to promote transparency and accountability.[39]

Agencies should exercise their judgment to ensure that the methods and media used to provide mitigation and monitoring information are commensurate with the importance of the action and the resources at issue, taking into account any risks of harm to affected resources. In some cases, agencies may need to balance competing privacy or confidentiality concerns (e.g., protecting confidential business information or the location of sacred sites) with the benefits of public disclosure.

III. REMEDYING INEFFECTIVE OR NON-IMPLEMENTED MITIGATION

Through careful monitoring, agencies may discover that mitigation commitments have not been implemented, or have not had the environmental results predicted in the NEPA and decision documents. Agencies, having committed to mitigation, should work to remedy such inadequacies. It is an agency's underlying authority or other legal authority that provides the basis for the commitment to implement mitigation and monitor its effectiveness. As discussed in Section I, agencies should not commit to mitigation considered in an EIS or EA unless there are sufficient legal authorities and they expect the resources to be available to perform or ensure the performance of the mitigation. In some cases, as discussed in Section II, agencies may exercise their authority to make

---

[37] 42 U.S.C. § 4332(2)(G).

[38] Presidential Memorandum for Heads of Executive Departments and Agencies Concerning the Freedom of Information Act, 74 Fed. Reg. 4,683 (Jan. 21, 2009); *accord* DOJ, "Memorandum for Heads of Executive Departments and Agencies Concerning the Freedom of Information Act" (Mar. 19, 2009), *available at* www.usdoj.gov/ag/foia-memo-march2009.pdf.

[39] Office of Mgmt. & Budget, Executive Office of the President, "Open Government Directive" (Dec. 8, 2009), *available at* www.whitehouse.gov/open/documents/open-government-directive.

relevant funding, permitting, or other agency approvals and decisions conditional on the performance of mitigation commitments by third parties. It follows that an agency must rely on its underlying authority and available resources to take remedial steps. Agencies should consider taking remedial steps as long as there remains a pending Federal decision regarding the project or proposed action. Agencies may also exercise their legal authority to enforce conditions placed on funding, grants, permits, or other approvals.

If a mitigation commitment is simply not undertaken or fails to mitigate the environmental effects as predicted, the responsible agency should further consider whether it is necessary to prepare supplemental NEPA analysis and documentation.[40] The agency determination would be based upon its expertise and judgment regarding environmental consequences. Much will depend upon the agency's determination as to what, if any, portions of the Federal action remain and what opportunities remain to address the effects of the mitigation failure. In cases where an EIS or a supplementary EA or EIS is required, the agency must avoid actions that would have adverse environmental impacts and limit its choice of reasonable alternatives during the preparation of an EIS.[41]

In cases where there is no remaining agency action to be taken, and the mitigation has not been fully implemented or has not been as effective as predicted, it may not be appropriate to supplement the original NEPA analysis and documentation. However, it would be appropriate for future NEPA analyses of similar proposed actions and relevant programs to consider past experience and address the potential for environmental consequences as a result of mitigation failure. This would ensure that the assumed environmental baselines reflect true conditions, and that similar mitigation is not relied on in subsequent decisions, at least without more robust provisions for adaptive management or analysis of mitigation alternatives that can be applied in the event of mitigation failure.

IV. CONCLUSION

This guidance is intended to assist Federal agencies with the development of their NEPA procedures, guidance, and regulations; foster the appropriate use of Findings of No Significant Impact; and ensure that mitigation commitments are appropriately and effectively documented, implemented, and monitored. The guidance also provides Federal agencies with recommended actions in circumstances where mitigation is not

---

[40] 40 CFR § 1502.9(c) (requiring an agency to prepare supplements to draft or final EISs if the agency makes substantial changes in the proposed action that are relevant to environmental concerns, or if there are significant new circumstances or information relevant to environmental concerns and bearing on the proposed action or its impacts).

[41] Id. § 1506.1(a) (providing that until an agency issues a Record of Decision, no action concerning the proposal may be taken that would have an adverse environmental impact or limit the choice of reasonable alternatives).

15

implemented or fails to have the predicted effect. Questions regarding this guidance
should be directed to the CEQ Associate Director for NEPA Oversight.

APPENDIX

Case Study: Existing Agency Mitigation Regulations & Guidance

A number of agencies have already taken actions to improve their use of mitigation and their monitoring of mitigation commitments undertaken as part of their NEPA processes. For example, the Department of the Army has promulgated regulations implementing NEPA for military installations and programs that include a monitoring and implementation component.[42] These NEPA implementing procedures are notable for their comprehensive approach to ensuring that mitigation proposed in the NEPA review process is completed and monitored for effectiveness. These procedures are described in detail below to illustrate one approach agencies can use to meet the goals of this Guidance.

a.   *Mitigation Planning*

Consistent with existing CEQ guidelines, the Army's NEPA implementing regulations place significant emphasis on the planning and implementation of mitigation throughout the environmental analysis process. The first step of mitigation planning is to seek to avoid or minimize harm.[43] When the analysis proceeds to an EA or EIS, however, the Army regulation requires that any mitigation measures be "clearly assessed and those selected for implementation will be identified in the [FONSI] or the ROD," and that "[t]he proponent must implement those identified mitigations, because they are commitments made as part of the Army decision."[44] This is notable as this mitigation is a binding commitment documented in the agency NEPA decision. In addition, the adoption of mitigation that reduces environmental impacts below the NEPA significance threshold is similarly binding upon the agency.[45] When the mitigation results in a FONSI in a NEPA analysis, the mitigation is considered legally binding.[46] Because these regulations create a clear obligation for the agency to ensure any proposed mitigation adopted in the environmental review process is performed, there is assurance that mitigation will lead to a reduction of environmental impacts in the implementation stage and include binding mechanisms for enforcement.

Another important mechanism in the Army's regulations to assure effective mitigation results is the requirement to fully fund and implement adopted mitigation. It is acknowledged in the regulations that "unless money is actually budgeted and manpower

---

[42] The Department of the Army promulgated its NEPA implementing procedures as a regulation.

[43] *See* 40 CFR § 1508.2.

[44] 32 CFR § 651.15(b).

[45] *Id.* § 651.35(g)

[46] *Id.* § 651.15(c).

assigned, the mitigation does not exist."[47] As a result, a proposed action cannot proceed until all adopted mitigation is fully resourced or until the lack of funding is addressed in the NEPA analysis.[48] This is an important step in the planning process, as mitigation benefits are unlikely to be realized unless financial and planning resources are committed through the NEPA planning process.

b.   *Mitigation Monitoring*

The Army regulations recognize that monitoring is an integral part of any mitigation system.[49] The Army regulations require monitoring plans and implementation programs to be summarized in NEPA documentation, and should consider several important factors. These factors include anticipated changes in environmental conditions or project activities, unexpected outcomes from mitigation, controversy over the selected alternative, potential impacts or adverse effects on federally or state protected resources, and statutory permitting requirements.[50] Consideration of these factors can help prioritize monitoring efforts and anticipate possible challenges.

The Army regulations distinguish between implementation monitoring and effectiveness monitoring. Implementation monitoring ensures that mitigation commitments made in NEPA documentation are implemented. To further this objective, the Army regulations specify that these conditions must be written into any contracts furthering the proposed action. In addition, the agency or unit proposing the action is ultimately responsible for the performance of the mitigation activities.[51] In a helpful appendix to its regulations, the Army outlines guidelines for the creation of an implementation monitoring program to address contract performance, the role of cooperating agencies, and the responsibilities of the lead agency.[52]

The Army's effectiveness monitoring addresses changing conditions inherent in evolving natural systems and the potential for unexpected environmental mitigation outcomes. For this monitoring effort, the Army utilizes its Environmental Management System (EMS) based on the standardized ISO 14001 protocols.[53] The core of this

---

[47] *Id.* § 651.15(d).

[48] *Id.* § 651.15(d).

[49] *Id.* § 651.15(i).

[50] *Id.* §§ 651.15(h)(1)-(4) Appendix C to 32 CFR § 651, 67 Fed. Reg. 15,290, 15,326-28 (Mar. 29, 2002).

[51] *Id.* § 651.15(i)(1).

[52] *See* Appendix C to 32 CFR § 651, 67 Fed. Reg. 15,290, 15,326-28 (Mar. 29, 2002).

[53] *See also* CEQ, "Aligning NEPA Processes with Environmental Management Systems" (2007), *available at*

program is the creation of a clear and accountable system for tracking and reporting both quantitative and qualitative measures of the mitigation efforts. An action-forcing response to mitigation failure is essential to the success of any mitigation program. In the context of a mitigated FONSI, the Army regulations provide that if any "identified mitigation measures do not occur, so that significant adverse environmental effects could be reasonably expected to result, the [agency actor] must publish a [Notice of Intent] and prepare an EIS."[54] This is an essential response measure to changed conditions in the proposed agency action. In addition, the Army regulations address potential failures in the mitigation systems indentified through monitoring. If mitigation is ineffective, the agency entity responsible should re-examine the mitigation and consider a different approach to mitigation. However, if mitigation is required to reduce environmental impacts below significance levels are found to be ineffective, the regulations contemplate the issuance of a Notice of Intent and preparation of an EIS.[55]

The Army regulations also provide guidance for the challenging task of defining parameters for effectiveness monitoring. Guidelines include identifying a source of expertise, using measurable and replicable technical parameters, conducting a baseline study before mitigation is commenced, using a control to isolate mitigation effects, and, importantly, providing timely results to allow the decision-maker to take corrective action if necessary.[56] In addition, the regulations call for the preparation of an environmental monitoring report to determine the accuracy of the mitigation impact predictions made in the NEPA planning process.[57] The report is essential for agency planning and documentation and promotes public engagement in the mitigation process.

c.   *Public Engagement*

The Army regulations seek to integrate robust engagement of the interested public in the mitigation monitoring program. The regulations place responsibility on the entity proposing the action to respond to inquiries from the public and other agencies regarding the status of mitigation adopted in the NEPA process.[58] In addition, the regulations find that "concerned citizens are essential to the credibility of [the] review" of mitigation

---

ceq.hss.doe.gov/nepa/nepapubs/Aligning_NEPA_Processes_with_Environmental_Manag ement_Systems_2007.pdf.

[54] 32 CFR § 651.15(c).

[55] *See id.* § 651.35(g) (describing the implementation steps, including public availability and implementation tracking, that must be taken when a FONSI requires mitigation); *id.* § 651.15(k).

[56] *See* subsections (g)(1)-(5) of Appendix C to 32 CFR § 651, 67 Fed. Reg. at 15,327.

[57] 32 CFR § 651.15(l).

[58] *Id.* § 651.15(b).

effectiveness.[59] The Army specifies that outreach with the interested public regarding mitigation efforts is to be coordinated by the installation's Environmental Office.[60] These regulations bring the public a step closer to the process by designating an agency source responsible for enabling public participation, and by acknowledging the important role the public can play to ensure the integrity and tracking of the mitigation process. The success of agency mitigation efforts will be bolstered by public access to timely information on NEPA mitigation monitoring.

# # #

---

[59] *Id.* § 651.15(k).

[60] 32 CFR § 651.15(j).

20

NEPA Deskbook

Appendix 28 **Final Guidance for Federal Departments and Agencies on Establishing, Applying, and Revising Categorical Exclusions Under the National Environmental Policy Act**

75628 Federal Register / Vol. 75, No. 233 / Monday, December 6, 2010 / Rules and Regulations

COUNCIL ON ENVIRONMENTAL QUALITY

40 CFR Parts 1500, 1501, 1502, 1503, 1504, 1505, 1506, 1507, and 1508

Final Guidance for Federal Departments and Agencies on Establishing, Applying, and Revising Categorical Exclusions Under the National Environmental Policy Act

AGENCY: Council on Environmental Quality.

ACTION: Notice of availability.

SUMMARY: The Council on Environmental Quality (CEQ) is issuing its final guidance on categorical exclusions. This guidance provides methods for substantiating categorical exclusions, clarifies the process for establishing categorical exclusions, outlines how agencies should engage the public when establishing and using categorical exclusions, describes how agencies can document the use of categorical exclusions, and recommends periodic agency review of existing categorical exclusions. A categorical exclusion is a category of actions that a Federal agency determines does not normally result in individually or cumulatively significant environmental effects. This guidance clarifies the rules for establishing, applying, and revising categorical exclusions. It applies to categorical exclusions established by Federal agencies in accordance with CEQ regulations for implementing the procedural provisions of the National Environmental Policy Act. The guidance was developed to assist agencies in making their implementation of the National Environmental Policy Act (NEPA) more transparent and efficient.

DATES: The guidance is effective December 6, 2010.

FOR FURTHER INFORMATION CONTACT: The Council on Environmental Quality (ATTN: Horst Greczmiel, Associate Director for National Environmental Policy Act Oversight), 722 Jackson Place, NW., Washington, DC 20503. Telephone: (202) 395–5750.

SUPPLEMENTARY INFORMATION: This guidance applies to categorical exclusions established by Federal agencies in accordance with § 1507.3 of the CEQ Regulations for Implementing the Procedural Provisions of the National Environmental Policy Act, 40 CFR parts 1500–1508.

Enacted in 1970, the National Environmental Policy Act (NEPA), 42 U.S.C. 4321–4370, is a fundamental tool used to harmonize our environmental, economic, and social aspirations and is a cornerstone of our Nation's efforts to protect the environment. NEPA recognizes that many Federal activities affect the environment and mandates that Federal agencies consider the environmental impacts of their proposed actions before deciding to adopt proposals and take action.[1] Many Federal actions do not normally have significant effects on the environment. When agencies identify categories of activities that do not normally have the potential for individually or cumulatively significant impacts, they may establish a categorical exclusion for those activities. The use of categorical exclusions can reduce paperwork and delay, so that more resources are available to assess proposed actions that are likely to have the potential to cause significant environmental effects in an environmental assessment (EA) or environmental impact statement (EIS). This guidance clarifies the rules for establishing categorical exclusions by describing: (1) How to establish or revise a categorical exclusion; (2) how to use public involvement and documentation to help define and substantiate a proposed categorical exclusion; (3) how to apply an established categorical exclusion; (4) how to determine when to prepare documentation and involve the public when applying a categorical exclusion; and (5) how to conduct periodic reviews of categorical exclusions to assure their continued appropriate use and usefulness.

On February 18, 2010, the Council on Environmental Quality announced three proposed draft guidance documents to modernize and reinvigorate NEPA, in conjunction with the fortieth anniversary of the statute's enactment.[2] This guidance document is the first of those three to be released in final form. With respect to the other two guidance documents, one addresses when and how Federal agencies should consider greenhouse gas emissions and climate change in their proposed actions, and the other addresses when agencies need to monitor commitments made in EAs and EISs, and how agencies can appropriately use mitigated "Findings of No Significant Impact." The **Federal Register** notice announcing the draft categorical exclusion guidance and requesting public comments was published on February 23, 2010.[3] CEQ appreciates the thoughtful responses to its request for comments on the draft guidance. Commenters included private citizens, corporations, environmental organizations, trade associations, and State agencies. CEQ received fifty-eight comments, which are available online at *http://www.whitehouse.gov/ administration/eop/ceq/initiatives/ nepa/comments* and at *http:// www.nepa.gov*. The comments that suggested editorial revisions and requested clarification of terms are addressed in the text of the final guidance. Comments that raised policy or substantive concerns are grouped into thematic issues and addressed in the following sections of this notice.

Process for Developing and Using Categorical Exclusions

Many commenters expressed support for CEQ's categorical exclusion guidance and for the timely and efficient use of categorical exclusions in the NEPA environmental review process to inform agency decisionmaking. Some commenters favored guidance that would limit the use of categorical exclusions. Others expressed concern that this guidance will discourage the appropriate use of categorical exclusions or make the NEPA process more difficult for agencies, and thereby delay agency decisionmaking.

This guidance was developed to provide for the consistent, proper, and appropriate development and use of categorical exclusions by Federal agencies. It reinforces the process required to establish categorical exclusions by explaining methods available to substantiate categorical exclusions. It also seeks to ensure opportunities for public involvement and increasing transparency when Federal agencies establish categorical exclusions and subsequently use those categorical exclusions to satisfy their NEPA obligations for specific proposed actions. Additionally, this guidance affords Federal agencies flexibility in developing and implementing categorical exclusions while ensuring that categorical exclusions are administered in compliance with NEPA and the CEQ Regulations. When appropriately established and applied, categorical exclusions expedite the environmental review process for proposals that normally do not require additional analysis and documentation in an EA or an EIS.

---

[1] A discussion of NEPA applicability is beyond the scope of this guidance. For more information see CEQ, *The Citizen's Guide to the National Environmental Policy Act, available at ceq.hss.doe.gov/nepa/Citizens_Guide_Dec07.pdf*.

[2] For more information on this announcement, see *http://www.whitehouse.gov/administration/eop/ ceq/initiatives/nepa*.

[3] National Environmental Policy Act (NEPA) Draft Guidance, Establishing, Applying, and Revising Categorical Exclusions under the National Environmental Policy Act, 75 FR 8045, Feb. 23, 2010.

Federal Register / Vol. 75, No. 233 / Monday, December 6, 2010 / Rules and Regulations   **75629**

Applicability and Limitations

Some commenters expressed concern that the guidance creates additional limitations and constraints on the establishment of categorical exclusions, while others expressed unqualified support for using text that constrains the scope of the actions to which a categorical exclusion could apply. The discussion in the guidance of physical, temporal, or environmental factors that would constrain the use of a categorical exclusion is consistent with NEPA and past CEQ guidance.

Federal agencies that identify physical, temporal, or environmental constraints in the definition of a proposed category of actions may be able to better ensure that a new or revised categorical exclusion is neither too broadly nor too narrowly defined. Some information regarding implementation of mitigation measures that are an integral part of the proposed actions and how those actions will be carried out may be necessary to adequately understand and describe the category of actions and their projected impacts. A better and more comprehensive description of a category of actions provides clarity and transparency for proposed projects that could be categorically excluded from further analysis and documentation in an EA or an EIS.

Public Involvement

Some commenters expressed concern over the timeliness and burden of NEPA reviews when there is greater public involvement. The final guidance makes it clear that CEQ strongly encourages public involvement in the establishment and revision of categorical exclusions. As the guidance explains, engaging the public in the environmental aspects of Federal decisionmaking is a key policy goal of NEPA and the CEQ Regulations. Public involvement is not limited to the provision of information by agencies; it should also include meaningful opportunities for the public to provide comment and feedback on the information made available. Considering recent advances in information technology, agencies should consider employing additional measures to involve the public beyond simply publishing a **Federal Register** notice as required when an agency seeks to establish new or revised categorical exclusions.[4]

The perceived environmental effects of the proposed category of actions are

[4] See 40 CFR 1506.6(a) (requiring agencies to make diligent efforts to involve the public in preparing and implementing their NEPA procedures).

a factor that an agency should consider when it decides whether there is a need for public involvement in determining whether to apply a categorical exclusion. Accordingly, the guidance clarifies that agencies have flexibility when applying categorical exclusions to focus their public involvement on those proposed actions and issues the agency expects to raise environmental issues and concerns that are important to the public.

In the final guidance, CEQ uses the terms "encourage" and "recommend" interchangeably. The language of the guidance relating to public engagement reflects CEQ's authority under NEPA and the CEQ regulations to guide agency development and implementation of agency NEPA procedures. It also reflects the importance of allowing agencies to use their expertise to determine the appropriate level of engagement with the public.

Substantiating and Documenting Categorical Exclusions

Some commenters raised the concern that the requirement to substantiate and document categorical exclusions would be burdensome and cause delay. One commenter recommended that the guidance should encourage consultation with State agencies, other Federal agencies with special expertise, and other stakeholders. Another commenter suggested that the guidance permit agencies to consult with industry project proponents that possess information that would be useful in substantiating a categorical exclusion. Along the same lines, another commenter stated that agencies should be encouraged to seek information from the most relevant and reliable sources possible.

The guidance has been revised to reflect that, when substantiating and documenting the environmental effects of a category of actions, a Federal agency need not be limited to its own experiences. Instead, the agency should consider information and records from other private and public entities, including other Federal agencies that have experience with the actions covered in a proposed categorical exclusion. The guidance acknowledges that the reliability of scientific information varies according to its source and the rigor with which it was developed, and that it is the responsibility of the agency to determine whether the information reflects accepted knowledge, accurate findings, and experience with the environmental effects relevant to the actions that would be included in the proposed categorical exclusion.

The guidance addresses the concerns over timeliness and undue burdens by explaining that the amount of information required to substantiate a proposed new or revised categorical exclusion should be proportionate to the type of activities included in the proposed category of actions. Actions that potentially have little or no impact should not require extensive information or documentation. Determining the extent of substantiation and documentation is ultimately the responsibility of the agency and will vary depending on the nature of the proposed action and the effects associated with the action. The guidance encourages agencies to make use of agency Web sites to provide further clarity and transparency to their NEPA procedures. It also recommends using modern technology to maintain and facilitate the use of documentation in future evaluations and benchmarking.

Extraordinary Circumstances

Several commenters requested clearer and more detailed guidance on the application of extraordinary circumstances. Extraordinary circumstances are appropriately understood as those factors or circumstances that will help an agency identify the situations or environmental settings when an otherwise categorically-excludable action merits further analysis and documentation in an EA or an EIS. Specific comments noted that the determination that an extraordinary circumstance will require additional environmental review in an EA or an EIS should depend not solely on the existence of the extraordinary circumstance but rather on an analysis of its impacts. CEQ agrees with this perspective. For example, when an agency uses a protected resource, such as historic property or threatened and endangered species, as an extraordinary circumstance, the guidance clarifies that whether additional review and documentation of a proposed action's potential environmental impacts in an EA or an EIS is required is based on the potential for significantly impacting that protected resource. However, CEQ recognizes that some agency NEPA procedures require additional analysis based solely on the existence of an extraordinary circumstance. In such cases, the agencies may define their extraordinary circumstances differently, so that a particular situation, such as the presence of a protected resource, is not considered an extraordinary circumstance per se, but a factor to consider when determining if there are extraordinary circumstances, such as a significant impact to that resource. This

75630 **Federal Register**/Vol. 75, No. 233/Monday, December 6, 2010/Rules and Regulations

way of structuring NEPA procedures is also appropriate. What is important is that situations or circumstances that may warrant additional analysis and documentation in an EA or an EIS are fully considered before a categorical exclusion is used.

The guidance was also revised to clarify how agencies can use the factors set out in the CEQ Regulations to determine significance. The Federal agencies are ultimately responsible for the determination of specific extraordinary circumstances for a category of actions, as well as the determination of whether to use the significance factors set out in the CEQ Regulations when establishing extraordinary circumstances.[5] Agency determinations are informed by the public and CEQ during the development of the categorical exclusions.

Documenting the Use of Categorical Exclusions

Commenters were most concerned over the potential for delay and the creation of administrative burdens for projects and programs. The guidance makes it clear that the documentation prepared when categorically excluding an action should be as concise as possible to avoid unnecessary delays and administrative burdens for projects and programs. The guidance explains that each agency should determine the circumstances in which it is appropriate to prepare additional documentation. It also explains that for some activities with little risk of significant environmental effects, there may be no practical need for, or benefit from, preparing any documentation beyond the existing record supporting the underlying categorical exclusion and any administrative record for that activity. The guidance makes it clear that the extent of the documentation prepared is the responsibility of the agency and should be tailored to the type of action involved, the potential for extraordinary circumstances, and compliance requirements of other laws, regulations, and policies.

Cumulative Impacts

Some commenters were concerned that the guidance overlooked the importance of cumulative effects. As specifically set out in the CEQ Regulations and the final guidance, the consideration of the potential cumulative impacts of proposed actions is an important and integral aspect of the NEPA process. The guidance makes

[5] See 40 CFR 1508.27 (defining "significantly" for NEPA purposes in terms of several context and intensity factors for agencies to consider).

it clear that both individual and cumulative impacts must be considered when establishing categorical exclusions. With regard to the cumulative impacts of actions that an agency has categorically excluded, the guidance recommends that agencies consider the frequency with which the categorically-excluded actions are applied. For some types of categorical exclusions, it may also be appropriate for the agency to track and periodically assess use of the categorical exclusion to ensure that cumulative impacts do not rise to a level that would warrant further NEPA analysis and documentation.

Monitoring

Commenters voiced concerns that the guidance would create a new requirement for monitoring. The final guidance makes it clear that any Federal agency program charged with complying with NEPA should develop and maintain sufficient capacity to ensure the validity of NEPA reviews that predict that there will not be significant impacts. The amount of effort and the methods used for assessing environmental effects should be proportionate to the potential effects of the action that is the subject of a proposed categorical exclusion and should ensure that the use of categorical exclusions does not inadvertently result in significant impacts.

As the guidance explains, agencies seeking to substantiate new or revised categorical exclusions can rely on the information gathered from monitoring actions the agency took in the past, as well as from monitoring the effects of impact demonstration projects. Relying solely on completed EAs and Findings of No Significant Impact (FONSIs) is not sufficient without information validating the FONSI which was projected in advance of implementation. The guidance makes it clear that FONSIs cannot be relied on as a basis for establishing a categorical exclusion unless the absence of significant environmental effects has been verified through credible monitoring of the implemented activity or other sources of corroborating information. The intensity of monitoring efforts for particular categories of actions or impact demonstration projects is appropriately left to the judgment of the agencies. Furthermore, the guidance explains that in some cases monitoring may not be appropriate and agencies can evaluate other information.

Review of Existing Categorical Exclusions

Several commenters advocated "grandfathering" existing categorical

exclusions. Two other commenters voiced support for the periodic review of agency categorical exclusions and specifically requested that the guidance call for rigorous review of existing categorical exclusions. Two commenters requested that the guidance explicitly provide for public participation during the review process. Several verbal comments focused on the recommended seven year review period and suggested alternative review periods ranging from two to ten years. Several commenters also requested that the guidance describe with greater clarity how the periodic review should be implemented.

CEQ believes it is extremely important to review the categorical exclusions already established by the Federal agencies. The fact that an agency's categorical exclusions were established years ago is all the more reason to review them to ensure that changes in technology, operations, agency missions, and the environment do not call into question the continued use of these categorical exclusions. The guidance also explains the value of such a review. Reviewing categorical exclusions can serve as the impetus for clarifying the actions covered by an existing categorical exclusion. It can also help agencies identify additional extraordinary circumstances and consider the appropriate documentation when using certain categorical exclusions. The guidance states that the review should focus on categorical exclusions that no longer reflect current environmental circumstances or an agency's policies, procedures, programs, or mission.

This guidance recommends that agencies develop a process and timeline to periodically review their categorical exclusions (and extraordinary circumstances) to ensure that their categorical exclusions remain current and appropriate, and that those reviews should be conducted at least every seven years. A seven-year cycle allows the agencies to regularly review categorical exclusions to avoid the use of categorical exclusions that are outdated and no longer appropriate. If the agency believes that a different timeframe is appropriate, the agency should articulate a sound basis for that conclusion, explaining how the alternate timeframe will still allow the agency to avoid the use of categorical exclusions that are outdated and no longer appropriate. As described in the guidance, agencies should use their Web sites to notify the public and CEQ about how and when their reviews of existing categorical exclusions will be conducted. CEQ will perform oversight of agencies' reviews, beginning with those agencies currently reassessing or experiencing difficulties with implementing their categorical exclusions, as well as with agencies facing challenges to their application of categorical exclusions.

The Final Guidance

The final guidance is provided here and is available on the National Environmental Policy Act Web site (*http://www.nepa.gov*) specifically at, ceq.hss.doe.gov/ceq_regulations/ guidance.html. For reasons stated in the preamble, above, CEQ issues the following guidance on establishing, applying, and revising categorical exclusions.

MEMORANDUM FOR HEADS OF FEDERAL DEPARTMENTS AND AGENCIES

FROM: NANCY H. SUTLEY
Chair
Council on Environmental Quality
SUBJECT: *Final Guidance for Federal Departments and Agencies on Establishing, Applying, and Revising Categorical Exclusions under the National Environmental Policy Act*

The Council on Environmental Quality (CEQ) is issuing this guidance for Federal departments and agencies on how to establish, apply, and revise categorical exclusions in accordance with section 102 of the National Environmental Policy Act (NEPA), 42 U.S.C. 4332, and the CEQ Regulations for Implementing the Procedural Provisions of NEPA (CEQ Regulations), 40 CFR Parts 1500–1508.[6] This guidance explains the requirements of NEPA and the CEQ Regulations, describes CEQ policies, and recommends procedures for agencies to use to ensure that their use of categorical exclusions is consistent with applicable law and regulations.[7] The guidance is based on

NEPA, the CEQ Regulations, legal precedent and agency NEPA experience and practice. It describes:

• How to establish or revise a categorical exclusion;

• How to use public involvement and documentation to help define and substantiate a proposed categorical exclusion;

• How to apply an established categorical exclusion, and determine when to prepare documentation and involve the public;[8] and

• How to conduct periodic reviews of categorical exclusions to assure their continued appropriate use and usefulness.

This guidance is designed to afford Federal agencies flexibility in developing and implementing categorical exclusions, while ensuring that categorical exclusions are administered to further the purposes of NEPA and the CEQ Regulations.[9]

I. Introduction

The CEQ Regulations provide basic requirements for establishing and using categorical exclusions. Section 1508.4 of the CEQ Regulations defines a "categorical exclusion" as

a category of actions which do not individually or cumulatively have a significant effect on the human environment and which have been found to have no such effect in procedures adopted by a Federal agency in implementation of these regulations (§ 1507.3) and for which, therefore, neither an environmental assessment nor an environmental impact statement is required.[10]

Categories of actions for which exclusions are established can be limited by their terms. Furthermore, the application of a categorical exclusion can be limited by "extraordinary circumstances." Extraordinary circumstances are factors or circumstances in which a normally excluded action may have a significant environmental effect that then requires further analysis in an environmental

assessment (EA) or an environmental impact statement (EIS).[11]

Categorical exclusions are not exemptions or waivers of NEPA review; they are simply one type of NEPA review. To establish a categorical exclusion, agencies determine whether a proposed activity is one that, on the basis of past experience, normally does not require further environmental review. Once established, categorical exclusions provide an efficient tool to complete the NEPA environmental review process for proposals that normally do not require more resource-intensive EAs or EISs. The use of categorical exclusions can reduce paperwork and delay, so that EAs or EISs are targeted toward proposed actions that truly have the potential to cause significant environmental effects.[12]

When determining whether to use a categorical exclusion for a proposed activity, a Federal agency must carefully review the description of the proposed action to ensure that it fits within the category of actions described in the categorical exclusion. Next, the agency must consider the specific circumstances associated with the proposed activity, to rule out any extraordinary circumstances that might give rise to significant environmental effects requiring further analysis and documentation in an EA or an EIS.[13] In other words, when evaluating whether to apply a categorical exclusion to a proposed activity, an agency must consider the specific circumstances associated with the activity and may not end its review based solely on the determination that the activity fits within the description of the categorical exclusion; rather, the agency must also consider whether there are extraordinary circumstances that would warrant further NEPA review. Even if a proposed activity fits within the definition of a categorical exclusion and does not raise extraordinary circumstances, the CEQ Regulations make clear that an agency can, at its discretion, decide "to prepare an environmental assessment * * * in order to assist agency planning and decisionmaking."[14]

Since Federal agencies began using categorical exclusions in the late 1970s,

---

[6] The Council on Environmental Quality (CEQ) Regulations for Implementing the Procedural Provisions of NEPA (CEQ Regulations), *available on* www.nepa.gov at ceq.hss.doe.gov/ceq_regulations/ regulations.html. This guidance applies only to categorical exclusions established by Federal agencies in accordance with section 1507.3 of the CEQ Regulations, 40 CFR 1507.3. It does not address categorical exclusions established by statute, as their use is governed by the terms of specific legislation and subsequent interpretation by the agencies charged with the implementation of that statute and NEPA requirements. CEQ encourages agencies to apply their extraordinary circumstances to categorical exclusions established by statute when the statute is silent as to the use and application of extraordinary circumstances.

[7] This guidance is not a rule or regulation, and the recommendations it contains may not apply to a particular situation based upon the individual facts and circumstances. This guidance does not change or substitute for any law, regulation, or any other legally binding requirement and is not legally

enforceable. The use of non-mandatory language such as "guidance," "recommend," "may," "should," and "can," is intended to describe CEQ policies and recommendations. The use of mandatory terminology such as "must" and "required" is intended to describe controlling requirements under the terms of NEPA and the CEQ regulations, but this document does not establish legally binding requirements in and of itself.

[8] The term "public" in this guidance refers to any individuals, groups, entities or agencies external to the Federal agency analyzing the proposed categorical exclusion or proposed activity.

[9] 40 CFR 1507.1 (noting that CEQ Regulations intend to allow each agency flexibility in adapting its NEPA implementing procedures to requirements of other applicable laws).

[10] *Id.* at § 1508.4.

[11] *Id.*

[12] *See id.* at §§ 1500.4(p) (recommending use of categorical exclusions as a tool to reduce paperwork), 1500.5(k) (recommending categorical exclusions as a tool to reduce delay).

[13] 40 CFR 1508.4 (requiring Federal agencies to adopt procedures to ensure that categorical exclusions are not applied to proposed actions involving extraordinary circumstances that might have significant environmental effects).

[14] 40 CFR 1501.3(b).

the number and scope of categorically-excluded activities have expanded significantly. Today, categorical exclusions are the most frequently employed method of complying with NEPA, underscoring the need for this guidance on the promulgation and use of categorical exclusions.[15] Appropriate reliance on categorical exclusions provides a reasonable, proportionate, and effective analysis for many proposed actions, helping agencies reduce paperwork and delay. If used inappropriately, categorical exclusions can thwart NEPA's environmental stewardship goals, by compromising the quality and transparency of agency environmental review and decisionmaking, as well as compromising the opportunity for meaningful public participation and review.

II. Establishing and Revising Categorical Exclusions

A. Conditions Warranting New or Revised Categorical Exclusions

Federal agencies may establish a new or revised categorical exclusion in a variety of circumstances. For example, an agency may determine that a class of actions—such as payroll processing, data collection, conducting surveys, or installing an electronic security system in a facility—can be categorically excluded because it is not expected to have significant individual or cumulative environmental effects. As discussed further in Section III.A.1, below, agencies may also identify potential new categorical exclusions after the agencies have performed NEPA reviews of a class of proposed actions and found that, when implemented, the actions resulted in no significant environmental impacts. Other categories of actions may become appropriate for categorical exclusions as a result of mission changes. When agencies acquire new responsibilities through legislation or administrative restructuring, they should propose new categorical exclusions after they, or other agencies, gain sufficient experience with the new activities to make a reasoned determination that any resulting environmental impacts are not significant.[16]

Agencies sometimes employ "tiering" to incorporate findings from NEPA environmental reviews that address broad programs or issues into reviews that subsequently deal with more specific and focused proposed actions.[17] Agencies may rely on tiering to make predicate findings about environmental impacts when establishing a categorical exclusion. To the extent that mitigation commitments developed during the broader review become an integral part of the basis for subsequently excluding a proposed category of actions, care must be taken to ensure that those commitments are clearly presented as required design elements in the description of the category of actions being considered for a categorical exclusion.

If actions in a proposed categorical exclusion are found to have potentially significant environmental effects, an agency can abandon the proposed categorical exclusion, or revise it to eliminate the potential for significant impacts. This can be done by: (1) Limiting or removing activities included in the categorical exclusion; (2) placing additional constraints on the categorical exclusion's applicability; or (3) revising or identifying additional applicable extraordinary circumstances. When an agency revises an extraordinary circumstance, it should make sure that the revised version clearly identifies the circumstances when further environmental evaluation in an EA or an EIS is warranted.

B. The Text of the Categorical Exclusion

In prior guidance, CEQ has generally addressed the crafting of categorical exclusions, encouraging agencies to "consider broadly defined criteria which characterize types of actions that, based on the agency's experience, do not cause significant environmental effects," and to "offer several examples of activities frequently performed by that agency's personnel which would normally fall in these categories."[18] CEQ's prior guidance also urges agencies to consider whether the cumulative effects of multiple small actions "would cause sufficient environmental impact to take the actions out of the categorically-excluded class."[19] This guidance expands on CEQ's earlier guidance, by advising agencies that the text of a

proposed new or revised categorical exclusion should clearly define the eligible category of actions, as well as any physical, temporal, or environmental factors that would constrain its use.

Some activities may be variable in their environmental effects, such that they can only be categorically excluded in certain regions, at certain times of the year, or within a certain frequency. For example, because the status and sensitivity of environmental resources varies across the nation or by time of year (*e.g.,* in accordance with a protected species' breeding season), it may be appropriate to limit the geographic applicability of a categorical exclusion to a specific region or environmental setting. Similarly, it may be appropriate to limit the frequency with which a categorical exclusion is used in a particular area. Categorical exclusions for activities with variable impacts must be carefully described to limit their application to circumstances where the activity has been shown not to have significant individual or cumulative environmental effects. Those limits may be spatial (restricting the extent of the proposed action by distance or area); temporal (restricting the proposed action during certain seasons or nesting periods in a particular setting); or numeric (limiting the number of proposed actions that can be categorically excluded in a given area or timeframe). Federal agencies that identify these constraints can better ensure that a categorical exclusion is neither too broadly nor too narrowly defined.

When developing a new or revised categorical exclusion, Federal agencies must be sure the proposed category captures the entire proposed action. Categorical exclusions should not be established or used for a segment or an interdependent part of a larger proposed action. The actions included in the category of actions described in the categorical exclusion must be stand-alone actions that have independent utility. Agencies are also encouraged to provide representative examples of the types of activities covered in the text of the categorical exclusion, especially for broad categorical exclusions. These examples will provide further clarity and transparency regarding the types of actions covered by the categorical exclusion.

C. Extraordinary Circumstances

Extraordinary circumstances are appropriately understood as those factors or circumstances that help a Federal agency identify situations or environmental settings that may require

---

[15] *See* CEQ reports to Congress on the status and progress of NEPA reviews for Recovery Act funded projects and activities, *available on http:// www.nepa.gov at ceq.hss.doe.gov/ceq_reports/ recovery_act_reports.html.*

[16] When legislative or administrative action creates a new agency or restructures an existing agency, the agency should determine if its decisionmaking processes have changed and ensure that its NEPA implementing procedures align the

NEPA review and other environmental planning processes with agency decisionmaking.

[17] 40 CFR 1502.4(d), 1502.20, 1508.28.

[18] Council on Environmental Quality, "Guidance Regarding NEPA Regulations," 48 FR 34,263, 34,265, Jul. 28, 1983, *available on http:// www.nepa.gov at ceq.hss.doe.gov/nepa/regs/1983/ 1983guid.htm.*

[19] *Id.*

Federal Register / Vol. 75, No. 233 / Monday, December 6, 2010 / Rules and Regulations **75633**

an otherwise categorically-excludable action to be further analyzed in an EA or an EIS. Often these factors are similar to those used to evaluate intensity for purposes of determining significance pursuant to section 1508.27(b) of the CEQ Regulations.[20] For example, several agencies list as extraordinary circumstances the potential effects on protected species or habitat, or on historic properties listed or eligible for listing in the National Register of Historic Places.

When proposing new or revised categorical exclusions, Federal agencies should consider the extraordinary circumstances described in their NEPA procedures to ensure that they adequately account for those situations and settings in which a proposed categorical exclusion should not be applied. An extraordinary circumstance requires the agency to determine how to proceed with the NEPA review. For example, the presence of a factor, such as a threatened or endangered species or a historic resource, could be an extraordinary circumstance, which, depending on the structure of the agency's NEPA implementing procedures, could either cause the agency to prepare an EA or an EIS, or cause the agency to consider whether the proposed action's impacts on that factor require additional analysis in an EA or an EIS. In other situations, the extraordinary circumstance could be defined to include both the presence of the factor and the impact on that factor. Either way, agency NEPA implementing procedures should clearly describe the manner in which an agency applies extraordinary circumstances and the circumstances under which additional analysis in an EA or an EIS is warranted.

Agencies should review their existing extraordinary circumstances concurrently with the review of their categorical exclusions. If an agency's existing extraordinary circumstances do not provide sufficient parameters to limit a proposed new or revised categorical exclusion to actions that do not have the potential for significant environmental effects, the agency should identify and propose additional extraordinary circumstances or revise those that will apply to the proposed categorical exclusion. If extensive extraordinary circumstances are needed to limit a proposed categorical exclusion, the agency should also consider whether the proposed categorical exclusion itself is appropriate. Any new or revised extraordinary circumstances must be

issued together with the new or revised categorical exclusion in draft form and then in final form according to the procedures described in Section IV.

III. Substantiating a New or Revised Categorical Exclusion

Substantiating a new or revised categorical exclusion is basic to good decisionmaking. It serves as the agency's own administrative record of the underlying reasoning for the categorical exclusion. A key issue confronting Federal agencies is how to substantiate a determination that a proposed new or revised categorical exclusion describes a category of actions that do not individually or cumulatively have a significant effect on the human environment.[21] Provided below are methods agencies can use to gather and evaluate information to substantiate proposed new or revised categorical exclusions.

A. Gathering Information To Substantiate a Categorical Exclusion

The amount of information required to substantiate a categorical exclusion depends on the type of activities included in the proposed category of actions. Actions that are reasonably expected to have little impact (for example, conducting surveys or purchasing small amounts of office supplies consistent with applicable acquisition and environmental standards) should not require extensive supporting information.[22] For actions that do not obviously lack significant environmental effects, agencies must gather sufficient information to support establishing a new or revised categorical exclusion. An agency can substantiate a categorical exclusion using the sources of information described below, either alone or in combination.[23]

---

[21] *See id.* at §§ 1508.7, 1508.8, 1508.27.

[22] Agencies should still consider the environmental effects of actions that are taken on a large scale. Agency-wide procurement and personnel actions could have cumulative impacts. For example, purchasing paper with higher recycled content uses less natural resources and will have lesser environmental impacts. *See* "Federal Leadership in Environmental, Energy, and Economic Performance," E.O. No. 13,514, 74 FR 52,117, Oct. 8, 2009.

[23] Agencies should be mindful of their obligations under the Information Quality Act to ensure the quality, objectivity, utility, and integrity of the information they use or disseminate as the basis of an agency decision to establish a categorical exclusion. *See* Information Quality Act, Pub. L. No. 106–554, section 515 (2000), 114 Stat. 2763, 2763A–153 (codified at 44 U.S.C. 3516 (2001)); *see also* "Guidelines for Ensuring and Maximizing the Quality, Objectivity, Utility, and Integrity of Information Disseminated by Federal Agencies, Republication," 60 FR 8452, Feb. 22, 2002, *available at http://www.whitehouse.gov/omb/inforeg/infopoltech.html.* Additional laws and regulations that establish obligations that apply or may apply

1. Previously Implemented Actions

An agency's assessment of the environmental effects of previously implemented or ongoing actions is an important source of information to substantiate a categorical exclusion. Such assessment allows the agency's experience with implementation and operating procedures to be taken into account in developing the proposed categorical exclusion.

Agencies can obtain useful substantiating information by monitoring and/or otherwise evaluating the effects of implemented actions that were analyzed in EAs that consistently supported Findings of No Significant Impact. If the evaluation of the implemented action validates the environmental effects (or lack thereof) predicted in the EA, this provides strong support for a proposed categorical exclusion. Care must be taken to ensure that any mitigation measures developed during the EA process are an integral component of the actions considered for inclusion in a proposed categorical exclusion.

Implemented actions analyzed in an EIS can also be a useful source of substantiating information if the implemented action has independent utility to the agency, separate and apart from the broader action analyzed in the EIS. The EIS must specifically address the environmental effects of the independent proposed action and determine that those effects are not significant. For example, when a discrete, independent action is analyzed in an EIS as part of a broad management action, an evaluation of the actual effects of that discrete action may support a proposed categorical exclusion for the discrete action. As with actions previously analyzed in EAs, predicted effects (or lack thereof) should be validated through monitoring or other corroborating evidence.

Agencies can also identify or substantiate new categorical exclusions and extraordinary circumstances by using auditing and implementation data gathered in accordance with an Environmental Management System or other systems that track environmental performance and the effects of particular actions taken to attain that performance.[24]

---

to the processes of establishing and applying categorical exclusions (such as the Federal Records Act) are beyond the scope of this guidance.

[24] An EMS provides a systematic framework for a Federal agency to monitor and continually improve its environmental performance through audits, evaluation of legal and other requirements, and management reviews. The potential for EMS to support NEPA work is further described in CEQ's

Continued

---

[20] *Id.* at § 1508.27(b).

75634   **Federal Register** / Vol. 75, No. 233 / Monday, December 6, 2010 / Rules and Regulations

Agencies should also consider appropriate monitoring or other evaluation of the environmental effects of their categorically-excluded actions, to inform periodic reviews of existing categorical exclusions, as discussed in Section VI, below.

2. Impact Demonstration Projects

When Federal agencies lack experience with a particular category of actions that is being considered for a proposed categorical exclusion, they may undertake impact demonstration projects to assess the environmental effects of those actions. As part of a demonstration project, the Federal agency should monitor the actual environmental effects of the proposed action during and after implementation. The NEPA documentation prepared for impact demonstration projects should explain how the monitoring and analysis results will be used to evaluate the merits of a proposed categorical exclusion. When designing impact demonstration projects, an agency must ensure that the action being evaluated accurately represents the scope, the operational context, and the environmental context of the entire category of actions that will be described in the proposed categorical exclusion. For example, if the proposed categorical exclusion would be used in regions or areas of the country with different environmental settings, a series of impact demonstration projects may be needed in those areas where the categorical exclusion would be used.

3. Information From Professional Staff, Expert Opinions, and Scientific Analyses

A Federal agency may rely on the expertise, experience, and judgment of its professional staff as well as outside experts to assess the potential environmental effects of applying proposed categorical exclusions, provided that the experts have knowledge, training, and experience relevant to the implementation and environmental effects of the actions described in the proposed categorical exclusion. The administrative record for the proposed categorical exclusion should document the experts' credentials (*e.g.,* education, training, certifications, years of related experience) and describe how the experts arrived at their conclusions.

Scientific analyses are another good source of information to substantiate a

new or revised categorical exclusion. Because the reliability of scientific information varies according to its source and the rigor with which it was developed, the Federal agency remains responsible for determining whether the information reflects accepted knowledge, accurate findings, and experience relevant to the environmental effects of the actions that would be included in the proposed categorical exclusion. Peer-reviewed findings may be especially useful to support an agency's scientific analysis, but agencies may also consult professional opinions, reports, and research findings that have not been formally peer-reviewed. Scientific information that has not been externally peer-reviewed may require additional scrutiny and evaluation by the agency. In all cases, findings must be based on high-quality, accurate technical and scientific information.[25]

4. Benchmarking Other Agencies' Experiences

A Federal agency cannot rely on another agency's categorical exclusion to support a decision not to prepare an EA or an EIS for its own actions. An agency may, however, substantiate a categorical exclusion of its own based on another agency's experience with a comparable categorical exclusion and the administrative record developed when the other agency's categorical exclusion was established. Federal agencies can also substantiate categorical exclusions by benchmarking, or drawing support, from private and public entities that have experience with the actions covered in a proposed categorical exclusion, such as State and local agencies, Tribes, academic and professional institutions, and other Federal agencies.

When determining whether it is appropriate to rely on another entity's experience, an agency must demonstrate that the benchmarked actions are comparable to the actions in a proposed categorical exclusion. The agency can demonstrate this based on: (1) Characteristics of the actions; (2) methods of implementing the actions; (3) frequency of the actions; (4) applicable standard operating procedures or implementing guidance (including extraordinary circumstances); and (5) timing and context, including the environmental settings in which the actions take place.

B. Evaluating the Information Supporting Categorical Exclusions

After gathering substantiating information and determining that the category of actions in the proposed categorical exclusion does not normally result in individually or cumulatively significant environmental effects, a Federal agency should develop findings that demonstrate how it made its determination. These findings should account for similarities and differences between the proposed categorical exclusion and the substantiating information. The findings should describe the method and criteria the agency used to assess the environmental effects of the proposed categorical exclusion. These findings, and the relevant substantiating information, should be maintained in an administrative record that will support: Benchmarking by other agencies (as discussed in Section III.A.4, above); applying the categorical exclusions (as discussed in Section V.A, below); and periodically reviewing the continued viability of the categorical exclusion (as discussed in Section VI, below). These findings should also be made available to the public, at least in preliminary form, as part of the process of seeking public input on the establishment of new or revised categorical exclusions, though the final findings may be revised based on new information received from the public and other sources.

IV. Procedures for Establishing a New or Revised Categorical Exclusion

Pursuant to section 1507.3(a) of the CEQ Regulations, Federal agencies are required to consult with the public and with CEQ whenever they amend their NEPA procedures, including when they establish new or revised categorical exclusions. An agency can only adopt new or revised NEPA implementing procedures after the public has had notice and an opportunity to comment, and after CEQ has issued a determination that the procedures are in conformity with NEPA and the CEQ regulations. Accordingly, an agency's process for establishing a new or revised categorical exclusion should include the following steps:

• Draft the proposed categorical exclusion based on the agency's experience and substantiating information;

• Consult with CEQ on the proposed categorical exclusion;

• Consult with other Federal agencies that conduct similar activities to coordinate with their current procedures, especially for programs

---

Guidebook, "Aligning National Environmental Policy Act Processes with Environmental Management Systems" (2007), *available on http:// www.nepa.gov* at *ceq.hss.doe.gov/publications/ nepa_and_ems.html.*

[25] *See* 40 CFR 1500.1(b), 1502.24.

requesting similar information from members of the public (*e.g.*, applicants);

• Publish a notice of the proposed categorical exclusion in the **Federal Register** for public review and comment;

• Consider public comments;

• Consult with CEQ on the public comments received and the proposed final categorical exclusion to obtain CEQ's written determination of conformity with NEPA and the CEQ Regulations;

• Publish the final categorical exclusion in the **Federal Register**;

• File the categorical exclusion with CEQ; and

• Make the categorical exclusion readily available to the public through the agency's Web site and/or other means.

A. Consultation With CEQ

The CEQ Regulations require agencies to consult with CEQ prior to publishing their proposed NEPA procedures in the **Federal Register** for public comment. Agencies are encouraged to involve CEQ as early as possible in the process and to enlist CEQ's expertise and assistance with interagency coordination to make the process as efficient as possible.[26]

Following the public comment period, the Federal agency must consider the comments received and consult again with CEQ to discuss substantive comments and how they will be addressed. CEQ shall complete its review within thirty (30) days of receiving the final text of the agency's proposed categorical exclusion. For consultation to successfully conclude, CEQ must provide the agency with a written statement that the categorical exclusion was developed in conformity with NEPA and the CEQ Regulations. Finally, when the Federal agency publishes the final version of the categorical exclusion in the **Federal Register** and on its established agency Web site, the agency should notify CEQ of such publication so as to satisfy the requirements to file the final categorical exclusion with CEQ and to make the final categorical exclusion readily available to the public.[27]

B. Seeking Public Involvement When Establishing or Revising a Categorical Exclusion

Engaging the public in the environmental aspects of Federal decisionmaking is a key aspect of NEPA

---

[26] 40 CFR 1507.3(a) (requiring agencies with similar programs to consult with one another and with CEQ to coordinate their procedures).

[27] *Id.*

and the CEQ Regulations.[28] At a minimum, the CEQ Regulations require Federal agencies to make any proposed amendments to their categorical exclusions available for public review and comment in the **Federal Register**,[29] regardless of whether the categorical exclusions are promulgated as regulations through rulemaking, or issued as departmental directives or orders.[30] To maximize the value of comments from interested parties, the agency's **Federal Register** notice should:

• Describe the proposed activities covered by the categorical exclusion and provide the proposed text of the categorical exclusion;

• Summarize the information in the agency's administrative record that was used to substantiate the categorical exclusion, including an evaluation of the information and related findings;[31]

• Define all applicable terms;

• Describe the extraordinary circumstances that may limit the use of the categorical exclusion; and

• Describe the available means for submitting questions and comments about the proposed categorical exclusion (for example, e-mail addresses, mailing addresses, Web site addresses, and names and phone numbers of agency points of contact).

---

[28] National Environmental Policy Act of 1969, § 2 *et seq.*, 42 U.S.C. 4321 *et seq.; see, e.g.,* 40 CFR 1506.6(a) (requiring agencies to make diligent efforts to involve the public in preparing and implementing their NEPA procedures); 40 CFR 1507.3(a) (requiring each agency to consult with CEQ while developing its procedures and before publishing them in the **Federal Register** for comment; providing that an agency's NEPA procedures shall be adopted only after an opportunity for public review; and providing that, once in effect, the procedures must be made readily available to the public).

[29] *See* 40 CFR 1507.3 (outlining procedural requirements for agencies to establish and revise their NEPA implementing regulations), 1506.6(a) (requiring agencies to involve the public in rulemaking, including public notice and an opportunity to comment).

[30] NEPA and the CEQ Regulations do not require agency NEPA implementing procedures, of which categorical exclusions are a key component, to be promulgated as regulations through rulemaking. Agencies should ensure they comply with all appropriate agency requirements for issuing and revising their NEPA implementing procedures.

[31] This step is particularly beneficial when the agency determines that the public will view a potential impact as significant, as it provides the agency the opportunity to explain why it believes that impact to be presumptively insignificant. Whenever practicable, the agency should include a link to a Web site containing all the supporting information, evaluations, and findings. Ready access to all supporting information will likely minimize the need for members of the public to depend on Freedom of Information Act requests and enhance the NEPA goals of outreach and disclosure. Agencies should consider using their regulatory development tools to assist in maintaining access to supporting information, such as establishing an online docket using *http://www.regulations.gov.*

When establishing or revising a categorical exclusion, agencies should also pursue additional opportunities for public involvement beyond publication in the **Federal Register** in cases where there is likely to be significant public interest and additional outreach would facilitate public input. The extent of public involvement can be tailored to the nature of the proposed categorical exclusion and the degree of expected public interest.

CEQ encourages Federal agencies to engage interested parties such as public interest groups, Federal NEPA contacts at other agencies, Tribal governments and agencies, and State and local governments and agencies. The purpose of this engagement is to share relevant data, information, and concerns. Agencies can involve the public by using the methods noted in section 1506.6 of the CEQ Regulations, as well as other public involvement techniques such as focus groups, e-mail exchanges, conference calls, and Web-based forums.

CEQ also strongly encourages Federal agencies to post updates on their official Web sites whenever they issue **Federal Register** notices for new or revised categorical exclusions. An agency Web site may serve as the primary location where the public learns about agency NEPA implementing procedures and their use, and obtains efficient access to updates and supporting information. Therefore, agencies should ensure that their NEPA implementing procedures and any final revisions or amendments are easily accessed through the agency's official Web site including when an agency is adding, deleting, or revising the categorical exclusions and/or the extraordinary circumstances in its NEPA implementing procedures.

V. Applying an Established Categorical Exclusion

When applying a categorical exclusion to a proposed action, Federal agencies face two key decisions: (1) Whether to prepare documentation supporting their determination to use a categorical exclusion for a proposed action; and (2) whether public engagement and disclosure may be useful to inform determinations about using categorical exclusions.

A. When To Document Categorical Exclusion Determinations

In prior guidance, CEQ has "strongly discourage[d] procedures that would require the preparation of additional paperwork to document that an activity has been categorically excluded," based on an expectation that "sufficient information will usually be available

75636   **Federal Register** / Vol. 75, No. 233 / Monday, December 6, 2010 / Rules and Regulations

during the course of normal project development" to determine whether an EIS or an EA is needed.[32] Moreover, "the agency's administrative record (for the proposed action) will clearly document the basis for its decision." [33] This guidance modifies our prior guidance to the extent that it recognizes that each Federal agency should decide—and update its NEPA implementing procedures and guidance to indicate—whether any of its categorical exclusions warrant preparation of additional documentation.

Some activities, such as routine personnel actions or purchases of small amounts of supplies, may carry little risk of significant environmental effects, such that there is no practical need for, or benefit from, preparing additional documentation when applying a categorical exclusion to those activities. For those activities, the administrative record for establishing the categorical exclusion and any normal project development documentation may be considered sufficient.

For other activities, such as decisions to allow various stages of resource development after a programmatic environmental review, documentation may be appropriate to demonstrate that the proposed action comports with any limitations identified in prior NEPA analysis and that there are no potentially significant impacts expected as a result of extraordinary circumstances. In such cases, the documentation should address proposal-specific factors and show consideration of extraordinary circumstances with regard to the potential for localized impacts. It is up to agencies to decide whether to prepare separate NEPA documentation in such cases or to include this documentation in other project-specific documents that the agency is preparing.

In some cases, courts have required documentation to demonstrate that a Federal agency has considered the environmental effects associated with extraordinary circumstances.[34] Documenting the application of a categorical exclusion provides the agency the opportunity to demonstrate why its decision to use the categorical exclusion is entitled to deference.[35]

---

[32] "Guidance Regarding NEPA Regulations," 48 FR 34,263, 34,265, Jul. 28, 1983, *available on http://www.nepa.gov_at ceq.hss.doe.gov/nepa/regs/1983/1983guid.htm.*
[33] *Id.*
[34] *See, e.g., California v. Norton,* 311 F.3d 1162, 1175–78 (9th Cir. 2002).
[35] The agency determination that an action is categorically excluded may itself be challenged under the Administrative Procedure Act, 5 U.S.C. 501 *et seq.*

Documentation may be necessary to comply with the requirements of other laws, regulations, and policies, such as the Endangered Species Act or the National Historic Preservation Act. When that is the case, all resource analyses and the results of any consultations or coordination should be incorporated by reference in the administrative record developed for the proposed action. Moreover, the nature and severity of the effect on resources subject to additional laws or regulations may be a reason for limiting the use of a categorical exclusion and therefore should, where appropriate, also be addressed in documentation showing how potential extraordinary circumstances were considered and addressed in the decision to use the categorical exclusion.

For those categorical exclusions for which an agency determines that documentation is appropriate, the documentation should cite the categorical exclusion being used and show that the agency determined that: (1) The proposed action fits within the category of actions described in the categorical exclusion; and (2) there are no extraordinary circumstances that would preclude the proposed action from being categorically excluded. The extent of the documentation should be tailored to the type of action involved, the potential for extraordinary circumstances and environmental effects, and any applicable requirements of other laws, regulations, and policies. If lengthy documentation is needed to address these aspects, an agency should consider whether it is appropriate to apply the categorical exclusion in that particular situation. In all circumstances, any documentation prepared for a categorical exclusion should be concise.

B. When To Seek Public Engagement and Disclosure

Most Federal agencies do not routinely notify the public when they use a categorical exclusion to meet their NEPA responsibilities. There are some circumstances, however, where the public may be able to provide an agency with valuable information, such as whether a proposal involves extraordinary circumstances or potentially significant cumulative impacts that can help the agency decide whether to apply a categorical exclusion. CEQ therefore encourages Federal agencies to determine—and specify in their NEPA implementing procedures—those circumstances in which the public should be engaged or notified before a categorical exclusion is used.

Agencies should utilize information technology to provide the public with access to information about the agency's NEPA compliance. CEQ strongly recommends that agencies post key information about their NEPA procedures and implementation on a publicly available Web site. The Web site should include:
• The text of the categorical exclusions and applicable extraordinary circumstances;
• A synopsis of the administrative record supporting the establishment of each categorical exclusion with information on how the public can access the entire administrative record;
• Those categorical exclusions which the agency determines are and are not likely to be of interest to the public; [36] and
• Information on agencies' use of categorical exclusions for proposed actions, particularly in those situations where there is a high level of public interest in a proposed action.

Where an agency has documented a categorical exclusion, it should also consider posting that documentation online. For example, in 2009, the Department of Energy adopted a policy to post documented categorical exclusion determinations online.[37] By adopting a similar policy, other agencies can significantly increase the quality and transparency of their decisionmaking when using categorical exclusions.

VI. Periodic Review of Established Categorical Exclusions

The CEQ Regulations direct Federal agencies to "continue to review their policies and procedures and in consultation with [CEQ] to revise them as necessary to ensure full compliance with the purposes and provisions of [NEPA]." [38] Many agencies have categorical exclusions that were established many years ago. Some Federal agencies have internal procedures for identifying and revising categorical exclusions that no longer reflect current environmental circumstances, or current agency policies, procedures, programs, or mission. Where an agency's categorical exclusions have not been regularly

---

[36] Many agencies publish two lists of categorical exclusions: (1) Those which typically do not raise public concerns due to the low risk of potential environmental effects, and (2) those more likely to raise public concerns.
[37] *See* Department of Energy, Categorical Exclusion Determinations, *available at http://www.gc.energy.gov/NEPA/categorical_exclusion_determinations.htm.*
[38] 40 CFR 1507.3.

Federal Register / Vol. 75, No. 233 / Monday, December 6, 2010 / Rules and Regulations   **75637**

reviewed, they should be reviewed by the agency as soon as possible.

There are several reasons why Federal agencies should periodically review their categorical exclusions. For example, a Federal agency may find that an existing categorical exclusion is not being used because the category of actions is too narrowly defined. In such cases, the agency should consider amending its NEPA implementing procedures to expand the description of the category of actions included in the categorical exclusion. An agency could also find that an existing categorical exclusion includes actions that raise the potential for significant environmental effects with some regularity. In those cases, the agency should determine whether to delete the categorical exclusion, or revise it to either limit the category of actions or expand the extraordinary circumstances that limit when the categorical exclusion can be used. Periodic review can also help agencies identify additional factors that should be included in their extraordinary circumstances and consider whether certain categorical exclusions should be documented.

Agencies should exercise sound judgment about the appropriateness of categorically excluding activities in light of evolving or changing conditions that might present new or different environmental impacts or risks. The assumptions underlying the nature and impact of activities encompassed by a categorical exclusion may have changed over time. Different technological capacities of permitted activities may present very different risk or impact profiles. This issue was addressed in CEQ's August 16, 2010 report reviewing the Department of the Interior's Minerals Management Service's application of NEPA to the permitting of deepwater oil and gas drilling.[39]

Agencies should review their categorical exclusions on an established timeframe, beginning with the categorical exclusions that were established earliest and/or the categorical exclusions that may have the greatest potential for significant environmental impacts. This guidance recommends that agencies develop a process and timeline to periodically

review their categorical exclusions (and extraordinary circumstances) to ensure that their categorical exclusions remain current and appropriate, and that those reviews should be conducted at least every seven years. A seven-year cycle allows the agencies to regularly review categorical exclusions to avoid the use of categorical exclusions that are outdated and no longer appropriate. If the agency believes that a different timeframe is appropriate, the agency should articulate a sound basis for that conclusion, explaining how the alternate timeframe will still allow the agency to avoid the use of categorical exclusions that are outdated and no longer appropriate. The agency should publish its process and time period, along with its articulation of a sound basis for periods over seven years, on the agency's Web site and notify CEQ where on the Web site the review procedures are posted. We recognize that due to competing priorities, resource constraints, or for other reasons, agencies may not always be able to meet these time periods. The fact that a categorical exclusion has not been evaluated within the time established does not invalidate its use for NEPA compliance, as long as such use is consistent with the defined scope of the exclusion and has properly considered any potential extraordinary circumstances.

In establishing this review process, agencies should take into account factors including changed circumstances, how frequently the categorical exclusions are used, the extent to which resources and geographic areas are potentially affected, and the expected duration of impacts. The level of scrutiny and evaluation during the review process should be commensurate with a categorically-excluded activity's potential to cause environmental impacts and the extent to which relevant circumstances have changed since it was issued or last reviewed. Some categorical exclusions, such as for routine purchases or contracting for office-related services, may require minimal review. Other categorical exclusions may require a more thorough reassessment of scope, environmental effects, and extraordinary circumstances, such as when they are tiered to programmatic EAs or EISs that analyzed activities whose underlying circumstances have since changed.

To facilitate reviews, the Federal agency offices charged with overseeing their agency's NEPA compliance should develop and maintain sufficient capacity to periodically review their existing categorical exclusions to ensure

that the agency's prediction of no significant impacts is borne out in practice.[40] Agencies can efficiently assess changed circumstances by utilizing a variety of methods such as those recommended in Section III, above, for substantiating new or revised categorical exclusions. These methods include benchmarking, monitoring of previously implemented actions, and consultation with professional staff. The type and extent of monitoring and other information that should be considered in periodic reviews, as well as the particular entity or entities within the agency that would be responsible for gathering this information, will vary depending upon the nature of the actions and their anticipated effects. Consequently, agencies should utilize the expertise, experience, and judgment of agency professional staff when determining the appropriate type and extent of monitoring and other information to consider. This information will help the agency determine whether its categorical exclusions are used appropriately, or whether a categorical exclusion needs to be revised. Agencies can also use this information when they engage stakeholders in developing proposed revisions to categorical exclusions and extraordinary circumstances.

Agencies can also facilitate reviews by keeping records of their experiences with certain activities in a number of ways, including tracking information provided by agency field offices.[41] In such cases, a Federal agency could conduct its periodic review of an established categorical exclusion by soliciting information from field offices about the observed effects of implemented actions, both from agency personnel and the public. On-the-ground monitoring to evaluate environmental effects of an agency's categorically-excluded actions, where appropriate, can also be incorporated into an agency's procedures for conducting its oversight of ongoing projects and can be included as part of regular site visits to project areas.

Agencies can also conduct periodic review of existing categorical exclusions through broader program reviews. Program reviews can occur at various levels (for example, field office, division office, headquarters office) and on various scales (for example, geographic location, project type, or areas identified in an interagency agreement). While a

---

[39] Council on Environmental Quality, *Report Regarding the Mineral Management Service's National Environmental Policy Act Policies, Practices, and Procedures as They Relate to Outer Continental Shelf Oil and Gas Exploration,* available at ceq.hss.doe.gov/current_developments/ docs/CEQ_Report_Reviewing_MMS_OCS_ NEPA_Implementation.pdf (Aug. 2010) at 18–20 (explaining that MMS NEPA review for the Macondo Exploratory Well relied on categorical exclusions established in the 1980s, before deepwater drilling became widespread).

[40] 40 CFR 1507.2.

[41] Council on Environmental Quality, *The NEPA Task Force Report to the Council on Environmental Quality—Modernizing NEPA Implementation,* p. 63 (Sept. 2003), *available on http://www.nepa.gov* at ceq.hss.doe.gov/ntf/report/index.html.

75638 **Federal Register** / Vol. 75, No. 233 / Monday, December 6, 2010 / Rules and Regulations

Federal agency may choose to initiate a program review specifically focused on categorical exclusions, it is possible that program reviews with a broader focus may yield information relevant to categorical exclusions and may thus substitute for reviews specifically focused on categorical exclusions. However, the substantial flexibility that agencies have in how they structure their review procedures underscores the importance of ensuring that the review procedures are clear and transparent.

In working with agencies on reviewing their existing categorical exclusions, CEQ will look to the actual impacts from activities that have been subject to categorical exclusions, and will consider the extent and scope of agency monitoring and/or other substantiating evidence. As part of its oversight role and responsibilities under NEPA, CEQ will contact agencies following the release of this guidance to ascertain the status of their reviews of existing categorical exclusions. CEQ will make every effort to align its oversight with reviews being conducted by the agency and will begin with those agencies that are currently reassessing their categorical exclusions, as well as with agencies that are experiencing difficulties or facing challenges to their application of categorical exclusions.

Finally, it is important to note that the rationale and supporting information for establishing or documenting experience with using a categorical exclusion may be lost if an agency has inadequate procedures for recording, retrieving, and preserving documents and administrative records. Therefore, Federal agencies will benefit from a review of their current practices for maintaining and preserving such records. Measures to ensure future availability could include greater centralization of records, use of modern storage systems and improvements in the agency's electronic and hard copy filing systems.[42]

VII. Conclusion

This guidance will help to guide CEQ and the agencies when an agency seeks to propose a new or revised categorical exclusion. It should also guide the agencies when categorical exclusions are used for proposed actions, when reviewing existing categorical exclusions, or when proposing new categorical exclusions. Questions regarding this guidance should be directed to the CEQ Associate Director for NEPA Oversight.

Nancy H. Sutley,
Chair.
[FR Doc. 2010–30017 Filed 12–3–10; 8:45 am]
BILLING CODE 3125–W0–P

---

[42] Agencies should be mindful of their obligations to maintain and preserve agency records under the Federal Records Act for maintaining and preserving agency records. 44 U.S.C. 3101 *et seq.*

NEPA Deskbook

Appendix 29 Reporting Cooperating Agencies in Implementing the Procedural Requirements of NEPA

December 23, 2004

MEMORANDUM FOR THE HEADS OF FEDERAL AGENCIES

FROM: JAMES L. CONNAUGHTON

SUBJECT: REPORTING COOPERATING AGENCIES IN IMPLEMENTING THE
            PROCEDURAL REQUIREMENTS OF THE NATIONAL ENVIRONMENTAL
            POLICY ACT

The January 30, 2002, Memorandum for Heads of Federal Agencies, Subject: Cooperating Agencies in Implementing the Procedural Requirements of the National Environmental Policy Act[1], consistent with the President's commitment to increase local participation and facilitate cooperative conservation, established a reporting requirement for all EISs and EAs. The purpose of this Memorandum is to establish a revised report to ensure that all Federal agencies are consistently reporting designation of Federal and non-federal cooperating agencies in the preparation of analyses and documentation required by the National Environmental Policy Act (NEPA).[2]

This memorandum ends the six month reporting requirement and establishes an improved reporting mechanism. We developed the new report format based on recommendations from your agencies to more accurately measure our progress in assuring cooperating agency status to federal and non-federal governmental bodies that qualify for such status. CEQ will convene an interagency work group to develop metrics applicable to all agencies for using the reports to improve agency NEPA processes and decisionmaking.

Agencies of the Federal government responsible for preparing NEPA analyses will now report once each fiscal year (FY). The report will be due three months after the close of the FY. For example, the first such report for October 1, 2004 through September 30, 2005 will be due on January 3, 2006.

For EISs with a Notice of Intent published between October 1, 2004 and September 30, 2005, the lead agency will report: (1) the title of the EIS; (2) the names of the cooperating agencies for the EIS; (3) the names of agencies who declined an invitation to participate as a cooperating agency or who requested but failed to reach agreement on establishing cooperating agency status and agencies whose cooperating agency status was ended, and the reason(s)

---

[1] Available at http://ceq.eh.doe.gov/nepa/regs/guidance.html

[2] Cooperating agency status under NEPA is not equivalent to other requirements calling for an agency to engage another governmental entity in a consultation or coordination process (e.g., Endangered Species Act section 7, National Historic Preservation Act section 106). Agencies are urged to integrate NEPA requirements with other environmental review and consultation requirements (40 C.F.R. § 1500.2(c)); and reminded that establishing or ending cooperating agency status does not satisfy or end those other requirements.

cooperating agency status was not established or was ended; and (4) the current status of the EIS. Reports after FY 05 would include updates to previous reports on EISs.

For EAs, the lead agency will report: (1) the number of EAs completed between October 1, 2004 and September 30, 2005; (2) the number of those EAs which included participation of one or more cooperating agencies; and (3) the reasons agencies did not accept invitations or reach agreement to participate as cooperating agencies, or ended the cooperating agency status prior to completing the EA.

The form for submitting the annual report is attached (Attachment 1). Also attached are Frequently Askcd Questions and Answers developed with the agencies to address common issues and be used in conjunction with the report form (Attachment 2).

If you have any questions concerning this memorandum, please contact Horst G. Greczmiel, Associate Director for NEPA Oversight at 202-395-5750, Horst_Greczmiel@ceq.eop.gov, or 202-456-0753 (fax).

# # #

INSERT NAME OF AGENCY SUBMITTING THE REPORT

Cooperating Agency Report to the Council on Environmental Quality

October 1, 2004 to September 30, 2005

I.   **Environmental Impact Statements:**

EIS TITLE *(Insert Title of each EIS for which your agency published a NOI during the fiscal year)*	COOPERATING AGENCIES *(Insert names of agencies that were invited and agreed to participate in the EIS process as Cooperating Agencies or that requested Cooperating Agency status and reached agreement with the lead agency to participate in the EIS process as Cooperating Agencies)*	CA STATUS NOT ESTABLISHED OR ENDED *(Insert the name(s) of any agency(ies) that: declined in writing –required for federal agencies, see 40 CFR 1501.6(c) – or verbally to participate as a Cooperating Agency; requested Cooperating Agency status but was unable to reach agreement to participate as a Cooperating Agency; or that assumed Cooperating Agency status which was subsequently ended and the reason Cooperating Agency status was not established or was ended – see 5 listed reasons below)*	STATUS OF EIS *(Insert the following dates as mm/dd/yyyy)*
			NOI: DEIS NOA:

		FEIS NOA: ROD:
		NOI: DEIS NOA: FEIS NOA: ROD:
		NOI: DEIS NOA: FEIS NOA: ROD:
		NOI: DEIS NOA: FEIS NOA: ROD:

Reasons CA status was not established or why it ended:

1. Potential Cooperating Agency lacked special expertise and jurisdiction by law.

2. Potential Cooperating Agency lacked authority to enter into an agreement to be a CA.

3. Potential or active CA lacked agreement with the agency.
(e.g., unable to accept the scope of the analysis or the purpose and need for the proposed action; unable to accept responsibilities and/or milestones for analysis and documentation; unable to develop information/analysis of all reasonable alternatives; unable to prevent release of predecisional information; misrepresents the process or the findings presented in the analysis and documentation).

4. Potential or active CA lacked capacity (training or resources) to participate.
(e.g., unable to participate during scoping and/or throughout the preparation of the analysis and documentation as necessary to meet process milestones; unable to identify significant issues, eliminate minor issues, identify issues previously studied, or identify conflicts with the objectives of regional, State and local land use plans, policies and controls in a timely manner; unable to assist in preparing portions of the review and analysis and help resolve significant environmental issues in a timely manner; unable to provide resources to support scheduling and critical milestones).

5. Other (specify).

Attachment 1

II.   Environmental Assessments:

	Total
Number of EAs completed by your agency during the fiscal year	
Number of those EAs your agency prepared with CAs	
The reason(s) from the list below that cooperating agency status was not established or was ended (NOTE: agencies may replace this row of the report with a paragraph describing the most frequent reasons)	(number) EAs – reason #1 (number) EAs – reason #2 (number) EAs – reason #3 (number) EAs – reason #4 (number) EAs – reason #5

Reasons CA status was not established or why it ended:

1.   Potential Cooperating Agency lacked special expertise and jurisdiction by law.

2.   Potential Cooperating Agency lacked authority to enter into an agreement to be a CA.

3.   Potential or active CA lacked agreement with the agency.
(e.g., unable to accept the scope of the analysis or the purpose and need for the proposed action; unable to accept responsibilities and/or milestones for analysis and documentation; unable to develop information/analysis of all reasonable alternatives; unable to prevent release of predecisional information; misrepresents the process or the findings presented in the analysis and documentation).

4.   Potential or active CA lacked capacity (training or resources) to participate.
(e.g., unable to participate during scoping and/or throughout the preparation of the analysis and documentation as necessary to meet process milestones; unable to identify significant issues, eliminate minor issues, identify issues previously studied, or identify conflicts with the objectives of regional, State and local land use plans, policies and controls in a timely manner; unable to assist in preparing portions of the review and analysis and help resolve significant environmental issues in a timely manner; unable to provide resources to support scheduling and critical milestones).

5.   Other (specify).

Attachment 1

Cooperating Agency Report to the Council on Environmental Quality

Frequently Asked Questions and Answers

1.   What are the major changes between the reporting requirement established in January 2002 and this reporting requirement?

The major changes: (1) increase the reporting period from six to twelve months; (2) align the reporting period with the fiscal year; (3) decrease the amount of information reported; (4) simplify the identification of challenges or barriers to establishing cooperating agency status; and (5) report completed rather than initiated environmental assessments.

2.   Do agencies report Environmental Impact Statements (EISs) and Environmental Assessments (EAs) if they are a Cooperating Agency (CA)?

No. Report only those EAs and EISs that the agency is responsible for preparing. When more than one federal agency has NEPA responsibilities (e.g. one funds or approves a project that another implements) then the agencies should work together, either as joint-leads or as lead and cooperating agencies, to avoid duplicative NEPA work. The lead agency responsible for preparing the EA or EIS is responsible for submitting the CA report.

3.   Who reports the EIS or EA when there are joint lead agencies responsible for preparing the EIS or EA?

Joint lead agencies can be involved when a Tribe, State or local agency with a requirement comparable to NEPA, or another federal agency either (1) proposes or is involved in the same action, or (2) is involved in a group of actions directly related to each other because of their functional interdependence or geographical proximity [see 40 CFR §§1501.5 and 1506.2]. When a federal agency is a joint-lead agency with a Tribal, State or local government, the federal agency will report the EA or EIS. When more than one federal agency is a joint-lead, the federal joint-lead agencies should agree on which one federal agency will report the EA or EIS. Although a formal document to establish Cooperating Agency Status is not required, the agencies involved need to clearly understand their respective roles and a formal document or exchange of letters may be helpful in correcting misunderstandings brought on by changing personnel and priorities. When a formal document or an exchange of letters is used, the agency with reporting responsibility should be identified.

4.   Which EAs and EISs are reported?

The report will provide information on EISs <u>begun</u> during the fiscal year reporting period, and on EAs <u>completed</u> during the fiscal year reporting period. For purposes of this report, an EIS is begun when the Notice of Intent (NOI) is published in the Federal Register, and an EA is completed when a Finding of No Significant Impact (FONSI) is completed or a NOI to prepare an EIS is published.

5.   What is required for an agency to be reported as a Cooperating Agency?

Agencies with either "jurisdiction by law" or "special expertise" are eligible to be cooperating agencies. When they are invited and agree to be cooperating agencies or their request for cooperating agency status is granted, then they qualify and should be reported as cooperating agencies. When more than one federal agency has NEPA responsibilities – or in the case of tribal, state or local governments, responsibilities for requirements in addition to but not in conflict with those in NEPA – then the agencies should work together, either as joint-leads or as lead and cooperating agencies, to avoid redundant, duplicative NEPA work and cooperating agency status is one way to accomplish these responsibilities. Agencies with a permitting or approval role, often referred to as consulting agencies, can be invited to be cooperating agencies and lead agencies are encouraged to actively consider extending cooperating agency status to such agencies.

6.   Does the cooperating agency's name go on the EA or EIS?

Yes. For an EIS, the cover must list all cooperating agencies (federal and non-federal) as required by Section 1502.11 of the CEQ NEPA regulations [see http://ceq.eh.doe.gov/nepa/regs/000925letter.html]. An EA must list the agencies consulted [see 40 CFR §1508.9] and agencies with cooperating agency status can be listed as a subset of those consulted.

7.   Which agencies must be reported when Cooperating Agency status is not established or is ended?

Agencies should be reported in the EIS column "CA Status not Established or Ended" and in the EA report's third row or optional explanatory paragraph when:
  (1) An agency declines an invitation to participate as a Cooperating Agency in writing or verbally. Federal agencies are required to decline in writing and to provide a copy of their reply to the invitation to the Council on Environmental Quality (see 40 CFR §1501.6(c)).
  (2) An agency requests cooperating agency status but an agreement to participate as a Cooperating Agency is not reached with the agency responsible for the NEPA analysis and documentation.
  (3) An agency whose Cooperating Agency status was established but ended prior to completion of the NEPA analysis and documentation.
The reporting agency must indicate the reason that the Cooperating Agency status was not established or was ended. Five main categories of reasons, with examples, are provided on the report form. When there are several reasons, provide the primary reason(s) for not establishing or ending the Cooperating Agency status.

8.   How will agencies update the EIS information in subsequent fiscal years?

The reporting agency will provide updated information (for example: new cooperating agencies; new EIS status) in subsequent FYs by submitting the previous EIS report with new information inserted and highlighted.

Attachment 2   3

NEPA Deskbook

Appendix 30 Other Helpful CEQ Publications

Other Helpful CEQ Publications

The following documents, too lengthy to reproduce in this Deskbook, may be helpful in your research:

CEQ, Incorporating Biodiversity Considerations Into Environmental Impact Analysis Under the National Environmental Policy Act (Jan. 1993)

CEQ, The National Environmental Policy Act, A Study of Its Effectiveness After Twenty-Five Years (Jan. 1997)

CEQ, Environmental Justice, Guidance Under the National Environmental Policy Act (Dec. 1997).

CEQ & OMB Memorandum on Environmental Collaboration and Conflict Resolution, 7 September 2012 (available at http://energy.gov/sites/prod/files/OMB_CEQ_Env_Collab_Conflict_Resolution_20120907-2012.pdf)

Memorandum for Heads of Federal Departments and Agencies: Emergencies and the National Environmental Policy Act, 12 May 2010 (available at http://energy.gov/sites/prod/files/nepapub/nepa_documents/RedDont/G-CEQ-Emergencies.pdf)

Memorandum for Heads of Departments and Federal Agencies Reporting on NEPA Status for Activities and Projects Receiving American Recovery and Reinvestment Act Funding, 20 November 2009 (with 4 attachments)

Memorandum for Heads of Departments and Federal Agencies: Reporting NEPA Status and Progress for Recovery Act Activities and Projects, 3 April 2009 (this replaced the 11 March 2009 Memorandum for Heads of Departments and Federal Agencies: Reporting NEPA Status and Progress for Recovery Act Activities and Projects; and is supplemented by the 20 November 2009 Memorandum for Heads of Departments and Federal Agencies Reporting on NEPA Status for Activities and Projects Receiving American Recovery and Reinvestment Act Funding) (available at http://www.osec.doc.gov/oam/archive/docs/Recovery%20Act%20and%20NEPA%20Apr%203%2009.pdf)

CEQ Exchange of Letters with Secretary of Energy: Application of NEPA Categorical Exclusions to the Auto Loan Program under section 136 of the Energy Independence and Security Act of 2007, March 2009 Part 1, Part 2

Memorandum for Heads of Departments and Federal Agencies: Department and Agency NEPA Contacts and Capacity, 12 February 2009

CEQ, OSTP, OMB memo on National Environmental Status and Trends Indicators, June 2008

CEQ & OMB Memorandum on Environmental Conflict Resolution, 28 November 2005 - This memorandum has been replaced by the CEQ & OMB memorandum of 7 September 2012.

Memorandum for Federal NEPA Contacts: Emergency Actions and NEPA, 8 September 2005 (available at http://energy.gov/sites/prod/files/nepapub/nepa_documents/RedDont/G-CEQ-EmergencyGuidance.pdf).

Guidance on the Consideration of Past Actions in Cumulative Effects Analysis, 24 June 2005 (available at http://energy.gov/sites/prod/files/nepapub/nepa_documents/RedDont/G-CEQ-PastActsCumulEffects.pdf)

NEPA Deskbook

Appendix 31 Policy and Procedures for the Review of Federal Actions Impacting the Environment

Policy and Procedures for the Review of Federal Actions Impacting the Environment

October 3, 1984

TABLE OF CONTENTS

7. Providing Guidance as a Cooperating Agency
8. EPA as Lead Agency
    o A. Determining Lead Agency
9. Reporting and Control

CHAPTER 4 - REVIEW OF DRAFT ENVIRONMENTAL IMPACT STATEMENTS

1. Policy
2. Draft EIS Review Management
    o A. Establishing Deadlines and Time Extensions
    o B. Categorization and Agency Notification System for Draft EIS's
3. Scope of Comments on the Draft EIS
    o A. General
    o B. Mitigation (40 CFR 1508.20)
    o C. Statutory Authorities
    o D. Alternatives
    o E. Purpose and Need
    o F. Projects Subject to Section 404(r) of the Clean Water Act
    o G. Projects Potentially Affecting a Designated "Sole Source" Aquifer Subject to Section
    o 1424(e) of the SDWA
4. Rating System Criteria
    o A. Rating the Environmental Impact of the Action
    o B. Adequacy of the Impact Statement
5. Approving and Distributing Comments on Draft EIS's
    o A. Categories LO, EC, EO, 1, or 2
    o B. Categories EU or 3
    o C. Checklist for Distribution of Agency Comments on the Draft EIS
6. Reporting and Control

CHAPTER 5 - POST-DRAFT EIS FOLLOW-UP

1. Policy
2. Post-Draft Consultations
3. Status Reports
4. Reporting and Control

CHAPTER 6 - REVIEW OF FINAL EIS'S

1. Policy
2. Final EIS Review Management
    o A. Designating Lead Responsibility and Principal and Associate Reviewers
    o B. Establishing Deadlines and Time Extensions

Summary of Rating Definitions and Follow-up Action

CHAPTER 1 - PURPOSE, POLICY, AND MANDATES

1. PURPOSE.

A. This manual establishes policies and procedures for carrying out the Environmental Protection Agency's (EPA's) responsibilities to review and comment on Federal actions affecting the quality of the environment. EPA has general statutory authority under the National Environmental Policy Act of 1969 and the Council on Environmental Quality's implementing regulations, and has specific authority and responsibility under Section 309 of the Clean Air Act to conduct such reviews, comment in writing, and make those comments available to the public. These responsibilities have been combined into one process and are referred to throughout this Manual as the Environmental Review Process.

B. This manual contains EPA's policies and procedures for carrying out the Environmental Review Process, assigns specific responsibilities, and outlines mechanisms for resolving problems that arise in the Environmental Review Process. This Manual is supplemented by, and should be read in conjunction with, the following manuals, which are also prepared, distributed, and maintained by the Office of Federal Activities:

1. Office of Federal Activities Policies and Procedures Manual. Contains current guidance and detailed information related to the Environmental Review Process; and

2. Environmental Review Process Data Management Manual. Contains detailed guidance and reporting requirements for the national level computerized tracking system.

2. STATUTORY AUTHORITIES

A. The National Environmental Policy Act of 1969 (NEPA), as amended, (42 U.S.C. 4321 et seq., Public Law 91-190, 83 Stat. 852), requires that all Federal agencies proposing legislation and other major actions significantly affecting the quality of the human environment consult with other agencies having jurisdiction by law or special expertise over such environmental considerations, and thereafter prepare a detailed statement of these environmental effects. The Council on Environmental Quality (CEQ) has published regulations and associated guidance to implement NEPA (40 CFR Parts 1500-1508).

B. Section 309 of the Clean Air Act, as amended, (42 U.S.C. 7609, Public Law 91-604 12(a), 84 Stat. 1709), requires the EPA to review and comment in writing on the environmental impact of any matter relating to the duties and responsibilities granted pursuant to the Act or other provisions of the authority of the Administrator, contained in any: (1) legislation proposed by a Federal department or agency; (2) newly authorized Federal projects for construction and as major Federal action, or actions, other than a project for construction, to which Section 102(2)(C) of Public Law 91-190 applies; and (3) proposed regulations published by any department or agency of the Federal Government. Such written comments must be made public at the conclusion of any review. In the event such legislation, action, or regulation is determined to be unsatisfactory from the standpoint of public health, welfare, or environmental quality, the determination will be published and the matter referred to the CEQ.

C. Federal environmental laws require, in most circumstances, facilities of the Executive Branch of the Federal Government to comply with Federal, State, and local pollution control requirements promulgated pursuant to, or effective under, those statutes. The review of proposed Federal projects for compliance with these national environmental standards is the responsibility of the EPA through the Environmental Review Process and the Federal Facilities Compliance Program. In addition to these general statutory authorities, the reviews required under Section 1424(e) of the Safe Drinking Water Act (42 U.S.C. 300 h-3, Public Law 93-523, 88 Stat. 1678) and Section 404(r) of the Federal Water Pollution Control Act (Clean Water Act) (33 U.S.C. 1344(r), Public Law 92-500, Public Law 95-217, 86 Stat. 884, 91 Stat 1600) are integrated into the Environmental Review Process.

3. POLICY.

A. The objective of the Environmental Review Process is to foster the goals of the NEPA process by ensuring that the EPA's environmental expertise, as expressed in its comments on Federal actions and other interagency liaison activity, is considered by agency decision makers. It is EPA's policy to carry out the Environmental Review Process in conjunction with EPA's other authorities to:

1. Participate in interagency coordination early in the planning process to identify significant environmental issues that should be addressed in completed documents;

2. Conduct follow-up coordination on actions where EPA has identified significant environmental impacts to ensure a full understanding of the issues and to ensure implementation of appropriate corrective actions; and

3. Identify environmentally unsatisfactory proposals and consult with other agencies, including the CEQ, to achieve timely resolution of the major issues and problems.

B. In implementing this policy, EPA will assist Federal agencies in:

1. Achieving the goals set forth in the NEPA;

2. Meeting the objectives and complying with the requirements of the laws and regulations administered by the EPA; and

3. Developing concise, well-reasoned decision documents which identify project impacts, a range of project alternatives, and mitigation measures that will avoid or minimize adverse effects on the environment.

CHAPTER 2 - MANAGEMENT OF THE ENVIRONMENTAL REVIEW PROCESS

1. GENERAL RESPONSIBILITIES.

The EPA Administrator has delegated responsibility for carrying out the Environmental Review Process to the Assistant Administrator for External Affairs and the Regional Administrators but has retained the responsibility to refer matters to the CEQ. The Assistant Administrator, Office of External Affairs, has in turn delegated program management to the Director, Office of Federal Activities, but has retained the responsibility for concurring on proposed comment letters that have the potential for referral to the CEQ.

2. OFFICE OF FEDERAL ACTIVITIES.

The Office of Federal Activities (OFA) within with' n the Office of External Affairs (OEA) is the program manager for the Environmental Review Process and for the overall coordination and policy development for activities associated with this process. To carry out these responsibilities, the OFA will maintain management support functions consisting of Federal Agency Liaison staff assigned to coordinate with the Headquarters offices of all Federal agencies and a Management Information Unit. The Director, Federal Agency Liaison Division, working through the Director, OFA, has overall policy development and management oversight responsibility for the Environmental Review Process.

A. Federal Agency Liaisons. Each Federal Agency Liaison (FAL), working through their Division Director and other appropriate elements within the OFA, has the following responsibilities:

1. Conduct Headquarters-level liaison with other Federal agencies to identify those actions that should be reviewed and to provide information on how the EPA can most effectively review other agencies' proposed actions pursuant to the Environmental Review Process;

2. Provide management oversight of regional review actions carried out under the requirements of this Manual, and provide policy guidance on the Environmental Review Process to Headquarters program offices and regional EIS reviewers;

3. Ensure appropriate Headquarters involvement and support for actions that are elevated under

these Procedures: and

4. Coordinate the EPA review of proposed regulations, national level Environmental Impact Statements (EIS's), and other national level activities and other national level actions.

B. Management Information Unit.

1. The Management Information Unit (MIU) is responsible for the operation of a centralized data management and reporting system for the Environmental Review Process, and for the public availability of comments pursuant to Section 309 of the Clean Air Act. The procedures and requirements for this centralized data system are described in the Environmental Review Process Data Management Manual. The MIU is also responsible for the official filing of all EIS's in accordance with 40 CFR Section 1506.9.

2. The MIU is responsible for preparing the following reports to inform EPA officials and the public of EIS's and other Federal actions received by the EPA for review and comment.

   o **COMDATE.** This weekly computerized report contains a list of all EIS's filed, pursuant to 40 CFR Section 1506.9, during the previous week. COMDATE lists, in part, the EIS title, official filing date, EPA control numbers, location, Federal Register notice date (40 CFR 1506.10(a)), date comments are due to the lead agency, and regional assignment. Other relevant information is also noted such as overall extensions of time granted by lead agencies and EPA ratings of previously filed draft EIS's.

   o **CEQ Notice of EIS Availability.** A Notice of Availability is published in the Federal Register each Friday for EIS's filed during the previous week, pursuant to 40 CFR Section 1506.10(a). The minimum periods for review of the EIS's are calculated from the Federal Register date of this notice.

   o **Notice of Availability of EPA Comments.** A notice will be published weekly announcing the availability of EPA comments on EISs, regulations, and any other action for which an unsatisfactory determination has been made. The notice will include, in part, the title, a summary of comments, and the rating (if applicable) of each review completed.

3. REGIONAL OFFICE.

Each EPA regional office is responsible for carrying out the Environmental Review Process in accordance with the policies and procedures of this Manual for proposed Federal actions affecting its region. Each EPA regional office will designate a regional environmental review coordinator who has overall management responsibility for the Environmental Review Process in that region. It is the responsibility of the regional environmental review coordinator to:

A. Ensure that the region is maintaining effective liaison with other Federal agencies at the regional level;

B. Carry out lead responsibilities for the review of proposed EIS's and other Federal actions assigned to the coordinator's region or other actions for which it has lead responsibility (see paragraph 6 of this chapter); and

C. Ensure that the region is maintaining the official agency files and is properly tracking correspondence generated under the regional Environmental Review Process.

4. PROGRAM OFFICES.

EPA program offices are responsible for providing technical assistance and policy guidance on review actions directly related to their areas of responsibility. When acting as principal or associate reviewer in accordance with paragraph 5 of this chapter, program offices will follow the policies and procedures set forth in this Manual.

5. SPECIFIC REVIEW MANAGEMENT RESPONSIBILITIES.

A. Headquarters and Regional Environmental Review Coordinators. The term Environmental Review Coordinator (ERC) is used in this Manual to mean either a regional environmental review coordinator or the OFA Division Director managing FAL responsibilities for a particular action agency. It is the ERC's responsibility to manage the environmental review of actions to ensure EPA compliance with the procedures in this Manual and to:

1. Ensure the timely receipt of all assigned EIS's listed in COMDATE, and ensure completion of MIU reporting requirements;

2. Designate a principal reviewer for each assigned action;

3. Coordinate determination of the level of participation in EIS scoping efforts and manage participation efforts;

4. Coordinate determination of EPA's involvement as a cooperating agency under Section 1501.6 of the CEQ regulations;

5. Determine the case-by-case need for reviewing the adequacy of the contents of draft EIS's;

6. Determine the case-by-case need for preparation of comments on final EIS's;

7. Determine the appropriate rating to be assigned to each draft EIS in the comment letter;

8. Determine the need for preparation of comments on non-EIS actions;

9. Ensure timely distribution and public availability of comments; and

10. Initiate and manage agency follow-up efforts on comment letters identifying significant Problem areas.

B. Principal Reviewer. The principal reviewer (PR) within a person designated by the ERC to coordinate the review of the action and to prepare the EPA comment letter on the proposed Federal action. The PR will be responsible for ensuring that the views of other EPA offices are adequately represented in the comment letter, and that the comment letter is consistent with agency policy and reflects all applicable EPA environmental responsibilities. In general, the PR for Headquarters lead reviews will be the FAL assigned to the lead agency. The PR will have the responsibility to:

1. Select associate reviewers (AR's) ensuring that all appropriate regional and Headquarters EPA offices are asked to participate;

2. Set due dates for AR comments that will ensure adequate time for review by the signing official;

3. Coordinate with AR's to ensure timely receipt of comments and timely receipt on of disagreements or inconsistencies between reviewers;

4. Review and assure the validity of all comments included in the final EPA response;

5. Resolve and record the disposition of any disagreements with or between AR comments in accordance with subparagraph d, below;

6. Ensure consistency of EPA comments with any previous comments on the action;

7. Recommend the most appropriate rating of the environmental impacts of the proposal and/or the adequacy of the EIS, and include the rating in all draft EIS comment letters; and

8. Ensure the distribution of copies of the signed comment letter to all AR's and other appropriate parties.

C. Associate Reviewer. The associate reviewer (AR) is a person designated by the PR to provide technical and policy advice in specific review areas and to provide the views of the office in which the AR is located. AR's will have the responsibility to:

1. Review assigned actions within their areas of responsibility taking into account the policies and procedures of this Manual;

2. Submit comments to the PR on actions in a timely manner;

3. Obtain the appropriate level of concurrence on comments submitted;

4. If significant issues are identified, assist the PR in determining the most appropriate rating for the proposed action; and

5. Upon the request of the PR and within the limits of available resources, provide liaison with, and technical assistance to, the agency that initiated the EIS or other Federal action.

D. Consolidation of Comments. The PR will consider all AR comments during preparation of the EPA comment letter. If the PR disagrees with substantive AR comments, the PR will attempt to resolve the differences directly with the AR. If this is not possible, the ERC will be informed and will coordinate resolution of the issue. On comment letters where substantive changes are made to comments generated by an AR, the PR will obtain AR concurrence on the final letter. If major policy issues are involved, the ERC should be .informed and policy level concurrence by the AR off ice should be obtained. All AR comments, with applicable PR notations on disposition of the specific issue, will be retained in the official project file.

6. ROUTING AND LEAD RESPONSIBILITY OF EIS'S AND OTHER FEDERAL ACTIONS.

A. Distribution of EIS's should be accomplished by lead agencies on or before the EIS filing date. To ensure that all EIS's are properly distributed, the ERC will check the weekly COMDATE report to make sure that all assigned EIS's have been received. If the ERC has not received an EIS identified in COMDATE, the ERC will inform the MIU immediately and work with the MIU to obtain the EIS. If appropriate, a request for a time extension due to lack of availability of the EIS will be coordinated by the MIU at that time. The following table represents the normal routing and lead responsibility assignment of review actions.

Action	Directed to
Legislation (not accompanied by EIS)	Office of Legislative Analysis
Policy statements, regulations, procedures, and legislation accompanied by an EIS	Office of Federal Activities
Actions that embody a high degree of national controversy or significance, or pioneer Agency policy	Office of Federal Activities
All other actions	Appropriate regional office

B. In general, a regional office will have the lead responsibility for reviewing all EIS's and other Federal actions it receives. Specific exceptions occur where:

1. The EIS or other Federal action pertains to an action that is to take place in another region. In such cases, that regional office will have the lead, the MIU will be informed immediately, and the EIS will be forwarded to the lead region.

2. The EIS pertains to more than one region. In this case, the affected regions should refer to COMDATE to determine which is the lead region and which is an AR. If there is a disagreement with the COMDATE assignments, the designated lead region will inform the MIU.

3. The EIS or other Federal action pertains primarily to national EPA policy, regulations, or procedures, or to an action which does not have a geographical focus (e.g., overlapping several regions), or to an action concerning areas in which the regional office does not have adequate expertise. If the ERC suspects this to be the case, the ERC will contact the appropriate FAL to determine lead responsibility. Unless otherwise agreed upon, such cases will be forwarded immediately to the MIU for reassignment of the action.

C. A regional or Headquarters office may at any time request that a particular EIS or other Federal action be evaluated by the OFA to determine lead responsibility.

CHAPTER 3 - PRE-EIS REVIEW ACTIVITIES

1. POLICY.

It is EPA's policy to participate early in the NEPA compliance efforts of other Federal agencies to the fullest extent practicable in order to identify EPA matters of concern with proposed agency actions and to assist in resolving these concerns at the earliest possible stage of project development. The ERC will make a concerted effort to resolve project concerns through early coordination, where possible, rather than rely on submission of critical comments on completed documents.

2. GENERAL LIAISON.

A. The regional environmental review coordinator and the FAL's will establish and maintain contact at the appropriate levels of other agencies in order to foster an effective working relationship between agencies, to understand the agencies' programs and policies, and to be kept informed of projects of interest to the EPA.

B. To the fullest extent practicable, the ERC will assist the action agencies in:

1. Early identification of potential project impacts and the need to prepare assessments or EIS's;

2. Identification of appropriate environmental assessment techniques and methodologies; and

3. Incorporation of all reasonable alternatives and impact mitigation measures in the planning and development of projects.

3. EPA'S PARTICIPATION IN SCOPING.

A. General. Scoping is the formal early coordination process required by CEQ's 1979 Regulations (40 CFR 1501.7) and is intended to ensure that problems are identified early and are properly studied, that issues of little significance do not consume time and effort, that the draft EIS is thorough and balanced, and that delays occasioned by an inadequate draft EIS are avoided. To help achieve these objectives, EPA will participate in scoping processes to the fullest extent practicable, emphasizing attendance at scoping meetings.

B. Responding to Scoping Requests.

1. The ERC will review and respond by letter to all scoping requests specifically mate to the EPA. Although Federal Register Notices of Intent to prepare an EIS are not considered specific, the ERC is responsible for being aware of all relevant scoping requests and for participating in those of special interest to the EPA. Responses to these non-EPA specific scoping requests may be made by telephone, but a record of the communication must be kept in the official project file.

2. Scoping letters can be either a form letter of acknowledgment with a list of generic concerns (related to project type or project area), or a letter with detailed action-specific comments. A generic scoping letter or telephone response must define EPA's anticipated level of participation in the scoping process and include at least the following information:

    1. For the general type of project being proposed:
        1. *A list of all EPA permits that might be required;*
        2. *Significant environmental issues that should be emphasized in preparation of the EIS; and*
        3. *References to publications, including guidelines and current research, that would be useful in analyzing the environmental impacts of various alternatives.*

    2. A statement regarding EPA's intention to carry out its independent environmental review responsibilities under Section 309 of the Clean Air Act; and

    3. The name, title, and telephone number of the appropriate working-level contact in the EPA.

3. (3) The level of EPA participation in scoping processes will be determined by the ERC on a case-

by-case basis, taking into account the following factors:

- ○ EPA's statutory responsibility;
- ○ Severity of potential environmental impacts;
- ○ Priority concerns identified in the Administrator's Agency Operating Guidance; and
- ○ Available staff and travel resources.

C. Input to the Scoping Process. For those scoping requests where the ERC determines that more substantive EPA participation is warranted, the generic information listed in subparagraph 3b(2) should be supplemented with further detailed guidance to the lead agency. Such guidance will, to the extent possible, include:

1. Specific environmental issues that should be analyzed;

2. Specific information or data related to the area of interest;

3. Specific assessment techniques and methodologies that EPA program offices use or have approved for use;

4. Reasonable alternatives to the proposed action that may avoid potential adverse impacts, including suggestions for an environmentally preferred alternative: and

5. Mitigation measures that should be considered to reduce or substantially eliminate adverse environmental impacts.

4. EPA AS A COOPERATING AGENCY.

A. General. Under 40 CFR 1501.6, the lead agency may request any other Federal agency to serve as a cooperating agency if it has jurisdiction or special expertise (statutory responsibility, agency mission, or related program experience) regarding any environmental issue that should be addressed in the statement. EPA may also request that the lead agency designate it as a cooperating agency. The ERC is responsible for determining whether the EPA will become a cooperating agency. The ERC is encouraged to accept cooperating agency status as often as possible, taking into account the criteria in subparagraph 3b(3).

B. Responding to Requests To Be a Cooperating Agency.

1. If EPA determines in response to a formal request or makes an independent request to be a cooperating agency, the ERC must inform the lead agency of this decision in writing. The response must clearly state that every effort will be made to raise and resolve issues during scoping and EIS preparation, but that EPA has independent obligations under Section 309 of the Clean Air Act to review and comment on every draft EIS. EPA's response to a request to become a cooperating agency should clearly outline EPA's role in the

preparation of the EIS. EPA's participation may range from participation in the scoping process and reviewing the scope of work, any preliminary drafts, or technical documents to assuming responsibility for developing information, preparing environmental analyses, and actually drafting portions of the EIS.

2. If the ERC determines that resource limitations preclude any involvement in the preparation of another agency's EIS, or preclude the degree of involvement requested by the lead agency, it must inform the lead agency in writing (40 CFR 1501.6(c)). The letter should clearly state that EPA's status as a cooperating agency does not affect its independent responsibilities under Section 309 of the Clean Air Act to review and comment on other agencies' EIS's. A copy of this reply will be submitted to the CEQ.

C. Providing Guidance as a Cooperating Agency. Information and/or guidance should be given to the lead agency in those areas where the EPA has special expertise as related to EPA's duties and responsibilities and in those subject areas described in subparagraph 3C. Specific guidance will be given in those areas where the EPA intends to exercise regulatory responsibility.

5. EPA AS LEAD AGENCY.

Determining Lead Agency . When, in accordance with 40 CFR Part 6, EPA has an action which is subject to 102(2)(C) of NEPA and the action involves another Federal agency, the ERC and the other Federal agency will determine the lead agency status in accordance with the guidance contained in 40 CFR 1501.5(c), taking into account any relevant Memorandum of Understanding which EPA has executed with the Federal agency in question. Selection of the lead agency should be made at the earliest possible time. If the EPA is the lead agency, EPA will not review the EIS under the Environmental Review Process.

6. REPORTING AND CONTROL.

All responses related to scoping, cooperating, or lead agency issues, together with follow-up correspondence must be made a part of the official project file. Copies of letters in which EPA declines an agency's request to become a cooperating agency must be sent to the CEQ.

CHAPTER 4 - REVIEW OF DRAFT ENVIRONMENTAL IMPACT STATEMENTS

I. POLICY.

It is EPA's policy to review and comment in writing on all draft EIS's officially filed with the EPA, to provide a rating of the draft EIS which summarizes EPA's level of concern, and to meet with the lead agency to resolve significant issues. The EPA review will be primarily concerned with identifying and recommending corrective action for the significant environmental impacts associated with the proposal. Review of the adequacy of the information and analysis contained in the draft EIS's will be done as needed to support this objective.

2. DRAFT EIS REVIEW MANAGEMENT.

Except as noted below, the review management procedures and responsibilities given in chapter 2 apply to the review of draft EIS's.

A. Establishing Deadlines and Time Extensions.

1. Deadlines. Unless a different deadline is officially established for receiving comments, EPA will provide comments on a draft EIS to the lead agency within 45 days from the start of the official review period. The official EIS due dates are listed in COMDATE. The PR will set internal deadlines to ensure EPA's comments are received within the official comment period.

2. Time Extensions. Requests for extensions of review periods on draft EISs's should be kept to a minimum. In general, review period extensions O.E.M. on draft EIS's should not be requested unless important environmental issues are involved, and detailed substantive comments are being prepared. Time extensions should normally not exceed 15 days.

B. Categorization and Agency Notification System for Draft EIS's.

1. After completing the review of a draft EIS, the PR will categorize or rate the EIS according to the alpha numeric system described below and in paragraph 4 of this chapter, and include the designated rat in the comment letter. In general, the rating will be based on the lead agency's preferred alternative. If, however, a preferred alternative is not identified, or if the preferred alternative has significant environmental problems that could be avoided by selection of another alternative, or if there is reason to believe that the preferred alternative may be changed at a later stage, the reviewer should rate individual alternatives. The purpose of the rating system is to synthesize the level of EPA's overall concern with the proposal and to define the associated follow-up that will be conducted with the lead agency.

2. The alphabetical categories LO, EC, EO, and EU signify EPA's evaluation of the environmental impacts of the proposal. Numerical categories 1, 2, and 3 signify an evaluation of the adequacy of the draft EIS. A summary of the rating definitions and the associated follow-up action is given in figure 4-1 at the end of this chapter. This figure

should be attached to draft EIS comment letters when the lead agency may be unfamiliar with the EPA rating system. To the maximum extent possible, assignments of the alphabetical rating will be based on the overall environmental impact of the proposed project or action, including those project impacts that are not adequately addressed in the draft EIS. When there is insufficient information in the draft EIS, the determination of potential project impact may be based on other documents, information, or on-site surveys. The comment letter should clearly identify the source of information used by the EPA in evaluating the proposal.

3. The rating of a draft EIS will consist of one of the category combinations shown in the table below. As noted in the table and described in chapter 5, the ERC must follow up with the lead agency in those cases where significant problem areas are identified.

Category	Lead Agency Pre-Notification	Follow-up on Draft EIS Comment Letter
LO	None	None
EC-1, EC-2	None	Phone Call
EO-1, EO-2	Phone Call	Meeting
EO-3, EU-1, EU-2, EU-3, 3	Meeting	Meeting

4. For categories EO, EU, or 3, the ERC will ensure that the lead agency is notified of the general EPA concerns prior to receipt of EPA's comment letter. For categories EU and 3, the ERC must attempt to meet with the lead agency to discuss EPA's concerns prior to submission of the comment letter to the lead agency. The purposes of such a meeting are to describe the specific EPA concerns and discuss ways to resolve those concerns, to ensure that the EPA review has correctly interpreted the proposal and supporting information, and to become aware of any ongoing lead agency actions that might resolve the EPA concerns. To assure the objectivity and independence of the EPA review responsibility, the EPA comment letter itself and the assigned rating are not subject to negotiation and should not be changed on the basis of the meeting unless errors are discovered in EPA's understanding of the issues. However, the reviewer may add in the letter an acknowledgment of any relevant new lead agency activities that the reviewer believes could resolve the EPA concerns.

3. SCOPE OF COMMENTS ON THE DRAFT EIS

A. General. In general, EPA's comments will focus on the proposal but will, if necessary, review the complete range of alternatives, identifying those that are environmentally unacceptable to EPA and identifying EPA's preferred alternative. EPA's comment letter on the draft EIS will reflect all of EPA's environmental responsibilities that may bear on the action. The review will include EPA's assessment of the expected environmental impacts of the action and, if substantive impacts are identified, an evaluation of the adequacy of the supporting information presented in the EIS with suggestions for additional information that is needed. The EPA comment letter on draft EIS's will:

1. Explicitly reference EPA's review responsibilities under NEPA/Section 309;

2. Acknowledge positive lead agency responses to EPA scoping suggestions or early coordination efforts;

3. Provide a clear and concise description of EPA's substantive concerns and recommendations with supporting details given in attachments;

4. Include a rating of the proposal and, if appropriate, the adequacy of the EIS in accordance with the criteria established in paragraphs 2 and 4 of this chapter; and

5. Give the name and phone number of an appropriate EPA contact person.

B. Mitigation (40 CFR 1508.20). EPA's comments should include measures to avoid or minimize damage to the environment, or to protect, restore, and enhance the environment. Suggestions for mitigation should be oriented towards selection of mitigation measures that are technically feasible, of long-term effectiveness, and have a high likelihood of being implemented.

C. Statutory Authorities Special efforts should be made to identify project impacts that may lead to possible violation of national environmental standards or that might preclude or bias future issuance of EPA related environmental permits. EPA comments regarding potential violations of standards must be clearly stated in the letter, and an offer should be made to work with the proposing agency to develop appropriate measures to reduce impacts.

D. Alternatives. If significant impacts are associated with the proposal and they cannot be adequately mitigated, EPA's comments should suggest an environmentally preferable alternative, including if necessary, a new alternative. The suggested alternatives should be both reasonable and feasible. In this context, such an alternative is one that is practical in the technical, economic, and social sense, even if the alternative is outside the jurisdiction of the lead agency.

E. Purpose and Need. If a detailed review of alternatives is required, the reviewer may have to address the purpose of and need for the proposed action in order to determine to what degree an alternative would meet project objectives. In these cases, the reviewer may comment on the technical adequacy and accuracy of the EIS's methods for estimating the need for the proposed action in cases where this affects the definition of reasonable and feasible alternatives. Within the context of reviewing purpose and need, the EPA may also comment on the economic justification of the project, and the relationship between the lead agency's economic analysis and any unquantified environmental impacts, values, and amenities. The comments may also address the technical validity and adequacy of the supporting data for the EIS's economic analyses.

F. Projects Subject to Section 404(r) of the Clean Water Act. The Section 404 Coordinator will serve as an associate reviewer for those projects for which an agency is seeking an exemption under Section 404(r), and shall concur with the EPA comment letter. Section 404(r) provides that discharges of dredged or fill material which are part of Federal construction projects specifically authorized by Congress are not subject to regulation under Sections 301, 402, or 404 of the Clean Water Act if the information on the effects of such discharge including consideration of the Section 404(b)(1) Guidelines, is included in the EIS for the project, and the EIS has been submitted to Congress before the discharge occurs and before the authorization for the project occurs. In accordance with the CEQ's guidance of November 17, 1980, EPA's comments on the EIS will serve as the vehicle for informing the agency of EPA's determination whether the proposed Section 404(r) exemption will be in compliance with the requirements of the Section 404(b)(1) Guidelines. The comments should reference the CEQ Memorandum for Heads of Agencies, which provides guidance on applying Section 404(r) and should include EPA's determination regarding:

1. Whether the EIS contains requisite information on the proposed discharges and other effects; and

2. Whether the proposal is consistent with Section 404(b)(1) Guidelines.

G. Projects Potentially Affecting a Designated "Sole Source" Aquifer Subject to Section 1424(e) of the Safe Drinking Water Act.

1. The regional office responsible for implementing the Safe Drinking Water Act (SDWA) will act as an AR on any EIS for a project potentially affecting a sole source aquifer designated under Section 1424(e) of the SDWA. EPA's comments on the draft EIS will serve as EPA's preliminary comments for the groundwater impact evaluation required under Section 1424(e), which stipulates that no commitment to a project of Federal financial assistance may be made, if the Administrator determines that a project has the potential to contaminate a designated aquifer, so as to create a significant hazard to public health. (Rules proposed to implement 1424(e) are found at 42 FR 51620, September 29, 1977.)

2. If it is determined that a project may contaminate the aquifer through the recharge zone so as to create a significant hazard to public health, the ERC will, in consultation with the drinking water staff, prepare a briefing memorandum and comment letter for the Regional Administrator. Copies of the briefing memorandum and the proposed comment letter shall first be sent to the appropriate FAL, who will coordinate concurrence by the appropriate Headquarters offices. The comment letter should cite EPA's authorities under Section 309/NEPA and Section 1424(e) of SDWA, and state that the project is a candidate for both referral to the CEQ and a Section 1424(e) determination.

4. RATING SYSTEM CRITERIA.

A. Rating the Environmental Impact of the Action.

1. LO (Lack of Objections). The review has not identified any potential environmental impacts requiring substantive changes to the preferred alternative. The review may have disclosed opportunities for application of mitigation measures that could be accomplished with no more than minor changes to the proposed action.

2. EC (Environmental Concerns). The review has identified environmental impacts that should be avoided in order to fully protect the environment. Corrective measures may require changes to the preferred alternative or application of mitigation measures that can reduce the environmental impact.

3. EO (Environmental Objections). The review has identified significant environmental impacts that should be avoided in order to adequately protect the environment. Corrective measures may require substantial changes to the preferred alternative or consideration of some other project alternative (including the no action alternative or a new alternative). The basis for environmental Objections can include situations:

    1. *Where an action might violate or be inconsistent with achievement or maintenance of a national environmental standard;*

    2. *Where the Federal agency violates its own substantive environmental requirements that relate to EPA's areas of jurisdiction or expertise;*

    3. *Where there is a violation of an EPA policy declaration;*

    4. *Where there are no applicable standards or where applicable standards will not be violated but there is potential for significant environmental degradation that could be corrected by project modification or other feasible alternatives; or*

    5. *Where proceeding with the proposed action would set a precedent for future actions that collectively could result in significant environmental impacts.*

4. EU (Environmentally Unsatisfactory). The review has identified adverse environmental impacts that are of sufficient magnitude that EPA believes the proposed action must not proceed as proposed. The basis for an environmentally unsatisfactory determination consists of identification of environmentally objectionable impacts as defined above and one or more of the following conditions:

    1. *The potential violation of or inconsistency with a national environmental standard*

is substantive and/or will occur on a long-term basis;

2. *There are no applicable standards but the severity, duration, or geographical scope of the impacts associated with the proposed action warrant special attention; or*

3. *The potential environmental impacts resulting from the proposed action are of national importance because of the threat to national environmental resources or to environmental policies.*

B. Adequacy of the Impact Statement.

1. 1 (Adequate). The draft EIS adequately sets forth the environmental impact(s) of the preferred alternative and those of the alternatives reasonably available to the project or action. No further analysis or data collection is necessary, but the reviewer may suggest the addition of clarifying language or information.

2. 2 (Insufficient Information). The draft EIS does not contain sufficient information to fully assess environmental impacts that should be avoided in order to fully protect the environment, or the reviewer has identified new reasonably available alternatives that are within the spectrum of alternatives analyzed in the draft EIS, which could reduce the environmental impacts of the proposal. The identified additional information, data, analyses, or discussion should be included in the final EIS.

3. 3 (Inadequate). The draft EIS does not adequately assess the potentially significant environmental impacts of the proposal, or the reviewer has identified new, reasonably available, alternatives, that are outside of the spectrum of alternatives analyzed in the draft EIS, which should be analyzed in order to reduce the potentially significant environmental impacts. The identified additional information, data, analyses, or discussions are of such a magnitude that they should have full public review at a draft stage. This rating indicates EPA's belief that the draft EIS does not meet the purposes of NEPA and/or the Section 309 review, and thus should be formally revised and made available for public comment in a supplemental or revised draft EIS.

5. APPROVING AND DISTRIBUTING COMMENTS ON DRAFT EIS'S.

A. Categories LO, EC, EO, 1, or 2. For draft EIS's rated LO, EC, EO, 1, or 2 the comments will be signed by the appropriate regional or Headquarters official and the ERC will distribute EPA's comments in accordance with subparagraph 5c of this chapter.

B. Categories EU or 3. For draft EIS's where the ERC is proposing a rating of EU or 3, the EPA comment letter must be cleared by the Assistant Administrator for External Affairs prior to release. If the review within a reg regional action, the draft letter will be submitted through the

OFA for clearance. The draft comment letter must be submitted at least 5 working days prior to the due date and the proposed rating must have been approved by the regional signing official. In every case where a draft statement has been rated EU or 3, the Assistant Administrator, OEA, will send a copy of the EPA comment letter to the CEQ. In addition, where the EPA has commented to a regional office of the originating agency, appropriate officials within the headquarters office of the originating agency will also be informed. If a communications strategy has been developed for the action, the release of information should follow that strategy.

C. Checklist for Distribution of Agency Comments on the Draft EIS.*

Addressee	Number of Copies
Agency submitting statement	Original
CEQ (if EU or 3) with transmittal letter	1 copy
Office of Public Affairs (if comments are rated EU or 3)	1 copy
EPA offices which served as associate reviewers	1 copy
Office of Federal Activities Attn: MIU	2 copies

6. REPORTING AND CONTROL.

All draft EIS's under review, all time extensions, and all comment letters on draft EIS's will be entered in the MIU data management system. All EPA comment letters and associated correspondence on draft EISs will he retained fn the official project file.

To the maximum extent practicable, the comment letter should not be distributed to parties outside of the EPA until after the original has been received by the lead agency.

CHAPTER 5 - POST-DRAFT EIS FOLLOW-UP

I. POLICY.

It is EPA's policy to conduct follow-up discussions with the lead agency to ensure that EPA's concerns raised at the draft EIS stage are fully understood and considered by the lead agency. To the extent resources allow, follow-up efforts should exceed the min mum required red by this chapter and paragraph 2b(3) of chapter 4.

2. POST-DRAFT CONSULTATIONS.

In cases where a draft EIS is rated EO, EU, or 3, the ERC must initiate consultation with the lead agency. Agency consultation will continue at increasing levels of management, through the EPA Assistant Administrator level, as appropriate, until EPA's concerns are resolved or further negotiations are pointless. For those actions where the region is the PR, the ERC will work through the appropriate FAL to coordinate the consultation efforts at the regional and Headquarters levels. The ERC and/or FAL should be prepared to review the project in the field, to develop additional information, and/or to work with the agency to improve the proposed action and the supporting final EIS. When substantive consultation meetings are held, the ERC must document the outcome and, as appropriate, respond in writing to the lead agency to acknowledge any points of agreement, and to restate any unresolved issues.

3. STATUS REPORTS.

A. After consulting or meeting with the lead agency concerning draft EIS's rated EU or 3, the ERC will prepare a status memorandum for the Assistant Administrator, OEA, through the Director, OFA, and, if it is a regional action, for the Regional Administrator. This memorandum should summarize: (1) the progress of the consultations; (2) the remaining unresolved issues; (3) the positions of other affected Federal agencies; and (4) a prognosis for the resolution of remaining issues.

B. The ERC will periodically assess the lead agency's progress in respond to EPA's concerns on draft EIS's rated EU or 3. It s the ERC's responsibility to anticipate, and make early preparation for, those final EIS's which will be so unresponsive ve to EPA's concerns that a recommendation on for referral of the final EIS to the CEQ will be required.

4. REPORTING AND CONTROL.

All correspondence regarding post-draft consultations and agreements must be retained in the official project file. For all draft EIS's which have been rated EU or 3, the official file must also contain all material that may be needed for a formal referral package.

CHAPTER 6 - REVIEW OF FINAL EIS'S

I. POLICY.

It is EPA's policy to conduct detailed reviews of those final EIS's which had significant issues raised by the EPA at the draft EIS stage. Each final EIS will be checked to determine whether the statement adequately resolves the problems identified in the EPA review of the draft EIS, or whether there has been a substantive change in the proposal. A detailed review and submission of comments on the final EIS will be done for those actions rated EO, EU, or 3 at the draft stage. A detailed review on other f; final EIS's may be done if the ERC determines that conditions warrant it.

2. FINAL EIS REVIEW MANAGEMENT.

Except as noted below, the review management procedures and responsibilities given in chapter 2 apply to the review of final EIS's.

A. Designating Lead Responsibility and Principal and Associate Reviewers. Lead responsibility for the final EIS will be the same as for the draft EIS unless other arrangements have been made with the MIU. If possible, the same principal and associate reviewers who dealt with the draft EIS will be assigned to review the final EIS.

B. Establishing Deadlines and Time Extensions.

1. Deadlines. Unless a different deadline is officially established for receiving comments, EPA will respond to a final EIS within 30 days from the start of the official review period. The official EIS due dates are listed in COMDATE. The PR will set internal deadlines to ensure EPA's comments are received within the official comment period. All final EIS's which are candidates for referral to the CEQ, will be given priority review in accordance with the internal deadlines specified in chapter 9.

2. Time Extensions. Requests for extensions of review periods on final EIS's should be kept to a minimum. In general, review period extensions on final EIS's should not be requested unless important environmental issues are involved and detailed substantive comments are being prepared. Time extensions should normally not exceed 15 days. Time extensions for a referral 8 linc will be requested in accordance with the procedures in chapter 9.

C. Categorizing Final EIS's. The alpha numeric rating system used for draft EIS's will be applied to final EIS's for internal management purposes only (see chapter 4, paragraph 4). The EPA rating is not to be included in comment letters on final EIS's. Instead, the comments will rely wholly on narrative explanations to describe the environmental impact of the proposed action or the responsiveness or unresponsiveness of the EIS. The PR will include the assigned rating when entering the action into the MIU data management system.

3. SCOPE OF COMMENTS ON FINAL EIS'S.

A. General.

1. Except in unusual circumstances, the review of final EIS's will be directed to the maj or unresolved issues, focusing on the impacts of the project rather than on the adequacy of the statement. Except in unusual circumstances, the scope of review will be limited to issues raised in EPA's comments on the draft EIS that have not been resolved in the final EIS, and any new, potentially significant impacts that have been identified as a result of information made available after publication of with the draft EIS.

2. Within 5 days after the start of the review period for the final EIS, the PR will make a preliminary determination as to whether the action meets the criteria for "environmentally unsatisfactory" as set forth in chapter 4, paragraph 4 of this Manual. If the action is determined to be environmentally unsatisfactory, the procedures set forth in chapter 9 of this Manual will be followed.

3. For final EIS's which had drafts categorized as LO, the PR may decide that no formal comments on the final EIS will be submitted to the lead agency. Written comments will be prepared in other cases and when the agency has made substantive modifications in the proposed action in comparison to the draft EIS. In addition, written comments will be prepared for final EIS's that involve Section 404(r) or Section 1424(e) issues.

4. In those cases involving significant mitigation requirements or where the proposed agency action is not clear, EPA's comments on the final EIS will also include a request for a copy of the Record of Decision.

B. Mitigation Measures. If a final EIS identifies for the first time, or modifies the agency's preferred alternative, EPA's review should include consideration of any additional specific mitigation measures necessary to reduce any adverse impacts of that alternative. When mitigation measures are recommended, the comment letter should suggest that the lead agency include these measures in their Record of Decision as specific conditions on their permits or grants. Where mitigation measures are directly related to the acceptability of the action, the comment letter should include a request that the lead agency keep EPA informed of progress in carrying out the mitigation measures proposed by the EPA.

C. Projects Under Section 404(r) of the Clean Water Act.

1. The Section 404 Coordinator will serve as an associate reviewer on all final EIS's involving a potential 404 permit. In order to satisfy the provisions of Section 404(r), the EIS process must be completed before Congress approves requests for authorizations and appropriations. Pursuant to the CEQ Memorandum for Heads of Agencies, November 17, 1980, completion of the EIS process includes resolution of any pre-decision referrals.

2. The comment letter on a final EIS seeking a 404(r) exemption will include EPA's determination regarding: (a) whether the EIS contains requisite information on the

proposed discharges and other effects, and (b) whether the proposal is consistent with the 404(b)(1) Guidelines.

3. If a negative determination on either (2)(a) or (b) is made, the appropriate FAL will be informed and will coordinate with the lead agency to ensure that the required statement of EPA's determination is included in the lead agency's congressional submission. The FAL will also ensure that EPA's views regarding an exemption are effectively represented in the Office of Management and Budget's (OMB's) legislative and budget processes.

D. Projects Subject to Groundwater Evaluation Under Section 1424(e) of the SDWA.

1. The regional drinking water program staff will serve as an AR on the review of any EIS for a project potentially affecting a designated "sole source" aquifer and will be responsible for the preliminary determination of project compliance with the requirements of Section 1424(e) of the SDWA.

2. If the regional drinking water program staff determines that a project may contaminate the aquifer through the recharge zone so as to create a significant hazard to public health, the ERC will, in consultation with the regional drinking water staff and appropriate Headquarters FAL, prepare a briefing memorandum and comment letter for the Regional Administrator. Upon approval, the Regional Administrator shall submit the package to the Director, OFA, who shall coordinate the appropriate Headquarters approval and submission to the Administrator for action.

4. UNRESPONSIVE FINAL EIS.

1. If the lead agency prepares a final EIS rather than a supplement or revised draft EIS in response to an EPA "3" rating, or if there are significant new circumstances or information relevant to areas of significant environmental impact, the review should follow the procedures of chapter 4 to determine if the proposal is either "environmentally unsatisfactory" or "inadequate." If it is determined that either of these situations apply, the procedures of chapter 9 should be initiated to determine if a referral of the proposal to the CEQ is warranted.

2. If a referral is not warranted, but the EIS contains insufficient information to assess potentially significant environmental impacts of the proposed action, a request should be made for the agency to prepare a supplemental EIS. In such cases, the EPA comment letter must demonstrate that the final EIS is unresponsive to EPA's comments on the draft EIS and state EPA's belief that the final EIS is inadequate to meet the purposes of the NEPA and/or the EPA review, and therefore should be formally supplemented (40 CFR 1502.9(c)).

5. DISTRIBUTION OF THE FINAL EIS COMMENT LETTER.

The ERC will coordinate distribution of the final EIS comment letter in accordance with chapter 4, paragraph 5 of this Manual (or in the case of a referral, chapter 9, paragraph 5) and any applicable communications strategy. To the maximum extent practicable, the comment letter will not be distributed externally until after the lead agency has received the original.

6. REPORTING AND CONTROL.

All final EIS's, comment letters, no comment memoranda, and correspondence related to time extensions will be entered in the MIU data management system and retained in the official project file. The final EIS rating must also be entered into the MIU system (even if no comment letter was sent).

CHAPTER 7 - MONITORING AND FOLLOW-UP

1. POLICY.

It is EPA's policy to conduct, on a selected basis, follow-up activities on comments on final EIS's to ensure that: (1) the EPA participates as fully as possible in any post-EIS efforts designed to assist agency decision making; (2) agreed upon mitigation measures are identified in the Record of Decision; and (3) the agreed upon mitigation measures are fully implemented (e.g., permit conditions, operating plan stipulations, etc.).

2. MONITORING AND FOLLOW - UP.

A. After transmittal of EPA's comments on the final EIS, the PR will, as appropriate, ensure that:

1. EPA receives a copy of the Record of Decision;

2. The lead agency has incorporated into the Record of Decision all agreed upon mitigation and other impact reduction measures; and

3. The lead agency has included all agreed upon measures as conditions in grants, permits, or other approvals, where appropriate.

B. Officials who could be subsequently involved in the proposed action should be informed of the final EPA position on the EIS (e.g., regional or State enforcement officials for NPDES permitting, regional enforcement officials for Section 404 enforcement, regional air program or enforcement officials for transportation control strategy compliance and State implementation plan requirements).

C. Where resources allow, the ERC is encouraged to assess the level of compliance and effectiveness of Federal agency mitigation measures. The ERC is responsible for determining when and how EPA's final EIS follow-up and monitoring should be carried out.

3. REVIEW OF THE RECORD OF DECISION.

A. The PR should review the Record of Decision on all final EIS's on which the EPA has expressed environmental Objections, and/or those where the EPA has negotiated mitigation measures or changes in project design.

B. The ERC will bring problems or discrepancies between the Record of Decision and agreed upon mitigation measures to the attention of the lead agency. Any unresolved issues should be coordinated with the appropriate FAL, and, through the FAL, with the lead agency's headquarters office, and if appropriate, with the CEQ.

4. REPORTING AND CONTROL.

All correspondence regarding the Record of Decision will be recorded in the official project file.

CHAPTER 8 - REVIEW OF DOCUMENTS OTHER THAN EIS'S

1. POLICY.

The Environmental Review Process will include review of those proposed Federal agency actions, legislation, regulations, and notices which may not be contained in an EIS, but which could lead to or have significant environmental, impacts.

2. GENERAL REVIEW PROCEDURES.

A. Lead Responsibility for Review of Other Actions. Lead responsibilities for non-EIS actions are, in general, as defined below but may be adjusted ,n accordance with the procedures in chapter 2 of this Manual.

   1. The OFA will have lead responsibility on all regulation reviews and the appropriate FAL

With will determine which proposed regulations should be reviewed:

2. The Office of Legislative Analysis (OLA), within the Office of External Affairs, will have lead responsibility on all non-EIS legislation reviews and will determine when the EPA will prepare formal comments on legislation; and

3. Overall management of the review of non-EIS agency actions, including environmental assessments and Findings of No Significant Impact (FONSI's), license applications, etc., is the responsibility of the ERC managing the liaison activity that involves the action.

B. Conducting Reviews of Other Actions. The ERC will follow the review coordination procedures of chapter 2 to ensure that EPA's comments are coordinated and comprehensive and are received by the originating agency within its decision making period. If the ERC believes that an EIS is needed on the proposed action, the procedures found in paragraph 6 of this chapter should be followed.

C. Rating Other Federal Actions. Except for the referral criteria, the rating system for draft impact statements pursuant to chapter 4 of this Manual will not be used for non-EIS actions. If the PR determines that a Federal agency action covered by this chapter is environmentally unsatisfactory in accordance with.th the criteria listed in chapter 4, thus warranting a referral to the CEQ, then the procedures found in paragraph 7 of this chapter will apply.

3. LEGISLATION REVIEWS.

The OLA has lead responsibility on all proposed legislation not accompanied by an EIS. The OLA is responsible for coordinating with other EPA program and regional offices, and for preparing EPA's comments on all legislation. Any ERC receiving proposed legislation from another Federal agency should forward it directly to the OLA for action.

4. REGULATION REVIEWS.

The FAL's will monitor the Federal Register regularly to determine which environmental regulations proposed by their assigned Federal agencies are significant and should be reviewed. FAL's will normally act as PR's for regulations proposed by the agencies assigned to them. The Director, OFA, will be the signatory official for comments on these regulations. The FAL will be responsible for ensuring that the regions and EPA program offices impacted by the regulations will be designated as AR's.

5. OTHER AGENCY ACTION REVIEWS.

The ERC may determine that other non-EIS Federal actions such as environmental assessments (40 CFR 1508.9), FONSI's (40 CFR 1508.13), issue papers, or technical support documents should be reviewed. The ERC's decision to review these actions will take into account the relationship of the proposed action to other Federal actions and how the document fits into the overall decision making process.

6. DETERMINING THE NEED FOR AN EIS.

Whenever the ERC determines on the basis of investigating a public inquiry, reviewing a regulation or environmental assessment/FONSI, or by other means, that a Federal agency has not or does not intend to prepare an EIS on an action that the EPA believes could significantly affect the quality of the human environment, the following procedures pertain.

A. If it is a regional action, the ERC will immediately contact the appropriate FAL and develop a coordinated regional/headquarters approach for working with the lead agency.

B. The ERC will initiate consultation with the Federal agency responsible for the major action to explore the necessity for EIS preparation. Discussions with the agency will be couched in terms of suggested action for the Federal agency's consideration rather than as an EPA requirement. It is the lead agency's responsibility to decide if an EIS will be prepared.

C. If, after such consultation, the ERC believes that the requirements of Section 102(2)(C) of NEPA are applicable, the PR will prepare a comment letter to the Federal agency responsible for the proposed action. The comment letter should include EPA's assessment of the action and reasons why the EPA believes the agency should prepare an EIS.

7. ENVIRONMENTALLY UNSATISFACTORY ACTIONS.

If the ERC determines that a non-EIS action is environmentally unsatisfactory at the draft stage (in accordance with the EU criteria specified in chapter 4), the proposed comment letter must be cleared by the Assistant Administrator, OEA, prior to release. The procedures of chapter 4 must be followed in obtaining this clearance. At the time of the clearance request, or if the non-EIS action is a final action, the ERC and/or appropriate FAL will set up internal consultation and referral procedures similar to those outlined in chapter 9 of this Manual. The procedures will also consider the option of request an EIS. The procedures will ensure that the referral will take place no later than 5 days before the "final" lead agency action. For example, in the case of proposed regulations, the referral must occur prior to publication of the final rule.

8. REPORTING AND CONTROL.

Regulations under review and the resulting comment letters, as well as comment letters on any other non-EIS action determined to be environmentally unsatisfactory, will be entered into the MIU data management system. All agency comment letters and official agency actions related to the Environmental Review Process will be retained in the official project file.

CHAPTER 9 - REFERRALS TO THE COUNCIL ON ENVIRONMENTAL QUALITY

1. POLICY.

The EPA authority for referring proposed regulations or major Federal actions to the Council on Environmental Quality (40 CFR 1504 and Section 309 of the Clean Air Act) will be used only when significant environmental issues are involved and only after every effort to resolve these issues at the agency level has been exhausted.

2. CRITERIA FOR REFERRAL.

In order to meet a determination of "unsatisfactory from the standpoint of public health or welfare or environmental quality," the proposed action must satisfy the "environmentally unsatisfactory" criteria given in chapter 4.

3 . REFERRAL PROCEDURES.

A. The CEQ has established a 25-day time period, starting from the date of the Notice of Availability of the final EIS Jn the Federal Register, for referring final EIS's (40 CFR 1504.3(b)). Extensions of EIS referral periods can be granted only by the lead agency (40 CFR 1504.3(b)) and must be specific to the 25-day referral period rather than the overall comment period.

B. Since EPA has author quality under Section 309 of the Clean Air Act to refer proposed regulations and maj or Federal actions for which no EIS has been prepared, the intent of the 25 day deadline is incorporated in the procedures of this section by requiring all EPA referrals to be made no later than 5 days before the end of the comment period or, in any case, 5 days before the final action takes place.

4. REFERRAL PACKAGE DEVELOPMENT SEQUENCE.

A. The objective of the referral package development sequence requirements in this section is to ensure that the referral package is ready within the rigid 25-day time limit and, simultaneously, allow for a final attempt to resolve EPA's concerns with the lead agency. The key elements in this sequence are:

    1. Early identification of the potential referral action by the PR/ERC;

2. Approval of the referral action by the Regional Administrator (if a regional action) and the Assistant Administrator, OEA;

3. An attempt to meet with the lead agency and work out EPA's concerns; and

4. Preparation of the referral package to preserve the referral option if discussions with the lead agency do not resolve EPA's concerns.

B. Specific procedures for the referral development sequence are described below. To facilitate this description, it is assumed that the referral action is taken by a region. The same procedures apply where Headquarters has the referral action except there would be no regional requirements.

1. Within 5 days after the beginning of the review period the PR, in consultation with the ERC, will make a preliminary determination as to whether the action is unsatisfactory from the standpoint of public health, welfare, or environmental quality in accordance with the EU criteria in chapter 4. If a referral is indicated, the ERC will notify the appropriate FAL and proceed with development of the materials described below.

2. Within 10 days from the start of the 25-day referral period, the ERC, in consultation with the FAL, will prepare and submit to the Regional Administrator and the Assistant Administrator, OEA, through the Director, OFA, a briefing memorandum and interim response to the lead agency. The interim response will state that the EPA is considering a referral to the CEQ and will request a meeting and time extension to allow for a resolution of EPA's concerns. The briefing memorandum will contain the following information:

   1. *Brief description of the proposed action;*
   2. *Reason the action is environmentally unsatisfactory;*
   3. *Description of the attempts to resolve differences with the lead agency;*
   4. *Positions of other affected Federal agencies, groups, and public officials; and*
   5. *Recommended strategy for resolution of remaining issues.*

3. If the lead agency grants a time extension, EPA negotiations will take place and, if necessary, the referral package will be developed according to the extended referral time period. If the lead agency grants a time extension of the referral period by phone, the ERC will immediately prepare a letter to the lead agency documenting the agreement. If a time extension is not granted, the referral preparation will proceed on the basis of the original referral deadline.

4. No later than 10 days before the referral deadline, the FAL will prepare a short information memorandum for the Administrator describing potential referral and the status of unresolved issues; a one page "talking points" paper; and an outline of a communication

strategy for notifying all interested groups of EPA's action. Development of the communication strategy is to be coordinated with the immediate Office of the Assistant Administrator for External Affairs.

5. No later than 7 days before the referral deadline, the final referral package, prepared in accordance with paragraph 6 of this chapter and approved by the Regional Administrator, will be forwarded to the Director, OFA.

6. No later than 5 days before the referral deadline, the Director, OFA, will ensure that the referral package is in final form with all letters and appropriate concurrences ready for the Administrator's signature, and working through the Assistant Administrator for OEA, to ensure that a briefing has been arranged for the Administrator.

5. CONTENT AND ORGANIZATION OF THE REFERRAL PACKAGES.

A. Administrator's Referral Package. The referral package for the Administrator will include the package to be submitted to the CEQ and the lead agency, and the following:

1. An action memorandum to the Administrator (not to exceed two pages) briefly outlining the proposed action, EPA's concerns with the proposed action, and positions of other affected Federal agencies, public interest groups, and congressional delegations.

2. A communications strategy for notifying all interested groups of the referral. This strategy will be coordinated with the immediate Office of the Assistant Administrator for External Affairs and will follow the established strategy development format.

B. CEQ Referral Package. The CEQ referral package will consist of a letter for the Administrator's signature to the Chairman of the CEQ setting forth the basis of EPA's determination and the lead agency referral package described below.

C. Lead Agency Referral Package. This package will consist of the following:

1. A letter for the Administrator's signature to the head of the lead agency informing the lead agency of EPA's unsatisfactory determination, and of the referral of the matter to the CEQ. The letter should request that no action be taken on the proposed action until the CEQ acts on the matter.

2. Detailed comments supporting EPA's conclusion that the matter is unsatisfactory from the standpoint of public health, welfare, or environmental quality. The detailed comments will include the following information:

    1. *The unacceptable impacts related to EPA's areas of jurisdiction or expertise;*

2. *The reasons EPA believes the matter is unsatisfactory;*
3. *Description of those national resources or environmental policies that would be adversely affected;*
4. *Identification of environmentally preferable alternatives;*
5. *Identification of agreed upon facts;*
6. *Identification of material facts in controversy; and*
7. *Brief review of attempts by the EPA to resolve the concerns with the lead agency.*

6. APPROVING AND DISTRIBUTING THE REFERRAL PACKAGE.

After the Administrator signs the referral comment letters to the lead agency and to the CEQ, the letters will be hand carried to the addressees. The appropriate FAL will then ensure follow-up distribution of the CEQ referral package as follows and/or in accordance with the communications strategy:

Addressee	Number of Copies
Lead agency	3 copies
CEQ	4 copies
EPA Administrator	2 copies
Assistant Administrator, OEA	2 copies
Headquarters Office of Public Affairs	2 copies
Appropriate regional office	3 copies
Appropriate regional Office of Public Affairs	2 copies
Director, OFA	1 copy
Management Information Unit, OFA	1 copy
EPA offices which served as associate reviewers	1 copy
Appropriate elected officials	Determined by the Office of Congressional Liaison

7. REPORTING AND CONTROL.

The referral package, all related correspondence, and documentation of time extensions will be retained in the official project file. Time extensions will be entered into the MIU data management system.

Appendix

SUMMARY OF RATING DEFINITIONS AND FOLLOW-UP ACTION*

Environmental Impact of the Action

LO -- Lack of Objections The EPA review has not identified any potential environmental impacts requiring substantive changes to the proposal The review may have disclosed opportunities for application of mitigation m measures that could be accomplished with no more than minor changes to the proposal.

EC--Environmental Concerns The EPA review has identified environmental impacts that should be avoided in order to fully protect the environment. Corrective measures may require changes to the preferred alternative or application of mitigation measures that can reduce the environmental impact EPA would like to work with the lead agency to reduce these impacts.

EO--Environmental Objections The EPA review has identified significant environmental impacts that must be avoided in order to provide adequate protection for the environment. Corrective measures may require substantial changes to the preferred alternative or consideration of some other project alternative (including the no action alternative or a new alternative). EPA intends co work which with the lead agency to reduce these impacts.

EU--Environmentally Unsatisfactory The EPA review has identified adverse environmental impacts chat are of sufficient magnitude that they are unsatisfactory from the standpoint of public health or welfare or environmental quality EPA intends to work with the lead agency co reduce these impacts. If the potential unsatisfactory impacts are not corrected at the final EIS stage this proposal will be recommended for referral to the CEQ.

Adequacy of the Impact Statement

Category 1--Adequate EPA believes the draft EIS adequately sets forth the environmental impact(s) of the preferred alternative and those of the alternatives reasonably avail able to the project or action No further analysis or data collection is necessary but the reviewer may suggest the addition of clarifying language or information.

Category 2--Insufficient Information The draft EIS does not contain sufficient information for EPA to fully assess environ _ impacts that should be avoided Ln order co fully protect the environment or the EPA reviewer has identified new reasonably available alternatives that are within the spectrum of alternatives analyzed in the draft EIS which could reduce with the environmental impacts of the action The identified additional information data analyses or discussion should be included in with the final EIS.

Category 3--Inadequate EPA does not believe that with the draft EIS adequately assesses potentially significant environmental impacts of the action, or with the EPA reviewer his identified new reasonably available alternatives that are outside of the spectrum of alternatives analyzed in the draft EIS, which should be analyzed in order to reduce the potentially significant environmental impacts. EPA believes that the identified additional information data analyses or discussions are of such a s magnitude that they should have full public review at a draft stage. EPA does not believe that the draft EIS is adequate for the purposes of the NEPA and/or Section 309 review, and thus should be formally revised and made available for public comment in a supplemental or revised draft EIS. On the basis of the potential significant impacts involved, this proposal could be a candidate for referral to the CEQ.

*From EPA Manual 1640 Policy and Procedures for the Review of Federal Actions Impacting with the Environment.

NEPA Deskbook

Appendix 32 Amended Environmental Impact Statement Filing System Guidance for Implementing 1506.9 and 1506.10 of the CEQ Regulations Implementing the Procedural Provisions of NEPA

51530   Federal Register / Vol. 77, No. 165 / Friday, August 24, 2012 / Notices

ENVIRONMENTAL PROTECTION AGENCY

[ER–FRL9004–7]

Amended Environmental Impact Statement Filing System Guidance for Implementing 40 CFR 1506.9 and 1506.10 of the Council on Environmental Quality's Regulations Implementing the National Environmental Policy Act

1. Introduction

On October 7, 1977, the Council of Environmental Quality (CEQ) and the Environmental Protection Agency (EPA) signed a Memorandum of Agreement (MOA) that allocated the responsibilities of the two agencies for assuring the government-wide implementation of the National Environmental Policy Act of 1969 (NEPA). Specifically, the MOA transferred to EPA the administrative aspects of the environmental impact statement (EIS) filing process. Within EPA, the Office of Federal Activities has been designated the official recipient in EPA of all EISs. These responsibilities have been codified in CEQ's NEPA Implementing Regulations (40 CFR Parts 1500–1508), and are totally separate from the substantive EPA reviews performed pursuant to both NEPA and Section 309 of the Clean Air Act.

Under 40 CFR 1506.9, EPA can issue guidelines to implement its EIS filing responsibilities. The purpose of the EPA Filing System Guidelines is to provide guidance to Federal agencies on filing EISs, including draft, final, and supplemental EISs. Information is provided on: (1) How to file EISs; (2) the steps to follow when a Federal agency is adopting an EIS, or when an EIS is withdrawn, delayed or reopened; (3) public review periods; (4) issuance of notices of availability in the **Federal Register**; and (5) retention of filed EISs.

The guidelines published today update the previous guidelines, which were first published in the **Federal Register** on March 7, 1989. These updated guidelines have been modified to incorporate changes necessary to implement the *e-NEPA* electronic filing system.

2. Purpose

Pursuant to 40 CFR 1506.9 and 1506.10, EPA is responsible for administering the EIS filing process, and can issue guidelines to implement those responsibilities. The process of EIS filing includes the following: (1) Receiving and recording of the EISs, so that information in them can be incorporated into EPA's computerized data base; (2) establishing the beginning and ending dates for comment and review periods for draft and final EISs, respectively; (3) publishing these dates in a weekly Notice of Availability (NOA) in the **Federal Register**; (4) retaining the EISs in a central repository; and (5) determining whether time periods can be lengthened or shortened for "compelling reasons of national policy."

Under 40 CFR 1506.9, lead agencies are responsible for distributing EISs, and for providing additional copies of already distributed EISs, to the interested public for review. However, EPA will assist the public and other Federal agencies by providing agency contacts on, and information about, EISs.

3. Filing Draft, Final, and Supplemental EISs

Federal agencies are required to prepare EISs in accordance with 40 CFR part 1502, and to file the EISs with EPA as specified in 40 CFR 1506.9. As of October 1, 2012, Federal agencies file an EIS by submitting the complete EIS, including appendices, to EPA through the *e-NEPA* electronic filing system.

To sign up for *e-NEPA*, register for an account at: *https://cdx.epa.gov/ epa_home.asp*

Select "NEPA Electronic Filing System (*e-NEPA*)" when prompted to add a program. Inquiries can also be made to: (202) 564–7146 or (202) 564–0678 or by email to: *EISfiling@epa.gov*.

Please note that if a Federal agency prepares an abbreviated Final EIS (as described in 40 CFR 1503.4(c)), it should include copies of the Draft EIS when filing the Final EIS.

The EISs must be filed no earlier than they are transmitted to commenting agencies and made available to the public (40 CFR 1506.9). This will assure that the EIS is received by all interested parties by the time EPA's NOA appears in the **Federal Register**, and, therefore, allows for the full minimum comment and review periods.

If EPA receives a request to file an EIS and transmittal of that EIS is not complete, it will not publish a NOA in the **Federal Register** until assurances have been given that the transmittal process is complete. Similarly, if EPA discovers that a filed EIS has not been transmitted, EPA will issue a notice with the weekly Notices of Availability retracting the EIS from public review of the EIS until the transmittal process is completed. Once the agency has fulfilled the requirements of 40 CFR 1506.9, and has completed the transmittal process, EPA will reestablish the filing date and the minimum time

period, and will publish this information in the next NOA. Requirements for circulation of EISs appear in 40 CFR 1502.19. Please note that the EIS submitted to the Office of Federal Activities through *e-NEPA* is only for filing purposes.

EPA must be notified when a Federal agency adopts an EIS in order to commence the appropriate comment or review period. If a Federal agency chooses to adopt an EIS written by another agency, and it was not a cooperating agency in the preparation of the original EIS, the EIS must be re-circulated and filed with EPA according to the requirements set forth in 40 CFR 1506.3(b). In turn, EPA will publish a NOA in the **Federal Register** announcing that the document will have an appropriate comment or review period. When an agency adopts an EIS on which it served as a cooperating agency, the document does not need to be circulated for public comment or review; it is not necessary to file the EIS again with EPA. However, EPA should be notified in order to ensure that the official EIS record is accurate. Notifications can be sent by email to: *EISfiling@epa.gov*. EPA will publish an amended NOA in the **Federal Register** that states that an adoption has occurred. This will not establish a comment period, but will complete the public record.

EPA should also be notified of all situations where an agency has decided to withdraw, delay, or reopen a review period on an EIS. Notifications can be sent by email to: *EISfiling@epa.gov*. All such notices to EPA will be reflected in EPA's weekly Notices of Availability published in the **Federal Register**. In the case of reopening EIS review periods, the lead agency should notify EPA as to what measures will be taken to ensure that the EIS is available to all interested parties. This is especially important for EIS reviews that are being reopened after a substantial amount of time has passed since the original review period closed.

Once received by EPA, each EIS is assigned an official filing date and checked for completeness and compliance with 40 CFR 1502.10. If the EIS is not "complete" (*i.e.*, if the documents do not contain the required components), EPA will contact the lead agency to obtain the omitted information or to resolve any questions prior to publishing the NOA in the **Federal Register**.

Agencies often publish (either in their EISs or individual notices to the public) a date by which all comments on an EIS are to be received; such actions are encouraged. However, agencies should

ensure that the date they use is based on the date of publication of the NOA in the **Federal Register**. If the published date gives reviewers less than the minimum review time computed by EPA, EPA will send the agency contact a letter explaining how the review period is calculated and the correct date by which comments are due back to the lead agency. This letter also encourages agencies to notify all reviewers and interested parties of the corrected review periods.

4. Notice in the Federal Register

EPA will prepare a weekly report of all EISs filed during the preceding week for publication each Friday under a NOA in the **Federal Register**. If the Friday is a Federal holiday the publication will be on Thursday. At the time EPA sends its weekly report for publication in the **Federal Register**, the report will also be sent to the CEQ. Amended notices may be added to the NOA to include corrections, changes in time periods of previously filed EISs, withdrawals of EISs by lead agencies, and retraction of EISs by EPA.

5. Time Periods

The minimum time periods set forth in 40 CFR 1506.10 (b), (c), and (d) are calculated from the date EPA publishes the NOA in the **Federal Register**. Comment periods for draft EISs, draft supplements, and revised draft EISs will end 45 calendar days after publication of the NOA in the **Federal Register**; review periods for final EISs and final supplements will end 30 calendar days after publication of the NOA in the **Federal Register**. If a calculated time period would end on a non-working day, the assigned time period will be the next working day (*i.e.*, time periods will not end on weekends or Federal holidays). While these time periods are minimum time periods, a lead agency may establish longer time periods. If the lead agency employs a longer time period, it must notify EPA of the extended time period when either filing the EIS through *e-NEPA* or by email to: *EISfiling@epa.gov* when the lead agency extends the time period. It should be noted that 40 CFR 1506.10(b) allows for an exception to the rules of timing. An exception may be made in the case of an agency decision which is subject to a formal internal appeal. Agencies should assure that EPA is informed so that the situation is accurately reflected in the NOA.

Moreover, under 40 CFR 1506.10(d), EPA has the authority to both extend and reduce the time periods on draft and final EISs based on a demonstration of "compelling reasons of national

51532 Federal Register / Vol. 77, No. 165 / Friday, August 24, 2012 / Notices

policy." A lead agency request to EPA to reduce time periods or another Federal agency (not the lead agency) request to formally extend a time period should be submitted in writing to the Director, Office of Federal Activities, and outline the reasons for the request. These requests can be submitted by email to: *EISfiling@epa.gov.* EPA will accept telephone requests; however, agencies should follow up such requests in writing so that the documentation supporting the decision is complete. A meeting to discuss the consequences for the project and any decision to change time periods may be necessary. For this reason, EPA asks that it be made aware of any intent to submit requests of this type as early as possible in the NEPA process. This is to prevent the possibility of the time frame for the decision on the time period modification from interfering with the lead agency's schedule for the EIS. EPA will notify CEQ of any reduction or extension granted.

6. Retention

Filed EISs are retained in the *e-NEPA* Filing system for two years. After two years the EISs are sent to the National Records Center. After a total of twenty (20) years the EISs are transferred to the National Archives Records Administration (NARA).

Please note that EPA maintains a Web site that will make available copies of the filed EISs to the public. The retention schedule does not affect the availability of these electronic copies.

Dated: August 21, 2012.

Cliff Rader,

Director, NEPA Compliance Division, Office of Federal Activities.

[FR Doc. 2012–20914 Filed 8–23–12; 8:45 am]

DILLING CODE 6660 60–P

ENVIRONMENTAL PROTECTION AGENCY

[ER–FRL–9004–6]

Environmental Impacts Statements; Notice of Availability

AGENCY: Office of Federal Activities, General Information (202) 564–7146 or *http://www.epa.gov/compliance/nepa/*

Weekly receipt of Environmental Impact Statements Filed 08/13/2012 Through 08/17/2012 Pursuant to 40 CFR 1506.9.

Notice

Section 309(a) of the Clean Air Act requires that EPA make public its comments on EISs issued by other Federal agencies. EPA's comment letters

on EISs are available at: *http://www.epa.gov/compliance/nepa/eisdata.html.*

SUPPLEMENTARY INFORMATION: Starting October 1, 2012, EPA will not accept paper copies or CDs of EISs for filing purposes; all submissions on or after October 1, 2012 must be made through e-NEPA. While this system eliminates the need to submit paper or CD copies to EPA to meet filing requirements, electronic submission does not change requirements for distribution of EISs for public review and comment. To begin using e-NEPA, you must first register with EPA's electronic reporting site— *https://cdx.epa.gov/epa_home.asp.*

EIS No. 20120268, Draft EIS, USFWS, WV, Proposed Issuance of an Incidental Take Permit for the Beech Ridge Energy Wind Project Habitat Conservation Plan, Implementation, Greenbrier and Nicholas Counties, WV, Comment Period Ends: 10/23/2012, Contact: Laura Hill 304–636–6586, ext 18.

EIS No. 20120269, Final EIS, FHWA, CA, State Route 91 Corridor Improvement Project, Widening SR 91 from SR 91/State Route 241 Interchange in Orange County to Pierce Street in Riverside County, Orange and Riverside Counties, CA, Review Period Ends: 09/24/2012, Contact: Aaron Burton 909–388–2841.

EIS No. 20120270, Final Supplement, FHWA, MN, Trunk Highway 60 between Windom and St. James, Implementation of Transportation System Improvements, Funding, USACE Section 404 Permit, Cottonwood and Watonwan Counties, MN, Review Period Ends: 09/24/2012, Contact: Philip Forst 651–291–6110.

EIS No. 20120271, Final EIS, USFWS, NV, Sheldon National Wildlife Refuge Project, Draft Resource Conservation Plan, Implementation, Humboldt and Washoe Counties, NV and Lake County, OR, Review Period Ends: 09/24/2012, Contact: Aaron Collins 541–947–3315, ext. 223.

EIS No. 20120272, Final EIS, USN, CA, Marine Corps Base Camp Pendleton Project, Base wide Water Infrastructure, Construction and Operation, San Diego County, CA, Review Period Ends: 09/24/2012, Contact: Jesse Martinez 619–532–3844.

EIS No. 20120273, Final EIS, FHWA, CO, Breckenridge Ski Resort Peak 6 Project, Implementation, White River National Forest, Summit County, CO, Review Period Ends: 09/24/2012, Contact: Joe Foreman 970–262–3443.

EIS No. 20120274, Draft EIS, USFS, AZ, Prescott National Forest Land and Resource Management Plan, Implementation, Yavapai and Coconino Counties, AZ, Comment Period Ends: 10/08/2012, Contact: Mary C. Rasmussen 928–443–8265.

EIS No. 20120275, Draft EIS, USFS, MT, Wild Cramer Forest Health and Fuels Reduction Project, Swan Lake Ranger District, Flathead National Forest, Flathead County, MT, Comment Period Ends: 10/08/2012, Contact: Richard Kehr 406–837–7500.

Amended Notices

EIS No. 20120201, Draft Supplement, USACE, IN, Indianapolis North Flood Damage Reduction, Modifications to Project Features and Realignment of the South Warfleigh Section, Marion County, IN, Comment Period Ends: 08/31/2012, Contact: Michael Turner 502–315–6900.

Revision to FR Notice Published 07/20/2012; Extending Comment Period from 08/31/2012 to 09/28/2012.

EIS No. 20120227, Draft EIS, USMC, GA, Proposed Modernization and Expansion of Townsend Bombing Range, Acquiring Additional Property and Constructing Infrastructure to Allow the Use of Precision-Guided Munitions, McIntosh and Long Counties, GA, Comment Period Ends: 09/27/2012, Contact: Veronda Johnson 571–256–2783.

Revision to FR Notice Published 7/13/2012; Extending Review Period from 8/27/12 to 09/27/2012.

EIS No. 20120247, Final EIS, USACE, 00, Mississippi River Gulf Outlet Ecosystem Restoration, To Develop a Comprehensive Ecosystem Restoration Plan To Restore the Lake Borgne Ecosystems, LA and MS, Review Period Ends: 09/06/2012, Contact: Tammy Gilmore 504–862–1002.

Revision to FR Notice Published 7/27/2012; Extending Review Period from 08/27/2012 to 09/06/2012.

Dated: August 21, 2012.

Cliff Rader,

Director, NEPA Compliance Division, Office of Federal Activities.

[FR Doc. 2012–20913 Filed 8–23–12; 8:45 am]

BILLING CODE 6560–50–P

NEPA Deskbook

Other Helpful Materials

Appendix 33 Abstracts of Selected Supreme Court Litigation Under NEPA

Abstracts of Selected U.S. Supreme Court Cases

Monsanto Co. v. Geertson Seed Farms, 130 S. Ct. 2743 (June 21, 2010)

The U.S. Supreme Court held that a district court abused its discretion in enjoining the Animal and Plant Health Inspection Service (APHIS) from effecting a partial deregulation of Roundup Ready Alfalfa (RRA), a variety of alfalfa genetically engineered to tolerate the herbicide Roundup, and in prohibiting the planting of RRA pending the Agency's completion of an EIS under NEPA. Petitioners and the government do not dispute that APHIS' deregulation decision violated NEPA, but they challenge the scope of the relief granted. None of the four factors for granting permanent injunctive relief supports the district court's order enjoining APHIS from partially deregulating RRA during the pendency of the EIS process. Most importantly, respondents cannot show that they will suffer irreparable injury if APHIS is allowed to proceed with any partial deregulation. And because it was inappropriate for the district court to foreclose even the possibility of a partial and temporary deregulation, it follows that it was inappropriate to enjoin planting in accordance with such a deregulation decision. An injunction is a drastic and extraordinary remedy that should not be granted as a matter of course. If, as respondents concede, a less drastic remedy (such as partial or complete vacatur of APHIS' deregulation decision) was sufficient to redress their injury, no recourse to the additional and extraordinary relief of an injunction was warranted. The Court, therefore, reversed and remanded the Ninth Circuit decision affirming the district court.

Winter v. Natural Resources Defense Council, 555 U.S. 7 (Nov. 12, 2008)

The U.S. Supreme Court vacated a lower court's preliminary injunction concerning the Navy's use of "mid-frequency active" (MFA) sonar during integrated training exercises in the waters off southern California (SOCAL). The plaintiffs—groups and individuals devoted to the protection of marine mammals and ocean habitats—assert that MFA sonar causes serious injuries to these animals. The Navy disputes that claim, noting that MFA sonar training in SOCAL waters has been conducted for 40 years without a single documented sonar-related injury to any marine mammal. Plaintiffs sued the Navy, seeking declaratory and injunctive relief on the grounds that the training exercises violated NEPA and other federal laws; in particular, plaintiffs contend that the Navy should have prepared an environmental impact statement before

conducting the latest round of SOCAL exercises. The district court entered a preliminary injunction prohibiting the Navy from using MFA sonar during its training exercises. The Court of Appeals held that this injunction was overbroad and remanded to the district court for a narrower remedy. The district court then entered another preliminary injunction, imposing six restrictions on the Navy's use of sonar during its SOCAL training exercises. The Navy then sought relief from the Executive Branch, and the CEQ authorized the Navy to implement "alternative arrangements" to NEPA compliance in light of "emergency circumstances." The CEQ allowed the Navy to continue its training exercises under voluntary mitigation procedures that the Navy had previously adopted. In light of the CEQ's actions, the Navy moved to vacate the district court's preliminary injunction. The district court refused to do so, and the Court of Appeals affirmed. The Court of Appeals held that there was a serious question whether the CEQ's interpretation of the "emergency circumstances" regulation was lawful, that plaintiffs had carried their burden of establishing a "possibility" of irreparable injury, and that the preliminary injunction was appropriate because the balance of hardships and consideration of the public interest favored the plaintiffs. But the Supreme Court disagreed, vacating the preliminary injunction to the extent challenged by the Navy. The balance of equities and the public interest tip strongly in favor of the Navy. The Navy's need to conduct realistic training with active sonar to respond to the threat posed by enemy submarines plainly outweighs the interests advanced by the plaintiffs.

Norton v. Southern Utah Wilderness Alliance, 542 U.S. 55 (June 14, 2004)

The U.S. Supreme Court held that a district court lacked subject matter jurisdiction to review an environmental group's claims that the Bureau of Land Management (BLM) violated the Federal Land Policy and Management Act (FLPMA) and NEPA by not properly managing off-road vehicle (ORV) use on federal lands classified as wilderness study areas (WSAs). The Tenth Circuit reversed the district court's dismissal of the claims, but the Supreme Court held that BLM's alleged failures to act are not remediable under the APA. An APA §706(1) claim can proceed only where a plaintiff asserts that an agency failed to take a discrete agency action that it is required to take. Here, the group claims that BLM violated FLPMA's nonimpairment mandate by permitting ORV use in certain WSAs. But while FLPMA §1782(c) is mandatory as to the object to be achieved, it leaves BLM discretion to decide how to achieve that object. The group also claimed that BLM's failure to comply with provisions of its land use plans contravenes the requirement that the Secretary manage public lands in accordance with such plans. But the land use plan statements at issue here are not a legally binding commitment enforceable under APA §706(1). Last, the group argued that BLM did not fulfill its obligation under NEPA to take a "hard look" at whether to supplement its EIS to take increased ORV use into account. But since BLM's approval of its land use plan was the "action" that required the EIS; and since that plan has already been approved; there is no ongoing "major federal action" that could require supplementation. The Court, therefore, reversed and remanded the Tenth Circuit's decision.

Department of Transportation v. Public Citizen, 541 U.S. 752 (June 7, 2004)

The U.S. Supreme Court held that the Federal Motor Carrier Safety Administration (FMCSA) did not violate NEPA, relevant CEQ regulations, or the CAA when it failed to evaluate the environmental impact of increased cross-border operations of Mexican motor carriers in its EA because any environmental impact would be the effect of lifting a 19-year moratorium against Mexican motor carriers from operating within the United States, not of the regulations' implementation. The issue was whether increased cross-border operations of Mexican motor carriers and correlative release of emissions was an effect of the FMCSA's rules and, if not, then the FMCSA's failure to address environmental effects in the EA was proper. The Court also held that the group forfeited any objection to the EA on the ground that it did not adequately discuss potential alternatives to the proposed action because respondents never identified in their comments to the rules any alternatives beyond those the EA evaluated. Finally, the FMCSA's purpose is to register any motor carrier willing and able to comply with various safety and financial responsibility rules. Thus, since the FMCSA has no ability to prevent such cross-border operations, it lacks the power to act on whatever information might be contained in an EIS and could not act on whatever input the public could provide. The FMCSA did not violate the CAA by failing to make a conformity determination which considered direct and indirect emissions in a nonattainment or maintenance area. Trucks' emissions were not direct because they will not occur at the same time or place as the promulgation of the regulations nor were they considered indirect because the FMCSA cannot practically control or maintain control over the emissions: the

FMCSA has no ability to countermand the president's decision to lift the moratorium or to act categorically to prevent Mexican carriers from registering and Mexican trucks from entering the country; and once the regulations are promulgated, the FMCSA will not be able to regulate any aspect of vehicle exhaust from those trucks. Although the lower court held that the EA was deficient because it failed to give adequate consideration to the overall environmental impact of lifting the moratorium, the Court rejected an environmental group's challenge to the procedures used in promulgating these regulations and remanded the case for further proceedings.

Robertson v. Methow Valley Citizens Council, 490 U.S. 332 (May 1, 1989)

The U.S. Supreme Court rules that an EIS need not include a final detailed mitigation plan or a worst case analysis. The U.S. Forest Service had issued a development permit based on an EIS that, in discussing mitigation of off-site effects, mostly recommended general steps that state and local agencies might take. The Court first rules that NEPA and regulations issued by CEQ establish a procedural requirement that an EIS discuss mitigation in enough detail to ensure that environmental consequences have been fairly evaluated, but not a substantive requirement that it formulate and adopt a complete mitigation plan. Moreover, the off-site effects of this development cannot be mitigated unless state and local agencies act, and the Court holds that the Forest service need not delay action until those agencies have decided on mitigation measures. The Court rules that NEPA does not require that measures be taken to mitigate the adverse effects of major federal actions, or that every EIS include a detailed explanation of those measures. The Court next holds that NEPA does not require that an EIS address uncertainty through worst case analysis. A CEQ regulation requiring such analysis has been rescinded, and the Court holds that the regulation is not still applicable as a codification of previous judicial decisions. Those decisions merely required agencies to describe uncertain environmental impacts, not to conduct worst case analyses. Moreover, the regulation replacing the worst case requirement is entitled to substantial deference because there appear to have been good reasons for the change. The prior regulation was much criticized, and the new regulation is designed to focus the EIS process on significant rather than speculative risks. The Court also holds that failure to develop a complete mitigation plan did not violate Forest Service regulations requiring permits to include mitigation measures. The on-site mitigation recommendations were sufficiently clear, and the Court holds that the regulations do not condition permit issuance on consideration and implementation of off-site mitigation measures. The regulations are based on recreational land use authorities, not environmental quality concerns. The Court holds that the Forest Service could reasonably construe its regulations not to extend to potential off-site state or county actions, and that this interpretation is controlling.

Marsh v. Oregon Natural Resources Council, 490 U.S. 360 (May 1, 1989)

The Court rules that an agency's decision on whether to prepare a supplemental EIS should be reviewed under the arbitrary and capricious standard, and upholds the Army Corps of Engineers' decision not to supplement an EIS for a dam in Oregon. The Court first holds that the EIS was not defective for failure to include a complete mitigation plan or a worst-case analysis. The Court then holds that EIS supplementation based on new information is sometimes required by the purposes of NEPA and by regulations issued by the Council on Environmental Quality and the Corps. Applying a rule of reason, an agency must supplement an EIS when new information shows that future major federal action on the project will significantly affect the quality of the human environment in a manner or to an extent not previously considered. The Court next holds that review of an agency's decision on whether to supplement an EIS is governed by the arbitrary and capricious standard of APA §706(2)(A). The dispute over the significance of the new information is factual, not legal, so the Court will review the decision carefully but give deference to the agency's expertise and discretion. The Court notes that the difference between the arbitrary and capricious standard and the reasonableness standard applied by some courts is not of great practical consequence, and that its ruling therefore will not require substantial changes in established NEPA law. The Court then holds that the Corps did not act arbitrarily and capriciously in deciding not to supplement the EIS based on receipt of an internal state agency memorandum arguing that the dam would adversely affect fishing and a soil survey suggesting that it might increase turbidity. The Corps carefully considered these materials and responded to the claim that they required EIS supplementation. Moreover, there are indications that they did not convey significant new information. No one suggested that the information was highly significant until this lawsuit was filed. The agency whose staff wrote the memorandum did not adopt its position or deem it significant enough to transmit to the Corps, and independent experts found it significantly flawed. Moreover, despite the soil survey, the Corps legitimately concluded that the existing turbidity predictions were accurate. It was not arbitrary and capricious for the Corps to find that the information which was new and accurate was not significant and that the information which was significant was not new or accurate.

Baltimore Gas & Electric v. Natural Resources Defense Council, Inc., 462 U.S. 87 (June 6, 1983)

The Supreme Court, reversing the D.C. Circuit's decision, rules that the Nuclear Regulatory Commission (NRC) complied with NEPA and was not arbitrary and capricious in adopting generic rules — the "S-3 Table" — dictating how nuclear reactor licensing decisions take into account the environmental impacts of the nuclear fuel cycle. The D.C. Circuit had ruled that the NRC violated NEPA by determining, in spite of substantial uncertainty, that licensing boards should assume that the long-term storage of nuclear wastes has no significant environmental impact and thus should not be considered in individual licensing decisions. The Court rules that the NRC reasonably evaluated the environmental impacts of the fuel cycle. It is clear from the record that the NRC considered all the data on long-term storage and disclosed the substantial uncertainty concerning its safety. Furthermore, the NRC reasonably chose to prepare a generic rather than a plant-specific EIS of long-term storage, since the environmental impacts of much of the fuel cycle are not plant-specific but are common to all nuclear power plants. The NRC also did not act arbitrarily or capriciously in generically deciding that the uncertainties surrounding fuel storage were insufficient to affect individual licensing decisions. The Court points out that the S-3 Table and the "zero-release assumption" were developed for the limited purpose of considering the risks of the most likely long-term waste disposal method as they affect individual licensing decisions. Furthermore, the uncertainties concerning the zero-release assumption, a single figure in the entire table, are offset by conservative assumptions reflected in other values in the table. Finally, the Court notes that it must generally defer to agency expertise at the frontiers of science. The Court rules that the NRC's zero-release assumption was not arbitrary and capricious under the Administrative Procedure Act. The NRC considered and revealed the uncertainties of long-term storage and even those commissioners dissatisfied with the zero-release assumption were convinced that the environmental impacts should be considered in other proceedings. In addition, the Court rules that the S-3 Table does not preclude consideration in individual licensing decisions of the human health, socioeconomic, or cumulative impacts of fuel cycle activities. Although ambiguities existed in earlier regulations, the

Court finds no basis for the D.C. Circuit's conclusion that the NRC ever precluded a licensing board from considering these effects.

Metropolitan Edison Co. v. People Against Nuclear Energy, 460 U.S. 766 (Apr. 19, 1983)

The Supreme Court, reversing the D.C. Circuit, rules that NEPA does not require the Nuclear Regulatory Commission to consider the potential psychological harm to local residents before authorizing the resumption of power generation at the sister unit to the damaged Three Mile Island nuclear reactor. The Court finds that NEPA's sweeping goals to enhance human health and welfare are ends that Congress chose to pursue by means of protecting the physical environment. NEPA requires a reasonably close causal relationship between a change in the physical environment and the effect at issue. Although the Court agrees that human health is cognizable under NEPA and that human health includes psychological health, agencies need only consider such effects when caused by federally induced changes in the physical environment. The Court rules that the risk of nuclear accident is not an effect on the physical environment and thus NEPA does not apply to any resulting damage to psychological health. In addition, it is unreasonably difficult for agencies to distinguish between disagreement with governmental policies that cause severe anxiety and stress and "genuine" claims of psychological health damage. The D.C. Circuit erred in concluding that the unusual severity of the psychological impacts of Three Mile Island made a distinction possible, because the key question is whether the impacts are environmental in nature, not how serious they may be. Moreover, NEPA does not address past effects of past federal actions, only future effects of future actions. Finally, the Court rules that since there were no environmental effects requiring NEPA consideration, the agency was not required to consider secondary community effects

Weinberger v. Catholic Action of Hawaii/Peace Education Project, 454 U.S. 139 (Dec. 1, 1981)

Reversing a decision of the Ninth Circuit, the Supreme Court upholds the Navy's failure to prepare an EIS for a classified nuclear weapons storage project. The Court first holds that the Ninth Circuit incorrectly interpreted NEPA §102(2)(C) by requiring preparation of a "hypothetical" EIS. It notes that public disclosure of an EIS is expressly governed by the Freedom of Information Act (FOIA). Exemption 1 of FOIA exempts from disclosure national defense or foreign policy matters that are properly classified pursuant to executive order. Since information on whether nuclear

weapons will be stored at the project site is classified, an EIS premised on nuclear weapons storage would be exempt from disclosure. The Court also holds that the Navy is not required to prepare, for internal use only, an EIS premised on nuclear weapons storage at the facility. The obligation to prepare an EIS requires a proposal for action. Because of security regulations, however, the storage of nuclear weapons at the site was not shown to have been formally proposed. Thus, for practical purposes the Navy's compliance with NEPA in this case is beyond judicial scrutiny. In a concurring opinion, two members of the court emphasize that classified proposals are not exempt from NEPA's EIS requirement. Where feasible, EISs should be organized so that unclassified portions can be made available to the public.

Strycker's Bay Neighborhood Council, Inc. v. Karlen, 444 U.S. 223 (Jan. 7, 1980)

In a per curiam order, the Supreme Court reverses the decision of the Second Circuit Court of Appeals in Karlen v. Harris, 590 F.2d 39 (2d Cir. 1978). At issue was a plan by the Department of Housing and Urban Development (HUD) to redesignate a site in New York City for a proposed low-income housing project. The Court concludes that HUD complied with NEPA in considering the environmental consequences of its decision. In addition, the Court, relying on its decision two years ago in Vermont Yankee Nuclear Power Corp. v. NRDC, 435 U.S. 519 (U.S. 1978), rejects the Second Circuit's conclusion that NEPA required the agency, in selecting a course of action, to elevate environmental concerns over other appropriate considerations. In dissent, Justice Marshall rejects the notion that a reviewing court's duty under NEPA is limited to ensuring that an agency has followed the requisite procedures in considering environmental consequences, arguing that the questions of whether HUD's decision was arbitrary, capricious, or an abuse of discretion and whether the agency gave a "hard look" at the environmental consequences are sufficiently difficult and important to merit plenary consideration.

Andrus v. Sierra Club, 442 U.S. 347 (June 11, 1979)

The Supreme Court rules that NEPA does not require federal agencies to prepare EISs to accompany appropriations requests. Unanimously reversing a decision of the U.S. Court of Appeals for the D.C. Circuit, 581 F.2d 895 (D.C. Cir. 1978), the Court holds that neither "routine" budget requests nor those which result from a "painstaking review of an ongoing program" are to be considered "proposals for legislation" within the meaning of §102(2)(C) of NEPA for which an EIS must be prepared. In reaching this conclusion, the Court relies on the Council on Environmental Quality's new NEPA implementation regulations, which interpret the phrase "proposals for legislation" to exclude appropriations requests, and the traditional congressional distinction between "legislation" and "appropriation." The Court likewise rejects the court of appeals' conclusion that appropriations requests which envision significant revisions in ongoing programs constitute proposals for "major Federal action" under NEPA. Such requests do not themselves propose actions but instead seek funding for actions already proposed. Moreover, a contrary ruling would lead to unnecessary redundancy since an EIS must in any event be prepared for the underlying programmatic decision. Because § 102(2)(C) of NEPA has no application to appropriations requests, the court of appeals' further ruling requiring the Office of Management and Budget to adopt regulations for the implementation of its NEPA obligations was also incorrect.

Vermont Yankee Nuclear Power Corp. v. Natural Resources Defense Council, Inc., 435 U.S. 519 (Apr. 3, 1978)

On review of two cases in which plaintiffs challenged the Nuclear Regulatory Commission's (NRC's) licensing of two nuclear power plants, the Supreme Court unanimously reverses the court of appeals' invalidation of the licenses, announcing that the role of the judiciary in the nuclear licensing process must be carefully limited to avoid unauthorized intrusions into the domain of the administrative agency. In the first case (No. 419), the U.S. Court of Appeals for the District of Columbia Circuit had sustained respondent's contention that NRC provided for an inadequate ventilation of the issues under NEPA when it decided to consider the issue of nuclear waste disposal in a separate, non-adjudicatory hearing, the results of which would be applied retroactively to petitioner's license, rather than in the licensing proceeding itself. Disagreeing with that holding, the Supreme Court held the case law and the legislative history of the APA to support the proposition that as long as an agency complies with the APA's minimum requirements, as had the NRC in this case, it is free to adopt or to decline to adopt additional, more complex procedures. The lower court's invalidation, for procedural inadequacy, of the spent fuel cycle rule which emerged from the separate hearing is also rejected by the Court. Because of the absence from this case of circumstances compelling judicial imposition of more exacting procedural safeguards, the court of appeals erred in not judging the procedural adequacy of that proceeding by the rule-making standards set

out in §553 of the APA. This issue is remanded, not for a reassessment of procedures, but for a determination whether, under the APA, the adopted rule is supported by substantial evidence produced at the hearing. With respect to the second case (No. 528) the Court holds that the court of appeals was again wrong in reversing the issuance of the construction license because of the NRC's refusal to explore the question of energy conservation as an alternative to construction of the plant. Where, as in this case, the adoption of a project alternative is merely suggested by a party without at least a minimal showing as to the advantages or wisdom of adopting it, the agency is not required to research and analyze exhaustively the issue; the agency was justified in requiring a showing of sufficient force to require reasonable minds to inquire further. The Court also reverses the appellate court's holding that the Atomic Safety and Licensing Appeals Board should have returned the safety report submitted by the Advisory Committee on Reactor Safeguards for analysis of other issues in terms understandable to a layman. This ruling misinterpreted the Committee's purpose and function and demonstrates an inadequate regard for the resources and time that have been invested in this project. In conclusion, the Court notes that the nation's experiment with nuclear power represents a legislative policy decision which cannot be second-guessed by the judiciary, and that NEPA does not authorize the courts to substitute their judgment for that of Congress or the executive branch.

Kleppe v. Sierra Club, 427 U.S. 390 (June 28, 1976)

The Supreme Court reverses the Court of Appeals for the D.C. Circuit, 514 F.2d 856 (D.C. Cir. 1975), and holds that NEPA does not require preparation of an environmental impact statement for coal leasing in the Northern Great Plains region absent an agency proposal for regional coal development. There has been no regional proposal; all proposals have been of local or national scope. Nor can a regional impact statement be prepared for practical reasons, since there would be no factual predicate for analysis. The court of appeals erred in holding that agency contemplation of controlling coal development requires an impact statement. The agencies' procedural duty to prepare impact statements for proposals is precise; the court of appeals mistakenly departed from the statutory language by requiring a four-part balancing test for impact statement preparation. In addition, the court of appeals improperly enjoined further coal leasing pending preparation of an impact statement since the equities lay on the side of the lessees and their consumers. Although comprehensive impact statements are often necessary for related proposals, the determination of the relevant geographical region covered by the statement falls within the informed discretion of the responsible agency. A partial concurrence and dissent argues that the court of appeals' four-part balancing test would implement NEPA's goals by allowing court intervention prior to solidification of an agency's environmental position, rather than fostering wasted effort through belated injunctive relief. The lower court's test merely restricts judicial review to a small number of proper instances where the agency is violating NEPA through nonpreparation of an impact statement. It is no answer to say that such a test invites litigation, if that litigation is brought to redress agency non-compliance with NEPA's mandates. Furthermore, NEPA's legislative history belies the majority's assertion that the Act's requirements are "precise."

Flint Ridge Development Co. v. Scenic Rivers Ass'n of Oklahoma, 426 U.S. 776 (June 24, 1976)

In a challenge to the Department of Housing and Urban Development (HUD) for allowing a disclosure statement required by the Interstate Land Sales Disclosure Act to become effective without first filing an environmental impact statement, the Supreme Court holds that NEPA's impact statement requirement is inapplicable whenever a "clear and unavoidable conflict" between the requirements of NEPA and another statute occurs. Moreover, HUD's action on the disclosure statement is not a "major federal action significantly affecting the human environment" because HUD has no "ability to react to the environmental consequences" of the disclosure. Absent incompleteness in the statement, the Secretary of HUD has no discretion to extend the 30-day time period after which disclosure statements automatically become effective. The court of appeals decision, 520 F.2d 240 (10th Cir. 1975), is reversed.

Aberdeen & Rockfish R.R. Co. v. Students Challenging Regulatory Agency Procedures (SCRAP II), 422 U.S. 289 (June 24, 1975)

The Supreme Court reverses a three-judge district court decision that held inadequate the ICC's compliance with NEPA in assessing the environmental impact of a general railroad freight rate increase on the recycling industry. Relying on the long-established and limited character of the ICC's "general revenue

proceeding" at which such increases are approved, and emphasizing that the ICC was investigating in a "more appropriate proceeding" the existing rate structure's discrimination against recyclables which the general increase exacerbated, the court finds that the ICC was justified in limiting the scope of the impact statement largely to the effect of the increase rather than including an extended environmental examination of the underlying rate structure. The across-the-board percentage increase in freight rates is facially neutral in its environmental effect, and the ICC need not "start over again" its decisionmaking process in order to reflect a wholly new environmental assessment. In a case such as this where a federal agency is not proposing an action but is instead considering a proposal by a non-federal party which requires federal approval, the first point at which an impact statement must be prepared is when a recognizable "recommendation or report" for federal action (i.e., approval) appears. Justice Douglas dissents, arguing that the majority's ruling excuses a history of foot-dragging by the ICC on NEPA compliance, and pointing out that the "more appropriate proceeding" investigating the environmental effects of the underlying rate structure may go on indefinitely while irreparable environmental damage occurs.

United States v. Students Challenging Regulatory Agency Procedures (SCRAP I), 412 U.S. 669 (June 18, 1973)

The U.S. Supreme Court holds that an environmental group is sufficiently aggrieved by the temporary rate increase allowed by the ICC on the rail shipment of recycled goods to have standing, but the district court lacks the power to interfere with the Commission's discretionary decision or to suspend the rate increase itself. The allegations of SCRAP that the use and enjoyment of natural resources by its members would be disturbed by the results of the nonuse of recycled goods caused by the rate increase show injury in fact sufficient to maintain standing, although many others may have suffered the same harm, and the causal connection between the act complained of and the eventual damage to petitioners is somewhat attenuated. In §15 (7) of the Interstate Commerce Act Congress vested complete power to suspend rate increases pending a final decision as to their lawfulness solely in the ICC to the complete exclusion of the courts. NEPA cannot be construed to repeal this policy. The judgment of the district court is reversed and the case remanded.

NEPA Deskbook

Appendix 34 Model NEPA Complaint

Model Complaint

Model NEPA Complaint[1]
(for failure to prepare environmental impact statement)

Civil Action No.

Caption	)
_____	)
_____	)

COMPLAINT FOR DECLARATORY
AND INJUNCTIVE RELIEF

Introduction

[The introductory paragraph should describe the nature of the action.]

Jurisdiction

This action arises under the National Environmental Policy Act of 1969, as amended ("NEPA"), 42 U.S.C. §44321 *et seq.*, and its implementing regulations, adopted by the Council on Environmental Quality ("CEQ") and applicable to all agencies "CEQ NEPA Regulations"), 40 C.F.R. Parts 1500-1508. [Here you may cite any applicable agency NEPA procedures. Also cite the legal authority for the action alleged to be subject to NEPA.] Judicial review is sought pursuant to §10 of the Administrative Procedure Act ("APA"), 5 U.S.C. §§701-706, authorizing judicial review of all agency actions. This Court has jurisdiction over this action pursuant to 28 U.S.C. §§1311 and 1361, and may grant declaratory judgment and further relief pursuant to 28 U.S.C. §§2201 and 2202.

Plaintiffs

Plaintiff _____ is a non-profit, public benefit membership corporation organized under the laws of the State of _____. Its principal office is located at _____ _____. Its other offices are located in _____. [Plaintiff's] members are scientists and other citizens of the United States. [Plaintiff] has a nationwide membership in excess of _____ persons, including some _____ members in the State of _____, many of whom use [the affected area—here a water body] for swimming, fishing, boating, birdwatching, and scientific studies, and whose uses of [the water body] will be damaged and impaired by [the action alleged to cause significant environmental impact]. [Plaintiff] exists to promote research and action, and to take action itself, to protect and enhance the environment, including the preservation of estuaries, rivers, wetlands, and fish and wildlife resources. Through participation in numerous legislative, administrative, and judicial proceedings, [plaintiff] has demonstrated its strong interest in the effective conservation of the nation's estuarine and coastal resources and the proper administration of laws designed to protect these resources.

[Follow with an appropriate paragraph for each plaintiff.]

Members of each of the Plaintiff organizations (hereinafter referred to collectively as "members" live in the vicinity of [the water body] (hereinafter sometimes referred to as the "affected waters"). Plaintiffs' members use and enjoy the resources in and around [the affected waters] for [food, sportfishing, wildlife viewing and education, photography, scientific study, recreation, boating, swimming, other beach and water-related activities, and general aesthetic and spiritual enjoyment]. Plaintiffs and their members will be adversely affected and injured by Defendants' actions in issuing a permit for [the action alleged to cause significant environmental impact], as set forth more fully below. Plaintiffs' representatives and members have taken part in administrative proceedings concerning [the action alleged to case significant environment impact] in the affected area, including testifying at the public hearings held by [the agency]. Plaintiff's interests in this action fall squarely within the zone of interests protected by the laws sought to be enforced in this action.

---

1.   Compliant drafted by Nicholas C. Yost. *Ed.*

Defendants

Defendant [U.S. official] is sued in his official capacity as [position occupied]. In that capacity, he is responsible for the activities of [the agency] in [taking the action alleged to require NEPA compliance]. [Cite the legal authority for the agency action.]

[Follow with a similar paragraph for each defendant.]

The Proposals

[Describe the proposed action alleged to require an EIS, giving both a chronology and a description of the alleged environmental impacts. These paragraphs form the heart of your factual showing.]

Applicable Laws

The National Environmental Policy Act §102(2)(C), 42 U.S.C. §4322(2)(C), requires "responsible [federal] officials" to prepare environmental impact statements ("EISs") on proposals for legislation and other "major Federal actions significantly affecting the quality of the human environment."

It is this section and this requirement which are the heart of this case. As described in detail below, permitting by a federal agency (here [the agency]), is a "Federal action" subject to the EIS requirement. Under NEPA, an agency must prepare an EIS when an "action" may have a significant environmental effect. 40 C.F.R. §1508.3. It is Plaintiffs' contention that in this case [the agency's] action may, and indeed in some cases will, have a significant environmental effect and that therefore as a matter of law an EIS must be prepared.

The National Environmental Policy Act established a national policy to "prevent or eliminate damage to the environment and biosphere." NEPA §2, 42 U.S.C. §4321. The Act recognizes "the critical importance of restoring and maintaining environmental quality," declares that the federal government has a continuing responsibility to use "all practicable means" to minimize environmental degradation, and directs that "to the fullest extent possible . . . the policies, regulations and public laws of the United States shall be interpreted and administered in accordance with the policies set forth in this Act." NEPA §§101(a), 102(1), 42 U.S.C. §§4331(A), 4332(1). The Act further recognizes the right of each person to enjoy a healthful environment. NEPA §101(c), 42 U.S.C. §4331(c).

Under Executive Order No. 11514 (March 5, 1970), as amended by Executive Order No. 11991 (May 24, 1977), §§2(g) and 3(h), the CEQ has issued regulations binding on all federal agencies for the implementation of the procedural provisions of NEPA. Those regulations (fully entitled "Regulations for Implementing the Procedural Provisions of the National Environmental Policy Act") became effective in 1979 and binding upon [the agency] as of that date. 43 Fed. Reg. 55978-56007 (1978), 40 C.F.R. Parts 1500-1508. Each agency was required by the CEQ NEPA Regulations to adopt "procedures" to supplement those regulations. 40 C.F.R. §1507.3.

Pursuant to the CEQ's directive, [the agency] adopted _____ C.F.R. Part ____. [Here cite any applicable agency NEPA procedures.]

[Add paragraphs discussing any particular statutory or regulatory provisions specifically applicable to the particular case. For instance, it may be appropriate to cite to the applicable subsections of 40 C.F.R. §1508.27, which set out the criteria for "significance" of environmental impact and therefore determine the need for an EIS.]

For the reasons stated in paragraphs ____ above, Defendants' proposals may and in some cases will significantly affect the quality of the human environment.

For the reasons stated in paragraphs ____ above and ____ below, Defendants' proposals will cause irreparable injury.

Violations of Law

Count I

Violation of §102(2)(C) of NEPA, 42 U.S.C. §4332(2)(C)—Failure to Prepare EIS

Plaintiffs repeat and incorporate by reference the allegations contained in paragraphs _____ through _____ above.

The National Environmental Policy Act of 1969, as amended, 42 U.S.C. §4321 *et seq.*, requires all federal agencies to prepare a detailed EIS on every proposal for a major federal action significantly affecting the quality of the human environment. 42 U.S.C. §4332(2)(C). That EIS must always contain a detailed discussion of environmental impacts (40 C.F.R. §1502.16) and of alternatives (40 C.F.R. §1502.14).

The proposal to [describe the action alleged to require NEPA compliance] is a major federal action significantly affecting the quality of the human environment for which Defendants must prepare an EIS. It is an action requiring an EIS because:

The [action] may or will have a significant environmental effect.

By the criteria set out in the CEQ NEPA Regulations (see [paragraphs following paragraph 9 above]), there may or will be such significant effects.

Count II

Violations of Administrative Procedure Act, 5 U.S.C. §§701-706

Plaintiffs repeat and incorporate by reference the allegations contained in paragraphs _____ through _____ above.

Due to Defendants' knowing and conscious failure to comply with NEPA, Plaintiffs have suffered legal wrongs because of agency action and are adversely affected and aggrieved by agency action within the meaning of the APA, 5 U.S.C. §702.

Defendants' knowing and conscious failure to comply with NEPA is arbitrary, capricious, and an abuse of discretion, not in accordance with law, in excess of statutory jurisdiction, and without observance of procedure required by law within the meaning of the APA, 5 U.S.C. §706(2), and should therefore be declared unlawful and set aside by this Court.

Prayer For Relief

WHEREFORE, Plaintiffs respectfully request that this Court:

Declare that Defendants' actions in [taking the action alleged to require an EIS] without first having prepared a detailed statement on the environmental impacts of an alternatives to the [action taken] constitute violations of NEPA and of the APA and are therefore null and of no legal force and effect;

Issue a mandatory injunction requiring Defendants to rescind the [decision made] and prohibiting any activities to be conducted pursuant to [that decision] until such time as Defendants have complied with NEPA and have prepared an adequate environmental impact statement and have come to a decision in light of the statement;

Allow Plaintiffs to recover the costs of this action, including attorneys fees;

Grant such other and further relief as the Court deems just and proposal.

Dated: _____   **(Signature Block)**

_____

NEPA Deskbook

Appendix 35 List of Agency NEPA Contacts

List of Agency NEPA Contacts

Access Board

Kathy Roy Johnson
Office of the General Counsel
1331 F Street, N.W.
Washington, DC 20004
(202) 272-0042
(202) 272-0081 (fax)
Johnson@access-board.gov

Advisory Council on Historic Preservation

Charlene D. Vaughn
Office of Federal Programs
Assistant Director for Federal Program Development
1100 Pennsylvania Avenue, N.W.
Washington, DC 20004
(202) 606-8533
(202) 606-8672 (fax)
cvaughn@achp.gov

Department of Agriculture

Charles L. Walthall
Agriculture Research Service
National Program Leader, Office of National Programs
5601 Sunnyside Avenue, Room 4-2288
Beltsville, MD 20705-5140
(301) 504-4634
(301) 504-6231 (fax)
charlie.walthall@ars.usda.gov

Elizabeth (Wendy) Nelson
Animal and Plant Health Inspection Service
Environmental Services
Environmental Protection Specialist
4700 River Road, Unit 149
Riverdale, MD 20737-1238
(301) 734-3089
(301) 734-3640 (fax)
elizabeth.e.nelson@aphis.usda.gov

Dr. Mary Ann Rozum
Cooperative State Research, Education and Extension
Service
Natural Resources and Environmental Unit
1400 Independence Ave, SW
Washington, DC 20250-2210
(202) 401-4533
(202) 401-1706 (fax)
mrozum@crees.usda.gov

Matthew Ponish
Farm Service Agency
National Environmental Compliance Manager
1400 Independence Ave., S.W., Room 4617-S
Washington, DC 20250
(202) 720-6221
(202) 720-4619 (fax)
matthew.ponish@wdc.usda.gov

Andrée DuVarney
Natural Resources Conservation Service
National Environmental Coordinator
1621 N. Kent Street
Arlington, VA 22209
(703) 235-8091
(202) 720-2646 (fax)
andree.duvarney@wdc.usda.gov

Frank Mancino
Rural Housing Service and Rural Business-Cooperative Service
Senior Environmental Protection Specialist
1400 Independence Ave., S.W., Room 6900
Washington, DC 20250-0700
(202) 720-1827
(202) 690-4335 (fax)
frank.mancino@wdc.usda.gov

Mark Plank
Rural Utilities Service
Engineering and Environmental Staff
Senior Environmental Scientist
1400 Independence Ave., S.W., Room 2240
Washington, DC 20250-0700
(202) 720-1649
(202) 720-0820 (fax)
mark.plank@usda.gov

Joe Carbone
U.S. Forest Service
Ecosystem Management Coordination
201 14th Street, S.W.
Washington, DC 20250-1100
(202) 205-0884
(202) 205-0102 (fax)
jcarbone@fs.fed.us

Alaska Natural Gas Office of the Federal Coordinator

Joseph M Oglander
Transportation Projects
General Counsel
1717 H St., NW
Washington, DC 20006
(202) 478-9754
(202) 254-0692 (fax)
joglandere@arcticgas.gov

Armed Forces Retirement Home

Justin Seffens
Chief, Campus Operations
3700 North Capitol Street, Room 310
Washington, DC 20011-8400
(202) 730-3508
(202) 730-3539 (fax)
justin.seffrens@afrh.gov

Board of Governors of the Federal Reserve System

Keith Bates
Engineering and Facilities
Chief
20th and C Street, N.W.
Washington, DC 20551
(202) 452-3720
(202) 728-5800 (fax)
keith.bates@frb.gov

Department of Commerce

Genevieve Walker
Department of Commerce
Environmental Programs Manager
1401 Constitution Avenue, N.W., Room 1036
Washington, DC 20230
(202) 482-2345
gwalker@doc.gov

Steve Leathery
National Marine Fisheries Service
National NEPA Coordinator
1315 East-West Highway
Silver Spring, MD 20910-0001
(301) 713-2239
(301) 713-1940 (fax)
steve.leathery@noaa.gov

Steve Kokkinakis
National Oceanic and Atmospheric Administration
NEPA Policy & Compliance
1315 East West Highway, Room 15723
Silver Spring, MD 20910
(301) 713-1622
(301) 713-0585
steve.kokkinakis@noaa.gov

David Raymond Ives
Economic Development Administration
Sustainability Coordinator
14th and Constitution Avenue, N.W.
Washington, DC 20230-0001

202-482-0529

202-482-0995 (fax)
david.raymond.ives@eda.doc.gov

Committee for Purchase From People Who Are Blind or Severely Disabled

Dennis Lockard
General Counsel
Crystal Square 3, Suite 10800
1421 Jefferson Davis Highway
Arlington, VA 22202-3259
(703) 603-7740
(703) 603-0655 (fax)
dlockard@abilityone.gov

Consumer Product Safety Commission

Robert Franklin
Directorate for Economic Analysis
4330 East West Highway
Bethesda, MD 20814
(301) 504-7708
(301) 504-0109
rfranklin@cpsc.gov

Department of Defense

Terry Bowers
Department of Defense
Office of Deputy Undersecretary Defense (Installations and Environment)
Director, Environmental Security - EQ
3400 Defense, Pentagon, Room 5C646
Washington, DC 20314-3400
(703) 696-9447
(703) 693-2659 (fax)
terry.bowers@osd.mil

Jack Bush
Department of Air Force
Senior Planner/NEPA Program Manager
1260 Air Force, Pentagon, Room 4C-950
Washington, DC 20330-1260
(703) 614-0237
(703) 604-5260 (fax)
jack.bush@pentagon.af.mil

Cheryl Antosh
Department of Army
Army Secretariat POC
110 Army, Pentagon, Room 3D453
Washington, DC 20310
(703) 614-1234
cheryl.c.antosh@mail.mil

John C. Furry
Army Corps of Engineers
Senior Policy Advisor, Planning and Review Division
441 G Street, N.W., Room CECW-PC
Washington, DC 20314-1000
(202) 761-5875
(202) 761-8957
john.c.furry@usace.army.mil

Chip Smith
Army Corps of Engineers
Assistant for Environmental, Tribal and Regulatory
Affairs
108 Army Pentagon
Washington, DC 20310-0108
(703) 693-3655
(703) 697-8433(fax)
charles.r.smith567.civ@mail.mil

Thomas Egeland
Department of Navy
NEPA Liaison
1777 North Kent Street
Rosslyn, VA 22209
(703) 588-6671
(703) 588-8428
tom.egeland@navy.mil

Karen Foskey
United States Navy
Office of the Chief of Naval Operations
Environmental Planning/NEPA Lead, Operational
Environmental Readiness & Planning
Chief of Naval Operations (N45) Navy, Pentagon,
Suite 2000
Washington, DC 22202-3735
(703) 602-2859
(703) 602-5364 (fax)
karen.foskey@navy.mil

Sue Goodfellow
United States Marine Corps
Natural and Cultural Resources Division
Cultural Resources Specialist
2 Navy Annex
Washington, DC 20380-1775
(703) 695-8240
(703) 695-8550 (fax)
sue.goodfellow@usmc.mil

Randy Chambers
National Guard Bureau
office of General Counsel
Chief Environmental Law/Real Estate
1411 Jefferson Davis Highway
Arlington, VA 22202-3231
(703) 607-2729
(703) 607-3682 (fax)
randy.chambers@ngb.ang.af.mil

Ann Engelberger
Defense Logistics Agency
Environmental Protection Specialist
8725 John J. Kingman Road
Ft. Belvoir, VA 22060-6221
(703) 767-0705
(703) 767-6093 (fax)
ann.engelberger@dla.mil

Defense Threat Reduction Agency
NEPA Coordinator - Position vacant [*waiting to hear
whether position yet filled*]
1680 Texas Street, S.E.
Kirkland Air Force Base, NM, 87111

Delaware River Basin Commission

Carol Collier
Executive Director
P.O. Box 7360
West Trenton, NJ 08628-0360
(609) 883-9500
(609) 883-9522 (fax)
ccollier@drbc.state.nj.us

Denali Commission

Adison Wetzel
Program Specialist
510 L Street, Suite 410
Anchorage, AK 99501
(907) 271-1640
(907) 271-1415 (fax)
awetzel@denali.gov

Department of Energy

Carol M. Borgstrom
Office of Environment, Safety and Health
Director, Office of NEPA Policy and Compliance
1000 Independence Avenue, S.W., Room 3E-094
Washington, DC 20585-0119
(202) 586-4600
(202) 586-7031 (fax)
carol.borgstrom@hq.doe.gov

Katherine Semple Pierce
Bonneville Power Administration
Office of Energy Resources
NEPA Compliance Officer
P.O. Box 3621
Portland, OR 97208-3621
(503) 230-3962
(503) 230-5699 (fax)
kspierce@bpa.gov

Shane Collins
Western Area Power Administration
Natural Resources Manager
P.O. Box 281213
Lakewood, CO 80228-8213
(720) 962-7252
(720) 962-7263 (fax)
collins@wapa.gov

Environmental Protection Agency

Cliff Rader
Office of Federal Activities
Director of NEPA Compliance Division
1200 Pennsylvania Avenue, N.W..
Ariel Ross Bldg., Mail Code 2252-A
Washington, DC 20460
(202) 564-7159
(202) 564-0072 (fax)
rader.cliff@epa.gov

Export-Import Bank of the United States

Tracey Braun
Office of the General Counsel
Senior Counsel
811 Vermont Avenue, N.W.
Washington, DC 20571
(202) 565-3437
(202) 565-3586 (fax)
tracey.braun@exim.gov

Farm Credit Administration

Gaylon Dykstra
Office of Regulatory Policy
Assistant to the Director
1501 Farm Credit Drive
McLean, VA 22102
(703) 883-4322
(703) 883-4477 (fax)
dykstrag@fca.gov

Federal Communications Commission

Aliza Katz
FCC NEPA Contact
445 12th Street, S.W., Room 8-B525
Washington, DC 20554
(202) 418-1720
(202) 418-7540 (fax)
akatz@fcc.gov

Lee Martin
Administrative Law Division
Counsel, Office of General Counsel
445 12th Street, S.W., Room 8-A523
Washington, DC 20554
(202) 418-1754
lee.martin@fcc.gov

Michael Wagner
Mass Media Bureau
NEPA Contact
445 12th Street, S.W., Room 2-A523
Washington, DC 20554
(202) 418-2775
(202) 418-1410 (fax)
mwagner@fcc.gov

Dan Abeyta
Wireless Telecommunications Bureau
NEPA Contact
445 12th Street, S.W.
Washington, DC 20554
(202) 418-1538
(202) 418-7447 (fax)
dabeyta@fcc.gov

Federal Deposit Insurance Corporation

Brian Yellin
Facilities Operations Section
Assistant Director
3501 North Fairfax Drive, E-3112
Arlington, VA 22226
(703) 562-2249
(703) 562-2519 (fax)
byellin@fdic.gov

Federal Energy Regulatory Commission

Timothy Konnert
Office of Energy Projects, Fish Biologist
888 First Street, N.E., Room 6A-01
Washington, DC 20426
(202) 502-6359
(202) 219-2152 (fax)
mark.robinson@ferc.gov

Ann Miles
Office of Energy Projects, Division of Hydropower-
Environment and Engineering
Director
888 First Street, N.E.
Washington, DC 20426
(202) 502-6769
(202) 219-0205 (fax)
ann.miles@ferc.gov

Lauren H. O'Donnell
Division of Gas - Environmental Engineering
Director
888 First Street, N.E., Room 62-23
Washington, DC 20426
(202) 502-8325
(202) 502-0353 (fax)
lauren.odonnell@ferc.gov

Federal Maritime Commission

Karen Gregory
Assistant Secretary
800 North Capitol Street, N.W.
Washington, DC 20573
(202) 523-5725
(202) 523-0014 (fax)
kgregory@fmc.gov

Federal Trade Commission

John Daly
Assistant General Counsel, Litigation
600 Pennsylvania Avenue, N.W., Room 580
Washington, DC 20580
(202) 326-2244
(202) 326-2477 (fax)
jdaly@ftc.gov

General Services Administration

Nathan Smith
Public Buildings Service, Office of Applied Science
Director, Environmental Program
1800 F Street, N.W., Room 4209
Washington, DC 20405
(202) 208-1116
(202) 501-0143 (fax)
nathan.smith@gsa.gov

Department of Health and Human Services

Edward Pfister
Office for Facilities Management and Policy, Division
of Programs
DHHS Environmental Program Manager
200 Independence Avenue, S.W., Room 318E, #45
Washington, DC 20201
(202) 619-0788
(202) 205-4751 (fax)
edward.pfister@hhs.gov

Sharunda Buchanan
Centers for Disease Control and Prevention
National Center for Environmental Health
Director, Division of Emergency and Environmental
Health Services
Chamblee Bldg. Room 6007
Chamblee, GA 30341-3717
(770) 488-7362
(770) 488-4820 (fax)
sdb4@cdc.gov

George Chandler
Centers for Disease Control and Prevention
Director, Building and Facilities Office
CDC Mailstop MS-75
1600 Clifton Road, N.E.
Atlanta, GA 30333
(404) 498-2650
(404) 498-2596 (fax)
gec2@cdc.gov

Suzanne Fitzpatrick
Food and Drug Administration
Office of Commissioner
Senior Science Policy Officer, OSHC
1735 Parklawn (14C-06)
5600 Fishers Lane
Rockville, MD 20857
(301) 827-4591
(301) 827-3042 (fax)
sfitzpat@oc.fda.gov

Keith Webber
FDA Center for Drug Evaluation and Research
5515 Security Lane
Rodwell II, Room 7231
Rockville, MD 20852
(301) 594-2847
(301) 827-3698 (fax)
webber@cder.fda.gov

Raanan (Ron) A. Bloom
FDA Center for Drug Evaluation and Research
Office of Pharmaceutical Science
10903 New Hampshire Avenue
Building 21, Room 3515
Silver Spring, MD 20993
(301) 796-2185
(301) 796-9734 (fax)
raanan.bloom@fda.hhs.gov

Holly Zahner
FDA, Center for Veterinary Medicine
Office of New Animal Drug Evaluation
Environmental Safety Team
7500 Standish Plae
Mail Code HFV-103
Rockville, MD 20855
(240) 276-8181
(240) 276-8175 (fax)
holly.zahner@fda.hhs.gov

Barry Hooberman
FDA Center for Veterinary Medicine
7500 Standish Place
HFV-103
Rockville, MD 20855
(240) 453-6835
(240) 453-6880 (fax)
barry.hooberman@fda.hhs.gov

Annette McCarthy
FDA, Center for Food Safety and Applied Nutrition
5100 Paint Branch Parkway, 3048-US
College Park, MD 20740
(240) 402-1057
(301) 436-2973 (fax)
annette.mccarthy@fda.hhs.gov

Ann Piesen
Health Resources Services Administration
Office of Federal Assistance Management
Analyst, Division of Grants Policy
5600 Fishers Lane
Rockville, MD 20857
(301) 594-4258
(301) 443-5461 (fax)
apiesen@hrsa.gov

Stephen S. Aoyama
Indian Health Service
Office of Division of Sanitation Facilities Construction
Environmental Engineer
801 Thompson Avenue, Suite 120
Rockville, MD 20852-1627
(301) 443-1046
(301) 443-7538 (fax)
stephen.aoyama@ihs.gov

Valerie Nottingham
National Institutes of Health
Division of Environmental Protection, ORF
Chief, Environmental Quality Branch
9000 Rockville Pike, Building 13, Room 2S11
Bethesda, MD 20892
(301) 496-7775
(301) 480-8056 (fax)
nottingv@ors.od.nih.gov

Department of Homeland Security

David Reese
Environmental Protection Specialist
301 Seventh Street, S.W., Room 3522-24
Washington, DC 20528
(202) 306-5687
(202) 772-9749 (fax)
david.reese@dhs.gov

Kristin Leahy
Federal Emergency Management Agency
Environmental Officer
1800 S. Bell St.
Arlington, Va 22202
(202) 646-2741
(202) 646-2577 (fax)
kristin.leahy@dhs.gov

Marin A. Fife
Federal Law Enforcement Training Center
Environmental Protection Specialist
1131 Chapel Crossing Road, Building 681, EVS
Glynco, GA 31524
(912) 261-4038
(912) 544-4231 (fax)
martin.fife@dhs.gov

Paige Tucker
Immigration and Customs Enforcement
Environmental Manager
500 12th St. NW
Washington DC 20536
(202) 732-6003
paige.tucker@dhs.gov

Kathryn Jones
Transportation Security Administration
Office of Occupational Safety, Health and Environment
Environmental Protection Specialist
601 South 12th Street, TSA-17, W11-332N
Arlington, VA 22202
(571) 227-1116
(571) 227-2906 (fax)
kathryn.jones@dhs.gov

Ed Wandelt
U.S. Coast Guard
Environmental Management Division (G-SEC-3)
Chief
2100 2nd Street, S.W.
Washington, DC 20593-0001
(202) 475-5687
(202) 267-4219 (fax)
edward.f.wandelt@uscg.dhs.gov

Christopher Oh
U.S. Customs and Border Protection
Environmental Programs Branch
Branch Chief
1300 Pennsylvania Avenue, N.W.
Washington, DC 20227
(202) 344-2448
christopher.oh@dhs.gov

Department of Housing and Urban Development

Danielle Schopp
Office of Environment and Energy
Community Planner
451 7th Street, S.W.
Washington, DC 20410-7000
(202) 402-4442
(202) 708-3363 (fax)
danielle.l.schopp@hud.gov

Department of Interior

David Sire
Office of Environmental Policy and Compliance
Team Leader, Natural Resources Management
1849 C Street, N.W.
Mailstop 2342, Main Interior
Washington, DC 20240-0001
(202) 208-6661
(202) 208-6970 (fax)
david_sire@ios.doi.gov

Marv Keller
Bureau of Indian Affairs
Chief, Division of Environmental and Cultural
Resources Management
2051 Mercator Drive, Room 247
Reston, VA 20191
(703) 390-6470
(703) 390-6304 (fax)
marv.keller@bia.gov

Kerry Rodgers
Bureau of Land Management
Division of Decision Support, Planning, and NEPA
Senior NEPA Specialist
1849 C Street, N.W.
Washington, DC 20240
(202) 912-7158)
kerodgers@blm.gov

Catherine Cunningham
Bureau of Reclamation
Environmental Specialist
Denver Federal Center, P.O. Box 25007
Building 67 (D-500)
Denver, CO 80225
(303) 445-2875
(303) 445-6465 (fax)
ccunningham@do.usbr.gov

James Bennett
Minerals Management Service
Chief, Environmental Assessment Branch
381 Elden Street, Mail Stop 4042
Herndon, VA 20170-4842
(703) 787-1660
(703) 787-1026 (fax)
jfbennett@mms.gov

Patrick Walsh
National Park Service
Chief, Environmental Planning and Compliance
Branch
P.O. Box 25287
Denver, CO 80225-0287
(303) 987-6620
(303) 987-6782(fax)
patrick_walsh@nps.gov

Andy DeVito
Office of Surface Mining
Regulatory Analyst
381 Constitution Avenue, S.W., SIB MS 202
Washington, DC 20240-0001
(202) 208-2802
(202) 219-3276 (fax)
adevito@osmre.gov

Larry Bright
United States Fish and Wildlife Service
Acting Federal NEPA Contact
4401 North Fairfax Drive, MS-400
Arlington, VA 22203
(703) 358-2440
(703) 358-1869 (fax)
pat_carter@fws.gov

Esther Eng
United States Geological Survey
Chief, Environmental Affairs Program
12201 Sunrise Valley Drive, Mail Stop 423
Reston, VA 22092-0002
(703) 648-7550
(703) 648-7475 (fax)
eeng@usgs.gov

International Boundary and Water Commission, US & Mexico

Gilbert Anaya
International Boundary and Water Commission, US
& Mexico
Chief, Environmental Management
4171 North Mesa Street, C-100
El Paso, TX 79902-1441
(915) 832-4749 direct: 4118
(915) 832-4195 (fax)
carlospena@ibwc.state.gov

Department of Justice

Beverly Li
Environmental and Natural Resources Division
NEPA Coordinator, General Litigation Section
P.O. Box 7611
Washington, DC 20004
(202) 353-9213
(202) 305-0506 (fax)
guillermo.montero@usdoj.gov

Department of Justice Facilities and Administration
Services
Staff Environmental Protection Specialist
1331 Pennsylvania Avenue, NW, Suite 1050
Washington, DC 20531
(202) 307-6486
(202) 307-1915 (fax)
chip.love@usdoj.gov

Melissa Fieri-Fetrow
Community Oriented Policing Services
Counsel, Office of General Counsel
1100 Vermont Avenue, N.W.
Washington, DC 20531-0001
(202) 514-1873
(202) 514-3456 (fax)
melissa.fierifetrow@usdoj.gov

Ellen Harrison
Drug Enforcement Administration
Senior Attorney, Civil Litigation Section (CCL)
2401 Jefferson Davis Highway
Alexandria, VA 22301-1055
(202) 307-8041
(202) 307-8046 (fax)
ellen.harrison@usdoj.gov

Bridgette L. Lyles
Federal Bureau of Prisons
Site Selection and Environmental Review Branch
Environmental Protection Specialist
320 First Street, N.W.
Washington, DC 20534-2025
(202) 514-6470
(202) 616-6024 (fax)
blyles@bop.gov

Chau Tran
Justice Management Division
Supervisory Program Manager
1331 Pennsylvania Avenue, Suite 1050
Washington, DC 20530
(202) 353-0761
(202) 307-5157 (fax)
chau.h.tran@usdoj.gov

Catherine Shaw
Federal Bureau of Investigation
Environmental Program Specialist
320 First Street, N.W.
Washington, DC 20534
(202) 962-9181
(202) 616-6024 (fax)
catherine.shaw@ic.fbi.gov

Laura Kelso
U.S. Marshals Service
Associate General Counsel, Office of General Counsel
1535 Jefferson Davis Highway
Arlington, VA 22202
(202) 307-9054
(202) 307-9456 (fax)
laura.kelso@usdoj.gov

Department of Labor

Hong Kim
Office of the Assistant Secretary for Policy, Senior
Economist
200 Constitution Avenue, N.W.
Washington, DC 20210
(202) 693-5953
kim.hong@dol.gov

Robert Stone
Mine Safety and Health Administration
Economist, Office of Standards, Regulations and
Variances
1100 Wilson Boulevard
Arlington, VA 22209
(202) 693-9445
(202) 693-9441 (fax)
stone.robert@dol.gov

Occupational Safety and Health Administration
Position Vacant
200 Constitution Avenue, N.W.
Washington, DC 20210-0002

Marine Mammal Commission

Michael L. Gosliner
General Counsel
4340 East-West Highway, Room 905
Bethesda, MD 20814
(301) 504-0087
(301) 504-0099 (fax)
mgosliner@mmc.gov

Millennium Challenge Corporation

Thomas P. Schehl
Director, Environmental and Social Assessment
875 15th Street, N.W.
Washington, DC 20005
(202) 521-2618
(202) 521-3701 (fax)
schehltp@mcc.gov

National Aeronautics and Space Administration

Tina Norwood
Environmental Management Division
Environmental Protection Specialist
300 E Street, S.W., Room 5E39
Washington, DC 20546
(202) 358-7324
(202) 358-3948 (fax)
tina.norwood-1@nasa.gov

National Capital Planning Commission

Shane L. Dettan
Office of Urban Design and Plan Review
Senior Urban Planner, Urban Design and Plan Review
401 9th Street, N.W., Suite 500
(202) 482-7267
(202) 482-7272 (fax)
shane.dettman@ncpc.gov

National Credit Union Administration

Frank Kressman
National Credit Union Administration
Office of General Counsel, Division of Operations
Staff Attorney
1775 Duke Street
Alexandria, VA 22314-3428
(703) 518-6558
(703) 837-2770 (fax)
fkressman@ncua.gov

National Indian Gaming Commission

Dawn Houle
Executive Chief of Staff
1441 L Street, N.W.
Washington, DC 20005
(202) 632-7003

(202) 632-7066 (fax)
dawn_houle@nigc.gov

Nuclear Regulatory Commission

Kevin R. O'Sullivan
Division of Intergovernmental Liaison and
Rulemaking
Branch Chief, Intergovernmental Liaison Branch
Nuclear Regulatory Commission, Mail Stop T-8-F-42
Washington, DC 20555
(301) 415-8112
(301) 415-5955 (fax)
kevin.osullivan@nrc.gov

National Science Foundation

Caroline M. Blanco
Office of General Counsel
Assistant General Counsel - Environmental
4201 Wilson Boulevard, Room 1265.27
Arlington, VA 22230
(703) 292-4592
(703) 292-9041 (fax)
cblanco@nsf.gov

Overseas Private Investment Corporation

Mary Boomgard
Director, Environmental Affairs Department
1100 New Hampshire Avenue, N.W.
Washington, DC 20527
(202) 336-8614
(202) 218-0177 (fax)
mboom@opic.gov

Presidio Trust

John Pelka
Manager, NEPA Compliance
34 Graham Street, P.O. Box 29052
San Francisco, CA 94129-0052
(415) 561-5365
(415) 561-2790 (fax)
jpelka@presidiotrust.gov

Securities and Exchange Commission

Geoffrey Aronoa
General Counsel
100 F. Street N.E.
Washington, DC 20549
(202) 5512-5100
(202) 772-9260 (fax)
aronowg@sec.gov

Small Business Administration

Gary Fox
Office of the General Counsel, Department of Litigation and Claims
Assistant General Counsel
409 3rd Street, S.W.
Washington, DC 20416
(202) 205-6862
(202) 481-2122 (fax)
gary.fox@sba.gov

Darryl A. Hairston
Office of Administration
Assistant Administrator
409 3rd Street, S.W., Room 5000
Washington, DC 20416
(202) 205-6630
(202) 205-6821 (fax)
darryl.hairston@sba.gov

Department of State

Alexander Yuan
Bureau of Oceans and International Environmental and Scientific Affairs
Office of Environmental Policy
Foreign Affairs Officer, Development
2201 C Street, N.W., Suite 2657
Washington, DC 20520
(202) 647-4284
(202) 647-1051 (fax)
YuanAW@state.gov

John Matuszak
Bureau of Oceans and International Environmental and Scientific Affairs
2201 C Street, N.W., Suite 4325
Washington, DC 20520
(202) 647-9278
(202) 647-5947 (fax)
matuszakjm@state.gov

Tennessee Valley Authority

Charles Nicholson
Environemntal Policy and Planning
Manager, NEPA Administration
400 West Summit Hill Drive, Mail Stop WT 8C-K
Knoxville, TN 37902-1499
(865) 632-3582
(865) 632-6855 (fax)
cpnicholson@tva.gov

Department of Transportation

Camille Mittelholtz
Office of Assistant Secretary for Transportation Policy
Environmental Policies Team Leader
1200 New Jersey Avenue, S.E., W84-314
Washington, DC 20590-0001
(202) 366-4861
(202) 366-0263 (fax)
camille.mittelholtz@ost.dot.gov

Rhonda Solomon
Federal Aviation Administration
Office of Environmental and Energy (AEE-200)
Environmental Protection Specialist
800 Independence Avenue, S.W., Room 902
Washington, DC 20591
(202) 366-3021
(202) 267-5594 (fax)
rhonda.solomon@faa.gov

Gerald Solomon
Federal Highway Administration
Office of Project Development and Environmental Review
Acting Director
1200 New Jersey Avenue, S.E.
Washington, DC 20590
(202) 366-2037
(202) 366-3409 (fax)
gerald.solomon@dot.gov

Elaine Walls
Federal Motor Carrier Safety Administration
Chief Counsel, Office of the Chief Counsel
400 7th Street, S.W., Room 3103 (MC-CC)
Washington, DC 20590
(202) 366-1394
(202) 366-7041 (fax)
elaine.walls@fmcsa.dot.gov

David Valenstein
Federal Railroad Administration
Office of Railroad Development
Environmental Program Manager
1200 New Jersey Avenue, S.E., MS-20, Room W38-303
Washington, DC 20590
(202) 493-6368
(202) 493-6401 (fax)
david.valenstein@dot.gov

Antoinette Quagliata
Federal Transit Administration
Office of Planning and Environment
Director, Office of Human and Natural Environment
1200 New Jersey Avenue, S.E., Room E45-333
Washington, DC 20590
(202) 366-1626
(202) 493-2478 (fax)
antoinette.quagliata@dot.gov

Kris Gilson
Maritime Administration (MAR-820)
Office of Environmental Activities
Environmental Protection Specialist
1200 New Jersey Ave S.E. (Southeast Federal Center, West. Bldg)
Washington, DC 20590
(202) 366-0714
(202) 366-6988 (fax)
kristine.gilson@dot.gov

Angel Jackson
National Highway Traffic Safety Administration
Office of International Policy, Fuel Economy, and Consumer Programs
1200 New Jersey Avenue, S.E., Room W43-446
Washington, DC 20590-0003
(202) 366-0154
(202) 493-2990 (fax)
angel.jackson@dot.gov

Sherri Pappas
Pipeline and Hazardous Materials Safety Administration
Counsel, Office of the Chief Counsel
400 7th Street, S.W., Room 8407 (DCC-20)
Washington, DC 20590
(202) 366-4400
(202) 366-7041 (fax)
sherri.pappas@dot.gov

Cassandra Allwell
Research and Innovative Technology Administration
Office of Planning and Policy Analysis
Community Planner
55 Broadway, Room DTS-30
Cambridge, MA 02142-1093
(617) 494-3997
(617) 494-3260 (fax)
allwell@volpe.dot.gov

Paul Valihura
Research and Innovative Technology Administration
Environmental Engineering Division, Volpe Center
Senior Environmental Scientist
55 Broadway, Kendal Square
Cambridge, MA 02142-1093
(617) 494-2918
(617) 494-2789 (fax)
paul.valihura@volpe.dot.gov

Brian P. Cromie
Saint Lawrence Seaway Development Corporation
Industrial Hygienist
P.O. Box 520, 180 Andrews Street
Massena, NY 13662-0520
(315) 764-3234
(315) 764-3243 (fax)
brian.cromie@sls.dot.gov

Victoria Rutson
Surface Transportation Board
Chief, Section of Environmental Analysis
1925 K Street, N.W.
Washington, DC 20423
(202) 245-0295
(202) 565-9000 (fax)
rutsonv@stb.dot.gov

Department of Treasury

Eric R. Bradley
Office of Environment, Safety, and Health
Environmental Protection Specialist
1500 Pennsylvania Avenue, S.W. (Annex 6400)
Washington, DC 20220
(202) 622-0728
(202) 622-5334 (fax)
eric.bradley@do.treas.gov

United States Postal Service

Asif Ansari
Environmental Compliance/Risk Management
Manager
P.O. Box 6599377
North Metro, GA 30026-9377
(770) 717-3721
(651) 661-0400 (fax)
ansif.a.ansari@usps.gov

United States Institute for Environmental Conflict Resolution

Mark Schaefer
Acting Director
130 South Scott Avenue
Tucson, AZ 85701
(520) 901-8513
(520) 670-5530
schaefer@udall.gov

Valles Caldera Trust

Marie E. Rodriguez
Natural Resources Coordinator
P.O. Box 359 C
Jemez Springs, NM 87025
(505) 428-7728
(505) 661-0400
mrodriguez@vallescaldera.gov

Department of Veteran Affairs

Michelle DeGrandi
Veterans Health Administration
Environmental Counsel, Office of General Counsel
14312 Hayes Street
Overland Park, KS 6622
(913) 400-2106
(202) 273-9384 (fax)
michelle.degrandi@va.gov

NEPA Deskbook

Appendix 36 NEPA Documents Available

NEPA Documents Available Through the ELR Document Service

The following documents are available from ELR—The Environmental Law Reporter's Guidance and Policy Collection website at http://www.elistore.org. Documents are arranged in reverse chronological order.

Consideration of Cumulative Impacts in EPA Review of NEPA Documents	(EPA 5/99) (20 pp.)	ELR No. AD-4220
Proposed Changes to the Voluntary Environmental Impact Statement Policy, 62 Fed. Reg. 6334	(EPA 11/28/97) (4 pp.)	ELR No. AD-3600
National Park Service's Draft NEPA Guidelines	(DOI 5/22/97) (132 pp.)	ELR No. AD-3468
The National Environmental Policy Act: A Study of Its Effectiveness After Twenty-Five Years	(CEQ 1/97) (50 pp.)	ELR No. AD-3182
Environmental Impact Analysis Process Desk Reference	(Air Force 5/95) (338 pp.)	ELR No. AD-1219
National Environmental Policy Act Compliance Program	(DOE 11/10/94) (17 pp.)	ELR No. AD-642
Environmental Assessment Checklist	(DOE 8/16/94) (24 pp.)	ELR No. AD-644
Lessons Learned in the Preparation of NEPA Documents	(DOE 8/12/94) (12 pp.)	ELR No. AD-655
Directory of Potential Stakeholders for Department of Energy Actions Under the National Environmental Policy Act	(DOE 7/94) (84 pp.)	ELR No. AD-654
Secretarial Policy on National Environmental Policy Act	(DOE 6/94) (12 pp.)	ELR No. AD-640
Questions and Answers on the Secretarial Policy Statement on the National Environmental Policy Act	(DOE 6/94) (15 pp.)	ELR No. AD-641
Report of the Environmental Assessment Process Improvement Team (Environmental Assessment Process Improvement Team	1/19/94 (28 pp.)	ELR No. AD-653
Environmental Report Checklist (Revision 9) and Staff's Recommended Mitigation Procedures	(FERC 7/22/93) (59 pp.)	ELR No. AD-1215
National Environmental Policy Act Review Process	(Nat'l Institutes of Health 6/4/93) (21 pp.)	ELR No. AD-1222
Guidance on Incorporating EPA's Pollution Prevention Strategy Into the Environmental Review Process	(EPA 2/24/93) (20 pp.)	ELR No. AD-659
Pollution Prevention and the National Environmental Policy Act	(CEQ 1/12/93) (18 pp.)	ELR No. AD-638
Incorporating Biodiversity Considerations Into Environmental Impact Analysis Under the National Environmental Policy Act	(CEQ 1/93) (54 pp.)	ELR NO. AD-637
Habitat Evaluation: Guidance for the Review of Environmental Impact Assessment Documents	(EPA 1/93) (74 pp.)	ELR No. AD-660
Procedures for Compliance With Floodplain/Wetlands Environmental Review Requirements (10 C.F.R. Part 1022)	(DOE 10/16/92, modified 9/94) (11 pp.)	ELR No. AD-652
Integrating Pollution Prevention With NEPA Planning Activities	(DOE 10/15/92) (4 pp.)	ELR No. AD-651
Appendix A Categorical Exclusions	(DOE 8/7/92) (2 pp.)	ELR No. AD-650

Title	Source	ELR No.
Recommendations on Alternative Actions for Analysis in Site-Wide NEPA Reviews	(DOE 5/26/92) (4 pp.)	ELR No. AD-649
Frequently Asked Questions on the Department of Energy's NEPA Regulations	(DOE 5/92, amended 9/94) (11 pp.)	ELR No. AD-639
Guidance on Implementation of the DOE NEPA/CERCLA Integration Policy	(DOE 11/15/91) (9 pp.)	ELR No. AD-647
Environmental Review Procedures	(NOAA 8/6/91) (31 pp.)	ELR No. AD-1217
Site Development Planning	(DOE 1/7/91, amended 3/26/92) (24 pp.)	ELR No. AD-648
Facilities Environmental Handbook	(U.S. Postal Service 1/91) (80 pp.)	ELR No. AD-1216
Department of the Treasury Environmental Quality Program	(Treasury Dep't 9/25/90) (17 pp.)	ELR No. AD-1214
Environmental Decision Record Instructions	(TVA 11/89) (12 pp.)	ELR No. AD-1210
Environmental Effects of Army Actions: Army Regulation 200-2	(Dep't of the Army 12/23/88) (46 pp.)	ELR No. AD-1223
Guidance Related to Analysis of Impacts to Workers in NEPA Documentation	(DOE 6/10/88) (4 pp.)	ELR No. AD-646
Airport Environmental Handbook	(FAA 10/8/85) (124 pp.)	ELR No. AD-1228
Procedures for Considering Environmental Impacts	(DOT Maritime Administration 7/23/85) (3 pp.)	ELR No. AD-1226
National Environmental Policy Act Implementing Procedures and Policy for Considering Environmental Impacts	(U.S. Coast Guard 7/12/85) (100 pp.)	ELR No. AD-1227
Procedures for Compliance With the National Environmental Policy Act	(TVA 4/12/83) (15 pp.)	ELR No. AD-1211
Guidance Material for the Preparation of Environmental Documents	(FHWA 2/24/82) (34 pp.)	ELR No. AD-1225
Operational Procedures for Implementing Section 102 of the National Environmental Policy Act of 1969, Other Laws Pertaining to Specific Aspects of the Environment and Applicable Executive Orders, 46 FR 44083	(U.S. Int'l Boundary Waters Comm'n 9/2/81) (12 pp.)	ELR No. AD-1212
Environmental Considerations in Defense Logistics Agency Actions Abroad	(DLA 7/14/81) (10 pp.)	ELR No. AD-1221
Environmental Considerations in Defense Logistics Agency Actions in the United States	(DLRA 6/1/81) (74 pp.)	ELR No. AD-1220
Implementation of Executive Order No. 12114 Environmental Effects Abroad of Major Federal Actions; Final Guideline	(DOE 1/5/81) (5 pp.)	ELR No. AD-847
Guidance on Applying Section 404(r) of the Clean Water Act to Federal Projects Which Involve the Discharge of Fill Materials Into Waters of the U.S., Including Wetlands	(CEQ 11/17/80) (4 pp.)	ELR No. AD-632

Analysis of Impacts on Prime and Unique Agricultural Lands in Implementing NEPA; Interagency Consultation to Avoid or Mitigate Adverse Effects on Rivers in the Nationwide Inventory	(CEQ 9/8/80) (4 pp.)	ELR No. AD-631
Unified Procedures Applicable to Major Federal Actions Relating to Nuclear Activities Subject to Executive Order No. 12114	(U.S. State Department 11/13/79) (5 pp.)	ELR No. AD-656
Procedures for Considering Environmental Impacts	(DOT 9/18/79) (37 pp.)	ELR No. AD-1224
Environmental Policies and Procedures	(Nat'l Capital Planning Comm'n 9/13/79, amended 9/3/81 and 10/21/82) (20 pp.)	ELR No. AD-1213
Environmental Effects Abroad of Major Federal Actions	(CEQ 3/21/79) (3 pp.)	ELR No. AD-630
Compliance With Floodplain/Wetlands Environmental Review Requirements	(DOE 3/7/79) (7 pp.)	ELR No. AD-645
Programmatic Environmental Analysis: "Where the National Environmental Policy Act and Weapons System Management Processes Meet"	(Air Force undated) (21 pp.)	ELR No. AD-1218

Notes

Notes

Notes

Notes

Notes